SAGE Handbook of
Mixed Methods in Social
& Behavioral Research
Second Edition

SAGE Handbook of
Mixed Methods in Social & Behavioral Research
Second Edition

Edited by

Abbas Tashakkori
University of North Texas

Charles Teddlie
Louisiana State University, Baton Rouge

Los Angeles | London | New Delhi
Singapore | Washington DC

For information:

SAGE Publications, Inc.
2455 Teller Road
Thousand Oaks, California 91320
E-mail: order@sagepub.com

SAGE Publications India Pvt. Ltd.
B 1/I 1 Mohan Cooperative Industrial Area
Mathura Road, New Delhi 110 044
India

SAGE Publications Ltd.
1 Oliver's Yard
55 City Road
London EC1Y 1SP
United Kingdom

SAGE Publications Asia-Pacific Pte. Ltd.
33 Pekin Street #02-01
Far East Square
Singapore 048763

Printed in the United States of America

Library of Congress Cataloging-in-Publication Data

SAGE handbook of mixed methods in social & behavioral research / editors, Abbas Tashakkori, Charles Teddlie. — 2nd ed.
    p. cm.
Rev. ed. of: Handbook of mixed methods in social and behavioral research.
Includes bibliographical references and index.
ISBN 978-1-4129-7266-6 (cloth)
    1. Social sciences—Research—Methodology—Handbooks, manuals, etc. I. Tashakkori, Abbas. II. Teddlie, Charles. III. Handbook of mixed methods in social & behavioral research.

H62.T244 2010
300.72—dc22   2010006465

This book is printed on acid-free paper.

10   11   12   13   14   10   9   8   7   6   5   4   3   2   1

Acquisitions Editor:	Vicki Knight
Associate Editor:	Lauren Habib
Editorial Assistant:	Ashley Dodd
Production Editor:	Astrid Virding
Copy Editor:	Jackie Tasch, Alison Hope, Mary Tederstrom
Typesetter:	C&M Digitals (P) Ltd.
Proofreader:	Dennis W. Webb, Scott Oney
Indexer:	William Ragsdale
Cover Designer:	Glenn Vogel
Marketing Manager:	Stephanie Adams

CONTENTS

PART III. CONTEMPORARY APPLICATIONS OF MIXED METHODS RESEARCH

PREFACE

Working on the two editions of the *Handbook of Mixed Methods in Social and Behavioral Research* has been an interesting intellectual journey through time for us. As the two volumes have evolved, we have experienced the excitement of the growth and diversification of a field of social research methodology that has become known as the *third methodological movement,* taking its place alongside the two more traditional approaches over the past decade.

We initiated the *Handbook* in the late 1990s, immediately following our first book on mixed methods (Tashakkori & Teddlie, 1998) with some trepidation and uncertainty about its salience to the social and behavioral sciences. From our point of view, combining qualitative and qualitative approaches for answering complex social research questions seemed a nonissue (or in many cases, a *no-brainer*). We asked ourselves: "Doesn't everyone do this? Don't most practitioners in applied research or evaluation areas already use mixed methods?"

We had both graduated with degrees in "experimental" social psychology in the late 1970s (and you do not get much more post-positivistic than that), but we also had both deviated almost immediately from the mainstream quantitative research tradition in our own research and evaluation endeavors. Our research questions in areas such as the motives for child bearing, consequences of psychosocial modernity, and other issues in cultural anthropology (Tashakkori) and of the factors that generate effectiveness in schools serving disadvantaged and minority students (Teddlie) could be answered only using a combination of qualitative and quantitative methods, which we adopted almost intuitively (i.e., how else would we study these complex issues without using all the methodological tools available to us?).

The idea of producing a *Handbook of Mixed Methods* gradually emerged from our teaching and research together at Louisiana State University, where our students' dissertations often called for mixed methods; yet, their flexibility in using those methods was still somewhat constrained by the residues of the paradigm wars (e.g., the attitudes of some of their committee members). Among other activities, we held a mock debate between the qualitative and quantitative points of view for colleagues and students at a seminar in the mid-1990s, which resulted in a "split decision" with mixed methods carrying the day.

We became keenly aware of the controversial nature of pulling together emerging and diverse ideas about integrating the qualitative and quantitative approaches (camps) in a *Handbook*, and of its possible impact on social science methodology. We hoped that the *Handbook* would encourage those who were doing integrated research in social and behavioral sciences to "come out of the closet" and start a community of scholars to support themselves. We must confess that the rate and scope of development of the mixed methods community has far exceeded what we would have predicted or expected as we began to put the first *Handbook* together.

The first edition of the *Handbook* provided a platform for scholars to discuss the merits of mixed methods research, its feasibility, and its limitations. The field of mixed methods research has expanded in a number of ways since the publication of that first edition, which has been cited as one of the major catalysts for that growth. That volume provided a viable third alternative to the traditional approaches, and it was written by a talented group of authors who were already practicing mixed methods in their own diverse fields. Probably more than any other source at that point in time, the first edition of the *Handbook* demonstrated the diversity and richness of ideas about mixed methods, both within and across disciplines.

We faced a welcome, but formidable challenge when we started organizing the second edition of the *Handbook*, which is now in front of you, within the context of an exciting and at times controversial history in which the field has been both widely praised and strongly criticized. This second edition of the *Handbook* will, we hope, provide an even stronger platform for the field than the first because it is based on numerous inclusive and diverse theoretical and practical pillars, which support a community of scholars across the globe and across disciplines.

An exciting outcome of our efforts to put this second edition together is that it is both similar to, and highly different from, the first edition in many aspects. Although it is composed of a completely different set of chapters than the first edition, this edition is also squarely anchored in its predecessor. We will summarize some of these similarities and differences in the following sections of this preface.

◆ Similarities and Differences Between the Two Editions of the Handbook

Similar to our approach in the first edition, we decided to deliberately keep a balance between the number of emerging scholars and more "established" authors in this volume. We have tried to maintain a balance between new and old ideas in the second edition by asking the authors of the two groups/generations of scholars to write chapters together, suggesting possible co-authors when needed, and encouraging more established colleagues to team up with emerging scholars. We believe that these efforts have been rewarded by the results: Although the chapters in this edition are well anchored in the first one, they dramatically expand those older frameworks. Furthermore, we have been able to substantially expand the community of mixed methods scholars by incorporating many new authors from across the globe and across disciplines in the *Handbook,* which we further comment on later in this Preface.

In the first edition of the *Handbook*, one of our main objectives was to encourage as much diversity in the generation of ideas and methods as possible. Since that time, the field of mixed methods has expanded with an increasing trajectory. Although that expansion is healthy, indicating strong growth in a new field, we may also be approaching a point of entropy that makes it increasingly difficult to keep the diverse ideas connected and together under the heading of mixed methodology. We have been more mindful of the need to create connections between disparate conceptualizations in mixed methods and have encouraged our authors to attempt to create such bridges, especially in chapters aimed at synthesizing broad areas of concern (e.g., design, analysis).

After much deliberation, we invited authors to write about given aspects or topics in mixed methods that we knew they were interested in, but which we also knew they had not written extensively about (see comments below regarding steps in developing the second edition). We asked these identified scholars to team up with others whom they chose and to try to create overarching/superordinate frameworks that could bridge current ideas within those topical areas (e.g., in conceptualization, research questions, design type, data analysis, quality audits). Although there are varying degrees of success in achieving these goals, the second edition of the *Handbook* presents many innovative new understandings that resulted from syntheses of the diverse current ideas in the field. We are hoping that these new understandings (gestalts) will help discussions toward a more connected field of mixed methods.

We have to confess that despite our success in resolving some of the old controversies and contradictions in mixed methodology, many new ones have also emerged in the second edition. We discuss these old and new dilemmas and controversies in detail in Chapters 1 and 31 of the second edition.

◆ *Emergence of Pedagogy as a Challenge to the Community*

Although we were concerned about pedagogy when we put the first edition of the *Handbook* together, it has received much more attention since then, emerging as one of the most difficult and controversial areas in mixed methods (and research methodology, in general). Before the publication of the first edition, mixed methodology seemed to be

largely self-taught.[1] We experienced this "self-teaching" process many years before, as described in the first section of the Preface. We were very fortunate to have had mentors who were themselves struggling with, learning about, and using the best tools to answer complex research questions (note comments in the Acknowledgments section).

While we were fortunate in our own development as researchers, it has become increasingly apparent that the "failure of pedagogy" in social research methodology (Teddlie & Tashakkori, 2003) and mixed methods must be addressed, as noted by several authors (e.g., Creswell, Tashakkori, Jensen, & Shapley, 2003). Several insightful chapters and articles have been written recently describing in detail the advances that have been made in the pedagogy of mixed methods since the publication of the first edition of the *Handbook* (e.g., Christ, 2009; Earley, 2007).

We attend to issues of pedagogy much more closely in this second edition of the *Handbook* by (a) including the experiences and emerging work of "first generation" instructors teaching graduate students how to actually do integrated research during their formal training; and (b) asking all the authors to include chapter objectives and discussion questions that would provide pedagogical tools for professors of research methodology. Thus, those wanting to use this *Handbook*, or parts of it, when developing their own mixed methods courses, will have access to learning objectives and discussion/research questions that the authors of each chapter believed were important as they developed their chapters.

We have also asked the authors to cross-reference each other, as an additional pedagogical tool. At the least, these cross-references offer three distinct clusters of chapters that instructors and students may want to examine more closely:

- Four chapters in Section I that discuss how conceptual orientations can affect the way researchers conduct and interpret their mixed studies (Greene

& Hall, Chapter 5; Maxwell & Mittapalli, Chapter 6; Hesse-Biber, Chapter 7; Mertens and her colleagues, Chapter 8)

- Three chapters in Section II that provide a major focal point by presenting examples of the latest developments in mixed methods data analysis and display (Onwuegbuzie & Combs, Chapter 17; Bazeley, Chapter 18; Dickinson, Chapter 19)

- Four chapters in Section II that provide guiding frameworks and principles for mixed methods research with regard to design, sampling, data analysis, and making inferences from results (Nastasi, Hitchcock, & Brown, Chapter 13; Collins, Chapter 15; Onwuegbuzie & Combs, Chapter 17; O'Cathain, Chapter 21)

◆ *Our Journey:*
Steps in Developing
the Second Edition

When putting together the first edition of the *Handbook,* we were very fortunate to have recruited a talented group of scholars whose collective contributions resulted in a "declaration of independence" of mixed methods as a third methodological movement separate from the traditional qualitative and quantitative approaches. That edition necessarily included reactions to the paradigm wars (and their aftermath), plus extended justifications for the value and feasibility of mixed methods.

When recruiting authors for the second edition, we were more interested in describing where mixed methods as a field is now and what the next generation of research will encompass; we believe that the viability of mixed methods as a third methodological approach is now firmly established. To that end, we used a two-step process to generate the content for the new *Handbook:* (1) soliciting input to a questionnaire sent to a wide ranging group of authors

(our Informal Advisory Board) requesting information regarding the most important topics in the field as it now exists and (2) generating a list of chapters that reflected the ideas that emerged from the survey results and also represented the diversity of authors (e.g., philosophical, methodological, geographical) who are currently writing in the field. The remainder of this section provides a few more details on these two processes.

We sent questionnaires to about 30 leaders in the field asking them to propose issues (up to five) that they considered essential for inclusion in the *Handbook:* to list authors (together with topics if possible) who would make important contemporary contributions, and to make other suggestions that would result in a successful volume. We also asked each respondent to propose two chapters they might be willing to contribute to the volume, thereby allowing us to begin to stockpile ideas for the book.

We included a list of sample topics for the book in the questionnaire directions to initiate the dialogue, and this list was expanded considerably based on responses from our Informal Advisory Board. Altogether, we received valuable feedback from about 20 individuals, who provided us with more than 75 topics ranging from the very specific to the very general. One of our most interesting challenges as co-editors of the *Handbook* was to develop a final set of chapters that coherently tied together as many of these diverse issues as possible into one volume. The respondents to our questionnaire then served as an *ad hoc* committee that continued to advise us on various issues as we further developed the volume. The members of this Informal Advisory Board are acknowledged later in this chapter.

After we developed a list of potential authors and topics, we sent a communication to all, describing our expectations for the further development of their chapters. In a communication to all authors, we provided a series of general expectations for the second edition of the *Handbook* that were quite different from the first. First, each chapter in the new volume should concentrate on theoretical and applied literature from the past decade only (with even closer emphasis on the past few years) because earlier writings (with the exception of occasional "classic" texts) have limited relevance to descriptions of the rapidly expanding field.

Second, each chapter should set the stage for a unified field of mixed methods with clear definitions of methodological concepts and innovations that would provide overall guidance for the next generation of scholars. We wanted the second edition of the *Handbook* to establish common characteristics of mixed methods that set it apart from other approaches. Third, we suggested that each chapter should strive to bring ideas together, rather than generating as many diverse concepts as possible for further development. The second edition of the *Handbook* calls for convergence around a unified set of concepts without sacrificing the potential for new ideas, designs, and applications. Fourth, we asked the authors to advance the field by emphasizing how to actually conduct mixed methods studies step by step within real world settings.

We identified and communicated several general goals for the new edition of the *Handbook*:

- to provide a platform for discourse and integration of current ideas among a variety of scholars;

- to recognize the achievement and contributions of the leaders in the field;

- to provide a stage for the emergence of a new generation of scholars in mixed methods;

- to encourage the development of new mixed methods techniques and applications; and

- to further reduce artificial boundaries between the qualitative and quantitative approaches by encouraging research aimed at answering important questions in the social and behavioral sciences using the most appropriate approach, which will often be mixed methods, especially in applied areas.

◆ The Authors of the Handbook

As we discussed above, while the first edition of the Handbook included a wide variety of authors and topics, we wanted to make this volume even more diversified. This is one of the reasons that we consulted with many leaders in the field to be sure that the final lineup of topics covered the field as broadly as possible.

We believe that the *Handbook* chapters do represent a wide range of opinions. While there was agreement among the authors on many points, there were also important differences between them. Ironically, one of these disagreements is about whether the field is ready to come to consensus on important issues! Another important example of the disagreements is on the possibility of universal social science research principles that are devoid of paradigm considerations, as opposed to the belief that any study must adhere to one (or multiple) paradigm perspective(s).[2]

The second edition offers the perspectives of a very diverse group of scholars. In addition to gender diversity (58% female, 42% male), the authors represent a wide range of expertise and educational/training backgrounds, with virtually all being bilingual in qualitative and quantitative methods. The geographic backgrounds of the authors in this edition of the *Handbook* is more diverse than that of the first one in that about one third (16/52) either are from universities or research organizations outside the United States or are involved in research and evaluation for international agencies such as the World Bank. As we will discuss in Chapters 1 and 31, we believe that this represents a significant undercount of the actual number of scholars practicing mixed methods internationally and that the percentage of authors from outside the boundaries of the United States (and Europe) is expanding rapidly. One possible reason for this expansion is that their research often involves the examination of crucial applied issues that are explicitly situated within/across cultural contexts, best investigated by a combination of methods.

One final note on diversity concerns the number of authors in the second edition of the *Handbook* who also contributed to the first one. As we began developing this volume, our goal was to have at least 50% of the authors to be new contributors who did not have a chapter in the first edition. As it turns out, only 25% of the contributors to the first edition (13/52) also have chapters in this edition, and several of these authors (e.g., Burke Johnson, John Creswell, Joseph Maxwell) were explicitly asked to write about very different topics the second time around. We are pleased with our success in expanding the community of mixed methods scholars, encouraging a wider and more emergent "intellectual gene pool," which we hope will benefit the community.

◆ Acknowledgments

We briefly noted the influence of our mentors and colleagues in our own development as mixed methods researchers. Among them, we include Amir H. Mehryar, Asghar Razavieh, Vaida Thompson, John Thibaut, Chester A. Insko, David Heise, and Dick Udry. We are forever indebted to them. Many other social science scholars have influenced our thoughts and our drive to seek mixed methods, although they remain nameless here.

We would also like to gratefully acknowledge the members of our Informal Advisory Board, many of whom also contributed to the *Handbook:* Pat Bazeley, Manfred Max Bergman, Thomas W. Christ, John W. Creswell, Mark Earley, Joseph L. Gallo, Stephen Gorard, Jennifer C. Greene, Natalyia V. Ivankova, Burke Johnson, Joseph A. Maxwell, Donna M. Mertens, Steven Miller, David Morgan, Isadore Newman, Katrin Niglas, Alicia O'Cathain, Anthony J. Onwuegbuzie, and Vicki L. Plano Clark. Their initial comments on our plan and the

author line-up were influential on our final structure. We would like our readers to know that at times we have strayed from some of their advice. So any shortcomings are ours, not theirs.

Needless to say, the second edition of the *Handbook* would have not been possible without the encouragement and hard work of the Sage editors and production crew. We are grateful to the Sage team, which included Vicki Knight, Lauren Habib, and Ashley Dodd, for their support and advice throughout this lengthy and often difficult process. We are especially indebted to our acquisitions editor, Vicki Knight, who put this project on the fast track and made sure we completed it on time (or close to it). Thanks also to production editor Astrid Virding and the copy editing team, which included Jacqueline Tasch, Alison Hope, and Mary Tederstrom. Although not directly involved in this edition, we are grateful for C. Deborah Laughton's support of our initial idea to develop a *Handbook* in 1999. Without her encouragement and support, the idea of a *Handbook of Mixed Methods Research* might have been lost, or at least substantially delayed. Last, but not the least, we are indebted to our families who have suffered through our frustrations, put up with our distractions, and supported us throughout the process. We are deeply indebted to you: Marylyn, Ariana, and Susan!

◆ Notes

1. Up until around the time of the publication of the first *Handbook,* scholars had been largely self-taught as chronicled in Nancy Leech's (Chapter 11) interviews with early developers of the field. Leech's chapter describes how early developers trained in the 1970s or thereabouts were taught almost exclusively quantitative methods in graduate school and then learned how to conduct qualitative research on their own, typically while involved in conducting studies of complex social phenomena. Another, more

recent trend involves researchers schooled in qualitative traditions beginning in the mid-1980s or thereabouts, who picked up some quantitative skills through graduate coursework, but who were introduced to mixed methods research mainly through "on the job" training. A later trend currently ongoing involves "first generation" instructors teaching graduate students how to actually do integrated research during their formal training (e.g., Christ, Chapter 25).

2. An example of the latter is the point of view that each mixed methods study has an identifiable and dominant "theoretical drive" and a supplementary component, which must be kept as separate as possible so that the strengths of each paradigmatic position can be realized (see Morse, Chapter 14.).

◆ References

Christ, T. W. (2009). Designing, teaching, and evaluating two complementary mixed methods research courses. *Journal of Mixed Methods Research, 3*(4), 292–325.

Creswell, J., Tashakkori, A., Jensen, K., & Shapley, K. (2003). Teaching mixed methods research: Practice, dilemmas and challenges. In A. Tashakkori & C. Teddlie (Eds.), *Handbook of mixed methods in social & behavioral research* (pp. 619–638). Thousand Oaks, CA: Sage.

Earley, M. A. (2007). Developing a syllabus for a mixed methods research course. *International Journal of Social Research Methodology, 10*(2), 145–162.

Tashakkori, A., & Teddlie, C. (1998). *Mixed methodology: Combining the qualitative and quantitative approaches.* Thousand Oaks, CA: Sage.

Teddlie, C., & Tashakkori, A. (2003). Major issues and controversies in the use of mixed methods in the social and behavioral sciences. In A. Tashakkori & C. Teddlie (Eds.), *Handbook of mixed methods in social & behavioral research* (pp. 3–50). Thousand Oaks, CA: Sage.

1

OVERVIEW OF CONTEMPORARY ISSUES IN MIXED METHODS RESEARCH

◆ Charles Teddlie and Abbas Tashakkori

Objectives

The objectives of this chapter are:

- to present the organizational structure of the *Handbook,* both in words and visually in terms of three overlapping circles corresponding to the three parts of the volume;

- to summarize the core characteristics of MMR, which are widely acknowledged by many, if not most, scholars writing in the field;

- to present an overview of issues or controversies that are important to the contemporary field of MMR; and

- to describe each of these issues, explaining why each is important and providing information on diverse points of view regarding them;

This is the second edition of the *SAGE Handbook of Mixed Methods in Social & Behavioral Research* (subsequently referred to as the *Handbook*). While only 7 years have passed since the publication of the first edition, the landscape of mixed methods research (MMR) has changed remarkably due to the large number of significant works that have been published in the interim (e.g., Bergman, 2008; Brannen, 2005; Creswell & Plano Clark, 2007; Gorard & Taylor, 2004; Greene, 2007, 2008; Johnson & Onwuegbuzie, 2004; Johnson, Onwuegbuzie, & Turner, 2007; Mertens, 2007; Morgan, 2007; Morse & Niehaus, 2010; Plano Clark & Creswell, 2008; Ridenour & Newman, 2008; Teddlie & Tashakkori, 2009).

In the first edition, published in 2003, we asked two basic questions: (1) Why do we need a *Handbook* in this field at this point in time? (2) What major issues and controversies will this *Handbook* address? The question regarding why we need a *Handbook* was important in 2003 when MMR was just formally emerging as a distinct methodological field: We needed a *Handbook* at that time to help legitimize the field as an alternative to qualitative and quantitative methods. With regard to the current *Handbook,* the answer to the "why" question is twofold: (1) to chronicle the advances made in the field over the past 7 years and (2) to present a comprehensive snapshot of the field of MMR as the decade of the 2010s begins. Therefore, we have carefully selected the chapters contained in the current *Handbook* to generate a diverse and representative overview of what the field has accomplished and what it looks like now in terms of a wide variety of topical areas.[1]

Answering the second question (what major issues and controversies will this *Handbook* address?) is complicated, given the broad range of important topics now facing the field. Which issues and controversies are most salient and pervasively written about in 2010? Some of these issues might include:

- What are the boundaries of MMR as a field, especially as it is being adapted in one form or another into virtually all the pure and applied social and behavioral sciences? As adaptation occurs differentially across these disciplines, what are the basic core characteristics of MMR? Should these basic core characteristics be broadly defined so that the field can serve as a "big tent," or do we need a narrowly defined set of attributes that more precisely define the field? What constitutes the structure or "map" of MMR (Creswell, 2009, 2010 [this volume])?

- What is the relative importance of conceptual issues as opposed to issues of method and methodology in MMR? Should contemporary writing continue to stress both, or is it time for another phase of MMR, perhaps focusing more on issues of method and methodology? What is the relationship between conceptual orientation and how we conduct MMR?

- What is the relationship of MMR to the other broadly defined methodological areas: qualitative (QUAL) research and quantitative (QUAN) research? Is MMR an amalgamation or mixture of the other basic approaches, or does it constitute a distinct approach toward social science inquiry itself (e.g., Greene, 2008)? Should it have its own unique language, should we develop a common language that allows us to talk across methodological boundaries, or should it be a combination of the two (e.g., Teddlie & Tashakkori, 2003)?

We engage these and other issues in this chapter by first presenting the organizational structure for the *Handbook,* which can also be seen as an evolving blueprint for the field of MMR. Following this discussion, we turn our attention to the nature and general characteristics of MMR, examining seemingly common elements that have emerged as the field has developed over the past 30 years. Identification of these common or core characteristics is important as the field matures. We then examine issues and challenges of contemporary MMR, which we believe are the most important areas currently being discussed or debated in the field.

◆ *Organization of the SAGE Handbook of Mixed Methods in Social & Behavioral Research, 2nd Edition*

THE THREE PARTS OF THE HANDBOOK

The volume is divided into three separate parts, depicted as overlapping circles in Figure 1.1:

- Part I. Conceptual Issues: Philosophical, Theoretical, Sociopolitical

- Part II. Issues Regarding Methods and Methodology

- Part III. Contemporary Applications of Mixed Methods Research

As we were organizing the *Handbook,* it seemed to us that chapters could be divided into three basic categories: (1) those dealing with conceptual issues such as philosophical assumptions or beliefs, theoretical frameworks, sociopolitical concerns, historical perspectives, and so forth; (2) those concerned with the "how to" of MMR, both in terms of specific methods (strategies and procedures) and broader approaches to scientific inquiry using mixed methods; and (3) applications of mixed methods within and across specific academic disciplines and with regard to special topical areas (e.g., pedagogy, collaborative

Figure 1.1 Overlapping Components of an Emerging "Map" of Mixed Methods Research

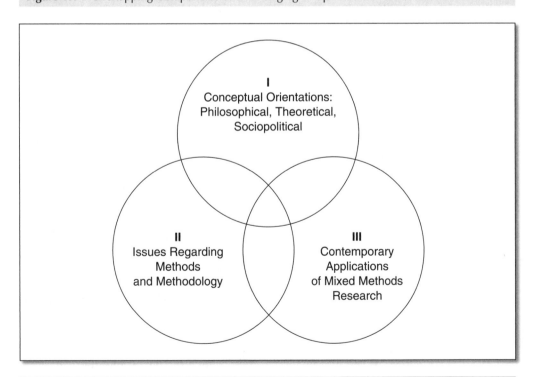

Note: These circles portray the information contained in the three parts of this volume.

research strategies). Although these broad domains overlap, it is obvious from reading the chapters in each part as a group that each part has a distinctive emphasis.

AN OVERVIEW OF PART I OF THE HANDBOOK

The section of the *Handbook* titled "Conceptual Issues: Philosophical, Theoretical, Sociopolitical" (Chapters 2 through 11)[2] has a deliberately broad title to cover the numerous topics contained within it. Although some authors in Part I avoid the use of the term *paradigm,* they address issues intrinsic to the philosophical foundations of social inquiry such as *epistemology* (beliefs about the nature of knowledge, including those related to the objectivity/subjectivity dualism); *axiology* (beliefs about the role of values or ethics in conducting research), *ontology* (beliefs about the nature of reality), and others (e.g., the possibility of generalizations, the nature of causality). Chapter 9 by Niglas catalogs many of the philosophical dimensions discussed in Part I, portraying them as continua rather than dichotomies, which is an oft repeated distinction in the mixed methods literature.

Issues related to the epistemological foundations have been central to MMR since its inception and continue to be featured in this volume. These issues link the nature of knowledge and the most appropriate ways of producing that knowledge, which for MMR has included the synergy of combining the QUAL and QUAN approaches. Biesta's Chapter 4 in Part I engages epistemological issues by positing *intersubjectivity* (a common world that we create from our individual subjective worlds) as an alterative to the either-or of subjectivism and objectivism. Similarly, the chapters by Johnson and Gray, Greene and Hall, Maxwell and Mittapalli, and others in Part I address epistemological issues in their perspectives on the nature and kinds of knowledge that can be produced using MMR.

While epistemological considerations have been prominent throughout the history of MMR, axiological issues are featured foremost in the Part I chapters by Hesse-Biber (the importance of *axiological practice* in her feminist theoretical approach) and Mertens, Bledsoe, Sullivan, and Wilson (the *axiological assumption,* which has precedence in their transformative paradigm). These chapters emphasize what Greene (2008) calls the *sociopolitical commitments domain* of MMR, which she describes as the "location of social science in society" (p. 10). Greene considers sociopolitical issues as a distinct domain in MMR, yet one that is related to philosophical issues. Creswell (2010 [this volume]) also discusses these issues as part of what he calls the *politicization* of MMR, an area in which he includes topics such as deconstructing and justifying mixed methods. For us, the sociopolitical domain of MMR is an area where the individual axiological orientations of researchers are applied to the concerns and problems of the real world contexts within which they work.

Ontological considerations per se do not feature as prominently in the mixed methods literature, or in this *Handbook,* as those of epistemology or axiology. In Chapter 3, Johnson and Gray characterize what they consider the mixed methods position on this issue as *ontological pluralism* or *multiple realism,* which "fully acknowledges the 'realities' discussed in QUAL and in QUAN and . . . rejects singular reductionisms and dogmatisms" (**p. 72**). The Maxwell and Mittapalli chapter in Part I presents their version of critical realism, which combines a *realist ontology* (a "real" world exists independent of our perceptions) with a constructivist epistemology (our understanding of this "real" world is a construction based on our own perspectives and points of view). Critical (or scientific) realism is endorsed by others in the *Handbook* (e.g., Christ's chapter in Part III), and is one of the philosophical orientations considered by the hypothetical researcher "Michelle" in Greene and Hall's Chapter 5 description of how the dialectic stance informs practice.

Another component of Circle I in Figure 1.1 concerns *theoretical frameworks,* which operate at a different level of abstraction than philosophical considerations (e.g., Creswell, 2010; Crotty, 1998). A theoretical perspective,[3] such as feminism or attribution theory or the contingency theory of leadership, refers to a "unified, systematic explanation of a diverse range of social phenomena" (Schwandt, 1997, p. 54). Greene's (2007) description of the *substantive theory stance* in MMR states, "What matters most in guiding inquiry decisions are the substantive issues and conceptual theories relevant to the study being conducted, not philosophical paradigms in and of themselves" (p. 69). Creswell (2010) similarly distinguishes between philosophical assumptions and a theoretical lens, concluding that we need a better understanding of how distinct theoretical perspectives can be used in MMR. The only example of an explicitly stated theoretical framework in Part I is Hesse-Biber's chapter on how the feminist theoretical perspective affects the manner in which MMR is conducted. As MMR expands throughout various disciplines in the human sciences, it could be that theoretical perspectives indigenous to those fields of inquiry (or cutting across them) will strongly influence how mixed methods are employed within them.

Chapter 5 by Johnson and Gray is an important contribution because it grounds MMR within the history of the philosophy of science. It traces prior attempts to integrate QUAL and QUAN research by identifying *proto-mixed methods thinkers* (e.g., Aristotle, Abelard, Kant) and discussing how their work exhibited the *spirit* of MMR. It is important for practitioners of MMR to understand that the conceptual foundation for this approach has been a de facto part of the philosophy of science for as long as that of the (supposedly) more traditional approaches (Johnson & Gray, 2010 [this volume]; Teddlie & Johnson, 2009a, 2009b).

AN OVERVIEW OF PART II OF THE HANDBOOK

The section of the *Handbook* titled "Issues Regarding Methods and Methodology" (Chapters 12 through 21) includes information related to (1) *methods,* which are specific strategies and procedures for implementing MMR designs, including those associated with design, sampling, data collection, data analysis, and interpretation of findings, and (2) *methodology,* which connotes a broad inquiry logic or general approach to MMR inquiry that guides the selection of specific methods. The commonly used term *methodology* has a variety of slightly different meanings depending on the source (e.g., Crotty, 1998; Greene, 2008; Morgan, 2007; Schwandt, 1997).

In this chapter, we define the *methodology of mixed research* as follows: the broad inquiry logic that guides the selection of specific methods and that is informed by conceptual positions common to mixed methods practitioners (e.g., the rejection of "either-or" choices at all levels of the research process). For us, this definition of methodology distinguishes the MMR approach to conducting research from that practiced in either the QUAN or QUAL approach.

Rejection of the "either-or" leads to a guiding methodological principle of MMR: *methodological eclecticism,* which means that practitioners of mixed methods select and then synergistically integrate the most appropriate techniques from a myriad of QUAL, QUAN, and mixed strategies to thoroughly investigate a phenomenon of interest (Teddlie & Tashakkori, in press). As we continue our discussion in this chapter (and Chapter 31), we will be looking for other guiding principles that mixed methods researchers use as they conduct their work. More details regarding *methodological eclecticism* are presented in a later section on the common core characteristics of MMR.

Before briefly previewing chapters in Part II, we should note that some authors (e.g., Guba & Lincoln, 2005; Lincoln &

Guba, 2000; Mertens, 2007; Mertens, Bledsoe, Sullivan, & Wilson, 2010 [this volume]) define paradigms as consisting of sets of interlocking philosophical assumptions: epistemological, axiological, ontological, and methodological.[4] We discussed the first three of these basic belief systems in Part I on conceptual issues in MMR, but we situate the fourth (methodological assumptions) in Part II. This distinction is an important one, consistent with our belief that conceptual and methodological issues are separable on several dimensions, but that there is an extremely important interface between the two, which we later describe as one of the major contemporary issues in MMR.

The linkage of specific methods with interconnected philosophical beliefs (e.g., Guba & Lincoln, 2005; Lincoln & Guba, 2000; Sale, Lohfeld, & Brazil, 2002) results in the *incompatibility thesis*, which has been widely rejected by the MMR community. The inclusion of methodological issues as part of paradigm considerations also leads to unfortunate and misleading terms such as quantitative paradigm, qualitative paradigm, and mixed methods paradigm, as noted by others (e.g., Gorard, 2010 [this volume]; Gorard & Taylor, 2004). Mixing these terms contributes to conceptual fuzziness in MMR.

Several Part II chapters are concerned with specific methodological topics or techniques in MMR: the generation of research questions (Plano Clark & Badiee), computer-assisted data analysis (Bazeley), visual displays (Dickinson), hermeneutic content analysis (Bergman), and Q methodology/ Q factor analysis (Newman & Ramlo). Other chapters in Part II attempt the difficult task of synthesizing the current MMR literature in broad areas such as research designs (Nastasi, Hitchcock, & Brown), sampling (Collins), data analysis (Onwuegbuzie & Combs), and quality of inferences (O'Cathain). The authors of these chapters search for methodological principles (or synthesizing frameworks) that guide the conduct of MMR in specific research settings.

AN OVERVIEW OF PART III OF THE HANDBOOK

The section of the *Handbook* titled "Contemporary Applications of Mixed Methods Research" (Chapters 22 through 30) includes (1) cross-disciplinary and cross-cultural applications of MMR and (2) practical issues in the applications of MMR (e.g., pedagogy, collaboration, funding). The first edition of the *Handbook* summarized MMR in broad areas such as sociology, psychology, and evaluation research, whereas this volume contains chapters in more specialized areas such as international development evaluation (Bamberger, Rao, & Woolcock), action research (Christ), biographical research (Nilsen & Brannen), educational effectiveness research (Sammons), and intervention research in the health sciences (Song, Sandelowski, & Happ).

The Lieber and Weisner chapter in this section presents an overview of the practical issues that mixed research practitioners face, while the Dahlberg, Wittink, and Gallo chapter discusses funding and publishing issues, and the Christ chapter summarizes issues in MMR pedagogy. In Chapter 29, Harden and Thomas describe how mixed methods techniques can be used in systematic reviews of specific research areas (e.g., children's perspectives and experiences regarding healthy eating). In Chapter 23, Ivankova and Kawamura present an up-to-date analysis of the utilization of MMR from 2000 to 2008 across disciplines, chronicling the sharp increase in incidence rates.

OVERLAPS OR INTERFACES BETWEEN THE THREE PARTS

We recognize that the three circles in Figure 1.1 overlap; in fact, a handful of the *Handbook* chapters could arguably have been placed in more then one section, given that they cover diverse, yet interrelated topics. For example, Gorard's chapter on "Research Design as Independent of

Methods" could have been placed in Part II, but we put it in Part I because of its argument for universal social science research principles devoid of paradigm considerations or schisms between the QUAL and QUAN approaches (see also Onwuegbuzie & Leech, 2005).

We think that the overlaps or interfaces among the three *Handbook* sections, as depicted in Figure 1.1, are among the most valuable characteristics of the organizational structure of this volume. The topics within those overlapping areas are in the "border land" between conceptual issues and methods (Circles I and II), between methods and applications (Circles II and III), and between conceptual issues and applications (Circles I and III). As such, these topics tend to be dynamic and fluid. For instance, how are conceptual issues different from and similar to issues regarding methods and methodology? What does the overlap between these two sections consist of in terms of specific topics? How do conceptual orientations affect the selection of methods, or do they?

Authors of three Part I chapters address the overlap between Circles I and II directly by demonstrating how conceptual orientations are inextricably linked to how MMR is conducted (Greene & Hall; Hesse-Biber; Mertens et al.). On the other hand, Leech (Chapter 11), who interviewed four of the early developers of the field, reported that two of them did not include "philosophy" (or conceptual orientation) in their definitions of MMR (Alan Bryman, Janice Morse), while a third (John Creswell) included it in his 2009 interview with Leech but not in a definition given 2 years earlier (Johnson et al., 2007). The interaction (or lack of it) between conceptual and methodological issues in MMR is a complex and evolving one, which we detail later in this chapter.

Topics in the overlap between methods and applications include issues such as why and how mixed methods are differentially applied across different disciplines. For example, why are mixed methods more

easily accepted in some disciplines or specialty areas than others? Why are academic disciplines reluctant to embrace mixed methods (e.g., psychology)? Are mixed methods techniques applied similarly across disciplinary lines, or are there differences?

The overlap between conceptual orientations and applications of MMR also contains some interesting topics. Foremost among these are sociopolitical commitments, which we characterized earlier as the interaction between concerns and problems of the real world and the axiological orientations of researchers.

WHAT IS THE STRUCTURE OR "MAP" OF MIXED METHODS RESEARCH?

The *structure* or "map" of MMR emerged as an important issue as a result of Creswell's (2009, 2010) recent insightful reflections on the topic. He bases the importance of a current map of MMR on a very practical consideration: Authors submitting articles to publications such as the *Journal of Mixed Methods Research* have needed such a structure "so that they could position their study within the existing discussions" ongoing in the field (Creswell, 2009, p. 96).

Creswell (2010) compares three perspectives regarding the current field of MMR (Creswell, 2009; Greene, 2008; Tashakkori & Teddlie, 2003c) that were useful in developing the general domains in his map of MMR. He compares each of these three sources in terms of specific issues and questions that were addressed in their perspectives on MMR. (See Table 2.1 in Creswell, 2010.) The five general domains that Creswell identified are: the essence of mixed methods domain, the philosophical domain, the procedures domain, the adoption and use domain, and the political domain.

Creswell (2009) used a similar set of domains to categorize specific topics (e.g., the use of the QUAL theoretical lens in MMR, joint displays of QUAN and QUAL data) within the literature. We believe that the generation of a structure or map of MMR, *containing general domains and specific topic areas (or lines of inquiry) within those domains,* would be highly beneficial. We perceive that this structure or map would constantly evolve as new topics (or lines of inquiry) emerge and that the general domains would also be subject to change over time.

From a practical perspective, such a structure or map would allow investigators from various disciplines to situate their projects within a specific line of inquiry associated with MMR. Such a map could have great heuristic value because lines of inquiry can guide investigators toward studies similar to their own areas of interest, which could then help them in further framing their research purposes and questions. Lines of inquiry result in progressively more complex findings and serve as fertile breeding grounds for new research projects that often cross disciplinary boundaries.[5]

THE ORGANIZATIONAL STRUCTURE OF THE HANDBOOK APPLIED TO THE MAP OF MIXED METHODS RESEARCH

The three broad areas depicted in Figure 1.1 (conceptual orientations, methods and methodology, applications of MMR) *serve as the domains in our structure or map of the field of MMR.* We further this discussion in Chapter 31 where we compare the perspectives of Creswell (2010) and Greene (2008) in relation to our map of the field of MMR. Chapter 31 also describes examples of specific lines of inquiry within the broad domains that could guide future MMR studies.

◆ The Nature and General Characteristics of Mixed Methods Research

An issue discussed by Leech (2010 [this volume]), based on her interviews with early developers of MMR, concerns whether the field is ready to become more "organized and systematic"; that is, are we ready to come to consensus with regard to some basic characteristics about the nature of the field. There was disagreement on this issue, with some sentiment toward seeking greater agreement on basic issues such as language and some concern about moving to convergence too quickly.

We believe that there is general agreement on some characteristics of MMR, and we recently summarized those in a chapter in the forthcoming fourth edition of the *Handbook of Qualitative Research* (Teddlie & Tashakkori, in press). By necessity, these characteristics are very broad (and, even so, we do not expect consensus regarding them), but they at least represent a place to start the dialogue.

The first general characteristic of MMR is what we call *methodological eclecticism,* a term that has only occasionally been used in the literature (e.g., Hammersley, 1996; Yanchar & Williams, 2006). We defined methodological eclecticism earlier in this chapter as selecting and then synergistically integrating the most appropriate techniques from a myriad of QUAL, QUAN, and mixed methods to more thoroughly investigate a phenomenon of interest. This definition goes beyond simply combining QUAL and QUAN methods to cancel out respective weaknesses of one or the other. A researcher employing methodological eclecticism is a *connoisseur of methods,*[6] who knowledgeably (and often intuitively) selects the best techniques available to answer research questions that frequently evolve as a study unfolds.

While this characteristic of MMR may seem so fundamental that it need not be stated, its origins are of importance. Methodological eclecticism stems from rejection of *the incompatibility of methods thesis,* which stated that it is inappropriate to mix QUAL and QUAN methods due to fundamental differences (*incommensurability*) between the paradigms (i.e., postpositivism, constructivism) supposedly underlying those methods. The alternative to this point of view, the *compatibility thesis*, contends that combining QUAN and QUAL methods is appropriate in many research settings, denying that such "a wedding of methods is epistemologically incoherent" (Howe, 1988, p. 10). The rejection of the incommensurability of paradigms thesis[7] is a major point of demarcation between advocates of MMR and others advocating purist methodological stances.

Methodological eclecticism means that we are free to combine methods and that we do so by choosing what we believe to be the best tools for answering our questions. We have called this choice of "best" methods for answering research questions "design quality"[8] and have included it as an essential part of our framework for determining the inference quality of MMR (Tashakkori & Teddlie, 2008). While we endorse methodological eclecticism, it is also important to recognize that:

1. The best method for any given study in the human sciences may be purely QUAL or purely QUAN, rather than mixed.

2. Most seemingly purist QUAL or QUAN studies might actually include shades of the other approach (i.e., studies that may be placed on multiple continua, each including a shade of QUAL and QUAN approaches. We will discuss this later under the fourth characteristic of MMR).

3. The terms QUAL and QUAN are often proxies for different concepts/attributes across studies (i.e., QUAN approach might mean different things in different studies).

The second contemporary characteristic of MMR is *paradigm pluralism,* or the belief that a variety of paradigms may serve as the underlying philosophy for the use of mixed methods. A variety of conceptual orientations associated with mixed methods are represented in this volume, including pragmatism, critical theory, the dialectic stance, critical realism, and so forth (e.g., chapters by Biesta; Greene & Hall; Maxwell & Mittapalli; Hesse-Biber; Mertens et al.).

We believe that contemporary MMR is a kind of "big tent" and that it is both unwise and unnecessary to exclude individuals from the MMR community because their conceptual orientations are different. We agree with Denzin's (2008) paraphrase of a theme originally stated by Guba (1990): "A change in paradigmatic postures involves a personal odyssey; that is, we each have a personal history with our preferred paradigm and this needs to be honored" (p. 322). Paradigm pluralism calls for practitioners of mixed methods to honor a variety of philosophical or theoretical stances among their colleagues.

The third characteristic of contemporary MMR is *an emphasis on diversity at all levels of the research enterprise,* from the broader, more conceptual dimensions to the narrower, more empirical ones. This characteristic extends to issues beyond the aforementioned methodological eclecticism and paradigm pluralism. For example, MMR can simultaneously address a diverse range of confirmatory and exploratory questions, while single-approach studies often address only one or the other. Properly conducted MMR also provides the opportunity for an assortment of divergent conclusions and inferences due to the complexity of the data sources and analyses involved in the research.

MMR emerged partially out of triangulation literature, which has commonly been associated with the *convergence* of results. Nevertheless, there is a growing awareness that an equally important result of combining information from different sources is *divergence* or dissimilarity (e.g., Erzberger & Kelle, 2003; Greene, 2007; Johnson & Onwuegbuzie, 2004; Tashakkori & Teddlie, 2008). This emphasis on divergent results often provides greater insight into complex aspects of a phenomenon, which can then lead to more in-depth investigation of previously unexplored aspects of that phenomenon.

The fourth characteristic of contemporary MMR is *an emphasis on continua rather than a set of dichotomies* (e.g., Newman, Ridenour, Newman, & DeMarco, 2003; Niglas, 2004; Patton, 1990, 2002; Tashakkori & Teddlie, 2003c). A hallmark of MMR is its replacement of the either-or from the paradigm debates with continua that describe a range of options from across the methodological spectrum. Johnson and Gray (2010) refer to this antidualistic stance as *synechism,* which involves replacing binaries with continua.

For example, we have applied what we called the QUAL-MIXED-QUAN multidimensional continuum to a variety of research issues, including statement of research questions, designs, data analysis, and validity or inference quality (Teddlie & Tashakkori, 2009). Niglas (2010 [this volume]) has extended this discussion through her multidimensional model of research methodology, which presents a variety of philosophical and methodological continua within a multidimensional space and the placement of specific research methods within that space.

The fifth characteristic of contemporary MMR is *an iterative, cyclical approach to research,* which includes both deductive and inductive logic[9] in the same study (e.g., Krathwohl, 1993, 2004; Tashakkori & Teddlie, 1998). The cycle of research may be seen as moving from grounded results (facts, observations) through inductive logic to general inferences (abstract generalizations or theory), then from those general inferences (or theory) through deductive logic to tentative hypotheses or predictions of particular events/outcomes. Research may start at any point in the cycle: Some researchers start from theories or abstract generalizations whereas others start from observations or other data points. We believe that all MMR projects go through a full cycle at least once, regardless of their starting point (e.g., Teddlie & Tashakkori, 2009).

This cyclical approach to research may also be conceptualized in terms of the distinction between the *context of justification*

(associated with deductive logic) and the *context of discovery* (associated with inductive logic), which has recently been discussed in MMR (e.g., Johnson & Gray, 2010; Hesse-Biber, 2010 [this volume]; Teddlie & Johnson, 2009a). While practitioners of MMR recognize the logic of justification as a key part of their research, they also acknowledge the importance of the context of discovery, which involves creative insight possibly leading to new knowledge. This discovery component of MMR often, but not always, comes from the emergent themes associated with QUAL data analysis.

The sixth characteristic endorsed by many writing in MMR is *a focus on the research question (or research problem) in determining the methods employed within any given study* (e.g., Bryman, 2006; Johnson & Onwuegbuzie, 2004; Niglas, 2010; Tashakkori & Teddlie, 1998). This *centrality of the research question* was initially intended to move researchers (particularly novices) beyond intractable philosophical issues (e.g., epistemological, ontological) associated with the paradigms debate and toward the selection of methods that were best suited to investigate phenomena of interest to them.

Much has been written about the starting point for research in the past decade; that is, do researchers start with a worldview or conceptual problem, a general purpose for conducting research, a research question, or some combination thereof? Newman et al. (2003) have argued convincingly that during the past four decades, the research purpose has gained in importance relative to the research question. We maintain, however, that once researchers have decided what they are interested in studying (e.g., what motivates the study, purpose, personal/political agenda), the specifics of their research questions will determine the choice of the best tools to use, which may be QUAL, QUAN, or mixed.

The seventh characteristic of contemporary MMR is a *set of basic "signature" research designs and analytical processes,* which are commonly agreed upon, although they go by different names and diagrammatic illustrations. For example, we defined *parallel mixed designs* (Teddlie & Tashakkori, 2009) as

> a family of MM designs in which mixing occurs in an independent manner either simultaneously or with some time lapse. The QUAL and QUAN *strands* are planned and implemented in order to answer related aspects of the same questions. (p. 341, italics in original)

These designs have also been called concurrent, simultaneous, and triangulation designs, but there is much commonality across their definitions.

We call these design and analysis processes "signature" terms because they are unique to MMR and help set that approach apart from QUAL and QUAN research. Other signature design and analysis terms include sequential mixed designs, conversion mixed designs, quantitizing, qualitizing, and inherently mixed data analysis.

While there is general agreement about the existence of these unique MMR design and analytical processes, there is considerable disagreement about terminology and definitions, which increase as more complex typologies are generated. For example, many believe that a complete typology of MMR designs is impossible due to the emergent nature of the QUAL component of the research and the ability of MMR designs to mutate, while others seek agreement on a basic set of designs for the sake of simplicity and pedagogy. This disagreement is another manifestation of the tension between those who want MMR to become more systematic and organized (e.g., Tashakkori, 2009) and those who believe we are not ready for consensus (e.g., as noted in Leech, 2010).

The eighth contemporary characteristic of MMR is *a tendency toward balance and compromise that is implicit within the "third methodological community."* MMR is based on rejecting the either-or of the incompatibility thesis; therefore, we as a community are inclined toward generating a balance between the excesses exhibited by scholars at either end of the methodological spectrum, while forging a unique MMR identity. In their survey of Western thinking, Johnson and Gray (2010) similarly depict balance and compromise as one of the core principles of MMR, tracing that characteristic back to several philosophers.

In a similar vein, Denzin (2008) recapitulated three of Guba's (1990) themes regarding paradigms as follows:

- "There needs to be decline in confrontationalism by alternative paradigm proponents"

- "Paths for fruitful dialog between and across paradigms need to be explored"

- "The three main interpretive communities . . . must learn how to cooperate and work with one another." (p. 322)

We believe that most mixed methods researchers are in agreement with these themes, which call for compromise in dialogues among the three methodological communities.

The ninth characteristic of MMR is *a reliance on visual representations (e.g., figures, diagrams) and a common notational system.* MMR designs, data collection procedures, and analytical techniques lend themselves to visual representations, which can simplify the complex interrelationships among elements inherent in those processes (e.g., Creswell & Plano Clark, 2007; Dickinson, 2010 [this volume]; Ivankova, Creswell, & Stick, 2006; Maxwell & Loomis, 2003; Niglas, 2010; Onwuegbuzie & Combs, 2010 [this volume]; Tashakkori & Teddlie, 2003c; Teddlie & Tashakkori, 2009). QUAN methodologists sometimes graph experimental designs (e.g., Cook & Campbell, 1979), but MMR seems particularly prone to this form of communication. An important characteristic of these diagrams and figures is their ability to incorporate more dimensions as the processes they describe evolve.

Adding to these graphic communication devices, MMR has a common notation system that was developed early on (Morse, 1991, 2003) and continues to expand (e.g., Morse, 2010 [this volume]). This notation system has allowed practitioners of mixed methods to communicate in a convenient, shorthand manner.

◆ ## Issues and Challenges of Contemporary Mixed Methods Research

While there is some general agreement on the characteristics summarized in the previous section, there is ongoing debate about a number of important issues and controversies in MMR, which are discussed throughout the *Handbook*. Table 1.1 lists nine of these issues, which are elaborated on in this chapter and Chapter 31. In this chapter, the focus is on the general description and current status of each

issue, in addition to considerations of why the topic is important to the field. The emphasis in the last chapter is on recent developments related to some of these issues, focusing on contributions from this *Handbook* and other current sources.

Like many typologies in an evolving field, the issues in Table 1.1 are neither exhaustive nor mutually exclusive: We could discuss more topics (and do in Chapter 31), and there are obvious overlaps across some of the areas. Nevertheless, we offer these particular issues as avenues for furthering the conversation about mixed methods and encourage readers to develop their own sets of issues as they read this volume

Five of the issues in Table 1.1 were also discussed in the first edition of the *Handbook* and are explored further in this edition (i.e., conceptual issues, language, design, inference quality, and practical issues in MMR applications). Four other issues added to this edition of the *Handbook* have either emerged since the publication of the first edition or were not

Table 1.1   Nine Important Issues or Controversies in Contemporary Mixed Methods Research

Issues	Continued from first edition/ New to this volume
Conceptual stances in mixed methods research (MMR)	Continuation of paradigmatic foundations theme
The conceptual/methodological/methods interface in MMR	New
The research question or research problem in MMR	New
The language of MMR	Continuation of nomenclature and basic definitions theme
Design issues in MMR	Continuation
Analysis issues in MMR	New
Issues in drawing inferences in MMR	Continuation
Practical issues in the applications of MMR (e.g., pedagogy, collaboration, and other models, funding)	Continuation of logistics of MMR theme
Cross-disciplinary and cross-cultural applications of MMR	New

as important 7 years ago. For example, analysis issues have become more important over time: They were emphasized in only one chapter of the first edition, whereas five chapters in the second edition address these topics.

CONCEPTUAL STANCES IN MIXED METHODS RESEARCH

Issues related to conceptual stances in MMR evolved from what we labeled the "Paradigmatic Foundations of Mixed Methods Research" in the first *Handbook*. This change in title reflects a transformation in MMR thought away from paradigms as monolithic interlocking sets of philosophical assumptions and toward a more practical orientation that emphasizes individual components of philosophy and theory as guiding research activities. This change emerged from critiques of what Morgan (2007) called the *metaphysical paradigm* (e.g., Guba & Lincoln, 1994, 2005; Lincoln & Guba, 1985), which is described later in this chapter.

The following section first presents information on the purist stance and how its underlying metaphysical paradigm has been deconstructed. Then, it defines and updates recent information regarding six other conceptual stances, which practitioners of mixed methods have employed in their research. Because these conceptual stances have been presented in detail elsewhere (Greene, 2007; Teddlie & Tashakkori, 2003), we focus on contemporary developments in this discussion.

The Purist Stance and Deconstruction of the Metaphysical Paradigm

The purist stance, described initially by Rossman and Wilson (1985), states that paradigms (e.g., constructivism, postpositivism) play the leading role in determining how research studies are conducted.

Incommensurability of paradigms is assumed under this stance; research must be conducted within the guidelines established by constructivism, postpositivism, or some other monolithic paradigm. According to the purist stance, MMR as described throughout this volume is not possible because mixing methods is allowed only within a given paradigm (e.g., Greene, 2007).

An important development since the last edition of the *Handbook* has been a detailed critique of the concept of *paradigm* as used by purists, who link assumptions (e.g., epistemology, ontology) of their chosen paradigm with methodological traditions (QUAL, QUAN). While rejection of the incompatibility thesis has been a part of the mixed methods literature going back to Howe (1988), an explicit, nuanced rationale for this rejection has been more forthcoming only recently. This rejection is based on criticism of the interlinking of heterogeneous assumptions under the umbrella of what constitutes a paradigm (e.g., Biesta, 2010 [this volume]; Greene, 2007; Morgan, 2007). For example, Biesta (2010) refers to "clusters" of assumptions in his critique of paradigms, while Greene and Hall (2010 [this volume]) reiterate Biesta's conclusion that theorists should focus on individual philosophical assumptions rather than paradigm "packages."

Morgan (2007, pp. 50–54) presented the most explicit deconstruction of the term *paradigm* in the MMR literature, positing four alternative (and non-mutually exclusive) interpretations:

- paradigms as worldviews (ways of perceiving and experiencing the world)

- paradigms as epistemological stances, which Morgan called the metaphysical paradigm, which in his analysis is composed of the tripartite linkage of ontology, epistemology, and methodology

- paradigms as model examples (i.e., exemplars demonstrating how research is conducted in a field of study)

• paradigms as "shared beliefs among a community of researchers" (Morgan, 2007, p. 53) about the nature of questions, the methods of study, and so forth.

Morgan further argued that now is the time to move away from what he called the "exhausted" concept of the metaphysical paradigm to paradigms as shared beliefs in a research community. He argued that there were conceptual problems with the former position (e.g., a *strong* stand on incommensurability) and that the latter

position is a more accurate interpretation of Kuhn's (1970) use of the term. Morgan's focus on shared beliefs in a research field has contributed to an increasing emphasis on the "community of scholars" perspective (e.g., Creswell, 2010; Tashakkori & Creswell, 2008), a position that has been reinforced by Denscombe's (2008) discussion of the nature that such a community might take. Other details regarding Morgan's pragmatic approach to methodology in the social sciences are found in Box 1.1.

BOX 1.1

Morgan's Pragmatic Approach to Methodology in the Social Sciences

Morgan (2007) substitutes what he calls the *pragmatic approach* for the metaphysical paradigm as a new guiding approach to methodology in the social sciences. This pragmatic approach focuses on "methodology as an area that connects issues at the abstract level of epistemology and the mechanical level of actual methods" (p. 68). Thus, he places methodology at the center of his pragmatic approach diagramming it as the link between epistemology and methods: epistemology↔methodology↔methods (p. 69).

Furthermore, Morgan (2007) proposed an organizational framework for understanding his "pragmatic approach to social science methodology" (p. 73). This framework refers to key "pragmatic" concepts such as *abduction, intersubjectivity,* and *transferability,* which supersede the QUAL/QUAN dichotomies of induction/deduction, subjectivity/objectivity, and context/generality. Further development of these pragmatic concepts "creates a range of new opportunities for thinking about classic methodological issues in the social sciences" (p. 72).

Review of Conceptual Stances Associated with Mixed Methods Research

Each of the remaining six conceptual stances from Table 1.2 has been used (explicitly or implicitly) by groups of scholars who are practicing MMR. While the term paradigm is used in the names of some of the conceptual stances described in this section, we do not use this term in the sense of the metaphysical paradigm but rather as "shared beliefs in a research field," which "usually describes smaller research groups" (Morgan, 2007, p. 51).

The *a-paradigmatic stance* states that, for many studies conducted within real world settings especially in applied fields, paradigms or conceptual stances are unimportant to practice (e.g., Teddlie & Tashakkori, 2003). Patton (2002) expressed this stance as follows: "in real-world practice, methods can be separated from the epistemology out of which they emerged" (p. 136; quote was boldface in original).

Greene (2007) concluded from her observations in the field that much of MMR and evaluation is implemented within the frameworks of either the a-paradigmatic or purist stances. Because these two stances are almost polar opposites, a schism exists among practitioners of MMR on the importance of paradigms (or conceptual stances, to use the language employed in this section) in terms of how research is practiced in real world settings. This schism exists between individuals who might be called methods oriented as opposed to those who are conceptually oriented. Leech (2010) states that her interview with one of the early developers of MMR (Creswell) indicated that he was concerned about the growing gulf or divide between these "methodological types" and "philosopher types."

The *substantive theory stance* was discussed earlier in this chapter in the "Overview of Part I of the Handbook." Both Greene (2007) and Creswell (2010) refer to this as a position in which theoretical orientations (e.g., critical race theory, attribution theory) relevant to the research study being conducted are more important than philosophical paradigms.

Researchers who subscribe to the *complementary strengths stance* believe that MMR is possible but that the different methods must be kept as separate as feasible so that the strength of each paradigmatic position (e.g., constructivism, postpositivism) can be realized (e.g., Brewer & Hunter, 2006; Morse, 2003). Morse (2010) presents an extension of this position, which is also described later in this chapter as it relates to design issues.

Some scholars believe that *multiple paradigms* may serve as the foundation for MMR. For instance, Creswell, Plano Clark, Gutmann, and Hanson (2003) presented six advanced mixed methods designs and then argued that a single paradigm does not apply to all the designs. Creswell and his colleagues gave several examples: postpositivism might be the best paradigm for a sequential design predominantly using quantitative methods; interpretivism might be the best paradigm for a sequential design that is predominantly qualitative; and so forth.

The *dialectic stance* assumes that all paradigms have something to offer and that the use of multiple paradigms in a single study contributes to greater understanding of the phenomenon under investigation (e.g., Greene & Caracelli, 2003). Researchers employing this stance think dialectically, which involves consideration of opposing viewpoints and interaction with the "tensions" caused by their juxtaposition. Greene (2007) believes that "important paradigm differences should be respectfully and intentionally used together ... to achieve dialectical discovery of enhanced, reframed, or new understandings" (p. 69). For example, Greene and Hall (2010) present a hypothetical investigator (Michelle), whose mental model is a blend of constructivist epistemology and feminist ideology.

The *single paradigm stance* (Teddlie & Tashakkori, 2003) was initially formulated to provide a philosophical underpinning for MMR in the same manner that constructivism did for QUAL methods and postpositivism did for QUAN methods. Greene (2007) refined this position and renamed it the "alternative paradigm stance," which she described as one that "welcomes or even requires a mix of methods" and was "not troubled by issues of incommensurable philosophical assumptions" (p. 82).

Candidates for the alternative paradigm currently include *pragmatism* (e.g., Biesta, 2010; Greene & Hall, 2010; Johnson & Onwuegbuzie, 2004), *critical realism* (Maxwell & Mittapalli, 2010 [this volume]), and the *transformative paradigm* (Mertens, 2007; Mertens et al., 2010). Although pragmatism is the most popular alternative paradigm for many practitioners of MMR, there are several versions of it, ranging from Johnson and Onwuegbuzie's (2004) synthesis, which included more than 20 general characteristics, to Biesta's (2010) depiction of Deweyan pragmatism as what we might call an "*un*paradigm":

Pragmatism should not be understood as a philosophical position among others, but rather as a set of philosophical tools that can be used to address problems— not in the least problems created by other philosophical approaches and positions. One of the central ideas in pragmatism is that engagement in philosophical activity should be done in order to address problems, not to build systems. (p. 97)

Chapter 31 presents further details on these alternative conceptual stances drawing from various chapters in this volume.

THE CONCEPTUAL/ METHODOLOGICAL/ METHODS INTERFACE IN MMR

There are many differences among practitioners of mixed methods, but perhaps the most basic one is between those who are conceptually oriented (represented by Circle 1 in Figure 1.1) and those who are methods oriented (represented by Circle 2). Johnson et al. (2007) and Tashakkori (2006) have referred to this distinction as that between a "top-down" approach, in which research is driven by the conceptual or philosophical orientation of the researcher, and a "bottom-up" approach, in which research questions and methods related to those questions drive the research process.

While many conceptual and methods issues can be addressed separately, we believe that they are linked in a number of important ways, which we portray as the overlap or interface between Circles 1 and 2 in Figure 1.1. We call this overlap the "conceptual/methodological/methods interface in MMR" and put it forward as an important new issue that has emerged explicitly since the publication of the first *Handbook* in 2003.

We defined the *methodology of mixed research* earlier in this chapter as the broad inquiry logic that guides the selection of specific methods (represented by Circle 2) and which is informed by conceptual positions common to mixed methods practitioners (represented by Circle 1). We propose that the methodology of mixed research is the overlap or interface that links conceptual issues (Circle 1) and issues of methods (Circle 2) in MMR. In other words, the *methodology of mixed research* can be characterized as the mediator between conceptual and methods issues within the field, or as the point of integration between the two.[10]

Our characterization of the methodology of mixed research as the mediator or point of integration between conceptual and methods issues highlights the importance of delineating the basic principles of that methodology. What are the methodological principles that bind practitioners of MMR together regardless of differences on other issues? What are the methodological principles of MMR that set us apart as a community of scholars? At this point in the development of MMR, we believe that at least two methodological principles set it apart from other approaches, both of which were described earlier as general characteristics of MMR.

1. *Rejection of the either-or at all levels of the research process,* which leads to methodological eclecticism (i.e., the researcher as a connoisseur of methods). Practitioners of mixed methods are constantly looking for other methods to explore a research problem or answer a research question through a synergistic process that Sammons (2010 [this volume]) refers to as *mutual illumination.* We believe that MMR in the future will feature a more exotic mix of methods as researchers become more comfortable with crossing traditional methodological boundaries in answering research questions or furthering our knowledge regarding a particular research problem. Mixed methods researchers are "shamelessly eclectic" as described by Rossman and Wilson (1994), and the future of the field should feature increasingly interesting mixtures of methods (e.g., mixing geographical information systems and qualitative software; Fielding & Cisneros-Puebla, 2009). Several authors in this volume describe MMR that integrates more advanced techniques from

the QUAL and QUAN approaches, inherently mixed techniques (Teddlie & Tashakkori, 2009), and other methods unique to MMR (e.g., Bazeley; Bergman; Hesse-Biber; and Newman & Ramlo, all in this volume).

2. *Subscription to the iterative, cyclical approach to research.* Fully integrated MMR mixes top-down deductive and bottom-up inductive processes in the same study, using both confirmatory and exploratory research questions in a search for relationships between entities, the processes that underlie these relationships, and the context of these occurrences. It involves as many diverse data collection and analysis procedures as the researchers think appropriate and results in thoroughly integrated findings and inferences. These inductively and deductively based findings and inferences then generate another cycle of research as the phenomenon under study is explored at deeper levels of understanding. All truly mixed research studies go through this full cycle at least once, regardless of the initial starting point.

We believe that other methodological principles of mixed research will emerge as the field progresses and that a crucial mission for the MMR community is to discover or generate these principles over the next several years. In putting together the *Handbook*, we asked ourselves a series of questions about these methodological principles of, or frameworks for, mixed research, including the following:

- What are the methodological principles or frameworks for *research design* that distinguishes MMR from the traditional QUAL or QUAN approaches? (see Chapter 13 by Nastasi, Hitchcock, & Brown for some answers to this question)
- What are the methodological principles or frameworks for *sampling* that distinguish MMR from the traditional

QUAL or QUAN approaches? (see Chapter 15 by Collins for some answers to this question)

- What are the methodological principles or frameworks for *data analysis* that distinguish MMR from the traditional QUAL or QUAN approaches? (see Chapter 17 by Onwuegbuzie and Combs for some answers to this question)
- What are the methodological principles or frameworks for *determining the quality of inferences* that distinguishes MMR from the traditional QUAL or QUAN approaches? (see Chapter 21 by O'Cathain for some answers to this question)

We realize that these are difficult questions that are confounded by the fact that there are a number of strong voices in the field and that diversity of opinion has always been a trademark of MMR. Nevertheless, we also believe that our collective efforts in this *Handbook* mark the beginning of the delineation of methodological principles for mixed research.

THE RESEARCH QUESTION OR RESEARCH PROBLEM IN MIXED METHODS RESEARCH

While the methodological principles discussed in the previous section guide the general conduct of studies employing MMR, the research question (or research problem) determines the specific methods (QUAN, QUAL, or MMR) used within any given study. The following section briefly summarizes recent dialogue concerning the role of the research question (or problem) in MMR.

We initially referred to the "dictatorship of the research question" over a decade ago (Tashakkori & Teddlie, 1998) in an effort to bring the importance of the research question to the center of the ongoing discourse and to move researchers beyond the paradigm debate. Since then, much has been written about the importance and the attributes of MMR questions (Creswell & Plano Clark, 2007), the importance of purpose and political agenda in MMR (Mertens, 2007; Newman et al., 2003), and the necessity of correspondence between these elements and the research design, data analysis, and inferences (Tashakkori & Teddlie, 2008).

Currently, there seems to be a pervasive acknowledgment that a mixed methods project must start with a research question (or a set of questions) that drives all later stages/components of the project (even though it might get modified as the research proceeds). Consequently, the crucial question becomes: What shape should the mixed methods research question take? We have always asserted that a *mixed methods question* is one that clearly calls for a *mixed methods study*. In other words, we have favored an overarching question that potentially requires a structured quantitative approach *and* an emergent and holistic qualitative type of approach. A consequence of such a question is that it may be broken into subquestions, each requiring a different (QUAL or QUAN) approach to answer.

Such an umbrella question may lead the researcher to any one of the families of mixed designs (parallel, sequential, conversion, or a combination of these three families, as we discuss later). In some emergent sequential studies, the questions of a later phase develop as a reaction to the inferences of the previous one. In these designs, the new components are added to the initial question, forming an emergent umbrella question that incorporates all aspects of the events or behaviors under study. This is a necessary augmentation, making it possible to make integrated, meta-inferences as answers to these revised umbrella questions.

Some discussions of research questions (e.g., Creswell & Plano Clark, 2007) in

mixed methods have focused on questions about the nature of integration (i.e., how do the findings of the two strands relate to each other?). Although these questions are essential, and should be asked during the course of a mixed methods study, we do not consider them research questions. Our rationale for this assertion is that researchers do not conduct research with the purpose of finding out if components of a study agree or disagree with, or complement, each other (unless the study's main problem is to solve a methodological problem by comparing the QUAL and QUAN approaches).

A variety of issues remain to be fully explored and discussed in mixed methods community:

- the shape/format of the questions (overarching, inquiring about the nature of mixing, and so forth)

- general attributes of MMR questions (emergent, preplanned, etic, emic, exploratory, explanatory, understanding, etc.)

- components of MMR questions (one overarching question, two separate questions, other)

- functional utility of asking and answering MMR questions (i.e., the stated need for using mixed methods), and

- consequences of asking and answering MMR questions (e.g., call for social-political change)

We have included a chapter (Plano Clark & Badiee, Chapter 12) on this issue in this *Handbook* and will re-examine some of the controversies again in Chapter 31.

THE LANGUAGE OF MIXED METHODS RESEARCH

The language of MMR is a broadly defined term that we labeled "nomenclature and basic definitions" in the first edition of the *Handbook*. Language issues in MMR include both the names and definitions of the most important concepts in the field. These issues have become progressively more complex as the number of terms has increased, and the variations (often subtle) of definitions associated with those terms have multiplied. Language is very important in an emergent field such as MMR because the words we use to define the field ultimately shape how we make sense of it (e.g., Creswell, 2010). We are now at the point of needing greater precision in our construction of the language of MMR.

The following section is divided into two areas: (1) issues in creating a new language for MMR and (2) issues in creating a common language across methodological approaches (QUAN, QUAL, MMR). Taken together, these two subsections address a basic question: Should we create a new language for MMR, should we be more interested in creating a common language across methodological approaches, or should our approach be a combination of the two? We have seen evidence for both approaches over the past few years (unique MMR language; common language across the three approaches) which we detail throughout this section.

Issues in Creating a New Language for MMR

Many practitioners of MMR believe we need a language unique to the field, one that would define and describe those concepts that differentiate it from QUAL or QUAN research. For instance, as the field has developed, several authors have labored to identify and define exactly what mixed methods research is (e.g., Creswell & Plano Clark, 2007; Greene, 2007, 2008; Johnson et al., 2007; Tashakkori & Teddlie, 1998, 2003a). There has been continued debate over what the field should be called, with

variants including, but certainly not limited to: multimethod research (a historical term not used much now), multiple methods, mixed methods, mixed methodology, mixed research, integrated or integrative research, blended research, and so forth.

Fortunately, there appears to be some consensus around *mixed methods research* as the de facto term due to common usage (e.g., the name of this *Handbook* and of the leading journal in the field). We suspect that this term will endure because it now has the trappings of a brand name, widely disseminated and commonly used throughout the social and behavioral sciences.

As for the definition of MMR, Johnson et al. (2007) presented 19 alternative meanings from leaders in the field, which varied considerably in terms of specificity and content. Their constant comparative analysis of these definitions resulted in five themes, which they then incorporated into a composite definition:

> Mixed methods research is the type of research in which a researcher or team of researchers combines elements of qualitative and quantitative research approaches (e.g., use of qualitative and quantitative viewpoints, data collection, analysis, inference techniques) for the broad purposes of breadth and depth of understanding and corroboration. (Johnson et al., 2007, p. 123)

While a reader may disagree with some aspects of this definition (e.g., it is too generic or does not include a component of interest to the reader), it is difficult to criticize the process that Johnson and his colleagues employed to generate it. This systematic approach for defining terms with multiple meaning in MMR is a valuable one, which we discuss again later in this chapter.

The first step in creating a vocabulary for MMR is to identify the terms to include in it. It appears that there are at least three potential sources for a vocabulary of MMR:

• Terms that are in widespread use throughout the literature, such as the names for the signature design and analytical processes (e.g., sequential designs, quantitizing). Some of these mixed methods processes have multiple names and definitions, thereby requiring procedures such as that employed by Johnson et al. (2007) to generate composite terms and definitions.

• Blended or amalgamated terms describing MMR concepts that are a combination of QUAL and QUAN terminology, such as *inference transferability,* a term that subsumes the QUAN terms external validity and generalizability, plus the QUAL term transferability (e.g., Tashakkori & Teddlie, 1998). Such MMR blended terms emerge as typologies are generated that combine elements of the QUAN and QUAL research processes.

• Terms that describe particular research processes indigenous or unique to MMR, such as *fused data analysis* (Bazeley, 2003) or *inherently mixed data analysis* (Teddlie & Tashakkori, 2009). These terms are used to identify MMR processes that are discovered or generated by practitioners as they employ mixed methods in their research.

Box 1.2 presents a partial list of unique terms related to mixed methods data analysis that have emerged since the 1990s. The emergence of new analytical processes constitutes one of the most creative areas in MMR and often comes from researchers working on practical solutions for answering their research questions using available QUAL and QUAN data.

BOX 1.2

Partial List of Data Analysis Terms Indigenous to Mixed Methods Research

A partial list of MMR data analysis terms includes:

- crossover track analysis
- data conversion or transformation
- data importation
- fully integrated mixed data analysis
- fused data analysis
- inherently mixed data analysis
- integrated data display
- integrated data reduction
- iterative sequential mixed analysis
- morphed data analysis

- multilevel mixed data analysis
- narrative profile formation
- parallel mixed data analysis
- parallel track analysis
- quantitizing
- qualitizing
- single track analysis
- sequential mixed data analysis
- typology development
- warranted assertion analysis

The vocabulary of MMR will constantly expand as additional blended and indigenous terms are generated. Some terms will be proposed and defined, but then discarded due to lack of common usage or conceptual clarity. The term *multimethod,* for instance, has been largely discarded in MMR because it connotes a limited type of mixing of methods (i.e., keeping the QUAL and QUAN components largely separated until the end of the study), which has been superseded by approaches that emphasize the integration of methods across the entire research process.

Other terms will survive because they find common usage and there is general agreement about what they mean. For example, the term *iterative sequential mixed analysis* has been used (e.g., Teddlie & Tashakkori, 2009) to describe the analysis of data from a sequential study with more than two phases (e.g., QUAL→ QUAN→QUAL). Examples of iterative sequential mixed analysis are found throughout the literature (e.g., Kumagai, Bliss, Daniels, & Carroll, 2004; Tolman & Szalacha, 1999) and the concept has been applied specifically to research conducted over the Internet (Teddlie, Tashakkori, & Johnson, 2008). The term iterative sequential mixed analysis will most likely become a part of the lexicon of MMR, or another more inclusive term will evolve that describes the types of analyses associated with complex sequential mixed designs.

Glossaries of MMR terms have begun appearing (e.g., Morse & Niehaus, 2010; Tashakkori & Teddlie, 2003a; Teddlie & Tashakkori, 2009). The compilation of these glossaries has revealed a problem that MMR has faced since its emergence as a separate methodological approach: inconsistency in terminology and definitions (e.g., Bryman, 2008). These inconsistencies have included (1) having a number of different definitions for the same term and (2) having a number of different names for the same concept. For example, we included a glossary in the first edition of the *Handbook* with some 150 terms, many of which had multiple definitions (e.g., mixed methods had four different meanings) indicating that different authors thought the term was important, yet disagreed as to its exact meaning.

As noted in the introduction to this section, we need greater precision and consistency in the language of MMR, which we as a community of scholars are currently constructing. While such precision and consistency entails hard work, such as that expended by Johnson and his colleagues (2007) in developing their composite definition of *mixed methods research,* we believe that such work will yield great benefits for the field. One suggestion[11] for accomplishing this is the generation of a dictionary of MMR terms similar to that developed for qualitative inquiry by Schwandt (1997). Such a dictionary could go into detail regarding the etiology and various meanings associated with MMR terms. Chapter 31 presents more details on this suggestion and other issues related to the further development of the language of MMR.

Generating a Common Language Across Methodological Approaches

If there are unique languages for QUAN research, QUAL research, and MMR, then researchers need to be *trilingual* to converse across methodological boundaries. Although this trilingualism may be necessary for the time being, we believe that a long-term goal of mixed methods practitioners should be to generate a language that identifies common processes across the methodological approaches. Such a language would encompass those processes that are highly similar to one another across multiple applications.

At this stage in the development of thought about this language, it is unclear how many common processes there are and the extent of their similarities. It is clear, however, that many specific methods or techniques are not subsumable (i.e., cannot be placed into a broader or more comprehensive cross-methodological category) because they have no equivalent in the other languages, or equivalents have not yet been developed. The search for terms for this common language involves looking for what Gorard (2010) calls the universal logic of all research.

The belief that some limited vocabulary of common terms is possible stems from the rejection of either-or dualisms, which is at the heart of MMR. Practitioners of MMR replace these dualisms with continua that describe a range of options from one end of the methodological spectrum to the other. Once a set of multidimensional continua has been substituted for the dichotomy, it is possible to look for the commonality that binds each continuum (dimension, aspect) together. For example, Sandelowski, Voils, and Knafl (2009), in discussing the nature of data, concluded that "qualitative and quantitative data are not so much different kinds of data as *these data are experiences* formed into, for example, words or numbers, respectively" (p. 209, italics added). The commonality that binds the dichotomy of QUAL and QUAN data together is the "something experienced" that generated the data in the first place. We believe that as mixed methods data analysis evolves, "researchers will think of data less in terms of words or numbers and more in terms of transferable units of information that happen to be initially generated in one form or the other" (Teddlie & Tashakkori, 2009, p. 283).

Practitioners of MMR are in a unique position because their approach to research allows them to look across diverse methodological applications for the commonalities that bind similar processes together. For example, one of the distinguishing characteristics of MMR discussed earlier in this chapter is the "iterative, cyclical approach to research," which combines the inductive processes typically associated with QUAL research and the deductive processes typically associated with QUAN research. This cycle of research is a term that could be included in a common methodological language because it contains elements associated with all three approaches.

We recently (Teddlie & Tashakkori, 2009, p. 282) generated a list of common analytical processes used in both QUAL and QUAN research. These processes are cognitively interchangeable, although one uses numbers and the other employs words as data. For example, a practitioner of MMR

knows that cluster analysis employs the same modus operandi as the categorizing process of the constant comparative method: that is, maximizing between-group variation and minimizing within-group variation. Other examples include: comparing analyses from one part of a sample with analyses from another part of the sample; comparing actual results with expected results; and contrasting components of research design or elements to find differences. Recognition of these common processes is a step in the direction of developing a language that crosses methodological lines.

DESIGN ISSUES IN MIXED METHODS RESEARCH

Design typologies have long been an important feature of MMR, starting with Greene, Caracelli, and Graham (1989) writing in the field of evaluation and Morse (1991) in nursing. The reasons for the importance of MMR design typologies include their role in (1) establishing a common language for the field, (2) providing possible blueprints for researchers who want to employ MM designs, (3) legitimizing MMR by introducing designs that are clearly distinct from those in QUAN or QUAL research, and (4) providing useful tools for pedagogical purposes (i.e., having students compare and contrast alternative typologies).

In the context of these calls for developing mixed methods design typologies or prototypes, a number of frameworks have been proposed by the community of mixed methods scholars, often with both overlapping and divergent components and/or different names/labels. For example, we discussed a signature design type earlier in this chapter, which we called the *parallel mixed design* (e.g., Teddlie & Tashakkori, 2009) and which has had a number of different names over time (e.g., concurrent, simultaneous, triangulation designs). These designs have been defined similarly yet have differed on key particulars such as whether or not the QUAL and QUAN phases of the study occurred at the same time, or with some time lapse, or both.

It is apparent that the conceptualization of mixed methods designs has undergone substantial changes over the past decade. For example, our typology of mixed designs has evolved considerably from the initial version (Tashakkori & Teddlie, 1998) up through the latest edition (Tashakkori, Brown, & Borghese, 2009; Tashakkori & Newman, 2010; Tashakkori & Teddlie, in progress). We discuss particulars of our latest framework later in this section.

Recently, some authors have contended that there is an overemphasis on research design typologies (e.g., Adamson, 2004; Bazeley, 2009), arguing that other areas (e.g., data analysis) should be stressed more. Some have suggested a need for a set number of prespecified designs, while others contend that MMR design typologies can never be exhaustive due to the iterative nature of MMR projects (i.e., new components or strands might be added during the course of a project). This is an important point; many inexperienced researchers want a design "menu" from which to select the "correct" one, similar to the menus provided in QUAN research (e.g., Shadish, Cook, & Campbell, 2002). In contrast, researchers using mixed methods are encouraged to continuously re-examine the results from one strand of a study compared to the results from another and to make changes both in the design and data collection procedures accordingly.

Although some find the lack of consensus regarding the specific number and types of designs disconcerting, others believe that this is a healthy sign of the growth of the mixed methods community. The ultimate value of these typologies lies in their ability to provide researchers with viable design options to choose from and build on (i.e., modify, expand, combine) when they are planning or implementing their MMR studies. We acknowledge the fact that this diversity makes it more difficult to teach and to learn mixed methodology. Students often

complain that there are too many design types, or too many suggestions about how to plan a mixed methods study. However, we are confident that over time, useful and common components of different frameworks will be identified and reconciled by the MMR community, especially by the same group (doctoral students and young scholars) that is currently critical of what members consider to be unnecessary complexities.

Perhaps, these differences would be made more salient if we briefly review three different frameworks for planning and implementing mixed methods designs: those of Janice Morse, Jennifer Greene, and our own. Although other perspectives are equally valuable, we chose these three because they represent the diversity of ideas underlying almost all design frameworks and demonstrate many of the ongoing issues related to MMR designs.

We discussed Morse's (1991, 2003, 2010) design typology earlier in this chapter with regard to the common notational system and the complementary strengths stance. In Morse's system, the priority of one method over the other is an important dimension predetermined before data collection starts. Each study has a theoretical or primary drive (inductive or deductive) that determines the overall purpose of the study, a core component (primary or main study), and a supplementary component (which is incomplete by itself and is regarded as complementary to the core component). Morse argues that MMR is possible, but that the QUAN and QUAL components must be kept as separate as possible so that the strengths of each paradigmatic position can be realized.

In Morse's system, there is no mixing of primary drives. This position is, of course, quite different from that generally endorsed in the contemporary field of MMR, where a more thorough mixing of methods is a given. Morse's (2010) latest version of her typology includes the "point of interface" (where the two components join in either the data analysis or narrative of the results) and contains interesting diagrams of the relationships between the core and supplementary components of the research project, designated as left and right pathways.

Greene (2007) contends that researchers cannot divorce method from "assumptive frameworks" when designing MMR studies; therefore, she encourages mixing those frameworks in single research studies. Her designs are anchored in mixing methods for five basic purposes, which emerged from Greene et al. (1989): triangulation, complementarity, development, initiation, and expansion. Caracelli and Greene (1997) distinguished between *component designs,* in which the methods are connected or mixed only at the level of inference, and *integrated designs,* in which the methods are integrated throughout the course of the study.

Greene (2007) presented two examples of component designs (convergence, extension) and four examples of integrated designs (iteration, blending, nesting or embedding, mixing for reasons of substance or values). These six examples of MMR designs map onto the five basic purposes for mixing, with each example aligned with one or two of the original purposes. Greene (2007) concludes that designing an MMR study does *not* involve following a formula or set of prescriptions, but rather is "an artful crafting of the kind of mix that will best fulfill the intended purposes for mixing within the practical resources and contexts at hand" (p. 129).

In our approach to MMR, we have always treated design as separable from research purpose. That is not to deny the importance of purpose; obviously, if you did not have a purpose for doing a study, you would not have research questions, and you would probably not be conducting research at all. We think purpose is a complex, psycho-socio-political concept that motivates any given research project, and we believe each individual has a multiplicity of purposes for doing research, ranging from advancing his or her career to understanding complex phenomena, to improving society.

As noted above, our design typology has evolved as MMR has developed over the past decade (Tashakkori & Teddlie, 1998, 2003c; Teddlie & Tashakkori, 2009). In the latest edition of our typology (Tashakkori et al., 2009; Tashakkori & Newman, 2010; Tashakkori & Teddlie, in progress), we have made an effort to simplify it, while also incorporating as many recent developments in the field as possible. We have identified four *families* of designs in our typology, three of which are basic: parallel, sequential, and conversion. The fourth one, fully integrated, is a complex and iterative type that potentially includes combinations of the other three. These families are based on what we call "type of implementation process"; that is, how does the integration of the QUAL and QUAN strands actually occur when conducting a study.

We have subdivided each of the three basic families of designs into three variations based on the data sources: multiple samples, same/subsample, and multilevel samples/data. In the first variation, QUAL and QUAN data are collected from different individuals or are not linked. In the second variation, both data types are available for at least some individuals and are linked in one form or another (this includes the conversion of some data to another type). In the third, qualitative data are collected at one level of a social structure (e.g., parents), while quantitative data are collected at another (e.g., children), and are linked during analysis and inference.

This 3 × 3 combination produces nine basic design options. The fourth family of designs (fully integrated) incorporates multiple forms of these nine options, often in an iterative and emergent manner. Increasingly, MMR studies appear to be using this last design family by combining the basic configurations, often with multiple types/sources of data.

We conclude this section by re-iterating a few characteristics of the three typologies we have discussed. All three reflect coherent and internally consistent perspectives, which remain viable as they have evolved over time, will continue to change in interesting ways related to developments in the field, and are heuristic in terms of informing MMR dissertations and other projects.

Our perspective is similar to Greene's orientation in that we distinguish between whether integration occurs at only one stage of the process (for us, the experiential stage) or throughout the study. Our latest solution to this thorny issue is the distinction between mixed and *quasi-mixed designs,* defining the latter as designs in which two types of data are collected and analyzed, but there is little or no integration of findings and *inferences* from the study. On the other hand, we differ with Morse's typology in that we do not believe in the necessity of pre-specifying a priority/dominance of QUAL or QUAN approaches because we believe that any single study is composed of multiple criteria, each conceptualized as a continuum, rather than a single dichotomy between core and supplementary components.

We should also note that although there are differences among the three typologies in terms of how they conceptualize MMR design, it is possible to select components of each and graft them on to the others. For example, in each of the 10 possible variations of design in our framework, one might make decisions about priority of QUAL or QUAN approach, if that is deemed useful in answering the research questions. For example, in the sequential family of designs with multiple samples, one might have a predominantly QUAN study with a less important QUAL strand that involves the collection of data on a different group of individuals.

One way of making sense out of the myriad of design typologies is to consider the criteria or dimensions on which designs differ (e.g., Greene, 2007; Teddlie & Tashakkori, 2009). Most theorists differentiate MMR designs on the basis of sequence (e.g., independent phases, or phases that are rooted in each other on a pre-planned or emergent manner). Some believe in the necessity of specifying the dominance or priority of a QUAL or QUAN approach, while others see little value in it. We recently identified seven criteria that are used in MMR typologies together with the design questions they address (Teddlie & Tashakkori, 2009).

We have suggested that when planning projects, researchers should consider these criteria, select those most salient to their particular study within its specific context, and then emphasize those dimensions in their selection of a specific design. For instance, if the researcher anticipates that his or her research question is best answered using primarily QUAL methods, but that QUAN methods may also meaningfully contribute to the project, then priority of approach is a salient design characteristic. If it is unclear whether the QUAL or QUAN sources will ultimately be most important in the results and inferences, which is more often the case at least in the MMR we have conducted, then priority of approach is not a salient design dimension.

ANALYSIS ISSUES IN MIXED METHODS RESEARCH

Analysis issues were not included as a major issue in the first edition of the *Handbook,* but there has been a growing awareness of their importance since then. Bazeley (2009) recently concluded that an indicator of the maturation of MMR would come when it moves from "a literature dominated by foundations and design typologies" toward a field "in which there are advances in conceptualization and breakthroughs derived from analytical techniques that support integration" (p. 206). Using that definition, MMR appears to be headed toward greater maturity. There are several trends in the literature that indicate the growing attention that is being paid to analytical issues in MMR.

The first trend involves the publication of a number of syntheses of analytical techniques in MMR, including Onwuegbuzie and Teddlie's (2003) chapter in the first

Handbook. These authors presented a framework for analyzing mixed data, which identified 12 pre-analysis considerations and a seven-stage generic MMR analysis model. This chapter was an important step in that it followed up on previous descriptions of mixed methods data analysis (e.g., Caracelli & Greene, 1993; Li, Marquart, & Zercher, 2000; Sandelowski, 2000; Tashakkori & Teddlie, 1998) and helped to generate a dialogue regarding MMR data analysis as a separate issue. Additional frameworks for mixed methods data analysis have been published recently, but they are often linked to specific design typologies (e.g., Creswell & Plano Clark, 2007; Greene, 2007; Morse & Niehaus, 2010; Teddlie & Tashakkori, 2009).

A second trend in MMR data analysis has been a dramatic increase in the identification of data analysis processes indigenous to MMR as exemplified by Box 1.2. These processes include general analytical procedures (e.g., data conversion); specific techniques within more general analytical processes (e.g., crossover track analysis within parallel mixed data analysis); and complex iterative mixed data analyses (e.g., iterative sequential data analysis, Teddlie & Tashakkori, 2009). The discovery or generation of these MMR data analysis procedures is a manifestation of the creative energy that is being expended in this area.

A third trend is the generation of new MMR analyses that borrow from or adapt existing procedures in the QUAL or QUAN traditions. There are two examples in this volume: Bergman's adaptation of QUAL and QUAN content analysis strategies in what he calls hermeneutic content analysis (Chapter 16) and Newman and Ramlo's mixed methods adaptation of Q methodology and Q factor analysis (Chapter 20).

A fourth trend involves MM researchers applying the analytical frameworks that have previously been used in either the QUAL or QUAN tradition in developing analogous techniques within the other tradition (e.g. Greene, 2007; Teddlie & Tashakkori, 2009). This requires both appropriate training in the QUAN and QUAL approaches and the ability to creatively see analogous processes from the mixed methods perspective.

The final trend is probably the most important: computerized analysis of MMR data sources and analyses (e.g., Bazeley, 2003, 2010). Bazeley (2003) has called this process *fused data analysis,* which she describes as follows:

> Software programs for statistical analysis and for qualitative data analysis can be used side-by-side for parallel or sequential analyses of mixed form data. In doing so, they offer . . . the capacity of qualitative data analysis (QDA) software to incorporate quantitative data into a qualitative analysis, and to transform qualitative coding and matrices developed from qualitative coding into a format which allows statistical analysis. . . . The "fusing" of analysis then takes the researcher beyond blending of different sources to the place where the same sources are used in different but interdependent ways in order to more fully understand the topic at hand. (p. 385)

Bazeley (2010) continues this discussion by presenting a variety of strategies in which computer software programs foster the integration of QUAL and QUAN data by either combining them or converting them.

There are several interesting questions related to analysis issues in MMR including the following:

1. Are MMR data analysis issues separate from research design issues, or are the two processes inextricably bound? What is the relationship between the design and analysis decisions that practitioners of mixed methods make as they conduct their research?

2. Can the diverse indigenous and adapted MMR data analysis procedures (e.g., those listed in Box 1.2) be incorporated within a single mixed data analysis

framework, or are the criteria that practitioners of MMR have used to create their mixed analysis typologies too divergent for a single framework? As Greene (2008) asked, is "integrated analysis . . . a mixed methods methodological area in which practice may always take the lead?" (p. 15).

3. If an inclusive framework for mixed methods data analysis is possible, what shape will it take? Onwuegbuzie and Combs (2010) have furthered the discussion by proposing a "meta-framework of mixed analysis strategies," which we discuss along with other analysis issues in Chapter 31.

ISSUES IN DRAWING INFERENCES IN MIXED METHODS RESEARCH

Scholars in both the QUAL and QUAN traditions have used the term *inference* to denote the process of making sense of the results, or the outcomes, of the research process (i.e., conclusions, constructions, etc.). We initially used the term in an attempt to differentiate three distinct components of research projects (Tashakkori & Teddlie, 1998): *data* (as an input to the process of meaning making in research), *data analysis* (as the process of applying a set of tools to summarize the data and link its components), and *inference* (as the outcome of the process of meaning making). These distinctions emerged from the need to differentiate between standards/audits for assessing quality in research: We called for distinguishing (1) data quality from (2) data analysis quality/adequacy from (3) the quality of conclusions that are made on the basis of the findings or results. (In Chapter 31, we refer to this as a systems approach to assessing the quality of research projects). Although some scholars still confuse data with results/findings or with the final outcome of research, there is growing awareness that inferences are clearly separate from the other two and must be explicitly evaluated for quality.

Aside from the research methodology literature, in cognitive psychology, the term inference has been used in discussions of inductive and deductive reasoning that results in causal and noncausal conclusions in everyday life (i.e., by "everyday pragmatists," as labeled by Biesta, 2010). For example, Sternberg (2009) suggests that "one approach to studying inductive reasoning is to examine **causal inferences**— how people make judgments about whether something causes something else" (p. 515, bold in original). He also discusses inference as a complex process of making conclusions about relationships (causal or otherwise) in everyday life: "The great puzzle of inductive reasoning is how we manage to infer useful general principles based on the huge number of observations of covariation to which we are constantly exposed" (Sternberg, 2009, p. 515). Smith and Kosslyn (2007) present a slightly different view of inference which links it to "category knowledge" in reasoning and cognition:

Indeed, the whole point of categorizing is to allow you to draw *inferences*, namely, to allow you to derive information not explicitly present in a single member of a category but available because of knowledge of the characteristics of the group or groups to which it belongs. Once you categorize a perceived entity, many useful inferences can follow. (p. 149, italics in the original)

Our definition of inference has roots in cognitive psychology, philosophy, and research methodology. We have defined it as "a researcher's construction of the relationships among people, events, and variables as well as his or her construction of respondents' perceptions, behaviors, and feelings and how these relate to each other in a coherent and systematic manner" (Tashakkori & Teddlie, 2003c, p. 692).

Although inferences are the most important aspects or outcomes of any study, little has been written about their characteristics, the process of making them, and possible standards for assessing their quality. An interesting and complex question to answer in MMR is: How do we make inferences on the basis of the results of QUAL and QUAN analyses of our data? This question is closely related to one that has been asked about the naïve analysis of events and behaviors. Discussing the process of inference in everyday human problem solving, Sternberg (2009) asks, "On what basis do people draw inferences? People generally use both bottom-up strategies and top-down strategies for doing so" (p. 519). Bottom-up strategies are "based on observing various instances and considering the degree of variability across instances" (p. 519). Top-down cognitive strategies, on the other hand, include "selectively searching for constancies within many variations, and selectively combining concepts and categories" (p. 519). We believe that the process of making inferences in research follows a similar model, but it is more formal and systematic. We will expand this idea in Chapter 31, when we refer to mixed methods as a *humanistic methodology*.

How do we make inferences in MMR? We have made an effort to identify possible steps in generating inferences in MMR (see Teddlie & Tashakkori, 2009, pp. 289–293). A major part of that process includes keeping one's research questions in the foreground because at the most basic level, inferences are answers to research questions. At the most abstract level, inferences are mini-theories and explanations for explaining events and behaviors. From this point of view, inferences fall on a continuum from the more specific to the more general; that is, they include conclusions that range from the meaning of a specific event, behavior, or relationship to global explanations of why events, behaviors, or relationships occur. Obviously, the former is more concrete, and the latter is more abstract. By virtue of being concrete, the former is more specific to the context in which the behaviors or events were observed, whereas the latter is much less situation specific.

Perhaps the most fundamental step in making inferences is to examine each part of a set of data analysis outcomes (results) separately and then evaluate how effectively it answers a research question/purpose set forth earlier. These results might be themes obtained from content analysis, numerical summaries of observed/measured variables, or complex outcomes of inferential statistics. In each case, one might ask: What does this mean? What does this tell me about the behavior or event under investigation? How does this answer my research (specific) question? In MMR, these initial queries are made from the results of both QUAL and QUAN data analyses, which are compared and contrasted on an ongoing basis, then integrated to create a more general answer to each specific research question. After going through this first stage of making inferences, one needs to compare and contrast the answers to different questions (actually, aspects of the same overarching mixed methods question) and to assess conceptual variations and similarities between them. This is the stage in which the more abstract/global explanations are found for the events and behaviors.

How do we know that our inferences are credible or believable, and not merely a function of our imaginations? This question has received more attention in the literature than the question regarding how to make inferences in MMR. At least three broad types of answers have been offered so far in the literature (Dellinger & Leech, 2007; Onwuegbuzie & Johnson, 2006; Tashakkori & Teddlie, 2003c). We have used social cognition as a model by focusing on the similarities between the researcher and the naïve analyst of behaviors and events in everyday life (the "everyday pragmatist"). In this model, quality of inferences is assessed simultaneously by examining (a) the process of reaching the results that they are based on (i.e., *design quality,* Tashakkori & Teddlie, 2003c) and (b) the attributes of the conclusions themselves (i.e., *interpretive rigor*). The degree of confidence that one has in a conclusion is impacted by evaluations of these two components of the study.

The first criterion (design quality) asks if a suitable design was used and implemented adequately, if the components of the design fit together seamlessly, and if the data were analyzed in an efficacious and comprehensive manner. The second criterion (interpretive rigor) examines the degree of consistency of conclusions within the study, consistency with the state of knowledge about the phenomenon or behavior, consistency of conclusions reached by multiple interpreters of the same findings, distinctiveness of a specific (preferred) conclusion from other plausible explanations of the same results, and the degree of correspondence between the conclusions and the research questions of a mixed methods study. Consistent with this last point (correspondence with initial mixed methods questions) is the assessment of the degree to which the findings of various strands of a study are effectively integrated toward developing a more advanced understanding of the phenomenon or behavior under investigation.

A second answer to the question of how we know if our inferences are credible or believable concerns the legitimacy of the conclusions. Onwuegbuzie and Johnson's (2006) *legitimation model* searches for quality by examining the consistency within various components of the study (including the consistency between the questions, design, and inferences), adequacy of representing both an emic and an etic view, and adequacy of integrating the QUAL and QUAN components of design (e.g., sampling, analysis). The authors also add a consequential component by examining the degree to which the consumers of MMR value the meta-inferences that are obtained from the results of QUAL and QUAN findings.

This consequential element is also present in the third answer to the question of inference quality, proposed by Dellinger and Leech (2007). Their *validation framework* is heavily rooted in the idea of construct validity, which they perceive as

"encompassing all validity evidence" (Dellinger & Leech, 2007, p. 316).

In a previous section, we discussed language issues in MMR, including the development of a common language across methodological approaches. Perhaps, the term inference is being increasingly used as a common or "bridge" term within the QUAL, QUAN, and MMR literatures.[12]

PRACTICAL ISSUES IN THE APPLICATIONS OF MIXED METHODS RESEARCH

This section on practical issues in MMR evolved from what we called the "logistics of conducting mixed methods research" in the first *Handbook,* which included two issues: pedagogy and models for professional competency/collaboration. These two topics are again featured in this edition of the *Handbook,* plus other practical issues that have emerged, including the funding of MMR projects. All of these issues are discussed in Part III of the *Handbook,* which is depicted as Circle III in Figure 1.1.

Many of the practical topics discussed in Part III of the *Handbook* revolve around how a researcher practices methodological eclecticism, or how one becomes a *connoisseur of methods.* How does a researcher learn how to select and integrate the most appropriate techniques from a myriad of strategies (QUAL, QUAN, mixed) to thoroughly investigate a research question or problem of interest? The experienced practitioner of mixed methods seems to almost intuitively select the design and procedures that best fit the research question/problem under study, but how does he or she get to that point?

In the recent past (before the turn of the 21st century), there was only one answer to that question: through the process of applying research tools, which individuals had acquired from a patchwork of graduate and undergraduate coursework and prior experiences, to answer complex questions or problems that could be not be addressed properly within the QUAN or QUAL traditions alone. Leech's (2010) description of how the early developers of MMR began to combine QUAL and QUAN components in their work describes how this sometimes happened: Researchers were often trained in traditions that emphasized numerical data collection and statistical analysis, picked up some skills in narrative data collection and thematic analysis as their careers developed (due to their interest in those topics), and then found themselves applying all that they knew about research methods in studies of complex social phenomena. In the preface to this volume, we also shared with you our own experiences and struggles in this process of learning MMR through a "bottom-up approach" to research. This process of intuitively using a variety of methods and techniques and drawing conclusions based on syntheses of the various types of evidence available is also described by Gorard (2010).

In the first *Handbook,* we described the lack of formal training in mixed methods as "the failure of pedagogy" and briefly described the handful of textbooks that covered mixed methods at that time and the even smaller number of articles that addressed pedagogical issues (e.g., Creswell, Tashakkori, Jensen, & Shapley, 2003; Tashakkori & Teddlie, 2003b). As detailed throughout this *Handbook,* there has been an explosion in the number of texts devoted to mixed research since that time, and a corresponding upsurge in the number of universities offering formal courses in mixed research as chronicled by Christ (2009, 2010 [this volume]), Earley (2007), and Niglas (2007).

Recent articles on pedagogical practice have been quite valuable, such as Earley's (2007) account of the 12-step process he used to develop a syllabus for his MMR course and Christ's (2009) description of the generation for his students of a research proposal process with eight interactive features. Nevertheless, the first generation of instructors of mixed methods courses must still face some problematic areas, including the complexity of teaching the numerous design typologies that were discussed earlier in this chapter (e.g., Earley, 2007, reported that students in his classes counted a total of 52 different design possibilities). Several of these pedagogical issues are discussed in this volume by Christ (Chapter 25), including a detailed description of how he used action research to improve his introductory and advanced mixed methods courses.

Nevertheless, pedagogy tells only part of the story regarding how a researcher becomes a *methodological connoisseur.* In the previous *Handbook,* we presented three models for what we called professional competency and collaboration:

- A single researcher develops dual competencies in both QUAL and QUAN methods to the point that he or she can conduct "solo" mixed methods investigations. This dual competency is the ultimate goal for the *connoisseur of methods* we have been discussing, but critics are skeptical that this is a realistic goal for most researchers, who do not have the training or field experiences to be competent in both QUAL and QUAN methods. We will discuss this in more detail in Chapter 31.

- The second model solved the problem of dual competency by proposing a collaborative team approach to mixed research consisting of members with competency in one of the two traditions (i.e., collaborative teams consisting of one or more qualitatively oriented researchers and one or more quantitatively oriented researchers). Such collaborative efforts are not uncommon in large-scale studies in the health sciences or in studies conducted in complex educational or evaluation settings.

- The third model calls for each team member in a mixed study to have a *minimum level of competency* in QUAL and QUAN methods, plus expertise in one or the other (e.g., Shulha & Wilson, 2003; Teddlie & Tashakkori, 2003). A problem with the second approach (teams consisting of qualitatively and quantitatively oriented researchers) is that without minimum competency in both types of research, team members may not be able to communicate effectively because they lack a "common" methodological language (discussed earlier in this chapter). We concluded that the third model (minimum competency model) is probably prerequisite for the second one (the team approach) to actually work in practice.

Lieber and Weisner (2010 [this volume]) discuss the value of collaborative teams consisting of colleagues with different training and experiential backgrounds in terms of generating a "respectful environment" in which team members can struggle to design and carry out the best mixed research possible given the context of the study. They also describe the CHILD project, a longitudinal family and child developmental study, conducted by a team consisting of members from the fields of education, anthropology, psychology, statistics, family studies, and so forth.

Similarly one of the co-editors of this volume (Teddlie) participated in a longitudinal educational effectiveness project (Louisiana School Effectiveness Study) with a core team of 11 investigators from education, psychology, statistics, nursing, and research methods. Five of the team members were self-identified as mixed methods practitioners, while three maintained a primarily QUAN orientation, and three were primarily QUAL in orientation. These varieties of disciplinary/training backgrounds and research orientations led to lively group interchanges in which individual schools were discussed. These discussions were tape-recorded and were a primary source for six extensive mixed methods case studies, which appeared in Teddlie and Stringfield (1993).

Experiences on such mixed methods research teams can do much to create and enhance methodological connoisseurship. Researchers become more competent in various research methodologies as they work collaboratively on projects where they see others applying problem-solving skills to research issues from a methodological perspective at least slightly different from their own. For instance, the Jang, McDougall, Pollon, Herbert, and Russell (2008) study of "schools in challenging circumstances" quoted one of the graduate students involved in the study as follows:

> My participation in a mixed methods project expanded my horizons from research methodology as a debate between paradigms that dealt with "people versus numbers" and from an understanding that abstract debates between "either/or" actually, and quite compellingly, dialectically resolve into an "and." (p. 243)

This qualitatively oriented graduate researcher had originally been concerned about how she could contribute to the QUAN part of the study. She commented that her "rich" understanding of the QUAL data led her to seek a better understanding of the statistical analyses and graphic displays, which she discovered to be "full of life." This novice researcher appears to be in the beginning stages of becoming a methodological connoisseur.

Other practical issues presented in this edition of the *Handbook* include funding and writing mixed methods, both of which are discussed by Dahlberg, Wittink, and Gallo (Chapter 30). The Dahlberg et al. approach to both topics stresses practical considerations: they see their mission as providing "the reader with tangible strategies at the point where the epistemological rubber meets the road—to publication and grant funding" (p. 777, this volume). Creswell (2010) provides further information on funding opportunities for MMR. These and other practical issues are discussed further in Chapter 31.

CROSS-DISCIPLINARY AND CROSS-CULTURAL APPLICATIONS OF MIXED METHODS RESEARCH

Cross-disciplinary and cross-cultural applications of MMR were not included as a major issue in the first edition of the *Handbook,* but the recent diffusion of mixed research throughout the human sciences and across academic communities around the world is a topic of growing interest in the field. Much of the dynamic energy within MMR comes from this expansion into other disciplines and cultures. There are several interesting trends in this cross-disciplinary and cross-cultural dispersion, which we briefly introduce in this section, including the wide variance in adoption rates of MMR that is apparent within academic discipline and specialty areas.

MMR has been rapidly expanding into all disciplines in the social and behavioral sciences over the past decade, as indicated by several studies of *incidence rates* (counts of the absolute number of MMR articles published per year) and *prevalence rates* (the proportion of research studies published in a given field that are mixed in nature). Although several incidence and prevalence rates studies have been published (e.g., Hart, Smith, Swars, & Smith, 2009), we briefly review information from two recent analyses (Alise & Teddlie, in press; Ivankova & Kawamura, 2010 [this volume]) as evidence of trends in the cross-disciplinary adoption of MMR.

Ivankova and Kawamura's Chapter 23 documents three interesting trends in the incidence rates of empirical mixed research published in several major databases from 2000 to 2008. First, there was a dramatic increase in the number of articles that were identified as "mixed methods" from only 10 in 2000 to 243 in 2008. This sharp increase was especially noticeable after 2003, when the first edition of the *Handbook* was published and the term *mixed methods* became more widely used. Second, there was a wide variance in the use of mixed methods across disciplines, with the health and medical fields accounting for 47% of the total number of mixed articles published, education accounting for 21%, and the rest of the fields accounting for the remaining 32%. Altogether mixed research studies were

published in 70 specific fields within broader disciplines, indicating the utility of MMR across a wide spectrum of academic specialty areas. Third, when looking at national origin of the first author of the articles, researchers from more than 30 countries contributed to the database, with over half of those from the United States, another 20% from the United Kingdom, and a significant number of the remainder from Canada and Australia (compared to all the other countries).

The prevalence rates study conducted by Alise and Teddlie (in press) compared the proportion of articles employing QUAL, QUAN, or mixed methods within "elite" journals in four disciplines. Education and nursing were selected to represent applied disciplines, while sociology and psychology were chosen to represent "pure" or basic disciplines using the Biglan (1973) classification system. The prevalence rates for mixed methods studies was considerably higher (16%) in the applied disciplines compared to the pure or basic disciplines (6%). The higher prevalence rates for MMR in applied fields were expected because MMR originated in areas such as nursing, education, and evaluation. The prevalence rate for QUAN studies in elite journals in psychology was 93%, with the other 7% classified as mixed.

Incidence and prevalence rates studies are crucial at this time for practitioners of mixed methods because they describe how MMR techniques are spreading across a variety of disciplines and how they are evolving as they expand into areas where other methodologies have previously dominated. A number of interesting questions emerge from information that has accumulated thus far. What can be done to encourage greater use of mixed methods in applied areas where they already used? What remaining barriers exist to their greater use? How can mixed methods be introduced into applied research fields where the QUAN or QUAL tradition is still dominant? Chapters 27 and 28, by Sammons and by Song and her colleagues, respectively, address the last question by discussing how mixed methods have been successfully introduced into fields of study that have been dominated by the traditional QUAN approach.

How can mixed methods be introduced into "pure" or basic disciplines such as psychology, which has long been dominated by the QUAN tradition (especially experimental/quasi-experimental methods)? A promising sign for the use of MMR in psychology was the recent publication of an article in *Developmental Psychology* on mixing QUAL and QUAN research (Yoshikawa, Weisner, Kalil, & Way 2008). Yoshikawa and colleagues described research settings in development science, where mixed methods might be especially appropriate, including studies that explore causal associations and their mechanisms (for an excellent earlier review of these applications, see Waszak & Sines, 2003).

It is obvious that researchers working within specific disciplines and fields will shape MMR to fit the context within which they work. Ivankova and Kawamura (2010) provide insightful descriptions of how researchers in the fields of health and medicine, education, computer science, and social work have applied MMR within their fields. As MMR disperses throughout the human sciences, one challenge will be to ascertain if practitioners of mixed methods can develop and maintain a "core identity" (e.g., a set of commonly understood methodological principles) that cuts across disciplinary lines.

While researchers from a few countries have dominated the academic discourse, there is evidence that MMR is attracting scholars from a wide variety of national and cultural backgrounds. For example, the literature review by Ivankova and Kawamura (2010) indicated that scholars from more than 30 countries generated articles employing mixed methods between 2000 and 2008. In the past decade, the mixed methods community has enjoyed an increasingly lively geographic and national diversity. Much writing, research reports, and lively scholarly debates have emerged from the United States, Europe, Canada, Australia, and to some extent, New Zealand and Japan. Although scholars from other parts of the world are publishing mixed methods research articles and methodological papers, the number and scope of these writings is still small. We see indications of accelerating growth in trans-cultural mixed methods studies.

One of the advantages of mixed methods has been its flexibility to use cultural knowledge and systematic/anecdotal field observations as research data/evidence in different types of research. Use of QUAL observations and cultural/linguistic knowledge in interpreting QUAN research and measurement results is not new in cultural/cognitive anthropology, cross-cultural psychology, and related disciplines (for example, see Hambleton, Merenda, & Spielberger, 2005; Waszak & Sines, 2003). However, there is a need for a systematic set of procedures that help in summarizing and presenting both the QUAL and the QUAN results (e.g., QUAL observations and field notes and QUAN questionnaires and structured data). Mixed methods provide such an impetus while also legitimizing the integration of QUAL and QUAN methods, data, and results.

Currently, the developing world is not highly visible in publications regarding or involving mixed methods. This, however, is not an indication of lack of feasibility or use of mixed methods in these countries. There are many indications that researchers are taking a bottom-up path to mixed methods in many areas of the world by creatively integrating QUAL and QUAN methods/approaches (also see our preface to this volume). An examination of cross-cultural research books (e.g., Smith, Bond, & Cagitcibasi, 2006) provides ample examples of integrating cultural knowledge, field notes, and qualitative observations/interviews in interpretation of survey results (or vice versa).

◆ *Conclusions*

This chapter introduced the reader to the organizational structure of the *Handbook*, which consists of three parts, devoted to conceptual issues, issues of methods and methodology, and contemporary applications of MMR. The overlaps among these three parts, were also discussed, and the methodology of mixed methods research was defined as the point of integration between the conceptual and methods levels. The concept of an overall "map" for the field of MMR was discussed, and its potential importance for the development of the field was further delineated.

Nine common core characteristics of MMR were discussed, including methodological eclecticism, paradigm pluralism, an emphasis on diversity at all levels of the research enterprise, and an iterative, cyclical approach to research. The value of having these common characteristics in

terms of setting MMR apart from the two traditional approaches to research was emphasized.

Nine issues or controversies in contemporary MMR were discussed in detail because they involve topics that are debated throughout the *Handbook*. Four of these topics were presented as new issues that had emerged since the first edition of the *Handbook*. Analysis issues and cross-disciplinary/cross-cultural applications were highlighted as important topics for the future of MMR.

An overall goal for the *Handbook* was introduced: the delineation of methodological principles or frameworks for MMR. Two such principles were discussed, and the reader was informed that other chapters of the *Handbook*, especially those in Part II, would explore these principles/frameworks in more detail.

Chapters in the *Handbook* were briefly previewed so that readers could envision the breadth of the topics that are discussed in the volume.

Research Questions and Exercises

1. Consider the three general sections of the *Handbook*. How are topics within those sections different from and similar to one another? Discuss points of overlap among them.

2. Discuss the importance of developing a "map" of the field of MMR, including specific lines of inquiry. (You may want to reconsider this question after reading Chapter 2 by John Creswell.)

3. Which of the nine common characteristics presented is the most important in terms of setting MMR apart from the two traditional approaches to research? Why?

4. Which of the nine issues or controversies currently being debated in MMR do you consider the most important? Why?

5. What is meant by the terms methodological eclecticism and connoisseur of methods (or methodological connoisseur)?

6. What are two principles of mixed methodology? Describe how they set practitioners of mixed methods apart from researchers who use QUAL or QUAN methods exclusively.

7. What are some of the issues in developing a language for MMR?

8. Select two of the following topics and write a short essay comparing their importance for the future of MMR: design issues, analysis issues, issues in drawing inferences.

9. Select two of the following topics and write a brief essay comparing their importance for the future of MMR: pedagogy, collaborative teams, cross-disciplinary applications, and cross-cultural applications.

◆ Notes

1. In developing this chapter, we were informed by numerous scholars who have made significant contributions to MMR since 2003. The selection and treatment of the issues discussed in this chapter were particularly influenced by the work of Pat Bazeley, John Creswell, Jennifer Greene, Burke Johnson, David Morgan, and Tony Onwuegbuzie.

2. We cite chapters in this *Handbook* by either their chapter number (e.g., Chapter 2) or by their appropriate 2010 reference with authors' names (e.g., Creswell, 2010). Chapter numbers are used in the Overview sections and in instances where we are discussing the chapter within the context of the *Handbook*. Citations to 2010 publications are used elsewhere in the document. First citations using authors' names include a reference to this volume (e.g., Creswell (2010 [this volume]), while following references do not (e.g., Creswell, 2010). References for many of the chapters are located at the end of the document.

3. The distinction between what constitutes a paradigm or a theory is sometimes controversial, as exemplified by Mertens and her colleagues' (2010) delineation of why their conceptual orientation is a paradigm rather than a theory.

4. Guba and Lincoln (2005; also Lincoln & Guba, 2000) added axiology to their set of basic beliefs associated with paradigms although it was not included in earlier versions. They added axiology because it would "begin to help us see the embeddedness of ethics within, not external to, paradigms" (Guba & Lincoln, 2005, p. 200). Morgan (2007) excludes axiology from his portrayal of paradigms as *epistemological stances* (retaining epistemology, ontology, and methodology) because it is a "poor fit with the emphasis on the *philosophy of knowledge* that Lincoln and Guba originated" (Morgan, 2007, p. 58, italics in original).

5. See Teddlie and Tashakkori (2009, pp. 117–118) for a more detailed discussion of lines of research or inquiry including examples.

6. Denzin and Lincoln (2005, p. 4) similarly refer to QUAL researchers as bricoleurs, who use a variety of methodological practices associated with QUAL research.

7. At the time that MMR emerged, numerous researchers in the social and behavioral sciences believed that QUAN and QUAL research should not be mixed due to the link between epistemology and methodology. Lincoln (2010) has argued that the incommensurability thesis operates not at the methods level, but rather at the paradigmatic level. She further contends that she and her co-authors (e.g., Guba & Lincoln, 1981) have consistently argued for the use of mixed methods, and she presented several quotes illustrating that position. Nevertheless, other authors have linked ontology, epistemology, and methodology, as described by Morgan (2007) and elaborated on later in this chapter. We believe that the linkage of epistemological positions with methodological orientations led to the incompatibility thesis (Howe, 1988), which has been rejected by practitioners of mixed methods.

8. *Design quality* is the degree to which the investigator has used the most appropriate procedures for answering the research question(s) and implemented them effectively. It consists of *design suitability, fidelity, within-design consistency,* and *analytic adequacy* (Tashakkori & Teddlie, 2008).

9. Abductive logic is a third type of logic, which occurs when a researcher observes a surprising event and then tries to determine what might have caused it (e.g., Peirce, 1974). It is the process whereby a hypothesis is generated, so that the surprising event may be explained. Morgan (2007) included abduction as part of his pragmatic approach to methodology in the social sciences.

10. Our conceptual/methodological/methods interface is similar to the epistemology↔methodology↔methods connection that characterizes Morgan's (2007) pragmatic approach to methodology in the social sciences (refer to Box 1.1). The ultimate goal for his pragmatic approach is to generate a "properly integrated methodology for the social sciences" (p. 73). Our immediate goal for this *Handbook* is to delineate some methodological principles that integrate the conceptual and methods levels of MMR.

11. Burke Johnson influenced our thoughts with regard to the value of generating a dictionary for MMR.

12. Creswell (2010) has concluded that our use of the terms *inference* or *meta-inference*

seems to lean in the direction of QUAN research, rather than a language for MMR. We caution our readers that the way we use the term *inference* is not the same as *statistical inference,* which is used in a very specific context within QUAN data analysis. As noted in the text, our definition of inference is much broader and is based on an extensive literature with origins in cognitive psychology (social cognition), philosophy, and research methodology, including QUAL research traditions.

◆ References

Adamson, J. (2004). [Review of the book *Handbook of mixed methods in social and behavioral research*]. *International Journal of Epidemiology, 33*(6), 1414–1415.

Alise, M. A., & Teddlie, C. (in press). A continuation of the paradigm wars? Prevalence rates of methodological approaches across the social/behavioral sciences. Manuscript accepted for publication in the *Journal of Mixed Methods Research.*

Bazeley, P. (2003). Computerized data analysis for mixed methods research. In A. Tashakkori & C. Teddlie (Eds.), *Handbook of mixed methods in social and behavioral research* (pp. 385–422). Thousand Oaks, CA: Sage.

Bazeley, P. (2009). Integrating data analyses in mixed methods research. *Journal of Mixed Methods Research, 3*(3), 203–207.

Bazeley, P. (2010). Computer assisted integration of mixed methods data sources and analysis. In A. Tashakkori & C. Teddlie (Eds.), *SAGE handbook of mixed methods in social & behavioral research* (2nd ed.). Thousand Oaks, CA: Sage.

Bergman, M. M. (Ed.). (2008). *Advances in mixed methods research: Theories and applications.* London: Sage.

Biesta, G. (2010). Pragmatism and the philosophical foundations of mixed methods research. In A. Tashakkori & C. Teddlie (Eds.), *SAGE handbook of mixed methods in social & behavioral research* (2nd ed.). Thousand Oaks, CA: Sage.

Biglan, A. (1973). The characteristics of subject matter in different academic areas. *Journal of Applied Psychology 57*(3), 195–203.

Brannen, J (2005). Mixed methods: The entry of qualitative and quantitative approaches into the research process. *International Journal of Social Research Methodology, 8*(3), 173–184.

Brewer, J., & Hunter, A. (2006). *Foundations of multimethod research: Synthesizing styles* (2nd ed.). Thousand Oaks, CA: Sage.

Bryman, A. (2006). Paradigm peace and the implications for quality. *International Journal of Social Research Methodology Theory and Practice, 9*(2), 111–126.

Bryman, A. (2008). Why do researchers combine quantitative and qualitative research? In M. M. Bergman (Ed.), *Advances in mixed methods research: Theories and applications* (pp. 87–100). London: Sage.

Caracelli, V. J., & Greene, J. C. (1993). Data analysis strategies for mixed-method evaluation designs. *Educational Evaluation and Policy Analysis, 15*(2), 195–207.

Caracelli, V. J., & Greene, J. C. (1997). Crafting mixed-method evaluation designs. In J. C. Greene & V. J. Caracelli (Eds.), *Advances in mixed-method evaluation: The challenges and benefits of integrating diverse paradigms* (New Directions for Evaluation, No. 74, pp. 19–32). San Francisco: Jossey-Bass.

Christ, T. W. (2009). Designing, teaching, and evaluating two complementary mixed methods research courses. *Journal of Mixed Methods Research, 3*(4), 292–325.

Christ, T. (2010). Teaching mixed methods and action research: Pedagogical, practical, and evaluative considerations. In A. Tashakkori & C. Teddlie (Eds.), *SAGE handbook of mixed methods in social & behavioral research* (2nd ed.). Thousand Oaks, CA: Sage.

Cook, T. D., & Campbell, D. T. (1979). *Quasiexperimentation: Design and analysis issues for field settings.* Boston: Houghton Mifflin.

Creswell, J. W. (2009). Mapping the field of mixed methods research. *Journal of Mixed Methods Reseach 3*(2), 95–108.

Creswell, J. W. (2010). Mapping the developing landscape of mixed methods research. In A. Tashakkori & C. Teddlie (Eds.), *SAGE handbook of mixed methods in social & behavioral research* (2nd ed.). Thousand Oaks, CA: Sage.

Creswell, J., & Plano Clark, V. (2007). *Designing and conducting mixed methods research*. Thousand Oaks, CA: Sage.

Creswell, J., Plano Clark, V., Gutmann, M., & Hanson, W. (2003). Advanced mixed methods research designs. In A. Tashakkori & C. Teddlie (Eds.), *Handbook of mixed methods in social and behavioral research* (pp. 209–240). Thousand Oaks, CA: Sage.

Creswell, J., Tashakkori, A., Jensen, K., & Shapley, K. (2003). Teaching mixed methods research: Practice, dilemmas and challenges. In A. Tashakkori & C. Teddlie (Eds.), *Handbook of mixed methods in social and behavioral research* (pp. 619–638). Thousand Oaks, CA: Sage.

Crotty, M. (1998). *The foundations of social research: Meaning and perspective in the research process*. London: Sage.

Dellinger, A. B., & Leech, N. L. (2007). Toward a unified validation framework in mixed methods research. *Journal of Mixed Methods Research, 1*(4), 309–332.

Denscombe, M. (2008). Communities of practice: A research paradigm for the mixed methods approach. *Journal of Mixed Methods Research, 2*, 270–283.

Denzin, N. K., & Lincoln, Y. S. (2005). Introduction: The discipline and practice of qualitative research. In N. K. Denzin & Y. S. Lincoln (Eds.), *Handbook of qualitative research* (3rd ed., pp. 1–32). Thousand Oaks, CA: Sage.

Denzin, N. K. (2008). The new paradigm dialogs and qualitative inquiry. *International Journal of Qualitative Studies in Education, 21*, 315–325.

Dickinson, W. B. (2010). Visual displays for mixed methods findings. In A. Tashakkori & C. Teddlie (Eds.), *SAGE handbook of mixed methods in social & behavioral research* (2nd ed.). Thousand Oaks, CA: Sage.

Earley, M. A. (2007). Developing a syllabus for a mixed methods research course. *International Journal of Social Research Methodology, 10*(2), 145–162.

Erzberger, C., & Kelle, U. (2003). Making inferences in mixed methods: The rules of integration. In A. Tashakkori & C. Teddlie (Eds.), *Handbook of mixed methods in social and behavioral research* (pp. 457–490). Thousand Oaks, CA: Sage.

Fielding, N., & Cisneros-Puebla, C. A. (2009). CAQDAS-GIS Convergence: Toward a new integrated mixed method research practice? *Journal of Mixed Methods Research, 3*(4), 349–370.

Gorard, S. (2010). Research design as independent of methods. In A. Tashakkori & C. Teddlie (Eds.), *SAGE handbook of mixed methods in social & behavioral research* (2nd ed.). Thousand Oaks, CA: Sage.

Gorard, S., & Taylor, C. (2004). *Combining methods in educational and social research*. Buckingham, UK: Open University Press.

Greene, J. C. (2007). *Mixing methods in social inquiry*. San Francisco: Jossey-Bass.

Greene, J. C. (2008). Is mixed methods social inquiry a distinctive methodology? *Journal of Mixed Methods Research, 2*(1), 7–22.

Greene, J. C., & Caracelli, V. J. (2003). Making paradigmatic sense of mixed-method practice. In A. Tashakkori & C. Teddlie (Eds.), *Handbook of mixed methods in social and behavioral research* (pp. 91–110). Thousand Oaks, CA: Sage.

Greene, J. C., Caracelli, V. J., & Graham, W. F. (1989). Toward a conceptual framework for mixed-method evaluation designs. *Educational Evaluation and Policy Analysis, 11*, 255–274.

Greene, J., & Hall, J. (2010). Dialectics and pragmatism: Being of consequence. In A. Tashakkori & C. Teddlie (Eds.), *SAGE handbook of mixed methods in social & behavioral research* (2nd ed.). Thousand Oaks, CA: Sage.

Guba, E. G. (1990). Carrying on the dialog. In E. G. Guba (Ed.), *The paradigm dialog* (pp. 368–378). Thousand Oaks, CA: Sage.

Guba, E. G., & Lincoln, Y. S. (1981). *Effective evaluation*. San Francisco: Jossey-Bass Inc.

Guba, E. G., & Lincoln, Y. S. (1994). Competing paradigms in qualitative research. In N. K. Denzin & Y. S. Lincoln (Eds.), *Handbook of qualitative research* (pp. 105–117). Thousand Oaks, CA: Sage.

Guba, E. G., & Lincoln, Y. S. (2005). Paradigmatic controversies, contradictions, and emerging confluences. In N. K. Denzin & Y. S. Lincoln (Eds.), *Handbook of qualitative research* (3rd ed., pp. 191–215). Thousand Oaks, CA: Sage.

Hambleton, R. K., Merenda, P. F., & Spielberger, C. D. (2005). *Adapting educational and psychological tests for cross-cultural assessment*. Mahwah, NJ: Lawrence Erlbaum.

Hammersley, M. (1996). The relationship between qualitative and quantitative research: Paradigm loyalty versus methodological eclecticism. In J. T. E. Richardson (Ed.), *Handbook of qualitative research methods for psychology and the social sciences* (pp. 159–174). Leicester, UK: BPS Books.

Hart, L. C., Smith, S. Z., Swars, S. L., & Smith, M. E. (2009). An examination of research methods in mathematics education (1995–2005). *Journal of Mixed Methods Research, 3*(1), 26–41.

Hesse-Biber, S. (2010). Feminist approaches to mixed methods research: Linking theory and praxis. In A. Tashakkori & C. Teddlie (Eds.), *SAGE handbook of mixed methods in social and behavioral research* (2nd ed.). Thousand Oaks, CA: Sage.

Howe, K. R. (1988). Against the quantitative-qualitative incompatibility thesis or dogmas die hard. *Educational Researcher, 17,* 10–16.

Ivankova, N. V., Creswell, J. W., & Stick, S. (2006). Using mixed methods sequential explanatory design: From theory to practice. *Field Methods, 18*(1), 3–20.

Ivankova, N., & Kawamura, Y. (2010). Emerging trends in the utilization of integrated designs in the social, behavioral, and health sciences. In A. Tashakkori & C. Teddlie (Eds.), *SAGE handbook of mixed methods in social & behavioral research* (2nd ed.). Thousand Oaks, CA: Sage.

Jang, E. E., McDougall, D. E., Pollon, D., Herbert, M., & Russell, P. (2008). Integrative mixed methods data analytic

strategies in research on school success in challenging circumstances. *Journal of Mixed Methods Research, 2*(2), 221–247.

Johnson, B., & Gray, R. (2010). A history of philosophical and theoretical issues for mixed methods research. In A. Tashakkori & C. Teddlie (Eds.), *SAGE handbook of mixed methods in social & behavioral research* (2nd ed.). Thousand Oaks, CA: Sage.

Johnson, R. B., & Onwuegbuzie, A. (2004). Mixed methods research: A research paradigm whose time has come. *Educational Researcher, 33*(7), 14–26.

Johnson, R. B., Onwuegbuzie, A. J., & Turner, L. A. (2007). Toward a definition of mixed methods research. *Journal of Mixed Methods Research, 1*(2), 112–133.

Krathwohl, D. R. (1993). *Methods of educational and social science research: An integrated approach*. White Plains, NY: Longman.

Krathwohl, D. R. (2004). *Methods of educational and social science research: An integrated approach* (2nd ed.). Long Grove, IL: Waveland Press.

Kuhn, T. S. (1970). *The structure of scientific revolutions*. Chicago: University of Chicago Press.

Kumagai, Y., Bliss, J. C., Daniels, S. E., & Carroll, M. S. (2004). Research on causal attribution of wildfire: An exploratory multiple-methods approach. *Society and Natural Resources, 17,* 113–127.

Leech, N. L. (2010). Interviews with the early developers of mixed methods research. In A. Tashakkori & C. Teddlie (Eds.), *SAGE handbook of mixed methods in social & behavioral research* (2nd ed.). Thousand Oaks, CA: Sage.

Li, S., Marquart, J. M., & Zercher, C. (2000). Conceptual issues and analytic strategies in mixed-method studies of preschool inclusion. *Journal of Early Intervention, 23,* 116–132.

Lieber, E., & Weisner, T. S. (2010). Meeting the practical challenges of mixed methods research. In A. Tashakkori & C. Teddlie (Eds.), *SAGE handbook of mixed methods in social & behavioral research* (2nd ed.). Thousand Oaks, CA: Sage.

Lincoln, Y. S. (2010). "What a long strange trip it's been . . . ": Twenty-five years of qualitative and new paradigm research. *Qualitative Inquiry, 16*(1), 3–9.

Lincoln, Y. S., & Guba, E. G. (1985). *Naturalistic inquiry.* Beverly Hills: Sage.

Lincoln, Y. S., & Guba, E. G. (2000). Paradigmatic controversies, contradictions, and emerging confluences. In N. K. Denzin & Y. S. Lincoln (Eds.), *Handbook of qualitative research* (2nd ed., pp. 163–188). Thousand Oaks, CA: Sage.

Maxwell, J., & Loomis, D. (2003). Mixed methods design: An alternative approach. In A. Tashakkori & C. Teddlie (Eds.), *Handbook of mixed methods in social and behavioral research* (pp. 241–272). Thousand Oaks, CA: Sage.

Maxwell, J. A., & Mittapalli, K. (2010). Realism as a stance for mixed method research. In A. Tashakkori & C. Teddlie (Eds.), *SAGE handbook of mixed methods in social & behavioral research* (2nd ed.). Thousand Oaks, CA: Sage.

Mertens, D. M. (2007). Transformative paradigm: Mixed methods and social justice. *Journal of Mixed Methods Research, 1*(3), 212–225.

Mertens, D. M., Bledsoe, K. L., Sullivan, M., & Wilson, A. (2010). Utilization of mixed methods for transformative purposes. In A. Tashakkori & C. Teddlie (Eds.), *SAGE handbook of mixed methods in social & behavioral research* (2nd ed.). Thousand Oaks, CA: Sage.

Morgan, D. (2007). Paradigms lost and pragmatism regained: Methodological implications of combining qualitative and quantitative methods. *Journal of Mixed Methods Research, 1*(1), 48–76.

Morse, J. M. (1991). Approaches to qualitative-quantitative methodological triangulation. *Nursing Research, 40*(2), 120–123.

Morse, J. M. (2003). Principles of mixed methods and multimethod research design. In A. Tashakkori & C. Teddlie (Eds.), *Handbook of mixed methods in social and behavioral research* (pp. 189–208). Thousand Oaks, CA: Sage.

Morse, J. M. (2010). Procedures and practice of mixed method design: Maintaining control, rigor, and complexity. In A. Tashakkori & C. Teddlie (Eds.), *SAGE handbook of mixed methods in social & behavioral research* (2nd ed.). Thousand Oaks, CA: Sage.

Morse, J., & Niehaus, L. (2010). *Mixed method design: Principles and procedures.* Walnut Creek, CA: Left Coast Press.

Newman, I., Ridenour, C., Newman, C., & DeMarco, Jr., G. M. P. (2003). A typology of research purposes and its relationship to mixed methods research. In A. Tashakkori & C. Teddlie (Eds.), *Handbook of mixed methods in social and behavioral research* (pp. 167–188). Thousand Oaks, CA: Sage.

Niglas, K. (2004). *The combined use of qualitative and quantitative methods in educational research.* Tallinn, Estonia: Tallinn Pedagogical University Series, Dissertations on Social Sciences.

Niglas, K. (2007). Introducing the qualitative-quantitative continuum: An alternative view of teaching research methods courses. In M. Murtonen, J. Rautopuro, & P. Vaisanen (Eds.), *Learning and teaching of research methods at university* (pp. 185–203). Turku, Finland: Finnish Educational Research Association.

Niglas, K. (2010). The multidimensional model of research methodology: An integrated set of continua. In A. Tashakkori & C. Teddlie (Eds.), *SAGE handbook of mixed methods in social & behavioral research* (2nd ed.). Thousand Oaks, CA: Sage.

Onwuegbuzie, A., & Combs, J. (2010). Emergent data analysis techniques in mixed methods research: A synthesis. In A. Tashakkori & C. Teddlie (Eds.), *SAGE handbook of mixed methods in social & behavioral research* (2nd ed.). Thousand Oaks, CA: Sage.

Onwuegbuzie, A. J., & Johnson, R. B. (2006). The validity issue in mixed research. *Research in the Schools, 13*(1), 48–63.

Onwuegbuzie, A. J., & Leech, N. L. (2005). Taking the "Q" out of research: Teaching research methodology courses without the divide between quantitative and qualitative paradigms. *Quality & Quantity: International Journal of Methodology, 39,* 267–296.

Onwuegbuzie, A. J., & Teddlie, C. (2003). A framework for analyzing data in mixed methods research. In A. Tashakkori & C. Teddlie (Eds.), *Handbook of mixed methods in social and behavioral research* (pp. 351–384). Thousand Oaks, CA: Sage.

Patton, M. Q. (1990). *Qualitative research and evaluation methods* (2nd ed.). Thousand Oaks, CA: Sage.

Patton, M. Q. (2002). *Qualitative research and evaluation methods* (3rd ed.). Thousand Oaks, CA: Sage.

Peirce, C. S. (1974). *Collected papers* (C. Hartshore, P. Weiss, & A. Burks, Eds.). Cambridge, MA: The Belknap Press of Harvard University Press.

Plano Clark, V. L., & Creswell, J. W. (2008). *The mixed methods reader.* Thousand Oaks, CA: Sage.

Ridenour, C. S., & Newman, I. (2008). *Mixed methods research: Exploring the interactive continuum.* Carbondale: Southern Illinois University Press.

Rossman, G., & Wilson, B. (1985). Numbers and words: Combining quantitative and qualitative methods in a single large scale evaluation study. *Evaluation Review, 9,* 627–643.

Rossman, G., & Wilson, B. (1994). Numbers and words revisited: Being "shamelessly eclectic." *Quality and Quantity, 28,* 315–327.

Sale, J., Lohfeld, L., & Brazil, K. (2002). Revisiting the qualitative-quantitative debate: Implications for mixed-methods research. *Quality and Quantity, 36,* 43–53.

Sammons, P. (2010). The contribution of mixed methods to recent research on educational effectiveness. In A. Tashakkori & C. Teddlie (Eds.), *SAGE handbook of mixed methods in social & behavioral research* (2nd ed.). Thousand Oaks, CA: Sage.

Sandelowski, M. (2000). Combining qualitative and quantitative sampling, data collection, and analysis techniques in mixed-method studies. *Research in Nursing Health, 23,* 246–255.

Sandelowski, M., Voils, C. I., & Knafl, G. (2009). On quantitizing. *Journal of Mixed Methods Research, 3*(3), 208–222.

Schwandt, T. (1997). *Qualitative inquiry: A dictionary of terms.* Thousand Oaks, CA: Sage.

Shadish, W., Cook, T., & Campbell, D. (2002). *Experimental and quasi-experimental designs for general causal inference.* Boston: Houghton Mifflin.

Shulha, L., & Wilson, R. (2003). Collaborative mixed methods research. In A.Tashakkori and C. Teddlie (Eds.), *Handbook of mixed methods in social and behavioral research* (pp. 639–670). Thousand Oaks, CA: Sage.

Smith, E. E., & Kosslyn, S. M. (2007). *Cognitive psychology: Mind and brain.* Upper Saddle River, NJ: Pearson.

Smith, P. B., Bond, M. H., & Cagitcibasi, C. (2006). *Understanding social psychology across cultures: Living and working in a changing world.* London: Sage.

Sternberg, R. J. (2009). *Cognitive psychology.* Belmont, CA: Wadsworth.

Tashakkori, A. (2006, July). *Growing pains? Agreements, disagreements, and new directions in conceptualizing mixed methods.* Keynote address presented at 2nd annual Mixed Methods Conference, Humerton School of Health Sciences, Cambridge, UK.

Tashakkori, A. (2009). Are we there yet? The state of the mixed methods community. *Journal of Mixed Methods Research, 3*(4), 287–291.

Tashakkori, A., Brown, L. M., & Borghese, P. (2009). Integrated methods for studying a systemic conceptualization of stress and coping. In K. Collins, A. J. Onwuegbuzie, & Q. G. Jiao (Eds.), *Toward a Broader understanding of stress and coping: Mixed methods approaches* (Research on Stress and Coping in Education Series, Volume V). New Age Publishing.

Tashakkori, A., & Creswell, J. (2008). Envisioning the future stewards of the social-behavioral research enterprise. *Journal of Mixed Methods Research, 2*(4), 291–295.

Tashakkori, A., & Newman, I. (2010). Mixed methods: Integrating quantitative and qualitative approaches to research. In B. McGaw, E. Baker, & P. P. Peterson (Eds.), *International encyclopedia of education* (3rd ed.). Oxford, UK: Elsevier.

Tashakkori, A., & Teddlie, C. (1998). *Mixed methodology: Combining the qualitative and quantitative approaches.* Thousand Oaks, CA: Sage.

Tashakkori, A., & Teddlie, C. (Eds.), (2003a). *Handbook of mixed methods in social and behavioral research.* Thousand Oaks, CA: Sage.

Tashakkori, A., & Teddlie, C. (2003b). Issues and dilemmas in teaching research methods courses in social and behavioral sciences: U.S. perspective. *International Journal of Social Research Methodology, 6,* 61–77.

Tashakkori, A., & Teddlie, C. (2003c). The past and future of mixed methods research: From data triangulation to mixed model designs. In A. Tashakkori & C. Teddlie (Eds.), *Handbook of mixed methods in social and behavioral research* (pp. 671–702). Thousand Oaks, CA: Sage.

Tashakkori, A., & Teddlie, C. (2008). Quality of inference in mixed methods research: Calling for an integrative framework. In M. M. Bergman (Ed.), *Advances in mixed methods research: Theories and applications* (pp. 101–119). London: Sage.

Tashakkori, A., & Teddlie, C. (in progress). *A practical guide for planning and conducting integrated research in human, behavioral, and social research.* New York: Guilford Press.

Teddlie, C., & Johnson, B. (2009a). Methodological thought before the twentieth century. In C. Teddlie & A. Tashakkori (Eds.), *The foundations of mixed methods research: Integrating quantitative and qualitative techniques in the social and behavioral sciences* (pp. 40–61). Thousand Oaks, CA: Sage.

Teddlie, C., & Johnson, B. (2009b). Methodological thought since the twentieth century. In C. Teddlie & A. Tashakkori (Eds.), *The foundations of mixed methods research: Integrating quantitative and qualitative techniques in the social and behavioral sciences* (pp. 62–82). Thousand Oaks, CA: Sage.

Teddlie, C., & Stringfield, S. (1993). *Schools make a difference: Lessons learned from a 10-year study of school effects.* New York: Teachers College Press.

Teddlie, C., & Tashakkori, A. (2003). Major issues and controversies in the use of mixed methods in the social and behavioral sciences. In A. Tashakkori & C. Teddlie (Eds.), *Handbook of mixed methods in social and behavioral research* (pp. 3–50). Thousand Oaks, CA: Sage.

Teddlie, C., & Tashakkori, A. (2009). *The foundations of mixed methods research: Integrating quantitative and qualitative techniques in the social and behavioral Sciences.* Thousand Oaks, CA: Sage.

Teddlie, C., & Tashakkori, A. (in press). Mixed methods: Contemporary issues in an emerging field. In N. K. Denzin & Y. S. Lincoln (Eds.), *Handbook of qualitative research* (4th ed.). Thousand Oaks, CA: Sage.

Teddlie, C., Tashakkori, A., & Johnson, B. (2008). Emergent techniques in the gathering and analysis of mixed methods data. In S. Hesse-Biber & P. Leavy (Eds.), *Handbook of emergent methods in social research* (pp. 389–413). New York: Guilford Press.

Tolman, D., & Szalacha, L. (1999). Dimensions of desire: Bridging qualitative and quantitative methods in a study of female sexuality. *Psychology of Women Quarterly, 23,* 7–39.

Waszak, C., & Sines, M. C. (2003). Mixed methods in psychological research. In A. Tashakkori & C. Teddlie (Eds.), *Handbook of mixed methods in social and behavioral research* (pp. 557–576). Thousand Oaks, CA: Sage.

Yanchar, S. C., & Williams, D. D. (2006). Reconsidering the compatibility thesis and eclecticism: Five proposed guidelines for method use. *Educational Researcher, 35*(9), 3–12.

Yoshikawa, H., Weisner, T. D., Kalil, A., & Way, N. (2008). Mixing qualitative and quantitative research in developmental science: Uses and methodological choices. *Developmental Psychology, 33*(7), 344–354.

PART I

CONCEPTUAL ISSUES: PHILOSOPHICAL, THEORETICAL, SOCIOPOLITICAL

2

MAPPING THE DEVELOPING LANDSCAPE OF MIXED METHODS RESEARCH

◆ John W. Creswell

Objectives

From this chapter, readers should obtain:

- a current understanding of the field of mixed methods research that has developed, especially within the last 7 years;

- a view of varied perspectives on the essence of mixed methods, its definitions, and the language that has developed about the field;

- an overview of the current discussion about the philosophical assumptions and theoretical lenses used in mixed methods research;

- a perspective about the emerging detailed procedures for conducting mixed methods; and

- knowledge about recent developments in the field of mixed methods, including disciplinary, international, and funding initiatives.

In the approximate 20-year history of mixed methods (Greene, 2008), the landscape of this field has developed dramatically, especially so in the years since the publication of the first edition of this *Handbook* (Tashakkori & Teddlie, 2003). The growth in interest can be documented through various social and health science disciplines that have embraced this form of research, new journals exclusively devoted to this approach, conferences hosting symposia and paper presentations on using this form of research, and support from funding agencies for mixed methods projects (Creswell, in press). The circle of scholars and fields embracing mixed methods continues to expand and expand. In light of these developments, it is time to reflect on this developing landscape and to map discussions about issues, priorities, and topics that have emerged. Such a mapping can provide a status report of the field of mixed methods, provide new scholars to the field of mixed methods with a general guide for positioning their studies within the mixed methods literature, and help encourage focused discussions among experienced researchers familiar with the literature on mixed methods.

This chapter maps key developments in mixed methods research and suggests future issues that need to be addressed. This mapping will address developments since 2003 and build on three recent discussions about the status of mixed methods. It will then concentrate on four key domains of topics that have emerged from these status discussions: the essence of mixed methods, the philosophical foundations, the procedures for conducting a mixed methods study, and the adoption and use of mixed methods. The intent of mapping the field of mixed methods is not to "fix" the content or to provide definitive statements about each domain. Instead, it will be to suggest multiple perspectives that have emerged, to raise further questions that need to be addressed, and to offer my voice in the conversation. This chapter will not be an exhaustive treatment of issues and topics, but rather a dialogue about key domains that cross the issues, priorities, and topics in the field, and that I hope will capture recent threads of conversation in the mixed methods community.

◆ Three Recent Discussions About the Current State of Mixed Methods Research

Three discussions have appeared in recent years that help to map the current state of the field of mixed methods: Tashakkori and Teddlie (2003), Greene (2008), and Creswell (2008, 2009a). Issues, topics, and questions being raised in these discussions are listed in Table 2.1. The first was presented by Tashakkori and Teddlie (2003) in the beginning and ending chapters of the first edition of this *Handbook*. It detailed six major unresolved issues and controversies in the use of mixed methods in social and behavioral research.

A few years later, Greene (2008) published an analysis of key domains in mixed methods in the *Journal of Mixed Methods Research* (JMMR) based on a keynote address presented to the Mixed Methods Special Interest Group at the American Educational Research Association in 2007. In setting forth her domains, Greene (2008) asked "what important questions remain to be engaged?" and she raised questions about "priorities for a mixed methods research agenda" (p. 8).

My discussion of topics in the field of mixed methods (Creswell, 2008) was first presented as a keynote address to the 2008 Mixed Methods Conference at Cambridge University in England. My mapping of the field was an attempt to align papers being presented at the conference with my developing understanding of the field, which I had culled from more than 300 submissions during 3 years as co-editor and co-founder of JMMR. From this conference presentation,

Table 2.1 Issues/Priorities/Topics About Mixed Methods Suggested by Tashakkori and Teddlie (2003), Greene (2008), and Creswell (2008, 2009a)

General Domain	Areas/Domains Tashakkori & Teddlie (2003)	Specific issues and questions	Areas/Domains for Greene (2008)	Specific priorities	Areas/Domains for Creswell (2008, 2009a)	Specific topics
Essence of mixed methods domain	• The nomenclature and the basic definitions used in mixed methods research • The utility of mixed methods research (why do we do it?)	• Should we use QUAN and QUAL terms or develop new mixed methods terms? • What are the reasons for conducting mixed methods research?			Nature of mixed methods	• Definition • Bilingual language • Incorporation of mixed methods into existing designs
Philosophical domain	The paradigmatic foundations for mixed methods research	• What are the paradigm perspectives in mixed methods research (dialectical, single paradigm, multiple paradigm)?	Philosophical assumptions and stances	• What actually does influence inquirers' methodological decisions in practice? • How do the assumptions and stances of pragmatism influence inquiry decisions?	Philosophical and theoretical issues	• Combining philosophical positions, worldviews, and paradigms • Philosophical foundation of mixed methods • Use of qualitative theoretical lens in mixed methods • False distinction between qualitative and quantitative research • Thinking in a mixed methods way; mental models

(Continued)

Table 2.1 (Continued)

General Domain	Areas/Domains Tashakkori & Teddlie (2003)	Specific issues and questions	Areas/Domains for Greene (2008)	Specific priorities	Areas/Domains for Creswell (2008, 2009a)	Specific topics
Procedures domain	• Design issues in mixed methods research • Issues in drawing inferences in mixed methods research	• How can mixed methods design be conceptualized? (stages of research as conceptualization, method, and inference) • How monostrand designs differ from multistrand • What are the types of multistrand designs? • What are the rules and procedures for forming inferences? • What are the standards for evaluating and improving the quality of inferences?	Inquiry logics	• What are the particular strengths and limitations of various methods of data collection? • How do we choose particular methods for a given inquiry purpose and design? • Around what does mixing occur? (constructs? questions? purposes?) • What does a methodology of mixed methods look like?	Techniques of mixed methods	• Unusual blends of methods • Joint displays of quantitative and qualitative data • Longitudinal, evaluation studies • Transforming qualitative data into counts • Process steps of research (theory, questions, sampling, interpretation) • New thinking about research designs • Methodological issues in using designs • Notations for designs • Visual diagrams for designs • Software applications • Integration and mixing issues • Rationale for mixed methods • Validity • Ethics

General Domain	Areas/Domains Tashakkori & Teddlie (2003)	Specific issues and questions	Areas/Domains for Greene (2008)	Specific priorities	Areas/Domains for Creswell (2008, 2009a)	Specific topics
Adoption and use domain	The logistics of conducting mixed methods research	• What is involved in collaborating on a mixed methods project? • What are some of the unresolved pedagogical issues in teaching mixed methods research?	Guidelines for practice	• What are the unique aspects of mixed methods practice that deal specifically with mixing? • What can be learned from conversations across disciplines and fields of applied inquiry practice?	Adoption and use of mixed methods	• Fields and disciplines using it • Team approaches • Linking mixed methods to discipline techniques • Teaching mixed methods to students • Writing up and reporting
Political domain			Sociopolitical commitments	• Who is the audience? • What perspective is represented? • Whose voice is heard? • Who is being advocated for?	Politicization of mixed methods	• Funding of mixed methods research • Deconstructing mixed methods • Justifying mixed methods

I then drafted a shorter version as an editorial for JMMR focusing on a few specific issues (Creswell, 2009a).

As shown in Table 2.1, although each discussion is slightly different, there are common thoughts across all three writings, and these ideas will form the domains to be used in mapping the field of mixed methods in this chapter. All three writings address philosophical issues, the procedures in conducting a mixed methods study, and the adoption and use of mixed methods. As for the philosophical issues, all three discussions point to understanding the philosophical foundations of mixed methods, with the two more recent writings (Creswell, 2008, 2009a; Greene, 2008) focusing much more on the *practice* of using philosophical perspectives in mixed methods studies (e.g., how to combine them, how they influence inquiry decisions). That philosophical issues continue to be debated in mixed methods indicates that the paradigm debate of the 1990s is far from over; it continues to occupy discussions about the foundations for mixed methods.

In terms of procedures, Tashakkori and Teddlie (2003) focus on the broader design issues, whereas Greene (2008) and my writings (Creswell, 2008, 2009a) go into detailed areas of methods. This analysis might suggest that our discussions are becoming much more detailed and analytic about how to conduct a study in recent years. This reinforces the assumption that many of us hold that the techniques of conducting mixed methods research have received considerable attention in the field. Regarding the adoption and use of mixed methods, whereas the earlier discussions by Tashakkori and Teddlie (2003) focused on collaboration and teaching mixed methods, the more recent writings by Greene (2008) and Creswell (2008, 2009a) have examined increased use of mixed methods by new disciplines and across fields of inquiry practice. This analysis does suggest the trend of mixed methods spreading to many fields and being adapted to suit unique discipline approaches to research methodology.

The essence of mixed methods and the political domain received uneven treatment in the three writings. For some, the questions about the meaning of mixed methods and the nature of the language it uses continue to resurface, as illustrated in the issues and topics presented by Tashakkori and Teddlie in 2003 and my topics detailed in 2008 and 2009a. Political issues also have an uneven assessment in that they surfaced more recently in the Greene (2008) and the Creswell (2008, 2009a) discussions. Perhaps with the evolving establishment of the field, critics and concerns about mixed methods are beginning to surface with increased frequency, a topic that I attempt to squarely address in another chapter (see Creswell, in press). Also, in the discussion to follow, I will integrate these political issues and concerns into commentary about the other domains, recognizing that these domains often overlap and can be sorted out for discussion only as a heuristic to promote the conversation.

This discussion, then, is an attempt to look across these three discussions and to focus on specific issues, priorities, and topics that require extended discussion and elaboration. In this discussion, I recognize that many perspectives have emerged and new questions have arisen.

THE ESSENCE OF MIXED METHODS

Although Tashakkori and Teddlie (2003) were concerned about the language being used in mixed methods, and they briefly mentioned definitions as one area of interest, they did not anticipate fully the rather extensive discussions that would follow about the core definition for mixed methods, the critique to follow, and the varied language that has emerged.

On the definition of mixed methods. A rather extensive discussion has developed in the last few years about how mixed methods should be defined. The definition of mixed methods has undergone considerable revision since the early definition by Greene, Caracelli, and Graham (1989), who focused on the use of multiple "methods." Then, the conversation moved on to a "methodology" orientation (Tashakkori & Teddlie, 1998) reflected in the title of their book, *Mixed Methodology*. *Methods* differed from *methodology* in that the former focused on the procedures of data collection, data analysis, and possibly interpretation, whereas methodology involved everything from the worldview at the start of the research process to the last procedures of inquiry (Guba & Lincoln, 1989). At the center of this recent discussion has been the article on definitions of mixed methods research by Johnson, Onwuegbuzie, and Turner (2007). They asked 21 researchers to define mixed methods and obtained 19 definitions. These definitions differed in terms of what was being mixed (e.g., methods or methodologies, or types of research), the stage of the research process in which mixing occurred (e.g., data collection, data analysis), the breadth of the mixing (e.g., from data to worldviews), the purpose for mixing (e.g., breadth, corroboration), and the drive for the research (e.g., bottom-up, top-down, the core component). As a result of their review, Johnson et al. (2007) offered a composite definition:

> Mixed methods research is the type of research in which a researcher or team of researchers combines elements of qualitative and quantitative research approaches (e.g., use of qualitative and quantitative viewpoints, data collection, analysis, inference techniques) for the purposes of breadth and depth of understanding and corroboration. (p. 123)

Whether one agreed with this definition or not, a reading of the different perspectives illustrated how the definition of mixed methods has been contested territory. An interesting analysis of the nature of mixed methods comes from Elliot (2005), who took the position that to view mixed methods from a "methods" perspectives provided a clean way to view this form of research.

In my own work, I view mixed methods primarily as a method approach (see Creswell & Plano Clark, 2007) because of the difficulty of convincing many individuals that mixing of philosophical foundations is possible (an implicit assumption from the methodological perspective). In my writings and workshops, I suggest that mixed methods is more than simply the collection of two independent strands of quantitative (QUAN) and qualitative (QUAL) data, and I draw a line down between the two approaches. I then mention that mixed methods involves the connection, integration, or linking of these two strands, and I create another line that intersects the QUAN and QUAL data strands. On this line that intersects, I then construct a circle and say that we call this circle *mixed methods*. I continue on by saying that different groups of scholars have entered this circle. Some come from a methods orientation, others from a methodology orientation, still others from a philosophical orientation, and then some who use mixed methods procedures within their traditional designs, such as experiments, narrative studies, evaluation projects, and so forth. A visual of this diagram, once completed, is shown in Figure 2.1.

Figure 2.1 The Essence of Mixed Methods Research Diagram

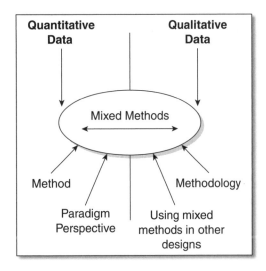

This last group to enter the circle needs further elaboration. For lack of a better term, I call this group those who bring in a framework for mixed methods procedures. Some larger framework becomes a placeholder within which the researcher gathers QUAN and QUAL data (or conducts mixed methods procedures). This idea first surfaced when a participant at a workshop asked, "Is ethnography mixed methods research?" The sense of this question was that ethnographers traditionally collect both QUAN and QUAL data and may link the two sets of data as well. Morse and Niehaus (2009) briefly discuss this question and conclude that many ethnographers see their methodology as a distinct approach, and accordingly, ethnography needs to be viewed as independent of mixed methods. But this certainly is a debatable point. I see researchers using mixed methods within larger frameworks of many different types. Evidence for these frameworks comes from several fields, such as using mixed methods procedures within narrative studies (Elliot, 2005), within experiments (Sandelowski, 1996), and within case studies (Luck, Jackson, & Usher, 2006). Other frameworks could also be advanced, such as using mixed methods within a network analysis framework (Quinlan & Quinlan, 2010)) or in the context of an overarching problem or research question (Yin, 2006), a feminist lens (Hesse-Biber & Leavy, 2007), an action research project (Christ, 2009), or visual methodology, such as documentary development (Creswell & McCoy, in press). If the nature of mixed methods can be expanded to include these different applications, then the potential for extending the reach of mixed methods is staggering. Assuming that some see mixed methods as a "new" idea, the way for researchers to adopt a new idea is for it to be integrated into existing practices.

Turning this argument in a different direction, we can see that a broad conceptualization of mixed methods raises the potential problem of the misappropriations of other designs as mixed methods. Where does the mixed methods approach end and other designs and methodologies begin? The prior example about ethnography raises this question. Several other examples illustrate this potential dilemma as well. For example, as one type of mixed methods design, we have written about a sequential QUAL followed by QUAN design for the purposes of developing and testing an instrument (Creswell & Plano Clark, 2007). Is this procedure misappropriating the idea of scale development (DeVellis, 1991), which has been in the literature for some years, or it is an appropriate adaptation of mixed methods research? The early stages of scale development call for an initial exploration, even though this may take the form of a review of the literature rather than a detailed QUAL data collection procedure, such as the use of focus groups (Vogt, King, & King, 2004). Unquestionably, studies calling themselves "mixed methods" studies are being published with the aim of developing an instrument based on QUAL data collection (Myers & Oetzel, 2003). Another example of potential misappropriation involves collecting QUAL data and transforming it into QUAN counts in a mixed methods study. This is the procedure used in traditional content analysis. Have mixed methods researchers misappropriated content analysis for their own ends (a question raised by Sandelowski, Voils, & Knafl, 2009)? I can see arguments on both sides, but as frameworks within which mixed methods procedures are being used take on more importance, the boundaries of mixed methods move well beyond a simple discussion of the definition of the nature of this form of research.

On the language of mixed methods research. Tashakkori and Teddlie (2003) perceptively identified as an important issue the question of the nomenclature that was becoming part of the language of mixed methods research. Vygotsky and Cole's (1978) sociocultural perspective on language proposed that language shapes how individuals made sense of the world and that the learning process consists of a gradual internalization of this language. So, it is appropriate to ask: What is the language of mixed methods? The issue being raised by Tashakkori and Teddlie (2003) was whether we needed a "bilingual" or new language for mixed methods research so terms did not favor QUAN or QUAL research. I am reminded of the language that emerged in QUAL research in the early 1980s around the topic of QUAL validity, and how terms such as trustworthiness and authenticity created a distinct new language for QUAL inquiry (Lincoln & Guba, 1985).

As mixed methods research develops, similar questions have emerged, and I see a distinct mixed methods language of research emerging. For example, in writing about validity, Onwuegbuzie and Johnson (2006) intentionally called validity *legitimation,* to create a separate, distinct term in mixed methods. In our work on research designs, we referred to one of our designs as an *exploratory sequential design* not only to advance a new, distinct name for a design but also to signify that the research would first explore qualitatively and then follow up quantitatively (Creswell & Plano Clark, 2007). When Teddlie and Tashakkori (2009) speak of *inference transferability* (p. 311), they have created a blended term with both QUAN (inference) and QUAL (transferability) meanings. These examples illustrate the creation of a bilingual language.

There are counterexamples of names in mixed methods that provide a less bilingual picture. For example, Teddlie and Tashakkori (2009) have used the term *inferences* or *meta-inferences* to denote when the results are incorporated into a coherent conceptual framework to provide an answer to the research question. The word *inferences* is often associated with QUAN research and drawing conclusions from a sample to a population. Another example of a QUAN-leaning term is *construct validity,* used by Leech, Dellinger, Brannagan, and Tanaka (2010) as an umbrella validity concept for mixed methods research. This term is drawn from long-established QUAN research and measurement ideas and is not a term used by QUAL researchers. On the QUAL side in

mixed methods discussions, we have a term such as *transformative* (Mertens, 2009, p. v), which is typically associated with QUAL research.

Even the terms for the overall approach to inquiry being discussed here are open to debate. Should it be called *mixed methods,* which suggests a methods orientation; *mixed methodology,* conveying more of the process of research; or simply *mixed research* (Johnson et al., 2007), signifying the mixing of research but not necessarily only methods? With the *Handbook* (Tashakkori & Teddlie, 2003) and the *Journal of Mixed Methods Research,* a convincing case could be made that *mixed methods,* especially since 2003, has been widely adopted in the literature.

Unquestionably, the language that has emerged is both bilingual and oriented toward QUAN or QUAL inquiry. The use of glossaries in recent books on mixed methods is an attempt to establish the language of mixed methods (see Morse & Niehaus, 2009; Teddlie & Tashakkori, 2009). I am inclined to support the conclusion reached by Tashakkori and Teddlie (2003): that ultimately a bilingual language will win the day in mixed methods research. If mixed methods is to be considered a "third methodological movement" (Tashakkori & Teddlie, 2003, p. 697), one could argue that it needs it own distinct language.

This being said, this discussion raises important questions for further discussion about who controls the language of mixed methods, how it is conveyed, and what the language should be as the field moves forward. Freshwater (2007) asks: Who is dominating the discourse? Is it a "fixed" discussion, not open to alternative perspectives? Are individuals merely adopting mixed methods as a mantra without thinking through the possibilities? Is mixed methods becoming another metanarrative that needs to be deconstructed? This postmodern line of questioning has emerged recently, and it can be viewed as a healthy critique of mixed methods. A related philosophical critique is that mixed methods favors a postpositivist orientation, elevates QUAN experimental methods to the top of the methodological hierarchy, and constrains QUAL research to a largely auxiliary role of "what works" (Howe, 2004). This hierarchy also promotes mixed methods practice as evidence-based approaches, attractive to funding agencies (Giddings, 2006). In addition, mixed methods research inappropriately mixes different paradigms based on different realities (Sale, Lohfeld, & Brazil, 2002).

THE PHILOSOPHICAL AND THEORETICAL FOUNDATIONS OF MIXED METHODS

The philosophical issues surrounding mixed methods have received and continue to receive considerable discussion in the field of mixed methods. Extensive discussions are to be found in both Tashakkori and Teddlie (2003) and Greene (2008) about the paradigmatic or philosophical foundations for mixed methods research. Tashakkori and Teddlie (2003) discussed the different perspectives that have emerged (e.g., dialectical, single paradigm, and multiple paradigm), whereas Greene (2008) focused her attention on pragmatism and on the practical question of how the philosophical perspectives influenced the actual practice of research.

Recent developments in the philosophy discussion. Both Tashakkori and Teddlie (2003) and Greene (2008) reconstructed for readers what is now becoming a well-known litany of different stances about the philosophical foundations of mixed methods (also see Greene & Hall, 2010 [this volume]). One stance holds that paradigms are different (incommensurable stance) and cannot be mixed; thus, mixed methods research is an untenable proposition. Another stance is that the paradigms are independent and can be mixed and matched in various combinations (an aparadigmatic stance). A further perspective is that the paradigms are not incompatible, but they are different and should be kept separate in mixed methods research (complementary strengths stance).

Also, the paradigms are different in important ways, and this difference can lead to useful tensions and insights (a dialectic stance) and should be honored. In addition, a single paradigm provides the foundation for mixed methods, and this foundation may be found in pragmatism or a transformative-emancipatory perspective (an alternative paradigm stance). And finally, paradigms can be mixed in a study and linked to the type of design being used (design stance). These varied stances suggests a lively conversation about paradigms in the mixed methods field, differences of opinions, and a continuation of the paradigm debate that was discussed in the literature during the 1990s (see Greene & Caracelli, 1997).

Adding to the perspectives is the perception that paradigms represent rigid categories of information. This seemed to be reinforced by the discrete boxes around different paradigm stances (see Creswell, 2009b; Lincoln & Guba, 2000). Such rigid boundaries were not suggested by Kuhn (1970), who many scholars turn to as the major architect of the paradigm discussion. For the mixed methods community, the issue now becomes identifying whether or how the field has moved beyond the different paradigms and the stances.

Recently, mixed methods writers have returned to Kuhn's (1970) idea of a community of practitioners. Kuhn defined paradigms as "what members of a scientific community share" (p. 176). Two key articles appeared in 2007 and 2008 in the *Journal of Mixed Methods Research* by an American author, David Morgan, and a British author, Martin Descombe. Morgan's (2007) article is a fascinating piece of scholarship, and it was first presented in 2005 as the keynote address at the Mixed Methods Conference in Cambridge, England. Morgan (2007) saw paradigms as "shared belief systems that influence the kinds of knowledge researchers seek and how they interpret the evidence they collect" (p. 50). He also saw four versions of the concept of paradigms and asserted that these versions had different levels of generality. First, paradigms can be seen as worldviews, all-encompassing perspectives on the world, or second, they can be seen as epistemologies incorporating ideas from the philosophy of science such as ontology, methodology, and epistemology. Third, paradigms can viewed as the "best" or "typical" solutions to problems, and fourth, paradigms may represent shared beliefs of a research field. Morgan strongly endorsed this last perspective. Researchers, he said, share a consensus in specialty areas about what questions are most meaningful and which procedures are most appropriate for answering the questions. In short, many practicing researchers understand paradigms from a "community of scholars" perspective (p. 53). According to Morgan, this was the version of paradigms that Kuhn (1970) most favored.

Denscombe (2008) reinforced Morgan's thoughts and added more details about the nature of the community. He outlined how communities work using such ideas as shared identity, common research problems, social networks, knowledge formation, and informal groupings. These ideas seem to begin formulating an answer to Greene's (2008) question about how philosophy actually influences researchers' decisions. It also speaks to Greene's (2008) interest in learning from conversations across disciplines and fields of practice. The mixed methods field is becoming fragmented by discipline orientation, and it will ultimately be shaped, I believe, by strong subject matter interests. For example, when I hear my colleagues in the health sciences at the Veterans Administration Health Services Research Center in Ann Arbor, Michigan, talk about mixed methods as "formative" and "summative" evaluation procedures, I recognize that a unique field or discipline orientation to mixed methods is being applied (Forman & Damschroder, 2007).

On theoretical orientations. Neither Tashakkori and Teddlie (2003) nor Greene (2008) addressed directly the theoretical perspectives discussion that has developed in the mixed methods field in recent years. To place this topic in perspective, I have often found useful Crotty's (1998) conceptualization of the different hierarchical levels of perspectives that might be incorporated into a research study: from the broad epistemological perspective (e.g., objectivism, subjectivism) to the theoretical perspective (e.g., feminism, critical inquiry), to methodology (e.g., experimental research, ethnography), and on to the methods (e.g., sampling, observation). Theory, in this placement, resided immediately below the epistemology level, and it helped to inform the methodology and the methods. The question that is emerging is: How does one use theory in a mixed methods study? My conceptualization of an answer to this question is to consider how theory might be drawn either from a social sciences theory (e.g., a theory of attribution, a theory of leadership, a theory of diffusion and adoption) or from an advocacy theory. A social science theory is positioned at the beginning of mixed methods studies, and it provides a framework for asking questions and gathering data. An advocacy (or emancipatory) theoretical lens has been part of the discussion in QUAL research for some time. It involves taking a theoretical position for underrepresented or marginalized groups, such as a feminist theory, a racial or ethnic theory, a sexual orientation theory, or a disability theory (Mertens, 2009). With one goal of QUAL research being to address issues of social justice and the human condition (Denzin & Lincoln, 2005), this emphasis has come to be expected from some scholars in mixed methods research. However, we noted a couple of years ago that few studies incorporated the advocacy/emancipatory lens in mixed methods studies (Creswell & Plano Clark, 2007). Some writers have criticized mixed methods for not being interpretive enough and not honoring ends associated with social justice, such as understanding people in their own terms, engaging stakeholders in dialogue, and encouraging a democratic role for participants (Howe, 2004). Denzin and Lincoln (2005) discussed how the mixed methods movement has taken "qualitative methods out of their natural home, which is within the critical, interpretive framework" (p. 9). These concerns have raised my awareness of the need for more mixed methods studies with an advocacy/emancipatory theoretical lens. However, such studies are appearing in the mixed methods literature, such as a study of African American women's interest in science and an investigation of women's social capital in Australia (Buck et al., 2009; Hodgkin, 2008). Recent writings have linked feminist standpoint epistemology to mixed methods (Hesse-Biber & Leavy, 2007).

With these developments, it is important to begin thinking about how to incorporate an advocacy/emancipatory theoretical lens into a mixed methods study. A recent paper analyzed 12 mixed methods studies (Sweetman, Badiee, & Creswell, in press) incorporating an advocacy theoretical lens and made suggestions for incorporating this lens into a study. It suggested including the theoretical lens in the beginning of the study as a framework, discussing the literature using the lens, making explicit the research problem and advocacy issue, writing research questions using advocacy language, collecting data to not further marginalize the community, positioning oneself in the research, and suggesting a plan of action or change. Despite these suggestions, more work needs to be done to establish how the procedures of mixed methods might change depending on the type of advocacy lens (e.g., feminist, racial) being used.

PROCEDURES FOR CONDUCTING MIXED METHODS RESEARCH

As Greene (2008) states, no area has been discussed more in the mixed methods literature than the methods and procedures. In research procedures, the techniques seem to be developing at a rapid pace from the larger questions of research designs to the more detailed areas of data collection and the steps in the research process.

Research designs. Tashakkori and Teddlie (2003) point to the use and types of research

designs as important issues to address. When we wrote about mixed methods in 2007, my colleague, Plano Clark, and I reviewed 12 different typologies of design drawn from writing in diverse fields such as evaluation, public health, education, and primary medical care (Creswell & Plano Clark, 2007). Authors of these typologies used different terms, advanced different diagrams of procedures, and suggested different purposes for the types of designs. In addition, new mixed methods books have advanced their own preferred typologies (e.g., Morse & Niehaus, 2009; Teddlie & Tashakkori, 2009).

In the spirit of helping beginning mixed methods researchers, we suggested in 2007 a parsimonious set of designs that were most prevalent, and we advanced four designs—triangulation, embedded, explanatory, and exploratory—and variations of them, amounting to 10 different designs (Creswell & Plano Clark, 2007). The lesson we immediately learned from feedback has been that the designs actually being used are often much more complex. For example, in the field of evaluation, the multiphase procedures may involve an initial needs assessment, the development of a program, the testing and administering of an instrument to assess the efficacy of the program, and the revisions and continued development of the program. This procedure calls for several phases of both QUAN and QUAL data collection. A good illustration is the longitudinal evaluation and intervention study of youth in Sri Lanka (Nastasi et al., 2007). In one table, the authors present five phases of the research involving both concurrent and sequential phases of data collection. This combination of both concurrent and sequential phases of data collection can be found today in published studies (e.g., see Woolley, 2009). In sum, the discussion of typologies of design has moved beyond simple two-phase projects (e.g., QUAN followed by QUAL) to multiphase programs of inquiry stretching over many years and incorporating many elements.

Still, to figure out the designs, a rather simple logic prevails that has been a mainstay of mixed methods for several years.

Greene (2008) elegantly summarizes the primary dimensions that distinguish among the designs and their typologies: the degree to which different methods are implemented independently or interactively (independence/interaction), the priority or dominance given to one methodology or another versus equality (status), and whether the different methods are implemented concurrently or in sequence (timing). For a novice mixed methods researcher, thinking about these three dimensions certainly provides a strong foothold into interpreting the many designs available.

Along with these designs, we now have an ever-expanding notation system (Creswell & Plano Clark, 2007; Morse, 1991; Morse & Niehaus, 2009). As shown in Table 2.2, the notation has developed beyond the use of capital letters, lower-case letters, arrows, and plus signs to include the embedding of one form of data within a larger design (e.g., a QUAL component added to an experiment); the inclusion of a purpose or rationale in the notation system; and the use of symbols that help to explain multiphase, interrelated studies in a program of inquiry. Diagrams of procedures are now comment elements in mixed methods studies, appearing in published empirical articles along with written instructions as to how to draw diagrams (Ivankova, Creswell, & Stick, 2006).

As shown in Figure 2.2, these authors provided a figure of their procedures in a mixed methods study of students' persistence

Table 2.2 Notation for Mixed Methods Studies

Notation	Explanation for Notation	Key References Citing Notation
QUAL, QUAN	Shorthand labels for *qualitative* and *quantitative* that denote equality between the two approaches because of an equal number of letters	Morse (1991)
QUAL + QUAN	Both the quantitative and qualitative methods occur at the same time (concurrently)	Morse (1991)
QUAL→quan	The methods occur in a sequence, with the qualitative methods occurring before the quantitative methods and building on them	Morse (1991)
QUAN→qual	Capital letters indicates theoretical drive or priority (core methods) given in a study; lower case indicates (supplemental methods)	Morse (1991); Morse & Niehaus (2009)
QUAN(qual)	The qualitative methods are embedded within a quantitative design	Creswell & Plano Clark, 2007; Plano Clark & Creswell, 2008
QUAN + QUAL = convergence	The equal sign identifies the purpose or rationale for the design	Morse & Niehaus (2009)
QUAL→ [QUAN→qual] →[QUAN + qu]	Square brackets indicate a self-contained project within a series of interrelated studies. The larger font indicates core methods or theoretical drive; smaller font indicates supplemental methods	Morse & Niehaus (2009)

Figure 2.2 An Example of a Diagram of Mixed Methods Procedures

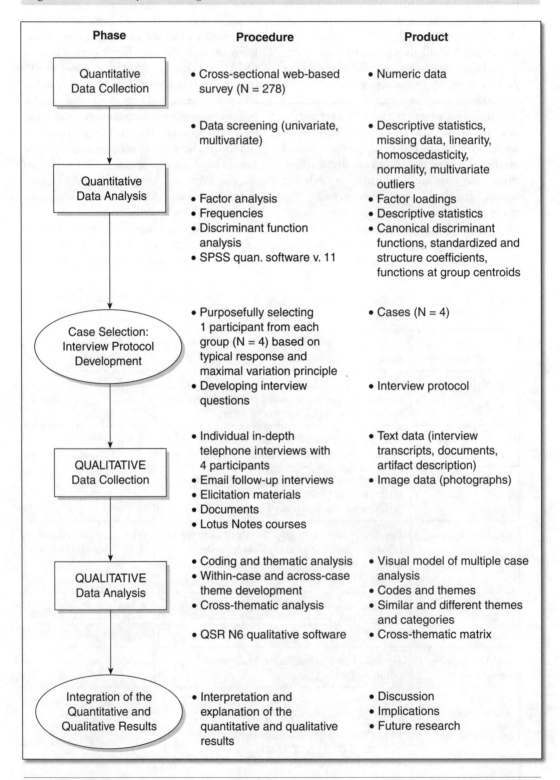

SOURCE: Ivankova, Creswell, & Stick, 2006, p. 981. Used with permission from Sage Publications.

in a distributed doctoral program in educational leadership in higher education. Their diagram illustrated several elements in designing a figure to portray mixed methods procedure. Boxes and circles indicated the general flow of data collection and analysis, arrows showed sequence, bulleted points in a column detailed the procedures for each stage in the sequence, and additional bulleted points in another column identified products to emerge in each phase (which funding agencies like to see). In my experience, these figures are being adopted with increasing frequency in mixed methods writings, and they are a welcome relief for readers who recognize the complex procedures of multiple data collection and analysis that is central to mixed methods.

In addition, mixed methods designs have begun to incorporate unusual blends of methods. For example, in Singer, Ryff, Carr, and Magee (2002), the study of the mental health of individuals was formed using longitudinal-survey data to create rich life-history narratives. Articles are beginning to explore results (e.g., confirming, diverging, complementary) that emerge when synthesizing QUAL and QUAN data (Voils, Sandelowski, Barroso, & Hasselblad, 2008). The representation of designs has also advanced with joint displays of QUAN and QUAL data in the same table (see the joint display provided by Lee & Greene, 2007).

A fascinating trend to watch is the reconceptualization of research designs away from typologies to other ways of thinking about designs. Three examples illustrate this recent trend. First, using systems theory, Maxwell and Loomis (2003) conceptualized the interactive five dimensions of the research process consisting of the purpose, the conceptual framework, the questions, the methods, and the issue of validity. Thus, design, in their approach, gave way to the process of research for a fuller, more expansive view of the way to conceptualize and design mixed methods research.

Another approach has been the innovative thinking of Hall and Howard (2008). They advanced a synergistic approach in which two or more options interacted so that their combined effect was greater than the sum of the individual parts. Translated into mixed methods, this means that the sum of QUAN and QUAL research is greater than either approach alone. Instead of looking at mixed methods as the priority of one approach over the other, or of a weighting of one approach, the researchers consider the equal value and representations of each. Instead of unequal importance of the two approaches, the two are viewed from an ideology of multiple points of view rather than differences. Collaboration on a mixed methods project means that researchers share their areas of expertise. The researchers also balance objectivity with subjectivity. In sum, the synergistic approach, along with other challenges to typological perspectives, has contributed to a softening of the differences between QUAL and QUAN research, has provided answers to questions about dominance of one method over the other (e.g., Denzin & Lincoln, 2005), and has honored the formation of research teams with diverse expertise.

A final approach to designs is somewhat of a blend of traditional thinking and a reconceptualization. Morse and Niehaus (2009) called attention to the *theoretical drive* of a study, which informed the type of design used. They defined theoretical drive as the core methods component in a study and indicated that researchers could identify this component by whether their study was approached inductively or deductively. Thus, they saw all designs as having a core component and a supportive component.

Validity and evaluation discussions. Validity concerns have become much more a part of the discussion of mixed methods research. The traditional approach is to talk about validity from a QUAN perspective and from a QUAL perspective but not to mix the two (Tashakkori & Teddlie, 1998). More recently, several perspectives have developed to conceptualize validity. First, a framework for viewing validity has been assembled by Leech et al. (2010). They used the term *construct validity* as the overarching framework and felt that validity permeated all phases of the research process, including a review of the literature, the design and evaluation of a study, inferences drawn, the use of the findings, and the consequences of the findings. This perspective clearly built on ideas about construct validity that emerged from QUAN research in recent years (e.g., Messick, 1995).

Second, an attempt has been made to link evaluation standards with validity concerns. For example, Teddlie and Tashakkori (2009) addressed the inference process of research and how mixed methods research needed should be assessed for design quality (suitability, adequacy/fidelity, consistency, and analytic adequacy) and interpretive rigor (interpretive consistency, theoretical consistency, interpretive agreement, interpretive distinctiveness, and integrative efficacy). Again, this perspective drew on the close connection between inferences and validity standards; the idea that validity (construct) is the drawing of inferences to make generalizations is a QUAN perspective.

Third, a new set of validity terms unique to mixed methods research has been developed by Onwuegbuzie and Johnson (2006). To create a bilingual language for mixed methods, they called validity *legitimation,* and they advanced a typology of nine forms of legitimation in mixed methods research. These forms related to such factors as sampling designs the sequence of phases in the design, the blending of paradigmatic assumptions, and the quality of the inferences. A fourth and final stance has been to view validity concerns as related to types of designs, a connection that was established by Campbell and Stanley (1966) when they discussed types of internal and external validity threats to experimental and quasi-experimental designs. We have taken this perspective (Creswell, Plano Clark, & Garrett, 2008) and have called these concerns methodological and validity threats. For example, in a convergent parallel design in which the researcher collects both QUAN and QUAL data (Creswell & Plano Clark, in press), issues that might pose a validity threat to drawing meaningful and useful conclusions relate to whether the same constructs (or questions) are being assessed with both forms of data, whether the unequal sample sizes pose threats to drawing conclusions, and whether conclusions drawn from assessing discrepancies in merging the results favor the QUAL or the QUAN data results.

In summary, the discussions about the procedures of mixed methods have moved the conversation beyond a justification for this form of inquiry (Tashakkori & Teddlie, 2003) and into detailed suggestions for how to proceed with conducting a mixed methods project. In terms of design, Kelle ((2006) seems on target when he suggested that there is currently no canonization of mixed methods designs. Perhaps, as Greene (2008) mentioned, practice will lead the way toward a consensus around designs. Indeed, in the last couple of years, there have been detailed discussions about the procedures used by research teams and individuals as they negotiated issues in completing a mixed methods project. For example, a recent article by Brady and O'Regan (2009) discussed a mixed methods study of a youth mentoring program in Ireland and highlighted the journey of the team through adopting a type of design, establishing an epistemological position, and conducting data analysis using various methods and sources.

The future bodes well for further developments in procedures (as when Greene, 2008, called for understanding mixed methods practice). One of these is a need to better understand the steps in data analysis, especially how, when, why, and where the data are "mixed," or what Morse and Niehaus (2009) call the "point of interface" (p. 25). Knowing data analysis procedures will lead to the potential for more useful software applications for analysis extending current discussions (see Kuckartz's 2009 paper on realizing mixed-methods approaches with MAXQDA). Continued discussions of potential stances about validity are also needed (Dellinger & Leech, 2007) as well as conversations about ethical issues (see Mertens & Ginsberg, 2009). The writing phase of the procedures needs further discussion as journal editors call for articles within a 3,000- or 5,000-word limit, especially in the health sciences (see the discussion on this subject in Dahlberg, Wittink, and Gallo, 2010 [this volume]). For example, Stange, Crabtree, and Miller (2006) have discussed writing forms such as publishing separate QUAN and QUAL papers from a mixed methods study, staging their papers as separate articles in a single issue of a journal, or integrating their methods into a single article.

ADOPTION AND USE OF MIXED METHODS

It is difficult to accurately gauge the extent to which mixed methods research has developed, especially since 2003. Neither Tashakkori and Teddlie (2003) nor Greene (2008) specifically discussed the emerging adoption of this approach, although Greene (2008) pointed to the issue that we needed to learn more from conversations across disciplines and fields of applied inquiry practice. Tashakkori and Teddlie included chapters in the first edition of the *Handbook* that addressed mixed methods within the context of evaluation, management and organizational research, the health sciences, nursing, psychology, sociology, and education. We can see evidence of development through such indicators as the numerous journal articles from many disciplines mentioned in the books on mixed methods research (Creswell & Plano Clark, in press; Morse & Niehaus, 2009; Teddlie & Tashakkori, 2009). Also, the term *mixed methods* is now appearing in titles of mixed methods empirical journal articles with increased frequency (e.g., Slonim-Nevo & Nevo, 2009). Numerous books now exist about the procedures of mixed methods, and new books are coming out each year. Discipline- or field-based books are now available, such as the book on mixed

methods in nursing and the health sciences (Andrew & Halcomb, 2009).

Several journals are now devoted to publishing methodology discussions and empirical mixed methods studies, such as the *Journal of Mixed Methods Research* (JMMR), *Quality and Quantity, Field Methods,* and the online journal, *International Journal of Multiple Research Approaches.* For *JMMR,* the reception has been impressive during the publication of three volumes of publications, and the receipt of more than 300 manuscripts. Still, within this broader picture, three trends are noteworthy that will likely shape the future of mixed methods research: disciplinary developments, international growth, and funding opportunities.

On disciplinary developments. Over the years, an emerging trend has been for authors to summarize the published mixed methods studies in a given discipline or field of study. This began with the classic article by Greene et al. (1989), who reviewed 57 studies in the field of evaluation. It continued on with the analysis of design decisions for studies reported in the field of higher education (Creswell, Goodchild, & Turner, 1996); interviews with scholars in the fields of family medicine, physics education, and counseling psychology (Plano Clark, 2005); reviews of 232 mixed methods studies in four social sciences disciplines (Bryman, 2006a), and more recently, a review of 75 mixed methods studies in marketing (Harrison, unpublished). Within specific disciplines, mixed methods research has been the focus of special issues of journals such as the *Annals of Family Medicine* (see Creswell, Fetters, & Ivankova, 2004) and the *Journal of Counseling Psychology* (see Hanson, Creswell, Plano Clark, Petska, & Creswell, 2005). An openness is being expressed by journals traditionally oriented toward QUAN research, such as a cardiology journal (see Curry, Nembhard, & Bradley, 2009), a psychology trauma journal (see Creswell & Zhang, 2009), and a school psychology publication

(Powell, Mihalas, Onwuegbuzie, Suldo, & Daley, 2008). New discipline-based groups and conferences are emerging with a special interest in mixed methods, such as the Special Interest Group in the American Educational Research Association, which is now 4 years old, and the special session on QUAL and mixed methods research that was held at the American Psychological Association meeting in Toronto in August 2009.

What factors are contributing to this disciplinary dispersion of mixed methods? Plano Clark (2005) assessed factors that signaled the acceptance of a new method within a discipline and found that it involved graduate students asking to use the methods in their research, disciplinary leaders advocating for the use of the new method, and researchers publishing studies that apply the new method. She concluded that mixed methods in the fields of physics education, primary care, and counseling psychology had not yet reached mainstream status.

Increased study of how different fields and disciplines have embraced mixed methods needs to be undertaken. In addition to learning more about factors that facilitate acceptance, we also need to learn more about how disciplines *shape* mixed methods to fit their needs. Studying, for example, how intervention researchers incorporate QUAL data into their clinical trials can portray an adaptation of mixed methods to traditional evidenced-based medicine (see the discussion about mixed methods intervention trials in Creswell, Fetters, Plano Clark, & Morales, 2009). Although such experimental trials have raised questions about the subversion of QUAL research to the dominant QUAN methodology in the health sciences (see Howe, 2004), the use of mixed methods does serve to bring QUAL research into the health sciences in an acceptable manner where it has not gained much entry. Also, discipline-based approaches, such as geographical information systems (GIS), are being seen as applications of mixed methods

procedures in fields such as sociology (Fielding & Cisneros-Puebla, 2009).

On international growth. That mixed methods research is moving out beyond the disciplines to many countries around the world cannot be disputed. Recent publications in *JMMR* attest to strong international participation, for example, from Sri Lanka (Nastasi et al., 2007), Germany (Bernardi, Keim, & von der Lippe, 2007), Japan (Fetters, Yoshioka, Greenberg, Gorenflo, & Yeo, 2007), and the United Kingdom (O'Cathain, Murphy, & Nicholl, 2007). The Mixed Methods Conference, now hosted by Leeds University in the United Kingdom, has completed 5 years with growing numbers each year, and in 2010, the conference will come to the United States for the first time. Over the years, American scholars have been involved in this conference, thus lessening the "Atlantic gap" that often occurs between U.S. academics and those from other countries. An international community is forming around mixed methods, with discussions about the QUAN and QUAL skills needed to undertake this form of inquiry and the need, especially in countries such as South Africa, for involvement of individuals with QUAN skills amid the preponderance of QUAL talent.

What may encourage more international cooperation is the advent of courses in mixed methods. Mixed methods courses have been part of the conversation about mixed methods over the years, with discussion about the content and instructional approaches of the courses (Creswell, Tashakkori, Jensen, & Shapley, 2003); about teaching graduate students to learn, use, and appreciate both QUAN and QUAL research within a mixed methods framework (Onwuegbuzie & Leech, 2009); and about identifying the strengths, challenges, and lessons learned from teaching mixed methods courses (see Christ, 2009). Several international online mixed methods courses are now available, offered in the United States at the University of Nebraska-Lincoln and at the University of Alabama-Birmingham. Articles such as Christ's (2009) highlight the importance of examining pedagogical issues, which was suggested by Tashakkori and Teddlie (2003), as well as understanding the practical application of mixed methods, as indicated by Greene (2008). However, as with discipline developments, it remains to be seen how different countries (some with much less of a pedagogical orientation than the United States) embrace mixed methods, train individuals outside of coursework in QUAN and QUAL skills, and adapt the inquiry methods to best fit current local problems and issues.

On funding opportunities. A concern is sometimes raised that mixed methods is simply a response to funding sources (Giddings, 2006) and the need to develop proposals that respond to funding agencies (see Dahlberg et al., 2010 [this volume]). Despite these concerns, neither Tashakkori and Teddlie (2003) nor Greene (2008) raised this concern or touched on the topic of funding and mixed methods research. Funding could be viewed as a stimulus for mixed methods research as well as an inhibiting force. I am inclined to view it as a helpful stimulus. In the United States, the National Institutes of Health (NIH, 1999) took the initiative several years in developing guidelines for combined QUAN and QUAL research, although these guidelines are in need of drastic revision today based on recent mixed methods developments. In 2004, NIH held a workshop titled, "Design and Conduct of Qualitative and Mixed-Methods Research in Social Work and Other Health Professions," sponsored by seven NIH institutes and two research offices. In 2003, the U.S. National Science Foundation held a workshop on the scientific foundations of QUAL research, with several papers devoted to the topic of combining QUAL and QUAN methods (Ragin, Nagel, & White, 2004). Private U.S. foundations, such as the Robert Wood Johnson Foundation and the W. T. Grant Foundation have had workshops on mixed methods research (Creswell & Plano Clark, 2007). In the United Kingdom, the Economic and Social Research Council's (ESRC) has funded inquiries into the use of mixed methods research through its Research Methods Programme (Bryman, 2006b).

On the U.S. side, and in light of the interest expressed in mixed methods research, Plano Clark (2009) has examined funded projects by NIH and their use of the term *mixed methods* in the abstracts for funded projects. Examining only the new funding awards (identified in the first year of funding) and using the search terms *mixed methods* or *multimethod*, Plano Clark obtained 272 hits from the NIH RePORTER (http://projectreporter.nih.gov/reporter.cfm) for the period of 1997 to 2008. Her review of these projects showed a steady increase in the use of the terms *mixed methods* and *multimethods* in funded project abstracts during this time period. Funding for the projects came from 25 different NIH agencies (with the National Institute of Mental Health funding the largest percentage of projects at 24%), one indicator of the widespread interest in this approach. As might be expected, 27% of the projects included an experimental or control trial component, and many projects revealed complex designs and design names, such as a "mixed methods prospective randomized controlled study" or a "longitudinal mixed methods descriptive study," or an "equivalent, sequential, transformative, mixed-methods study." The names alone present the immense variation that exists in undertaking health science mixed methods projects. In my own work with the RePORTER database, I have explored the K01 awards given to new scholars who present both a plan for career development as well as a substantive project. Looking solely at the funded projects for 2007, a number of these projects funded included a training component related to QUAL research and mixed methods.

Looking broadly at this area of funding, I feel that our understanding of adoption and use of mixed methods by funding agencies still deserves increased attention. Little seems to be known about funding from agencies in international countries, funding specific to disciplines, and funding that incorporates mixed methods into existing methodologies and designs, such as the substantial use of mixed methods within a clinical, experimental context at NIH.

◆ **Conclusions**

There are certainly parallels among the four themes I have discussed and the issues and important questions identified by Tashakkori and Teddlie (2003), Greene (2008), and myself. The perspective advanced in this chapter has perhaps expanded and added to the discussion the work of new authors, especially authors publishing in the *Journal of Mixed Methods Research*. My domain discussions have focused less on the justification for mixed methods and more on the stages of mixed methods procedures, such as inferences, as stated by Tashakkori and Teddlie (2003). It has addressed less the sociopolitical commitments suggested by Greene (2008), although I have included a number of references to critiques of mixed methods and the emerging postmodern perspective. My assessment suggests the numerous stances that have emerged in the etiology of mixed methods, and I have characterized these stances as a healthy indicator of the field. I have incorporated recent writings that suggest new developments and new insights that are beginning to shape the field, and, by raising questions throughout this discussion, I hope to stimulate further inquiries and new threads of thinking. Where mixed methods will be in 10 years is anyone's guess; I can only hope that my discussion has highlighted several themes—about the nature of mixed methods, the philosophical and theoretical debates, the procedures in conducting mixed methods research, and the adoption and use of it—that will be taken up later and expanded on with future new developments in mixed methods.

Research Questions and Exercises

1.   What common features do you see in the issues/priorities/topics advanced in Table 2.1 by Tashakkori and Teddlie (2003), Greene (2008), and Creswell (2008, 2009a)?

2.   How has the definition of mixed methods research changed over the years?

3.   Should the field of mixed methods research establish its own language, a bilingual language of its own?

4.   How has the discussion about the philosophical foundations for mixed methods changed in recent years?

5.   How has the discussion about the research designs in mixed methods developed in recent years?

6.   What are the trends in international and discipline adoption of mixed methods to surface recently?

◆ References

Andrew, S., & Halcomb, E. J. (Eds.). (2009). *Mixed methods research for nursing and the health sciences*. Chichester, West Sussex, UK: Blackwell.

Bernardi, L., Keim, S., & von der Lippe, H. (2007). Social influences on fertility: A comparative mixed methods study in Eastern and Western Germany. *Journal of Mixed Methods Research, 1*(1), 23–47.

Brady, B., & O'Regan, C. (2009). Meeting the challenge of doing a RCT evaluation of youth mentoring in Ireland: A journey in mixed methods. *Journal of Mixed Methods Research, 3*(3), 265–280.

Bryman, A. (2006a). Integrating quantitative and qualitative research: How is it done? *Qualitative Research, 6*(1), 97–113.

Bryman, A. (2006b). Paradigm peace and the implications for quality. *International Journal of Social Research and Methodology, 9*(2), 111–126.

Buck, G., Cook, K., Quigley, C., Eastwood, J., & Lucas, Y. (2009). Profiles of urban, low SES, African-American girls' attitudes toward science: A sequential explanatory mixed methods study. *Journal of Mixed Methods Research, 3*(4), 386–410.

Campbell, D. T., & Stanley, J. C. (1966). Experimental and quasi-experimental design for research on teaching. In N. L. Gage (Ed.), *Handbook of research on teaching* (pp. 1–80). Chicago: Rand McNally.

Christ, T. (2009). Designing, teaching, and evaluating two complementary mixed methods research courses. *Journal of Mixed Methods Research, 3*(4), 292–325.

Creswell, J. W. (in press). Controversies in mixed methods research. In N. K. Denzin & Y. S. Lincoln (Eds.), *SAGE handbook on qualitative research* (4th ed.). Thousand Oaks, CA: Sage.

Creswell, J. W. (2008, July 21). *How mixed methods has developed*. Keynote address for the 4th Annual Mixed Methods Conference, Fitzwilliam College, Cambridge University, UK.

Creswell, J. W. (2009a). Mapping the field of mixed methods research [Editorial]. *Journal of Mixed Methods Research, 3*(2), 95–108.

Creswell, J. W. (2009b). *Research design: Qualitative, quantitative, and mixed methods approaches* (3rd ed.). Thousand Oaks, CA: Sage.

Creswell, J. W., Fetters, M., & Ivankova, N. (2004, January/February). Designing a mixed methods study in primary care. *Annals of Family Medicine, 2*(1), 7–12.

Creswell, J. W., Fetters, M. D., Plano Clark, V. L., & Morales, A. (2009). Mixed methods intervention trials. In S. Andrew & E. J. Halcomb (Eds.), *Mixed methods research for nursing and the health sciences* (pp. 161–180). Chichester, West Sussex, UK: Blackwell.

Creswell, J. W., Goodchild, L., & Turner, P. (1996). Integrated qualitative and quantitative research: Epistemology, history, and designs. In J. Smart (Ed.), *Higher education: Handbook of theory and research* (Vol. 9, pp. 90–136). New York: Agathon Press.

Creswell, J. W., & McCoy, B. R. (in press). The use of mixed methods thinking in documentary development. In S. N. Hesse-Biber (Ed.), *The handbook of emergent technologies in social research*. Oxford, UK: Oxford University Press.

Creswell, J. W., & Plano Clark, V. L. (2007). *Designing and conducting mixed methods research*. Thousand Oaks, CA: Sage.

Creswell, J. W., & Plano Clark, V. L. (in press). *Designing and conducting mixed methods research* (2nd ed.). Thousand Oaks, CA: Sage.

Creswell, J. W., Plano Clark, V. L., & Garrett, A. L. (2008). Methodological issues in conducting mixed methods research designs. In M. M. Bergman (Ed.), *Advances in mixed methods research* (pp. 66–83). London: Sage.

Creswell, J. W., Tashakkori, A., Jensen, K., & Shapley, K. (2003). Teaching mixed methods research: Practice, dilemmas, and challenges. In A. Tashakkori & C. Teddlie (Eds.), *Handbook of mixed methods in social and behavioral research* (pp. 619–637). Thousand Oaks, CA: Sage.

Creswell, J. W., & Zhang, W. (2009). The application of mixed methods designs to trauma research. *Journal of Traumatic Stress* 22(6), 612-621.

Crotty, M. (1998). *The foundations of social research: Meaning and perspective in the research process.* London: Sage.

Curry, L. A., Nembhard, I. M., & Bradley, E. H. (2009). Qualitative and mixed methods provide unique contributions to outcomes research. *Circulation, 119,* 1442–1452.

Dahlberg, B., Wittink, M., & Gallo, J. (2010). Funding and publishing integrated studies: Writing effective mixed methods manuscripts and grant proposals. In A. Tashakkori & C. Teddlie (Eds.), *SAGE handbook of mixed methods in social & behavioral research* (2nd ed., pp. 775-802). Thousand Oaks, CA: Sage.

Dellinger, A. B., & Leech, N. L. (2007). Toward a unified validation framework in mixed methods research. *Journal of Mixed Methods Research, 1*(4), 309–332.

Denscombe, M. (2008). Communities of practice: A research paradigm for the mixed methods approach. *Journal of Mixed Methods Research, 2,* 270–283.

Denzin, N. K., & Lincoln, Y. S. (Eds.). (2005). *The SAGE handbook of qualitative research* (3rd ed.). Thousand Oaks, CA: Sage.

DeVellis, R. F. (1991). *Scale development: Theory and application.* Newbury Park, CA: Sage.

Elliot, J. (2005). *Using narrative in social research: Qualitative and quantitative approaches.* London: Sage.

Fetters, M. D., Yoshioka, T., Greenberg, G. M., Gorenflo, D. W., & Yeo, S.A. (2007). Advance consent in Japanese during prenatal care for epidural anesthesia during childbirth. *Journal of Mixed Methods Research, 1*(4), 333–365.

Fielding, N. G., & Cisneros-Puebla, C. A. (2009). CAQDAS-GIS convergence: Towards a new integrated mixed methods research practice? *Journal of Mixed Methods Research, 3*(4), 349–370.

Forman, J., & Damschroder, L. (2007, February). *Using mixed methods in evaluating intervention studies.* Presentation at the Mixed Methodology Workshop, VA HSR&D National Meeting, Arlington, VA.

Freshwater, D. (2007). Reading mixed methods research: Contexts for criticism. *Journal of Mixed Methods Research, 1*(2), 134–145.

Giddings, L. S. (2006). Mixed-methods research: Positivism dressed in drag? *Journal of Research in Nursing, 11*(3), 195–203.

Greene, J. C. (2008). Is mixed methods social inquiry a distinctive methodology? *Journal of Mixed Methods Research, 2*(1), 7–22.

Greene, J. C., & Caracelli, V. J. (Eds.). (1997). *Advances in mixed-method evaluation: The challenges and benefits of integrating diverse paradigms* (New Directions for Evaluation, Vol. 74). San Francisco: Jossey-Bass.

Greene, J. C., Caracelli, V. J., & Graham, W. F. (1989). Toward a conceptual framework for mixed-method evaluation designs. *Educational Evaluation and Policy Analysis, 11*(3), 255–274.

Greene, J., & Hall, J. (2010). Dialectics and pragmatism: Being of consequence. In A. Tashakkori & C. Teddlie (Eds.), *SAGE handbook of mixed methods in social & behavioral research* (2nd ed., pp. 119-143). Thousand Oaks, CA: Sage.

Guba, E., & Lincoln, Y. S. (1989). *Fourth generation evaluation.* Newbury Park, CA: Sage.

Hall, B., & Howard, K. (2008). A synergistic approach: Conducting mixed methods research with typological and systemic design considerations. *Journal of Mixed Methods Research, 2*(3), 248–269.

Hanson, W. E., Creswell, J. W., Plano Clark, V. L., Petska, K. S., & Creswell, J. D. (2005). Mixed methods research in counseling psychology. *Journal of Counseling Psychology* 52(2), 1–12.

Harrison, R. L. (unpublished paper). *Mixed methods designs in marketing research.* University of Nebraska-Lincoln, Department of Marketing.

Hesse-Biber, S. N., & Leavy, P. L. (2007). *Feminist research practice: A primer.* Thousand Oaks, CA: Sage.

Hodgkin, S. (2008). Telling it all: A story of women's social capital using a mixed methods approach. *Journal of Mixed Methods Research, 2*(4), 296–316.

Howe, K. R. (2004). A critique of experimentalism. *Qualitative Inquiry, 10,* 42–61.

Ivankova, N. V., Creswell, J. W., & Stick, S. L. (2006). Using mixed methods sequential explanatory design: From theory to practice. *Field Methods, 18*(1), 3–20.

Johnson, R. B., Onwuegbuzie, A. J., & Turner, L. A. (2007). Toward a definition of mixed methods research. *Journal of Mixed Methods Research, 1*(2), 112–133.

Kelle, U. (2006). Combining qualitative and quantitative methods in research practice: Purposes and advantages. *Qualitative Research in Psychology, 3,* 293–311.

Kuckartz, U. (2009). *Realizing mixed-methods approaches with MAXQDA.* Unpublished manuscript, Department of Education, Phillipps-Universitaet, Marburg, Germany.

Kuhn, T. S. (1970). *The structure of scientific revolutions* (2nd ed.) Chicago and London: University of Chicago Press.

Lee, Y-J, & Greene, J. (2007). The predictive validity of an ESL placement test: A mixed methods approach. *Journal of Mixed Methods Research, 1*(4), 366–389.

Leech, N. L, Dellinger, A. B., Brannagan, K. B., & Tanaka, H. (2010). Evaluating mixed research studies: A mixed methods approach. *Journal of Mixed Methods Research. 4*(1), 17-31.

Lincoln, Y. S., & Guba, E. (1985). *Naturalistic inquiry.* Beverly Hills, CA: Sage.

Lincoln, Y. S., & Guba, E. G. (2000). Paradigmatic controversies, contradictions, and emerging confluences. In N. K. Denzin & Y. S. Lincoln (Eds.), *Handbook of qualitative research* (2nd ed., pp. 163–188). Thousand Oaks, CA: Sage.

Luck, L., Jackson, D., & Usher, K. (2006). Case study: A bridge across the paradigms. *Nursing Inquiry, 13*(2), 103–109.

Maxwell, J., & Loomis, D. (2003). Mixed methods design: An alternative approach. In A. Tashakkori & C. Teddlie (Eds.), *Handbook of mixed methods in social & behavioral research* (pp. 241–272). Thousand Oaks, CA: Sage.

Mertens, D. M. (2009). *Transformative research and evaluation.* New York: Guilford Press.

Mertens, D. M., & Ginsberg, P. E. (2009). *Handbook of social research ethics.* Thousand Oaks, CA: Sage.

Messick, S. (1995). Validity of psychological assessment: Validation of inferences from persons' responses and performances as scientific inquiry into score meaning. *American Psychologist, 50*(9), 741–749.

Morgan, D. L. (2007). Paradigms lost and pragmatism regained: Methodological implications of combining qualitative and quantitative methods. *Journal of Mixed Methods Research, 1*(1), 48–76.

Morse, J. M. (1991). Approaches to qualitative-quantitative methodological triangulation. *Nursing Research, 40,* 120–123.

Morse, J., & Niehaus, L. (2009). *Mixed method design: Principles and procedures.* Walnut Creek, CA: Left Coast Press.

Myers, K. K., & Oetzel, J. G. (2003). Exploring the dimensions of organizational assimilation: Creating and validating a measure. *Communication Quarterly, 51*(4), 438–457.

Nastasi, B. K., Hitchcock, J., Sarkar, S., Burkholder, G., Varjas, K., & Jayasena, A. (2007). Mixed methods in intervention research: Theory to adaptation. *Journal of Mixed Methods Research, 1*(2), 164–182.

National Institutes of Health, Office of Behavioral and Social Sciences Research (1999). *Qualitative methods in health research: Opportunities and considerations in application and review.* Washington, DC: Author.

O'Cathain, A., Murphy, E., & Nicholl, J. (2007). Integration and publications as indicators of "yield" from mixed methods studies. *Journal of Mixed Methods Research, 1*(2), 147–163.

Onwuegbuzie, A. J., & Johnson, R. B. (2006). Types of legitimation (validity) in mixed methods research. *Research in the Schools, 13*(1), 48–63.

Onwuegbuzie, A., & Leech, N. (2009). Lessons learned for teaching mixed research: A framework for novice researchers. *International Journal of Multiple Research Approaches, 3*(1). (on-line journal)

Plano Clark, V. L. (2005). Cross-disciplinary analysis of the use of mixed methods in physics education research, counseling psychology, and primary care. (Doctoral dissertation, University of Nebraska-Lincoln, 2005). *Disssertation Abstracts International, 66,* 02A.

Plano Clark, V. L. (2009, July 10). *Recent trends in federally funded mixed methods projects in the United States*. A contributed paper presentation for the 5th Annual Mixed Methods Conference, Harrogate, UK, 2009.

Plano Clark, V. L., & Creswell, J. W. (2008). *Mixed methods reader*. Thousand Oaks, CA: Sage.

Powell, H., Milhalas, S., Onwuegbuzie, A. J., Suldo, S., & Daley, C. E. (2008). Mixed methods research in school psychology: A mixed methods investigation of trends in the literature. *Psychology in the Schools, 45*(4), 291–308.

Quinlan, E. & Quinlan, A. (2010). Representations of rape: Transcending methodological divides. *Journal of Mixed Methods Research 4* (2), 127–143.

Ragin, C. C., Nagel, J., & White, P. (2004). *Workshop on scientific foundations of qualitative research* (Report). Retrieved April 8, 2006 from http://www.nsf.gov/pubs/2004/nsf04219/nsf04219.pdf.

Sale, J. E. M., Lohfeld, L. H., & Brazil, K. (2002). Revisiting the quantitative-qualitative debate: Implications for mixed-methods research. *Quality and Quantity, 36*, 43–53.

Sandelowski, M. (1996). Using qualitative methods in intervention studies. *Research in Nursing & Health. 19*(4), 359–364.

Sandelowski, M., Voils, C. I., & Knafl, G. (2009). On quantitizing. *Journal of Mixed Methods Research, 3*(3), 208–222.

Singer, B., Ryff, C. D., Carr, D., & Magee, W. J. (2002). Linking life histories and mental health: A person-centered strategy. *Sociological Methodology, 28*, 1–51.

Slonim-Nevo, V., & Nevo, I. (2009). Conflicting findings in mixed methods research: An illustration from an Israeli study on immigration. *Journal of Mixed Methods Research, 3*(2), 109–128.

Stange, K.C., Crabtree, B.F., & Miller, W.L. (2006). Publishing multimethod research. *Annals of Family Medicine, 4*, 292–294.

Sweetman, D., Badiee, M., & Creswell, J. W. (in press). Use of the transformative framework in mixed methods studies. *Qualitative Inquiry.*

Tashakkori, A., & Teddlie, C. (1998). *Mixed methodology: Combining qualitative and quantitative approaches*. Thousand Oaks, CA: Sage.

Tashakkori, A., & Teddlie, C. (2003). The past and future of mixed methods research: From data triangulation to mixed model designs. In A. Tashakkori & C. Teddlie (Eds.), *Handbook of mixed methods in social & behavioral research* (pp. 671–701). Thousand Oaks, CA: Sage.

Teddlie, C., & Tashakkori, A. (2009). *Foundations of mixed methods research: Integrating quantitative and qualitative approaches in the social and behavioral sciences*. Thousand Oaks, CA: Sage.

Vogt, D. S., King, D. W., & King, L.A. (2004). Focus groups in psychological assessment: Enhancing content validity by consulting members of the target population. *Psychological Assessment, 16*, 231–243.

Voils, C. I., Sandelowski, M., Barroso, J., & Hasselblad, V. (2008). Making sense of qualitative and quantitative findings in mixed research synthesis studies. *Field Methods, 20*(3), 3–25.

Vygotsky, L. S., & Cole, M. (1978). *Mind in society the development of higher psychological processes*. Cambridge, MA: Harvard University Press.

Woolley, C. (2009). Meeting the mixed methods challenge of integration in a sociological study of structure and agency. *Journal of Mixed Methods Research 3*(1), 7–25.

Yin, R. K. (2006). Mixed methods research: Are the methods genuinely integrated or merely parallel? *Research in the Schools, 13*(1), 41–47.

3

A HISTORY OF PHILOSOPHICAL AND THEORETICAL ISSUES FOR MIXED METHODS RESEARCH

◆ Burke Johnson and Robert Gray

Objectives

To be able to

- define the major philosophical concepts discussed and articulate/justify your position on the concepts;

- explain the similarities between ancient and current debates about knowledge;

- describe how the Self has been viewed over history and explain how and why QUAL and QUAN writers might differ in their assumptions and views of the Self;

- explain the debate between Plato/Socrates and the Sophists about knowledge;

- describe what is meant by "MM-like thinking";

- describe the history of scientific methods;

(Continued)

(Continued)

- describe the philosophy of positivism and contrast it with today's postpositivism;
- describe the six major influences on the development of the QUAL worldview;
- explain what is meant by the "two-cultures" in academia;
- describe the recent articulation and formalization of MM; and
- explain the "pragmatic maxim" and the philosophy of dialectical pragmatism.

The purpose of this chapter is to provide an intellectual history of some key ideas and debates dividing qualitative and quantitative research, and to examine prior attempts at integration. We believe it is important to dialogue not only with contemporary writers, but also with writers of past times, for if we ignore them, we might falsely believe we invented "the debate" or "the science wars" or "the knowledge problem" (Goldman, 2006). Furthermore, many past arguments are still highly relevant. Our narrative is necessarily perspectival, but our aim is to provide some context and to connect readers to additional writers and literatures that are helpful in understanding qualitative (abbreviated QUAL in this chapter), quantitative (abbreviated QUAN in this chapter), and the third methodological paradigm of mixed methods research (abbreviated MM in this chapter).[1]

Before beginning our historical tour of key ideas, we present in Table 3.1 several concept pairs that have divided thinkers for much of Western history and underlie current methodological and philosophical paradigm differences. Although the pairs of concepts might be viewed as metaphysical dichotomies, they should be viewed only as distinctions (Putnam, 2004). That's because the mixed methods research perspective, following the classical pragmatists, takes an antidualistic stance called *synechism*. The idea is to view the world in terms of continua rather than binaries (See Box 3.1).

BOX 3.1

On Synechism

In the words of Charles Sanders Peirce (1839–1914)

The word synechism is the English form of the Greek (*synechismos*), from (*syneches*), continuous........Thus, *materialism* is the doctrine that matter is everything, *idealism* is the doctrine that ideas are everything, *dualism* is the philosophy which splits everything in two. In like manner, I have proposed to make *synechism* mean the tendency to regard everything as continuous. (Peirce 1893/1998, p. 1).

Thinking *synechistically* helps one avoid the error of "false choice," which is too commonly used in our journals and books as a way of describing the world and as an argument form. Mixed methods research also favorably views the principle of *syncretism,* which, as used here, involves attempting to reconcile opposing principles and viewpoints in particular research studies to answer particular research questions and meet particular social needs and purposes. It acknowledges weak, moderate, and strong forms of concepts, and avoids the category of necessity.

Table 3.1 Selected Concepts Dividing Academics

Concepts	Definitions
Physicalism/ materialism versus idealism	*Physicalism* is the newest instantiation of classical materialism, which said the world and reality are most essentially composed of matter. The newer name, physicalism, is preferred because some physical reality is nonmaterial (e.g., light, gravity, relationships, structure). Physicalism reduces all reality to physics. *Idealism* holds that ideas and the mental (including social and cultural) are the most fundamentally real.
Empiricism versus rationalism	*Empiricism* is the doctrine that knowledge comes from experience. *Rationalism* is the doctrine that knowledge comes from reasoning and thought.
Deduction versus induction versus abduction and dialectics	Classically speaking (Aristotle), *deduction* referred to reasoning from the general to the particular, *induction* referred to reasoning from the particular to the general, and *dialectics* involved questioning and consideration of different sides, hypothetical reasoning, and rhetorical persuasion. In current philosophy, deductive reasoning refers to drawing a conclusion that is necessarily true if the premises are true, and inductive reasoning refers to the process of drawing a conclusion that is probably true. Some view *abduction* as a form of inductive reasoning; others view it as a separate type involving (a) creative, back-and-forth reasoning or (b) reasoning to the best explanation.
Absolutism versus relativism	*Absolutism* is the doctrine that there are many natural laws and unchanging truths concerning the world. Relativism, in contrast, rejects making broad generalizations and holds that true or warranted knowledge can vary by person, group, place, and time.
Scientific naturalism versus humanism	*Scientific naturalism* is the doctrine that the focus of science should be on the natural/physical world and that any justification needed for modern science comes from science itself rather than from foundational philosophy (e.g., Quine, Kuhn). *Humanism* is the stance that writers should focus on the distinctly human characteristics of people, such as their feelings, emotions, free will, autonomy, creativity, morality, love for beauty, and uniqueness. Humanism is seen throughout history in the works of the poets and other literary writers.
Scientific explanation versus human understanding	*Scientific explanation* is the view that scientific knowledge should explain how the natural world operates. Traditionally, this focused on descriptive laws; more recently, with a revival of scientific realism, it focuses on causes and effects. *Human understanding* is the view that knowledge about humans must focus on subjective meanings.
Nomothetic knowledge versus ideographic knowledge	*Nomothetic knowledge* is the goal of traditional science; it includes scientific laws or at least strong generalizations of how the world is from an objective standpoint. *Ideographic knowledge* is focused on understanding particular individuals, groups, places, and settings. The distinction is between the general and particular knowledge.

SOURCE: Adapted from Johnson, 2008a.

In our survey of Western thinking, we identify what we see as important proto-QUAL ideas, important proto-QUAN ideas, and important proto-MM ideas. These are ideas that foreshadow current forms of QUAL, QUAN, and MM. We also provide six boxes tracing the history of the Self.[2] These boxes will help situate some of the assumptions of historical writers about humans and provide an understanding of one key battleground of QUAL and QUAN (i.e., what is the Self?). Before getting started, however, we discuss our "biases" and vision for MM.

First, we believe the human world (which is the focus of human and social science) is composed of many and multiple realities. We agree with QUAL that our thoughts and experiences and feelings and emotions are real. We agree with sociologists and anthropologists that languages, institutions, and cultures are real. We agree with QUAN that there are objective realities that can impact us. In short, we embrace *subjective reality* (e.g., individual, personal, experiential), *intersubjective reality* (e.g., social structures, languages, institutions, nonmaterial cultures), and *objective reality* (i.e., material/physical things, physical/causal processes) (Johnson & Onwuegbuzie, 2004). One might label our metaphysical position *ontological pluralism*. One might view our ontological pluralism as a new sort of realism (we will label it *multiple realism*); it fully acknowledges the "realities" discussed in QUAL and in QUAN, and it rejects singular reductionisms and dogmatisms. We believe that one principle of MM is to take seriously multiple types of realities, concurrently, and to attempt to interconnect the subjective, intersubjective, and objective parts of our world.

Second, rather than viewing differences in concepts and positions as "incompatible," we literally *thrive* on learning from differences and creating new syntheses. Conceptually speaking, it is important to acknowledge that there is no singular descriptive or explanatory conceptual system that, as Plato would say, "carves nature at its joints" (i.e., a perfect conceptual scheme that is a natural kind, precisely matching reality). Multiple disciplinary perspectives have much to add to our understanding of our world and, often, they need to be interconnected. The same claim operates at the level of philosophy.

Third, we believe that recognition of the benefits of balance and compromise are at the core of MM. Fourth, we believe that another core principle of MM is to dialectically examine multiple perspectives (in their strong versions) and create workable solutions in addressing important research questions and social problems. Finally, we are biased toward "a pragmatism of the middle" (Johnson, Onwuegbuzie, & Turner, 2007) or "dialectical pragmatism" (Johnson, 2009; Teddlie & Johnson, 2009b) as a useful philosophical partner for MM. As we dialogue with past writers, the reader will now perhaps understand what motivated our selection of writers.

◆ Ancient Debates Over Knowledge and Meaning

Many of deepest divisions fueling today's paradigm differences have been with us since ancient times,[3] where many of the concepts shown in Table 3.1 originated. Dogmatic/strong forms of the concepts are seen as well as early attempts at moderation, balance, and synthesis. At the core of the paradigm debates between today's QUAN, QUAL, and MM researchers are the issues of relativism and the nature of knowledge and reality.

Plato (429–347 BCE) and Socrates (470–399 BCE) famously disliked the Sophists (and the poets) because of the latter's relativism. Plato's view of knowledge was quite similar to philosophers of today following the JTB theory of truth (i.e., knowledge is justified true belief). Plato argued for essentialism in our concepts and certainty in what we claim to be true. Statements are (a) true or (b) false; today, this is known as the principle of bivalence, and it is at the heart of deductive logic and is relied on in much philosophical argumentation.[4] Because *knowledge* for Plato must be true, any knowledge claim was considered true or false. Plato also saw truth as unchanging. This can be seen in his theory of the forms. The forms are the true and eternal realities existing beyond the changing particulars we see in this world. Plato was a proto-rationalist because the route to truth was through a priori reasoning; he stressed deductive logic (certainty) and, sometimes, recollection of ideas to understand Truth as it existed in the universal forms (which are only approximated in empirical particulars). As discussed in his book the *Republic,* knowledge for Plato was most likely to be obtained by philosophers and other wise men (and possibly women).[5]

Plato and Socrates' nemeses, the Sophists, had a very different view of reality and truth and knowledge. Plato/Socrates rejected (as false) arguments by Presocratic Heraclitus (540–470 BCE) that reality is fluid and always changing. Plato/Socrates rejected the sophist Protagoras's (490–420 BCE) claim that "man is the measure of all things" (i.e., that humans, rather than some objective reality or god, decide what reality is, what is valuable, and what an idea means). Plato/Socrates rejected Sophist arguments that truth depends on the situation, the context, the issue, one's purpose, or one's perspective. In short, the nemesis of Plato and Socrates' position was ontological *relativism.* That's because Plato and Socrates were absolutists (see Table 3.1), and the Sophists were relativists.

Aristotle (384–322 BCE) is another of the great ancient philosophers who addressed the ideas discussed thus far. If we view Plato as a proto-rationalist seeking certainty in ideas and in the forms, Aristotle was, perhaps, a proto-empiricist seeking to develop understandings of what we see and experience in this world. Aristotle was somewhat of a direct realist, in that he thought what we see is what we can believe as real (i.e., he solved the problem of realism by denying that it was a problem). Although Aristotle, like Plato, wanted certainty, Aristotle knew it was not forthcoming in some realms (e.g., psychology, poetics, politics, and ethics), and he placed faith in the *endoxa* (reputable opinions) of wise people who had carefully studied phenomena and issues for a long time. Aristotle seemed to accept intersubjectivity as an indicator of

truth, rather than just the deductive/geometric-like proof desired by Plato. Aristotle's reliance on deduction, induction, dialectics, and opinion as potentially complementary approaches to understanding is in the spirit of MM. Aristotle merged Plato's other-worldly forms with matter seen here on Earth.

Aristotle's four causes (i.e., material, efficient, formal, and final) integrate earlier ideas of the times. His material and efficient causes are similar to natural science approaches to causation (and QUAN thinking); his formal and final/purposive causes might be viewed as related to idealism and free will/agency found in some QUAL writings. Last, in his emphasis on *balance* between the extremes of "excess and deficiency" (i.e., the "golden mean"), Aristotle (and many others in ancient times) puts forward a thoroughly MM epistemological virtue. Integrative strategies such as these are in the spirit of MM, and we will point out multiple historical examples of the spirit of MM in the remainder of this chapter.[6]

We briefly note a third view of reality present in the ancients, but different from Plato/Socrates and the Sophists. According to several Presocratics, reality could be reduced to fundamental *material* things. For Thales (640–546 BCE), all things come from and reduce to water (ontological monism); for Empedocles (493–433 BCE), all things come from earth, air, fire, and water (ontological pluralism); and for Leucippus (500–450 BCE) and Democritus (460–370 BCE), everything is composed of atoms and void (i.e., empty space). Although the atomists were not correct that the atom is indivisible (or uncuttable), the idea is fundamentally similar to today's physicalists. *Physicalism* (see Table 3.1) is perhaps more common in the natural sciences, but it also is present with some cognitive scientists holding the position of eliminative materialism (and related positions).[7] In the philosophy of mind, physicalists see the mind-body problem as solved: The mind (including *qualia*, or subjective experiences) is nothing but the body. Finally, according to physicalists, folk psychology (i.e., commonsense psychological theory and the classical concepts of psychology) is false and needs to be replaced with the true concepts of physics (Churchland, 1981). Most social scientists today, however, do not appear to hold this view because their research still largely relies on the concepts of sociology, psychology, phenomenology, and so on, rather than reduction to the concepts of physics and chemistry.

Before leaving the ancients, we note some key points. First, Plato/Socrates can be viewed as proto-QUAN, and the Sophists can be viewed as proto-QUAL in their views about knowledge. This intellectual conflict is Western Civilization's beginning of the paradigm wars! We believe the paradigm debates are largely about knowledge (and power and personality). Second, since the time of Plato, most Western philosophers have viewed truth as something that is certain and unchanging, much like Euclidian geometry.[8] According to current paradigm constructions, "capital T truth" (i.e., Truth) remains the goal of the QUAN paradigm, and the position of the QUAL paradigm is that truth is relative. One can safely conclude that this is a long-standing debate, and it is not likely to be resolved any time soon. Third, the ancients gave us the dialectical approach to knowledge and a proto-critical theory. Fourth, the Sophists' relativity of truth and emphasis on rhetoric and language gave us an early form of what would be called, about 2,400 years later, postmodernism and interpretivism. In short, we can see in ancient times the early origins of QUAL, QUAN, and MM ways of thinking, and many of the current debates have been with us since these ancient times (appearance vs. reality, relativism vs. invariantism, knowledge and ethics).

BOX 3.2

The Self in Ancient Times

Concern with the Self in the ancient world had to do with what happens after death. *Socrates* believed that his Self was contained in his rational soul, not his body, and that his soul would live on unencumbered by his body. *Plato* believed the immortal intellect constitutes the essence of a person. *Aristotle* differed from Plato in that he didn't appear to believe in the immortality of the intellect. For Aristotle, achieving full selfhood requires engaging in philosophical speculation and working with others for the common good. The Greeks saw truth to be a higher, unchanging reality, and the philosopher was someone with a passion to seek truth; despite this passion, however, the philosopher was ruled by reason and knowledge, not belief or intuition.

In Christian thought, the apostle *Paul* believed full selfhood was paradoxically realized in the sacrifice of Self to the service of Christ. *Augustine* believed that truth was not found outside of the Self, but rather from deep within it, in what he called the "inner self." For Augustine, the Self gained its continuity through memory, but that memory of earthly life is lost in heaven. For all of these philosophers, reality was to be perceived, not constructed, and an accurate understanding and representation of reality was at the heart of their purpose.

Unlike the philosophers, ancient poets were more concerned with inspiration than with reason. *Homer* was revered by the philosophers but also feared because poetic inspiration derives from the imagination, not from reason. For Homer and other writers, such as *Sophocles*, the concept of Self was problematic in that the characters in their writing were governed by fate. The Hebrew writers of the *psalms* wrote strictly from imagination derived from divine inspiration. Heavy use of metaphor and emphasis on the personal suggest an intensely passionate sense of individual selfhood. The Roman poet *Virgil*, unlike Homer and Sophocles, developed more self-aware epic heroes, who wrestled with the tension between reason and passion. While each of these poets endeavored to provide an understanding and illustration of the real world, their representations made no attempts to be "realistic."

The ancient philosophers and poets held similar conceptions of Self and universal truth, and both groups believed truth was derived from a divine entity; however, philosophers accused the poets of working from inspiration rather than reason, suggesting the philosophers were more proto-QUAN than the poets. Both groups would likely have considered themselves to lean heavily toward the proto-QUAN end of the spectrum, but their reliance on abstract truths to ground their empiricism suggests they were not as QUAN as they might have believed. We classify the poets as leaning in the proto-QUAL direction and providing some opposition to the exclusively rational thought of the ancient philosophers.

◆ **Medieval Debates Over Knowledge and Meaning**

During the Middle Ages, Europe was organized along the lines of "the great chain of being" (Lovejoy, 1936/1976). Everything, human and nonhuman, had its proper place in the organized cosmos. This was supported by Aristotle's similar cosmos, and Aristotle was known simply as "the philosopher," during this time. From a proto-QUAN perspective, we note the efforts of Roger Bacon (1214–1294 CE) to advocate the teaching of natural philosophy (i.e., science) in universities and for increased use of experiments. From a proto-QUAL perspective, we note the biblical exegesis movement and founding of hermeneutics (i.e., interpretation of text) by Johann Dannhauser in 1654 (Vessey, 2009) and Friedrich Schleiermacher (1760–1834). We see the MM perspective in the careful arguing of opposing sides by the scholastics, and in Peter Abelard's (1079–1142 CE) solution to the problem of universals. On one side of the debate were the realists (claiming that universals exist), and on the other side were the nominalists (claiming that only particulars exist). Abelard's solution was a middle position of conceptualism, which is the idea that universals exist in minds, but particulars exist in particular objects. A proto-MM approach to knowledge is seen in the title of Abelard's book, *Sic et Non* (i.e., yes and no). Today, we believe *both* QUAL and QUAN include "some truth," and our assessment of each on most issues is *sic et non*.

BOX 3.3

The Self in Medieval Times

The medieval concept of Self placed reason at the top and the passions below; the will suppressed the passions so that reason could be served. Mind and body were indivisibly linked, so the state of the body, and therefore the mind, was determined by the proportional relationship of the four bodily "humors" (black bile, yellow bile, phlegm, and blood). According to this "scientific" theory, a balanced mind required a balanced body, and an individual's personality was believed to be based on the type of balance/imbalance of the humors. *Averroës* believed that one part of the human soul is mortal, but the other part is immortal and part of the single divine soul. *Thomas Aquinas* disagreed with Averroës, arguing that the intellectual soul is immortal and that individuals remain distinct in eternity. Most medieval philosophers were principally theologians, who sought truth through scripture, and earlier religious writers such as Augustine; however, due to the work of Averroës, Aristotle was much esteemed.

(Continued)

(Continued)

Medieval poets held worldviews and conceptions of the Self that were similar to philosophers of their day, but the style was different. *Dante Alighieri's The Divine Comedy* is a first-person narrative that attempts to explain the Christian conception of the afterlife. It is a work of intense imagination, employing rich, descriptive imagery and making use of several figures from Greek, Roman, and Hebrew history and mythology. The Christian humanist *Petrarch* was devoutly Catholic, but he emphasized the importance of human imagination and achievement in the betterment of the human world. He was inspired by Augustine to move his attention from the natural world to a contemplation of Self in order to find truth from within. *Geoffrey Chaucer* built on Petrarch's humanist inclinations by developing characters who were notably flawed and conspicuously worldly. He anticipated the development of the novel with his use of unreliable narrators and unique characters from all walks of life, each of whom provided different perspectives on reality, morality, and truth, leading to an emergent sense of selfhood as relative and authentic.

Medieval philosophers and poets sought to understand and represent reality as it was mediated by universal truths. These truths, grounded in scripture, provided a theoretical framework for their worldview, suggesting that these philosophers and poets tended more toward the QUAL end of our spectrum.

◆ Scientific Revolution and Enlightenment

The 14th century is our candidate for perhaps the worst time to live in Europe because of weather, famine, and most importantly, the plague of 1348, which reduced the population between 30% and 70%. For descendents of survivors, the 15th and 16th centuries were better. The Italian and then Northern Renaissance brought a humanistic revival and a more positive attitude about the future. The scientific revolution of the 16th and 17th centuries and the 18th-century Enlightenment followed and marked a turning point in scientific and intellectual history, away from the Earth-centered universe, away from the great chain of being, and away from near complete control by the church of intellectual history. In the battle of ancients versus moderns, the moderns usually won, and a new rational attitude that the human world can be continually improved spread.

Francis Bacon (1561–1626) became a spokesperson for a new empirical, inductive, observational and experimental science as the way to discover knowledge. His methodological book, *The New Organon*, was meant to replace Aristotle's *The Organon*. The Greek word *organon* meant "instrument or tool," and Bacon claimed his new organon involved unvarying application of the empirical method via hard work (not creative work); the removal of the researcher from the research process was key because of human biases. According to Bacon, researchers must avoid the idols of the tribe (errors inherent in the human mind and ways of perception), the idols of the cave (resulting from researchers' idiosyncratic biases based on their backgrounds), the idols of the marketplace (resulting from ambiguities in language use), and idols of the theater (resulting from prior teachings of the authorities). The proto-QUAN idea was to remain value free and study the world systematically. Creativity was not needed.

In contrast to the early empiricist approach of Bacon, René Descartes (1596–1650) was a rationalist. His method was deductive, a priori reasoning. He played the skeptic only long enough to find the firm foundation on which geometric-like certain knowledge could be deduced. He claimed that "clear and distinct" ideas must be true (such as "I think therefore I am" and "God would not deceive me"), and he claimed to have found the way to deductive, necessary, certain, eternal truth. He was Plato revisited and founded modern *rationalism* (Table 3.1).

A generation later, the classical empiricists formalized the philosophy of *empiricism* (Table 3.1). John Locke (1632–1704) argued that humans' minds begin as *tabula rasa,* a blank tablet or slate to be written on by impressions entering the mind from the external world. David Hume (1711–1776) continued Locke's associationistic psychology and hoped to become the Newton of psychology, showing how the mind is deterministic (e.g., following the laws of physical contiguity, temporal precedence, and constant conjunction). Hume was skeptical of causation and deductive certainty and concluded that we can *know* very little. Ultimately, he relied on a biological-like determinism and suggested that we should follow social conventions and our passions when they feel correct. Hume identified the "problem of induction," which still haunts empirical scientists who hope to conclusively verify their theories. According to the problem of induction, observation and experimentation can never produce certainty because researchers can never observe all phenomena, and it is always possible that phenomena of tomorrow will be different from what has been the case in the past.[9] Researchers can empirically identify regularities; they cannot identify universal certainties. Despite Hume's skepticism, later writers including the positivists took from Hume a scientific naturalism as the approach to studying the human world and followed Hume's suggestion that facts and values must remain separate. This latter idea came to be known as Hume's law (i.e., we can never logically draw an *ought* from an *is*), and this became one of the core tenets of logical positivism.

The empiricists were QUAN thinkers. In contrast, Giambattista Vico (1668–1744) was a proto-MM thinker. Vico (1709/1990) identified two major approaches to understanding: the ancients, who interconnected different disciplines, and the moderns, who sundered that interconnectivity into different disciplines and focused on philosophical criticism at the expense of the creative insights, wisdom, and eloquence often found in the ancient approach (e.g., especially as seen in the ancient Cicero versus the modern Descartes). For Vico, both ancients and moderns had strengths and weaknesses.

Vico wanted people to use reason and imagination. He recognized the importance of continuums rather than dichotomies; of formal learning and practical experience; and of common sense, eloquence (*ars tropica*), and critical reasoning. Vico understood the importance of constructivism (*verum ipsum factum*) and nature and mathematics/logic for producing knowledge. He was a prototypical MM thinker because he relied on multiple standpoints and approaches to gaining fuller, complementary knowledge rather advocating a "one way" dogmatic view of knowledge. A cardinal rule of MM is antidogmatism.

Another core principle of MM is checks and balances. This idea is seen historically in the governments of ancient Athens and Sparta and the Roman Republic, it is present in Aristotle's political theory and was formalized and used later in history and government. Montesquieu (1689–1755) coined the phrase "checks and balances" and expanded Locke's executive and legislative governmental components by adding the judiciary. This thinking became part of the U. S. Constitution in 1787. From an MM perspective, checks and balances are important in research communities as a way of balancing the operation of perspectives, knowledge, and power. Checks and balances also are important for helping MM researchers to conduct research that meets exploratory and confirmatory needs and that produces MM knowledge (i.e., knowledge that has survived multiple-perspective development, examination, and warranting).

BOX 3.4

The Self in Early Modern Times

The Renaissance and Enlightenment mark the beginning of the development of the modern Self. While humanism and secular thought were becoming more prominent, theologians were still influential, especially early in the Renaissance. *Martin Luther* initiated the Protestant Reformation, transforming the relationship between God and humanity into an unmediated relationship between God and the Self. As philosophers became more secular, however, they developed a more empirical approach to the study of reality and the search for truth. *René Descartes*, with his *cogito ergo sum*, rationalistically proved the existence of a Self. *Thomas Hobbes* considered the Self as continually engaged in the struggle for power, as egotistical and selfish, and as never acting out of concern for others. *John Locke* attempted to reduce the mind to an atomized mechanical process and believed each human is born as a blank slate that gains knowledge through external influences. *David Hume* believed that we can be aware of things only as they relate to our consciousness, not as they exist in themselves. He argued that the Self can be known only as a series of perceptions and that a continuous Self that links those perceptions together is illogical, but he viewed the Self as potentially happy and social, enjoying engagements with others rather than concerning itself about its own deep structure. The empiricist philosophers' views of the Self as deterministic would become the essence of the Enlightenment Self.

The poets of this period held worldviews similar to the philosophers of their day, but their views of the Self were more nuanced and more complex, and compared to philosophers of the age, they began to show more tensions within the Self and in Self-to-other interactions. *Sir Philip Sydney* argued that Plato hated the poets because he knew poets had a more direct path to the truth. *William Shakespeare* developed complex characters confronted with difficult problems of ambiguous origin, yet these characters are shown to operate with free will. *John Bunyan* provided a model of how the individual Self must develop his or her own agency to find the path to salvation and forsake the outward temptations of the world. *Daniel Defoe's Moll Flanders* was one of the earliest openly feminist texts and presented a concept of Self as something that is constructed and changeable. *Voltaire* and *Samuel Johnson* showed a surface or empirical sense of Self throughout their work, focusing on the things people do rather than what motivates them. *James Boswell* identified the lack of authenticity in social situations, which brought an awareness of the divide between the projected Self and what was considered a "true" Self.

Philosophers and poets both believed that reason was the only legitimate intellectual pursuit and that passion and imagination were evils that led one away from virtue and truth. By the early 1700s, the philosophers had moved to the extreme proto-QUAN end of the spectrum, and the poets were not far behind, despite their tendency to show some complexity and nuance. The foundation of current QUAN thought lies firmly in Enlightenment values that came from this period.

◆   *19th-Century Developments*

Romanticism, which began in the late 18th century and continued into the 19th century,[10] was a dialectical reaction to what was seen as the excesses of the Enlightenment. The Enlightenment stood for positive progress; the new science and universal rationality could solve all social problems. But Enlightenment natural philosophers also viewed the individual as little more than a material being determined by natural and environmental influences.

The emphasis on universal rationality left little room for spirituality and human passions, emotions, imagination, and differences among individuals and cultures. Romantic writers attempted to bring the more human side of people back into focus, rejecting the idea of "man as machine." We view romanticism as a major early influence on QUAL; it was a proto-QUAL movement from the perspective of this chapter. Its focus on difference also is similar to 20th-century postmodernism. From an MM perspective, romanticism corrected an imbalance, and when taken together with Enlightenment views, it provides a fuller understanding of humans.

The next major philosophical/intellectual movement, *idealism* (Table 3.1), also developed in the late 18th century and continued throughout the 19th century, especially in Germany. The philosophy of idealism is usually attributed to the German philosopher/physicist Immanuel Kant (1724–1804), who attempted what he called a new Copernican revolution. His goal was to resolve the conflict between Descartes' rationalism (rational, deductive thought is the foundation for knowledge) and Hume's empiricism (sense experience is the foundation for all knowledge). Kant was especially uncomfortable with Hume's skepticism and sought to bring back the Platonic-like certainty required for True knowledge.

Kant's "solution" was that we can have universal knowledge about *phenomena* (things knowable by the senses), but we cannot have knowledge of *noumena* (things as they are in themselves; the world as it really is). This distinction lies at the heart of many current debates about realism. Kant also was a "constructivist" because, when working out his solution, he concluded that the mind plays an active role in constructing experience and knowledge. Unlike QUAL constructivists, however, Kant was a transcendental constructivist; his thinking required the mind to provide the same experience to everyone and to allow universal knowledge. Kant's desire for universal understanding and knowledge seems

misguided from the current perspective that different cultures and individuals can construct different understandings and different subjective and intersubjective realities. Nonetheless, from an MM perspective, we view Kant as a proto-MM thinker because he searched for integrative solutions between conflicting positions. We also like Kant's argument that quantity *and* quality are both necessary categories of human understanding. Aristotle made the same claim in ancient times. The importance of quantity *and* quality is another core principle of MM. Because most writers emphasize Kant's epistemology, we sometimes forget that Kant also found a place for ethics and freedom (in his third book, *Practical Knowledge*), and he concluded that freedom exists. From an MM perspective, current science seems misguided to the degree that it ignores freedom, choice, and intentionality as key parts of human constitution, motivation, and meaning.

Kant's transcendental idealism contrasts with other German idealists, who were somewhat closer to today's QUAL thinking. These thinkers included Johann Fichte (1762–1814), Friedrich Schelling (1775–1854), Friedrich Schiller (1759–1805), Johann Herder (1744–1803), and G. W. F. Hegel (1770–1831). These thinkers emphasized the dominance and separate reality of human mind and thought, in contrast to the materialist, reductionist, natural science position. They also helped pave the way for the coexistence of alternative conceptual frameworks, social constructivism, subjectivism, and culture as nonuniversal phenomena (Solomon, 1988). These idealists were important for the later development of the discipline of anthropology and, subsequently, QUAL (and MM) thinking.

The 19th century also was an important QUAN transition period for the development of scientific methods. First, the English word *scientist*, with its modern meaning, was coined by William Whewell (1794—1866) during this period.[11] At the same time, hypothesis testing became formalized as the key QUAN scientific method (Proctor & Capaldi, 2006). Although the terms *context of discovery* (the inductive/abductive method) and *context of justification* (the deductive, hypothesis-testing method) would not formally appear until the 20th century, these two concepts can be seen in John Herschel's (1792–1871) theory of scientific method (Losee, 2001). The context of discovery was relegated to psychology and was not part of "science proper," and this expulsion continued throughout the 20th century in QUAN research. The narrower scientific method (which eliminated the QUAL-like context of discovery) would become known in QUAN as the *hypothetico-deductive method* (Achinstein, 2004; Teddlie & Johnson, 2009a, 2009b). Although Whewell excluded a context of discovery, he emphasized that science relies on creative acts, which most 20th-century writers (e.g., logical positivists, falsificationists) would exclude from the hypothetico-deductive method. From the MM perspective, the generative, inductive nature of the context of discovery (which includes *construction* as well as discovery) *and* the context of justification (theory/hypothesis testing) are *both* very important (as well as abduction, dialectic, and criticism) to the practice of science. It is a core tenet of MM that multiple logical and creative methods should be used in MM-inspired science (Johnson, 2009).

Continuing with 19th-century developments that led to QUAN, classical positivism was born during the 1830s, thanks to Auguste Comte (1797–1857). Comte claimed that society and thought progress historically through three stages, the theocratic (i.e., simplistic, superstitious stage), the metaphysical (i.e., philosophical and transition stage), and the positive (i.e., the time of positive, certain knowledge). Unfortunately, Comte's positivism was *scientistic* because science was the only way to knowledge. All other forms of knowledge were denigrated. Comte believed that science is based on facts and lawful relationships. He viewed "causation" (which is important in contemporary QUAN) as a metaphysical concept that was unnecessary for science (Laudan, 1971). Because of his fear of metaphysics, he was an antirealist, similar to later logical positivists (i.e., all we

can scientifically talk about is what we can experience). Comte's positivism was important for QUAN, but it is somewhat dissimilar to QUAL descriptions of "positivism" (e.g., Guba, 1990).

A 19th-century movement of importance to QUAL is seen in the ideas of Wilhelm Dilthey (1833–1911) and Max Weber (1864–1920). Dilthey, a philosopher, emphasized the importance of hermeneutics, which is the interpretation of text, and he generalized this concept to the human sciences. He also articulated the difference between natural and human sciences (*naturwissenschaften* vs. *geisteswissenschaften*), which would be important for the separation of QUAN (which has since the Enlightenment tried to model itself on the natural sciences) and QUAL (which rejected the natural science model and developed a human science of subjectivity). This distinction also is seen in the contrast between explanation and understanding (Table 3.1). The former is about laws; the latter is about subjective meaning. Both Weber, an early sociologist, and Dilthey advocated the method of *verstehen,* which involves the empathetic understanding of the actors of history. Understanding of values and context also were important for these writers. Weber and Dilthey advocated the importance of both natural and human sciences, and they were interested in objectivity *and* subjectivity. Weber was especially interested in using his *interpretive sociology* to link the macro (social-structural) level with the micro (subjective/intersubjective) level. The bipartite division of science is of importance not only to QUAL but also to MM. A difference is that QUAL often defines itself in opposition to QUAN, but a core tenet of MM is to explicitly and deeply examine both QUAL and QUAN standpoints (Onwuegbuzie & Johnson, 2006).

The Darwin-Wallace theory of evolution is a final 19th-century development that was important in the QUAN/QUAL dispute. This theory showed how new species could emerge through natural selection (i.e., an interaction of chance and the environment over long periods of time). The scientific theory provided a powerful impetus that fueled a new fight between religion and science, and this continues to be one branch of the "science wars" (e.g., Does natural knowledge replace religious knowledge about the species?). Although it was a QUAN scientific theory, QUAL thinkers especially liked its implications for dynamic reality and for nonstatic truth. The Darwin-Wallace theory challenged the fixity of Platonic Truths and the natural scientific reductionist assumption that all phenomena are ultimately subject to unchanging physical laws. An MM perspective is pluralistic; it accepts multiple kinds of knowledge, it views both order and change as important parts of reality, and it accepts that some domains are more lawful than others.

BOX 3.5

The Self in the 19th Century

The Romantic Period privileged emotion and imagination over the emphasis on reason and empiricism that characterized the Enlightenment. This led to a revolutionary new sense of the Self. *Jean Jacques Rousseau*'s development of confessional discourse was influential in the development of Romanticism, with its combination of the revelation of Self with a conspicuous representation of Self. *Immanuel Kant* argued that our knowledge of an object does not stem from the object itself but rather from the way our understanding shapes that object, leading him to focus on how we have to think about the Self rather than the Self itself. *Georg Friedrich Hegel* contended that the certainty of Self is confirmed only by the opposition of another individual consciousness that negates it (i.e., an "other"). The Romantic period was also notable for widespread, subversive political writing. *Thomas Paine* and others wrote in favor of democratic revolution, while *Mary Wollstonecraft*, a pioneer of the feminist movement, argued that women deserve the same rights as men, and therefore equal access to selfhood.

The Romantic poets took these philosophical shifts to their extreme. *William Wordsworth* built on Rousseau's models of autobiography and confessional discourse as carefully constructed representations. His insistent focus on the subjectivity of the Self in communion with the subjectivity of Nature is central to the development of Romanticism. Wordsworth is also famous for his "spots of time," which are moments of epiphany and heightened (or transcendent) awareness, which he believed led to poetic inspiration; he thought the creative imagination produced a more sophisticated knowledge of Self and glimpses into universal truth. Later Romantics, such as *Walt Whitman*, believed that poetic inspiration could lead to a better world. *Ralph Waldo Emerson*'s concepts of transcendentalism and self-reliance grew out of the work of Kant and Wordsworth. Transcendentalism rejected empiricism and intellectualism, seeking truth within the human mind and spirit, while self-reliance built on the idea that truth is found only within oneself in opposition to society. For Emerson, the Self is fully human only when it rejects conformity and custom.

While the philosophers of the Romantic Period moved away from the strict empiricism of the Enlightenment, the poets made a much more significant shift. Their insistence on passion over reason and on imagination over knowledge is a complete reversal of Enlightenment values, and their belief that truth resides in the Self's response to outside stimuli places them squarely in the proto-QUAL camp. The Romantic Period was relatively short, however, and by the middle of the 19th century, poets and philosophers, while clearly influenced by Romantic thought, began to move back toward the middle of the spectrum.

◆ 20th-Century Developments

New developments in the pursuit of knowledge increased markedly in the 20th century. Paradigm-changing theories in natural science were Albert Einstein's (1879–1955) theories of quantum mechanics and relativity, which shifted physics away from an absolute, mechanistic, clockwork world to a new probabilistic and sometimes paradoxical natural world. Partially in response to Einstein's insights about the relativity of simultaneity, Percy Bridgman (1882–1961) developed his measurement theory of operationism, which in its early version literally equated a concept with the empirical operations used in measurement. This idea went hand in hand with the bourgeoning behaviorism movement in psychology (which later would become the dominant paradigm). It also went hand in hand with the logical positivists' verifiability principle.

Logical positivism was the second and last positivism, except for today's postpositivism which is popular in QUAN. Hacking (1983, pp. 41–42) concisely summarized the tenets of positivism as including an emphasis on verification, taking a pro-observation stance, taking an anti-cause stance (preferring lawful relationships), downplaying explanations, and taking an antitheoretical stance toward entities. If some of these seem surprising, it is because of the staunchly antimetaphysical position of the positivists. The logical positivists' verifiability principle stated that the only meaningful statements are (a) analytic statements (such as in mathematics and deductive logic) and (b) statements that can be verified through experience; all other statements (such as statements about values) were cognitive *nonsense*. This was a radical claim, and it supported the scientism of positivism. Scientism is the idea that scientific knowledge is the *only* true knowledge. It is aggressive and excessive. We will mention two key problems with logical positivism (for more problems, see Johnson, 2009). First, it relied on the logic of verification, which presupposed that a universal proposition (e.g., a hypothesis of a law) could be verified (as in

"proved") by empirical research (e.g., through experimentation). The problem is that support of the hypothesis by data does not provide proof of a scientific hypothesis or theory because the deductively *fallacious* argument of affirming the consequent (if p then q; q; therefore p) is used. Second, logical positivism's reliance on the distinction between theory statements/sentences and observation statements/sentences could not be maintained.

Karl Popper (1902–1994) tried to discredit logical positivism by exposing the logical problem of verificationism just mentioned; in its place, Popper recommended his concept of falsificationism. This is the idea that one cannot deductively (i.e., conclusively) verify a scientific proposition, but one *can* deductively (i.e., conclusively) *falsify* a proposition because falsificationism relies on the valid argument form of *modus tollens* (if p then q; not q; therefore not p). Falsificationism also had serious problems, such as the fact that a hypothesis cannot be tested in isolation from other required assumptions and conditions (this is known as the Duhem-Quine principle or the principle of holism in hypothesis testing) (Teddlie & Johnson, 2009b).

Not surprisingly, logical positivism was modified, becoming first logical empiricism (which replaced strong verification with a weaker condition called confirmation), and today it has become *postpositivism* (which is an extensively revised and more moderate philosophy of science) (Campbell, 1994; Phillips & Burbules, 2000). Today's QUAN researchers are, philosophically speaking, mostly postpositivists. This philosophy of science has incorporated many of the criticisms of positivism and accepts the following positions: (a) theory-ladenness of facts, (b) fallibility of knowledge, (c) underdetermination of theory by fact, (d) value-ladenness of facts, and (e) social construction of parts of reality. Because of advances made by postpositivism, we consider it unfortunate that some writers still attribute positivism to QUAN and continue to debate with the long-dead philosophy of positivism (Johnson, 2009).

BOX 3.6

The Self in the Early 20th Century

In the aftermath of Darwin, belief in an infinite, eternal reality was rejected. This removal of the primary basis of Western Thought created a "decentering" of subjectivity that dominated the concept of Self during this period. *Friedrich Nietzsche* rejected concepts like "mind" and "body" as linguistic constructs intended to help us understand our lives. For Nietzsche, the Self is a unity of urges driven by an unconscious will and subject to generations of attitudes and practice. He also introduced the MM concept of perspectivism, which contends that ideas can come only from a particular perspective. Since other perspectives hold a different relationship to truth, all perspectives must be partial. *Sigmund Freud*, unlike Descartes, saw the mind as a physical entity, and his famous conception of the three-part mind as id, ego, and superego decentered subjectivity and individual agency. His concept of the unconscious rejects the notion of free will. *William James* believed that individuals have multiple selves, that the Self is the conglomeration of all we can be said to possess—the body and psyche, as well as all physical possessions, relations, accomplishments, and so on. *Martin Heidegger* defined the existence of the Self as *Dasein* (being-in-the-world), which makes our presence intelligible. For Heidegger, existence of Self takes precedence over essence of Self. *Erving Goffman* argued that humans perform many roles in interaction and that "frontstage" and "backstage" behavior are usually different (Goffman, 1959). The truth or falsity of the interaction is extremely difficult to determine. Feminist writers such as *Sojourner Truth* also gained widespread recognition and influence during this period.

Mid- to late-19th-century novelists like *George Eliot* and *Mark Twain* rejected Romanticism and sought to represent life as realistically as possible. Writers at the turn of the century like *Stephen Crane* strove to present realistic and believable works of fiction that depict a harshly deterministic reality where human agency is an impossibility. Poets of the early 20th century, like *Rainer Maria Rilke*, combined Romantic influences with a contemporary humanist worldview. Modern novelists such as *James Joyce* attempted to represent the content of the human psyche with their stream of consciousness narrative technique. In the shift from modernism to postmodernism, *Jean-Paul Sartre* is considered the model existentialist and believed the Self is constructed by itself.

THE EMERGENCE OF QUAL

For the QUAL worldview, we consider six paramount 20th-century influences. First is the development of phenomenology in the 1920s and 1930s in Germany. Phenomenology is the human scientific study of the life worlds (*Lebenswelt*) or consciousness of individuals. The split between behaviorism and phenomenology became especially wide in academic psychology during the 20th century (cf. Brody & Oppenheim, 1966; Zaner, 1967). Phenomenology started in a transcendental form with Edmund Husserl (1859–1938), who assumed there were invariant structures of experiences that are common to all individuals. Phenomenology was transformed by Husserl's student, Martin Heidegger (1889–1976), through his discussions of deep concepts such as being-in-the-world, *Dasein*, equipment, presence, concern, fallenness, facticity, authenticity, and existence preceding essence. Phenomenological work was extended in Jean-Paul Sartre's (1905–1980) existentialism, which focused on the radical freedom of every individual, and in Alfred Schutz's

(1899–1959) socially oriented version of phenomenology. Later, phenomenologist Thomas Luckman teamed up with sociologist Peter Berger in the theoretically integrative 1966 book entitled *The Social Construction of Reality*. This book is important for MM because the authors interconnect the macro, meso, and micro, and they interconnect objective, intersubjective, and subjective. It is a general principle in MM that multiple levels and types of reality should be routinely considered and interrelated.

A second influence on QUAL included the early 20th-century developments of cultural relativism in anthropology and the linguistic-relativity hypothesis. Cultural relativism states that different groups have different but equally valuable nonmaterial and material cultures; methodologically speaking, it stands in contrast to ethnocentrism. Cultural relativism was popularized by Franz Boas (1858–1942), who was one of the founders of the discipline of anthropology. His approach to anthropology was especially popular until a scientific, materialist reaction in the 1950s (by Leslie White and Julian Steward). The relativist approach is again quite popular in today's anthropology (although multiple perspectives coexist). The linguistic-relativity hypothesis states that people see and understand their worlds through the lens of local language. In its strong form, it states that thoughts are fully bounded by language.

A third influence on QUAL is symbolic interactionism (most popular in sociological social psychology). Symbolic interactionism is a micro/meso-level theory showing how mind, Self, society, symbols, language, and meaning emerge through everyday situations and interactions. It tends to focus on intersubjectivity but can be used to connect the objective and the subjective. Early contributors were Charles Horton Cooley (1864–1929) (some of his key ideas were the looking-glass Self and primary and secondary groups), George Herbert Mead (1863–1931) (some of his key ideas were his conceptualizations of

mind, Self , and society and the *me* versus the *I*), Herbert Blumer (1900–1987) (who coined the term *symbolic interactionism* and emphasized empirical reasoning), and Erving Goffman (1922–1982) (two of his key ideas were dramaturgical analysis and impression management). More recent symbolic interactionists include Norman Denzin (2001), who takes a QUAL perspective, and Sheldon Stryker (2003), who takes a more QUAN perspective.

A fourth influence on QUAL is the theoretical perspective known in sociology as conflict theory and known more broadly in education and literary circles as *critical theory*. Conflict/critical theory builds on the classical writings of Karl Marx (1818–1883) and the 20th-century Frankfurt School and argues that society is built on power relationships and should be analyzed critically. The goal of conflict/critical theory is to reduce inequalities, traditionally focusing on class inequality, but now including many other inequalities such as gender stratification, ethnicity/"race" stratification, sexual identity discrimination, age discrimination, and international inequalities (between and within nations). It is important to understand, however, that conflict and critical theory are popular in QUAL, QUAN (especially in sociology), and MM. Recent advances in critical MM are seen in Hesse-Biber (2010) and Mertens (2007).

The fifth major 20th-century set of influences on QUAL includes the theoretical movements of post-structuralism and postmodernism. Structuralism is the early 20th-century theory emphasizing that a system cannot be understood without understanding its underlying structure. Structuralism began with the work of Ferdinand de Saussure (1857–1913) in linguistics/ semiotics in the early 20th century, but it also appeared in other fields such as anthropology and psychoanalysis. In contrast, post-structuralism was a 1960s and 1970s movement rejecting universal truth and emphasizing differences, deconstruction, and the connectedness of knowledge and power. Its most prolific theoreticians were Michel

Foucault (1926–1984) and Jacques Derrida (1930–2004). Postmodernism was more of an artistic, literary movement and focused its critique on modernism and its symbols and forms. In this movement, the word *modernism* often operates as a synonym for the Enlightenment. Two prominent postmodernists were Jean Baudrillard (1929–2007) and Jacques Lacan (1901–1981). These writers reminded scholars of the *differences* among individuals and other forms of representation. They also emphasized the importance of continual interpretation and the historicity of intellectual and social concepts. From an MM perspective, poststructuralism and postmodernism added some needed balance to the previously QUAN-dominated paradigm, which was becoming too scientistic

and gave little recognition to differences and particulars because of the goal of universal generalization.

The sixth 20th-century influence on QUAL is found in science studies.[12] Specifically, the "strong program" (e.g., Knorr-Cetina, 1981; Latour & Woolgar, 1986) has many similarities with the philosophy of QUAL. According to the strong program, scientific practice should be studied much the way sociologists and anthropologists study any cultural group. This involves examination of status, power, roles, norms, prestige, and other interpersonal factors in relationship to scientific practice. When done this way, scientific facts can be seen as socially constructed. For the perspective of a prominent QUAN methodologist on science studies, see Box 3.7.

BOX 3.7

QUAN and Science Studies

Perhaps the most prominent QUAN methodologist of the 20th century, Donald T. Campbell (1916–1996), viewed science studies surprisingly positively. In his later years, Campbell was open to and excited about the sociological study of science (Campbell, 1994). For example, he said "I heartily endorse science's status as a social product" (p. 131). According to this 1994 chapter, Campbell would agree with this core tenet of MM: Scientific practice and outcomes are influenced by both natural *and* social influences. Science is not just objective, and it is not just subjective. We commend Campbell for calling for a "more balanced synthesis" (p. 132).

KUHN AND SCIENTIFIC PARADIGMS

In 1962, Thomas Kuhn (1922–1996) published one of the most significant books for the philosophy of science in the 20th century. The book, entitled *The Structure of Scientific Revolutions,* integrated philosophical ideas from earlier writers (e.g., Polanyi, Hanson, and Fleck), and provided a new sort of history of science, one that focused on actual social practices and values of scientists (rather than rational reconstructions or happy stories of the uniform progress of science offered by logical positivists, falsificationists, and general science

writers). For Kuhn, a paradigm is an agreed upon theory, worldview, or methodology embodied in the beliefs, practices, and products of a group of scientists. Kuhn was a historicist because he believed that theories define scientific reality and theories change. According to his principle of paradigm incommensurability, communities of scientists literally lived in different worlds and were unable to communicate or understand each other. Kuhn articulated most of the philosophical ideas we mentioned earlier in reference to postpositivism. Kuhn's thinking had a profound effect on both QUAL and QUAN.

Unlike many thinkers in the natural sciences, Kuhn thought the social sciences were pre-paradigmatic because of the coexistence of multiple miniparadigms. Kuhn thought a successful science must spend long periods in normal science, where one paradigm dominates and practitioners focus on puzzle solving and extending the paradigm as far as it can go. I (BJ) have argued (in Johnson et al., 2007) that, at least for the social and behavioral sciences, a multiple paradigmatic condition is preferred, and the three major methodological paradigms (QUAN, QUAL, and MM) can and should coexist and provide healthy contrasts and dialogues. We are uncomfortable when any discipline is controlled by "one-way thinking." It is a tenet of MM that some research is best pursued via QUAN, some is best pursued via QUAL, and some research is best pursued via MM.

TWO CULTURES IN ACADEMIA

In 1959, an important book was written that documented the schism in the academy between natural scientific (QUAN) and literary intellectual (QUAL) cultures. The book, entitled *The Two Cultures and the Scientific Revolution,* was written by a prominent physicist *and* novelist Charles Percy Snow (1905–1980), who had earlier hoped to help bridge the split. Unfortunately, he found the differences to be far too great. He noted (a) "They have a curious distorted image of each other" (Snow, 1959, p. 4), (b) "The non-scientists have a rooted impression that the scientists are shallowly optimistic, unaware of man's [sic] condition. On the other hand, the scientists believe that the literary intellectuals are totally lacking in foresight, peculiarly unconcerned with their brother men [sic]" (pp. 5–6), (c) "This polarisation is sheer loss to us all" (p. 12), (d) "There seems then to be no place where the cultures meet" (p. 17), "The clashing point of two subjects, two disciplines, two cultures . . . ought to produce creative chances" (p. 17); note that Snow was a liberal/critical thinker: "The world can't survive half rich and half poor" (p. 44). Snow was in agreement with a tenet of MM that these cultures in the academy should more frequently work together for common purposes.

More recently, philosopher Simon Critchley (2001) also observed a split in the academy. He sees it emanating from a historical divide of "Continental" and "Anglo American" philosophers. When speaking of the strengths of the two broad groups, Critchley views Continental philosophy (QUAL) as more concerned with *wisdom* and Anglo American philosophy (QUAN) as more concerned with *scientific knowledge.* When speaking of the weaknesses of these groups, he is disturbed by the excesses of both groups when they become dogmatic, with Continental philosophy focusing on "nihilisms and obscurantisms" and analytic philosophy focusing on "scientisms." It is a core tenet of MM that both wisdom *and* science are important and should be integrated and that *both* QUAL (humanistic, poetic, freedom, passions) and QUAN (traditional objective and intersubjective) viewpoints are essential for the advancement of academia. Pragmatist philosopher Susan Haack (2000) labels this middle position well, for many of us, when she calls herself a "passionate moderate."

◆ Formal Emergence of MM

We have tried to show in this chapter that the spirit of MM has existed in many places and times. Other writers in this *Handbook* explicate the recent MM literature, so we will point out only a few current highlights here. In one sense, MM was present in the early 20th century before QUAN became the dominant paradigm in social science. For example, many social scientific works used mixed or multiple methods, as seen in the work of field sociologists, applied psychologists, and anthropologists (Gans, 1963; Hollingshead, 1949; Jahoda, Lazarsfeld, & Zeisel, 1931/2003; Lynd &

Lynd, 1929/1959; Roethlisberger & Dickson, 1939; Warner & Lunt, 1941). After examining about 10 psychology and sociology methods books written before 1935, we found one book (Fry, 1934) that included the following chapters: "Combining Methods of Study," "Qualitative Analysis," and "Quantitative Analysis." Fry stated the following:

> The summary of the methods of investigation employed in *Middletown* makes it clear that research work usually requires more than proficiency in one particular technique. Time and again the really creative part of a social inquiry is deciding how different approaches should be combined to yield the most fruitful results. (p. 136)

Soon after 1935, the social and behavioral sciences became increasingly dominated by a QUAN approach because it seemed to have the most promising future. The post-1935 period also was a time of increasing disciplinary crystallization instead of disciplinary integration of earlier times (Klein, 2007; Ogburn & Goldenweiser, 1927), and most emerging disciplines wanted to become a "science." MM would not rebound or be conceived formally until many decades later.

In 1959, the concept of *multiple operationalism* (or use of more than one method of measurement) was introduced by Campbell and Fiske. In 1966, the idea of *triangulation* appeared in a methods book by Webb, Campbell, Schwartz, and Sechrest. Triangulation was broadened and further developed by Jick (1979) and Denzin (1978). Cook (1985) advocated the concept of *critical multiplism* (or use of different methods to gain different perspectives). Slowly, MM concepts and practices were developed and used more commonly, especially by program evaluators, and related articles and books appeared (e.g., Brannen, 1992; Brewer & Hunter, 1989; Bryman, 1988; Cook, 1985; Creswell, 1994; Greene & Caracelli, 1997; Greene,

Caracelli, & Graham, 1989; Lincoln & Guba, 1985; Morgan, 1998; Morse, 1991; Newman & Benz, 1998; Reichardt & Cook, 1979; Rossman & Wilson, 1985; Tashakkori & Teddlie, 1998). MM was developed by many important scholars, and we have mentioned only a few here.

During the emergence of MM as a third methodological paradigm (along with QUAN and QUAL), MM has struggled somewhat to develop a corresponding philosophical paradigm. Many or perhaps most leaders in the field are advocating some form of philosophical pragmatism (e.g., Creswell & Plano Clark, 2006; Johnson & Christensen, 2008; Johnson & Onwuegbuzie, 2004; Morgan, 2006; Tashakkori & Teddlie, 1998, 2003; Teddlie & Tashakkori, 2009). Johnson et al. (2007) suggested different versions of pragmatism for different types of MM (an antirealist/constructivist version for QUAL-dominant MM, a realist/naturalist version for QUAN-dominant MM, and an intermediate version for equal-status MM). Because full chapters are devoted in this *Handbook* to pragmatism and realism (see Biesta, 2010; Greene & Hall, 2010; Maxwell & Mittapalli, 2010), we explicate here only the pragmatism most recently advocated by the lead author of this chapter and some of his colleagues.[13]

Johnson and Onwuegbuzie (2004) stated the pragmatic maxim as follows: "The meaning or instrumental or provisional truth of a concept, expression, or practice is determined by the experiences or consequences following from belief or use of the concept or practice."[14] In other words, the "small t" truths (i.e., warranted beliefs) that we use in our many human situations are obtained when our values and evidence provide warrants, and these small truths continually change. This philosophical assumption, if one is willing to make it, provides some "philosophical justification" for the practices of mixing concepts and approaches.[15] The mixing is justified at the end when it helps researchers obtain valued outcomes (e.g., understanding, description, explanation, prediction, improved practices, improved lives, reductions in inequalities, social justice) and when researchers obtain useful answers to their research questions. But pragmatism for MM also is a sophisticated philosophy.

Johnson and Onwuegbuzie (2004) constructed a composite pragmatism of 22 tenets selected from the often overlapping ideas of Charles Sanders Peirce (1839–1914), who coined the term *pragmatism* and offered the perspective of a creative philosophical logician; William James (1842–1910), who offered a pluralist, individually oriented pragmatism; and John Dewey (1859–1952), who offered a socially conscious and experimentally oriented version of pragmatism. Taken together, the principles selected from the three classical pragmatists produce a *complementary whole,* which Johnson and Onwuegbuzie believe can work well as a partner philosophy for MM. Here are several principles of classical pragmatism selected from the Johnson and Onwuegbuzie composite: (a) rejects dichotomous either-or thinking; (b) agrees with Dewey that knowledge comes from person-environment interaction (dissolving subject-object dualism) (Biesta & Burbules, 2003); (c) views knowledge as both constructed *and* resulting from empirical discovery; (d) takes the ontological position of pluralism (i.e., reality is complex and multiple); (e) takes the epistemological position that there are multiple routes to knowledge and that researchers should make "warranted assertions" rather than claims of unvarying Truth; (f) views theories instrumentally (i.e., theories are not viewed as fully True or false, but as more or less useful for predicting, explaining, and influencing desired change); and (g) incorporates values directly into inquiry and endorses equality, freedom, and democracy.[16]

I (Johnson) have recently articulated what I currently call *dialectical pragmatism.* Here is my explanation published in (2009; also see Johnson, 2008a, 2008b):

I recently coined the term *dialectical pragmatism* (in Teddlie & Johnson, 2009b) to provide a supportive philosophy for mixed methods research that combines Jennifer Greene's (2007) dialectical approach to mixed methods research and the philosophy of pragmatism. It requires listening and careful consideration of multiple viewpoints. Here's a formal definition. Dialectical pragmatism is a pragmatism tailored for mixed methods research. The base word (pragmatism) refers to the applicability of the core tenets of philosophical and methodological pragmatism (see Table 1 in Johnson & Onwuegbuzie, 2004, or, for a shorter list, Table 4.1 in Teddlie & Johnson, 2009b). The adjective "dialectical" emphasizes that mixed methods researchers must carefully listen to, consider, and dialogue with QUAL and QUAN perspectives, and learn from the natural tensions between these perspectives, when developing a workable solution for a mixed methods research study. Dialogue continues at every phase of the research study. Dialectical pragmatism is most important in equal-status mixed methods designs because in these designs the researcher or team of researchers attempt to give equal weight to the concepts, assumptions, and practices of qualitative and quantitative research (Johnson, Onwuegbuzie, & Turner, 2007). Most generally, the point is to dialectically listen to multiple standpoints and produce an approach to research that synthesizes insights from QUAL and QUAN and any other relevant perspectives. (p. 456)

Generally speaking, QUAN partners with the philosophical paradigm of postpositivism, and QUAL partners with the philosophical paradigm of constructivism. We recommend dialectical pragmatism as a partner for MM. We believe it can operate effectively as a "middle philosophy" that emphasizes continual interaction with multiple philosophical standpoints. Dialectical pragmatism is both a philosophy and an antiphilosophy because it rejects dualisms and philosophical quagmires. It can free researchers to *creatively* construct new research approaches and designs and sets of working assumptions that can help answer many research questions. It is a dynamic standpoint with a perspectival epistemology; it rejects monisms, reductionisms, and *dogmatisms* and suggests that we search for "workable solutions" to what we consider problematic in our world. It operates as a hermeneutical (interpretative) circle that focuses on continual improvement of the human condition. It suggests eliminating philosophical quagmires by continually examining and reconstructing our assumptions and philosophical commitments, but at the same time, dialectical pragmatism, if it is to work well, must learn from tensions and take multiple other philosophical and paradigmatic positions seriously. Always, dialectical pragmatism requires respecting and listening to others, and continually modifying our webs-of-belief in the pursuit of usable knowledge and social justice.

BOX 3.8

The Self in Late 20th Century

In the late 20th century, the concept of Self came to be understood as socially constructed and therefore became further distanced from a notion of truth. *Michel Foucault* posited that discourses are linguistic formations and practices that govern cultural activity, and the Self (or subjectivity) is a discursive formation that is mediated by social structures of power and normalization. For *Roland Barthes*, texts are produced not by authors but by language itself (i.e., discourse); therefore, the act of reading can become an act of writing, an act of producing the reader's own meanings, which can become not only an act of self-assertion, but also an act of resistance to discourse and power. *Gayatri Chakravorty Spivak* contended that Western views and discourses exclude members of groups from outside the mainstream power structure, particularly people from colonized or developing nations, and that this exclusion diminishes or negates the selfhood of these individuals, particularly women.

Postmodern/post-structural writers are difficult to pin down, but appear to be moving the concepts of selfhood, meaning, feeling, and what was once called truth back toward a more conceptual, less empirical place. These philosophers and poets have become primarily concerned with issues of representation and significance, but no individual writer could embody the multiple postmodernisms, although novelists *Thomas Pynchon* and *Umberto Eco* capture many elements that define postmodernism. Contemporary poets such as *Nikki Giovanni* tend toward the political side, while *Charles Bernstein* takes an experimental approach to language informed by the post-structuralism of Foucault and Barthes. The majority of contemporary poets dangle somewhere in between, aware of the epistemological shifts that underlie the contemporary worldview, hoping that in the absence of truth they can somehow represent the beauty of an authentic Self.

Although many QUAL writers have post-structural and postmodern leanings, the Self also is heavily researched in the largely QUAN discipline of social psychology. This QUAN literature, relying on correlational and experimental research, has addressed many complexities of the Self and its relationships to other constructs. Future thinking and research on the Self should be ripe for MM research/integration in the future.

◆ Conclusions

The paradigm wars over knowledge have their roots in ancient philosophy and have been present since those times. One can see proto-QUAL, proto-QUAN, and proto-MM ideas throughout history (ancient, medieval, early modern, modern, current), especially in debates over knowledge. Assumptions about the Self and the natural world have fueled the debates, but differences in temperament and struggles over power also are closely related to the knowledge wars. A QUAN-like worldview has generally dominated Western thinking since ancient times; however, QUAL-like pockets of thought have continued to trouble the dominant view for most of recorded history.

Over time, QUAN-like writers have advocated ideas and concepts such as deduction and certainty as a requirement for true knowledge, materialism/physicalism, scientific naturalism, empiricism and rationalism, positivism, hypothesis testing, causal explanation, and the production of nomothetic/universal knowledge. In contrast, QUAL-like writers have advocated ideas and concepts such as relativism, humanism, idealism, constructivism, and a focus on human understanding, culture, and ideographic/particularistic knowledge.

MM-like writers have since early times relied more on a dialectical approach of considering conflicting positions and attempting to provide a third or alternative position that synthesizes important parts of the different positions. This is done because different positions usually have something important to say about human concerns. The MM standpoint has emphasized ideas such as synechism/antidualism, syncretism, pluralism, multiple realism, balance of extremes, compromise, checks and balances, respect and coexistence, antidogmatism, complementarity, "integration" (e.g., of theory *and* practice, determinism *and* free will, interdisciplinary positions, multiple sources of evidence/truth, multiple epistemological standpoints, facts *and* values, knowledge *and* wisdom, reason *and* emotion, idealism *and* materialism, quantity *and* quality, objectivity *and* subjectivity, constructivism *and* postpositivism). The immediate goal of MM is to make warranted assertions and to produce pragmatic/workable "solutions" for valued ends.

Many philosophers and literary writers were discussed in the chapter to give voice to important ideas and to position QUAN, QUAL, and MM styles of thought as having always been with us. The chapter ends with a brief outline of the pragmatic maxim and the philosophy of dialectical pragmatism.

Research Questions and Exercises

1. Do you think it is important to take a historical approach to the examination of current debates? Explain why or why not?

2. What definition and theory of knowledge do you believe is most warranted for social and behavioral research?

3. What do you consider to be the primary strengths and weaknesses of QUAN?

4. What do you consider to be the primary strengths and weaknesses of QUAL?

5. What do you consider to be the primary strengths and weaknesses of MM?

6. How long do you think the QUAL versus QUAN debates will exist in academia? Why?

7. How can be QUAL versus QUAN debates be made more productive? What next step do you recommend?

◆ Notes

1. We rely on Greene's (2007) broad view of *methodology* as including (a) philosophical assumptions and stances, (b) inquiry logics, (c) guidelines for practice, and (d) sociopolitical commitments. Building on Greene's 2006 article, we refer to mixed methods research as a *methodological paradigm*, and we refer to the types of paradigms discussed by Guba (1990) as *philosophical paradigms*. Both are quite important, and they overlap substantially. We think it is best to include an adjective in front of the word *paradigm* to specify one's particular meaning.

2. Key references used for the Self boxes are Atkins (2005), Baumeister (1999), Damrosch (2003), Sorabji (2006), and Taylor (1989).

3. We relied on many sources for our discussion of the ancients. In addition to the original sources, here are some helpful secondary sources: Bakalis (2005), Brunschwig and Lloyd (2000), Lindberg (2007), Principe (2002), Robinson (1998), Roochnik (2004), Stumpf (1988).

4. Note the contrast between either/or practices and synechism.

5. Plato was less sexist than Aristotle.

6. We are ignoring the many ways that Aristotle was radically *unlike* the spirit of MM (e.g., his distrust of emotions, his cosmology of everything having its natural place including women and slaves).

7. Eliminative materialism is the radical position that there is no mind; there is only the material, physical body. *Mind* is a word that humans made up, in this view; it's analogous to a superstition or belief in something that we now know doesn't exist.

8. The 19th-century founding of non-Euclidian geometries required modification of the assumption that the world was perfectly logical (like Euclidian geometry).

9. Bertrand Russell likened the problem to a chicken that, for every day of its life, like clockwork, obtained feed from the farmer in the morning. The chicken generalized that the good farmer would continue the morning feeding process in the future; however, one morning, the farmer wringed the chicken's neck.

10. Hundred-year markers often are imprecise for delineating historical periods.

11. Up until this time, what we call scientists were known as natural philosophers (e.g., Yeo, 2003).

12. Science studies taken as a whole is balanced by QUAL and QUAN perspectives. For an overview, see Hackett, Amsterdamska, Lynch, & Wajcman, 2007.

13. Here's a link to a Library of Living Pragmatists: http://www.pragmatism.org/library/library.htm

14. Although Peirce originally formulated "the pragmatic maxim," the version provided here is a composite of the classical pragmatists.

15. See Johnson (2009) for a set of guidelines designed to include QUAN, QUAL, and MM standpoints.

16. Johnson (2009) also suggests an explicit value theory for MM. It involves making one's web of values explicit, determining how well valued outcomes are met, and starting the process anew in each situation (although some core values will always be present).

◆ References

Achinstein, P. (2004). *Science rules: A historical introduction to scientific methods*. Baltimore, MD: Johns Hopkins Press.

Atkins, K. (2005). *Self and subjectivity*. Malden, MA: Blackwell.

Bakalis, N. (2005). *Handbook of Greek philosophy: From Thales to the Stoics, Analysis and fragments.* Victoria, BC: Trafford.

Baumeister, R. F. (Ed.). (1999). *The self in social psychology.* Ann Arbor, MI: Psychology Press.

Biesta, G. (2010). Pragmatism and the philosophical foundations of mixed methods research. In A. Tashakkori & C. Teddlie (Eds.), *SAGE handbook of mixed methods in social & behavioral research* (2nd ed.). Thousand Oaks, CA: Sage.

Biesta, G. J. J., & Burbules, N. C. (2003). *Pragmatism and educational research.* Lanham, MD: Rowman & Littlefield.

Brannen, J. (1992). *Mixing methods: Quantitative and qualitative research.* Aldershot, UK: Avebury.

Brewer, J., & Hunter, A. (1989). *Multimethod research: A synthesis of styles.* Newbury Park, CA: Sage.

Brody, N., & Oppenheim, P. (1966). Tensions in psychology between the methods of behaviorism and phenomenology. *Psychological Review, 4,* 295–305.

Brunschwig, J., & Lloyd, G. (Eds.). (2000). *Greek thought: A guide to classical thought.* Cambridge, MA: Belknap Press.

Bryman, A. (1988). *Quantity and quality in social research.* London: Unwin Hyman.

Campbell, D. T. (1994). The social psychology of scientific validity: An epistemological perspective and a personalized history. In W. R. Shadish & S. Fuller, *The social psychology of science* (pp. 124–161). New York: Guilford.

Campbell, D. T., & Fisk, D. W. (1959). Convergent and discriminant validation by the multitrait-multimethod matrix. *Psychological Bulletin, 56,* 81–105.

Churchland, P. M. (1981). Eliminative materialism and the propositional attitudes. *Journal of Philosophy, 78*(2), 67–90.

Cook, T. D. (1985). Postpositivist critical multiplism. In L. Shotland & M. M. Mark (Eds.), *Social science and social policy* (pp. 21–62). Beverly Hills, CA: Sage.

Creswell, J. W. (1994). *Research design: Qualitative and quantitative approaches.* Thousand Oaks, CA: Sage.

Creswell, J. W., & Plano Clark, V. I. (2006). *Designing and conducting mixed methods research.* Thousand Oaks, CA: Sage.

Critchley, S. (2001). *Continental philosophy: A very short introduction.* Oxford, UK: Oxford University Press.

Damrosch, L. (2003). *The enlightenment invention of the modern self.* Chantilly, VA: The Teaching Company.

Denzin, N. K. (1978). *The research act: A theoretical introduction to sociological methods.* New York: Praeger.

Denzin, N. K. (2001). *Interpretative interactionism.* Thousand Oaks, CA: Sage.

Fry, C. L. (1934). *The technique of social investigation.* New York: Harper.

Gans,H. J. (1963). *Urban villagers: Group life and class in the life of Italian-Americans.* New York: Free Press.

Goffman, E. (1959). *The presentation of self in everyday life.* Garden City, NY: Anchor Books.

Goldman, S. L. (2006). *Science wars: What scientists know and how they know it.* Chantilly, VA: The Teaching Company.

Greene, J. C. (2007). *Mixed methods in social inquiry.* San Francisco: Jossey-Bass.

Greene, J. C., & Caracelli, V. J. (Eds.). (1997). *Advances in mixed-method evaluation: The challenges and benefits of integrating diverse paradigms* (New Directions for Evaluation, No. 74). San Francisco: Jossey-Bass.

Greene, J. C., Caracelli, V. J., & Graham, W. F. (1989). Toward a conceptual framework for mixed-method evaluation designs. *Educational Evaluation and Policy Analysis, 11, 255–274.*

Greene, J., & Hall, J. (2010). Dialectics and pragmatism: Being of consequence. In A. Tashakkori & C. Teddlie (Eds.), *SAGE handbook of mixed methods in social & behavioral research* (2nd ed.). Thousand Oaks, CA: Sage.

Guba, E. G. (1990). *The paradigm dialog.* Newbury Park, CA: Sage.

Haack, S. (2000). *Manifesto of a passionate moderate: Unfashionable essays.* Chicago: University of Chicago Press.

Hackett, E. J., Amsterdamska, O, Lynch, M., & Wajcman, J. (Eds.). (2007). *The handbook of science and technology studies.* Boston, MA: MIT Press.

Hacking, I. (1983). *Representing and intervening: Introductory topics in the philosophy of natural science.* Cambridge, UK: Cambridge University Press.

Hesse-Biber, S. (2010). *Mixed methods research: Merging theory with practice.* New York: Guilford Press.

Hollingshead, A. B. (1949). *Elmtown's youth.* New York: John Wiley.

Jahoda, M, Lazarsfeld, P. E., & Zeisel, H. (1931/2003). *Marienthal: The sociography of an unemployed community.* New Brunswick, NJ: Transaction.

Jick, T. D. (1979). Mixing qualitative and quantitative methods: Triangulation in action. *Administrative Science Quarterly, 24,* 602–611.

Johnson, R. B. (2008a). Editorial: Living with tensions. *Journal of Mixed Methods Research, 2,* 203–207.

Johnson, R. B. (2008b). Knowledge. In L. M. Given (Ed.), *The Sage encyclopedia of qualitative research methods* (pp. 478–482). Thousand Oaks, CA: Sage.

Johnson, R. B. (2009). Toward a more inclusive "scientific research in education." *Educational Researcher, 38,* 449-457.

Johnson, R. B., & Christensen, L. B. (2008). *Educational research: Quantitative, qualitative, and mixed approaches.* Thousand Oaks, CA: Sage.

Johnson, R. B., & Onwuegbuzie, A. J. (2004). Mixed methods research: A research paradigm whose time has come. *Educational Researcher, 33,* 14–26.

Johnson, R. B., Onwuegbuzie, A. J., & Turner, L. A. (2007). Toward a definition of mixed methods research. *Journal of Mixed Methods Research, 1,* 112–133.

Klein, J. T. (2007). Interdisciplinary approaches in social science research. In W. Outhwaite & S. P. Turner (Eds.), *The Sage handbook of social science methodology* (pp. 32–49). Thousand Oaks, CA: Sage.

Knorr-Cetina, K. D. (1981). *The manufacture of knowledge: An essay on the constructivist and contextual nature of science.* Oxford, UK: Pergamon.

Kuhn, T. S. (1962). *The structure of scientific revolutions.* Chicago: University of Chicago Press.

Latour, B., & Woolgar, S. (1986). *Laboratory life: The construction of scientific facts.* Princeton, NJ: Princeton University Press.

Laudan, L. (1971). Towards a reassessment of Comte's "Methode Positive." *Philosophy of Science, 38*(1), 35–53.

Lincoln, Y. S., & Guba, E. G. (1985). *Naturalistic inquiry.* Beverly Hills, CA: Sage.

Lindberg, D. C. (2007). *The beginnings of Western science: The European scientific tradition in philosophical, religious, and institutional context, prehistory to A. D. 1450.* Chicago: University of Chicago Press.

Losee, J. (2001). *A historical introduction to the philosophy of science.* Oxford, UK: Oxford University Press.

Lovejoy, A. O. (1976). *The great chain of being: A study of the history of an idea.* Cambridge, MA: Harvard University Press. (Original work published 1936)

Lynd, R. S., & Lynd, H. M. (1929/1959). *Middletown: A study in modern American culture.* Orlando, FL: Harcourt Brace.

Maxwell, J. A., & Mittapalli, K. (2010). Realism as a stance for mixed method research. In A. Tashakkori & C. Teddlie (Eds.), *SAGE handbook of mixed methods in social & behavioral research* (2nd ed.). Thousand Oaks, CA: Sage.

Mertens, D. M. (2007). Transformative paradigm: Mixed methods and social justice. *Journal of Mixed Methods Research, 1,* 212–225.

Morgan, D. L. (1998). Practical strategies for combining qualitative and quantitative methods: Applications to health research. *Qualitative Health Research, 3,* 362–376.

Morgan, D. L. (2006). Paradigms lost and pragmatism regained: Methodological implications of combining qualitative and quantitative methods. *Journal of Mixed Methods Research, 1,* 48–76.

Morse, J. M. (1991). Approaches to qualitative-quantitative methodological triangulation. *Nursing Research, 40,* 120–123.

Newman, I., & Benz, C. R. (1998). *Qualitative-quantitative research methodology: Exploring the interactive continuum.* Carbondale: Southern Illinois University Press.

Ogburn, W. F., & Goldenweiser, A. (Eds.). (1927). *The social sciences and their interrelations.* Boston: Houghton Mifflin.

Onwuegbuzie, A. J., & Johnson, R. B. (2006). The validity issue in mixed research. *Research in the Schools, 13*(1), 48–63. (Also available at http://www.msera.org/rits_131.htm)

Peirce, C. S. (1998). Immortality in the light of synechism. In *The essential Peirce* (pp. 1–10). Bloomington: Indiana University Press. (Original work published 1893)

Phillips, D. C., & Burbules, N. C. (2000). *Postpositivism and educational research*. New York: Rowman & Littlefield.

Principe, L. M. (2002). *History of science: Antiquity to 1700*. Chantilly, VA: The Teaching Company.

Proctor, R. W., & Capaldi, E. J. (2006). *Why science matters: Understanding the methods of psychological research*. Malden, MA: Blackwell.

Putnam, H. (2004). *The collapse of the fact/value dichotomy and other essays*. Cambridge, MA: Harvard University Press.

Reichardt, C. S., & Cook, T. D. (1979). Beyond qualitative versus quantitative research. In T. D. Cook & C. S. Reichardt (Eds.), *Qualitative and quantitative methods in evaluation research* (pp. 7–32). Newbury Park, CA: Sage.

Robinson, D. (Ed.). (1998). *The mind*. Oxford, UK: Oxford University Press.

Roethlisberger, F. J., & Dickson, W. J. (1939). *Management and the worker*. Cambridge, MA: Harvard University Press.

Roochnik, D. (2004). *Retrieving the ancients: An introduction to Greek philosophy*. Malden, MA: Blackwell.

Rossman, G. B., & Wilson, B. (1985). Numbers and words: Combining quantitative and qualitative methods in a single large scale evaluation study. *Evaluation Review, 9*, 627–643.

Snow, C. P. (1959). *The two cultures and the scientific revolution*. New York: Cambridge University Press.

Solomon, R. C. (1988). *Continental philosophy since 1750: The rise and fall of the self*. Oxford, UK: Oxford University Press.

Sorabji, R. (2006). *Self: Ancient and modern insights about individuality, life, and death*. Chicago: University of Chicago Press.

Stryker, S. (2003). *Symbolic interactionism: A social structural version*. Caldwell, NJ: Blackburn.

Stumpf, S. E. (1988). *Socrates to Sartre: A history of philosophy*. New York: McGraw-Hill.

Tashakkori, A., & Teddlie, C. (1998). *Mixed methodology: Combining qualitative and quantitative approaches*. Thousand Oaks, CA: Sage.

Tashakkori, A., & Teddlie, C. (2003). *Handbook of mixed methods in social and behavioral research*. Thousand Oaks, CA: Sage.

Taylor, C. (1989). *Sources of the self: The making of the modern identity*. Cambridge, MA: Harvard University Press.

Teddlie, C., & Johnson, R. B. (2009a). Methodological thought before the 20th century. In C. Teddlie & A. Tashakkori, *Foundations of mixed methods research: Integrating quantitative and qualitative techniques in the social and behavioral sciences* (pp. 40–61). Thousand Oaks, CA: Sage.

Teddlie, C., & Johnson, R. B. (2009b). Methodological thought since the 20th century. In C. Teddlie & A. Tashakkori, *Foundations of mixed methods research: Integrating quantitative and qualitative techniques in the social and behavioral sciences* (pp. 62–82). Thousand Oaks, CA: Sage.

Teddlie, C., & Tashakkori, A. (2009). *Foundations of mixed methods research: Integrating quantitative and qualitative approaches in the social and behavioral sciences*. Thousand Oaks, CA: Sage.

Vessey, D. (2009). Philosophical hermeneutics. In J. R. Shook & J. Margolis (Eds.), *A companion to pragmatism* (pp. 209–214). Malden, MA: Blackwell.

Vico., G. (1990). *On the study of methods of our time* (E. Gianturco, Trans). Ithaca, NY: Cornell University Press. (Original work published 1709)

Warner, W., & Lunt, P. S. (1941). *The social life of a modern community* (Yankee City series, Vol. 1). New Haven, CT: Yale University Press.

Webb, E. J., Campbell, D. T., Schwartz, R. D., & Sechrest, L. (1966). *Unobtrusive measures*. Chicago: Rand McNally.

Yeo, R. (2003). *Defining science: William Whewell, natural knowledge and public debate in early Victorian Britain*. Cambridge, UK: Cambridge University Press.

Zaner, R. M. (1967). Criticism of "tensions in psychology between the methods of behaviorism and phenomenology." *Psychological Review, 74*, 318–324.

4

PRAGMATISM AND THE PHILOSOPHICAL FOUNDATIONS OF MIXED METHODS RESEARCH[1]

◆ Gert Biesta

The purpose of this chapter is to review the claim that pragmatism can provide a philosophical framework for mixed methods research. In the literature, there are stronger and weaker versions of this claim, ranging from the suggestion that pragmatism provides *the* philosophical foundation for mixed methods research to the idea that pragmatism could provide philosophical support for mixed methods approaches. In this chapter, I review the case for pragmatism in three steps. I begin with some conceptual clarification in the discussion about the philosophical dimensions of social and behavioral research. I then focus on mixed methods research and

indicate seven different levels at which ideas about mixing occur in discussions about mixed methods research. I do this to indicate at what levels mixing is relatively unproblematic and where issues become more complex and serious. In the third step, I bring in pragmatism through a reconstruction of the main elements of John Dewey's theory of knowing. In the concluding section of the chapter, I bring these elements together to evaluate in what ways and to what extent pragmatism can provide philosophical support for mixed methods research. The intention of the chapter is not to promote pragmatism but to help readers to come to an informed judgment about the utility of pragmatism as a framework for the justification and development of mixed approaches in social and behavioral research. My own view is that Dewey's pragmatism is helpful in overcoming some of the dualisms that continue to stifle discussions about social and behavioral research (see also Biesta, 2007). Dewey's pragmatism can help us to see, for example, that realist assumptions do not necessarily have to go together with an objectivist conception of truth; that intervention plays a crucial role in the ways in which we obtain knowledge; and that because our knowing is always a result of our actions, knowledge can provide us only with information about possible connections between actions and consequences, not with once-and-for-all truths about a world independent from our lived lives. In this regard, Dewey's ideas can help to break down alleged epistemological hierarchies between the different methods and methodologies that make up mixed methods approaches in the social and behavioral sciences.

◆ Introduction

There appears to be a rather broad consensus within the field of mixed methods research that the rationale for a mixed approach has to be a pragmatic one. Rather than starting from particular philosophical assumptions or convictions, the choice of a mixed approach is seen as one that should be driven by the very questions that research seeks to answer. Johnson and Onwuegbuzie (2004) formulate this as the idea that one should "choose the combination or mixture of methods and procedures that works best for answering your research questions" (p. 17), while Tashakkori and Teddlie (1998) express the same line of thinking with the even stronger principle of the "*dictatorship* of the research question" (p. 20; italics added) (see also Bryman, 2006). There is, of course, nothing wrong with the suggestion

that the methods one uses for research should be appropriate for what one wishes to achieve (although, as I will argue below in discussing how we formulate the purposes of research, there is an issue whether the research question itself is the level at which the purpose of research gets articulated). This is just sound pragmatism of the kind that would argue that a screwdriver is generally a better tool for fixing a screw than a hammer (unless one is very impatient, of course).

While the pragmatic justification for mixed methods research is fairly unproblematic—it simply relies on an argument for the utility of research means for research ends—things become more complicated when the claim for *everyday* pragmatism[2] is taken as an argument for *philosophical* pragmatism to the extent that the latter is seen as the philosophical "paradigm" for mixed methods research. The latter has, for example, been argued by Tashakkori and Teddlie when they suggest that "the paradigm of pragmatism can be employed as the philosophical underpinning for using mixed methods and mixed models (Tashakkori & Teddlie, 1998, p. 167, see also pp. 20–39; for a similar view, see, for example, Johnson & Onwuegbuzie, 2004; Morgan, 2007; for a more cautious approach, see Gorard with Taylor, 2004, p. 144). It is also the suggestion made by Greene (2008), who identifies pragmatism as a "leading contender for the philosophical champion of the mixed methods arena" (p. 8). Although some work has been done on introducing ideas from pragmatism to the field of mixed methods research (see Johnson & Onwuegbuzie, 2004; Maxcy, 2003; Morgan, 2007; Tashakkori & Teddlie, 1998; and the chapters in this volume by Johnson & Gray, 2010; Greene & Hall, 2010), I believe that the challenge formulated by Greene still stands, in that we need not only to achieve a better and more precise[3] understanding of what pragmatism entails but also to engage in more detail with the question of how ideas from pragmatism might be relevant for mixed methods research.

The thesis that I will put forward in this chapter is that we should not expect that pragmatism—and from now on I will use this word to refer to *philosophical* pragmatism—can provide *the* philosophical framework for mixed methods research. The main reason for this is that, perhaps unlike many other philosophies, pragmatism should not be understood as a philosophical position among others, but rather as a set of philosophical tools that can be used to address problems—not in the least problems created by other philosophical approaches and positions. One of the central ideas in pragmatism is that engagement in philosophical activity should be done to address problems, not to build systems (see Biesta, 2009b). John Dewey (1922) explicitly warned against system building in philosophy by characterizing the tendency to conflate the outcomes of specific inquiries with antecedent ontological conditions as "*the* philosophical fallacy" (p. 123; italics in original). This is not to suggest that pragmatism has nothing to offer to the field of mixed methods research, but it is important to see that what it has to offer is not a paradigmatic underpinning or wholesale justification of mixed methods research, but rather a set of insights that can help us to have a more precise discussion about the strengths and weaknesses of mixed methods approaches. This is why this chapter is organized around issues and problems, not the defense of pragmatism as a philosophical position or paradigm.

I begin this chapter with brief comments on three (sets of) concepts which, although very prominent in the discussion about mixed methods research, are in my view rather unhelpful. Having cleared the ground a little, I then present seven levels at which discussions about the pros and cons and strengths and weaknesses of mixed methods approaches have taken place or are still taking place. My aim in distinguishing the different levels in the discussion is not to add to an already substantial body of literature devoted to characterizing the different

possible designs for mixed methods research (see, e.g., Creswell & Plano Clark, 2007; Plano Clark & Creswell, 2008; Tashakkori & Teddlie, 2003a). I rather aim to identify where, when, and how problems arise in the discussion and where issues are actually straightforward and unproblematic. I then turn to pragmatism and, more specifically, to the work of John Dewey, which I take to be the most detailed and developed form of pragmatism where it concerns questions about knowledge, reality, and the conduct of inquiry (for a more detailed account, see Biesta & Burbules, 2003). His work has also been the most influential strand of pragmatism in the development of 20th-century philosophy of science (see, for example, Schillp, 1951), although for a long time—that is, until the influential contributions by Rorty (1980, 1982)—the "necessity" of pragmatism (Sleeper, 1986) has not been acknowledged. I provide a reconstruction of Dewey's main ideas, with a particular focus on the epistemological, ontological, and methodological dimensions of his work. I then discuss what pragmatism has to offer to the field of mixed methods research. This will allow me to indicate in a more precise manner to what extent pragmatism can indeed be a "philosophical champion" (Greene, 2008) for mixed methods research and also to suggest some of the limitations of pragmatism. By organizing the chapter in this way, I hope to make some "thoughtful progress" (Greene 2008, p. 13) with regard to exploring the potential of pragmatism in the context of mixed methods research and also to identify those parts of the discussion that cannot that easily be covered by pragmatist philosophy.

It is important to bear in mind that although discussions continue in many countries around the world about virtues and vices of mixed methods approaches, such discussions happen against the background of very different and very particular histories of the field of social and behavioral research. Whereas the epistemological, ontological, and methodological dimensions of these discussions may to a large extent be the same across different contexts, the political significance of such discussions may work out radically differently. Unlike Denzin (2008), I believe, therefore, that it is important not to take an entirely global perspective on the politics of social and behavioral research, but to be aware that while the intervention of mixed methods research can be a progressive development in one context or at one particular point in time, it can well have regressive effects at other points in time or in other contexts.

◆ Unhelpful Concepts

I wish to make some brief comments on three (sets of) concepts that figure prominently in discussions about the philosophical justification of research in the social and behavioral sciences—at least, that is, in the English-speaking world. In my view, they are rather unhelpful, mainly because they are rather imprecise.

The first set of concepts, which is pervasive in the literature on research methods and methodologies, concerns the notions of *qualitative research* and *quantitative research*. The simple problem here is that research *in itself* can be neither qualitative nor quantitative; only *data* can properly be said to be qualitative or quantitative. Data can either be *quantities* (expressed in numbers) or *qualities* (usually expressed in text, although numbers can be used to stand for qualities as well). The problem is that in many discussions, the notions of qualitative research and quantitative research stand for much more than just the kind of data being used. The terms tend to stand for a whole cluster of aspects of research, such as methods, designs, methodologies, epistemological and ontological assumptions, and so on. To use the words *quantitative* and *qualitative* to refer to such *clusters* is not only imprecise but also unhelpful because what often is at stake in discussions between proponents of

the different approaches is precisely *not* the nature of the data being used but bigger issues such as views about the nature of reality, the limits of knowledge, or the purpose and politics of research. The notions qualitative research and qualitative research tend to obscure those aspects that really matter in the discussion and can even create quasi-problems and oppositions, for example, when researchers who use numbers and researchers who use text assume that they have nothing to share, even if their research is actually informed by similar assumptions about the nature of social reality or driven by similar ambitions about knowledge creation.

The fact that, in most discussions, the notions of qualitative research and quantitative research actually stand for a whole cluster of assumptions brings me to a second unhelpful concept, which is the notion of *paradigm*. David Morgan (2007) has done an excellent job in unraveling the different ways in which this concept is being used in discussions about the philosophical foundations of research. One particularly helpful point is his distinction between four ways in which the idea of paradigm has been used in such discussions: as worldviews, as epistemological stances, as shared beliefs in a research field, and as model examples (Morgan, 2007, p. 54). One of the main problems with the notion of paradigm is that it tends to bring under one heading a range of different ideas and assumptions that do not *necessarily* have to go together. This tends to make the notion of paradigm into a container concept and leads to a situation in which paradigms have to be embraced or rejected in a wholesale manner rather than letting the discussion focus on smaller elements, such as ontological, epistemological, or methodological views and assumptions. The so-called "incompatibility thesis" (see Howe, 1988) is an example of how positions can become ossified when articulated in terms of paradigms rather than in terms of the parts that make up a particular point of view. At a social level, the lumping together of heterogeneous assumptions tends to lead to fractions, oppositions, and a polarization of the discussion rather than interaction and exchange. Paradigm thinking also tends to give research students (but not only them) the impression that they need to adopt a particular paradigmatic stance—as in "I am a qualitative researcher"—before they can start doing research. Although it is true that research questions are not neutral but depend on, for example, the assumptions one holds about the nature of reality or the nature of knowledge, it would be a mistake to think that such assumptions are just a matter of belief—of conversion to a particular paradigm. The idea of paradigm, then, becomes an excuse for not having to engage in discussions about the assumptions that underpin research.

The third unhelpful concept in the discussion is that of positivism. One problem is that the label tends to be used to cover a cluster of ideas that do not necessarily belong together. Lincoln and Guba (1985), for example, characterize positivism—or actually positiv*ists*—as believing that there is a single reality, that the knower and the known are independent, that inquiry is value free, that time- and context-free generalizations are possible, and that real causes are temporally precedent to or simultaneous with effects (see Lincoln & Guba, quoted in Tashakkori & Teddlie, 1998, p.7). Although such ideas can all play a role in discussions about research, it is unhelpful to cluster them together as one position, thereby suggesting that someone who would want to make a case for, say, the independence of the knower and the known, would automatically have to commit herself to all other aspects of positivism. As with the idea of paradigm, positivism becomes an excuse for not having to engage with the real issues. It becomes a rhetorical strategy that simply brands positivists as bad—or the "baddies" as positivists—rather than trying to understand when and where and why it might matter to think of, say, the knower and the known as dependent and when and where

and why it might matter to think of them as independent. The pejorative use of the term *positivism* also gives a bad name to what is, in principle, a very important question: whether, how, and to what extent it might be possible to make a distinction between positive knowledge and speculative knowledge. This is not to suggest that the distinction can be made easily, nor that the answer to the question is the same in all situations, but to highlight that the question in itself is an important one, even if one would come to the conclusion that all our knowledge is, in a sense, speculative, that is, that a sharp distinction between observation and theory—or between facts and values—is actually very difficult to defend.

The main problem with these concepts, therefore, is not that they carry no meaning but that, to a large extent, they are just not precise enough to promote meaningful discussions. I believe, therefore, that a discussion on mixing methods in social and behavioral research should at least try to bracket the concepts mentioned above, which is what I will attempt to do in the discussion that follows.

◆ Seven Levels in the Discussion on Mixed Methods Research

An interesting aspect of the development of mixed methods research is that, in addition to discussion about the ways in which research can use a combination of different approaches, an increasing number of studies are actually using a mixed approach (for an exemplary overview of both strands, see particularly Plano Clark & Creswell, 2008). This has resulted in sophisticated typologies of mixed methods design (see particularly the contributions by Creswell, Plano Clark, Gutmann, & Hanson, 2003; Greene, Caracelli, & Graham 1989; Tashakkori & Teddlie, 1998, 2003b) and in a much better understanding of what mixed methods research can actually achieve (see also Onwuegbuzie & Johnson, 2006). One of the more encompassing typologies currently available is the one developed by Creswell et al. (2003). Building on earlier typologies, they distinguish between sequential explanatory design, sequential exploratory design, sequential transformative design, concurrent triangulation design, concurrent nested design, and concurrent transformative design. Their typology is quite sophisticated, taking into consideration different sequences of data collection (implementation), the balance between a quantitative and a qualitative perspective within the overall approach (priority), the phase of the research in which mixing takes place (stage of integration), and the question whether research aims for change or not (theoretical perspective). However, it is predominantly structured in terms of the distinction between quantitative research and qualitative research. As a result, their typology reinforces the rather crude distinction between the two approaches, and little work is done to unpack the cluster of ideas behind these notions. This may explain why Creswell et al. (2003, p. 231) have very little to say about the theoretical and philosophical perspectives that might inform if not justify mixed approaches, ending up with a rather eclectic view about the paradigms researchers might select for their research.

For these reasons, in this section, I will approach the question of mixing in a slightly different way, focusing at the different levels within the discussion on mixed methods research. This will allow me to indicate in a more precise manner where (philosophical) problems arise and where they do not, which, in turn, will allow me to say with more precision where pragmatism has something to offer in addressing these problems.

Seven Levels in the Discussion on Mixed Methods Research

I distinguish between seven levels of the discussion. I refer to these as 'levels' rather than 'dimensions' because, to a certain extent, the levels build upon each other.

Level 1: data (Is it possible to have numbers and text within the same research?)

Level 2: methods (Is it possible to have data collection methods that generate numbers and data collection methods that generate text within the same research? Is it possible to have data analysis methods for the analysis of numbers and text within the same research?)

Level 3: design (Is it possible to have interventionalist and noninterventionalist designs within the same research?)

Level 4: epistemology (Which epistemological set of ideas is most appropriate to account for the knowledge generated through a mixed approach?)

Level 5: ontology (Is it possible to combine different assumptions about reality within the same research?)

Level 6: purposes of research (Is it possible to combine the intention to explain with the intention to understand?)

Level 7: practical roles of research (Can research be orientated toward both a technical and a cultural role?)

DATA

The first level in the discussion concerns the *data* of research. Here a mixed approach would make use of both numbers and text. Combining these does not raise any particular problems, neither of a philosophical nor of a more practical nature. We can just see numbers and text as two forms of information and, more generally, as two modes of representation.

METHODS

The second level concerns the methods of data collection and data analysis. Here a mixed approach would make use, for example, of a combination of closed questionnaires and interviews; it would use statistical techniques to analyze the data generated through the questionnaires and interpretative approaches to analyze the data generated through interviews. At the level of data collection, this is, again, unproblematic as it would just be an extension of the combination of numbers and text. At the level of analysis, we can characterize this mixing as a combination of measurement and interpretation. Again, combining the two does not, in itself, raise any philosophical or practical issues. It is simply about analyzing data in ways that are data-adequate. One could even add that measurement is itself a form of interpretation, in which case at the level of analysis, the distinction would disappear.

DESIGN

The third level concerns the *design* of research. Here things become slightly more complicated. The distinction I wish to make here is between *interventionalist* and *noninterventionalist* designs. Experimental designs are a main example of the first and naturalistic designs a main example of the latter. Combining the two within one study is, in itself, not problematic; one can envisage a

project that contains both interventionalist and noninterventionalist elements. Problems arise when both strategies have to feed into one knowledge claim because to know something through intervention is different from knowing something through observation. In the first case, our knowledge is about the relationships between interventions and the consequences of these interventions on a particular phenomenon, whereas in the second, our knowledge is about the phenomenon as observed. The practical question here is *how* the two approaches feed into one knowledge claim, that is, whether this is done through triangulation, through a sequential design (with either the interventionalist or the noninterventionalist approach first), or in a concurrent design (for these terms, see Creswell et al., 2003). The more fundamental question, however, is whether one believes that it is possible to make a distinction between interventionalist and noninterventionalist ways of knowing, or whether one would hold that any attempt to know always already constitutes an intervention of some kind. As I will show below, pragmatism denies that knowledge can be gained in any other way than through intervention. While in terms of design there are therefore no particular problems in combining interventionalist and noninterventionalist strategies within the same project, there is an underlying epistemological issue that has to do with the question whether pure observation is possible or not. I will return to this.

EPISTEMOLOGY

The fourth level concerns the epistemological assumptions informing research. It is at this level that there has been a substantial amount of discussion. This is not surprising, given that the ideas one holds about what can be known and what it means to know something—which I take to be the two central questions of epistemology— are of crucial importance if we understand research first and foremost as a process through which we generate knowledge.[4]

Within the context of mixed methods research, the question here is not whether it is possible to combine different epistemological assumptions or positions—this is obviously not possible. The question rather is which epistemological beliefs one wishes to use for the design and justification of one's research. One point I wish to make here is that we should begin by treating the epistemological question as a *separate* question rather than to assume, as is done in paradigm thinking, that the question always comes as part of a cluster of elements that are necessarily related to each other. To put it simply: The suggestion that research which uses numbers or statistics is necessarily committed to, say, an objectivist epistemology is both wrong and unhelpful.

There are three further points to consider. The first is that although I am suggesting we *begin* by treating epistemological questions separately from, say, questions about data, methods, methodology or ontology, this does not mean that *any* combination of these elements is possible, just that there are more combinations than what is commonly assumed in paradigm thinking. Second, there is, of course, the important question of which epistemological position one wishes to endorse. This, third, should not be seen as just a matter of choice, personal conviction, or even conversion. The philosophical discussion about what can be known and what it means to know something is first and foremost about *arguments*. This is an ongoing discussion to which, as I will show below, pragmatism has made an important and original contribution. What we cannot expect from pragmatism in relation to mixed methods research is that it will provide the paradigm for such designs. It can, however, help to clarify some of the issues about what it means to claim knowledge on the basis of mixed methods designs and approaches. Because the views of pragmatism offer alternatives to some of the traditional positions in the discussion, I will not attempt to discuss those positions here in any detail but will return to this in my reconstruction of pragmatism below. (I also refer readers to the chapter by Johnson and Gray, 2010 [this volume].) At this stage, I wish to mention two radically different views about knowledge that can often be found in the discussion, one holding that it is possible to gain objective knowledge about how the world really—that is, independent from knowers—is and one holding that all knowledge contains at least a subjective element or, in the most extreme case, is entirely produced by the knower. It is this distinction between an objectivist and a subjectivist epistemology that sometimes results in a sharp division within the social and behavioral research community and is one manifestation of what is known as the 'incompatibility thesis' (see Howe, 1988).

ONTOLOGY

The fifth level of the discussion is that of ontology, that is, of the assumptions and beliefs we hold about reality and, more specifically, about the reality that is the object of research. With regard to social and behavioral research one of the most important distinctions is that between what we might refer to as a *mechanistic ontology* and a *social ontology*. Whereas the first would approach the world in deterministic terms, that is, as a system in which there are causes and effects and deterministic connections between the two, the second would see the world as a world of meaning and interpretation. The distinction between the two ontologies is basically a simple one, although the underlying discussions and the implications of these discussions are far more complicated (I refer the readers to the chapter by Maxwell and Mittapalli, 2010 [this volume]; see also Maxwell, 2004). Let's look at this through a simple example: someone raising her hand. If we see this as an event occurring in a universe with causes and effects and deterministic connections, the event can be known through identifying all the causes that lead to the event. Whereas this would allow us to know what *caused* the event, it would not allow us to generate any knowledge about the *meaning* of the event, that is, the fact that this was a student who put up her hand because she wanted to ask a question. It is only when we approach the event within the context of a social ontology—that is, within a world of intentions and reasons—that we can come to know the event as a *meaningful* event. Viewed in this way, it matters a lot what kind of ontological assumptions we bring to our research because this, to a large extent, determines what kind of knowledge we would be looking for. Those who make a case for a social ontology would not necessarily deny the existence of a world of causes and effects but would argue that to understand individual and social action as *meaningful* rather than as mechanically caused, another set of ontological assumptions needs to be introduced. The extreme position at the other end of the spectrum is one holding that all social phenomena can ultimately be reduced to natural or physical phenomena so that, at least in principle but eventually also in practice, the only knowledge that counts is the knowledge formulated on the basis of a mechanistic ontology. This view is known as reductionism and also as physicalism. What matters in the context of social and behavioral research is first and foremost the question of *causality,* that is, whether we should assume that human action is *caused* and should therefore look for the causes of action and the laws that govern causality in order to be able to predict and control human action, or whether we should assume that human action is *motivated* so that we need to look for intentions and reasons for action in order to provide an answer to the question why people act as they act.

It is important to note that the idea of simple, mechanistic causality has been questioned from a number of angles (for the contribution from critical realism to this discussion, see Maxwell, 2004; Maxwell & Mittapalli, 2010). One important contribution

has come from complexity theory (see Prigogine & Stengers, 1985), in which it has been argued that strong, deterministic causality is likely to occur only in closed, nonrecursive systems, that is, systems that do not interact with outside factors or conditions and where the interactions within the system do not feed back into the system itself. As soon as systems become more open and/or recursive, the interactions between factors become (far) more complex and (far) less predictable. In dynamic open systems, interruptions do not so much lead to predictable outcomes as to a disturbance that, under particular conditions, can lead to a reorganization of the system. Although there are causes and effects in such interactions, the causes do not operate deterministically, and although the ways in which systems respond and self-organize may be limited, several different outcomes are more likely than only one. Because social and biological systems tend to be open systems, complexity theory provides us with a different way to think about actions and consequences than what is often assumed in discussions about causality in social and behavioral research.

PURPOSES OF RESEARCH

The controversies around the (im)possibility of mixed methods research—particularly as articulated in terms of an alleged opposition between qualitative and quantitative research or paradigm—seem to focus particularly on epistemological questions about the objectivity or subjectivity of knowledge and ontological questions about causality and the specific nature of social phenomena. What is remarkably absent is a discussion in terms of the *purposes* of the research—and it is important to acknowledge that decisions about the wider purposes of research provide the framing for specific research questions, not the other way around. With regard to this, an important distinction must be made between research that seeks to *explain* and research that seeks to *understand*.[5] The ambition of explanatory research is to identify causes, factors, or correlations and, through this, generate knowledge that can be used to influence the course of future events. The ambition of interpretative research is to generate understanding through an articulation of the intentions and reasons for action. The distinction between explanation and understanding maps relatively neatly onto the distinction between a mechanistic and a social ontology to the extent that a choice for explanation assumes the existence of a reality that is explainable in causal or correlational terms, whereas a choice for interpretation starts from a social ontology. It is important, however, to separate the purposes of research from the ontological assumptions. One reason for this is that the connection between the purposes of research and the ontological assumptions informing research is not as strong as it has long been assumed. The fact that research in the social and the behavioral domain can find regularities and correlations that give the impression of a degree of causal connectedness does not automatically commit the researcher to the adoption of a mechanistic ontology, because many of the connections that exist in the social domain are actually achieved through interpretative acts. This can, for example, be seen in research on teaching and learning. Although such research can find connections between teaching and learning, this does not mean that these connections are achieved in a mechanistic or physicalistic way. Rather, when teaching and learning are connected, it is because those who learn have, in some way, interpreted and made sense of the teaching. The link between teaching and learning is thus established through *interpretation*— which means that to make sense of research that finds such correlations, one needs to bring in a social ontology rather than a mechanistic one (see Vanderstraeten & Biesta, 2006).

PRACTICAL ROLES

The final level of the discussion concerns the relationships between research and practice. Because much social and behavioral research intends to have practical significance for (aspects or domains of) human action—something to which Greene and Caracelli (1997) refer as the *transformation* dimension of research; see also Creswell et al. (2003)—one important question is how this practical intention can best be understood. In this regard, de Vries (1990) has made a helpful distinction between two ways in which research can connect with practice. In one way, research provides means, techniques, and technologies that practitioners can use to achieve their ends. De Vries refers to this as the technical role of research. In the other way, research provides practitioners with different ways of seeing and understanding their practice, to which he refers as the cultural role of research. Although these are distinct roles that rely on different kinds of research knowledge, De Vries has argued that the two roles can work together. When research is successful in its technical role, in that practitioners take up the techniques and technologies provided by the research, this may also influence their understanding of the situation in which the outcomes of the research are being used. The success of behaviorist psychotherapy, for example, may convince people that mental problems are actually the result of learned patterns of behavior rather than deeper psycho-dynamic origins. Similarly, when research is successful in its cultural role of providing practitioners with new ways of understanding their practices and the problems that occur, this may create a situation in which research can subsequently perform its technical role more effectively or productively.

CONCLUDING REMARKS

The purpose of this section has been to present the different dimensions that play a role in discussions about mixed methods research. Rather than assuming that this discussion is one of paradigms—of tightly clustered sets of assumptions—I have suggested that it is more productive to look at all the elements and dimensions of the discussion separately, first and foremost to be able to identify with much more precision which aspects of mixed methods research are unproblematic and which aspects raise further questions. I have done this primarily to create a situation in which I can then indicate with more precision where pragmatism may have something to offer to the field of mixed methods research, although I do hope that by opening up the paradigms, I have also helped to create more clarity about the extent to which there is compatibility and the areas in which there is likely to be incompatibility. My perception is that the issues that seem to generate most discussion have to do with the status of knowledge and with questions about causality; there are strong and opposed views in these areas—although such views are often not presented in a very precise manner. Having identified some of the key issues and problems in the discussion about the philosophical underpinnings of mixed methods research, I will now turn to pragmatism and, more specifically, the work of John Dewey.

◆ Knowing as a Way of Doing: John Dewey's Pragmatism

The contribution of Deweyan pragmatism lies first and foremost in the domain of epistemology. To characterize Dewey's ideas as an epistemology is, however, not entirely correct as Dewey did not so much offer new answers to old epistemological questions as he replaced the very assumptions on which modern epistemology had been based. According to Stephen Toulmin (1984), Dewey's philosophy actually offers a "radical dismantling of the epistemological tradition" displaying "farsightedness, perception

and originality" of a kind that could hardly be recognized at the time (pp. ix–x).

MODERN EPISTEMOLOGY AND THE 'MIND-WORLD SCHEME'

In modern epistemology, the question of knowledge is often phrased as the question how the human mind can acquire knowledge of a world outside of itself. Robert Nozick (1981, pp. 161–171) put the challenge most succinctly when he asked whether we can ever know that we are *not* a brain suspended in a vat full of liquid, wired to a computer that is feeding our current experiences. Nozick is part of a long tradition in which the nature of knowledge is examined from a *skeptical* point of view, that is, starting from the assumption that knowledge may *not* be possible because we may not be able to get outside of our own mind. The first philosopher to place skepticism at the heart of modern epistemology was René Descartes. In the *Second Meditation,* he used the "method of doubt" to arrive at the conclusion that although we can doubt everything, we cannot, when doing so, doubt that we are engaged in a process of doubting. Whereas this provided Descartes with certainty about the existence of the thinking self, it did *not* provide any certainty about the existence of a world *beyond* our experience, and this issue has troubled modern epistemology ever since. It eventually led David Hume to the conclusion that the existence of an external world of enduring objects is a "very useful hypothesis" but not something that can ever be proven.

What unites the ideas of Nozick, Descartes, and Hume is their reliance on a dualistic view of reality. They assume that reality consists of two totally different substances, mind and matter, and that the question of knowledge has to begin with the mind in order then to ask how the mind can get in touch with the material world outside of itself. The dualism between mind and matter set the agenda for modern epistemology by giving it the task of answering the question about how the mind can get in touch with the world (see, e.g., Dancy, 1985). It has also provided the framework for the distinction between objectivity and subjectivity. After all, on the basis of the dualism between a knowing subject and objects to be known, knowledge can be objective if it depicts how objects are in themselves. If this is considered impossible, then the only other option is for knowledge to be subjective, that is, produced by the activities of the human mind. The implications of this way of thinking go well beyond technical questions about the quality of knowledge. Many recent discussions about culture, ethics, morality, science, rationality and even Western civilization appear to be informed by the idea that the only choice we have is between the two options presented through the "mind-world scheme." More important, many participants in these discussions seem to fear that if we give up objectivity, the only thing left is chaos. Richard Bernstein (1983) aptly refers to this as the "Cartesian anxiety," the idea that *either* there is "a fixed foundation for our knowledge" *or* we cannot escape "the forces of darkness that envelop us with madness, with intellectual and moral chaos" (p. 18).

The mind-world scheme offers only two options: objectivity or subjectivity. The crucial question, however, is not which option to choose. The far more important question is whether the underlying mind-world scheme is itself inevitable or whether it is possible to think about knowledge and reality in a different way, starting from different assumptions. John Dewey's theory of knowledge—which, for reasons that will become clear below would better be called a theory of *knowing*—does precisely this. It offers an understanding of knowing that is *not* premised on the dualistic mind-world scheme. It offers an understanding of knowing that does *not* start from what he saw as the "impossible question" as to how "a knower who is purely individual or 'subjective,' and whose being is wholly psychical and immaterial . . . and a world to be known which is purely universal or 'objective,' and

whose being is wholly mechanical and physical" can ever reach each other (Dewey, 1911, p. 441). Instead, Dewey (1929) put forward a framework that starts with *interactions*—or, as he later preferred to call it, *transactions*—taking place in nature and in which nature itself is understood as "a moving whole of interacting parts" (p. 232). This is Dewey's self-confessed "Copernican turn," in which "(t)he old center was mind" while "(t)he new center is indefinite interactions" (p. 232). The key concept in this Copernican turn is experience.

EXPERIENCE

Whereas *transaction* refers to interactions taking place in nature more generally, *experience* refers to the transactions of *living* organisms and their environments. What is distinctive about these transactions is that they constitute a *double* relationship.

> The organism acts in accordance with its own structure, simple or complex, upon its surroundings. As a consequence the changes produced in the environment react upon the organism and its activities. The living creature undergoes, suffers, the consequences of its own behavior. This close connection between doing and suffering or undergoing forms what we call experience. (Dewey, 1920, p. 129)

Experience is, therefore, the way in which living organisms are implicated in their environment. Contrary to what is suggested in the mind-world scheme, experience is not "a veil that shuts man off from nature" but rather "a means of penetrating continually further into the heart of nature" (Dewey, 1925, p. 15).

Dewey saw knowing as the mode of experience that in some way supports action. It is concerned with grasping the *relationship* between our actions and their consequences. As a result, knowing can help us to get more control over our actions, at least more than if we used blind trial and error. It is important to see that *control* here does not mean complete mastery but rather the ability to plan intelligently and direct our actions. This ability is first of all important in those situations in which we are not sure how to act—which is expressed in one of Dewey's (1929) definitions of knowing as having to do with "the transformation of disturbed and unsettled situations into those more controlled and more significant" (p. 236). Knowing is also important to achieve more control, a more intelligent approach in the other domains of experience, which is expressed in Dewey's claim that knowing "facilitates control of objects for purposes of non-cognitive experience" (p. 79).

FROM ACTION TO INTELLIGENT ACTION

The framework for Dewey's theory of knowing lies in his theory of action, the outlines of which he developed early on in his career in a landmark paper called "The Reflex Arc Concept in Psychology" (Dewey, 1896). One way to summarize Dewey's theory of action is to say that it amounts to *a theory of experimental learning*. Dewey characterizes living organisms—including human organisms—as capable of establishing and maintaining a dynamic coordination with their environment. Through this process, the predispositions—or *habits* as Dewey preferred to call them—of the organism become more focused and more specific, more attuned to ever changing environing conditions, which is another way of saying that through the tentative, experimental way in which living organisms maintain coordinated transaction with their environment, they *learn*. This learning, however, is *not* the acquisition of information about how the world "out there" is. It is a learning process through which living organisms acquire a complex and flexible set of predispositions for action.

Learning is, therefore, basically a process of trial and error, and in one sense, this is indeed how Dewey argues that living organisms learn. But there is a difference between blind trial and error and what Dewey called "intelligent action." The difference has to do with the intervention of thinking: "dramatic rehearsal (in imagination) of various competing possible lines of action" (Dewey, 1922, p. 132). The choice for a specific line of action should be understood as "hitting in imagination upon an object which furnishes an adequate stimulus to the recovery of overt action" (p. 134). Whether this choice will actually lead to coordinated transaction will become clear only when the organism actually acts. This is why thinking can never guarantee that our actions will result in coordinated transactions. But what it can do is make the process of choosing more intelligent than would be the case with blind trial and error.

THE REALITY OF EXPERIENCE

One important implication of Dewey's transactional definition of experience is that it puts an end to the idea that it is only through knowledge that we can obtain a hold on reality. For Dewey, all modes of experience are equally real because they are all modes of the transaction of living organisms and their environments. From this, Dewey (1905) concluded that "things—anything, everything, in the ordinary or non-technical use of the term 'thing'—are what they are experienced as" (p. 158). This first of all means that everyone's experience is equally real. The horse trader, the jockey, the zoologist, and the paleontologist will all have their own experience of a horse. If their accounts turn out to be different, there is, however, no reason for assuming that the content of only one of them can be real and that the experiences of the others must necessarily be any less accurate or real. It simply reflects the fact that a horse trader will have a different experience of the horse than a zoologist does because the trader enters the transaction from a different standpoint, from a different background, from a different history, and with different purposes and intentions. This also implies that what is experienced is itself real. If someone is flustered by a noise, then that noise *is* fearsome. This claim must, of course, be understood transactionally. If someone is frightened by a sound, then the fear is the immediate response of the organism. The sound *is* frightening because the organism reacts to the sound as being a frightening sound. This implies, however, that *being* frightened is not the same as *knowing* that one is frightened. Knowing what *caused* the fearsome noise is a different experience. While the latter experience may be more true than the former, in Dewey's view, it is not more *real.* "The question of truth is not as to whether Being or Non-Being, Reality or mere Appearance is experienced, but as to the *worth* of a certain concretely experienced thing" (Dewey, 1905, p. 163). One important implication of this is that experience in itself does not provide us with any knowledge. Dewey rejected, in other words, the view that experience provides us with elementary "bits" of knowledge which, when put together in a systematic of logical manner, result in knowledge.[6]

FROM EXPERIENCE TO KNOWLEDGE

For Dewey, the difference between experience and knowledge is that knowledge is concerned with the *occurrence* of experience. The office of knowledge signifies a search "for those relations upon which the *occurrence* of real qualities and values depends" (Dewey, 1929, p. 83). In this respect, knowledge is intimately and necessarily connected with action because—and this is the most crucial point in Dewey's theory of knowing—the discovery of the conditions and consequences of experience "can take place *only* by modifying the given

qualities in such ways that *relations* become manifest" (Dewey, 1929, p. 84; italics added). The shift from understanding knowledge as being concerned with the world "as it is" to understanding knowledge as being concerned with *conditions* and *consequences,* is a very important element of Dewey's approach. It represents a shift from a concern with things as they are to a concern with "the history to which a given thing belongs" (Dewey, 1925, p. 243). It is a shift from "knowing as an aesthetic enjoyment of the properties of nature as a world of divine art, to knowing as a means of secular control—that is, a method of purposefully introducing changes which will alter the direction of the course of events" (Dewey, 1929, p. 81). This implies that, for Dewey, knowledge is concerned with the relations between actions and consequences. This introduces the dimension of *time* into Dewey's theory of knowing—a reason for arguing that Dewey has a temporal conception of knowledge.

THE TEMPORAL DEVELOPMENT OF EXPERIENCE

In Dewey's (1916) view, the question of knowledge—or to be more precise: the issue of knowing—arises

> because of the appearance of incompatible factors within the empirical situation. . . . Then opposed responses are provoked which cannot be taken simultaneously in overt action, and which accordingly can be dealt with, whether simultaneously or successively, only after they have been brought into a plan of organized action. (p. 326)

The problem here is one of the *meaning* of the situation—and for Dewey *situation* refers to organism and environment in transaction. The only way to solve the problem in an *intelligent* manner and not by simple trial and error is by means of a systematic inspection of the situation. On the one hand, we need to identify and state the problem. On the other hand, we need to develop suggestions for addressing the problem, for finding a way to act, and hence find out what the meaning of the situation actually is. Although thought or reflection must play an important part in this process, they will, in themselves, not result in knowledge. Only when action follows can the value of both the analysis of the problem and the suggested solution be established. We need overt action to determine the worth and validity of our reflective considerations. Otherwise we have, at most, a hypothesis about the problem and a hypothesis about its possible solution.

This means that to get knowledge, we need action. But although action is a necessary condition for knowledge, it is not a sufficient one. We also need thinking or reflection. The *combination* of reflection and action leads to knowledge. From this, it follows that knowing, the acquisition of knowledge, is not something that takes place somewhere deep down inside the human mind. Knowing is itself an activity, it is "literally something which we do" (Dewey, 1916, p. 367). The meaning that emerges from the restoration of coordinated action is a meaning "which is contemporaneously aware of meaning something beyond itself" (Dewey, 1906, p. 113). This "beyond" is not simply present or will not simply become present in the future. It will become present *only* "through the intervention of an operation" (Dewey, 1906, pp. 113–114), that is, through what we *do*. When experience is *cognitional,* as Dewey puts it, it means that we perceive something as meaning-something-else-which-we-will-experience-when-we-act-in-a-specific-way. It is along these lines that knowledge is intimately connected to the possibility of control. "In knowledge," Dewey (1929) argued, "causes become means and effects become consequences, and thereby things having meaning" (p. 236). Knowledge has, in other words, to do with *inference*: a reaction to something distant in time or place. Because inference is a step into an unknown future, it is a precarious journey. Inference always involves uncertainty and risk. A stone, Dewey argued, can react to stimuli only of the present, not of the future, and for that reason cannot make mistakes. Because inference entails the possibility of mistake, it introduces truth and falsity into the world (see Dewey, 1915, p. 70).

THE OBJECTS OF KNOWLEDGE

Dewey's approach has important implications for how we understand the objects of knowledge. Whereas in the dualistic approach the objects of knowledge are seen as "things" that exist in a world "out there" and are there for us to discover and depict, Dewey's transactional view sees the objects of knowledge as the outcomes of processes of inquiry. Because the habits we acquire through such processes provide us with more specific predispositions for action, habits in a sense embody the ways in which our environment becomes more meaningful for us. The experimental transformation of organism-environment transactions transforms the environment in which and through which we act into what Dewey (1922) referred to as "a figured framework of objects" (p. 128). This is the reason why Dewey (1925) referred to objects of perception not as things but as "events with meaning" (p. 240). In the case of spoken language, it is relatively easy to see that words—or "sound-events" do not have a meaning of their own, but that they have *become* meaningful over time. It is far more difficult to draw the same conclusion with respect to physical objects, such as chairs, tables, trees, stones, hills, and flowers, "where it seems as if the union of intellectual meaning with physical fact were aboriginal" (Dewey, 1933, p. 231). Yet, chairs and tables are as much events with meaning as words are. And their meaning has a strictly transactional origin, in that it has to be understood as the outcome of the specific ways in which successful relationships between our actions and their consequences have been established over time. It is not, therefore, that through a process of inquiry, we can find out what the possible meanings of, for example, a chair are. Rather, a chair specifies a particular way in which the transaction with the environment has become meaningful. For this reason, Dewey argued that we should think of objects as tools. "The character of an object is like that of a tool . . . ; it is an order of determination of sequential changes terminating in a foreseen consequence" (Dewey, 1925, p. 121)[7]

TRUTH AND CORRESPONDENCE

The final element of Dewey's theory of knowing has to do with the question of truth. We have already seen that, for Dewey, there is no sense in asking about the truth of our immediate experience. Immediate experience simply is what it is. Truth and falsity enter the scene only when we raise questions about the *meaning* of experience.

> Truth and falsity are not properties of any experience or thing, in and of itself or in its first intention; but of things where the problem of assurance consciously enters in. Truth and falsity present themselves as significant facts only in situations in which specific meanings are intentionally compared and contrasted with reference to the question of worth, as to the reliability of meaning. (Dewey, 1906, p. 118; italics in original)

Truth and falsity are, therefore, not concerned with things as such, but with the relationship between our experience of a thing on the one hand and our possible actions or responses on the other. We approach a piece of paper as if we can write on it; the piece of paper means "being able to write on it." But only when we act can we know whether this inferred meaning can

become actual—or, in more day-to-day terms, whether what we expected the situation to be was indeed the case. This means that truth is always contextual and related to action; it also means that truth is itself temporal. Truth does not refer to an alleged correspondence between a proposition and reality. It has to do with the correspondence between suggested meaning and realized meaning, that is, meaning "put into practice." "The agreement, correspondence, is between purpose, plan, and its own execution, fulfillment" (Dewey, 1907, p. 84).

This does not mean that truth becomes disconnected from reality. The contrary is the case, because of the transactional framework that informs Dewey's theory of knowing and because of the *indispensable* role of action in the process that results in knowledge. The upshot of this is that knowledge is not a passive registration of reality "out there." Our intervention, our action, is a crucial, necessary, and constitutive part of knowledge. In this sense, we can say that knowledge is always a human construction, just as the objects of knowledge are. But it does *not* mean that anything is possible. We always intervene in an existing course of events and although our intervention introduces change, it will always be change of an existing course of events. We cannot create out of nothing. For Dewey, the only possible construction is a *reconstruction*.

THE CONSEQUENCES OF PRAGMATISM

One of the most important implications of Dewey's transactional approach is that knowledge does *not* provide us with a picture of reality as it is in itself—an idea to which Dewey referred as the "spectator theory of knowledge." For Dewey, knowledge always concerns the *relationship* between (our) actions and (their) consequences. This, in essence, is what a transactional conception of knowledge implies. It means that knowledge is a construction or, to be more precise, that the objects of knowledge are constructions. But contrary to how constructivism is often understood under the mind-world scheme (as purely mental and hence subjective), Dewey's constructivism is a *transactional* constructivism, a constructivism that holds that knowledge is at the very same time constructed *and* real. This is why we can call Dewey's position a form of realism, albeit *transactional realism* (Sleeper, 1986).

Given that knowledge concerns the relationship between (our) actions and (their) consequences, knowledge will ever offer us only *possibilities* but not certainty. The conclusions we draw on the basis of careful observation of what follows from how we act on the world show what has been possible in this particular transactional situation. Sometimes what was possible in one situation turns out also to be possible in another situation; but in other situations, the transactional determinants of the situation are different, so that what was possible in one case is no longer possible in another case (see also Biesta, 2007). This is why Dewey preferred to refer to the outcomes of inquiry and research as "warranted assertions" instead of truth. The assertions we make about the consequences of our actions are warranted on the basis of careful observation and control. But they are only warranted in relation to the particular situation in which they were produced, and we shouldn't make the mistake—for example, by putting the label *true* on them—of thinking that they will be warranted for all time and all similar situations. This does not mean that conclusions from one situation cannot be useful for other situations. But knowledge from one situation transfers to another situation by guiding our observation and perception and suggesting possible ways for resolving problems, for finding ways forward. Whether these possibilities will address the specific problems in the specific new transactional situation can be discovered only when we act.

A more general feature of Dewey's transactional approach to knowing is that, contrary to mainstream modern philosophy, his approach is not a skeptical one. For Dewey, there is no gap between human beings and the world. This does not mean that everything we experience is simply true. While Dewey does hold that things are what they are experienced as, there is a crucial difference between experience and knowledge. Whereas experience simply "is," knowledge, because it has to do with inference, can always be fallible. In this respect, we have to conclude that Dewey's transactional theory of knowing is a form of fallibilism. But it is important to see that, for Dewey, knowledge is fallible *not* because of an alleged gap between ourselves and the world but simply because we can never be sure what the future will bring, not in the least because what the future will look like depends also on our own ongoing actions. According to the transactional approach, we are not spectators of a finished universe but participants in an ever evolving, unfinished universe.

Dewey's transactional approach also cuts across the either/or of objectivism and subjectivism. From a transactional point of view, the world always appears as a function of what we do. Objectivity, understood as a depiction of a world completely independent from and untouched by us, is therefore simply impossible. If we want to know the world, we *must* interact, and as a result, we will know the world only in the way in which it responds to us. The world we construct emerges out of the doing-undergoing-doing dynamics of what Dewey calls experience. One could argue—and many critics of Dewey have done so—that although Dewey rejects objectivism, he thus ends up in a situation of complete subjectivism. Dewey simply acknowledges that this is the case—but he adds that there is no problem with this at all, as long as we see that the worlds we construct are constructed for our own individual purposes, for our own attempts to address the problems we face. It is only when we start to interact with others that the need for some form of coordination of our subjective worlds with the subjective worlds of others arises. What happens in this case is that, through interaction, cooperation, coordination, and communication, we construct an *intersubjective* world out of our individual, subjective worlds. By showing that objectivity is simply not possible, that subjectivity is not always a problem, and that intersubjectivity addresses those instances where the subjectivity of knowledge does become a problem, Dewey presents us with a position that helps us to overcome the stalemate between objectivism and subjectivism. He also hints at a way in which we can overcome the Cartesian anxiety by showing that we do not have to give up the world when we want to acknowledge that knowledge is always plural, changing, and open. Knowing, most important, is always a thoroughly *human* endeavor.

◆ Discussion: Pragmatism and Mixed Methods Research

The first thing to note is that pragmatism offers a very specific view of knowledge, one claiming that the only way we can acquire knowledge is through *the combination of action and reflection*. This approach has, first of all, implications for the status of knowledge in that knowledge according to the pragmatist view is always about relationships between actions and consequences, never about a world "out there." This approach also has implications for the objects of knowledge, which appear as constructions out of the relationships between actions and consequences, not as isolated entities that pre-exist the act of knowing. These implications lie at the heart of Dewey's transactional constructivism, which itself follows from Dewey's transactional realism, which holds that there is no structural gap between human beings and their environments because we are participants in

an ever evolving universe. At the level of design, Dewey's transactional approach seems to connect most closely with what I have referred to as interventionalist designs. Whereas *methodologically*, therefore, pragmatism seems to be on the side, so to speak, of interventionalist designs and not on the side of noninterventionalist designs—and in this respect cannot be seen to provide a philosophical foundation for an approach that would combine the two—at an *epistemological level*, Dewey would deny that it is possible to gain knowledge other than through action. This should not be understood as the claim that noninterventionalist designs are not possible or that naturalistic research does not exist. It rather means that even in those cases, the act of observation is not a neutral registration of reality "out there" but always already involves particular selections from an infinite number of possibilities. Although this can be read as a version of the idea that all observation is theory laden (Hanson, 1958; see also Popper, 1959/2002), for Dewey, this is less a question of how theory plays a role in observation than the more basic claim that observation is itself a transaction and not, as he put it somewhere, a "Kodak picture." In precisely this way, Dewey offers an interesting set of arguments for the possibility of combining interventionalist and noninterventionalist designs.

This same point works out differently with regard to the purposes of research. In relation to this, I have made a distinction between explanation and understanding. Whereas understanding aims to identify intentions of and reasons for (social) action, the main orientation of explanation is to identify causes or, in more open definitions, to find correlations between events. The latter orientation is clearly the one that is central in Dewey's transactional theory of knowing, which claims that knowing is always about relationships between actions and consequences. In this respect, Deweyan pragmatism is able to offer philosophical support for explanatory research but not for interpretative research. This is partly connected to Dewey's ontology, which is on the causal end of the spectrum (although see below). After all, Dewey characterizes the universe as a "moving whole of interacting parts," and because the parts interact, knowledge about actions and consequences and particular histories and trajectories is possible, not through observation but by connecting with these connections, so to speak. Dewey's universe is, however, not a deterministic universe. It is more an evolutionary universe in which human beings are a creative factor and in which new things can emerge, not unlike the way in which complexity theory views reality (see Osberg, Biesta, & Cilliers, 2008).

It is important to mention at this point that Dewey does not assume that human beings are robots. The idea that human action is meaningful and that meaning-guided action, with regard to our transactions both with the natural and with the social world, plays an absolutely central role in Dewey's thinking (see, e.g., Biesta, 2006). It is, however, not something that plays a prominent role in his theory of knowing, not even in his views on knowing in the social and educational domain (see Biesta & Burbules, 2003; see also Biesta, 2009a), or at least not in a way that would be recognizable as interpretative research from the standpoint of those who argue for a fundamental distinction between the natural and the social domain.

Whereas Deweyan pragmatism is, therefore, not really able to provide support for attempts to combine explanation and understanding or to bring a mechanistic and a social ontology together, this works out differently when we turn to the level of epistemology. The major contribution Dewey has made in relation to this is his dismantling of the very framework that has created one of the most persistent dualisms in the discussion about knowledge and the role of research in the production of knowledge: that between objectivism and subjectivism, between the position that true knowledge

has to be objective knowledge—knowledge about how objects in themselves "really" are—and the position that knowledge can ever be only subjective because we can never be certain that our minds can really access the world "out there." This dualism, and all the different varieties of the opposition expressed in these two positions, relies on what I have referred to as the mind-world scheme. The major contribution of Dewey is that he engages with this discussion from a different starting point so that the either/or of objectivism and subjectivism loses its meaning. This is tremendously liberating as it does away with an alleged hierarchy between different knowledges. Dewey thus shows that no knowledge can claim to provide us with a deeper, more real, or more true account of the world. Different knowledges are simply the result of different ways in which we engage with the world. They are, in other words, the consequences of different actions. This is tremendously important for the field of mixed methods research as it does away with alleged hierarchies between different approaches and rather helps to make the case that different approaches generate *different* outcomes, *different* connections between doing and undergoing, between actions and consequences, so that we always need to judge our knowledge claims pragmatically, that is in relation to the processes and procedures through which the knowledge has been generated so as not to make any assertions that cannot be warranted on the basis of the particular methods and methodologies used. Dewey's pragmatism particularly helps us to think in a radically different way about the notion of truth and emphasizes that research can ever provide us only with insights into what has been possible, not about what is or will be the case (for a concrete example of such an application of Deweyan pragmatism, see Biesta, 2007). Dewey's pragmatism does not provide us with a blanket justification for all forms of mixed methods research but helps the field to ask more precise questions about the strength, status, and validity of the knowledge claims developed on the basis of particular designs. Here Deweyan pragmatism opens the way for a much more specific discussion about the worth of different knowledge claims in relation to different research designs and strategies, a discussion no longer crippled by unhelpful epistemological dichotomies.

I conclude that although pragmatism is unable to provide *the* philosophical foundation for mixed methods research, it has some important things to offer particularly in helping mixed methods researchers to ask better and more precise questions about the philosophical implications and justifications of their designs.

Research Questions and Exercises

1. What different conceptions of pragmatism are being used in discussions about mixed methods research and to what extent do they express core ideas from philosophical pragmatism?

2. Explore, using concrete examples of mixed methods research, to what extent the distinction between seven levels in discussions about mixed methods research is helpful to get a better sense of what is actually being mixed or combined.

3. Pragmatism makes a distinction between the reality of experience and the truth of experience. You may wish to reflect on this distinction, particularly to appreciate the difference between a transactional understanding of reality and truth and a dualistic understanding.

4. How does pragmatism go beyond both objectivism and subjectivism?

5. How can pragmatism bridge the difference between interventionalist and noninterventionalist research designs?

6. Why is pragmatism less suited for providing philosophical support for combining explanatory and interpretative research strategies?

7. How does Dewey's pragmatism overcome an alleged hierarchy between different knowledges?

8. How can pragmatism contribute to the justification of mixed methods research? What are its limitations?

◆ Notes

1. I wish to express my gratitude to Charles Teddlie, Abbas Tashakkori, Burke Johnson, and Joseph Maxwell for their extremely helpful feedback and suggestions on earlier versions of my chapter.

2. My use of the term *everyday pragmatism* is not meant in a derogatory way; it is simply a term useful for making a distinction between a pragmatic justification for mixed methods approaches as the most suitable approaches

given particular research aims and objectives and pragmatism as a philosophical tradition.

3. Although I believe that any discussion about philosophical foundations or frameworks should focus on issues rather than abstract questions about what the most accurate understanding of a particular philosophical position is, I do think that precision in such reconstructions is very important. For that reason, I would argue that the 22 "general characteristics of pragmatism" outlined by Johnson and Onwuegbuzie (2004) are not precise enough, particularly not their depiction of notions of truth and "what works."

The main issue here has to do with two different arguments for why we should think of our knowledge as always provisional: one based on the assumption that we can never really "get hold" of the world and another based on the assumption that our knowledge is always the result of our actions and interventions. This difference leads to radically different views about the fallibility of knowledge, and it is precisely at this point that, unlike what has been claimed by Phillips and Burbules (2000), there is a fundamental difference between postpositivists such as Popper and transactional realists like Dewey.

4. It is important to bear in mind that this assumption is not unproblematic and that to simply understand the practice of research through an epistemological lens at least narrows our perception of what research does and perhaps even leads to a fundamental misunderstanding of how research works and what the role of knowledge in the practice of research is. Bruno Latour's *Science in Action* (1987) is a challenging example of how one can understand the practice of science without starting from epistemological assumptions. See also Latour and Woolgar, 1979.

5. The discussion about explanation and understanding has a long history in the social sciences (see Frisby, 1972). In the 1960s, there was an intensive discussion between Karl Popper and Theodor W. Adorno and, later, between Hans Albert and Jürgen Habermas, on the question of whether there was one method for all scientific research or whether social research required its own methods, given the different nature of social reality.

6. The latter view was the one put forward by logical positivism and, although philosophically discredited, still lives on in the idea that knowledge acquisition is an inductive process starting from the collection of basic facts and working "upward" toward general statements (see Ayer, 1959; Achinstein & Barker, 1969).

7. Dewey's approach is sometimes characterized as instrumentalism, also by Dewey himself. Whereas instrumentalism is generally taken as the view that *theories* are instruments or tools, Dewey's instrumentalism is about the instrumental character of objects-of-knowledge (see Biesta, 1992).

♦ References

Achinstein, P., & Barker, S. F. (1969). *The legacy of logical positivism: Studies in the philosophy of science.* Baltimore: Johns Hopkins Press.

Ayer, A. J. (1959). *Logical positivism.* Glencoe, IL: Free Press.

Bernstein, R. J. (1983). *Beyond objectivism and relativism: Science, hermeneutics, and praxis.* Oxford, UK: Basil Blackwell.

Biesta, G. J. J. (1992). *John Dewey: Theorie en praktijk.* Delft: Eburon.

Biesta, G. J. J. (2006). "Of all affairs, communication is the most wonderful": Education as communicative praxis. In D. T. Hansen (Ed.), *John Dewey and our educational prospect: A critical engagement with Dewey's Democracy and Education* (pp. 23–37). Albany: SUNY Press.

Biesta, G. J. J. (2007). Why 'what works' won't work: Evidence-based practice and the democratic deficit of educational research. *Educational Theory, 57*(1), 1–22.

Biesta, G. J. J. (2009a). Building bridges or building people? On the role of engineering in education. *Journal of Curriculum Studies, 41*(1), 13–16.

Biesta, G. J. J. (2009b). How to use pragmatism pragmatically? Suggestions for the 21st century. In A. G. Rud, J. Garrison, & L. Stone (Eds.), *John Dewey at one hundred-fifty* (pp. 30–39). Lafayette, IN: Purdue University Press.

Biesta, G. J. J., & Burbules, N. C. (2003). *Pragmatism and educational research.* Lanham, MD: Rowman & Littlefield.

Bryman, A. (2006). Paradigm peace and the implications for quality. *International Journal of Social Research Methodology, Theory and Practice, 9*(2), 111–126.

Creswell, J. W., & Plano Clark, V. L. (2007). *Designing and conducting mixed methods research.* Thousands Oaks, CA: Sage.

Creswell, J. W., Plano Clark, V. L., Gutmann, M. L., & Hanson, W. E. (2003). Advanced mixed method research designs. In A. Tashakkori & C. Teddlie (Eds.), *Handbook of mixed methods in social and behavioral research*. Thousands Oaks, CA: Sage.

Dancy, J. (1985). *An introduction of contemporary epistemology*. Oxford, UK: Basil Blackwell.

Denzin, N. K. (2008). The new paradigm dialogs and qualitative inquiry. *International Journal of Qualitative Studies in Education, 21*(4), 315–325.

Dewey, J. (1896). The reflex arc concept in psychology. In J. A. Boydston (Ed.), *The early works (1882–1898)* (Vol. 5, pp. 96–109). Carbondale and Edwardsville: Southern Illinois University Press.

Dewey, J. (1905). The postulate of immediate empricism. In J. A. Boydston (Ed.), *The middle works (1899–1924)* (Vol. 3, pp. 158–167). Carbondale and Edwardsville: Southern Illinois University Press.

Dewey, J. (1906). The experimental theory of knowledge. In J. A. Boydston (Ed.), *The middle works (1899–1924)* (Vol. 3, pp. 107–127). Carbondale and Edwardsville: Southern Illinois University Press.

Dewey, J. (1907). The control of ideas by facts. In J. A. Boydston (Ed.), *The middle works (1899–1924)* (Vol. 4, pp. 78–90). Carbondale and Edwardsville: Southern Illinois University Press.

Dewey, J. (1911). Epistemology. In J. A. Boydston (Ed.), *The middle works (1899–1924)* (Vol. 6, pp. 440–442). Carbondale and Edwardsville: Southern Illinois University Press.

Dewey, J. (1915). The logic of judgements of practice. In J. A. Boydston (Ed.), *The middle works (1899–1924)* (Vol. 8, pp. 14—82). Carbondale: Southern Illinois University Press.

Dewey, J. (1916). Introduction to *Essays in experimental logic*. In J. A. Boydston (Ed.), *The middle works (1899–1924)* (Vol. 10, pp. 320–369). Carbondale and Edwardsville: Southern Illinois University Press.

Dewey, J. (1920). *Reconstruction in philosophy*. In J. A. Boydston (Ed.), *The middle works (1899–1924)* (Vol. 12, pp. 77–201). Carbondale and Edwardsville: Southern Illinois University Press.

Dewey, J. (1922). *Human nature and conduct*. In J. A. Boydston (Ed.), *The middle works*

(1899–1924) (Vol. 14). Carbondale and Edwardsville: Southern Illinois University Press.

Dewey, J. (1925). *Experience and nature*. In J. A. Boydston (Ed.), *The later works (1925–1953)* (Vol. 1). Carbondale and Edwardsville: Southern Illinois University Press.

Dewey, J. (1929). *The quest for certainty*. In J. A. Boydston (Ed.), *The later works (1925–1953)* (Vol. 4). Carbondale and Edwardsville: Southern Illinois University Press.

Dewey, J. (1933). How we think: A restatement of the relation of reflective thinking to the educative process. In J. A. Boydston (Ed.), *The later works (1925–1953)* (Vol. 8, pp. 105–352). Carbondale and Edwardsville: Southern Illinois University Press.

Frisby, D. (1972). The Popper-Adorno controversy: The methodological dispute in German sociology. *Philosophy of the Social Sciences, 2*, 105–119.

Gorard, S. with Taylor, C. (2004). *Combining methods in educational and social research*. Maidenhead, UK: Open University Press.

Greene J. C. (2008). Is mixed methods social inquiry a distinctive methodology? *Journal of Mixed Methods Research, 7*(2), 7–22.

Greene, J. C., & Caracelli, V. J. (Eds.). (1997). *Advances in mixed-method evaluation: The challenges and benefits of integrating diverse paradigms*. San Francisco: Jossey-Bass.

Greene, J. C., Caracelli, V. J., & Graham, W. F. (1989). Toward a conceptual framework for mixed-method evaluation designs. *Educational Evaluation and Policy Analysis, 11*(3), 225–274.

Greene, J. C., & Hall, J. (2010). Dialectics and pragmatism: Being of consequence. In A. Tashakkori & C. Teddlie (Eds.), *SAGE handbook of mixed methods in social & behavioral research* (2nd ed.). Thousand Oaks, CA: Sage.

Hanson, N.R. (1958). *Patterns of discovery: An inquiry into the conceptual foundations of science*. Cambridge, UK: Cambridge University Press.

Howe, K. (1988). Against the quantitative-qualitative incompatibility thesis, or,

Dogmas die hard. *Educational Researcher,* *17,* 10–16.

Johnson, B., & Gray, R. (2010). A history of philosophical and theoretical issues for mixed methods research. In A. Tashakkori & C.Teddlie (Eds.), *SAGE handbook of mixed methods in social & behavioral research* (2nd ed.). Thousand Oaks, CA: Sage.

Johnson, R. B., & Onwuegbuzie, A. J. (2004). Mixed methods research: A research paradigm whose time has come. *Educational Research, 33*(7), 14–26.

Latour, B. (1987). *Science in action: How to follow scientists and engineers through society.* Cambridge, MA: Harvard University Press.

Latour, B., & Woolgar, S. (1979). *Laboratory life: The social construction of scientific facts.* Beverley Hills, CA: Sage.

Lincoln, Y., & Guba, E. (1985). *Naturalistic inquiry.* Beverly Hills, CA: Sage.

Maxcy, S. (2003). Pragmatic threads in mixed methods research in the social sciences: The search for multiple modes of inquiry and the end of the philosophy of formalism. In A. Tashakkori & C. Teddlie (Eds.), *Handbook of mixed methods in social and behavioral research.* Thousands Oaks, CA: Sage.

Maxwell, J. A. (2004). Causal explanation, qualitative research, and scientific inquiry in education. *Educational Researcher, 33*(2), 3–11.

Maxwell, J. A., & Mittapalli, K. (2010). Realism as a stance for mixed method research. In A. Tashakkori & C. Teddlie (Eds.), *SAGE handbook of mixed methods in social & behavioral research* (2nd ed.). Thousand Oaks, CA: Sage.

Morgan, D. L. (2007). Paradigms lost and pragmatism regained: Methodological implications of combining qualitative and quantitative methods. *Journal of Mixed Methods Research, 1*(1), 48–76.

Nozick, R. (1981). *Philosophical explanations.* Oxford, UK: Oxford University Press.

Onwuegbuzie, A. J., & Johnson, R. B. (2006). The validity issue in mixed research. *Research in Schools 13*(1), 48–63.

Osberg, D. C., Biesta, G. J. J., & Cilliers, P. (2008). From representation to emergence: Complexity's challenge to the epistemology of schooling. *Educational Philosophy and Theory, 40*(1), 213–227.

Phillips, D. C., & Burbules, N. C. (2000). *Postpositivism and educational research.* Lanham, MD: Rowman & Littlefield.

Plano Clark, V. L., & Creswell, J. W. (2008). *The mixed methods reader.* Thousand Oaks, CA: Sage.

Popper, K. (2002). *The logic of scientific discovery.* London: Routledge. (Original work published 1959)

Prigogine, I., & Stengers, I. (1985). *Order out of chaos: Man's new dialogue with nature.* London: Flamingo.

Rorty, R. (1980). *Philosophy and the mirror of nature.* Oxford, UK: Blackwell.

Rorty, R. (1982). *Consequences of pragmatism.* Minneapolis: University of Minnesota Press.

Schillp, P. A. (1951). *The philosophy of John Dewey.* New York: Open Court.

Sleeper, R. W. (1986). *The necessity of pragmatism: John Dewey's conception of philosophy.* New Haven, CT: Yale University Press.

Tashakkori, A., & Teddlie, C. (1998). *Mixed methodology. Combining qualitative and quantitative approaches.* London: Sage.

Tashakkori, A., & Teddlie, C. (Eds.). (2003a). *Handbook of mixed methods in social and behavioral research.* Thousands Oaks, CA: Sage.

Tashakkori, A., & Teddlie, C. (2003b). The past and future of mixed methods research: From data triangulation to mixed model design. In A. Tashakkori & C. Teddlie (eds), *Handbook of mixed methods in social and behavioral research* (pp. 671–701). Thousands Oaks, CA: Sage.

Toulmin, S. (1984). Introduction. In J. A. Boydston (Ed.), *The later works (1925–1953)* (Vol. 4, pp. vii–xxii). Carbondale and Edwardsville: Southern Illinois University Press.

Vanderstraeten, R., & Biesta, G. J. J. (2006). How is education possible? A pragmatist account of communication and the social organisation of education. *British Journal of Educational Studies, 54*(2), 160–174.

Vries, G. H. de (1990). *De ontwikkeling van wetenschap.* Groningen: Wolters Noordhoff.

5

DIALECTICS AND PRAGMATISM

Being of Consequence

◆ Jennifer C. Greene and Jori N. Hall

Objectives

The authors of this chapter aspire that readers will:

- enhance their understanding of the important role of philosophical, disciplinary, and value assumptions in social inquiry.

- Develop a practice-oriented understanding of two different stances on mixing at the level of philosophical assumptions in mixed methods inquiry: the dialectic and the pragmatic stances.

- Arrive at a position of respect for both the dialectic and pragmatic stances as legitimate frameworks for mixed methods inquiry.

Amixed methods approach to social inquiry has clearly arrived on the methodological catwalks that showcase the latest in both conceptual vogue and practical fashion. There are now dozens of books on mixed methods inquiry, along with a highly successful new *Journal of Mixed Methods Research*. In addition to an annual international conference devoted to mixed methods inquiry, mixed methods strands are appearing in many other varied conference venues, from the annual International Congress on Qualitative Inquiry (http://www.icqi.org/) to the 2009 conference of the International Society for the Quality of Life Studies (http://www.isqols2009.istitutodeglinnocenti.it/). Workshops on mixed methods inquiry are regular features of preconference professional development offerings, for example, at the meetings of the American Educational Research Association and the European Evaluation Society. Mixed methods empirical studies have also appeared in multiple fields, including education, evaluation, nursing, social work, and international development, as well as anthropology, geography, political science, and sociology.

The increasing popularity of mixed methods ideas, especially in applied social science domains, is fully understandable, as the overall rationale for mixing methods in social inquiry is "better understanding" of the inherent complexities and contingencies of human phenomena. Better understanding, mixed methods advocates maintain, can be importantly attained by using a plurality of our ways of seeing, interpreting, and knowing. And who does not want to better understand the important phenomena she or he is studying? Who does not want to claim better understanding as part of a research or evaluation proposal or a paper submitted for publication? Moreover, from a pragmatic and practitioner standpoint, social inquirers have long been mixing methods, as it simply made practical sense to measure both the frequency and experiential significance of an important phenomenon, or to juxtapose etic, theory-derived, standardized measures of human activity with emic, contextual, individualized narratives of meaning. The more recent conceptual development of the mixed methods field is built on these accomplishments of practice. A major purpose of mixed methods theory is to help practitioners make the mixing of methods more intentional, multilevel, and thoughtful and thus yield more compelling results.

In the first *Handbook of Mixed Methods Research,* editors Abbas Tashakkori and Charles Teddlie presented in their introductory chapter a set of six issues of currency at that time in the mixed methods field (Teddlie & Tashakkori, 2003). The present chapter engages one of those six issues, around which considerable conversation and controversy persist. This was dubbed the paradigm issue in mixed methods inquiry by Tashakkori and Teddlie, and it pertains to the possibility and defensibility of mixing at the level of philosophical assumptions, commonly bundled as paradigms. That is, when one mixes methods, what else can be legitimately mixed? And what alternatives exist for thinking well about mixing philosophical stances and assumptions? Specifically, this chapter presents and probes two mixed methods stances on these issues (Greene, 2007): (1) the dialectic stance, which advances the mixing of different philosophical frameworks and assumptions in dialogic fashion, and (2) the alternative paradigm stance, through which proponents overwhelmingly advance some form of American pragmatism as an enticingly good fit to the dynamics of mixing methods in social inquiry.

A modest elaboration of the paradigm issue in mixed methods inquiry is offered next, punctuated with our own positions on the critical dimensions that define this issue. We then take up each of the two major stances in turn—the dialectic stance and the stance of pragmatism. We present a description and conceptual rationale for the stance and then snapshots from an empirical example. We seek in the examples to translate general conceptual thinking to the actual methodological deliberations and decisions of the practitioner. We conclude the chapter with a critical comparison of these two stances, underscoring the consequences of mixing methods either dialectically or pragmatically. We perceive both stances to be of consequence, albeit with different meanings of the term.

◆ *The Paradigm Issue in Mixed Methods Inquiry*

The paradigm issue in mixed methods social inquiry is a complicated one, as it entangles the following issues among others. What is a paradigm? Is the construct of a paradigm the most useful lens with which to engage the role of philosophical assumptions and conceptual stances in mixed methods inquiry? Are traditional paradigms—many still actively used in most social science communities—relevant to an emerging field like mixed methods inquiry? Or might the field of mixing methods be unnecessarily constricted, even distorted by such traditions? What promising alternatives exist? And, whatever the paradigm or framework, what important role, if any, does it play in inquiry practice? We begin with this last question.

APPRECIATING PHILOSOPHY

This chapter is anchored in a straightforward and, we believe, uncontroversial premise. We maintain that—like all professionals, or perhaps even like all forms of work or even all forms of intentional human activity—social inquirers conduct their craft from within a particular understanding of the nature, texture, and role of social inquiry in society. It is simply not possible to conduct social inquiry without some self-understanding of what it means to be an inquirer, what the purpose and role of such

activity is in society, and what a competent study looks like. For many inquirers this self-understanding may be implicit, but it is present nonetheless. Just as master teachers of literature are continuously examining their teaching decisions, assessing the worth of their guidance, say, to a particular student who is struggling to make sense of *Angela's Ashes* (McCourt, 1999), and in turn evaluating the validity of their initial diagnosis of the problem, accomplished social inquirers make ongoing practice decisions based on an image of what it means and what it looks like to conduct social inquiry, including what defensible methods look like and what constitutes warranted knowledge.

Thus, the philosophy of science matters to social inquiry (Biesta, 2010 [this volume], Maxwell & Mittapalli, 2010 [this volume]). Yet, it matters less how this philosophy is packaged.[1]

DODGING DEFINITIONS

Understanding that there are multiple conceptualizations of what constitutes a philosophical paradigm from Thomas Kuhn forward, we do not assert any one particular definition. Consistent with most discussions about the philosophy that matters in social science, we maintain that the paradigm concept includes the philosophical issues of ontology or what is the nature of the social world we study, epistemology or what counts as warranted knowledge, methodology or how to generate and justify such knowledge, and axiology or what is the nature and role of values in social inquiry. We further agree with many that paradigms are social constructions, historically and culturally embedded discourse practices, and therefore neither inviolate nor fixed. A defensible and useful paradigm offers a coherent and internally consistent set of assumptions relevant to the practice of social science, but no particular bundles of assumptions are sacrosanct. Notably, one of the most brilliant and influential social science theorists of the last century, Donald T. Campbell (1984), was an ontological realist and an epistemological relativist, combining attributes—realism and relativism—typically allocated to different paradigms.

Attention to the philosophical assumptions of paradigms remains critically important to social scientific inquiry, because—as indicated above—these assumptions importantly guide social inquiry decisions on the ground. Yet, the character of social inquiry practice is shaped and molded by more than abstract philosophical assumptions. What one studies and how one makes sense of data and analysis results are also influenced by disciplinary ways of thinking; by the particular theories favored by the inquirer; by life experience, both professional and personal; by the dynamics of the context; by political factors and personal values; and more. This broader constellation of inquirer predispositions and responses to context has been called a *mental model* by Denis Phillips (1996) and Mary Lee Smith (1997).

A mental model is the set of assumptions, understandings, predispositions, and values and beliefs with which all social inquirers approach their work. Mental models influence how we craft our work in terms of what we choose to study and how we frame, design, and implement a given inquiry. Mental models also influence how we observe and listen, what we see and hear, what we interpret as salient and important, and indeed what we learn from our empirical work. (Greene, 2007, p. 12)

This broader and more multifaceted concept of mental model—which includes philosophical assumptions, alongside disciplinary perspectives, substantive theories, experience, values, and beliefs—works for us as a more robust frame for social inquiry than the concept of philosophical paradigm. And it is particularly useful when engaging the paradigm issue in mixed methods social inquiry

because it focuses attention on a multiplicity of assumptions, stances, beliefs, and commitments that are not inherently incompatible or incommensurable. The challenges of assumptive incommensurability are integral to the paradigm issue in mixed methods inquiry and are taken up in the next section.

MAPPING STANCES ON MIXING PARADIGMS IN MIXED METHODS INQUIRY

Because the paradigm issue in the mixed methods conversation has remained contested, participants in the mixed methods conversation have endeavored to map the various issues involved and positions taken. Not surprising for a young and dynamic field like mixed methods, this mapping is an ever evolving exercise, aiming—like all good conceptualizations—for spareness and parsimony. One current version of this map is presented in Table 5.1, intended to represent the most popular contending stances at this time. This presentation highlights varying beliefs in the importance of paradigmatic and assumptive beliefs to inquiry practice (second column) and in the possibility and desirability of mixing assumptions from different traditions (third column). In the first three stances, paradigms are viewed as important guides to inquiry practice, in contrast to the aparadigmatic stance in which theory and context are advanced as more important guides to practical inquiry decisions. The role of philosophical assumptions in a mixed methods study framed by pragmatism depends on the particular pragmatic perspectives of the inquirer. The stances further differ in their views on the possibility and practicality of mixing assumptions from different philosophical traditions.

Clearly, complicating this table are other issues, including varying definitions of the construct of paradigm and controversies internal to the philosophy of science. One such controversy—directly germane to mixing paradigms in mixed methods inquiry—is

Table 5.1 Stances on Mixing Paradigms While Mixing Methods

Stance	What is the importance and role of philosophical assumptions in inquiry practice?	Can assumptions from different philosophical traditions usefully and meaningfully inform the same study?
Purist	High: Assumptions importantly guide and direct inquiry decisions.	No, because assumptions from different traditions are incompatible.
Complementary strengths	High: Assumptions, along with context and theory, importantly guide and direct inquiry decisions.	Yes, but they must remain separate so that paradigmatic and methodological integrity can be maintained.
Dialectic	*High: Assumptions, along with context and theory, importantly guide and direct inquiry decisions.*	*Yes, assumptions from different traditions can be respectfully and dialectically engaged in dialogue toward enhanced, reframed, or new understandings.*
Aparadigmatic	Low: Assumptions importantly inform our understanding of methodology, but inquiry practice is more directly informed by theory, context, and/or ideology.	One can mix and match assumptions from different traditions as required by the inquiry context and theory, but they exert little influence on inquiry decisions.
Alternative paradigm: Pragmatism	*Mixed: This can range from "high" where transactional assumptions about human action can importantly guide human action to "low" where the focus is reoriented instrumentally to developing workable solutions to ongoing social problems.*	*Because pragmatism, even in its various forms, presents a coherent system of thought, there is no mixing of assumptions from different traditions.*

SOURCE: Adapted from Greene (2007) and Teddlie and Tashakkori (2009).

whether or not the assumptions in different paradigms are radically incommensurable[2] such that one cannot simultaneously believe, for example, that the social world is real and that the social world is constructed or that science should be values-free and science should be values-critical (Karlsson Vestman & Conner, 2006). Clearly, a strong belief in paradigmatic incommensurability precludes the possibility of mixing at this most abstract level of methodology, as represented by the purist stance in Table 5.1 and with the label of the *incompatibility thesis* by Teddlie and Tashakkori (2009).[3] Most mixed methods proponents reject this premise in its strongest

form and have argued instead for a reframing of incommensurability in ways that accept multiple standpoints. To illustrate, following Michael Patton (2002) and many others, Teddlie and Tashakkori (2009) reframe paradigm attributes—for example, inductive and deductive, value neutral and value involved—as continua rather than dualisms. And Maxwell and Mittapalli (2010 [this volume]), following Lawrence Mohr, promote a reframing around a variance and a process perspective on human activity. This is akin to Charles Ragin's (2008) variable-oriented and case-oriented approach to social inquiry. This reframing well serves a mixed methods agenda.

REPRISE

In short, we believe that the key assumptions and lofty discourse of postpositivism, constructivism, phenomenology, critical social science, action research, feminist inquiry, postmodernism, *and* pragmatism, along with other philosophical paradigms, remain integral to the ongoing development and justification of a mixed methods approach to social inquiry. This is most importantly because these abstractions, along with other strands of inquirers' mental models, critically guide inquiry practice decisions.

In an argument for the contributions of complexity theory to policy-oriented evaluation studies, Gill Callahan (2008) asserted that "the real potential for using social scientific knowledge [for policy development and implementation] lies in a critical awareness of the nature of the knowledge produced" (p. 400). We agree with Callahan and further believe that mindfulness of the contours of one's own philosophical assumptions and mental model makes for better social inquiry, although we recognize that this is an empirical question. At minimum, social inquirers today need to be mindful and intentional in learning about the plurality of frameworks for research and evaluation and then in justifying the choices they make in particular inquiry contexts.

Our discussion now turns to an elaboration of two contrasting paradigm stances—highlighted with italics in Table 5.1—the dialectic stance and the stance favoring pragmatism.

◆ Thinking Dialectically

A dialectic stance actively welcomes more than one paradigmatic tradition and mental model, along with more than one methodology and type of method, into the same inquiry space and engages them in respectful dialogue one with the other throughout the inquiry. A dialectic stance "seeks not so much convergence as insight . . . the generation of important understandings and discernments through the juxtaposition of different lenses, perspectives, and stances" (Greene, 2005, p. 208). A dialectic stance thereby affords a meaningful engagement with difference, an engagement intended to be fundamentally generative of insight and understanding that are of conceptual and practical consequence.

RATIONALE

A dialectic stance for mixed methods inquiry rests on several standpoints and commitments, best captured in the first author's promotion of a "mixed methods way of thinking" (Greene, 2007). First, this stance recognizes the legitimacy of multiple paradigmatic traditions, as they represent "multiple ways of seeing and hearing, multiple ways of making sense of the social world, and multiple standpoints on what is important and to be valued and cherished" (Greene, 2007, p. 20). Any one tradition provides but one perspective, inevitably partial, on human phenomena. Because human phenomena are extraordinarily complex, better understanding of this complexity can be attained with the use of more than one perspective.

Related to the legitimacy granted to multiple paradigmatic traditions, a dialectic stance underscores the importance and richness of this multiplicity. Too often, and in fact increasingly so, the mixed methods philosophical conversation is framed as a choice among three paradigms: the qualitative paradigm, the quantitative paradigm, and pragmatism. We find this array of options misleading and limiting. The terms *qualitative* and *quantitative* refer to types of data and methods and perhaps to clusters of methodological traditions but not to philosophical paradigms (Biesta, 2010 [this volume]). To use the qualitative and quantitative labels for paradigms is to reify and essentialize them and thereby disregard their constructed nature and discount the diverse histories and social locations of different kinds of qualitative and quantitative inquiry. To illustrate, survey research and experimental research both rely on standardized, mostly quantitative data but have very different rationales, histories, strengths and weaknesses, and roles in society. And ethnography and narrative inquiry both rely on the inquirer's presence on site and reflexive attention to emerging issues of salience but again have different rationales, histories, strengths and weaknesses, and roles in society. Perhaps more important, limiting social inquiry to just three paradigmatic choices overlooks other traditions of long-standing stature and significant contributions to the social good. These prominently feature action research and critical social science (including various feminist approaches to inquiry, participatory inquiry, transformative inquiry), among others. A dialectic stance legitimizes and therefore actively welcomes perspectives and insights from the full array of traditions of social inquiry theory and practice.

Second, the character of better understanding as a primary goal of mixed methods inquiry should not be equated with convergence or consonance, as in triangulation. Certainly, triangulation is a worthy mixed methods (and multiple methods) purpose, as congruent results from more than one method afford greater confidence in the inferences to be made. At the same time, the dialectic stance holds with equal regard inquiry results that are divergent or dissonant (Mathison, 1988). In fact, divergent or dissonant results invoke Thomas Cook's (1985) "empirical puzzles," and as such, they require further analysis and careful scrutiny of data patterns and warrants, ideally leading to new insights, perspectives, and understandings. As identified by Greene (2007), a number of classic studies in the mixed methods literature well illustrate this potential (Jick, 1983; Louis, 1981; Maxwell, Bashook, & Sandlow, 1986; Phelan, 1987; Trend, 1979).

Third, a mixed methods way of thinking, as well exemplified by the dialectic stance, offers opportunities to meaningfully engage with difference as we encounter it in the contexts we study—difference of culture, ethnicity, gender, religion, tradition, and so forth. Because the dialectic stance invites a multiplicity of ways of seeing and ways of knowing into the same study, a multiplicity of different perspectives is engaged, as are diversity and variation in the substance of what is being studied. These differences encompass knowledge claims and value claims alike, because different paradigmatic and methodological traditions embrace different value commitments or, in some cases, eschew a place for values in science all together. Our globalized world is getting smaller as technology enables each of us to travel to other places and experience, even if just in a brief YouTube video, the rhythms and culture of life elsewhere. A form of social inquiry that legitimizes and engages respectfully with difference may be well positioned to advance cross-place understanding and acceptance. There are few challenges of greater consequence than such understanding and acceptance for the sustainability of our humanity and our planet.

DIALECTIC THINKING IN PRACTICE

The mixed methods dialectic stance in action will be illustrated with excerpts from an inquirer's journal as she conducts an educational study in a middle school in a small urban community in the United States.[4] This format underscores the importance of the cognitive, analytic, and intuitive character of mixing. That is, we use concepts from mixed methods theory to conceptualize, design, and implement our mixed methods study. But the actual dialectic mixing of consequence lies in the construction or composition of inferences, drawn from purposeful conversations among and integrations of different threads of data patterns.

Such composition is a cognitive process, conducted in dialogue by an inquiry team and in internal dialogue by a sole inquirer. The example that follows is made up, based on our experiences as inquirers in middle schools. The journal entries are imagined.

The study, funded by the W. T. Grant Foundation, is designed to map the complex interactions that occur among middle school children as they go through their school day. With this study, the foundation seeks to contribute to our collective understanding of the factors and experiences that matter in positive youth development in the critical context of schooling. The researcher, Michelle, has particular interests in peer interactions that cross traditional demographic markers of difference, specifically, family income, race and ethnicity, and gender. The study is funded for 2 years at a modest level.

Study purpose and framework. The study aims to develop a descriptive portrayal of peer interactions in particular school contexts, along with selected youth's accounts of the nature and meaning of various types of interactions in diverse school contexts. Context is the primary sampling unit, drawing from research that identifies a number of dimensions of school contexts that matter for youth interactions, for example, the presence of an adult, the demographic diversity of the peer group, and expectations for academic versus social behavior. Interactions that occur in diverse contexts will be further sampled, along with the youth participating in these interactions, for data gathering.

Michelle's mental model is a blend of constructivist epistemology and feminist ideology. Her recent doctoral training was in the sociology of education, and her mentor is a renowned ethnographer in education, whose work focuses on the microcultures that inhabit urban secondary schools. Michelle has also found the perspectives of critical race theory and of Pierre Bourdieu's (1984) social capital and *habitus* useful to her program of research on the intersections of school culture and youth peer relationships. Michelle has more experience and comfort with unstructured, emergent qualitative methodologies than with structured, a priori quantitative methodologies, but she is open to all ways of gathering and interpreting information.

Michelle records her preliminary thinking about what could serve as appropriate and useful frameworks for her study. The interplay of thinking about research question, method, and framework (Maxwell, 1996) are evident in the journal entry in Box 5.1.

BOX 5.1

Michelle's Journal Entry on Study Framework

The study purposes call for a systematic portrayal of youth interactions in context and for some inside understanding of what these interactions signify for the youth involved. Clearly, different kinds of methods are needed for these different purposes. But I will also want to connect the data from the different methods, rather than just present separate sets of findings. Such connections between the etic and emic perspectives on peer interactions are a key agenda for this study. Hey, that reminds me of that mixed methods article I read last week. Maybe I should consult some references on mixing methods?

Open-ended interviews will certainly be needed to gather information on how youth make meaning of their peer interactions. I think my training and experience with constructivist inquiry will serve me well for these interviews. But the sampling for these interviews should not be purposeful; rather some systematic and representative sampling will be needed.[5] Except, of course, for gender; because of my feminist commitments, I will want to pay particular attention to the gendered character of all interactions studied.

Some kind of structured observations will be needed to develop the descriptive portrait of peer interactions in different kinds of contexts. The observation instrument will need a consistent set of a priori definitions, grounded in relevant theory, regarding who is interacting with whom and what they are doing. Such standardization is critical to this method. I am hopeful that the work being done in New York by Aaron and his colleagues on observations of youth groups could be modified for my purposes. And I am thinking that a critical realist framework for these observations might be most useful, especially in contrast to more traditional postpositivism. As I think I understand it, critical realism offers a process view of causality, which may be an excellent framework for studying underlying causal mechanisms at work in contextualized peer interactions among youth, which are anything but "regular"!

Michelle locates some references on mixed methods and also contacts her colleagues in New York about their work on observing peer interactions among youth. She is pleased she is conducting this study in a school she knows well from prior research, as she already has relevant data on the overall school culture and climate.

Study design. Michelle continues to plan to use some combination of open-ended interviews and structured observations in her study, assessing with these methods both overlapping and distinct facets of the complex phenomenon of youth peer group interactions in a school setting. The design questions become (a) how to organize this mix of methods and also (b) how to think well about mixing different assumptive frameworks—notably, feminist constructivism and critical realism—along with the mix of methods. From the mixed methods readings, Michelle determines that her primary purpose for mixing methods is *complementarity,* and a secondary purpose is *initiation* (Greene, 2007). She wants to use the different methods to develop a more comprehensive and inclusive understanding of peer interactions in a middle school context (than is possible with just one method), but she is also open to surprises and to paradoxical patterns in the data that warrant further pursuit.

In service of these particular mixed methods purposes, it is clear that this will be in integrative study, with the different methods and data sets conversing with and informing one another as the study proceeds. Michelle further decides that her two primary methods—interviews and observations—should be relatively equal in weight or importance, rather than have one dominant method/methodology. Michelle also plans an iterative design, where the methods are used sequentially. The reasons for this are both practical and substantive. On the practical side, she wants to draw her (mostly) representative interview sample from the structured observation data, so she needs to do the observations first.[6] Specifically, Michelle aims to use the most salient dimensions of the observation data as a sampling frame for the interviews and also to contribute to her interview questions. For example, if a significant portion of youth interactions in academic contexts—such as small-group work in a classroom—are characterized by strong cooperation, Michelle intends that her interview sample includes youth from these observations to learn more about the dynamics of such cooperation and the school climate factors that make it possible. More substantively, she also plans to conduct a second round of structured observations after the interviews—although of a smaller sample of contexts and interactions than the first round. In this second round, she plans to follow up on key dimensions of the interview data with more intensive observation of selected contexts and interactions. In this way, the design is iterative—first structured observations, then open-ended interviews, then additional structured observations, with the results from each method contributing to the data collection for the subsequent method.

Michelle reflects on her design decisions in the next journal entry, Box 5.2.

BOX 5.2

Michelle's Journal Entry on Study Design

I like this design. I think it will work well to generate good and useful data. Yet, I am still puzzled about how to "mix" the different lenses I will be using for the different methods. What does such mixing look like? I assume that when collecting and analyzing the observation data, I can don my critical realist lens, and when working the interview data, I can don my feminist constructivist lens. But when I am connecting one data set to another or analyzing both sets of data together, how do I honor the stances and commitments of each lens?

Data collection. Here (Box 5.3) is one of Michelle's journal entries from the field. The first round of observation data have been collected and are being analyzed, in part, as preparation for selecting the interview sample and conducting the interviews.

BOX 5.3

Michelle's Journal Entry on Data Collection

Hmmm . . . I wonder if this is what is meant by mixing frameworks or lenses or paradigms in mixed methods studies? While analyzing the observation data, I found myself looking for gender in the interactions observed, even though the gender lens is part of the framework within which the interviews are being planned. I don't mean gender as in male or female, but gender as in dynamics of power, voice, and privilege in interactions among mixed groups of youth. The observation instrument does not define power, voice, and privilege as understood from a feminist stance. But I am looking for them anyway. I also found myself questioning some of the variables in the observation data. I realize that the items and scales are intended to capture "real" dimensions of the context and the interactions taking place. But I can't help but wonder about the socially constructed character of such interactional events and processes. I am already eager to collect the interview data and continue this conversation across frameworks and lenses.

Data analysis. Michelle has now completed the data collection for her study. She found the sequential design helpful in progressively focusing in on the diverse yet bounded character of peer interactions in the middle school. And the analysis of one data set to inform the development (sampling and instrumentation) of the next method was quite straightforward and simultaneously illuminating.

Now, however, it is time to conduct more integrative analyses. Michelle is experimenting with two analytic ideas suggested in the mixed methods literature. First, she is "importing" midstream results from the analysis of one type of data into the analysis of the other type of data. In particular, she is using major themes from a descriptive analysis of the interview data to inform the analysis of the two sets of observation data. She is endeavoring to cluster the observation data by these major themes, assess patterns of interactions (primarily via correlations) within each cluster, and then compare such patterns across clusters. The question being pursued in this analysis is: What can be learned when the observation data are clustered or grouped by the structure of meaning identified in the interview data, as represented by the descriptive themes? To give a concrete example, one descriptive theme relates to the presence and the character of humor and playfulness in peer interactions. The observation data could be clustered by the extent of humor and playfulness observed and then each

cluster analyzed for number, types, and diversity of youth present; location of interaction; primary content of conversation; and other relevant variables—looking for markers that do and do not differentiate among the clusters. Interesting findings could then be taken back to the interview data and pursued in analyses thereof. Michelle expects that cognizance of the emic and constructed nature of the interview data, juxtaposed with the etic and realist nature of the observation data, will enhance this cross-data set analysis.

Second, Michelle is also constructing several matrices in which data of multiple types can be arrayed and then analyzed for patterns and insights. Michelle is finding the matrix display idea especially challenging and creative. Along what dimensions can the data in this study be meaningfully arrayed is the important question in constructing an analytic matrix. Here are two data analysis journal entries, Boxes 5.4 and 5.5.

BOX 5.4

Michelle's Early Journal Entry on Data Analysis

Aaargh!! What was I thinking? This mixed methods analytic work is confusing. I can't seem to make any meaningful linkages or connections among the various sets of data that I have. Each has something to say, but the connections remain elusive. I keep trying to identify meaningful dimensions along which both data sets can be arrayed, but with little success so far. Maybe the paradigm purists had it right?

BOX 5.5

Michelle's Later Journal Entry on Data Analysis

Hey, what a difference a day makes, no? The matrix display of today was wonderfully successful. The key was finding some way to order the contexts in which the observations took place because matrix dimensions need to be ordered. And I found the key to that order in the interview data—a very complex key related to place and density of space. Contexts of peer interactions can be ordered on how centrally they are located in the school and how dense the interactions are in that place. Provisionally, I think density means both intensity and

(Continued)

(Continued)

importance—the latter from the youth's point of view. The interview data can help further unpack these concepts of centrality and density, but meanwhile, the concepts are providing a wonderfully provocative frame for conducting some analyses of the two sets of data together.

I am working on two different matrices right now. In the first, which is actually a 2×2 table formed by the dimensions of high versus low centrality and density, I am trying to assess key aspects of the observation data that show up in various combinations of these dimensions. This one will be especially interesting because it will analyze the structured observation data within a framework generated by youth's own constructions of meaning in their peer interactions. I will also add a lens of gender to this analysis and maybe even conduct it separately for boys and girls. In the second matrix analysis, I will select observed contexts at the extremes of the identified dimensions (high versus low centrality and density) and record in the cells of the matrix the salient themes from the interviews that occurred in those contexts. I am very much looking forward to seeing what differences show up and especially what they look like.

Peer interactions in this school appear to be framed importantly by geography—space and place matters in these interactions. I wonder how the meanings of space and place are related to the school and the peer cultures.

Interpretation, inference, and warrant. Michelle pursued these and other mixed methods data analysis toward a rich portrait of peer interactions in school contexts, a portrait transected by the multiple assumptions afforded by her multiple lenses. She felt comfortable weaving together these assumptions in patterns indicated by the data, her analyses, and, of course, her own perspectives and interpretations. She had high confidence in the quality of each data set, judged by its own methodological criteria. She also had high confidence in the integrative inferences she developed from her analyses and was currently developing an integrated argument for the quality and warrant of these inferences. Here is a final journal entry, Box 5.6.

BOX 5.6

Michelle's Journal Entry on Interpretation and Inference

My argument for inference quality and warrant will be anchored in the value of the *multiple* ways of looking at and understanding peer interactions in school contexts that I included in this study. I will trace the analytic conversations I conducted among the interview and observation data sets and identify the critical contributions of each conversation along the way. I will further argue that it is because I mixed assumptions and stances along with methods and data that I have generated such rich and compelling results.

◆ Thinking Pragmatically

The pragmatic stance argues for the use of mixed and multiple methods to meaningfully generate information to address inquiry questions (Morgan, 2007). This is a commonly known and articulated view of pragmatism. Biesta (2010 [this volume]) characterizes this perspective as "everyday pragmatism" referring to the "utility of research means for research ends." Akin to the position taken by Biesta, Patton (2002), an ardent supporter of pragmatism, describes being pragmatic as emphasizing practical issues of "methodological appropriateness" (p. 72). Burke Johnson and Tony Onwuegbuzie (2004) further explicate Patton's point by noting that pragmatism has a "logic of inquiry" that primarily focuses on problem solving and outcomes, allowing one to make use of a myriad of methods for the practical purposes of induction, deduction, and abduction. Yet, as underscored by Biesta and other authors in this *Handbook,* pragmatism encompasses philosophical attributes that have important implications for social inquiry in general and mixed methods inquiry specifically.

RATIONALE

The rationale for the pragmatic stance for mixed methods lies in its response to the traditional epistemological stances that purport issues of paradigmatic incommensurability when conducting mixed methods inquiry (Greene, 2008). Although the pragmatic stance disputes the traditional a priori assumption of incommensurability, it does not fully eschew philosophical traditions. Rather, the pragmatic stance positions philosophical traditions and multiple perspectives in service of the inquiry problem at hand.

Because of its epistemological and methodological flexibility, the popularity of and potential for pragmatism to become the paradigm of choice for mixed methods inquiry comes as no surprise (Greene, 2008). Yet, recent mixed methods discourse draws attention to the tendency of some social inquirers to "adopt MMR [mixed methods research] as a mindless mantra" (Freshwater, 2007, p. 135), thus raising issues related to the thoughtful integration of methods and the paradigmatic assumptions being used when making use of the pragmatic stance (Bryman, 2006; Freshwater, 2007). Indeed, mixing methods should not be viewed as a magical methodological solution for the complexities of social inquiry. Similarly,

pragmatism, as a philosophical paradigm, should not be blindly taken up by mixed methods inquirers as the paradigm of choice without a proper understanding of the characteristics that constitute the paradigm (see Biesta, 2010 [this volume]).

Pragmatism is an American philosophy developed primarily from the writings of Charles Sanders Peirce, William James, and especially John Dewey (Biesta & Burbules, 2003). It is important to note that there are multiple versions of pragmatism, primarily drawn from the work of these prolific thinkers. The mixed methods literature also provides a characterization of pragmatism (Johnson & Onwuegbuzie, 2004). From these two literatures, major tenets of the pragmatic philosophical framework were synthesized (Biesta & Burbules, 2003; Johnson & Onwuegbuzie, 2004) to include:

- a rejection of the traditional mind and matter dualism

- a view of knowledge as both constructed and as a function of organism-environment transactions

- a recognition that knowledge is fallible because we can never be certain that our current knowledge will be appropriate for future inquiry problems

- a belief that truth comes from experience, and that absolute truth will be determined at the end of history

- a problem-solving, action-focused inquiry process

- an advancement of the term *warranted assertions* to underscore the point that assertions can be warranted only in specific inquiry contexts and that their value must be re-established in new inquiries

- a commitment to values of democracy, freedom, equality, and progress

It is important to note that the pragmatic philosophy, particularly from a Deweyan perspective, is perhaps more accurately described as an anti-philosophy in the sense that it shifts the focus from traditional issues of epistemology to an emphasis on the inter-actions between humans and their environment (both natural and social) (Biesta & Burbules, 2003). These interactions—or more accurately *transactions*—represent the change process an individual undergoes as he or she adapts to the environment (Biesta & Burbules, 2003). These individual adaptive transactions are continuously informed by previous experiences through which an individual creates his or her own world. However, when an individual works with others, his or her individual world is altered to accommodate a group response to accomplish common goals. Both the indi-vidual and social responses to the environ-ment represent experiences from which knowledge is acquired and refined (Biesta & Burbules, 2003; Johnson & Onwuegbuzie, 2004). Dewey's ideas about knowledge con-struction depart from the subjectivism and objectivism dualism and introduce a unique pragmatic perspective: *intersubjectivity.* An intersubjective world is a "world in which we live and act together and for which we have a shared responsibility" (Biesta & Burbules, 2003, p. 108). Within the context of social inquiry, this shared responsibility includes thinking (considering varying lines of action), cooperating (conducting actions together), and communicating (developing mutual understandings) (Biesta & Burbules, 2003; Johnson & Onwuegbuzie, 2004; Morgan, 2007).

The philosophical pragmatic stance advanced by Dewey also has consequences for the way in which we think about inquiry (science) as well as the relationship between inquiry and practice and their results. Science or the "social practice called science," from a pragmatic perspective, is not deemed superior to common sense or our everyday knowledge; it is considered one form of inquiry, with possibilities for different problems or experiences (Biesta & Burbules, 2003, p. 88). Furthermore,

Dewey's pragmatic perspective rejects the idea that science and practice are different in an epistemological sense in which "science is purely concerned with knowl-edge and practice is purely concerned with action" (Biesta & Burbules, 2003, p. 105). This reasoning advocates an informative relationship between inquiry and practice rather than a linear relationship where inquiry simply informs practice. Dewey's pragmatic view of inquiry also "rejects the need to choose between a pair of extremes where inquiry results are either completely specific to a particular context or an instance of some more generalized set of principles" (Morgan, 2007, p. 72). The fun-damental idea here is *transferability* or the ways in which findings can be used in other settings and the warrants for making those assertions (Morgan, 2007).

The pragmatic stance has no set methodological requirements for social inquiry but rather has a consequential action-knowledge framework to guide inquiry. Pragmatic inquirers may select any method based on its appropriateness to the situation at hand. Through the inquiry process, the inquirer attempts to be aware of his or her assumptions with the goal of using knowledge gathered from multiple methods in service of work-able solutions (Johnson & Onwuegbuzie, 2004). That is, the pragmatic stance advances mixing multiple sources of evi-dence to attain and modify knowledge, which in turn is used to inform potential solutions or varying lines of action and to consider their consequences. Possible solu-tions to problems or the results of prag-matic inquiry are viewed as assertions that become warranted in terms of their trans-ferability in different situations (Johnson & Onwuegbuzie, 2004). From a prag-matic stance, this requires inquirers to work back and forth between the specific results and their general implications (Morgan, 2007). And so, mixed methods inquiry with a pragmatic stance is an active and iterative process of establishing warranted assertions as they are applied in new experiences. With this pragmatic philosophical paradigm framework in mind, we now present an example of mixing methods with a pragmatic stance.

PRAGMATIC THINKING IN PRACTICE

The example illustrates how some of the assumptions from the pragmatic framework show up in mixed methods practice. Like the previous mixed methods dialectic stance illustration, the mixed methods pragmatic example will be presented in the form of excerpts from an inquirer's journal. The study used in the example is loosely based on a study of educational accountability conducted by the second author (Hall, 2008). The journal entries are fictitious but are grounded in the practical, contextual, and consequential character of pragmatic mixed methods research in action (Datta, 1997).

The study was framed primarily to respond to concerns related to schools struggling to meet the needs of their diverse student body while simultaneously working to meet the external accountability mandates of the U.S. federal educational policy, No Child Left Behind (NCLB). NCLB relies heavily on annual mandated tests and sanctions[7] for purposes of school improvement. However, test score data provide little information about the specific curricula being taught or the contexts within which schools operate and therefore remain insufficient to improve teaching and learning. Furthermore, many school staff do not have the skills and knowledge necessary to respond effectively to both external accountability of NCLB and their local needs (Desimone, Garet, Birman, Porter, & Yoon, 2002; Elmore, 2004; Rallis & MacMullen, 2000). This is particularly true of those schools that serve a high proportion of minority and low-income learners (students eligible to receive free or reduced lunch) (Sunderman, Kim, & Orfield, 2005).

As a former teacher in a Chicago public middle school that served a high population of students who were economically disadvantaged, Juan has experience with NCLB and has dealt with the consequences of not meeting annual yearly progress (AYP) on performance standards. In his current position as an assistant professor, Juan studies educational accountability focusing on a school's *collective capacity;* that is, the areas in which schools need to work collectively for school improvement purposes (i.e., leadership, decision making, resources, instruction) (Abelmann & Elmore, 1999; Carnoy, Elmore, & Siskin, 2003; Newmann, King, & Rigdon, 1997; Rallis & MacMullen, 2000).

Study purpose and framework. Informed by his personal experiences with NCLB and previous accountability studies, Juan seeks to better understand the complex interplay between a public school's unique contextual features and the NCLB policy. Finding practical ways to assist schools in need of improvement (as defined by NCLB) is the overall purpose of his study. Specifically, the study aims to examine the collective capacity of a high-poverty middle school to hold itself internally accountable to the external accountability mandates of NCLB. Guided by his study purpose, Juan contemplates possible inquiry questions. While pondering inquiry questions, it occurs to Juan that part of the solution to the problem of educational accountability lies in refining the conceptualization of collective capacity to make better decisions about how it should look in practice. With this in mind, Juan concludes that he wants his study to inform current understandings of collective capacity in addition to exploring how it is actually enacted. Juan's thinking about how to best frame his research project, with this dual purpose in mind, is reflected in this journal entry, Box 5.7.

BOX 5.7

Juan's Journal Entry on Study Framework

The NCLB policy does not pay a lot of attention to the particular contextual features of schools, and as far as I'm concerned, it is the inner working of schools that matters most when it comes to school improvement efforts. I need a framework that allows me to engage the school context and school members' perspectives, which I certainly value. Perhaps a case study might be in order. Although, I really don't want to conduct a case study in the traditional sense because my goal is not to learn about the school per se, but to use it as more of a context for refining the conceptual collective capacity framework. Is there a case study framework appropriate for this purpose?

Also, because of severe budget cuts, I will have limited assistance on this project and can dedicate only one academic year to this study. I need a framework that will allow me to conduct this study in a meaningful yet manageable way. What to do?

Juan begins to investigate different case study frameworks and finds Robert Stake's (2000, 2005) ideas about *instrumental* case study equally reasonable and intriguing. He finds that instrumental case study research, in particular, is uniquely positioned to enhance explanation of phenomena (Stake, 1995) as it "plays a supportive role" in understanding the researcher's "external interest" (Stake, 2000, p. 437). The knowledge gathered is valuable to inform how similar phenomena might be considered in different contexts (Stake, 1978). Based on his understanding of instrumental case study research, Juan then identifies a middle school appropriate for his study: Negola Middle School (NMS). Juan selects NMS because it has been able to met AYP goals despite its high percentage of students from a low socioeconomic background (68%). Against this contextual background, Juan aims to target his primary research interest: collective capacity. Juan thinks this particular case will provide descriptions of successful collective capacity strategies based on evidentiary data. Juan also thinks this case will be useful to inform, expand, challenge, or modify current understandings of collective capacity.

Also, because mathematics is an NCLB-tested content area,[8] Juan seeks to investigate the collective capacity of the school's mathematics program as part of his study. He thinks the study of collective capacity within the context of the mathematics program will provide an opportunity for an in-depth study.

Study design. With his research questions in mind, Juan reflects about the design of the study. He likes the idea of a case study that incorporates various kinds of methods to examine collective capacity on both the school and program levels. Juan aims to conduct informal interviews and observations to learn about the school context and to understand the language used within this particular school. Then, he plans to use a questionnaire, informed by the qualitative data gathered, to understand how collective capacity is perceived by NMS teachers and administrators. After the questionnaire data are collected and analyzed, Juan plans to conduct in-depth interviews and observations to examine collective capacity within the context of the school's mathematics program in more detail. In this way, the study design is helping to extend understandings of how collective capacity is experienced and enacted on different levels (Mason, 2006).

Based on his readings, Juan knows that his case study framework is well suited to carry out mixed methods inquiry as it has "epistemological, ontological, and methodological flexibility" (Luck, Jackson, & Usher, 2006, p. 103), and he doesn't take issue with this. Furthermore, from a more practical perspective, he determines that case studies provide a nice bounded system of inquiry (Stake, 2000) within which to apply mixed methods inquiry.

Juan continues to think about his mixed methods design. After perusing the multiple typologies of mixed methods designs, Juan finds John Creswell's (2003) discussion most helpful to organize his data collection and analysis strategy. Juan previously determined that the methods in his study would be implemented sequentially, but he now considers which data source will be given priority, particularly during the data analysis stage of the research, and how the qualitative and quantitative data will be mixed or integrated. He sketches out a graphic visual of his sequential design (Box 5.8), adapted from Creswell's discussion, in his journal.

BOX 5.8

Juan's Mixed Methods Study Design

	QUAN		→		QUAL
qual	QUAN	QUAN	QUAL	QUAL	Interpretation
Data →	Data →	Data →	Data →	Data →	of Entire
Collection	Collection	Analysis	Collection	Analysis	Analysis

Juan is pleased with his mixed methods design because he thinks the sequential design is clear and straightforward. He thinks he can even share a modified version with NMS teachers and administrators during a faculty meeting as part of his presentation to communicate his research plans. In Juan's mixed methods design variation, quantitative and qualitative sources of data are given equal status during collection and analysis as denoted by the use of capital letters. But priority is given to qualitative data at the stage of interpretation. After making decisions about the study design, Juan reflects on some of the implications of his study design.

Juan gives priority to understanding collective capacity and the ways in which it is enacted. Juan's idea is to use the questionnaire, in-depth interviews, and observations within a single case study to inform future studies conducted on a larger scale. This is the practical analytical thrust of his study. Yet, because Juan is conducting a single case study, he is concerned about his ability to provide generalizable information that face difficult circumstances. Juan discusses his frustration in his journal, Box 5.9.

BOX 5.9

Juan's Journal Entry on Study Design

Okay, I really like the case study framework and I think using a mixed methods approach will target lived experiences and realities, yielding a more comprehensive understanding of collective capacity, which is what I'm after. Yet, I need to consider the consequences of using this form of inquiry. For example, my questionnaire will be administered to approximately 50 NMS faculty.

(Continued)

(Continued)

From a statistical standpoint, this does not provide any basis for making generalizations. But, at the same time, I'm not interested in statistical significance. I do think, however, that inferences can be drawn from the themes and patterns identified from this single case study which, in turn, can add to the existing accountability literature and advance the way schools in need of improvement think about collective capacity.

Data collection. Juan's sequential design will be conducted in two main phases. In Part 1, Juan conducts informal interviews with administrators and some teachers as a way to learn about the school and to also have the faculty learn more about him and the purpose of his study. Juan then uses the data collected informally and the conceptual framework of collective capacity that emerged from his extensive review of the literature to develop questionnaire items. Juan pilots the questionnaire with middle school teachers from his former school, makes modifications, and then administers the instrument to the 45 NMS teachers and administrators present that day.

In Part 2 of the case study, Juan asks about and observes collective capacity as perceived and enacted in the daily rhythms and routines of the school's mathematics program. Juan includes the perspectives of all six mathematics teachers (two at each grade level: sixth, seventh, and eighth) and administrators (principal, assistant principal, and the dean of students). In addition, he believes that the student perspective is particularly important to studies on accountability because they are most impacted by accountability mechanisms. In response to

this, he solicits the assistance of the school counselor to identify participants for student focus group interviews.

Data analysis. Juan begins his analysis with a parallel form of mixed analysis in which the quantitative and qualitative data are analyzed separately, and each analysis is accorded equal importance in the study. The questionnaire analysis consists of computing descriptive statistics for each collective capacity dimension. On average, the questionnaire results show that NMS faculty reported an overall positive perception of collective capacity.

To analyze the interviews and observations from the mathematics program, Juan uses a form of modified induction as identified in the mixed methods literature. First, he analyzes the interview and observation data with the original collective capacity framework in mind. Then, Juan analyzes the data with intentional sensitivity to discovering new insights. This procedure is iteratively conducted multiple times, with the results used to refine the collective capacity framework. As he continues, Juan reflectively identifies initial impressions and attempts to flesh them out in his journal. One such impression is featured in this journal entry, Box 5.10.

BOX 5.10

Juan's Journal Entry on Data Analysis

The original conceptual framework did provide the means to examine collective capacity as relevant to the case. It was extremely practical in terms of organizing both the quantitative data and the qualitative data sets. In particular, this organization helped to me to rethink the conceptualization of the leadership collective capacity dimension. Initially, I thought of leadership in terms of school building-level administrators (principal, assistant principal, and the dean of students). This definition was reflected in the questionnaire. However, the interview and observational data provided deeper insights as to role and practices of teacher leaders and district-level content coordinators. It appears that these leaders provide essential multilevel support and reinforcement of teachers' pedagogical-content knowledge. As a result, the leadership collective capacity dimension has been expanded to importantly include leaders in the form of teacher leaders and district-level administration.

Interpretation, inferences, and warrant. After Juan analyzes each data set separately, he analyzes them together for purposes of generating inferences. Juan continues to pay considerable attention to the connections between the school-level quantitative results and the math program-level qualitative data. With some hunches in mind, he decides to conduct a more systematic analysis of the qualitative data to confirm or disconfirm his preliminary inferences. For the most part, Juan notices consistency across the data sources. Yet, there are some instances where the data sets diverge. When attempts to reconcile data divergence are futile, Juan decides to check his interpretations of the data during informal conversations with administrators and mathematics teachers. Juan perceives this tactic as a way to advance mutual understandings of the data via reflecting with school members about observed events or clarifying what was stated during an interview. In a practical yet meaningful way, Juan perceives this process as providing an opportunity to summarize his inferences.

After member checking and considerable modification, Juan feels more confident about his inferences. Now, Juan considers how he will organize the write-up of the case. Here is one of Juan's write-up journal entries, Box 5.11.

BOX 5.11

Juan's Journal Entry on Interpretation and Inference

I think I will include an opening vignette to provide contextual description of the case. Assertions about collective capacity will be included with sufficient warrant. These assertions will be supported by the evidentiary data including multiple perspectives, my experiences with NCLB, and previous accountability research.

Perhaps I should use a two-circle Venn diagram with one circle representing dimensions of collective capacity at the school level and the other representing dimensions of collective capacity at the program level. The overlapping area would then represent the dimensions of collective capacity that are shared at both levels. I'm not too sure about this idea, but it might provide a nice visual representation to complement the other sections included in the write-up.

Ultimately, I aim to have my final write-up convey collective capacity strategies in such a way that other schools in need of improvement will be able to consider the degree to which the inferences from this particular case will inform their options for action.

◆ Conclusions

This chapter is an argument for *not* closing down the conversation about the paradigm issue in mixed methods social inquiry, for *not* trying to settle it by delineating *the* mixed methods paradigm. In 1986, Smith and Heshusius made an impassioned argument for *not* closing down the conversation regarding the substantive differences between qualitative and quantitative inquiry traditions. Smith and Heshusius were worried that valued differences—especially differences in underlying logics of inquiry (paradigms, mental models)—would be buried under some hegemonic consensual framework for social inquiry and that rich and meaningful diversity in social inquiry would be reduced. We share this worry. We perceive that the mixed methods field is vitally alive, in part, because it welcomes a diversity of perspectives and thought. We value this liveliness and believe that it is important for the continued productive development of the field.

Among the differences of generative value are the stances that diverse inquirers in distinct contexts take on the paradigm issue when conducting a mixed methods study.

This chapter has articulated and illustrated two of these stances—the dialectic and the pragmatic paradigm stance for mixing methods in social inquiry. Consistent with the emphases in this chapter, Table 5.2 offers a comparative display of what matters most in *practical inquiry decisions* for each stance, of what mattered to Michelle and Juan as they were conducting their respective studies. It is important to note that both stances attend to underlying philosophical assumptions as important frameworks for inquiry, but these assumptions direct the practitioner along quite different pathways. That is, the major difference is the orientation of each stance, of what the inquirer's antennae are attuned to in the inquiry environment, of what the inquirer is especially mindful of during the

inquiry. The dialectic inquirer's antennae are specifically attuned to philosophy and to the assumptions, stances, and values underlying the multiple philosophical frameworks that are guiding the inquiry. Mindfulness of and respect for the differences in these frameworks constitute the core of the dialectic attitude. The pragmatic inquirer's antennae are attuned to generating useful practical solutions to the important problem being studied. The pragmatist attends to context, practicality, and instrumentality—not to philosophy—in service of this overall commitment to problem solutions. This major difference in orientation is reflected in each inquirer's decisions about frameworks, methodology, and design.

Both inquirers are mindful and critically reflective during the study, although with antennae oriented somewhat differently. The dialectic inquirer is especially attentive to the importance of surprises and paradoxes across the different data sets, valuing and even seeking dissonance as a means to deeper insight. The pragmatic inquirer is especially attentive to the actionable value of the different data sets, privileging inquiry results of direct practical application in addressing important problems in the world. Critical reflection is used by both inquirers as a means of maintaining vigilance regarding the generation of warranted assertions. For both inquirers, redirection of the inquiry is needed if the desired assertions are not being generated.

The character of warrant for study inferences is significantly different for these two mixed methods stances. The dialectic inquirer aspires to generate deep, insightful, comprehensive understandings—woven from an integration of the various methods used and data sets collected. The pragmatic inquirer seeks actionable knowledge of direct practical value in the context being studied. The actionable knowledge generated is continuously warranted through its application elsewhere. Across these differences, the dialectic and pragmatic inquirer share a commitment akin to "intelligent inquiry," from Dewey. For both inquirers,

Table 5.2 Critical Influences on Inquiry Decisions for the Dialectic and Pragmatic Stances

Inquiry Decision	*Dialectic Stance*	*Pragmatic Stance*
What concept, issue, or problem is important to study?	The inquiry focus preferably comes from a troubling problem of some importance in the world.	The inquiry focus comes from a problem of some importance in the world.
What frameworks—philosophical, theoretical, other—should guide the study?	More than one philosophical, theoretical, and/or mental model framework intentionally guides the study.	Context and practicality—not philosophical frameworks—are useful guides for practice. And information from everyday experience is as important as information from prior research and from theory.
What inquiry approach (methodology) should be used?	Decisions about inquiry approaches follow from inquiry questions and frameworks. A mixed methods approach is often the best match.	Whatever works; whatever can best engage and usefully inform the important practical problem at hand.
How should the study be designed?	The preferred design is interactive and recursive, featuring intentional "conversations" among the data sets from the different methods at multiple points in the study.	The preferred design is instrumentally effective in gathering information and inclusive of multiple perspectives to inform the practical problem at hand.
What is important to be mindful of in data collection and analysis?	It is important to be respectful of the multiple frameworks guiding the study and to be alert to surprises and dissonance in data patterns.	It is important to reflect on outcomes, goals, assumptions and values and to consider the ways in which the data inform and support possible actions.
What are important inquirer activities and stances during the inquiry process?	The dialectic inquirer engages in an ongoing dialogue among the various data sets in the study, repeatedly and critically assessing the merit of inquiry decisions and results in terms of generating more comprehensive and insightful results. The dialectic inquirer also considers more generative directions for the study on an ongoing basis.	The pragmatic inquirer engages in ongoing reflection on inquiry decisions and results, assessing their practical worth and actionable value. The pragmatic inquirer further engages in ongoing communications with those in the inquiry context, seeking support for the practical value of what is being learned.
What constitute warranted inferences?	Warranted inferences represent respectful integrations of diverse lenses on the phenomena studied, possibly including jagged points of dissonance. Warranted inferences represent more comprehensive and insightful understandings than could be attained with one framework/method alone.	Warranted inferences represent actionable knowledge, that is, knowledge that can be acted upon, in this context and others, or knowledge that is directly actionable for improving the important practical problem being studied.
What is the hoped-for contribution of the study?	Consequential in terms of meaningful engagement with differences that matter.	Consequential in terms of contributions to workable solutions to important problems.

inquiry is directly linked to context, to practice, to everyday life, and to lived experience. For both inquirers, the goal of inquiry is the improvement of life conditions through reflective articulation of an inquiry agenda of especially practical value and a thorough consideration of the means to address it.

Finally, both the dialectic and the pragmatic mixed methods stances aim to be of consequence, albeit in different ways. An inquirer with a dialectic stance aspires to surface, engage, and legitimize difference in the social world, toward greater understanding and acceptance of difference. Dialectic consequentiality is an easing of the tensions, the violence, and the hatred that divide different peoples, one from another. An inquirer with a pragmatic stance aspires to contribute to workable solutions to ongoing and pressing problems in the world. The pragmatist seeks actionable knowledge, knowledge laced with guidance about what to do. Pragmatic consequentiality is the direct improvement of life conditions and life chances for those in need, a touchable change in the "real world."

Research Questions and Exercises

1. What is the paradigm issue in mixed methods social inquiry?

2. What issues define the different stances on this issue? What are your own views on this issue?

3. What are distinctive characteristics and aspirations of the dialectic stance on mixing assumptions and values while mixing methods?

4. What are your own views on the conceptual merits and practical value of this stance? What else did you want to know about Michelle's thinking and reasoning in conducting her mixed methods study?

5. What are distinctive characteristics and aspirations of the stance of pragmatism for mixed methods inquiry?

6. What are your own views on the conceptual merits and practical value of this stance? What else did you want to know about Juan's thinking and reasoning in conducting his mixed methods study?

7. What further learning do you wish to do to help identify and develop your own stance on mixing assumptions and values while mixing methods?

◆ Notes

1. We find Biesta's (2010 [this volume]) argument—for focusing on individual philosophical assumptions, notably ontology and epistemology, rather than paradigm packages— practical and likely to advance the mixed methods discussion on paradigms in productive and meaningful directions.

2. See Howe (1988) for an excellent discussion on the incommensurability thesis.

3. Janice Morse's (2003) requirement that all studies have just one dominant theoretical "thrust" is also consistent with this stance, although she welcomes mixing at the assumptive level across studies in a program of research.

4. Small urban communities have many of the characteristics of large cities, but with less

intensity and less isolation due to the smaller scale.

5. This use of a methodological strategy—representative sampling—that comes from a different methodology from that being used—open-ended interviews within a constructivist framework—is an interesting type of mixing at the design stage of inquiry.

6. The use of data from one method to inform the development or implementation of a second method—including sampling decisions—is also recognized as a *development* purpose in mixed methods inquiry.

7. Schools that fail to make AYP over time face corrective action; the amount of federal funds that they receive may be reduced, they may be restructured or converted into charter schools, or they may be taken over by their district or state (U.S. Department of Education, 2009).

8. NCLB mandates that all states annually test Grades 3 to 8 in reading, math, and science to hold them accountable for the academic achievement of their students. Schools must show AYP based on the aggregate test scores of all students and disaggregated scores by selected subgroups. By the end of the 2013–2014 school year, all students must meet or exceed state standards in tested subject areas (U.S. Department of Education, 2009).

◆ References

Abelmann, C., & Elmore, R. F. (1999). *When accountability knocks, will anyone answer?* (Research Report RR42). Madison, WI: Consortium for Policy Research in Education.

Biesta, G. (2010). Pragmatism and the philosophical foundations of mixed methods research. In A. Tashakkori & C. Teddlie (Eds.), *SAGE handbook of mixed methods in social & behavioral research* (2nd ed.). Thousand Oaks, CA: Sage.

Biesta, G. J. J., & Burbules, N. (2003). *Pragmatism and educational research*. Lanham, MD: Rowman & Littlefield.

Bordieu, P. (1984). *Distinction: A social critique of the judgment of taste* (R. Nice, Trans.). Cambridge, MA: Harvard University Press.

Bryman, A. (2006). Paradigm peace and the implications for quality. *International Journal of Social Research Methodology, 9*(2), 111–126.

Callahan, G. (2008). Evaluation and negotiated order: Developing the application of complexity theory. *Evaluation, 14*(4), 339–411.

Campbell, D. T. (1984). Can we be scientific in applied social research? In R. F. Conner, D. G. Altman, & C. Jackson (Eds.), *Evaluation studies review annual* (Vol. 9, pp. 26–48). Thousand Oaks, CA: Sage.

Carnoy, M., Elmore, R., & Siskin, L. (2003). *The new accountability: High school and high-stakes testing.* New York: Routledge Falmer.

Cook, T. D. (1985). Postpositivist critical multiplism. In R. L. Shotland & M. M. Mark (Eds.), *Social science and social policy* (pp. 21–62). Thousand Oaks, CA: Sage.

Creswell, J. (2003). *Research design: Qualitative, quantitative, and mixed methods approaches.* Thousand Oaks, CA: Sage.

Datta, L. (1997). A pragmatic basis for mixed-method designs. In J. C. Greene & V. J. Caracelli (Eds.), *Advances in mixed-method evaluation: The challenges and benefits of integrating diverse paradigms* (pp. 53–70). San Francisco: Jossey-Bass.

Desimone, L., Garet, M., Birman, B., Porter, A., & Yoon, K. (2002). How do district management and implementation strategies relate to the quality of the professional development that districts provide to teachers? *Teachers College Record, 104*(7), 1265–1312.

Elmore, R. (2004). *School reform from the inside out: Policy, practice, and performance.* Cambridge, MA: Harvard Education Press.

Freshwater, D. (2007). Reading mixed methods research: Contexts for criticism. *Journal of Mixed Methods Research, 1*(2), 134–146.

Greene, J. C. (2005). The generative potential of mixed methods inquiry. *International Journal of Research & Method in Education, 28*(2), 207–211.

Greene, J. C. (2007). *Mixed methods in social inquiry.* San Francisco: Jossey-Bass.

Greene, J.C. (2008). Is mixed methods social inquiry a distinctive methodology? *Journal of Mixed Methods Research, 2*(1), 7–22.

Hall, J. (2008). *Educational accountability: Investigating the collective capacity of a middle school* (Doctoral dissertation). Available from ProQuest Dissertations and Theses database (AAT No. 3314784)

Howe, K. R. (1988). Against the quantitative-qualitative incompatibility thesis (or dogmas die hard). *Educational Researcher, 17*(8), 10–16.

Jick, T. D. (1983). Mixing qualitative and quantitative methods: Triangulation in action. In J. VanMaanen (Ed.), *Qualitative methodology* (pp. 135–148). Thousand Oaks, CA: Sage.

Johnson, R. B., & Onwuegbuzie, A. J. (2004). Mixed methods research: A research paradigm whose time has come. *Educational Researcher, 33*(7), 14–26.

Karlsson Vestman, O., & Conner, R. E. (2006). The relationship between evaluation and politics. In I. F. Shaw, J. C. Greene, & M. M. Mark (Eds.), *The Sage handbook of evaluation* (pp. 225–242). London: Sage.

Louis, K. S. (1981, April). *Policy researcher as sleuth: New approaches to integrating qualitative and quantitative methods.* Paper presented at the annual meeting of the American Educational Research Association, Los Angeles. (ED 207 256)

Luck, L., Jackson, D., & Usher, K. (2006). Case study: A bridge across paradigms. *Nursing Inquiry, 13,* 103–109.

Mathison, S. (1988). Why triangulate? *Educational Researcher, 17*(2), 13–17.

Mason, J. (2006). Mixing methods in a qualitatively-driven way. *Qualitative Research 6*(1), 9–25.

Maxwell, J. A. (1996). *Qualitative research design: An interactive approach.* Thousand Oaks, CA: Sage.

Maxwell, J. A., Bashook, P. G., & Sandlow, C. J. (1986). Combining ethnographic and experimental methods in educational evaluation. In D. M. Fetterman & M. A. Pittman (eds.), *Educational evaluation: Ethnography in*

theory, practice, and politics (pp. 121–143). Thousand Oaks, CA: Sage.

Maxwell, J. A., & Mittapalli, K. (2010). Realism as a stance for mixed method research. In A. Tashakkori & C. Teddlie (Eds.), *SAGE handbook of mixed methods in social & behavioral research* (2nd ed.). Thousand Oaks, CA: Sage.

McCourt, F. (1999). *Angela's ashes.* New York: Touchstone.

Morgan, D. (2007). Paradigms lost and pragmatism regained: Methodological implications of combining qualitative and quantitative methods. *Journal of Mixed Methods Research, 1*(1), 48–76.

Morse, J. M. (2003). Principles in mixed methods and multimethod research design. In A. Tasakkori & C. Teddlie (Eds.), *Handbook of mixed methods in social and behavioral research* (pp. 167–188). Thousand Oaks, CA: Sage.

Newmann, F. M., King, M. B., & Rigdon, M. (1997). Accountability and school performance: Implications from restructuring schools. *Harvard Educational Review, 67*(1), 41–74.

Patton, M. Q. (2002). *Qualitative research and evaluation methods* (3rd ed.). Thousand Oaks, CA: Sage.

Phelan, P. (1987). Compatibility of qualitative and quantitative methods: Studying child sexual abuse in America. *Education and Urban Society, 20*(1), 35–41.

Phillips, D. C. (1996). Philosophical perspectives. In D. C. Berliner & R. C. Calfee (Eds.), *Handbook of educational psychology* (pp. 1005–1019). Old Tappan, NJ: Macmillan.

Ragin, C. C. (2008). *Redesigning social inquiry. Fuzzy sets and beyond.* Chicago: University of Chicago Press.

Rallis, S., & MacMullen, M. (2000, June). Inquiry-minded schools: Opening doors for accountability. *Phi Delta Kappan,* 766–773.

Smith, J. K., & Heshusius, L. (1986). Closing down the conversation: The end of the quantitative-qualitative debate among educational inquirers. *Educational Researcher, 15*(1), 4–12.

Smith, M. L. (1997). Mixing and matching: Methods and models. In J. C. Greene & V. J. Caracelli (Eds.), *Advances in mixed-method evaluation: The challenges and benefits of integrating diverse paradigms* (New Directions for Evaluation, No. 74, pp. 73–85). San Francisco: Jossey-Bass.

Stake, R. E. (1978, February). The case study method in social inquiry. *Educational Researcher, 7*(2), 5–8.

Stake, R. E. (1995). *The art of case study research.* Thousand Oaks, CA: Sage.

Stake, R. E. (2000). Case studies. In N. K. Denzin & Y. S. Lincoln (Eds.), *Handbook of qualitative research* (2nd ed.). Thousand Oaks, CA: Sage.

Stake, R. E. (2005). Case studies. In N. K. Denzin & Y. S. Lincoln (Eds.), *Handbook of qualitative research* (3rd ed.). Thousand Oaks, CA: Sage.

Sunderman, G. L., Kim, J. S., & Orfield, G. (2005). *NCLB meets school realities: Lessons from the field.* Thousand Oaks, CA: Corwin Press.

Teddlie, C., & Tashakkori, A. (2003). Major issues and controversies in the use of mixed methods in the social and behavioral sciences. In A. Tashakkori & C. Teddlie (eds.), *Handbook of mixed methods in social and behavioral research* (pp. 3–50). Thousand Oaks, CA: Sage.

Teddlie, C., & Taskakkori, A. (2009). *Foundations of mixed methods research.* Thousand Oaks, CA: Sage.

Trend, M. G. (1979). On the reconciliation of qualitative and quantitative analyses: A case study. In T. D. Cook & C. S. Reichardt (Eds.), *Qualitative and quantitative methods in evaluation research* (pp. 68–86). Thousand Oaks, CA: Sage.

U.S. Department of Education. (2009). *Elementary & secondary education: No Child Left Behind: A desktop reference.* Washington, DC: Author. Retrieved August 10, 2009, from http://www.ed.gov/admins/lead/account/nclbreference/html

REALISM AS A STANCE FOR MIXED METHODS RESEARCH

◆ Joseph A. Maxwell and Kavita Mittapalli

Objectives

Upon finishing this chapter you should be able to:

- understand the main characteristics of critical realism, as the term is used in this chapter;

- identify some of the important differences between realism, positivism, constructivism, and pragmatism that are relevant to mixed methods research;

- understand why the view of paradigms as logically unified sets of premises that are shared by members of a research community is problematic; and

- identify some of the aspects of mixed methods research for which realism can provide a useful perspective.

Philosophical realism, a currently prominent approach in the philosophy of science, is gaining increased attention as an alternative to both positivism/empiricism and constructivism as a stance for research and evaluation in the social sciences (Campbell, 1988; House, 1991; Mark, Henry, & Julnes, 2000; Maxwell, 1990, 1992, 2004a, 2008; Pawson, 2006; Pawson & Tilley, 1997; Sayer, 1992, 2000). Contemporary versions of realism have presented sophisticated approaches to some of the contentious philosophical issues involved in the paradigm wars over qualitative and quantitative research.

Although there are now a considerable number of substantive mixed methods studies that have employed a realist perspective, realism has received relatively little notice in discussions of mixed methodology (exceptions include Greene, 2007; Greene & Hall, 2010 [this volume]; Lipscomb, 2008; McEvoy & Richards, 2006). We argue that, as a philosophical perspective that validates and supports key aspects of both qualitative and quantitative approaches while identifying some specific limitations of each, realism can constitute a productive stance for mixed methods research and can facilitate a more effective collaboration between qualitative and quantitative researchers.

There are many diverse versions of realism across the philosophical landscape, but a common feature of the realist positions that we discuss here is an integration of a realist ontology (there is a real world that exists independently of our perceptions, theories, and constructions) with a constructivist epistemology (our *understanding* of this world is inevitably a construction from our own perspectives and standpoint, and there is no possibility of attaining a "God's eye point of view" that is independent of any particular viewpoint). In addition, these versions of realism acknowledge the reality of mental phenomena and the value of an interpretive perspective for studying these (Putnam, 1990, 1999; Sayer, 1992, 2000).

Different terms have been used for such versions of realism, including critical realism (Archer, Bhaskar, Collier, Lawson, & Norrie, 1998; Bhaskar, 1989), experiential realism (Lakoff, 1987), subtle realism (Hammersley, 1992), emergent realism (Henry, Julnes, & Mark, 1998; Mark et al., 2000), natural realism (Putnam, 1999), innocent realism (Haack, 1998, 2003), and agential realism (Barad, 2007). We will use the term critical realism in a broad sense to include all of these versions of realism. (We provide a more detailed description of realism later in this chapter.)

There is a widespread view within mixed methods research that the appropriate philosophical partner for qualitative research is constructivism and for quantitative research, postpositivist empiricism (Johnson & Gray, 2010 [this volume]). This view would seem to make mixed methods research a philosophical oxymoron, or at least a problematic union. Postpositivism and constructivism disagree on major issues concerning the nature of the objects of research and our knowledge of these (Guba & Lincoln, 1989), and these disagreements played a major role in what have been called the paradigm wars between qualitative and quantitative approaches.

In response, methodological pragmatists (e.g., Patton, 2001; Reichardt & Cook, 1979; Tashakkori & Teddlie, 1998) have claimed that these philosophical disagreements are not fundamental and that research methods are not intrinsically linked to specific philosophical positions. They have argued that methods can be combined on the basis of their practical utility and that paradigmatic conflicts can be ignored. This view has gained substantial acceptance within the mixed methods research community, and pragmatism has been promoted as the appropriate philosophical stance for mixed methods research (Biesta, 2010 [this volume]; Johnson & Gray, 2010 [this volume]; Maxcy, 2003; Tashakkori & Teddlie, 2003).

We agree with pragmatists that research practices are not determined by, or dependent on, philosophical paradigms. A research strategy or method is not necessarily linked to a single philosophical stance, and any approach may be informed by one or more of a number of paradigms (Greene, 2000; Pitman & Maxwell, 1992). However, we believe that the pragmatist position underestimates the actual *influence* of philosophical assumptions on research methods, an influence that is particularly significant for combining qualitative and quantitative approaches. Ontological, epistemological, and axiological assumptions are real properties of researchers and evaluators, part of what Henry et al. (1998; Mark et al., 2000) call values. These assumptions inevitably influence researchers' purposes and actions to some degree and are often implicit and not easily abandoned or changed.

For example, mainstream quantitative research has traditionally presupposed a Humean, regularity view of causation (Mohr, 1996; cf. Johnson & Gray, 2010), although this is rarely explicit. This philosophical assumption leads to, and supports, a variable-oriented approach to research, an emphasis on replicability and general laws, and a validity strategy based on experimental or statistical controls. These characteristics, and the philosophical position that informs them, *inherently* relegate qualitative research to a secondary role in investigating causality. This restricts the range of questions for which qualitative methods are seen as appropriate and makes mixed methods research both more difficult and less productive (Maxwell, 2004a). On the other hand, qualitative researchers who accept a "strong" constructivist philosophy reject quantitative researchers' characteristic assumption that objective, verifiable knowledge about the world is possible (Schwandt, 1997, p. 20) and the view of the world as analyzable in terms of causes (Guba & Lincoln, 1989). This prevents these qualitative researchers from accepting (let alone using) some central features of quantitative design, data collection, and analysis.

Urging researchers to simply set aside these assumptions is not just unrealistic, but counterproductive. Paradigmatic assumptions function not simply as constraints on methods but as lenses for viewing the world, revealing phenomena and generating insights that would be difficult to obtain with other lenses. This idea is at the heart of Greene's (2007, pp. 79–80; Greene & Hall, 2010 [this volume]) dialectic stance for doing mixed methods research, in which the goal is to create a dialogue between diverse perspectives on the phenomena being studied, so as to deepen, rather than simply broaden or triangulate, the understanding gained. Greene considers this the most valuable stance for mixed methods research because the juxtaposition of different lenses or "mental models" that it requires is the most likely to produce generative insights and depth of understanding and also because it promotes a meaningful engagement with difference and a dialogue across paradigm boundaries.

In this chapter, we argue that realism—in particular, what we call critical realism—can contribute to such a dialogue and can help resolve some of the problems created by other perspectives. Realism provides a philosophical stance that is compatible with the essential methodological characteristics of *both* qualitative and quantitative research, and it can facilitate communication and cooperation between the two (Greene, 2000; Mark et al., 2000). However, we also argue that realism has some specific implications that challenge certain practices in both qualitative and quantitative research and that point to new ways of addressing some important issues in mixed methods research.

We are not arguing for realism as an alternate paradigm (Greene, 2007, pp. 82–86) that is the preferred stance for mixed methods research. In fact, we are skeptical of the entire concept of unified paradigms in research, a concept that has dominated the discussion of the relationship between philosophical assumptions and research methods. So before we discuss what we see as the potential contributions of a realist perspective, we want to address the larger issue of paradigms in mixed methods research.

◆ Paradigms in Mixed Methods Research

The main argument for combining qualitative and quantitative paradigmatic positions, as well as methods, in mixed methods research has traditionally been their complementarity—that they have different strengths and limitations and that using them together allows the researcher to draw conclusions that would not be possible using either method alone. However, this argument usually assumes that the quantitative and qualitative traditions embody different paradigms—ontological, epistemological, and value assumptions, as well as methodological differences—that are, even if compatible, distinctly different from one another and that these differences are straightforward and easily categorized. Most textbooks or other general presentations of mixed methods research list the relative strengths and limitations of qualitative and quantitative research and use these to develop strategies for combining the two. These lists of strengths are typically dichotomous, and the characteristics of each approach are presented as uniform, polar, and complementary.

This dichotomous and polar view of the two approaches has been challenged by Hammersley (1992) and Howe (2003), and more recently by Bergman (2008a), Biesta (2010 [this volume]), Hammersley (2008), and Fielding (2008), who argue for a more complex and contextualized understanding of the potential contributions of each approach. Many of the contributors to the volume edited by Bergman (2008b) have serious reservations about the way mixed methods research has been conceptualized and see the qualitative/quantitative distinction as much more problematic than has traditionally been assumed. Bergman (2008a) claims that the assumption of generic "strengths" of each approach, based on paradigm differences, is fallacious and that the conventional divide between qualitative and quantitative methods is to a considerable degree related to "delineating and preserving identities and ideologies rather than to describe possibilities and limits of a rather heterogeneous group of data collection and analysis techniques" (p. 29).

In addition to the critiques by Bergman, Hammersley, and others of the view that paradigms constitute a set of logically consistent assumptions that have necessary connections to methods, the view that paradigms are generally shared by members of a community of researchers is problematic. While prominent advocates of this view (e.g., Denzin & Lincoln, 2005) now concede that qualitative researchers don't all share the same epistemological assumptions, they still assume, or at least write as if, qualitative researchers can be divided into distinct "camps" or "moments," including postpositivist, constructivist, and postmodern, that do share a particular paradigm.

This view is supported by the assumption that all communities are united by shared beliefs, values, and practices, a theory exemplified in the anthropological concept of culture. However, this assumption has frequently been challenged in anthropology by authors who argue that it denies or ignores the existence of substantial intracultural diversity in communities and misrepresents the actual processes that generate and maintain social solidarity (Hannerz, 1992; Maxwell, 1999; Wallace, 1970). It has also been challenged by postmodern scholars, who generally consider diversity—within individual identities, as well as within social communities—to be fundamental rather than superficial (e.g., Bernstein, 1992; Rosenau, 1992). Studies have demonstrated substantial and often unrecognized diversity in the supposedly paradigmatic assumptions held by linguists (McCawley, 1982) and qualitative evaluators (Pitman & Maxwell, 1992). This issue will be addressed in more general terms below, in considering the importance of diversity as a real phenomenon.

A perspective that makes little mention of postmodernism (and is critical of specific aspects of postmodern theory when it does so), but that is strikingly compatible with postmodernism's overall insistence on the pervasive significance of diversity, as well as with a dialectic stance for mixed methods research, has been presented by Abbott (2001, 2004). Abbott argued that ontological and epistemological positions, rather than being unified, foundational sets of premises that strongly shape the practices of particular communities of scholars, function instead as heuristics—conceptual tools that are used to solve specific problems in theory and research. He stated that if we take any of a large number of debates between polar positions, such as positivism versus interpretivism, analysis versus narrative, realism versus constructivism, and so on, we find that these issues can play out at many different levels, even within communities of scholars that have adopted one or the other of these positions as characterizing their field at a broader level. Thus, within the community of sociologists of science, which is generally seen as constructivist in orientation, there are internal debates that can be seen as involving realist versus constructivist assumptions, and the debates often employ both realist and constructivist theoretical "moves" by particular scholars within that community.

One of the many examples that Abbott analyzed was Chambliss's study of competitive swimming (Chambliss, 1989; see Example 1). Abbott argued that the debate over Chambliss's work shows the power of making a realist or constructivist move, even within a largely constructivist field, creating new leads for research. He stated that "the idea of heuristics is to open up new topics, to find new things. To do that, sometimes we need to invoke constructivism, as have the students of occupational prestige. Sometimes we need a little realism" (Abbott, 2004, p. 191). This position is quite compatible with Hacking's (1999) detailed and incisive analysis of constructivism, uncovering the ways in which particular phenomena (mental illness, child abuse, nuclear weapons, rocks) can be usefully seen as both real and social constructs.

Example 1

On the basis of 5 years of ethnographic research, including coaching swimming teams at different levels and observing and interviewing swimmers, Chambliss argued that there is no such thing as talent as an explanation of high performance; it is a myth that romanticizes and mystifies what he called "the mundanity of excellence." He supported this claim with detailed evidence from his observations and interviews, showing that high performance is simply the result of dozens of specific skills, learned or stumbled upon, that are repeatedly practiced and synthesized into a coherent whole. Abbott saw this as a constructivist move in the debate over sports performance; it asserted that talent is a social construction that does not refer to any real causal factor but is simply a vacuous explanation for high performance.

This move was consistent with the field of sociology of sport, which was generally seen as constructionist in orientation. However, underlying Chambliss's argument for a constructivist interpretation of talent was a realist move, identifying actual skills and practices and excellence as the outcome of these, as real phenomena rather than simply constructions. As a result, his work was attacked by others in this field for not treating winning, and the skills that led to this, as themselves social constructions. Chambliss's reply was that while selecting winners on the basis of elapsed times, rather than the beauty or precision of their strokes, was certainly a social construction, once that construction was made, the factors that lead to success in terms of that standard, and the outcomes of races, have a real existence independent of how they are construed by participants and judges.

From this perspective, epistemological positions look less like the traditional view of paradigms and more like tools in a toolkit. Logical consistency is the wrong standard to apply to a toolkit. You don't care if the tools are all consistent with some axiomatic principle; you care if, among them, they enable you to do the job, to create something that can meet your needs or accomplish your goals. In the same way, consistency is the wrong standard to apply to an individual's or a community's ontological and epistemological views. These views, seen as heuristics, are resources for getting your work done. This approach is similar to Greene's dialectic stance but puts more emphasis on the dialectic use of discrete conceptual tools, rather than paradigms in a more global sense.

The rest of this chapter explores some of the specific uses of realist conceptual tools in social research. First, however, we need to describe realism in more detail as a general approach in both the natural and social sciences.

◆ *What Is Realism?*

In the philosophy of science, including the philosophy of the social sciences, realism has been an important, if not the dominant, approach for more than 30 years (Baert, 1998, pp. 189–190); realism has been a prominent position in other areas of philosophy as well (Kulp, 1997). The proliferation of realist positions has led one realist philosopher to claim that "scientific realism is a majority position whose advocates are so divided as to appear a minority" (Leplin, 1984, p. 1). The idea that there is a real world with which we interact, and to which our concepts and theories refer, has proved to be a resilient and powerful one that has attracted increased philosophical attention following the demise of positivism.

Philosophic realism in general is defined by Phillips (1987) as "the view that entities exist independently of being perceived, or

independently of our theories about them" (p. 205). More specifically, Lakoff (1987) lists the following characteristics of what he terms *experiential realism*:

(a) a commitment to the existence of a real world, (b) a recognition that reality places constraints on concepts, (c) a conception of truth that goes beyond mere internal coherence, and (d) a commitment to the existence of stable knowledge of the world. (p. xv)

In the social sciences, the most important manifestation of realism is the *critical realist* tradition most closely associated with the work of Bhaskar (1978, 1989) and others in this tradition (Archer et al., 1998). However, we also draw substantially from other versions of realism that we see as compatible with the key ideas of this tradition, in particular those of the philosophers Haack (1998, 2003), Manicas (2006), and Putnam (1990, 1999), the physicist and historian of science Barad (2007), the linguist Lakoff (1987; Lakoff & Johnson, 1999), and the evaluation researchers Pawson and Tilley (1997).

The distinctive feature of these forms of realism is that they deny that we have any objective or certain knowledge of the world, and accept the possibility of alternative valid accounts of any phenomenon. All theories about the world are grounded in a particular perspective and worldview, and all knowledge is partial, incomplete, and fallible. Lakoff (1987) states this distinction between *objectivist* and *realist* views as follows:

Scientific objectivism claims that there is only one fully correct way in which reality can be divided up into objects, properties, and relations. . . . Scientific realism, on the other hand, assumes that "the world is the way it is," while acknowledging that there can be more than one scientifically correct way of understanding reality in terms of conceptual schemes with different objects and categories of objects. (p. 265)

In taking this position, critical realism retains an ontological realism while accepting a form of epistemological relativism or constructivism. This position has achieved widespread, if often implicit, acceptance as an alternative both to naïve realism and to radical constructivist views that deny the existence of any reality apart from our constructions. Shadish, Cook, and Campbell (2002) argued that "all scientists are epistemological constructivists and relativists" in the sense that they believe that *both* the ontological world and the worlds of ideology, values, and so forth play a role in the construction of scientific knowledge (p. 29). Conversely, Schwandt (1997) stated that

> many (if not most, I suspect) qualitative researchers have a common-sense realist *ontology*, that is, they take seriously the existence of things, events, structures, people, meanings, and so forth in the environment as independent in some way from their experience with them. (p. 134)

Schwandt (1997) also noted that most social constructivists in the sociology of science "do not conclude that there is no material reality 'out there'" (p. 20; see also Shadish et al., 2002, pp. 28–31). Ezzy (2002, pp. 15–18) argued similarly that while some postmodernists deny that reality exists, others simply want to problematize our assumptions about reality in light of the complexity of our process of understanding it. He cites Kvale's (1995) claim that while moderate postmodernism rejects the idea of universal truth, it "accepts the possibility of specific, local, personal, and community forms of truth with a focus on daily life and local narrative" (p. 21).

Example 2

A particularly detailed and sophisticated statement of the sort of realism we adopt here was presented by the physicist and historian of science Evelyn Fox Keller (1992), with the assumption that this viewpoint is so widely shared that it needs no explicit defense. She stated, "I begin with a few philosophical platitudes about the nature of scientific knowledge upon which I *think* we can agree, but which, in any case, will serve to define my own point of departure":

Scientific theories neither mirror nor correspond to reality.

Like all theories, they are models, in Geertz's (1973) terms, both models of and models for, but especially, they are models *for*; scientific theories represent in order to intervene, if only in search of confirmation. And the world in which they aim to intervene is, first and foremost, the world of material (that is, physical) reality. For this reason, I prefer to call them tools. From the first experiment to the latest technology, they facilitate our actions in and on that world, enabling us not to mirror, but to bump against, to perturb, to transform that material reality. In this sense scientific theories are tools for changing the world.

Such theories, or stories, are invented, crafted, or constructed by human subjects, interacting both with other human subjects and with nonhuman subjects/objects.

But even granted that they are constructed, and even abandoning the hope for a one-to-one correspondence with the real, the effectiveness of these tools in changing the world has something to do with the relation between theory and reality. To the extent that scientific

(Continued)

(Continued)

theories do in fact "work"—that is, lead to action on things and people that, in extreme cases (for example, nuclear weaponry), appear to be independent of any belief system—they must be said to possess a kind of "adequacy" in relation to a world that is not itself constituted symbolically—a world we might designate as "residual reality."

I take this world of "residual reality" to be vastly larger than any possible representation we might construct. Accordingly, different perspectives, different languages will lead to theories that not only attach to the real in different ways (that is, carve the world at different joints), but they will attach to different parts of the real—and perhaps even differently to the same parts. (pp. 73–74)

Such versions of realism share many characteristics with philosophical pragmatism. It is worth noting, therefore, that some of the major figures in pragmatism were also ontological realists (Maxcy, 2003, p. 56; see also Biesta, 2010). Buchler (1940) said of Peirce, the founder of American pragmatism, that

> Underlying every phase of Peirce's thought is his realism. The supposition that there are real things—the real is "that whose characters are independent of what anybody may think them to be"—he regards as the "fundamental hypothesis" of science, for it alone explains the manner in which minds are compelled to agreement. (p. xiv).

Contemporary philosophers who integrate pragmatism and realism include Haack (2006) and Putnam (1990; Conant & Zeglen, 2002); Putnam once commented that he should have called his version of realism *pragmatic realism.*

Despite the widespread commonsense acceptance of combining ontological realism and epistemological constructivism, the application of this perspective to qualitative research, as advocated by Hammersley (1992) and Maxwell (1992), was challenged by Smith and Deemer (2000), who asserted that the ontological concept of a reality independent of our theories can serve no useful function because there is no way to employ this that will avoid the constraints of a relativist epistemology. They concluded that "Maxwell is unable to show us how to get reality to do some serious work" (p. 883). In what follows, therefore, we attempt to show how a realist ontology *can* do useful work in the methodology and practice of mixed methods research, if it is taken seriously and its implications systematically developed. We do so by describing some specific implications of critical realism for quantitative, qualitative, and mixed methods research, showing how a realist perspective can provide new and useful ways of approaching problems and important insights into social phenomena.

Given the prominence of realist views in philosophy, it is puzzling that realism has not had a greater influence on research methodology. Despite the contributions to a realist approach to social research by Campbell (1988), Huberman and Miles (1985), Sayer (1992, 2000), Hammersley (1992), House (1991), and others, philosophic realism seems still to be largely unnoticed by most researchers (one exception is the field of program evaluation, where realist approaches developed by Pawson and Tilley (1997) and Henry et al. (1998; Mark et al., 2000) have had a significant impact). Even when realism is noticed, it tends to be seen by quantitative researchers as a commonsense truism with no important implications and dismissed by qualitative researchers as simply positivism in another guise (Mark et al., 2000, p. 166).

However, realism is strikingly different from positivism in many of its premises and implications (Baert, 1998, pp. 192–193). One of the most significant of these is the realist understanding of causality. Realists have been among the strongest critics of the "regularity" view of causation, which was typical of positivism and is still dominant in quantitative research (Maxwell, 2004a). In addition, most critical realists accept the reality of mental states and attributes and the importance of these for causal explanation in the social sciences, positions rejected by both traditional positivism and constructivism. Both of these aspects of realism are discussed in more detail below and constitute two areas in which critical realism can make an important contribution to mixed methods research.

Although some realists have been critical of quantitative and experimental research (e.g., Pawson & Tilley, 1997; Sayer, 1992), we believe that realism is a productive stance for both quantitative and qualitative research (cf. Mark et al., 2000). Donald Campbell, a major figure in the development of experimental methods in social research and an important influence on quantitative methodology in general, was an explicit critical realist in the broad sense we use here (Campbell, 1988; cf. Maxwell, 1990), and his realist perspective was acknowledged by Weisner (2005, p. 6) as an influence on the mixed methods studies in which he was involved.

Realism is also compatible with some of the assumptions and implications of constructivism and postmodernism, including the idea that difference is fundamental rather than superficial, a skepticism toward "general laws," an antifoundationalist stance, and a relativist epistemology (Maxwell, 1995, 1999). It differs from these approaches primarily in its realist ontology—a commitment to the existence of a real, although not an objectively knowable, world—and its emphasis on causal explanation (although a fundamentally different concept of causal explanation than that of the positivists) as intrinsic to social science.

Such an ecumenical approach is so characteristic of realism that Baert (1998, p. 194) accuses realists of ruling out almost nothing but extreme positivism. It is true that realism is pragmatic in that it does not discard *a priori* those approaches that have shown some ability to increase our understanding of the world. However, the value of realism does not derive simply from its compatibility with different approaches to research or from its pragmatic orientation to methods. Realism has important implications for the conduct of research. In the remainder of this chapter, therefore, we want to take seriously a realist ontology and to outline some of its most important implications for mixed methods research.

◆ Potential Contributions of Realism to Mixed Methods Research

There are many aspects of mixed methods research for which realism provides a valuable perspective. For example, it is useful to view research designs as real entities—not simply as models *for* research but also as the actual conceptualizations and practices employed in a specific study. The latter approach helps a reader of a research publication to understand the *real* design of a study, its "logic-in-use," which may differ substantially from its "reconstructed logic" (Kaplan, 1964, p. 8) presented in publications (Maxwell, 2005; Maxwell & Loomis, 2003). This conception of design as a model of, as well as for, research is exemplified in a classic qualitative study of medical students (Becker, Geer, Hughes, & Strauss, 1961/1977; see Example 3).

Example 3

Becker et al. (1961/1977) begin their chapter on the "Design of the Study" by stating:

In one sense, our study had no design. That is, we had no well-worked-out set of hypotheses to be tested, no data-gathering instruments purposely designed to secure information relevant to these hypotheses, no set of analytic procedures specified in advance. Insofar as the term "design" implies these features of elaborate prior planning, our study had none.

If we take the idea of design in a larger and looser sense, using it to identify those elements of order, system, and consistency our procedures did exhibit, our study had a design. We can say what this was by describing our original view of the problem, our theoretical and methodological commitments, and the way these affected our research and were affected by it as we proceeded. (p. 17)

A second example of the application of a realist perspective to research design is to view the relationships that a researcher establishes with participants and other stakeholders in a study as a real component of the "design-in-use" of a study, one that is rarely addressed in discussions of research design and that often is critical to the actual functioning of a study (Maxwell, 2002, 2005).

In what follows, we focus on four issues for which we feel realism can make a particularly important contribution to mixed methods research: causal explanation, mind and reality, validity, and diversity.

A PROCESS APPROACH TO CAUSALITY

For most of the 20th century, the dominant conception of causality in the philosophy of science was based on David Hume's analysis, generally known as the regularity theory of causation (House, 1991; Salmon, 1989). Hume argued that we can't directly perceive causal relationships, only the observed regularities in associations of events, and he rejected any reference to hypothesized or inferred

entities and mechanisms. This view treats the actual process of causality as unobservable, a "black box," and focuses simply on discovering whether there is a systematic relationship between inputs and outputs. This conception of causality is "the basis of ordinary quantitative research and of the stricture that we need comparison in order to establish causality" (Mohr, 1996, p. 99).

In quantitative research, the regularity theory of causation is intrinsic to an approach to explanation that Mohr (1982) called *variance theory*. Variance theory deals with variables and the correlations among them; it is based on an analysis of the contribution of differences in measured values of particular variables to differences in values of other variables. The comparison of conditions or groups in which the presumed causal factor takes different values, while other factors are held constant or statistically controlled, is central to this approach to causation. Thus, variance theory tends to be associated with research that employs experimental or correlational designs, quantitative measurement, and statistical analysis. As Mohr (1982) noted, "the variance-theory model of explanation in social science has a close affinity to statistics. The archetypal rendering of this idea of causality is the linear or nonlinear regression model" (p. 42).

In philosophy, the most widely accepted alternative to the regularity approach to causality is a realist approach that sees causality as fundamentally referring to the actual causal mechanisms and processes that are involved in particular events and situations. For the philosophy of science in general, this approach was most systematically developed by Salmon (1984, 1989, 1998), who referred to it as the *causal/mechanical* view. This approach

> makes explanatory knowledge into knowledge of the . . . mechanisms by which nature works. . . . It exhibits the ways in which the things we want to explain come about. (Salmon, 1989, pp. 182–183)

For the social sciences, this approach to explanation closely resembles what Mohr (1982) called *process theory*. Process theory deals with *events* and the processes that connect them; it is based on an analysis of the causal *processes* by which some events influence others. It is fundamentally different from variance theory as a way of thinking about scientific explanation. Sayer (1992) argued:

> Much that has been written on methods of explanation assumes that causation is a matter of regularities in relationships between events, and that without models of regularities we are left with allegedly inferior, "ad hoc" narratives. But social science has been singularly unsuccessful in discovering law-like regularities. One of the main achievements of recent realist philosophy has been to show that this is an inevitable consequence of an erroneous view of causation. Realism replaces the regularity model with one in which objects and social relations have causal powers which may or may not produce regularities, and which can be explained

independently of them. In view of this, less weight is put on quantitative methods for discovering and assessing regularities and more on methods of establishing the qualitative nature of social objects and relations on which causal mechanisms depend. (pp. 2–3)

This approach is quite different from variance theory. Pawson and Tilley (1997), in their realist approach to program evaluation, stated:

> When realists say that the constant conjunction view of one event producing another is inadequate, they are not attempting to bring further "intervening" variables into the picture . . . The idea is that the mechanism is responsible for the relationship itself. A mechanism is . . . not a variable but an *account* of the makeup, behaviour and interrelationship of those processes which are responsible for the regularity. (pp. 67–68)

Similar distinctions to that between variance and process theory have been presented by many other writers, including the distinctions between variable-oriented and case-oriented approaches (Ragin, 1987), propositional knowledge and case knowledge (Shulman, 1986), and factor theories and explanatory theories (Yin, 1993, pp. 15–21). Sayer (1992, pp. 241–251) similarly distinguished between extensive and intensive research designs; extensive designs address regularities, common patterns, and distributions of features of populations, whereas intensive designs focus on how processes work in particular cases.

These arguments suggests that realist, process-oriented qualitative investigations deserve a more prominent place in social research, including experimental research, where they complement regularity-based quantitative research. Shadish et al. (2002), in what is arguably the most detailed and sophisticated presentation of the case for experimental research, stated:

> The unique strength of experimentation is in describing the consequences attributable to deliberately varying a treatment. We call this *causal description*. In contrast, experiments do less well in clarifying the mechanisms through which and the conditions under which that causal relationship holds—what we call *causal explanation*. (p. 9)

Referring to a "delicate balance" between causal descriptions and causal explanations, they assert that "most experiments can be designed to provide better explanations than is the case today" (p. 12) and describe several studies in which qualitative methods were used to substantially strengthen the understanding of causal mechanisms in experimental investigations (pp. 390–392).

Realist social researchers also place considerable emphasis on the context dependence of causal explanation (e.g., Huberman & Miles, 1985, p. 354; Sayer, 1992, pp. 60–61). Pawson and Tilley (1997) sum up this position in their formula "mechanism + context = outcome" (p. xv). They maintain that "the relationship between causal mechanisms and their effects is not fixed, but contingent" (p. 69); it depends on the context within which the mechanism operates. This is not simply a claim that causal relationships vary across contexts; it is a more fundamental claim, that the context within which a causal process occurs is, to a greater or lesser extent, intrinsically involved in that process, and often cannot be "controlled for" in a variance-theory sense without misrepresenting the causal mechanism (Sayer, 2000, pp. 114–118). For the social sciences, the social and cultural contexts of the phenomenon studied are crucial for understanding the operation of causal mechanisms.

We argue that a realist alternative to the dominant regularity model of causality can provide a way out of the somewhat polarized confrontation between qualitative and quantitative researchers on this issue of causal investigation (Maxwell, 2004a, 2004b, 2008). It recognizes the explanatory importance of the *context* of the phenomena studied and does so in a way that does not simply reduce this context to a set of "extraneous variables." It relies fundamentally on an understanding of the *processes* by which an event or situation occurs, rather than simply a comparison of situations involving the presence and absence of the presumed cause. Finally, it legitimates a concern with understanding *particular* situations and events, rather than addressing only general patterns. A process theory of causation does not require abandoning quantitative, variance-based methods for investigating causality; it simply requires recognition that process-based approaches are as legitimate as, and often complementary to, variance-based ones.

MIND AS PART OF REALITY

The neglect of mental phenomena, or the attempt to deal with these solely within a behavioral, variable-oriented framework, is one of the main problems that qualitative researchers attribute to quantitative research, and one of the main arguments that qualitative researchers make for adopting a constructivist or interpretivist stance for research is that these approaches inherently recognize the important of the mental realm. However, the types of realism that we discuss here treat mental entities as equally real to physical ones and as relevant to causal explanations of individual and social phenomena. Sayer (1992) stated that "social phenomena are concept-dependent . . . What the practices, institutions, rules, roles, or relationships *are* depends on what they mean in society to its members" (p. 30). Emotions, beliefs, values, and so on are part of reality; they are not simply abstractions from behavior or constructions of the observer. Realism in this sense, therefore, does *not* entail materialism, nor is it simply a cover for a reductionist agenda that would attempt to eliminate mental concepts from scientific discourse (Putnam, 1999, p. 74 ff.).

However, realists are not dualists, postulating two different realms of reality, the physical and the mental. In our view, the clearest and most credible analysis of this issue has been that of Putnam (1990, 1999), who argued for the legitimacy of both mental and physical ways of making sense of the world. He advocated a distinction between mental and physical *perspectives* or languages, both referring to reality, but from different conceptual standpoints. He argued that "the metaphysical realignment we propose involves an acquiescence in a plurality of conceptual resources, of different and mutually irreducible vocabularies . . . coupled with a return not to dualism but to the 'naturalism of the common man.'" (1999, p. 38)

Thus, while realism rejects the idea of "multiple realities" in the sense of independent and incommensurable *worlds* in which different individuals or societies live, it is quite compatible with the idea that there are different valid *perspectives* on the world. However, it holds that these perspectives, as held by the people we study as well as ourselves, are *part of* the world that we want to understand, and that our understanding of these perspectives can be more or less correct (Phillips, 1987).

A realist approach thus recognizes the reality and importance of *meaning*, as well as of physical and behavioral phenomena, as having explanatory significance, and the essentially *interpretive* nature of our understanding of the former (Sayer, 2000, pp. 17–18). Combining this view with a process-oriented approach to causality can resolve the long-standing perceived contradiction between "reason" explanations and "cause" explanations and integrate both in explanatory theories. Weber's (1905/1949) sharp distinction between causal explanation and interpretive understanding obscured the importance of reasons as causal influences on actions, and

thus their role as essential components of any full explanation of human action. Realism can deal with the apparent dissimilarity of reason explanations and cause explanations by showing that reasons can plausibly be seen as real events in a causal nexus leading to the action.

Realism also supports the idea that individuals' social and physical contexts have a causal influence on their beliefs and perspectives. While this proposition is widely accepted in everyday life, constructivists have tended to deny the reality of such influences, while positivism and some forms of postpositivist empiricism tend to simply dismiss the reality or importance of individuals' perspectives, or to "operationalize" these to behavioral variables. From a realist perspective, not only are individuals' perspectives and their situations both real phenomena, but they are *separate* phenomena that causally interact with one another.

Thus, a realist perspective can provide a framework for better understanding the relationship between individuals' perspectives and their actual situations. This issue has been a prominent concern in the philosophy of social science for many years (e.g., MacIntyre, 1967/1970; Menzel, 1978), and is central to "critical" approaches to qualitative research. Critical realism treats both individuals' perspectives and their situations as real phenomena that causally interact with one another. In this, realism supports the emphasis that critical theory places on the influence that social and economic conditions have on beliefs and ideologies. Sayer (1992, pp. 222–223) stated that the objects of "interpretive" understanding (meanings, beliefs, motives, and so on) are influenced both by the material circumstances in which they exist and by the cultural resources that provide individuals with ways of making sense of their situations. However, critical realism approaches the understanding of this interaction without assuming any *specific* theory of the relationship between material and ideational phenomena, such as Marxism.

A realist perspective also legitimates and clarifies the concept of "ideological distortion"—that cultural forms may obscure or misrepresent aspects of the economic or social system or the physical environment—while affirming the causal interaction between the physical and social environment and cultural forms. In particular, realism is compatible with what have been called ideological or non-reflectionist approaches to culture, in which cultural forms that contradict aspects of social structure may serve ideological functions that act to sustain the social system or constitute adaptive responses to the physical or social environment (e.g., Maxwell, 1978). An emphasis on causal processes rather than regularities or laws in explaining sociocultural phenomena also allows explanations to be tailored to single cases and unique circumstances, so that different individuals or social groups may have different responses to similar situations, depending on differences in specific personal or cultural characteristics that are causally relevant to the outcome.

VALIDITY AND INFERENCE QUALITY

Validity and quality are issues about which qualitative and quantitative researchers have had substantial disagreements. The types of validity (many qualitative researchers don't even use this term) employed in each tradition have little overlap (Teddlie & Tashakkori, 2003), and the basic assumptions involved in the two approaches are radically different. Teddlie and Tashakkori went so far as to recommend abandoning the term *validity* entirely in mixed methods research, arguing that the term has taken on such diverse meanings that it is losing its ability to communicate anything (pp. 12, 36–37).

Despite these differences, there is an important similarity between the typical quantitative and qualitative approaches to validity. Both focus largely on the *procedures* used in collecting data and drawing inferences from these data. This is particularly obvious in the movement for evidence-based research, which relies almost entirely on the type of research design as the basis for assessing the validity of the results, with randomized experiments as the gold standard for design quality. However, it also characterizes prominent approaches to validity (or its analogues) in qualitative research.

A realist concept of validity is quite different from these procedure-based approaches. Validity, from a realist perspective, is not a matter of procedures, but of the relationship between the claim and the phenomena that the claim is about (Hammersley, 1992; House, 1991; Maxwell, 1992; Norris, 1983). Shadish et al. (2002), in what is currently the definitive work on experimental and quasi-experimental research, state:

> Validity is a property of inferences. It is *not* a property of designs or methods, for the same designs may contribute to more or less valid inferences under different circumstances. . . . No method guarantees the validity of an inference. (p. 34; italics in original)

Also, as argued by Keller in the passage quoted in Example 2, a realist approach to validity does not entail that concepts, theories, or claims "reflect" or "correspond to" reality, only that whether these claims "work" depends on their relationship to a reality independent of our constructions (cf. Barad, 2007). While critical realism denies that we can have any objective perception of these phenomena to which we can compare our claims, it does not abandon the possibility of *testing* these claims against evidence about the nature of the phenomena.

We see this process of testing claims against the evidence that is relevant to the claims as fundamental to a scientific approach in general. However, the types of evidence that are relevant to a claim depend on the nature of the claim. A claim about a person's beliefs requires a different sort of evidence from a claim about the outcome of a randomized trial of a new drug. Specifically, claims about meanings and perspectives, which fall under the general category of interpretive claims, require quite different sorts of evidence from claims about behavior, let alone claims about the relationships between variables. A realist approach to validity also entails that a valid description, explanation, or interpretation not only must not be supported by evidence, but must address plausible *alternative* descriptions, explanations, or interpretations of the phenomenon about which the claim is made.

For these reasons, the main approach to validity in experimental research (e.g., Shadish et al., 2002) is grounded in the concept of a validity threat—a possible way that a conclusion might be wrong—and ways to address these threats. However, the emphasis has largely been on the designs and methods used to deal with these threats. This has been facilitated by the fact that this literature has, consistently with a regularity view of causality as inherently general, dealt mainly with *types* of validity threats, rather than emphasizing the actual ways a specific conclusion might be wrong in a given study. The importance of the latter point is implicit in the realist argument above, that validity is not simply determined by procedures (although procedures are obviously relevant to the validity of a conclusion) but must be assessed in the specific context of a particular study. It is also an implication of a realist view of causality as inherently local rather than general.

A realist perspective on validity can thus be of value to mixed methods researchers by focusing attention on the specific plausible threats to the conclusions drawn in a given study, which depend on the context and purposes of that study as well on the methods used.

DIVERSITY AS A REAL PHENOMENON

Finally, realism implies that diversity is itself a real phenomenon. This fact is most obvious in evolutionary biology, where variation among organisms is the precondition of evolutionary change. Lewontin (1973) argued that the Darwinian revolution replaced a Platonic, idealist view of variation (that variations were simply imperfect approximations to the ideal or type of a species) with a realist view that saw actual variation as the fundamental fact of biology and the cornerstone of evolutionary theory. Mayr (1982), arguing against the prevailing view that the most important characteristic of a species is the normal type of the organism, stated that "the most interesting parameter in the statistics of natural populations is the actual variation, its amount, and its nature" (p. 47).

Similar arguments about diversity have been made for the social sciences, as described above in discussing paradigms. However, both qualitative and quantitative research have tendencies, theoretical as well as methodological, to ignore or suppress diversity in their goal of seeking general accounts, although in different ways (Maxwell, 1995). Quantitative research often aggregates data across individuals and settings and ignores individual and group diversity that cannot be subsumed into a general explanation (Shulman, 1986). Because of its emphasis on *general* descriptions and causal theories, it tends to impose or generate wide-ranging but simplistic models that do not take account of individual variation, unique contextual influences, diverse meanings, and idiosyncratic phenomena.

However, qualitative researchers also tend to neglect diversity. Theoretically, this is often the result of social theories that emphasize uniformity; such theories include a definition of culture as beliefs or practices that are shared by members of a society, and approaches to community and social order that assume a dichotomy between consensus and conflict

(Maxwell, 1999). Methodologically, the sample size and sampling strategies used in qualitative studies are often inadequate to fully identify and characterize the actual diversity that exists in the setting or population studied and can lead to simplistic generalizations or the assumption of greater uniformity or agreement than actually exists.

Mixed methods research provides one way to help overcome the theoretical and methodological characteristics that lead to the neglect of diversity. Qualitative methods and approaches, which focus on particular phenomena and processes and their unique contexts, can help to overcome the biases inherent in universalizing, variable-oriented quantitative methods. Conversely, quantitative methods can provide systematic evidence for diversity and can help to correct a tendency to ignore complexity and to focus on typical characteristics and shared concepts and themes. However, doing so effectively requires recognizing the reality of diversity.

To sum up this section, we are not simply claiming that realism is a productive stance for mixed method research because it is compatible with both qualitative and quantitative research and treats the two perspectives as equally valid and useful. We have also argued that realism has important implications for both approaches, ones that push both qualitative and quantitative researchers to examine more closely some issues that they typically dismiss or ignore. Realism can therefore not only help to integrate the two approaches into a more coherent combination, and promote closer and more equal cooperation between qualitative and quantitative researchers, but can serve to increase the usefulness of both approaches.

◆ Applications of Critical Realism in Mixed Methods Practice

Explicit use of realist perspectives in mixed methods research is still relatively uncommon and sometimes involves little more than an acknowledgment that realism has informed the research. For example, Weisner (2005), in his introduction to a collection of papers on mixed methods studies of children's development and family life, paid homage to Campbell's realist and multiplist approach, saying that this skeptical realism and holism "provides the context and tradition for much of our work" (pp. 5–6), but he doesn't discuss how, specifically, realism did so.

As noted above, the one area in which realist perspectives have had a major influence on mixed methods studies is in program evaluation. The work of Tilley (described in Pawson & Tilley, 1997) and Mark et al. (2000; Henry et al., 1998), much of which combined qualitative and quantitative approaches, has provided a realist alternative to traditional ways of conceptualizing program evaluations. In addition, Pawson's (2006) analysis of literature reviews for evidence-based policy constitutes a major critique of standard ways of integrating qualitative and quantitative results in a literature synthesis, and presents a realist alternative to these approaches.

There is also the potential within realist approaches for incorporating features highlighted by an emancipatory paradigm and promoting social justice (House, 1991); this is a significant aspect of Bhaskar's version of critical realism, which has been more prominent in Europe than in the United States. Some important advances based on critical realism have recently been made in mixed methods research in accounting (Brown & Brignall, 2007; Covaleski & Dirsmith, 1983, 1990), operations management (Mingers, 2000, 2006; Reed, 2005), economics (Downward, Finch, & Ramsay, 2002; Fleetwood, 1999; Lawson, 1989, 1997, 1998, 2001; Olsen, 2004), political science (Patomäki, 2002), medicine (Clark, MacIntyre, & Cruikshank, 2007), and nursing (Lipscomb, 2008; Stickley, 2006).

Modell (2007) used critical realism to develop a unified approach for validating mixed methods research in accounting management. He argues that whereas critical realism shows many similarities to, and has indeed borrowed key concepts from, the pragmatist tradition, it constitutes a more relevant philosophical foundation to this end. Based on examples from the field of management accounting and budgeting in the U.S. nursing area and the jute industry in Bangladesh (see Covaleski & Dirsmith, 1983; Hoque & Hopper, 1994, 1997), Modell's work explicates how critical realism may inform management accounting research by effectively integrating qualitative and quantitative methods. The examples illustrate the role of context-specific conditions that may be captured only through deeper empirical probing and reconceptualization. In a later study, Covaleski and Dirsmith (1990) conceded that their quest for a deeper understanding of budgeting was derived from a growing realization of the problematic nature of the traditional, positivist approach. The authors describe "freeing" themselves from a priori theories to develop a more contextualized understanding of the lived experiences of interviewees, and to produce a more multifaceted conceptualization of budgeting (Covaleski & Dirsmith, 1990).

In economics, critical realism points to the main limitations of neoclassical economics (based on econometrics principles that are reductionist in nature and presuppose that concepts can be measured, counted, manipulated, and cross-classified), and it provides a philosophical and methodological foundation for a broad set of alternative approaches (see Downward et al., 2002; Downward & Mearman, 2007; Fleetwood, 1999; Lawson, 1989, 1997, 1998, 2001). In this regard, within economics, critical realism supports Lawson's view that the exclusive dependence on mathematical/statistical modeling in economics is misguided (Castellacci, 2006).

Olsen (2004) illustrated some of the limitations of the latter approach in two studies of Indian grain markets and peasant farmers, focusing on distress sales in the first and the gendered nature of poverty in the second. She used both theoretical and methodological triangulation in these studies. Theoretically, she combined neoclassical, Marxist political economy, and feminist political economy perspectives; methodologically, she used a survey of a random sample of farmers, ethnographic observations, in-depth interviews, family histories, and the analysis of documents and secondary data. Her results exposed deficiencies in both the neoclassical and Marxist approaches and showed the necessity of adding qualitative to quantitative methods to understand the phenomena studied. She concludes with three rules of thumb for realist research: a complex and stratified ontology, explicit value analysis, and getting behind the numbers and mathematical models to causal mechanisms.

Within the field of psychiatry, where hierarchy and control prevail, a critical realist perspective offers a model that does not submit to the dominant discourse but rather recognizes that service users now possess decision-making power, especially in terms of being able to provide services that statutory services providers now require (Stickley, 2006). Based on a power/knowledge discourse, Stickley suggested a critical realist framework that offers a theoretical explanation for *cause* and *change* with an argument for an alternative to accepted models of service user involvement. He argued that because mental health nurses are often the workers who have the most contact with service users, it is essential that they give consideration to the philosophies and approaches that underpin these models, which are emancipatory for people who use mental health services.

McEvoy and Richards (2006) justified using a critical realist framework for mixed methods in a case study in nursing of how and why gatekeeping decisions emerge at the interface between primary care and community mental health teams. The quantitative survey helped them to identify patterns of practice, which were confirmed and elaborated by the findings from semistructured interviews. Using mixed methods gave the inquiry a "better sense of balance and perspective" (p. 66). In addition, the findings from both approaches stimulated retroductive reasoning, a process that involves the construction of *hypothetical* models as a way of uncovering the *real* structures, contexts, and mechanisms that are presumed to produce empirical phenomena (Bhaskar, 1978, 1986, 1989). In addition, reliance on retroduction necessitates that the researcher is being explicit about what is being done during the process, including data collection and

analysis (Bollingtoft, 2007), leading to the development of a theoretical model that explained why gatekeeping decisions tended to emerge in the way they did.

In summary, we believe that realist perspectives and approaches can make important contributions to mixed methods research. These contributions involve not simply an overall perspective within which qualitative and quantitative methods and assumptions can be better integrated, but also specific insights and strategies that can enable mixed methods researchers to better understand the contexts and processes they study.

Research Questions and Exercises

1. How does the realist perspective presented in this chapter fit with your own assumptions about qualitative, quantitative, and mixed methods research? Has the chapter changed your thinking about any of these? Do you disagree with any of the chapter's arguments? Why?

2. How could you apply the specific realist approaches described here to an actual study that you might conduct? What difference would these make in how you design and carry out the study?

3. How does the perspective on mixed methods research presented in this chapter differ from that in other chapters of the *Handbook*? How are these different views helpful to you in understanding mixed methods research publications or thinking about how to do mixed methods research?

◆ References

Abbott, A. (2001). *Chaos of disciplines.* Chicago: University of Chicago Press.

Abbott, A. (2004). *Methods of discovery: Heuristics for the social sciences.* New York: W. W. Norton.

Archer, M., Bhaskar, R., Collier, A., Lawson, T., & Norrie, A. (Eds.). (1998). *Critical realism: Essential readings.* London: Routledge.

Baert, P. (1998). *Social theory in the twentieth century.* New York: New York University Press.

Barad, K. (2007). *Meeting the universe halfway: Quantum physics and the entanglement of matter and meaning.* Durham, NC: Duke University Press.

Becker, H. S., Geer, B., Hughes, E. C., & Strauss, A. L. (1977). *Boys in white: Student culture in medical school.* Piscataway, NJ: Transaction Books. (Original work published 1961)

Bergman, M. M. (Ed.). (2008a). *Advances in mixed methods research.* London: Sage.

Bergman, M. M. (2008b). The straw men of the qualitative-quantitative divide and their influence on mixed methods research. In

M. Bergman (Ed.), *Advances in mixed methods research* (pp. 11–21). London: Sage.

Bernstein, R. (1992). *The new constellation: The ethical-political horizons of modernity-postmodernity.* Cambridge MA: MIT Press.

Bhaskar, R. (1978). *A realist theory of science* (2nd ed.). Brighton, UK: Harvester.

Bhaskar, R. (1986). *Scientific realism and human emancipation.* London: Verso.

Bhaskar, R. (1989). *Reclaiming reality: A critical introduction to contemporary philosophy.* London: Verso.

Biesta, G. (2010). Pragmatism and the philosophical foundations of mixed methods research. In A. Tashakkori & C. Teddlie (Eds.), *SAGE handbook of mixed methods in social and behavioral research* (2nd ed.). Thousand Oaks, CA: Sage.

Bollingtoft, A. (2007). A critical realist approach to quality in observation studies. In H. Neergaard & J. P. Ulhoi (Eds.), *Handbook of qualitative research methods in entrepreneurship.* Northampton MA: Edward Elgar.

Brown, R., & Brignall, S. (2007). Reflections on the use of a dual-methodology research design to evaluate accounting and management practice in UK university central administrative services, *Management Accounting Research, 18,* 32–48.

Buchler, J. (1940). Introduction. In J. Buchler (Ed.), *The philosophy of Peirce: Selected writings.* New York; Routledge & Kegan Paul.

Campbell, D. T. (1988). *Methodology and epistemology for social science: Selected papers* (S. Overman, Ed.). Chicago: University of Chicago Press.

Castellacci, F. (2006). A critical realist interpretation of evolutionary growth theorizing. *Cambridge Journal of Economics, 30,* 861–880.

Chambliss, D. (1989). The mundanity of excellence: An ethnographic report on stratification and Olympic swimmers. *Sociological Theory 7,* 70–86.

Clark, A. M., MacIntyre, P. D., & Cruickshank, J. (2007). A critical realist approach to understanding and evaluating heart health programmes. *Health, 11*(4), 513–539.

Conant, J., & Zeglen, U. M. (2002). *Hilary Putnam: Pragmatism and realism.* London: Routledge.

Covaleski, M. A., & Dirsmith, M. W. (1983). Budgets as a means of control and loose coupling. *Accounting, Organizations and Society, 8,* 323–340.

Covaleski, M. A., & Dirsmith, M. W. (1990). Dialectical tension, double reflexivity and the everyday accounting researcher: On using qualitative methods. *Accounting, Organizations and Society, 15,* 543–547.

Denzin, N. K., & Lincoln, Y. S. (2005). Introduction: The discipline and practice of qualitative research. In N. K. Denzin & Y. S. Lincoln (Eds.), *Handbook of qualitative research* (3rd ed., pp. 1–42). Thousand Oaks, CA: Sage.

Downward, P., Finch, J. H., & Ramsay, J. (2002). Critical realism, empirical methods and inference: A critical discussion. *Cambridge Journal of Economics, 26,* 481–500.

Downward, P., & Mearman, A. (2007). Retroduction as mixed-methods triangulation in economic research: Reorienting economics into social science. *Cambridge Journal of Economics, 31,* 77–99.

Ezzy, D. (2002). *Qualitative analysis: Practice and innovation.* London: Routledge.

Fielding, N. (2008). Analytic density, postmodernism, and applied multiple method research. In M. Bergman (Ed.), *Advances in mixed methods research* (pp. 37–52). London: Sage

Fleetwood, S. (1999). *Critical realism in economics: Development and debate.* London: Routledge.

Geertz, C. (1973). *The interpretation of cultures.* New York: Basic Books.

Greene, J. (2000). Understanding social programs through evaluation. In N. K. Denzin & Y. S. Lincoln (Eds.), *Handbook of qualitative research* (2nd ed., pp. 981–1000). Thousand Oaks, CA: Sage.

Greene, J. (2007). *Mixed methods in social inquiry.* San Francisco: Jossey-Bass.

Greene, J., & Hall, J. (2010). Dialectics and pragmatism: Being of consequence.

In A. Tashakkori & C. Teddlie (Eds.), *SAGE handbook of mixed methods in social & behavioral research* (2nd ed.). Thousand Oaks, CA: Sage.

Guba, E. G., & Lincoln, Y. S. (1989). *Fourth generation evaluation.* Thousand Oaks, CA: Sage.

Haack, S. (1998). *Manifesto of a passionate moderate.* Chicago: University of Chicago Press.

Haack, S. (2003). *Defending science—within reason.* Amherst, NY: Prometheus Press.

Haack, S. (2006). *Pragmatism, old and new: Selected writings.* Amherst, NY: Prometheus Books.

Hacking, I. (1999). *The social construction of what?* Cambridge, MA: Harvard University Press.

Hammersley, M. (1992). Ethnography and realism. In M. Hammersley, *What's wrong with ethnography? Methodological explorations* (pp. 43–56). London: Routledge.

Hammersley, M. (2008). Troubles with triangulation. In M. Bergman (Ed.), *Advances in mixed methods research* (pp. 22–36). London: Sage.

Hannerz, U. (1992). *Cultural complexity: Studies in the social organization of meaning.* New York: Columbia University Press.

Henry, G., Julnes, J., & Mark, M. (1998). *Realist evaluation: An emerging theory in support of practice* (New Directions for Evaluation, No. 78). San Francisco: Jossey-Bass.

Hoque, Z., & Hopper, T. (1994). Rationality, accounting, and politics: A case study of management control in a Bangladeshi jute mill. *Management Accounting Research, 5,* 5–30.

Hoque, Z., & Hopper, T. (1997). Political and industrial relations turbulence, competition and budgeting in the nationalised jute mills of Bangladesh. *Accounting and Business Research, 27,* 125–143

Howe, K. (2003). *Closing methodological divides.* Boston: Kluwer Academic.

House, E. (1991). Realism in research. *Educational Researcher, 20*(6), 2–9.

Huberman, A. M., & Miles, M. B. (1985). Assessing local causality in qualitative research. In D. N. Berg & K. K. Smith (Eds.), *Exploring clinical methods for social research* (pp. 351–382). Beverly Hills, CA: Sage.

Johnson, B., & Gray, R. (2010). A history of philosophical and theoretical issues for mixed methods research. In A. Tashakkori & C. Teddlie (Eds.), *SAGE handbook of mixed methods in social & behavioral research* (2nd ed.). Thousand Oaks, CA: Sage.

Kaplan, A. (1964). *The conduct of inquiry.* San Francisco: Chandler.

Keller, E. F. (1992). *Secrets of life, secrets of death: Essays on language, gender, and science.* New York: Routledge.

Kulp, C. B. (Ed.). (1997). *Realism/antirealism and epistemology.* Lanham MD: Rowman and Littlefield.

Kvale, S. (1995). *Interviews: An introduction to qualitative research interviewing.* Thousand Oaks, CA: Sage.

Lakoff, G. (1987). *Women, fire, and dangerous things: What categories reveal about the mind.* Chicago: University of Chicago Press.

Lakoff, G., & Johnson, M. (1999). *Philosophy in the flesh: The embodied mind and its challenge to western thought.* New York: Basic Books.

Lawson, T (1989). Abstraction, tendencies and stylized facts: A realist approach to economic analysis. *Cambridge Journal of Economics, 13,* 59–78.

Lawson, T. (1997). *Economics and reality.* London, Routledge.

Lawson, T. (1998). Transcendental realism. In J. Davis, D. W. Hands, & U. Mäki (Eds.), *The handbook of economic methodology.* Cheltenham, UK: Edward Elgar.

Lawson, T. (2001). *Reorienting economics.* London, Routledge.

Leplin, J. (1984). Introduction. In J. Leplin (Ed.), *Scientific realism.* Berkeley: University of California Press.

Lewontin, R. C. (1973). Darwin and Mendel—The materialist revolution. In J. Neyman (Ed.), *The heritage of Copernicus: Theories "more pleasing to the mind."* Cambridge: MIT Press.

Lipscomb, M. (2008). Mixed method in nursing studies: A critical realist critique. *Nursing Philosophy, 9*, 32–45.

MacIntyre, A. (1970). The idea of a social science. In B. R. Wilson (Ed.), *Rationality* (pp. 112–130). New York: Harper & Row. (Reprinted from *Aristotelian society Supplement 41*, 1967).

Manicas, P. T. (2006). *A realist philosophy of social science: Explanation and understanding.* Cambridge, UK: Cambridge University Press.

Mark, M. M., Henry, G. T., & Julnes, G. (2000). *Evaluation: An integrated framework for understanding, guiding, and improving policies and programs.* San Francisco: Jossey-Bass.

Maxcy, S. (2003). Pragmatic threads in mixed method research in the social sciences: The search for multiple modes of inquiry and the end of the philosophy of formalism. In A. Tashakkori & C. Teddlie (Eds.), *Handbook of mixed methods in social and behavioral research* (pp. 51–89). Thousand Oaks, CA: Sage.

Maxwell, J. A. (1978). The evolution of Plains Indian kin terminologies: A non-reflectionist account. *Plains Anthropologist 23*, 13–29.

Maxwell, J. A. (1990). Up from positivism (essay review of DT Campbell, *Methodology and epistemology for social science). Harvard Educational Review, 60*, 497–501.

Maxwell, J. A. (1992). Understanding and validity in qualitative research. *Harvard Educational Review, 62*, 279–300.

Maxwell, J. A. (1995). Diversity and methodology in a changing world. *Pedagogía 30*, 32–40.

Maxwell, J. A. (1999). A realist/postmodern concept of culture. In E. L. Cerroni-Long (Ed.), *Anthropological theory in North America* (pp. 143–73). Westport, CT: Bergin & Garvey.

Maxwell, J. A. (2002). Realism and the role of the researcher in qualitative psychology. In M. Kiegelmann (Ed.), *The role of the researcher in qualitative psychology.* Tuebingen, Germany: Verlag Ingeborg Huber.

Maxwell, J. A. (2004a). Causal explanation, qualitative research, and scientific inquiry in education. *Educational Researcher 33*(2), 3–11.

Maxwell, J. A. (2004b). Using qualitative methods for causal explanation. *Field Methods 16*(3), 243–264.

Maxwell, J. A. (2005). *Qualitative research design: An interactive approach* (2nd ed.). Thousand Oaks, CA: Sage.

Maxwell, J. A. (2008). The value of a realist understanding of causality for qualitative research. In N. Denzin (Ed.), *Qualitative research and the politics of evidence* (pp. 163–181). Walnut Creek, CA: Left Coast Press.

Maxwell, J. A., & Loomis, D. (2003). Mixed methods design: An alternative approach. In A. Tashakkori & C. Teddlie (Eds.), *Handbook of mixed methods in social and behavioral research* (pp. 241–271). Thousand Oaks, CA: Sage.

Mayr, E. (1982). *The growth of biological thought: Diversity, evolution, and inheritance.* Cambridge, MA: Harvard University Press.

McCawley, J. D. (1982). *Thirty million theories of grammar.* Chicago: University of Chicago Press.

McEvoy, P., & Richards, D. (2006). Rationale for using a combination of quantitative and qualitative methods. *Journal of Research in Nursing, 11*, 66–78.

Menzel, H. (1978). Meaning—who needs it? In M. Brenner, P. Marsh, & M. Brenner (Eds.), *The social contexts of method* (pp. 140–171). New York: St. Martin's Press.

Mingers, J. (2000). The contribution of critical realism as an underpinning philosophy for OR/MS and systems, *Journal of the Operational Research Society, 51*, 1256–1270.

Mingers, J. (2006). A critique of statistical modelling in management science from a critical realist perspective: Its role within multimethodology, *Journal of the Operational Research Society, 57*, 202–219.

Modell, S. (2007). *Integrating qualitative and quantitative methods in management accounting research: A critical realist approach.* Unpublished manuscript, Manchester Business School (Manchester) and School of Accounting, University of Technology, Sydney.

Mohr, L. B. (1982). *Explaining organizational behavior.* San Francisco: Jossey-Bass.

Mohr, L. B. (1996). *The causes of human behavior: Implications for theory and method in the social sciences.* Ann Arbor: University of Michigan Press.

Norris, S. P. (1983). The inconsistencies at the foundation of construct validation theory. In E. R. House (Ed.), *Philosophy of evaluation* (New Directions for Program Evaluation, No. 19, pp. 53–74). San Francisco: Jossey-Bass.

Olsen, W. (2004). Methodological triangulation and realist research: An Indian exemplar. In B. Carter & C. New, *Making realism work: Realist social theory and empirical research* (pp. 135-150). London: Routledge.

Patomäki, H. (2002). *After international relations: critical realism and the (re)construction of world politics.* London: Routledge.

Patton, M. Q. (2001). *Qualitative research and evaluation methods* (3rd ed.). Thousand Oaks, CA: Sage.

Pawson, R. (2006). *Evidence-based policy: A realist perspective.* London: Sage.

Pawson, R., & Tilley, N. (1997). *Realistic evaluation.* London: Sage.

Phillips, D. C. (1987). *Philosophy, science, and social inquiry: Contemporary methodological controversies in social science and related applied fields of research.* Oxford, UK: Pergamon Press.

Pitman, M. A., & Maxwell, J. A. (1992). Qualitative approaches to evaluation. In M. D. LeCompte, W. L. Millroy, & J. Preissle (Eds.), *The handbook of qualitative research in education* (pp. 729–770). San Diego: Academic Press.

Putnam, H. (1990). *Realism with a human face* (J. Conant, ed.). Cambridge, MA: Harvard University Press.

Putnam, H. (1999). *The threefold cord: Mind, body, and world.* New York: Columbia University Press.

Ragin, C. C. (1987). *The comparative method: Moving beyond qualitative and quantitative strategies.* Berkeley: University of California Press.

Reed, M. (2005). Reflections on the "realist turn" in organization and management studies. *Journal of Management Studies,* 42, 1621–1644.

Reichardt, C. S., & Cook, T. D. (1979). Beyond qualitative versus quantitative methods. In T. D. Cook & C. S. Reichardt (Eds.), *Qualitative and quantitative methods in program evaluation* (pp. 7–32). Thousand Oaks, CA: Sage.

Rosenau, P. M. (1992). *Post-modernism and the social sciences.* Princeton, NJ: Princeton University Press.

Salmon, W. C. (1984). *Scientific explanation and the causal structure of the world.* Princeton, NJ: Princeton University Press.

Salmon, W. C. (1989). Four decades of scientific explanation. In P. Kitcher & W. C. Salmon (Eds.), *Scientific explanation* (pp. 3–219). Minneapolis: University of Minnesota Press.

Salmon, W. C. (1998). *Causality and explanation.* New York: Oxford University Press.

Sayer, A. (1992). *Method in social science: A realist approach* (2nd ed.). London: Routledge.

Sayer, A. (2000). *Realism and social science.* London: Sage.

Schwandt, T. A. (1997). *Qualitative inquiry: A dictionary of terms.* Thousand Oaks, CA: Sage.

Shadish, W. R., Cook, T. D., & Campbell, D. T. (2002). *Experimental and quasi-experimental designs for generalized causal inference.* Boston: Houghton Mifflin.

Shulman, L. (1986). *Paradigms and programs.* In M. C. Wittrock (Ed.), *Handbook of research on teaching* (3rd ed.). New York: Macmillan.

Smith, J. K., & Deemer, D. K. (2000). The problem of criteria in the age of relativism. In N. K. Denzin & Y. S. Lincoln (Eds.), *Handbook of qualitative research* (2nd ed., pp. 877–896). Thousand Oaks, CA: Sage.

Stickley, T. (2006). Should service user involvement be consigned to history? A critical realist perspective. *Journal of Psychiatric and Mental Health Nursing, 13,* 570–577.

Tashakkori, A., & Teddlie, C. (1998). *Mixed methodology: Combining qualitative and quantitative approaches.* Thousand Oaks, CA: Sage.

Tashakkori, A., & Teddlie, C. (2003). The past and future of mixed methods research: From data triangulation to mixed model designs. In A. Tashakkori & C. Teddlie (Eds.), *Handbook of mixed methods in social and behavioral research* (pp. 671–701). Thousand Oaks, CA: Sage.

Teddlie, C., & Tashakkori, A. (2003). Major issues and controversies in the use of mixed methods in the social and behavioral sciences. In A. Tashakkori & C. Teddlie (Eds.), *Handbook of mixed methods in social and behavioral research* (pp. 3–50). Thousand Oaks, CA: Sage.

Wallace, A. F. C. (1970). *Culture and personality* (2nd ed.). New York: Random House.

Weber, M. (1949). Critical studies in the logic of the social sciences. In M. Weber, *The methodology of the social sciences.* New York: The Free Press. (Reprinted from *Archiv fuer Sozialwissenschaft und Sozialpolitik,* 1905)

Weisner, T. S. (2005). *Discovering successful pathways in children's development: Mixed methods in the study of childhood and family life.* Chicago: University of Chicago Press.

Yin, R. (1993). *Applications of case study research.* Thousand Oaks, CA: Sage.

7

FEMINIST APPROACHES TO MIXED METHODS RESEARCH

Linking Theory and Praxis[1]

◆ Sharlene Nagy Hesse-Biber

Objectives

The objectives of this chapter are:

- To familiarize you with a feminist approach to mixed methods. I point to the set of core assumptions that encompass most feminist approaches to research: a centering of women's concerns and issues as well as those of other oppressed groups and a commitment to social change and social justice. Feminist approaches stress the importance of difference by taking into account the intersections and interconnections of gender with race, ethnicity, class, sexual preference, and so on. I take up a brief history of contemporary feminist research approaches and discuss the basic themes contained in each. I stress the importance of thinking about feminist approaches as multi; there is no one feminist approach and likewise there is a range of definitions of what it means to practice feminist research.

(Continued)

(Continued)

- To provide you with an in-depth look at a variety of applications of a feminist approach to mixed methods research. I offer a set of case studies to illustrate the rationale and the practice of a mixed methods project from a feminist lens.

- To provide you with a sense of the contributions a feminist approach brings to mixed methods research and in turn how a mixed methods approach can serve to promote feminist goals.

Feminist researchers hail from many different theoretical perspectives, ask a variety of questions, and pursue a wide spectrum of methodologies and methods. Some use quantitative methods, others qualitative, and still others combine these methods or even invent new emergent methods in the service of their research goals. What draws these strands of feminist inquiry together is their common pursuit of knowledge building that centers the lives of women and other oppressed groups. Feminists dig down into the knowledge landscape to uncover new voices and perspectives. Mixed methods research provides feminists with an important set of knowledge excavation tools. Yet, not all mixed methods research that purports to study women's lives is feminist in its purpose, spirit, or design. This chapter will examine how feminist researchers practice mixed methods research; it provides an opportunity to center feminist knowledge building, which has traditionally been marginalized from mainstream research methods accounts.

Mixed methods are not inherently feminist or nonfeminist; they are tools or techniques researchers employ to answer specific research questions. Qualitative methods are often more associated with feminist research than quantitative methods; however, feminist researchers have debated the appropriateness of using different methods in studying women's lives (Bowles & Duelli Klein, 1984; Roberts, 1981). Some feminists argue that only qualitative methods can capture the subtleties and nuances of women's lived experiences. Others go further and note that qualitative methods are "better" and "more feminist" than quantitative approaches (for a fuller discussion of this, see Miner-Rubino & Jayaratne, 2007, p. 300). Those who advocate a "qualitative methods only" approach see quantitative methods as tools that reinforce the status quo; in the words of Audre Lorde (1984), "the master's tools will never dismantle the master's house" (p. 13). Indeed, some feminist researchers claim that, in effect, quantitative methods are patriarchal tools that serve only to undermine steps toward social change on behalf of women's issues and concerns (for a discussion of this issue, see Reinharz, 1985).

Feminist praxis refers to the varied ways feminist research proceeds. In the case study section of this chapter, feminist researchers draw on a variety of traditional and emergent methods, as they have done historically (Hesse-Biber, 2007). Feminist researchers cross cultural as well as disciplinary boundaries. They borrow research methods from a range of disciplines, including the arts and humanities (Hesse-Biber & Leavy, 2006). Quantitative research methods *are not antithetical to* feminist inquiry, per se, but careful attention needs to be paid to the types of questions researchers ask, who is the subject of inquiry, how these methods are practiced, and to what extent their data analysis findings and interpretation reinforce

the status quo or are in fact used to promote social change and social justice goals
(see Chafetz, 2004, who provides specific
examples of postpositivism working for
feminist ends). Reinharz (1992), in her classic text, *Feminist Methods in Social
Research*, notes that "feminism supplies the
perspective and the disciplines supply the
method. The feminist researcher exists at
their intersection" (p. 243).

Being cognizant of our *research standpoint* is an important characteristic of a
feminist approach to research, and this
requires a careful attention to *axiological
practice*. Axiology means being cognizant
of our values, attitudes, and biases and
acknowledging how this might play out in
research praxis in terms of (a) what questions are asked or not asked in our
research; (b) what type of data is or is not
collected; and (c) the type of methods,
measurement, analysis, and interpretation
that shape our understanding of the research
process. For a further discussion of axiology, see Hesse-Biber (2010) and Mertens
et al. (2010 [this volume]). This relationship can be explored with a helpful
model. We can see in Figure 7.1 that the
research question implies a particular
worldview or paradigmatic standpoint—
the set of assumptions researchers make
about the nature of the social world (ontology) and who can know this world (epistemology). This paradigmatic viewpoint lends
itself to the selection of particular types of
methodologies. These paradigmatic assumptions are either conscious (the solid arrow)
or unconscious (the broken arrow). The
types of methods a researcher selects and the
methods, analysis, and interpretation of
data also are shaped by the researcher's
overall paradigmatic research standpoint.

Feminist research practice creates a
tight link between the elements of the
research process—ontology, epistemology, methodology, and method—often
shaping new research work that is
"greater than the sum of its parts."[2] We
see this synergy unfolding by looking at

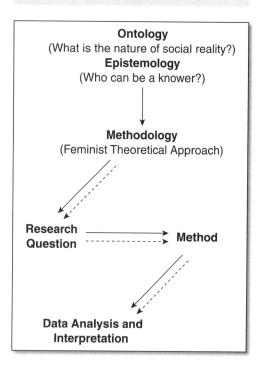

Figure 7.1   Axiology and Feminist
Research Praxis

how feminist researchers engage with the
research process, starting with the research
questions they ask and how research methods are practiced, especially addressing
issues of power, authority, reflexivity,
ethics, and difference. Methods in the
hands of feminist researchers begin to
take on a new *context of practice*. For
instance, feminists practice survey methods by interrogating the male bias of
some survey questions as well as the
power differentials between researcher
and researched in the survey interview
(see Hesse-Biber, 2007; Hesse-Biber &
Leavy, 2007). Feminists question whether
a survey's sampling frame is responsive to
issues of difference, ensuring that survey
findings are interpreted in a way that also
includes the experiences of marginalized
populations. Increasingly, feminists are
tweaking old methods and inventing new
ones to get at marginalized knowledge
(Hesse-Biber & Leavy, 2006).

◆ Feminist Approaches to Research: What Makes Research Feminist?

Research becomes "feminist" when one applies theoretical perspectives that focus on women's lives—their concerns and experiences. A feminist perspective expands understanding of gender differences on social problems and issues not by adding women and stirring them into the same old questions, but by including gender as a distinct category of analysis. In addition, there is the understanding that not all women are the same, and feminists seek to understand how gender intersects with race, ethnicity, class, sexual preference, disability, nationality, and so on. There is growing awareness, as well, of the global issues facing women, particularly with respect to imperialism, colonialism, and national identity (Biccom, 2009; Mohanty, 1988). Linda Smith's (1999) work on decolonizing methodologies demonstrates how colonial power has both the influence and authority to simultaneously define legitimate knowledge and dismiss the knowledge base of the indigenous peoples. She notes:

> It is research which is imbued with an "attitude" and a "spirit" which assumes a certain ownership of the entire world, and which has established systems and forms of governance which embed that attitude in institutional practices. These practices determine what counts as legitimate research and who counts as legitimate researchers. (p. 56)

Adrien Katherine Wing (2000) highlights another important emerging epistemology called *global critical race feminism*. Feminists working from this perspective are creating a new feminism of difference drawing on postmodern conceptualizations of power and knowledge in a global and increasingly interconnected context. Wing explains that feminists working in this new tradition must account for the context of global postmodern forms of power when considering the nature and impact of intersectionality, which is the standpoint based on a combination of locations within the social structure (i.e., race, class, gender, sexuality, geography, and so on).

A feminist approach to research is also "connected in principle to feminist struggle" (Sprague & Zimmerman, 1993, p. 266), often with the intent of changing the basic structures of oppression. By tackling research problems that expose power, difference, silence, and oppression, feminist researchers seek to promote social justice by moving toward a more just society for women and other oppressed groups. Patti Lather (1991) notes that the practice of a feminist approach to research means that feminists "consciously use our research to help participants understand and change their situations" (p. 226).

A SHORT HISTORY OF CONTEMPORARY FEMINIST RESEARCH: THEORY AND PRACTICE

During the 1970s and 1980s, feminist researchers worked to "deconstruct" what they perceived as errors within their disciplines, such that feminist researchers' insights on male bias in science cascaded across disciplines including psychology, philosophy, history, sociology, education, anthropology, and the fields of language and communications, with the goal of eradicating sexist research. A fundamental argument of these researchers was that women were "left out" of existing knowledge and that their issues, needs, and concerns needed to be included in the research process. *Feminist empiricists*, as they were referred to, embraced a postpositivist methodology but were mindful of the importance of not simply "adding and stirring" women into postpositivist research projects (Hundleby, 2007). Margrit Eichler and Jeanne Lapointe's classic research primer *On the Treatment of the Sexes in Research* (1985) provides a critique of the lack of inclusion of gender in traditional empirical research as well as a checklist for integrating gender as a category of analysis in social research. Some of their most profound suggestions include advice concerning what *not* to do when women are included in a research project (Eichler & Lapointe, 1985, p. 9), such as:

- Treat Western sex roles as universal

- Transform statistical differences into innate differences

- Fail to recognize that difference does not mean inferiority.

Feminist researchers also challenged the viability of generally accepted postpositivist concepts like objectivity. They questioned this traditional tenet of scientific knowledge building by unpacking postpositivism's claim to being scientifically objective. Feminist philosopher Donna Haraway (1988) posited instead the concept of "situated knowledge" to counter postpositivism's claim of a value-free science. By this, she meant that *all knowledge and truth claims are partial, socially situated, subjective, power-imbued, and relational* (see also Hesse-Biber, 2007, 2008). With this understanding, denying the existence of values, biases, and politics in academia and research is undesirable, and many suggest that knowledge is "achieved" by acknowledging the specificity and unique aspects of women's experiences. Feminist philosopher Sandra Harding (1993) introduced the concept of "strong objectivity," by which she meant the recognition that all knowledge comes from a particular point of view. Harding notes that it is in acknowledging our situated location and being reflexive of our position within it that we become more objective:

Strong objectivity requires that the subject of knowledge be placed on the same critical, causal plane as the objects of knowledge. Thus, strong objectivity requires what we can think of as "strong reflexivity." . . . The subject of knowledge—the individual and the historically located social community whose unexamined beliefs its members are likely to hold "unknowingly," . . . must be considered as part of the object of knowledge from the perspective of scientific method. (p. 69)

Strong objectivity, as advocated by Harding, requires an axiological awareness; researchers must self-reflect on their values, attitudes, and agenda. For example, they should ask themselves: How do my history and research standpoint influence the questions I ask?

FEMINIST STANDPOINT THEORIES

Feminist researchers have developed knowledge building models rooted in the research of women's lives, targeting women's everyday experiences as the subject of inquiry. Dorothy Smith (1987), one of the early pioneers of feminist standpoint perspectives, stresses the necessity of starting research from women's lives and taking into account women's *everyday experiences,* especially by finding and analyzing the gaps that occur when women try to fit their lives into the dominant culture's way of conceptualizing women's situations. By looking at the difference between two perspectives, the researcher gains a more accurate and theoretically richer set of explanations of the lives of the oppressors and the oppressed. Some standpoint theorists collapse all of women's experiences into one defining experience. Other versions of standpoint theory are open to comparing and understanding the interlocking relationships between racism, sexism, heterosexism, and class oppression as additional starting points for understanding social reality (see Harding, 2007; Naples, 2007; Wylie, 2007).

Feminist empiricists as well as early standpoint theorists advocate for the development of new questions that serve to unearth women's subjugated knowledge. Both feminist approaches often assume a perspective on sex as a universal and historical category of analysis (this was replicated in studying other differences, such as race, for example: Harding, 1991; Mohanty, 1988). Such a view obviates the idea that categories of difference interconnect with one another (see Zinn, Hondagneu-Sotelo, & Messner, 2008, pp. 6–7).

THE TURN TOWARD DIFFERENCE AND GLOBALIZATION RESEARCH

The shift towards difference and globalization began when feminists of color criticized early feminist researchers for perpetuating essentialist thinking about gendered experience. They instead argued for a view of gender as inflected by categories of difference in terms of ethnicity and class (see Anzaldua, 1990; hooks, 1984; Mohanty, 1988). As Hirsch and Keller (1990) state, "feminists of color have revealed to white middle-class feminists the extent of their own racism" (p. 379). In addition, the voices of feminist researchers of color had largely gone unheard; sociologist Patricia Hill Collins (1990) stressed the importance of black feminist thought as "the ideas produced by black women that clarify a standpoint of and for Black women" (p. 37). It is through listening to the experiences of the "other" that one obtains a more complete understanding of knowledge. White sociologists, because of their privileged standpoint, are "in no position to notice the specific anomalies apparent to Afro-American women, because these same sociological insiders produced them" (Hill Collins, 1990, p. 53).

There is also a growing awareness among feminist researchers of the importance of women's experiences in a globalized context with respect to issues of imperialism, colonialism, and national identity (see Bhavnani, 2007; Kim, 2007; Mendez & Wolf, 2007). Very often, analyses of difference with regard to race, class, and gender ignore differences among women with regard to their particular geographical/cultural placement across the globe. How do we study these differences? What are some models of difference that allow for an understanding of women's experiences within a global context, models that serve to empower women and promote social change?

Intersectionality considers women's differences as locations or roads taken and notes that where their differences "cross" or match, there exists an intersection of women's experience. Although locating the intersections at which women's differences cross is one way that some feminists have begun to capture these linkages, Kum-Kum Bhavnani (2007) argues that this metaphor does not work well to empower women. In fact, the concept of an intersection implies the image of a crossroads, whereby those who meet are coming from and going to a given destination, which is defined by the route these roads take. This metaphor does not provide a way for new roads to be charted; all the "roads" are fixed. Bhavnani (2007) notes:

A discourse of intersectionality that draws on a crossroads metaphor . . . directs the gaze to the intersections of the roads and the directions in which they travel and meet . . . This matters because if we are not only to analyze the world but also to change it, then the easiest way to imagine the shifts in the relationships between race/ethnicity and gender is to imagine the roads being moved to form new intersections. (pp. 640–641)

Bhavnani suggests a more empowering metaphor, interconnections that configure, which "connotes more movement and fluidity than lies in the metaphor of intersection, as well as offering a way of thinking about how not only race and gender but also nation, sexuality, and wealth all interconnect, configure, and reshape each other" (p. 641).

What remains a challenge for feminist research is linking different strands of knowledge building in order to gather a more complex understanding of the workings of racism, imperialism, and neocolonialism across historical and cultural current scholarships in a way that emphasizes the simultaneous operation of race, class, gender, sexuality, and other differences. At the structural level, hierarchies of oppression are connected and embedded in all social institutions. We can each exist at different locations along all dimensions, leading to the possibility that we can be both dominant and subordinate at the same time. (For a more extended discussion of the contributions of feminist research, see Hesse-Biber, 2007, 2008).

◆ Case Studies of Feminist Approaches to Mixed Methods Research

This section presents some in-depth case studies of how feminists use mixed methods research. Some feminists might choose mixed methods for the same reasons that nonfeminist researchers do. While qualitative methods and the use of multiple qualitative methods are an important part of feminist research praxis, mixed methods (qualitative and quantitative) research designs lend themselves to the following feminist research goals:

• Exploring women's subjugated knowledge by giving voice to women's experiences, in particular, knowledge ignored by traditional research approaches, which leave out gender as a category of inquiry

• Exploring multiple understandings of the nature of social reality, as this particularly pertains to women's issues and standpoints

• Studying across differences in terms of race, class, gender, and so on

• Fostering social justice and social change on behalf of women and other oppressed groups

There are often multiple objectives contained within any given feminist research project, and as we shall see feminists use a variety of mixed methods designs. The Greene and Hall (2010 [this volume]) chapter also demonstrates how (a) a dialectical stance and (b) pragmatism can also affect how a mixed methods study is planned, conducted, and interpreted. These case studies explore how feminist researchers tackle some of the major dimensions of feminist research and specifically how mixed methods can serve to further feminist research problems and perspectives.

As you approach each of these case studies, there are several sensitizing questions you might apply to each, namely:

• What particular research problems lend themselves to mixing methods?

• What specific mixed methods research designs are used and why?

• At what stage in the process of a research project are the methods mixed, if at all?

• What are the specific advantages and disadvantages of using a mixed methods approach?

• What makes this research case an example of a feminist approach to mixed methods?

In the first case study, we will join Andrea Nightingale as she describes her mixed methods journey studying land usage in Nepal.

CASE STUDY 1. UNCOVERING SUBJUGATED KNOWLEDGE: FOREST LAND USAGE IN NEPAL[3]

Geographic feminist researcher Andrea Nightingale (2003) placed women's concerns at the center of her research project on the use of a community forest in Nepal. She employed a mixed methods research design to explore the heretofore silenced voices of women from specific caste systems, whose work and family lives compose an integral part of land forest usage.

Her feminist methodological perspective was based on Donna Haraway's (1988) idea that all knowledge is "situationally based." Feminist objectivity asserts that knowledge and truth are partial, situated, subjective, power imbued, and relational. It also dissuades the denial of values, biases, and politics, which, if ignored, would lead to a replication of dominant cultural understandings of a given social phenomenon.

Nightingale (2003) notes that many feminist geographers were feminist empiricists prior to the 1990s, engaged in making women visible in geographical studies and "adding and stirring" them into their research projects with little attention to differences among women in their analysis and interpretation of research findings. Instead, Nightingale's *feminist standpoint* research perspective placed women's issues as a central point of data collection and analysis in understanding land forest usage. Her specific research questions sought to reveal how the forest was used by those whose voices had been left out of traditional quantitative geographical methods and how, in turn, those voices shaped the landscape of the forest and the way the environment was understood and used by those groups.

For Nightingale (2003), a mixed methods approach allowed her to get at "the silences and discrepancies" in her research findings (p. 81). Nightingale's reasoning for using a mixed methods approach stemmed directly from a feminist epistemology on knowledge building, which considers all knowledge to be socially situated. The data she collected from women's experiences with forest usage went against dominant quantitative

interpretations, which relied on aerial photos alone. She notes:

> In my own work on community forestry in Nepal, I used qualitative, ethnographic techniques, such as oral histories, participant-observation and in-depth interviewing as well as aerial photo interpretation and quantitative vegetation inventory. In addition to highlighting the situatedness and partiality of knowledge, the Nepali case study also helps to show the importance of challenging "dominant" representations of forest change—in this case, aerial photo interpretation—not by rejecting them outright, but by demonstrating explicitly how they provide only one part of the story of forest change. (p. 80)

In an interview I conducted with the researcher, Nightingale explained the initial tension in employing a mixed methods design when her committee wanted her to use aerial interpretations to validate the interviews; however, she considered findings from both methods equally valid:

> And certainly triangulation was part of the agenda in terms of the kind of work I was doing . . . but I really felt very strongly that there were different ways of understanding what was happening with forest change. And I didn't want to privilege one of those understandings over the other but rather I wanted to kind of put them side-by-side and see what they said to one another.

Nightingale's perspective on land usage combined a feminist perspective with a more traditional quantitative geographic approach. Traditional approaches to geography demand a "correct" interpretation of land cover and landforms by checking areas on each photo with areas on the ground. This seemingly straightforward method of comparison raised a central question for Nightingale's research, namely, *Do the individual life histories of forest usage and the aerial photos tell the same story?* Using a feminist standpoint perspective, Nightingale set out to explore how the forest landscape and the changes perceived in the snapshot photos were understood by those whose voices have often been left out of the traditional understandings of land usage over time.

Nightingale employed both quantitative and qualitative methods to explore her research questions. She used ethnographic techniques, specifically ecological oral histories, to ascertain landscape change from the lived experience of individuals who used the land over time. She conducted field observations and interviews with one community of villagers within the Mugu district of northwest Nepal. She asked her respondents to talk about their past and present perceptions of the forest with regard to their experiences with and assessment of ecological conditions of the forest environment. Nightingale also conducted a quantitative aerial photo analysis (from 1978 and 1996) by systematically categorizing land by texture, color, and shade within the photos. For a look at the use of geographical information systems (GIS) in mixed methods, see Bazeley (2010 [this volume]). Nightingale displayed some trepidation in employing a mixed methods design because, while she felt both methods were equally valid in that they "correctly" relayed the story of forest use, she continued to grapple with two questions:

- What if the histories and the photos did not tell the same story?

- If they did not, what would that reveal about both oral histories and aerial photo interpretation?

A feminist lens also led Nightingale to look at the nature-society boundary, which is socially constructed through the everyday interactions of individuals with the natural landscape. In another part of the same interview with Nightingale, she reflected on this:

Hesse-Biber: It sounds to me as if the way in which you thought of these issues entails an interaction of the environment with its surrounding social context of people using it and their ideas about it. The forest becomes part of kind of a living space, right? Where people are interacting in many different ways that deal with issues of power and social control and gender and all of those things to create the forest that you see in any given picture.

Nightingale: Absolutely, that's a really nice way to put it. And I was very much influenced by some kind of postmodern thinking around class... Thinking not so much rigidly and linearly about class as something you were born into but rather that class is performed. And so the kinds of economic activities you engage in determine your class position. And those things change over time and for many people they can be involved in multiple class processes... ummm... even in one given day.

Nightingale's insights reveal a new conceptual space to rethink the nature-society interface. What appears hidden in the aerial photos of the forest is a set of societal relationships embedded especially in caste, class, and gendered relationships as well as cultural beliefs about the natural environment. Nightingale finds that the forest usage is a space of contention among various gender and caste groupings that serve to shape how the forest is managed and ecological decisions are made. For the most part, such social interactions serve to reproduce traditionally gendered and especially caste norms, perpetuating the power of high-caste males within these forest communities. These power imbalances are most evident in Nightingale's (2003) observations of forest-usage community meetings:

> Women and low-caste men are largely excluded from the management decision making process in multi-caste user-groups. Caste and gender norms require that they sit away from the high-caste men who run the meeting, literally and symbolically dimming their voices at meetings . . . By understanding ecological conditions in . . . relationship with social relations and cultural practices, the complex and often contradictory effects of each on the others is revealed. (pp. 536–537)

The following diagram (Figure 7.2) depicts how the various methods she used intersected and affected her overall interpretation.

Nightingale mixes not only methods in data collection but also the analysis of her data (QUAL and QUAN data analysis). She uses one type of data to inform the other and compares inconsistencies rather than trying to triangulate the data to fit a given story or "truth." Nightingale (2003) uses both data sets, including aerial photos and oral histories of forest usage, "on equal terms" to answer questions "at roughly the same scale" (p. 86). Both data sets are equally important, and one does not preempt the other. She notes:

> A different research design might have used photos merely to set the context for forest change and then used the histories to detail the cultural and political aspects of that change. Instead, by setting the data sets in relation to each other, I have allowed for both to be acknowledged as partial and situated. (p. 86)

What seems hidden in the aerial photos of the forest is a set of societal[4] and cultural[5] factors that make for a richer understanding of the forest landscape and its transformation over time than using only the traditional

Figure 7.2   Nightingale's (2003) Mixed Methods Research Design: Beyond Triangulation

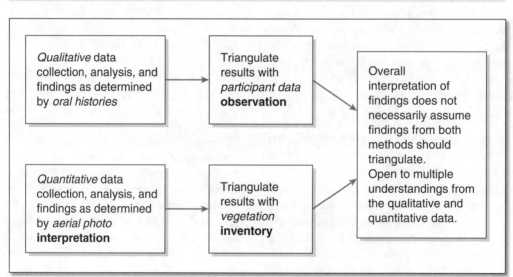

quantitative method of analyzing the aerial photos. Nightingale's feminist research approach was in the service of seeking out women's varying experiences with forest usage. In addition, she was cognizant of social justice/social transformation goals as she sought to use the knowledge gained for a "feminist political ecology."[6] Nightingale is aware of the need to take her research to the social activism level through the integration of women's voices into forestry planning and development, noting:

> To take this work further it is necessary to ask: what opportunities for positive ecological and social change are produced by understanding the complexities of these processes? Recognizing the mutual constitution of social relations and environment requires that planners reevaluate how they formulate development programmes. Rather than having separate gender, basic needs, or environmental programmes, it is necessary to reconceptualise these not as additive process but as embedded within each other . . . This analysis points to the need for more attention to how projects are implemented and the importance of allowing for sufficient flexibility and attention to the shifting relationships between environment, development, and difference. (Nightingale, 2006, p. 181–182)

CASE STUDY 2. GETTING AT SUBJUGATED KNOWLEDGE: SEX WORK IN TIJUANA

Yasmina Katsulis is a feminist geographer who, like Andrea Nightingale, focuses on women's lived experiences. In this specific case study, she is interested in understanding the situation of girls and women who work in the sex industry in Tijuana, Mexico (Katsulis, 2009). As a feminist, she focuses on women's lives and seeks to uncover knowledge of their day-to-day experiences in order to address issues of

violence against women and confront the stereotypes that surround women who work in the sex trade industry. In her initial literature review, she found that previous research studies of sex workers assumed a deviant model of understanding their plight and labeled and stigmatized them as prostitutes and "disease vectors" (p. 3). Her research embodied a variety of feminist research goals that ranged from uncovering subjugated knowledge to transforming the social situation of women's lives with regard to the sex work industry.

Katsulis's feminist theoretical framework guided her choice of methods. She did not select a mixed methods design a priori; rather, the shape of her study evolved over time in an iterative fashion. She notes that although she started off with a primarily qualitative study, after a few months her priorities began to change. Katsulis (2009) notes:

> It was not until I had been living in Tijuana for a number of months that I realized how structurally diverse the commercial sex industry is. My goal of writing a purely qualitative study shifted as I began to strategize about how to incorporate this diversity and, more specifically, to identify patterns in the relationships between social diversity, social hierarchy, and health outcomes. (p. 12)

We can see that her research questions began to incorporate a more quantitative perspective in terms of inquiring about the macrolevel social and economic power hierarchies within sex work as an occupation. This moved Katsulis to adopt a mixed methods design that included a quantitative component in addition to her original qualitative-only design. Her overall research question was: What are "the experiences of a diverse range of sex workers who live and work on the U.S-Mexican border?" (Katsulis, 2009, p. 1)

As depicted in Figure 7.3, Katsulis did not have a pre-planned mixed methods

Figure 7.3 Katsulis's (2009) Exploratory Sequential Mixed Methods Research Design

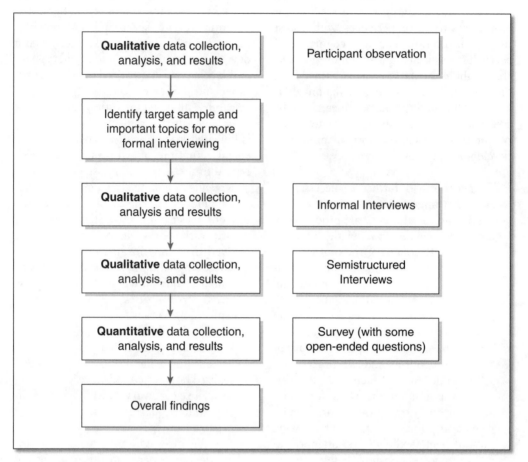

design. She interviewed women who came to a clinic in Tijuana for HIV/AIDS prevention; these women, for the most part, were working in the legal sector of the sex trade. Their experiences made her more fully aware of the fact that she had a very select pool of women, who were not representative of the majority of sex workers from the illegal sector of this industry. To reach this particular segment of the sex worker population, survey interviews were added to the research design as a quantitative component. Katsulis explains her design as follows: "I used a combination of participant observation, informal conversational interviews, semistructured interviews, and surveys conducted in a variety of settings" (p. 12).

Her initial field observations at several sites led her to gather a targeted, purposive sample that "allowed [her] to explore potential themes within a broad range of diverse work experiences" (p. 12). This sample consisted of "customers, professionals, researchers, and policymakers" (p. 12). The bulk of her in-depth data collection consisted of "talking with sex workers themselves." As she notes, she "carried out 251 formal interviews with sex workers, 88 of whom worked legally (86 females, 2 transgendered females), and 160 of whom worked illegally (107 females, 14 transgendered females, 42 males)" (Katsulis, 2009, p. 12).

Katsulis's (2009) data analysis is a good example of how mixed methods data can be integrated at different stages of the research process. Let's follow her exploratory sequential mixed methods design. She first began with participant observation at several research sites over the course of 18 months, and the findings from these observations were integrated in her study in two ways: (1) they informed a target sample for more semistructured interviewing and (2) they provided guidance for questionnaire items for the in-depth interviews, which composed the next qualitative phrase of her study. Semistructured interviews were then conducted with legal sex workers within a clinic setting. The data she gathered from these interviews with legal sex workers propelled her to expand her study to illegal sex workers covering a range of different work in Tijuana (including strippers, brothel workers, street hookers, massage parlor workers, and call/escort services). Serendipity also played a part in her research design, as she received additional funding from the National Science Foundation to carry out this broader survey. The final component of her mixed methods design consisted of surveying illegal workers, who form the majority of sex workers (the ratio of illegal to legal workers is 2 to 1). In addition, her grant allowed her to provide free HIV testing to all participants.

Katsulis's (2009) integrated analysis allowed room for multiple sets of data to dialogue with each other. By using a feminist approach to mixed methods research, beyond getting at the lived experiences of sex workers, she was able to tap into the different types of sex work, a distinction that is most often missed. Her research goals were in the service of social justice. The quantitative component of her study provided Katsulis with a "dualistic perspective" that combined women's lived experiences (from interviews) with a broader set of findings (from the survey). With the quantitative findings, she was able to broaden and generalize her qualitative findings in a way that helped make arguments for social change and social policy initiatives.

Somehow, numbers seem to connote "scientific method" and "rigor," which often is appealing to policymakers (see Spalter-Roth & Hartmann, 1996).

CASE STUDY 3. UNCOVERING SUBJUGATED KNOWLEDGE AND GENERATING/TESTING THEORIES OF INEQUALITY: STUDYING THE GENDER GAP IN PUBLIC OPINION IN CANADA

Brenda O'Neill's (2009) research deals with the interface between feminism, religion, and women's political opinions. She is a feminist empiricist researcher whose goals are similar to those of early feminist empiricists (whom I noted earlier in the introduction). O'Neill sought to uncover subjugated knowledge regarding women's political opinions, which had been left out of academic research in her field of political science. She notes her postpositivist leanings and feminist perspective, which, early on in the process of formulating her study, elicited an abrupt negation of the validity of her work at a research workshop she attended. She notes:

> In short, I believe that the research question ought to dictate the appropriate method to employ. The dominance of quantitative techniques in my work stems from my statistical training in the disciplines of economics and political science. I additionally identify as a feminist and my openness to qualitative methods stems from independent learning, research and reading. My first academic invitation to contribute to an edited collection involved writing a chapter on the use of quantitative methods within feminist research (O'Neill, 1995). At the workshop where we were asked to deliver the papers, my presentation was interrupted by a researcher who turned to the editors and asked why my chapter was included in the volume given that feminists had

largely discredited quantitative research methods. That experience galvanized my interest in methods, methodology and epistemology. (O'Neill, 2009, p. 1)

One of the roadblocks to carrying out this type of research is that the quantitative data sets available in her field, which she might use for a secondary data analysis, do not contain information by gender. O'Neill found that she had to gather her own data to tap into women's opinions on the variety of issues she wished to address. In addition, she notes that the lack of information makes it difficult to perform mixed methods research projects; this was especially true in the early stages of her professional career because of the enormous upfront costs of acquiring a quantitative data set and the difficulty of obtaining funding.

O'Neill's research sought to answer the following question: What is the role of religious beliefs and feminist identification in shaping women's political attitudes? She employed an exploratory sequential mixed methods design, starting out with a qualitative focus group component. She gathered data from nine ethnic- and age-diverse focus groups of women (8 to 10 women each) from a sample of Canadian cities that varied in size and region. She nested a short quantitative survey into the focus groups, which gathered demographic data on the participants (age, social class, religious affiliation).

She followed the qualitative component with a quantitative telephone survey of a random sample of 1,264 women age 18 or older drawn from 10 Canadian provinces. The survey was intended to gather data on women's attitudes and beliefs regarding politics, feminism, and religion. In addition, standard demographic data was also collected (socioeconomic status, religious denomination, etc.). The sequence of methods used in her study is depicted in Figure 7.4.

Let's examine O'Neill's (2009) rationale for conducting her exploratory sequential mixed methods design and how this particular design lent itself to her particular research question both derived from her feminist perspective. Her overall goal was to "set the record straight" regarding

Figure 7.4 O'Neill's (2009) Exploratory Sequential Mixed Methods Research Design

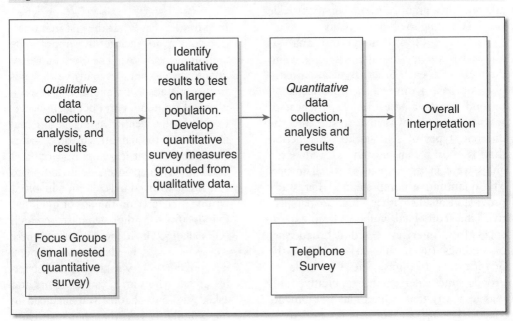

women's political attitudes and beliefs, and to do so, she needed to unearth women's subjugated knowledge. She also sought to transform research methods, measures, and concepts to include women's voices. She arrived at her research question because she was unhappy with the way in which the concept of religion had been measured previously. One of the issues that arose in her focus groups was that "faith needed to be conceptualized beyond the narrow concepts of membership in a religious denomination and attendance at services" which is "how more quantitative approaches to the study of political behavior have conceptualized religion: denomination (including a measure for evangelicalism), salience and attendance at services" (p. 11).

In addition, O'Neill (2009) sought to generate a theory from the qualitative data about women's political participation and its relation to religion and feminism; she then wanted to "test out" the theory on the quantitative data. She inductively created a set of quantitative measures using information she obtained from the qualitative component of her study to ground her quantitative measures in women's lived experiences. She wanted, in effect, to develop nonandrocentric measures of participation and a more robust understanding of religion and feminism to inform the questions she developed for her quantitative survey. Her qualitative data component was directly in the service of these feminist research goals. O'Neill also used the qualitative and quantitative studies to complement one another. She notes:

> By starting with a more qualitative method, I was able [to] incorporate the rich discussions into the construction of survey questions. And indeed, the ability to better capture the multidimensionality of concepts by using the Qual/Quant design has been identified by others (Leckenby & Hesse-Biber, 2007). More than this, however, the focus groups

established the importance of a concept that I would have completely missed had I jumped immediately into the more quantitative method (e.g. the importance of spirituality). The focus groups also provided assistance with the choice of vocabulary and the phrasing of new questions that deviated from those employed in existing surveys. (pp. 11–12)

CASE STUDY 4.
THE POTENTIAL CONUNDRUMS
AND MISSED OPPORTUNITIES
IN USING A MIXED METHODS
EXPLANATORY DESIGN FOR
FEMINIST RESEARCH INQUIRY:
A CAUTIONARY CASE STUDY

The case studies we presented thus far do not employ a sequential explanatory mixed methods design. This design is often used in research with the intention of complementarity, whereby information gained from a qualitative study, which is second in sequence, is said to enhance understanding of the quantitative, which is often seen as the primary component of this mixed methods design.

The advantages of complementarity cannot be taken at face value and need to be problematized in the context of feminist research goals. A feminist approach to research is cognizant of the use of male-biased measures, which are a critical issue when employing this type of design. A researcher cannot assume that the quantitative study's questions are unbiased, especially if taken from a standard (mainstream) set of measures, even when their validity coefficients are said to make them highly valid. One must ask: *valid with respect to whom or what?* O'Neill's (2009) case study questioned the male bias of most of the measurements of political opinion research used in her discipline. There is a lean toward androcentric measures within her discipline, and instead of using existing measures, O'Neill began with a qualitative study to provide a grounded understanding of women's feelings with regard to a range of political opinion issues. She created her measures "from the ground up." This was also the case with her measures of feminism and religiosity. Beginning with a grounded approach that informs quantitative measures, then, helps to deal with androcentric bias. The same logic must also be applied when one deals with other differences, understanding that they may not be part of preexistent mainstream measures.

In her mixed methods project, Suzanne Hodgkin (2008) tackles an important and often neglected set of research questions regarding women's acquisition of social capital, an important resource with which women negotiate their social worlds. She applies a feminist transformative approach whose overall research goal is to promote social justice (see Mertens et al., 2010 [this volume]). Two questions guided her study:

• "Do men and women have different social capital profiles?"

• "Why do women participate more in social and community activities than in civic activities?" (p. 301)

More specifically, Hodgkin wanted to show the synergistic impact of using a mixed methods design; she applies this design to show that mixed methods can be used in and "bring both depth and texture to" feminist research (p. 297). To do

this, she centered gender as a major variable of analysis. Like feminist empiricists before her, she sought to address the lack of gender focus in studies of social capital—defined as "the norms and networks that enable people to work collectively together to address and resolve problems they face in common" (p. 297)—as well as to make visible women's motivations for investing in particular types of social capital acquisition. Her goal was "to develop an understanding of what motivates women's involvement in social, civic, and community life and the social realities of their experiences" (p. 304).

Hodgkin selected an explanatory sequential mixed methods research design to demonstrate how mixed methods research can be complementary to feminist research. She began with a quantitative component and ended with a qualitative component, which was used to help explain complexities in the quantitative data (see Figure 7.5).

In the quantitative phase, Hodgkin (2008) sent a survey to 4,000 random households in Australia. The majority of respondents were employed, living in a household as a couple, and educated at least through secondary school (p. 302). The goal of the study was to identify any gender differences between men and women's social capital profiles. Hodgkin used a previously generated measure of social capital developed by the South Australian Community Research Unit, which she notes

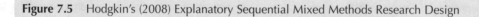

Figure 7.5   Hodgkin's (2008) Explanatory Sequential Mixed Methods Research Design

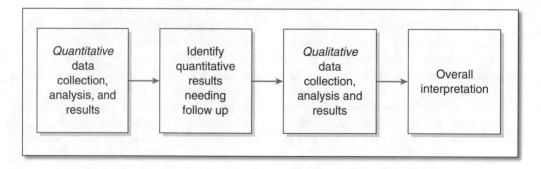

could "make a distinction between informal and formal types of participation" that would highlight women's involvement in nonpublic activities (p. 301). The instrument was "sufficiently sensitive to gender issues, particularly its focus on caring . . . The researcher particularly favored the distinction made between [social and civic activities]" (p. 303). However, unlike O'Neill, as discussed above, Hodgkin did not interrogate in more detail the androcentric biases that might be present in these measurements.

The next step in her research was a qualitative phase involving interviews. Using random cluster sampling, 12 women ages 29 to 49 were selected from among the women who had agreed to interviews when completing the questionnaire. The first six participants within the age range to respond were chosen; in addition, six more participants were interviewed, after which "the researcher felt comfortable that saturation had been achieved" (p. 302). The qualitative data collection component was extensive and allowed Hodgkin to explore women's viewpoints regarding their participation in social, community, and civic activities. The data collection phase consisted of an interview, one week of diary writing (or written reflections), and a second interview.

In analyzing her mixed methods data, however, Hodgkin (2008) incorporated little dialogue between the quantitative and qualitative elements, except that the qualitative findings were in the service of the quantitative findings. Quantitative data were analyzed to determine differences in types of participation based on gender. Here, gender was employed as a nominal variable, with no differentiation among women in terms of specific differences that might matter, such as social class, age, and number of children. She notes that women as a categorical variable "reported higher levels of informal social participation, social participation in groups, and community group participation" (p. 307). In addition, women were involved more in informal sociability and activities with a

group/community focus or focus on children. Men were more involved with civic and "formal" activities (e.g., sporting clubs and trade union groups) (p. 308).

Analysis of the qualitative data revealed women's motivations to participate in social, community, and civic activities. Hodgkin (2008) notes: "The quantitative findings provide evidence of women's predominance in formal sociability and to a lesser extent men's predominance in associational life. . . . The researcher used the narratives to delve more into the motivations behind the range of participation" (p. 313).

Within her analysis, each method played a distinct role, with one level layered on top of the other. She notes that the quantitative data provided "the big picture, revealing a different pattern of participation for men and women. The qualitative data assists in developing and sharpening this picture" (p. 313). There is no back and forth analytical tension between the two data sets or any questioning of findings from either data set.

The author explicitly states that her research project was "located in the transformative paradigm" and was conducted in the tradition of feminist empiricist research (p. 299). Her research question was transformative in that it sought to obtain subjugated knowledge regarding women's motivations and degree of social capital. However, Hodgkin's study misses an important opportunity in that she does not push on the boundaries of this paradigm enough, nor does she use mixed methods to their full social justice potential in this study. There is no attempt to discuss how her findings can be transformative in our understanding of women's social participation and its implications for social policy to actually improve women's lived conditions.

In addition, the category of woman is treated as a universal/essentialist category with no discussion of differences among the women and men in her study (i.e., with regard to differences in race, class, age, and so on). To what extent did the quantitative measures of the survey actually capture gender differences? When gender is treated as a variable with little attention to other differences among women and men, can we assume that the measures of her two most important variables capture the range of women's and men's lived experiences? Those researchers working from a postpositivistic tradition may unwittingly assume that their measure of sex or gender does not need to take into account the types of women in their study (for example, women of a certain class or race). However, to what extent is this traditional way of measuring sex or gender in fact stereotyping our perception of women and men by lumping them into a nominal level measure, with only two categories to choose from: men and women? (See Ravanera & Rajulton, 2010, for a discussion and empirical example of exploring differences in social capital among women).

◆ Conclusions

Mixed methods research designs hold out promise for enabling feminists to test out their theories and generalize their findings through integrating and contextualizing women's lived experiences at the macro level (placing them into a larger socio-historical context). O'Neill's (2009) study of women's political opinions did this by placing her research findings from both methods in conversation with each other. She notes,

> By starting with a more qualitative method, I was able incorporate the rich discussions into the construction of survey questions. And indeed, the ability to better capture the multi-dimensionality of concepts by using the Qual/Quant design has been identified by others. (p. 11)

The knowledge generated from a mixed methods study can empower feminist researchers by providing the information they need to pursue social justice goals for women and other oppressed groups. Mixed methods are tools for social transformation in women's lives. Numbers plus words are a powerful combination in speaking to that segment of social policy decision makers (see Gottfried, 1996) who expect the researcher to have both types of data. We observed the strong social change/social justice mission that runs through the case studies we presented.

Feminist perspectives can also enrich the praxis of mixed methods by adding to the validity of the mixed methods process by stressing the importance of reflecting on our standpoint—the values and attitudes we bring to our research. Feminist praxis, for example, interrogates mainstream measurement practices, providing strategies for dealing with gender bias when using the "master's tools," tending to issues of androcentrism, racism, classism, and so on throughout the research process. O'Neill's (2009) case study is an excellent example of reflection on the bias of measurement tools in her discipline. O'Neill interrogated a standard measurement of religiosity from her discipline but decided against employing a secondary measure in her study because she felt it did not take women's viewpoints into account. Instead, she started out with a qualitative focus group component to develop her own measures. The focus group component gave her the language to access women's experiences with regard to the concept of religion, specifically their sense of spirituality. Her feminist approach to measurement informed her mixed methods design by providing "assistance with the choice of vocabulary and the phrasing of new questions that deviated from those employed in existing surveys" (O'Neill, 2009, p. 12).

Feminist praxis of mixed methods research centers the research question in the selection of a specific method or methods to employ. The choice of a mixed methods research design is not methods centric. There usually is no pre-programmed mixed methods design at the beginning of a research project, but the design unfolds iteratively as the feminist researcher gathers information, analyzes and interprets it, and decides what to do next. Yasmina Katsulis's (2009) case study of the sex industry in Tijuana, Mexico, started out with a qualitative component that consisted of ethnographic observations and in-depth interviews at a clinic; however, the information she gathered and analyzed led her to expand her study to other subgroups of sex workers through a quantitative survey.

Feminist researchers trouble dualistic categorical variables like sex/gender by contextualizing and destabilizing them through the examination of the interconnections between differences that might be important to their research question. There is emphasis on the socially constructed nature of the sex/gender category and a high awareness of differences within the research process.

Feminist researchers also challenge mixed methods research to go beyond triangulation as a primary mixed methods rationale. Andrea Nightingale's (2003) research study employed a range of mixed methods designs to explore the silenced voices of women from different caste rankings. She did this by collecting oral histories from women as well as collecting forestry documents to uncover women's experiences. She sought to integrate this knowledge with a more quantitative approach that employed an aerial photo analysis.

Feminist approaches to mixed methods provide some important strategies for researchers who want to mix methods at the data analysis and data interpretation stage. Each level of data analysis is brought into conversation with the other. Nightingale notes that using GPS data alone as primary evidence of forest usage, as practiced by traditional geographic researchers, provides only one type of lens with which to view forest usage. While GPS provides a snapshot over time, it does not get at processes underlying forest changes.

Feminist perspectives are multimethodological and traverse views of reality from postpositivism to postmodernism. Likewise, feminism encourages mixed methods researchers to think beyond triangulation as the model of mixing methods and instead to prioritize strong objectivity and accept the tensions and ambiguities of diverse mixed methods findings. Researchers should not prematurely shut down inquiry because research findings are ambiguous, for that is where new knowledge is discovered

and marginalized knowledge is brought to the foreground.

THE CHALLENGE OF MIXED METHODS RESEARCH FOR FEMINIST RESEARCHERS

The case studies also reveal that feminist approaches to mixed methods research can encounter troubled waters when traversing quantitative and qualitative methods. Sometimes in spite of the best of intentions on the part of some feminist researchers, they too may introduce bias into their own research projects by relying on androcentric measures. They may not have the time or money to obtain their own measures. We noted in O'Neill's (2009) study that she was able to address her concern in this regard, given the fortuitous timing of obtaining grant monies, which allowed her to develop measures grounded in women's experiences. Other feminists need to work with the master's measures and in doing so may in fact inadvertently reinforce the very gender stereotypes they seek to upend.

In addition, we have also seen a failure of some feminist research projects to go the extra mile of connecting their quantitative and qualitative components and thereby missing the possible synergy of dialoguing across the tensions and ambiguities that might arise within their data. They may also miss the opportunity to follow through on the promise of social change and transformation that is contained within their research project.

THE IMPORTANCE OF MINDING THE CONTEXT OF DISCOVERY AND THE CONTEXT OF JUSTIFICATION

Early feminist researchers talked about the overall research process as having to take account of two important components, each with its own set of conundrums. The *context of discovery* is that part of the research process that asks questions and formulates hypotheses. The *context of justification* is the component that carries out the project-specific measures and methods tools (Sprague & Zimmerman, 1993). For the historical context of these terms, see Johnson and Gray (2010 [this volume]).

Especially left out of consideration in many mixed methods projects in general is a lack of reflexivity with regard to the context of discovery. It is within the problem formation and question asking stage of research that researchers' values and attitudes first enter the research process, often determining what questions are asked (and not asked); what individuals/groups are included (and excluded); and which specific hypotheses are tested (or not tested). This set of potential biases can impact the validity of research findings no matter how well the context of justification component is carried out.

The practice of "strong objectivity"—having researchers disclose their values, attitudes, and biases in their approach to a particular set of research questions and engage in strong reflexivity throughout the research process—can often offset these biases. Several aspects of awareness are particularly important. First, be conscious of difference and how it is or is not integrated in your research project. The extent to which you will tend to difference depends on the specific research question. A feminist researcher is cognizant of difference and is aware of how specific women's experiences will differ due to their divergent locations in a social structure and the historic trends and events that characterize their lives. To engage with difference within a feminist approach means that gender is located at the intersections of other differences such as race, class, and sexuality.

TOOLS FOR MAINTAINING THE SYNERGISTIC PROMISE OF MIXED METHODS RESEARCH: THE NEED FOR REFLEXIVITY

Reflexivity is an important tool for navigating your research project across the mixed methods landscape. Feminist researchers practice strong reflexivity by being conscious of how their assumptions affect their research practices, including the specific ways in which their own agendas impact their research—from the selection of the research problem and method to the ways they analyze and interpret their data (Hesse-Biber & Piatelli, 2007). Practicing *reflexivity* helps researchers get in touch with their research assumptions. This makes the researcher more conscious of what values, attitudes, and research concerns can be brought to any given research project. Consider the following reflexive questions as you embark on your own mixed methods research project:

- How does your position in society affect the way you observe and perceive others in your daily life?

- What particular values and biases do you bring to and/or impose on your research?

- What particular ideas on the nature of knowledge/reality do you bring to your research?

- What specific research questions guide your choice of research methods?

THE NEED FOR DIALOGUE AND COMMUNICATION SKILLS

Mixed methods research holds out great promise to traverse macro- and micro-layered understandings of women's lived experiences and brings forth diverse understandings of women's lives. To do so will also require dialogue and listening skills across these layers of meaning. To dialogue means to develop good communication and listening skills and to listen across our differences with the goal of understanding, not "winning." To truly dialogue, we must (a) confront our assumptions (especially traditional assumptions concerning the role of women in society), (b) suspend judgment, (c) accept/embrace differences, and (d) internally listen as a means toward building a new set of shared assumptions and culture.

Honing all these research skills will keep the synergistic promise of mixed methods research alive. Their increasing acquisition by social researchers also serves to promote an increasing awareness of the importance of the research question. In addition, tending to the context of discovery will guide the rationale of methods selection. Two methods may not be better than one. Feminist researchers more specifically will seek out tools that are flexible and fluid with new awareness that even the master's tools, to paraphrase from Audre Lorde, can become unbound from patriarchal ends and be put into the service of feminist research goals.

Research Questions and Exercises

1. What are some common errors that feminists believe are present in traditional research, and how are feminists currently working to change these biases?

2. What are specific advantages of using mixed methods for feminist researchers?

3. How would you define standpoint theory? How does standpoint theory lend itself to mixed methods research?

4. What is Sandra Harding's definition of "strong objectivity," and how does it apply to both feminist research and mixed methods research?

5. How do the following researchers, coming from a feminist worldview, use mixed methods to their advantage? What do their research designs look like?

   - Nightingale's forest usage study in Nepal
   - Katsulis's sex work study in Tijuana, Mexico
   - O'Neill's study of political views in Canada
   - Hodgkin's work on social capital in Australia

6. What is reflexivity, and why is it important for feminist research?

◆ Notes

1. The author wishes to acknowledge the outstanding research assistance, editorial advice, and editing of this chapter by Alicia Johnson, Boston College undergraduate, class of 2011. Thanks also to Astrid Virding and Jacqueline Tasch from Sage Publications for their editorial assistance at the final stage of publication.

2. An *ontology* can be thought of as the basic assumptions about the nature of the reality, whereas an *epistemology* is "a theory of knowledge" that contains specific assumptions about the knowledge building process and asks questions such as: Who can know? What can be known? (Harding, 1987, p. 3). Reseachers' ontological and epistemological assumptions are tightly linked to their specific *methodology*—the theoretical perspectives they employ, the specific research questions they pursue, the types of *methods* they select, and how they go about their research praxis—how they carry out the practice of knowledge building using specific methods. There is, then, a tight link between these aspects of the research process, whether they are consciously held by the researcher or are assumptions that the researcher is not aware of.

3. Part of this case study example is adapted from Sharlene Hesse-Biber, *Mixed methods research: Merging theory with practice* (Guilford Publications, 2010).

4. The web of social relations and interweaving of caste, class, race, and gender relationships with regard to the natural environment.

5. The set of beliefs about nature and how the natural environment is conceptualized by individuals; factors that interface with the forest landscape.

6. Nightingale (2006) notes: "Feminist political ecology provides tools for political ecologists to examine gender and emphasizes the importance of considering gender in the context of a variety of natural-resource issues" (p. 169).

◆ References

Anzaldua, G. E. (1990). *Making face, making soul/Haciendo caras: Creative and critical perspectives by feminists of color*. San Francisco: Aunt Lute Books.

Bazeley, P. (2010). Computer assisted integration of mixed methods data sources and analysis. In A. Tashakkori & C. Teddlie (Eds.), *SAGE handbook of mixed methods in social & behavioral research* (2nd ed.). Thousand Oaks, CA: Sage.

Bhavnani, K. (2007). Interconnections and configurations: Toward a global feminist ethnography. In S. Hesse-Biber (Ed.), *Handbook of feminist research: Theory and praxis* (pp. 639–649). Thousand Oaks, CA: Sage.

Biccom, A. (2009). *Global citizenship and the legacy of empire: Marketing development*. New York: Routledge.

Bowles, G., & Duelli Klein, R. (1983). *Theories of women's studies*. London: Routledge & Kegan Paul.

Chafetz, J. S. (2004). Some thoughts by an unrepentant "positivist" who considers herself a feminist nonetheless. In S. Hesse-Biber & M. L. Yaiser (Eds.), *Feminist perspectives on social research* (pp. 302–329). NewYork: Oxford University Press.

Eichler, M., & Lapointe, J. (1985). *On the treatment of the sexes in research*. Ottawa: Social Sciences and Humanities Research Council of Canada.

Gottfried, H. (Ed.). (1996). *Feminism and social change*. Urbana: University of Illinois Press.

Greene, J., & Hall, J. (2010). Dialectics and pragmatism: Being of consequence. In A. Tashakkori & C. Teddlie (Eds.), *SAGE handbook of mixed methods in social & behavioral research* (2nd ed.). Thousand Oaks, CA: Sage.

Haraway, D. (1988). Situated knowledges: The science question in feminism and the privilege of partial perspectives. *Feminist Studies, 14*(3), 575–599.

Harding, S. (1991). *Whose science? Whose knowledge?* Ithaca, NY: Cornell University Press.

Harding, S. (1993). Rethinking standpoint epistemology: What is "strong objectivity"?. In L. Alcoff & E. Potter (Eds.), *Feminist epistemologies* (pp. 49–82). New York: Routledge.

Harding, S. (2007). Feminist standpoints. In S. Hesse-Biber (Ed.), *Handbook of feminist research: Theory and praxis* (pp. 45–69). Thousand Oaks, CA: Sage.

Hesse-Biber, S. N. (2007). *Handbook of feminist research: Theory and praxis*. Thousand Oaks, CA: Sage.

Hesse-Biber, S. N. (2008). Feminist research. In L. M. Given (Ed.), *The Sage encyclopedia of qualitative research methods* (Vol. 1, pp. 335–338). Thousand Oaks, CA: Sage.

Hesse-Biber, S. N. (2010). *Mixed methods research: Merging theory with practice*. New York: Guilford.

Hesse-Biber, S. N., & Leavy, P. (Eds.). (2006). *Emergent methods in social research*. Thousand Oaks, CA: Sage.

Hesse-Biber, S. N., & Leavy, P. (2007). *Feminist research practice: A primer*. Thousand Oaks, CA: Sage.

Hesse-Biber, S., & Piatelli, D. (2007). From theory to method and back again: The synergistic praxis of theory and method. In S. Hesse-Biber (Ed.), *Handbook of feminist research: Theory and praxis* (pp. 143–153). Thousand Oaks, CA: Sage.

Hill Collins, P. (1990). *Black feminist thought: Knowledge, consciousness, and the politics of empowerment.* New York: Routledge.

Hirsch, M., & Keller, E. F. (1990). *Conflicts in feminism.* New York: Routledge.

Hodgkin, S. (2008). Telling it all: A story of women's social capital using a mixed methods approach. *Journal of Mixed Methods Research, 2,* 296–316.

hooks, b. (1984). *Feminist theory from margin to center.* Boston: South End Press.

Hundleby, C. (2007). Feminist empiricism. In S. Hesse-Biber (Ed.), *Handbook of feminist research: Theory and praxis* (pp. 29–44). Thousand Oaks, CA: Sage.

Johnson, B., & Gray, R. (2010). A history of philosophical and theoretical issues for mixed methods research. In A. Tashakkori & C. Teddlie (Eds.), *SAGE handbook of mixed methods in social & behavioral research* (2nd ed.). Thousand Oaks, CA: Sage.

Katsulis, Y. (2009). *Sex work and the city: The social geography of health and safety in Tijuana, Mexico.* Austin: University of Texas Press.

Kim, H. S. (2007). The politics of border crossings: Black, postcolonial, and transational feminist perspectives. In S. Hesse-Biber (Ed.), *Handbook of feminist research: Theory and praxis* (pp. 107–122). Thousand Oaks, CA: Sage.

Lather, P. (1991). *Getting smart: Feminist research and pedagogy with/in the postmodern.* New York: Routledge.

Leckenby, D., & Hesse-Biber, S. N. (2007). Feminist approaches to mixed-methods research. S. N. Hesse-Biber & P. L. Leavy (Eds.), *Feminist research practice: A primer* (pp. 249–291). Thousand Oaks, CA: Sage.

Lorde, A. (1984). *Sister outsider: Essays and speeches.* Berkeley, CA: The Crossing Press.

Mendez, J. B., & Wolf, D. L. (2007). Feminizing global research/globalizing feminist research: Methods and practice under globalization. In S. Hesse-Biber (Ed.), *Handbook of feminist research: Theory and praxis* (pp. 651–659). Thousand Oaks, CA: Sage.

Mertens, D. M., Bledoe, K. L., Sullivan, M., & Wilson, A. (2010). Utilization of mixed methods for transformative purposes. In A. Tashakkori & C. Teddlie (Eds.), *SAGE handbook of mixed methods in social & behavioral research* (2nd ed.). Thousand Oaks, CA: Sage.

Miner-Rubino, K., & Jayaratne, T. E. (2007). Feminist survey research. In S. Hesse-Biber (Ed.), *Feminist research practice: A primer* (pp. 293–325). Thousand Oaks, CA: Sage.

Mohanty, C. T. (1988). Under Western eyes: Feminist scholarship and colonial discourses. *Feminist Review, 30,* 61–88.

Naples, N. (2007). Standpoint epistemology and beyond. In S. Hesse-Biber (Ed.), *Handbook of feminist research: Theory and praxis* (pp. 579–589). Thousand Oaks, CA: Sage.

Nightingale, A. (2003). A feminist in the forest: Situated knowledges and mixing methods in natural resource management. *ACME: An International E-Journal for Critical Geographers, 2*(1), 77–90.

Nightingale, A. (2006). The nature of gender: Work, gender, and environment. *Society and Space, 24,* 165–185.

O'Neill, B. (1995). The gender gap: Re-evaluating theory and method. In S. Peterborough (Ed.), *Changing methods: Feminists reflect on practice* (pp. 327–355). Ontario: Broadview Press.

O'Neill, B. (2009). *A mixed methods approach to studying women's political opinions.* Paper presented at the First European Conference on Politics and Gender, Queen's University of Belfast, UK.

Ravanera, Z. R., & Rajulton, F. (2010). Measuring social capital and its differentials by family structure. *Social Indicator Research, 95*(1), 63–89.

Reinharz, S. (1985). Feminist distrust: Problems of context and content in sociological work. In D. Berg & K. Smith (Eds.), *Exploring clinical methods for social research* (pp. 63–84). New York: Wiley.

Reinharz, S. (1992). *Feminist methods in social research.* New York: Oxford University Press.

Roberts, H. (1981). *Doing feminist research.* Boston: Routledge & Kegan Paul.

Smith, D. (1987). *The everyday world as problematic: A feminist sociology.* Boston: Northeastern University Press.

Smith, L. T. (1999). *Decolonizing methodologies: Research and indigenous peoples.* New York: St. Martin's Press.

Spalter-Roth, R., & Hartmann, H. (1996). Small happinesses: The feminist struggle to integrate social research with social activism. In H. Gottfried (Ed.), *Feminism and social change* (pp. 206–224). Urbana: University of Illinois Press.

Sprague, J., & Zimmerman, M. (1993). Overcoming dualisms: A feminist agenda for sociological methodology. In P. England (Ed.), *Theory on gender/feminism on theory* (pp. 255–280). New York: Aldine DeGruyter.

Sullivan, G. (2010). *Art practice as research: Inquiry in visual arts* (2nd ed.). Thousand Oaks, CA: Sage.

Wing, A. K. (2000). *Global critical race feminism: An international reader.* New York: New York University Press.

Wylie, A. (2007). The feminism question in science: What does it mean to "do science as a feminist"? In S. N. Hesse-Biber (Ed.), *The handbook of feminist research: Theory and praxis* (pp. 567–577). Thousand Oaks, CA: Sage.

Zinn, M. B., Hondagneu-Sotelo, P., & Messner, M. A. (2008). *Gender through the prism of difference.* New York: Allyn & Bacon.

8

UTILIZATION OF MIXED METHODS FOR TRANSFORMATIVE PURPOSES

◆ Donna M. Mertens, Katrina L. Bledsoe,
Martin Sullivan, and Amy Wilson

Objectives

Specific objectives for this chapter are to

- describe the events based on history, changes in ethical codes, and passage of multilateral human rights declarations that contribute to the rationale for the transformative paradigm;

- discuss the underlying philosophical belief systems of the transformative paradigm and their implications for use of mixed methods approaches to research;

- explain how a transformative perspective can be used to understand and account for culture, power, and social justice in conducting research with diverse populations;

- understand how the use of mixed methods within the transformative paradigm can be used to provide a better understanding of the context in which communities and individuals reside;

- analyze examples of mixed methods studies to determine facets that reflect the use of a transformative paradigm; and

- identify challenges encountered in conducting transformative mixed methods research.

I f a program is designed to increase the diversity of the teaching profession with the ultimate goal of improving achievement for racial or ethnic minority students who are deaf, with additional disabilities, then is a design that focuses on the number and characteristics of teachers recruited and trained sufficient? What would a mixed methods design offer to enhance understanding of the dynamics involved in this complex and challenging scenario? What is the potential for enhancement of understanding if a transformative lens is used to frame the study with the consideration of culture, power, diversity, and social justice as central concerns?

In this chapter, we explore answers to questions about the use of the transformative paradigm as an overarching philosophical framework for addressing such issues in a variety of research contexts, such as teacher preparation, obesity prevention, inclusive education for people with disability, and poverty reduction in Africa. We examine mixed methods research for each of these aforementioned topics by illuminating the underlying assumptions from the transformative paradigm that disrupt commonly held beliefs that stigmatize members of these communities and brings focus to their lived experiences and resilience.

The transformative paradigm builds on the seminal work of Guba and Lincoln (1989, 2005), which explicated the basic belief systems that constitute major worldviews in the research community. Guba and Lincoln contributed to the understanding of how paradigms function in the research world by identifying four fundamental belief systems that define a research paradigm: axiological beliefs about the nature of ethics; ontological beliefs about the nature of reality; epistemological beliefs about the nature of knowledge and the relationship between the knower and that which would be known; and methodological beliefs about the appropriate methods for systematic investigation to yield warrantable assertions. We use these belief systems to explain the meaning of the transformative paradigm and its implications for mixed methods research. Box 8.1 displays communications initiated by Mertens and her graduate students with Lincoln and Denzin; it illustrates how the transformative paradigm fits into the taxonomy of paradigms that appears in Guba and Lincoln (2005). The transformative paradigm is offered as an integrated set of beliefs that is at the same level as the postpositivist and constructivist paradigms and that is commensurate with critical theory and other theories such as feminist (see Hesse-Biber, 2010 [this volume]) and disability rights theories.

BOX 8.1

Paradigms and Theories

For the interested reader, Guba and Lincoln provide detailed analyses of these belief systems for several paradigms: positivism, postpositivism, constructivism, critical theory et al., and participatory. My students and I were perplexed as to why critical theory et al. would be included at the level of paradigm when it is a theory. Hence, we wrote and asked Lincoln and Denzin about this. In personal communication (March 19, 2006), they acknowledged that critical theory et al. is not at the same level as a paradigm. They wrote:

First, with respect to the paradigm-theory distinction: For us, a paradigm is a metaphysics, an integrated philosophical statement which encompasses positions on ontology (what we believe the nature of reality to be), epistemology (what we believe can be known about that reality, how the reality "works," and the best ways for coming-to-know), axiology (the role of values, aesthetics within any inquiry), and teleology (what we believe the ends of inquiries might provide to us by way of knowledge, and what form the ends might take). Paradigms are the overarching cosmological statements to which we subscribe when we engage in research, although there might be other paradigms which we employ or deploy in other realms of our lives, such as faith (a theological paradigm), the law (a judicial paradigm), or simple social description (a demographic paradigm, for instance).

Theories are statements, usually integrated statements, within paradigms that give us some model or format for thinking about a phenomenon. A theory might have one such statement, or many connected statements, but theories describe some aspect of "reality." The reason for collapsing paradigms and theories (besides saving space!) is that theories and paradigms are commensurate; that is, they exhibit resonance, such that theories are nested within and under paradigms. Paradigms do not contain theories which violate the paradigms' cosmological assumptions, and theories do not grow from cosmological assumptions which do not support the theory. Thus, they are related, as "parent" and "child"; that is, paradigms and theories belong in ontological and epistemological and axiological "families." So that is why we have joined them.

◆ Transformative Paradigm

The philosophical assumptions of the transformative paradigm lead to consideration of approaches to research that reflect explicit recognition of values and knowledge of self and community that form a basis for methodological decisions (Mertens, 2009). The transformative paradigm arose partially because researchers and members of marginalized communities expressed dissatisfaction with the dominant research paradigms and practices and because of limitations in the research associated with these paradigms that were articulated by feminists; people of color; indigenous and postcolonial peoples; people with disability; members of the lesbian, gay, bisexual, transsexual, and queer communities; and others who have experienced discrimination and oppression, as well as other advocates for social justice (see Creswell, 2010 [this volume]; Hesse-Biber, 2010).

Of the four belief systems identified by Guba and Lincoln (2005), the axiological assumption takes precedence and serves as a basis for articulating the other three belief systems because the transformative paradigm emerged from the need to be more explicit about how researchers can address issues of social justice. The transformative paradigm's axiological assumption rests on the recognition of power differences and ethical implications that derive from those differences in terms of discrimination, oppression, misrepresentation, and being made to feel and be invisible (marginalized) (Mertens, Holmes, & Harris, 2009). As Brooks (2006) notes,

Racism contributes to local and international racial disparities. These disparities are commonly found throughout virtually all areas of health, education, income, imprisonment, and the like. Given the magnitude of the gaping racial disparities both within and between nations, the question needs to be asked: Why is it those who implement societal programs seeking to reduce today's racial disparities generally fail to include serious investigations of racism as a potential contributor to such disparities?

Brooks (2006) limits her concerns to racism, yet there are many bases for discrimination and oppression, such as sexism, classism, able-ism, and others that are used as barriers to accessing privilege in society. People are born into circumstances that are associated with a greater or lesser probability of access to privilege, whether that is on the basis of physical, economic, social, historical, or other factors. The transformative paradigm offers a broad scope with regard to dimensions of diversity that are related to access to greater or lesser privilege, acknowledging that the relevant dimensions of diversity are contextually dependent and may encompass characteristics and life circumstances such as homelessness, body odor, or being drunk. The transformative paradigm emerged as a way to bring visibility to members of communities who have been pushed to societal margins throughout history and to bring their voices into the world of research in order to enhance social justice.

Given the central focus of the transformative paradigm on issues of social justice, the axiological assumption is key to framing the foundation of the transformative paradigm and provides the basis for the development of the other defining belief systems of this paradigm. The transformative axiological assumption reflects the need for ethical choices in research to include the realization that discrimination and oppression are pervasive and that researchers have a moral responsibility to understand the communities in which they work in order to challenge societal processes that sustain the status quo.

Principles of ethics (respect, beneficence, and justice) are defined in codes such as those that guide ethical review boards. Within this legalistic ethical framework, respect is defined in terms of courtesy and autonomy and is operationalized through the informed consent process. Beneficence is defined in terms of maximizing good outcomes and minimizing harm, without explicit acknowledgement of the furtherance of social justice as a potential benefit for participants. Justice is defined in terms of ensuring that benefits of the research accrue to those who accept the risks involved in participating in the research, again without specific reference to the broader implications for social justice.

Researchers who situate their work in the transformative paradigm value these legalistic definitions of ethical principles; however, their transformative axiological assumption leads them to extend and reframe these principles. Thus, respect includes the critical examination of cultural norms of interaction in diverse communities and across cultural groups. Transformative beneficence is defined in terms of the promotion of human rights and improvement of social justice. An explicit connection is made between the process and outcomes of research and the furtherance of a social justice agenda.

Researchers who work within the transformative paradigm find that there is an intertwining of interests with multilateral organizations and professional associations that share similar values in the promotion of human rights. For example, the United Nations passed the International Convention on the Elimination of All Forms of Racial Discrimination (1969), the Convention on the Elimination of All Forms of Discrimination against Women (1979), Convention on the Rights of the Child (1990), the International Convention of the Protection of the Rights of All Migrant Workers and Members of Their Families (1990), the Declaration of the Rights of Indigenous Peoples, and the Convention on the Rights of Persons with Disabilities (2006). The list of UN declarations reinforces the need for the transformative paradigm to be responsive to violations of human rights associated with relevant dimensions of diversity.

In addition, several professional organizations have revised their codes of ethics to reflect the need to be more culturally aware and responsive, including the American Psychological Association, American Educational Research Association, American

Sociological Association, American Anthropological Association, American Evaluation Association, the International Organization for Cooperation in Evaluation (IOCE), and the International Development Evaluation Association (IDEAS). The *zeitgeist* that surrounds revisions to professional associations' codes of ethics stands in testimony for the need for researchers to be more aware of the implications of the transformative paradigm for their work.

The synergy between the professional associations and multilateral organizations on this topic of human rights is illustrated by the map for the future priorities for evaluation in an international context with an emphasis on human rights, developed by the UN International Children's Emergency Fund's (UNICEF), with the endorsement of IOCE and IDEAS:

> Within a human rights approach, evaluation should focus on the most vulnerable populations to determine whether public policies are designed to ensure that all people enjoy their rights as citizens, whether disparities are eliminated and equity enhanced, and whether democratic approaches have been adopted that include everyone in decision-making processes that affect their interests. (Segone, 2006, p. 12)

This ethical impetus supports the need for a way of thinking about research that focuses on social justice and human rights as a starting point. The need for the transformative paradigm is also evidenced in the headlines of newspapers, scholarly literature, and the voices of those with unequal access to privileges. For example, the HIV/AIDS epidemic presents challenges around the world from Washington, D.C., to parts of Africa. Gang violence is a problem in many parts of the world and is often connected with the trafficking and use of illegal drugs. Indigenous peoples who still suffer from a legacy of oppressive colonialism are more often given prison sentences

instead of preventive social supports when they are found to be associated with such activities. Impaired people, subjected to the medical gaze, re-created as "the disabled," and labeled dangerous or deviant, are either incarcerated in institutions or excluded from the mainstream and generally subjected to regimes of cure, care, or observation.[1]

Scholars write about these headlineworthy problems and the difficulties of addressing them. However, solutions to the problems are elusive. If a transformative lens is brought to such topics and the focus is on human rights and social justice, then researchers can raise questions that are directly relevant to the life experiences and contexts of those whose quality of life is most impacted by inequality, discrimination, and oppression. Chilisa (2005, 2009) has used a transformative lens to shape research in Botswana; Battiste (2000) offers ideas for Native American Indians; Cram (2009) and Smith (2005) provide insights into working with the Maori people in New Zealand; Wilson (2005) introduced a paradigm shift for international development researchers in the field of deafness and disability; Bledsoe and Hopson (2009; Bledsoe, 2007) developed transformative research frameworks for working in African American communities; and Sullivan (2009) suggests ways of working creatively and ethically with people with disability.

Sullivan (2009) documented the paradigm shift that began in the early 1970s in the understanding of disability with the development of the social model in opposition to the hegemonic individual medical model of disability. The former locates disability in social structures and attitudes whereas the latter locates disability in individuals (Oliver, 1990; Union of the Physically Impaired Against Segregation, 1976). From this perspective, disability is no longer a personal tragedy but a basis for social oppression. Furthermore, what counts as disability research is no longer the cause and cure of disability in individuals, but the uncovering and transformation of the disabling society and institutionalized disablism. In short, disability research has become a matter of human rights and social justice. Thus, the transformative paradigm for research is viewed as being commensurate with this shift in the model of disability from a medical problem that needs to be fixed to a sociocultural basis for oppression.

The use of disability rights as a theoretical lens is one illustration of the theoretical frameworks that are commensurate with research conducted within the transformative paradigm. Others include, but are not limited to, feminist theory, critical theory, critical race theory, and queer theory. Feminist researchers who link feminist standpoint with mixed methods research include Hollingsworth (2004), Hesse-Biber and Leavy (2007), and Stewart and Cole (2007). Sweetman, Badiee, and Creswell (2009) cite the following illustrative examples of using a feminist lens with mixed methods research conducted within the transformative paradigm: Cartwright, Schow, and Herrera 's (2006) study advocating for poor Hispanic female immigrants; Tolman and Szalacha's (1999) study of girls in high school; Hollingsworth's (2004) study of custody cases involving older women with children; and Shapiro, Setterlund, and Cragg's (2003) study of policy related to drug use with regard to the experiences of older women. Sweetman et al. also identified transformative mixed methods studies that focused on people with disability (Boland, Daly, & Staines, 2008), families facing eviction (Hill, Dillane, Bannister, & Scott, 2002), feminist-based family therapy (Freeman, 2000), drug users (Kumar et al., 2000), people of low socioeconomic class (Newman & Wyly, 2006), and couples with children (Nordenmark & Nyman, 2003).

The axiological assumption provides grounding for the other belief systems (ontology, epistemology, and methodology) that constitute a unified worldview. Recall that the ontological assumption is used as a basis for answering the question: what is

the nature of reality? The transformative ontological assumption rejects cultural relativism and recognizes the influence of privilege in determining what is accepted as real and the consequences of accepting one version of reality over another (Mertens, 2010). Versions of reality are socially constructed and shaped by a variety of factors, including social, political, cultural, economic, ethnic, gender, disability, or other cultural lenses. However, "Truths are not relative. What are relative are opinions about truth" (Nicolás Gómez Dávila, 2005). There are versions of truth that are harmful for groups who are characterized in negative terms and stereotypes by those with power (e.g., deaf people are immature and impulsive; "welfare moms" have babies to get more money). When these versions of truth (often based on stereotypes, prejudices, and biases) are interrogated through a transformative lens, they can be rejected as having no truth value.

The transformative paradigm recognizes the danger of accepting multiple socially constructed realities as having equal legitimacy. Damage is done when differences of perceptions of what is real are accepted, and when factors are ignored that give privilege to one version of reality over another, such as the influence of social, political, cultural, economic, ethnic, gender, and disability lenses in the construction of reality. In addition, the transformative ontological belief emphasizes that which seems "real" may instead be reified structures that are taken to be real because of historical situations. Thus, what is taken to be real, needs to be critically examined via an ideological critique of its role in perpetuating oppressive social structures and policies.

The transformative axiological and ontological assumptions lead to the epistemological assumption that the relationship between researchers and participants is a critical determinant in achieving an understanding of valid knowledge within a transformative context. Therefore, the nature of the relationship is characterized by close collaboration between researchers and participants with specific attention given to issues of communication and power. Christians (2005) criticized the notion that a "morally neutral, objective observer will get the facts right" (p. 148). Hence, implications from the axiological assumption surface in the epistemological assumption in that ethical ways of knowing must be cognizant of power relations associated with gender, sexual orientation, class, ethnicity, race, nationality, disability, and other dimensions of diversity. These inequities in power relations lead to the epistemological assumption in the transformative paradigm that "understanding the culture and building trust are deemed to be paramount" (Mertens, 2009, p. 57).

The transformative methodological assumption reflects the three previously discussed assumptions and leads to support for mixed methods approaches.

> Inclusion of a qualitative dimension in methodological assumptions is critical in transformative research and evaluation as a point of establishing a dialogue between the researchers and the community members. Mixed methods designs can be considered to address the informational needs of the community. However, the methodological decisions are made with a conscious awareness of contextual and historical factors, especially as they relate to discrimination and oppression. Thus the formation of partnerships with researchers and the community is an important step in addressing methodological questions in research. (Mertens, 2009, p. 59)

Methodologically, the transformative paradigm reframes the researcher's worldview in terms of establishing the focus of the research, development of research questions, and decisions about data collection, analysis, interpretation, and use. The examples of mixed methods research that follow in this chapter illustrate a variety of design options in mixed methods that are grounded in the transformative paradigm.

◆ Transformative Mixed Methods Designs

Researchers who situate themselves within the transformative worldview do not necessarily use mixed methods (Mertens & Ginsberg, 2008, 2009). However, mixed methods research that is reflective of the transformative paradigm is identified by adherence to a social justice agenda; explicit acknowledgment of factors that are culturally based in the definition of what is perceived to be real; recognition and challenging of power differences in relationships in the research context and wider society; and the need to develop methodological approaches that are responsive to the aforementioned complexities. A transformative model for mixed methods research suggests the need for community involvement, as well as the cyclical use of data to inform decisions for next steps, whether those steps related to additional research or to program changes (Mertens, 2007, 2009).

Some, but not all, researchers whose work exemplifies the transformative belief systems explicitly identify the transformative paradigm as their worldview (Mertens, 2009; Sweetman et al., 2009). Yet, it is possible to analyze mixed methods research in terms of the underlying belief systems and examine those studies that do illustrate the transformative mixed methods approach. Hence, the remainder of this chapter provides examples of a variety of mixed methods designs with illustrations drawn from the authors' research studies as well as relevant literature. We present these examples to illustrate how the transformative paradigm plays out in mixed methods research with a goal of enhancing readers' understandings of how to conduct similar research. The examples were chosen to reflect options for mixed methods designs, such as the sequential and concurrent designs (see Creswell, 2009; Mertens, 2010; and Teddlie and Tashakkori, 2009; for more on mixed methods designs).

TRANSFORMATIVE SEQUENTIAL DESIGNS

A transformative sequential design is one in which researchers ground their work in the transformative paradigm's belief systems and then use quantitative methods first, followed by qualitative methods or the converse (qualitative methods followed by quantitative methods). We present examples of this approach taken from teacher preparation, obesity prevention programs, inclusive education for disabled people in New Zealand, and poverty reduction in Rwanda.

Teacher Preparation

The scenario that appeared at the beginning of this chapter is based on an evaluation of a teacher preparation project that was conducted at Gallaudet University's Department of Education (Mertens, 2008; Mertens, Holmes, Harris, & Brandt, 2007). Gallaudet is the only university in the world with the specific mission of providing higher education for deaf people and for hearing people who intend to work with the deaf population. Gallaudet's Department of Education obtained a grant from the U.S. Department of Education to recruit and train students of color and students who were deaf or hard of hearing to prepare teachers for students who are deaf or hard of hearing and who have an additional disability. The program director contacted Mertens and indicated that the project was coming to an end and that they were contractually obligated to conduct a summative evaluation.

Using a transformative lens, Mertens questioned the director about the history of the project and its current status, as well as requested documents such as the request for proposals, the proposal submitted to the U.S. Department of Education, and the annual reports that the project had submitted. Thus, the evaluation began with qualitative data collection strategies of interviewing and document review. Based on analysis of these data, Mertens decided to invite members of the deaf community to join her as co-evaluators, deliberately selecting individuals who reflected important dimensions of diversity in the deaf community. Diversity considerations of relevance to deaf community include a person's choice of language (signed or spoken; American Sign Language or Pidgin Signed English) and use of assistive listening technology (such as hearing aids or cochlear implants). Two of the co-evaluators were culturally deaf, meaning that they used American Sign Language and did not speak while they were signing. One of the co-evaluators was a deaf woman who was raised orally (i.e., she used supportive technology to capitalize on her residual hearing, read lips, and spoke English.) At the time of the study, she used a cochlear implant to enhance her hearing.

As a team, Mertens and colleagues reviewed the documents and discussed how to approach the study. Graduates of the program were scheduled to attend a reflective seminar the following month; we agreed this would be a good venue for data collection. We observed the seminar proceedings for 2 days, taking careful field notes, and comparing our notes at the end of each day. On the third day, with agreement of the seminar coordinator, we interviewed all of the participants, using questions that were based on our observations and document reviews. Several issues of social justice surfaced from our preliminary data collections and analyses, and we used the interviews to explore these further. For example, the issue of marginalization of teachers who teach students with multiple disabilities, as well as the marginalization of the students themselves, was noted in our field notes of interviews with program graduates in May 2007:

- I feel teachers in the mainstream resist our students, especially students with multiple disabilities.

- It's almost like multiple disabilities/ special needs section is totally separate, an island opposed to the regular deaf school. I hate the separation. I've worked there 2 years, and many teachers at the regular deaf school building look at me as if I'm a visitor. When I tell them I've been teaching here for 2 years, they look at me in awe.

In addition, the field notes and interviews revealed concerns about how to address the diversity within the population of deaf and hard of hearing students with multiple disabilities in terms of:

- diverse home languages (e.g., Spanish, Arabic);

- diagnosing and teaching disability groups other than those with severe disabilities (e.g., learning disabilities, autism);

- multiple communication modes used in their classrooms; and

- diverse settings and teacher's roles.

Mertens and colleagues pursued these issues in the May 2007 interviews with program graduates, which yielded such comments as:

- When the home language is Spanish and the kid has very limited language and no sign, no English. Now I have a student who is deaf with another disability from another country.

- My students are under 5 years old, and they come with zero language and their behavior is awful. They can't sit for even a minute. Kids come with temper tantrums and run out of the school building. I have to teach these kids language;

I see them start to learn to behave and interact with others. My biggest challenge is seeing three kids run out of school at the same time. Which one do I run after? One kid got into the storm drain. I'm only one teacher, and I have an assistant, but that means there is still one kid we can't chase after at the same time as the other two.

We then used the data from the qualitative part of the study to construct a Web-based quantitative survey, which was sent to all the program graduates. This gave us access to a broader base of participants to determine if the issues, attitudes, and concerns expressed by those in attendance at the seminar were shared by other program graduates. The quantitative data confirmed the concerns that were raised by the seminar participants: that they felt marginalized as teachers and they needed more support for dealing with the diversity of their students.

The final cycle of data collection involved preparing interview questions for the university faculty who participated in the program and the cooperating school administrators and teachers. The interview questions were based on the data that were collected from program graduates and were designed to present the findings to the faculty and school staff members in order to determine their thoughts about these challenges. For example, the final quote from the teacher about the students who run out of the classroom was used to inquire about the need for additional preparation and/or support for the new teachers. Mertens and Holmes (2008) made a presentation of these results to an audience of faculty from 70 different universities in the United States and Canada that have programs to prepare teachers of the deaf and hard of hearing. The presentation was followed by lively discussion about the challenges involved in this type of teacher preparation and the need to give attention to the multiple-disability students that are increasingly attending mainstream schools. The Gallaudet Department of Education set up an online mentoring system for new program graduates, which was so popular that they opened it up to all teacher candidates in the department, not just those in the multiple disabilities program.

Adolescent Obesity Prevention

Bledsoe (2005) evaluated a program designed to address adolescent obesity in a Trenton, New Jersey, high school. The program was a response to what the faculty and administration recognized as a growing problem among adolescents within the school community: that black and Latino high school students were at a higher risk for obesity than the national average.

Teachers and administrators worked to conceptualize the program, informally known as the Obesity Project Study (TOPS), to combat the growing number of overweight students (Bledsoe, 2005). TOPS was considered part of a larger agenda to provide information and actionable strategies focused on health and well-being for high school students and their families and the Trenton community at large. The desire of the faculty and administration to have an evidenced-base intervention led them to seek collaboration with the city's local liberal arts college.

The evaluation addressed two objectives:

• To understand the needs and challenges of an increasingly diverse community by providing scientific evidence of an associative link between cultural identity (how one identifies with their culture) and physical health behavior outcomes

• To make sure that the health promotion program not only educated, but also addressed the dynamics (e.g., attitudes and behaviors) that encourage and discourage healthy nutrition behavior

To address these objectives, the program consisted of three components: (1) physical (teaching students to exercise regularly), (2) psychological (encouraging students to understand their eating habits), and (3) educational (teaching students to make healthy food and eating choices). Initial evaluation activities focused on gathering information that would inform the design of the program and the strategies to accurately assess the effectiveness of the intervention within the cultural context.

Despite the good intentions of school officials, there was a tremendous gap between the program developers and researchers, on the one hand, and the student body population. Most, if not all, researchers and school officials were white (except for Bledsoe, the lead evaluator, who is African American), were middle to upper-middle class, and were not living within the city's limits. The program consumers and research participants were students of color, living in a city with a median income of $36,000, and considered impoverished and underserved. It became clear to the research team that views of nutrition, health, and obesity were influenced by power and privilege: those in the most powerful positions making decisions and determining lifestyle choices for those in less powerful positions.

For example, many of the assumptions concerning the rationale behind perceived high rates of obesity among urban high school students were based on high-level stakeholders' (e.g., teachers, researchers, community partners) theory that was loosely informed by the literature. This "theory" emphasized an individual deficit model anchored by variables such as low self-esteem, poverty, and educational deficiency. The research team sought to close the gap in the power structure by engaging in more qualitative (in addition to quantitative) and/or unusual methods that would help provide an understanding of the students and the community in which they resided (Mertens, 2007).

The first approach of the evaluation team was to meet with students regularly via the use of focus groups. These focus groups were used to gather information about the kind of intervention to which student participants would respond. The group discussions served two purposes. First, they served to connect the evaluation team (made up of college-age research assistants) to the students. Second, they served to provide needed context of any possible intervention design and future evaluation strategies. These groups were used throughout the project to bring the student voice into the planning of the program, as well as the evaluation process.

A second approach was to gather baseline data via survey from the students and their teachers, families, and the general environment. The team, with feedback from the students, designed surveys (students provided feedback on the wording of questions and the general concepts that should be covered) for students, parents, and teachers. The team also conducted a site mapping of the city to identify the environmental and community factors that encouraged or discouraged unhealthy eating patterns.

The third approach, based on the results obtained from the focus groups, surveys, and site mapping, involved the evaluation team meeting regularly with faculty, staff, and administration. These meetings served as a conduit to present information obtained from student, teacher, and parent surveys. As information from key consumers and participants was brought to light, the composition of the program collaborators changed. Instead of private and local general medical practitioners, new collaborators, such as a municipal land use group, a community environmental housing development organization, and the department of health were included. In addition, the evaluation team brought on an urban planner who used Geographical Information Systems to provide a Web-based mapping of the city's eateries and grocery and convenience stores.

By using the transformative paradigm, the team was able to diminish the power differential by fostering regular dialogue with students, teachers, and staff members in every planning aspect. In this case, using focus groups first and then using quantitative methods allowed for the creation of a bond with the students who began to feel (a) that they had some control over what they would be asked to disclose and in what manner and (b) that they had ownership in the development of the program and research (Bledsoe & Hopson, 2009). Finally, this approach allowed for a more accurate understanding of health and well-being in the city in a collective and community-based manner, as opposed to a deficit model of human imperfection and blame (Bledsoe & Hopson, 2009).

Disability Studies in New Zealand

A good example of disability research in New Zealand using mixed methods is Alison Kearney's (2009) research into the exclusion of disabled children from and within their neighborhood schools, despite legislation guaranteeing their right to inclusion. In this research, Kearney sets out to explore the nature of this exclusion to provide some answers as to why this was happening and to make recommendations that may reduce this exclusion. She developed a three-phase mixed methods study: Phase 1 involved an online questionnaire for parents whose children had experienced barriers, followed by a semistructured interview with a random stratified sample of these parents; Phase 2 involved a postal questionnaire to principals in three regions of New Zealand, followed by a semistructured interview with a sample of these principals; Phase 3 involved interviews with teachers in one school and a focus group interview with a group of teacher aides in the school. Kearney concludes her study with some powerful and compelling recommendations to (a) schools on how they might reduce and eliminate the exclusion of disabled students and (b) to government and government agencies on how they might develop truly inclusive education in New Zealand.

Although Kearney does not claim this research to be within the transformative paradigm, it clearly fits within it. The exclusion of disabled people from schools constitutes a violation of their human and legal rights; the need to rectify this situation is a matter of social justice—not just for the individuals involved but for their families and *whanau* (extended family) as well. A genuinely inclusive education system will result in the transformation of the lives not only of the disabled students involved but of all students who must learn to work with and within a community in which difference and diversity is a valued given.

International Development and Health Services in Zambia

Mbwili-Muleya, Lungu, Kabuba, Zulu Lishandu, and Loewenson (2008) used a transformative, sequential mixed methods design to investigate the effectiveness of a health intervention program in Zambia over a 3-year period. As demonstrated in other transformative studies, one of the most important considerations centered on relational issues between service providers and recipients that challenged effective service delivery. They described their research approach as follows:

The design was an intervention study using the spiral model concept of participating, reflecting, and acting by the targeted groups in an iterative manner (Loewenson et al., 2006). Identification of issues and areas targeted for change and baseline data on these change areas were collected through qualitative techniques— focus group discussions (FGDs) and participatory tools—during an orientation workshop. This was followed by an implementation phase of the activities that were planned during the workshop on planning and budgeting at the participating health centres. Regular review meetings were held to reflect on the activities and outputs achieved, followed by

the further action identified to be necessary. A pre and post intervention questionnaire was administered to assess change in the new HCs [Health Committee] involved. (p. 5)

Mbwili-Muleya et al. (2008) found that pre-post test questionnaires allowed them to document that the health intervention program was successful. More important, they reported that the participatory action research process demystified and removed suspicions between stakeholders, strengthened dialogue between communities and health workers, and increased the community involvement in planning and in resolving community issues, increasing the efficacy of the program.

TRANSFORMATIVE PARALLEL DESIGN FOR MIXED METHODS

A transformative parallel design involves the use of both quantitative and qualitative methods at essentially the same time during the study. In this section, we use examples of this mixed methods approach from an evaluation of a crime prevention program, a study on spinal cord injury, and a study on an international development poverty reduction program.

The Peace Campaign Crime Prevention Program

Bledsoe (2001) evaluated an East Los Angeles community's efforts to reduce bullying and intimidation in school and in the community. The Peace Campaign was a response to a growing situation in which school-age children in the East Los Angeles community were being bullied and intimidated into giving up material goods and property and were also being "jumped" or forced into early gang membership and violence (Bledsoe, 2001). The program was a collaborative effort, with the school administration, parents, a local community service organization, and the Los Angeles Police Department (LAPD), designed to provide services that focus on the bullies and intimidators, as well as the bullied and intimidated, and the parents and community members who were at a loss about how to deal with the situation. Services included providing communication skills training for parents and children, as well as sponsoring activities that encouraged students to project their energies toward more fruitful avenues such as sports, academics, and the arts.

The evaluation team was asked to help determine the extent of bullying and intimidation within the community and to evaluate the effectiveness of the campaign. The team used focus groups and interviews of key constituents, as well as surveys, to help provide a well-rounded understanding of (a) the extent to which students were being bullied and engaging in bullying and intimidation; (b) the community's general context, which served both to protect and to place at risk children and their families; and (c) appropriate strategies to address the situation.

Members of each stakeholder group were asked to participate in either a survey or focus group. The choice of method was determined by the participants and their perceived comfort level, and survey and focus group data were combined to give a comprehensive picture. The team felt that this approach—to provide participants a choice of the measures in which they would like to participate—would result in more accurate data collection (Mertens, 2007).

Several perspectives emerged from the use of qualitative and quantitative measures. First, the team discovered that part of the problem was exacerbated by aspects such as culture (bullying and intimidation were considered an extension of the artifact of *machismo,* a characteristic considered indicative of manhood within the immigrant Latino community), socioeconomic status (the community was of low socioeconomic status, and employment was temporary or consisted of low-level service

profession jobs), and community population (the community had a high percentage of monolingual, Spanish-only immigrants who had recently come to the East Los Angeles area with little knowledge of the surrounding city).

Participants noted that increasing daily communication and improving communication skills between students and parents seemed to reduce bullying and intimidation. The increase in communication seemed not only to help students develop strategies that could keep them safe from bullying but also to lessen the use of bullying techniques.

In addition, data from student-level focus groups indicated that students felt they had outlets and support from many sources, not just one. Their data, as well as data from parents, teachers, the LAPD, and other key constituents, found that bullying and intimidation was not a family issue or a school issue. It was a community issue and the problem needed to be addressed using a community-based perspective, rather than using an individual deficit model (Bledsoe, 2001). Thus, the community program designers included aspects in which the LAPD and other community members were active as a community in their response to potentially violent situations, developed partnership-like interactions, and sponsored community-building activities. The transformative perspective also allowed for the consideration of the close relationship between the researcher and participants, the values of the community, and the general context in which participants resided (Bledsoe, 2001).

Spinal Cord Injury Research in New Zealand

Sullivan and colleagues (2007) are currently undertaking research in New Zealand on the first 2 years of spinal cord injury (SCI) and the transition from spinal unit to community. Anecdotal evidence suggests that many people with SCI in New Zealand waste their lives away existing on accident compensation, once they leave the spinal unit[2]. To test this, the *SCI: The First Two Years* longitudinal study was designed to find out what actually happened to people with SCI, once they left the spinal unit. Funding was obtained from the New Zealand Health Research Council (New Zealand HRC) and the 4-year study began in August 2007. This study is nationwide and includes both tetraplegics and paraplegics.

The aims of the research are (a) to explore how the interrelationship(s) of body, self, and society have shaped the life chances, life choices, and subjectivity of a cohort of people with SCI; and (b) to investigate how entitlement to rehabilitation and compensation through the Accident Compensation Commission (ACC) affects socioeconomic and health outcomes. All new SCI-people with neurological damage to their spinal cord, but without serious cognitive injury, admitted to one of New Zealand's two spinal units will be eligible to participate if they are New Zealand citizens or permanent residents aged between 16 and 65.

At the beginning of research design, Sullivan and colleagues consulted with the directors of the spinal units to seek their permission and support for the research. They then entered a partnership arrangement with the consumer groups at each of the spinal units: the Association of Spinal Concerns (TASC) at Auckland and the Burwood Academy of Independent Living (BAIL) at Christchurch. In close consultation with these groups, the study was designed and questionnaires developed. To ensure the research was culturally sensitive and in line with the Treaty of Waitangi principles,[3] a representative from Ranga Hauora, Maori Health Services, Burwood Hospital, took part in these discussions. The final proposal was also scrutinized by the Ngai Tahu Research Consultation Committee (the local tribal authority for research in the Christchurch area) and the Maori Health Research Unit of the Counties-Manukau District Health Board

(which has tribal authority over research located in the Auckland area).

The research uses a transformative parallel design using quantitative and qualitative methods concurrently. Quantitative material will be collected in three structured interviews with all participants recruited over a 2-year period. The first interview is at 4 months following SCI. This is a face-to-face interview undertaken by the trained on-site interviewers (who themselves have an SCI) prior to participants' discharge from the spinal unit. The second and third structured follow-up interviews will be undertaken by telephone at 12 and 24 months after SCI. The timing of these interviews complies with international recommendations for follow-up times in injury outcome studies (van Beeck et al., 2007). These three structured interviews are designed to collect factual evidence on the "what" of the world SCI people inhabit: their life chances, attitudes, health status, support services, work and income, personal and social relationships, and life satisfaction, as this constitutes the framework in which they create their subjectivity. Two qualitative, face-to-face interviews with a subsample of 20 participants explore in greater depth the meanings participants now attach to these phenomena and how these phenomena and meanings are shaping their life choices and subjectivity. On the advice of BAIL and TASC, these qualitative interviews will be held at 6 and 18 months after discharge from the spinal units for specific reasons. At 6 months, the person ought to be settled in at home with alterations complete and the necessary personal supports in place to be thinking about venturing out into the broader world if he or she has not already done so. At 18 months, any neurological recovery that is going to occur will have occurred and the person will be thinking "so this is it for the rest of my life." Inferences derived from facts and personal perspectives will be triangulated to enrich understandings of what actually happens to SCI people in the first 2 years post-injury.

In summer 2009, recruitment is continuing, and the second round of quantitative interviews is being conducted. A different questionnaire is being used, which while repeating a number of questions from the first interview, includes a new set of questions on issues such as what has changed for participants since the first interview and their use and satisfaction with support services generally and with personal careers and ACC in particular. These later questions are yielding some interesting data, which will be followed up in-depth in the second qualitative interview.

This exemplifies the beauty of using mixed methods within a transformative paradigm. The quantitative data provide the raw numbers, which are processed into the frequency tables that constitute the skeleton of what happens to SCI people as they transition from spinal unit to community. A skeleton, while providing a useful model, does not provide the how, the why, or the "where to from here" detail necessary for transforming lives. Quantitative data are useful for promoting policy change, but the qualitative data, the subjective meanings of the individuals concerned, reveal the appropriate color, texture, and direction of that policy if it is to transform the lives of the target population on the ground.

While seeking and obtaining transformation at the macro policy level is very important, what happens to individuals on the ground provides the "proof of the (policy) pudding." At this stage of the research, participants are so newly paralyzed that most of their energy is directed at their personal situation of learning to live in new bodies and new lives. Notwithstanding, we have had a high response rate to this study, as most want to contribute their experience in order to improve or transform the lot of all people with SCI. In terms of the study having a transformative effect on the immediate lives of participants, to date, this has been achieved in two ways.

First, one of the key aims of the study was to involve newly paralyzed people as part of

the research team.[4] To this end, a number of people with SCI were recruited through TASC and BAIL, trained in research and interviewing techniques, and included as paid members of the team to recruit and carry out the quantitative interviews. They will also be used in the analysis of data.

Second, at a more prosaic level, the research is transformative insofar as it provides the opportunity for those newly paralyzed participants in the qualitative side of the study with the opportunity to speak confidentially with someone with at least 30 years experience of living successfully with SCI.

In summary, the transformative paradigm uses mixed methods to bring about social justice for minority groups by researching with them their conditions of existence and deconstructing these so that they can eliminate barriers and build better lives for themselves. Participants in the *SCI: The First Two Years* study are motivated by the desire to move beyond anecdote and find out what actually happens to people with SCI once they leave the spinal unit. Has this population been adequately prepared to manage living productively with SCI in their communities? If not, what might be done better or differently, what might be added to or eliminated from the rehabilitation programs in the spinal units? Is this population getting the ongoing supports necessary for living in the community? If so, is there room for improvement? If not, why not? How can this be rectified? Only when we have the answers to these questions will we be in a position to know if and what barriers impede SCI New Zealanders from reaching their full potential in terms of living productive and fulfilling lives.

International Development and Poverty

The United Nations' Millennium Development Goals (MDGs) place emphasis on and expectation of results from organizations delivering development assistance to communities in poor countries. Impact assessments have traditionally been used to report movement toward the MDGs, but quantitative data does not always accurately reflect what is observed on the ground, nor offer practical recommendations for improving practice. When specifically studying poverty itself, quantitative measures have not been able to accurately capture the dynamics of poverty and why it occurs (Addison, Hulme, & Kanbur, 2008). Howe and McKay (2007) found in Rwanda that using quantitative measures limited their understanding of chronic poverty (poverty that lasts over a long period of time) and that these measures were ineffective in discovering the factors and processes that caused it. Historically, random sample household surveys and structured interviews were commonly used and then analyzed using statistical techniques to describe the demographics of poverty, but the qualitative dimension necessary to answer the why and how questions about chronic poverty were missing.

For the past 15 years, the World Bank has included a Participatory Poverty Assessment (PPA) in poverty measurement and assessment, employing purposive sampling and semistructured and interactive interviews to collect data related to "people's judgments, attitudes, preferences, priorities, and/or perceptions about a subject—and analyzes it usually through sociological or anthropological research techniques" (Carvalho & White, 1997, p. 1). (See Bamberger, Rao, & Woolcock, 2010 [this volume] for more details on mixed methods research conducted by the World Bank.)

PPA, designed by the World Bank in the mid-90s, includes poor people in the process of analyzing poverty and in creating strategies for influencing national policy (Norton, Bird, Brock, Kakande, & Turk, 2001). PPA uses a variety of participatory tools and activities that encourage information sharing, analysis, and action. PPAs are usually done in a community with collaboration of representatives from universities, nongovernment organizations (NGOs), government officials, or local development agencies. During many PPAs, the stakeholders develop community action plans, which are later supported by local governments or development organizations.

To study chronic poverty, researchers use a "Q-squared" approach (quantitative + qualitative sources) where economic factors found in government household surveys are analyzed simultaneously with well-being and quality of life factors found in the PPAs (Addison et al. 2008). For example, in Rwanda (Howe & McKay, 2007), household surveys (Q1) described the assets owned by poor families, their living conditions, their annual income, and consumption over time. The addition of qualitative methods (Q2) allowed for a clearer understanding of the "extent, pattern, and nature of chronic poverty" because measures such as human development and well-being gave deeper insight into factors overlooked by Q1. The results of the Q-squared approach, shared with all stakeholders, gave the Rwandan participants a better understanding of their poverty, a tool to use for social mobilization, and the ability to identify factors that affect their welfare at the household level. Supplemental qualitative methods in studying chronic poverty have been critical to attain social justice for the poor who are typically marginalized because of lack of access and exclusion.

International Development and Mixed Methods

International organizations send billions of dollars in development aid to economically poor countries for development programs targeted to better the lives of people living in poverty. External experts routinely monitor and evaluate programs using single-method approaches to measure the effectiveness/efficiency of projects and to discern whether accountability demands of donor agencies are being met (Mayoux &

Mosedale, 2005). Development research institutes have noted many development projects are unsustainable and make minimal impact on improving communities. Debates have emerged about the cost/benefit of the impact assessments as they take considerable time and resources away from the development programs. Questions have arisen concerning the validity of assessments that measure the economic impact of projects but ignore the multidimensionality of poverty and the social, political, and cultural factors that also influence economics (Mayoux & Chambers, 2005). Exclusively measuring "development" through an economic lens is insufficient in designing policies to truly make a positive impact on poor people's well-being (Cobb, 2002). Poor populations and minority groups have been nearly voiceless in the evaluation process and excluded from participating in making decisions and policies on their own behalf (Turk, 1999). Rather than assessments that "proved impacts" and held limited practical relevance to the beneficiaries, development organizations and stakeholders have requested assessments that aid them in "improving their practice" (Hulme, 2000).

Researchers conducting development studies now recognize that their work is improved when they use qualitative participatory assessment tools in which stakeholders participate fully in the evaluation and consequently learn about their needs and opportunities (Hulme, 2007). Participatory techniques include case studies, participant observation, focus groups, semistructured interviews with key informants, and Participatory Learning and Actions where program stakeholders participate in the study in a variety of ways (drawing resource maps, developing timelines, ranking their well-being, prioritizing challenges to resolve, or sketching seasonal diagrams). Participatory activities raise the stakeholders' awareness of their right to a voice in the evaluation process and inform and empower them to take actions they can make to improve their program.

Currently, it is difficult to locate development studies using mixed methods that share the study's results with all stakeholders (other than PPA—see below). Many researchers have wholeheartedly embraced Chambers (1997) and Narayan's (1996) call for a more inclusive, qualitative methodology of putting the "first last" and the "last first." Some practitioners work with stakeholders to create knowledge that is socially useful and contributes to advocating for the attainment of human rights using qualitative means, yet they omit using quantitative tools. Wilson and Kakiri (2005) used case studies, focus groups, and individual interviews to learn what development assistance deaf beneficiaries desired from their Kenyan government and foreign NGOs. The results of the study were used by the deaf community to obtain government funding for several national and international activities; the study also was a tool to identify their needs when discussing policy with their government ministries, yet no quantitative data collection tools were used in the study.

Other development studies that use mixed methods tend not to be transformative, as the resulting data are not shared with the stakeholders. Hulme (1999) studied 13 Microfinance Institutions in East Africa to understand why individuals dropped out of these small business programs meant to bring income into homes of the moderately poor. Quantitative data were collected and analyzed from computerized dropout records as well as spreadsheets detailing each individual's account statements. About 1,400 people were interviewed, from bank employers who made loans to those who borrowed money. Results show banks tended to adhere to strict bank policies that did not fit the clients' needs, which varied according to:

> seasons, stage of life, means of gaining a livelihood and a host of contingencies. Clients need loans for emergency medical and health bills, savings to pay

school fees, insurance in case of the death of an adult income earner, a mortgage to build a house, a savings plan so they have a small retirement income, and many, many other needs. (Hulme, 1999, p. ii)

Qualitative methods have the express purpose of empowering the beneficiaries, yet similar to other final reports using mixed methods in development, this study makes no mention of sharing results with stakeholders.

◆ Conclusions

The work discussed in this chapter highlights the use of mixed methods research methodology within a transformative framework. In particular, the authors demonstrate how engaging with communities that are often marginalized has produced powerful results for the questions and issues of interest to those communities.

In addition, the transformative paradigm allows for the inclusion of important contextual factors such as social justice (or lack thereof), power, and oppression to be addressed in (a) the type of questions asked; (b) the types of designs used; (c) the manner in which those designs are used; and (d) the kind of information that can be gathered that can both benefit and accurately represent the cultural communities. This chapter discusses issues in conducting transformative mixed methods research that can be used to expand on and complement earlier work. It also brings to visibility domains of social inquiry in which transformative mixed methods can be fruitfully applied, such as participatory action research, dissertation research, program evaluation, and international development. Framing research with philosophical components from the transformative paradigm allows the researcher to focus on how that perspective plays out in mixed methods research. Such a focus should help others decide how to conduct similar research.

Research Questions and Exercises

1. Analyze one of the examples in this chapter in terms of the philosophical assumptions of the transformative paradigm. Present evidence from the study that supports the claim that it is reflective of the transformative belief systems.

2. Visit the U.S. Agency for International Development's Web page, "Telling Our Story" (http://www.usaid.gov/stories/index.html), and read examples of development assistance projects the U.S. supports worldwide. Select one project and list all of the stakeholders you think should participate in an evaluation of the project and why. What kinds of supports might be necessary to involve the stakeholders in appropriate ways?

3. Howe and McKay (2007) used qualitative methods, such as focus groups, to understand the "extent, pattern, and nature of chronic poverty" in Rwanda. What information do you imagine they were able to gather from focus group discussions that they were unable to capture using quantitative methods? How could this imagined collected data be used by poor people themselves?

4. Visit the United Nation's Web page, "About the Millennium Development Goals" (http://www.undp.org/mdg/basics.shtml), and select one of the eight goals. Describe the measures (indicators) the United Nations uses to measure achievement of that goal. Derive implications for mixed methods research based on your review of these documents.

5. How did the qualitative data enhance quantitative data in Bledsoe's (2001, 2005) evaluation of the obesity program or the peace campaign program? By using the transformative paradigm in her work with the high school obesity prevention program, what does Bledsoe feel she accomplishes with the participants?

6. What are the transformative elements of Sullivan et al.'s (2007) research in the SCI community?

7. What are the challenges of using transformative mixed methods in the context in which you conduct your own research?

◆ Notes

1. As when living in group homes owned by an agency contracted by the state to provide accommodation and to enforce attendance at life-skills, educational, vocational, and various training programs designed to keep "clients" safely occupied.

2. In 1974, New Zealanders gave up the right to sue for compensation if they incurred injury in an accident. In return, a state-run Accident Compensation Commission (ACC) was established to provide all people in New Zealand 24-hour, no-fault compensation. Compensation includes a cash lump sum, all rehabilitation costs including aids and appliances, any necessary home and workplace alterations, ongoing home care and support, a motor vehicle, and 80% earnings-related compensation (ERC) for the period of rehabilitation (this might be extended for life if one cannot return to work). It is funded from levies on employers, wages, petrol, and motor vehicle registration. If, however, one's SCI is congenital or caused through illness, one is not covered by ACC and must rely on the far less generous and means-tested Invalid Benefit and Ministry of Health Disability Support Services (DSS) for rehabilitation, aides and appliances, and so on.

3. The Treaty of Waitangi is the founding document of New Zealand. It was signed between *iwi* Maori (tribes) and representatives of the British Crown in 1840 and allowed for the annexation and establishment of British law in New Zealand. Maori and English texts of the treaty were circulated throughout New Zealand, with the overwhelming majority of chiefs signing the Maori text. Later-day debates over translation have seen the principles of the treaty—partnership, participation and protection—rather than the actual clauses incorporated in New Zealand law.

4. Martin Sullivan, a paraplegic himself and first researcher on the team, was philosophically committed to including people with SCI on the research team. Happily, this coincided with the Health Research Council of New Zealand (funding body) policy to build research capacity within the disability community and the important tenet of transformative research to include appropriately in the research process people from marginalized communities.

◆ References

Addison, T., Hulme, D., & Kanbur, R. (2008, Spring). *Poverty dynamics: Measurement and understanding from an interdisciplinary perspective*. Retrieved May 13, 2009, from http://www.q-squared.ca/papers52.html

Bamberger, M., Rao, V., & Woolcock, M. (2010). Using mixed methods in monitoring and evaluation: Experiences from international development evaluation. In A. Tashakkori & C. Teddlie (Eds.), *SAGE handbook of mixed methods in social & behavioral research* (2nd ed.). Thousand Oaks, CA: Sage.

Battiste, M. (Ed.). (2000). *Reclaiming indigenous voice and vision.* Vancouver: University of British Columbia Press.

Bledsoe, K. L. (2001, October). One community's efforts to protect its children from a life of violence: What we learned from The Peace Campaign of Highland Park. *The Flame: The Magazine of the Claremont Graduate University, 2*(2), 4–5. Claremont, CA: Claremont Graduate University.

Bledsoe, K. L (2005). Trenton Central High School Obesity Prevention Program: Democracy through inclusion. *Harvard Family Research Project Evaluation Exchange, 9*(3), 17.

Bledsoe, K. L. (2007). Summary of the Fun with Books Program. *American Journal of Evaluation, 28,* 522–524

Bledsoe, K. L., & Hopson, R. H. (2009). Conducting ethical research in underserved communities. In D. M. Mertens & P. Ginsberg (Eds), *Handbook of ethics for research in the social sciences* (pp. 391–406). Thousand Oaks, CA: Sage.

Boland, M., Daly, L., & Staines, A. (2008). Methodological issues in inclusive intellectual disability research: A health promotion needs assessment of people attending Irish disability services. *Journal of Applied Research in Intellectual Disabilities, 21*(3), 199–209.

Brooks, P. (2006, July). *Racism, ethics, and research.* Paper presented at the International Sociological Association World Congress, Durban, South Africa.

Cartwright, E., Schow, D., & Herrera, S. (2006). Using participatory research to build an effective type 2 diabetes intervention: The process of advocacy among female Hispanic farmworkers and their families in southeast Idaho. *Women & Health, 43*(4), 89–109.

Carvalho, S., & White, H. (1997). *Combining the quantitative and qualitative approaches to poverty measurement and analysis approaches to poverty measurement and analysis* (World Bank Technical Paper No. 366). Washington, DC: World Bank.

Chambers, R. (1997). *Whose reality counts? Putting the first last.* London: ITDG.

Chilisa, B. (2005). Educational research within postcolonial Africa: A critique of HIV/AIDS research in Botswana. *International Journal of Qualitative Studies in Education, 18,* 659–684.

Chilisa, B. (2009). Indigenous African-centered ethics: Contesting and complementing dominant models. In D. M. Mertens & P. E. Ginsberg (Eds.), *Handbook of social research ethics* (pp. 407–425). Thousand Oaks, CA: Sage.

Christians, C. (2005). Ethics and politics in qualitative research. In N. K. Denzin & Y. S. Lincoln (Eds.), The *SAGE handbook of qualitative research* (3rd ed., pp. 139–164). Thousand Oaks, CA: Sage.

Cobb, J. (2002, May). *A Buddhist-Christian critique of neo-liberal economics.* Buddhist Eastern Conference, Kyoto, Japan.

Cram, F. (2009). Maintaining indigenous voices. In D. M. Mertens & P. E. Ginsberg (Eds.), *Handbook of social research ethics* (pp. 308–322). Thousand Oaks, CA: Sage.

Creswell, J. W. (2009). *Research design: Qualitative, quantitative, and mixed methods approaches* (3rd ed.). Thousand Oaks, CA: Sage.

Creswell, J. W. (2010). Mapping the developing landscape of mixed methods research. In A. Tashakkori & C. Teddlie (Eds.), *SAGE handbook of mixed methods in social & behavioral research* (2nd ed.). Thousand Oaks, CA: Sage.

Davila, N. G. (2005). *Escolios a Un Texto Implicito: Obra completa.* Bogota: Villegas Editores.

Freeman, M. L. (2000). Incorporating gender issues in practice with the Satir growth model. *Families in Society, 81*(3), 256–268.

Guba, E. G., & Lincoln, Y. S. (1989). *Fourth generation evaluation.* Newbury Park, CA: Sage.

Guba, E. G., & Lincoln, Y. S. (2005). Paradigmatic controversies, contradictions, and emerging confluence. In N. K. Denzin & Y. S. Lincoln (Eds.), *The SAGE handbook of qualitative research* (3rd ed., pp. 191–215). Thousand Oaks, CA: Sage.

Hesse-Biber, S. (2010). Feminist approaches to mixed methods research: Linking theory and praxis. In A. Tashakkori & C. Teddlie (Eds.), *SAGE handbook of mixed methods in social & behavioral research* (2nd ed.). Thousand Oaks, CA: Sage.

Hesse-Biber, S. N., & Leavy, P. (Eds.) (2007). *Feminist research practice.* Thousand Oaks, CA: Sage.

Hill, M., Dillane, J., Bannister, J., & Scott, S. (2002). Everybody needs good neighbours: An evaluation of an intensive project for families facing eviction. *Child & Family Social Work, 7*(2), 79–89.

Hollingsworth, L. D. (2004). Child custody loss among women with persistent severe mental illness. *Social Work Research, 28*(4), 199–209.

Howe, G., & McKay, A. (2007). Combining quantitative and qualitative methods in assessing chronic poverty: The case of Rwanda. *World Development, 35*(2), 197–211.

Hulme, D. (2007, January). *Integrating quantitative and qualitative research for country case studies of development.* Comparative Analysis: Methodological Workshop, Beijing, China.

Hulme, D. (2000). Impact assessment methodologies for microfinance: Theory, experience and better practice. *World Development, 28*(1), 79–88.

Hulme, D. (1999). *Client drop-outs from East African microfinance institutions.* Nairobi, Kenya: MicroSave.

Kearney, A. (2009) *Barriers to school inclusion: An investigation into the exclusion of disabled students from and within New Zealand schools.* Unpublished PhD dissertation in education, Massey University, Palmerston North, New Zealand.

Kumar, M. S., Mudaliar, S. M., Thyagarajan, S. P., Kumar, S., Selvanayagam, A., Daniels, D. (2000). Rapid assessment and response to injecting drug use in Madras, south India. *International Journal of Drug Policy, 11*, 83–98.

Mayoux, L., & Chambers, R. (2005). Reversing the paradigm: Quantification, participatory methods and pro-poor impact assessment. *Journal of International Development, 17*, 271–298.

Mayoux, L., & Mosedale, S. (2005). Impact assessment for pro-poor accountability: Innovations and challenges. *Journal of International Development, 17*, 187–193.

Mbwili-Muleya C., Lungu M., Kabuba I., Zulu Lishandu I., & Loewenson R. (2008). Consolidating processes for community—health centre partnership and accountability in Zambia, Lusaka District Health Team and Equity Gauge Zambia, EQUINET Participatory Research Report An *EQUINET PRA project report.* Harare, Zimbabwe: EQUINET.

Mertens, D. M. (2007). Transformative considerations: Inclusion and social justice. *American Journal of Evaluation, 28*, 86–90.

Mertens, D. M. (2008, April). *Transformative mixed methods research in an educational context.* Invited presentation at the annual meeting of the American Educational Research Association, New York.

Mertens, D. M. (2009). *Transformative research and evaluation.* New York: Guilford Press.

Mertens, D. M. (2010). *Research and evaluation in education and psychology: Integrating diversity with quantitative, qualitative, and mixed methods* (3rd ed.). Thousand Oaks, CA: Sage.

Mertens, D. M., & Ginsberg, P. (2008). Deep in ethical waters: Transformative perspectives for qualitative social work research. *Qualitative Social Work, 7*, 484–503.

Mertens, D. M., & Ginsberg, P. (Eds.). (2009). *Handbook of social research ethics.* Thousand Oaks, CA: Sage.

Mertens, D. M., & Holmes, H. (2008, February). *Preparation of teachers for students who are deaf and have a disability.* Presentation at the annual meeting of the Association of College Educators-Deaf and Hard of Hearing, Monterey, CA.

Mertens, D. M., Holmes, H., & Harris, R. (2009). Transformative research and ethics. In D. M. Mertens & P. Ginsberg (Eds.), *Handbook of social research ethics* (pp. 85–102). Thousand Oaks, CA: Sage.

Mertens, D. M., Holmes, H., Harris, R., & Brandt, S. (2007). *Project SUCCESS:*

Summative evaluation report. Washington, DC: Gallaudet University.

Narayan, D. (1996). *Toward participatory research* (World Bank Technical Paper). Washington, DC: World Bank.

Newman, K., & Wyly, E. K. (2006). The right to stay put, revisited: Gentrification and resistance to displacement in New York City. *Urban Studies, 43*(1), 23–57.

Nordenmark, M., & Nyman, C. (2003). Fair or unfair? Perceived fairness of household division of labour and gender equality among women and men: The Swedish case. *European Journal of Women's Studies, 10*(2), 181–209.

Norton, A., Bird, B., Brock, K., Kakande, M., & Turk, C. (2001). *A rough guide to PPAs: Participatory poverty assessments: An introduction to theory and practice.* London: Overseas Development Institute.

Oliver, M. T. (1990). *The politics of disablement.* Basingstoke, UK: Macmillan.

Segone, M. (Ed.). (2006). New trends in development evaluation. Geneva: UNICEF Regional Office for CEE/CIS and IPEN, Issue No. 5. Retrieved February 14, 2010, from www.unicef.org/ceecis/resources_1220.html

Shapiro, M., Setterlund, D., & Cragg, C. (2003). Capturing the complexity of women's experiences: A mixed-method approach to studying incontinence in older women. *Affilia, 18,* 21–33.

Smith, L. T. (2005). On tricky ground: Researching the native in the age of uncertainty. In N. K. Denzin & Y. S. Lincoln (Eds.), *The SAGE handbook of qualitative research* (3rd ed., pp. 85–108). Thousand Oaks, CA: Sage.

Stewart, A. J., & Cole, E. R. (2007). Narratives and numbers: Feminist multiple methods research. In S. N. Hesse-Biber (Ed.), *Handbook of feminist research: Theory and praxis* (pp. 327–344). Thousand Oaks, CA: Sage.

Sullivan, M. (2009). Philosophy, ethics, and the disability community. In D. M. Mertens &

P. G. Ginsberg (Eds.), *Handbook of social research ethics* (pp. 69–84). Thousand Oaks, CA: Sage.

Sullivan, M., Derrett, S., Crawford, M., Beaver, C., Fergusson, P., Paul, C., & Herbison, P. (2007). *SCI: The first two years* (Unpublished Research Application GA 207). Auckland: Health Research Council of New Zealand.

Sweetman, D., Badiee, M., & Creswell, J. (2009, May). *Use of the transformative framework in mixed methods studies.* Paper presented at the Congress of Qualitative Inquiry, University of Illinois, Champaign-Urbana.

Teddlie, C., & Tashakkori, A. (2009). *Foundations of mixed methods research.* Thousand Oaks, CA: Sage.

Tolman, D., & Szalacha, L. (1999). Dimensions of desire: Bridging qualitative and quantitative methods in a study of female adolescent sexuality. *Psychology of Women Quarterly, 23,* 7–39.

Turk, C. (1999, November). *Linking participatory poverty assessments to policy and policymaking: Experience from Vietnam* (Policy Research Working Paper No. 2526). Washington, DC: World Bank.

Union of the Physically Impaired Against Segregation. (1976). *Fundamental principles of disability.* London: Author.

Van Beeck, E., Larsen, C., Lyons R., Meerding, W., Mulder, S., & Essink-Bot, M. (2007). Draft guidelines for the conduction of empirical studies into injury-related disability. *Journal of Trauma-Injury Infection & Critical Care, 62*(2), 534–550.

Wilson, A. (2005). The effectiveness of international development assistance from American organizations to deaf communities in Jamaica. *American Annals of the Deaf, 150*(3), 202–304.

Wilson, A., & Kakiri, N. (2005, November). *Final report for the Kenyan Ministry of Education: A survey of the development assistance desired by Deaf Kenyans.* Washington DC: Gallaudet University.

9

THE MULTIDIMENSIONAL MODEL OF RESEARCH METHODOLOGY

An Integrated Set of Continua

◆ Katrin Niglas

Objectives

The detailed objectives of the chapter are to

- present a brief history describing how the idea of philosophical research paradigms (and essential attributes of those paradigms) were converted from dualisms into continua;

- present a brief history describing how the QUAN-QUAL methodological dichotomy (and its constituent components) was converted into a set of QUAN-MM-QUAL methodological continua;

- present the multidimensional model of research methodology and describe its constituent parts as illustrated in Figure 9.2;

- describe in more detail the philosophical continuum in the model;

- describe in more detail the methodological continuum in the model;

(Continued)

(Continued)

- discuss how the philosophical and methodological continua interact in the model;

- describe in more detail the continuum in the multidimensional model of research methodology that positions the natural and technical sciences on one end and the arts on the other; and

- discuss how specific research methods and genres can be situated within the space generated by the model.

In contemporary thinking, the historical paradigm wars about the methodology of social sciences are often declared to be over. The integration of *qualitative* and *quantitative* aspects of research has gained immense popularity. Ongoing debates about the relationship between these two approaches seem to have taken a turn from issues related to philosophical worldview toward more pragmatic aspects of using various mixed methods designed for studies in all the fields of social sciences (Niglas, 2009; also see Creswell, 2010, and Teddlie & Tashakkori, 2010 [both in this volume]).

What does this pragmatic point of view mean, and what will be its impact on the context of research practice? Has time closed the gap between the old conflicting quantitative and qualitative paradigms, and can they now coexist peacefully with a new one called the mixed methods (MM) paradigm? Or should we abandon the paradigmatic picture of social sciences altogether and, along with that, lay aside philosophical questions as well? If not in terms of paradigms, how then should we conceptualize research methodology in the social sciences?

This chapter argues that instead of classifying research methodology into a small number of clearly separate paradigms or movements, it is more appropriate and helpful to conceptualize methodology as a *multidimensional set of continua*. This kind of antidualistic stance (i.e., the tendency to regard everything as continuous) is called *synechism* by Johnson and Gray (2010 [this

volume]). The main aim of the current chapter is to elaborate on the synechistic view by integrating numerous *continua*, which describe various aspects of research studies, into one holistic *multidimensional model of research methodology*. Relevant developments in the social sciences since the 1970s will be reviewed in the first part of the chapter to show how the idea of incommensurable paradigms, prevalent at the end of the last century, has gradually given way to the conceptualization of research methodology as a continuum, or more correctly as a set of continua.

◆ **From Dichotomies to Continua in Philosophies and Methodologies: Current Trends in the Literature**

As mentioned above, the main goal of the chapter is to introduce and discuss the model of research methodology that integrates multiple continua relevant in defining the nature of a research study. The following section discusses the evolution of thought regarding philosophical and methodological continua, both of which are the main building blocks of the multidimensional model of research methodology. Although conceptually related, their evolution was distinct. Therefore, the development of the ideas will be addressed in two separate subsections.

FROM PHILOSOPHICAL DICHOTOMIES TO PHILOSOPHICAL CONTINUA

During the final decades of the last century, the paradigm shift from positivist-quantitative to interpretivist-qualitative ways of doing research was advocated by many writers and methodologists as a desirable goal. This paradigmatic view of research methods proposed that there are a limited number of competing paradigms—sets of basic beliefs (or metaphysics)—in social research, which the researcher follows or should follow (e.g., Guba & Lincoln, 1989, 1994; Lincoln & Guba, 1985). Even though the paradigms were called by various labels until the beginning of the 1990s, most authors referred to two incommensurable research paradigms (see Table 9.1).[1]

In that context, paradigms were defined by a set of philosophical dichotomies like *realism* versus *relativism* (as ontological stances) or *objectivism* versus *subjectivism* as epistemologies of conventional-positivist and new-interpretive paradigms, respectively (e.g., Guba & Lincoln, 1989). However, it is clear from most accounts of paradigmatic programs that these philosophically based paradigms were seen to have considerable methodological implications. For example, Lincoln and Guba (1985) write, "We call such a systematic set of beliefs, together with

Table 9.1   Different Labels Used for Inquiry Paradigms (Adapted From Niglas, 1999)

Positivist	Interpretive		Bassey, 1995; Ericson, 1986; Howe, 1988
Positivist/postpositivist	Constructivist	Critical theoretical	Guba & Lincoln, 1994
Objective-quantitative	Interpretive-qualitative	Critical theoretical	Gage, 1989
Normative (positivist)	Interpretive (anti-positivist)		Cohen & Manion,1989
Positivist	Naturalistic-ethnographic		Hoshmand, 1989
Empiricist	Humanistic		Smith, 1989
Quantitative	Qualitative		Smith & Heshusius, 1986
Positivist	Phenomenological		Bryman, 1984; Firestone, 1987
Quantitative-realist	Qualitative-idealist		Smith, 1983
Rationalistic	Naturalistic		Guba & Lincoln, 1982
Dominant	Innovative		Hudson, 1975
Social facts	Social definition	Social behavior	Ritzer, 1975
Agricultural-botany	Social anthropology		Parlett & Hamilton, 1972

their accompanying methods, a *paradigm*" (p. 15, italics in original).

Very commonly, the positivistic or conventional paradigm was seen to designate the quantitative approach and the interpretive paradigm, the qualitative approach. The underlying assumption here is that particular methods follow from the general methodological positions, which themselves follow from or are part of the "(meta)-theoretical positions" (Platt, 1986, p. 502).

The idea of philosophy-based research paradigms has been persistently criticized for neglecting the multiplicity of approaches there are on the philosophical level and for not acknowledging their internal inconsistency and overlapping nature (e.g., Keat & Urry, 1975). Therefore, the early views were soon reviewed and elaborated. In her reflection on the process of "making of a constructivist" paradigm, Yvonna Lincoln (1990) admits that there were many things about the new paradigm, as well as about the ways the paradigms were defined, that she and her coauthors took for granted too readily and therefore need to be reshaped. Furthermore, it is acknowledged that the landscape of social scientific inquiry is continuously changing so that the paradigm system cannot be seen as fixed but as evolving through time (Guba & Lincoln, 2005, p. 191).

In accordance with this evolution, there are several important developments in the way in which the idea of philosophically based research paradigms is used today. First

of all, the proponents of the paradigmatic view have argued that qualitative and quantitative methods may be used appropriately with any research paradigm (Guba & Lincoln, 1989, p. 195). More important, many authors now write about the blurring of genres and a multiparadigmatic era (e.g., Geertz, 1993) in which "practitioners of the various new and emergent paradigms continue either to look for common ground or to find ways in which to distinguish their forms of inquiry from others" (Guba & Lincoln, 2005, p. 211). Thus, even radical proponents of the paradigmatic view extend their lists of research paradigms to four or five and accept that there is an overlap between them (see Table 9.2). However, having moved from two philosophy-based worldview paradigms to a flexible and evolving five-paradigm picture, proponents of the paradigmatic view still argue for two broad but incommensurable sets of belief systems:

> So, . . . *positivism* and *post-positivism* are clearly commensurable. In the same vein, elements of *interpretivist/postmodern* critical theory, constructivist and participative inquiry, fit comfortably together. Commensurability is an issue only when researchers want to "pick and choose" among the axioms of positivist and interpretivist models, because the axioms are contradictory and mutually exclusive. (Guba & Lincoln, 2005, p. 201, italics in original)

Table 9.2 The Evolution of the Paradigm System in the Texts by Guba and Lincoln (Adapted From Niglas, 2004a)

1985/1989	1990/1994	2000/2005
Conventional (positivist)	Positivism	Positivism
Constructivist	Postpositivism	Postpositivism
	Critical theory	Critical theory
	Constructivism	Constructivism
		Participatory

Not only the number of proposed paradigms has changed over time, but also the views about what the critical aspects or issues are that define those paradigms. The three main dualisms (i.e., realist vs. relativist ontology, objective vs. subjective epistemology, and interventionist vs. hermeneutic methodology) have gradually been amended by a whole set of critical and practical issues characteristic of paradigms such as *nature of knowledge, values, voice,* and *inquirer posture* (Guba & Lincoln, 2005, Tables 8.1 to 8.5). Most of the paradigm positions on these issues are now described as partly overlapping and forming a continuum rather than a dichotomy. For example, the ontological positions of the paradigms vary from naive realism to relativism, including critical realism, historical realism, and participative subjective-objective reality (Guba & Lincoln, 2005, p. 195). Similarly, several other authors have converted the original philosophical dualisms into a number of continua like *deduction–induction, objective inquiry–subjective inquiry, value-bound inquiry–value-free inquiry, ideographic understandings–nomothetic understandings,* and so forth, which are relevant in the context of research practice (Tashakkori & Teddlie, 1998; Teddlie & Tashakkori, 2009).

Regardless of these developments, many texts on methodology do not adequately present the complexity and variability of diverse ideas about positivism, constructivism, pragmatism, or other philosophical traditions (Bergman, 2008). Furthermore, critics conclude that the philosophical views of most researchers do not clearly belong to any single philosophical tradition, as the paradigmatic model assumes. In the real world, the philosophical positions of most investigators can be most appropriately represented by a number of philosophical continua (Teddlie & Tashakkori, 2009, p. 94). It is, therefore, a complex and multifaceted individual mental model, which is formed by many factors like education and training, personal values, disciplinary perspectives,

philosophy of science, and so forth, rather than a formalized paradigm, that guides the work of social inquirers (e.g., Greene, 2007; Phillips, 1996; Smith, 1997).

This short overview demonstrates that even though some influential texts about methodology still advocate incommensurability between two broad worldview positions, there has been a gradual move toward the idea of continuum in discussions about philosophical research paradigms. Critics believe that the ontological and epistemological contradistinction of research traditions, as proposed by the paradigmatic view, is based on false premises. They argue that philosophical schools of thought are internally diverse and overlap with each other forming a continuum, rather than a set of clearly discernible paradigms. As a result, their influence on research methodology is not as direct or entrenched as is suggested by the proponents of the paradigmatic view.

FROM METHODOLOGICAL DICHOTOMIES TO METHODOLOGICAL CONTINUA

During the 1970s and 1980s, the critique against quantitative research, which had dominated the field of social sciences for several decades, became very extensive. There was often fundamental disagreement between quantitative and qualitative methodologists on many aspects of research methodology and principles, which should be the basis of social and educational research (Gage, 1989; Hammersley, 1992b).

Since then, the terms *quantitative* and *qualitative research* have been very widely used in methodological texts, but exact definitions for these terms have seldom been proposed. The original meaning of the word *quantitative* (from Latin *quantitās*) refers to numerical accounts and mathematical methods, while the meaning of the word *qualitative* (from Latin *quālitās*) refers to the nature, character, and properties of the phenomenon. From there follows one of the most common ways of understanding the essence of quantitative and qualitative research:

> The study is quantitative if it makes use of structured numerical data and statistical analysis techniques and qualitative if the argumentation is not based on numbers and calculations but on the substantial analysis of unstructured data. (Niglas, 2004a, p. 163)

The nature of data and data collection procedures has a central position in this common definition. However, in methodological texts, the terms *quantitative* and *qualitative research* were often seen to signify more than different ways of collecting data: They were taken to denote divergent assumptions about the nature and purpose of research in the social sciences (Bryman, 1988). Thus, the methods dichotomy was only one of many related dichotomies by which qualitative and quantitative research were characterized. Long lists of dimensions of differences between qualitative and quantitative methodologies were proposed in textbooks and in academic discussion (see Table 9.3).[2]

In the early days of the debates between proponents of qualitative and quantitative approaches, the issues were often technical in nature, concerning the precision, generalization, relevance, or practical value of research findings. Subsequently, some methodologists started to argue that to see the distinction between quantitative and qualitative methodologies only as a technical matter and to accept the complementary nature of different approaches is misleading because these methodologies represent fundamentally different epistemological and worldview positions (i.e., incommensurable paradigms) (e.g., Smith, 1983, 1989; Smith & Heshusius, 1986).

The tendency to bind qualitative and quantitative methodologies with particular antagonistic worldview positions has been

Table 9.3 Common Dichotomies in Methodological Literature

Qualitative	Quantitative
narrative	numeric
subjective	objective
inductive	deductive
descriptive	predictive
detailed/deep	generalizable
teleological	causal
open	standardized
finalistic	mechanistic
understanding	explanation
exploratory	confirmatory
empiricism	rationalism
value laden	value neutral
atheoretical	theoretical
naturalism	positivism
relativism	realism
anthropology	sociology
micro	macro
art	science

widely criticized in the methodological literature. Since the beginning of the 1980s, several papers have been published arguing that quantitative and qualitative approaches to research are not mutually exclusive (e.g., Bryman, 1988; Eckeberg & Hill, 1980; Hammersley, 1992b; Howe, 1988; McNamara, 1979; Reichardt & Cook, 1979). Based on this premise, the new methodological approach, often called *mixed methods,* emerged. For example, as early as 1980, Patton added a chapter on "methodological mixes" to his widely used textbook on qualitative evaluation methods. Foundations of mixed methods research were elaborated by Tashakkori and Teddlie in their book published in 1998. Since then, mixed methods research has flourished and has been accepted by many writers as the third methodological movement (Teddlie & Tashakkori, 2003) or the third research paradigm (Johnson & Onwuegbuzie, 2004; Ridenour & Newman, 2008).

While giving prominence to methodological issues, leaders of the mixed methods community systematically looked for a suitable philosophical framework for mixed methods research. Most often, the third methodological movement has been attuned to the framework of the pragmatist paradigm (e.g., Tashakkori & Teddlie, 2003, p. 679; Johnson & Onwuegbuzie, 2004), but postpositivism, some form of scientific realism, and the transformative-emancipatory paradigm have also been promoted as alternative philosophical frameworks for mixed methods research (e.g., House, 1994; Maxwell, 2004; Mertens, 2003; Miller, 2003; Ridenour & Newman, 2008).

The idea of mixed methods as the third paradigm has not been accepted by all the proponents of the combined use of qualitative and quantitative approaches. Since the beginning of the so-called paradigm wars, many authors have challenged the view that divides social research into a limited number of paradigms, whether based on philosophical categories (e.g., positivism, constructivism) or methodological distinctions (i.e., qualitative, quantitative, and mixed methods) (e.g., Eckeberg & Hill, 1980; Freidheim, 1979; McNamara, 1979; Platt, 1986; Snizek, 1975). While various philosophical frameworks favor mixed methods research approaches, several authors believe that "mixed methods research works far better in practice than in theory" (e.g., Bergman, 2008).

Furthermore, opponents of the paradigmatic view argue that there are major differences in philosophical as well as methodological preferences within the camp of qualitative researchers, as well as within the ranks of quantitative researchers, and that research practice is much more variegated and complicated than that proposed by a paradigmatic view (Niglas, 2004a). Hammersley (1992a) represents the latter position, writing that "even an expansion to six paradigms would still not satisfactorily cover the potential, or even actual, range of methodological views to be found amongst educational and social researchers" (p. 134). Thus, the plurality of methodological views and approaches could be better modeled using the idea of a continuum (e.g., Niglas, 2001; Tesch, 1990).

Among the first advocates of the concept of the QUAL-QUAN continuum were Newman and Benz in 1998. Elaborating their ideas, Ridenour and Newman (2008) describe the QUAL-QUAN "interactive continuum" as the third and most beneficial category of mixed methods, which is argued to be different from the other two categories. Instead of dichotomizing quantitative and qualitative methods, it "rejects the dichotomy and relies on a continuum in which research may be predominantly qualitative or predominantly quantitative" (Ridenour & Newman, 2008, p. 27). The interactive continuum is seen as a holistic approach to research, which encompasses theory building as well as theory testing as common purposes for qualitative and quantitative research. However, the authors remain unconvinced regarding the simultaneous use of qualitative and quantitative methods for a common purpose because they hold to the view that underlying assumptions of qualitative and quantitative research are incongruent with each other.

The incongruence point of view has been criticized by several authors for being based on misperceptions regarding the existence of two distinct and often opposite sets of qualities related to the two large families of methods (Bergman, 2008; Niglas, 1999). Criticism of this incongruence point of view is well stated by Bergman (2008):

QL [qualitative] and QN [quantitative] methods are two large and heterogeneous families of methods, which are difficult to describe such that the characteristics attributed to the methods of one family are attributable to all of its members, and that are clearly differentiable from the members of the other family of methods. (p. 17)

No matter how hard we try to define clear-cut boundaries between quantitative research and qualitative research, there always seem to be studies that are more similar to studies in the other group than to studies in their own (e.g., Bryman, 1988; Hammersley, 1992b; Howe, 1988; Niglas, 2004a, 2004b). From this perspective, qualitative and quantitative approaches should be seen as proxies for the polar ends of the multidimensional QUAL-MM-QUAN continuum, which runs from the purist qualitative tradition to the purist quantitative tradition, encompassing variants of mixed methods research in the middle (Teddlie & Tashakkori, 2009, p. 28).

To illustrate this perspective, the model in Figure 9.1 consists of three arbitrarily chosen dimensions.[3] According to the conventional understanding, quantitative studies aim to be confirmatory, objective, and generalizable in nature. Thus, they should be located in the lower left-hand corner of the cube, whereas qualitative ones (which are exploratory, descriptive, and subjective in nature) should be located in the upper right-hand corner of the cube. The paradigmatic view assumes the rest of the cube to be empty. However, today most of the methodological thinking celebrates the plurality of designs throughout the cube, which represents the multidimensional continuum of methodological approaches.

Figure 9.1 Quantitative and Qualitative Research as a Multidimensional Continuum (Adapted From Niglas, 2004b)

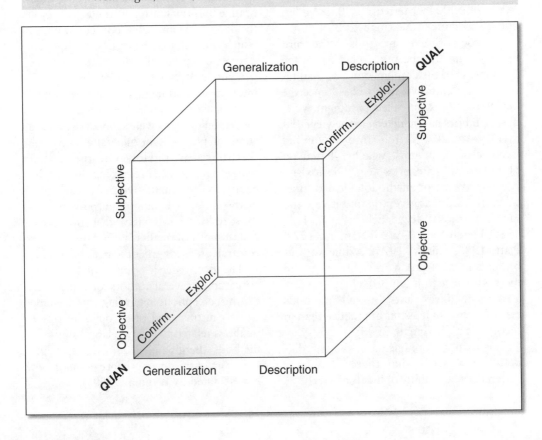

This conceptualization of research methodology can be elaborated by deconstructing research designs into methodological components such as purposes, strategy, sampling, data collection, data analysis, and inferences. Concrete methods and techniques belonging to any of the methodological components can be placed along the continuum from purely qualitative to purely quantitative orientation (Niglas, 2004a). Alternatively, methodological components of a research project can be characterized by using a number of properties, each forming a separate continuum.

Teddlie and Tashakkori (2009) have identified the most important of these properties of methodological components in generating an elaborated framework they call the "multidimensional continuum of research projects" (pp. 94–95; see Table 9.4). In general, the methodological aspects of quantitative projects are closer to the left side of Table 9.4, while qualitative projects are closer to the right side of this multidimensional continuum. Most studies, however, can be considered mixed at least to some degree because various combinations of properties from the left and right sides are possible, and there are many methodological aspects of research projects that are best located toward the middle of the continua in Table 9.4 (Teddlie & Tashakkori, 2009).

By defining mixed methods research using a holistic set of methodological aspects and

Table 9.4 Multidimensional Continuum of Research Projects (Teddlie & Tashakkori, 2009)

Sphere of Concepts: Purposes, Questions, Objectives	
Deductive questions	← ——————→ Inductive questions
Objective purpose	← ——————→ Subjective purpose
Value neutral	← ——————→ Value involved
Confirmation	← ——————→ Understanding
Explanatory	← ——————→ Exploratory
Sphere of Concrete Processes (Experiential Sphere)	
Numeric data	← ——————→ Narrative data
Structured/closed-ended	← ——————→ Open-ended
Preplanned design	← ——————→ Emergent design
Statistical analysis	← ——————→ Thematic analysis
Probability sample	← ——————→ Purposive sample
Sphere of Inferences and Explanations	
Deductive inference	← ——————→ Inductive inference
"Objective" inferences	← ——————→ "Subjective" inferences
Value neutral	← ——————→ Value rich
Politically noncommittal	← ——————→ Transformative
Etic representation	← ——————→ Emic representation
Nomothetic	← ——————→ Ideographic

NOTE: Most QUAN research is closer to the left side of this table, whereas most QUAL research is closer to the right side. For the sake of diversity, we intentionally put QUAN on the left side, whereas most other tables and figures in this text have QUAN on the right side.

properties, instead of drawing only on the nature of data collection and analysis, the range of mixed methods approaches and research designs is considerably broadened.

The discussion above shows that the concept of a paradigm is still frequently used when methodologically different research approaches (e.g., QUAL, QUAN, and MM) are introduced or discussed. Today, however, methodological paradigms are increasingly portrayed as three broad and overlapping methodological traditions, rather than as incommensurable approaches that compete for dominance.

◆ The Multidimensional Model of Research Methodology

The methodological QUAN-MM-QUAL continua presented in Table 9.4 significantly advance thought regarding methodological issues and help members of the research community in putting together the most suitable designs for their research projects. Nevertheless, there is a need for a holistic framework that would integrate the methodological continua with the philosophical continua discussed earlier in the chapter, and illustrating the influences that each has on the other. The aim of this section of the chapter is to introduce and discuss in detail the holistic multidimensional model of research methodology, which is presented in Figure 9.2.

The holistic model integrates three main continua: philosophy, methodology, and arts-sciences. These main continua interact with each other and form a multidimensional space for specific methodologies and research techniques. To better grasp the main ideas grounding the model, one could interpret the two-dimensional schema in Figure 9.2, which presents the multidimensional model of research methodology, as a bird's-eye perspective into a cylinder. Imagine the outer circle of keywords (i.e., the philosophical continuum) as being the *top* of the cylinder, and the methodological continuum being the *bottom* of the cylinder. Specific methodological techniques and approaches fit within the multidimensional space between the top and bottom of the cylinder (i.e., between the philosophical continuum and the methodological continuum).

To best facilitate the comprehension of the model, all its essential components will be discussed in five subsequent subsections of the chapter. These components are: the philosophical continuum, the methodological continuum, the interaction between the methodological and philosophical continua, the interaction with the continuum between the arts and sciences, and the placement of the specific methods within the multidimensional space created by the model.

THE PHILOSOPHICAL CONTINUUM

The philosophical continuum of the multidimensional model of research methodology (Figure 9.2) is represented by the outer circle of keywords that form arcs at the top and bottom of the figure (e.g., positivism, phenomenology, pragmatism). The model suggests that in the context of research studies, philosophy, taken more generally, imposes "how to think about" social phenomena.

The philosophical continuum can be seen as an elaboration of the ideas presented and discussed in connection with Table 9.2 earlier in this chapter. First, it must be noted that instead of a few paradigms, the model includes labels for nine schools of thought on the philosophical level. Even this is an obvious simplification; several other traditions could be added, but their inclusion would make the schema too complex and confusing.[4] Second, by connecting the ovals surrounding the keywords, the model hints at the overlap and mutual influence between different traditions and schools of thought. If one were to imagine the outer oval as the overlay of the cylinder where the traditions are spread all over the surface, the overlap between the traditions in the

Figure 9.2 The Multidimensional Model of Research Methodology (Adapted From Niglas, 2001)

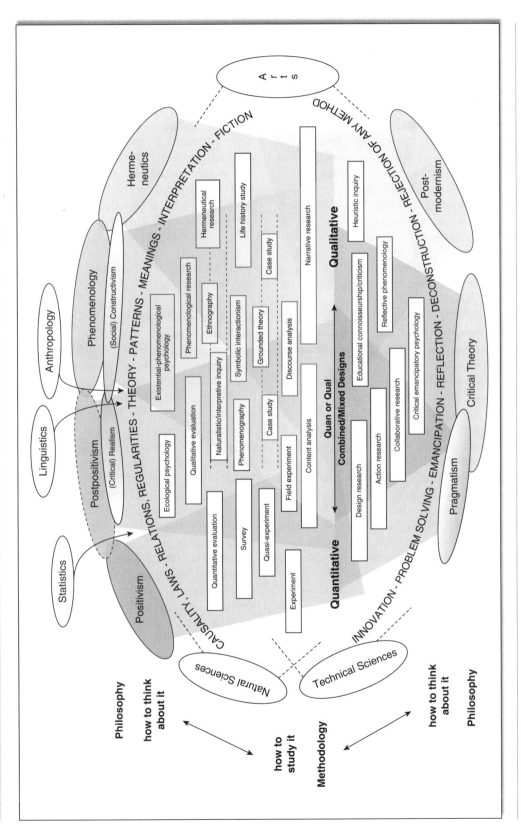

NOTE: The original model uses colors, which are transformed into gray shadings for technical reasons. You can find the original model at www.tlu.ee/~katrin/mmrm/

upper and lower edge of the schema (e.g., the overlap between phenomenological and critical theoretical traditions) becomes perceptible as well. Finally, it is important to understand that the philosophical continuum (and also the other two main continua of the multidimensional model of research methodology) incorporates a number of more specific dimensions like *realism-relativism, subjective-objective, emic-etic,* and so forth.

The placement of philosophical orientations in the continuum is best explained by the keywords in caps (e.g., causality, regularities, problem solving), which illustrate the change in the main focus and the purposes of inquiry along the multidimensional continuum of research traditions. It can be seen that there is no paradigmatic leap but rather gradual transformation of characteristic concepts and purposes.[5]

Other chapters in this volume refer to various philosophical orientations that favor mixed methods research. Some of them are easy to find from the schema in Figure 9.2. For example, pragmatism, often referred to as the most suitable philosophical orientation for the mixed methods research tradition (see Biesta, 2010; Greene & Hall, 2010; Johnson & Gray, 2010 [all in this volume]), can be found in the lower edge next to the keyword *problem solving,* and critical realism (see Maxwell & Mittapalli, 2010 [this volume]) approximately at the same spot in the upper edge, next to the keywords *relations* and *regularities.* Missing orientations can be mentally located using their propinquity with the traditions and keywords the schema depicts. For example, feminism (see Hesse-Biber, 2010 [this volume]), participatory stance (see Christ, 2010 [this volume]; Mertens, 2003), and transformative orientation (see Mertens, Bledsoe, Sullivan, & Wilson, 2010 [this volume]) have their roots in the ideas that originate from various branches of critical theory but have

some obvious influences from other research traditions as well. With somewhat different emphasis, they establish the emancipation of collaborative problem solving and transformative innovation as main goals for research endeavors. The model suggests that these orientations are partly overlapping and could be located, respectively, in the space from the center to the lower-left edge of the two-dimensional representation of the multidimensional model of research methodology in Figure 9.2.

THE METHODOLOGICAL CONTINUUM

The methodological continuum of the multidimensional model of research methodology (Figure 9.2), which imposes the concept of "how to study" social phenomena, runs in the bottom of the imaginary cylinder and is visualized in the center of the schema (i.e., the quantitative↔qualitative dimension). There is a large space between the QUAN and QUAL ends of the continuum where quantitative and qualitative research approaches are both valued and used either alternatively or in combination, thus forming various mixed methods research designs.

Like the philosophical continuum of the model, the methodological continuum incorporates a number of more specific dimensions (e.g., deductive-inductive, numeric-narrative, probabilistic-purposive) relevant to various methodological aspects of research projects. As such, the methodological continuum of the multidimensional model of research methodology is similar to the models presented in Figure 9.1 and Table 9.4. Therefore, a lengthy discussion is unnecessary here, and the reader is advised to revisit the earlier subsections of the chapter for a more detailed discussion of the methodological continuum.

THE INTERACTION BETWEEN THE PHILOSOPHICAL AND METHODOLOGICAL CONTINUA

The methodological literature review in the first part of this chapter demonstrated that most contemporary methodologists reject the idea that there is a tight bond between philosophical worldview paradigms and certain research methodologies. This does not mean that the relationship between philosophical traditions and methodological approaches should be neglected, or that the "everything goes" mentality should be adopted by practicing researchers.

On the contrary, the multidimensional model of research methodology emphasizes that the ideas, traditions, and influences from both the philosophical and methodological levels, as well as the relationship between them, are more varied and complicated than often depicted in methodological texts. These ideas become evident when one looks at the *philosophy-methodology dimension* of the schema in Figure 9.2, which runs from top to bottom of the imaginary cylinder (i.e., from the outer circle to the center of the two-dimensional schema). The shadings originating from the continuum of philosophical orientations represent the influence of different schools of thought on the ways in which we study social phenomena. It is important to notice that the closer we move to the continuum of methodology, the more diffuse and mixed these influences become. On the other hand, looking from the methodological continuum toward the philosophical continuum, the same effect demonstrates the tendency of particular methodologies and methods to be used by various research traditions, as well as within many different philosophical frameworks.

Furthermore, one of the most important aims of the multidimensional model of research methodology is to show that the interaction between philosophy and methodology is not direct but *mediated* by both the research community and the particular researcher or research project under consideration. This idea from the model is based on the premise that the concrete purpose, or the research problem, rather than the philosophical position of the researcher determines the design of the study (e.g., Bryman, 2007; Tashakkori & Teddlie, 1998). The type of problems and questions we choose to study depends in turn on several things, including the ways we are accustomed to thinking about the role of scientific endeavor and the ways the phenomena are conceptualized in particular research traditions (see Figure 9.3). Therefore, in the schema in Figure 9.2, the circle of keywords below the philosophical continuum (e.g., causality, laws, innovation), which illustrates the change in main focus and purposes for inquiry along the multidimensional continuum of research traditions, has a key role in understanding the relationship between philosophical schools of thought and methodological practices of researchers.

It is argued that philosophical orientation and traditions, as well as some more pragmatic aspects (e.g., the need to improve practice, methodological skills that the researchers have, resources such as time and money), influence how we choose to study social phenomena in the framework of particular research projects. Nevertheless, these influences on the choice of methodology are (or should be) *indirect*; that is, they are *mediated* by our research purposes and questions (e.g., Bryman, 2007; Niglas, 2009). The multidimensional model of research methodology emphasizes that inquirers should not base their methodological decisions on the simplified assumptions of a paradigmatic bond between philosophical positions and certain research techniques; rather, they should demonstrate far more directly and explicitly the consistency of chosen techniques with the purpose and design of the study, as well as theoretical considerations (Bergman, 2008).

Figure 9.3 The Choice of Methodology and Methods for a Study in Practice (Adapted From Niglas, 1999)

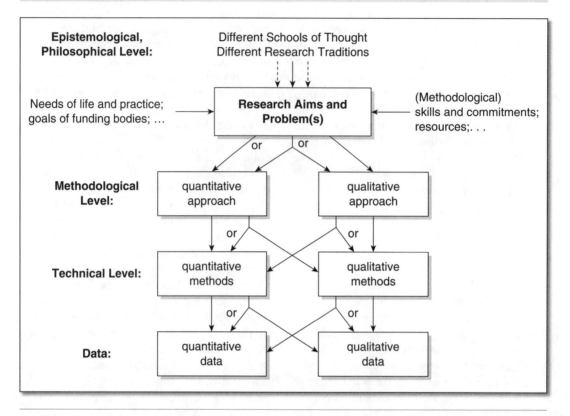

NOTE: This figure illustrates the centrality of the research problem in determining the choice of methodology and methods. The other influences, such as theoretical framework, practical needs, or resources, should be mediated by the choice of research purposes and questions.

THE CONTINUUM BETWEEN THE ARTS AND SCIENCES

We saw that the interaction between philosophical schools of thought and methodological practices is mediated by research purposes and questions set for particular research projects. In addition, there is another important mediator between the philosophical and methodological continua in the multidimensional model of research methodology: the continuum of neighboring disciplines, with natural and technical sciences on one end and the arts on the other. This continuum is represented in Figure 9.2 by keywords on the outer circle that have a transparent background (e.g., natural sciences, statistics, arts). It is obvious that disciplinary influences are important with regard to both "how we think about" social phenomena and "how we study" them. The continuum between the arts and sciences is based on historical events and illustrates most clearly the evolution of social sciences as a discipline.

The institutionalization of the social sciences in the first half of the last century happened when *logical positivism*, proposed by the Vienna Circle, was the dominant influence among philosophers and social scientists in defining what science was. This view was modeled on the assumption that there were no critical differences between the natural sciences and social sciences. Therefore, subjectivity was eschewed and "objective" methods were employed to identify "objective" facts about social life. This view of social science has been criticized severely, but some aspects of the positivist and empiricist traditions are still prevalent in mainstream thinking in the social sciences (e.g., Manicas, 2007).

This historically dominating view has been challenged by many authors writing from various positions, from pragmatism to hermeneutics and from structuralism to post-structuralism and postmodernism, who have redefined social science in non-positivist terms. Some of these alternative interpretative and activist approaches have moved the conceptualization of phenomena in the social sciences closer to the ways of thinking that are characteristic of the arts (e.g., Denzin & Lincoln, 2005; Eisner, 1991). Thus, some techniques and methods that we consider as belonging to different genres of arts have been "borrowed" for social scientific inquiry.

Narrative turn in the social sciences, demonstrated by the "memoir boom" in literature and popular culture (Langellier, 2001) and other trends, is a good example of the influence of the arts in contemporary social sciences. The idea of collecting and using *personal stories* (and other narratives) as data was informed by well-developed traditions in literary studies, social linguistics, and other academic disciplines. Instead of providing objective descriptions of the world, narrative studies position the investigator as a part of the field, simultaneously mediating and interpreting the "other" in dialogue with the self (Reissman, 2008). Today, narrative accounts are used in the context of qualitative research and also mixed or integrated with various types of quantitative data. Furthermore, narrative inquirers have pushed the boundaries further by working more directly with artistic forms such as photography, poetry, drama, and video when collecting field texts or composing their own research text (Mello, 2007).

The infusion of the arts into social sciences can also be witnessed in extensive lists of new approaches for conducting postmodern social research. Carol Grbich (2003) displays numerous examples of innovative and creative textual forms in social research, taking advantage of literary and dramatic approaches, as well as artistic techniques like juxtaposition, layering, pastiche, vignette, poetry, and so forth. She also refers to creative visual and aural forms such as photography, paintings, computer imaging, music, and other sounds, which can have great potential for use in social research.

Authors (e.g., Finley, 2005) have argued that the arts-based methodologies open up a whole galaxy of new possibilities for socially responsible, politically activist, and locally useful social research. These new ways of presenting and representing data interweave findings from research with the voices of the researcher(s), participants, and audience, and sometimes also with voices of the writer and performer of research-laden artistic text, thereby blurring the boundaries between the arts and sciences.

Mello (2007) explored the borders between the genres, poetically summarizing her thoughts about the role of art in social research as follows:

> The language of arts in a narrative inquiry landscape
>
> art as a tool to promote reflection
>
> art for the sake of aesthetic experience
>
> photography images poems fiction novels films drama theatre music dance whatever
>
> / . . . /
>
> multiple aesthetic perspectives
>
> empowerment inclusion construction of knowledge
>
> changing the qualitative research landscape
>
> pushing boundaries . . . (p. 220)

The acceptance of arts-based and arts-informed research in the landscape of qualitative inquiry is corroborated by the inclusion of many chapters in *The SAGE Handbook of Qualitative Research* (Denzin & Lincoln, 2005) that discuss the usefulness of various artistic forms like performance ethnography, visual sociology, cultural poesis, or investigative poetry within the field of social research (see Alexander, 2005; Finley, 2005; Harper, 2005; Hartnett & Engels, 2005; Stewart, 2005).

In parallel with the growing utilization of various forms of art, there has been a move toward the acceptance of the principles of design science as a useful resource for advancing our understanding in the field of education and social sciences (e.g., Edelson, 2002). The *design research* approach, which offers methodological means for problem solving and innovation, has turned out to be especially promising in advancing ideas in the field of *e-learning* and in more traditional areas of educational and social sciences.

These trends exemplify why the multidimensional model of research methodology in Figure 9.2 is visualized as having roots in sciences at one end of the continuum, while blending with the arts at the other end.

THE PLACEMENT OF THE SPECIFIC METHODS WITHIN THE MULTIDIMENSIONAL MODEL OF RESEARCH METHODOLOGY

The main continua of the integrated model and their interaction dimension create multidimensional space for research traditions and specific research methods, which fills the imaginary cylinder between the philosophical and methodological continua. In Figure 9.2, this space is represented by the area within the outer circles of keywords on the two-dimensional schema of the multidimensional model of research methodology. This schema locates different concepts and labels related to the methodology of social and behavioral sciences such that more abstractly defined approaches (e.g., ecological psychology, critical emancipatory psychology) are closer to the philosophical continuum (i.e., to the outer circle of terms), whereas more concrete research methods or techniques (e.g., narrative research, design research) are located more closely to the QUAN-MM-QUAL continuum, which runs in the middle of the schema. The location of the concepts from left to right is determined by the propinquity of the particular concept with the keywords representing the philosophical and methodological continua as well as the main focuses of the research.

Following these principles, the school of critical emancipatory psychology, for example, is located right under the philosophical continuum in the sphere defined by the philosophical orientation of critical theory, where the main focus of research is emancipation. Similarly, the tradition of qualitative evaluation is close to the philosophical continuum in the spheres most clearly influenced by postpositivist and phenomenological thought, and by some newer or less influential orientations as well as by critical theory from the other edge of the philosophical continuum. The (true) experiment, on the other hand, as a concrete research design, is closer to the methodological continuum and located in the sphere where the main focus of research is on discovering causal laws.

The precise location and size of the boxes surrounding the terms should not be compared in a very rigid manner, either from the philosophical level to the methodological level (i.e., from the outer circle to the middle) or from left to right. Nevertheless, some of the boxes are intentionally stretched out to stress that these concepts are rather general labels embracing various ways of conceptualizing and doing research. A good example here is the case study, which is contemporaneously used to denote very different types of studies.

Although the aim of the multidimensional model of research methodology is to offer an overall holistic framework and clear principles for the placement of the methodological concepts into the multidimensional space created by the model, the schema in Figure 9.2 includes only a few of the methodological techniques actually used in the field of social sciences. This is partially due to the space limitations within Figure 9.2 itself. For example, the more concrete methodological techniques (e.g., various methods and techniques for data collection and analysis) are not currently located in Figure 9.2 but can be easily assumed to best fit along the QUAN-MM-QUAL continuum, with highly standardized and structured practices on the left and emergent open-ended approaches on the right, leaving ample space for semistructured and mixed techniques in the middle. Given the framework and the principles introduced above, the reader is encouraged to find appropriate locations for concepts relevant to her or his particular research practice.

When interpreting the location of the methodological concepts within the multidimensional space of the integrated model, it is important to understand that the closer we move to the level of concrete methods, the more diffuse and mixed will be the influence of philosophical schools of thought. This in turn means that particular methods and techniques can be and are used in the context of various research traditions and philosophical frameworks.

◆ Conclusion

In the first part of this chapter, the development of the methodological discourse in the field of social sciences since the 1970s was briefly reviewed. This demonstrated how the idea of incommensurable paradigms, based on a metaphysical belief system on the one hand and on methodologically different research approaches on the other (both prevalent at the end of the last century), has gradually given way to the conceptualization of research as a multidimensional continuum. Based on the idea of multidimensional continua, it was argued that the best understanding of the different possibilities for generating a design for an empirical research study can be achieved through an open and creative, yet at the same time a systematic and organized, perspective on the relationships between different philosophical orientations, methodological approaches, and aspects of design. This perspective presupposes the deconstruction of the design of an empirical study into methodological aspects, which are then scrutinized in terms of numerous philosophical and methodological continua defined by polar properties like numeric-narrative, preplanned-emergent, inductive-deductive, objective-subjective, value neutral–value rich, and so forth.

In the second part of the chapter, these ideas were elaborated and brought together to create a holistic multidimensional model of research methodology, which integrates the philosophical and methodological continua and creates a multidimensional space for methodological concepts (see Figure 9.2). On the one hand, this model can be seen as a dynamic, visual means for arguing against the paradigmatic approach to methodology. On the other hand, it can be used for pedagogical purposes as an artifice that helps to organize thinking about methodological concepts. It is assumed that scrutinizing the multidimensional model of research methodology will facilitate the comprehension of the essential issues in recent methodological thought and thereby help practicing researchers to base their research designs on stronger grounds than the simplified assumptions of a paradigmatic view.

It should be noted that regardless of its abundance of detail, the integrated model is not static or all-inclusive. Characteristic of any given schema, it offers a general framework that does not include all the details actually available at the time (i.e., particular schools of thought, methodological movements, research strategies). Nevertheless, the reader, cognizant that terms close to each other on the schema have similar roots and share contexts, should find it easy to fit the new concepts into the existing framework and see the relationships that there are between different schools of thought and research approaches.

On the other hand, the ideas on both layers of the model (i.e., "how to think about" social phenomena as well "how to study" them) are evolving rapidly. New philosophical schools of thought emerge, and old ones are modified; new methodologies, methods, and techniques are elaborated and experimented; new influences bring novel focuses and viewpoints; and so forth. Thus, the details included and placed into the model need to be reviewed and renewed over time. However, it is assumed that the framework offered by the integrated multidimensional model of research methodology can accommodate natural development in the field and will stay viable over time.

Research Questions and Exercises

1. Describe the development of the methodological discourse starting from the idea of the QUAN-QUAL dichotomy and ending with the QUAN-MM-QUAL methodological continuum.

2. Write a short essay describing the positive effects the promotion of two research paradigms had on social research and the research community, using additional references if necessary.

3. List several of the polar properties (e.g., numeric-narrative) and explain your understanding of how research practice is related to them. Use the references given in the text, and find original sources if you need further clarification.

4. What are the main constituent components of the multidimensional model of research methodology, and how are they visualized in Figure 9.2?

5. How are the natural and technical sciences and the arts related to the social sciences?

6. Select three methodological concepts from different parts of the model and give a reason for their location on the schema.

7. Select three methodological concepts that you cannot find from the model and explain where they would fit best in the model.

◆ Notes

1. Some of the authors referred to in Table 9.1, like Bryman and Howe, describe the paradigms in order to criticize the paradigmatic view and do not therefore subscribe to the paradigmatic view.

2. See, for example, Cook and Campbell (1979, p. 10), who used Bogdan and Taylor (1975) as their source; see also Evered and Louis, 1981; Patton, 1986.

3. Three dimensions were chosen because visual models with more than three dimensions are not easy to grasp. However, readers are advised to mentally add a number of other dimensions presented earlier to this model.

4. There are several other simplifications and omissions in the model, which are characteristic of any schematic presentation. The terms and concepts included are those which, according to the author's experience, are most central and/or influential in the methodological discussions in the fields of educational and

behavioral research. However, depending on the field of social science and the particular point in time, the details in the schema could be somewhat different, while the main framework and ideas holds.

5. It has to be noted that the keywords *theory, meanings,* and *interpretation,* used on the figure, are relevant concepts throughout all research approaches, no matter what tradition. However, the location of the keyword *theory* denotes the specific context where the primary focus of empirical research is on creating theory. Similarly, the keywords *meanings* and *interpretation* are located in the context where the primary focus of research is on finding out how people create meaning for and interpret the aspects of their social life.

◆ References

Alexander, B. K. (2005). Performance ethnography: The reenacting and inciting of culture. In N. K. Denzin & Y. S. Lincoln (Eds.), *The SAGE handbook of qualitative research* (3rd ed., pp. 411–442). Thousand Oaks, CA: Sage.

Bassey, M. (1995). *Creating education through research: A global perspective of educational research for the 21st century.* England: Kirklington Moor Press/BERA.

Bergman, M. M. (2008). The straw men of the qualitative-quantitative divide and their influence on mixed methods research. In M. M. Bergman (Ed.), *Advances in mixed methods research: Theories and applications* (pp. 11–21). Thousand Oaks, CA: Sage.

Biesta, G. (2010). Pragmatism and the philosophical foundations of mixed methods research. In A. Tashakkori & C. Teddlie (Eds.), *SAGE handbook of mixed methods in social & behavioral research* (2nd ed.). Thousand Oaks, CA: Sage.

Bogdan, R., & Taylor, S. K. (1975). *Introduction to qualitative research methods: A phenomenological approach to the social sciences.* New York: Wiley.

Bryman, A. (1984). The debate about quantitative and qualitative research: A question of method or epistemology? *The British Journal of Sociology, 35*(1), 75–93.

Bryman, A. (1988). *Quantity and quality in social research.* London: Unwin Hyman.

Bryman, A. (2007). The research question in social research: What is its role? *International Journal of Social Research Methodology, 10*(1), 5–20.

Christ, T. (2010). Teaching mixed methods and action research: Pedagogical, practical, and evaluative considerations. In A. Tashakkori & C. Teddlie (Eds.), *SAGE handbook of mixed methods in social & behavioral research.* Thousand Oaks, CA: Sage.

Cohen, L., & Manion, L. (1989). *Research methods in education* (3rd ed.). London: Routledge.

Cook, T. D., & Campbell, D. T. (1979). *Quasi-experimentation: Design and analysis issues for field settings.* Chicago: Rand McNally.

Creswell, J. W. (2010). Mapping the developing landscape of mixed methods research. In A. Tashakkori & C. Teddlie (Eds.), *SAGE handbook of mixed methods in social & behavioral research* (2nd ed.). Thousand Oaks, CA: Sage.

Denzin, N. K., & Lincoln Y. S. (Eds.). (2005). *The SAGE handbook of qualitative research* (3rd ed.). Thousand Oaks, CA: Sage.

Eckeberg, D. L., & Hill, L. (1980). The paradigm concept and sociology: A critical review. In G. Guttin (Ed.), *Paradigm and revolutions: Apprisals and applications of Thomas Kuhn's philosophy of science* (pp. 117–136). Notre Dame, London: University of Notre Dame Press.

Edelson, D. C. (2002). Design research: What we learn when we engage in design. *The Journal of the Learning Sciences, 11*(1), 105–121.

Eisner, E. W. (1991). *The enlightened eye: Qualitative inquiry and the enhancement of educational practice.* New York: Macmillan.

Ericson, F. (1986). Qualitative methods in research on teaching. In M. C. Wittrock (Ed.), *Handbook of research on teaching* (3rd ed., pp. 119–161). London: Collier Macmillan.

Evered, R., & Louis, M. R. (1981). Alternative perspectives in the organisational sciences: "Inquiry from the inside" and "inquiry from the outside." *Academy of Management Review, 6*(3), 385–395.

Finley, S. (2005). Arts-based inquiry: Performing revolutionary pedagogy. In N. K. Denzin & Y. S. Lincoln (Eds.), *The SAGE handbook of qualitative research* (3rd ed., pp. 681–694). Thousand Oaks, CA: Sage.

Firestone, W. (1987). Meaning in method: The rhetoric of quantitative and qualitative research. *Educational Researcher, 16*(7), 16–22.

Freidheim, E. A. (1979). An empirical comparison of Ritzer's paradigms and similar metatheories. *Social Forces, 58*(1), 59–66.

Gage, N. L. (1989). The paradigm wars and their aftermath: A "historical" sketch of research on teaching since 1989. *Educational Researcher, 18*(7), 4–10.

Geertz, C. (1993). *Local knowledge: Further essays in interpretive anthropology.* London: Fonatana.

Grbich, C. (2003). *New approaches in social research.* Thousand Oaks, CA: Sage.

Greene, J. C. (2007). *Mixing methods in social inquiry.* San Francisco: Jossey-Bass.

Greene, J., & Hall, J. (2010). Dialectics and pragmatism: Being of consequence. In A. Tashakkori & C. Teddlie (Eds.), *SAGE handbook of mixed methods in social & behavioral research* (2nd ed.). Thousand Oaks, CA: Sage.

Guba, E. G., & Lincoln, Y. S. (1982). Epistemological and methodological bases of naturalistic inquiry. *Educational Communication and Technology Journal, 30*(4), 233–252.

Guba, E. G., & Lincoln, Y. S. (1989). *Fourth generation evaluation.* London: Sage.

Guba, E. G., & Lincoln, Y. S. (1994). Competing paradigms in qualitative research. In N. K. Denzin & Y. S. Lincoln (Eds.), *Handbook of qualitative research* (pp. 105–117). Thousand Oaks, CA: Sage.

Guba, E. G., & Lincoln, Y. S. (2005). Paradigmatic controversies, contradictions, and emerging confluences. In N. K. Denzin & Y. S. Lincoln (Eds.), *The SAGE handbook of qualitative research* (3rd ed., pp. 191–216). Thousand Oaks, CA: Sage.

Hammersley, M. (1992a). The paradigm wars: Reports from the front. *British Journal of Sociology of Education, 13*(1), 131–143.

Hammersley, M. (1992b). *What's wrong with ethnography? Methodological explorations.* London: Routledge.

Harper, D. (2005). What's new visually? In N. K. Denzin & Y. S. Lincoln (Eds.), *The SAGE handbook of qualitative research* (3rd ed., pp. 747–762). Thousand Oaks, CA: Sage.

Hartnett, S. J., & Engels, J. D. (2005). "Aria in time of war": Investigative poetry and the politics of witnessing. In N. K. Denzin & Y. S. Lincoln (Eds.), *The SAGE handbook of qualitative research* (3rd ed., pp. 1043–1068). Thousand Oaks, CA: Sage.

Hesse-Biber, S. (2010). Feminist approaches to mixed methods research: Linking theory and praxis. In A. Tashakkori & C. Teddlie (Eds.), *SAGE handbook of mixed methods in social & behavioral research* (2nd ed.). Thousand Oaks, CA: Sage.

Hoshmand, L. S. T. (1989). Alternate research paradigms: A review and teaching proposal. *The Counseling Psychologist, 17*(1), 3–79.

House, E. R. (1994). Inegrating the quantitative and qualitative. In C. S. Reichardt & S. F. Rallis (Eds.), *The qualitative-quantitative debate: New perspectives* (New Directions for Evaluation, No. 61). San Francisco: Jossey-Bass.

Howe, K. (1988). Against the quantitative-qualitative incompatibility thesis or dogmas die hard. *Educational Researcher, 17*(8), 10–16.

Hudson, G. (1975). Two paradigms of educational research? *Research Intelligence, 1*(2), 68–71.

Johnson, B., & Gray, R. (2010). A history of philosophical and theoretical issues for mixed methods research. In A. Tashakkori & C. Teddlie (Eds.), *SAGE handbook of mixed methods in social & behavioral research* (2nd ed.). Thousand Oaks, CA: Sage.

Johnson, R. B., & Onwuegbuzie, A. J. (2004). Mixed methods research: A research paradigm whose time has come. *Educational Researcher, 33*(7), 14–26.

Keat, R., & Urry, J. (1975). *Social theory as science*. London: Routledge & Kegan Paul.

Langellier, K. M. (2001). Personal narrative. In M. Jolly (Ed.), *Encyclopedia of life writing: Authobiographical and biographical forms* (Vol. 2, pp. 699–701). London: Fitzroy Dearborn.

Lincoln, Y. S. (1990). The making of a constructivist: A remembrance of transformations past. In E. G. Guba (Ed.), *The paradigm dialog* (pp. 67–87). Thousand Oaks, CA: Sage.

Lincoln, Y. S., & Guba, E. G. (1985). *Naturalistic inquiry*. Beverly Hills, CA: Sage.

Manicas, P. (2007). The social sciences since World War II: The rise and fall of scientism. In W. Outhwite & S. P. Turner (Eds.), *The Sage handbook of social science methodology* (pp. 7–31). London: Sage.

Maxwell, J. A. (2004). *Realism as a stance for mixed methods research*. Paper presented at the annual meeting of the American Educational Research Association, Chicago.

Maxwell, J. A., & Mittapalli, K. (2010). Realism as a stance for mixed method research. In A. Tashakkori & C. Teddlie (Eds.), *SAGE handbook of mixed methods in social & behavioral research* (2nd ed.). Thousand Oaks, CA: Sage.

McNamara, D. R. (1979). Paradigm lost: Thomas Kuhn and educational research. *British Educational Research Journal, 5*(2), 167–173.

Mello, D. M. (2007). The language of arts in a narrative inquiry landscape. In D. J. Clandini (Ed.), *Handbook of narrative inquiry: Mapping a methodology* (pp. 203–223). Thousand Oaks, CA: Sage.

Mertens, D. M. (2003). Mixed methods and the politics of human research: The transformative-emancipatory perspective. In A. Tashakkori & C. Teddlie (Eds.), *Handbook of mixed methods in social and behavioral research* (pp. 135–164). Thousand Oaks, CA: Sage.

Mertens, D. M., Bledsoe, K. L., Sullivan, M., & Wilson, A. (2010). Utilization of mixed methods for transformative purposes. In A. Tashakkori & C. Teddlie (Eds.), *SAGE handbook of mixed methods in social & behavioral research* (2nd ed.). Thousand Oaks, CA: Sage.

Miller, S. (2003). Impact of mixed methods and design on inference quality. In A. Tashakkori & C. Teddlie (Eds.), *Handbook of mixed methods in social and behavioral research* (pp. 423–456). Thousand Oaks, CA: Sage.

Newman, I., & Benz, C. R. (1998). *Qualitative-quantitative research methodology: Exploring the interactive continuum*. Carbondale: Southern Illinois University Press.

Niglas, K. (1999, September 22–25). *Quantitative and qualitative inquiry in educational research: Is there a paradigmatic difference between them?* Paper presented at ECER99, Lahti, Finland; *Education Line*. Retrieved from http://www.leeds.ac.uk/educol/

Niglas, K. (2001, September 5–8). *Paradigms and methodology in educational research*. Paper presented at ECER2001, Lille, France; *Education Line*. Retrieved from http://www.leeds.ac.uk/educol/

Niglas, K. (2004a). *The combined use of qualitative and quantitative methods in educational research*. Tallinn, Estonia: Tallinn Pedagogical University.

Niglas, K. (2004b). Kvalitatiivsete ja kvantitatiivsete meetodite vahekorrast sotsiaal- ja kasvatusteaduslikus uurimistöös. In A. Lepik & M. Pandis (Eds.), *Interdistsiplinaarsus sotsiaal- ja kasvatusteadustes. Sotsiaal- ja kasvatusteaduste doktorantide II teaduskonverents 25.–26. aprillil 2003 TPÜ-s. Artiklite kogumik* (pp. 28–43). Tallinn, Estonia: Tallinn Pedagogical University.

Niglas, K. (2009). How the novice researcher can make sense of mixed methods designs. *International Journal of Multiple Research Approaches, 3*(1), 34–46.

Parlett, M., & Hamilton, D. (1972). *Evaluation as illumination: A new approach to the study of innovatory programs* (Occasional Paper 9). Edinburgh: University of Edinburgh.

Patton, M. Q. (1980). *Qualitative evaluation and research methods*. Newbury Park, CA: Sage.

Patton, M. Q. (1986). *Utilization-focused evaluation* (2nd ed.). Beverly Hills, CA: Sage.

Phillips, D. C. (1996). Philosophical perspectives. In D. C. Berliner & R. C. Calfee (Eds.), *Handbook of educational psychology* (pp. 1005–1019). Old Tappan, NJ: Macmillan.

Platt, J. (1986). Functionalism and the survey: The relation of theory and method. *Sociological Review, 34*(3), 501–536.

Reichardt, C. S., & Cook, T. D. (1979). Beyond qualitative versus quantitative methods. In T. D. Cook & C. S. Reichardt (Eds.), *Qualitative and quantitative methods in evaluation research* (pp. 7–32). Beverly Hills, CA: Sage.

Reissman, C. K. (2008). *Narrative methods for the human sciences.* Thousand Oaks, CA: Sage.

Ridenour, C. S., & Newman, I. (2008). *Mixed methods research: Exploring the interactive continuum.* Carbondale: Southern Illinois University Press.

Ritzer, G. (1975). Sociology: A multiple paradigm science. *The American Sociologist, 10*(3), 156–157.

Smith, J. K. (1983). Quantitative versus qualitative research: An attempt to clarify the issue. *Educational Researcher, 12*(3), 6–13.

Smith, J. K. (1989). *The nature of social and educational inquiry.* Norwood, NJ: Ablex.

Smith, J. K., & Heshusius, L. (1986). Closing down the conversation: The end of the quantitative-qualitative debate among educational inquirers. *Educational Researcher, 15*(1), 4–12.

, M. L. (1997). Mixing and matching: Methods and models. In J. C. Greene & V. J. Caracelli (Eds.), *Advances in mixed-Method evaluation: The challenges and benefits of integrating diverse paradigms* (New Directions for Evaluation, No. 74, pp. 73–85). San Francisco: Jossey-Bass.

Snizek, W. E. (1975). The relationship between theory and research: A study in the sociology of sociology. *The Sociological Quarterly, 16*(Summer), 415–428.

Stewart, K. (2005). Cultural poesis: The generativity of emergent things. In N. K. Denzin & Y. S. Lincoln (Eds.), *The SAGE handbook of qualitative research* (3rd ed., pp. 1027–1042). Thousand Oaks, CA: Sage.

Tashakkori, A., & Teddlie, C. (1998). *Mixed methodology: Combining qualitative and quantitative approaches* (Applied Social Research Methods, No. 46). Thousand Oaks, CA: Sage.

Tashakkori, A., & Teddlie, C. (2003). The past and future of mixed methods research: From data triangulation to mixed model designs. In A. Tashakkori & C. Teddlie (Eds.), *Handbook of mixed methods in social and behavioral research* (pp. 671–702). Thousand Oaks, CA: Sage.

Teddlie, C., & Tashakkori, A. (2003). Major issues and controversies in the use of mixed methods in the social and behavioral sciences. In A. Tashakkori & C. Teddlie (Eds.), *Handbook of mixed methods in social and behavioral research* (pp. 3–50). Thousand Oaks, CA: Sage.

Teddlie, C., & Tashakkori, A. (2009). *Foundations of mixed methods research: Integrating quantitative and qualitative approaches in the social and behavioral sciences.* Thousand Oaks, CA: Sage.

Teddlie, C., & Tashakkori, A. (2010). Overview of contemporary issues in mixed methods research. In A. Tashakkori & C. Teddlie (Eds.), *SAGE handbook of mixed methods in social & behavioral research* (2nd ed.). Thousand Oaks, CA: Sage.

Tesch, R. (1990). *Qualitative research: Analysis types and software tools.* New York: Falmer Press.

10

RESEARCH DESIGN, AS INDEPENDENT OF METHODS

◆ Stephen Gorard

Objectives

Readers of this chapter should be in a better position to

- understand the process of research design;

- place their own and other's work within a full cycle or program of ongoing research;

- understand why good research almost always involves a mixture of evidence;

- defend themselves from those who want numbers and text to be enemies rather than allies; and

- argue that good research is more ethical for society than poor research.

The term *mixed methods* is generally used to refer to social science research that combines in one study evidence (or techniques or approaches) deemed both quantitative and qualitative (e.g., Creswell & Plano Clark, 2007; Johnson & Onwuegbuzie, 2004). However mixed methods work is described, the key element seems to be this combination of quantitative and qualitative work at some level. It also appears that social science researchers as a body, and commentators on mixed methods in particular, view quantitative research as involving numbers, measurement, and often forms of analysis based on sampling theory. Qualitative research, on the other hand, is viewed as almost anything not involving numbers, commonly text and discourse, but also images, observations, recordings, and, on rare occasions, smell and other sensory data. Each type of research has a specialist vocabulary and an underlying philosophy purportedly making it a paradigm incommensurable with the other. Mixed methods approaches are therefore seen as complex, difficult, and innovative because they seek to combine both of the q-word paradigms in the same study or research program.

I was not fully aware of these paradigms and their attendant beliefs, like positivism and interpretivism, when I started my PhD study as an educational practitioner. In that early study of school choice, I naturally used a variety of methods and techniques, from simple re-analysis of existing data sets, documents, and archives through complex modeling of a new survey, to in-depth observations and interviews (Gorard, 1997b). This seems to me what any novice researcher would do naturally (unless contaminated by the nonsense peddled in mainstream methods resources). Doing so seemed to cause me no problems, other than the time and effort involved, and I felt that my conclusions were drawn logically from an unproblematic synthesis of the various forms of evidence. It was only once I was under way that I discovered that methods experts

believed what I was doing was wrong, impossible, or at least revolutionary in some way. In fact, what I did was none of those things. It seemed quite normal for any who genuinely wanted to find out the answers to their research questions, and from that time, I began to try and explain to these experts and authorities why (Gorard, 1997a). In the 12 years since my PhD, I have completed about 60 projects large and small and had about 600 publications of all types. In nearly all cases, I have continued to mix the methods known to others as quantitative and qualitative, both in the "new political arithmetic" style of my PhD and in a variety of different styles including Bayesian syntheses, complex interventions, and design studies (e.g., Gorard, Taylor, & Fitz, 2003; Gorard, 2007; Selwyn, Gorard, & Furlong, 2006). I have also continued to write about methods, including why quantitative work is misunderstood, both by its advocates and by its opponents (e.g., Gorard, 2006, 2010a); how misuse of the term *theory* by advocates of qualitative research has become a barrier to mixed methods (e.g., Gorard, 2004b, 2004c); the ethics of mixing methods (e.g., Gorard, 2002a; Gorard, 2004a); and most important, the underlying universal logic of all research (e.g., Gorard, 2002b, 2002c).

Yet, postgraduate students and new researchers in the United Kingdom are still routinely (mis-)taught about the incommensurable paradigms and how they must elect one or the other approach. Subsequently, they may be told that they can mix methods (if that is not a contradiction) and perhaps even that a mixed methods approach is a third paradigm they can choose (a bit like a fashion accessory). But the damage has been done by then. These new researchers may now view research evidence as a dichotomy of numbers and everything that is not numbers, and they will reason that even if they can mix the two, the fact of mixing suggests separate ingredients in the first place. If they are hesitant to work with numbers, they will tend to select the qualitative paradigm, and so convert their prior weakness in handling an essential form of evidence into a pretend bulwark and eventually a basis for criticizing those who *do* use numbers. Those less hesitant with numbers will tend to find that the system both forces them to become quantitative (because it is only by opposites that the paradigms can be protective bulwarks) and positively encourages them as well, because there is a widespread shortage of social scientists willing and able to work with numbers in U.K. education research. For example, I review papers for around 50 journals internationally, and I rarely get papers to review in my own work areas. The common denominator to what I am sent is numbers. Editors send me papers with numbers, not because I ask for them but because, unlike the majority of people in my field, I am prepared to look at them. Thus, I become, in their minds, a quantitative expert even though I am nothing of the sort and have done as many interviews and documentary, archival, video, and other in-depth analyses as most qualitative experts.

I believe that there is a different way of presenting the logic of research, not involving this particular unhelpful binary, through consideration of design and the full cycle of research work. I illustrate such an approach in this chapter, first looking at the relationship between methods and design and then between methods and the cycle. The chapter continues with a consideration of the differences between the q-word approaches. It ends with a consideration of the possible implications, if the argument thus far has been accepted, for the conduct of research, its ethics, and the preparation of new researchers. Of course, to my mind, the law of parsimony should mean that it is not necessary for me to argue in favor of an overall logic to social science research with no schism and no paradigms (as that term is used here, rather than as the fluid conversion of questions into puzzles as discussed by Kuhn and others). But it may be

interesting for those imbued with "isms" at least to understand my point of view.

◆ **Research Design in Social Science: The Forgotten Element?**

Research design in the social sciences, as elsewhere, is a way of organizing a research project or program from inception to maximize the likelihood of generating evidence that provides a warranted answer to the research questions for a given level of resource. The emphasis is less on how to conduct a type of research than on which type is appropriate in the circumstances (Hakim, 2000). In the same way that research questions can evolve as a project unfolds, so can research design(s). The structure of a standard design is not intended to be restrictive because designs can be easily used in combination; nor is it assumed that any off-the-shelf existing design is always or ever appropriate. Instead, consideration of design at the outset is intended to stimulate early awareness of the pitfalls and opportunities that will present themselves and, through knowledge of prior designs, to simplify subsequent analysis and so aid warranted conclusions.

There are many elements to consider in a research design; they commonly include the treatment or program to be evaluated (if there is one), the data collected, the groups and subgroups of interest, the allocation of cases to groups or to treatments (where appropriate), and what happens over time (unless the study is a snapshot). Any design or project may have only some of these elements. Perhaps the most common type of design in social science involves no treatment, no allocation to groups, and no consideration of time. It is cross-sectional with one or more pre-existing groups. It is also often described as qualitative in the sense that no measurements are used, and the data are often based on interviews. It is this design that makes it hardest to warrant any claims because there is usually no comparison between groups or over time or place. But actually this design does not entail any specific kind of data, any more than any other design. In fact, nothing about consideration of treatments, data collection, groups, allocation, and time entails a specific kind of evidence. Most designs seem to me to be an encouragement to use a variety of data. Standard designs can be classified in a number of ways, such as whether there is a treatment or intervention (active) or not (passive). Active designs include

- Randomized control trials (with or without blinds)

- Quasi-experiments—including interrupted time series

- Natural experiments

- Action research

- Design studies

and some might say

- Participant observation

Passive designs include

- Cohort studies (time series and retrospective)

- Other longitudinal designs

- Case control studies

- New political arithmetic

- Cross-sectional studies

and some might say

- Systematic reviews (including Bayesian)

The choice depends largely on the kind of claims and conclusions to be drawn and, to a lesser extent, on the practicalities of the situation and resources available. I say these are lesser considerations because if it is not possible, for financial, ethical, or other reasons, to use a suitable design, then the research should not be done at all (as opposed to being done badly and perhaps leading to inappropriate claims to knowledge). The need for warranted conclusions requires the researcher to identify the kind of claims to be made—such as descriptive, associative, correlational, or causal—and then ensure that the most appropriate possible design is used. Put simply, a comparative claim must have an explicit and suitable comparator, for example. The warranting principle is based on this consideration—if the claim to be drawn from the evidence is not actually true, then how else could the evidence be explained? The claim should be the simplest explanation for the available evidence. What the design should do is eliminate (or at least test or allow for) the greatest possible number of alternate explanations. In this way, the design eases the analysis process and provides part of the warrant for the research claims.

What all of these standard designs and variants of them have in common is that they do not specify the kind of data to be used or collected. At the level of an individual study, the research design used by social scientists will be independent of, and logically prior to, the methods of data collection and analysis employed. No kinds of data and no particular philosophical predicates are entailed by common existing design structures such as longitudinal, case study, randomized controlled trial, or action research. A good intervention, for example, could and should use a variety of data collection techniques to understand whether something works, how to improve it, or why it does not work. Experiments can use any kind of data as outcomes and collect any kind of data throughout to help understand why the outcomes are as they are. Longitudinal studies can collect data of all types over time. Case studies involve immersion in one real-life scenario, collecting data of any kind, ranging from existing records to *ad hoc* observations. And so on.

Mixed methods approaches are, therefore, not a kind of research design; nor do they entail or privilege a particular design. Of course, all stages in research can be said to involve elements of design. The sample design is one example, and the design of instruments for data collection another. But research design, as usually defined in social science research and as discussed here, is a prior stage to each of these (de Vaus, 2001).

◆ **The Cycle of Research**

At the meta-level of a program of research conducted by one team, or a field of research conducted by otherwise separate teams, the overarching research design will incorporate most methods of data collection and analysis. Figure 10.1 is a simplified description of a full cycle for a research program (for a fuller description and discussion, see Middleton, Gorard, Taylor, & Bannan-Ritland, 2008). It is based on a number of sources, including the genesis of a design study (Gorard, 2004a), the U.K. Medical Research Council (MRC) model for undertaking complex medical interventions (MRC, 2000), and one OECD conception of what useful policy research looks like (Cook & Gorard, 2007). The cycle is more properly a spiral that has no clear beginning or end, in which activities

Figure 10.1 An Outline of the Full Cycle of Social Science Research and Development

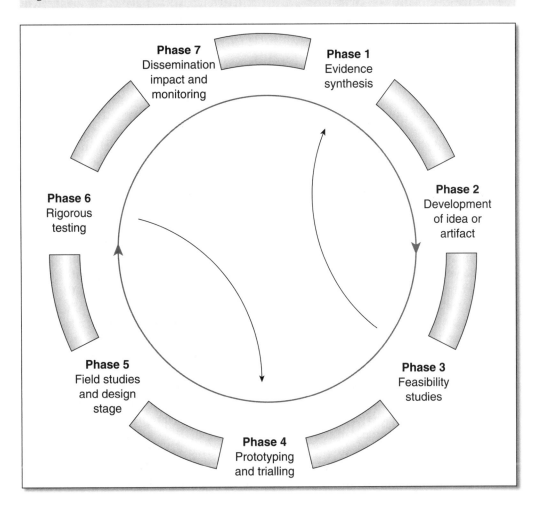

(phases) overlap, can take place simultaneously, and iterate. Nevertheless, the various phases should be recognizable to anyone working in areas of applied social science, like public policy. Starting with draft research questions, the research cycle might begin with a synthesis of existing evidence (Phase 1 here). Ideally, this synthesis would be an inclusive review of the literature, both published and unpublished (perhaps combining the different kinds of evidence via a Bayesian approach—Gorard, Roberts, & Taylor, 2004), coupled with a re-analysis of relevant existing data sets of all kinds (including data archives and administrative data sets), and related policy/practice documents. It is not possible to conduct a fair appraisal of the existing evidence on almost any real topic in applied social science without naturally combining evidence involving text, numbers, pictures, and a variety of other data forms. Anyone who excludes relevant data because of its type (such as text or numeric) is a fake researcher, not really trying to find anything out.

Currently, the kind of comprehensive synthesis outlined above is rare. If more took place, one consequence might be that research programs would more often end at Phase 1, where the answers to the research questions are already as well established as social science answers can be. Another consequence might be that researchers would more often revise their initial questions suitably before continuing to other phases of the cycle (White, 2008). For example, there is little point in continuing to investigate why the attainment gap between boys and girls at school is increasing if initial work shows that the gap is actually decreasing (Gorard, Rees, & Salisbury, 2001). The eclectic reuse of existing evidence would often be more ethical than standard practice (a patchy literature review), making better and more efficient use of the taxpayer and charitable money spent on the subsequent research.

Similarly, where a project or program continues past Phase 1, every further phase in the cycle would tend to involve a mixture of methods. Each phase might lead to a realization that little more can be learned and that the study is over, or that the study needs radical revision and iteration to an earlier phase(s) or progression to a subsequent phase. The overall program might be envisaged as tending toward an artifact or product of some kind. This product might be a theory (if the desired outcome is simply knowledge), a proposed improvement for public policy, or a tool/resource for a practitioner. For any of these outcomes to be promoted and disseminated in an ethical manner, they must have been tested (or else the dissemination must merely state that they seem a good idea, but that we have no real idea of their value). A theory, by definition, will generate testable propositions. A proposed public policy intervention can be tested realistically and then monitored *in situ* for the predicted benefits and for any unwanted and undesirable side effects. Therefore, for that minority of programs that continue as far as Phase 6 in Figure 10.1, rigorous testing must usually involve a mixture of methods and types of evidence in just the same way as Phase 1. Even where a purely numeric outcome is envisaged as the benefit of the research program (such as a more effective or cost-efficient service), it is no good knowing that the intervention works if we do not also know that it is unpopular and likely to be ignored or subverted in practice. Similarly, it would be a waste of resources, and therefore unethical simply to discover that an intervention did not work in Phase 6 and so return to a new program of study in Phase 1. We would want to know why it did not work, or perhaps how to improve it, and whether it was effective for some regular pattern of cases but not for others. So in Phase 6, as in Phase 1, the researcher or team who genuinely wants to find something out will naturally use a range of methods and approaches including measurement, narrative, and observation.

The same kind of conclusion could be reached for every phase in Figure 10.1. Even monitoring and evaluation of the rollout of the results (Phase 7) is best done by using all and any data available. Even in simple academic impact terms, a citation count for a piece of research gives no idea of the way in which it is used (just mentioned or fundamental to the new work of others), nor indeed whether the citation is critical of the research and whether it is justified in being critical. On the other hand, for a widely cited piece of research, reading in-depth how the research has been cited in a few pieces gives no idea of the overall pattern. Analyzing citation patterns *and* reading some of the citing pieces—perhaps chosen to represent features of the overall pattern—gives a much better indication of the impact of this research. Methods of data collection and analysis are not alternatives; they are complementary. Specific methods might be used to answer a simple, perhaps descriptive research question in one phase, but even then, the answer will tend to yield more complex causal questions, which require more attention to research design (Cook & Gorard, 2007).

Across all stages of the cycle up to definitive testing, engineering of results into useable form, and subsequent rollout and monitoring, different methods might have a more dominant role in any one stage, but the overall process for a field of endeavor requires a full range of research techniques. It is indefensible for researchers, even those limited in expertise to one technique (and so admitting that they are not competent to conduct even something as basic as a comprehensive literature review, for example), to imagine that they are not involved in a larger process that mixes methods naturally and automatically.

◆ Reconsidering the Schism

The q-word dichotomy has, as illustrated, no relevance to design or indeed to entire programs of research. We may consider that surveys and interviews, for example, are quite different, but even here, there may

be a continuum through structured interview schedules to open-ended survey items delivered face-to-face. The q-word division is not helpful even with methods. Is there such a thing as a qualitative interview *and* a quantitative interview? I doubt it. Interview, as a general category, is enough. The q-words add nothing. So what lies beneath the schism? I consider here three general propositions—that the schism arises from important differences in paradigm, scale, and methods of data analysis.

THE Q-WORDS ARE NOT PARADIGMS

In the sociology of science, the notion of a paradigm is a description of the sets of socially accepted assumptions that tend to appear in "normal science" (Kuhn, 1970). A paradigm is a set of accepted rules within any field for solving one or more puzzles—where a puzzle is defined as a scientific question that it is possible to find a solution to in the near future, to distinguish it from the many important and interesting questions that do not have an answer at any particular stage of progress (Davis, 1994). Normal science, in Kuhnian terms, is held together, rightly or wrongly, by the norms of reviewing and acceptance that work in a taken-for-granted theoretical framework. A paradigm shift occurs when the framework changes, perhaps through the accumulation of evidence, perhaps due to a genuinely new idea, but partly through a change in general acceptance. Often, a new paradigm emerges because a procedure or set of rules has been created for converting another more general query *into* a puzzle. But what Kuhn saw as normal science could also be simply passive and uncritical rather than genuinely cumulative in nature. It could be based on practices that differ from those stated because of deceit, either of the self or of the audience (Lakatos, 1978, p. 44), and because researchers conceal their actual methodological divergence in practice (Gephart, 1988).

However, instead of using *paradigm* to refer to a topic or field of research (such as traditional physics), which might undergo a radical shift on the basis of evidence (to quantum physics, for example), some commentators now use it to refer to a whole approach to research including philosophy, values, and method (Perlesz & Lindsay, 2003). The most common of these approaches are qualitative and quantitative, even though the q-words make sense, if they make sense at all, only as descriptions of data. These commentators tend to use the term *paradigm* conservatively, to defend themselves against the need to change, or against contradictory evidence of a different nature to their own. Their idea of paradigm appears to defend them because they pointlessly parcel up unrelated ideas in methodology (as explained in Biesta, 2010 [this volume]). The idea of normal science as a collection of individuals all working toward the solution of a closely defined problem has all but disappeared. Instead, we have paradigm as a symptom of scientific immaturity. The concept of paradigm has, thus, become a cultural cliché with so many meanings it is now almost meaningless. And many of the terms associated with paradigms—the "isms" such as positivism—are used almost entirely to refer to others, having become intellectually acceptable terms of abuse and ridicule (see also Hammersley, 2005).

Unfortunately, some novice research students can quickly become imprisoned within one of these fake qualitative and quantitative paradigms. They learn, because they are taught, that if they use any numbers in their research then they must be positivist or realist in philosophy, and they must be hypothetico-deductive or traditional in style (see, for example, such claims by Clarke, 1999). If, on the other hand, students disavow the use of numbers in research, then they must be interpretivist, holistic, and alternative, believing in multiple perspectives rather than truth, and so on. Sale, Lohfeld, and Brazil (2002), for example, claim that "the

quantitative paradigm is based on positivism. Science is characterized by empirical research" (p. 44), whereas, "in contrast, the qualitative paradigm is based on . . . multiple realities. [There is] no external referent by which to compare claims of truth" (p. 45). Such commentators "evidently believe that the choice of a research method represents commitment to a certain kind of truth and the concomitant rejection of other kinds of truth" (Snow, 2001, p. 3). They consider that the value of their methods can be judged completely separately from the questions they are used to answer.

What is ironic about this use of the term *paradigm* to refer to a methods- and value-based system in social research is that it has never been intended to be generally taken for granted, in the way that "normal science" is. Rather, it splits the field into two noncommunicating parts. Therefore, a paradigm of this kind cannot be shifted by evidence, ideas, or the fact that others reject it. It becomes divisive and conservative in nature, leading to "an exaggeration of the differences between the two traditions" (Gray & Densten, 1998, p. 419) and an impoverishment of the range of methods deployed to try and solve important social problems.

It is somewhat impractical to sustain an argument that all parts of all methods, including data collection, carry epistemological or ontological commitments anyway (Bryman, 2001; Frazer, 1995). So, researchers tend to confuse the issues, shuttling from technical to philosophical differences and exaggerating them into a paradigm (Bryman, 1988). No research design implies either qualitative or quantitative data even though reviewers commonly make the mistake of assuming that they do—that experiments can collect only numeric data, observation must be non-numeric, and so on. Observation of how work is conducted shows that, in practice, qualitative and quantitative work are *not* conducted in differing research paradigms. The alleged differences between research paradigms (in this sense) prevail in spite of good evidence, not because of it ("Quack Theories," 2002).

Mixed methods have been claimed to be a third paradigm (Johnson & Onwuegbuzie, 2004), but this seems to add to the confusion by apparently confirming the validity of the first two, instead of simply blowing them all away by not mentioning any of them in the development of new researchers. Worldviews do not logically entail or privilege the use of specific methods (Guba, 1990) but may be thought to do so only due to a common confusion between the logic of designing a study and the method of collecting data (according to de Vaus, 2001; Geurts & Roosendaal, 2001). "The researcher's fidelity to principles of inquiry is more important than allegiance to procedural mechanics. . . . Research should be judged by the quality and soundness of its conception, implementation and description, not by the genre within which it is conducted" (Paul & Marfo, 2001, pp. 543–545). In real life, methods *can* be separated from the epistemology from which they emerge, so that qualitative work is not tied to a constructivist paradigm, and so on (Teddlie & Tashakkori, 2003). The paradigm argument for the q-word approaches is a red herring and unnecessarily complex to boot (as evidenced in some of the other chapters in Part I of this collection).

NOT JUST AN ISSUE OF SCALE

Some authorities suggest that a clear difference between the q-word approaches is their scale (e.g., Creswell & Plano Clark, 2007), with qualitative data collection necessarily involving small numbers of cases, whereas quantitative relies on very large samples to increase power and reduce the standard error. This is misleading for two reasons. First, it is not an accurate description of what happens in practice. Both Gorard and Rees (2002) and Selwyn et al. (2006) interviewed 1,100 adults in their own homes, for example, and treated the data gathered as individual life histories.

This is larger scale than many surveys. On the other hand, Smith and Gorard (2005) conducted a field trial in one school with only 26 students in the treatment group, yielding both attainment scores and contextual data. The number of cases is not necessarily related to methods of data collection or to either of the q-words. Second, issues such as sampling error and power relate only to a tiny minority of studies where a true and complete random sample is used or where a population is randomly allocated to treatment groups. In the much more common situations—working with incomplete samples with measurement error or dropout; convenience, snowball, and other nonrandom samples; and the increasing amount of population data available to us—the constraints of sampling theory are completely irrelevant. Also, the standard error/power theory of analysis is fatally flawed in its own terms, even when used as intended (Gorard, 2010a). The accounts of hundreds of interviewees can be properly analyzed as text, and the account of one case study can properly involve numbers. The supposed link between scale and paradigm is just an illusion.

THE LOGIC OF ANALYSIS IS SIMILAR

Another possible distinction between the q-word approaches is their method of analysis. Qualitative work is supposed to be subjective and so closer to a social world (Gergen & Gergen, 2000). Quantitative work is supposed to help us become objective (Bradley & Schaefer, 1998). This distinction between quantitative and qualitative analysis is exaggerated, largely because of widespread error by those who handle numbers (Gorard, 2010a) and ignorance of the subjective and interpretivist nature of numeric analysis by those who do not (Gorard, 2006). The similarities of the underlying procedures used are remarkable (Onwuegbuzie & Leech, 2005). Few analytical techniques are restricted by data gathering methods, input data, or sample size. Most methods of analysis use some form of number, such as *tend, most, some, all, none, few,* and so on (Gorard, 1997a). Whenever one talks of things being *rare, typical, great,* or *related,* this is a numeric claim and can only be so substantiated, whether expressed verbally or in figures (Meehl, 1998). Similarly, quantification does not consist of simply assigning numbers to things but of relating empirical relations to numeric relations (Nash, 2002). The numbers themselves are valuable only insofar as their behavior is an isomorph of the qualities they are summarizing. Statistical analysis is misunderstood by observers if they do not consider also the social settings in which it takes place and the role of qualitative factors in reaching a conclusion (MacKenzie, 1999). Normal statistical textbooks describe ideal procedures to follow, but several studies of actual behavior have observed different common practices among researchers. "Producing a statistic is a social enterprise" (Gephart, 1988, p. 15), and the stages of selecting variables, making observations, and coding the results take place in everyday settings where subjective influences arise. It would be dishonest to pretend otherwise.

Even such an apparently basic operation as the measurement of a length involves acceptance of a series of theories and judgments about the nature of length and the isomorphic behavior of numbers (Berka, 1983). As with *number* and *length,* so also with many of our basic concepts and classifications for use in social science—*sex, time, place, family, class,* or *ethnicity* (Gorard, 2003). Measurement is an intrinsically interpretivist process (Gorard, 2010b). Personal judgment(s) lie at the heart of all research—in our choice of research questions, samples, questions to participants, and methods of analysis— regardless of the kinds of data to be collected. The idea that quantitative work is objective and qualitative is subjective is based on a misunderstanding of how research is actually conducted.

◆ Implications (If the Argument So Far Is Accepted)

FOR THE CONDUCT OF RESEARCH

Mixed methods are not a design. Nor do they represent some kind of paradigm, separate from those traditionally termed qualitative and quantitative. How could mixed methods be incommensurable with the two elements supposed to be mixed within them? Mixed methods are, then, just a description of how most people would go about researching any topic that they really wanted to find out about. The results of research if taken seriously affect the lives of real people and lead to genuine expenditure and opportunity costs. We should be (nearly) as concerned about research as we are about investigations and decisions in our lives. It is instructive to contrast how we, as researchers, generally behave when conducting research professionally and how we behave when trying to answer important questions in our everyday lives. When we make real-life decisions about where to live and where to work, as well as the care and safety of our children, the health of our loved ones, and so on, many of us behave very differently from researchers.

No one, on buying a house, refuses to discuss or even know the price, the mortgage repayments, the room measurements, or the number of bathrooms. No one, on buying a house, refuses to visit the house, look at pictures of it, walk or drive around the neighborhood, or talk to people about it. All rational actors putting a substantial personal investment into their own house would naturally, and without any consideration of paradigms, epistemology, identity, or mixed methods, use all and any convenient data to help make up their minds. We will believe that the house is real even though external to us and that it remains the same even when we approach it from different ends of the street. Thus, we would not start with "isms." We would not refuse to visit the house or talk to the neighbors about it because we were quantitative researchers and did not believe that observation or narratives were valid or reliable enough for our purposes. We would not refuse to consider the interest rate for the loan or the size of the monthly repayments because we were qualitative researchers and did not believe that numbers could do justice to the social world. And we would naturally, even unconsciously, synthesize the various forms of data to reach a verdict. I do not mean to say that such real-life decisions are easy; the difficulties do not stem from paradigms and epistemology, however, but from weighing up factors like cost, convenience, luxury, safety, and so on. People would use the same naturally mixed approach when making arrangements for the safety of their children or loved ones and for any information-based task about which they really cared. For important matters, we behave sensibly, eclectically, critically, skeptically, but always with that final leap of faith because research, however carefully conducted, does not provide the action—it only informs the action. We collect all and any evidence available to us as time and resources allow and then synthesize it naturally, without consideration of mixing methods as such.

Thus, I can envisage only two situations in which social science researchers would not similarly use mixed methods in their work. Perhaps they might not care about the results and are simply pretending to do research (and wasting people's time and money in the process). This may be a common phenomenon in reality. Or their research question could be peculiarly specific, entailing only one method. However, the existence of this second situation, analogous to using only one tool from a larger toolbox, is not any kind of argument for separate paradigms of the two q-words and mixed methods. Mixed methods, in the sense of having a variety of tools in the toolbox and using them as appropriate, is the only sensible way to approach research. Thus, a central premise of mixed methods is

that "the use of quantitative and qualitative approaches in combination provides a better understanding of research problems than either approach alone" (Creswell & Plano Clark, 2007, p. 5). This is what I have always argued, but without the need to create a new paradigm (Gorard, 1997b; Gorard, 2004a). Mixed methods (the ability to use any appropriate methods) is the only sensible and ethical way to conduct research.

FOR ETHICAL CONSIDERATION OF PROJECTS

A key ethical concern for those conducting or using publicly funded research ought to be the quality of the research, and so the robustness of the findings, and the security of the conclusions drawn. Until recently, very little of the writing on the ethics of education research has been concerned with quality. The concern has been largely for the participants in the research process, which is perfectly proper, but this emphasis may have blinded researchers to their responsibility to those not participating in the research process. The taxpayers and charity donors who fund the research, and members of the general public who use the resulting public services, for example, have the right to expect that the research has been conducted in such a way that it is possible for the researcher to test and answer the questions asked. People are shocked to discover that they are funding the work of social scientists who either believe that everything can be encompassed in numbers or much more often believe that nothing can be achieved using numbers (or that nothing is true, or that there is no external world, or . . .).

Generating secure findings for widespread use in public policy should involve a variety of factors including care and attention, skeptical consideration of plausible alternatives, independent replication, transparent prior criteria for success and failure, use of multiple complementary methods, and explicit rigorous testing of tentative explanations. The q-word paradigms are just a hindrance here, and so are unethical as originally suggested in Gorard (2002a, 2003), with this second principle of research ethics slowly filtering into professional guidelines (e.g., Social Research Association, 2003).

FOR THE DEVELOPMENT OF NEW RESEARCHERS

As I explained at the start of the chapter, I was lucky enough to be undamaged by supposed research methods development of the kind now compulsory for publicly funded new researchers in the United Kingdom. Or perhaps I was critical and confident enough to query what methods experts were saying and writing. Methods text, courses, and resources are replete with errors and misinformation, such that many do more damage than good. Some mistakes are relatively trivial. I remember clearly being told by international experts that triangulation was based on having three points of view, or that the finite population correction meant that a sample must be smaller than I proposed, for example. I have heard colleagues coteaching in my own modules tell our students that regression is a *test* of causation (see also Robinson, Levin, Thomas, Pituch, & Vaughn, 2007) or that software like NVivo will analyze textual data for them. Some examples are more serious. There is a widespread error in methods texts implicitly stating that the probability of a hypothesis given the data is the same as, or closely related to, the probability of the data, given that the hypothesis is true. However, probably the most serious mistakes currently made in researcher development are the lack of awareness of design and the suggestion that methods imply values and are a matter of personal preference rather than a consequence of the problems to be overcome via research.

Much research methods training in social science is predicated on the notion that there are distinct categories of methods such as qualitative or quantitative. Methods are then generally taught to researchers in an isolated way, and this isolation is reinforced by sessions and resources on researcher identities, paradigms, and values. The schism between qualitative and quantitative work is very confusing for student researchers (Ercikan & Wolff-Michael, 2006). It is rightly confusing because it does not make sense. These artificial categories of data collection and analysis are not paradigms. Both kinds of methods involve subjective judgments about less than perfect evidence. Both involve consideration of quantity and of quality, of type and frequency. Nothing is gained by the schism, and I have been wrong in allowing publishers to use the q-words in the titles of some of my books (altering "the role of numbers made easy" to "quantitative methods," for example). Subsequently, many of the same methods training programs taken by new researchers refer to the value of mixing methods, such as those deemed qualitative or quantitative. Perhaps, unsurprisingly, this leads to further confusion. Better to leave paradigms, schisms, and mixing methods for later, or even leave them out of training courses altogether.

It is not enough merely to eliminate the q-words from module headings and resources. The change has to be adopted by all tutors respecting every kind of evidence for what it is, and following this respect through in their own teaching and writing. This is what I have implemented successfully in both previous universities in which I have worked. It is what I am trying to implement in my current institution—encouraged as ever by national funding bodies, supported by the upper echelons of the university, and opposed by the least research-active of my colleagues, who seem to want to cling to their comforting paradigms, perhaps as an explanation for their unwillingness to conduct relevant, rigorous, and ethical research. This is part of the reason why I would want research methods development for new researchers to be exclusively in the hands of the most successful practical researchers, who are often busy doing research, rather than in the hands of those supposed methods specialists, who are often unencumbered by research contracts and so free to corrupt the researchers of the future. Busy practical researchers will tend to focus on the craft, the fun, the importance, *and* the humility of research. They will want new researchers to help them combat inequality, inefficiency, and corruption in important areas of public policy like health, education, crime, and social housing. There is just no time to waste on meaningless complications and the unworkable philosophy of the q-word paradigms.

◆ *Conclusions*

This chapter looks at the idea of mixed methods approaches to research and concludes that this is the way new researchers would naturally approach the solution of any important evidence-informed problem. This means that a lot of the epistemology and identity routinely taught to new researchers is not just pointless; it may actually harm their development. The chapter reminds readers of the importance of research design and how this neglected stage of the research cycle is completely independent of issues like methods of data collection and analysis. The schismic classifications of qualitative and quantitative work are unjustifiable as paradigms. They are not based on the scale of the work or on different underlying logic of analysis. They are pointless. The chapter ends with some considerations of the implications for the conduct of publicly funded research, for the ethics of social science, and for the preparation of new researchers.

Research Questions and Exercises

1. If the first principle of research ethics is not to harm research participants, how would you summarize the second principle discussed in this chapter?

2. Can all issues of research ethics be classified under these two principles, or are there more?

3. Why do you think so many professional researchers think it is possible to claim that researchers should ignore either evidence in the form of text or evidence in the form of numbers?

4. Try to imagine a real-life situation that is important to you in which you had to make an evidence-informed decision. What reason could you have for ignoring relevant evidence simply because it was numeric (or textual)?

5. Look at some journals in your area of interest and consider how many papers use techniques based on random sampling theory (such as significance tests, standard errors, confidence intervals). How many of these actually had random samples, and how many were using these techniques erroneously?

6. Look at some journals in your area of interest and consider how many papers using purportedly qualitative methods make either explicit or implicit comparative claims (over time, place, or social group) without presenting any data from a comparator group.

7. Examine the meaning and use of the term *warrant* in social science research. How useful is it for your own work?

◆ References

Berka, K. (1983). *Measurement: Its concepts, theories, and problems*. London: Reidel.

Biesta, G. (2010). Pragmatism and the philosophical foundations of mixed methods research. In A. Tashakkori & C. Teddlie (Eds.), *SAGE handbook of mixed methods in social & behavioral research* (2nd ed.). Thousand Oaks, CA: Sage.

Bradley, W., & Shaefer, K. (1998). *Limitations of measurement in the social sciences*. Thousand Oaks, CA: Sage.

Bryman, A. (1988). *Quantity and quality in social research*. London: Unwin Hyman.

Bryman, A. (2001). *Social research methods*. Oxford, UK: Oxford University Press.

Clarke, A. (1999). *Evaluation research*. London: Sage.

Cook, T., & Gorard, S. (2007). What counts and what should count as evidence. In Organization for Economic Cooperation and Development (Ed.), *Evidence in education: Linking research and policy* (pp. 33–49). Paris: OECD.

Creswell, J., & Plano Clark, V. (2007). *Designing and conducting mixed methods research*. London: Sage.

Davis, J. (1994). What's wrong with sociology? *Sociological Forum, 9*(2), 179–197.

de Vaus, D. (2001). *Research design in social science*. London: Sage.

Ercikan, K., & Wolff-Michael, R. (2006). What good is polarizing research into qualitative and quantitative? *Educational Researcher, 35*(5), 14–23.

Frazer, E. (1995). What's new in the philosophy of science? *Oxford Review of Education, 21*(3), 267.

Gephart, R. (1988). *Ethnostatistics: Qualitative foundations for quantitative research*. London: Sage.

Gergen, M., & Gergen, K. (2000). Qualitative inquiry, tensions, and transformations. In N. Denzin & Y. Lincoln (Eds.), *The landscape of qualitative reserach: Theories and issues*. Thousand Oaks, CA: Sage.

Geurts, P., & Roosendaal, H. (2001). Estimating the direction of innovative change based on theory and mixed methods. *Quality and Quantity, 35*, 407–427.

Gorard, S. (1997a). A choice of methods: The methodology of choice. *Research in Education, 57*, 45–56.

Gorard, S. (1997b). *School choice in an established market*. Aldershot, UK: Ashgate.

Gorard, S. (2002a). Ethics and equity: Pursuing the perspective of non-participants. *Social Research Update, 39*, 1–4.

Gorard, S. (2002b). Fostering scepticism: The importance of warranting claims. *Evaluation and Research in Education, 16*(3), 136–149.

Gorard, S. (2002c). The role of causal models in education as a social science. *Evaluation and Research in Education, 16*(1), 51–65.

Gorard, S. (2003). *Quantitative methods in social science: The role of numbers made easy*. London: Continuum.

Gorard, S. (with Taylor, C.). (2004a). *Combining methods in educational and social research*. London: Open University Press.

Gorard, S. (2004b). Scepticism or clericalism? Theory as a barrier to combining methods. *Journal of Educational Enquiry, 5*(1), 1–21.

Gorard, S. (2004c). Three abuses of "theory": An engagement with Nash. *Journal of Educational Enquiry, 5*(2), 19–29.

Gorard, S. (2006). Towards a judgement-based statistical analysis. *British Journal of Sociology of Education, 27*(1), 67–80.

Gorard, S. (with Adnett, N., May, H., Slack, K., Smith, E., & Thomas, L.). (2007). *Overcoming barriers to HE*. Stoke-on-Trent, UK: Trentham Books.

Gorard, S. (2010a). All evidence is equal: The flaw in statistical reasoning. *Oxford Review of Education, 36*(1), 63–77.

Gorard, S. (2010b). Measuring is more than assigning numbers. In G. Walford, E. Tucker, & M. Viswanathan (Eds.), *Handbook of measurement*. Thousand Oaks, CA: Sage.

Gorard, S., & Rees, G. (2002). *Creating a learning society?* Bristol, UK: Policy Press.

Gorard, S., Rees, G., & Salisbury, J. (2001). The differential attainment of boys and girls at school: Investigating the patterns and their determinants. *British Educational Research Journal, 27*(2), 125–139.

Gorard, S., Roberts, K., & Taylor, C. (2004). What kind of creature is a design experiment? *British Educational Research Journal, 30*(4), 575–590.

Gorard, S., Taylor, C., & Fitz, J. (2003). *Schools, markets and choice policies.* London: Routledge.

Gray, J., & Densten, I. (1998). Integrating quantitative and qualitative analysis using latent and manifest variables. *Quality and Quantity, 32*, 419–431.

Guba, E. (1990). The alternative paradigm dialog. In E. Guba (Ed.), *The paradigm dialog* (pp. 17–27). London: Sage.

Hakim, C. (2000). *Research design.* London: Routledge.

Hammersley, M. (2005). Countering the "new orthodoxy" in educational research: A response to Phil Hodkinson. *British Educational Research Journal, 31*(2), 139–155.

Johnson, R., & Onwuegbuzie, A. (2004). Mixed methods research: A research paradigm whose time has come. *Educational Researcher, 33*(7), 14–26.

Kuhn, T. (1970). *The structure of scientific revolutions.* Chicago: University of Chicago Press.

Lakatos, I. (1978). *The methodology of scientific research programmes.* Cambridge, UK: Cambridge University Press.

MacKenzie, D. (1999). The zero-sum assumption. *Social Studies of Science, 29*(2), 223–234.

Medical Research Council. (2000). *A framework for development and evaluation of RCTs for complex interventions to improve health.* London: Author.

Meehl, P. (1998, May 23). *The power of quantitative thinking.* Speech delivered on receipt of the James McKeen Cattell Fellow award at the American Psychological Society, Washington DC.

Middleton, J., Gorard, S., Taylor, C., & Bannan-Ritland, B. (2008). The "compleat" design experiment: From soup to nuts. In A. Kelly, R. Lesh, & J. Baek (Eds.), *Handbook of design research methods in education: Innovations in science, technology, engineering and mathematic learning and teaching* (pp. 21–46). New York: Routledge.

Nash, R. (2002). Numbers and narratives: Further reflections in the sociology of education. *British Journal of Sociology of Education, 23*(3), 397–412.

Onwuegbuzie, A., & Leech, N. (2005). Taking the "Q" out of research: Teaching research methodology courses without the divide between quantitative and qualitative paradigms. *Quality and Quantity, 38*, 267–296.

Paul, J., & Marfo, K. (2001). Preparation of educational researchers in philosophical foundations of inquiry. *Review of Educational Research, 71*(4), 525–547.

Perlesz, A., & Lindsay, J. (2003). Methodological triangulation in researching families: Making sense of dissonant data. *International Journal of Social Research Methodology, 6*(1), 25–40.

Quack theories. (2002). *Russell Turpin's "Characterization of quack theories."* Retrieved September 5, 2002, from http://quasar.as.utexas.edu/billinfo/quack.html

Robinson, D., Levin, J., Thomas, G., Pituch, K., & Vaughn, S. (2007). The incidence of "causal" statements in teaching-and-learning research journals. *American Educational Research Journal, 44*(2), 400–413.

Sale, J., Lohfeld, L., & Brazil, K. (2002). Revisiting the quantitative-qualitative debate: Implications for mixed-methods research. *Quality and Quantity, 36*, 43–53.

Selwyn, N., Gorard, S., & Furlong, J. (2006). *Adult learning in the digital age.* London: Routledge Falmer.

Smith, E., & Gorard, S. (2005). "They don't give us our marks": The role of formative feedback in student progress. *Assessment in Education, 12*(1), 21–38.

Snow, C. (2001). Knowing what we know: Children, teachers, researchers. *Educational Researcher, 30*(7), 3–9.

Social Research Association. (2003). *Ethical guidelines.* Retrieved August 17, 2009, from www.the-sra.org.uk

Teddlie, C., & Tashakkori, A. (2003). Major issues and controversies in the use of mixed methods. In A. Tashakkori & C. Teddlie (Eds.), *Handbook of mixed methods in social & behavioral research.* Thousand Oaks, CA: Sage.

White, P. (2008). *Developing research questions: A guide for social scientists.* London: Palgrave.

11

INTERVIEWS WITH THE EARLY DEVELOPERS OF MIXED METHODS RESEARCH[1]

◆ Nancy L. Leech

Objectives

This chapter has the following learning objectives:

- to understand the thoughts of the early developers of mixed methods research on the field;

- to explore how the initial developers became interested in mixed research, their personal passions and hopes for mixed research, ideas or thoughts they had/have that are not readily reflected in the writings, and where they see the field moving, among other areas; and

- to compare and contrast the thoughts from the interviews of the early developers.

AUTHOR'S NOTE: Correspondence should be addressed to Nancy L. Leech, University of Colorado Denver, School of Education and Human Development, Campus Box 106, PO Box 173364, Denver, Colorado 80217, phone: 303-315-6327, or e-mail: nancy.leech@ucdenver.edu

Mixed methods research is not a new phenomenon. According to Johnson, Onwuegbuzie, and Turner (2007), "Although mixed methods research is not new, it is a new movement, or discourse, or research paradigm (with a growing number of members) that has arisen in response to the currents of *quantitative research* and *qualitative research*" (p. 113, italics in original). Yet, even though it is not a new phenomenon, it is moving, evolving, and changing. Therefore, it is important and interesting to understand where the movement started, where it is at present, and where it may be going.

The goal of this chapter is to provide a forum to share the thoughts of the developers of mixed methods research on the field. This chapter starts with a brief discussion of the historical roots of three research genres: quantitative, qualitative, and mixed.[2] Next, the interviews with the early developers of mixed methods research are presented, along with quotes gathered from the interviews. The interview questions explored the past, present, and future of mixed methods research, specifically in the following areas: how the initial developers became interested in mixed research, their personal passions and hopes for mixed research, ideas or thoughts they had/have that are not readily reflected in their writings, and where they see the field moving. Finally, distinctions and connections (differences and similarities) across the interviews are described. Having more understanding of the thoughts of the early developers of mixed methods research may help the field develop a stronger foundation and, thus, a firmer sense of where it came from and where it may be moving.

◆ Identifying the Beginning of a Research Genre[3]

To assess when a research genre began is tricky. First, it is necessary to explicate how the beginning of a movement could be identified. For purposes of this chapter, the beginning of a movement in research will be defined as the point at which researchers began to formalize and promote the approach. While quantitative research has roots going back to antiquity, its origins in the social sciences were delayed until those fields of study began to emerge midway through the 19th century. Thus, for the quantitative research approach, 19th-century methodologists could be identified as beginning the movement (Teddlie & Johnson, 2009). Researchers such as August Comte (1798–1857) in sociology and Wilhelm Wundt in psychology (1832–1920) paved the way for the quantitative approach. These authors were writing about quantitative research in their specific fields at a time when others were not; furthermore, these authors were promoting the use of quantitative research. These methods dominated in the social and behavioral sciences through the 1960s. Seminal quantitative works of the 20th century include Campbell and Stanley (1963) and Cook and Campbell (1979).

Regarding qualitative research, Denzin and Lincoln (2005) suggest the history of the qualitative approach in North America began in the early 1900s and incorporates eight phases. According to these authors, the second phase, from the post–World War II period to the 1970s, was when textbook authors (e.g., Bogdan & Taylor, 1975; Glaser & Strauss, 1967; Lofland & Lofland, 1994) attempted to formalize the qualitative approach. Yet, Denzin and Lincoln (2005) do not delineate founders of the qualitative approach; therefore, we could presume that those who published during the second phase and who helped to move the field forward were the initial developers of qualitative research in the social and behavioral sciences. A second wave of important contributors to qualitative research in the social and behavioral sciences emerged in the 1980s and early 1990s and included Norman Denzin, Yvonna Lincoln and Egon Guba, Matthew Miles and Michael Huberman, Michael Quinn Patton, Robert Stake, and Robert Yin.

To learn about the history of mixed methods research in the social sciences and how it has blossomed into the movement that it is today, I started by completing a literature search. Two major search engines (PsycINFO and ERIC) were used to find articles. With these search engines, the key words *mixed methods* and *history* were combined using the Boolean logical operator AND. I searched for articles between the years of 1960 and 2009. The initial search using PsycINFO yielded 185 articles, and using ERIC only 3 articles. False hits (i.e., articles not reporting on mixed methods research), duplicates between databases, empirical articles, dissertations, books, book chapters, and unpublished papers were deleted. A further criterion used for inclusion included the following: The article needed to include specific information on the history or the beginning of mixed methods research. After this deletion, only six remained (i.e., Capraro & Thompson, 2008; Gelo, Braakmann, & Benetka, 2008; Giacobbi, Poczardowski, & Hager, 2005; Greene, Benjamin, & Goodyear, 2001; Leahey, 2007; Plano Clark, Huddleston-Casas, Churchill, Green, & Garrett, 2008). Of these articles, none discussed the beginnings of mixed methods research beyond the qualitative and quantitative incompatibility thesis (Howe, 1988). A few articles did not come up in the search (i.e., Johnson et al., 2007), even though they include information on the history of mixed methods. Thus, information from these articles is incorporated throughout this chapter.

Recently, a few texts (Creswell & Plano Clark, 2007; Greene, 2007; Ridenour & Newman, 2008; Teddlie & Tashakorri, 2003, 2009) have included a chapter or two exploring the history of mixed methods research. None of these authors explain in depth what really happened to spark the widespread interest in mixed methods research. After reading these histories, I was left feeling that more detective work was needed; specifically, I was interested in learning more about the

past, present, and future of mixed methods research from those who were involved in the early days.

I decided to search for and interview individuals who made major contributions to developing mixed methods research in the last 10 to 15 years of the 20th century, when the field was emerging. Therefore, I began a search for authors from both the United States and Europe whose mixed methods works from that period were cited frequently.

◆ The Early Developers— Who They Are

Working with the co-editors of this *Handbook,* I identified the following scholars as individuals who significantly contributed to the beginning of the field of mixed methods research: Julia Brannen, Alan Bryman, John Creswell, Jennifer Greene, David Morgan, and Janice Morse. Each of these individuals was contacted via e-mail and asked to interview for this chapter. Dr. Morgan and Dr. Brannen were not available to participate in the interviews. (Brannen's viewpoints may be seen in Chapter 26 of this volume, which she co-authored). To better understand who the early developers are, a short biography of each is presented in the remainder of this section.

Alan Bryman graduated from the University of Kent at Canterbury in 1971. He has taught several different content courses (e.g., organization studies, sociology of work) along with research methods. As early as 1984, he had an article in which he discussed the debate between quantitative and qualitative research. In 1988, Professor Bryman authored *Quantity and Quality in Social Research.* Since August 2005, Professor Bryman has been professor of organizational and social research, School of Management, University of Leicester. Recently, he has written two chapters on mixed methods research (Bryman, 2008a, 2008b).

John Creswell graduated with a doctorate from the University of Iowa in 1974.

In 1994, he authored *Research Design: Qualitative and Quantitative Approaches*. He is currently professor of educational psychology and was the founding director of the Office of Qualitative and Mixed Methods Research at the University of Nebraska–Lincoln. He has taught several topics, including content courses (e.g., administration, higher education) and research methods, including qualitative research, survey methods, and mixed methods research. He is the founding co-editor of the *Journal of Mixed Methods Research* (*JMMR*). In 2007, Dr. Creswell co-wrote one of the best-selling texts on mixed methods research (Creswell & Plano Clark, 2007).

Jennifer Greene received her doctorate from Stanford University in 1976. In 1985, she published two articles on mixed methods research, both on triangulation (Greene & McClintock, 1985; McClintock & Greene, 1985). In 1989, she published one of the most cited early articles on mixed methods inquiry: the article discussed conceptual frameworks for mixed methods evaluation designs and reviewed a sample of 57 empirical evaluation studies to assess the empirical warrant for and meaningfulness of these frameworks (Greene, Caracelli, & Graham, 1989). Since 1999, she has been professor in the Department of Educational Psychology at the University of Illinois at Urbana-Champaign. Dr. Greene has taught inquiry methods (including mixed methods inquiry), measurement, and evaluation courses. In 2007, she published a book on mixed methods social inquiry.

Janice Morse graduated in 1981 from the University of Utah with two PhDs, one in nursing and one in anthropology. In 1991, Dr. Morse published one of the first articles focusing on triangulation in mixed methods research, developing the notation for describing mixed method designs. She learned mixed methods by doing research—both qualitatively and quantitatively driven—and has held research career awards. In 1997, she founded the International Institute for Qualitative Methodology (IIQM) at the

University of Alberta, Canada, and she has taught a large number of workshops internationally on various mixed method designs. From these courses, she published (with Linda Niehaus and others) a number of articles that developed the principles and processes of mixed methods research. Since 2007, Dr. Morse has been professor in the College of Nursing and holds the Barnes Presidential Endowed Chair. In 2009, she co-authored a book on mixed methods research entitled *Principles and Procedures of Mixed-Method Design*.

◆ Interviews With the Early Developers

Table 11.1 presents the questions that were asked in the interviews. The questions were focused into four general areas: orienting questions and queries about the past, the present, and the future of mixed methods research. On request, the initial questions were e-mailed to the participants. A few follow-up questions came up during the interviews, and some of these questions were then asked in subsequent interviews with others. All of the participants were given the opportunity to read early drafts of the chapter and make appropriate changes so that their viewpoints are accurately portrayed.

The responses from the early developers are presented in no specific order. Quotes from the interviews are included to give the reader a flavor of each of the interviews.

ORIENTING QUESTIONS

Question 1. What is your definition of mixed methods research?

Interestingly, two of the early developers used the word *philosophy* in their definition. Creswell stated that mixed methods research starts with understanding that a person's method is tied to that person's

Table 11.1 Interview Questions

	Interview Questions
Orienting questions	What is your definition of mixed methods research?
	Do you feel like a founder of mixed methods research?
Past	How did you become interested in mixed research?
	What was your education like? How long ago was your education? Were both qualitative and quantitative methods valued? After learning about (qualitative/quantitative) research, how did you learn about the other approach?
	What was/is your passion for mixed research?
Present	What ideas or thoughts regarding mixed research have you had that are not readily reflected in the writings?
Future	Where do you see the field of mixed research moving?
	What problems do you see in mixed methods research?
	What are your hopes for the field of mixed research?

NOTE: Questions that were added after the initial planning of the interviews are in italics.

philosophy. He thinks it is the reflection and analysis of both quantitative and qualitative data and the integration of these two data sources. The design is framed within a larger philosophical foundation that is made.

Similarly, Greene defined mixed methods research as the

intentional use of more than one method, methodology, and/or methodological tradition in the same study or program of research. Methodological traditions include the assumptions of philosophical paradigms, as well as disciplinary and theoretical perspectives. And mixing can occur on some or all of these levels, although I believe that mixing at multiple levels offers the greatest possibilities for deeper, broader, and more insightful understanding. My mixed methods ideal is to catalyze respectful conversations across these different ways of generating and valuing knowledge.

The other two initial developers, Morse and Bryman, did not mention philosophy in regard to the definition of mixed methods research. Morse stated that mixed methods research can be defined as

using one method that's very solid and complete and a second supplementary component [that] is not complete and won't stand alone to solve a research problem. Some others may call *mixed methods* what I call *multiple methods*— where both methods are complete in themselves and could be published as two articles, each in a separate journal. Mixed methods may be qualitative and quantitative, or both qualitative, or both quantitative.

Bryman, later in his interview, implied that philosophy and paradigms do not really play a role in mixed methods research because it is strictly a method. Thus, his definition of mixed methods research was "research that entails the collection and analysis of quantitative and qualitative data within a single project."

Question 2. Do you feel like a founder of mixed methods research?

Initially, we (the co-editors and I) thought to call those who helped originate mixed methods research *founders*. Based on feedback from the participants, we changed the name to *early developers*. Some participants said they did not feel like a *founder* because the mixing of methods had occurred prior to their writings.

THE PAST—WHY THEY BECAME INVOLVED WITH MIXED METHODS RESEARCH

Question 3. How did you become interested in mixed methods research?

After the interviews began, other questions were added so that more specific information could be obtained. Thus, this question turned into the following five questions:

How did you become interested in mixed research?

What was your education like?

How long ago was your education?

Were both qualitative and quantitative methods valued?

After learning about (qualitative/ quantitative) research, how did you learn about the other approach?

Morse started her research career as a student at Penn State, working on a master's degree in a program that was exclusively quantitative. She had a project that would have been best completed using a qualitative or mixed methods approach, but because of the program's quantitative

focus, she conducted the project from that perspective. At the University of Utah, where she worked on her PhDs in nursing and in anthropology, there was a high level of both statistics and qualitative methods in the programs. She considers her grounding to be initially in quantitative, but then she learned qualitative shortly thereafter. One of her dissertations is quantitative with a minor qualitative component (anthropology), and the other is qualitative with a minor quantitative component (nursing). When she graduated with her two doctorates, she was adept at both methods, believing that there was a fit between the research question and the method, and the methods were simply tools for conducting inquiry. She tried not to "prefer" either quantitative or qualitative, and her students also used mixed method designs when studying such topics as infant behavior, touch, or styles of nursing care.

"By accident" is how Bryman says he became interested in mixed methods research. In the 1980s, he was writing his acclaimed book, *Quantity and Quality in Social Research,* where he outlined both quantitative and qualitative approaches, discussed philosophical issues, and talked about paradigms.

As I was reading, I realized I was encountering quite a number of significant studies where people had combined quantitative and qualitative research, so I thought, "Ah, it would be a good idea to have a chapter in the book that discussed the findings of studies where the two had been combined and to examine the different ways in which they had been combined."

The chapter included an outline of 10 different ways quantitative and qualitative research had been combined in past research studies. According to Bryman, "although that chapter was very much an afterthought, it was actually the chapter that attracted the most attention." Even though he did not take any research methods courses, Bryman feels that he was brought up in the quantitative research tradition. In the early 1970s, his first job was as a research assistant using quantitative methods. When he obtained his first teaching position in sociology in 1974, he was asked to teach research methods and became an expert on research methodology. In the late 1970s, he began introducing qualitative research in his courses.

Creswell received his PhD in 1974 at the University of Iowa in quantitative methods and used those methods in his dissertation. In 1983, he began teaching a course on developing the dissertation. For the first 5 years, more and more students wanted information on both qualitative and quantitative research methods, so he incorporated both into the course, which led him to think about how to combine the two methods. In 1985, he learned how to do qualitative methods by teaching a qualitative methods course. Between 1988 and 1989, he wrote a chapter on combining the two, which came out in his 1994 research text (Creswell, 1994). In 1991, at the American Education Research Association's conference, he went to a presentation by a graduate student who used "mixed-methods research" (with a hyphen between mixed and methods). He was the only person in the audience, and he thought, "this will be the research of the future" and will "bridge/span across qualitative and quantitative research." Creswell's book, *Research Design: Qualitative and Quantitative Approaches,* became a best seller in 1995; he believes its popularity was due to the chapter on mixed methods research.

For Greene, "It's been my own intellectual journey" to probe the possibilities of mixed methods social inquiry. She attended graduate school in the 1970s, when there was only one type of methodology to learn (i.e., objectivist quantitative research methodologies). Her first job was in a research and evaluation center, and the quantitative methodologies she had learned

in graduate school did not "work very well in the real world." At the same time, qualitative research methodologies were becoming more popular, so, on her own, she learned qualitative methodologies and their accompanying philosophical frameworks. When she got a job where she had to teach qualitative methodologies, she had to "really learn" them and became a "convert and champion of qualitative methods for a number of years." Being an evaluator, she appreciated qualitative methods; yet, she came to realize that "they don't claim much voice on the policy stage, so I wanted to speak louder, retain the promise and potential of qualitative methods, but speak more loudly." After working with colleagues where she undertook the qualitative portion of the evaluation study and the others did the quantitative portion (Greene & McClintock, 1985; McClintock & Greene, 1985), she was intrigued and realized the value of mixing the two methods. She found that "this is really fun!"

Question 4. What was/is your passion for mixed methods research?

When asked about passion for mixed methods research, Bryman stated,

I am not actually passionate about mixing the two [qualitative and quantitative methods]. There is a sense in which I tend to view that you should always consider what is the most appropriate methodological approach for the research problem. . . . For many research problems, mixed methods approach is either unnecessary or even inappropriate.

He does feel passionate about "the neglect of qualitative research by some social scientists who ignore it and treat it as some kind of lesser form of life." He states that his thought about research methods is summed up in the British expression of "horses for courses," which means one should use the right horse for the right course. Professor Bryman is a pragmatist: "It's all to do with tailoring your methodological approach to the research problem."

Morse put it very simply: Her passion for mixed methods research came from having research problems that fit mixed methods research.

Greene feels "intellectually passionate but cautious" regarding mixed methods social inquiry. She is "cautious of somehow advancing mixed methods as better than any other way to do inquiry . . . we should be very mindful of the times when we should not do a mixed methods study." She feels we should be modest in championing a mixed methods inquiry approach and "careful about claiming some promised potential, wonderful things about mixing methods that we don't really know ourselves at this point." She feels mixed methods researchers and evaluators need to remain respectful of other traditions. According to Greene, "I do not think mixed methods is going to take over all social research. We are joining a long respected family, and we are the newcomer and we should be respectful of our elders."

Creswell's work focused on "the types of mixed methods designs that are out there." When he wrote a chapter for the first edition of the *Handbook of Mixed Methods Research* on types of advanced mixed methods designs (Creswell, Plano Clark, Guttmann, & Hanson, 2003), he was motivated by the concept of visual diagrams for the designs and challenges in designs; he wanted to encourage researchers to think in terms of designs for mixed methods research studies. After working as an editor of *JMMR*, his interest has "shifted to a broader picture . . . to look at the topic within the field of mixed methods research, not necessarily the empirical area but the broader topic of methodological topics . . . that have begun to emerge and to map that area."

REFLECTIONS ON THE PRESENT OF MIXED METHODS RESEARCH

Question 5. What ideas or thoughts regarding mixed research have you had that are not readily reflected in the writings?

In general, Jennifer Greene feels her ideas are well reflected in her writings. One reason she feels passionate about mixed methods is that

> mixed methods is an important opportunity to engage with difference. I draw a parallel between intellectual engagement with different ways of knowing and different philosophical and methodological traditions and a political or value-based engagement with differences that exist in the phenomena we study. . . . That's the source of my passion.

Professor Bryman feels that we have a good understanding of how to conduct mixed methods research. He cited many leading mixed methodologists (i.e., Creswell, Tashakkori, Morgan, Brannen, Teddlie) and how these methodologists have advanced the field of mixed methods research. Yet, he believes that we still do not have a good understanding regarding how to present and write about mixed methods research:

> What we need now is really to get a good understanding of what good mixed methods research articles are supposed to look like and develop some exemplars of what the right kind of way of writing up mixed methods research might be.

Professor Bryman feels that the arrival of *JMMR* has been a good beginning, which has increased our understanding of what a mixed methods article should look like.

Creswell identified three areas of concern. First, many of the articles submitted to *JMMR* are lacking information on how the article will add to the discussion of mixed methods research literature. Most people "are just not familiar with the literature." The issue, then, is how to educate authors regarding the existing literature in mixed methods research. Second, authors struggle with the writing of mixed methods research. He said, "I see myself as a writer" and "I have a strong interest in the writing of mixed methods research," including how to propose and stage a study. Furthermore, he is intrigued by "writing with a transformational lens." Finally, having watched the evolution of qualitative research in the 1980s and the differences that arose between scholars within and outside the United States (what he calls the Atlantic divide), we should try to avoid the creation of an Atlantic divide for mixed methods researchers. His solution to this issue is to go to all conferences on mixed methods research, inside the United States and abroad, and to collaborate with colleagues from around the world. He feels it is important to "not view mixed methods as an American methodology; it is a worldwide language."

According to Morse, there is not enough information telling researchers how to "actually do mixed methods" research. The current mixed methods research texts do not "provide you with principles, strategies, or guidance." As a solution to this, she recently wrote a book on mixed methods research that is, "at last, a book that hopefully tells you what to do."

THOUGHTS ABOUT THE FUTURE OF MIXED METHODS RESEARCH

Question 6. Where do you see the field of mixed research moving?

Bryman replied,

I really find that a difficult question . . . in a sense I don't regard it as a field, I kind of think of it as a way of thinking about how you go about research. So, I don't have a strong feel or a strong sense

of where it ought to be going or might be going. . . . People, perhaps, need to be more kind of innovative in their thinking about the methods that can be combined.

Bryman sees most mixed methods research as including some type of survey with a semistructured interview/focus group. His content analysis indicated that "55 to 60% of all of the articles included that combination . . . that really is quite a restriction." He wonders why we do not have more mixed methods research articles with discourse analysis or experimental design. He says "there are numerous possibilities out there." He hopes that researchers will begin to think more innovatively about available combination possibilities. Some of this "will have to come from people who are not necessarily in the mixed methods community." He uses the example of researchers who use discourse analysis in their research, who may come up with a quantification that can stem from the discourse analysis. This addition of the quantification will enhance the discourse analysis.

Morse believes there "has to be some kind of agreement about terminology, and the language of mixed methods needs to be further developed." Furthermore, research designs need to be agreed upon and clarified.

Greene shared her fear of where mixed methods inquiry is moving:

We are moving toward some kind of convergence. Some kind of settling of difference . . . and will emphasize a technical level of methodology. It will be about technique—step one, step two, step three—it will be that kind of technique. It will be reduced . . . the wonder that is possible in mixed methods will be reduced to procedures and techniques.

She hopes we are not moving in that direction, but she is fearful that we may be.

Creswell, who has been conducting mixed methods research workshops for the past 7 years, has recently observed a change in what the workshop attendees are seeking. In the initial workshops that he conducted, everyone wanted simply to be introduced to mixed methods research. Recently, there has been a "dramatic shift": The workshop attendees want to know "how do I do this study." They need good examples of mixed methods studies, where they can see the procedures for conducting the study and understand the challenges of doing mixed methods research. He likens the stage that mixed methods research is currently in with the development of a textbook. Using the example of Keppel and Wickens (2004), Creswell explains that the first edition was not presented as well as the later editions:

> With each edition, they build in a little bit more technical competence . . . the understanding of how to do it, clarifying examples are much better. To me that is an example of where mixed methods is going. Our technique will become better and become clearer.

Creswell also speaks of "the possibility of a growing gulf between the methodologist type and the philosopher type." As the methodologists become more adept and the philosophers come up with more assumptions, there may be more of a divide between these two groups. Also, whoever develops a software package to do mixed methods research "will have a gold mine," he says. The prime movers in the field of mixed methods research are graduate students, as they are the majority of the people who are attending mixed methods research workshops and are "looking for new ways of doing research and are not afraid of trying out new methodology." He believes that graduate students will then be helping existing faculty, "who are more steeped in their traditional ways of doing research," understand and learn mixed methods research.

Question 7. What problems do you see in mixed methods research?

Initially, this was not one of the questions for the interviews. After starting the interviews, it was clear that this issue was on each of the early developers' minds. Therefore, it was added as a question for subsequent interviews.

Morse identified several problems with mixed methods research. First, "why can't we have a singular language? . . . [W]e have the opportunity to develop something that is cohesive." Second, "people think it is hard—it's not hard. It's so easy it's like falling off a log." To make it easy, according to Morse, mixed methods researchers need to attend to sampling, understand their "theoretical drive"—whether they are working inductively and deductively—and focus on the "point of interface," which is where the researcher brings the components of the study together. She feels that "we are moving into chaos. We, who are in the field, should have enough sense to say, 'Let's pull together on this.'"

Greene does not necessarily see problems with mixed methods inquiry, but she does believe the "range of views in the field make it full of rich conversations, but messy." She is not sure if Teddlie and Tashakkori's (2003) perception of mixed methods research being in its adolescence is quite right; she feels that the field of mixed methods inquiry may not be that far along yet. Greene thinks we are still in a stage where things will be challenging, and we should "frame the differences and challenges as opportunities for further learning and further conversation and further discourse." She uses the example of pragmatism:

> [It] would be very much too bad, [though] not a problem [per se,] . . . if everybody agreed that pragmatism was *the* paradigm for mixed methods research. . . . [W]e don't have very much enough information *at all* on what it means to do a study from a philosophically pragmatic standpoint. . . . What does it mean to have a

transactional view of reality? What does it mean to have a consequential view of truth? What does that look like in the studies that we do? Because I think the mixing of different ways of knowing and the engagement with difference is the most fun part of mixed methods, I think it would be too bad if we closed down that conversation already and everybody just agreed. . . . Let's not try to settle everything. Let's keep this conversation open and dynamic and respectful of the different positions that exist.

She has observed that some federal agencies are open to mixed methods research studies in their requests for proposals, which gives mixed methods inquiry more legitimacy.

The problems that Creswell identified throughout the interview included that authors seem not to know the mixed methods literature and not to have computer software that can conduct mixed methods analysis. When directly asked the question about problems in mixed methods research, he stated that there are many controversies. The first is how to conduct mixed methods research with an interpretive approach and attempt to ensure that "qualitative researchers do not feel marginalized" in mixed methods research. Another controversy, according to Creswell, is how mixed methods will be used in "gold standard," experimental, randomized studies.

When asked about problems in mixed methods research, Bryman said "ghetto-ization":

[It] is the possibility that the mixed methods community [might] seal itself off from the wider social science community and end up talking to each other rather than beyond. The arrival of specialist journals and conferences raises this prospect. I'm not saying it is something that will or would happen but that there is that possibility. It can be seen, for example, in the field of conversation analysis (CA) where CA practitioners have to a very significant

extent become like a cult with sacred texts (e.g., Harvey Sacks's lecture notes) and specialist journals, conferences, and online communities.

He feels that the idea of a "mixed methods movement" is a good term, as there should be "proselytizing": We should try to get more converts to mixed methods research by giving papers and publishing in mainstream journals. He says,

I like the idea of construing mixed methods as a *movement*, but on the other hand, I would not like it to become like a cult, where people only talk to each other. And I do see that as a potential danger. . . . [T]here is so much that mixed methods offers in terms of enhancing the social sciences and methodological understanding more generally, that really we ought to make sure that we don't just talk to each other, but we talk more widely.

Question 8. What are your hopes for the field of mixed methods research?

Greene stated that she hopes that the "interest and growth in [the] field will continue in a divergent way for a while." She has enjoyed reading the conceptual and empirical work of those researchers and evaluators who are mixing in new ways and with new types of data (e.g., GIS mapping with census data analysis). She suspects that it may be uncomfortable for those who are uneasy with "ambivalence and messiness. . . . [M]y hope is that it will continue to be messy for some time."

Bryman's hopes for mixed methods research include that "more and more people realize its potential and that it becomes more mainstream." An issue for mixed methods researchers that he has found is to answer the question "What constitutes good quality mixed methods research?"

I came across [articles] and it was dire, it really was atrocious . . . where you would get "here are my quantitative findings and here are my qualitative findings, would you mind, please Mr. and Mrs. Reader to work out yourself what the overall meaning of this is? . . . do the mixing for me." . . . I think that is unacceptable.

Bryman is not suggesting that the problem is specific to mixed methods research (quantitative and qualitative research also have articles that are "dire"). He believes that it would be helpful for emerging and established scholars to "have some articulation of what the . . . basic requirements are of a mixed methods article." There has been some writing in this area (Bryman, Creswell and Plano Clark, Tashakkori and Teddlie). He does not think the matter needs to be "slavish conformity to strict criteria," but we need to explain what we are looking for in regard to a good mixed methods article. Bryman thinks "we are making some headway, but we are reaching a point where we perhaps need to synthesize this and think a little bit more about what constitutes a good, rigorous, mixed methods article."

Morse started her answer this way: "I am sorry it has ended up in this kind of a mess" due to "books that . . . are not peer reviewed." This misinformation causes confusion for students and researchers and promotes researchers to conduct studies that are called "mixed methods research" but do not have steps that are clearly delineated. She hopes the field, in the future, figures out how to conduct mixed methods research.

Creswell suggests, "If you view mixed methods as a method, collecting qualitative and quantitative data . . . people are using other designs, collecting both qualitative and quantitative data and using them" in many types of research, including case study research, experimental research, and narrative research. He states that "if you want to get a person to adopt a new idea, or adapt your approach, it should be an add-on to what they are already doing. The potential now for mixed methods is streaming across many methods."

◆ The Early Developers: Distinctions and Connections

After completion of the interviews, I found there were interesting results and surprising findings: It was clear that the early developers of mixed methods research agreed on some topics and that they viewed some matters differently. From these thoughts, five main distinctions and eight connections were identified. In a few cases, content differed in the interviews; thus, comparisons are at times only between a subset of the participants.

DISTINCTIONS

Five main distinctions were readily apparent after completion of the interviews. These included definitions of mixed methods research, whether to stay in a "messy" place or to find agreement, whether to keep our conversations among ourselves, what philosophical viewpoint mixed methods researchers should adopt, and guidance for conducting mixed methods research. Each of the five distinctions will be briefly discussed.

Distinction 1. Definitions of mixed methods research. Before the interviews, I had a few assumptions about what kind of information I would find. One of my assumptions was that the early developers would define mixed methods research similarly. Johnson et al. (2007) found similarities and differences in their investigation of how leaders in the mixed methods field defined mixed methods research. These authors said, "We hoped to find some consensus about the core of mixed methods research, and we did" (p. 123). I thought that the early developers might not have the exact same definition but that the foundation of their definitions would be similar enough there would be no need to include a question about their definition of mixed methods research. Yet, a few minutes into the first interview, it was evident that there was a need to step back and find out exactly how each participant defined mixed methods. As this question was not planned, the participants did not have the question in advance. Therefore, interestingly, many of the early developers had to stop and think before responding.

As previously noted, two of the early developers (Creswell and Greene) used the word *philosophy* in their definition, whereas Morse and Bryman did not. This is intriguing, as one issue that was striking between the initial developers was that some viewed mixed methods as mixing in all areas, including philosophy (i.e., Greene), whereas Bryman viewed it solely as a methodology. Furthermore, whether multiple forms of data (both qualitative and quantitative data) are necessary stood out in the definitions. Both Bryman and Creswell indicated that both types of data are needed in a mixed methods study. Morse's definition of mixed methods was even more different from the others' definitions, in that with her definition a mixed methods study could have two qualitative components (and thus, only qualitative data), two quantitative components (with only quantitative data), or a qualitative and a quantitative component. Greene's definition mentions mixing at many levels. Although she did not explicate the type of data needed, her definition implies the mixing of different kinds of data—spatial and numeric, or graphic and textual—that are gathered with different kinds of methods.

In 2007, three of the early developers (i.e., Greene, Morse, and Creswell) contributed their definitions of mixed methods as part of a research project conducted by Johnson and his colleagues. When I asked Greene for her definition, her first reply was, "What did I say when they did that article?" From this, I thought it may be interesting to compare the definitions of mixed methods research in the Johnson et al.

(2007) article with the definitions gathered during the interviews. Greene's and Morse's definitions were very similar in both the article and my interviews. Conversely, Creswell's definition was somewhat different. In the 2007 article, his definition was "Mixed methods research is a research design (or methodology) in which the researcher collects, analyzes, and mixes (integrates or connects) both quantitative and qualitative data in a single study or a multiphase program of inquiry" (p. 119). The striking difference from his interview definition is that *philosophy* is not included in 2007, yet, it seems to play an important role in his definition in the interview. This difference speaks to the possible change in trends in the field of mixed methods research. Philosophy and its role in mixed methods research has been a topic of discussion for quite some time (Greene & Caracelli, 2003; Maxcy, 2003; Tashakkori & Teddlie, 1998) and has continued to be discussed in the literature (Bazeley, 2009; Greene, 2009; Perla & Carifio, 2009). Perla and Carifio (2009) said, "Without some understanding and appreciation for the epistemic and philosophic issues that surround a particular methodology or paradigm, it becomes easy to create superficial distinctions of method that upon careful examination migrate to one end of the same spectrum" (p. 41). Recently, Bazeley (2009) concluded that we need to move "on from a literature dominated by foundations and design typologies" to focus on "advances in conceptualization and breakthroughs derived from analytic techniques that support integration" (p. 206). Yet, there was not agreement on this issue when talking with the early developers; some are ready to move on, while others are not.

Distinction 2: To stay in a "messy" place or to find agreement. All of the early developers stated, in one fashion or another, that currently the field of mixed methods research is "messy." Yet, interestingly, there was no agreement on whether the field is ready to become more organized and systematic. Greene believes that the field of mixed methods research is not ready to come to consensus. Furthermore, she believes that if we did arrive at some type of agreement any time soon, we would lose important facets of mixed methods research. On the other side is Morse, who would like the field to come to consensus, in particular with terminology, and thinks we need to work together to do so.

Distinction 3: Whether to keep our conversations among ourselves. One distinction between the early developers that was curious to me was where conversations should take place and who should be included. Morse, Creswell, and Bryman discussed the need to involve researchers from across the world. Creswell outlined how he is attending all conferences on mixed methods and believes in the need for an international mixed methods association. From her role in the IIQM, Morse has presented internationally; her articles have been translated into Japanese; and her co-authored book is already being translated into Korean. In contrast, Bryman is concerned about the field becoming a cult, where only the members are included in discussions.

Distinction 4: What philosophical viewpoint mixed methods researchers should adopt. As noted earlier, there has been discussion regarding philosophical viewpoints and mixed methods research (Bazeley, 2009; Greene, 2009; Perla & Carifio, 2009). A striking difference between Greene and Bryman was that the latter clearly stated that he is a pragmatist[4] and that he conducts research (including mixed methods studies) from this standpoint. One of Greene's major concerns is the current press to adopt a philosophical stance of pragmatism as the mixed methods paradigm or framework. She is unsure that we currently know enough about the pragmatic viewpoint and what it means for mixed methods research.

Distinction 5: Guidance for conducting mixed methods research. An additional point of dissension among the early developers of mixed methods research was where the field of mixed methods research stands regarding agreement of how to conduct a mixed methods study and the language used in mixed methods research. Creswell and Morse stated clearly their belief that mixed methods researchers need guidance, including a step-by-step process for how to conduct a mixed methods study. Greene agrees with this in that students and novice researchers would benefit from this type of information; yet, she feels that experienced mixed methods researchers should be creative in their studies and should not be locked into a checklist of steps to conduct a study. Bryman also thinks we should be innovative in our designing of mixed methods research, and he believes we are past needing step-by-step guidance, as many in the field of mixed methods (he mentioned Creswell, Tashakkori, Morgan, Brannen, and Teddlie) have already clearly articulated how mixed methods studies can be conducted.

CONNECTIONS

After the interviews with the early developers of mixed methods research, eight connections, or similarities, emerged. The connections were training, the popularity of early mixed methods chapters, when to conduct a mixed methods study, the need for innovative ideas, reaching researchers in other disciplines and countries, the maturity (or lack thereof) of mixed methods research, how to write about mixed methods research, and the need for exemplars. Each of these eight connections will be briefly discussed.

Connection 1: Training. All of the early developers of mixed methods research were initially trained in the quantitative tradition and three (Greene, Creswell, and Bryman) learned how to conduct qualitative research on their own. This similarity could be based on the fact that they were all learning research in the same decade (i.e., the 1970s). During this time, quantitative research was the main type of research conducted, as the qualitative approach still "lacked a history within educational research" (Howe & Eisenhart, 1990, p. 2). Morse, coming from the disciplines of nursing and anthropology, had the fortune of taking courses in qualitative methods.

In addition, it is fascinating that all the initial developers learned qualitative methods very early in their careers. This information is evidence that having a strong foundation in both quantitative and qualitative research methods is necessary and important for conducting mixed methods research, providing support for many scholars' beliefs regarding educating graduate students in research methods (Creswell & Plano Clark, 2007; Greene, 2007; Johnson & Onwuegbuzie, 2004; Ridenour & Newman, 2008; Teddlie & Tashakkori, 2009).

Connection 2: The popularity of early mixed methods chapters. Both Bryman and Creswell thought their research books, published in the late 1980s and early 1990s, became popular due to the inclusion of a chapter on mixed methods research. This phenomenon suggests that social science researchers more than a decade ago were curious about and wanting more information regarding mixed methods research. It is unfortunate that this cue was not taken more seriously so that texts on mixed methods research could have been written and available more quickly. If texts had been available, the field of mixed methods research might be in a very different place today.

Connection 3: When to conduct a mixed methods study. Bryman, Greene, and Morse share a belief that researchers should be cautious about when they use mixed methods in

studies. These early developers maintain that mixed methods are not always the best choice for a given study. Mixed methods research should not be categorized as the "catch-all" method for any given study. Thus, from the information learned in these interviews, it appears that researchers should be conscientious about the research question and choosing the best research approach (i.e., quantitative, qualitative, or mixed methods) to answer the research question at hand.

Connection 4: The need for innovative ideas. Many of the early developers believe that mixed methods research will benefit from new and innovative ideas, designs, areas of inquiry, and research strategies. Bryman believes that researchers should be innovative with mixed methods research. Creswell believes graduate students are the future of mixed methods and will create and develop innovative strategies for the mixed methods field. Greene thinks we should not limit the mixing of methods to techniques and procedures, but rather mix at levels of methodology and framework as well. She feels the magic of mixed methods research occurs when a study goes beyond the step-by-step approach. From these thoughts from the early developers, it is clear that mixed methods researchers should look beyond the available data collection, design, and analysis strategies: Mixed methods researchers should be creative and pioneering. The field of mixed methods research has room to grow and expand—we have yet to arrive at the limit of the capacity and potential of mixed methods research.

Connection 5: Reaching researchers in other disciplines and countries. Both Creswell and Bryman indicated the need for the field of mixed methods to include researchers from other disciplines and encouraged care not to exclude researchers from other countries. As Bryman so aptly stated, we do not want mixed methods research to become a cult where there are gatekeepers who determine who can participate. Creswell's thoughts about the Atlantic divide brought up a valid and important concern in that mixed methods research is not a U.S.-based phenomenon; researchers from all over the world are conducting mixed methods research and should be included in the discussions as the field grows and changes.

Connection 6: The maturity (or lack thereof) of mixed methods research. In the first edition of the *Handbook of Mixed Methods in Social and Behavioral Research*, Teddlie and Tashakkori (2003) state, "The field is just entering its 'adolescence' and . . . there are many unresolved issues to address before a more mature mixed methods research area can emerge. Nevertheless, we also believe that the handbook . . . will stimulate greater maturity in the field" (p. 3). Six years later, all of the early developers of mixed methods research believe that the field of mixed methods research is still emerging, evolving, and messy. In some respects, this seems healthy, as the field of mixed methods research is relatively young. Yet, until the field becomes more mature and stable (i.e., terms, definitions, and designs become commonplace and similarly understood by researchers), mixed methods research will be difficult, especially for novice mixed methods researchers.

Connection 7: How to write about mixed methods research. One of the major needs for the field of mixed methods research is examples of how to write and present a mixed methods research study. Many of the initial developers mentioned that as editors or reviewers for journals, they have had manuscripts submitted that are supposedly presentations of mixed methods studies. In many of these, it can be difficult to know what the authors are attempting to convey, as these manuscripts are not well written. According to the early developers, areas that need attention in the writing include, but are not limited to, (a) presenting the author's definition of mixed methods research, (b) having an understanding of how the study fits within the extant mixed methods literature, (c) explicitly stating the researcher's philosophy, and (d) explicating where the mixing occurred.

Connection 8: The need for exemplars. Most of the early developers felt that both emerging and established mixed methods researchers would benefit from exemplars of mixed methods studies. Based on this similarity across the interviews, as a follow-up question, the participants were asked to provide a citation for a published mixed methods article that is exemplary. Greene suggested the article by Li, Marquart, and Zercher (2000) as an example of a good mixed methods study and presentation in an article because

> it demonstrates the value of careful and intentional planning of the mixing of methods. It explicates and illustrates the multiple levels on which methods can be mixed—paradigm, methodology, method/technique. It offers highly creative and innovative methods of data analysis and interpretation, which is where the important mixes actually happen.

Morse suggested her 1989 article as an exemplar mixed methods study. She diagrams this study as QUAL + *qual* + *quan*→*qual* + *qual*→*quan*. The mixing of qualitative and quantitative methods, or what she calls the point of interface, is in the results section. "The phenomena is so complex that it could not have been accessed using a single method," she said during the interview. The study is evaluated in her book (Morse & Niehaus, 2009). Creswell pointed to the mixed methods studies evaluated in Plano Clark and Creswell (2008). These articles include Luzzo (1995); Idler, Hudson, and Leventhal (1999); Donovan et al. (2002); Victor, Ross, and Axford (2004); Messer, Steckler, and Dignan (1999); Way, Stauber, Nakkula, and London (1994); Thøgersen-Ntoumani and Fox (2005); Milton, Watkins, Studdard, and Burch (2003); and Richter (1997).

◆ *Conclusions*

Having the opportunity to converse with the early developers of mixed methods research was a chance of a lifetime. Being able to have an understanding of who these people are and begin to unravel each of their unique views of mixed methods research was an amazing experience. I found the initial developers to be genuine, caring people who are scholars who have worked tirelessly to promote our field of mixed methods research.

After concluding each interview, I found certain statements made by the participants to stand out and be especially memorable. Morse's comment that "we are into *p* values" is a great example of how quantitative research is overvalued, and how we need to move further in our thinking about what kind of results are helpful. After speaking

with Bryman, his statement, "Methods can serve different masters," summed up much of our interview as well as his point of view of mixed methods research. Creswell's statement, "If you want to get a person to adopt a new idea, or adapt your approach, it should be an add-on to what they are already doing," was beneficial in that this viewpoint may assist researchers in understanding how to promote mixed methods research. Finally, Greene's thought, "Let's keep this conversation open and dynamic and respectful of the different positions that exist," clearly explicates that as the early developers see it, the field is still emerging; most of the initial developers believe conversations need to continue. The conversations from these interviews were just the beginning; the future of mixed methods research will have continued conversations that include scholars from multiple disciplines from varied areas of the world.

Research Questions and Exercises

1. What is your definition of mixed methods research? Is it helpful to have multiple definitions, or would it be more beneficial to have one specific definition that all researchers use?

2. How has the field been enriched by the varying perspectives of the early developers? Are there negative aspects to this diversity of viewpoints?

3. In what ways (if any) does a researcher's philosophical viewpoint impact his or her research?

4. Should there be specific guidelines that researchers follow when conducting a mixed methods research study, or should researchers be creative and develop new and innovative methods?

◆ *Notes*

1. The co-editors of this volume encouraged me to conduct the interviews presented in this article and were available for further dialogue throughout the process.

2. Including only these three traditions does not indicate that other traditions (e.g., action research, participatory research, and critical social science) are not important. These

three traditions were specified to simplify the discussion.

3. The terms *genre, movement,* and *approach* are used interchangeably throughout this chapter.

4. Johnson et al. (2007) identify three types of pragmatists: pragmatism of the right (those who have a "strong form of realism, and a weak form of pluralism," p. 125); pragmatism of the left (those who believe in "antirealism and strong pluralism," p. 125); and pragmatism of

the middle. Bryman did not state a preference for a specific type of pragmatism.

◆ References

Bazeley, P. (2009). Editorial: Integrating data analyses in mixed methods research. *Journal of Mixed Methods Research, 3,* 203–207.

Bogdan, R., & Taylor, S. J. (1975). *Introduction to qualitative research methods: A phenomenological approach to the social sciences.* New York: John Wiley.

Bryman, A. (1984). The debate about quantitative and qualitative research: A question of method or epistemology? *British Journal of Sociology, 35,* 75–92.

Bryman, A. (1988). *Quantity and quality in social research.* London: Unwin Hyman.

Bryman, A. (2008a). The end of the paradigm wars? In P. Alasuutari, L. Bickman, & J. Brannen (Eds.), *The SAGE handbook of social research methods* (pp. 13–25). Thousand Oaks, CA: Sage.

Bryman, A. (2008b). Why do researchers integrate/combine/mesh/blend/mix/merge/fuse quantitative and qualitative research? In M. M. Bergman (Ed.), *Advances in mixed methods research* (pp. 87–100). Thousand Oaks, CA: Sage.

Campbell, D. T., & Stanley, J. (1963). Experimental and quasi-experimental designs for research on teaching. In N. L. Gage (Ed.), *Handbook of research on teaching.* Chicago: Rand McNally. (Also published as *Experimental and quasi-experimental designs for research.* Chicago: Rand McNally, 1966.)

Capraro, R. M., & Thompson, B. (2008). The educational researcher defined: What will future researchers be trained to do? *Journal of Educational Research, 101,* 247–253.

Cook, T. D., & Campbell, D. T. (1979). *Quasiexperimentation: Design and analysis issues for field settings.* Boston: Houghton Mifflin.

Creswell, J. W. (1994). *Research design: Qualitative and quantitative approaches.* Thousand Oaks, CA: Sage.

Creswell, J. W., & Plano Clark, V. L. (2007). *Designing and conducting mixed methods research.* Thousand Oaks, CA: Sage.

Creswell, J. W., Plano Clark, V. L., Guttmann, M. L., & Hanson, E. E. (2003). Advanced mixed methods research design. In A. Tashakkori & C. Teddlie (Eds.), *Handbook of mixed methods in social and behavioral research* (pp. 209–240). Thousand Oaks, CA: Sage.

Denzin, N. K., & Lincoln, Y. S. (2005). Introduction: The discipline and practice of qualitative research. In N. K. Denzin & Y. S. Lincoln (Eds.), *The SAGE handbook of qualitative research* (3rd ed., pp. 1–32). Thousand Oaks, CA: Sage.

Donovan, J., Mills, J., Smith, M., Brindle, L., Jacoby, A., Peters, T., et al. (2002). Improving design and conduct of randomized trials by embedding them in qualitative research: ProteT (prostate testing for cancer and treatment) study. *British Medical Journal, 325,* 766–769.

Gelo, O., Braakmann, D., & Benetka, G. (2008). Quantitative and qualitative research: Beyond the debate. *Integrative Psychological & Behavioral Science, 42*(3), 266–290.

Giacobbi, P. R., Poczardowski, A., & Hager, P. (2005). A pragmatic research philosophy for applied sport psychology. *Sport Psychologist, 19,* 18–31.

Glaser, B. G., & Strauss, A. L. (1967). *The discovery of grounded theory: Strategies for qualitative research.* Chicago: Aldine.

Greene, J. C. (2007). *Mixed methods in social inquiry.* San Francisco: Jossey-Bass.

Greene, J. C. (2009). Is mixed methods social inquiry a distinctive methodology? *Journal of Mixed Methods Research, 2,* 7–22.

Greene, J. C., Benjamin, L., & Goodyear, L. (2001). The merits of mixing methods in evaluation. *Evaluation, 7*(1), 25–44.

Greene, J. C., & Caracelli, V. J. (2003). Making paradigmatic sense of mixed methods practice. In A. Tashakkori & C. Teddlie (Eds.), *Handbook of mixed methods in social and behavioral research* (pp. 91–110). Thousand Oaks, CA: Sage.

Greene, J. C., Caracelli, V. J., & Graham, W. F. (1989). Toward a conceptual framework for mixed-method evaluation designs. *Educational Evaluation and Policy Analysis, 11,* 255–274.

Greene, J. C., & McClintock, C. (1985). Triangulation in evaluation: Design and analysis issues. *Evaluation Review, 9,* 523–545.

Howe, K. R. (1988). Against the quantitative-qualitative incompatability thesis or dogmas die hard. *Educational Researcher, 17,* 10–16.

Howe, K. R., & Eisenhart, M. (1990). Standards for qualitative (and quantitative) research: A prolegomenon. *Educational Researcher, 19,* 2–9.

Idler, E. L., Hudson, S. V., & Leventhal, H. (1999). The meanings of self-ratings of health: A qualitative and quantitative approach. *Research on Aging, 21*(3), 458–476.

Johnson, R. B., & Onwuegbuzie, A. J. (2004). Mixed methods research: A research paradigm whose time has come. *Educational Researcher, 33*(7), 14–26.

Johnson, R. B., Onwuegbuzie, A. J., & Turner, L. A. (2007). Toward a definition of mixed methods research. *Journal of Mixed Methods Research, 1,* 112–133.

Keppel, G., & Wickens, T. D. (2004). *Design and analysis: A researcher's handbook* (4th ed.). Upper Saddle River, NJ: Prentice Hall.

Leahey, E. (2007). Convergence and confidentiality? Limits to the implementation of mixed methodology. *Social Science Research, 36*(1), 149–158.

Li, S., Marquart, J. M., & Zercher, C. (2000). Conceptual issues and analytic strategies in mixed-method studies of preschool inclusion. *Journal of Early Intervention, 23,* 116–132.

Lofland, J., & Lofland, L. H. (1994). *Analyzing social settings: A guide to qualitative observation and analysis* (3rd ed.). Belmont, CA: Wadsworth.

Luzzo, D. A. (1995). Gender differences in college students' career maturity and perceived barriers in career development. *Journal of Counseling and Development, 73,* 319–322.

Maxcy, S. J. (2003). Pragmatic threads in mixed methods research in the social sciences: The search for multiple modes of inquiry and the end of the philosophy of formalism. In A. Tashakkori & C. Teddlie (Eds.), *Handbook of mixed methods in social and behavioral research* (pp. 51–90). Thousand Oaks, CA: Sage.

McClintock, C., & Greene, J. C. (1985). Triangulation in practice. *Evaluation and Program Planning, 8,* 351–357.

Messer, L., Steckler, A., & Dignan, M. (1999). Early detection of cervical cancer among Native American women: A qualitative supplement to a quantitative study. *Health Education and Behavior, 8*(26), 547–562.

Milton, J., Watkins, K. E., Studdard, S. S., & Burch, M. (2003). The ever widening gyre: Factors affecting change in adult education graduate programs in the United States. *Adult Education Quarterly, 54*(1), 23–41.

Morse, J. M. (1989). Cultural responses to parturition: Childbirth in Fiji. *Medical Anthropology, 12*(1), 35–44.

Morse, J. M. (1991). Approaches to qualitative-quantitative methodological triangulation. *Nursing Research, 40*(2), 120–123.

Morse, J. M., & Niehaus, L. (2009). *Principles and procedures of mixed-method design.* Walnut Creek, CA: Left Coast Press.

Perla, R. J., & Carifio, J. (2009). Toward a general and unified view of educational research and educational evaluation. *Journal of MultiDisciplinary Evaluation, 6,* 38–55.

Plano Clark, V. L., & Creswell, J. W. (2008). *The mixed methods reader.* Thousand Oaks, CA: Sage.

Plano Clark, V. L., Huddleston-Casas, C. A., Churchill, S. L., Green, D. O., & Garrett, A. L. (2008). Mixed methods approaches in family science research. *Journal of Family Issues, 29*(11), 1543–1566.

Richter, K. (1997). Child care choice in urban Thailand: Qualitative and quantitative evidence of the decision-making process. *Journal of Family Issues, 18*(2), 174–204.

Ridenour, C. S., & Newman, I. (2008). *Mixed methods research: Exploring the interactive continuum.* Carbondale: Southern Illinois University Press.

Tashakkori, A., & Teddlie, C. (1998). *Mixed methodology: Combining the qualitative and quantitative approaches.* Thousand Oaks, CA: Sage.

Teddlie, C., & Johnson, B. (2009). Methodological thought since the 20th century. In C. Teddlie & A. Tashakkori (Eds.), *Foundations of mixed methods research: Integrating quantitative and qualitative approaches in the social and behavioral sciences* (pp. 62–82). Thousand Oaks, CA: Sage.

Teddlie, C., & Tashakkori, A. (2003). Major issues and controversies in the use of mixed methods in the social and behavioral sciences. In A. Tashakkori & C. Teddlie (Eds.), *Handbook of mixed methods in social and behavioral research* (pp. 3–50). Thousand Oaks, CA: Sage.

Teddlie, C., & Tashakkori, A. (2009). *Foundations of mixed methods research: Integrating quantitative and qualitative approaches in the social and behavioral sciences.* Thousand Oaks, CA: Sage.

Thøgersen-Ntoumani, C., & Fox, K. R. (2005). Physical activity and mental well-being typologies in corporate employees: A mixed methods approach. *Work and Stress, 19*(1), 50–67.

Victor, C. R., Ross, R., & Axford, J. (2004). Capturing lay perspectives in a randomized control trial of a health promotion intervention for people with osteoarthritis of the knee. *Journal of Evaluation in Clinical Practice, 10*(1), 63–70.

Way, N., Stauber, H. Y., Nakkula, M. J., & London, P. (1994). Depression and substance use in two divergent high school cultures: A quantitative and qualitative analysis. *Journal of Youth and Adolescence, 23*(3), 331–357.

PART II

ISSUES REGARDING METHODS AND METHODOLOGY

12

RESEARCH QUESTIONS IN MIXED METHODS RESEARCH

◆ Vicki L. Plano Clark and Manijeh Badiee

Objectives

After completing this chapter, you should be able to

- articulate your definition of research questions within mixed methods research;

- distinguish between two prominent perspectives about how a mixed methods study is designed in response to its research questions;

- identify the major influences to which researchers attribute the origins of their mixed methods research questions;

- describe four dimensions useful for writing mixed research questions and give examples of the different options for each;

- apply criteria for evaluating research questions in mixed methods studies; and

- write good research questions for your mixed methods study.

Research questions play a central role in the process of conducting research, particularly the decision to use a mixed methods approach. The mixed methods literature is uniform in its position that mixed methods research is appropriate when a study's purpose and research questions warrant a combination of quantitative and qualitative approaches. Although much has been written about the link between purposes and mixed methods, comparatively little work has explicitly addressed research questions in mixed methods research. Because of their importance, however, scholars need to critically consider the decisions that shape and are shaped by research questions within mixed methods research. In addition, researchers need practical guidance about how to conceptualize and write research questions when conducting mixed methods studies.

The intent of this chapter, therefore, is to advance a framework for research questions in mixed methods research that builds on methodological discussions as well as researchers' practice for conceptualizing and stating their research questions. We begin by briefly defining what we mean by research questions and reviewing their importance. Next, we discuss two prominent perspectives about the role of research questions in designing mixed methods studies. From there, we advance a model that explains the origins of research questions within the dynamic mixed methods research process as it is experienced in practice. From this model, we describe how mixed methods researchers write their research questions. We delineate the dimensions of these questions and provide examples from practice to illustrate the range of approaches that researchers use across each dimension. We conclude with recommendations for researchers formulating research questions that call for and fit within a mixed methods approach.

◆ Defining Research Questions

At its most basic level, researchers conduct research to answer questions, and therefore, research questions are of central importance for all approaches to research. Despite their importance, research questions are not easily defined, and scholars do not always agree as to what constitutes a research question. We begin with a brief discussion of how research questions differ from other aspects of research studies and why they are important. These two concepts convey our definition of research questions and serve to clarify the scope of this chapter.

Three key elements define the focus for any study: the content area, the purpose, and the research questions. As depicted in Figure 12.1, these elements are viewed in a hierarchy that spans from the general and broad (the content area) to the specific and narrow (the research questions) (Creswell, 2008; Punch, 2005; Ridenour & Newman, 2008). The content area, also referred to as the topic or research problem, represents the broad substantive subject matter of a study. For example, a study's content area might be online interactions, diabetes prevention, management styles, or any other topics that pique the interest of researchers. Due to the broad nature of content areas, one can imagine a wide range of possible purposes and use of methods within any particular area.

A study's purpose falls within the content area. The purpose describes the researcher's primary intent, objectives, and goals for the study. The purpose provides a guide to the researcher's thinking about the study (Punch, 2005) and sets the overall direction for the research (Creswell, 2008). Many research purposes are possible, as illustrated by Newman, Ridenour, Newman, and DeMarco (2003), who advanced a typology of more than 40 distinct purposes and demonstrated their application within one content area. They noted that certain methods are best suited for or traditionally linked to studies with certain purposes. The general purpose for a mixed methods study indicates the need for and use of both quantitative and qualitative methods (Teddlie & Tashakkori, 2009). For example, a researcher's complementary purpose may be to develop a complete understanding of

Figure 12.1 Focusing a Study From the Topic to Research Questions

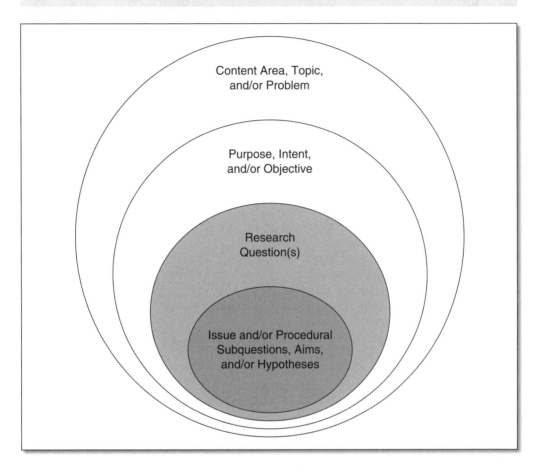

online interactions, which includes qualitatively describing how individuals interact with others online and quantitatively assessing the trends of different interaction types. As such, the researcher moves from the purpose to research questions.

Research questions are derived from and extend a study's purpose (Ridenour & Newman, 2008). Compared with the purpose, research questions are more specific and represent the actual questions that the researcher is working to answer (Creswell, 2008). Research questions set boundaries to a research project, clarify its specific directions, and keep a study from becoming too large (Punch, 2005; Teddlie & Tashakkori, 2009). Research questions also are important in the reporting of research. As literary devices, they provide

a framework for organizing a report and help the author link the study's purpose to the study's methods and results (Creswell, 2008).

Researchers typically state multiple research questions and often subquestions that further narrow larger questions. These questions and subquestions are often content or issue focused. For example, a researcher may ask: How do user characteristics relate to different types of online interactions? Researchers may also pose procedural subquestions that emphasize the procedures to be used to address a more general question (Creswell, 2008; Randolph, 2008; Stake, 1995). That is, the same researcher may pose procedural questions such as these: What statements describe users' online interactions? What themes emerge from the statements? What is the prevalence of the themes? How does the prevalence of themes relate to users' characteristics? Procedural questions are more common in research studies using emergent designs where the content results are not predictable at the start of the study.

In addition to using different question types, researchers also use different forms for writing their research questions. Researchers may state their research questions explicitly as questions, that is, as interrogative statements complete with question mark: for example, What online interactions occur in distance courses? Researchers also state research questions in the form of study aims. Aims are declarative sentences that express what a researcher means to accomplish: for example, This study aims to describe the online interactions that occur in distance courses. Finally, researchers may state research questions in the form of hypotheses. Hypotheses are statements that predict the outcome of research questions and are best used in preset designs when a researcher has a sound reason to be able to make a prediction (Johnson & Christensen, 2008). For example, a researcher might offer this hypothesis: Successful distance courses include a richer set of interactions among students and the instructor than those rated as unsuccessful.

In this chapter, we define research questions as the specific questions that the researcher is attempting to answer when conducting a mixed methods study. As indicated by the shaded regions of Figure 12.1, our definition includes both issue and procedural questions and subquestions. Although we primarily use the term *research question,* our use of this term includes statements made as questions, aims, and hypotheses.

◆ The Role of Research Questions for Designing Mixed Methods Research Studies

Because research questions provide the narrow focus for a study, they provide a direct link from the study's purpose to its design and methods. The role of research questions within the process of designing mixed methods research has received extensive attention within the literature. In these writings, scholars have advanced two models: Research questions dictate methods and research questions are the hub of the research process. While commonalities exist between these models, there are also differences in their emphases and the relationships contained within them, as represented in Figure 12.2.

RESEARCH QUESTIONS DICTATE METHODS

Several scholars have discussed research questions as the driving force for mixed methods research (e.g., Greene, 2007; Johnson & Onwuegbuzie, 2004; Onwuegbuzie & Leech, 2006; Ridenour & Newman, 2008; Teddlie & Tashakkori, 2009). They argue that researchers should start with research questions, and all methods decisions should follow directly from these questions. Writers advocating this perspective invoke strong language to convey the dominating role of the research question. Greene (2007) noted that "methodology is ever the servant of purpose [and questions], never the master" (p. 97). Similarly, Tashakkori and Teddlie (1998) described this perspective as the "dictatorship of the research question" (p. 20). We depict a simplified view of this model in Figure 12.2a.

From this dictatorship model, a researcher's choice of methods becomes analogous to selecting the best tools from the repertoire of tools available in the researcher's methods toolbox to answer the stated questions. For example, Onwuegbuzie and Leech (2006) discuss how research questions drive the choice of a specific mixed methods design, sampling procedures, and data analysis techniques. In addition, the use of mixed methods becomes appropriate if, and only if, it is called for by the research questions, such as when a researcher has both exploratory and confirmatory questions (Bryman, 2006b; Teddlie &

Figure 12.2 Two Models of How Mixed Methods Research Studies Are Designed in Response to Research Questions

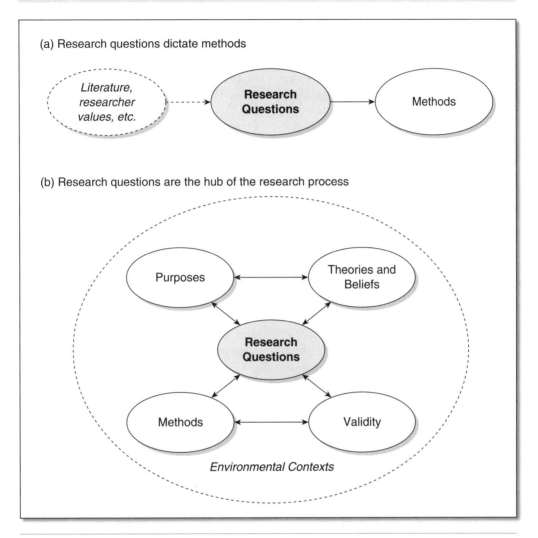

(a) Research questions dictate methods

Literature, researcher values, etc. - - - → **Research Questions** → Methods

(b) Research questions are the hub of the research process

Purposes ←→ Theories and Beliefs

Research Questions

Methods ←→ Validity

Environmental Contexts

SOURCE: Adapted from Maxwell & Loomis (2003, p. 246) with permission of Sage Publications.

Tashakkori, 2009). This pragmatic perspective relegates considerations such as the worldviews commonly associated with certain methods and a researcher's preference for certain methods to positions of secondary importance (Tashakkori & Teddlie, 1998), as portrayed by the dotted lines in Figure 12.2a.

There are many advantages to using a model in which the research questions dictate the methods for mixed methods research. This model fits a pragmatic perspective well where designs and methods are selected based on "what works" for answering the stated research questions (see Biesta, 2010; Greene & Hall, 2010 [both in this volume] for a more in-depth discussion of pragmatism). By de-emphasizing the link between methods and paradigms and placing the emphasis on research questions, this model also helps to defuse debates about whether paradigms can be mixed. In addition, this model fits well with a traditional and largely linear process of research that encourages researchers to minimize contextual influences on designing a research study, such as personal preferences for using certain methods. Writers discussing this model do acknowledge that the research process is more complex than a simple dictatorship. They note that questions are guided by personal value systems; may emerge or change during a study; and interact with purpose, theory, and methods (Greene, 2007; Onwuegbuzie & Leech, 2006; Tashakkori & Teddlie, 1998). The emphasis on a pragmatic, linear model of the process of research, however, provides little guidance for researchers who are using different worldviews (e.g., see discussions of the transformative paradigm, Mertens, Bledsoe, Sullivan, & Wilson, 2010; critical realism, Maxwell & Mittapalli, 2010 [both in this volume]) or who are navigating the dynamic process by which research questions develop, are refined, or emerge within the conduct of some mixed methods studies.

RESEARCH QUESTIONS ARE THE HUB OF THE RESEARCH PROCESS

Maxwell and Loomis's (2003) interactive model is an alternative model of the role of research questions within mixed methods design. This systemic model, pictured in Figure 12.2b, directly relates a study's research questions to four study components—its purposes, guiding theories and beliefs, methods, and validity considerations—and emphasizes the interrelationships among these components. In this model, research questions also play a central role, but this model views them as interacting and integrated with other components of the research process instead of in a linear process. Research questions are considered central to this model because they inform and are informed by the other components, not because they are a starting point. That is, they are the hub of the interactive model. When Maxwell and Loomis (2003) apply this model to mixed methods studies, the research questions include both questions of variance (e.g., how true, present, much, or correlated?) that are associated with quantitative data and questions of process (e.g., how and why?) that are associated with qualitative data. The combination of variance and process questions informs and is responsive to the purposes, conceptual frameworks, methods, and validity considerations within the design of the study.

Maxwell and Loomis (2003) offer several advantages of this dynamic model for mixed methods research. They argue that individuals can develop a more nuanced understanding of the integrated nature of a mixed methods study by examining each of the five components because the integration of the quantitative and qualitative aspects may occur across components. In addition, they argue that this model provides a more responsive tool for considering how to design a mixed methods study because it better considers the context and process by which a particular mixed methods study unfolds in practice, instead of overemphasizing preset design typologies. Although the focus of their discussion is on the five components, Maxwell and Loomis also present a model of the contextual factors that influence these components in mixed methods design, which is symbolized here by the dotted line in Figure 12.2b. They note that funding goals and research paradigm are contexts that directly influence one's research questions, and they provide numerous other contexts that indirectly influence the research questions through the beliefs and theories, purposes, methods, and validity components salient to the study.

Both models provide useful frameworks for designing a mixed methods study in response to research questions that call for understandings developed through quantitative and qualitative approaches. In both cases, the writings focus on the implications of the research questions on other decisions, such as methods, as opposed to focusing on the development of the research questions themselves. Therefore, these models prove most useful for demonstrating how research questions link to the rest of the mixed methods research process, but they do not provide a specific framework for considering how researchers arrive at their mixed research questions in practice, and they do not suggest guidelines for how these questions are composed.

◆ A Framework for Describing the Origins of Research Questions in Mixed Methods Research

To examine the origins of research questions within mixed methods research, we read relevant literature and examined practice-based sources for insight into how researchers compose research questions in practice as they plan, conduct, and report mixed methods studies. We studied the research questions reported within (a) the abstracts from 226 U.S. federally funded health-related proposals that self-identified as using mixed methods research within the CRISP Database (crisp.cit.nih.gov/)[1] (Plano Clark, in press), (b) 25 dissertations that self-identified as using mixed methods within the Dissertation Abstracts database, and (c) numerous manuscripts that reported the results from mixed methods studies. In addition, our sources included studies that reported the results of interviews with mixed methods researchers (Bryman, 2006b, 2007; O'Cathain, Murphy, & Nicholl, 2007; Plano Clark, 2005).

We offer the model in Figure 12.3, which emphasizes the development, refinement, and emergence of research questions within mixed methods studies and delineates the dimensions of these questions. The rectangular boxes represent the general research process. That is, this model considers

how research questions are generated at three stages of research: (1) at the start of the study from the literature and practice, (2) in conjunction with the decisions about and implementation of the methods, and (3) in response to specific results and interpretations that emerge from the study. It also acknowledges the role of the environment by placing this process within communities of practice and tying it to the personal fit with the researcher. We do not offer this model as a replacement for the other models. Instead, we argue that this model emphasizes different aspects of the research process and therefore seeks to further our thinking about research questions within mixed methods studies. The role of each of these categories in the generation of mixed research questions is considered in this section. The next section focuses on the dimensions for writing questions generated within mixed methods studies (the central circle in Figure 12.3).

RESEARCH QUESTIONS ARE SUGGESTED BY PROBLEMS FOUND IN THE DISCIPLINARY LITERATURE AND PRACTICE

The most traditional approach to generating research questions is for the researcher to develop them in response to problems as identified within the literature and practice. This development process includes identifying a topic, reviewing literature, defining terms, and stating a general purpose or objective for the research (Ridenour & Newman, 2008). Researchers develop questions based on deficiencies within the literature about a topic, such as a gap in the literature or voices of individuals who have not been heard or who have been silenced, or practice that needs to be improved (Creswell, 2008). As such, research questions in mixed methods are about what is *not* known about a phenomenon (Teddlie & Tashakkori, 2009). Deficiencies in the literature that point to a need for both quantitative and qualitative approaches call for a researcher to develop a

Figure 12.3 A Model of the Origin of Research Questions Within the Process of Mixed Methods Research

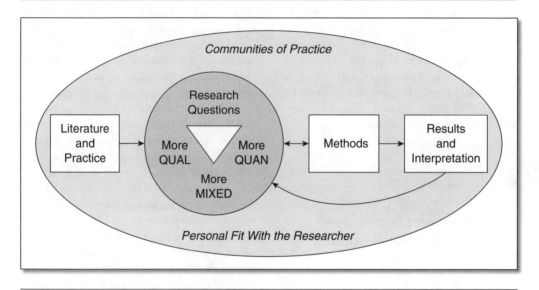

NOTE: QUAN = quantitative; QUAL = qualitative.

mixed methods purpose and research questions (Creswell & Plano Clark, 2007). Examples of researchers' considerations about relevant literature and practices when formulating research questions include the following:

• What is known about the topic from prior qualitative, quantitative, and mixed methods research?

• What is not known? What knowledge is needed?

• Is one type of question and method inadequate for addressing the needed knowledge?

• What theories or conceptual frameworks inform thinking about the topic? Do aspects of the theory need to be generated and tested?

Research questions in mixed methods research also require two types of information (e.g., narrative and numerical) to be answered (Teddlie & Tashakkori, 2009). For example, after an extensive discussion

of the literature, Feldon and Kafai (2008) noted inconsistencies in prior quantitative and qualitative research conducted on the personal meanings and social functions of avatars (graphic self-representations within online environments) and argued that there is a need to develop "contextualized understanding of broader trends" (p. 580). From this literature-derived need, they stated a combination of questions about quantitative trends in online user activity related to the avatars and about qualitative descriptions of the meaning of the user activities. As another example, Bernardi, Keim, and von der Lippe (2007) concluded from the literature that there are two specific problems related to the study of social influences on fertility. They linked these problems to the study's aims by noting, "We regard a combination of qualitative and quantitative approaches as best suited to tackle the two problems" (p. 24). The identification of gaps in understanding as a source of research questions is also common practice within mixed methods proposals. Bradley (2007) noted in her proposal that "the lack of evidence about what accounts for hospital-level variation in risk-adjusted mortality rates is a critical gap in our current knowledge about how to improve outcomes" (Paragraph 1). To address this gap, she proposed two aims, one to generate hypotheses about hospital-level practices and a second to test these hypotheses in terms of specific mortality rate outcomes.

RESEARCH QUESTIONS ARE INFLUENCED BY COMMUNITIES OF PRACTICE

With the exception of Maxwell and Loomis (2003), little of the mixed methods literature has examined the influence of social factors on the research process in general, and the generation of research questions in particular. Recent discussions by Morgan (2007) and Denscombe (2008), however, highlight the importance of disciplines and research groups as influential contexts for the mixed methods research process. Both discussions draw heavily on Kuhn's (1970) work and emphasize a definition of paradigm that is based on research practice and research communities. Morgan (2007) defines a paradigm as a community of researchers who "share a consensus about which questions are most meaningful" (p. 53). Denscombe (2008) links this idea to "communities of practice" and argues that evidence from practice supports the conclusion that social factors significantly affect researchers' methodological decisions when conducting mixed methods research. Maxwell and Loomis (2003) also described social factors as part of the environment in which all aspects of research design take place. Therefore, while this discussion focuses on the influence of communities of practice on the origin of research questions, we acknowledge that it plays a contextual role for the entire research process in Figure 12.3.

There are many ways that communities of practice influence the generation of research questions within mixed methods studies. Denscombe (2008) describes the power of

these influences by stating, "Researchers who have regards to careers and research funding will find it hard, probably impossible, to ignore such an influence to conform to group norms" (p. 279). That is, when researchers develop research questions for a study, they often consider (consciously or subconsciously) issues such as these:

- Are mixed research questions of interest to or preferred by the larger discipline?

- Will my doctoral committee approve or require mixed questions?

- Do mixed questions need to be asked to satisfy different audiences?

- What questions will be publishable in disciplinary journals?

- How can my questions match the priorities of funders?

Due to the ubiquitous nature of social influences and the general practice to forgo discussion of these influences within published research reports, their role within individual studies is often hidden and unexamined. Interviews with mixed methods researchers, however, highlight the importance of communities-of-practice influences. Bryman (2007) uncovered significant influences that he attributed to the "predispositions and preferences of . . . disciplines and funding agencies" (p. 20). Plano Clark (2005) also noted examples of researchers describing the nature of these influences, such as the perception that individuals are influenced to choose their questions and use of mixed methods based on perceived fads within disciplines. Although we found no published report in which a researcher claimed to use mixed questions in response to a current fad, recent trends in the growing use of mixed methods give credence to this claim. For example, when searching the Dissertation Abstracts database, we found that the number of dissertations that self-report as mixed methods has increased exponentially from 23 to 718 between the years of 1997 and 2007. Clearly, there is growing interest in asking questions associated with this approach.

Researchers interviewed by Plano Clark (2005) identified additional types of influences from research communities. Counseling psychology researchers described being more apt to pose mixed research questions because "counseling psychologists were now more interested in process questions in addition to outcome-based questions" (p. 116). Researchers from the discipline of physics education research reported the need to pose two types of questions (quantitative and qualitative) to satisfy the different expectations of their researcher and practitioner audiences. Evidence for the influence of community norms on research questions can also be found within published studies. This influence ranges from the presentation style used to the types of questions deemed acceptable. Our examination of different venues for reporting mixed methods research found that dissertation authors usually stated their research questions as questions, whereas investigators usually stated specific aims instead of questions in their proposal abstracts. Journal article authors varied in the rhetorical style in their mixed methods reports, including the use of questions, hypotheses, and aims.

The influence of funding agencies is particularly important in mixed methods research (O'Cathain et al., 2007; Plano Clark, 2005, in press) and goes beyond the style used to state research questions within proposals. Researchers may specifically adapt their questions to meet funding guidelines calling for certain types of questions or methods. For example, in one successful funding proposal, the investigator noted the tie between the agency's goals and her proposed study: "Further, in using a mixed methods approach to accomplish this task, this research will address a second goal by the [funding agency]: to use a variety of qualitative and quantitative methods as a vehicle for collecting data" (Owen-Smith, 2007, Paragraph 1). As another example of the magnitude of funders' influence, Miall and March (2005) changed their research questions

and subsequent methods to satisfy their funders' view that qualitative questions should be studied before quantitative questions. They noted, "We had intended to draw an interview sample from the larger telephone survey. In reviewing our research proposal, the funding agency mandated a qualitative study followed by a survey" (p. 407).

RESEARCH QUESTIONS FIT WITH A RESEARCHER'S BELIEFS AND PRIOR EXPERIENCES

The choice to develop mixed research questions also reflects personal aspects of the researcher. Anyone who has worked with graduate students has probably heard students claim that they consider only certain types of research questions because they are "quantitative researchers" or "qualitative researchers." As much as methodologists would like to discourage this methods-first thinking, the reality is that most of us have also heard similar statements from very experienced and successful researchers, who say they are interested only in cause-and-effect questions that call for quantitative experimental methods or in process questions that call for the use of grounded theory methods. Researchers generate questions that are consistent with their personal worldview and mental models for conducting research. Researchers' choices and statements of mixed research questions are also shaped by their personal goals, value systems, preferred styles of research, and expertise (Creswell & Plano Clark, 2007; Maxwell & Loomis, 2003; Tashakkori & Teddlie, 1998). That is, researchers may want to actively examine how their personal beliefs are influencing a mixed methods study's research questions, by asking questions such as the following:

• Are questions associated with mixed methods research consistent with my worldview and/or mental models for research?

- Is my prior training helping me to be open to mixed research questions?

- Do my personal goals call for mixed research questions?

- Are my prior experiences encouraging me to consider mixed research questions?

Certain worldviews and standpoints are considered conducive for researchers to pose mixed research questions. These include pragmatic (Johnson & Onwuegbuzie, 2004), dialectical (Greene & Hall, 2010), transformative (Mertens et al., 2010), and feminist (Hesse-Biber, 2010 [this volume]) perspectives. Researchers may identify the perspective that shapes their questions in their reports. Edwards and Lopez (2006) stated that their study of the development of a critical consciousness "was conceptualized from a pragmatic theoretical paradigm" (p. 281). Hodgkin (2008) discussed how she conceptualized her study of women's social capital from the transformative research paradigm and feminist perspectives, which led her to pose mixed methods research questions "to highlight issues of need (quantitative data) and to give voice to these issues (qualitative data)" (p. 299).

As with the community-of-practice context, researchers seldom discuss how personal considerations influenced their research questions in their reports beyond possibly identifying the worldview framing the study. In interviews, however, mixed methods researchers readily discussed the importance of their personal history and prior methods training in influencing the development of mixed research questions (Plano Clark, 2005). Likewise, in her mixed methods book, Greene (2007) describes how her personal "mixed methods story" (p. 60) developed through formal schooling, tenure expectations, personal dissatisfaction with mono-method approaches, professional development, and a belief in the value of diverse perspectives. She encourages other researchers to reflect on how their personal history influences the research that they conduct, including the questions they ask.

Some researchers also explicitly tie their questions and methods to personal goals. For example, the U.S. National Institutes of Health offer "K" awards where investigators propose training activities to develop expertise with particular methods, such as mixed methods, including a research study that will provide them the opportunity to apply and practice the new skill. An example of the personal aspect from one of many such successful proposals is, "The applicant is proposing funding . . . to conduct a program of training and research that will develop skills in mixed-methods research strategies. . . . The proposed research projects will complement the training program by providing opportunities to implement the mixed-methods strategies" (Stirman, 2007, Paragraph 1). Researchers also pose mixed questions based on their personal interests and experiences. For example, Green (2003) describes how her experiences as the mother of a daughter with disabilities led her to pose questions that mattered to her, and she reported her mixed methods study to answer them.

RESEARCH QUESTIONS SHAPE AND ARE SHAPED BY METHODS

As the models in Figure 12.2 illustrate, researchers select methods that are best suited for addressing their research questions. In addition to questions informing researchers' methods choices, issues particular to the methods element of the research process can also influence a mixed methods study's research questions. The double-headed arrow between research questions and methods in Figure 12.3 indicates this back-and-forth relationship. Research questions may be refined or new questions stated as the researcher considers whether initially stated questions are researchable with known methods and available resources (Punch, 2005). In addition, Onwuegbuzie and Leech (2006) discuss how research questions are shaped depending on whether the researcher is using a concurrent or sequential mixed methods approach. Creswell and Plano Clark (2007) also suggest that questions be refined within the context of the selected mixed methods design variant. They recommend that researchers develop a specific mixed methods question (using an issue or procedural format) that will be answered by the process of integrating the quantitative and qualitative strands within the design being used. Therefore, research questions may emerge or be modified as a researcher considers method issues such as the following:

• What questions are consistent with the planned mixed methods design?

• What question will be answered by integrating the quantitative and qualitative strands?

• Are the stated research questions researchable?

• Can the research questions be addressed with the available participants?

• Are there ethical implications that call for mixed research questions?

• Does the need for tools or materials suggest additional research questions?

In practice, researchers pose questions that call for and are adapted to fit within specific mixed methods approaches, such as mixed methods research questions that researchers tie to the integration procedures of their selected design. For example, after stating quantitative and qualitative research questions in her concurrent study about long-term effects of traumatic brain injury, Curry (2006) asked a question to guide the comparison of the two sets of results: "How do the qualitative findings corroborate or give meaning to the quantitative results, and vice versa?" (p. 23). Penn (2008) chose a sequential design where he first addressed quantitative research questions and then qualitatively

followed up on these initial results for further explanation. Within the context of this design, he stated two mixed methods questions: "1. In what ways does the qualitative multicase study help to explain the quantitative results? 2. How do the quantitative and qualitative data together reveal faculty approaches to improving teaching at a large Midwestern research institution?" (p. 13).

Issues with the research setting or related to the intended participants may lead a researcher to modify mixed research questions or add new questions that turn a previously quantitative or qualitative study into a mixed methods study. For example, a much-needed randomized control trial investigation to answer questions about the relative effectiveness of different treatments for prostate cancer faced great difficulty in adequately recruiting participants to the randomization process. The research team added exploratory questions about the recruitment process, and Donovan et al. (2002) reported what was learned qualitatively and how these qualitative results were used to improve the conduct of the experimental trial. Brady and O'Regan (2009) also describe how their research questions had to change to accommodate methods issues that emerged in relation to participant sampling constraints and ethical considerations within their mixed methods study of the impact of a youth mentoring program. In addition, they reported how methods concerns about how to effectively integrate their data sources led to a new research question focused on the integration procedures. They asked, "What results emerge regarding the potential of this youth mentoring program from comparing the outcome data from the impact study with the case study data from the mentoring pairs?" (p. 276).

We also found that researchers state research questions in response to the need for specific data collection tools, such as a valid instrument. In her National Institutes of Health (NIH) proposal, McWayne (2007) aims to assess the association between Latino family involvement and school readiness outcomes for preschool children. To quantitatively address this question, she needs to first develop a culturally sensitive instrument to measure Latino family involvement. Therefore, she states a preliminary aim to understand family involvement during the preschool period as conceptualized by Latino parents. She plans to address this aim qualitatively and then use the information to develop the needed quantitative instrument. In this way, she expects to be able to study the topic in a culturally sensitive way and draw culturally relevant conclusions from the overall study.

RESEARCH QUESTIONS MAY EMERGE FROM A STUDY'S RESULTS AND INTERPRETATIONS

Within some mixed methods studies, questions emerge or are refined based on results and the researcher's interpretations of the results. The curved arrow in Figure 12.3 indicates the emergence of questions in response to initial results. Simply because of their complexity, mixed methods studies have the potential for initial results to suggest new research questions, particularly related to the integration of the methods that go beyond the researcher's initial intentions (Bryman, 2006a). In fact, an advantage of using mixed methods is that the researcher can be responsive to unanticipated results and not be confined to predetermined questions or methods (Christ, 2007). This flexibility is useful in exploratory and longitudinal studies where the researcher is unsure of the direction of the study at the start of the research process (Christ, 2007), in sequential designs where questions in subsequent phases are informed by the results of an earlier phase (Teddlie & Tashakkori, 2009), and in concurrent studies where questions calling for new integration procedures are suggested by preliminary results (Plano Clark, Garrett, & Leslie-Pelecky, 2009). Several kinds of interpretations may propel the researcher to modify or develop research questions,

including results that are unexpected, are contrary to the study's theoretical framework, point to the existence of extreme or outlier cases, bring into question issues of validity, or are divergent and cannot be readily explained (Creswell & Plano Clark, 2007). Therefore, another set of issues that mixed methods researchers consider in regard to generating research questions includes the following:

- Are initial results required before subsequent research questions can be developed?

- Is there sufficient information to interpret the results?

- Do unexpected or surprising results suggest a new kind of question?

- Are the results and interpretations valid, and if not, what questions does this raise?

There are many examples of mixed methods studies where research questions emerged or were modified based on initial results and interpretations. For example, Aldridge, Fraser, and Huang (1999) identified an anomaly in their quantitative results, in that Taiwanese students, compared with Australian students, had more favorable attitudes toward science despite having less favorable perceptions about their science learning environments. This finding led the researchers to pose new questions about the science learning environments in the two countries for a second qualitative phase to explain the anomalous result. Ras (2009) found that she was having trouble interpreting the findings in her qualitative case study of a school undergoing a self-imposed curricular change process, and thus the preliminary findings raised new questions of interpretation that required quantitative methods. As she addressed these new questions, her qualitative study became a mixed method study. As a final example, Barroso and Sandelowski (2001) describe how a question emerged in regard to the validity of the quantitative scores they obtained from a depression measure in a study of fatigue with participants who were HIV positive. They then used qualitative comments from participants to better understand how they were interpreting the instrument's items.

◆ *Writing Research Questions in Mixed Methods Research*

We now turn our attention to how researchers write the research questions found within mixed methods research. The triangle in the center of Figure 12.3 illustrates a three-ended continuum of the questions that researchers pose and interpret as more quantitative, more qualitative, or more mixed. Rather than viewing research questions as dichotomized neatly into distinct categories, we recognize that researchers make interpretations within the context of their research endeavor as to whether the questions they have generated are best addressed with quantitative, qualitative, or a combination of information. That said, writers generally agree on common attributes of the questions that researchers interpret as being associated with quantitative, qualitative, or mixed methods, and, like many other writers, we use terms such as *quantitative questions* or *mixed questions* as a shorthand for questions that have these characteristics and are answered with the corresponding forms of data. We begin with a brief review of quantitative and qualitative questions before discussing mixed research questions.

RESEARCH QUESTIONS ASSOCIATED WITH QUANTITATIVE METHODS

Quantitative researchers tend to use prespecified research questions derived from the literature. This allows quantitative studies to unfold in a linear fashion, from literature to questions to methods. Quantitative questions involve variables, which are characteristics or attributes of individuals and organizations that vary in the sample and that the researcher will measure using numeric scores. They are associated with a wide range of purposes for research, including describing trends and patterns, assessing variances, identifying differences, measuring outcomes, and testing theories. Quantitative questions may be descriptive and focus on participants' responses to individual variables. They often involve more than one variable and fall within two broad categories: questions about relationships among variables or questions about comparisons among groups. In any case, the researcher decides that the descriptions, relationships, or comparisons are assessed best using quantitative data and statistical procedures.

Methodologists offer considerable advice for writing good quantitative questions (e.g., Creswell, 2008; Johnson & Christensen, 2008; Onwuegbuzie & Leech, 2006). Researchers should formulate quantitative research questions in highly specific terms to specify the data and analyses needed to answer them. When stated as questions, they should begin with *how, what,* or *why* and use signal terms such as *differ, compare,* and *relate* to indicate links between variables. Researchers using deductive logic are more likely to state their quantitative research questions as hypotheses because they may be able to make predictions based on prior research or existing theories. Consider the following example of a quantitative research question: What is the relationship between engineers' ability to work on teams and work satisfaction? This question can be answered by quantitatively measuring the two variables (ability to work on teams and work satisfaction) for many participants and determining the association between them. Research questions that share these attributes fall within the "more QUAN" dimension of Figure 12.3.

RESEARCH QUESTIONS ASSOCIATED WITH QUALITATIVE METHODS

Researchers who ask qualitative questions are usually working from an inductive perspective. Therefore, although qualitative research questions can be prespecified, they often emerge and are shaped as the study develops and the researcher learns more about the phenomenon under study (Corbin & Strauss, 2008; Punch, 2005). Qualitative researchers use their research questions to determine where to focus their attention, but not to prescribe the direction of their research (Ridenour & Newman, 2008). The inductive purpose of qualitative inquiry differs from quantitative research. Qualitative questions are often associated with purposes for research that call for developing understanding, uncovering meaning, explaining processes, and generating theories. A qualitative research question asks a general, open-ended question about a single phenomenon, process, or issue and provides the researcher with sufficient flexibility and freedom to explore a topic in depth (Corbin & Strauss, 2008).

Good qualitative research questions are broad, but narrow enough to focus on the issues most relevant to the individuals under investigation. A qualitative question identifies the topic area and gives the reader information on what is of interest to the investigator. Creswell (2008) recommends stating qualitative questions in neutral, nondirectional language; identifying only one phenomenon; beginning with the words *what* or *how;* and considering the use of issue or procedural subquestions. The following is an example of a qualitative research question: What is the experience of being part of a team for engineers in a midwestern electric company? The question provides a focus for methods decisions to understand and describe participants' experiences in their own words. Questions that researchers interpret as having these attributes fall toward the "more QUAL" dimension of Figure 12.3.

RESEARCH QUESTIONS ASSOCIATED WITH MIXED METHODS

Studies that include questions that the researcher associates with *both* quantitative and qualitative approaches fall along the "more MIXED" dimension of Figure 12.3. Although Newman et al. (2003) explained that one cannot develop an effective typology of research questions for mixed methods, there are typologies of research purposes for which a researcher may state a combination of questions and choose to use a mixed methods approach (e.g., Greene, Caracelli, & Graham, 1989; Newman et al., 2003). Recently, Bryman (2006a) assembled a list of 16 reasons for combining quantitative and qualitative research to address mixed research questions based on the methodological literature and researchers' practice. This list includes triangulation, offset weaknesses, completeness, structure and process, different research questions, explanation, unexpected results, instrument development, sampling, credibility, context, illustration, utility of results, confirm and discover, diversity of views, and enhancement.

Across these many reasons for mixed methods research, our examination of the literature and researchers' practice identified four dimensions that describe how researchers write research questions within the context of their mixed methods studies. These dimensions are summarized in Table 12.1 along with hypothetical examples from studies about online interactions. The first two dimensions relate to the rhetorical style used to write the questions and the last two identify how the questions relate to other questions in the study and to the overall research process.

Dimension 1—Rhetorical style: Question format. As discussed at the beginning of this chapter, we were open to considering research questions that investigators stated in different formats. In our review of mixed

Table 12.1 Dimensions for Writing Research Questions in Mixed Methods Studies

Dimension	Options	Description	Hypothetical Examples From Studies About Online Interactions
Rhetorical style: Format	Question	The researcher writes an interrogative sentence complete with question mark.	1. What online interactions occur in successful and unsuccessful distance courses?
	Aim	The researcher writes a declarative sentence that expresses what is to be accomplished.	1. This study aims to describe the online interactions that occur in successful and unsuccessful distance courses.
	Hypothesis	The researcher writes a statement that predicts an outcome for a research question.	1. Successful distance courses include a richer set of interactions among students and the instructor than those rated as unsuccessful.
Rhetorical style: Level of integration[a]	Separate questions only	The researcher writes separate questions for the qualitative and quantitative strands of the study.	1a. How does online game play relate to study strategies? [QUAN] 1b. What is the process of studying for online game players? [QUAL] 2a. What is the meaning of online friendships? [QUAL] 2b. What factors play a role for people who have meaningful online friendships? [QUAN]
	General, overarching mixed methods question	The researcher writes a broad question that is addressed with both quantitative and qualitative approaches.	1. How can the impact of online dating sites be understood? 2. What is community within an online network?
	Hybrid mixed methods issue question	The researcher writes one question with two distinct parts and uses a quantitative approach to address one part and a qualitative approach to address the other part.	1. How is an effective online course developed and tested? 2. Does hours spent online affect intimacy between romantic couples? If yes, how?

Dimension	Options	Description	*Hypothetical Examples From Studies About Online Interactions*
	Mixed methods procedural/ mixing question	The researcher writes a narrow question that directs the integration of the qualitative and quantitative strands of the study.	1. What is the relationship between the case studies of online professors and the survey data about their attitudes? 2. How do the follow-up narrative results extend, refute, or illuminate the survey findings about students' experiences of online classes?
	Combination	The researcher combines at least one mixed methods question with separate quantitative and qualitative questions.	1a. How do adolescents use social networking sites? [MM] 1b. What theory explains adolescents' process of using social networking sites? [QUAL] 1c. How are the identified factors related? [QUAN] 1d. To what extent do the quantitative correlational results generalize the qualitative grounded theory model? [MM]
The relationship of questions to other questions	Independent	The researcher writes two or more research questions that are related, and one question does not depend on the results of the other question.	1a. How do pre-teenagers perceive online bullying? 1b. How frequently do pre-teenagers experience acts of online bullying? 2a. What are managers' perceptions of teleconferencing? 2b. What factors play a role in employee satisfaction with teleconferencing?
	Dependent	The researcher writes a question that depends on the results of another research question.	1a. Which strategies do blog writers employ to widen their audience? 1b. What influences the use of these strategies? 2a. What themes emerge to describe the experience of online dating? 2b. How frequently do each of these themes occur for online daters?

(Continued)

Table 12.1 (Continued)

Dimension	Options	Description	Hypothetical Examples From Studies About Online Interactions
The relationship of questions to the research process	Predetermined	The researcher writes a question based on literature, practice, personal tendencies, and/or disciplinary considerations at the outset of the study.	1. How do college students perceive the impact of Web sites like YouTube? 2. What ways has online chatting affected work productivity?
	Emergent	The researcher formulates a new or modified question during the design, data collection, data analysis, or interpretation.	1. To what extent do people who are not part of online global communities experience the themes that emerged from the qualitative data? 2. What are the most effective online educational tools for first graders?

NOTE: QUAN = quantitative; QUAL = qualitative; MM = mixed methods.

a. *Level of integration* refers to the rhetorical style of the written research questions. As mixed methods studies, the expectation is that *all* of the hypothetical studies would integrate the qualitative and quantitative strands.

methods practice, we found that mixed methods researchers use each of the described formats. That is, mixed methods researchers state their research questions in the form of

- questions,

- aims, and/or

- hypotheses.

The question format was common in dissertations and used in many mixed methods journal articles. This use may reflect audience expectations across disciplines and publication venues as well as an overall emphasis on the research question in mixed methods research. In addition, we found that study aims were used extensively in the proposal abstracts that we reviewed and that this use occurs in response to requirements set by funding agencies. Although less common, we also found examples of questions stated as hypotheses in a few articles and dissertations, and they were usually paired with qualitative questions. For example, Myers and Oetzel (2003) wrote one qualitative research question (RQ) and four quantitative hypotheses (H1–H4), which included the following:

RQ: What are the dimensions of organizational assimilation? (p. 440)

H1: The dimensions of organizational assimilation correlate positively with job satisfaction. (p. 441)

Dimension 2—Rhetorical style: Level of integration. Any research approach can use research questions written in different formats, but there is an additional dimension specific to the rhetorical style of questions found within mixed methods studies. This dimension describes the level of integration conveyed in the writing of the questions. Keep in mind that we expect *all* mixed methods studies to meaningfully integrate the quantitative and qualitative strands of the study. Therefore, rather than indicate the extent to which results are integrated, the level-of-integration dimension assesses the extent to which the research questions are written in an integrated style. Broadly speaking, mixed methods researchers state either separate quantitative and qualitative questions or mixed methods research questions or both. A mixed methods research question is defined as a single question that "embeds both a quantitative research question and a qualitative research question within the same question" (Onwuegbuzie & Leech, 2006, p. 483). The concept of mixed methods research questions is relatively new and thus far has received only minimal attention in the literature (Creswell & Plano Clark, 2007; Onwuegbuzie & Leech, 2006; Tashakkori & Creswell, 2007). Drawing from the literature and available reports, we found several style options in use by researchers: (a) separate quantitative and qualitative questions only; (b) general, overarching mixed methods questions; (c) hybrid mixed methods issue questions; and (d) mixed methods procedural/mixing questions.

• *Researchers may state separate quantitative and qualitative questions only.* As Teddlie and Tashakkori (2009) discuss, all mixed methods studies include at least two questions—one qualitative, one quantitative. Therefore, it is natural for researchers to write separate questions. Separate questions are two or more questions that the researcher associates with at least two different methods. For example, *What is this?* and *What is that?* reflect separate questions if *this* is explored qualitatively and *that* is examined quantitatively. Researchers distinguish their qualitative and quantitative questions through formatting or phrasing.

Differentiating questions through formatting includes the use of labels (i.e., *qualitative* or *quantitative*) in headings or parenthetical comments. The phrasing of the questions, such as using language traditionally associated with one approach, can also indicate their nature. For example, Webster (2009) wrote two quantitative and two qualitative questions, and one of each is mentioned here:

> Is there a statistically significant difference in nursing student empathy, as measured by the Interpersonal Reactivity Index (IRI), after a psychiatric nursing clinical experience? What are student perceptions of working with mentally ill clients during a psychiatric nursing clinical experience? (pp. 6–7)

The language of the first question makes it clear that it is quantitative because the researcher uses the term *statistically significant.* The second question was explored qualitatively through interviews. Some researchers state separate questions but do not provide clear indications that they are associating different questions with different methods. In these cases, the qualitative or quantitative nature of the question can be inferred only in the context of the entire study.

• *Researchers may state an overarching mixed methods question.* An overarching mixed methods question is one broad issue-focused question such as *What is this?* which the researcher interprets as requiring *both* quantitative and qualitative information to answer. As such, these questions emphasize the overall integrated nature of the study as opposed to breaking questions into separate components (Yin, 2006). From our review, we share three examples of researchers stating overarching mixed methods questions. Plano Clark et al. (2009) asked:

> How do the alumni of the [nontraditional science] graduate education program perceive the impact of their participation? (pp. 5–6)

They considered the word *perceive* as a neutral word and explained that their question is best suited to a mixed methods design because they required qualitative and quantitative information to adequately describe the perceptions of impact. A study by Igo, Kiewra, and Bruning (2008) is more explicit:

How do different copy-and-paste note-taking interventions affect college students' learning of Web-based text ideas? The first two words in this question indicate that a mixed methods approach is warranted, with *do* indicating the need for an experiment and *how* indicating the need for a qualitative follow-up. (p. 150, italics in original)

The first phase of the study was an experimental design in which quantitative data were collected in the form of scores on learning tasks. In the second phase, the authors analyzed student notes and interviews to extend the findings from the experiment. Thus, the authors justify the use of mixed methods and state how their language indicates the different types of data. As another interesting example, Fitzpatrick (2008) stated four overarching questions labeled as quantitative and qualitative. Each question was associated with data collected with both methods. One such question was the following:

What specialized skills do urban teachers rely upon to be successful within the urban setting? (p. 23)

• *Researchers may state a hybrid mixed methods issue question.* Hybrid questions are single questions about the content of the study that include two distinct parts, with each part associated with either a qualitative or quantitative approach. *What is this and that?* and *How and why does that occur?* are examples of hybrid questions. For example, Nakagami (2006) stated a hybrid aim in a proposal for funding:

The proposed study will examine the relationship and explore the causal ordering between consumer working alliance, hope, and psychosocial functioning outcomes. (Paragraph 1)

In the initial phase of this study, the investigator plans to gather quantitative structured interviews from participants to assess the interactions of working alliance, hope, and psychosocial outcomes for schizophrenic patients. The subsequent phase consists of qualitative open-ended interviews to further explore the quantitative results. Another hybrid question was found in a dissertation by Emert (2008). The question was this:

Does participation in the Fulbright Teacher Exchange Program impact the intercultural competence of participants? If yes, how? (p. 6)

The first part is more quantitative in nature because the researchers assessed intercultural development through a pretest and posttest survey. The second part indicates a more qualitative orientation because they explored the impact through interviews.

• *Researchers may state a mixed methods procedural/mixing question.* The final rhetorical style occurs when authors state a question about the study's integration using a procedural focus. These questions are written so that they explicitly direct the procedures for mixing the strands of a mixed methods study, and they are tied to the specific design being used (Creswell & Plano Clark, 2007). Example formats include the following: *What is the congruence between this and that? What is a culturally sensitive instrument based on that? How does this explain that?* Keep in mind that researchers using procedural questions do not conduct their studies for the purpose of employing certain procedures. Instead, procedural questions are one rhetorical option for writing research questions in mixed methods research. Procedural questions may be particularly useful for providing initial direction to a study where topics are expected to emerge, highlighting the use of an integrated design, foreshadowing integration procedures for audiences unfamiliar with mixed methods, and conveying the complexity inherent in mixed methods designs.

We found numerous examples of mixed methods procedural questions. LaPrairie, Slate, Schulte, and Onwuegbuzie (2009) conducted a concurrent study where they gathered qualitative information about student perceptions of best and poor college professors as well as quantitative information about student characteristics. They asked the following question, which indicates how they will link their two data sets in a sequential analysis:

What is the difference in endorsed themes of best college professors as a function of gender, ethnicity, student status, and generation status? (p. 9)

In addition to the four general questions noted earlier, Fitzpatrick's (2008) dissertation about urban music teaching included one procedural question:

In what ways do the survey and case study align with one another? (p. 23)

She gathered survey data from music teachers in one strand of her study and conducted case studies consisting of interviews and observations with four music teachers in the other strand. The two sets of results were compared and integrated to answer the procedural question. McWayne (2007) stated three aims in her proposal to conduct a sequential study that begins with a qualitative phase and builds to a second quantitative phase. Between her qualitative and quantitative aims, she stated a procedural mixing aim that highlights how she plans to connect the two phases:

(b) [to] create a culturally relevant, multidimensional quantitative instrument with items that capture the specific behaviors Latino parents engage in to support their preschool children's early educational success [as identified in the qualitative phase] (Paragraph 1)

In a sequential study starting with a quantitative phase, Starker's (2008) mixing question was this:

How do the qualitative responses enhance the interpretation of preservice teachers' [quantitative Web-based instruments] scores? (p. 28)

The quantitative component of this study assessed effectiveness of delivering content using a Web-based tool. Qualitative data were collected in a second phase to enhance the interpretation of the quantitative results as foreshadowed in the mixing question.

• *Researchers may combine rhetorical styles.* Although we have focused on separate rhetorical options, researchers may find they are confronted with a tension between wanting to state questions that emphasize the integrated nature of study and those that emphasize the connection between questions and methods. Therefore, many researchers combine multiple styles. Combinations work well because the different styles emphasize different aspects of a mixed methods study including the content issue, the specific questions that call for different methods, and the integration procedures. For example, Scott and Sutton (2009) combined an overarching question, separate quantitative questions, and a procedural mixed methods question when they wrote:

The overarching question was what trends appear in teachers' emotions during professional development and how do these emotions relate to acceptance of the writing process based on a mixed methods design. Subquestions included

Phase 1

1. What are the trends in teachers' emotions during the year in which they are asked to use the writing process?

2. What changes do teachers report in their teaching practices?

3. How are trends in emotions related to changes in practices?

Phase 2

4. How do teachers' reflections on emotions and changes in teacher practices illuminate understanding of the relationships between emotions and change in teacher practices as found in Phase 1? (p. 153)

Dimension 3—The relationship of questions to other questions. Because mixed methods researchers state at least two research questions, another important dimension is how the questions relate to each other. The relationship among the questions is important because it shapes (and may be shaped by) the overall design and the relationship between the quantitative and qualitative components of the study. Two alternatives are available: The questions may be related, but independent of each other, or one question may depend on the results of another question.

• *The research questions may be independent of each other.* Research questions are considered as independent when Question B does not depend on the results of Question A and vice versa. That is, asking *What is this?* and *What is that?* is the same as asking *What is that?* and *What is this?* Although the questions relate to the same larger content topic, there is no implied order to the questions, and as such, the quantitative and qualitative components of the study may be implemented in parallel and independently from each

other. Two of Brady and O'Regan's (2009) research questions provide a good example of independent questions:

> What is the impact of the BBBS [Big Brothers Big Sisters] program on the participating youth? How is the program experienced by stakeholders? (p. 273)

Both questions relate to understanding the BBBS mentoring program. The first research question was addressed through surveys of youth that related to the impact of the program, and the second question was answered through interviews with stakeholders.

• *One research question may be dependent on the results of another question.* Dependent questions occur when one question depends on the results of another question within the study. Asking *What is this?* and then *What is that?* is not the same as asking *What is that?* and then *What is this?*; one needs to know the *this* before one can study the *that.* Dependent questions generally call for the use of sequential designs (Creswell & Plano Clark, 2007) or sequential analytic techniques, such as data transformation, where one type of data is dependent on the other type, such as when qualitative themes are transformed into quantitative counts (Onwuegbuzie & Teddlie, 2003). Biddix's (2009) two-phase study represents an example of using dependent questions:

> (1) What career paths for women lead to the community college SSAO [Senior Student Affairs Officer]? (2) What influences path decisions to change jobs or institutions? (p. 3)

In the first phase of the study, SSAO résumés were the primary source of data, informing an initial network analysis. The second phase consisted of interviews with SSAOs, which sought to explain the paths identified from the network analysis. Eli and Mohr-Schroeder (2009) also stated dependent questions in their study of math teachers:

> What types of mathematical connections do prospective middle grades teachers make while completing investigative tasks meant to probe mathematical connections? What is the relationship between prospective middle grades teachers' mathematics knowledge for teaching geometry and the types of mathematical connections made while completing investigative mathematical tasks? (p. 16)

The authors qualitatively described the types of mathematical connections and then used data transformation to quantitatively score the results about connections and relate them to other quantitative variables. Thus, the second research question depended on the results of the first question.

Dimension 4—The relationship of questions to the research process. As summarized in Figure 12.3, research questions are often generated at the start of a study's research process, but they also may emerge as the study's method decisions and results come into play. Teddlie and Tashakkori (2009) suggest that questions in concurrent/parallel studies are generated at the project's onset. That is, they are predetermined or preset at the start. Emergent questions are also possible and even probable in many mixed method studies. Tashakkori and Creswell (2007) discuss the practice of writing research questions for each phase of a sequential study as it evolves. Plano Clark et al. (2009) discussed how they addressed their overarching question with a concurrent design, but new mixing questions emerged as they examined initial results in their study. Therefore, broadly speaking, research questions within mixed methods studies are either predetermined or emergent within the process of research.

● *Research questions may be predetermined.* When research questions are predetermined, Question X is stated at the beginning of the study based on the researcher's understanding of the literature and practice, personal tendencies, or disciplinary considerations. Wade (2008) asked a predetermined question:

> What affect did learning styles of children with autism have on improving their behavior? (p. 7)

The author collected pretest and posttest qualitative and quantitative data to address this question in a concurrent design. From the outset, this researcher determined that qualitative data were intended to provide more in-depth understanding, and thus the research questions were predetermined.

● *Research questions may be emergent.* Emergent questions are formed during the design, data collection, data analysis, and interpretation aspects of the research process. They emerge due to issues such as complications with the implementation of methods, an unexpected finding, or a new understanding. For example, Way, Stauber, Nakkula, and London (1994) described the questions that emerged from their unexpected quantitative result, namely that students from two schools had different patterns in the relationship between substance use and depression. They formulated two new questions, one qualitative and one mixing:

> (a) How might students with similarly high depression levels across the two schools differ in their perspectives on substance use? (b) How might these possible differences in perspectives begin to explain why depression and substance use are differentially related across the schools? (p. 343)

Christ (2007) also illustrated how new questions emerge within an exploratory, longitudinal mixed methods study. Taking advantage of unforeseen circumstances of a budget reduction at one of his study sites, he added new questions to a third phase of his study when he asked:

(1) How have disability support services at an institutional level changed as a result of declining funds? and (2) Are there differences in the way students and staff view the effectiveness of disability support services? (p. 232)

That is, he posed a new set of mixed questions within the context of an ongoing mixed methods study.

As the set of dimensions and corresponding options illustrate, mixed methods researchers have alternatives for writing research questions in the context of their studies. Together, they provide a framework of the evolving conventions for writing mixed research questions. In addition, researchers frequently combine two or more options for each dimension in their published reports. For example, an author may write questions and hypotheses or have both predetermined and emergent questions. Based on these dimensions, we offer a list of recommendations for writing research questions for mixed methods research in Box 12.1.

BOX 12.1

Recommendations for Writing Mixed Research Questions for Mixed Methods Studies

1. When conducting a mixed methods study, keep your research questions central to your design process. Use methods that are best suited to answering your questions, but also ensure that your questions are responsive to important design and interpretation issues.

2. Reflect critically on the origins of your research questions when conducting a mixed methods study. Discuss the varied contexts that influenced your questions as you report your study to share the challenges that are inherent in conducting mixed methods research.

3. When writing your mixed research questions, select the format that matches the norms of your audience. If there is a choice of format, use the question format to highlight their importance within the conduct of mixed methods research.

4. Use consistent terms to refer to variables or phenomena examined across multiple questions.

5. Use a combination of rhetorical styles to convey the larger question guiding the study, the specific subquestions associated with quantitative and qualitative methods, and an issue or procedural mixed methods question that directs and foreshadows how and why the strands will be integrated.

6. Relate the question style and content to the specific mixed methods design being used. For example, dependent questions should be associated with either a sequential design or sequential procedures (such as data transformation).

7. If the questions are independent, list them in their order of importance. If the questions are dependent, list them in order of what has to be answered first.

8. Determine whether the study is best addressed with predetermined or emergent questions or both. Even if starting with predetermined questions, be open to the possibility of emergent questions. When questions emerge, explicitly discuss the process by which they emerged and the considerations that led to posing new questions.

◆ Evaluating Mixed Research Questions

Issues of quality in mixed methods research are receiving increased attention (see O'Cathain, 2010 [this volume]). Due to the varied nature and intent of quantitative, qualitative, and mixed research questions, it is a challenge to specify specific criteria useful for evaluating each of these forms. Methodologists have discussed general criteria that indicate good research questions (e.g., Creswell, 2008; Punch, 2005; Teddlie & Tashakkori, 2009), and these can apply equally well to the context of questions within mixed methods research. Building from these ideas, we suggest the following considerations as pertinent to mixed research questions.

• *Mixed questions should be researchable.* The questions should be answerable using a combination of available methods and integration techniques. The questions should also be manageable given the resources and expertise of the researcher or research team.

• *Mixed questions should be important.* Recognizing that mixed research questions are shaped by many influences, the questions still need to be substantively relevant and contribute to knowledge about phenomena that are salient within our communities of practice. Their importance should be at least partly documented through multiple references to the literature.

• *Mixed questions should have conceptual clarity.* Questions should be stated in ways that make them easy to understand and clarify what the researcher wants to answer in the study. This may warrant a great deal of reflection on the part of researchers to truly understand what they are attempting to address. With mixed research questions, this also means that researchers should make it clear how they are interpreting the questions in terms of the quantitative/qualitative/mixed continua.

This clarity can be aided by using signal terms that are readily identified with each approach (e.g., *statistically significant, narrative,* or *integration*) or by including an explanation of how the questions are being interpreted within the study's context.

• *There should be congruence among the mixed questions, overall mixed methods design, and results.* Research questions need to have a good fit with the methods and results of the study. That is, the underlying logic of what questions are being asked and how the researcher goes about answering them with mixed methods should be apparent, understandable, and defendable. This congruence can be enhanced in a report by organizing the structure of the methods, results, and interpretation sections to match the statement of the questions.

• *Mixed questions should convey the need for integration or foreshadow an integrated approach or both.* The issue of integration has become central to thinking about all aspects of mixed methods research (Teddlie & Tashakkori, 2006). Mixed methods research requires that the quantitative and qualitative aspects of a study be meaningfully related to each other, and the research questions should facilitate this process. The level of integration conveyed by the questions can be enhanced through the use of mixed methods research questions (overarching, hybrid, procedural, or a combination of these forms). Mixed methods researchers should avoid the use of only separate quantitative and qualitative questions, which may work to keep the methods separate in the implementation of the study (Yin, 2006).

◆ Conclusions

In conclusion, this chapter has attempted to take another step in the work to conceptualize how research questions are generated and stated within the context of mixed methods research. We described existing models of how mixed methods studies are designed in response to research questions and then specified a model that focused on how such questions are generated in the research process and in response to personal and disciplinary contexts. We also delineated a set of dimensions that describe how researchers write the questions for their mixed methods studies as well as criteria for evaluating the quality of these questions.

Like the process of conducting mixed methods research itself, mixed research questions are necessarily complex and dynamic. The field of mixed methods is only beginning to think about the nature of these questions. Researchers will continue to expand the types of questions they ask and the ways that they choose to combine questions and methods. As with quantitative and qualitative methods, conventions for developing and writing mixed questions are starting to form within communities of practice and will continue to become established as methodologists and researchers alike further examine the practice of mixed methods research. We encourage all scholars working in the area of mixed methods to report their reflections about their mixed research questions so that the entire community of mixed methods practice can better understand and consider this essential element of our research endeavors.

Research Questions and Exercises

1. Define research questions and discuss their importance for conducting mixed methods research.

2. Discuss the two models of mixed methods research design in Figure 12.2. Which model best fits with your own process for designing a mixed methods study? Explain your ideas.

3. Examine the research questions in a recent mixed methods study. How did the author link the research questions to the methods in the study?

4. Consider a mixed methods study that you are planning to conduct or have conducted. How did you generate the research questions? List the salient contexts that influenced these questions. In what ways do you find these influences to be supportive or unsupportive of your research efforts?

5. Find a published mixed methods study that used a concurrent design. Locate the authors' research questions and identify which options they used for each of the dimensions for writing mixed questions.

6. Find a published mixed methods study that used a sequential design. Locate the authors' research questions and identify which options they used for each of the dimensions for writing mixed questions.

7. Using the evaluation criteria outlined in this chapter, critique the research questions posed in a mixed methods study. What changes would you suggest?

8. Write good mixed questions for a study that you would like to conduct that calls for a mixed methods approach. How do these questions illustrate each of the dimensions in Table 12.1?

◆ Note

1. As of September 1, 2009, the CRISP database has been replaced by the Research Portfolio Online Reporting Tools Expenditures & Results (RePORTER) database found at http://project reporter.nih.gov/reporter.cfm

◆ References

Aldridge, J. M., Fraser, B. J., & Huang, T. I. (1999). Investigating classroom environments in Taiwan and Australia with multiple research methods. *Journal of Educational Research, 93*(1), 48–62.

Barroso, J., & Sandelowski, M. (2001). In the field with the Beck Depression Inventory. *Qualitative Health Research, 11,* 491–504.

Bernardi, L., Keim, S., & von der Lippe, H. (2007). Social influences on fertility: A comparative mixed methods study in Eastern and Western Germany. *Journal of Mixed Methods Research, 1*(1), 23–47.

Biddix, J. P. (2009, April). *Women's career pathways to the community college senior student affairs officer.* Paper presented at the meeting of the American Educational Research Association, San Diego, CA.

Biesta, G. (2010). Pragmatism and the philosophical foundations of mixed methods Research. In A. Tashakkori & C. Teddlie (Eds.), *SAGE handbook of mixed methods in social & behavioral research* (2nd ed.). Thousand Oaks, CA: Sage.

Bradley, E. H. (2007). *Hospital strategies to improve outcome performance* (Grant No. 1R01HS016929-01). Abstract retrieved from CRISP database: http://crisp.cit.nih.gov/

Brady, B., & O'Regan, C. (2009). Meeting the challenge of doing an RCT evaluation of youth mentoring in Ireland: A journey in mixed methods. *Journal of Mixed Methods Research, 3,* 265–280.

Bryman, A. (2006a). Integrating quantitative and qualitative research: How is it done? *Qualitative Research, 6,* 97–113.

Bryman, A. (2006b). Paradigm peace and the implications for quality. *International Journal of Social Research Methodology, 9*(2), 111–126.

Bryman, A. (2007). Barriers to integrating quantitative and qualitative research. *Journal of Mixed Methods Research, 1,* 8–22.

Christ, T. W. (2007). A recursive approach to mixed methods research in a longitudinal study of postsecondary education disability support services. *Journal of Mixed Methods Research, 1*(3), 226–241.

Corbin, J., & Strauss, A. (2008). *Basics of qualitative research* (3rd ed.). Thousand Oaks, CA: Sage.

Creswell, J. W. (2008). *Educational research: Planning, conducting, and evaluating quantitative and qualitative research* (3rd ed.). Upper Saddle River, NJ: Pearson.

Creswell, J. W., & Plano Clark, V. L. (2007). *Designing and conducting mixed methods research.* Thousand Oaks, CA: Sage.

Curry, E. M. (2006). *Long-term effects of traumatic brain injury as perceived by parental and spousal caregivers: A mixed methods study.* Retrieved from ProQuest Dissertations & Theses. (AAT 3222555)

Denscombe, M. (2008). Communities of practice: A research paradigm for the mixed methods approach. *Journal of Mixed Methods Research, 2*(3), 270–283.

Donovan, J., Mills, N., Smith, M., Brindle, L., Jacoby, A., Peters, T., et al. (2002). Improving design and conduct of randomised trials by embedding them in qualitative research: ProtecT (prostate testing for cancer and treatment) study. *British Medical Journal, 325,* 766–769.

Edwards, L. M., & Lopez, S. J. (2006). Perceived family support, acculturation, and life satisfaction in Mexican American youth: A mixed-methods exploration. *Journal of Counseling Psychology, 53,* 279–287.

Eli, J. A., & Mohr-Schroeder, M. J. (2009, April). *An exploratory study of prospective middle grades teachers' mathematical connections while completing tasks in geometry.* Paper presented at the meeting of the American Educational Research Association, San Diego, CA.

Emert, H. A. (2008). *Developing intercultural competence through teaching abroad with*

Fulbright: Personal experience and professional impact. Retrieved from ProQuest Dissertations & Theses. (AAT 3308069)

Feldon, D. F., & Kafai, Y. B. (2008). Mixed methods for mixed reality: Understanding users' avatar activities in virtual worlds. *Educational Technology Research and Development, 56*(5–6), 575–593.

Fitzpatrick, K. R. (2008). *A mixed methods portrait of urban instrumental music teaching.* Retrieved from ProQuest Dissertations & Theses. (AAT 3303647)

Green, S. E. (2003). "What do you mean 'what's wrong with her?'" Stigma and the lives of families of children with disabilities. *Social Science and Medicine, 57,* 1361–1374.

Greene, J. C. (2007). *Mixed methods in social inquiry.* San Francisco: Jossey-Bass.

Greene, J. C., Caracelli, V. J., & Graham, W. F. (1989). Toward a conceptual framework for mixed-method evaluation designs. *Educational Evaluation and Policy Analysis, 11*(3), 255–274.

Greene, J., & Hall, J. (2010). Dialectics and pragmatism: Being of consequence. In A. Tashakkori & C. Teddlie (Eds.), *SAGE handbook of mixed methods in social & behavioral research* (2nd ed.). Thousand Oaks, CA: Sage.

Hesse-Biber, S. (2010). Feminist approaches to mixed methods research: Linking theory and praxis. In A. Tashakkori & C. Teddlie (Eds.), *SAGE handbook of mixed methods in social & behavioral research* (2nd ed.). Thousand Oaks, CA: Sage.

Hodgkin, S. (2008). Telling it all: A story of women's social capital using a mixed methods approach. *Journal of Mixed Methods Research, 2*(3), 296–316.

Igo, L. B., Kiewra, K. A., & Bruning, R. (2008). Individual differences and intervention flaws: A sequential explanatory study of college students' copy-and-paste note taking. *Journal of Mixed Methods Research, 2*(2), 149–168.

Johnson, B., & Christensen, L. (2008). *Educational research: Quantitative, qualitative, and mixed methods approaches* (3rd ed.). Thousand Oaks, CA: Sage.

Johnson, R. B., & Onwuegbuzie, A. J. (2004). Mixed methods research: A research paradigm whose time has come. *Educational Researcher, 33,* 14–26.

Kuhn, T. S. (1970). *The structure of scientific revolutions* (2nd ed.). Chicago: University of Chicago Press.

LaPrairie, K., Slate, J. R., Schulte, D. P., & Onwuegbuzie, A. J. (2009, April). *A mixed analysis of college students' best and worst college professors.* Paper presented at the meeting of the American Educational Research Association, San Diego, CA.

Maxwell, J. A., & Loomis, D. M. (2003). Mixed methods design: An alternative approach. In A. Tashakkori & C. Teddlie (Eds.), *Handbook of mixed methods in social & behavioral research* (pp. 241–271). Thousand Oaks CA: Sage.

Maxwell, J. A., & Mittapalli, K. (2010). Realism as a stance for mixed method research. In A. Tashakkori & C. Teddlie (Eds.), *SAGE handbook of mixed methods in social & behavioral research* (2nd ed.). Thousand Oaks, CA: Sage.

McWayne, C. (2007). *Latino family involvement and children's school readiness: A mixed methods study* (Grant No. 1R03HD050363-01A2). Abstract retrieved from CRISP database: http://crisp.cit.nih.gov/

Mertens, D. M., Bledsoe, K. L., Sullivan, M., & Wilson, A. (2010). Utilization of mixed methods for transformative purposes. In A. Tashakkori & C. Teddlie (Eds.), *SAGE handbook of mixed methods in social & behavioral research* (2nd ed.). Thousand Oaks, CA: Sage.

Miall, C. E., & March, K. (2005). Open adoption as a family form. *Journal of Family Issues, 26*(3), 380–410.

Morgan, D. L. (2007). Paradigms lost and pragmatism regained: Methodological implications of combining qualitative and quantitative methods. *Journal of Mixed Methods Research, 1*(1), 48–76.

Myers, K. K., & Oetzel, J. G. (2003). Exploring the dimensions of organizational assimilation: Creating and validating a measure. *Communication Quarterly, 51*(4), 438–457.

Nakagami, E. (2006). *Treatment processes in psychosocial rehab services* (Grant No. 1F31MH078366-01). Abstract retrieved from CRISP database: http://crisp.cit.nih.gov/

Newman, I., Ridenour, C. S., Newman, C., & DeMarco, G. M. P., Jr. (2003). A typology of research purposes and its relationship to mixed methods. In A. Tashakkori & C. Teddlie (Eds.), *Handbook of mixed methods in social and behavioral research* (pp. 167–188). Thousand Oaks, CA: Sage.

O'Cathain, A. (2010). Assessing the quality of mixed methods research: Toward a comprehensive framework. In A. Tashakkori & C. Teddlie (Eds.), *SAGE handbook of mixed methods in social & behavioral research* (2nd ed.). Thousand Oaks, CA: Sage.

O'Cathain, A., Murphy, E., & Nicholl, J. (2007). Why, and how, mixed methods research is undertaken in health services research in England: A mixed methods study. *BMC Health Services Research, 7*(85): doi:10.1186/1472-6963-7-85.

Onwuegbuzie, A. J., & Leech, N. L. (2006). Linking research questions to mixed methods data analysis procedures. *The Qualitative Report, 11*(3), 474–498. Retrieved July 14, 2009, from http://www.nova.edu/ssss/QR/QR11-3/onwuegbuzie.pdf

Onwuegbuzie, A. J., & Teddlie, C. (2003). A framework for analyzing data in mixed methods research. In A. Tashakkori & C. Teddlie (Eds.), *Handbook of mixed methods in social and behavioral research* (pp. 351–383). Thousand Oaks, CA: Sage.

Owen-Smith, A. (2007). *Complementary and alternative medicine use among African-Americans with AIDS* (Grant No. 1F31AT004553-01). Abstract retrieved from CRISP database: http://crisp.cit.nih.gov/

Penn, J. D. (2008). *Faculty approaches to improving teaching: A mixed methods case study*. Retrieved from ProQuest Dissertations & Theses. (AAT 3331438)

Plano Clark, V. L. (2005). Cross-disciplinary analysis of the use of mixed methods in physics education research, counseling psychology, and primary care (Doctoral dissertation, University of Nebraska–Lincoln, 2005). *Dissertation Abstracts International, 66,* 02A.

Plano Clark, V. L. (in press). The adoption and practice of mixed methods: U.S. trends in federally funded health-related research. *Qualitative Inquiry.*

Plano Clark, V. L., Garrett, A. L., & Leslie-Pelecky, D. L. (2009). Applying three strategies for integrating quantitative and qualitative databases in a mixed methods study of a nontraditional graduate education program. *Field Methods.* doi: 10.1177/1525822X09357174

Punch, K. F. (2005). *Introduction to social research: Quantitative and qualitative approaches* (2nd ed.). London: Sage.

Randolph, J. J. (2008). *Multidisciplinary methods in educational technology research and development.* Hämeenlinna, Finland: HAMK University of Applied Sciences. Retrieved September 15, 2009, from http://justusrandolph.net/articles/multidisciplinary_methods.pdf

Ras, N. L. (2009, April). *Multidimensional theory and data interrogation in educational change research: A mixed methods case study.* Paper presented at the meeting of the American Educational Research Association, San Diego, CA.

Ridenour, C. S., & Newman, I. (2008). *Mixed methods research: Exploring the interactive continuum* (2nd ed.). Carbondale: Southern Illinois University Press.

Scott, C., & Sutton, R. E. (2009). Emotions and change during professional development for teachers: A mixed methods study. *Journal of Mixed Methods Research, 3*(2), 151–171.

Stake, R. E. (1995). *The art of case study research.* Thousand Oaks, CA: Sage.

Starker, T. V. (2008). *Examining preservice teachers' cognitive engagement, knowledge, and self-efficacy of culturally responsive teaching using a web-based case study module: A mixed methods approach.* Retrieved from ProQuest Dissertations & Theses. (AAT 3309208)

Stirman, S. (2007). *Influences on the sustainability of evidence-based psychotherapies*

(Grant No. 1K99MH080100-01A1). Abstract retrieved from CRISP database: http://crisp.cit.nih.gov/

Tashakkori, A., & Creswell, J. W. (2007). Exploring the nature of research questions in mixed methods research [Editorial]. *Journal of Mixed Methods Research, 1*(3), 207–211.

Tashakkori, A., & Teddlie, C. (1998). *Mixed methodology: Combining qualitative and quantitative approaches.* Thousand Oaks, CA: Sage.

Teddlie, C., & Tashakkori, A. (2006). A general typology of research designs featuring mixed methods. *Research in the Schools, 13*, 12–28.

Teddlie, C., & Tashakkori, A. (2009). *Foundations of mixed methods research.* Thousand Oaks, CA: Sage.

Wade, V. J. (2008). *Active intervention: Kinesthetic learning style leavens the lump of student achievement of autistic students.* Retrieved from ProQuest Dissertations & Theses. (AAT 3304141)

Way, N., Stauber, H. Y., Nakkula, M. J., & London, P. (1994). Depression and substance use in two divergent high school cultures: A quantitative and qualitative analysis. *Journal of Youth and Adolescence, 23*(3), 331–357.

Webster, D. (2009). *Creative reflective experience: Promoting empathy in psychiatric nursing.* Retrieved from ProQuest Dissertations & Theses. (AAT 3312911)

Yin, R. K. (2006). Mixed methods research: Are the methods genuinely integrated or merely parallel? *Research in the Schools, 13*(1), 41–47.

13

AN INCLUSIVE FRAMEWORK FOR CONCEPTUALIZING MIXED METHODS DESIGN TYPOLOGIES

Moving Toward Fully Integrated Synergistic Research Models

◆ Bonnie Kaul Nastasi,
John H. Hitchcock, and Lisa M. Brown

Objectives

After completing this chapter, you should be able to

- conceptualize existing mixed methods design typologies on a continuum from basic to complex;

- propose an inclusive framework to facilitate classification of mixed methods research and development of fully integrated designs;

- provide guidelines for critiquing and designing mixed methods research using the inclusive framework; and

- identify future directions.

Although there have been numerous attempts to develop typologies for classifying mixed methods designs, an inclusive typology remains elusive (Creswell, 2009; Tashakkori & Teddlie, 2003; Teddlie & Tashakkori, 2006, 2009). Given the difficulties, it seems reasonable to ask: Why even bother with the typology task in the first place? A follow-up question is: Why hasn't the mixed methods field brought some closure to this issue? After all, discussing typologies is as old as the notion that mixed methods is a distinctive third paradigm (i.e., a paradigm separate from qualitative and quantitative; Johnson, Onwuegbuzie, & Turner, 2007). And a third question: Why should we expect this chapter to be anything other than yet another addition to the burgeoning list of typologies, or put another way, do we need another typology?

To promote full disclosure, we believe typologies can offer important services to the mixed methods field and indeed view the first question—*Why do we need typologies?*—as a way to set up a straw man argument. Teddlie and Tashakkori (2003) cite the importance of typologies in establishing a common language and thereby promoting organizational structure within a field, promoting legitimacy of said field, thinking through designs, and supporting pedagogy (see also Teddlie & Tashakkori, 2006). One can appreciate, for example, how communication is facilitated if a manuscript reports a study used a sequential exploratory design using the typology proposed by Creswell and colleagues (Creswell, Plano Clark, Gutmann, & Hanson, 2003). Those who are unfamiliar with mixed methods work can learn a lot by deconstructing the terms *sequential* and *exploratory*, whereas those who are familiar with Creswell's work can readily glean important information about the researcher's likely goals. Certainly, other research traditions enjoy the benefits of fairly well-established nomenclatures. For example, those familiar with experimental design work can infer a lot when an author says a study employed a "retrospective two-armed quasi-experiment with baseline equating."[1] Similarly, those with qualitative training will typically glean a great deal of information about design goals from terms such as *ethnography, case study, discourse analysis, constant comparison analyses,* and so on. It is also the case that poorly thought out typologies and associated nomenclatures can undermine understanding. Consider, for example, the idea of causal modeling (i.e., structural equation modeling). This is essentially an analytic procedure using advanced regression techniques, and depending on the underlying design, it may or may not answer causal questions. But the fact that an analysis technique is sometimes thought of as some sort of design has probably led to some confusion about what structural equation modeling can and cannot do (Tabachnick & Fidell, 2007; Wegener & Fabrigar, 2000), a problem that the authors suspect could have been avoided given more careful thought about research typologies and associated naming conventions. In terms of promoting field legitimacy, there is a good argument for saying there are distinctive aspects of mixed methods research if one has to use fairly distinctive terms to describe a mixed methods design. Indeed, it would be interesting to see how well classic designs that used multiple methods (e.g., Rosenthal & Jacobson's [1968, 1992] work on the Pygmalion effect) reflect contemporary mixed methods terminology and thinking.[2] But one need only read about experimental validity, psychometric, and qualitative typologies to see how these systems can facilitate advanced thinking about what a given design can and cannot do (see, for example, Shadish, Cook, & Campbell, 2002). The overall point here is that design typologies and naming systems have implications for communication, pedagogy, organizing research, and so on. This makes continued wrestling with mixed methods typologies a useful endeavor, even if the issue remains problematic.

This segues to the second question, which can be rephrased as *Why has a mixed method design typology been elusive?* Mixed methods designs have been used to address highly diverse questions and appear to be continuously altered as methodologists have addressed questions in creative ways. Indeed, the perspective from the first *Handbook* on this issue remains reasonable today:

> Mixed model designs can be distinguished on a number of different dimensions (e.g., purpose, underlying paradigm) and developing a typology that would encompass all of those dimensions would be impossible. What is more, even if we could list all of the mixed method designs at one point in time, the types of designs would continue to evolve, thereby making the typology no longer exhaustive. (Teddlie & Tashakkori, 2003, pp. 26–27)

The remainder of this chapter deals in part with the last question, *Do we need another typology?* Before proceeding, there are three important points. First, any need to update design typologies is probably a form of good news, as this suggests innovation. Hence, we hope there will be a need to continually revisit the issue. Second, we do not view the current chapter as an introduction of a new typology so much as an attempt to integrate the body of work that has come before us into an inclusive framework that can help researchers identify a typology that suits their needs and proceed accordingly with the study design. Third, in formulating an inclusive framework of mixed methods designs, our goal is to provide a structure that both encompasses existing thinking about typologies and is flexible enough to accommodate innovation.

◆ Precursors to Design Decisions

Decisions about design selection and classification are influenced by considerations about research purpose, the researcher's theoretical perspective or worldview, and concerns about inference quality. In this section, we explore these three sets of precursors.

RESEARCH PURPOSE AND QUESTIONS

A primary assumption made here is that the research purpose and questions are interlinked and together guide the choice of research method—qualitative, quantitative, or mixed. Hence, any effort to classify a design should consider its underlying purpose, and this is considered within the proposed framework to integrate the various typologies. As is the case with design, the purposes of research have been classified in the literature. Newman, Ridenour, Newman, and DeMarco (2003) proposed nine categories of research purpose: (1) predict; (2) add to the knowledge base; (3) have a personal, social, institutional, and/or organizational impact; (4) measure change; (5) understand complex phenomena; (6) test new ideas; (7) generate new ideas; (8) inform constituencies; and (9) examine the past. Although these purposes have traditionally been associated with qualitative or quantitative research, Newman and colleagues suggest that mixed methods approaches can apply to many of them. One of the most important contributions of their thinking, consistent with the underlying theme of the first edition of *Handbook of Mixed Methods in Social and Behavioral Research* (Tashakkori & Teddlie, 2003), is that purpose is the driving force behind decision making about research methodology.

Greene, Caracelli, and Graham (1989) propose five categories of purposes for mixed-method evaluation designs: triangulation, complementarity, development, initiation, and expansion. In *triangulation* studies, researchers seek convergence or corroboration of results across different methods (e.g., combined use qualitative and quantitative). In *complementarity*, researchers seek elaboration or clarification of results for one method (e.g., quantitative) from another method (qualitative). In *development* studies, researchers seek to inform later phases of the research method based on findings of prior phases (e.g., results of qualitative study lead to subsequent quantitative study). In *initiation* studies, researchers seek new perspectives or contradictions by the use of mixed methods. In *expansion* studies, researchers seek to extend breadth and depth through use of mixed methods (e.g., qualitative to understand process and quantitative to examine outcomes).

Bryman (2006) proposes an alternative 16-type scheme for classifying research purpose to reflect the variety of research rationales in existing mixed methods literature. Tashakkori and Creswell (2007) extend this discussion and suggest the need for specific "mixed methods" research questions that reflect the typology; for example, sequential and concurrent designs may require different types of research questions (we return to their discussion in the design typologies sections).

THEORETICAL PERSPECTIVE

An important determinant of design selection is the theoretical or philosophical perspective of the researcher (also referred to as paradigm, worldview, or conceptual framework). Broadly conceived, this category addresses the theoretical foundations, paradigm, or worldview of the researcher that guides the research. Johnson et al. (2007) refer to the researcher's orientation or purpose in relationship to the needs of the researched (i.e., top-down vs. bottom-up orientation) as critical for distinguishing types of mixed methods. We also include context in which research is conceived or implemented or to which results will be applied. Perhaps the most common distinction, in addition to methods, among qualitative, quantitative, and mixed methods research is that of paradigmatic foundation. Quantitative and qualitative research, for example, can be characterized by respective paradigms of postpositivism and

constructivism.[3] Several paradigms or mental models for mixed methods research also have been proposed (Greene, 2007), including the purist (e.g., firmly rooted in postpositivism), aparadigmatic (driven by research purpose or demands of context), substantive theory (driven by the theory underlying the substantive aspect of the work, e.g., prevention theory), complementary strengths (combining the strengths of qualitative and quantitative methods), dialectical (emphasizing the differences in perspective reflected in researchers and methods), and alternative paradigms (pragmatism, realism, emancipation).

The most common alternative paradigm associated with mixed methods research appears to be *pragmatism* (Maxcy, 2003; Morgan, 2007; Tashakkori & Teddlie, 1998, 2003).[4] Morgan distinguishes quantitative, qualitative, and mixed methods on the basis of the connection between theory and data, the researcher's relationship to research process, and the inferences drawn from data. He distinguishes qualitative, quantitative, and mixed methods research (respectively) as follows: (a) The theory-data connection is inductive, deductive, and abductive (inductive and deductive). (b) The researcher's relationship to research process is subjective, objective, and intersubjective (emphasizing the interpersonal nature of research). (c) The basis of inference is context (context-specific), generality (generalizability), and transferability (applicable to other persons and contexts based on similarity of research-applied conditions). Morgan's distinctions portray the commensurability or complementarity of qualitative and quantitative methods within mixed methods research. Such distinctions are intended to overcome the perceived incommensurability or incompatibility of quantitative and qualitative methods as depicted in the early paradigm wars. Furthermore, pragmatism places emphasis on the practical aspects of research (e.g., what works best for answering the research question), the context (e.g., what is most appropriate given the contextual conditions), and potential consequences of the research (e.g., the social or political implications). Consistent with a pragmatic approach and in an effort to reflect current thinking about definitions of mixed methods research, Johnson and colleagues (2007) propose a *contingency theory* of research, in which qualitative, quantitative, and mixed methods research are valued, and decisions about choice and mixing of methods are dependent on the situational contingencies.

Although pragmatics is perhaps the most common paradigmatic foundation for mixed methods, others have been proposed. Greene (2007), for example, takes a *dialectical* position, which emphasizes the importance of differences and the tension created by those differences (e.g., between the perspectives of the researcher and researched). To illustrate application of dialectical stance, Greene uses participatory action research (PAR). The political and social change orientation that is the basis of PAR also is inherent in Mertens's (2003, 2007) *transformative(-emancipatory)* perspective. Mertens (2007) asserts that mixed methods research provides "a framework for examining assumptions that explicitly address power issues, social justice, and cultural complexity throughout the research process" (p. 212). As such, mixed methods designs can help researchers (a) address the cultural and political complexities inherent in the social settings in which research is conducted and (b) engage research participants as partners in creating social change. To achieve these goals, however, requires participation of community members (stakeholders, research participants) and a cyclical research process for building sustainable change.

A transformative paradigm is consistent with participatory models of research, practice, and capacity building (e.g., Eade, 1997; Nastasi et al., 2007; Nastasi, Moore, & Varjas, 2004; Nelson & Prilleltensky, 2005). The collaborative and applied nature of both dialectic and transformative stances is consistent with the *communities of practice* model proposed by Denscombe (2008), in which researchers and practitioners are partners in research that is practice driven and pragmatic. For mixed methods researchers adhering to the communities of practice model, "there is no clear distinction between practitioners and researchers. The practice is the research; the research is the practice" (Denscombe, 2008, p. 277).

Across the alternative perspectives, several commonalities are worth noting. These include tensions between researcher and researched, inductive and deductive thinking, and context-specific and universal applications. Such tensions are perhaps best resolved by using a participatory (e.g., community members) or collaborative (e.g., researcher-practitioner) process, assuming a critical-reflective stance, and focusing on the potential practical and political implications of research findings. Although we cannot resolve the question of the alternative paradigm for mixed methods, we consider the commonalities and strengths of pragmatist, transformative, and communities of practice approaches as critical to an inclusive model of mixed methods research.

INFERENCE QUALITY ISSUES

Design decisions related to inference quality address whether one evaluates quality on the basis of quantitative (e.g., internal and external validity) or qualitative (e.g., credibility, transferability) criteria or both. Some methodologists propose that inference quality be evaluated separately for qualitative and quantitative methods prior to mixing (e.g., Ridenour & Newman, 2008). Thus, the researcher must separately account for measurement validity (Messick, 1995) and internal and external validity for quantitative methods (Shadish et al., 2002) and trustworthiness for qualitative methods (Lincoln & Guba, 1985).

Using the concept of *legitimation* to convey validity in mixed methods, Onwuegbuzie and Johnson (2006) extend the consideration of validity to be inclusive of qualitative, quantitative, and mixed methods. Drawing on separate legitimation models for qualitative (Onwuegbuzie & Leech, 2007) and quantitative research (Onwuegbuzie, 2003), Onwuegbuzie and Johnson (2006) proposed a third legitimation model specific to mixed methods, which is intended to ensure or maximize the meta-inferences drawn from the combined methods. The typology of mixed methods legitimation includes the following types: (a) *sample integration,* referring to the relationship between qualitative and quantitative sampling and mixed methods inferences; (b) *inside-outside,* the balance of emic and etic perspectives; (c) *weakness minimization,* the extent to which strengths of qualitative or quantitative methods compensate for respective weaknesses; (d) *sequential,* minimizing the potential influence of sequencing of qualitative and quantitative phases; (e) *conversion,* the extent to which quantizing and qualitizing influences inferences from mixed methods; (f) *paradigmatic mixing,* the extent to which researchers' beliefs relative to qualitative and quantitative approaches are successfully integrated; (g) *commensurability,* the extent to which the meta-inferences reflect integration of qualitative and quantitative perspectives; (h) *multiple validities,* the influence of addressing legitimation from qualitative, quantitative, and mixed perspectives on meta-inferences; and (i) *political,* the value attributed by consumers to meta-inferences drawn from both qualitative and quantitative data.

Dellinger and Leech (2007) have proposed a *unified validation framework,* which incorporates criteria for ensuring validity from traditional quantitative (measurement, internal, external) and qualitative (e.g., trustworthiness) perspectives, with criteria specifically related to validation of mixed methods. Drawing on Messick's (1995) model of construct validity, which emphasizes the evidential and consequential basis for determining meaning of data with regard to its interpretation and use, they propose several elements of construct validation for mixed methods research that parallel the research process (from conceptualization to

inference): (a) The *foundational element* refers to the conceptual basis of the study (e.g., grounding in existing research and theory) and the links between conceptual, methodological, analytical, and inferential stages of the research process; (b) the *construct validation element* refers to respective validity of qualitative, quantitative, and mixed methods employed in the study (i.e., the methodological and analytical phases). In addition to the traditional criteria for validity of qualitative and quantitative methods, they proposed specific criteria relevant to the design quality, legitimation, and interpretive rigor of the mixed methods: (c) The *translation fidelity, or inferential consistency audit, element* refers to the links between inferences and the conceptual, methodological, and analytic processes; (d) the *utilization or historical element* refers to how the findings were used and the appropriateness of the utilization; (e) the *consequential element* refers to the social and political consequences of data use and the acceptability of these uses. Consistent with the notion of mixed methods as an alternative paradigm, Dellinger and Leech (2007) characterize construct validation as a "continuous process of negotiation of meaning" (p. 321).

Teddlie and Tashakkori (2009) provide an *integrative framework* for considering inference quality, particularly as it applies to more complex (integrated) typologies. The framework includes 10 criteria for evaluating quality as it relates to two broad aspects of research—design quality and interpretive rigor. For each criterion, specific questions are posed to guide the researcher and the critic/reviewer's decisions about inference quality (these questions are reflected parenthetically in the following description of the criteria). The four criteria relevant to *design quality* include (1) design suitability (Is the design appropriate to the research purpose and questions?); (2) design fidelity (Are the qualitative, quantitative, and mixed methods procedures implemented with adequate rigor?); (3) within-design consistency

(Is there consistency across all components of the design, e.g., sampling, data collection, analysis?); and (4) analytic adequacy (Are the analytic procedures appropriate and adequate to answer the research questions?). Six criteria pertaining to *interpretive rigor* include (1) interpretive consistency (Are interpretations consistent with findings?); (2) theoretical consistency (Are inferences consistent with existing theory and research?); (3) interpretative agreement (Are interpretations consistent across researchers or scholars in the field and with the interpretations of participants?); (4) interpretive distinctiveness (Are the interpretations the most credible, based on findings and alternative explanations?); (5) integrative efficacy (Are meta-inferences drawn from findings and inferences from various components or strands of the study? Do the meta-inferences account for consistencies and inconsistencies across these findings?); and (6) interpretive correspondence (Do inferences match the study purposes?). (See Teddlie & Tashakkori, 2009, for a more comprehensive explanation and examples of the criteria.) Of course, these criteria could apply to any research study. In the case of mixed methods research, however, one must consider the criteria as they relate to the qualitative, quantitative, and mixed methods components of the study and to the purpose for mixing. For example, in considering interpretive rigor, the researcher must account for the match between findings and interpretations not only with reference to qualitative and quantitative findings separately, but also with regard to inferences drawn from the mixed method findings (meta-inferences).

◆ Current Typologies: State of the Art

A review of the existing literature on mixed methods design typologies revealed a broad array of criteria or dimensions for classifying mixed methods studies (see Table 13.1). In the preceding section, we discussed several considerations that are relevant to classifying mixed methods designs, or what we might label as precursors to design selection. As reflected in Table 13.1, the aforementioned precursors to design selection address critical questions related to research purpose, researcher's worldview or context of the research, and inference quality. Design typologies, in contrast, provide classification schemes for depicting the framework related to the mixing of research approaches (qualitative, quantitative) and methods. We summarize the existing typologies as Types I through VI, with the ordering referring to complexity of mixing, ranging from decisions about the number of research strands and priority of methods and data (i.e., basic typologies I through III), to considerations about the integration or synthesis of research approaches (complex typologies IV through VI). Thus, the basic typologies classify designs on the basis of the following criteria, respectively: (I) number of strands or phases of research process; (II) types, mixing, and priority of data; and (III) stages in which mixing of methods/data occurs. The complex typologies classify designs on the basis of approach to integration of methods. For example, Typology IV, focusing on integrated approaches, involves the combination or mixing of precursors and basic design considerations. Typology V deals with iterative or changing approaches, in which the design evolves during multiple phases of research process, a process that is more likely to occur within a research program rather than single study. Typology VI deals with synergistic design approaches that involve attempts to resolve the dialectic nature of mixing methods across paradigms to achieve a true synthesis of qualitative and quantitative research.

Table 13.1 Precursors and Basic and Complex Typologies for Mixed Methods Research

Criteria	Definition/Key Features	Examples of Typologies for Precursors and Designs
Precursors to Design Decisions		
Research purpose/question	Purpose of the research, ranging from basic to translational	• Newman, Ridenour, Newman, & DeMarco (2003), typology of research purposes, link purpose to design/methods decisions • Tashakkori & Creswell (2007), driven by research question • Greene, Caracelli, & Graham (1989) • Bryman (2006)
Theory, worldview, paradigm, context	Theoretical foundations, paradigm or worldview of researcher; single vs. multiple paradigm & mixing of paradigms; context in which research is conceived, implemented, applied (i.e., conceptual or foundational considerations)	• Tashakkori & Teddlie (1998, 2003), pragmatism • Maxcy (2003), pragmatism • Morgan (2007), pragmatism • Johnson, Onwuegbuzie, & Turner (2007), contingency theory • Greene (2007), dialectical • Mertens (2003, 2007), transformative-emancipatory • Denscombe (2008), communities of practice
Inference quality	Extent to which validity issues are addressed along QUAL-MMR-QUAN continua	• Dellinger & Leech (2007), mixed methods construct validation framework • Onwuegbuzie & Johnson (2006), legitimation • Ridenour & Newman (2008), validity of quantitative and qualitative methods considered separately
Basic Design Typologies		
I. Strand/Phases of Research: Monostrand vs. Multistrand	Single vs. multiple phases, including single study vs. research program	• Tashakkori & Teddlie (2003) • Teddlie & Tashakkori (2009)

Criteria	Definition/Key Features	Examples of Typologies for Precursors and Designs
II. Methods/Data a. Types of data b. Mixing/sequencing/ implementation c. Priority/dominance	Based on the types, mixing, and priority given to different methods/data: a. Qual-Quan b. Concurrent, parallel, embedded c. Dominance of QUAL vs QUAN	• Morse (2003), a, b, c (notation system) • Johnson et al. (2007), continuum of mixing, Qual-MMR-Quan • Leech & Onwuegbuzie (2009), combinations of a, b, c • Creswell & Plano Clark (2007) • Greene et al. (1989)
III. Stage of research process	Points within the research process—research question, sampling, data collection, analysis, inference—where mixing occurs; some models deal only with particular stage	*Mixing across the research process* • Teddlie & Tashakkori (2009) • Ridenour & Newman (2008) • Johnson & Onwuegbuzie (2004) *Mixing at specific stages: Sampling* • Onwuegbuzie & Collins (2007) • Teddlie & Yu (2007) • Kemper, Stringfield, & Teddlie (2003) *Data collection* • Johnson & Turner (2003) *Data analysis* • Onwuegbuzie & Teddlie (2003) *Data inference/data representation* • Erzeberger & Kelle (2003) • Sandelowski (2003)
Complex Design Typologies		
IV. Integrated /Interactive/ Systemic	Some combination of criteria related to precursors and/or basic typologies	• Johnson et al. (2007), research purpose, theory; II, III • Greene (2007), research purpose, theory, inference quality; II, III

(Continued)

Table 13.1 (Continued)

Criteria	Definition/Key Features	Examples of Typologies for Precursors and Designs
		• Maxwell & Loomis (2003), research purpose, theory, inference quality; II, III • Creswell & Plano Clark (2007), research purpose, theory, inference quality; I–III • Creswell et al. (2003), theory, I–III • Onwuegbuzie & Collins (2007), purpose, II (a, b) & III (sampling) • Teddlie & Tashakkori (2009), research purpose, theory, inference quality; I–III (see also Tashakkori & Teddlie, 2003; Teddlie & Tashakkori, 2006)
V. Iterative	Evolving or changing designs—design changes throughout the research process; earlier phases and findings influence subsequent decision making	• Teddlie & Tashakkori (2009) • Nastasi et al. (2007)
VI. Synergistic	MMR > QUAL + QUAN QUAL = QUAN QUAL ~ QUAN Researcher(s) ~ Design Researcher(s) ~ Participants	• Hall & Howard (2008), synergistic approach • Nastasi et al. (2007), participatory • Shulha & Wilson (2003), collaborative models • Denscombe (2008), communities of practice • Chatterji (2005), extended-term evaluation designs • Mertens (2007), transformative, participatory

NOTE: QUAL = qualitative; MMR = mixed methods research; QUAN = quantitative.

◆ *Basic Design Typologies*

Basic design typologies deal with questions relevant to the number of research strands and how and at what stages of the research process the data are mixed. Although we characterize these as basic, the description that follows reflects the evolving complexity of even these most basic classification schemes.

TYPE I: RESEARCH STRANDS OR PHASES

Type I typologies address whether the research involves one or multiple phases. Teddlie and Tashakkori (2009; see also Tashakkori & Teddlie, 2003; Teddlie & Tashakkori, 2006) classify designs as monostrand or multistrand (one vs. multiple strands, respectively) and define strand or phase as encompassing three stages—conceptualization (theoretical foundations, purpose, research questions), experiential (data collection and analysis methods), and inferential (data interpretation, application). A *monostrand* design includes a single phase of the conceptualization-experiential-inferential process. *Multistrand* designs use multiple phases, each of which includes the conceptualization-experiential-inferential process. Teddlie and Tashakkori, of course, consider this criterion in the context of other design criteria and thus present strands within a complex integrated typology as well (see Type IV). *Strand* also might refer to distinctions with regard to single study (cf. monostrand) versus multiple studies or program of research (multistrand; e.g., see Nastasi et al., 2007). Such distinctions have influenced definitions of mixed methods research (see Johnson et al., 2007).

One of the specific typology issues described in Tashakkori and Teddlie's earlier work (1998) is whether to classify an investigation as confirmatory, exploratory, or both. Taking into account the above discussion of theoretical perspectives and inference quality issues behind mixed methods designs, this exemplifies much of the rationale behind typology work in the subfield because mixed methods almost routinely deal with both goals, often within the same design. Briefly, most confirmatory questions are determined on an a priori basis. If a statistical investigation is involved, related analysis plans also should be established at the outset and include adequate sample sizes (i.e., statistical power). Put another way, confirmatory questions largely follow the traditional scientific method one learns in secondary school or earlier on, where theory informs a hypothesis, which in turn is tested via data analysis and so on. By contrast, exploratory questions need not necessarily be specified in advance and often unfold as investigators learn more about the phenomena being investigated. Although these are often envisaged as a more qualitative issue, there are confirmatory qualitative questions (Maxwell, 2004) and certainly exploratory quantitative applications. From a mixed methods point of view, particularly in multistrand applications, it is possible that not all confirmatory questions can or should be specified in advance. This is especially the case with iterative design applications; thinking through this can be better understood via the Type II Typology, *Methods/Data*, and the Type III Typology, *Stage of the Research Process*. By contrast, more complex typologies, discussed later on, address designs with planned iteration and synergy, often to identify exploratory (and confirmatory) questions that can be articulated only after the context in which they will be asked is well understood, and mixing is done to facilitate interpretation of data.

TYPE II: METHODS/DATA

Type II typologies perhaps represent the most basic and earliest distinctions in mixed methods research, that is, the classification of mixed methods designs on the basis of the manner in which qualitative and quantitative methods or data are incorporated. This category of typologies encompasses three components: (a) the types of methods/data or respective use of qualitative and quantitative methods/data; (b) the manner in which the methods and data are mixed, sequentially, concurrently, or embedded; and (c) the priority or dominance given to qualitative and quantitative methods and data in the study design. Morse (2003) provides the basic notation system for depicting the type of methods

(Qual, Quan), mixing (simultaneous, qual + quan; sequential, qual → quan), and priority (dominant, QUAL; supplemental, qual) given to qualitative and quantitative methods in a research project or study.[5]

Greene et al. (1989) make distinctions on the basis of the relative status (dominance), independence (methods conceived and implemented independently or interactively), and timing (simultaneous, sequential) of qualitative and quantitative methods. Morse (2003) and Greene et al. (1989) link decisions about methods/data to purpose and paradigm, thus reflecting the difficulties in depicting the variations across mixed methods studies via basic typologies. As the mixed methods field has evolved, the complexity of even these simple distinctions (e.g., dominance or timing) necessitated more complex depictions of designs.

To better reflect the complexity of mixed methods design, Creswell and Plano Clark (2007) proposed four major design types (each with subtypes) that varied on the basis of timing (concurrent, sequential), weighting (equal vs. unequal; cf. dominance or priority), and mixing (during what phase of research process are data merged and how are they merged). The four major types include *triangulation* (depicted as QUAN + QUAL), *embedded* (QUAN [qual] or QUAL [quan]), *explanatory* (QUAN → qual), and *exploratory* (QUAL → quan). To guide decision making, Creswell and Plano Clark provide a decision tree using criteria of timing, weighting, and mixing. Of course, such decisions are ultimately guided by the researcher's purpose (e.g., an exploratory design for the purpose of instrument development).

In an attempt to provide a more integrated typology, and based on a review of published mixed methods research, Leech and Onwuegbuzie (2009) proposed a three-dimensional typology. The potential variations in level of mixing (partially, fully), time orientation (concurrent, sequential), and emphasis (equal, dominance) of qualitative and quantitative methods yielded

eight design types, with an accompanying notational system:

1. Partially mixed concurrent equal status designs (e.g., QUAN + QUAL)

2. Partially mixed concurrent dominant status designs (e.g., Quan + QUAL)

3. Partially mixed sequential equal status designs (e.g., QUAL → QUAN)

4. Partially mixed sequential dominant status designs (e.g., Qual → QUAN)

5. Fully mixed concurrent equal status designs (e.g., QUAN + QUAL)

6. Fully mixed concurrent dominant status designs (e.g., Quan + QUAL)

7. Fully mixed sequential equal status designs (e.g., QUAL → QUAN)

8. Fully mixed sequential dominant status designs (e.g., Qual → QUAN)

Leech and Onwuegbuzie (2009) assert that these eight designs are comprehensive enough to encompass most mixed methods research designs. Of course, one might consider the three dimensions as continua rather than dichotomous, thus potentially yielding an even broader array of mixed methods designs. Johnson et al. (2007) proposed a continuum for representing the three major paradigms, qualitative–mixed methods–quantitative, along which the subtypes of mixed methods research can be placed based on the mixing, timing, and emphasis (see Johnson et al., 2007, for further discussion and illustration of these distinctions).

TYPE III: STAGE OF THE RESEARCH PROCESS

Another way of classifying mixed methods research is based on the stage of the research process within which mixing occurs. Teddlie and Tashakkori (2009) characterized the stages broadly as conceptualization, experiential (methodological and analytical), and inferential. These three broad stages encompass more specific points in the research process: theory/worldview, research purpose/question, sampling, data collection, data analysis, inference, representation, and application.

Ridenour and Newman (2008) describe the research process as an *interactive continuum* and emphasize the importance of consistency across the stages. They depict mixed methods research as an iterative process along an interactive continuum of qualitative-quantitative research (i.e., as a continuum of theory building and theory testing, respectively). The critical features of their depiction are: (a) research as a process driven by research purpose and questions; (b) the research process (purpose, questions, data collection, analysis, inference, and application) as cyclical; (c) mixed methods as part of a continuum of qualitative-quantitative research; and (d) the self-correcting feedback loops within the research process (i.e., across stages), reflecting both the iterative and interactive nature of research. One might critique any research, but particularly mixed methods research, on the basis of the consistency across questions, methods, and inferences (i.e., does the research question drive methods and inferences); what Ridenour and Newman refer to as the *consistency-question model* (see also Newman et al., 2003). (We return to the consistency-question issue in our consideration of Type IV.)

The basis for classification of designs within Type III is the stage or stages at which mixing occurs. Although some proposed typologies or models suggest qualitative-quantitative mixing (i.e., mixed methods) at every stage of the process (e.g., Ridenour & Newman, 2008; Teddlie & Tashakkori, 2009), others propose typologies on the basis of mixing within a particular stage. For example, Onwuegbuzie and Collins (2007) propose a sampling design typology that includes 24 major sampling schemes for mixed methods research and guidelines for determining sample size.

A two-dimensional model of sampling, which combines time orientation (concurrent, sequential) with relationship between quantitative and qualitative samples (identical, parallel, nested, multilevel), provides the basis for making decisions about the sampling scheme and size.

In addition to typology for more traditional probability, purposive, and convenience sampling, Teddlie and Yu (2007) proposed and illustrated a mixed method typology of sampling that includes five types: (a) basic mixed methods sampling (purposive or quota sampling), (b) sequential mixed methods (sampling of first phase informs sampling decisions of the next, e.g., in QUAN → QUAL design, the qualitative sample is a subsample of the initial quantitative sample), (c) concurrent mixed methods sampling (i.e., through joint or independent probability and purposive sampling in QUAL + QUAN design), (d) multilevel mixed methods sampling (typically requiring multiple sampling techniques across organizational or system levels; e.g., probability sampling of students within schools selected via purposive or stratified sampling), and (e) combination of mixed methods sampling strategies. Teddlie and Yu also provide guidelines for mixed methods sampling that take into account the study's purpose, assumptions of respective qualitative and quantitative methods, inferential requirements, and ethical and practical issues.

Other mixed methodologists have proposed typologies related to data collection (e.g., Johnson & Turner, 2003), data analysis (Onwuegbuzie & Teddlie, 2003), and data inference/representation (Erzeberger & Kelle, 2003; Sandelowski, 2003). The critical question related to Type III typologies is whether we can classify mixed methods designs on the basis of the stage at which the mixing occurs. Alternatively, should mixing occur across the stages of the research process? We return to these questions as we consider the complex typologies and our proposed inclusive framework.

◆ Complex Typologies

The current status of typologies for mixed methods research is perhaps best depicted by complex-level typologies. These of course draw on the basic typologies and vary with regard to how the more specific criteria from Typologies I through III have been integrated or synthesized to reflect a mixed methods research process. This change has paralleled the evolution of mixed methods to the status of a third paradigm as distinct from quantitative and qualitative paradigms. In this section, we review three types of complex typologies: integrated (also labeled as interactive, systemic), iterative, and synergistic. The types represent increasing synthesis of basic typologies across the research process and evolution toward mixed methods research as a synergistic process.

TYPE IV: INTEGRATED, INTERACTIVE, OR SYSTEMIC

The first level of complexity, Type IV, reflects some combination of criteria reflected in the precursors and basic typologies (see Table 13.1), along with recognition of the importance of considering the context in which research is conceived and carried out and to which findings are likely to be applied. This group of typologies has been variously labeled as integrated, interactive, and systemic, to convey the interconnectedness of decision making within the overall research process (e.g., theory to application). For the sake of discussion, we refer to these collectively as *integrated typologies,* although we note terminology of specific authors.

The notion of integrated typology is perhaps best reflected in the definition of mixed methods research proposed by Johnson and colleagues (2007). Their definition resulted from a content analysis of definitions from several leaders in the field of mixed methods.

Mixed methods research is an intellectual and practical synthesis based on qualitative and quantitative research; it is the third methodological or research paradigm (along with qualitative and quantitative research). It recognizes the importance of traditional quantitative and qualitative research but also offers a powerful third paradigm choice that often will provide the most informative, complete, balanced, and useful research results. Mixed methods research is the research paradigm that (a) partners with the philosophy of pragmatism in one of its forms (left, right, middle); (b) follows the logic of mixed methods research (including the logic of the fundamental principle and any other useful logics imported from qualitative or quantitative research that are helpful for producing defensible and usable research findings); (c) relies on qualitative and quantitative viewpoints, data collection, analysis, and inference techniques combined according to the logic of mixed methods research to address one's research question(s); and (d) is cognizant, appreciative, and inclusive of local and broader sociopolitical realities, resources, and needs. Furthermore, the mixed methods research paradigm offers an important approach for *generating* important research questions *and* providing warranted answers to those questions. This type of research should be used when the nexus of contingencies in a situation, in relation to one's research question(s), suggests that mixed methods research is likely to provide superior research findings and outcomes. (p. 129)

Johnson and colleagues (2007) also identified five themes in the definitions proposed by mixed methods experts. These themes collectively reflect an integrated perspective with regard to precursors and basic design criteria: types of methods/data mixed, timing of mixing, breadth of mixing, rationale for mixing, and researcher orientation.

As Johnson et al. (2007) noted, this integrated typology closely corresponds to that proposed by Greene (2007), although we would extend the depiction of Greene's typology to include criteria related to inference quality. Greene describes *integrated mixed methods designs* as those in which "methods intentionally interact with one another during the course of the study [and thus] offer more varied and differentiated design possibilities" (p. 125). She contrasts these to component designs, in which the qualitative and quantitative methods remain separate during implementation of the research and are integrated only at the interpretation stage. Types of integrated designs include iteration, blending, nesting/embedding, and mixing for reasons of substance or value (Greene, 2007). *Iteration* refers to a situation in which methods from one phase of a study are used to inform subsequent phases. *Blending* refers to the use of complementary yet equal qualitative and quantitative methods throughout the research process, with integration occurring at data analysis. *Nesting* refers to the embedding of a secondary method within the primary study method (e.g., qual within QUAN), with the study design guided by the conceptual model of the primary method; in this case, mixing occurs also at data analysis. *Mixing for reasons of substance or value* (values/substance-based rationale) refers to those designs in which the substantive topic or research ideology mandates the mixing of methods, for example (as Greene notes), Mertens's (2003, 2007) transformative design. A distinct feature of the integrated designs identified by Greene is that the systematic mixing of methods within the research process is driven by the researcher's purpose.

Earlier work by Maxwell and Loomis (2003) reflects the interactive or systemic nature of integrated designs, in which the components of the research process (e.g., purpose, methods, validity) are interconnected via some linear or cyclical system. Thus, the relationships between components are just as important as the components themselves. The *interactive model* of mixed method design proposed by Maxwell and Loomis includes research purpose and questions, conceptual framework, methods, and validity; it emphasizes the importance of research as a process. Their model also encompasses contextual factors that influence the research design, for example, researcher skills, participant concerns, ethical standards, and research setting.

Although the typology proposed by Creswell and Plano Clark (2007; see also Creswell et al., 2003) is based primarily on the timing of implementation, priority/weighting, and stage of mixing, the differentiation of types also is linked to researchers' decisions at multiple stages in the research process, from purpose to validity. Thus, purpose or theoretical perspective can influence choice of design, which in turn influences methodological decisions (sampling, data collection, data analysis), decisions about inference quality, and inferential thinking. Similarly, the typology proposed by Onwuegbuzie and Collins (2007) is based primarily on sampling, yet assumes a more integrative perspective. Specifically, these methodologists connect decisions about sampling to considerations of research purpose as well as timing and type of data. Thus, one could consider the typologies proposed by Creswell and Plano Clark and Onwuegbuzie and Collins to be integrative in nature, even though the authors themselves may not label them as such.

Teddlie and Tashakkori (2009; see also Tashakkori & Teddlie, 2003; Teddlie & Tashakkori, 2006) proposed a typology of *mixed methods multistrand designs,* which they consider to be the most complex of mixed methods designs. The criteria for inclusion in this group are (a) mixing of qualitative and quantitative methods and (b) mixing within or across two or more research strands (with *strand* defined as a conceptualization-experiential-inferential cycle). These designs are thus more likely to be reflected in large-scale research projects of multiyear research programs than in single studies. In addition, the degree of *integration,* according to Teddlie and Tashakkori (2009), depends on the extent to which qualitative and quantitative data are integrated at analysis and inference stages of the research process. If qualitative and quantitative data are both collected but not integrated at analysis and inference stages, they are more appropriately labeled as *quasi-mixed* multistrand designs (see Teddlie & Tashakkori, 2009, for further discussion and illustration of these distinctions).

Teddlie and Tashakkori (2009) identify and define five design types or families, using the term *family* to portray the possible permutations of each type:[6] (1) *parallel mixed designs,* with application of qualitative and quantitative methods occurring in either simultaneous or lapsed parallel strands (i.e., conceptualization to inference occurs separately for QUAL and QUAN) to answer related parts of the same questions; (2) *sequential mixed designs,* with application of qualitative and quantitative methods in consecutive strands, with subsequent strands and questions developing out of the earlier strands (these can occur in an iterative manner); (3) *conversion mixed designs,* with qualitative and quantitative analysis and inference using one data type (e.g., qualitative data is analyzed qualitatively and quantitized, transformed to quantitative data) to answer related parts of the same questions; (4) *multilevel mixed designs,* with mixing across levels in a multilevel (e.g., organization, individuals) study conducted in parallel or sequentially to answer a set of related questions; and (5) *fully integrated mixed designs,* which is an iterative design and thus more appropriately discussed in the next section.

TYPE V: ITERATIVE

Mixed methods *iterative designs* are those in which mixing of qualitative and quantitative methods occurs in a dynamic,

changing, or evolving manner over the course of the research project or program, such that findings at one stage influence decisions about methods at parallel or subsequent stages. Such designs are perhaps best exemplified by Teddlie and Tashakkori's (2009) family of *fully integrated mixed designs,* in which "mixing occurs in an interactive or iterative manner at all stages of the study. At each stage, one approach [e.g., QUAN] affects the formulation of the other [e.g., QUAL], and multiple types of implementation [i.e., QUAL & QUAN data collection, analysis, and inference] processes occur" (p. 151).

Nastasi and colleagues (2007) have described a type of fully integrated mixed design characterized by a recursive (iterative) mixed method process depicted as Qual→←Quan, to depict multistrand research and development projects. This type of iterative design is one in which mixed methods are used to facilitate development and testing of theory, evaluation instruments, and intervention programs that are culturally and contextually appropriate. The mixing of qualitative and quantitative methods occurs in a recursive manner (with implementation of each research method informing the other, e.g., *Qual → Quan → Qual → Quan . . .*) throughout the research and development process. Consistent with other integrated designs, consistency across the research process/strand (conceptual-experiential-inferential) is required.

TYPE VI: SYNERGISTIC

The most complex of integrated or iterative designs are mixed methods designs characterized by synergism. Hall and Howard (2008) describe the synergistic approach as a combination of the basic typological and integrated approaches discussed thus far. Consistent with other complex types, the mixing of qualitative and quantitative research in synergistic approaches occurs at the conceptual as well as implementation levels, and thus requires consideration of what we have labeled *precursors* (see Table 13.1). Hall and Howard describe four core principles for synergistic approaches:

1. *Concept of synergy,* to depict the idea that the combined effect of mixing methods approaches results in both a research process and outcomes (findings) that are greater than those produced by the application of either the qualitative or quantitative approach alone. We depict this concept as *MMR > QUAL + QUAN.*

2. *Position of equal value,* to depict the corresponding or equivalent value of qualitative and quantitative approaches (conceptual, experiential, inferential) in a mixed methods approach. Despite variations in weighting given to either during any particular stage of the research process, overall the two approaches are considered equivalent. We depict this concept as *QUAL = QUAN.*

3. *Ideology of difference,* or dialectical perspective (e.g., Greene, 2007), which emphasizes the importance of multiple perspectives associated with mixing of qualitative and quantitative approaches. Consistent with the concept of dialectic, mixing of QUAL and QUAN requires attempts to reconcile conflicting points of view reflected at each stage of the research process (conceptual to inferential); the resulting synthesis is assumed to be necessary for achieving synergism. A dialectical process also is inherent in the integrated and iterative approaches. We depict this concept as *QUAL ~ QUAN.*

4. *Relationships among the researcher(s) and with study design.* This principle reflects (a) the likely necessity of collaboration among researchers, assuming few researchers have sufficient expertise in both qualitative and quantitative approaches; and (b) the importance of a reflective stance by the researchers (sole researcher with qualitative and quantitative expertise or team of researchers) in balancing the potentially opposing qualitative-quantitative views (e.g., subjectivity-objectivity) in reference to interpretation of data. We depict this concept as *Researcher(s) ~ Design* to reflect the synergism of researchers and design.

Although the emphasis on qualitative and quantitative methods and perspectives can vary across the research process or strands of research, the synergism resulting from mixing of research approaches must occur at the analysis and interpretation stages. This is consistent with expected outcomes of other complex design types (integrated or iterative), in which inferences drawn from qualitative and quantitative methods are integrated at what Teddlie and Tashakkori (2009) call the final *meta-inference* stage. The meta-inferences reflect a mixed-paradigm perspective resulting from the synthesis of qualitative and quantitative research perspectives applied to the findings. Also inherent in the synergistic approach is consideration of realities of the research context (the social, cultural, ethical, political); this also is consistent with other complex design types. The focus on the real-world context of research becomes critical in any attempts by researchers to bridge the gap between research and practice within the social and behavioral science disciplines. Research models presented by other mixed methodologists embody the synergistic approach (Chatterji, 2005; Mertens, 2007; Nastasi et al., 2007; readers are referred to their work for more detail).

As noted by Hall and Howard (2008), a fully integrated or synergistic approach to mixed methods research is likely to require collaboration among teams of researchers. Other methodologists have asserted requisite collaboration or partnerships for mixed methods research (e.g., Denscombe, 2008; Mertens, 2007; Nastasi et al., 2007; Shulha & Wilson, 2003). Shula and Wilson use a social constuctivist model (see also Nastasi et al., 2004) to explain the synergistic outcomes of researcher collaboration in mixed methods research for the research and the researcher (e.g., enhanced learning and thinking), what we depict as *Researcher(s) ~ Participants*. Denscombe describes the communities of practice as a paradigm for encompassing mixed methods research, emphasizing collaboration between researchers and practitioners. Mertens (2007) and Nastasi et al. (2007) further extend the concept of collaboration to include participation of stakeholders (the "researched" or research participants, practitioners, and representatives of other key stakeholder groups in the community) in the collaborative process.

Collaboration among researchers is intended to enhance the quality of mixed methods research process and outcomes. Participation of practitioners and community members as partners in the mixed methods research process is intended to enhance the application to real-world problems, the translation of research to practice, and the achievement of transformative goals. We contend that the integration of such collaboration (among researchers) and participation (of stakeholders) with the synergistic mixed method approach provides the basis for an inclusive model of mixed methods research that can encompass the basic typological and complex integrated models.

◆ An Inclusive Framework of Design Typologies: Extending Complex Typologies

Consistent with Hall and Howard's (2008) synergistic model, we propose an inclusive framework for envisioning the potential variations of mixed methods research designs that combine existing basic and complex typologies. This new framework, *synergistic partnership-based fully integrated mixed methods research*, incorporates the synergistic framework of Hall and Howard with professional collaborative and stakeholder participatory approaches to achieve

pragmatic and transformative goals as well as scientific goals. Thus, the framework encompasses all the criteria outlined in Table 13.1 and is intended to be comprehensive in its representation of variations in mixed methods research for achieving a range of purposes. The research process is depicted as cyclical (see Figure 13.1) to reflect the iterative nature of research for specific researchers as well as social and behavioral sciences. The cycle includes all stages of the research process, from conceptualization (research purpose, informed by worldview and existing theory, research, practice or policy) to implementation (sampling to data analysis) to inference (data inference, inference quality, data representation) and application. The framework necessitates answering questions about consistency across stages (cf. consistency-question; Newman et al., 2003; Ridenour & Newman, 2008). In addition, as Figure 13.1 suggests, completing the cycle of research requires considerations of applications to practice or policy as well as theory and research-based knowledge. The proposed framework addresses the critical question of the nature of mixing of methods: How does one combine qualitative and quantitative research in terms of priority and timing (cf. Creswell & Plano Clark, 2007)? In response to this question, the approach embodies a ubiquitous integration of qualitative and quantitative approaches, depicted as QUAL↔QUAN at each stage of the research process (see Figure 13.1). That is, mixing of qualitative and quantitative within mixed methods designs occurs at each stage of the cycle (from theory to application); thus each stage can be represented by QUAL↔QUAN. In this regard, the model incorporates a key characteristic of the fully integrated mixed methods model proposed by Teddlie and Tashakkori (2009) and the dialectical process proposed by Hall and Howard (2008), with allowance for variations in timing and priority across the stages. The question for researchers is how the mixing of qualitative and quantitative

Figure 13.1 Synergistic Partnership-Based Fully Integrated Mixed Methods Research: Cycle of Research

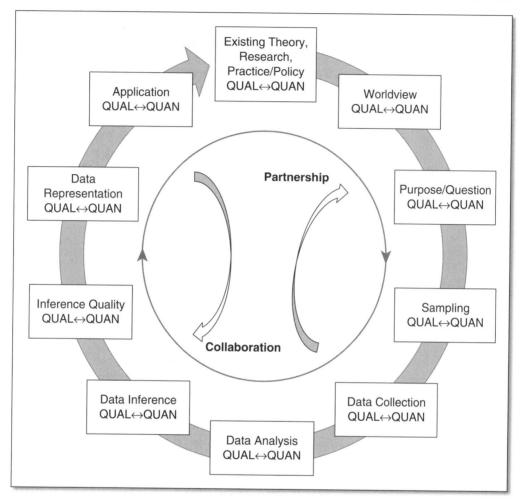

NOTE: This cycle reflects the proposed inclusive framework for conceptualizing, designing, and critiquing mixed methods research designs. The framework builds on existing design typologies and is intended to encompass considerations relevant to precursors and basic and complex typologies (depicted in Table 13.1). The key features of the cycle are (a) the centrality of partnership with stakeholders and collaboration among researchers; (b) the cyclical nature of research from conceptualization to application; (c) the iterative nature of the cycle, depicted by the central arrows (reflecting the potential return to earlier stages based on outcomes of subsequent stages; e.g., data inference leads back to more data collection); and (d) the ongoing mixing and attempts at synthesizing qualitative and quantitative perspectives, methods, and data at each stage in the cycle (depicted as QUAL⟵⟶QUAN).

approaches occurs at each stage of the process from theory to application. This continual attention to mixing is assumed to be requisite to achieving synergy (MMR > QUAL + QUAN).

The cycle depicted in Figure 13.1 reflects a complete strand, encompassing conceptual, experiential, and inferential stages (Teddlie & Tashakkori, 2009), and can be applied to monostrand (e.g., single study or cycle) or multistrand (or multiple studies within a research program; multiple cycles) research. Within a single strand, of course, data collection or analysis can lead the researcher back to further data collection. The assumption in multistrand studies is that the cycle would be repeated, for example, to address multiple purposes (e.g., theory development followed by theory testing). At a fully integrated level (cf. Teddlie & Tashakkori, 2009), the mixing of qualitative and quantitative research occurs at every stage.

Most important, the inclusive model reflects the synergism of Hall and Howard's (2008) model, depicted as MMR > QUAL + QUAN, suggesting that the most complex mixed methods designs are those that result in findings and applications that go beyond what either qualitative or quantitative research alone could produce. The synergism is best reflected in what Teddlie and Tashakkori (2009) refer to as meta-inferences that result from the integration of separate qualitative and quantitative inferences in a fully integrated model (and require reconciling discrepancies across findings). We extend the concept of synergism proposed by Hall and Howard (2008) in our inclusion of the participatory/collaborative components, or what we call partnership-based approaches. Consistent with a social constructivist perspective, we propose that the findings and applications of mixed methods research (and perhaps any research) are further enhanced by partnerships with professionals (researchers, practitioners) with multiple perspectives and expertise and other key stakeholders (e.g., research participants, community members, policymakers) who have vested interests in the outcomes. Thus, the outcomes of partnership-based approaches are greater than the outcomes resulting from sole researcher/perspective approaches. In addition, considerations of synergism affect decisions throughout the research process but are particularly important when planning for or evaluating inference quality. Consistent with the integrative framework of Teddlie and Tashakkori (2009), inference quality must take into account the basis and legitimacy of meta-inferences (i.e., Do meta-inferences reflect the synergism resulting from reconciliation of consistencies and inconsistencies based on different strands of research?). Fundamentally, the synergism of partnership-based fully integrated mixed methods research is assumed to be essential (*de rigueur*) for addressing the complex real-world problems in the social and behavioral sciences.

APPLYING THE INCLUSIVE FRAMEWORK FOR CONCEPTUALIZING DESIGN TYPOLOGIES

The partnership-based, synergistic, cyclical, and fully integrated model we propose might best be thought of as an ideal framework for designing and critiquing mixed methods research. We recognize, however, that its application requires considerations of the potential variations of designs reflected in the basic and integrated typologies. To facilitate discussion of application, we have depicted the process in a more linear (step-by-step) format in Figure 13.2. The research process (strand) includes 10 stages; thus, the process would recur in multistrand research. The participation and collaboration process is depicted as extending across the strand.

Within each stage, researchers must make decisions relevant to conducting mixed methods research, which then influence the type of mixed methods research that is achieved. To typify the research within an inclusive mixed methods framework requires consideration of both general process and stage-specific features of the research and the extent to which the

Figure 13.2 Synergistic Partnership-Based Fully Integrated Mixed Methods Research: Stages of Research Process

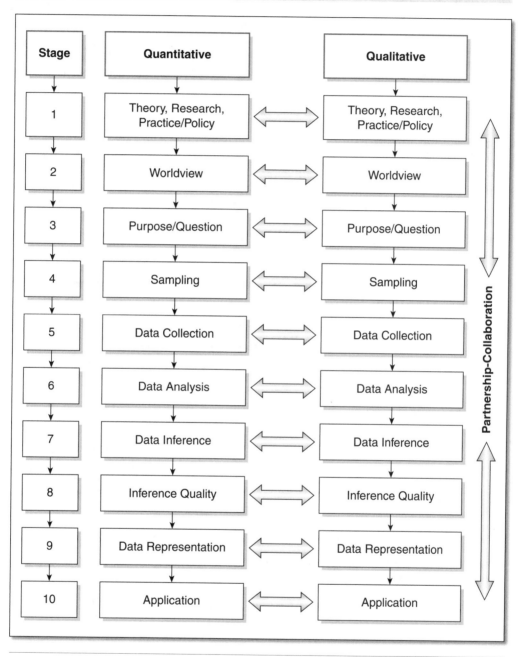

NOTE: The linear representation of research cycle (depicted in Figure 13.1) is intended to facilitate application of the proposed framework for conceptualizing, designing, and critiquing mixed methods research designs. The research cycle (strand) is depicted as a 10-stage process, requiring *stage-specific decisions* relevant to purpose, theory, methods of data collection and analysis, and so on; and *overall process decisions* relevant to iteration of the cycle, integration or synthesis of methods and data, respective roles of researchers and participants, and other complexities of the research design.

research meets criteria within the basic and complex typologies that are encompassed in an all-inclusive framework. The answers to these questions would thus provide the standards for designing, classifying, and critiquing mixed methods research. The potential variations, of course, are infinite, and the purpose of this discussion is to propose a framework for reflecting these variations within the context of an all-encompassing yet perhaps ideal framework for mixed methods research.

We propose a set of questions to guide design and classification of mixed methods research with our synergistic partnership-based fully integrated mixed methods framework. These include both general (overarching, process-oriented) and stage-specific questions. Responding to the questions requires an understanding of the precursors and continuum of typologies depicted in Table 13.1 and the inclusive framework and research process as depicted in Figures 13.1 and 13.2. The questions are posed in past tense

(to facilitate classification or critique of a design); however, the questions can be rephrased easily to guide design planning as well. We provide a set of exercises at the end of the chapter to facilitate understanding of mixed methods design typologies (depicted in Table 13.1) and the inclusive framework for classifying and designing mixed methods research (Figures 13.1 and 13.2).

We begin with 10 stage-specific questions in Table 13.2. These questions correspond to the focus of the respective research stages depicted in Figure 13.2 and are linked to respective precursor or typological criteria depicted in Table 13.1. Of course, the questions would need to be repeatedly applied to respective strands in multistrand designs. Thus, before proceeding with the series of questions, an initial question for the researcher or reviewer would be this: How many strands are involved in the research process (i.e., is this mono-strand or multistrand)?

Table 13.2 Stage-Specific Questions for Mixed Methods Research

Stage	Questions	Precursor or Typological Criteria (See Table 13.1)
Stage 1	What theory or theories, research, practice, and/or policy formed the basis for the research?	Precursor-theory
Stage 2	What worldview(s) guided the research?	Precursor-theory
Stage 3	What was the purpose of the research study or program?	Precursor-purpose
Stage 4	What types of sampling were used? Were these appropriate given the research purposes/questions?	Types III, IV
Stage 5	What data collection methods were used? How were the methods mixed with regard to weighting and timing? Were methods appropriate for answering the research questions?	Types II, III, IV

Stage	Questions	Precursor or Typological Criteria (See Table 13.1)
Stage 6	How were data analyzed? What were the relative weighting and timing of analysis for qualitative and quantitative data? Were data analysis techniques appropriate for addressing the research question and for the types of data collected? Did results of data analysis lead to collection of new data?	Types II–V
Stage 7	What was the process for data inference? Were inferences drawn separately from qualitative and quantitative data? How were the data mixed with regard to inferences? How were discrepancies resolved? Did the inferences lead to new data collection to answer the same or different questions? Were findings used to answer the research questions?	Types I–V
Stage 8	What techniques did the researchers use to ensure inference quality? Did these include those relevant to quantitative, qualitative, and mixed methods research? Did data quality findings lead to decisions to collect additional data?	Precursor-inference quality; Type V
Stage 9	How were data represented for presentation? Were both qualitative and quantitative data represented? How were they mixed within the presentation? Were data represented for the purpose of serving multiple audiences (specify audiences)? Were these audiences appropriate given the purposes of the research? Did data presentation result in decisions to continue data collection or initiate new strands of research?	Types I–V
Stage 10	To what extent were research findings used to inform theory, research, practice, and/or policy? Were the findings used in a way that was consistent with the conceptual foundations of the research? Did the findings lead to generation of new research questions and new research strands?	Types I and III–V

NOTE: These stages are repeated across strands in multistrand research.

Table 13.3 lists the overarching or general questions that apply to the research process, encompass more than a single stage, and may need to be addressed at multiple stages (e.g., questions about mixing could apply to both data collection and data analysis) and across strands in multistrand research. These questions are particularly important for determining if the research meets the criteria for the highest level of complexity in mixed methods research as reflected in the complex models (integrated, iterative, synergistic).

Table 13.3 Overarching (General) Design Questions: Research Process Questions

Question	Process Characteristic Addressed
Was the research process iterative? Did decisions in later phases result in revisiting earlier phases? (For example, after completing specific steps, did the researchers return to earlier steps before moving forward? Did the results of data inference suggest additional questions leading to further sampling, data collection, etc.?	Iteration
To what extent did earlier decisions influence subsequent decisions? Was there consistency across stages of the process?	Consistency, Integration
Was there coherence among the stages of the research process? (For example, were the questions linked to decisions about data collection and analysis? Did inferences follow from results of data analysis and address the research purpose or question?	Integration
What partners were involved in the research process? To what extent were they involved at each stage?	Partnership, Collaboration
To what extent did the research involve collaboration of different researchers (e.g., qualitative, quantitative; within or across disciplines)? Did the collaboration contribute to the synergism of mixed methods?	Synergism, Collaboration
To what extent were qualitative and quantitative perspectives or approaches used across the research process? What was the nature of the mixing of these approaches? Did qualitative and quantitative approaches have equal value in the research process?	Data Mixing, Equivalence, Synergism
To what extent did the research process involve consideration of multiple perspectives? To what extent did the research activity include a social constructivist process in order to achieve synergism?	Dialetic, Synergism
To what extent did the researchers move beyond inferences based on separate consideration of qualitative and quantitative data and integrate across approaches?	Meta-inference, Synergism
Was the research process cyclical? Did the researchers complete the cycle by applying findings to inform existing theory, research, and practice or policy? Did the researchers engage in a reflective process regarding etic-emic discrepancies (e.g., researcher's worldview vs. participants' worldview)? Was the researcher's worldview changed as a function of engaging in the research process?	Cyclical, Reflexive

◆ Conclusions

The proposed inclusive framework for mixed methods research, synergistic partnership-based fully integrated mixed methods research (Figure 13.1), is intended to extend the existing typologies by incorporating both precursors to and key features of the basic and complex typologies (depicted in Table 13.1). The critical elements of the proposed framework are its comprehensiveness, the cyclical nature of the research process, the emphasis on synergism resulting from mixed methods and partnerships among researchers and with other stakeholders, and the relevance to the complexities of real-world research and the application to solving real-world problems. The framework has potential application to the design and evaluation of mixed methods research across the disciplines in the social and behavioral sciences, and thus could be useful to researchers, reviewers of research, and faculty who teach research methods. The utility as a comprehensive typology that can accommodate the diversity of mixed methods designs, including future developments, is yet to be tested.

Future directions related to the proposed inclusive framework can address questions related to utility and validity of the identified critical elements. We recommend several possibilities:

- To test comprehensiveness and flexibility, apply the typology to classifying existing mixed methods research across social and behavioral science disciplines.

- To test the relevance to complexities of real-world research, develop and conduct mixed methods research studies within field settings influenced by a range of social, cultural, political, ethical, and practical realities.

- To test the relevance to solving real-world problems, develop and conduct applied mixed methods research studies that address social, cultural, and political problems (e.g., with emancipatory-transformative goals).

- To test the partnership-based component, examine application to mixed methods research studies that involve collaboration of researchers with diverse expertise in methods and substantive areas, collaboration of researchers and practitioners, and participation of other stakeholders such as community members, research participants, and policymakers.

- To test synergism, conduct mixed methods research studies with various levels of mixing (integration, iteration, synthesis) and examine differential outcomes with regard to the quality and application of findings.

We expect that attempts to bring structure and organization to the field of mixed methods research and the search for the all-inclusive typology will continue as the field evolves. We encourage mixed methodologists to consider our depiction of an inclusive framework as part of this evolution, and we welcome future developments.

Research Questions and Exercises

The following exercises are designed to facilitate understanding and application of the range of basic and complex typologies depicted in Table 13.1 and the research cycle and stages of the inclusive framework depicted in Figures 13.1 and 13.2.

(Continued)

(Continued)

Exercise 13.1. Application of Mixed Methods Research to Disaster Management

The following scenario depicts the intersection of the personal experiences of one individual with an ongoing mixed methods research project designed to address related needs. Following the scenario is a guided discussion of the application of the stages of the inclusive framework depicted in Figure 13.2.

Scenario

Maria Gonzales is a 55-year-old female who has been caring for her elderly mother since her father's death 3 years ago. Maria and her family immigrated to the United States from Cuba in the early 1980s and settled in the Miami area. Her mother, Lucinda, has been diagnosed with moderate stage Alzheimer's disease, which has slightly affected her daily functioning. Lucinda is dependent on Maria for driving, financial support, and medical decision making. In addition to living with and providing care for her mother, Maria is employed full-time as a housekeeper through a franchise company that coordinates her schedule for cleaning multiple homes each day throughout the Miami area.

Despite the growing burden of caring for her mother, Maria is committed to providing ongoing care and is strongly opposed to the idea of admitting her to a nursing home. However, to continue her full-time position as a housekeeper, she recently enrolled her mother in a Medicaid-funded adult day care program. Although Maria's employer has been relatively flexible in allowing her time off for her mother's doctors' appointments, she is worried that the company will eventually lose patience. She fears that her increasing requests for time off could jeopardize her employment.

When a hurricane recently struck the Miami area, Maria and her mother were forced to use a public shelter for 3 days, although it did not provide the services necessary to support her mother's physical and mental health needs. Lucinda did not fare well in the chaotic environment of a public shelter. Her cognitive functioning markedly decreased, and she easily became disoriented and confused. Lucinda also began to wander and need assistance with toileting. Her special needs created some tension among the shelter volunteers. Furthermore, Maria needed the assistance of shelter workers because she did not bring enough of her mother's cardiac medication to the shelter.

The hurricane caused significant damage to the Gonzales's home, including the loss of their car. Maria had significant problems interacting with the insurance company. She went nearly a month without reliable transportation to travel to work or her mother's medical appointments. Maria turned to her church as a primary source of support during these stressful times. It was through her church that Maria was introduced to university researchers, who sought to better understand the needs of individuals caring for their elderly parents during disasters.

Maria was asked to participate in a focus group to discuss her needs after disasters. During the focus group, several of her concerns and recent problems were brought to light, and she found that other local families encountered similar issues. Focus group participants discussed the ways in which they preferred to receive information about disaster preparedness, shelters, and recovery services. These themes were incorporated into a questionnaire that was later administered to a larger population of older adults and caregivers living in the Miami area. The questionnaire findings revealed that a number of people received information from their churches. It was unclear, however, why some churches provided the information about emergency special needs shelters, and others did not. For this reason, a third phase of research was implemented, where church leaders were interviewed to clarify current practices and how dissemination of this information could be improved.

Application of an Inclusive Mixed Methods Research Framework

Stage 1: Theory. The theoretical selection for the purposes of this exercise is the ecological framework (e.g., Bronfenbrenner, 1989). Ecological factors are organized into the following levels of influence: intrapersonal/individual (e.g., knowledge, attitudes, behaviors), interpersonal (e.g., family, social networks), institutional (e.g., voluntary organization, workplace), community (e.g., relationships between organizations, institutions, informal networks), and public policy (e.g., local, state, national laws and policies). Mixed methods can be used to examine both within- and between-factor questions (i.e., person × family × community × institutional).

Discussion Questions

1. How would you apply the ecological framework to this particular scenario? What are the implications for mixed methods research design?

2. What factors need to be considered in exploring disaster preparedness and recovery issues for the older population? Based on existing research? Based on the practical situation depicted in the scenario?

3. How might you involve stakeholders in this stage?

Stage 2: Worldview. Selection of data collection methods must consider cultural orientations and incorporate the language and phrasing for research instruments. Multiple phases of research (pilot testing instruments with different populations) can increase the accuracy of the findings and help to develop more meaningful policy recommendations and social marketing tools. For example, Maria's sense of responsibility for her family may be considered to be a cultural factor that should be taken into consideration. Her relationship with her church, the expectations placed on her as a member, and the support offered through the church can offer valuable insight into her service seeking behavior.

Discussion Questions

1. What cultural factors need to be considered in addressing the needs of an older population following a disaster? What cultural factors are likely to be most critical in this situation? In examining cultural perspectives (worldviews), which stakeholder groups need to be considered?

2. How might stakeholders contribute to this phase as partners or collaborators?

3. How can you apply mixed methods research to examine the worldview of participants and other stakeholders in this scenario?

(Continued)

(Continued)

Stage 3: Research Purpose. Research can be driven by multiple purposes such as addressing real-world applied problems of individuals or groups, attempting to influence government policies, or advancing knowledge in a specific discipline.

Discussion Questions

1. What is the purpose of the research described in this scenario?

2. How does the research purpose influence decisions about mixed methods design?

3. What role would stakeholders play in determining the purpose of the research?

Stage 4: Sampling. Postdisaster research can present logistical challenges related to sampling and other design features. In this scenario, the following sequence of data collection is proposed: Qualitative → Quantitative → Qualitative. The first phase may require a convenience sample of individuals currently living in emergency shelters or identified through community organizations such as churches. These organizations also could assist in identifying individuals who have elderly parents living at home with them, so that samples of elderly and caregivers could be identified to obtain a representative sample for the quantitative questionnaire. The third phase might include a subset of those completing the questionnaire.

Discussion Questions

1. How would you characterize the current design (as presented in the scenario) based on existing mixed methods typologies?

2. How would you approach sampling within this current scenario?

3. What populations would need to be represented?

4. How would the approach to sampling vary across the proposed phases of data collection: focus groups, quantitative questionnaires, and follow-up interviews?

5. How might stakeholder groups participate in decision making about sampling?

Stage 5: Data Collection. In this scenario, the first phase of data collection relies on focus groups and facilitates identification of central issues facing individuals caring for elderly parents. These data contribute to development of a questionnaire that is culturally and contextually meaningful. The questionnaire serves as the data collection tool for the second phase of the study. The third phase then consists of interviews to provide a deeper understanding of the patterns identified by the analysis of questionnaire data.

Discussion Questions

1. How do the data collection methods relate to the research purposes (or questions)?

2. What other data collection methods might be used in this scenario?

3. How would you characterize the study design in terms of the proposed methods?

4. What alternative mixed methods designs might be appropriate?

5. How would you involve stakeholders in decision making about methods or in the process of data collection?

Stage 6: Data Analysis. In the current scenario, the data collection methods yield textual data from focus group and follow-up interviews and quantitative data from questionnaires.

Discussion Questions

1. What procedures might you use to analyze the textual data? For example, how would you identify and select code categories? Would these differ for data generated from focus groups and follow-up interviews?

2. How would you analyze the quantitative data?

3. How will you integrate data from the three methods—focus groups, questionnaires, and follow-up interviews? How might findings from respective data sets influence decisions about analysis of other data sets (e.g., how will findings from questionnaires influence coding of follow-up interviews or re-analysis of focus group data)?

4. What role can stakeholders play in data analysis decisions and implementation?

Stage 7: Data Inference. Inferences or conclusions drawn from the data are likely to be influenced by data sets, considered both individually and collectively. Similarly, the three data sets might contribute differently to addressing research purposes or questions. For example, in this scenario, the focus group data will inform the development of the questionnaire, and the follow-up interview data can help to clarify findings from the questionnaire data.

Discussion Questions

1. How do decisions related to theory, research purpose, design, sampling, and data collection and analysis methods influence inferences that can be drawn from the resulting data?

2. In this scenario, what types of inferences are possible from the different data sets? For example, can one make generalizations to the population based on focus groups? Questionnaires? Follow-up interviews? Similarly, how can the different data sets contribute to decision making about programming for the elderly in this postdisaster context? How can data contribute to policy decisions?

3. How do the different data sets address the purposes of the research for this scenario?

4. What are the possible advantages and disadvantages of integrating data across the three data collection methods?

5. What are the advantages and disadvantages of mixed methods research (compared with qualitative or quantitative designs) when making inferential decisions? (Hint: Consider the added value for various research purposes.)

6. How can this phase contribute to the generation of new research questions—to be addressed within this study (i.e., recursive design) or in subsequent research?

7. How can the stakeholders contribute to this stage of the research process?

(Continued)

(Continued)

Stage 8: Inference Quality. One might assume that the triangulation of methods and subsequent data integration (e.g., in this scenario) can enhance the quality of inferences and researchers' confidence in the results and subsequent application to practice or policy making. Issues of inference quality have been addressed from qualitative, quantitative, and mixed methods design perspectives. Consider the different approaches to ensuring quality in mixed methods research discussed in this chapter.

Discussion Questions

1. What strategies for ensuring inference quality might you apply in this scenario?

2. For this scenario, how might considerations of inference quality change the mixed methods design, selection of methods, sampling, and so on?

3. How might inference quality influence decisions to return to earlier stages of the research process (e.g., conduct more data collection following analysis)?

4. How does the research purpose influence the selection of strategies for ensuring quality?

5. What role would stakeholders play in making decisions about inference quality?

Stage 9: Data Representation. Decisions about data representation are influenced by research purpose, design features, and intended audiences. In the current scenario, there are several potential audiences for data dissemination.

Discussion Questions

1. Identify the potential audiences relevant to this scenario.

2. What are the various ways in which the data from this scenario could be represented (consider data sets individually and collectively)?

3. How will the choice of audience influence the representation of data?

4. How can the stakeholders assist in decisions about data representation?

Stage 10: Application. The most likely applications of research findings for this scenario are identification of service needs for the population, development of relevant services in affected communities (including the immediate context), and recommendations for policy related to disaster management. Thus, mixed methods research can contribute to practice and policy. Furthermore, research findings can contribute to development of theory and the empirical knowledge about disaster management for the relevant social and health science fields.

Discussion Questions

1. What are the potential applications of findings in this scenario? How might we design the study differently to enhance application to science (theory, research), practice, or policy?

2. How can stakeholders participate as collaborators or partners in decisions about application of findings?

3. How are decisions about research purpose, theory, and design likely to influence potential applications of findings?

4. What are the advantages and disadvantages of mixed methods research for informing science, practice, and policy? How do we best integrate methods within mixed methods designs to maximize application to science, practice, and policy?

Exercise 13.2. Critique of Existing Research

Identify a mixed methods research study from literature in your discipline. Critique the article using the stage-specific and overarching process questions found in Tables 13.2 and 13.3.

Exercise 13.3. Designing Mixed Methods Research

Propose a mixed methods research study, using the stage-specific and overarching process questions found in Tables 13.2 and 13.3 to inform design decisions.

◆ Notes

1. This would be a design in which two study conditions, such as a treatment and control group, were formed prior to the start of the investigation using nonrandom procedures, so the researcher tried to establish that the groups were similar on a set of observed characteristics before treatment began.

2. This chapter ends with a discussion of future directions pertaining to the inclusive framework, one of which is to apply it to a series of studies to both test it and see what can be learned about the field. For example, would the Rosenthal and Jacobson (1968) work be classified as a mixed methods design using contemporary definitions? If so, would it be reliably classified into one of the typologies that informs the framework presented here?

3. Lincoln and Guba (1985) provide one of the early distinctions among the paradigmatic foundations of qualitative and quantitative methods.

4. For more comprehensive discussion of the paradigms relevant to mixed methods, see Greene (2007).

5. Less common notations depict recurring or iterative mixing, to reflect more complex designs; for example, Qual > Quan > Qual >

Quan, or Quan ←→ Qual (Nastasi et al., 2007; Sandelowski, 2003).

6. See also Teddlie & Yu's (2007) related sampling typology discussed in the Type III section of this chapter.

◆ References

Bronfenbrenner, U. (1989). Ecological systems theory. In R. Vasta (Ed.), *Annals of child development* (Vol. 6, pp. 187–249). Greenwich, CT: JAI Press.

Bryman, A. (2006). Integrating quantitative and qualitative research: How is it done? *Qualitative Research, 6*, 97–113.

Chatterji, M. (2005). Evidence on "What Works": An argument for extended-term mixed-method (ETTM) evaluation designs. *Educational Researcher, 34*, 14–24.

Creswell, J. W. (2009). Mapping the field of mixed methods research [Editorial]. *Journal of Mixed Methods Research, 3*, 95–108.

Creswell, J. W., & Plano Clark, V. L. (2007). *Designing and conducting mixed methods research*. Thousand Oaks, CA: Sage.

Creswell, J. W., Plano Clark, V. L., Gutmann, M. L., & Hanson, W. E. (2003). Advanced mixed methods research designs. In A. Tashakkori

& C. Teddlie (Eds.), *Handbook of mixed methods in social and behavioral research* (pp. 209–240). Thousand Oaks, CA: Sage.

Dellinger, A. B., & Leech, N. L. (2007). Toward a unified validation framework in mixed methods research. *Journal of Mixed Methods Research, 1,* 309–332.

Denscombe, M. (2008). Communities of practice: A research paradigm for the mixed methods approach. *Journal of Mixed Methods Research, 2,* 270–283.

Eade, D. (1997). *Capacity-building: An approach to people-centred development.* Oxford, UK: Oxfam.

Erzeberger, C., & Kelle, U. (2003). Marking inferences in mixed methods: The rules of integration. In A. Tashakkori & C. Teddlie (Eds.), *Handbook of mixed methods in social and behavioral research* (pp. 457–490). Thousand Oaks, CA: Sage.

Greene, J. C. (2007). *Mixed methods in social inquiry.* San Francisco: Jossey-Bass.

Greene, J. C., Caracelli, V. J., & Graham, W. F. (1989). Toward a conceptual framework for mixed-method evaluation designs. *Educational Evaluation and Policy Analysis, 11,* 255–274.

Hall, B., & Howard, K. (2008). A synergistic approach: Conducting mixed methods research with typological and systemic design considerations. *Journal of Mixed Methods Research, 2,* 248–269.

Johnson, B., & Turner, L. A. (2003). Data collection strategies in mixed methods research. In A. Tashakkori & C. Teddlie (Eds.), *Handbook of mixed methods in social and behavioral research* (pp. 297–320). Thousand Oaks, CA: Sage.

Johnson, R. B., & Onwuegbuzie, A. J. (2004). Mixed methods research: A research paradigm whose time has come. *Educational Researcher, 33*(7), 14–16.

Johnson, R. B., Onwuegbuzie, A. J., & Turner, L. A. (2007). Toward a definition of mixed methods research. *Journal of Mixed Methods Research, 1,* 112–133.

Kemper, E. A., Stringfield, S., & Teddlie, C. (2003). Mixed methods sampling strategies in social science research. In A. Tashakkori

& C. Teddlie (Eds.), *Handbook of mixed methods in social and behavioral research* (pp. 273–296). Thousand Oaks, CA: Sage.

Leech, N. L., & Onwuegbuzie, A. J. (2009). A typology of mixed methods research designs. *Quality and Quantity, 43,* 265–275.

Lincoln, Y. S., & Guba, E. G. (1985). *Naturalistic inquiry.* Thousand Oaks, CA: Sage.

Maxcy, S. J. (2003). Pragmatic threads in mixed methods research in the social sciences: The search for multiple modes of inquiry and the end of the philosophy of formalism. In A. Tashakkori & C. Teddlie (Eds.), *Handbook of mixed methods in social and behavior research* (pp. 51–90). Thousand Oaks, CA: Sage.

Maxwell, J. A. (2004). Using qualitative methods for causal explanation. *Field Methods, 16*(3), 243–264.

Maxwell, J. A., & Loomis, D. M. (2003). Mixed methods design: An alternative approach. In A. Tashakkori & C. Teddlie (Eds.), *Handbook of mixed methods in social and behavioral research* (pp. 241–272). Thousand Oaks, CA: Sage.

Mertens, D. M. (2003). Mixed methods and the politics of human research: The transformative-emancipatory perspective. In A. Tashakkori & C. Teddlie (Eds.), *Handbook of mixed methods in social and behavioral research* (pp. 135–166). Thousand Oaks, CA: Sage.

Mertens, D. M. (2007). Transformative paradigm: Mixed methods and social justice. *Journal of Mixed Methods Research, 1,* 212–225.

Messick, S. (1995). Validity of psychological assessment: Validation of inferences from persons' responses and performances as scientific inquiry into score meaning. *American Psychologist, 50,* 741–749.

Morgan, D. L. (2007). Paradigms lost and pragmatism regained: Methodological implications of combining qualitative and quantitative methods. *Journal of Mixed Methods Research, 1,* 48–76.

Morse, J. M. (2003). Principles of mixed methods and multimethod research design. In A. Tashakkori & C. Teddlie (Eds.),

Handbook of mixed methods in social and behavioral research (pp. 189–209). Thousand Oaks, CA: Sage.

Nastasi, B. K., Hitchcock, J., Sarkar, S., Burkholder, G., Varjas, K., & Jayasena, A. (2007). Mixed methods in intervention research: Theory to adaptation. *Journal of Mixed Methods Research, 1,* 164–182.

Nastasi, B. K., Moore, R. B., & Varjas, K. M. (2004). *School-based mental health services: Creating comprehensive and culturally specific programs.* Washington, DC: American Psychological Association.

Nelson, G., & Prilleltensky, I. (2005). *Community psychology: In pursuit of liberation and well-being.* New York: Palgrave Macmillan.

Newman, I., Ridenour, C. S., Newman, C., & DeMarco, G. M. P., Jr. (2003). A typology of research purposes and its relationship to mixed methods. In A. Tashakkori & C. Teddlie (Eds.), *Handbook of mixed methods in social and behavioral research* (pp. 167–188). Thousand Oaks, CA: Sage.

Onwuegbuzie, A. J. (2003). Expanding the framework of internal and external validity in quantitative research. *Research in the Schools, 10*(1), 71–90.

Onwuegbuzie, A. J., & Collins, K. M. T. (2007). A typology of mixed methods sampling designs in social science research. *The Qualitative Report, 12,* 281–316. Retrieved August 15, 2009, from http://www.nova .edu/ssss/QR/QR12-2/onwuegbuzie2.pdf

Onwuegbuzie, A. J., & Johnson, R. B. (2006). The validity issue in mixed research. *Research in the Schools, 13,* 48–63.

Onwuegbuzie, A. J., & Leech, N. L. (2007). Validity and qualitative research: An oxymoron. *Quality & Quantity, 41,* 233–249.

Onwuegbuzie, A. J., & Teddlie, C. (2003). A framework for analyzing data in mixed methods research. In A. Tashakkori & C. Teddlie (Eds.), *Handbook of mixed methods in social and behavioral research* (pp. 351–384). Thousand Oaks, CA: Sage.

Ridenour, C. S., & Newman, I. (2008). *Mixed methods research: Exploring the interactive continuum.* Carbondale: Southern Illinois University Press.

Rosenthal, R., & Jacobson, L. (1968). *Pygmalion in the classroom: Teacher expectations and pupils' intellectual development.* New York: Holt, Rinehart & Winston.

Rosenthal, R., & Jacobson, L. (1992). *Pygmalion in the classroom: Expanded edition.* New York: Irvington.

Sandelowski, M. (2003). Tables or tableaux? The challenges of writing and reading mixed methods studies. In A. Tashakkori & C. Teddlie (Eds.), *Handbook of mixed methods in social and behavioral research* (pp. 321–350). Thousand Oaks, CA: Sage.

Shadish, W. R., Cook, T. D., & Campbell, D. T. (2002). *Experimental and quasi-experimental designs for generalized causal inference.* Boston: Houghton- Mifflin.

Shulha, L. M., & Wilson, R. J. (2003). Collaborative mixed methods research. In A. Tashakkori & C. Teddlie (Eds.), *Handbook of mixed methods in social and behavioral research* (pp. 639–670). Thousand Oaks, CA: Sage.

Tabachnick, B. G., & Fidell, L. S. (2007). *Using multivariate statistics* (5th ed.). Pearson.

Tashakkori, A., & Creswell, J. W. (2007). Exploring the nature of research questions in mixed methods research [Editorial]. *Journal of Mixed Methods Research, 1,* 207–211.

Tashakkori, A., & Teddlie, C. (1998). *Mixed methodology: Combining quantitative and qualitative approaches.* Thousand Oaks, CA: Sage.

Tashakkori, A., & Teddlie, C. (Eds.). (2003). *Handbook of mixed methods in social and behavioral research.* Thousand Oaks, CA: Sage.

Tashakkori, A., & Teddlie, C. (2003). The past and future of mixed methods research: From data triangulation to mixed model designs. In A. Tashakkori & C. Teddlie (Eds.), *Handbook of mixed methods in social and behavioral research* (pp. 671–702). Thousand Oaks, CA: Sage.

Teddlie, C., & Tashakkori, A. (2003). Major issues and controversies in the use of mixed methods in the social and behavioral sciences. In A. Tashakkori & C. Teddlie

(Eds.), *Handbook of mixed methods in social and behavioral research* (pp. 3–50). Thousand Oaks, CA: Sage.

Teddlie, C., & Tashakkori, A. (2006). A general typology of research designs featuring mixed methods. *Research in the Schools, 13*, 12–28.

Teddlie, C., & Tashakkori, A. (2009). *Foundations of mixed methods research: Integrating quantitative and qualitative approaches in the social and behavioral sciences.* Thousand Oaks, CA: Sage.

Teddlie, C., & Yu, F. (2007). Mixed methods sampling: A typology with examples. *Journal of Mixed Methods Research, 1,* 77–100.

Wegener, D. T., & Fabrigar, L. R. (2000). Analysis and design of nonexperimental data: Addressing causal and noncausal hypotheses. In H. T. Reis & C. M. Judd (Eds.), *Handbook of research methods in social and personality psychology* (pp. 412–450). New York: Cambridge University Press.

PROCEDURES AND PRACTICE OF MIXED METHOD DESIGN

Maintaining Control, Rigor, and Complexity

◆ Janice Morse

Objectives

After completing this chapter, you should be able to

- define what mixed method design is and is not and to differentiate it from multiple method design;

- understand the importance of the armchair walkthrough and of diagramming;

- define the major components of mixed method design: the theoretical drive, the core component, the supplemental component, pacing, and the point of interface; and

- explain the major principles for maintaining rigor in mixed method design.

AUTHOR'S NOTE: Many ideas expressed in this chapter have been previously published in J. M. Morse and L. Niehaus, *Mixed method design: Principles and procedures*, Walnut Creek, CA: Left Coast Press, 2009. I thank Dr. Linda Niehaus and the pre- and postdoctoral students in the EQUIPP project (Enhancing Qualitative Understanding for Illness Processes and Prevention) at the International Institute for Qualitative Methodology, University of Alberta, Canada, for their insightful questions and enthusiasm for mixed methods design.

During the last 10 years, interest in mixed method design has escalated. Researchers consider mixed method design to be a way to work efficiently with the nuances of present-day research and to encapsulate quantitative variables with phenomena that cannot easily be quantified in the same project. They consider mixed method design to be efficient because it can incorporate both meaning and quantity into the same project; it is a method that acknowledges the progression of research as it moves inductively toward solving a puzzle or increases the scope of deductive inquiry, and it is a method that enables questions that normally would emerge at the end of a project to be addressed before closure. Researchers, granting agencies, and academics realize that, in mixed method design, the two paradigms, qualitative and quantitative—designs that have been quarreling for decades—may find a peaceful and mutually respectful region in which to coexist. There has been only one problem— researchers were uncertain about how to actually *do* mixed method research (see Bryman, 2006). In this chapter, I will present one way to approach the complexities of these designs.

◆ Clarifying What Mixed Method Design Is and Is Not

Some researchers consider mixed methods to be any project that involves both qualitative and quantitative methods (see Leech, 2010 [this volume]). The definition used here is not restricted to combinations of qualitative and quantitative projects—it also includes any research with different types of data, approaches to analysis, or research conducted on two different populations or groups, whether it be qualitative or quantitative. Mixed method design consists of one project, known as the *core* project, which is a complete method in itself, and a second project consisting of a different type of data or analysis, using a strategy (and there may be more than one) that is incomplete: that is, that is not comprehensible or publishable apart from the core project. This *supplemental strategy* provides a means to access another area that is pertinent to the research question and that cannot be included in the core component. Data for the supplemental component are collected and analyzed only until the researcher is *certain* that he or she has the answer to that particular part of the research question.

Note that the above definition of mixed method design differentiates mixed methods from multiple methods. *Multiple methods design* consists of two or more studies using different methods, which address the same research question or different parts of the same research question or programmatic goal. As each research project in a multiple method design is self-contained, complete, and publishable as a stand-alone article, there are no extraordinary methodological conundrums for researchers who are conducting a multiple method design. Often, a researcher conducts the projects and publishes them separately and then publishes a synthesizing article showing the complementary relationship between, or the complementary relationships in, the sets of findings in answering the overall question.

Once we consider mixed methods using the definition proposed by Morse and Niehaus (2009), the methodological difficulties of conducting research that consists of one complete plus one incomplete project become apparent. How does one do good science when the second component (or project)—an integral part of the project as a whole—is not complete? How does one maintain rigor when the qualitative supplemental strategy has an inadequate sample, or when the quantitative supplemental strategy (which was conducted on the qualitative sample) has an inadequate n and was chosen without randomization?

◆ The Significance of the Research Question

Initially, research design is directed by and extends from the research question. If the research question is asking about, for instance, relationships, co-occurrences, or even causation, then the research project is deductive and the theoretical drive is quantitative (indicted by uppercase letters, as QUAN). That is, the complete method is a quantitative method that best answers most of the research question. The part of the question that cannot be answered by the selected quantitative question is addressed by either a qualitative or quantitative strategy, conducted either at the same time (called *simultaneous*, shown with a + sign), or else immediately following the core component (called *sequential*, indicated with an arrow →). If the research question is inductive, and descriptive or interpretative, it is usually answered using a qualitative method (indicated as QUAL), and the strategy used to answer the other part of the question may be either qualitative or quantitative and conducted simultaneously or sequentially. Thus, we have eight types of research designs (see Table 14.1) with uppercase letters indicating the theoretical drive and lowercase indicating the supplemental strategy.

The theoretical drive is exceedingly important, for it reminds the researcher of the overall *direction* of the research project, even if the design includes a strategy from the other paradigm (for instance, in QUAL + *quan* or QUAN + *qual* design). However, this does not mean that the supplementary project is actually conducted using the principles of the core component of the other paradigm—it means that the results of the supplementary component will be integrated into the results of the core component, with the core component forming the theoretical base for the presentation of the results. This will be described more fully later.

Table 14.1 Major Types of Simultaneous and Sequential Mixed Method Designs

Different Paradigms	Same Paradigms
QUAL + *quan*	QUAL + *qual*
QUAL → *quan*	QUAL → *qual*
QUAN + *qual*	QUAN + *quan*
QUAN → *qual*	QUAN → *quan*

In this chapter, I will address three important aspects of mixed method design: How to *maintain control* of your project so that it is not overwhelming, how to *maintain rigor* so that methodological assumptions are not violated, and how to *maintain complexity* so that your end product has not oversimplified the research problem. I will do this using the techniques of mixed method design developed with Niehaus and others (Morse, 2003; Morse & Niehaus, 2007, 2009; Morse, Niehaus, Wolfe, & Wilkins, 2006; Morse, Wolfe, & Niehaus, 2006).

◆ Maintaining Control

The researcher must always remain in the driver's seat, even with the most complex problems. As soon as the project is conceived and the question written, we suggest that an armchair walkthrough (Mayan, 2009; Morse, 1994, 1999) be conducted. This is a technique that enables the researcher to envision how the project may be implemented by comparing the effectiveness of several methods to address the question. The researcher contemplates:

If I use this method, I could conduct the study *here* or *there*, with *these* subjects or participants, collecting data using *x* and *y*, and analysis doing *thus* and *so*. These results will look like *this*. The supplementary component could use these participants or subjects, with data pertaining to *this* and *that*, and analysis will be conducted using *whatever*. This supplementary component will fit into the *results point of interface* and should be able to provide a poor/satisfactory/appropriate/excellent contribution to the research question.

Doing an armchair walkthrough enables the researcher to envision, before investing in the project, the best core method and supplementary component and, most important, how the components fit together. The next step is to *diagram* your design.

DIAGRAMMING

Diagramming enables the research team to envision the core method, the supplemental component, and the *pacing* of the project (that is, how the two projects will be organized, i.e., simultaneously or sequentially); and to determine the *point of interface* (i.e., where they will link: either in the analysis section or the results section).

A diagram of a QUAL + *quan* project is shown in Figure 14.1 and a QUAN + *qual*

Figure 14.1 An Overview of QUAL-*quan* Mixed Method Designs

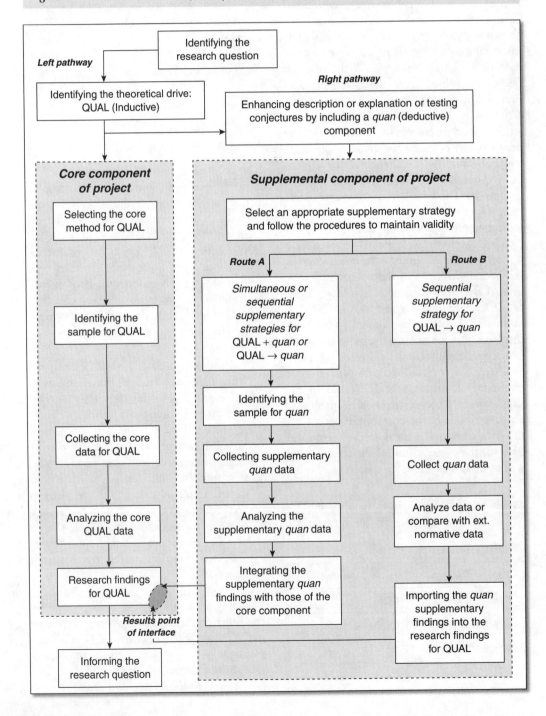

project in Figure 14.2. Always read these flow charts from the top down, whether or not they have an inductive or deductive theoretical drive. Although they may look complicated, these are not complex diagrams, once you start going through them bit by bit. The boxes represent basic steps in

the research project, and arrows lead from one step to the next. The most complex diagrams may have several research methods in one figure.

Once you have developed your diagram, place your project details on it—include the sample size, the instruments to be used, and

Figure 14.2 An Overview of QUAN-*qual* Mixed Method Designs

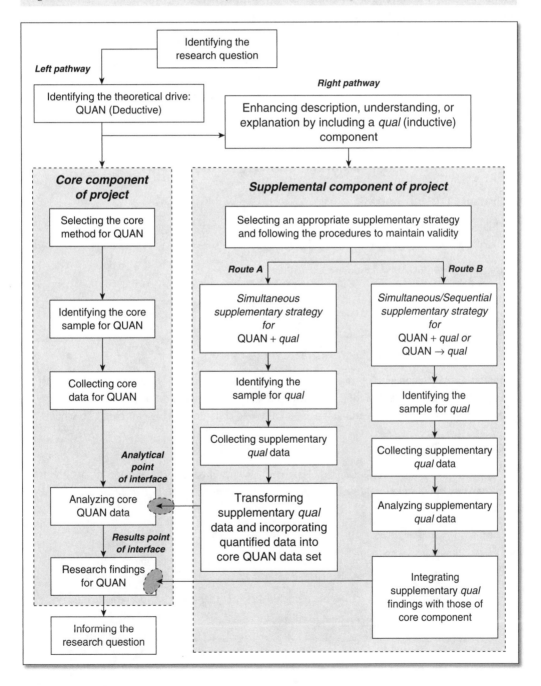

so forth—so that the diagram becomes a map depicting the course of the project.

Qualitatively driven designs: In Figure 14.1, qualitatively driven designs show the core component (QUAL) on the left pathway. By following this down, you will see that it does not differ from the procedures for any qualitative project until one reaches the *results point of interface.* By this time, the researcher will have completed the qualitative analysis. If the project is simultaneous, a QUAL (+) design, the supplemental *qual* or *quan* project (right pathway) will have been conducted alongside of the core project. If planned well, the findings from the supplemental project would then be integrated into the *results narrative,* and following the *discussion* section, the project is completed.

If the QUAL project is conducted sequentially, the QUAL core component is conducted in the normal way until the results are analyzed. At this time, the researcher may realize that another question arising from that analysis must be addressed, and he or she will design the supplemental component. The QUAL results are then put on hold until the supplemental component is completed. At that time, the results of both components are brought together at the point of interface, and the results of the supplemental component written into the results narrative of the core component.

Examples of Qualitatively Driven Designs

Example 1. QUAL→ *quan*

Habashi, J., & Worley, J. (2009). Child geopolitical agency: A mixed methods case study. *Journal of Mixed Methods Research, 3*(1), 42–64.

Design   Theoretical drive: Inductive

Pacing: Sequential

QUAL component: Focus groups and interviews

quan component: Instrument

Point of interface: Results narrative

In the QUAL component of this study, focus groups and interviews were conducted with Palestinian children to explore their political socialization. From these data, a quantitative instrument was developed. This instrument was submitted to children 9 to 14 years old at 30 schools.

Example 2. QUAL + *quan*

Wittink, M. N., Barg, F. K., & Gallo, J. J. (2006). Unwritten rules of talking to doctors about depression: Integrating qualitative and quantitative methods. *Annals of Family Medicine, 4*(4), 302–309.

Design   Theoretical drive: Inductive

Pacing: Simultaneous

QUAL component: Semistructured interviews

quan component: Coding of characteristics in interview and hypothesis testing

Point of interface: Results narrative

The purpose of this study was to determine patients' and physicians' perspectives on depression by assessing patients' views about interactions with their physicians. Four themes were identified from the interviews. Statistical analysis confirmed that two of the groups ("My doctor will just pick it up" and "They'll just send you to a psychiatrist") were rated as depressed by the physician. This technique allowed for both hypothesis generation and hypothesis testing.

Quantitatively driven designs (QUAN): Again, the core component (this time a quantitative component) is shown in the left-hand pathway (Figure 14.2). Tracing this down, for simultaneous (+) projects, again the steps in the core project appear as a normal quantitative project until one reaches the analysis and the results. Here you will notice that there are two *points of interface.* The *point of interface* is the position in which the two components meet. The first position, the *analytic point of interface,* is in the analysis section of the core component. It is for importing data that has been transformed from textual (in the *qual* component) to numerical; they are imported into the *analytic point of interface* as new variables and statistically analyzed as a part of the core data. The second position is the *results point of interface.* The textual results of the *qual* supplemental component are written into the QUAN results, with the QUAN results forming the framework, or base, of the results. With sequential (→) QUAN design, again the core project is placed on hold following analysis until the data from the *qual* or *quan* supplement component have developed to the point that they may be imported into the analysis in the results narrative.

If the *qual* data are to be transformed from textual to numerical in QUAN designs, these data *must* be in a special form. The textual data in the *qual* component must have an equivalent *n* to the core QUAN component. Furthermore, all participants in the *qual* sample *must have been asked the same question(s), in the same order.* These data are usually in the form of semistructured interviews, or from semistructured questions that are embedded, for instance, into the quantitative questionnaire (if used in the QUAN component).[1] New variables are then made to accommodate the imported transformed data, and these are statistically analyzed with the quantitative data set.

Examples of Quantitatively Driven Designs

Example 3. QUAN + *qual*

Brady, B., & O'Regan, C. O. (2009). Meeting the challenge of doing RCT evaluations of youth mentoring in Ireland: A journey of mixed methods. *Journal of Mixed Methods Research, 3*(3), 265–280.

Design   Theoretical drive: Deductive

Pacing: Simultaneous

QUAN component: Pre, during, and past survey

qual component: Observation, file analysis, case study interviews, and staff focus groups

Point of interface: Results

(Continued)

(Continued)

In this project, the program *Big Brothers Big Sisters* was evaluated using a QUAN + *qual* design. The quantitative portion was a series of surveys of youths, parents, mentors, and teachers to determine satisfaction data. The *qual* component consisted of a number of strategies—observations, file analysis case studies, interviews, and focus groups—to develop themes for the evaluation processes during the study.

Example 4. QUAN➔ *qual*

Hinton, D. E., Nguyen, L., & Pollack, M. H. (2007). Orthostatic panic events as a key Vietnamese reaction to traumatic events: The case of September 11, 2001. *Medical Anthropological Quarterly, 21*(1), 81–107.

Design Theoretical drive: Deductive

Pacing: Sequential

QUAN component: 4 instruments

qual component: Interviews

Point of interface: Results narrative

This quantitatively driven, sequential mixed method design examines trauma-related disorder in the cross-cultural perspective, including the model of orthostatic panic attacks (pp. 81–92) in Vietnamese immigrants. Participants were administered four structured interviews/ scales measuring the (1) orthostatic panic symptoms and, if present, (2) their severity, (3) their incidence in the past month, and (4) the degree of dissociation experienced every visit to the clinic. Data for this study were taken from 85 patient charts in the month prior to September 11, 2001, and one month after, and the scores for the two data points were compared. The sequential qualitative component consisted of interviews with 10 patients. Each patient was shown the orthostatic panic model, given an explanation of the condition's causation, and asked if "that explanation matched his or her understanding" (p. 93). The point of interface of the two components is in the results section, with the results of each component presented in separate sections.

SINGLE-PARADIGM MIXED METHOD DESIGNS

Mixed method designs are not solely "cross paradigm" designs but may also include QUAL +/➔ *qual* and QUAN +/➔ *quan* designs when the phenomenon demands it. Both QUAL +/➔ *qual* and QUAN +/➔ *quan* are used either when different types of data are used or when different levels of data (e.g., micro and macro) are used in the same project. The trickiest, however, is QUAL +/➔ *qual* .

QUAL +/➔ *qual* designs: Given that qualitative designs frequently contain more than one strategy (for instance, ethnography), is there such a design as QUAL +/➔ *qual*? Ethnography has always consisted of several different strategies, and that is what enables ethnography to "get below the surface." The QUAL component may consist of any standard qualitative method (e.g., focus groups, grounded theory, ethnography, phenomenology or participant observation), and the supplemental component may be interviews or observations from another person (e.g., caregivers' perspectives added to patients') added to obtain a different point of view from another group (e.g., another ethnic group) or from a different level for analysis (for instance, using conversational analysis or qualitative ethology). Sequential supplemental components may be for evaluation research, for instance, qualitatively derived assessment or qualitative outcome analysis (Morse & Penrod, 2000).

QUAN +/→ quan designs: An example of QUAN + *quan* may be a survey or some type of questionnaire as the QUAN component and the supplemental component *quan*, a physiological measure. An example of QUAN → *quan* may be a study that is separated by time or, for instance, an evaluation project. If the sample sizes are the same, the point of interface may be the *analytic point of interface* (in the analysis of the core component); if different, the comparison will be made in the *results point of interface*.

RESPECT THE THEORETICAL DRIVE

Why is the *theoretical drive* important? The theoretical drive reminds the researcher of the overall direction of the project. It assists the researcher to remain consistent with the principles of induction and qualitative inquiry (for QUAL projects) or with deduction and quantitative inquiry (for QUAN projects). This is particularly important with sampling.

Sampling for supplementary components: The greatest threat to validity in QUAL +/→ *quan* or QUAN +/→ *qual* designs is in sampling for the supplementary component. In both cases, the sample used in the core component is unsuitable—and invalid—if used in the supplementary component. Yet, despite the fact that the theoretical drive is inductive (for QUAL projects) and deductive

(for QUAN projects), the supplementary component must be conducted by adhering to the principles of the supplementary component's paradigm. Details will be discussed in the "Maintaining Rigor" section.

MAINTAIN PARSIMONY

Can you have more that one supplemental component? You can, but remember, every time you introduce another supplemental component, you are introducing more work. Your study will become more complicated, until your mind is spinning with data sets. Every time you add a supplemental component, you risk threats to validity and add costs and delays to your project. A good rule is that an answer to a question must be crucial to the project and urgently needed before you decide to add another component.

RECOGNIZE WHEN YOU ARE FINISHED

This sounds absurd, but knowing when to stop is not that easy. Because the supplemental component is not a complete method, the usual indicators of a project being finished are not available (i.e., for a *qual* component, indices of saturation, or for a *quan* component, perhaps statistical significance). The measure we use is that of researcher *certainty:* If the qualitative data provides the researcher with the confidence to understand whatever it is he or she is studying and make generalizing statements about it, the researcher usually has enough confidence to know when his or her questions have been answered, to be certain that it is probably correct, and to stop. In quantitative research, the researcher may use an instrument or scale with the qualitative sample—a purposeful, small sample. Using the sample is fine *provided* that the researcher has external norms or the physiological measures, or whatever, with which to interpret the scores. If the researcher does not have external norms and the qualitative sample is too small or unavailable, then he or she will have to draw another sample randomly from the population or use non-parametric statistics. The sample will be just large enough to provide a mean value, but not large enough to be considered completely "representative of the population."

Of course, the study is not completed at that point. The findings for the supplemental component must then be imported at the point of interface into the results narrative of the core component, and the study results and discussion sections written.

◆ Maintaining Rigor

KEEP THE QUAL-qual COMPONENTS QUALITATIVE, AND THE QUAN-quan COMPONENTS QUANTITATIVE

Regardless of the direction of the theoretical drive, the assumptions of each method must be respected. If the supplemental component is *qual,* then you must adhere to qualitative principles when conducting the supplemental component. Conversely, when the supplemental component is *quan,* adhere to quantitative principles. The researcher must keep each component separate until the point of interface—whether it is conducted in the same direction or against the theoretical drive. Mixed methods are not data soup!

ATTEND TO THE PRINCIPLES OF SAMPLING

It invalidates the QUAL +/→ *quan* project to use the QUAL sample for the quantitative component—the QUAL sample is inadequate: It is too small, and it has been purposively selected, so that from a quantitative perspective, it is biased. Similarly, it

invalidates the QUAN +/→ *qual* project to use the QUAN sample—the sample is too large, and it has been randomly selected.

QUAL +/→ quan designs: When sampling for the *quan* supplemental component in QUAL +/→ *quan* designs, the researcher is usually forced to draw a new sample from the population, one that is randomly selected and of the necessary size for analyzing the *quan* data. One exception: If the researcher has a quantitative instrument with external norms, and if the design is simultaneous, the researcher may give the instrument to the QUAL sample and use the normative data to interpret the participants' scores.

QUAN +/→ qual designs: When sampling for the *qual* supplemental component in QUAN +/→ *qual* designs, the researcher must be true to the principles of qualitative sampling. Some researchers draw the qualitative sample from the quantitative, using participants' scores as the basis for selection, or better, ask the research assistants who are collecting the data for the QUAN component to nominate the *qual* sample using qualitative criteria (i.e., select participants who are articulate, knowledgeable about the topic, and willing to participate). If the study is a sequential design, or if the task of drawing a sample from the QUAN sample is too awkward, a new qualitative sample should be selected from the population.

POINTS OF INTERFACE

One of the key aspects of mixed methods design is that although the two components are conducted separately, the supplemental component is imported into the core component for analysis (at the analytic point of interface) or into the results section to contribute to the narrative description of the results.

The analytic point of interface: As mentioned, there are only two research designs that are analyzed with the core data, and then only in special circumstances. The first is QUAN + *qual,* in which the qualitative data may be transformed to numerical data and these variables analyzed in the core statistical data set. Again, this may be performed only if in the *qual* component, the sample size is equivalent and the necessary data are available from all participants.

The second is QUAL + *quan* when everyone in the qualitative interviews has been asked a key question, one that can sort the entire set of interviews into groups, and then a chi-square can be used to determine significant differences according to these characteristics. For instance, in a study of health in the inner city, participants' definitions of health could be coded as either physical or psychological, and when compared with the participants' self-rating of health, there was a significant relationship between how the residents defined health and rated their own health (Morse, 1987).

The results point of interface: All research has a section in which the results are presented for the reader. This is primarily narrative, although it may contain some tables or figures to enhance the description.

So it is with mixed method research. Ideally, the researcher writes the results section, combining the findings from both components, although not paragraph by paragraph. The core component always forms the theoretical base or foundation for the results, and the findings from the supplemental core embellish this, adding important detail. While the reader should be able to identify which results came from each component, on no account should the two results be presented separately.

BE REFLEXIVE (USE INCREMENTAL VALIDITY)

The key to validity in qualitative inquiry is reflexivity (Finlay, 2002). This is because you are learning as you go

along and cannot entirely anticipate what you will find, even given the benefits of an armchair walkthrough. A single method study may, when nearing completion, become a mixed method study. A question may arise in the analysis that may appear relatively easy to answer, but in order to answer, it may be necessary to collect some data. In this case, you have a "designing on the run" sequential mixed method project. Of course, the additional method requires that you get approvals from your granting agency and from the institutional review board; even so, it is more efficient than publishing the first phase—and having the reviewers ask the obvious question—or conducting another study. Adding a sequential component (designing on the run) allows you to answer the questions that have emerged and places you in a better position to be funded for a subsequent study.

MISTAKES AND OTHER THREATS TO VALIDITY

The supplemental component precedes the core: Why can you *not* have designs in which the supplementary component precedes the core component? Well, everything is do-able, but it is not a good idea. Suppose you were conducting a project that you describe as *qual*→QUAN. The *qual* supplemental component may consist of "a few focus groups" from which you will develop a Likert scale, and because the Likert scale study appears to be the most work, you call it the core component. Now the hypothesized scale factors and the item wording will be obtained from the focus group data. Are you willing to skimp on a component that is so important to the success of your research program? This should NOT be *qual* → QUAN, but QUAL → *quan,* for the theoretical structure of the research program is resting on the qualitative component. Using "a few focus groups" is a threat to validity; as this component is so important to other research programs, it should be completed properly. As the second project will also be complete in itself, this will not be a mixed method project, but a multiple-method project. Subsequent complete projects are thus indicated by using small caps. The theoretical drive remains qualitative for the research program, because our programmatic question pertained to theory development.

A second common misconception for preceding the core project with the supplements is labeling the pilot project as a supplemental project. The purpose of a pilot project is to pretest an instrument, to see if one can get a sample for the main project, to learn how to use equipment or how to interview, and so forth. These purposes are steps in the process of preparing to do research, rather than steps that contribute to the theoretical progression of the project.

Using the supplemental component as the framework in the results: If you try this, you will immediately get into trouble because even in a QUAN +/→ *qual* design and the results point of interface, the qualitative findings are not rich enough to develop a theoretical base in which to place the findings. You *must* use the theoretical framework developed for the quantitative component at the beginning of the study. For QUAL +/→ *quan*, the quantitative measures are not cohesive and again cannot be used as the theoretical foundation into which you can write the results.

Writing up each component in separate paragraphs: This is not a serious problem, only a nuisance to the reviewers and readers. Writing the results from each component in separate paragraphs makes it difficult to show the complementary and integrated nature of the two components. Given that you have gone to all of that work to demonstrate that these two components are a part of the same

phenomenon, you should then respect your own perspective!

◆ Maintaining Complexity

The advantage of mixed method designs is that they allow the researcher to maintain the complexity of the phenomena within the research project. The splicing of reality to convert phenomena into researchable chunks is minimized. In QUAL designs, an accurate description of the interpretative prerogative is maintained. In QUAN designs, the representation or linking that measurement offers is retained. Mixed method designs can be as complex as the phenomena demand: There is no need to limit the number of supplementary projects to one. For example, in a QUAL project, you may have a simultaneous *quan* component and a sequential *qual* component. The notation for that project would be QUAL + *quan* → *qual*. Similarly with a QUAN project, you may have a simultaneous *qual* supplementary component and a sequential *quan* supplementary component: QUAN + *qual* → *quan*.

ADDING TO MULTIPLE METHOD PROJECTS

Mixed method projects may also be combined with single-method projects in a multiple methods design. If a complete single project is added to the chain of projects, it is presented in SMALL CAPS as it is still under the rubric of the *theoretical thrust* of the project. *Theoretical thrust* is the equivalent of the theoretical drive, except it refers to the research program or multiple method project. The first project planned from the research goal provides direction for the entire research program. For instance,

QUAN + *qual* → QUAN + QUAN

is a QUAN + *qual* mixed method project, followed by a quantitative project, followed by another quantitative project. A project

QUAL → *quan* + QUAL + *qual* → *quan*

is a mixed method qualitatively driven project with a sequential quantitative component. At the same time a qualitative mixed method project with a qualitative supplemental component is conducted, with a sequential quantitative supplemental component.

◆ **Conclusions**

In summary, when preparing a mixed method proposal, it is important to maintain control. Always do an armchair walkthrough to ensure that you have considered all optional designs and, given your context, have made the best choices, all things considered. Always diagram your study, and place as much information as possible on the diagram to make a map of your project.

When presenting or critiquing designs, or writing up your study, list details of the design, including

- Theoretical drive: Inductive or deductive
- Core component: QUAL or QUAN
  - Method: (identify/describe)
- Supplemental component(s): *qual* or *quan*
  - Strategy(ies): (identify/describe)
- Pacing: Simultaneous or sequential
- Point of interface: Analytic or results narrative

Delineating your mixed method design this way will enable the project to be conducted with minimal error and confusion, and writing will enable clear communication of what you did, when, why, and how, enabling the evaluation—and appreciation—of the results.

Research Questions and Exercises

1. Are there disadvantages in doing mixed method design? Identify studies in which multiple method design would be advantageous.

2. Are there disadvantages in doing multiple method design? Identify studies in which mixed method design would be advantageous.

3. Has mixed method design replaced triangulation? Can you use mixed method design to triangulate for validity?

4. What are the *dangers* of oversimplifying research design?

5. Why are semistructured interviews the most common qualitative method used in quantitatively driven mixed method design?

6. What are the risks of "maintaining complexity" in research design?

7. Pull some articles from the literature that have used mixed method design. Practice identifying the theoretical drive of these studies and diagramming their designs.

◆ Note

1. It is no surprise that Bryman (2006) found that semistructured interviews were the most common qualitative method when combined with quantitative. The reason is that this method produces the easiest data to transform.

◆ References

Brady, B., & O'Regan, C. O. (2009). Meeting the challenge of doing RCT evaluations of youth mentoring in Ireland: A journey of mixed methods. *Journal of Mixed Methods Research, 3*(3), 265–280.

Bryman, A. (2006). Integrating qualitative and quantitative research: How is it done? *Qualitative Research, 6*(1), 97–113.

Finlay, L. (2002). "Outing" the researcher: The provenance, process, and practice of reflexivity. *Qualitative Health Research, 12*(4), 531–545.

Habashi, J., & Worley, J. (2009). Child geopolitical agency: A mixed methods case study. *Journal of Mixed Methods Research, 3*(1), 42–64.

Hinton, D. E., Nguyen, L., & Pollack, M. H. (2007). Orthostatic panic events as a key Vietnamese reaction to traumatic events: The case of September 11, 2001. *Medical Anthropological Quarterly, 21*(1), 81–107.

Leech, N. L. (2010). Interviews with the early developers of mixed methods research. In A. Tashakkori & C. Teddlie (Eds.), *SAGE handbook of mixed methods in social & behavioral research* (2nd ed.). Thousand Oaks, CA: Sage.

Mayan, M. (2009). *The essentials of qualitative inquiry.* Walnut Creek, CA: Left Coast Press.

Morse, J. M. (1987). The meaning of health in an inner city community. *Nursing Papers/ Perspectives in Nursing, 19*(2), 27–41.

Morse, J. M. (1994). Designing qualitative research. In Y. Lincoln & N. Denzin (Eds.), *Handbook of qualitative inquiry* (pp. 220–235). Thousand Oaks, CA: Sage.

Morse, J. M. (1999). The armchair walkthrough [Editorial]. *Qualitative Health Research, 9*(4), 435–436.

Morse, J. M. (2003). Principles of mixed and multi-method research design. In A. Tashakkori & C. Teddlie (Eds.), *Handbook of mixed methods in social and behavioral research.* Thousand Oaks, CA: Sage.

Morse, J. M. (2010). Simultaneous and sequential qualitative mixed method designs. *Qualitative Inquiry, 16*(6).

Morse, J. M., & Niehaus, L. (2007). Combining qualitative and quantitative methods for mixed-method designs. In P. Munhall (Ed.), *Nursing research: A qualitative perspective* (4th ed., pp. 541–554). Boston: Jones & Bartlett.

Morse, J. M., & Niehaus, L. (2009). *Mixed method design: Principles and procedures.* Walnut Creek, CA: Left Coast Press.

Morse, J. M., Niehaus, L., Wolfe, R., & Wilkins, S. (2006). The role of theoretical drive in maintaining validity in mixed-method research. *Qualitative Research in Psychology, 3*(4), 279–291.

Morse, J. M., & Penrod, J. (2000). Qualitative outcome analysis: Evaluating nursing interventions for complex clinical phenomena. *Journal of Nursing Scholarship, 32*(2), 125–130.

Morse, J. M., Wolfe, R., & Niehaus, L. (2006). Principles and procedures for maintaining validity for mixed-method design. In L. Curry, R. Shield, & T. Wetle (Eds.), *Qualitative methods in research and public health: Aging and other special populations* (pp. 65–78). Washington, DC: GSA and APHA.

Wittink, M. N., Barg, F. K., & Gallo, J. J. (2006). Unwritten rules of talking to doctors about depression: Integrating qualitative and quantitative methods. *Annals of Family Medicine, 4*(4), 302–309.

15

ADVANCED SAMPLING DESIGNS IN MIXED RESEARCH

Current Practices and Emerging Trends in the Social and Behavioral Sciences

◆ Kathleen M. T. Collins

Objectives

Upon finishing this chapter, you should be able to

- define a sampling design;

- describe various probabilistic and purposive sampling schemes;

- discuss sample size recommendations appropriate for quantitative, qualitative, and mixed research designs;

- compare and contrast various forms of generalizations in terms of impacting sampling decisions;

- define and explain the sampling terms applicable to formulating sampling decisions in a mixed research inquiry;

(Continued)

(Continued)

- define and explain the existing sampling typologies for mixed research design;

- compare and contrast the characteristics of existing mixed research sampling typologies;

- discuss the five criteria comprising the integrative sampling typology;

- describe the seven steps of the mixed sampling process and understand the sampling issues associated with those steps;

- explain the role of interpretive consistency in formulating sampling decisions in a mixed research inquiry;

- explain the strategy of representativeness/saturation tradeoff in formulating sampling decisions in a mixed research inquiry;

- define and explain the four crises impacting sampling decisions in a mixed research inquiry; and

- understand the sampling issues related to the four crises impacting sampling decisions.

The process of selecting a sampling design for quantitative and qualitative studies requires two distinct yet interrelated decisions: decide on the strategy to select the participants (i.e., sampling scheme) and decide on the number of participants (i.e., sample size). The process of selecting a sampling design elevates in complexity when conducting mixed research that involves the concurrent or sequential combination of quantitative and qualitative approaches within one study or a program of research. In a mixed research context, the investigator must decide on a sampling design for the quantitative and qualitative phases of the study, and these decisions affect the quality of the researchers' meta-inferences and the degree to which the findings can generalize or transfer to other individuals, groups, and contexts.

To facilitate their selections of appropriate sampling schemes and sample sizes for the quantitative and qualitative phases, researchers who conduct mixed research, termed *mixed researchers* in this chapter, can access various sampling typologies, frameworks, and guidelines (e.g., Guest, Bunce, & Johnson, 2006; Onwuegbuzie & Collins, 2007; Onwuegbuzie & Leech, 2007a, 2007b; Sandelowski, 1995; Teddlie & Yu, 2007). A typology, which has been defined as the systemic classification of types, can provide novice and experienced mixed researchers alike specific recommendations to structure a study along with a professional language to facilitate communicating to consumers of research the processes, findings, and conclusions of a particular study (Collins & O'Cathain, 2009; Teddlie & Tashakkori, 2009). In addition, mixed researchers can compare and contrast various typologies, thereby leading to a broader understanding of the mixed research process (Teddlie & Tashakkori, 2009). However, typologies are criticized because they might describe only minimally the information deemed useful by the researcher, provide information that is overly complex or inconsistent, and be viewed inappropriately as a panacea for directing all of the researcher's efforts toward conducting mixed research (Collins & O'Cathain, 2009; Leech & Onwuegbuzie, 2009). Because a typology is not exhaustive, its parameters might artificially constrain mixed researchers' choices, given the wide range of mixed research designs implemented across the social and behavioral sciences (Maxwell & Loomis, 2003; Teddlie & Tashakkori, 2009). These limitations and other limitations (see Maxwell & Loomis, 2003, for an expanded discussion of limitations) have prompted methodologists to recommend that mixed researchers' use of typologies be complemented by using a systemic approach, an interactive model approach, or an integrative framework when planning and implementing mixed research (Hall & Howard, 2008; Maxwell & Loomis, 2003; Teddlie & Tashakkori, 2009). In response to these recommendations, the intent of this chapter is to present an inclusive approach to formulating sampling decisions that is applicable in the context of conducting mixed research, in particular, and monomethod research inquiries, in general.

In the context of sampling, a mixed researcher who is pursuing an inclusive approach to formulating sampling decisions recognizes that sampling decisions do not pertain only to procedures; rather, sampling decisions impact various interrelated steps of the research process. In addition, the mixed researcher's decisions pertaining to sampling design reflect the individual's values and assumptions about what constitutes credible data and what are the best mechanisms to collect data. These determinations regarding sampling decisions are shaped by the researcher's mental model, conceptualized "as the complex, multifaceted lens through which a social inquirer perceives and makes sense of the social world . . . [and it is the] inquirer's mental models that importantly

frame and guide social inquiry" (Greene, 2007, p. 13). Subsequently, in the context of this chapter, a sampling model that embraces an inclusive approach (a) builds on existing sampling typologies to provide a structure and a sampling lexicon, (b) guides the mixed researcher to reflect on the degree to which sampling decisions affect various steps in the mixed research process, and (c) incorporates a framework comprising quality indicators appropriate for assessing sampling decisions when conducting qualitative, quantitative, and mixed research.

The goal of this chapter is to present an inclusive sampling model that comprises three components. Component 1 presents an integrative typology composed of five criteria extracted from existing sampling typologies. Component 2 presents example questions to guide the researcher's reflections about the impact of sampling design at seven steps of the mixed research sampling process. Component 3 presents four criteria designed to address specific mixed-sampling issues pertinent to the implementation of sampling designs across the continuum of simple designs involving a small number of sampling schemes and advanced sampling designs encompassing multiple numbers and types of sampling schemes. These criteria are accompanied by reflective questions to document the extent to which the researcher has met these criteria when formulating a sampling design. Figure 15.1 illustrates the interconnections among the three components of the inclusive sampling model.

This chapter is divided into three sections. In the first section, the focus is on presenting topics specific to sampling, namely, identifying a sampling lexicon, describing the sampling process, and presenting common sampling schemes and sample size recommendations. The second section begins with a discussion of mixed sampling typologies. In addition, nine examples of published mixed research studies representing nine fields within the social and behavioral

Figure 15.1 Interrelationship of the Three Components of the Inclusive Sampling Model

Five Criteria
Comprising
Integrative
Typology

Seven Steps
Mixed
Sampling
Process

Four Criteria
Informing Sampling
Decisions

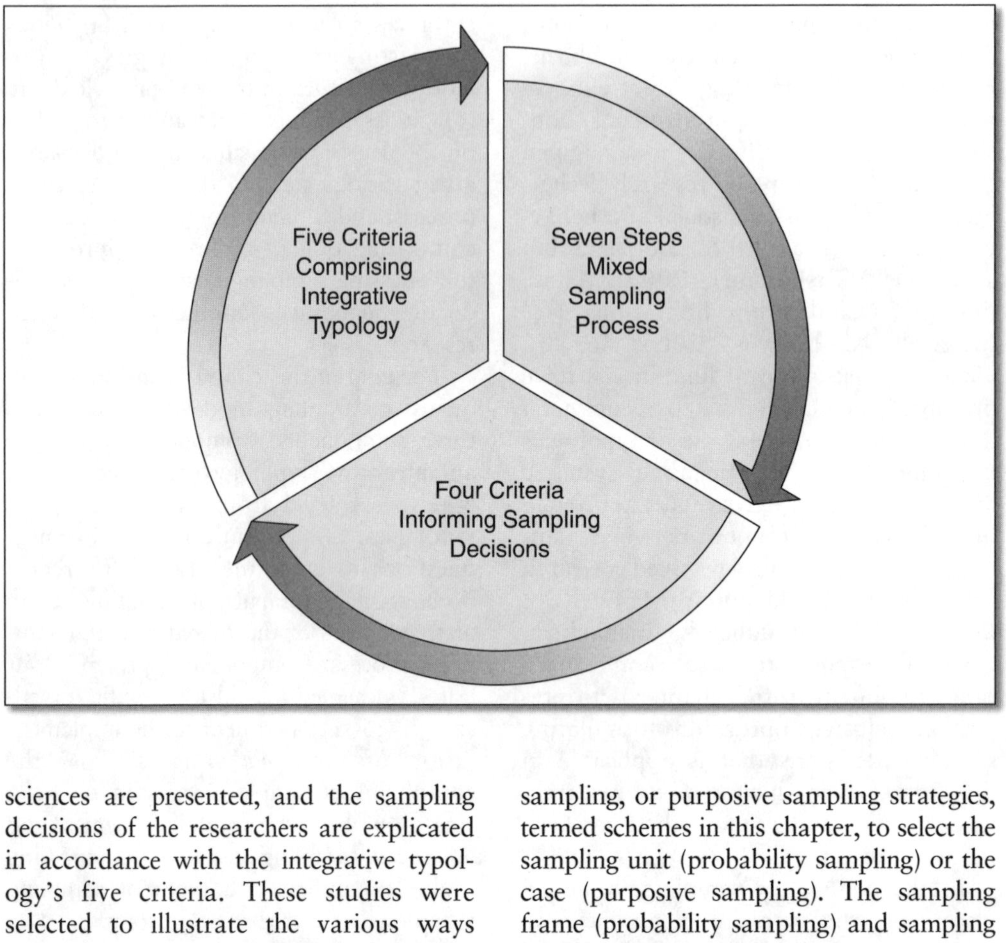

sciences are presented, and the sampling decisions of the researchers are explicated in accordance with the integrative typology's five criteria. These studies were selected to illustrate the various ways researchers are using sampling designs in mixed research. The third section presents the inclusive sampling model accompanied by reflective questions that researchers can use to document the extent to which they have met the inclusive model's criteria for determining advanced sampling designs.

◆ Topics Specific to Sampling

Sampling is the process of selecting a subset or sample unit from a larger group or population of interest, and its purpose is to address the study's research question (Tashakkori & Teddlie, 2003a). Traditionally, researchers employ probability sampling, nonprobability sampling, or purposive sampling strategies, termed schemes in this chapter, to select the sampling unit (probability sampling) or the case (purposive sampling). The sampling frame (probability sampling) and sampling boundary (purposive sampling) comprise the individuals, groups, contexts, observations, and activities that will provide the data source, either quantitative or qualitative, for a monomethod study or the data source for the phases (quantitative and qualitative) of a mixed research study. A sampling design is a framework that encompasses the sampling schemes (number of schemes × type of scheme) and the sample size for a single phase as in monomethod research or for two phases as in a mixed research study (Onwuegbuzie & Collins, 2007; Onwuegbuzie & Leech, 2007b).

Although choice of sampling schemes tends to be associated with a specific research design (e.g., purposive sampling is associated with qualitative design, and random sampling is associated with quantitative design), these associations tend not to be reflective of empirical practices (Bernard, 1995; Guest et al., 2006). For instance, Chiznik and Chiznik (2002) conducted a mixed research study to examine undergraduates' conceptions of the terms *privilege* and *oppression*. These investigators used a sample consisting of undergraduates enrolled in 10 randomly selected sections of a multicultural education course. The qualitative component consisted of the randomly selected sample's responses to an open-ended section of a questionnaire. More recently, Lopez and Tashakkori (2006) assessed the effect of two bilingual education programs on the attitudes and levels of academic achievement of fifth-grade students by selecting a random sample of interviewees for the qualitative phase of a mixed research study. The options of using purposive and random sampling singularly or as combined techniques in either or both the quantitative and qualitative phases expand the number of sampling schemes available to mixed researchers, thereby enhancing the diversity of mixed research designs.

◆ Types of Sampling Schemes

A researcher uses probability sampling schemes to select randomly the sampling units that are representative of the population of interest. Before the study commences, the researcher establishes a sampling frame and predetermines the number of sampling units, preferably based on a mathematical formula, such as a power analysis, and selects the units by using simple random sampling or other adaptations of simple random sampling, specifically, stratified, systematic, cluster, and two-stage or multi-stage random sampling (Johnson & Christensen, 2008). These methods meet the goals of ensuring that every member of the population of interest has an equal chance of selection and minimizing false positives in the statistical relationships among variables (Luborsky & Rubenstein, 1995). Typically,

the type of data collected is numeric, the analyses conducted are variable oriented, and the techniques executed are statistical techniques (Ragin, 1987); however, when conducting mixed research, the numeric data can be transformed, thereby providing narrative data that can be analyzed using case-oriented, qualitative techniques. When implementing probabilistic sampling designs, the researcher's objective is to make external statistical generalizations (i.e., generalizing conclusions to the population from which the sample was drawn).

Using the sampling frameworks compiled by Patton (1990) and Miles and Huberman (1994) as a base, more recently, Onwuegbuzie and Leech (2007a) identified 24 sampling schemes that can be used by qualitative, quantitative, and mixed researchers. Table 15.1 presents a description of five probabilistic sampling schemes and also provides descriptions of 19 purposive schemes.

When using a purposive sample, the goal is to add to or to generate new theories by obtaining new insights or fresh perspectives about the phenomenon of interest (Miles & Huberman, 1994). Purposive sampling schemes are employed by the researcher to choose strategically elite cases or key informants based on the researcher's perception that the selected cases will yield a depth of information or a unique perspective relative to the phenomenon of interest (Maxwell, 1997; Miles & Huberman, 1994; Sandelowski, 1995). This process tends to be nonrandom; however, to minimize key informant bias, a researcher can select randomly the key informants (Maxwell, 1996). Specifically, the researcher could use one of four probability schemes (simple random sampling, stratified random sampling, cluster random sampling, and systematic random sampling) to select the key informants. In some instances, the researcher implements a criterion sampling scheme to reflect a predetermined criterion or criteria to guide sample selection.

Two examples of potential criteria are illustrated by selection of either extreme

Table 15.1 Major Sampling Schemes in Mixed Research

Sampling Scheme	Description
Simple	Every individual in the sampling frame (i.e., desired population) has an equal and independent chance of being chosen for the study.
Stratified	Sampling frame is divided into subsections: groups that are relatively homogeneous with respect to one or more characteristics and a random sample from each stratum selected.
Cluster	Selecting intact groups representing clusters of individuals rather than choosing individuals one at a time.
Systematic	Choosing individuals from a list by selecting every kth sampling frame member, where k typifies the population divided by the preferred sample size.
Multistage random	Choosing a sample from the random sampling schemes in multiple stages.
Maximum variation	Choosing settings, groups, and/or individuals to maximize the range of perspectives investigated in the study.
Homogeneous	Choosing settings, groups, and/or individuals based on similar or specific characteristics.
Critical case	Choosing settings, groups, and/or individuals based on specific characteristic(s) because their inclusion provides the researcher with compelling insight about a phenomenon of interest.
Theory-based	Choosing settings, groups, and/or individuals because their inclusion helps the researcher to develop a theory.
Confirming/ disconfirming	After beginning data collection, the researcher conducts subsequent analyses to verify or contradict initial results.
Snowball/chain	Participants are asked to recruit individuals to join the study.
Extreme case	Selecting outlying cases and conducting comparative analyses.
Typical case	Selecting and analyzing average or normal cases.
Intensity	Choosing settings, groups, and/or individuals because their experiences relative to the phenomena of interest are viewed as intense but not extreme.
Politically important cases	Choosing settings, groups, and/or individuals to be included or excluded based on their political connection to the phenomena of interest.
Random purposeful	Selecting random cases from the sampling frame and randomly choosing a desired number of individuals to participate in the study.
Stratified purposeful	Sampling frame is divided into strata to obtain relatively homogeneous subgroups, and a purposeful sample is selected from each stratum.

Sampling Scheme	Description
Criterion	Choosing settings, groups, and/or individuals because they represent one or more criteria.
Opportunistic	Researcher selects a case based on specific characteristics (i.e., typical, negative, or extreme) to capitalize on developing events occurring during data collection.
Mixed purposeful	Choosing more than one sampling strategy and comparing the results emerging from both samples.
Convenience	Choosing settings, groups, and/or individuals that are conveniently available and willing to participate in the study.
Quota	Researcher identifies desired characteristics and quotas of sample members to be included in the study.
Multistage purposeful random	Choosing settings, groups, and/or individuals representing a sample in two or more stages. The first stage involves random selection and the following stages use purposive selection of participants.
Multistage purposeful	Choosing settings, groups, and/or individuals representing a sample in two or more stages in which all stages reflect purposive sampling of participants.

SOURCE: This table originally appeared in A. J. Onwuegbuzie & K. M. T. Collins (2007), A typology of mixed methods sampling designs in social science research. *The Qualitative Report, 12*(2), 281–316. Reprinted with permission of *The Qualitative Report*.

NOTE: There are five random (i.e., probabilistic) sampling schemes in this table: simple, stratified, cluster, systematic, and multistage random. All other schemes are nonrandom (i.e., purposive).

case or intensity scheme (Patton, 1990; Sandelowski, 2000) (cf. Table 15.1). Alternatively, to make certain that cases representative of specific characteristics (e.g., age, gender, level of variation relative to a phenomenon) are included in the sample, thereby enhancing "informational representativeness" (Sandelowski, 2000, p. 250), the researcher can use a stratified purposeful sampling scheme. In this context, the researcher subdivides a sampling frame into strata to obtain relatively homogeneous groups, selects a purposeful sample from each stratum, and conducts comparative analyses across cases (Miles & Huberman, 1994; Patton, 2002).

When using purposive sampling schemes, initially, the researcher establishes parameters or boundaries to delimit the specific cases or informant characteristics that will be assessed or observed and to identify what the researcher will examine in terms of environmental artifacts or individual characteristics. The sampling parameters or boundaries are accompanied by a sampling frame encompassing the theory and research question guiding the design along with the conceptual processes that structure the investigation (Miles & Huberman, 1994).

The selected case can refer to an individual, number of interviews, artifacts, observations, events, activities; once chosen, the selected cases are studied comprehensively (Sandelowski, 1995). Typically, when using a within-case sampling technique, cases are viewed individually, and multiple data points per case are accumulated and analyzed. Miles and Huberman (1994) note three characteristics of within-case sampling. First, individuals usually are viewed as nested within a larger context. Second, this selection process is based on a preselected theory or an emerging theory reflective of the study's analyses. Third, this form of sampling has an "*iterative* or 'rolling' quality working in progressive 'waves' as the study progresses" (Miles & Huberman, 1994, p. 29, italics in original).

When using a multiple-case sampling method, the researcher first establishes a detailed sampling frame that is linked to the study's research question and conceptual framework. This framework is employed to guide the examination of a range of convergent and divergent cases. These various cases are selected conceptually to explicate further the conclusions derived from the single within-case analysis (Miles & Huberman, 1994). As noted by Yin (1991), multiple-case sampling or cross-case sampling leads to replication and adds various analytical levels. Subsequently, using this approach increases the researcher's level of confidence pertaining to interpretation of findings (Miles & Huberman, 1994). In contrast to probability sampling, purposive sampling can occur at the initial stage or at multiple stages within a research study (e.g., multistage cluster sampling designs). Multistage cluster sampling occurs when the identification of the population is complex or the population is extremely large; subsequently, the researcher selects the sample in two or more stages (Creswell, 2005).

When using purposive sampling, the researcher can formulate internal statistical generalizations, which are derived from analyses of data obtained from a subset of elite informants who are representative of the sample from which they have been selected, and these generalizations are applied to this sample (Onwuegbuzie & Leech, 2007b). Internal statistical generalization is different than internal generalization. Maxwell (1992) defines internal generalization as conclusions derived from the sample as a whole—not based on elite informants—and these generalizations and conclusions derived from the entire sample are applicable only to the sample.

When using purposive sampling, other forms of generalization also are applicable, namely, analytic, case-to-case transfer, and naturalistic generalizations. When developing analytic generalizations, the researcher formulates multiple sampling decisions based on the evidential quality of data collected and draws "analytic conclusions" (Miles & Huberman, 1994, p. 29). According to Curtis, Gesler, Smith, and Washburn (2000), this form of generalization is "applied to wider theory on the basis of how selected cases 'fit' with general constructs" (p. 1002). In particular, "the investigator is striving to generalize a particular set of [case study] results to some broader theory" (Yin, 2009, p. 43).

In the context of multiple case sampling, the researcher formulates generalizations representing a case-to-case transfer supported by a theory (Firestone, 1993; Kennedy, 1979). Naturalistic generalizations are based wholly or in part on the perceptions of research consumers who reflect on their individual experiences and apply these experiences to filter the study's conclusions, thereby drawing their own conclusions pertaining to the degree to which the findings apply to other contexts or settings (Stake, 2005; Stake & Trumbull, 1982; Wehlage, 1981).

To determine the sample size for a purposive sample, the "gold standard" (Guest et al., 2006, p. 60) is saturation. To achieve saturation, a researcher collects and analyzes cases to the point that sampling additional cases does not provide any new information (i.e., informational redundancy) that can be incorporated into the thematic categories (i.e., theoretical saturation) (Glaser & Strauss, 1967; Lincoln & Guba, 1985; Sandelowski, 1995). However, determining an appropriate sample size to achieve the goal of saturation can be complex and is mediated by factors such as data quality in terms of amount and degree of complexity, sample heterogeneity, researcher's resources, and the number of individuals analyzing and interpreting the data (Guest et al., 2006; Ryan & Bernard, 2003). Sandelowski (1995) observed that often the reported sample sizes in a qualitative inquiry are too small to achieve informational redundancy and theoretical saturation, thereby reducing the trustworthiness of the findings and the transferability of the study's conclusions. Alternatively, the depth of data collected using a case-oriented approach might be jeopardized if the sample size is too large (Sandelowski, 1995). In addition, the sample's characteristics, in terms of degree of homogeneity versus heterogeneity, also impact the number of data points required to achieve saturation. The larger the degree of sample heterogeneity, the larger the number of cases recommended (Guest et al., 2006; Miles & Huberman, 1994; Sandelowski, 1995).

Guest et al. (2006) conducted a thematic analysis of interview data obtained from 60 in-depth interviews to determine the number of interviews required to reach theoretical saturation. The researchers employed a non-probabilistic sampling scheme to select participants who were at high risk for acquisition of HIV, thereby elevating the likelihood that they would be candidates for HIV prevention programs. To meet the criterion of being at high risk for acquisition of HIV, recruiters selected participants who were employed in some form of sex work. The researchers concluded that data saturation defined as "the point in data collection and analysis when new information produces little or no change to the codebook" (p. 65) occurred within the first 12 interviews. However, the criteria for selection produced a sample that was relatively homogeneous in terms of gender and manner of employment. The researchers noted the sample's homogeneity as a contributing factor to achieving data saturation at 12 interviews.

In addition, the type of purposive sampling scheme chosen by the researcher influences the sample size (Sandelowski, 1995). For example, if the researcher's goal is to assess a range of variability within a sample, both a maximum variation sampling scheme and an extreme case scheme (cf. Table 15.1) would address the goal; however, each scheme would require a different sample size. When using a maximum variation sampling scheme, the researcher likely would conduct a cross-case analysis involving a relatively large sample. In contrast, choosing an extreme case sampling scheme would likely lead the researcher to conduct an in-depth within-case analysis involving a small sample (Sandelowski, 1995). Sandelowski (1995) also observed that selecting cases representing a specific level of variation prior to data collection and analysis is shaped by achieving a "representative coverage of the variables likely to be important in understanding how diverse factors configure a whole" (p. 182). In this context, it is likely a researcher would select a criterion sampling strategy that would permit case selection prior to data collection and analysis based on a prespecified criterion (Sandelowski, 1995).

To guide researchers' decisions about sample size, various recommendations have been published. Attaining an adequate sample size is an important condition to be met when formulating sampling decisions because a small sample size reduces statistical power, thereby limiting the number of statistically significant relationships and differences that can be identified. In the qualitative phase, an inadequate sample size limits theoretical saturation, thereby compromising development of theory. In the context of a mixed research design, inadequate sample sizes limit the degree to which appropriate meta-inferences can be drawn from conclusions based on both phases of the study. In addition, in a sequential design (e.g., qualitative followed by quantitative, leading to a dependency between both components), a small qualitative sample limits the types of analyses that can be conducted (e.g., exploratory factor analysis, cluster analysis, correspondence analysis) in the quantitative data analysis phase.

Table 15.2 presents the minimum sample size recommendations pertaining to the most

Table 15.2 Minimum Sample Size Recommendations for Most Common Designs

Research Design/Method	Minimum Sample Size Suggestion
Correlational	64 participants for one-tailed hypotheses; 82 participants for two-tailed hypotheses (Onwuegbuzie, Jiao, & Bostick, 2004)
Causal-comparative	51 participants per group for one-tailed hypotheses; 64 participants for two-tailed hypotheses (Onwuegbuzie et al., 2004)
Experimental	21 participants per group for one-tailed hypotheses (Onwuegbuzie et al., 2004)
Case study	3–5 participants (Creswell, 2005)
Phenomenological	≤ 10 interviews (Creswell, 1998); ≥ 6 (Morse, 1994)
Grounded theory	15–20 (Creswell, 2005); 20–30 (Creswell & Plano Clark, 2007)
Ethnography	1 cultural group (Creswell, 2005); 30–50 interviews (Morse, 1994)
Ethnological	100–200 units of observation (Morse, 1994); 12 participants for a homogeneous sample (Guest, Bunce, & Johnson, 2006)
Data Collection Procedure	
Interview	6–9 participants (Krueger, 2000); 6–10 participants (Langford, Schoenfeld, & Izzo, 2002; Morgan, 1997); 6–12 participants (Johnson & Christensen, 2008)
Focus group	6–12 participants (Bernard, 1995); 8–12 participants (Baumgartner, Strong, & Hensley, 2002); 3 to 6 focus groups (Krueger, 1994; Morgan, 1997; Onwuegbuzie, Dickinson, Leech, & Zoran, in press)

SOURCE: This table originally appeared in A. J. Onwuegbuzie & K. M. T. Collins (2007), A typology of mixed methods sampling designs in social science research. *The Qualitative Report, 12*(2), 281–316. Reprinted with permission of *The Qualitative Report*.

NOTE: For correlational, causal-comparative, and experimental research designs, the recommended sample sizes represent those needed to detect a medium (using Cohen's [1988] criteria), one-tailed statistically significant relationship or difference with 0.80 power at the 5% level of significance.

common qualitative and quantitative designs. These recommended sizes are the result of a statistical power analysis undertaken by Onwuegbuzie, Jiao, and Bostick (2004).

This preceding section provided an overview of selective sampling terms,

examples of probability and purposive sample schemes, and sample recommendations. In the following section, sampling typologies are discussed, and this discussion is accompanied by a presentation of studies across nine fields representing the social and behavioral sciences to illustrate examples of current practices and emerging trends.

◆ Sampling Typologies in the Literature

When conducting mixed research, the researcher's choices pertaining to sampling techniques involve selecting sampling designs for the quantitative and qualitative components of the study. These selections often require that the mixed researcher use a combination of probability and purposive sampling designs. To facilitate these decisions, the mixed researcher can access mixed sampling typologies. The sampling typologies described below address the unique characteristics of mixed research design and data collection procedures.

CHARACTERISTICS OF MIXED SAMPLING TYPOLOGIES

Kemper, Stringfield, and Teddlie (2003) developed a theoretical matrix that crosses sampling technique (probability, purposive, and mixed) by the type of data produced (quantitative only, qualitative only, and a combination of both data forms). Each cell of the matrix indicates a level of frequency (e.g., happens often) measuring the degree to which a type of sampling strategy (e.g., probability or purposive) produces a type of data (e.g., quantitative data or qualitative). This typology alerts the mixed researcher to the relationship of the types of data produced and to the range of diversity of data that can be collected by combining probability and purposive sampling schemes within a single study.

Teddlie and Yu (2007) developed a typology that built on the theoretical matrix of Kemper et al. (2003) and delineated five types of mixed sampling techniques

applicable to the conduct of mixed research, namely, basic mixed sampling strategies, sequential mixed sampling, concurrent mixed sampling, multilevel mixed sampling, and a combination of mixed sampling strategies (p. 89). A key construct that underpins this typology's structure is the dependent relationship between the selection of a sample per phase and the strand of the research design (Teddlie & Tashakkori, 2006, 2009). Strand, defined by Tashakkori and Teddlie (2003b), is the component of the study that encompasses three stages: conceptualization, experiential, and inferential. Generally, strands are either qualitative or quantitative.

In the typology developed by Teddlie and Yu (2007), concurrent mixed sampling refers to the implementation sequence of the qualitative and quantitative strands of the study. Simultaneous or concurrent implementation occurs when the qualitative and quantitative components are implemented at the same time or within close proximity and are independent in terms of collection and analysis. Integration of data obtained from both samples occurs at the data interpretation stage of the mixed inquiry. Sequential implementation indicates that implementation of one component (e.g., quantitative) follows the other component (e.g., qualitative), and the relationship between the two components is dependent. Dependency occurs when the decisions made within the first phase (e.g., quantitative phase) influenced the decisions made in the subsequent phase (e.g., qualitative phase). Also, influencing this process is the trade-off between meeting the requirement of external generalizations versus meeting the requirement of transferability.

Onwuegbuzie and Collins (2007) conceptualized sampling design as encompassing two dimensions. Dimension 1 uses the base of most mixed research designs, namely the time orientation of the phases (concurrent or sequential) and the emphasis placed by the researcher on each phase (dominant, dominant-less, equal status)

(Johnson & Onwuegbuzie, 2004) in terms of selecting samples drawing appropriate inferences and generalizations. Dimension 1, time orientation of the phases, in this typology is analogous to the preceding typology's use of concurrent or sequential implementation of strands. However, Onwuegbuzie and Collins (2007) provide a second dimension; specifically, they identify the relationship between the quantitative and qualitative samples as a pivotal factor influencing the selection of the sampling unit per phase of the study. These relationships can be identical, parallel, nested, or multilevel.

Identical relationship indicates that the same sample participated in the study's quantitative phase and the qualitative phase. Parallel indicates that samples per phase are different but are selected from the same population of interest (e.g., both samples include elementary teachers, and different teachers participate in each component). Nested sample specifies that the sample participating in one phase (e.g., eight teachers selected randomly as key informants) represents a subset of the participants involved in the other phase (e.g., 40 teachers selected purposively). Multilevel samples specify that samples participating in the two phases are extracted from different populations (e.g., teachers, administrators, parents, students) and these selections can reflect various hierarchical levels of interaction with the variable of interest (e.g., student learning). This conceptualization of parallel, sequential, and multilevel differs from Teddlie and Yu (2007), who view the relationship between the strands as the inclusion of various sampling techniques (purposive and probability) within a single mixed research study or program of research, and the samples participating in the two phases are extracted from different populations.

INTEGRATIVE TYPOLOGY

A content analysis of the published mixed sampling typologies outlined earlier produced

the following five criteria as integral to formulating sampling decisions.

Criterion 1: The sampling unit selected for each phase of the study should reflect the dependent relationship between the samples selected per phase and the time orientation of the phases (concurrent or sequential) (Onwuegbuzie & Collins, 2007; Teddlie & Yu, 2007).

Criterion 2: The sampling unit selected for each phase of the study should reflect the relationship between the quantitative and qualitative samples (Onwuegbuzie & Collins, 2007).

Criterion 3: The sampling unit selected for each phase of the study should reflect the relationship between the specific combination of sampling schemes (probability, purposive) and the type of generalization selected by the researcher (Onwuegbuzie & Collins, 2007).

Criterion 4: The sampling unit selected for each phase of the study should reflect a minimum of one type of data collected (quantitative only, qualitative only) or a combination of both data types collected, thereby formulating a relationship between the varying types of data collected, subsequently optimizing the diversity of data available to analyze in response to the research question (Kemper et al., 2003; Teddlie & Yu, 2007).

Criterion 5: The researcher identifies the relationship between the emphasis of approach (dominant, dominant-less, equal) and the formulation of appropriate meta-inferences and generalizations (Onwuegbuzie & Collins, 2007) based on data collected from both phases of the study. This process is influenced by the trade-off between meeting the requirement of external generalizations versus meeting the requirement of transferability (Teddlie & Yu, 2007).

Addressing these five criteria leads the investigator to determine the appropriate sample size for each phase of the study. Figure 15.2 presents a visual depiction of the integrative typology.

The applicability of these five criteria is illustrated in the example studies outlined in the following section. In addition, the

Figure 15.2 Interrelationship of the Five Sampling Criteria Composing the Integrative Typology

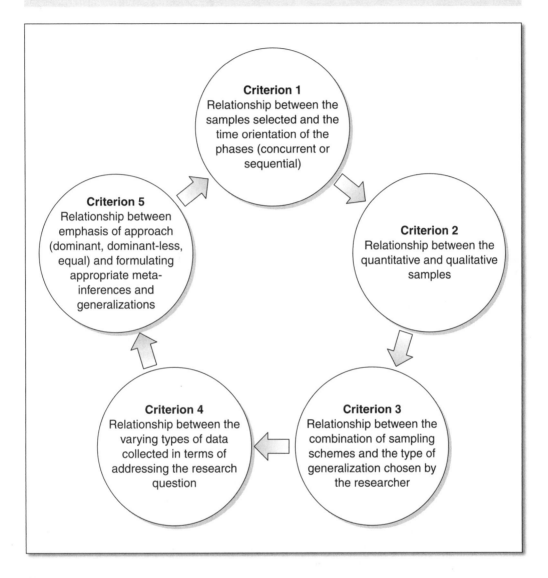

purpose of mixing in each study is identified to substantiate that the study is a mixed research study. The purpose of mixing methods within each of the example studies is classified using Greene, Caracelli, and Graham's (1989) typology. This typology lists five purposes of mixing (i.e., triangulation to obtain convergence of findings, complementarity to seek different dimensions of a single phenomenon, development to employ findings from one method to inform implementation of the second method, initiation to seek different dimensions of a single phenomenon to explore contradictions and inconsistencies, and expansion to seek different dimensions of different phenomena). The sampling characteristics of a criterion sample of nine empirical studies representing nine fields (i.e., library science, business, social psychology, social work, psychology, sociology, education, health science, medicine) of the social and behavioral sciences are presented in the next section.

EMPIRICAL STUDIES

To identify the sample of mixed research articles, specific criteria were followed. First, to obtain bibliographic records of empirical mixed research studies published recently, the databases of EBSCO, PRO-QUEST, and PSYCINFO were searched to obtain articles published during a 2½-year period from 2007 to mid-2009. Given this chapter's focus on advanced sampling designs, the keywords *stages* and *multistage* were used to locate studies that had multiple stages, thereby potentially identifying studies elevated in complexity (i.e., multiple numbers of samples and varying types of sampling schemes) in terms of sampling design. To obtain published studies using mixed research approaches, the keywords *mixed methods* and *mixed methods research* were used. In addition, the citations of the selected studies were scrutinized to ascertain if mixed research methodological sources were cited, such as textbooks (e.g., Creswell, 2003; Creswell & Plano Clark, 2007), handbooks (e.g., Tashakkori & Teddlie, 2003a), and published articles (e.g., Greene et al., 1989; Johnson & Onwuegbuzie, 2004). Last, the article was read, and the mixing purpose was identified and noted, thereby substantiating further that the studies were mixed research studies.

Study 1, Business. Kavanagh and Drennan (2008) conducted a concurrent design using multilevel samples (Onwuegbuzie & Collins, 2007) for the quantitative and qualitative phases of the study. The mixing purpose was complementarity (Greene et al., 1989). The student sample of 322 accounting students attending three universities in Australia was surveyed regarding their perceptions and expectations of appropriate work skills. Employers ($n = 28$) who hired accounting students were interviewed in the contexts of individual meetings and focus groups. The qualitative sample (employers) was selected purposively using a criterion scheme, and the

schools that participated in the quantitative phase were selected using a cluster scheme (Miles & Huberman, 1994; Patton, 1990). Both forms of data were produced. The authors did not identify explicitly the emphasis of approach in terms of formulating the conclusions and interpretations.

Study 2, Education. Black, Little, McCoach, Purcell, and Siegle (2008) conducted a 2-year program evaluation of a middle-level academic intervention program. The researchers conducted a concurrent design using multilevel samples (Onwuegbuzie & Collins, 2007). Student samples consisted of two different cohorts (51 students in each cohort) of sixth-grade students enrolled in two randomly selected intervention schools. The comparison sample consisted of 22 students who attended a third school and were taught using the standard curriculum. Quantitative data in the form of questionnaire responses designed to measure students' levels of affect pertaining to the curriculum, as well as report cards and standardized test scores as measures of academic performance levels, were collected from students attending the three schools. Qualitative data in the form of transcribed data obtained from interviews and focus groups were collected from program teachers, coordinators, and principals at the two intervention schools. The mixing purpose was complementarity (Greene et al., 1989). The samples were selected purposively using a multistage purposeful random sampling scheme (Miles & Huberman, 1994; Patton, 1990). The researchers emphasized the quantitative data in terms of formulating conclusions and interpretations.

Study 3, Library Science. Diederich, Dzbor, and Maynard (2007) employed a sequential design using nested samples (Onwuegbuzie & Collins, 2007) to evaluate a program designed to support digital library systems, specifically, semantic Web technologies. The mixing purpose was complementarity (Greene et al., 1989). In Phase 1, researchers administered a questionnaire to all registered users ($n = 240$) associated with 10 institutions (purposive;

self-selected sample) of the support program. In Phase 2, a volunteer sample ($n = 35$) associated with four institutions completed a series of tasks related to the application of the program. Samples for both phases were selected purposively (Miles & Huberman, 1994; Patton, 1990). Data from both phases were integrated and compared with the log files and also compared with evaluation results pertaining to other digital library systems. The authors did not identify explicitly the emphasis of approach in terms of formulating the conclusions and interpretations.

Study 4, Medicine. Craft Morgan and Konrad (2008) executed a concurrent design to conduct a program evaluation of a workforce development program for nursing assistants. The mixing purpose was complementarity (Greene et al., 1989). Data were collected in the forms of longitudinal semistructured interviews (qualitative phase) and survey data (quantitative phase) from multilevel samples (Onwuegbuzie & Collins, 2007). Eight program sites (i.e., purposive; criterion sample) were matched to comparison sites. At the eight program sites, 68 supervisors and 77 nursing assistants participated in the study. At the 10 comparison sites, 85 randomly selected supervisors participated in the study. Quantitative data consisted of responses to organizational questionnaires. Qualitative data were transcribed interviews from 84 managerial or key informants (i.e., purposive; critical case) at both sets of sites. Two forms of data were collected. The authors did not identify explicitly the emphasis of approach in terms of formulating the conclusions and interpretations.

Study 5, Nursing. Sargeant, Valli, Ferrier, and MacLeod (2008) conducted a sequential design using nested samples to assess the impact of a lifestyle counseling workshop on primary care clinicians' practice patterns in terms of attitudes, communication, and counseling skills. The mixing purpose was complementarity (Greene et al., 1989). The qualitative sample was extracted from the

larger sample, thereby representing a nested sample (Onwuegbuzie & Collins, 2007). Quantitative data consisted of questionnaire responses of 43 clinicians who volunteered to participate in the workshop (i.e., purposive; self-selected sample). The questionnaire, distributed at the conclusion of the workshop, asked respondents to identify changes that were being considered after completing the workshop and potential barriers to implementing these changes. Analyses of the questionnaires' responses indicated that 41 attendees intended to make changes in their practice patterns. Three months later, respondents ($n = 41$) were invited to participate in a telephone interview (qualitative phase) to assess specific changes that had been made and to identify factors influencing these changes. Twelve respondents accepted the invitation (purposive, convenience sample) (Miles & Huberman, 1994; Patton, 1990). Both forms of data were produced (quantitative; frequency counts and qualitative data; content analysis). The authors did not identify explicitly the emphasis of approach in terms of formulating the conclusions and interpretations.

Study 6, Public Health. Groleau, Pluye, and Nadeau (2007) conducted a sequential design to identify and assess a community's health status and health behaviors of the members. Groleau et al. used a multistage purposeful random sampling scheme (Miles & Huberman, 1994; Patton, 1990) to select the samples representing the major immigration groups residing in the community. The mixing purpose was development (Greene et al., 1989). The Phase 1 sample (quantitative phase) consisted of 2,400 members of a randomly selected community, who were surveyed by telephone concerning their use of mental health services and possible reasons for not using these services. Participants also completed a questionnaire designed to measure levels of stress. Results of the analyses of Phase 1 data were used to select the samples for the qualitative component. Phase 2 (qualitative phase) was designed to assess the degree to which social and contextual factors impacted health behaviors. Two qualitative studies were conducted. The sample for the first study (*n* = 18) was Vietnamese immigrants, and the second study's sample (*n* = 15) was West Indies immigrants (i.e., purposive critical case sampling scheme). Each participant was required to have experienced stress or a medically unexplained symptom (i.e., critical case). Participants in the Phase 2 sample were interviewed using a semistructured interview protocol. The qualitative sample was extracted from the larger sample, thereby representing a nested sample (Onwuegbuzie & Collins, 2007). A combination of schemes (multistage purposeful random and critical case) was used in the study, and two forms of data were collected (quantitative data, qualitative data). The authors did not identify explicitly the emphasis of approach in terms of formulating the conclusions and interpretations.

Study 7, Psychology. Suldo, Friedrich, White, Farmer, Minch, and Michalowski (2009) conducted a sequential study using nested samples (Onwuegbuzie & Collins, 2007) to assess (a) the types of teacher supports that were associated with adolescents' subjective well-being and (b) students' perceptions of teacher behaviors that were perceived as indicative of either high or low levels of social support. The mixing purpose was complementarity (Greene et al., 1989). Quantitative data consisted of the questionnaire responses of 401 middle school students enrolled in one school. Random selection was used to select students who represented each of the following tracks: gifted, advanced, and general education. The qualitative phase involved the purposive selection of a subset of the 401 students (*n* = 50 students) who were enrolled in either the gifted or general education tracks. The purposive selection of students ensured that both tracks were represented equally in the focus groups. The samples for both phases were selected using a multistage purposeful random sampling scheme (Miles &

Huberman, 1994; Patton, 1990). The authors did not identify explicitly the emphasis of approach in terms of formulating the conclusions and interpretations.

Study 8, Social Work. Waldrop (2007) conducted a two-stage concurrent-equal status design using identical purposive samples (Onwuegbuzie & Collins, 2007) to explore caregiver grief during end-stage care of a family member. The mixing purpose was triangulation (Greene et al., 1989). Quantitative data consisted of questionnaire responses of 30 caregivers who were caring for a terminally ill family member. The caregivers were contacted by the researchers and invited to participate in the study (i.e., purposive; criterion sample; Miles & Huberman, 1994; Patton, 1990). Two questionnaires were administered at Time 1 (during caregiving period) and at Time 2 (about 12 months following the care recipient's death). Qualitative data consisted of caregivers' responses to interview questions regarding the overall experience. Two forms of data were collected, and both forms of data were emphasized in the researcher's conclusions.

Study 9, Sociology. Anderson, Goe, and Weng (2007) used a sequential design using a multistage purposeful scheme (Miles & Huberman, 1994; Patton, 1990) for the quantitative and qualitative phases of a study designed to implement a change analysis of the working-poor population in the north central region of the United States. These researchers conducted a linear panel analysis (quantitative phase) to identify outlier counties (*n* = 1,055 counties) (i.e., purposive; extreme case). In-depth case studies (qualitative phase) of the selected counties (*n* = 112) were conducted. The mixing purpose was development (Greene et al., 1989). Multiple forms of data were collected and represented both quantitative and qualitative data. The authors did not identify explicitly the emphasis of approach in terms of formulating the conclusions and interpretations.

The integrative typology of five criteria was used to classify the nine studies. However, Criterion 3, specifying the type of generalization in terms of the combination of sampling schemes implemented, was not mentioned in the critiqued studies. Furthermore, only two studies (Black et al., 2008; Waldrop, 2007) explicitly met Criterion 5, by specifying clearly the researcher's emphasis on a specific data source in terms of formulating conclusions and interpretations. Omissions of responses to these two criteria compromise legitimation unless the samples are identical, as was the case in the Waldrop (2007) study. *Legitimation,* a term used by Onwuegbuzie and Johnson (2006), refers to the quality of inferences drawn by the researcher from each phase, which are then integrated to develop meta-inferences. *Sample integration,* a term conceptualized by Onwuegbuzie and Johnson (2006) as one of nine legitimation types particular to mixed research design, refers to the extent to which the relationship between the sampling designs for both phases allows the researchers to draw quality meta-inferences.

◆ *Introducing the Inclusive Sampling Model*

In this section, an inclusive sampling model consisting of three components is presented. Component 1 builds on existing sampling typologies to provide a structure and a sampling lexicon, leading to an integrative typology comprising five criteria derived from a content analysis of existing mixed research sampling typologies. These five criteria are presented in Figure 15.2.

Component 2 addresses the degree to which sampling decisions impact various steps of the research process. Onwuegbuzie and Collins (2007) conceptualized the mixed sampling process as including seven steps: (1) determine the mixed goal of the study, (2) formulate the mixed research objective, (3) determine the mixed research purpose, (4) determine the mixed research question, (5) select the mixed research design, (6) select the mixed sampling design, and (7) select the individual sampling schemes and sample sizes per phase.

The mixed researcher's selection of the long-term *goal* of the study (see Newman, Ridenour, Newman, & DeMarco, 2003, for details on the goals of mixing) identifies the type of information that will be collected based on the degree to which it addresses the various interests of stakeholders who will be impacted by the study's research question. Subsequently, the goal guides the mixed researcher to define explicitly a sampling design that will provide the data source for the study. These decisions can reflect one or more of the nine goals pertaining to mixing identified by Newman et al. (2003).

The choices of sampling scheme and sample size are influenced by the study's *objective* relative to the type of generalization pertaining to both external and internal generalizations (e.g., statistical generalization, analytic generalization; case-to-case transferability generalization, naturalistic generalization; Miles & Huberman, 1994; Stake, 2005; Yin, 2009). The researcher's selection of a type of generalization facilitates the choice of the sampling scheme and the determination of the sample size for each phase of the study. Next, the mixed researcher must determine the *purpose* of mixing methods within a study (Greene, 2007; Greene et al., 1989). When formulating sampling decisions, the purpose of mixing is addressed by deciding on the relationship of the samples (Onwuegbuzie & Collins, 2007). For example, addressing the purpose of triangulation likely would lead the mixed researcher to select an identical sample, whereby the same sample members participate in both phases of the study, or the researcher might select a parallel sample, whereby sample members are different, but the sample is drawn from the same population. Data generated by both samples can be analyzed to obtain convergence of findings. Sample selection relative to addressing the purposes of complementarity and initiation likely would lead the mixed researcher to select either a concurrent or sequential sampling design. However, addressing the purposes of development and expansion likely would lead the mixed researcher to include singularly or in various combinations a parallel sample, nested sample, or multilevel sample (Onwuegbuzie & Collins, 2007). The selection of a mixing purpose also should address the rationale for mixing approaches within a study. Collins, Onwuegbuzie, and Sutton (2006) identified the following four rationales for mixing: participant enrichment (recruiting participants appropriate for inclusion within a mixed inquiry), instrument fidelity (determining the appropriateness of existing instruments or development of new instruments within a mixed inquiry), treatment integrity (ensuring fidelity of the intervention within a mixed investigation), and significance enhancement (augmenting interpretation of findings within a mixed inquiry).

Addressing the *research question* by choosing carefully the sampling frame (quantitative) and the sampling boundary (qualitative) ensures that the sampling unit or case will generate an adequate and sufficient data source to enable the mixed researcher to formulate conclusions and interpretations in each phase of the study, which then are integrated into meta-inferences. A key component of mixed *design* is the time orientation of the phases of the study. Therefore, sampling decisions pertaining to the selection of the scheme and sample should reflect the dependent relationship between sampling decisions and the time orientation of the implementation of the phases. Decisions at each of the preceding steps lead the mixed researcher to the selection of the *sampling rationale(s), sampling scheme(s),* and *sample size(s)* per phase.

Concurrent sampling entails conducting the phases of the study independently, and data obtained from the sampling units or cases are collected at the same time or in a close proximal time frame. Sequential sampling involves selecting participants for the first phase (e.g., qualitative) of the study using purposive, or random, or a combination of both types of schemes and using the results to select criteria for selecting the sample of participants for the second phase (e.g., quantitative). Specifying the type of emphasis to be placed on each phase when selecting the sample scheme and sample size leads to informed decisions relative to drawing quality meta-inferences and appropriate generalizations. Table 15.3 presents the seven steps in the mixed research process, accompanied by example questions to guide the mixed researcher when formulating sampling decisions. These questions are not exhaustive; however, they are designed to prompt reflectivity on the part of the mixed researcher concerning the impact of sampling decisions within the mixed research process.

Component 3 presents four criteria addressing specific mixed sampling issues pertinent to the implementation of advanced sampling designs. Advanced sampling designs refer to studies that employ multiple samples and various combinations of sampling schemes, as in the cases of mixed purposeful, multistage purposeful, or random multistage purposeful sample schemes.

When selecting a sample for a mixed inquiry, mixed researchers address various crises, namely, the crises of representation, legitimation, integration, and politics (Collins, Onwuegbuzie, & Jiao, 2006; Onwuegbuzie & Collins, 2007). When selecting a probabilistic sample, representativeness refers to the "degree that the sample accurately represents the population" (Teddlie & Tashakkori, 2009, p. 344). However, statistical inference can be compromised by insufficient power based on

Table 15.3 Questions Relating Directly to Addressing Each Step of the Sampling Process

Goal of the study	What is the goal or long-term aim of this study?
	Who are the stakeholders who will be impacted by this study?
	What sample characteristics (e.g., age, culture, gender, social class) do you perceive will enable you to address the goal of this study?
Objective of the study	What level of generalization do you intend to form based on the conclusions and interpretations derived from both phases of the study?
	What level of emphasis or weight do you intend to place on the findings of each phase of the study?
	In what ways do you think the level of emphasis will impact the type of generalization?
Purpose of the study	To what degree do you think that sample characteristics (e.g., age, culture, gender, social class) will impact the purpose of mixing?
	What sampling design addresses optimally the purpose of mixing within the study?
Research question	To what degree do the samples for the qualitative and quantitative phases of the study generate a credible and sufficient data source, thereby enabling you to address the research question?
Research design	To what degree do the sampling schemes address optimally the design parameters in terms of time order of the approaches and emphasis of approach?
Sampling design	To what degree have you provided rationales for your selections of scheme and sample size per phase of the study?
Selection of sampling scheme	To what degree have you combined both purposive and probability sampling schemes in your study?
Selection of sample size	To what degree do the sample sizes per phase reflect adequate power (quantitative) and the generation of information-rich data (qualitative), thereby leading to formulation of quality inferences?

using sample sizes that are too small and using a sample scheme that limits external validity (Huck, 2000). When working with texts consisting of both words and numbers, representation refers to the researcher's ability to extract adequate information from the text, thereby extracting more meaning from the underlying data. The crisis of representation refers to the dilemma of effectively managing this process by encapsulating the meaning of the lived experiences. As noted by Denzin and Lincoln (2005),

Such experience, it is argued, is created in the social text written by the researcher. This is a representational crisis. It confronts the inescapable problem of representation, but does so within a framework that makes the direct link between experience and text problematic. (p. 19)

The crisis of representation refers to sampling problems that impact quantitative and qualitative sampling, and using both approaches within a single study exacerbates the impact of this crisis. Specifically, the crisis of representation in a mixed research study leads to compromised legitimation, specifically relevant to sample integration (extent to which the relationship between the sampling designs for both phases allows the researchers to draw quality meta-inferences) (Onwuegbuzie & Johnson, 2006). The challenge of achieving sample integration is exemplified by Sandelowski's (1995) observation of a potential dilemma faced by a researcher who has selected a representative sample for the purpose of statistical generalization and the selected sample does not address the "informational purposes" (p. 182) required in the qualitative component. In this scenario, sampling legitimation is compromised, leading to the crisis of integration (i.e., the degree to which the inferences formulated per phase are integrated into a "theoretically consistent meta-inference," thereby achieving integrative efficacy; Teddlie & Tashakkori, 2009, p. 305).

Interpretive consistency is another term used to denote the degree of consistency between the researcher's meta-inferences and the sampling design used in the study (Collins, Onwuegbuzie, & Jiao, 2006; Collins, Onwuegbuzie, & Jiao, 2007). Collins, Onwuegbuzie, and Jiao (2006) conducted a within-case analysis of 42 mixed research studies published in school psychology journals during a 5-year period (2001–2005) to ascertain the degree to which the researchers' meta-inferences were consistent with the sample sizes of each phase of the study. Their results indicated that irrespective of the sample size per phase and the discrepancy between sample sizes per phase, the majority of researchers formulated meta-inferences based on inferences drawn from both phases. Results of the qualitative analyses suggested a degree of interpretive inconsistency in many studies.

Collins et al. (2007) expanded the focus to examine 121 mixed research studies conducted in nine fields representing the social and behavioral sciences to determine the degree to which researchers are formulating appropriate meta-inferences, given the size of the samples. Their analyses revealed that the majority of researchers formulated meta-inferences based on inferences drawn from both phases. Results of the qualitative analyses indicated that sample sizes for the quantitative and qualitative phases were 30 or fewer, and 53.7% of the articles reported meta-inferences representing inappropriate statistical generalizations, thereby suggesting a degree of interpretive inconsistency in these specific studies.

One potential strategy to reconcile interpretive inconsistencies is to implement a "representativeness/saturation trade-off" (Teddlie & Tashakkori, 2009, p. 184). The trade-off occurs when the mixed researcher, for example, decides to place more weight on the representativeness of the quantitative sample to address the requirement of external validity and less weight on the qualitative sample, thereby limiting theoretical saturation. Subsequently, the emphasis on one approach enables the researcher to address either external generalization or transferability.

Last, the role of politics is bi-directionally associated with sampling decisions in terms of the degree to which the researcher's values and assumptions about framing the study and collecting credible data impact sampling decisions. The crisis of politics reflects the degree to which the findings of both phases are presented in a balanced manner and the degree to which these findings are viewed as applicable to other contexts by the consumers of the research (i.e., naturalistic generalization; Stake, 2005). Table 15.4 presents four crises of representation, legitimation, integration, and politics, accompanied by example questions to guide the mixed researcher when formulating sampling decisions for each phase. These questions are not exhaustive; however, they are designed to prompt reflectivity on the part of the mixed researcher concerning the impact of sampling decisions within the mixed research process.

Table 15.4 Possible Questions Relating to Criteria Informing Sampling Decisions

	Quantitative Phase	*Qualitative Phase*
Crisis of Representation	To what extent have you identified and, subsequently, selected a sample that has adequate power to detect statistically significant relationships or differences for the quantitative sample?	What types of techniques have you used to ensure that the qualitative sample's voice or constructions are presented clearly and are bias free? To what extent do the sampling schemes address theoretical validity (Maxwell, 1992) in terms of transference?
Crisis of Legitimation	To what extent do the sampling schemes address the study's objective in terms of generalizability?	To what extent do the sampling schemes address the study's objective in terms of transference?
Crisis of Integration	To what extent is the sample size pertaining to the quantitative phase balanced relative to the study's objective? To what extent is the sample size for the quantitative phase balanced relative to the sample size in the qualitative phase? To what extent does the sampling scheme or combination of schemes selected for the quantitative phase address the research goal, purpose, and research question?	To what extent is the sample size pertaining to the qualitative phase balanced relative to the study's objective? To what extent is the sample size for the qualitative phase balanced relative to the sample size in the quantitative phase? To what extent does the sampling scheme or combination of schemes selected for the qualitative phase address the research goal, purpose, and research question?
Crisis of Politics	To what extent are the findings from the quantitative phase presented clearly and in a balanced manner relative to addressing the goal of the study?	To what extent are the findings from the qualitative phase presented clearly and in a balanced manner relative to addressing the goal of the study?

◆ Conclusions

In this chapter, the reader was presented with guidelines and illustrative examples applicable for selecting sampling schemes and selecting a sample size for each phase of a mixed research study or a monomethod study. To facilitate the sampling process, an inclusive model was introduced. Three components form the inclusive model. Component 1 is an integrative typology, which comprises five criteria that are derived from published mixed sampling typologies. These criteria were used to critique nine mixed research studies representing nine fields in the social and behavioral sciences. Results of the critique indicated that two of the five criteria were not addressed in the majority of the critiqued studies. Specifically, the researchers' choices pertaining to the *type of generalization* in terms of the combination of sampling schemes implemented were not mentioned. In addition, only two of the nine studies stated explicitly the researchers' emphasis on a specific data source in terms of formulating conclusions and interpretations. These omissions are problematic due to the discrepancies in the sample sizes for the quantitative and qualitative phases across eight of the nine studies. Potentially, these omissions can compromise the quality of the researchers' meta-inferences and, subsequently, lead to compromised legitimation.

Although the sample size of the critiqued studies in this chapter is small, the fact that the sampling decisions shaping the nine studies could be categorized using the integrative typology introduced in this chapter begins the process of validating this typology as a useful means for clarifying researchers' sampling decisions. Furthermore, the fact that two

criteria were not addressed systematically in the selected studies provides incremental support for using an inclusive model to guide researchers' sampling decisions.

Component 2 outlined seven steps in the mixed research sampling process, and these steps were accompanied by questions to prompt the mixed researcher to reflect on the impact of sampling decisions at each step. Finally, four quality criteria (Component 3) were presented, and reflective questions were included to document the degree to which the researcher has met these criteria when formulating sampling decisions. It is hoped that this inclusive sampling model will present viable options to researchers when implementing advanced sampling designs encompassing multiple numbers and types of sampling schemes in the conduct of mixed research, in particular, and monomethod research, in general. It also is hoped that this model will contribute to and expand the conversation surrounding sampling decisions in mixed research, leading to an extension of this model by researchers interested in this topic.

Research Questions and Exercises

1. What are the components of a sampling design? Discuss the interrelationship between these components in terms of formulating sampling decisions in a quantitative, a qualitative, and a mixed research study.

2. Write a short essay describing the concept of generalization as a factor impacting sampling decisions. Include in your essay a section that compares and contrasts various forms of generalizations in terms of impacting sampling decisions in a research study.

3. Conduct a Web search and locate two mixed research studies published in the past 2 years that use different types of sampling schemes for the quantitative phase and the qualitative phase. Critique each study in terms of the degree to which the researcher has addressed the five criteria defining the integrative typology described in this chapter.

4. Develop a hypothetical mixed research study and discuss sampling issues at each of the seven steps of the mixed sampling process and strategies you will implement to address each of these issues at each step of the mixed sampling process.

5. Using your hypothetical mixed research study as a context, discuss how you will address each of the four crises impacting sampling decisions in a mixed research inquiry.

◆ References

Anderson, C. D., Goe, W. R., & Weng, C.-Y. (2007). A multi-method research strategy for understanding change in the rate of working poor in the north central region of the United States. *The Review of Regional Studies, 37*(3), 367–391.

Baumgartner, T. A., Strong, C. H., & Hensley, L. D. (2002). *Conducting and reading research in health and human performance* (3rd ed.). New York: McGraw-Hill.

Bernard, H. R. (1995). *Research methods in anthropology.* Walnut Creek, CA: AltaMira.

Black, A. C., Little, C. A., McCoach, D. B., Purcell, J. H., & Siegle, D. (2008). Advancement via individual determination: Method selection in conclusions about program effectiveness. *The Journal of Educational Research, 102*(2), 111–123.

Chiznik, E. W., & Chiznik, A. W. (2002). Are you privileged or oppressed? Students' conceptions of themselves and others. *Urban Education, 40*(2), 116–143.

Cohen, J. (1988). *Statistical power analysis for the behavioral sciences* (2nd ed.). Hillsdale, NJ: Lawrence Erlbaum.

Collins, K. M. T., & O'Cathain, A. (2009). Introduction: Ten points about mixed methods research to be considered by the novice researcher. *International Journal of Multiple Research Approaches, 3,* 2–7.

Collins, K. M. T., Onwuegbuzie, A. J., & Jiao, Q. G. (2006). Prevalence of mixed-methods sampling designs in social science research. *Evaluation & Research in Education, 19,* 83–101.

Collins, K. M. T., Onwuegbuzie, A. J., & Jiao, Q. G. (2007). A mixed methods investigation of mixed methods sampling designs in social and health science research. *Journal of Mixed Methods Research, 1,* 267–294.

Collins, K. M. T., Onwuegbuzie, A. J., & Sutton, I. L. (2006). A model incorporating the rationale and purpose for conducting mixed methods research in special education and beyond. *Learning Disabilities: A Contemporary Journal, 4,* 67–100.

Craft Morgan, J., & Konrad, T. R. (2008). A mixed-method evaluation of a workforce development intervention for nursing assistants in nursing homes: The case of WIN A STEP UP. *The Gerontologist, 48*(Special issue 1), 71–79.

Creswell, J. W. (1998). *Qualitative inquiry and research design: Choosing among five traditions.* Thousand Oaks, CA: Sage.

Creswell, J. W. (2003). *Research design: Qualitative, quantitative, and mixed methods approaches.* Thousand Oaks, CA: Sage.

Creswell, J. W. (2005). *Educational research: Planning, conducting, and evaluating quantitative and qualitative research* (2nd ed.). Upper Saddle River, NJ: Pearson Education.

Creswell, J. W., & Plano Clark, V. (2007). *Designing and conducting mixed methods research.* Thousand Oaks, CA: Sage.

Curtis, S., Gesler, W., Smith, G., & Washburn, S. (2000). Approaches to sampling and case selection in qualitative research: Examples in the geography of health. *Social Science and Medicine, 50,* 1001–1014.

Denzin, N. K., & Lincoln, Y. S. (2005). The discipline and practice of qualitative research. In N. K. Denzin & Y. S. Lincoln (Eds.), The SAGE *handbook of qualitative research* (3rd ed., pp. 1–32). Thousand Oaks, CA: Sage.

Diederich, J., Dzbor, M., & Maynard, D. (2007). REASE—The repository for learning units about the semantic web. *New Review of Hypermedia and Multimedia, 13*(2), 211–237.

Firestone, W. A. (1993). Alternative arguments for generalizing from data, as applied to qualitative research. *Educational Researcher, 2*(4), 16–23.

Glaser, B. G., & Strauss, A. L. (1967). *The discovery of grounded theory: Strategies for qualitative research.* Chicago: Aldine.

Greene, J. C. (2007). *Mixing methods in social inquiry.* San Francisco: Jossey-Bass.

Greene, J. C., Caracelli, V. J., & Graham, W. F. (1989). Toward a conceptual framework for mixed-method evaluation designs. *Educational Evaluation and Policy Analysis, 11,* 255–274.

Groleau, D., Pluye, P., & Nadeau, L. (2007). A mix-method approach to the cultural understanding of distress and the non-use of mental health services. *Journal of Mental Health, 16*(6), 731–741.

Guest, G., Bunce, A., & Johnson, L. (2006). How many interviews are enough? An experiment with data saturation and variability. *Field Methods, 18*(1), 59–82.

Hall, B., & Howard, K. (2008). A synergistic approach. *Journal of Mixed Methods Research, 2,* 248–269.

Huck, S. W. (2000). *Reading statistics and research* (3rd ed.). New York: Longman.

Johnson, R. B., & Christensen, L. (2008). *Educational research: Quantitative, qualitative, and mixed approaches* (3rd ed.). Thousand Oaks, CA: Sage.

Johnson, R. B., & Onwuegbuzie, A. J. (2004). Mixed methods research: A research paradigm whose time has come. *Educational Researcher, 33*(7), 14–26.

Kavanagh, M. H., & Drennan, L. (2008). What skills and attributes does an accounting graduate need? Evidence from student perceptions and employer expectations. *Accounting and Finance, 48,* 279–300.

Kemper, E., Stringfield, S., & Teddlie, C. (2003). Mixed methods sampling strategies in social science research. In A. Tashakkori & C. Teddlie (Eds.), *Handbook of mixed methods in social and behavioral research* (pp. 273–296). Thousand Oaks, CA: Sage.

Kennedy, M. (1979). Generalizing from single case studies. *Evaluation Quarterly, 3,* 661–678.

Krueger, R. A. (1994). *Focus groups: A practical guide for applied research* (2nd ed.). Thousand Oaks, CA: Sage.

Krueger, R. A. (2000). *Focus groups: A practical guide for applied research* (3rd ed.). Thousand Oaks, CA: Sage.

Langford, B. E., Schoenfeld, G., & Izzo, G. (2002). Nominal grouping sessions vs. focus groups. *Qualitative Market Research, 5,* 58–70.

Leech, N. L., & Onwuegbuzie, A. J. (2009). A typology of mixed methods research designs. *Quality and Quantity International Journal of Methodology, 43,* 265–275.

Lincoln, Y. S., & Guba, E. G. (1985). Emerging criteria for quality in quantitative and interpretive research. *Qualitative Inquiry, 1,* 275–289.

Lopez, M., & Tashakkori, A. (2006). Differentiated outcomes of TWBE and TBE on ELLs at different entry levels. *Bilingual Research Journal, 30*(1), 81–103.

Luborsky, M. R., & Rubenstein, R. L. (1995). Sampling qualitative research: Rationale, issues, and methods. *Research on Aging, 17*(1), 89–113.

Maxwell, J. A. (1992). Understanding and validity in qualitative research. *Harvard Educational Review, 62,* 279–299.

Maxwell, J. (1996). *Qualitative research design.* Newbury Park, CA: Sage.

Maxwell, J. (1997). Designing a qualitative study. In L. Bick & D. J. Rog (Eds.), *Handbook of applied social science methods* (pp. 69–100). Thousand Oaks, CA: Sage.

Maxwell, J. A., & Loomis, D. M. (2003). Mixed methods design: An alternative approach. In A. Tashakkori & C. Teddlie (Eds.), *Handbook of mixed methods in social & behavioral research* (pp. 241–272). Thousand Oaks, CA: Sage.

Miles, M. A., & Huberman, A. M. (1994). *Qualitative data analysis: An expanded source book* (2nd ed.). Thousand Oaks, CA: Sage.

Morgan, D. L. (1997). *Focus groups as qualitative research* (2nd ed.). (Qualitative Research Methods, No. 16). Thousand Oaks, CA: Sage.

Morse, J. M. (1994). Designing funded qualitative research. In N. K. Denzin & Y. S. Lincoln (Eds.), *Handbook of qualitative research* (pp. 220–235). Thousand Oaks, CA: Sage.

Newman, I., Ridenour, C. R., Newman, C., & DeMarco, G. M. P., Jr. (2003). A typology of research purposes and its relationship to mixed methods research. In A. Tashakkori & C. Teddlie (Eds.), *Handbook of mixed methods in social and behavioral research* (pp. 167–188). Thousand Oaks, CA: Sage.

Onwuegbuzie, A. J., & Collins, K. M. T. (2007). A typology of mixed methods sampling designs in social science research. *The Qualitative Report, 12*(2), 281–316. Retrieved May 15, 2009, from http://www.nova.edu/ssss/QR/QR12-2/Onwuegbuzie2.pdf

Onwuegbuzie, A. J., Dickinson, W. B., Leech, N. L., & Zoran, A. G. (in press). Toward more rigor in focus group research in stress and coping and beyond: A new mixed research framework for collecting and analyzing focus group data. In G. S. Gates, W. H. Gmelch, & M. Wolverton (Series Eds.) & K. M. T. Collins, A. J. Onwuegbuzie, & Q. G. Jiao (Vol. Eds.), *The research on stress and coping in education series: Vol. 5. Toward a broader understanding of stress and coping: Mixed methods approaches* (pp. 243–286). Charlotte, NC: Information Age Publishing.

Onwuegbuzie, A. J., Jiao, Q. G., & Bostick, S. L. (2004). *Library anxiety: Theory, research, and applications*. Lanham, MD: Scarecrow Press.

Onwuegbuzie, A. J., & Johnson, R. B. (2006). The validity issue in mixed research. *Research in the Schools, 13*(1), 48–63.

Onwuegbuzie, A. J., & Leech, N. L. (2007a). A call for qualitative power analyses. *Quality & Quantity, 41*, 105–121.

Onwuegbuzie, A. J., & Leech, N. L. (2007b). Sampling design in qualitative research: Making the sampling process more public. *The Qualitative Report, 12*(2), 238–254. Retrieved May 15, 2009, from http://www.nova.edu/ssss/QR/QR12-2/Onwuegbuzie1.pdf

Patton, M. Q. (1990). *Qualitative research and evaluation methods* (2nd ed.). Newbury Park, CA: Sage.

Patton, M. Q. (2002). *Qualitative research and evaluation methods* (3rd ed.). Thousand Oaks, CA: Sage.

Ragin, C. C. (1987). *The comparative method*. Berkeley: University of California Press.

Ryan, G., & Bernard, H. R. (2003). Techniques to identify themes. *Field Methods, 15*, 85–109.

Sandelowski, M. (1995). Focus on qualitative methods: Sample size in qualitative research. *Research in Nursing, 18*, 179–183.

Sandelowski, M. (2000). Focus on research methods: Combining qualitative and quantitative sampling, data collection, and analysis techniques in mixed-method studies. *Research in Nursing & Health, 23*, 246–255.

Sargeant, J., Valli, M., Ferrier, S., & MacLeod, H. (2008). Lifestyle counseling in primary care: Opportunities and challenges for changing practice. *Medical Teacher, 30*, 185–191.

Stake, R. E. (2005). Qualitative case studies. In N. K. Denzin & Y. S. Lincoln (Eds.), *The SAGE handbook of qualitative research* (3rd ed., pp. 443–466). Thousand Oaks, CA: Sage.

Stake, R. E., & Trumbull, D. J. (1982). Naturalistic generalizations. *Review Journal of Philosophy and Social Science, 7*, 3–12.

Suldo, S. M., Friedrich, A. A., White, T., Farmer, J., Minch, D., & Michalowski, J. (2009). Teacher support and adolescents' subjective well-being: A mixed-methods investigation. *School Psychology Review, 38*(1), 67–85.

Tashakkori, A., & Teddlie, C. (Eds.). (2003a). *Handbook of mixed methods in social & behavioral research*. Thousand Oaks, CA: Sage.

Tashakkori, A., & Teddlie, C. (2003b). The past and future of mixed methods research: From data triangulation to mixed model designs. In A. Tashakkori & C. Teddlie (Eds.), *Handbook of mixed methods in social and behavioral research* (pp. 671–702). Thousand Oaks, CA: Sage.

Teddlie, C., & Tashakkori, A. (2006). A general typology of research designs featuring mixed methods. *Research in the Schools, 13*(1), 12–28.

Teddlie, C., & Tashakkori, A. (2009). *Foundations of mixed methods research: Integrating quantitative and qualitative approaches in the social and behavioral sciences*. Thousand Oaks, CA: Sage.

Teddlie, C., & Yu, F. (2007). Mixed methods sampling: A typology with examples. *Journal of Mixed Methods Research, 1*, 77–100.

Waldrop, D. P. (2007). Caregiver grief in terminal illness and bereavement: A mixed-methods study. *Health & Social Work, 32*(3), 197–206.

Wehlage, G. (1981). The purpose of generalization in field-study research. In T. Popkewitz & R. Tabachnik (Eds.), *The study of schooling* (pp. 211–226). New York: Praeger.

Yin, R. K. (1991). *Applications of case study research*. Washington, DC: Cosmos Corp.

Yin, R. K. (2009). *Case study research: Design and methods* (4th ed.). Thousand Oaks, CA: Sage.

16

HERMENEUTIC CONTENT ANALYSIS

Textual and Audiovisual Analyses Within a Mixed Methods Framework

◆ Manfred Max Bergman

Objectives

After completing this chapter, you should be able to

- recognize the wealth of analytical potential in non-numerical data;

- describe the basics of qualitative and quantitative content analysis;

- explain why coding is a central component of qualitative and quantitative content analysis;

- describe how to apply a mixed methods design on textual material;

- explain the basic steps of hermeneutic content analysis (HCA);

- explain two special variants of HCA, thematic analysis with HCA (HCA-T) and causal analysis with HCA (HCA-C); and

- describe the limitations of HCA and recognize the potential for theoretical and empirical extension.

The two traditions of content analysis—qualitative and quantitative—have a long history in the social and related sciences, even though their individual potential, as well as their possible combination, within a mixed methods framework, has not been explored to date. This chapter introduces a mixed methods framework for content analysis, termed *hermeneutic content analysis* (HCA), in which the scope and applicability of content analysis is expanded to include explicitly the application of qualitative and quantitative methods to non-numerical data. The complex constructs *qualitative methods* and *quantitative methods* refer to data *analysis* techniques, that is, to research that applies theory-based and systematic analysis of data using nonstatistical and statistical analysis methods, respectively. Extending this terminology to data *collection* techniques, that is, interviews, focus groups, surveys, and so on, is inappropriate because data collection methods are predominantly independent from data analysis methods (see Bergman, 2008b, for an extended discussion). Ontological and epistemological positions to HCA are covered, as are two variants: thematic analysis with HCA (HCA-T) and causal analysis with HCA (HCA-C). As a family of mixed methods approaches, HCA can be applied within a constructivist, interpretive, or (post)-positivist framework. This form of mixed methods research illustrates innovative ways to combine qualitative and quantitative methods in a more integrated and consistent way. Furthermore, it outlines ways to analyze visual and other non-numerical and nontextual data in a mixed methods framework.

Endeavoring to differentiate qualitative from quantitative methods by claiming that qualitative methods are about words whereas quantitative methods are about numbers is an oft-cited, nicely parsimonious, but ultimately incorrect and misleading attempt to distinguish between the two families of research methods. The lesser problem with this statement is that it does not explicitly encompass the application of qualitative methods to pictures, audio and video data, architectural styles, symbols, and so on. More important, it incorrectly implies that quantitative methods cannot be applied to these types of data. The even more significant problem of this and other attempts to differentiate qualitative from quantitative methods (e.g., Creswell, 2003; Creswell & Plano Clark, 2006; Tashakkori &Teddlie, 1998, 2003) is that such conceptualizations delimit the possibilities of a greater and possibly more interesting range of methodological applications.[1] In addition, such differentiation attempts often lead to inconsistencies in that the theorizing about qualitative and quantitative methods, especially in relation to ontological and epistemological considerations, is often contradictory to their application in substantive research (see Bergman, 2008a, 2008b, for a more extensive discussion). In this regard, contemporary theorizations and applications of mixed methods designs may reveal innovative ways to integrate representatives of the two method families that have been considered incompatible in the past. From this perspective, mixed methods research has the potential for a radical reconceptualization of the range of applications of qualitative and quantitative methods. In other words, while mixed methods research designs are often considered a niche product in the social science research landscape, they may just revolutionize the conceptualization and execution of mono-method research in the social and related sciences.

In this chapter, I will summarize some of the central tenets of quantitative and qualitative content analysis, review initial attempts to integrate qualitative and quantitative content analysis, and then introduce HCA as a special form of mixed methods research. HCA essentially consists of a group of research designs that combine qualitative and quantitative analysis techniques to a single body of textual, audiovisual, and other non-numerical data. In this text, HCA will be explored in relation to two variants: thematic analysis (HCA-T) and causal analysis (HCA-C), although HCA can be easily extended to include social network analysis (HCA-N), ethnography (HCA-E), and discourse analysis (HCA-D).

◆ Content Analysis

The analysis of the content and its associated meaning of textual, audio, pictorial, and video data have a long and eminent history in the social sciences, possibly starting with Sigmund Freud's analyses of dreams, art, myths, religion, culture, and so on. At least since the 1940s, researchers have recognized the value of textual data from newspapers, political speeches, television, advertising, and other sources. In particular, communication studies established an important early tradition in content analysis, and even in its seminal stages, arguments raged for and against a qualitative or quantitative approach to textual content analysis.

The quantitative tradition was strongly influenced by the desire to apply reliability and validity criteria borrowed from psychometrics and adapted, sometimes unconvincingly, to the analysis of text. From this approach to textual analysis, reliability, especially inter-rater or intercoder reliability, became an important goal in the quest to objectively represent the meaning content of non-numerical data within a set of statistical frequencies and coefficients. Indeed, Berelson (1952) proposed that "by definition, content analysis must be objective" (p. 171), and, given that reliable and systematic analyses of textual content can be achieved only by the application of statistics, at least according to the author, the only objective analysis of content of text must be accomplished via quantitative analysis. This argument, of course, is circular. In response, Berelson's contemporary, Kracauer (1952), stated:

> Many quantitative investigations include frequency counts which rest on uncertain ground. . . . Probabilities are calculated; correlations are established and interpreted. Since these operations evolve on a mathematical plane—that is, without further recourse to the content analyzed—it is possible that their results are more inaccurate and oblique and less truly representative of the communication than are the doubtful counts from which they take root. (p. 633)

Yet even in the 1950s, the qualitative approach to content analysis was criticized as impressionistic, lacking in scientific rigor, and unobjective, although even the most quantitatively oriented researchers admitted that the initial stages of quantitative content analysis must rely on nonstatistical methods. Berelson and Lazarsfeld (1948), for example, admitted that "general subjective impressions" must be used to formulate the "categories" (pp. 115–117), that is, codes, which would be subsequently submitted to statistical analysis.

The goals of quantitative content analysis as outlined by Berelson in the 1950s are to a large extent still in operation in contemporary quantitative content analysis (e.g., Krippendorff, 2004). Developments in quantitative content analysis in the past decades focused mostly on the development of statistical analysis options in dedicated quantitative content analysis software packages (e.g., Concordance, Diction, DIMAP, General Inquirer, HAMLET, INTEXT, TEXTPACK, TextSmart, and WordStat), as well as on automated routines for words, phrases, or sentences in relation to disambiguation, that is, selecting the correct meaning from multiple possibilities in relation to homophony (different but similar sounding words), homography (different meanings of words with the same spelling), and polysemy (related meanings of identical words);

lemmatization, that is, grouping together different words or phrases that are similar or equal in meaning; grammatical tagging, that is, automatically assigning the correct grammatical class; and so on (Brekke, 1991; Butler, 1985). This theoretical and conceptual inertia produced a consistent approach to the quantitative analysis of text but also prevented quantitative content analysis from evolving and playing a more important role in contemporary social science research. With few exceptions (e.g., Mayring, 2000, 2002; Strauss & Corbin, 1998), most approaches in contemporary qualitative content analysis, in contrast, have integrated at least some postmodern and poststructural tenets from the 1980s onward and have thus become largely incompatible with quantitative approaches to content analysis, particularly in relation to their respective ontological and epistemological positions.

QUANTITATIVE CONTENT ANALYSIS

In quantitative content analysis, textual and audiovisual material is coded in order to subject counts of words, phrases, or images to statistical analysis. A number of reasons led researchers to apply statistical analyses to textual material. These included the desire to offer an objective description of text content; to describe communication trends over time, including topics and their shifting focus and relevance; to compare textual content internationally or across groups; to identify or compare communication styles; to compare actual with intended content; and to formally test hypotheses relating to symbolic and cultural issues (Berelson, 1952; cf. Holsti, 1969). For example, Kunkel and his colleagues (1999) coded and counted the number of "sexual situations" in a sample of 1,351 U.S. American television shows across 10 television channels between 1997 and 1998 (i.e., kissing, touching, using the word *sex* in the dialogue, implied or depicted sexual intercourse—one can only imagine

the intense discussions and attempts to operationally define what kind of kiss or touch must be clearly construed as sexual). Based on these counts, the researchers reported that 53% of all shows contain sexual material, averaging three "scenes with sex" per hour. These consisted of "passionate kissing" (50%), "physical flirting" (26%), "sexual intercourse implied" (12%), "intimate touching" (7%), and "sexual intercourse depicted" (3%). Soap operas, movies, and talk shows had the highest frequency of sexual content (85%, 83%, and 78%, respectively), while reality shows had the lowest frequency of sexual content (23%). Such data are often subjected to various bivariate and multivariate statistical analyses in an attempt to generalize findings to a larger population.

Apart from estimating population parameters, the main and highly problematic justification for using statistics on nonnumeric material includes the desire for scientific rigor in text analysis in the sense that statistical analyses, particularly in attempting to adapt reliability and validity measures as established in psychometrics, would automatically increase the scientific value of the work. In this context, terms such as *rigorous, objective,* and *scientific,* or Berelson's demand for objective analysis of the content of text, had a tremendous influence on subsequent endeavors in this vein (e.g., Holsti, 1969; Kelly & Stone, 1975; Krippendorff, 2004; Stone, Dunphy, Smith, & Ogilvie, 1966; Weber, 1990). Weber (1990), for example, states that "to make valid inferences from the text, it is important that the classification procedure be reliable in the sense of being consistent: Different people should code the same text in the same way" (p. 12). This is a good example of the bending of psychometric terminology: Inter-rater reliability is a necessary but insufficient condition for various forms of validity. A convergence of coding results in relation to the content of a text does in no way constitute a valid summary of the meaning of a text. Inter-rater reliability can easily be manipulated by, first, selecting raters who share a particular ideology or viewpoint of the researcher; second, training them carefully; and third, creating a simplistic coding framework. In addition, there are many forms of reliability that are not satisfied by a convergence of coding results. Finally, one could discuss the notion of validity in relation to making inferences from texts, not only because there are many forms of validity but also because of the questionable link between a statistical coefficient expressing the closeness of two or more raters to each other's coding and, if we were interested in construct validity, the degree to which a particular study assesses the specific concept that the researcher is attempting to measure.

Beyond attempts to validate the results of a quantitative analysis by using statistics, quantitative content analysts also stress the need for systematicity and standardized research processes. For instance, Krippendorff (2004), as one of the leading experts in quantitative content analysis, proposes five processes in the analysis of text content:

Unitizing: Identifying the units of analyses, such as words, phrases, sentences, responses to an interview question, texts, website content, blogs, articles, etc. In the study cited above, the units of analysis were television shows between 1997 and 1998.

Sampling: Selecting from a study population those units, which will be subjected to the analysis. As it would not have been feasible to study all shows across all television channels, Kunkel and his colleagues sampled among stations and television shows within a specific time period.

Reducing: The content of non-numerical data is reduced to its "essentials" by coding and statistical analysis. Sexual content was reduced to a few dimensions, which were, first, operationally defined,

second, coded, and, third, summarized by employing simple univariate statistics.

Inferring: The frequency counts of the coded material and other statistical information about the phenomena under investigation are linked to the research question and the context, within which the material is located.

Narrating: The results of the study are communicated narratively in reports, journals, and other outlets. In the above cited study, the results from the quantitative content analysis were published as a research report. (Kunkel et al., 1999)

It is of course possible to conduct far more complex studies within a quantitative content analysis framework. Brier's (2007) HAMLET II is a particularly sophisticated software package for quantitative content analysis in the social and related sciences. As with other packages of its kind, the initial task for the researcher is to subdivide the textual material into hermeneutic units (also referred to as context or analytic units; also unitizing as described above). Units can be paragraphs, Web sites, particular speeches or portions of speeches, interview responses to a specific question, and so on. Within these hermeneutic units are identified a set of significant words, phrases, or expressions, that is, text elements relevant to the research question or focus, which occur within the textual material to be studied. These are referred to as *codes* (also known as *indices* or *nodes*). The codes can be clustered into themes (also referred to as coding families or thematic categories). Codes and their corresponding themes are assembled in a dictionary or vocabulary list. For example, within an interview situation, interviewees may be asked about the differences in relationships between men and women. Responses may include statements such as "my husband never speaks to me about things that matter" or "when he is angry, he uses the silent treatment on me." The first step in analyzing this material with HAMLET II is to define the hermeneutic units, which, in this case, may be the responses to a particular question by each of the interviewees, including responses to probes associated with these questions. Based on the transcribed interview material, the researcher may then identify and attribute the keywords *speak* and *silent* to a theme relating to communication and consequently assign these codes to the thematic heading "communication" within the dictionary. A second theme may be "male," and the codes *husband* and *he* would be included in this coding theme. Thus, there are two themes, "male" and "communication," which, in this illustrative example, consist of the codes *husband* and *he,* as well as *speak* and *silent,* respectively. Dictionaries can become quite extensive; they may include hundreds of themes and subthemes, as well as thousands of codes. Obviously, the number of necessary themes will depend on the focus of the research, the quality of the non-numerical material to be analyzed, and the resources and personal style of the researcher. In the best cases, a coding scheme should be as parsimonious as possible, cover as much variation in relation to the research focus as necessary, and be replicable and interpretable. In the worst cases, researchers develop a tremendously complex coding scheme, which is confused with analysis and is more reflective of the intellectual capacity and idiosyncrasy of its creator.

HAMLET II, like other programs of its kind, trawls through text material to identify the occurrence of codes as prespecified within the dictionary. The strengths of this package, however, are its ability to work with themes that are not part of the explicit vocabulary in the text, that is, from the example above, "male" and "communication," and its analytic sophistication once the codes have been identified. HAMLET II does not simply transform the identified codes into variables for subsequent use in conventional statistical analysis, for example, measures of association and regression analyses. Instead, the identified occurrences can be transformed into a joint frequencies matrix or co-occurrence matrix, that is, a co-occurrence of the themes "male" and "communication" or its associated codes, which can be used for a large number of dimensional analyses, including many multidimensional scaling techniques from Coxon's (2004; Coxon, Brier, & Hawkins, 2004) NewMDSX program. In other words, a co-occurrence of codes or coding themes from a set of textual data can be transformed into multidimensional spatial or geometric relationships. The strength of this form of analysis is that it goes beyond the examination of the strength of associations between codes and themes by visualizing and dimensionalizing the complexity of meaning within non-numerical material.

Standard analytic routines in quantitative content analysis in HAMLET II include listing all words occurring in a specified text, sorting by frequency (WORDLIST), comparing lists of words shared by pairs of texts (COMPARE), displaying the word distribution and sentence length of a text (PROFILE), and providing keyword-in-context (KWIC). Beyond these, it is possible to examine the structure of word, phrase, or thematic joint frequencies with hierarchical and nonhierarchical cluster analysis, nonmetric multidimensional scaling procedures (MINISSA), an individual-differences scaling procedure (INDSCAL), and Procrustean individual-differences scaling (PINDIS), the latter comparing differences in occurrences and co-occurrences of codes and themes between different texts.

Although limited in relation to understanding and interpreting the meaning of text, quantitative content analyses, particularly in relation to modern visualization and scaling methods, provide a unique insight into the structure of the content of text that is not possible with qualitative analyses. This lengthy description of the quantitative content analysis software HAMLET II forms part of an analytic step in HCA, as will be discussed below.

QUALITATIVE CONTENT ANALYSIS

Initially, the goals of qualitative content analysis, as conceptualized by Kracauer (1952), were not far removed from those of quantitative content analysis: an accurate description of the content of text or, in the early stages, of communication messages. Kracauer, too, aimed for some form of objectivity in the assessment of the content of textual material. Where he differed with his quantitatively oriented colleagues was in the way to achieve this. He emphasized, for instance, that complex communications "reverberate with so many latent meanings that to isolate their manifest content and describe it in a 'straight' [i.e., statistical] manner is not only almost impossible, but can hardly be expected to yield significant results" (p. 638). In the same article, he wrote:

Unlike quantitative techniques, which draw guiltily upon hasty and incomplete impressionistic judgments, qualitative analysis is frankly and resolutely impressionistic. And it is precisely because of its resolute impressionism, that qualitative analysis may attain to an accuracy which quantitative techniques, with their undercurrent of impressionistic short cuts, cannot hope to achieve. Carrying its explorations beyond the point at which many content analysis investigations prematurely stop, as if fearful of drifting too far from the secure haven of statistics, qualitative exegesis is indeed capable of classifications and descriptions which conform far more closely to the text than those commonly produced by quantitative analysis. (p. 640)

In the past decades, qualitative content analysis has become quite heterogeneous in its assumptions, explicit goals, analytic process, and inference. Some qualitative approaches to content analysis attempt to get even closer to some "actual" meaning within a text, whereas other approaches recognize the inherently interpretive nature of textual analysis and have integrated post-structural and postmodern ideas into the qualitative research process, while concurrently and explicitly rejecting ontological and epistemological assumptions embedded in traditional quantitative content analysis.

Objectivist Traditions in Qualitative Content Analysis

Some variants of grounded theory are closely associated with the objectivist tradition of qualitative content analysis. Charmaz and Mitchell (2001) succinctly summarize the commonalities of all grounded theory traditions:

(a) simultaneous data collection and analysis, (b) pursuit of emergent themes through early data analysis, (c) discovery of basic social processes within the data, (d) inductive construction of abstract categories that explain and synthesize processes, (e) sampling to refine the categories through comparative processes, and (f) integration of categories into a theoretical framework that specifies causes, conditions, and consequences of the studies processes. (p. 160)

Connected to these, there are four stages of analysis: codes (identification of "anchors" within the data); concepts (grouping codes based on similarities to each other); categories (grouping concepts based on similarities to each other); and theory (explanations that may connect meaningfully the emergent categories).

The objectivist tradition of grounded theory, represented particularly by Strauss (e.g., Corbin & Strauss, 1990; Strauss & Corbin, 1998), who focused on systematicity and validation criteria for the coding and categorizing processes, assumed an ontological and epistemological position of data comparable to the postpositivistic tenets of quantitative content analysis: that data exist in an identifiable reality, an objectifiable world; that they represent knowable facts; and that they can be studied objectively. Although Straussian grounded theory is founded in symbolic interactionism, the interpretation of actors' situations and experiences is still understood as uniquely identifiable. By careful application of grounded theory and its associated research methods, the unbiased researcher ought to be able to uncover meaning correctly. In other words, while the sense-making process of Strauss's actors is framed within a constructivistic perspective—that actors construct meaning based on interpretations within particular interactions in situ—the identification of such meaning from a grounded theory perspective is believed to be uniquely identifiable by a rigorous application of systematic and validating research steps (e.g., Corbin & Strauss, 1990; Strauss & Corbin, 1998).

Beyond conventional attempts to apply validity and reliability criteria, quality of analysis in the qualitative tradition is often assessed with concepts such as credibility, trustworthiness, accountability, peer auditing, explicit coding frame and systematic coding, member checks, and reflexivity (e.g., Denzin & Lincoln, 2005; Flick, 2007; Seale, 1999).

Interpretive Traditions in Qualitative Content Analysis

Few qualitative research methods could be clearly identified as belonging to the family of content analysis. However, many qualitative approaches focus on the identification of meaning based on the content of the non-numerical material. Thus, the following examples will illustrate approaches that share similarities with an interpretive approach to qualitative content analysis.

In the latter part of their works on grounded theory, Strauss focused primarily on systematic and reliable coding techniques, while Glaser (1978, 1992) emphasized interpretation, context, the emergence of theory, and the influence of the researcher on the research results. Accordingly, coding and theory building in the Glaserian version of grounded theory is less procedurally constrained and prescriptive. The quality criteria

from this perspective are fit, the closeness of the relationship between the codes and categories; relevance, which addresses concerns of the participants beyond mere academic interests; workability, the ability of an emergent theory to explain or solve a problem under investigation; and modifiability, adjustability of the emergent theory to new data and theoretical insights (Glaser, 1978, 1992, 1998).

Interpretation of meaning is based not only on the content of text, but also on the context within which text was produced and within which the researcher studies the text. According to Van Dijk (1988), for example, "Textual dimensions account for the structures of discourse at various levels of description. Contextual dimensions relate these structural descriptions to various properties of context, such as cognitive processes and representations or sociocultural factors" (p. 25). Thus, truth claims embedded in the text, or discursive strategies employed to support or undermine truth claims—how factuality, order, and causality are manufactured rhetorically with words and language devices within text—can be the object of an interpretive content analysis, along with the actors within a narrative, the role that the narrative attributes to them, the identities allotted to them within the text, and their bounded agency within institutional or structural constraints. These possible foci must, of course, be tied to a specific theoretical framework and research theme or question, which would justify this type of approach and analysis.

Computer-Assisted Qualitative Data Analysis Software (CAQDAS)

Numerous software packages have emerged to simplify, organize, and systematize the almost inherently complex process of qualitative research (e.g., Atlas.ti, The Ethnograph, NUD*IST, now replaced by NVivo, winMAX, now MAXQDA). However, the coding process based on the increasing options and sophistication of computer-assisted qualitative data analysis software (CAQDAS)[2] may have inadvertent consequences. The increasing number of analytic features embedded in CAQDAS programs not only assist in organizing the emergent structure of the qualitative research process, but also influence the pre-results in the form of the systematization of the coding process of textual material, as well as the results from the coding process itself. In some applications, the research process and its output may share important characteristics with quantitatively oriented research. Some researchers have welcomed this development because it tends to introduce into the qualitative research process clear steps, procedures, rules, and so on, thus creating the impression that qualitative research, conducted in this way, is procedurally approaching quantitative. Approaching naïve positivism, a rule-based qualitative research process is believed by some to be more scientific. Such research, however, may simultaneously lose the flexibility, potential of discovery, and creativity that are usually qualitative research's greatest strength. In the end, the degree of systematization of the analytic process in qualitative content analysis—with or without CAQDAS—is strongly linked to the needs, habits, and style of the researcher, as well as the characteristics of the nonnumerical data to be analyzed and the research purpose and focus. But employing the numerous options of a CAQDAS program in the hope of rendering the analysis and its results more scientific, rigorous, and valid will not work. Instead, most programs are best used as an indexing and organizing tool, and most modern programs will indeed help organize and synthesize results, particularly for large, complex, or multimedia nonnumerical data sets. What may constrain a more in-depth qualitative analysis due to the way CAQDAS programs are structured and marketed also has an advantage in that it may create alternative analysis opportunities: Due in part to the systematization of coding, classifying, and categorizing with CAQDAS programs, combining qualitative and quantitative content analyses is beginning to find application in the social and related sciences.

◆ Content Analysis Within a Mixed Methods Framework

Qualitative and quantitative content analyses have been part of the social science methodology arsenal since at least the 1950s, but surprisingly, no systematic attempts have been made to bring the two traditions together within a mixed methods framework. This is due in part to different research traditions, which tend to be connected to incompatible ontological and epistemological positions often cited in the relevant literature. The considerable potential for a number of different forms of content analyses in a mixed methods framework remains yet undiscovered. One of such possibilities is presented here in the form of HCA.

CONVENTIONAL CONTENT ANALYSIS WITHIN A MIXED METHODS FRAMEWORK

A more conventional mixed methods application would proceed by initially conducting some form of thematic analysis of textual material. Once meaningful codes or taxonomies of codes have been identified according to the research question or theme, they are at least partially transformed into variables for statistical analysis. The most typical ways to transform codes into variables are the following:

Presence-absence coding or dichotomous coding: The most basic way to transform a coding scheme into variables is the identification of the presence or absence of a code or theme within a given hermeneutic unit. For instance, the absence of codes relating to the coding theme "communication" within a set of units could be coded as a *0*, while its presence in other hermeneutic units could be coded as a *1*. This type of coding would yield a dichotomous variable but it is insensitive to how often a code occurred within a hermeneutic unit.

Frequency coding or frequency axial coding (Strauss & Corbin, 1998): This type of transformation from codes into variables takes into consideration the frequency, or the number of occurrences of a particular code within a given hermeneutic unit. Although this form of coding may be more precise in measuring the occurrence of the code in a hermeneutic unit, it is not quite clear how significant the frequency of an occurrence is, compared with whether or not it occurred.

Intensity coding or intensity axial coding (Strauss & Corbin, 1998): At the basis of this transformation lies the subjective judgment of the coder. In this sense, a judge or a group of judges evaluates subjectively the intensity with which a code appears in the text. This usually takes the form of a 3- to 5-point ordinal scale.[3] Inter-rater or intercoder reliability measures are used to assess the degree of agreement between the judges, although it should be stated here that high inter-rater reliability is not an indication of validity (just because "expert" raters agree does not mean that they are right—cf. the flat earth theory a few centuries ago).

Beyond the concern about the significance of how often a code occurs, or whether the subjective assessment of judges yields precise and usable additional information in the analysis of textual material, one other limitation needs to be mentioned in this transformation process—that of decontextualization and the resulting loss of meaning. One of the particular strengths of qualitative research in understanding and interpreting non-numerical material is its potential closeness to the contexts within which research is conducted and within which non-numerical material is produced, analyzed, and interpreted. However, in the process of coding—selecting "relevant" occurrences from a text, grouping codes into themes, transforming themes into variables, and analyzing patterns between themes statistically—important aspects of the context may be neglected. In the worst case, the study may yield misleading results precisely because, in this reductionist approach,

many important aspects of the context have been neglected. Contextualization may be maintained to some degree when identification of codes and combination into themes are always conducted in explicit recognition of the context of the researcher, the research subject, and the nature of the non-numerical material. Recontextualization may be partially accomplished by interpreting the statistical results in conjunction with the complex textual material and its contexts as mentioned above. In other words, it would not make much sense to interpret the statistical coefficients or structures without returning to the non-numerical data and the conditions of their production and selection, which yielded the codes in the first place.

HERMENEUTIC CONTENT ANALYSIS

HCA is a group of analyses designed for non-numerical data. Its main characteristics are described here.

Hermeneutics as an ontological and epistemological framework. The guiding assumption of HCA is that the content and associated meanings of the non-numerical material may never be identified unequivocally. This is due in part to the fact that the textual material as a whole can be understood only by studying some of its parts, while the parts under study can be understood only in relation to the whole, yet, the meaning of the parts does not unequivocally represent the meaning of the whole. In addition, all research is bounded by the contextualized researcher and the contextualized research theme or question (e.g., Bergman & Coxon, 2005). All research activities, from conceptualization to interpretation of analytic results, are always linked and must therefore be understood in relation to their cultural, historical, political, and social contexts. Finally, there is no content and meaning within the data in the absence of a research focus or question, allowing for multiple contents and meanings of the same material.

An initial qualitative content analysis. In conjunction with a research focus, this analysis identifies, within the non-numerical material and in alignment with the hermeneutic limits as outlined above, themes, concepts, components, identities, agents, interactions, and structures relevant to the research focus or question. The results of the analysis are of value in themselves and, in principle, may not need further analysis.

A quantitative dimensional analysis. This may be based on a joint frequency matrix from a subsample of the elements identified in the initial qualitative content analysis. The selection of the subsample of elements to be analyzed quantitatively will depend (a) on a substantive justification, including exploration, theory building, and hypothesis testing; and (b) the suitability of the elements for statistical analysis. Various types of multidimensional scaling procedures can be performed from a relevant matrix, such as nonmetric multidimensional scaling procedures (MINISSA), individual-differences scaling procedures (INDSCAL), Procrustean individual-differences scaling (PINDIS), or any form of correspondence

analysis. This second research step clearly decontextualizes the elements identified in the previous step to examine the latent structure and patterns between them. Patterns identified in this way cannot usually be observed with qualitative methods, so this set of results is likely to add additional insights into the content and meaning structure embedded in the non-numerical data. Using mixed methods terminology, this second, quantitative part of the analysis may pursue aims relating to convergence between qualitative and quantitative results, but its particular interest will lie with complementarity, where the results from the quantitative analysis complement and provide additional insights to the interpretation of the results of the qualitative part.

A second recontextualizing qualitative analysis. This step will assist in the interpretation of the results from the dimensional analysis by (a) associating the findings and the context as identified in the first research step and (b) employing post hoc exploratory analyses in the original nontextual material.

Figure 16.1 Simplified Three-Step Analysis in Hermeneutic Content Analysis

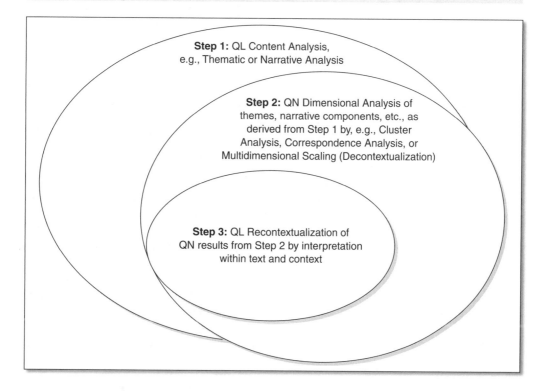

This step integrates the results from the qualitative content analysis with the patterns associated with the quantitative dimensional analysis of the codes identified in the first step. Furthermore, integration takes place within the context of the original textual material.

◆ *Conceptual and Philosophical Landscape*

Although HCA is somewhat connected to a particular ontological and epistemological position, in that the results of the analysis of the non-numerical material are by their nature hermeneutically framed, it is flexible enough to accommodate different positions within constructivist, interpretive, or (post)-positivist theory. One of its advantages in this regard is that HCA is not connected to a vague formulation of pragmatism but can be used consistently within different ontological and epistemological positions.

ONTOLOGICAL CONSIDERATIONS

Ontologically, mixed methods research is faced with a conundrum. Much of the literature on qualitative and quantitative research methods claims an incompatibility, often termed the Incompatibility Thesis and the thus resulting Paradigm War, in the sense that qualitative methods ostensibly are conducted with the idea that there is no reality, there are multiple realities, or reality is constructed or co-constructed by the researchers and their subject. Quantitative research, in contrast, ostensibly is conducted under the assumption that there is one single and objectifiable reality. Traditionally, mixed methods researchers get around this problem in three ways: They ignore the problem and get on with the research, they adopt a vague notion of pragmatism (e.g., Maxcy, 2003), or they invite tremendous inconsistencies into their design by claiming to work within the ontological constraint of one single

reality when they conduct their statistical analysis, and then switching to the no multiple-reality option when conducting the qualitative part. A fourth and least problematic solution would be to dissociate qualitative and quantitative methods from constructivism and post-positivism, as it is indeed possible to be either a constructivist or a (post)positivist and still conduct qualitative and quantitative research (e.g., Bergman, 2008a). So while HCA is designed to be conducted within a mild form of constructivism, there is nothing wrong with adapting the design to pursue more objectivistic and (post)positivistic research in this vein. It is indeed the researchers who decide on the truth value of the research data and results.

EPISTEMOLOGICAL CONSIDERATIONS

A similar conundrum exists in relation to epistemological concerns: Many texts on research methods draw a sharp line of demarcation between qualitative research, which ostensibly operates with the assumption that the researcher and the research subject are indivisible, and quantitative research, which assumes that it is not only possible but even necessary to separate the researcher from the research subject. From the latter perspective, all deviations are considered biases and threats to the validity and reliability of a study. As before, it is indeed up to the researcher to decide which position to take in relation to the subject. Personally, I take the position that there are a number of more or less obvious mistakes one can make in the conceptualizing, collecting, analyzing, and interpreting processes. Among them are issue framing or asking leading questions, asking context- or culture-insensitive questions, and using inappropriate language. However, once these obvious issues are dealt with, I would not claim that my research thus becomes free of bias, as I am aware that even the choice of topic, the phrasing of a research question, or the definitions of the key constructs in my research question are strongly related to the brainwashing that I have received during my years of study and research.

Another problem relates to the research subject. At first glance, it is quite easy to state that the research subject of content analysis should be the content of non-numerical data. However, there are at least two ways of conceptualizing the content of textual data. Interview transcripts, print and electronic media, and so on can be examined not only in terms of the content—what's "really" in the data—but also in relation to the data producers' intent or motivation. In this regard, Lasswell (1951) suggested that the objective of content analysis should be an inquiry into *who* says *what*, to *whom, why*, to *what extent* and with *what effect*. This has at least two shortcomings: First, it psychologizes the data, especially questions relating to the why and what effect, yet mostly, unless we are psychologists and have collected data that would allow us to examine these in detail, we do not really have sufficient information to begin to understand people's motivations or the effects that data have. Second, this approach focuses on the effects of data, which are difficult to assess if data do not explicitly yield effects or if other data, such as those in reception studies, are not available to study or even test its effects. Much safer would be an analysis that explores the non-numerical data as empirical material that was produced within a cultural, historical, political, economic, and social context. If at all necessary, the authors' intentions and motivations, for example, may be used as background information while the patterns, structure, dynamics, and substantive meaning within its context are usually the safer and more interesting focus of analysis.

VARIATIONS

HCA as a family of content analyses within a mixed methods framework can be applied in many ways. Two are introduced here: thematic analysis with HCA (HCA-T) and causal analysis with HCA (HCA-C). Other obvious extensions would include network analysis (HCA-N), ethnography

(HCA-E), or discourse analysis (HCA-D). HCA can be used on all non-numerical data, including visual and audio data, and its research steps can be expanded to include further qualitative and quantitative analyses not part of this introductory chapter. The number and forms of HCA variants will depend on the creativity and need of the researchers interested in analyzing content within a mixed methods framework.

Thematic Analysis

Possibly the most straightforward way of using HCA is to conduct a thematic analysis of texts such as newspaper articles, interview transcripts, policy documents, or advertisements (including pictures and videos). A thematic analysis would include but should not be limited to the identification of themes, where relevance is based on the research focus, question, context, and theoretical framework within which the research is conducted. Themes can be identified using either top-down coding, where researchers impose their coding scheme on a body of non-numerical material; bottom-up coding, where relevant elements are identified inductively, eventually leading to a set of relevant themes; or iterative coding, where coding takes place iteratively between bottom-up and top-down coding. Unfortunately, many qualitative researchers stop their analysis at this point, merely reporting the themes they identified in the data. Some researchers provide a quasi-quantification of themes (e.g., reporting on the most or least frequent occurrence of themes) or even a quantification thereof (e.g., providing a frequency count of themes). The latter is particularly problematic as the data under investigation are usually drawn from a nonrepresentative sample. Thus, a different subsample of a larger study population may yield a very different frequency count or even a different set of themes. Thus, quasi-quantification or quantification in this context should be at best illustrative of the characteristics of the material of the sample.

Depending on the material and focus of the research, additional analysis steps could be relevant, including the assessment of the relations between themes, the conditionality of themes within the material, shifting thematic boundaries and their fuzziness, and their substructure (subthemes). A combination of these could be quite revealing as well. For instance, one could study the content of poverty as presented by some media outlet as it pertains to whites and nonwhites, or men, women, and children, and then analyze how the conceptualization of poverty in such texts varies in terms of inclusiveness and fuzziness across different social groups.

Once themes, subthemes, combinations of themes, links between themes, or whatever is of relevance to the research project are identified in the first qualitative step, they will be analyzed statistically, using some form of dimensional analysis to examine structures and patterns, or differences of structures and patterns, as outlined above. This second quantitative step depends on the results of the first qualitative step, but it may reveal patterns that go beyond the qualitative analysis. Instead of merely interpreting the emergent structure according to the dimensional analysis, a third qualitative step links the results of the dimensional analysis with the source material. In other words, the patterns and structures from the statistical analysis will be connected or recontextualized to the source material in order to interpret the thematic elements under investigation within the context from which the codes were identified in the first place.

Causal Analysis

There are a number of ways to study causality in the social sciences. The most problematic and the least convincing is the attempt to identify general causal laws. More subtle ways to pursue causality may be valuable in their own right. The less ambitious version of a causal analysis would be limited to a theoretical or statistical model: that causality, causal relations, or causal directions are implied or explicitly stated by a theoretical or empirical model.

In this version, no overall claim of ultimate causes is made but, instead, they are either assumed or tested on a scale limited to the propositions embedded in theory or the empirical model. This second version would be compatible with HCA in that causal relations between phenomena may indeed be explained in terms of causality, if the researcher is thus inclined. A third and most appropriate way to incorporate causality in HCA would be to examine explicit or implicit causal claims or relations as embedded within text. This type of analysis would examine, first, the causes of a phenomenon *as presented within the narrative* of a text; second, the phenomenon itself and how it is presented in its dimensionality within the text; and third, the consequences of this phenomenon. A variety of interesting analyses could be imagined: For example, a study of narratives of local politicians about poverty among blacks in Soweto may reveal a variety of dimensions of how they understand poverty, what they see as the causes of poverty, and what the consequences are in relation to their beliefs about this causal chain within their narrative. Other applications could be a study of hospital quality among different groups of patients within a hospital, its causes and its consequences; a study of short-term and long-term unemployed about shame and depression; or an examination of sexual harassment among women varying in employment position across organizations. All these could be studied with HCA-C, first, by examining the themes and their content in relation to the phenomenon (poverty, quality of hospital treatment, unemployment, harassment), and then the causes and consequences as presented in the textual material. The qualitative analysis would provide partial information for various ways to examine the structure and patterns of the data from a multidimensional quantitative perspective. To better interpret the statistical results from the dimensional analysis, they would have to be recontextualized by connecting the identified geometric patterns and structure with the initial results from the qualitative analysis; a second, post-hoc qualitative analysis would explore statistical and geometrical patterns and structures within the original non-numeric data.

◆ Possibilities and Limitations of Hermeneutic Content Analysis

Limited possibilities for generalization and hypothesis testing: Researchers are unlikely to work with data that can be considered representative of a larger population, so generalizations and most hypothesis testing are not appropriate. However, there are some tests that can examine differences in patterns and structure, for example, differences in the structure of themes or in the attribution of causality of phenomena using various forms of multidimensional scaling or correspondence analysis techniques.

Difficult for large sets of data: As HCA has two important qualitative content analysis components, it is unlikely to be used for large data sets, simply because the available resources would not allow for a detailed qualitative analysis on this scale. However, it is conceivable that a subsample, using either probabilistic or nonprobabilistic sampling techniques, could be used for an initial, detailed qualitative analysis. Nevertheless, even if the initial qualitative analysis was performed on a subsample of the data, all data would have to be coded for the quantitative analysis, which still would devour considerable resources. In a narrower sense, however, HCA could be used to systematically develop dictionaries for more conventional quantitative content analyses.

HCA is most suitable for pursuing a complementarity mixed methods design: The quantitative results in Step 2 ought to complement the qualitative results from Step 1, while the qualitative results from Step 3 ought to complement the qualitative results

from Step 1 and the quantitative results from Step 2. It is indeed conceivable also to pursue convergence or convergent validity in these steps, but both the theoretical underpinning and the effort involved are likely to detract from this purpose.

Multifaceted exploration of content, structure, context, and meaning of non-numerical data: HCA is formidably suited for the exploration of meaning structures in a more comprehensive and holistic way than alternative approaches.

Debunking myths about qualitative and quantitative data analysis: Numerous myths about the possibilities and limits of qualitative and quantitative research methods are debunked, including that quantitative methods are about deductive research with large samples to identify general, causal laws or that qualitative research is about words, whereas quantitative research is about numbers.

◆ Conclusions

HCA is a special approach to mixed methods research, particularly focusing on the systematic analysis of data. Although this chapter focused primarily on textual data, all ideas presented herein are easily applicable to visual and other kinds of non-numerical data. A number of extensions of HCA can be imagined, such as its application in social network analysis (HCA-N), ethnography (HCA-E), and discourse analysis (HCA-D). In HCA and its derivatives, the same non-numerical material is analyzed qualitatively and quantitatively. The decontextualized quantitative part of HCA does not validate the initial qualitative analysis but adds different interpretive dimensions to the understanding of the content, structure, context, and meaning within the research material. The interpretation of the results of the quantitative analysis is enhanced by the post-hoc qualitative analysis, which recontextualizes the findings from the statistical analysis. Qualitative and quantitative aspects of HCA have equal status and are best explored in a complementarity mixed methods framework. HCA is illustrative of how sophisticated statistical analyses can be used in a hermeneutic interpretive framework and on equal footing with qualitative research methods. Given the symbiotic relations between qualitative and quantitative approaches in HCA, it could be argued that this design and method is a clear step toward mixed-mode research designs, i.e., research in which the boundaries between qualitative and quantitative frameworks are no longer clearly distinguishable. Finally, HCA demonstrates how some forms of multidimensional statistics can be used innovatively in a nonpositivistic way to contribute to qualitative methods, an interpretive research framework, and an exploration of innovative forms of analyses within a mixed methods design that are as yet underexplored.

Research Questions and Activities

1. What are the main differences between qualitative and quantitative content analyses?

2. Why are there so many ways to code a single text?

3. What advantages are there to analyzing non-numerical data, and what contribution could a mixed methods design make to an analysis of non-numerical data?

4. Explore the advertisements of a glossy journal (e.g., Cosmopolitan, Men's Health, House & Garden, etc.). What kind of research questions could you ask that could be answered by hermeneutic content analysis?

5. Can we assess causality with HCA-C?

◆ Notes

1. An interesting variant is outlined in Brewer and Hunter (2006), who propose four research "styles": fieldwork, survey research, experimentation, and nonreactive research. However, their conceptualization of the methods landscape poses similar problems as those attempts, which aim to transcend the incompatibility thesis in relation to qualitative and quantitative research (Bergman, 2006).

2. See http://caqdas.soc.surrey.ac.uk/ for an excellent review of the main CAQDAS packages.

3. Many researchers refer to such items as a Likert scale, which is incorrect. Likert scaling is a formal measurement process of a latent construct. It includes the subjective assessment of a panel of expert judges as well as a statistical analysis of their judgment, and it yields a multi-item measurement scale (e.g., Likert, 1932), constructed from a number of psychometrically validated items based on an ordinal measurement scale.

◆ References

Berelson, B. (1952). *Content analysis in communication research.* Glencoe, IL: Free Press.

Berelson, B., & Lazarsfeld, P. F. (1948). *The analysis of communication content.* New York: Bureau of Applied Social Research.

Bergman, M. M. (2008a). The straw men of the qualitative quantitative divide. In M. M. Bergman (Ed.), *Advances in mixed* methods research: Theories and applications. Thousand Oaks, CA: Sage.

Bergman, M. M. (2008b). Whither mixed methods? In M. M. Bergman (Ed.), *Advances in mixed methods research: Theories and applications*. Thousand Oaks, CA: Sage.

Bergman, M. M., & Coxon, A. P. M. (2005). The quality in qualitative methods. *Forum Qualitative Sozialforschung / Forum: Qualitative Social Research*, 6(2), Art. 34, http://nbn-resolving.de/urn:nbn:de:0114-fqs 0502344.

Brekke, M. (1991). Automatic parsing meets the wall. In S. Johansson & A. Stendström (Eds.), *English computer corpora: Selected papers and research guide*. Berlin: de Gruyter.

Brier, A. (2007). *Quantitative analysis of textual data with HAMLET II: A multidimensional scaling approach to quantitative textual analysis* (Software Manual and User Guide). Southampton, UK: ESRC National Centre for Research Methods.

Brewer, J., & Hunter, A. (2006). *Foundations of multimethod research: Synthesizing styles* (2nd ed.). Thousand Oaks, CA: Sage.

Butler, C. (1985). *Computers in linguistics*. Oxford, UK: Blackwell.

Charmaz, K., & Mitchell, R.G. (2001). Grounded theory in ethnography. In P. Atkinson, A. Coffey, S. Delamont, J. Lofland, & L. Lofland (Eds.), *Handbook of ethnography*. Thousand Oaks, CA: Sage

Corbin, J., & Strauss, A. (1990). Grounded theory research: Procedures, canons, and evaluative criteria. *Qualitative Sociology, 13*, 3–21.

Coxon, A. P. M. (2004). Multidimensional scaling. In M. S. Lewis-Beck, A. Bryman, & T. F. Liao (Eds.), *The Sage encyclopedia of social science research methods*. Thousand Oaks, CA: Sage.

Creswell, J. W., & Plano Clark, V. L. (2006). *Designing and conducting mixed methods research*. Thousand Oaks, CA: Sage.

Denzin, N. K., & Lincoln, Y. S. (Eds.). (2005). *The SAGE handbook of qualitative research* (3rd ed.). London: Sage.

Flick, U. (2007). *Managing quality in qualitative research*. London: Sage.

Glaser, B. G. (1978). *Theoretical sensitivity*. Mill Valley, CA: Sociology Press.

Glaser, B. G. (1992). *Basics of grounded theory analysis: Emergence vs. forcing*. Mill Valley, CA: Sociology Press.

Glaser, B. G. (1998). *Doing grounded theory: Issues and discussions*. Mill Valley, CA: Sociology Press.

Holsti, O. R. (1969). *Content analysis for the social sciences and humanities*. Reading, MA: Addison-Wesley.

Kelly, E. F., & Stone, P. J. (1975). *Computer recognition of English word senses*. Amsterdam: North Holland.

Kracauer, S. (1952, Winter). The challenge of qualitative content analysis. *International Communications Research, 631*–642.

Krippendorff, K. (2004). *Content analysis: An introduction to its methodology* (2nd ed.). Thousand Oaks, CA: Sage.

Kunkel, D., Cope, K. M., Farinola, W., Biely, E., Rollin, E., & Donnerstein, E. (1999). *Sex on TV*. Menlo Park, CA: Kaiser Family Foundation Report.

Lasswell, H. (1951). *The analysis of political behaviour: An empirical approach*. London: Routledge.

Likert, R. (1932). A technique for the measurement of attitudes. *Archives of Psychology, 140*, 1–55.

Maxcy, S. J. (2003). Pragmatic threads in mixed methods research in the social sciences: The search for multiple modes of inquiry and the end of the philosophy of formalism. In A. Tashakkori & C. Teddlie (Eds.), *Handbook of mixed methods in social and behavioral research*. Thousand Oaks, CA: Sage.

Mayring, P. (2000). Qualitative content analysis. Forum Qualitative Sozialforschung / Forum: Qualitative Social Research, 1, 2, Art. 20, http://nbn-resolving.de/urn:nbn:de: 0114-fqs0002204.

Mayring, P. (2002). *Qualitative Inhaltsanalyse: Grundlagen und Techniken* (9th ed.). UTB.

Seale, C. (1999). *The quality of qualitative research*. London: Sage.

Stone, P. J., Dunphy, D. C., Smith, M. S., & Ogilvie, D. M. (1966). *General inquirer: A computer approach to content analysis*. Cambridge, MA: MIT Press.

Strauss, A. L., & Corbin, J. (1998). *Basics of qualitative research: Techniques and procedures for developing grounded theory* (2nd ed.). London: Sage.

Tashakkori, A., & Teddlie, C. (1998). *Mixed methodology: Combining qualitative and quantitative approaches*. Thousand Oaks, CA: Sage.

Tashakkori, A., & Teddlie, C. (Eds.). (2003). *Handbook of mixed methods in social and behavioral research*. Thousand Oaks, CA: Sage.

Van Dijk, T. A. (1988). *News as discourse*. Hillsdale, NJ: Lawrence Erlbaum.

Weber, R. P. (1990). *Basic content analysis*. Thousand Oaks, CA: Sage.

17

EMERGENT DATA ANALYSIS TECHNIQUES IN MIXED METHODS RESEARCH

A Synthesis

◆ Anthony J. Onwuegbuzie and Julie P. Combs

Objectives

After completing this chapter, you should be able to

- describe the decisions that a mixed methods researcher makes during the quantitative data analysis process—from receipt of the quantitative data to the construction of inferences;

- describe the decisions that a mixed methods researcher makes during the qualitative data analysis process—from receipt of the qualitative data to the construction of inferences;

- describe the 13 criteria for conducting mixed analyses;

- compare and contrast parallel mixed analysis, cross-over mixed analysis, and non-cross-over mixed analysis; and

- identify which of the 13 criteria are involved in the mixed analysis of any given mixed methods study.

Analyzing data in mixed methods research is one of the most difficult steps—if not the most difficult step—of the mixed methods research process. This difficulty stems from the fact that a single analyst involved in the mixed methods study has to be competent in conducting an array of quantitative and qualitative data analysis techniques. Even when a team contains researchers who are competent in conducting both quantitative and qualitative research, those researchers must also be adept at integrating findings from both strands. Such effective integration is a necessity for coherent and meaningful meta-inferences (i.e., inferences from qualitative and quantitative findings being integrated into either a coherent whole or two distinct sets of coherent wholes; Tashakkori & Teddlie, 1998) such that increased *Verstehen* (i.e., understanding) can be achieved.

Because the analysis of data generated in mixed methods studies involves the use of one or more quantitative data analysis techniques and one or more qualitative data analysis techniques, we begin this chapter by presenting an overview of quantitative data analysis strategies and qualitative data analysis strategies. In so doing, we attempt to provide an inclusive framework for both analytical traditions. Inclusive frameworks are useful—if not essential—for reasons that include the following:

1. An inclusive framework helps to unite the field it represents (e.g., qualitative tradition) by providing a flexible organizational system that virtually every researcher in the field can use. As such, an inclusive framework has practical value.

2. An inclusive framework gives guidance and structure to researchers as to how to analyze data that have been collected in their studies. Such a framework would comprise typologies, models, paths, and the like from which researchers can choose optimally to address their research questions.

3. An inclusive framework helps to establish a common language (e.g., terminology, conventions, abbreviations) for labeling and describing analysis strategies for the field. Such consistency, in turn, likely would motivate future research methodologists to use the same language when developing new framework elements or modifying or expanding existing framework elements.

4. An inclusive framework helps to provide directions for future development of analytical strategies. Such a framework provides research methodologists with a foundation on which to build.

5. An inclusive framework helps to legitimate the field by facilitating rigor in the data analysis process by incorporating an optimal combination of typologies, models, paths, and the like.

6. An inclusive framework helps to legitimate the field by providing an accountability framework that researchers can use to conduct what we term *analysis audits*, which involve the comprehensive evaluation of both the product (i.e., findings that emerge) and the process of the analysis strategies used. Such an evaluation would lead to an assessment of the legitimacy (e.g., validity, credibility, trustworthiness, dependability, confirmability, transferability) of the inferences that emerge from the data analysis—what Teddlie and Tashakkori (2009) refer to as "inference quality" (p. 27). Foremost in analysis audits would be an attempt to assess the following four aspects of quality identified by Teddlie and Tashakkori (2009, pp. 302–303): (1) design suitability (i.e., to what extent are the selected analysis strategies reflective of the research questions?); (2) design fidelity (i.e., to what extent are the selected analysis strategies yielding an adequate representation of the data?); (3) within-design consistency (i.e., to what extent do the analytical components fit together in an integrated and coherent manner?); and (4) analytic adequacy (i.e., to what extent are the selected analysis

strategies appropriate and adequate to provide possible answers to research questions?) (see also O'Cathain, 2010 [this volume]).

7. An inclusive framework serves as a useful pedagogical tool. Research methodology instructors can use the framework to teach their students. Also, researchers from one tradition (e.g., qualitative) can use an inclusive framework to teach researchers from another tradition (e.g., quantitative).

For the remainder of this chapter, we refer to an inclusive framework as a meta-framework that incorporates frameworks, typologies, models, theories, paths, and the like.

◆ *Inclusive Framework for Quantitative Data Analysis Techniques*

The field of quantitative research contains several quantitative data analysis typologies. Figure 17.1 presents our meta-framework. This figure represents a concept map that outlines the major decisions that a quantitative analyst makes during the data analysis process—from receipt of the quantitative data to the construction of inferences. Specifically, once the quantitative data are available, depending on the research question(s), the analyst decides whether descriptive analyses or inferential analyses, or both, are appropriate. If descriptive analyses are pertinent, then the next decision is whether to use one or more of the single-quantity-based statistics (i.e., measures of central tendency, variability, position/relative standing, or distributional shape) or the exploratory-based statistics (e.g., exploratory factor analysis, cluster analysis, correspondence analysis, multidimensional scaling)—both of which yield descriptive statistics. In contrast, if inferential analyses are appropriate, then, depending

on the stated hypothesis, the sample size, and the assumptions underlying the data (e.g., linearity, independence, normality, equal variances), the analyst must decide whether to use parametric analyses or nonparametric analyses. If parametric analyses are deemed appropriate, then the quantitative analyst will select from among the numerous general linear model analyses (e.g., independent samples t test, analysis of variance, multiple regression) or the relatively few nongeneral linear model analyses (e.g., predictive discriminant analysis). In contrast, if nonparametric analyses are pertinent, then the analyst selects one or more of the measures of association, population tests, two-population comparisons, and/or several-population comparisons. All of these parametric and nonparametric analyses yield inferential statistics. Once the descriptive statistics or inferential statistics have been generated, the analyst chooses from among the four types of significance (i.e., statistical, practical, clinical, economic). Although the inferential statistics strand can generate all four indices of significance, the descriptive statistics strand has only three of the significance indices available (i.e., practical, clinical, economic) because descriptive statistics are not used to test hypotheses and thus do not involve the computation of p values. Each of the decision points for quantitative data analysis is displayed in Figure 17.1.

COMPONENTS OF QUANTITATIVE ANALYSES

Descriptive Analyses

As seen in Figure 17.1, two quantitative analysis components are used to analyze quantitative data: descriptive analyses and inferential analyses. These two analysis components yield descriptive statistics and inferential statistics, respectively. Descriptive analyses are techniques that are used to organize and summarize data for

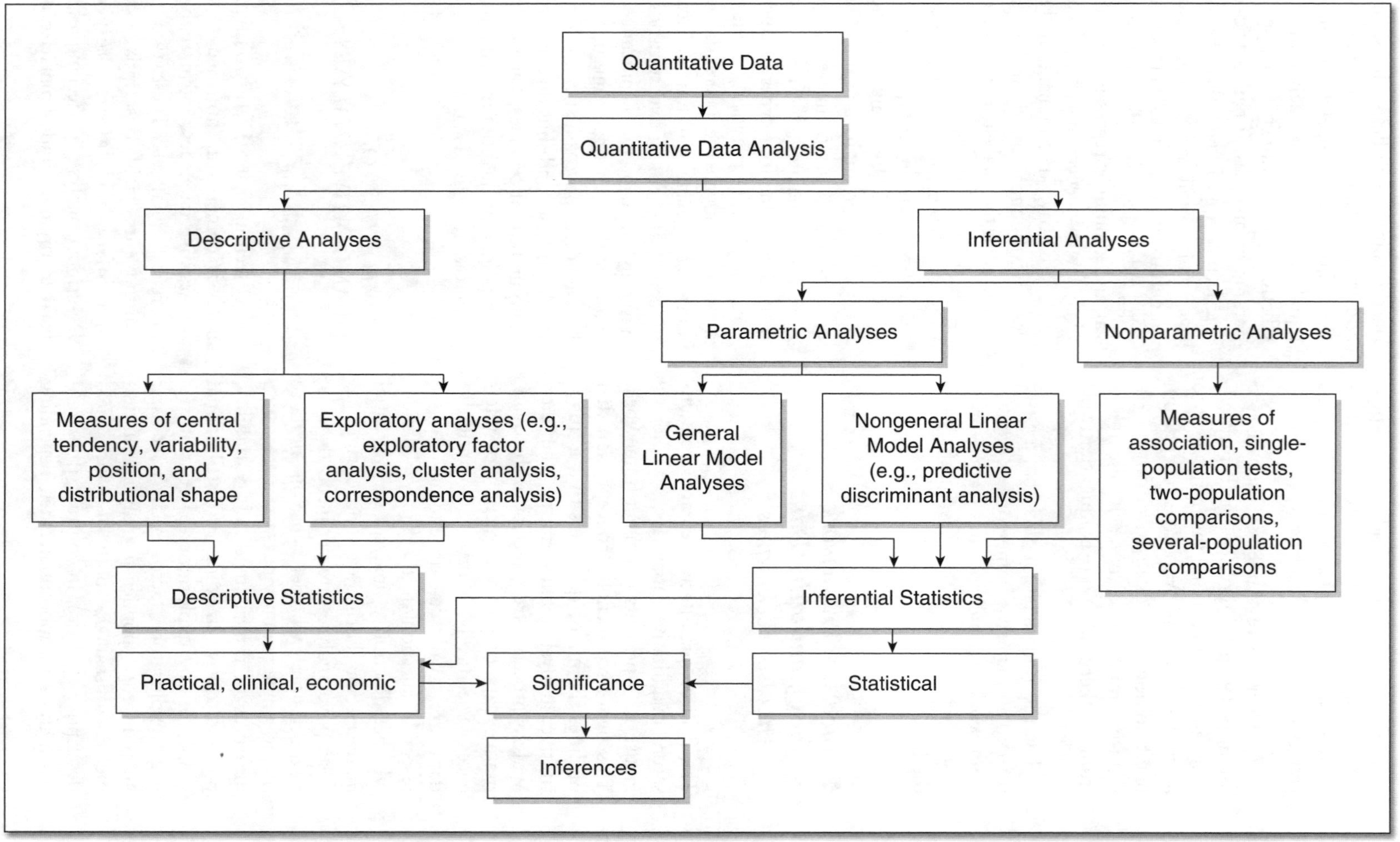

Figure 17.1 Meta-Framework of Quantitative Analysis Strategies

the purpose of enhancing understanding. In contrast, inferential analyses are techniques that are used to make predictions or judgments about a population based on the characteristics of a sample obtained from the population (i.e., making generalizations from a sample to the population from which the sample was selected). Descriptive analyses yield single-quantity-based statistics and exploratory-based statistics.

Single-quantity-based statistics. Descriptive statistics include measures of central tendency, measures of dispersion/variability, measures of position/relative standing, and measures of distributional shape. All of these types of descriptive statistics summarize data in a specific way. Measures of central tendency identify a single numerical value that is optimally representative of an entire distribution of scores. More specifically, the goal of measures of central tendency is to find the single number that is most typical or most representative of the entire distribution of scores. Measures of dispersion/variability provide an index of how spread apart the scores of the distribution are or how much the scores vary from each other. Measures of position/relative standing provide information about where a score falls relative to the other scores on the distribution of data. Finally, measures of distributional shape quantify how the shape of distribution of scores stemming from the sample differs from the shape of a normal distribution with the same mean and variance.

Exploratory-based statistics. Exploratory-based statistics are a class of statistical techniques that can be applied to data that represent *natural* clusters, factors, dimensions, or groupings. These techniques involve sorting the raw data into groups, such that each group represents units (e.g., cases, observations, or variables) that are relatively similar to each other and relatively dissimilar to units in the other group(s). Furthermore, exploratory-based statistics represent interdependence techniques, wherein no distinction is made between the dependent and independent variables; rather, the entire set of interdependent relationships is analyzed simultaneously. It is similar to multidimensional scaling in that both techniques assess interobject similarity by examining the complete set of interdependent relationships.

INFERENTIAL ANALYSES

Parametric Analyses Versus Nonparametric Analyses

Whereas descriptive analyses yield statistics, which are numerical properties that stem typically from the underlying sample, inferential analyses yield parameters, which are numerical properties of a population. Moreover, these parameters are used to provide information that helps the analyst make predictions (i.e., statistical generalizations) about the population of interest and assign probabilities to these predictions. An array of techniques is available for analyzing quantitative data for the purpose of making statistical generalizations. Each of these techniques can be classified as representing either parametric analyses or nonparametric analyses.

Parametric analyses are premised on certain assumptions about parameters being met. These assumptions include that the dependent variable is normally distributed, that each observation is independent of the other, that all populations being analyzed have the same variance, and that the data are measured with at least an interval level of measurement (Tabachnick & Fidell, 2006). However, in the field of social and behavioral sciences, these assumptions are not always met—in which case, nonparametric analyses might be considered.

Nonparametric analyses have much less stringent assumptions than do their parametric counterparts (Hollander & Wolfe, 1999). For example, nonparametric analyses do not require the assumption of normality to be met. Notwithstanding, nonparametric analyses are much less commonly used than are parametric analyses (Elmore & Woehlke, 1996) because nonparametric analyses, which typically involve the analysis of ranked data, make it more difficult for the analyst to make statistical generalizations about the actual difference between populations because there are no parameters to describe. Furthermore, the use of nonparametric analyses commonly leads to data being reduced or discarded (e.g., use of ranks maintain information about the order of the data but discard the raw values). Because information is discarded, nonparametric procedures can never be as statistically powerful (i.e., able to detect existing differences or relationships when these differences or relationships actually exist) as their parametric counterparts when the assumptions underlying parametric analyses actually hold (i.e., when parametric tests are valid).

General Linear Model

Perhaps the most important typology with respect to quantitative data analysis stems from the fact that *all parametric analyses* (i.e., univariate and multivariate techniques), with the exception of predictive discriminant analyses, are subsumed by a general linear model (GLM). Consequently, *all* analyses are correlational (Henson, 2000; Onwuegbuzie & Daniel, 2003; Thompson, 1998). Figure 17.2 illustrates how each analysis is subsumed by a GLM. From this figure, it can be seen that correlation analyses, for example, are a special type of regression analysis, which, in turn, is a special type of canonical correlation analysis, which, in turn, is a special type of path analysis. Thus, although not necessary, for instance, a regression analysis can be used to undertake a correlation analysis—although the converse cannot occur. Similarly, a canonical correlation analysis can be used to conduct a regression analysis or even a correlation analysis, and a path analysis can be used undertake a canonical correlation analysis, and so forth.

An important aspect that unites all members of the GLM family is that they all involve one or more independent (i.e., predictor) variables and one or more dependent

Figure 17.2   Members of the General Linear Model Family

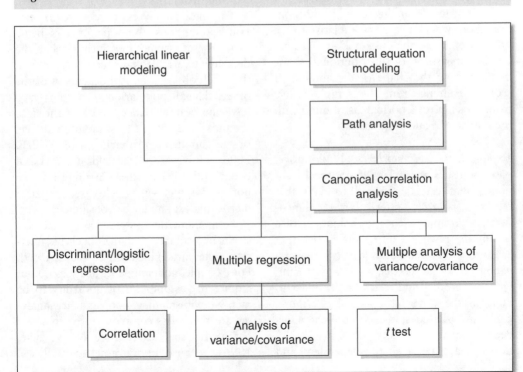

(i.e., criterion) variables. Thus, assuming the GLM assumptions are met (e.g., normality), knowledge of the number of independent and dependent variables, alongside their respective scales of measurement (i.e., nominal, ordinal, interval, ratio), will help researchers to select the most appropriate GLM analysis. This is illustrated in Table 17.1. For example, an independent samples *t* test is appropriate if there is one (nominal-level) independent variable with exactly two levels (i.e., dichotomous) and one (interval- or ratio-level) dependent variable.

Table 17.1 Framework for Selecting Appropriate General Linear Model Analysis

General Linear Model Analysis	*Number of Dependent Variables*	*Number of Independent Variables*	*Scale(s) of Measurement for Dependent Variable(s)*	*Scale(s) of Measurement for Independent Variable(s)*
Correlation coefficient	1	1	interval/ratio	interval/ratio
Independent samples t *test*	1	1	interval/ratio	dichotomous
Analysis of variance	1	≥ 1	interval/ratio	nominal
Analysis of covariance	1	≥ 1[a]	interval/ratio	nominal
Discriminant analysis	≥ 1	1	dichotomous/interval/ratio	nominal
Logistic regression	1	≥ 1	nominal	dichotomous/interval/ratio
Multiple regression	1	≥ 2	nominal	dichotomous/interval/ratio
Multiple analysis of variance	≥ 2	≥ 1	interval/ratio	nominal
Multiple analysis of covariance	≥ 2	≥ 1[a]	interval/ratio	nominal
Canonical correlation	≥ 2	≥ 2	dichotomous/interval/ratio	dichotomous/interval/ratio
Path analysis	≥ 1	≥ 1[b]	dichotomous/interval/ratio	dichotomous/interval/ratio
Structural equation modeling	≥ 1	≥ 1[b]	dichotomous/interval/ratio	dichotomous/interval/ratio
Hierarchical linear modeling	1	≥ 1[c]	nominal/interval/ratio	dichotomous/interval/ratio

a. Includes one or more covariates.

b. Includes one or more moderating variables and/or one or more mediating variables.

c. Includes two or more levels of data.

Typology of Significance

Leech and Onwuegbuzie (2004) identified the following four types of significance that aid in the interpretation of quantitative findings: statistical significance (i.e., probability of observed finding under the null hypothesis); practical significance (i.e., size of observed difference or relationship); clinical significance (i.e., the extent to which the intervention makes a real difference to the quality of life of the participants or to those with whom they interact); and economic significance (i.e., the economic value of the effect of an intervention). Although the first three types of significance have a long history, as noted by Leech and Onwuegbuzie, economic significance is underused in social and behavioral science research. These authors presented a typology of economic significance indices, comprising measures of cost-effectiveness (i.e., providing information about the effectiveness of an intervention per level of cost or the cost per level of effectiveness), cost-benefit (i.e., allowing comparisons of costs and benefits), cost-utility (i.e., providing information about the cost of the interventions relative to the estimated utility of their observed outcomes), cost-feasibility (i.e., providing information about the cost of an intervention to determine whether it is within boundaries of the budget or other available resources), and cost-sensitivity (i.e., incorporating uncertainty into the estimate of effectiveness, cost, benefit, utility, and/or feasibility). All of these measures provide indices based on monetary units.

◆ *Inclusive Framework for Qualitative Data Analysis Techniques*

Qualitative data analysis involves the analysis of various types of interpretive data (e.g., text, visual) that stem from an array of sources, including the following: interviews, surveys, observations, personal journals, diaries, permanent records, transcription of meetings, photographs, videos, and Web 2.0 tools (e.g., Facebook, MySpace.com, iTunes, iMovie, YouTube, Bebo, Friendster, Orkut, Flickr, Panoramio, Second Life). Definitions of qualitative data analysis abound. For example, Schwandt (2007) defines "analyzing qualitative data" as "the activity of making sense of, interpreting, or theorizing data. It is both art and science. . . . If data speak for themselves, analysis would not be necessary" (p. 6). Regarding qualitative analysis, Spradley (1979) states: "Analysis of any kind involves a way of thinking. It refers to the systematic examination of something to determine its parts, the relationship among parts, and their relationship to the whole" (p. 92). More recently, Creswell (2007) defined qualitative analysis as

> preparing and organizing the data (i.e., text data as in transcripts, or image data as in photographs) for analysis, then reducing the data into themes through a process of coding and condensing the codes, and finally representing the data in figures, tables, or a discussion. Across many books on qualitative research, this is the general process that researchers use. (p. 148)

Although qualitative research has been conducted since the early 20th century (Denzin & Lincoln, 2005), as noted by Johnson and Christensen (2008), qualitative data analysis

> is still a relatively new and rapidly developing branch of research methodology. . . . Over recent years, many qualitative researchers have realized the need for more systematic data analysis procedures, and they have started to write more about how to conduct qualitative research data analysis (e.g., Bryman & Burgess, 1994; Dey, 1993; Huberman & Miles, 1994; Lecompte & Preissle, 1993; Lofland & Lofland, 1995; Miles & Huberman, 1994; Patton, 1990; Silverman, 1993; Strauss & Corbin, 1990). (p. 530)

Furthermore, textbooks that describe qualitative data analysis techniques tend to focus on one data analysis technique (e.g., discourse analysis; Phillips & Jorgensen, 2002) or, at best, only a few techniques. Thus, despite the fact that there is currently an array of qualitative data analysis techniques, an inclusive framework of qualitative data analysis techniques does not appear to exist. Several useful frameworks have been developed. For example, Creswell (2007) conceptualized what he called a *data analysis spiral* (p. 150). This spiral represents the following data analysis phases, which the qualitative analyst undergoes during the data analysis process: data managing, reading/memoing,

describing, classifying, interpreting, and representing/visualizing. Although this is an excellent framework, we do not deem it to be optimally inclusive because it does not appear to incorporate the range of qualitative data analysis techniques. As noted by Teddlie and Tashakkori (2009), several taxonomies of qualitative data analyses have emerged (e.g., Dey, 1993); however, these taxonomies, although extremely useful, are not optimally inclusive.

With this in mind, Figure 17.3 represents our attempt to provide a meta-framework of qualitative analysis strategies. This figure

Figure 17.3   Meta-Framework of Qualitative Analysis Strategies

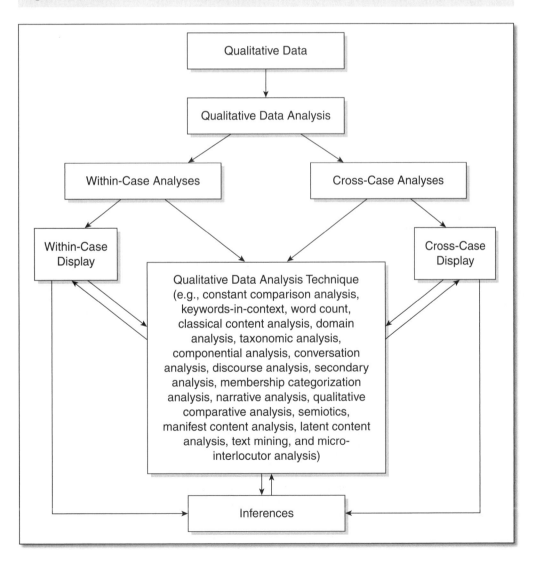

represents a concept map that outlines some of the major decisions that a qualitative analyst makes during the data analysis process—from receipt of the qualitative data to the construction of inferences. Specifically, once the qualitative data are available, depending on the research question(s), the analyst decides whether a within-case analysis or a cross-case analysis is appropriate, or both. Whichever of these classes of analyses is used, the analyst can decide which type(s) of qualitative analysis to use (e.g., constant comparison analysis) and whether or not to use one or more of Miles and Huberman's (1994) displays—which we will outline below. The displays can be used by themselves to analyze the data and yield inferences. Similarly, the selected qualitative data analysis technique(s) alone can be used to analyze the data, or a combination of the selected qualitative data analysis technique(s) and display(s) can be used. For example, findings from a constant comparison analysis can be represented graphically (i.e., the display[s] informing the qualitative analysis technique), or data contained in a display can be subjected to an analysis using one or more of the qualitative analysis techniques (i.e., the qualitative analysis technique informing the display).

WITHIN-CASE VERSUS CROSS-CASE DISPLAYS

Within-case analyses are qualitative analyses that are bounded within a single case. That is, data from cases are analyzed one case at a time. Conversely, cross-case analyses involve the simultaneous analysis of data yielded by multiple (i.e., two or more) cases (Miles & Huberman, 1994). An array of within-case and cross-case displays is presented in Table 17.2 and Table 17.3, respectively.

Table 17.2 Miles and Huberman's (1994) Within-Case Displays

Type of Display	Description
Partially ordered:	
Poem	Composition in verse
Context chart	Networks that map in graphic form the interrelationships among groups and roles that underlie the context of individual behavior
Checklist matrix	Way of analyzing/displaying one major concept, variable, or domain that includes several unordered components
Time-ordered:	
Event listing	Matrix or flowchart that organizes a series of concrete events by chronological time periods and sorts them into multiple categories
Critical incident chart	Maps a few critical events
Event-state network	Maps general states that are not as time-limited as events and might represent moderators or mediators that link specific events of interest
Activity record	Displays a specific recurring activity that is limited narrowly in time and space

Type of Display	Description
Decision modeling flowchart	Maps thoughts, plans, and decisions made during a flow of activity that is bounded by specific conditions
Growth gradient	Network that maps events that are conceptualized as being linked to an underlying variable that changes over time
Time-ordered matrix	Maps when particular phenomena occurred
Role-ordered:	
Role-ordered matrix	Maps the participant's "roles" by sorting data in rows and columns that have been collected from or about a set of data that reflect the participant's views, beliefs, expectations, and/or behaviors
Role-by-time matrix	Maps the participant's "roles," preserving chronological order
Conceptually ordered:	
Conceptually clustered matrix	Text table with rows and columns arranged to cluster items that are related theoretically, thematically, or empirically
Thematic conceptual matrix	Reflects ordering of themes
Folk taxonomy	Typically representing a hierarchical tree diagram that displays how a person classifies important phenomena
Cognitive map	Displays the person's representation of concepts pertaining to a particular domain
Effects matrix	Displays data yielding one or more outcomes in a differentiated manner, focusing on the outcome/dependent variable
Case dynamics matrix	Displays a set of elements for change and traces the consequential processes and outcomes for the purpose of initial explanation
Causal network	Displays the most important independent and dependent variables and their interrelationships

Table 17.3   Miles and Huberman's (1994) Cross-Case Displays

Type of Display	Description
Partially ordered:	
Partially ordered meta-matrices	Display descriptive data for each of several cases simultaneously
Case-ordered:	
Case-ordered descriptive meta-matrix	Contains descriptive data from all cases, but the cases are ordered by the main variable of interest

(Continued)

Table 17.3 (Continued)

Type of Display	Description
Two-variable case-ordered matrix	Displays descriptive data from all cases, but the cases are ordered by two main variables of interest that are represented by the rows and columns
Contrast table	Displays a few exemplary cases wherein the variable occurs in low or high form and contrasts several attributes of the basic variable
Scatterplot	Plots all cases on two or more axes to determine how close from each other the cases are
Case-ordered effects matrix	Sorts cases by degrees of the major cause of interest and shows the diverse effects for each case
Case-ordered predictor-outcome matrix	Arranges cases with respect to a main outcome variable and provides data for each case on the main antecedent variables
Predictor-outcome consequences matrix	Links a chain of predictors to some intermediate outcome, and then illustrates the consequence of that outcome
Time-ordered:	
Time-ordered meta-matrix	Table in which columns are organized sequentially by time period and the rows are not necessarily ordered
Time-ordered scatterplot	Displays similar variables in cases over two or more time periods
Composite sequence analysis	Permits extraction of typical stories that several cases share, without eliminating meaningful sequences
Conceptually ordered:	
Content-analytic summary table	Allows the researcher to focus on the content of a meta-matrix without reference to the underlying case
Substructing	Permits the identification of underlying dimensions
Decision tree modeling	Displays decisions and actions that are made across several cases
Variable-by-variable matrix	Displays two major variables in its rows and columns ordered by intensity with the cell entries representing the cases
Causal models	Network of variables with causal connections among them in order to provide a testable set of propositions or hunches about the complete network of variables and their interrelationships
Causal networks	Comparative analysis of all cases using variables deemed to be the most influential in explaining the outcome or criterion
Antecedents matrix	Display that is ordered by the outcome variable and displays all of the variables that appear to change the outcome variable

Coding

Virtually in every qualitative analysis, some form of coding typically takes place. Coding is a strategy that is used to find themes and patterns in qualitative data. Typically, the analyst codes meaning segments in the data, which can be utterances, words, phrases, sentences, lines of text, or paragraphs. The most common types of coding are (a) inductive coding (i.e., examining the data, identifying the meaning units, and attaching codes), (b) deductive coding (i.e., using a set of codes obtained from sources such as the literature or theory to examine the data to find instances of these codes), and (c) abductive coding (i.e., stemming from an interactive process of deductive and inductive reasoning).

TYPES OF QUALITATIVE ANALYSES

Qualitative researchers have an array of qualitative data analysis techniques from which to choose. Table 17.4 summarizes the 18 qualitative data analysis techniques identified by Leech and Onwuegbuzie (2007, 2008). These analysis techniques are organized around four major sources of qualitative data collected: talk, observations, drawings/photographs/videos, and documents (Leech & Onwuegbuzie, 2008).

Table 17.4 Most Common Qualitative Analyses

Type of Analysis	Short Description of Analysis
Constant comparison analysis	Systematically reducing data to codes, then developing themes from the codes
Classical content analysis	Counting the number of codes
Word count	Counting the total number of words used or the number of times a particular word is used
Keywords-in-context	Identifying keywords and using the surrounding words to understand the underlying meaning of the keyword
Domain analysis	Using the relationships between symbols and referents to identify domains
Taxonomic analysis	Creating a system of classification that inventories the domains into a flowchart or diagram to help the researcher understand the relationships among the domains
Componential analysis	Using matrices and/or tables to discover the differences among the subcomponents of domains
Conversation analysis	Using the behavior of speakers to describe people's methods for producing orderly social interaction
Discourse analysis	Selecting representative or unique segments of language use, such as several lines of an interview transcript, and then examining the selected lines in detail for rhetorical organization, variability, accountability, and positioning

(Continued)

Table 17.4 (Continued)

Type of Analysis	Short Description of Analysis
Secondary data analysis	Analyzing non-naturalistic data or artifacts that were derived from previous studies
Membership categorization analysis	Utilizing the role that interpretations play in making descriptions and the consequences of selecting a particular category (e.g., baby, sister, brother, mother, father = family)
Semiotics	Using talk and text as systems of signs under the assumption that no meaning can be attached to a single term
Manifest content analysis	Describing observed (i.e., manifest) aspects of communication via objective, systematic, and empirical means (Berelson, 1952)
Latent content analysis	Uncovering underlying meaning of text
Qualitative comparative analysis	Systematically analyzing similarities and differences across cases, typically being used as a theory-building approach, allowing the analyst to make connections among previously built categories, as well as to test and to develop the categories further
Narrative analysis	Considering the potential of stories to give meaning to individuals' lives, and treating data as stories, enabling researchers to take account of research participants' own evaluations
Text mining	Analyzing naturally occurring text to discover and capture semantic information
Micro-interlocutor analysis	Analyzing information stemming from one or more focus groups about which participants respond to each question, the order in which participants respond, the characteristics of each response, the nonverbal communication used, and the like

SOURCE: This table was adapted from Leech and Onwuegbuzie (2008).

◆ Mixed Data Analysis Techniques

THE NEED FOR AN INTEGRATIVE FRAMEWORK FOR CONDUCTING MIXED ANALYSES

Over the last few decades, several mixed analysis techniques have emerged. Specifically, there have been several articles (e.g., Bazeley, 1999, 2003, 2006; Caracelli & Greene, 1993; Chi, 1997; Datta, 2001; Greene, 2008; Greene, Caracelli, & Graham, 1989; Happ, DeVito Dabbs, Tate, Hricik, & Erlen, 2006; Jang, McDougall, Pollon, & Russell, 2008; Lee & Greene, 2007; Li, Marquart, & Zercher, 2000; Onwuegbuzie, 2003; Onwuegbuzie & Collins, 2009; Onwuegbuzie & Combs, 2009; Onwuegbuzie & Dickinson, 2008; Onwuegbuzie & Leech, 2004, 2006; Onwuegbuzie, Slate, Leech, & Collins, 2007, 2009; Onwuegbuzie & Teddlie, 2003; Sandelowski, 2000, 2001; Teddlie, Tashakkori, & Johnson, 2008; West & Tulloch, 2001) and chapters in seminal mixed research books (e.g., Bazeley, 2010 [this volume]; Bergman, 2010 [this volume]; Creswell & Plano Clark, 2007; Greene, 2007; Johnson & Christensen, 2008; Newman & Ramlo, 2010 [this volume]; Rao & Wolcock, 2003; Tashakkori & Teddlie, 1998; Teddlie & Tashakkori, 2009; Todd, Nerlich, McKeown, & Clarke, 2004). All of these articles and book chapters have made very important contributions to the mixed methods literature; however, surprisingly, to date, despite the extensiveness of the field of mixed analysis, as Greene (2008) concluded, "This work has not yet cohered into a widely accepted framework or set of ideas" (p. 14). Furthermore, as noted by Bazeley (2010), "there are surprisingly few published studies reporting results from projects which make more than very elementary use of the capacity to integrate data and analyses using computers" (p. 434). Thus, it is clear that an integrated framework is needed.

In recent years, although the list of works is not extensive, several authors have developed excellent typologies for classifying various mixed analysis strategies (e.g., Bazeley, 1999, 2003, 2006, 2009, 2010; Caracelli & Greene, 1993; Chi, 1997; Creswell & Plano Clark, 2007; Datta, 2001; Greene, 2007, 2008; Greene et al., 1989; Happ et al., 2006; Li et al., 2000; Onwuegbuzie, 2003; Onwuegbuzie, Collins, & Leech, in press; Onwuegbuzie & Dickinson, 2008; Onwuegbuzie & Leech, 2004; Onwuegbuzie, Slate, et al., 2007, 2009; Onwuegbuzie & Teddlie, 2003; Sandelowski, 2000, 2001; Tashakkori & Teddlie, 1998; Teddlie & Tashakkori, 2009; Teddlie et al., 2008; West & Tulloch, 2001). Our classical content analysis of these articles revealed 13 criteria that these authors have used to create their mixed analysis typologies:

1. Rationale/purpose for conducting the mixed analysis

2. Philosophy underpinning the mixed analysis

3. Number of data types that will be analyzed

4. Number of data analysis types that will be used

5. Time sequence of the mixed analysis

6. Level of interaction between quantitative and qualitative analyses

7. Priority of analytical components

8. Number of analytical phases

9. Link to other design components

10. Phase of the research process when all analysis decisions are made

11. Type of generalization

12. Analysis orientation

13. Cross-over nature of analysis

1. *Rationale/purpose for conducting the mixed analysis.* Greene et al. (1989), after examining a large number of mixed methods evaluation articles, conceptualized a typology for mixed methods purposes/designs. This typology involves the following five purposes, which, as noted by Collins, Onwuegbuzie, and Sutton (2006), could be used to make other mixed analysis decisions (e.g., which qualitative and quantitative data analysis strategies to use): triangulation (i.e., compare findings from the qualitative data with the quantitative results); complementarity (i.e., seek elaboration, illustration, enhancement, and clarification of the findings from one analytical strand [e.g., qualitative] with results from the other analytical strand [e.g., quantitative]); development (i.e., use the results from one analytical strand to help inform the other analytical strand); initiation (i.e., discover paradoxes and contradictions that emerge when findings from the two analytical strands are compared that might lead to a reframing of the research question); and expansion (i.e., expand breadth and range of a study by using multiple analytical strands for different study phases). For example, if triangulation is the rationale/purpose, then it would be appropriate for the analyst to make the analytical strands independent of one another (i.e., conduct the quantitative and qualitative analyses concurrently).

2. *Philosophy underpinning the mixed analysis.* As demonstrated by Bazeley (2009) and Onwuegbuzie, Johnson, and Collins (2009), it is difficult for researchers adhering to any paradigmatic tradition (e.g., postpositivism, constructivism) to claim justifiably a one-to-one correspondence between ontology/epistemology and type of analysis. For example, researchers who classify themselves as postpositivists are not restricted to quantitative analyses; nor are researchers who classify themselves as constructivists restricted to qualitative analyses (Onwuegbuzie, Johnson, et al., 2009). As such, researchers from all paradigmatic traditions potentially can use both quantitative and qualitative analyses (Bazeley, 2009), depending on their research questions. Indeed, as noted by Miles and Huberman (1994), "The question, then, is not whether the two sorts of data [qualitative and quantitative] and associated methods can be linked during study design, but whether it should be done, how it will be done, and for what purposes" (p. 41).

Notwithstanding, philosophical assumptions and stances of the mixed methods researcher can play a role in the analytical decisions made, which lie on a continuum from no philosophical assumptions (i.e., *aphilosophical*) to multiple philosophical assumptions. For instance, a mixed methods researcher might believe that paradigms are not necessarily incompatible but are substantively different and that, therefore, qualitative and quantitative approaches should be kept separate (i.e., *complementary strengths* orientation; Greene, 2007). Such a researcher likely would not integrate the qualitative and quantitative analyses to the same extent as might a mixed methods researcher with a transformative-emancipatory orientation (research that focuses on the lives, experiences, and worldviews of marginalized people; see Mertens, Bledsoe, Sullivan, & Wilson, 2010 [this volume]). Table 17.5 presents 11 mixed methods paradigms/worldviews identified by Onwuegbuzie, Johnson, et al. (2009).

Table 17.5 Mixed Research Paradigms and Worldviews and Their Mixed Analysis Assumptions

Paradigm/ Worldview	Stance	Core Mixed Analysis Strategies
Pragmatism-of-the-middle philosophy	Offers a practical and outcome-oriented method of inquiry that is based on action and leads, iteratively, to further action and the elimination of doubt; paradigms routinely are mixed (Johnson & Onwuegbuzie, 2004)	Sequential, concurrent, cross-over
Pragmatism-of-the-right	Holding a moderately strong form of realism and a weak form of pluralism (Johnson, Onwuegbuzie, & Turner, 2007)	Sequential, concurrent, cross-over
Pragmatism-of-the-left	Antirealism and strong pluralism (Johnson et al., 2007)	Sequential, concurrent, cross-over
Anti-conflationist	Methodology should not be conflated with technical aspects of method because the same method can be used by researchers with different ontological/epistemological stances; adoption of a more principled approach when combining	Sequential

Paradigm/ Worldview	Stance	Core Mixed Analysis Strategies
	methods—only appropriate to combine methods if a common ontological/epistemological stance can be maintained (McEvoy & Richards, 2003)	
Critical realist	Mix of critical theory and a multilevel, discursive social scientific realism (Onwuegbuzie, Johnson, & Collins, 2009)	Sequential, concurrent
Dialectical stance	Dialogical engagement with paradigm differences that generatively produce new knowledge and insights (Greene, 2007); use of "dialectical pragmatism" (i.e., examine qualitative and quantitative stances fully and dialectically and produce a combination solution that and works best for the research question) (Teddlie & Johnson, 2009)	Sequential, concurrent, cross-over
Complementary strengths	Paradigms are not necessarily incompatible but are substantively different; thus, methods used for different paradigms should be kept separate to preserve paradigmatic and methodological integrity (Greene, 2007)	Parallel
Transformative-emancipatory	Emancipatory, participatory, and antidiscriminatory research that focuses directly on the lives, experiences, and perceptions of marginalized persons or groups (Mertens, 2003)	Sequential, concurrent, cross-over
A-paradigmatic	Paradigms are logically independent and thus can be mixed; but although they are useful for reflection, they do not shape practical research decisions; rather, practical characteristics and issues related to the underlying context and problem drive these decisions (Greene, 2007)	Sequential, concurrent, cross-over
Substantive theory	Paradigms may be embedded or intertwined with substantive theories; yet, substantive issues and conceptual theories drive the mixed research, not paradigms (Greene, 2007)	Sequential, concurrent
Communities of practice	Consistent with pragmatist philosophy but accommodates variations and inconsistencies that prevail within mixed research by promoting a diversity of researchers, allowing paradigms to operate at different levels, incorporating group influences on methodological decisions, shifting debates about paradigms to the level of practice and research culture, and allowing methods to be chosen based on their practical value for addressing a research problem (Denscombe, 2008)	Sequential, concurrent, cross-over

SOURCE: Originally published in *International Journal of Multiple Research Approaches* (Onwuegbuzie, Johnson, & Collins, 2009, p. 134), http://www.ijmra.com; reproduced with permission.

3. *Number of data types that will be analyzed.* Whereas some mixed analysis typologies are based on the assumption that both qualitative and quantitative data are needed for a mixed analysis to occur, some typologies allow for the use of only one data type. Creswell and Plano Clark's (2007) typology is one that falls in the former camp. Indeed, Creswell and Plano Clark (2007) define mixed analysis as follows: "Data analysis in mixed methods research consists of analyzing the quantitative data using quantitative methods and the qualitative data using qualitative methods" (p. 128). In contrast, in Onwuegbuzie et al.'s (2007) typology, mixed analyses can occur even when only one data type is involved. According to these authors, if the data type is qualitative, then the first phase of the mixed analysis would be qualitative, and vice versa. Data that dictate the initial analysis then are converted into the other data type. For example, qualitative data, after being subjected to a qualitative analysis, can then be quantitized (i.e., transformed into numerical codes that can be analyzed statistically; Miles & Huberman, 1994; Tashakkori & Teddlie, 1998); or quantitative data, after being subjected to a quantitative analysis, can then be qualitized (i.e., transformed into narrative data that can be analyzed qualitatively; Tashakkori & Teddlie, 1998).

4. *Number of data analysis types that will be used.* There seems to be general agreement that mixed analyses involve the use of at least one qualitative analysis and at least one quantitative analysis—meaning that both data analysis types are needed to conduct a mixed analysis. Thus, the real question for mixed methods researchers to determine is how many qualitative analyses and quantitative analyses are needed.

5. *Time sequence of the mixed analysis.* Most typologies include time sequence as a dimension. Time sequence refers to whether the analytical strands occur in a chronological order (Creswell & Plano Clark, 2007). Specifically, the qualitative and quantitative

analyses can be conducted in no chronological order or concurrently (i.e., concurrent mixed analysis), or they can be conducted in chronological order or sequentially (i.e., sequential mixed analysis). When concurrent mixed analyses are employed, the analytical strands do not occur in any chronological order (Tashakkori & Teddlie, 1998). When sequential mixed analyses are conducted, either (a) the qualitative analysis phase is conducted first, which then informs the subsequent quantitative analysis phase (i.e., sequential qualitative-quantitative analysis); (b) the quantitative analysis phase is conducted first, which then informs the subsequent qualitative analysis phase (i.e., sequential quantitative-qualitative analysis); or (c) the qualitative and quantitative analyses occur sequentially in more than two phases (i.e., iterative sequential mixed analysis) (Teddlie & Tashakkori, 2009).

Teddlie and Tashakkori (2009) identified two types of sequential qualitative-quantitative analyses: (1) using the qualitative analysis to group study participants and then comparing these groups using quantitative analysis, and (2) using the qualitative analysis to group attributes, followed by a confirmatory quantitative analysis. Onwuegbuzie and Teddlie (2003) identified the following two types of sequential qualitative-quantitative analyses: (1) quantitative extreme case analysis (i.e., using quantitative analysis comparing extreme cases and non-extreme cases to examine extreme cases that emerged from the qualitative analysis) and (2) quantitative negative case analysis (i.e., using quantitative analysis comparing negative cases and non-negative cases to examine negative cases that emerged from the qualitative analysis).

With regard to sequential quantitative-qualitative analyses, Onwuegbuzie and Teddlie (2003) identified the following four types of sequential quantitative-qualitative analyses: (1) qualitative contrasting case analysis (i.e., conducting a quantitative descriptive analysis to identify a proportion or a specific number of those who obtained the lowest and highest scores on the quantitative measure and then using qualitative analysis of qualitative data to compare these two groups), (2) qualitative residual analysis (i.e., conducting an inferential analysis such as multiple regression and then qualitatively analyzing qualitative data pertaining to participants representing outlying cases to determine why these cases did not fit the chosen model), (3) qualitative follow-up interaction analysis (i.e., conducting an inferential analysis such as analysis of variance and then qualitatively analyzing qualitative data pertaining to selected participants to help explain any statistical interaction[s] that emerged), and (4) qualitative internal replication analysis (i.e., conducting an inferential analysis such as multiple regression, followed by internal replication analysis to assess the statistical stability of the selected model, and then qualitatively analyzing qualitative data pertaining to participants representing outlying cases in the internal replication model).

6. *Level of interaction between quantitative and qualitative analyses.* Another mixed analysis dimension that appears in some typologies is the point at which the analysis strands interact. Indeed, according to Teddlie and Tashakkori (2009), parallel mixed analysis is likely the most common mixed analysis technique. Thus, authors like Tashakkori and Teddlie (1998), Teddlie and Tashakkori (2009), and Onwuegbuzie and Leech (2004) have outlined the concept of parallel mixed analyses. In their earlier work, Tashakkori and Teddlie (1998) subsumed parallel mixed analysis under concurrent mixed analysis. However, in their most recent conceptualization, Teddlie and Tashakkori (2009), as do Onwuegbuzie and Leech (2004), distinguish parallel mixed analysis from concurrent mixed analysis. In their comprehensive discussion of parallel mixed analyses, Teddlie and Tashakkori (2009) define parallel mixed analysis, in its most basic and traditional form, as involving

two *separate* processes: QUAN [quantitative] analysis of data, using descriptive/inferential statistics for the appropriate

variables, and QUAL [qualitative] analysis of data, using thematic analysis related to the relevant narrative data. Although the two sets of analyses are independent, each provides an understanding of the phenomenon under investigation. These understandings are linked, combined, or integrated into meta-inferences. . . . These analyses can lead to convergent or divergent results. (p. 266, italics in original)

Li et al. (2000) refer to this basic parallel mixed analysis as a *parallel tracks* analysis. A more complex form of parallel mixed analyses are what Li et al. (2000) refer to as a *cross-over tracks* analysis, wherein "findings from the various methodological strands intertwine and inform each other throughout the study" (Datta, 2001, p. 34). According to Teddlie and Tashakkori (2009), these more complex forms of parallel mixed analyses are characterized by the following: (a) having more than two strands in the design, (b) allowing the analytical strands to inform each other before the meta-inference stage, (c) consolidating the qualitative and quantitative data such that these data are analyzed together, and (d) combining the parallel mixed analysis with other types of mixed analysis strategies (e.g., sequential) in studies that necessitate more complex designs.

7. *Priority of analytical components.* Another aspect of some mixed analysis typologies is the priority or emphasis given by the mixed methods research to the analytical strands. Specifically, the qualitative and quantitative strands can have approximately equal priority (i.e., equal status) with respect to addressing the research question(s), or one analytical strand can have significantly higher priority than does the other strand (i.e., dominant status). Although Teddlie and Tashakkori (2009) acknowledge that the priority of the strands cannot always be ascertained completely prior to the implementation of the study (i.e., at the research conceptualization stage),

the emphasis of the analytical strands is still an important consideration for some mixed methods researchers because it can potentially drive mixed analysis decisions. For example, a study in which the quantitative phase(s) has less priority than does the qualitative phase(s) is less likely to involve a complex quantitative-based research question that necessitates sophisticated quantitative data analysis techniques than is a study wherein the quantitative phase(s) has greater priority. Indeed, Morse (2003) has developed notations to designate the priority of the strands: QUAL indicates a qualitatively driven study, whereas QUAN denotes a quantitatively driven study.

8. *Number of analytical phases.* Some of the mixed analysis typologies are more phase-based in nature. In particular, Greene (2007, p. 155) identified the following four phases of analysis: (1) data transformation, (2) data correlation and comparison, (3) analysis for inquiry conclusions and inferences, and (4) using aspects of the analytic framework of one methodological tradition within the analysis of data from another tradition. Onwuegbuzie, Collins, Leech, Dellinger, and Jiao (in press) demonstrate how a mixed analysis can be undertaken at the literature review phase (i.e., research conceptualization stage), which they refer to as a mixed research synthesis. Mixed methods researchers using such a typology would then decide which analytical phases are pertinent for their studies. Another phase-based typology is represented by Onwuegbuzie and Teddlie (2003), who conceptualized a seven-step process for mixed data analysis: (1) data reduction, (2) data display, (3) data transformation, (4) data correlation, (5) data consolidation, (6) data comparison, and (7) data integration.

9. *Link to other design components.* Some mixed analysis typologies are design based; that is, the analyses are linked directly to the mixed methods designs for the study. In particular, Teddlie and Tashakkori (2009) link their mixed analysis

typology to their mixed design typology. Specifically, their typology contains the following six techniques: (1) parallel mixed data analysis, linked to parallel mixed designs; (2) conversion mixed data analysis (comprising quantitizing narrative data, qualitizing numeric data, and inherently mixed analysis techniques; i.e., researchers plan a priori to generate both qualitative and quantitative information from the same data source), which are linked to conversion mixed designs; (3) sequential mixed analysis techniques (i.e., sequential qualitative-quantitative analyses, sequential quantitative-qualitative analyses, and iterative sequential mixed analysis), which are linked to sequential mixed designs; (4) multilevel mixed data analysis (i.e., wherein the level of the unit of analysis is different for the qualitative [e.g., teachers] and quantitative [e.g., students]); (5) fully integrated mixed data analysis techniques (i.e., mixing of qualitative and quantitative approaches occurs interactively at all stages of the study), which are linked to fully integrated designs; and (6) application of analytical techniques of one tradition to the other (e.g., application of the traditional quantitative use of matrices and graphs to qualitative research, Miles & Huberman, 1994; use of effect sizes in qualitative research, Onwuegbuzie & Teddlie, 2003) (p. 264).

Similarly, Creswell and Plano Clark (2007) state that "the type of data analysis will vary depending on the type of mixed design used" (p. 135). These authors link four analysis techniques to their four major mixed methods designs: (1) concurrent data analysis with their triangulation design (i.e., wherein the qualitative and quantitative approaches are used to obtain different but complementary data within the same study); (2) concurrent data analysis with their embedded designs (i.e., wherein "one data set provides a supportive, secondary role in a study based primarily on the other data type" (p. 67); (3) sequential data analysis with embedded designs "in which the supportive data are collected before or after the primary dataset" (p. 142); and (4) sequential data analysis with the explanatory and the exploratory design, which involves two major sequential phases of qualitative and quantitative data collection and analysis.

10. *Phase of the research process when all analysis decisions are made.* Mixed analysis decisions can be made either a priori, a posteriori, or iteratively. Analytic decisions that are made a priori are more likely to occur in *quantitative-dominant* mixed analyses (cf. Johnson, Onwuegbuzie, & Turner, 2007), in which the analyst adopts a postpositivist stance, while simultaneously believing that the inclusion of qualitative data and approaches is likely to enhance the findings. Conversely, mixed analysis decisions that are made a posteriori are more likely to occur in *qualitative-dominant* mixed analyses (cf. Johnson et al., 2007), in which the researcher takes a constructivist-poststructuralist-critical stance with respect to the mixed analysis process, while simultaneously deeming the addition of quantitative data and approaches as helpful in providing richer data and interpretations. To say that mixed analysis decisions that are made iteratively means that some analytic decisions are made a priori, whereas the remaining analytic decisions are emergent. These represent the most common decisions in mixed methods research.

11. *Type of generalization.* The type of generalization also can inform the mixed analysis design. Onwuegbuzie, Slate, et al. (2009) identified five major types of generalizations that researchers can make: (1) external (statistical) generalizations, (2) internal (statistical) generalizations, (3) analytical generalizations, (4) case-to-case transfer, and (5) naturalistic generalization. External (statistical) generalizations involve making generalizations, predictions, or inferences on data yielded from a representative statistical (i.e., optimally random and large) sample to the *population* from which the sample was drawn (i.e., universalistic generalizability). In

contrast, internal (statistical) generalizations involve making generalizations, predictions, or inferences on data obtained from one or more representative or elite study participants (e.g., key informants, subsample members) to the *sample* from which the participant(s) was selected (i.e., particularistic generalizability). When making analytic generalizations, "the investigator is striving to generalize a particular set of [case study] results to some broader theory" (Yin, 2009, p. 43). That is, analytical generalizations are "applied to wider theory on the basis of how selected cases 'fit' with general constructs" (Curtis, Gesler, Smith, & Washburn, 2000, p. 1002) (i.e., particularistic generalizability). Case-to-case transfers involve making generalizations or inferences from one case to another (similar) case (Miles & Huberman, 1994) (i.e., particularistic generalizability). Finally, with naturalistic generalization, rather than the researcher making any form of generalization, it is the readers who make generalizations entirely, or at least in part, from their personal or vicarious experiences (Stake & Trumbull, 1982). Thus, Onwuegbuzie, Slate, et al. (2009) assert that mixed analysis—as is qualitative analysis and quantitative analysis—is guided by an attempt to analyze data in a way that yields one or more of these five types of generalizations, and they refer to this as the *fundamental principle of data analysis*. For example, whereas the quantitative analysis strand of a mixed analysis might justify external statistical generalizations under optimal conditions (e.g., large, random sampling), the qualitative analysis strand might justify analytical generalizations under optimal conditions (e.g., data saturation; Morse, 1995).

12. *Analysis orientation.* Onwuegbuzie, Slate, et al. (2009) conceptualized a typology for classifying mixed analysis techniques that is based on what they referred to as analysis orientations. Specifically, these authors identified the following three analysis orientations: case-oriented, variable-oriented, and process/experience-oriented analyses. This

conceptualization represents an extension of Ragin (1989), who originally contrasted variable-oriented and case-oriented research. According to Onwuegbuzie, Slate, et al. (2009), case-oriented analyses are analyses that focus mainly or exclusively on the selected case(s) in order to analyze and to interpret the meanings, experiences, perceptions, beliefs, or the like of one or more people—with a goal of particularizing and making analytical generalizations. As noted by Onwuegbuzie, Slate, et al. (2009), although case-oriented analyses are best suited for understanding phenomena pertaining to one or a relatively small number of cases and thus lend themselves better to qualitative research in general and qualitative analyses in particular, case-oriented analyses can be used for any number of cases and, therefore, can be used in quantitative research, yielding the use of quantitative analysis techniques such as single-subject analyses, descriptive analyses, and Q methodology (see Newman & Ramlo, 2010). Conversely, variable-oriented analyses involve identifying relationships— typically probabilistic in nature—among constructs that are treated as variables in a way that facilitates research that often is conceptual and theory-centered from the onset, and has a tendency toward external generalizations. As such, variable-oriented analyses, whose "'building blocks' are variables and their intercorrelations, rather than cases" (Miles & Huberman, 1994, p. 174), are more applicable for quantitative research in general and quantitative analyses in particular. However, although the use of large and representative samples often facilitates the identification of relationships among variables, small samples also can be used to identify such patterns, rendering variable-oriented analyses as also being pertinent for generating qualitative data and the use of qualitative analysis techniques (e.g., examining themes that emerge across cases). Finally, process/experience-oriented analyses involve evaluating processes or experiences relating to one or more cases within a specific context over time, with processes tending to be linked to variables and experiences tending to be associated with cases.

Figure 17.4 illustrates how both qualitative and quantitative analyses can represent case-oriented, variable-oriented, and process/experience-oriented analyses. This list is by no means exhaustive. However, this figure captures most of the major qualitative and quantitative analyses. Figure 17.4 reveals that with respect to quantitative analyses, some of the analyses (i.e., descriptive analyses, time series analysis, classical test theory, item response theory) can be used to conduct both case-oriented and variable-oriented analyses. For example, descriptive statistics can be used to describe characteristics (e.g., statistics anxiety) of one or more individuals on a case-by-case basis or as a single group of cases (i.e., case-oriented analysis). At the same time, descriptive statistics can be employed to assess the characteristics of variables (e.g., proportion of students with high levels of statistics anxiety) on a variable-by-variable basis or as a set of variables (i.e., variable-oriented analysis). Similarly, descriptive statistics can be used to assess how statistics anxiety evolves during a statistics course (i.e., process/experience-oriented analysis). With respect to qualitative analyses, several of the analyses (e.g., word count, keywords-in-context, classical content analysis, text mining, domain analysis, taxonomic analysis, componential analysis, qualitative comparative analysis, secondary data analysis, time-ordered matrix/network analysis) can be used for all three analysis orientations. For example, as noted by Miles and Huberman (1994), a time-ordered matrix/network analysis often can "produce 'generic narratives' that retain the 'plot line' of individual cases [i.e., case-oriented analysis], but show us principles that cut across them [i.e., variable-oriented analysis]" (p. 206). Also, a time-ordered matrix/network analysis also can be used to conduct process/experience-oriented analyses.

Figure 17.4 Three-Dimensional Matrix Indicating Analytical Techniques as a Function of Approach (i.e., Quantitative vs. Qualitative) and Analysis Emphasis (i.e., Case-Oriented vs. Variable-Oriented vs. Process/Experience-Oriented)

Phase	Case-Oriented	Variable-Oriented	Process/Experience-Oriented
Quantitative	Descriptive Analyses (e.g., measures of central tendency, variability, position) Cluster Analysis Q Methodology Time Series Analysis Profile Analysis Panel Data Analysis Single-Subject Analysis Classical Test Theory Item Response Theory Multidimensional Scaling Proportional Hazards Model	Descriptive Analyses Correlation Analysis Independent *t* tests Dependent *t* tests Analysis of Variance Analysis of Covariance Multiple Analysis of Variance Multiple Analysis of Covariance Multiple Regression (Multivariate) Logistic Regression Descriptive/Predictive Discriminant Analysis Log-Linear Analysis Canonical Correlation Analysis Path Analysis Structural Equation Modeling Hierarchical Linear Modeling Correspondence Analysis Multidimensional Scaling Exploratory/Confirmatory Factor Analysis Time Series Analysis Classical Test Theory Item Response Theory	Descriptive Analyses (e.g., measures of central tendency, variability, position) Dependent *t* tests Time Series Analysis Profile Analysis Panel Data Analysis Single-Subject Analysis Classical Test Theory Item Response Theory Repeated Measures Analysis of Variance Repeated Measures Analysis of Covariance Survival Analysis Path Analysis Structural Equation Modeling Hierarchical Linear Modeling
Qualitative	Method of Constant Comparison Word Count Keywords-in-Context	Word Count Keywords-in-Context Classical Content Analysis	Method of Constant Comparison Word Count Keywords-in-Context

(Continued)

Figure 17.4 (Continued)

Phase	Case-Oriented	Variable-Oriented	Process/Experience-Oriented
Qualitative	Classical Content Analysis Domain Analysis Taxonomic Analysis Componential Analysis Conversation Analysis Discourse Analysis Secondary Data Analysis Membership Categorization Analysis Narrative Analysis Semiotics Manifest Content Analysis Latent Content Analysis Text Mining Qualitative Comparative Analysis Micro-interlocutor Analysis Partially Ordered Matrix Analysis Time-Ordered Matrix/Network Analysis	Secondary Data Analysis Taxonomic Analysis Componential Analysis Text Mining Qualitative Comparative Analysis Semantic Network Analysis Cognitive Map Analysis Causal Network Analysis Conceptually Ordered Matrix Analysis Case-Ordered Matrix/Network Analysis Time-Ordered Matrix/Network Analysis Variable-by-Variable Matrix Analysis Predictor-Outcome Matrix Analysis Explanatory Effect Matrix Analysis	Classical Content Analysis Domain Analysis Taxonomic Analysis Componential Analysis Conversation Analysis Discourse Analysis Secondary Data Analysis Text Mining Narrative Analysis Manifest Content Analysis Latent Content Analysis Qualitative Comparative Analysis Semantic Network Analysis Cognitive Map Analysis Causal Network Analysis Time-Ordered Matrix/Network Analysis

SOURCE: Originally published in *International Journal of Multiple Research Approaches* (Onwuegbuzie, Slate, Leech, & Collins, 2009, p. 27). http://www.ijmra.com; reproduced with permission.

NOTE: All quantitative analyses above include nonparametric counterparts.

Thus, according to Onwuegbuzie, Slate, et al. (2009), the qualitative and quantitative analyses in Figure 17.4

can be used in an almost unlimited number of combinations, depending on the combination of case-oriented, variable-oriented analyses, and process/experience-oriented analyses needed to obtain interpretive consistency between the ensuing meta-inferences and the elements that characterize the study (i.e., the research goal, objective(s), mixing rationale and purpose,

mixed research question(s), mixed sampling design, and mixed research design). (p. 24)

Figure 17.5 represents Onwuegbuzie, Slate, et al.'s (2009) three-dimensional model for categorizing and organizing orientations for mixed analyses. The model's first dimension, variable-oriented analyses, can be conceptualized as falling on a particularistic-universalistic continuum, classifying the extent to which the meta-inferences stemming from the variable-oriented analysis can

Figure 17.5 A Three-Dimensional Model for Categorizing and Organizing Orientations for Mixed Analyses

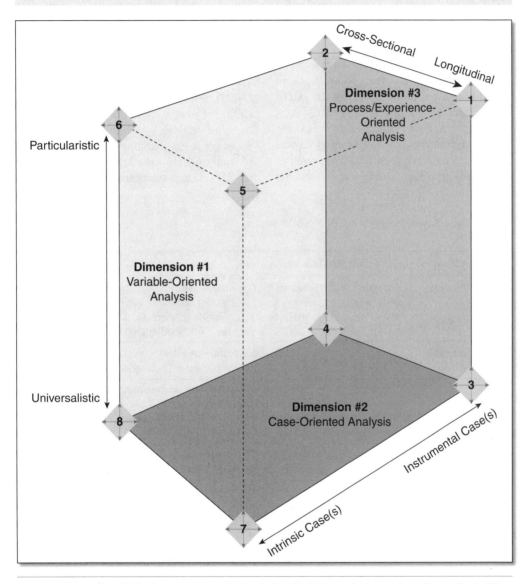

SOURCE: Originally published in *International Journal of Multiple Research Approaches* (Onwuegbuzie, Slate, Leech, & Collins, 2009, p. 28). http://www.ijmra.com; reproduced with permission.

NOTE: Directionality of the continua across each dimension is arbitrary. There is no intentionality of suggesting superiority of one continuum point or extreme over another. Rather, the appropriateness of the continuum point depends on the research goal, research objective(s), mixing rationale and purpose, mixed research question(s), mixed sampling design, and mixed research design. Encircled numbers represent eight possible combinations of the extreme points on the three dimensions of case-oriented, variable-oriented, and process/experience-oriented analyses.

be generalized. The second dimension, case-oriented analyses, ranges across an intrinsic-instrumental continuum, categorizing the purpose for selecting cases. The third dimension, process/experience-oriented analyses, categorizes the degree to which the study has

a temporal element, being represented by a cross-sectional-longitudinal continuum.

According to these authors, a mixed research study can be situated anywhere on the three-dimensional representation, demonstrating that quantitative and qualitative analyses can be mixed or embedded in almost unlimited ways. Furthermore, a given mixed analysis can be positioned within the three-dimensional space as a way of representing the mixed analytical design.

13. *Cross-over nature of analysis*. The final criterion that has been found to drive mixed analysis strategy represents an extension of Greene's (2007) "broad analytic concept" (p. 153) of "using aspects of the analytic framework of one methodological tradition in the analysis of data from another tradition" (p. 155). The example used by

Greene includes the use of visual displays (e.g., matrices and displays; cf. Miles & Huberman, 1994) to analyze qualitative data and the use of effect sizes in qualitative research (cf. Onwuegbuzie & Teddlie, 2003).

Building on the works of Greene (2007, 2008) and Onwuegbuzie and Teddlie (2003), we extend the concept of what we call *cross-over mixed analyses*, wherein one or more analysis types associated with one tradition (e.g., qualitative analysis) are used to analyze data associated with a different tradition (e.g., quantitative data). Table 17.6

Table 17.6   Cross-Over (Mixed) Analysis Strategies

Analysis Step	Cross-Case Analysis Strategy
Integrated data reduction	Reducing the dimensionality of qualitative data/findings using quantitative analysis (e.g., exploratory factor analysis of qualitative data) and/or quantitative data/findings using qualitative techniques (e.g., thematic analysis of quantitative data) (Onwuegbuzie, 2003; Onwuegbuzie & Teddlie, 2003)
Integrated data display	Visually presenting both qualitative and quantitative results within the same display (Lee & Greene, 2007; Onwuegbuzie & Dickinson, 2008)
Data transformation	Converting quantitative data into data that can be analyzed qualitatively (i.e., qualitizing data; Tashakkori & Teddlie, 1998), and/or qualitative data into numerical codes that can be analyzed statistically (i.e., quantitizing data; Tashakkori & Teddlie, 1998)
Data correlation	Correlating qualitative data with quantitized data and/or quantitative data with qualitized data (Onwuegbuzie & Teddlie, 2003)
Data consolidation	Combining or merging multiple data sets to create new or consolidated codes, variables, or data sets (Louis, 1982; Onwuegbuzie & Teddlie, 2003)
Data comparison	Comparing qualitative and quantitative data/findings (Onwuegbuzie & Teddlie, 2003)
Data integration	Integrating qualitative and quantitative data/findings into either a coherent whole or two separate sets (i.e., qualitative and quantitative) of coherent wholes (McConney, Rudd, & Ayres, 2002; Onwuegbuzie & Teddlie, 2003)
Warranted assertion analysis	Reviewing all qualitative and quantitative data to yield meta-inferences (Smith, 1997)
Data importation	Using follow-up findings from qualitative analysis to inform the quantitative analysis (e.g., qualitative contrasting case analysis, qualitative residual analysis, qualitative follow-up interaction analysis, and qualitative internal replication analysis; Li et al., 2000; Onwuegbuzie & Teddlie, 2003) or follow-up findings from quantitative analysis to inform the qualitative analysis (e.g., quantitative extreme case analysis, quantitative negative case analysis; Onwuegbuzie & Teddlie, 2003)

SOURCE: Originally published in *International Journal of Multiple Research Approaches* (Onwuegbuzie, Johnson, & Collins, 2009, p. 119), http://www.ijmra.com; reproduced with permission.

presents nine cross-over analysis types. As can be seen, cross-over analyses can be used to reduce, display, transform, correlate, consolidate, compare, integrate, assert, or import data. Cross-over mixed analyses are different from other types of mixed analyses (i.e., non-cross-over mixed analyses) such as parallel mixed analysis, because whereas non-cross-over mixed analyses involve collection of both types of data and the analysis conducted for each data set represents the same paradigmatic tradition (i.e., either traditional qualitative strategies used to analyze qualitative data or traditional quantitative strategies used to analyze quantitative data)—what Onwuegbuzie et al. (2007) call "within-paradigm analysis" (p. 12)—cross-over mixed analyses involve a between-paradigm analysis, which involves "an analysis technique that is more associated with one traditional paradigm (e.g., quantitative) to analyze data that originally represented the type of data collected that are more often associated with the other traditional paradigm (e.g., qualitative)" (Onwuegbuzie et al., 2007, p. 12). Thus, cross-over mixed analyses involve integration of qualitative and quantitative analyses to a greater extent than do other types of mixed analyses because they involve the mixing or combining of qualitative- and quantitative-based paradigmatic assumptions and stances. For example, a mixed methods researcher might use exploratory factor analysis to examine the structure of themes that emerged from a qualitative analysis (cf. Onwuegbuzie, 2003). In this instance, the researcher maintains either (a) an analytical-philosophical stance that the human mind/perception and mathematical/statistical algorithms can be used in a sequential manner to examine patterns in qualitative data or (b) an analytical-philosophical stance that transcends the stances that are associated with both paradigms (e.g., assuming that concepts of data saturation needed to extract trustworthy themes and reliability on which the exploratory factor analysis is based represent parallel concepts).

The distinction between cross-over mixed analyses and non-cross-over mixed analyses is important because certain epistemological, ontological, axiological, methodological, and rhetorical stances might be more appropriate for conducting cross-over mixed analyses than are other stances. Table 17.5 indicates 11 mixed methods paradigms/worldviews identified by Onwuegbuzie, Johnson, et al. (2009) that lend themselves to cross-over analyses. Teddlie and Tashakkori (2009) declared that applying aspects of analytical frameworks of one tradition to data analysis within another tradition—from which the concept of cross-over analysis stems—represents "one of the most fruitful areas for the further development of MM [mixed methods] analytical techniques" (p. 281).

◆ Meta-Framework of Mixed Analysis Strategies

Figure 17.6 represents our attempt to provide a meta-framework of mixed analysis strategies. This figure represents a concept map that depicts the 13 criteria that mixed method researchers might use at some point during the mixed analysis process. This meta-framework incorporates Collins et al.'s (2006) 13-step model of the mixed methods research process, which contains the following three stages: research formulation, research planning, and research implementation. The research implementation stage begins with the collection of data, which can be quantitative, qualitative, or both. At this point, the researcher can attempt to make all analysis decisions a priori, a posteriori, or iteratively (Criterion 10). Next, the analyst might determine the rationale/purpose of the mixed analysis (Criterion 1). The mixed analysis might be driven by the researcher's philosophy (Criterion 2) (cf. Biesta, 2010; Greene & Hall, 2010; Hesse-Biber, 2010; Maxwell & Mittapalli, 2010; Mertens et al., 2010 [all in this volume]) and/or the researcher's analysis orientation (Criterion 12). The analyst would decide on the number of data types (Criterion 3). Another criterion is deciding the level of interaction between the quantitative and qualitative analysis (Criterion 6), yielding either a parallel

Figure 17.6 Meta-Framework of Mixed Analysis Strategies

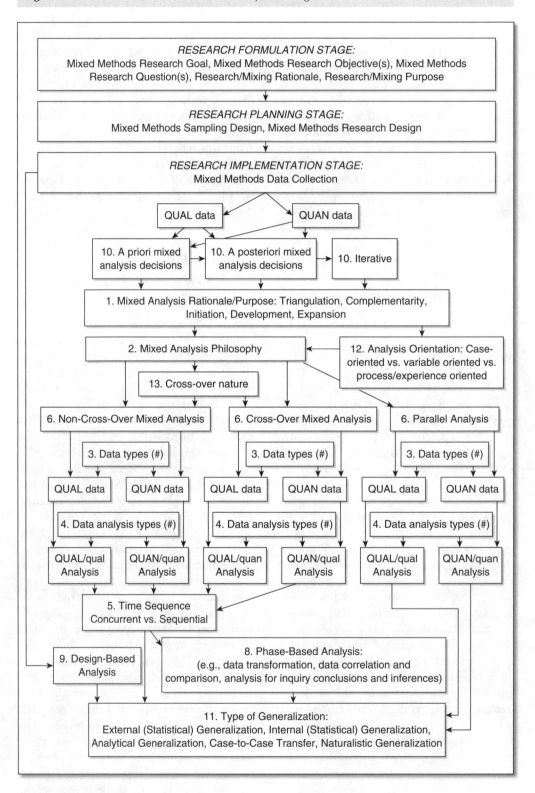

analysis or some form of interactive analysis. A parallel analysis in its most basic form would yield separate quantitative and qualitative analyses, which would generate one or more of the five types of generalization (Criterion 11). If an interactive analysis is of interest, the analyst might decide whether to use a cross-over (cf. Table 17.6, Figures 17.4 and 17.5) or non-cross-over mixed analysis (Criterion 13). Whichever of these types is used, the analyst would decide the number of data analysis types (Criterion 4). Furthermore, the analyst would decide on the specific quantitative (cf. Table 17.1, Figures 17.1 and 17.2) and qualitative (cf. Table 17.3, Figure 17.3) data analysis techniques to be used. Depending on the analysis used, the analyst could use quantitative (e.g., PASW, Excel, SAS), qualitative (e.g., NVivo8, Ethnograph, HyperResearch, Atlas.ti), or mixed analysis software (e.g., QDA Miner 3.2), or some combination, to conduct the mixed analysis (see Bazeley, 2010)—using visual displays as appropriate (Dickinson, 2010 [this volume]; Onwuegbuzie & Dickinson, 2008; Miles & Huberman, 1994; Tufte, 2001, 2006; Tukey, 1972, 1989; Wainer, 1990, 1992, 2005). The analyst also would decide the priority given to the quantitative and qualitative analysis phases (Criterion 7) and the time sequence of the mixed analysis (Criterion 5)—at which point, one or more of the five types of generalizations could be made (Criterion 11). Otherwise, the mixed analysis could be design-based (Criterion 9) or phase-based (Criterion 8), either of which would lead to at least one of the five types of generalizations (Criterion 11).

◆ *Conclusion: An Inclusive Definition of Mixed Method Analysis*

In this chapter, we presented several rationales for providing inclusive analytic frameworks. Next, we presented an inclusive framework for quantitative analyses, followed by an inclusive framework for qualitative analyses. In the remainder of the chapter, we moved toward an inclusive framework for mixed analyses. In particular, from the extant literature, we identified 13 criteria that authors have used to create their mixed analysis typologies.

From the 13 criteria that authors have used to create their mixed analysis typologies discussed above, we have developed a tentative and first approximation of a more comprehensive and inclusive definition or summary of what is called mixed analysis. Our new *inclusive definition* is as follows:

Mixed analysis involves the use of both quantitative and qualitative analytical techniques within the same framework, which is guided either a priori, a posteriori, or iteratively (representing analytical decisions that occur both prior to the study and during the study). It might be based on one of the existing mixed methods research paradigms (e.g., pragmatism, transformative-emancipatory) such that it meets one or more of the following rationales/purposes: triangulation, complementarity, development, initiation, and expansion. Mixed analyses involve the analyses of one or both data types (i.e., quantitative data *or* qualitative data; or quantitative data *and* qualitative data), which occur either concurrently (i.e., in no chronological order), or sequentially in two phases (in which the qualitative analysis phase precedes the quantitative analysis phase or vice versa, and findings from the initial analysis phase inform the subsequent phase), or more than two phases (i.e., iteratively). The analysis strands might not interact until the data interpretation stage, yielding a basic parallel mixed analysis, although more complex forms of parallel mixed analysis can be used, in which interaction takes place in a limited way before the data interpretation phase. The mixed analysis can be design based, wherein it is directly linked to the mixed methods design (e.g., sequential mixed analysis techniques used for sequential mixed methods designs). Alternatively, the mixed analysis can be phase based, in which the mixed analysis takes place in one or more phases (e.g., data transformation). In mixed analyses, either the qualitative or quantitative analysis strands might be given greater priority or approximately equal priority as a result of a priori decisions (i.e., determined at the research conceptualization phase) or decisions that emerge during the course of the study (i.e., a posteriori or iterative decisions). The mixed analysis could represent case-oriented, variable-oriented, and/or process/experience-oriented analyses. The mixed analysis is guided by an attempt to analyze data in a way that

yields at least one of five types of generalizations (i.e., external statistical generalizations, internal statistical generalizations, analytical generalizations, case-to-case transfer, naturalistic generalization). At its most integrated form, the mixed analysis might involve some form of cross-over analysis, wherein one or more analysis types associated with one tradition (e.g., qualitative analysis) are used to analyze data associated with a different tradition (e.g., quantitative data).

We hope that future mixed analysis typologies build on our inclusive framework, thereby further promoting mixed research as a distinctive methodology—consistent with the recommendation made by Greene (2008).

Research Questions and Exercises

1. Select a mixed methods research study, and identify the researcher's possible decision points for the quantitative data analysis phase(s) (see Figure 17.1).

2. Select a mixed methods research study, and identify the researcher's possible decision points for the qualitative data analysis phase(s) (see Figure 17.3).

3. Locate one example of a mixed method research study where the purpose for conducting the mixed analysis is identified.

4. Using Table 17.5, identify your mixed methods paradigms/worldviews.

5. Locate three mixed method research studies, and identify and compare the data types (i.e., qualitative, quantitative) and analysis techniques used.

6. Describe a hypothetical study that incorporates several of the criteria depicted on the meta-framework of mixed analysis strategies (see Figure 17.6). Note that not all criteria will be used in every study.

7. In your own words, define mixed analysis. What are the key attributes of mixed analyses?

8. What might be some challenges for the researcher conducting a mixed analysis?

9. What are some benefits for having an inclusive framework for mixed analysis?

◆ References

Bazeley, P. (1999). The *bricoleur* with a computer: Piecing together qualitative and quantitative data. *Qualitative Health Research, 9,* 279–287.

Bazeley, P. (2003). Computerized data analysis for mixed methods research. In A. Tashakkori & C. Teddlie (Eds.), *Handbook of mixed methods in social & behavioral research* (pp. 385–422). Thousand Oaks, CA: Sage.

Bazeley, P. (2006). The contribution of computer software to integrating qualitative and quantitative data and analyses. *Research in the Schools, 13*(1), 64–74.

Bazeley, P. (2009). Mixed methods data analysis. In S. Andrew & E. J. Halcomb (Eds.), *Mixed methods research for nursing and the health sciences* (pp. 84–118). Chichester, UK: Wiley-Blackwell.

Bazeley, P. (2010). Computer-assisted integration of mixed methods data sources and analysis. In A. Tashakkori & C. Teddlie (Eds.), *SAGE handbook of mixed methods in social & behavioral research* (2nd ed.). Thousand Oaks, CA: Sage.

Berelson, B. (1952). *Content analysis in communicative research.* New York: Free Press.

Bergman, M. M. (2010). Hermeneutic content analysis: Textual and audiovisual analyses within a mixed methods framework. In A. Tashakkori & C. Teddlie (Eds.), *SAGE handbook of mixed methods in social & behavioral research* (2nd ed.). Thousand Oaks, CA: Sage.

Biesta, G. (2010). Pragmatism and the philosophical foundations of mixed methods research. In A. Tashakkori & C. Teddlie (Eds.), *SAGE handbook of mixed methods in social & behavioral research* (2nd ed.). Thousand Oaks, CA: Sage.

Caracelli, V. W., & Greene, J. C. (1993). Data analysis strategies for mixed-method evaluation designs. *Educational Evaluation and Policy Analysis, 15,* 195–207.

Chi, M. T. H. (1997). Quantifying qualitative analyses of verbal data: A practical guide. *The Journal of the Learning Sciences, 6,* 271–315.

Collins, K. M. T., Onwuegbuzie, A. J., & Sutton, I. L. (2006). A model incorporating the rationale and purpose for conducting mixed methods research in special education and beyond. *Learning Disabilities: A Contemporary Journal, 4,* 67–100.

Creswell, J. W. (2007). *Qualitative inquiry and research design: Choosing among five approaches* (2nd ed.). Thousand Oaks, CA: Sage.

Creswell, J. W., & Plano Clark, V. L. (2007). *Designing and conducting mixed methods research.* Thousand Oaks, CA: Sage.

Curtis, S., Gesler, W., Smith, G., & Washburn, S. (2000). Approaches to sampling and case selection in qualitative research: Examples in the geography of health. *Social Science and Medicine, 50,* 1001–1014.

Datta, L. (2001). The wheelbarrow, the mosaic, and the double helix: Challenges and strategies for successfully carrying out mixed methods evaluation. *Evaluation Journal of Australia, 1*(2), 33–40.

Denscombe, M. (2008). Communities of practice: A research paradigm for the mixed methods approach. *Journal of Mixed Methods Research, 2,* 270–283.

Denzin, N. K., & Lincoln, Y. S. (2005). The discipline and practice of qualitative research. In N. K. Denzin & Y. S. Lincoln (Eds.), *The SAGE handbook of qualitative research* (3rd ed., pp. 1–32). Thousand Oaks, CA: Sage.

Dey, I. (1993). *Qualitative data analysis: A user-friendly guide for social scientists.* London: Routledge.

Dickinson, W. B. (2010). Visual displays for mixed methods findings. In A. Tashakkori & C. Teddlie (Eds.), *SAGE handbook of mixed methods in social & behavioral research* (2nd ed.). Thousand Oaks, CA: Sage.

Elmore, P. B., & Woehlke, P. L. (1996, April). *Research methods employed in "American Educational Research Journal," "Educational Researcher," and "Review of Educational Research" from 1978 to 1995.* Paper presented at the annual meeting of the American Educational Research Association, New York.

Greene, J. C. (2007). *Mixed methods in social inquiry.* San Francisco: Jossey-Bass.

Greene, J. C. (2008). Is mixed methods social inquiry a distinctive methodology? *Journal of Mixed Methods Research, 2,* 7–22.

Greene, J. C., Caracelli, V. J., & Graham, W. F. (1989). Toward a conceptual framework for mixed-method evaluation designs. *Educational Evaluation and Policy Analysis, 11,* 255–274.

Greene, J., & Hall, J. (2010). Dialectics and pragmatism: Being of consequence. In A. Tashakkori & C. Teddlie (Eds.), *SAGE handbook of mixed methods in social & behavioral research* (2nd ed.). Thousand Oaks, CA: Sage.

Happ, M. B., DeVito Dabbs, D. A., Tate, J., Hricik, A., & Erlen, J. (2006). Exemplars of mixed methods data combination and analysis. *Nursing Research, 55*(2, Suppl. 1), S43–S49.

Henson, R. K. (2000). Demystifying parametric analyses: Illustrating canonical correlation as the multivariate general linear model. *Multiple Linear Regression Viewpoints, 26,* 11–19.

Hesse-Biber, S. (2010). Feminist approaches to mixed methods research: Linking theory and praxis. In A. Tashakkori & C. Teddlie (Eds.), *SAGE handbook of mixed methods in social & behavioral research* (2nd ed.). Thousand Oaks, CA: Sage.

Hollander, M., & Wolfe, D. A. (1999). *Nonparametric statistical methods* (2nd ed.). New York: John Wiley.

Jang, E. E., McDougall, D. E., Pollon, D., & Russell, M. (2008). Integrative mixed methods data analytic strategies in research on school success in challenging environments. *Journal of Mixed Methods Research, 2,* 221–247.

Johnson, R. B., & Christensen, L. B. (2008). *Educational research: Quantitative, qualitative, and mixed approaches* (3rd ed.). Thousand Oaks, CA: Sage.

Johnson, R. B., & Onwuegbuzie, A. J. (2004). Mixed methods research: A research paradigm whose time has come. *Educational Researcher, 33*(7), 14–26.

Johnson, R. B., Onwuegbuzie, A. J., & Turner, L. A. (2007). Toward a definition of mixed methods research. *Journal of Mixed Methods Research, 1,* 112–133.

Lee, Y.-J., & Greene, J. C. (2007). The predictive validity of an ESL placement test: A mixed methods approach. *Journal of Mixed Methods Research, 1,* 366–389.

Leech, N. L., & Onwuegbuzie, A. J. (2004). A proposed fourth measure of significance: The role of economic significance in educational research. *Evaluation and Research in Education, 18,* 179–198.

Leech, N. L., & Onwuegbuzie, A. J. (2007). An array of qualitative data analysis tools: A call for qualitative data analysis triangulation. *School Psychology Quarterly, 22,* 557–584.

Leech, N. L., & Onwuegbuzie, A. J. (2008). Qualitative data analysis: A compendium of techniques and a framework for selection for school psychology research and beyond. *School Psychology Quarterly, 23,* 587–604.

Li, S., Marquart, J. M., & Zercher, C. (2000). Conceptual issues and analytical strategies in mixed-method studies of preschool inclusion. *Journal of Early Intervention, 23,* 116–132.

Louis, K. S. (1982). Sociologist as sleuth: Integrating methods in the RDU study. *American Behavioral Scientist, 26*(1), 101–120.

Maxwell, J. A., & Mittapalli, K. (2010). Realism as a stance for mixed method research. In A. Tashakkori & C. Teddlie (Eds.), *SAGE handbook of mixed methods in social & behavioral research* (2nd ed.). Thousand Oaks, CA: Sage.

McConney, A., Rudd, A., & Ayres, R. (2002). Getting to the bottom line: A method for synthesizing findings within mixed-method program evaluations. *American Journal of Evaluation, 23,* 121–140.

McEvoy, P., & Richards, D. (2003). Critical realism: A way forward for evaluation research in nursing? *Journal of Advanced Nursing, 43,* 411–420.

Mertens, D. (2003). Mixed methods and the politics of human research: The transformative-emancipatory perspective. In A. Tashakkori & C. Teddlie (Eds.), *Handbook of mixed methods in social & behavioral research* (pp. 135–164). Thousand Oaks, CA: Sage.

Mertens, D. M., Bledsoe, K. L., Sullivan, M., & Wilson, A. (2010). Utilization of mixed methods for transformative purposes. In

A. Tashakkori & C. Teddlie (Eds.), *SAGE handbook of mixed methods in social & behavioral research* (2nd ed.). Thousand Oaks, CA: Sage.

Miles, M. B., & Huberman, A. M. (1994). *Qualitative data analysis: An expanded sourcebook* (2nd ed.). Thousand Oaks, CA: Sage.

Morse, J. M. (1995). The significance of saturation. *Qualitative Health Research, 5,* 147–149.

Morse, J. (2003). Principles of mixed methods and multimethod research design. In A. Tashakkori & C. Teddlie (Eds.), *Handbook of mixed methods in social & behavioral research* (pp. 189–208). Thousand Oaks, CA: Sage.

Newman, I., & Ramlo, S. (2010). Using Q methodology and Q factor analysis in mixed methods research. In A. Tashakkori & C. Teddlie (Eds.), *SAGE handbook of mixed methods in social & behavioral research* (2nd ed.). Thousand Oaks, CA: Sage.

O'Cathain, A. (2010). Assessing the quality of mixed methods research: Toward a comprehensive framework. In A. Tashakkori & C. Teddlie (Eds.), *SAGE handbook of mixed methods in social & behavioral research* (2nd ed.). Thousand Oaks, CA: Sage.

Onwuegbuzie, A. J. (2003). Effect sizes in qualitative research: A prolegomenon. *Quality & Quantity: International Journal of Methodology, 37,* 393–409.

Onwuegbuzie, A. J., & Collins, K. M. T. (2009, March). *An innovative method for analyzing themes in mixed research: Introducing chi-square automatic interaction detection (CHAID).* Paper presented at the annual meeting of the American Educational Research Association, San Diego, CA.

Onwuegbuzie, A. J., Collins, K. M. T., & Leech, N. L. (in press). *Mixed research: A step-by-step guide.* New York: Taylor & Francis.

Onwuegbuzie, A. J., Collins, K. M. T., Leech, N. L., Dellinger, A., & Jiao, Q. G. (in press). A meta-framework for conducting mixed research syntheses. *The Qualitative Report.*

Onwuegbuzie, A. J., & Combs, J. P. (2009). *An innovative method for analyzing themes in mixed research: Introducing mixed thematic-exploratory factor analyses.* Manuscript submitted for publication.

Onwuegbuzie, A. J., & Daniel, L. G. (2003). Typology of analytical and interpretational errors in quantitative and qualitative educational research. *Current Issues in Education* [On-line], 6(2). Retrieved May 23, 2009, from http://cie.ed.asu.edu/volume6/number2/

Onwuegbuzie, A. J., & Dickinson, W. B. (2008). Mixed methods analysis and information visualization: Graphical display for effective communication of research results. *The Qualitative Report, 13,* 204–225. Retrieved March 28, 2009, from http://www.nova.edu/ssss/QR/QR13-2/onwuegbuzie.pdf

Onwuegbuzie, A. J., Johnson, R. B., & Collins, K. M. T. (2009). A call for mixed analysis: A philosophical framework for combining qualitative and quantitative. *International Journal of Multiple Research Approaches, 3,* 114–139.

Onwuegbuzie, A. J., & Leech, N. L. (2004). Enhancing the interpretation of "significant" findings: The role of mixed methods research. *The Qualitative Report, 9,* 770–792. Retrieved March 28, 2009, from http://www.nova.edu/ssss/QR/QR9-4/onwuegbuzie.pdf

Onwuegbuzie, A. J., & Leech, N. L. (2006). Linking research questions to mixed methods data analysis procedures. *The Qualitative Report, 11,* 474–498. Retrieved July 8, 2008, from http://www.nova.edu/ssss/QR/QR11-3/onwuegbuzie.pdf

Onwuegbuzie, A. J., Slate, J. R., Leech, N. L., & Collins, K. M. T. (2007). Conducting mixed analyses: A general typology. *International Journal of Multiple Research Approaches, 1,* 4–17.

Onwuegbuzie, A. J., Slate, J. R., Leech, N. L., & Collins, K. M. T. (2009). Mixed data analysis: Advanced integration techniques. *International Journal of Multiple Research Approaches, 3,* 13–33.

Onwuegbuzie, A. J., & Teddlie, C. (2003). A framework for analyzing data in mixed methods research. In A. Tashakkori & C. Teddlie (Eds.), *Handbook of mixed methods in social & behavioral research* (pp. 351–383). Thousand Oaks, CA: Sage.

Phillips, L. J., & Jorgensen, M. W. (2002). *Discourse analysis as theory and method.* Thousand Oaks, CA: Sage.

Ragin, C. C. (1989). *The comparative method: Moving beyond qualitative and quantitative strategies.* Berkeley: University of California Press.

Rao, V., & Wolcock, M. (2003). Integrating qualitative and quantitative approaches in program evaluation. In F. J. Bourguignon & L. Pereira de Silva (Eds.), *Evaluating the poverty and distribution impact of economic policies* (pp. 165–190). New York: The World Bank.

Sandelowski, M. (2000). Combining qualitative and quantitative sampling, data collection, and analysis techniques in mixed-method studies. *Research in Nursing Health, 23,* 246–255.

Sandelowski, M. (2001). Real qualitative researchers don't count: The use of numbers in qualitative research. *Research in Nursing and Health, 24,* 230–240.

Schwandt, T. A. (2007). *Sage dictionary of qualitative inquiry* (3rd ed.). Thousand Oaks, CA: Sage.

Smith, M. L. (1997). Mixing and matching: Methods and models. In J. C. Greene & V. J. Caracelli (Eds.), *Advances in mixed-method evaluation: The challenges and benefits of integrating diverse paradigms* (New Directions for Evaluation No. 74, pp. 73–85). San Francisco: Jossey-Bass.

Spradley, J. P. (1979). *The ethnographic interview.* Fort Worth, TX: Holt, Rinehart and Winston.

Stake, R. E., & Trumbull, D. J. (1982). Naturalistic generalizations. *Review Journal of Philosophy and Social Science, 7,* 3–12.

Tabachnick, B. G., & Fidell, L. S. (2006). *Using multivariate statistics* (5th ed.). New York: HarperCollins College.

Tashakkori, A., & Teddlie, C. (1998). *Mixed methodology: Combining qualitative and quantitative approaches* (Applied Social Research Methods Series, No. 46). Thousand Oaks, CA: Sage.

Teddlie, C., & Tashakkori, A. (2009). *Foundations of mixed methods research: Integrating quantitative and qualitative techniques in the social and behavioral sciences.* Thousand Oaks, CA: Sage.

Teddlie, C., Tashakkori, A., & Johnson, R. B. (2008). Emergent techniques in the gathering and analysis of mixed methods data. In S. N. Hesse-Biber & P. Leavy (Eds.), *Handbook of emergent methods* (pp. 389–414). New York: The Guilford Press.

Thompson, B. (1998, April). *Five methodological errors in educational research: The pantheon of statistical significance and other faux pas.* Paper presented at the annual meeting of the American Educational Research Association, San Diego, CA.

Todd, Z., Nerlich, B., McKeown, S., & Clarke, D. D. (2004). *Mixing methods in psychology: The integration of qualitative and quantitative methods in theory and practice.* New York: Psychology Press.

Tufte, E. R. (2001). *The visual display of quantitative information* (2nd ed.). Cheshire, CT: Graphics Press.

Tufte, E. R. (2006). *Beautiful evidence.* Cheshire, CT: Graphics Press.

Tukey, J. W. (1972). Some graphic and semigraphic displays. In T. A. Bancroft (Ed.), *Statistical papers in honor of George W. Snedecor* (pp. 293–316). Ames: The Iowa State University Press

Tukey, J. W. (1989). Data-based graphics: Visual display in the years to come. *Proceedings of the American Statistical Association, 84,* 366–381.

Wainer, H. (1990). Graphical visions from William Playfair to John Tukey. *Statistical Science, 5,* 340–346.

Wainer, H. (1992). Understanding graphs and tables. *Educational Researcher, 21*(1), 14–23.

Wainer, H. (2005). *Graphic discovery: A trout in the milk and other visual adventures.* Princeton, NJ: Princeton University Press.

West, E., & Tulloch, M. (2001, May). *Qualitising quantitative data: Should we do it, and if so, how?* Paper presented at the annual meeting of the Association for Social Research, Wollongong, New South Wales, Australia.

Yin, R. K. (2009). *Case study research: Design and methods* (4th ed.). Thousand Oaks, CA: Sage.

18

COMPUTER-ASSISTED INTEGRATION OF MIXED METHODS DATA SOURCES AND ANALYSES

◆ Pat Bazeley

Objectives

This chapter has one primary learning objective:

- to improve the level and quality of integration in, and thus inference from, mixed methods studies.

It also has a number of contributory sub-objectives:

- to stimulate readers to think more adventurously about the possibilities for analysis inherent in their mixed methods data;

- to introduce a range of software tools that will assist readers who wish to extend their practice and skills in data management and analysis; and

- to review approaches to, and ideas and suggestions for, ways of integrating data and analyses that are supported by software.

New tools within analysis software, developed in response to the growing interest in mixed methods research, facilitate and extend possibilities for working with mixed data types and analysis methods. This chapter considers the opportunities software presents the researcher working to integrate data and analyses in answering questions asked in the social and behavioral sciences.

◆ The Challenge of Integration

Integration of mixed data sources and approaches to analysis occurred in classic community studies and in evaluation research through much of the last century. All mixed methods studies, by definition, attempt some form of integration, but in the latter years of the last century, debates about commensurability of paradigms created anxiety for many researchers about integrating the various strands of a mixed (or multi-) method research project before they reached the point of drawing conclusions. Currently, specific disciplinary expectations (particularly evident in health and education) as to what constitutes "gold standard" scientific evidence continues to downplay the value of evidence derived from qualitative sources. These theoretical positions combine with practical difficulties involved in collecting, managing, and analyzing multiple sources to limit the extent to which researchers effectively integrate various components of their mixed methods studies (Bryman, 2007; O'Cathain, Murphy, & Nicholl, 2007). As noted by Greene (2007), the interaction challenge in integrated designs remains undertheorized and understudied; I would suggest that the level of integration in many (if not most) mixed methods studies remains underdeveloped.

This chapter takes as its starting point the assumption that integration of data and analyses is not only acceptable but often necessary for achieving project goals, and it looks at how such integration might be facilitated by use of computer software. For current purposes, and borrowing from previous work by Bryman (2007), Woolley (2009), Moran-Ellis et al. (2006), and Yin (2006), I define integration in mixed methods thus:

> Integration can be said to occur to the extent that different data elements and various strategies for analysis of those elements are combined throughout a study in such a way as to become interdependent in reaching a common theoretical or research goal, thereby producing findings that are greater than the sum of the parts.

My approach to integration recognizes "the reality that there can be many different 'mixes' or combinations of methods" (Yin, 2006, p. 41) and rejects a clear differentiation between qualitative and quantitative methods or approaches to research (Bergman, 2008). In describing their approach to concept analysis as an integrative mixed method, Kane and Trochim (2007) suggest:

> Rather than simply combining qualitative and quantitative methods, [concept analysis] challenges the distinction between these two and suggests that they may indeed be more deeply intertwined. In some sense it is a method that supports the notion that qualitative information can be well represented quantitatively and that quantitative information rests upon qualitative judgment. (p. 177)

This is an opinion that is somewhat reflective of a much earlier statement by Fielding and Fielding (1986):

> Ultimately all methods of data collection are analysed "qualitatively," in so far as the act of analysis is an interpretation, and therefore of necessity a selective rendering, of the "sense" of the available data. (p. 12)

If *quantitative* and *qualitative* are poles on a multidimensional continuum rather than distinct entities, as is now widely recognized, then emphasis on the separate definition of these components and a requirement for inclusion of both in a mixed methods study can create unhelpful boundary issues and further impede analytic integration.

The issue for researchers struggling in their attempt to integrate the different strands of their projects is compounded for those who also have a limited understanding of qualitative methodologies, such that they do little more than descriptively identify themes when working with text-based data, or simply use them to find "juicy quotes" to illustrate their statistical results (Bazeley, 2009a). Likewise, those with limited statistical understanding are prone to ignore the assumptions associated with particular statistical procedures and to draw inappropriate conclusions from their data, or they are simply unaware of the possibilities that statistical analyses can offer. Traditional research training in qualitative and/or quantitative methods, in addition, rarely engages with methodological developments that do not fit neatly into either of those boxes, such as Q methodology, social network analysis, or use of fuzzy logic or qualitative comparative analysis. One of the clear challenges in integrating data and analyses, therefore, is in having the breadth and depth of individual or team-based knowledge and skills on which to draw when undertaking a mixed methods study.

◆ Strategies for Integration

Analytic strategies, particularly decisions about the level of integration in mixed methods studies and the point at which it might occur, are very much related to issues of research design and purpose (Maxwell & Loomis, 2003). "Methodology is ever the servant of purpose, never the master" (Greene, 2007, p. 97). The primary purposes

for integrating methods, in Greene's analysis, are complementarity and initiation, with the latter being particularly served by dialectically integrated paradigmatic and methodological approaches.

In recent decades, mixed methods theorists have begun to identify a range of integrative design strategies for working with mixed data sources and complex questions (Creswell & Plano Clark, 2007; Greene, 2007; Teddlie & Tashakkori, 2009) and for integrating data specifically through analysis, rather than as a conclusion to analysis (Bazeley, 1999, 2006, 2009b, 2009c; Caracelli & Greene, 1993; Teddlie & Tashakkori, 2009). Two primary processes—combination and/or conversion—run through most integrative strategies (Bazeley, 2006), and computer software assists integration primarily through providing ways in which quantitative and qualitative data can be combined or converted.

◆ Software for Mixed Methods Analysis

Software for separately analyzed quantitative and qualitative components in a mixed methods study is widely available and can be used as suits the regular preferences of the researcher. Mixed methods researchers wanting to integrate different types of data within their analyses can find assistance also from a number of these software packages, as well as from some more specialist programs. Most of the software described below does not prescribe use of a particular methodology or method of analysis (within its broad domain) but rather provides tools for application to the researcher's chosen approach to analysis.

Available programs that are of assistance to the mixed methods researcher can be broadly classified into three groups: general purpose spreadsheets and databases; programs designed primarily for qualitative data analysis but which provide for combination or conversion of data; and add-on text-analysis modules for statistical programs, which categorize text data and then combine it into statistical analyses. In addition, there is an increasing range of software developed for specific purposes, often inherently involving mixed methods (Teddlie & Tashakkori, 2009).

Software developers respond to user demand. Recent developments in software reflect the growing acceptance of the integration of qualitative and quantitative data and analyses as a legitimate approach to handling data. These developments also offer exciting new possibilities for researchers wishing to explore the limits of what can be achieved with computer software as a tool. From a technical point of view, integrating qualitative and quantitative data is no longer difficult, providing one is reasonably comfortable with computers and with moving between a range of software packages. Yet, there are surprisingly few published studies reporting results from projects that make more than very elementary use of the capacity to integrate data and analyses using computers.

GENERAL PURPOSE SPREADSHEETS AND DATABASES

Spreadsheets and databases are widely available as components in general purpose office suites. Excel, for example, is often used in research as a data recording tool; as an intermediary for transferring numeric data from one program to another; for simple calculations such as sums, means, and percentages; for production of cross-tabulations (pivot tables); and for charting data. Often the handmaiden to other software, spreadsheets and databases also have some specific functions of value to mixed methods researchers.

Both text and numeric data can be recorded within a spreadsheet, making it a useful tool for mixed methods tasks that involve synthesis of varied forms of data from a range of sources, and one that is quite straightforward to use. A database can be used similarly, with the advantage of being able to handle larger text fields and queries across related tables, but it is somewhat more complex to set up and use. Columns are created to cover all issues to be explored and aspects of concern that might impinge on those, while numeric or summary data or brief quotes from each source or case are entered in each row. These do not need to be ordered in any particular way. Once entered, data can be sorted, resorted, or filtered on the basis of included numeric or categorical variables to reveal patterns across all responses (Bazeley, 2006; Niglas, 2007). New categories or issues can be added during the process if found to be necessary by adding an additional column, or additional categorization of the text summaries can be completed during analysis to allow further sorting and examination of relationships between categories.

STATISTICAL PACKAGES

Statistical software typically provides an extensive range of visualization tools to assist the quantitative researcher to see patterns in and interpret their data, including charts of various types, box plots, scatterplots, dendrograms, and dimensional plots.

Several statistical programs provide additional modules designed to auto-code responses to open-ended questions for statistical analysis. SPSS Text Analysis for Surveys (www.spss.com) creates modifiable categories based on regularly co-occurring words from short-answer text responses using natural language processing, allowing the researcher to rapidly categorize a large set of data and combine it with the precategorized or scaled responses from the same survey in regular statistical routines. WordStat (www.provalisresearch.com) can be used with either short answers or longer passages of unstructured text (up to 10 Mb). Starting from an automated content analysis of words in the text, the user sets up rules and so builds up dictionaries for categorizing the data. These rules can be stored for future use with further sets of data. Relationships between the coded content of documents and information stored in categorical or numeric variables can be rapidly explored using exploratory data analysis or graphical tools.

QUALITATIVE DATA ANALYSIS (QDA) SOFTWARE

Authors using manual methods for coding the qualitative data component of their mixed methods study typically describe an exhaustive process of reading, re-reading, and checking transcribed text to arrive at a series of themes and subthemes, with the description of these themes being presented as the analysis of the data. With computer-based coding, the researcher can separately identify, on the same passage, a range of contextual, action, responsive, or other factors, with any of these codes used in any combination, as appropriate, across any of the data. As soon as data are coded in this way, almost limitless possibilities for review, sorting, sifting, combination, and comparison of text segments become available, with original source context available as required (Bazeley, 2007).

Tools developed primarily (or initially) for analysis of qualitative data, but which have now developed specific capacities for integrative mixed methods analyses, include NVivo (www.qsrinternational.com) and MAXQDA (www.maxqda.com). QDA Miner (www.provalisresearch.com) has been developed as the qualitative coding component of a larger suite (including WordStat) purposively designed for application within mixed methods analyses. EthnoNotes (www.ethnonotes.com) is a multi-user, multiplatform Web-based application (purchased on a project/user/time basis), which has also been developed specifically for use in mixed methods applications.

Facilities currently offered to the mixed methods researcher by these programs include

- auto-coding tools to facilitate sorting of open-ended responses from structured surveys;

- integration of quantitative (variable) data with coded (thematic) qualitative data for matrix-based comparative analyses of coded text;

- conversion of qualitative coding to variable data;

- export of matrix-based data reflecting detail of associations between codes; and

- visualization tools.

PROGRAMS SUPPORTING PARTICULAR MIXED METHODS APPLICATIONS

These software programs are designed with particular methodological purposes in mind, rather than for general application to a broader range of projects and purposes.

QCA—Qualitative Comparative Analysis

QCA refers to a set of configurational comparative methods based on the logic of set theory and using Boolean algebra applied to small or moderate-size sets of categorized data. Data are organized as configurations in a "truth table," used to build explanatory models for a given outcome. The original QCA software, developed for dichotomized ("crisp set" or csQCA) data, remains DOS based. More recent developments, however, include and extend crisp set QCA analysis to analysis of multivalue data (TOSMANA, for mvQCA) and fuzzy-set data (FSQCA, for fsQCA). An overview of software on http://www.compasss.org/pages/resources/software.html provides links to (free) download sites for TOSMANA, FSQCA, and a QCA module in R, as well as other resources for users.

Software for Social Network Analysis

Raw data for social network analysis, generated from reports of specified types of contacts between members of a network, is entered into a simple matrix showing who connects with whom, which is then saved as a text file to be read by both statistical and graphical programs. Members of the network may be individuals or organizations or other entities that connect to each other in some way. Mathematical indices for centrality, density, and connectivity (among others) for networks or for the individuals within them can be calculated using, for example, UCINET6 (www.analytictech.com/ucinet6/ ucinet.htm). Pajek (http://pajek.imfm.si/doku .php?id=pajek)—Slovenian for spider—has been designed for analysis and visualization of large networks. NetDraw (packaged with UCINET) provides direct graphical representation of networks created using either UCINET or Pajek. Increasingly, researchers are developing a range of add-on modules for specialist analyses, for example, using analyses of triads to measure closure and brokerage as aspects of social capital (Prell & Skvoretz, 2008).

GIS Software

Software for geographic information systems (GIS) links physical, demographic, statistical, and social data by plotting them onto maps and so adds a spatial dimension to social science projects. Commercial GIS software suites appropriate for social science researchers include ArcGIS (www.esri.com) and MapInfo (www.mapinfo.com). Each of these suites provides core components with add-on modules for special purposes; additional specific purpose modules are often developed and made available free or at low cost from other users. Other programs such as Intergraph and Autodesk serve more specific industrial and commercial markets.

Some GIS freeware and add-ons, offering more limited functionality than the commercial programs, are also available: Lists can be found at http://opensourcegis.org; and www.freegis.org; with reviews at www .spatialserver.net/osgis.

The release of Google Earth (http://earth .google.com) has also brought a new visualization dimension to research, with the capacity to build links to locational images into any qualitative program that allows either external hyperlinks, or for images to be imported as data sources, or both (e.g., Atlas.ti, MAXQDA, NVivo).

◆ Data Management in an Integrated Project— Combining Diversity, Complexity, and Flexibility

Those working with mixed data sources are likely to be dealing with complex data sets in which there are multiple sources of varying types of data for each case, possibly from different time periods, and perhaps with cases embedded within cases. Computers come into their own when it comes to data management, as they can reliably keep track of sources, their content, and their connections (see Box 18.1). The range of data types that can be managed within analysis software is ever increasing. Until the turn of the century, few analysis programs could import and work with anything other than plain (ASCII) text or numbers, often with severe limitations on size of files. Many programs now have capacity to import and work with HTML, .pdf, audio, video, and image files as well as numeric, tabular, and rich-text data, within the one project, and to combine variable-based data with text records.

Along with managing complex data, exploratory research typically requires flexibility, for example, to modify coding, and even design, as it proceeds. Even in theory-testing projects, changes to design and coding frequently become necessary in response to data gathering. Qualitative software, in particular, allows for flexibility in developing and changing the structure and content of coding systems. In most programs, it is also possible to code on from already coded data, that is, to generate new, finer categories from material already coded at initial broad or automated coding categories, to identify and code additional aspects not previously noticed or considered, or to recode segments in response to development in conceptualization through the project. Typically, qualitative software also assists the researcher to keep a careful audit trail of the changes made.

BOX 18.1

Managing a Complex Set of Data in a 10-year Retrospective Longitudinal Evaluation Project

Green Valley was built as a public housing estate on the southwest fringe of Sydney in the 1960s. Now including a mix of public and privately owned houses, it remains an area of social and economic disadvantage close to a rapidly developing business center. For the past 10 years, the Centre for Health Equity, Training Research and Evaluation (CHETRE), jointly sponsored by the University of New South Wales and the Sydney South West Area Health Service, has been implementing and evaluating community development initiatives within this area. Over that period, results of regular surveys of residents, interviews with a range of stakeholders, and various sources of documentary evidence have been gathered. As part of my role in CHETRE, I have been asked to conduct a retrospective longitudinal study to examine the ebbs and flows of these varying initiatives over time and their impact on community capacity, health, and well-being through that period and to build a model that can guide future planning.

Starting from a box of reports, brochures, news clippings, and other documentary sources, along with a set of files comprising reports, interviews, and statistical databases, I am building a database in NVivo to manage and analyze this data, along with relevant literature. As a first step, every source of data will be recorded in the database, along with variable information pertaining to its type, date, and program and, where appropriate, with demographic data relating to the community role and other relevant aspects of the person(s) from whom it came (treated as attributes in NVivo). Word, .pdf, and multimedia files can be imported as internal sources; any documentary material that cannot be scanned and imported can be recorded as an external source, along with its attributes and its physical location. Hyperlinks to original sources and other files (e.g., SPSS databases or output files) can be stored for immediate access if needed.

The second step will be to work through this data, using NVivo's coding system to effectively index the contents of all the material (including external files). Coding will provide instant access to all material on each condition, action, person, issue, or outcome being considered. Essential components of this second step will be to keep an audit trail of processes used and changes made and to record in memos any queries or ideas prompted by reviewing the data.

The third step builds on the careful foundational work done during the previous two and is enormously facilitated by having done that work using software. Now, using query procedures in the software, conditions can be linked to actions and outcomes and issues arising by examining patterns in the intersections of coding categories; trends over time or differences in perspective depending on role or gender or age can be examined by examining the patterns

(Continued)

(Continued)

of intersection of coding categories with attribute data; analyses can be restricted to sub-groups of the population or particular periods of time by creating sets of data based on attribute values; exceptions can be examined; and so on—all tasks that would be extremely difficult to do using manual methods with such a large and diverse body of data. In addition, information from the qualitative database can be exported for use in other software applications to allow network analysis, locational analyses, or further statistical analyses.

◆ Integrating Numeric or Categorical Variables With Unstructured Data

The majority of mixed methods studies involve having more than one type of data, gathered concurrently or sequentially from the same sources or from different sources. The timing of collection and capacity for matching the sources both have implications for the degree to which analyses of the different components can be integrated. Responses obtained through surveys comprising both open and closed questions, for example, provide data where matching is readily available and integration during analysis is straightforward. Combinations of surveys or questionnaires with interviews or other separately gathered sources may be more problematic in this regard, and often, integration occurs only after completion of analysis of the separate sources, at the point of interpreting conclusions.

Whether one is using qualitative analysis software or software designed to automatically categorize text responses, the clear analytic advantage of using software is its capacity to sort coded text by categorized responses or background variables—whether these be demographic information, responses to questions asking for opinions or experience, or ratings given in response to scaled items. Linking these responses on an individual basis facilitates a richer and potentially more valid analysis (Box 18.2). Variations in responses can be better understood, and anomalies and alternative explanations examined. Matching in this way can assist, also, in scale validation, in exploring dimensionality in the data, and in theoretical development through better understanding the conditionality or consequences of responses.

BOX 18.2

Untapped Potential Impacts on Analysis Quality

The current distress levels of long-term survivors of lung cancer were investigated by Maliski, Sarna, Evangelista, and Padilla (2003). Those with lower levels of distressed mood spoke more positively as a group about five central themes of existential issues—health, self-care, physical ability, adjustment, and support (each described in detail)—than did those who scored higher on distress. Although this information is useful, the authors matched the qualitative data on a two-group basis only to depression scores, ignoring physiological measures such as spirometry results, even though these were described in detail in the method, and also ignoring a stated association of depression scores with racial and educational differences. A comparison of their five central themes using linked data that incorporated these variables may have led them to entirely different conclusions.

Permission to match data gathered at different times is increasingly an issue resulting from human ethics committees' requirements for preservation of anonymity for those responding to surveys or questionnaires. The best strategy is to ask respondents to provide necessary contact information at the end of the questionnaire or survey, if they are prepared to be followed up, along with permission to do so. If necessary, a code name can be used for matching. A critical element is that this issue has to be thought through *before* conducting the first data collection.

Methodological issues raised by combining categorical or numeric variables with text or visual data vary depending on the purpose—complementarity (the most common purpose) is generally unproblematic, for example—and are primarily related to issues raised by different sampling regimes, distributions, and sizes. Researchers interpreting the numeric output from a comparative analysis of text based on quantitatively defined groups must remain conscious of the sample size within each of the compared groups; otherwise, they risk misinterpreting the displayed results. It is also very easy to misinterpret the significance of differences when numbers are small, especially for those who have not had training in statistical procedures and assumptions.

COMBINING MIXED-FORM SURVEY DATA

Surveys or questionnaires employing both closed and open-ended questions are a common source of mixed data (Bryman, 2006). In its most elementary form, combination occurs where a closed question is followed up with a request to respondents to provide comment, explanation, or illustration of their answer. Matching categorical or numeric and text responses on an individual basis is not a problem in this setting, as the different forms of data are obtained at the same time. Comments can then be sorted by the categorized responses to provide illustrative material to assist in interpreting what each response really meant to the survey respondents. Researchers can use the open responses to provide illustrative quotes for their primary statistical analyses, and the direct link between the two data forms allows for a more detailed assessment of other relationships between the text and numeric components of the data, such as through comparative analyses (Box 18.3).

BOX 18.3

Linking Text and Numeric Data From a Survey

A combination of Stata and NVivo was used by Ford (2006) to analyze closed and open-ended responses to a survey instrument in her doctoral study of nurses' care of patients who use illicit drugs. Free text responses about the interpersonal constraints these patients imposed on their therapeutic nursing role were provided by 311 of the 1,605 respondents. Ford used this data in two different ways: She used the statistical data to compare those who wrote about their experience with those who didn't, and she then used demographic and other closed responses, imported into NVivo, as a basis for comparing the kinds of issues that these nurses raised.

Nurses who added free text responses were more likely than others to be in high-contact (i.e., clinical) areas of practice and reported more episodes of extended care for patients who

(Continued)

(Continued)

were illicit drug users; that is, the issues raised by the survey were more salient for them than for others. They were also younger and less experienced than the remainder of the study sample, and while they reported higher levels of role adequacy, they also reported lower motivation and satisfaction. The specific therapeutic concerns they expressed were about patient aggressiveness, manipulation, and irresponsibility, and they reported frustration with the patient, fear in their role, and pessimism about the usefulness of therapeutic interventions.

Those practicing in different areas expressed unique challenges in response to these patient behaviors, which required different nursing care and which engendered different attitudes. Midwives dealt with manipulative patients and aggressive partners but were particularly concerned about and frustrated with mothers' irresponsibility in the context of "putting a baby in the mix." The attitudes of those working in emergency to people coming into their care were impacted by the short-term nature of a relationship in which they also frequently experienced aggression and manipulation. They were most angered, however, by drug users' irresponsibility toward others harmed by their actions and were frustrated by not seeing any long-term outcomes for the patient from the experience or their care. In contrast, in a medical/surgical practice setting where there was an extended period of time-intensive contact, patients' continued aggressive and manipulative behavior created staffing and care issues.

Decisions about what software to use for linking and analyzing text and numeric data in surveys will depend on the volume and depth of the data, as well as on available or preferred programs. Simple comparative sorts of text responses to particular questions according to values on a categorical variable can be achieved in any spreadsheet or database, but researchers will be quickly overcome by large or complex data sets if that is their only tool. QDA software has the added advantage, for more complex responses, of allowing for revised coding of those responses to more detailed categories, perhaps revealing new concepts that are expressed across responses to a number of questions. Text at these new codes also is able to be compared across categorical variables, while the new categories generated can be exported as variable data back into the quantitative database. For large data sets, software that automates categorization of short-answer responses for inclusion in the statistical database, supplemented by reviewing a sample of responses in each category, may be the most appropriate solution.

COMBINING SURVEYS WITH INTERVIEWS OR OTHER UNSTRUCTURED DATA

Use of follow-up interviews to corroborate, illustrate, or elaborate on the meaning of categorized or scaled responses to survey questions continues to be the most common data-gathering strategy employed by mixed methods researchers (Bryman, 2006). Alternative quantitative sources, such as administrative data or biophysical measures, might be obtained in association with interview responses or with reports, filmed observations, or other unstructured data. Spreadsheets, databases, and auto-coding modules for statistical software are even less helpful for handling the qualitative material in these types of projects, however: Analysis of interview or other free text or visual data is a task that benefits particularly from use of QDA software. Coding of this data might proceed on an emergent basis, or it might be directed by the issues and categories raised in or by a prior survey; software can be used flexibly in either way.

The issues in relating quantitative to qualitative data are similar to those for mixed-form surveys. Benefits from these analyses extend beyond detecting simple patterns of association with subgroups to raising questions for further exploration about other relationships. In addition, such analyses provide insights regarding dimensionalization of concepts and the potential to validate scaled measures and to identify and explore deviant cases.

COMPARATIVE ANALYSES USING MIXED DATA

The assumption being tested through the comparative process is that a person's gender, or age, or role (or whatever it is that has been included) is relevant to whatever the person might say on the topic(s) of interest. Even in a primarily qualitative project, it is usually relevant to include at least some basic demographic variables in the analysis mix. In a simple extension of this principle, responses to precategorized questions (such as yes/no, or often/sometimes/never) or scaled measures (e.g., level of satisfaction, scores on a measure of social alienation) may also be relevant to the interpretive analysis of the qualitative data. Categorical or numeric variables can be set up and applied interactively within most QDA software, and often, they can be imported directly from table-based software (e.g., an Excel spreadsheet, or SPSS via Excel), making it very easy to include them in a database with text responses.

Integrative and analytic capacity might be enhanced where quantitative (e.g., demographic) information is simply available for viewing alongside retrieved text segments within a qualitative database, but the real comparative value from inclusion of quantitative data comes about through actual sorting of coded data according to values of a variable. QDA programs differ with regard to the ease with which these comparisons can be obtained, the kind of information generated by them, and the capacity to use the results from them in further analyses. Most, however, are moving to a standard where the comparative data for a range of values can be generated through a single query process, with results presented in a matrix display, rather than having to request data for each possible combination separately. Each alternative component of the information provided in a matrix resulting from this type of query (numeric display, found text) adds to the analytic picture, with numeric patterns showing "how many" and comparative texts showing "in what way."

Output from a comparative query in NVivo, for example, shows initially as a numeric display in which each cell of the matrix shows the number of sources containing text segment(s), which are identified at the same time by the code specified in that row and the attribute value specified for that column. The display can be changed to show the number of cases, passages, or words coded within each cell, if required. Shading can be used to highlight the relative density of coding across the cells. These tabular displays can be filtered by a row or column variable, exported in Excel format for further statistical analysis, or displayed (and exported) as a chart. Most critically, double-clicking on any cell will reveal the actual text passages meeting both row and column specifications (Figure 18.1).

Often, comparative analyses will simply reveal that some groups talk about a particular topic more often than others, or that different groups talk about different topics or raise different issues (as was the case in Ford's [2006] analysis discussed in Box 18.3). At times, however, a review of the sorted text reveals that different groups talk about the same topic in quite different ways—regardless of whether or not there were differences in how many talked about it. These differences may be revealing of dimensions within the concepts being coded or may suggest other conditions that are influencing the theme being examined. NVivo was used, for example, to compare expressions of satisfaction gained from doing research

Figure 18.1   Comparative Matrix Output From NVivo

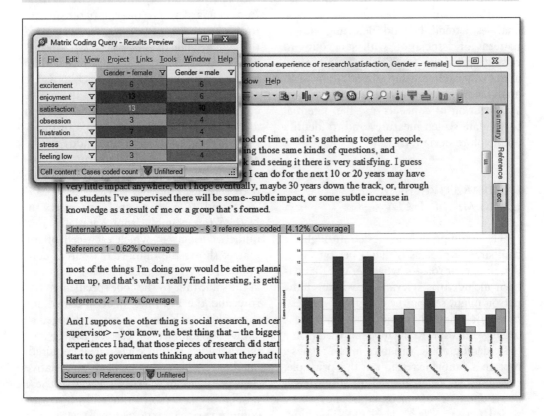

for male and female social scientists and scientists (Bazeley, 2007). About equal proportions within each gender and discipline group reported satisfaction. Whereas differences in the sorted text were not apparent for gender, comparisons across discipline suggested that scientists were likely to refer to the sense of agency they experienced in doing research, while most of those in the social sciences made reference to achieving a goal or a task when expressing satisfaction. These groups, therefore, gained satisfaction from different sources—a dimension of satisfaction not previously considered but one that is highly relevant to considerations of motivation for engaging in research.

In addition, instances where individuals go against a trend can be readily identified and explored in detail. From the examination of gender and discipline differences in satisfaction, two social scientists (one male, one female) also expressed agency, while

one scientist expressed neither agency nor achievement as a component of satisfaction. These cases could be identified, revealing that the two social scientists both worked in experimental psychology (more akin to science than social science), and the one scientist's current work was as much to do with recording the history of science and with designing educational materials as with being a scientist. It could be argued, then, that rather than contradicting the observed trend, these apparently discrepant cases added confirmation.

There are often marked inconsistencies in the way that people complete scaled items in questionnaires (Green, Statham, & Solomou, 2008). Where qualitative data can be gathered and used in association with scores derived from a quantitative scale, comparative analyses can make a contribution to understanding and verifying the meaning of the points on the scaled measure.

Using software, it is a straightforward task to identify whether differences in scores are reflected by comparable differences in the text. This adds a quite different approach to complement traditional validity testing of scales using confirmatory factor analysis or multiple correspondence analysis.

PATTERN ANALYSES INVOLVING MIXED DATA

Comparative analyses can be extended to include examining the pattern that emerges when, say, coded observational data is compared with interview data. Assuming the two sets of data can be linked on a case-by-case basis, and use of software, multiple comparisons can be quickly generated with a high degree of specificity. Thus, in an educational setting, the relationship between codes based on a teacher's observations about particular children and those based on the child's written or artistic work could be examined. Rather than seeking the combination of a code *and* a value of a variable or another code, in this case, the researcher would set up a query (or matrix query) seeking combinations of teachers' codes when they were *near* children's codes, with near being defined as "for the same case." The range of software capable of these types of analyses, which involve associations based on proximity between one code and another code, and of identifying and exploring converse cases, is more limited than for analyses that involve direct combination (intersection) of codes with other codes or variable data.

◆ *Transforming Qualitative Coding for Further Analysis*

Coding information derived from qualitative sources converts to numbers in a variety of forms, from simple counts to variable codes to measures of association, using a variety of methods. Text analysis modules linked to statistics programs are specifically designed to incorporate coded open responses into the statistical database, to be included with the quantitative variables. QDA software will generally provide counts; some will export document-based coding and/or case-based coding, while those that have a matrix function will usually also export results as shown in the matrix display. These exported data can then be imported, where appropriate, into a spreadsheet or statistical software.

When qualitative coding is used as the basis for statistical analysis, there is an advantage in that the researcher does not have to predetermine the categories to be used for that analysis, but when talk or text is reduced to categorical codes or numbers, the danger is that much of the meaning will be lost. With the use of software to generate codes for statistical analysis from qualitative material, text associated with those codes is retained in a readily accessible way. This assists interpretation of patterns during the process of analysis, validation of conclusions through checking findings back against the qualitative data, and initiation of further qualitative analyses or re-analyses.

Qualitative data might be transformed, or quantitized, to facilitate merging and comparison of different data sources or to allow exploratory, explanatory, comparative, predictive, or confirmatory statistical analyses (Sandelowski, Voils, & Knafl, 2009). Quantitizing data is not an end in itself, but "a means of making available techniques which add power and sensitivity to individual judgment when one attempts to detect and describe patterning in a set of observations" (Weinstein & Tamur, 1978, p. 140).

COUNTS FROM QUALITATIVE DATA

Simple frequencies generated from qualitative data have been used in a variety of ways in mixed methods projects, such as for counting themes, analyzing talk, and making comparisons. Counting is one form of description, reflecting the "numbered nature of phenomena" (Sandelowski, 2001, p. 231). Counts effectively communicate the frequency of occurrence of some feature in the text (Miles & Huberman, 1994) and summarize patterns in data (Morgan, 1993). Counts are the most common form in which numbers are introduced into primarily qualitative studies (Niglas, 2004), with frequencies seen by some as indicative of the relative importance of emergent themes (Onwuegbuzie & Teddlie, 2003). The use of numbers can help to maintain analytical integrity (countering biased impressions), with benefit also for identifying relationships and hypothesis testing (Miles & Huberman, 1994).

Using software for counting carries a range of benefits, the most obvious of which are the ease of obtaining counts and the increased accuracy of the counts obtained (Chi, 1997). Qualitative software routinely provides frequencies with which particular codes or themes occur in terms of the number of sources and separate passages coded. Some qualitative programs also provide case counts (useful where cases comprise partial or multiple sources), word counts, character counts, and proportions for coded data (Figure 18.2a). In addition, both specialist word-counting programs and most qualitative programs will provide simple frequency counts of the incidence of all words within in a body of text, along with keyword in context (KWIC) information and the possibility of direct access to more detailed context (Figure 18.2b).

Several theoretical and technical issues arise in using frequencies generated from qualitative coding that apply both when considering counts and when obtaining frequencies as a component of a more complex case- or matrix-based output:

- Whether one should base counts simply on the number of participants who mention something at all or on the overall frequency with which something is mentioned depends on the context in which counts are being obtained—did all cases have equal opportunity to mention the relevant item and so to be counted?—and the use to which they are being put—does volume signify relative importance? The possible meaning of a zero (0) count in those contexts is also relevant: 0 signifying something wasn't mentioned is meaningfully different from 0 signifying it didn't exist. Frequencies may be better regarded as ordinal rather than interval data, unless it can be ascertained that every instance is metrically comparable to every other instance. These issues are not exclusive to counts based on qualitative coding: There is no guarantee that every respondent in a survey, for instance, is interpreting and responding to the same categorical question in the same way.

- The specificity of what is being counted impacts on meaning and use of counts (Boyatzis, 1998). When a theme code is quantitized, its meaning tends to become fixed and single dimensional (Sivesind, 1999). Qualitative coding involving all occurrences, whether positive or negative, is a complication; even apparently factual descriptive codes are impacted by the reporting circumstances through which they are generated (Green et al., 2008; Sandelowski et al., 2009).

- The way in which (qualitative) texts are managed has implications for the generation of counts, particularly those reflecting volume. Say, for example, a passage of text is coded, and then the decision is made that the following text reflects the same code. Depending on whether the coding for the two passages is physically connected or not, that coding would be counted as one passage or as two. Similarly, when coding is removed from a passage, sometimes a blank character or line can be left behind, and so it is still counted for that code. Retrievals for all codes need to be checked before they are counted or exported.

- In using counts as part of the written report, issues arise through using percentages for small samples, relying on numbers to tell the whole story, and not providing sufficient context to allow the reader to properly interpret the numbers (Sandelowski, 2001).

Figure 18.2   Software Counts for Codes and Words

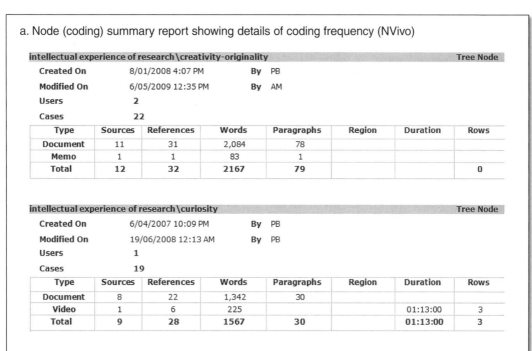

a. Node (coding) summary report showing details of coding frequency (NVivo)

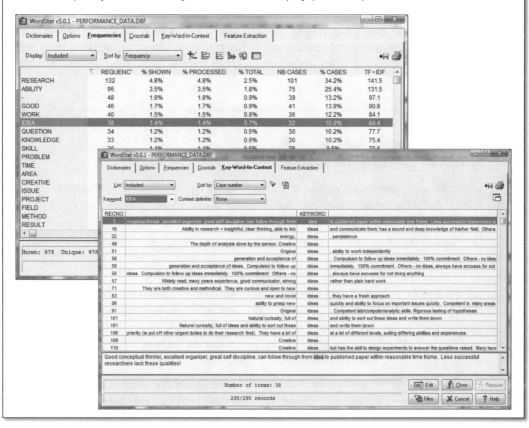

b. Word frequency counts and key-word-in-context display (WordStat)

QUANTITIZING CASE DATA

Quantitized data created as an export from qualitative software are transferred to a statistical package in the form of a regular case-by-variable matrix. Coding of text responses generated through QDA Miner or using text analysis modules for statistical software is automatically embedded in the statistical database. Quantitized data can be analyzed statistically on their own, or the new variables can be merged with an existing statistical database, even if some respondents have not provided both sources of data, providing there is a field on which the different sources can be matched for each case. Issues that were raised above regarding counts generally apply also to quantitized case-based coding.

Exported coding, once transferred to a statistical package, allows for a different type of examination of regularities and complex relationships in the data from that carried out within the qualitative database. Relationships within the data can be tested using standard bivariate and multivariate statistics (Box 18.4), predictive models can be built using regression-based techniques, or data might be explored using principal components or factor analysis. Meeting assumptions for valid inferential statistics of random or representative selection of cases is often an issue for qualitative projects (but increasingly also for quantitative surveys). Use of nonparametric statistics, simple visual displays, and techniques such as cluster or correspondence analysis to examine associations in the data might therefore be more appropriate with exported coding than procedures that assume a large, probabilistic, normally distributed sample. In situations where conclusions may not be generalizable to a larger population, use of statistical analyses nevertheless may be useful in making comparisons and in suggesting leads for further analysis.

MATRIX (PATTERN) DATA

Matrix data shows the pattern of relationship between two sets of items. In qualitative work, matrix displays can reduce information from complex field notes and interviews into a visual display that helps to make evident any patterns or regularities in the data. Cross-tabulations, or contingency tables, with their related statistical

---

BOX 18.4

Using Qualitative and Converted Coding to Test an Experimental Hypothesis

Converted qualitative coding was combined with an existing quantitative database in an experimental test of the impact of training through classroom discussions involving collaborative reasoning on children's argumentation (Reznitskaya et al., 2001). Following training, children wrote individual persuasive essays based on a different problem from that discussed in training. The essays were coded (using NUD*IST) for presence of formal argument devices and use of textual evidence. ANOVA and ANCOVA were used to demonstrate that having an argumentation schema developed through training enabled students to consider and present more arguments, independently of socioeconomic status or vocabulary skills. Detailed text analyses were then conducted on a purposive sample of essays to examine and illustrate argumentation strategies used by the children, revealing that "collaborative reasoning students are generally more successful at generating and articulating an argument, considering alternative perspectives, marshalling text information, and effectively utilizing certain formal argument devices" (p. 171).

procedures, have always been a basic tool within statistical software, for use in quantitative survey analysis. Similarly, codes from *exported* qualitative case data can be cross-tabulated within a statistical program, but with the risk that they may produce spurious connections simply as a consequence of both codes being found somewhere in the text from the same person, rather than because they have a particular association. If a matrix is generated *within* qualitative software, however, it is identifying only those connections that are likely to be meaningful, because both codes are present on the same segment(s) of data. Furthermore, the text associated with the count in each cell is available for checking, so that adjustments can be made, if necessary, and additional meaning ascertained.

A range of matrix query options is available in NVivo, MAXQDA, and QDA Miner. The numeric results of the matrix query can be exported, usually as an Excel table or a tab-delimited text file that can then be imported (more or less directly) into a selected statistics program. Matrix queries generally take one of three forms:

• A comparative matrix using attribute (e.g., demographic) data, as described above. A matrix, or cross-tabulation, can be generated equally well using exported coding or within the qualitative software (because attributes apply to whole cases), but the supporting text is available only if it is generated in the QDA software (cf. Figure 18.1).

• A pattern analysis of the relationship between one set of codes and another. The counts within each cell of the matrix might be based on intersections in coding, for example, when data are coded for the nature of the problem being experienced and also for the coping strategies that are adopted in relation to the specific problem. Alternatively, they might be based on proximities within the data, for example, when the researcher wants to relate some aspect of experience to an expressed attitude or behavior (or attitudes to behavior) and the codes for these do not necessarily intersect but can be found within a specified proximity, or in a particular sequence. Numbers in the resulting exported matrix from either the intersection or proximity query could be based on either case counts within each cell or frequency counts of how often these associations were found overall.

• A similarity matrix based on the association between a set of codes and itself. That is, the same set of codes is entered in both rows and columns with a request to find either intersections or proximities (within a specified distance) between the codes. The result shares some similarity to the more familiar correlation matrix: Frequencies within each cell represent the number of times each code is found in association with another (counting either cases or separate instances) and show as a reflected matrix with the diagonal giving the total number of finds for each code (Figure 18.3).

Those using matrix data generated from qualitative coding need to be aware of the basis on which the matrix was created. For example, comparative tables are usually more akin to multiple response data than to a cross-tabulation suitable for bivariate chi-squared analysis of differences, as the categories being compared across groups (i.e., row codes) are rarely mutually exclusive. In any matrices based on intersections of coding, there is a need to ensure that accidental hits are not included, where the tail end of one code overlaps the beginning of another—perhaps just by the blank character between them—without there being any meaningful association. And for matrices based on proximities, care needs to be exercised in specifying how the counts are constructed, to avoid irregular overcounting where a single co-occurrence could involve either one intersecting or two separate passages for the pair of codes.

Figure 18.3   Reflected (Similarity) Matrix

	commitment... ▽	organised, ... ▽	strategic ▽	methodologi... ▽	technical skill ▽	substantive ... ▽	analytic, thi... ▽	creative, inn... ▽
commitment, persist... ▽	133	20	8	7	4	15	27	22
organised, disciplined ▽	20	74	8	7	4	7	16	11
strategic ▽	8	8	63	5	4	7	12	10
methodologically so... ▽	7	7	5	96	12	19	37	27
technical skill ▽	4	4	4	12	44	6	9	8
substantive knowled... ▽	15	7	7	19	6	86	33	15
analytic, thinker ▽	27	16	12	37	9	33	151	43
creative, innovative ▽	22	11	10	27	8	15	43	138

NOTE: The cell entries on the diagonal show the total number of respondents using each concept; for example, *strategic* was used 63 times in total. Particular cells show the number of respondents who used that row-by-column combination when describing researchers who performed in particular ways; for example, *strategic* was used in the same context as *commitment* on eight occasions.

EXPLORATORY ANALYSES AND VISUAL DISPLAYS USING QUANTITIZED DATA

Exploratory statistical techniques with results presented as visual displays of relationships between codes (variables) are likely to be used to assist interpretive analysis of exported case and matrix data, rather than their being subject to statistical hypothesis testing. Multidimensional scaling, cluster analysis, and correspondence analysis are some of the exploratory techniques that have been applied to generate meta-themes, core dimensions, or comparative analyses—these techniques are particularly appropriate for data derived from qualitative coding as they do not assume that categories used are mutually exclusive or normally distributed. Specification of the type of distances to be calculated by the software for these types of analyses is impacted by the source and derivation of the data being used, however; that is, whether the data are binary, ordinal, or interval (Bartholomew, Steele, Moustaki, & Galbraith, 2002).

• Hierarchical cluster analysis is a classification technique based on case-by-variable data in which objects (cases or variables) are grouped on the basis of similarity in their pattern of distribution across the other axis. Clusters are progressively aggregated, with the results most commonly presented graphically as a dendrogram (Figure 18.4a).

• In multidimensional scaling (MDS), distances based on the similarity (or dissimilarity) of objects in a reflected matrix are used to generate dimensional plots of those objects. These plots and the associated dimensional statistics are used to reveal the structure of a set of data, where both the dimensions and any identifiable groupings of points in the plot are of interest (Figure 18.4b).

• Correspondence analysis generates a plot of data from cross-tabulated data, usually in two dimensions, providing an opportunity to see the relative ordering and spacing of categories across the rows and columns and the associations between row and column categories (Figure 18.4c).

Figure 18.4 Visual Displays Built From Quantitized Data

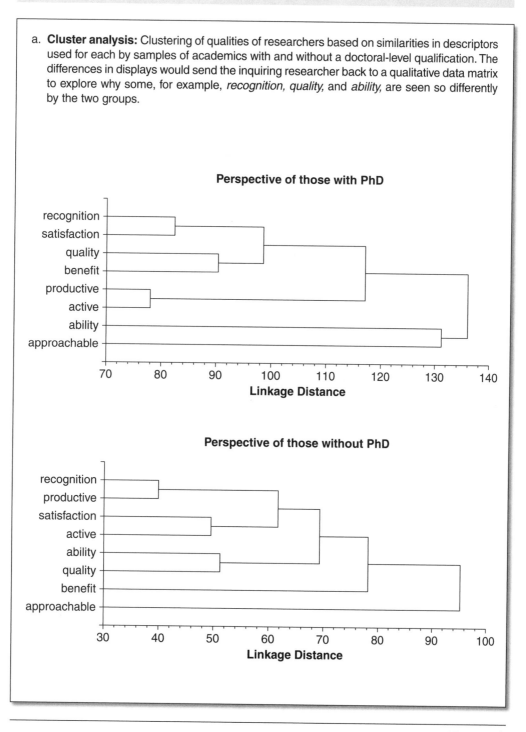

a. **Cluster analysis:** Clustering of qualities of researchers based on similarities in descriptors used for each by samples of academics with and without a doctoral-level qualification. The differences in displays would send the inquiring researcher back to a qualitative data matrix to explore why some, for example, *recognition, quality,* and *ability,* are seen so differently by the two groups.

(Continued)

Figure 18.4 (Continued)

b. **Multidimensional scaling:** Two-dimensional plot of key elements in research performance.

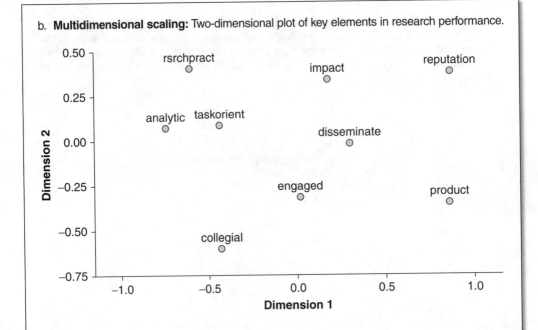

c. **Correspondence analysis:** Association between university and decile measures of emphasis on analytic/thinking skills in describing high-performing researchers.

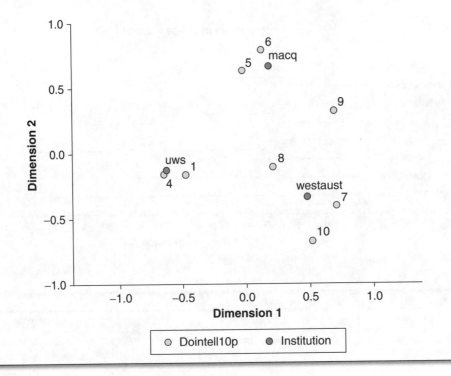

COMBINATION AND CONVERSION WORKING TOGETHER

One of the difficulties of presenting a range of analysis strategies is that it can appear that each of these strategies is applied in relative isolation when, in fact, an integrative mixed methods project working with complex data is much messier than that and quite likely to involve a mix of strategies that defies easy classification. Studies often involve both conversion and combination of data. This may occur concurrently or iteratively, as alternate analytic strategies and the programs that support them are used in multiple, sequenced phases where the conduct of each phase arises out of or draws on the analysis of the preceding phase (Greene, 2007). Blending or fusing of diverse data sources to create new, composite variables to feed back into an analysis is another way in which combination and conversion work together (Bazeley, 2006).

In an early example by Louis (1982), rating scales covering all relevant aspects of an evaluation of an educational innovation were developed and completed for each site on the basis of a combination of documented sources, statistical data, and researchers' holistic knowledge of the sites. The combined set of data was then analyzed statistically. More recently, Kane and Trochim (2007) have proposed a method of concept analysis in which participants first develop a series of (qualitative) statements about the topic of interest and then group and rate a refined list of these for importance and feasibility. Cluster analysis and multidimensional scaling are applied to the paired and rated statements to create a concept map and a range of visual displays. These are then used to effectively communicate back to the participants the key areas that need to be developed or evaluated and the relative importance and feasibility of working in each of those areas, as a stimulus for discussion.

◆ Interpreting Variable Data in Small to Medium N Samples

Inferential statistical procedures used for comparison, prediction, or explanation typically require large, normally distributed, probabilistically drawn samples. These are often not available to the mixed methods researcher, particularly when they are drawing on non-numeric sources or purposively selected samples for their data, and so they need to turn to other approaches.

USING STATISTICAL DATA TO EXAMINE TRENDS OR PATTERNS

Mixed methods researchers' samples might not meet the requirements for traditional statistical analyses such as regression, but they nevertheless have potentially useful qualitatively or quantitatively derived variable data. Nonparametric statistics can assist in interpretation of characteristics and comparisons, or Q methodology might be employed (Newman & Ramlo, 2010 [this volume]), while visual displays such as boxplots, graphs, and charts can be useful also in suggesting trends or patterns in data (Dickinson, 2010 [this volume]; see also Box 18.5).

In her book on narrative methods, Elliott (2005) describes using quantitative sources to build a single life-history narrative. Others have used cluster analysis to generate comparative narrative profiles. These approaches are referred to by Teddlie and Tashakkori (2009) as qualitizing data.

CONFIGURATIONAL COMPARATIVE METHODS

Configurational comparative methods, perhaps still better known as qualitative comparative analysis (QCA), encompass a set of procedures developed initially by Charles Ragin (1987) that specifically seek to bridge the divide between small-*N* and large-*N* studies (Rihoux & Ragin, 2009). By combining case- and variable-oriented approaches and using both deductive and inductive processes, QCA straddles quantitative and qualitative approaches to research.

QCA methods rely on close case-level knowledge, combined with good theoretical understanding, to identify relevant cases and a limited set of variables (quantitatively or qualitatively derived) to analyze in relation to the presence or absence of an identified outcome. For crisp set data (csQCA), variables are dichotomized and a "truth table" is built listing all the found configurations of variables, along with their positive, negative, or contradictory outcomes (e.g., Table 18.1). Drawing on the logic of set theory, Boolean algebra is applied to the table to generate potential necessary and/or sufficient conditions. A minimum set of interrelated "prime implicants" of general significance for a

given outcome from a small- or moderate-*N* database is then derived, usually with greater sensitivity and reliability than through using more traditional qualitative or quantitative techniques alone (Ragin, Shulman, Weinberg, & Gran, 2003). Unlike incremental additive statistical models, QCA may present multiple constellations of conjunctural factors that lead to the same result and, in so doing, rejects simplistic probabilistic models in favor of diversity that is more reflective of the complexity of the situation being studied (Berg-Schlosser, De Meur, Rihoux, & Ragin, 2009).

The basic method for QCA, which relied on dichotomizing all variables, has been extended to deal also with multivalue data (mvQCA) and fuzzy-set data (fsQCA). Analyses of crisp set (dichotomized) data are supported by TOSMANA and FSQCA; TOSMANA also supports mvQCA, and FSQCA supports fsQCA.

Table 18.1 Truth Table of Boolean Configurations With Five Conditions and One Outcome

CASEID	GNPCAP	URBANIZA	LITERACY	INDLAB	GOVSTAB	SURVIVAL
AUS	1	0	1	1	0	0
BEL, NET, UK	1	1	1	1	1	1
CZE	0	1	1	1	1	1
EST, FIN	0	0	1	0	1	C
FRA, SWE	1	0	1	1	1	1
GER	1	1	1	1	0	0
GRE,POR,SPA	0	0	0	0	0	0
HUN, POL	0	0	1	0	0	0
IRE	1	0	1	0	1	1
ITA, ROM	0	0	0	0	1	0

NOTE: Truth table from Rihoux and De Meur, 2009, p. 53, Table 3.7, based on conditions for the survival of democracy between the wars in Europe. The contradictory outcome for Estonia and Finland was resolved by adjusting the threshold for GNCAP, so that Finland and Czechoslovakia each changed value from 0 to 1 and consequently paired with other countries. (Used by permission, Sage Publications Ltd.)

◆ **Strategies That Combine Visual, Numeric, and Text Data**

Teddlie and Tashakkori (2009, p. 273) refer to social network analysis as "inherently mixed" in that, by default, it involves a mix of methods. The use of geographic information systems (GIS) in social research has those same characteristics of necessarily involving a mix of visual data with numeric or text data or both.

SOCIAL NETWORK ANALYSIS

The focus of social network analysis is on the ties that people (or other social objects) have, rather than on the attributes of the people in the networks. Either all of the ties within a defined population are considered or, when examining an egocentric network, ties for a specific person. Linkages between different organizations through their members might be examined at the level of the organization, for example, or the study might consider the way in which the structure of ties and an individual's place within that structure impacts on that individual and his or her relationships (Box 18.5).

In social network analysis, a visual display of network linkages is combined with mathematical and statistical analyses of the connections between nodes in the network (Scott, 2000). These analyses generate measures such as centrality, density, and connectivity of the network and of individual nodes within it. Cliques and bridges (a connecting node between two subnetworks) can be identified both visually and mathematically. Qualitative data relating to network connections and the way the network operates may be added to the mix, adding explanatory detail to the visual connections and measures provided by the network analysis software. Indeed, network relations are "embedded in particular social, cultural, temporal, and spatial contexts," and these are ignored at the peril of missing vital clues regarding the significance of the relationships (Clark, 2007, p. 20).

BOX 18.5

Mapping a Decision-Making Actor-Event-Process Across an Organizational Network

To systematically study the political decision-making process across a series of cases, using detailed narrative and documentary sources as a basis, Widmer, Hirschi, Serdült, and Vögeli (2008) first mapped actors by events, noting which actors were connected by an event, and how leadership in events progressed across actors over time. For each case, they then created a reflected matrix of participation by pairs of actors in the events (counting the number of events in which both had participated). A second matrix tabled process links between event leaders. These two matrices were multiplied (to give additional weight to the more sparse process matrix) to create a standard social network matrix reflecting connections between actors in the decision-making process, covering the range of decision-making events. This matrix could then be analyzed in UCINET, allowing visualization of the structure of actor networks (e.g., Figure 18.5) and providing scores for such things as network density, relative contact frequency, and actor degree centralization, for comparison with other decision-making cases.

(Continued)

(Continued)

Figure 18.5 Network Map of the Decision-Making Process for a Swiss International Treaty With Ghana

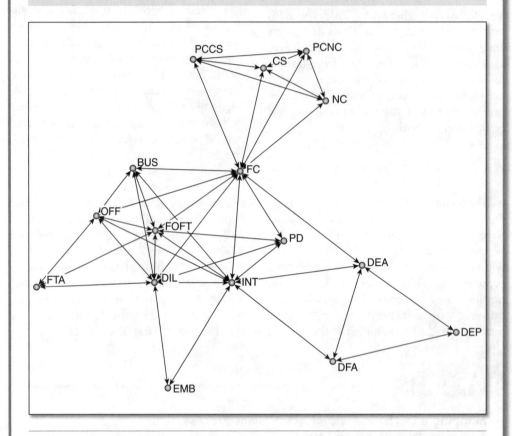

SOURCE: Widmer et al., 2008, p. 164, Figure 10.4 (b). This network demonstrated comparatively fewer actors than others, but that actor FC played a critical bridging role within it. The amount of contact between DIL and FOFT was also particularly heavy. (Used by permission, Thomas Widmer.)

GEOGRAPHIC INFORMATION SYSTEMS (GIS)

GIS technology provides an effective tool for integrating qualitative, quantitative, and visual data where social factors are related to physical locations or environments. Different types of information, or changes over time, or for different participant groups, are linked by being compared or overlaid on a series of maps or on the same map. Originally developed to analyze land use, GIS data is now being seen as an important component of any social science project that involves references to location, travel, or distance. Combining geographical or spatial data with social data in an analysis ensures a better awareness of contextual factors and how these might influence patterns of behavior (Box 18.6).

BOX 18.6

Combined Use of Mapping, Observation, Interviews, and Ratings Data to Evaluate Emergency Response to a Natural Hazard

To explore residents' preparedness to evacuate in the event of eruption of the Katla volcano in Iceland and consequent jökulhlaup (glacial outburst flooding) into the western hazard zone, Bird, Gisladottir, and Dominey-Howes (2009) used maps of the hazard zone, observed an evacuation trial, interviewed emergency workers, and survey-interviewed residents and tourists. Similar observation, mapping, interview, and survey methods were used also by Bird in the southern and eastern hazard zones (Figures 18.6 and 18.7). When these data are viewed in conjunction with each other and with resident comments, a clear picture emerges of some of the factors influencing residents' preparedness.

Figure 18.6   The Jökulhlaup (Glacial Meltwater) Hazard Zone to the South and East of Mýrdalsjökull Following Eruption of the Katla Volcano in Iceland

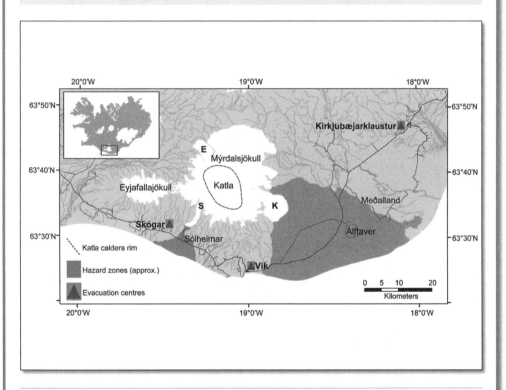

SOURCE: Deanne Bird, Department of Environment and Geography, Macquarie University, and Department of Geography and Tourism, University of Iceland, 2009. (Used with permission.)

(Continued)

(Continued)

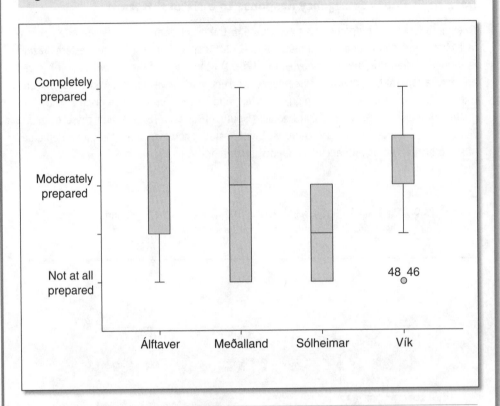

Figure 18.7 Resident Ratings of Preparedness to Evacuate in the Event of Jökulhlaup

SOURCE: Deanne Bird, Department of Environment and Geography, Macquarie University, and Department of Geography and Tourism, University of Iceland, 2009. (Used with permission.)

Residents in the farming communities of Sólheimar, Álftaver, and Meðalland are to be evacuated due to the risk of jökulhlaup, while houses in the low-lying coastal area of Vík are to be evacuated due to tsunami risk. Evacuation for the three farming communities is a more complex process involving disconnecting electric fencing and releasing livestock.

Very few residents across the region feel completely prepared for an evacuation. Residents in all areas other than Sólheimar will be given 30 minutes warning to complete preparations and evacuate; Sólheimar residents, who have to evacuate to the Vík centre, will be given only 15 minutes because if the flood flows from the southern catchment, they are located directly adjacent to the southern outlet glacier; hence, they feel less confident than others about their preparedness for evacuation. In contrast, Vík residents (of whom just 4% are farmers) have to travel only 5 minutes to reach the evacuation center, hence their generally higher level of preparedness. Residents in Álftaver are generally better prepared because they have worked on developing an alternative plan to the official one; the latter requires that they leave their higher homes and cross a low-lying area in the direct path of the flood to get to their evacuation center in Kirkjubæjarklaustur.

Social factors overriding geographic influences explain the marked exceptions within each area: The two unprepared people in Vík are recently arrived residents, and the completely prepared person in Meðalland keeps in constant touch with events and has actively sought information on previous eruptions from Katla and risk mitigation procedures.

Locational references within interviews or news stories or other qualitative sources might be mapped (Box 18.7), or alternatively, a large variety of factors related to a specific location might be gathered and managed in a database linked to GIS software in the process of undertaking a case study. The visual presentation of the data makes GIS a particularly powerful analytic and communication tool: Visual analysis can usefully precede more formal statistical analysis; GIS can bring previously ignored geographic variables into an analysis; and, by including many different contextual variables within the single integrated analysis, it provides a more holistic view of what is being considered (Jung, 2007; Steinberg & Steinberg, 2006).

BOX 18.7

Adding a Spatial Component to Ethnography With GIS

To understand how caregivers of children with disabilities navigate services, Skinner, Matthews, and Burton (2005) combined ethnographic data with GIS technology to create visual displays of when and where carers went (Figure 18.8):

> We use existing data sets, augment them with new and refined measures of spatial context and structure, integrate these geographic data sets with an array of ethnographic data products (i.e., field notes, recoded notes, family profiles, photographs, etc.), and then analyze the result with data visualization/mapping techniques and spatial statistical analysis. (p. 230)

They found the combination of methods helped them to better understand the contextual factors impacting on parents and carers as they attempted to access and use services for their children. As noted by one of the mothers: "You tell them that I don't just sit on my butt all day watching TV. I'm out there working for my children" (p. 235).

(Continued)

(Continued)

Figure 18.8 GIS Mapping of Daily Activities

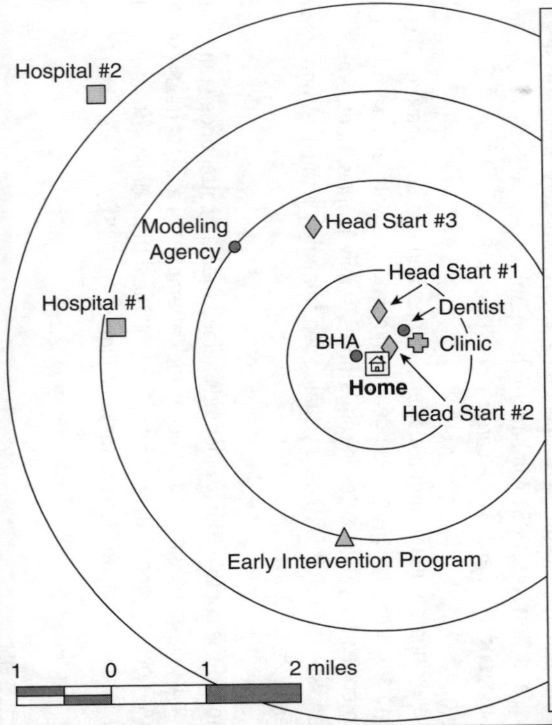

Calendar of events – November 2000

Monday	Tuesday	Wednesday	Thursday	Friday
		1 a. Travel to/from Early Intervention Program b. Counseling for BC	2	3 Travel to/from Early Intervention Program
6 Physical Therapy for BC	7 Counseling for BC	8 a. Policy Committee Meeting b. Progress Review for KC	9 Education Committee Meeting	10 Cablevision
13 a. Physical Therapy for BC b. Meeting at modeling agency	14 a. Dental visit b. Counseling for BC c. Travel to/from Orthopedic Appt.	15 a. Parent meeting b. Renewal of Lease (BHA)	16 Head Start 6-month checkup	17
20 a. Dental Appt for KC b. Physical Therapy for BC	21 a. Travel to/from Dr. b. Counseling for BC c. Travel to/from Town Policy Meeting	22 a. Dental Appt for DC b. Interview for WCF	23	24
27 Appt for DC Physical Therapy for BC	28 Counseling for BC	29 Parent Group Meeting	30	

NOTE: Skinner et al., 2005, p. 231, Map 7.1. The location of the meetings and appointments attended by the primary caregiver (November 2000). GIS is used to organize and map the data points. (Map produced by Stephen A. Matthews, December 2000.) (Used with permission, University of Chicago Press.)

◆ Synthesis and Metasynthesis

It is quite common in mixed methods research to need to bring together varied sources and forms of data to be synthesized in the process of analysis. In a study of recovery from lung transplantation, Happ, DeVito Dabbs, Tate, Hricik, and Erlen (2006) used Excel to record physiological data, supplemented by quantitized variables derived from observational and interview data, which they then analyzed graphically and statistically. In another analysis, also using Excel, Happ et al. took an alternative approach to synthesizing their data: They qualitized scaled data to combine it with information on key dimensions derived from qualitative analysis, and then again used Excel to sort the data.

The data entry, sorting, and filtering capacity of a spreadsheet makes it a useful tool to extend the researcher's capacity to build the kind of data matrices advocated and popularized by Miles and Huberman (1994). Although these strategies can be comparatively reductionist, they are also capable of delivering an overview of patterns in the data more rapidly than methods relying on working with full verbatim transcripts of data—and different types of data can be synthesized within the one matrix, with or without conversion of data from one type to another (Box 18.8). Spreadsheet matrices are particularly useful where time for analysis is limited, data is of varied types, or the data lacks "richness" and where relevant issues largely have been identified before analysis.

BOX 18.8

Research Opportunities for New Academic Staff

A spreadsheet was used with brief notes and key comments derived from semistructured interviews with 56 heads of academic departments, in six discipline areas across 12 Australian universities, regarding the research career opportunities afforded new academic staff in their departments (Bazeley et al., 1996; see Figure 18.9).

Data were sorted using categorical variables. Sorting of responses based on discipline revealed that at that time,

- New academic staff in physics had extensive opportunities given them—"honeymoon periods" from teaching, computer facilities, financial support—and that research activity was "expected."

- In nursing, the majority of new academic staff were still undergoing research training; support for research was more patchy and teaching demands were high.

- Staff in psychology had research qualifications, research was "supported," and necessary equipment was usually available, but teaching loads were a problem.

Interestingly, patterns were much more clearly defined by discipline than by the status of the university, and in general, the "pure" disciplines of physics and history had more in common than was shared with other disciplines; similarly, the practitioner-oriented disciplines of nursing and social work had much in common but differed from others.

(Continued)

(Continued)

Figure 18.9 Data Synthesis in Excel

	University Type	Department	Department-Infrastructure	Department-Finances	New Staff-Load	New Staff-Financial help	New Staff-Other help	New Staff-Mentoring
	A	B	O	P	Q	R	S	T
1								
32	1	PHYSICS	Very good	No problems	Considerably reduced	Generous	Provided eg courses	Formal scheme
33	3	PHYSICS	very good	good	lightened by casuals	plenty	study leave	attached to group
34	2	PHYSICS	good, but no maintenance money, computers outdated	"existing on small ARC"	lighter in first year	can shuffle extra money into new areas	Equipment provided by groups	responsibility of the groups
35	1	PSYCHOLOGY	Some dept money for unfunded projects. Space problems but equipment fine.	Money for equip., not staff	Heavy teaching -"a weakness"	Mech A money for grant applicants	Help with applics.(advice, pay for RA). Teaching relief first year.	Recently formalised for junior staff
36	1	PSYCHOLOGY	"Always tight" but hire only those they can support		"Overloaded", heavy load	Can access senior staff res.funds		Nothing formal. Many work with senior staff anyway
37	3	PSYCHOLOGY	More facilities than equipment	Problematic	Heavy teaching	Available	Encouragement and advice	Keeping a fairly close eye on postgrads and junior staff (informally)
	2	SOCIAL WORK	not needed		lot of indiv.	no dept	stats and	faculty

Shee ◄ ► ◄

Ready   NUM

Strategies for data synthesis can be applied not only to multiple sources of data within a study but also to results and conclusions drawn from multiple studies. The synthesis of results from differently conducted studies extends the more established concept of meta-analysis, a statistical technique developed to amalgamate and compare the results of a series of quantitative studies. When that technique was introduced, it was seen as beneficial where each individual study was not sufficiently strong in itself to establish a general conclusion. Meta-analyses and/or meta-syntheses are often called for in the context of evidence-based practice or when funding bodies expect a systematic review of previous research (Harden & Thomas, 2005; Pawson, 2006). As with single multimethod studies, meta-synthesis might involve separate, sequential, or integrated analyses, the latter avoiding the issue of having to classify component studies as quantitative or qualitative in the first place (Sandelowski, Voils, & Barroso, 2006).

Meta-analysis requires use of a common framework for measurement, such as an effect size, in order to be able to compare and combine the study results. Similarly, synthesis of components within a study, or meta-synthesis of results from multiple studies involving a variety of methodological approaches, requires application of a common conceptual framework (Box 18.9) to build a coherent analysis.

Integration of results from different studies often requires transformation of data in order to be able to effectively combine diverse sources. Coded data might be converted to variable data to allow synthesis using statistical techniques or, as with the Harden and Thomas example, the results of quantitative studies qualitized, for textual analysis in combination with the conclusions from qualitative studies. In a metasynthesis, the pooled data might then be analyzed using effect sizes or through identifying common themes.

Excel is a useful basic tool for synthesis and metasynthesis, where results of studies are reduced to brief summary statements or categorized variables, which can then be sorted on the basis of selected study components.

Excel has the advantage of simplicity of use and of being able to handle mixed forms of data within the one display. For more complex analyses, specialized statistical or qualitative software will be needed, depending on how the data are being treated.

◆ *Improving Rigor*

While there is general agreement that use of a computer improves (although never guarantees) rigor of coding and analysis, there is significant debate about what constitutes reliability and when it matters, especially in relation to qualitative coding and analysis. There are at least two situations, however, where transparency and consistency of coding is critical with relevance to mixed methods analysis: where multiple coders are working on the same set of data sources for the same purpose, and where qualitative data are being coded to facilitate conversion

---

BOX 18.9

Applying a Common Framework Based on Qualitative Data

A common framework is typically based on variable within trials data or quantitative studies, but when Harden and Thomas (2005) conducted a systematic review of studies on barriers to and facilitators of fruit and vegetable intake among children aged 4 to 10 years, they drew on the qualitative reports to create a framework. An initial meta-analysis of effect sizes from trials data on this topic had not shown any clear results relating interventions to outcomes. They then used NVivo to aggregate findings across qualitative "views" studies, from which they generated 13 themes. Six of these themes contributed to understanding the children's perspectives on what helped or hindered them from eating fruit and vegetables. These six themes were then used as the mechanism for combining the findings of the trials data with the qualitative data: A matrix was used to facilitate a constant comparative analysis that moved between the views data and narrative descriptions of interventions described in the trial reports. The authors noted that "the use of children's views to structure the final synthesis challenges traditional notions of who experts are and what constitutes expert opinion" (p. 264). They have since successfully applied this approach of using views data to structure a meta-synthesis in a number of other studies.

Figure 18.10 Coding Comparison Query (NVivo)

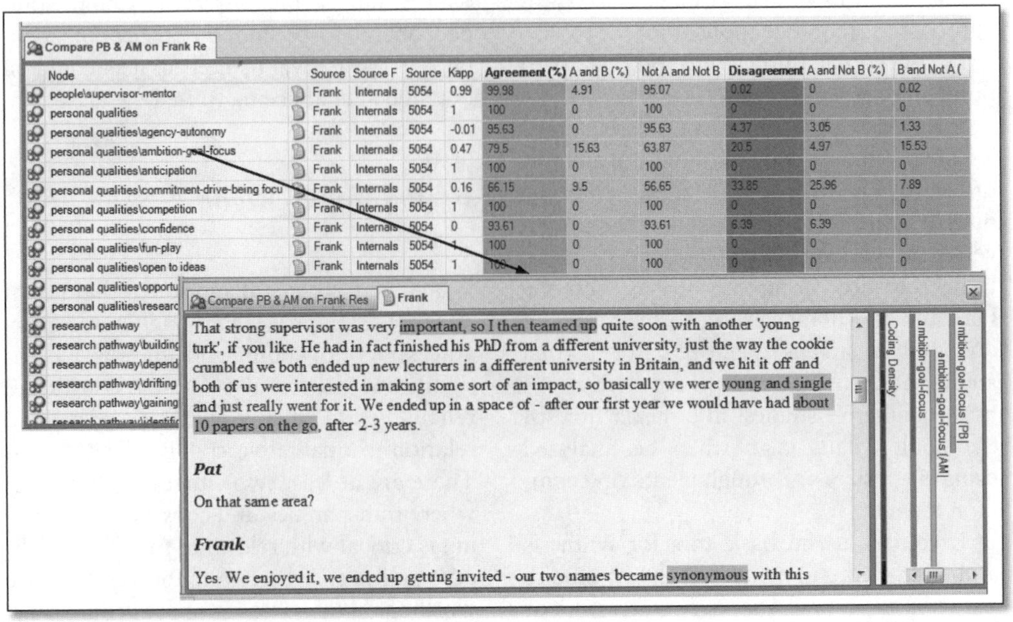

for statistical analysis (Boyatzis, 1998). Several programs, including EthnoNotes, Atlas.ti, and NVivo 8, now offer ways of carefully tracking the work of different coders (or the same coder at different times), providing both data for team discussion about coding strategies and, in EthnoNotes and NVivo, Cohen's Kappa indices of level of agreement in coding (Figure 18.10). A key advantage of this type of display is the opportunity for team researchers to see exactly how their coding agrees or disagrees, as a basis for discussion and refinement of practice.

◆ **Concluding Comments**

When those involved in the practical tasks of research work together with software specialists to resolve analysis problems, advances in methods result. Methodologists observing these developments become excited about new possibilities, yet sadly the "researcher in the street" often continues to struggle with pencil, scissors, and paper methods of analysis, largely oblivious to the increasing range of opportunities to improve extent, depth, and quality of integration in mixed methods analyses. As the mixed methods community moves on from debates about paradigms and typologies to practical strategies for working with mixed data, perhaps more attention will be given to methods of integrating data analyses and the technology that can support both separate and integrated analyses.

That is not to say that the solution to advancing mixed methods analyses is purely technical. As noted by Rihoux, Ragin, Yamasaki, and Bol (2009),

Just because a computing operation is *technically feasible doesn't mean that it is useful or even desirable.* Once again: the [software] should never be used in a "push-button" manner but rather in a reflexive way. Needless to say, the same should apply to any formal tool—statistical tools as well—in social science research. (p. 173, italics in original)

Software ever remains the tool and not the method, and fitness for purpose is a primary criterion in determining what to use of software's offerings and when to use it. Appropriate use of technology can increase the capacity of researchers to more rigorously examine the detail and consistency of the findings they present and so contribute to inference quality (Tashakkori & Teddlie, 2008), but perhaps more critically, it can help researchers to see data in new ways and so contribute to building understanding and refining theory.

Research Questions and Exercises

Questions to ask when you are planning an analysis:

1. Looking at qualitative data you are going to be working with, ask:

   - Are there ways in which I could combine quantitative variable data with this *during the analysis process* to facilitate comparisons?

   - Are there locational components that could be helpfully mapped?

   - Would it help to map the network of relationships between people (or other objects)?

   - Would using numbers help to clarify comparisons or reporting from the qualitative data?

   - Would there be any benefit in converting qualitative codes to variable data, for graphing, for statistical analyses, or perhaps, as input for QCA or social network analysis?

2. Looking at quantitative (variable, statistical) data you are working with, ask:

   - Are there ways in which these data tell a story, even if they are unable to be tested using inferential statistics? Would diagrams help to tell the story? Do the data together follow a common pattern, even though any one element is not significant?

   - Do I have any qualitative data that would help to explain the patterns revealed through the statistical analyses?

Exercises

1. Most software is available in free or 30-day trial versions, available for download from the Web sites indicated. Most also provide sample data or projects, and some provide tutorials and extensive electronic help files. Choose those that appear interesting to you and experiment with the sample data, or try importing some of your own (start with a small amount). Don't be disappointed if you don't become an instant expert, however, especially for mixed methods applications!

2. Identify an issue of interest to you in the domain you are studying or researching, for which you have a number of articles (say, 10 or more, preferably involving a range of analysis types). Create a spreadsheet in Excel, and list the articles in the first column (avoiding the first row). Now list various aspects of concern and some descriptor variables, related to the issue, across the tops of the columns. In the cells, type in or categorize each article with reference to the aspect for that column. (You might want to format the cells so that the text wraps and is top and left aligned, so that you can see it all. Also, use Freeze Panes or Split Panes to keep the header row and identification column visible as you work down and across.) Now select the whole sheet (click on the top left corner), and choose to Sort (Data menu) based on data in one of the categorized columns. Review the text to see if any pattern in another column has become evident.

(Continued)

(Continued)

3. If you have a data set from which you can choose a limited number of predictor variables (e.g., 4 to 5) for an assessed outcome, explore the difference in predictive outcomes derived using QCA methods compared with logistic regression modeling. Consider these differences in light of your understanding of the cases/participants you are investigating.

4. If you have some data that have been thematically coded, create a case-by-variable spreadsheet or statistical database from the coding and explore relationships in it using pivot tables (Excel), multiple-response cross-tabulations, nonparametric comparisons, or exploratory multivariate statistical analyses, or match with a continuous outcome variable and apply *t* tests or other predictive statistical analyses. Have you discovered any new associations or patterns in your data from these exercises? What issues are raised by the conversions? Return to the qualitative data to assist in understanding particular associations.

5. Take a set of variable data (or converted qualitative coding), and in a statistical database or Excel, explore the range of visual displays (charts and graphs) that might be created using it. Does this help to make trends or patterns any clearer?

6. Explore the possibilities for combining social network analysis with GIS principles by thinking about your own network of friends: With whom have you had contact over the past month? What form did that contact take (e.g., face-to-face, phone, text, Internet)? How frequent was the contact with each one? Where is the other person located? Who, among your network, is likely to be in contact with each other? Now, try plotting the various ties, but including as much as you can of the spatial and contact information through where you place your contacts and how you depict the links. How might such an ego-net look different for someone who is at a different stage in the life cycle?

◆ References

Bartholomew, D. J., Steele, F., Moustaki, I., & Galbraith, J. I. (2002). *The analysis and interpretation of multivariate data for social scientists*. Boca Raton, FL: Chapman & Hall/CRC.

Bazeley, P. (1999). The *bricoleur* with a computer: Piecing together qualitative and quantitative data. *Qualitative Health Research, 9*(2), 279–287.

Bazeley, P. (2006). The contribution of computer software to integrating qualitative and quantitative data and analyses. *Research in the Schools, 13*(1), 63–73.

Bazeley, P. (2007). *Qualitative data analysis with NVivo*. London: Sage.

Bazeley, P. (2009a). Analysing qualitative data: More than "identifying themes." *Malaysian Journal of Qualitative Research, 2*(2), 6–22. (Submitted copy available as a working paper on http://www.researchsupport.com.au)

Bazeley, P. (2009b). Integrating analyses in mixed methods research [Editorial]. *Journal of Mixed Methods Research, 3*(3), 203–207.

Bazeley, P. (2009c). Mixed methods data analysis. In S. Andrew & E. Halcomb (Eds.), *Mixed methods research for nursing and the health sciences* (pp. 84–118). Chichester, UK: Wiley-Blackwell.

Bazeley, P., Kemp, L., Stevens, K., Asmar, C., Grbich, C., Marsh, H., et al. (1996). *Waiting in the wings: A study of early career academic researchers in Australia* (National Board of Employment Education and

Training, Commissioned Report No. 50). Canberra: Australian Government Publishing Service.

Bergman, M. M. (2008). The straw men of the qualitative-quantitative divide and their influence on mixed methods research. In M. M. Bergman (Ed.), *Advances in mixed methods research* (pp. 11–21). London: Sage.

Berg-Schlosser, D., De Meur, G., Rihoux, B., & Ragin, C. (2009). Qualitative comparative analysis (QCA) as an approach. In B. Rihoux & C. Ragin (Eds.), *Configurational comparative methods* (pp. 1–18). Los Angeles: Sage.

Bird, D., Gisladottir, G., & Dominey-Howes, D. (2009). Resident perception of volcanic hazards and evacuation procedures. *Natural Hazards and Earth System Sciences, 9*(1), 251–266.

Boyatzis, R. E. (1998). *Transforming qualitative information: Thematic analysis and code development*. Thousand Oaks, CA: Sage.

Bryman, A. (2006). Integrating quantitative and qualitative research: How is it done? *Qualitative Research, 6*(1), 97–113.

Bryman, A. (2007). Barriers to integrating quantitative and qualitative research. *Journal of Mixed Methods Research, 1*(1), 8–22.

Caracelli, V., & Greene, J. (1993). Data analysis strategies for mixed-method evaluation designs. *Educational Evaluation and Policy Analysis, 15*(2), 195–207.

Chi, M. T. H. (1997). Quantifying qualitative analyses of verbal data: A practical guide. *The Journal of the Learning Sciences, 6*(3), 271–315.

Clark, A. (2007). *Understanding community: A review of networks, ties, and contacts* (NCRM Working Paper Series). University of Manchester, ESRC National Centre for Research Methods. Retrieved August 3, 2009, from http://eprints.ncrm.ac.uk/469/

Creswell, J. W., & Plano Clark, V. L. (2007). *Designing and conducting mixed methods research*. Thousand Oaks, CA: Sage.

Dickinson, W. B. (2010). Visual displays for mixed methods findings. In A. Tashakkori & C. Teddlie (Eds.), *SAGE handbook of*

mixed methods in social & behavioral research (2nd ed.). Thousand Oaks, CA: Sage.

Elliott, J. (2005). *Using narrative in social research: Qualitative and quantitative approaches*. London: Sage.

Fielding, N. G., & Fielding, J. L. (1986). *Linking data: The articulation of qualitative and quantitative methods in social research*. Beverly Hills, CA: Sage.

Ford, R. T. (2006). *Nursing attitudes and therapeutic capacity: What are the implications for nursing care of patients who use illicit drugs?* Unpublished thesis, Australian National University, Canberra.

Green, J., Statham, H., & Solomou, W. (2008). *Assessing satisfaction: Insights from a multi-methods study* (NCRM Working Paper Series). University of Manchester, ESRC National Centre for Research Methods. Retrieved December 11, 2008, from http://eprints.ncrm.ac.uk/462/

Greene, J. C. (2007). *Mixed methods in social inquiry*. San Francisco: Jossey-Bass.

Happ, M. B., DeVito Dabbs, A., Tate, J., Hricik, A., & Erlen, J. (2006). Exemplars of mixed methods data combination and analysis. *Nursing Research, 55*(2, Suppl. 1), S43–S49.

Harden, A., & Thomas, J. (2005). Methodological issues in combining diverse study types in systematic reviews. *International Journal of Social Research Methodology, 8*(3), 257–271.

Jung, J.-K. (2007). *Computer-aided qualitative GIS (CAQ-GIS) for critical researchers: An integration of quantitative and qualitative research in the geography of communities*. Unpublished thesis, State University of New York at Buffalo.

Kane, M., & Trochim, W. M. K. (2007). *Concept mapping for planning and evaluation*. Thousand Oaks, CA: Sage.

Louis, K. S. (1982). Sociologist as sleuth: Integrating methods in the RDU study. *American Behavioral Scientist, 26*(1), 101–120.

Maliski, S. L., Sarna, L., Evangelista, L., & Padilla, G. (2003). The aftermath of lung cancer: Balancing the good and bad. *Cancer Nursing, 26*(3), 237–244.

Maxwell, J., & Loomis, D. (2003). Mixed method design: An alternative approach. In A. Tashakkori & C. Teddlie (Eds.), *Handbook of mixed methods in social & behavioral research* (pp. 241–271). Thousand Oaks, CA: Sage.

Miles, M. B., & Huberman, A. M. (1994). *Qualitative data analysis: An expanded sourcebook.* Thousand Oaks, CA: Sage.

Moran-Ellis, J., Alexander, V. D., Cronin, A., Dickinson, M., Fielding, J., Sleney, J., et al. (2006). Triangulation and integration: Processes, claims and implications. *Qualitative Research, 6*(1), 45–59.

Morgan, D. L. (1993). Qualitative content analysis: A guide to paths not taken. *Qualitative Health Research, 3*(1), 112–121.

Newman, I., & Ramlo, S. E. (2010). Use of two multivariate techniques, Q methodology and Q factor analysis, to facilitate interpretation of mixed methods research. In A. Tashakkori & C. Teddlie (Eds.), *SAGE handbook of mixed methods in social & behavioral research* (2nd ed.). Thousand Oaks, CA: Sage.

Niglas, K. (2004). *The combined use of qualitative and quantitative methods in educational research.* Tallin, Estonia: Tallinn Pedagogical University.

Niglas, K. (2007). Review of: Microsoft Office Excel spreadsheet software. *Journal of Mixed Methods Research, 1*(3), 297–299.

O'Cathain, A., Murphy, E., & Nicholl, J. (2007). Integration and publications as indicators of "yield" from mixed methods studies. *Journal of Mixed Methods Research, 1*(2), 147–163.

Onwuegbuzie, A. J., & Teddlie, C. (2003). A framework for analyzing data in mixed methods research. In A. Tashakkori & C. Teddlie (Eds.), *Handbook of mixed methods in social and behavioral research* (pp. 351–384). Thousand Oaks, CA: Sage.

Pawson, R. (2006). *Evidence-based policy.* London: Sage.

Prell, C., & Skvoretz, J. (2008). Looking at social capital through triad structures. *Connections, 28*(2), 1–13.

Ragin, C. (1987). *The comparative method: Moving beyond qualitative and quantitative strategies.* Berkeley: University of California Press.

Ragin, C., Shulman, D., Weinberg, A., & Gran, B. (2003). Complexity, generality, and qualitative comparative analysis. *Field Methods, 15*(4), 323–340.

Reznitskaya, A., Anderson, R. C., McNurlen, B., Nguyen-Jahiel, K., Archodidou, A., & Kim, S.-Y. (2001). Influence of oral discussion on written argument. *Discourse Processes, 32*(2&3), 155–175.

Rihoux, B., & De Meur, G. (2009). Crisp set qualitative comparative analysis (csQCA). In B. Rihoux & C. Ragin (Eds.), *Configurational comparative methods* (pp. 33–68). Los Angeles: Sage.

Rihoux, B., & Ragin, C. (2009). Introduction. In B. Rihoux & C. Ragin (Eds.), *Configurational comparative methods* (pp. xvii–xxv). Los Angeles: Sage.

Rihoux, B., Ragin, C., Yamasaki, S., & Bol, D. (2009). Conclusions—the way(s) ahead. In B. Rihoux & C. Ragin (Eds.), *Configurational comparative methods* (pp. 167–178). Los Angeles: Sage.

Sandelowski, M. (2001). Real qualitative researchers do not count: The use of numbers in qualitative research. *Research in Nursing & Health, 24*(3), 230–240.

Sandelowski, M., Voils, C. I., & Barroso, J. (2006). Defining and designing mixed research synthesis studies. *Research in the Schools, 13*(1), 29–40.

Sandelowski, M., Voils, C. I., & Knafl, G. (2009). On quantitizing. *Journal of Mixed Methods Research, 3*(3), 208–222.

Scott, J. (2000). *Social network analysis: A handbook.* London: Sage.

Sivesind, K. H. (1999). Structured, qualitative comparison: Between singularity and single-dimensionality. *Quality and Quantity, 33,* 361–380.

Skinner, D., Matthews, S., & Burton, L. (2005). Combining ethnography and GIS technology. In T. S. Weisner (Ed.), *Discovering successful pathways in children's development.* Chicago: University of Chicago Press.

Steinberg, S. J., & Steinberg, S. L. (2006). *Geographic information systems for the social sciences: Investigating space and place.* Thousand Oaks, CA: Sage.

Tashakkori, A., & Teddlie, C. (2008). Quality of inferences in mixed methods research: Calling for an integrative framework. In M. M. Bergman (Ed.), *Advances in mixed methods research* (pp. 101–120). London: Sage.

Teddlie, C., & Tashakkori, A. (2009). *Foundations of mixed methods research.* Thousand Oaks, CA: Sage.

Weinstein, E. A., & Tamur, J. M. (1978). Meanings, purposes, and structural resources in social interaction. In J. G. Manis & B. N. Meltzer (Eds.), *Symbolic interaction* (3rd ed., pp. 138–140). Boston: Allyn & Bacon.

Widmer, T., Hirschi, C., Serdült, U., & Vögeli, C. (2008). Analysis with APES, the actor process event scheme. In M. M. Bergman (Ed.), *Advances in mixed methods research* (pp. 150–171). London: Sage.

Woolley, C. M. (2009). Meeting the mixed methods challenge of integration in a sociological study of structure and agency. *Journal of Mixed Methods Research, 3*(1), 7–25.

Yin, R. K. (2006). Mixed methods research: Are the methods genuinely integrated or merely parallel? *Research in the Schools, 13*(1), 41–47.

VISUAL DISPLAYS FOR MIXED METHODS FINDINGS

◆ Wendy B. Dickinson

Objectives

- Readers will be able to discuss the historical uses of graphical display.

- Readers will be able to explain how data visualization can serve as an important tool to improve data analysis.

- Readers will be familiar with Tufte's principles of visual display, and be able to identify and explain design excellence using the four elements of word, art, number, and image.

- Readers will be introduced to 2- and 3-dimensional graphing techniques, and will be able to appropriately apply these methods as indicated by the research questions.

◆ Introduction

In other research fields, there is an ever-increasing acknowledgment of the "increasing need for new methods and tools that support knowledge construction" from visual and geospatial data sets (Bhowmick, Griffin, MacEachern, Kluhsman, & Lengerich, 2008, p. 576). In educational research, this need for new methods and tools has been advanced by the creation of new ways to graphically represent the *procedures* in mixed methods studies, most notably Ivankova, Creswell, & Stick (2007); the visualization of the *findings* has not been fully addressed by contemporary researchers, however. This chapter provides an essential linkage between visual history, mixed research procedures, and graphical display to promote integration of all three elements, yielding a connected, panoramic visualization of research findings to aid in inference and decision making.

In Part I, we provide a historical overview of graphical display and discuss the narrative uses of visual display that have been used in the past to investigate and explain phenomena of interest.

◆ I. Historical Overview of Graphical Display

Symbolic imagery has been used since the earliest existence of mankind. Ancient cultures used symbols to convey ideas, record events such as battles or animals hunts, and teach their children the ways of their lives. Long before information was translated into formal written languages, "humans used images to communicate with each other and with a variety of imaginary creatures, worlds, and gods" (Burnett, 2004, p. 20; O'Donnell, 1998). For example, cave drawings in France still display a story quite effectively after several thousand of years.

"Maps, charts and diagrams at their simple best are not far removed from inscriptions on the walls of Lascaux, a Phoenician traders clay tally sheet, or a Sioux Indians buffalo hide summing up both a hunt and its yield" (Herdeg, 1974, p. 9). Lascaux, with its earliest cave images, is known as "the Sistine Chapel of Prehistory," with "the oldest artwork of mankind," displaying 600 drawings on the cave walls (Duckeck, 2009).

Beyond these earliest beginnings of pictorial representation, the marriage of information and image was preceded by centuries of separation. The "graphic explosion of the nineteenth century . . . had its origins in the intellectual turbulence of the eighteenth century," with the span between 1750 and 1850 showing "a shift in the language of science from words to pictures" (Wainer, 2005, p. 5). It took the arrival of William Playfair (1759–1823), the creator of all of the most well-known statistical graphics (the bar chart, the pie chart, and the time-series line graph; see Spence, 2005; Tufte, 1983, 2001), to "invent a universal language useful to science and commerce alike" that advanced the view "that a graph can help us formulate an understanding of nature by plotting data points and looking for patterns"—forever changing the way we would look at data (Wainer, 1997b, p. 35).

Graphs "achieve their success by capitalizing on the basic perceptual and cognitive capacities of human beings"; Playfair believed that "graphs would be a powerful aid to memory; intuitively, he appreciated that visual memory was more robust than memory for words or numbers" (Playfair, 1801 [2005], p. 29). Regarding the uniqueness and utility of his graphical inventions, Playfair wrote,

> As the eye is the best judge of proportion, being able to estimate it with more quickness and accuracy than any other of our organs, it follows, that whenever relative quantities are in question, . . . this mode of representing it is peculiarly applicable; it gives a simple, accurate and permanent

idea, by giving form and shape to a number of separate ideas, which are otherwise abstract and unconnected. (Playfair, 1801, p. *x*)

One of the earliest narrative uses of visual data display to connect ideas and investigate phenomena was the pioneering work of Dr. John Snow. In the year 1854, Dr. Snow was trying to determine the cause of a deadly outbreak of disease in central London. During this time in London's history, clean water was not readily available to the people who lived in the city. Instead, they had to walk with buckets to wells, located in their neighborhood, and pump up water from underground wells, then carry it back to their homes. A system of wells set up on a geographic grid served each street's inhabitants.

During this outbreak of disease, there was no readily available answer for what was actually causing the deaths for the people living in London, especially in one area. Dr. Snow believed that it had something to do with the water supply, so he began to investigate the deaths by plotting each death on a gridded map of the affected area by street and location. After plotting these deaths, he went door to door and spoke to the families living in the houses to determine if there were any other possible causes for the deaths. Snow reportedly was "knocking on doors, interrogating strangers in the street, asking anyone he encountered for anecdotal evidence about the outbreak and its victims" (Johnson, 2006, p. 135).

By using the results of both the quantitative data (the frequencies of death and location) and the results of his door-to-door interviews he was able to determine that most of the deaths were occurring in the area of the Broad Street pump. All told, approximately 700 people living within 250 yards of the Broad Street pump died in less than 2 weeks (Johnson, 2006). By removing the pump handle, which people used to access water from this particular well, he almost single-handedly stopped the

cholera epidemic and saved probably hundreds of lives.

Today, we recognize Dr. John Snow as one of the first people to use visual graphing methods to solve a medical mystery. In Figure 19.1, we see an updated version of Dr. Snow's famous Broad Street pump map (Frerichs, 2001). Many contemporary writers have examined early versions of the map including Tufte (1983), Frerichs (2001), and Onwuegbuzie and Dickinson (2008). By looking at the graph, we can easily see the underlying grid pattern, which includes the street names and major locations. We can identify major locations within the city including the Lion Brewery, workhouse, and Golden Square; but most importantly we can see the tiny line patterns that indicate the patterns of deaths observed and recorded in the city's residents. Each mark represented a death; the map has been referred to as "the Ghost Map" (Johnson, 2006) because of this portrayal of human mortality.

By looking at these line patterns, John Snow was able to determine that the majority of those deaths were indeed occurring by the Broad Street pump. John Snow incorporated multiple data sources, with multiple methods of inquiry (interview data, mortality counts [frequencies], mortality location, and narrative) to develop a solution to a deadly problem: the cholera epidemic. For mixed methods researchers, this provides the earliest example of an inquiry method that combined both quantitative analyses—the line pattern of deaths—and the qualitative aspect of the door-to-door interviews to solve a problem. And it is to this important application to mixed methods—complex problem solving—that visual data display is very well suited.

Part II provides an overview of visual imagery including principles of Gestalt theory, color theory, and communications, and the power and composition of the visual image as a whole. Part II also discusses graphical techniques based on the visual matrix selected to display the underlying phenomena.

Figure 19.1　John Snow's Map 1 (1854)

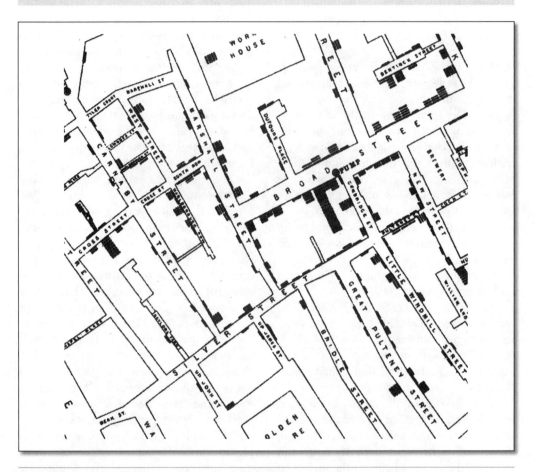

SOURCE: Frerichs, 2001. Reprinted with kind permission of Dr. R. Frerichs.

◆ II. Overview of Visual Imagery

Data visualization is the mapping of data into a Cartesian space—integrating a person's creativity and expertise into the knowledge discovery process, thus allowing a symbiosis of computational power with our visual potential (Bartke, 2005). Data visualization creates images—images whose content transcends the spoken word. For the viewer, this unspoken message can be more potent than spoken or written communication. Visual language is therefore an effective vehicle of both context and content.

Tapping our power of artistic imagery to transmit conceptual information is a natural extension of visual display. Indeed, "the ideals of science incorporate four major concerns: a reliance on evidence; a regard for both error and control; a need for publicness; and an interest in research generalizability" (Katzer, Cook, & Crouch, 1978, p. 14).

Thus, scientific communications, whether written, oral, or visual, can successfully address Katzer and colleagues' directives. Ideally, research data are summarized and displayed in such a way as to facilitate and maximize the transmission of research results. A visual summary of data can yield interesting information displaying patterns or trends that otherwise might remain unnoticed. Visual data sets also can show patterns of response not readily apparent as mere numbers. New research develops new methods and refines existing algorithms to graphically display multidimensional data, particularly with the addition of geographical (spatial) referents.

Many methods of multivariate graphical display attempt to simplify or reduce information in the data set to a relatively few variables. This reduction to two or three variables causes a loss of the original information and can cloud the interpretation of results or mask research findings. By creating multivariate graphical displays using all the original data, we enhance the user's ability to detect and comprehend important phenomena, communicate major conclusions, and provide practical methods to perform accurate calculations. Software packages commercially available today harness the power apparent in visual imagery, and merge seamlessly this visual power with the speed and storage capacity of the computer. Before we can utilize computer technology to draw our graphs (via algorithmic code), two important ideas must help create these strong visual images: the idea of overall form or shape (Gestalt), and the use of visual organization to accurately communicate information to the viewer.

GESTALT THEORY

What we "now refer to as Gestalt psychology began to develop in 1910" (Kohler, 1967, p. xviii). The German word *Gestalt* conveys form or shape. In the shadow of World War I, German researchers Koffka, Kohler, and Wertheimer formalized the tenets of Gestalt theory. Wertheimer (1923 [1938]) identified Gestalt factors as the figure-ground phenomena, proximity, similarity, common fate, and simplicity. Common fate or direction was described in this way: "[I]n most visual fields the contents of particular areas belong together as circumscribed units

from which their surroundings are excluded" (Kohler, 1967, pp. 80–81).

Within the next decade, Gestalt theorists would advance their ideas of figure-ground, common fate, proximity, similarity, and closure. Figure-ground refers to objects proceeding or moving forward together in a unified whole field, with the elements of an image seen as surrounded perceived as a figure, i.e., grouped into a whole, whereas the elements that are doing the surrounding will be perceived as a background (Wertheimer, 1923 [1938]). Physical location or proximity (closeness) determines which fields visually join together. Similarity of purpose or common fate also helps unify individual images into wholes. The closure phenomena occur when the figure is presented to the viewer with missing lines or spaces. The person viewing the uncompleted shape will tend to fill in the physical gaps conceptually to evaluate and complete the image. These individual factors of perception were subsumed under a common heading: the Law of Pragnanz. *Pragnanz* translates as compact yet significant, and this researcher refers to it as the "less is more" idea. The Law of Pragnanz frames psychological organization and perception as essential functions of good figures or good visual results.

VISUAL ORGANIZATION AND PERCEPTION

Gestalt theory introduced fundamental principles of visual organization: ideas that helped to explain the way humans view and respond to images. These principles explain the visual perception (message received) by the viewer in response to visual stimuli (images) and have "major influence on the perception of patterns," and "can be used as design principles in creating visualizations" (Zuk & Carpendale, 2006, p. 3). Viewer response to images is the basis for the power of graphical display; humans can recognize, perceive, and evaluate information more efficiently when presented as an image rather than as numbers or words.

The ability of humans to process visual information provides an advantage over data analysis utilizing only numbers or only words, because the human mind possesses the ability to discern objects and recognize patterns that still will confuse the current generation of computers. The Turing Test, created by Alan Turing in 1950, was an ingenious description of a way for a human judge to ask a series of questions and then decide, depending on the answers, whether the test subject is a human or a computer (von Ahn, Blum, & Langford, 2004).

One contemporary example of this human perceptual advantage, "object recognition in clutter," was explored by the use of CAPTCHAs, "completely automated public Turing test to tell computers and humans apart" (Mori & Malik, 2003, p. 1). CAPTCHAs are widely used to evaluate human perception of visual organization within computer programs (algorithms). One example is the use of CAPTCHAs by Yahoo and others to require potential users to solve a CAPTCHA test before they receive an email account—typically, by reading a visually distorted or deformed word (shape) on the screen and retyping it in a second text box provided on the screen. Most humans succeed at this test, while current computer programs fail (Mori & Malik, 2003). The interpretation of shape is crucial, since "shape incorporates aspects of both size and orientation," and its flexible nature allows for the creation of complex symbolism (Zuk & Carpendale, 2006, p. 2). In summary, this human ability to visually organize marks into discernible shapes and recognizable patterns provides strong theoretical and physiological support for the use of graphical display in both data exploration and the presentation of mixed methods findings.

POWER AND COMPOSITION OF THE VISUAL IMAGE

Visual images can be a powerful tool in data exploration and discovery. Exploratory data analysis is "like detective work: in it, data are examined and clues are uncovered . . . somehow we must examine data and look for suggestive patterns. Finding unexpected patterns is a path to discovery, and Tukey provided copious evidence that drawing a picture is the best way to do it" (Wainer, 2005, p. 119). Tukey created many unique display techniques, most notably the stem-and-leaf plot (Tukey, 1972, 1977). The stem-and-leaf plot displays the distribution of scores with the numbers themselves, making each element of the graph needed and effective.

In 1983, Bertin's framework for visualization, the Properties of the Graphic System, presented 8 visual variables: 2 planar dimension variables (x,y) and 6 retinal variables: size, value, grain (texture), color, orientation, and shape (Zuk & Carpendale, 2006, p. 2). The variable of *color* has "no implicit order, but is selective and associative"; therefore, we can use variations of color to represent both variable values and relationships between variables on the graph surface. When there are large amounts of variables, it may be impractical to assign a different color to portray each variable's value—we may want to use shades of gray, on a black-to-white continuum, to represent multiple values instead.

Tufte's principles of visual display (1990) spelled out specific visual consequences that governed the design, editing, analysis, and critique of data representations. Tufte believed these principles of data representations helped identify and explain design excellence, and defined the four elements of envisioned information as word, art, number, and image. Visual display is actually located at the intersection of all four elements: *word* is the labels on our graphs, *art* is the composition, *number* is the quantitative data, and *image* is the overall creation or communication of essential information. Figure 19.2 illustrates Tufte's four elements, representing the operational model for envisioning information.

Figure 19.2 Operational Model of Envisioning Information (Adapted From Tufte)

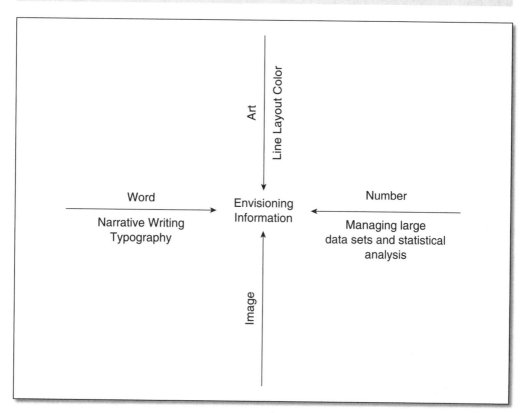

Lengler and Eppler (2007) provide a working definition of visualization methods for us: "A visualization method is a systematic, rule-based, external, permanent, and graphic representation that depicts information in a way that is conducive to acquiring insights, developing an elaborate understanding, or communicating experiences" (p. 1). By utilizing visualization in combination with mixed methods, we can acquire insights and understanding, and communicate our research findings to a wider audience of stakeholders.

Part III is a discussion of display techniques based on data type with numeric data typically generated from quantitative methods of analysis, text data typically generated from qualitative methods, and multiple data sources and types that are typically generated from mixed methods techniques.

◆ III. Procedures for Data Display Based on Data Type

The "graphic portrayal of quantitative data has deep roots": roots that reach into the histories of thematic cartography, statistical graphics, and data visualization, which are intertwined with each other, and roots that are connected with the rise of statistical thinking through the 19th century, and the technological developments in the 20th century (Friendly, 2008, p. 1). These technological advancements have enabled researchers to portray both quantitative and qualititative data in more efficacious ways. Today, data analysis of all data types begins with an examination of the observations. Original observations refer to data collected personally by the researcher, or collected by previous researchers, in the case of secondary analysis. Ware describes four stages of the data visualization process: "collection and storage of data itself; the preprocessing designed to transform the data into something we can understand; the display hardware and the graphics algorithms that produce an image on the screen; and the human perceptual and cognitive system of the perceiver" (Ware, 2000, p. 4).

Coding our data helps by grouping or sorting large numbers of variables into smaller, discrete categories. Once the original data set is coded and sorted and any necessary transformations have been accomplished, the researcher can examine it in its entirety. Special attention is given to missing data cases and outliers, and appropriate corrective procedures are performed. The resultant clean data file is then incorporated into a graphics program for multidimensional display. Once this entire data file has been graphed, a holistic feeling about the data set should emerge. Generally, the researcher will look for inconsistencies between and within groups, findings that conflict with established theory, and results that might suggest poor experimental control.

A good graph "lets the data tell their story clearly and completely" (Wainer, 1997a, p. 11). Therefore, when creating visual displays we start with our original data observations. We code, sort, and transform the data as needed, producing multidimensional graphical displays of information. From these displays of information we can conduct trend analyses and recognize patterns. Graphs may also be used as a visual summary of the research process: to "simplify complex information that would be difficult or lengthy to express in words, . . . to summarize or emphasize certain findings, illustrate complicated results such as interaction effects, and show patterns of data" (Nicol and Pexman, 2003, p. 2). We can more effectively communicate the results of our research to a wider research audience using graphical displays than we could just by showing tables of numbers or pages of

text alone. In fact, the greatest value of a graph is when it forces us to see what we never expected (Tukey, 1977).

When viewing a graphical display, especially one that is well constructed and clearly labeled, the results of the research are much clearer; people can see these results much more easily than they might be able to given only numbers or a highly technical report. Therefore, visual displays have become commonplace in contemporary print media: for example, newspapers, magazines, corporations, school districts, and testing companies all use visual displays.

Images can be visual renditions or representations of ideas, dimensions, and events (Dickinson, 2001). Representing data visually is a complex task, and Tufte recognized that "the world portrayed by our information displays is caught up in the 2-dimensionality of the endless flatland of paper" (Tufte, 1990, p. 12). One way to escape that "flatland" is to employ the use of a geospatial information system (GIS) within our data presentations, thus invoking the inherent geophysical relationship present in many of our contemporary research settings. Visual representation is the "depiction of objects in space" (Dickie, 1997, p. 59); commercially available graphing software, with GIS capacity, provides an opportunity to display research findings utilizing the one-to-one geographical correspondence of data to actual physical location.

Graphical display is an application of visual expression. By visually expressing data as an image, the underlying numerical observations can be communicated easily to the viewer. Contemporary inventions—the television, the computer, and the spread of the World Wide Web—have "dramatically changed the role of visual messages in communication" (Lester, 2006, p. vii). The concept of what constitutes communication is continually evolving to reflect changing social practice and inventions. For example, email is now commonly accepted and used for both social and professional functions.

GRAPHICAL COMMUNICATION: SUMMARY AND EXPOSURE

Graphs, like other communication forms, serve different purposes, with the most common goals being visual summary and exposure (Friendly, 1995). Per Friendly, summary refers to the visual inventory of created data which presents viewers with an informed understanding of the underlying information: Powsner and Tufte (1997) "advocated the creation of effective visual summaries, while advising researchers to retain multiple diverse methods for data representation" (Dickinson, Hines, & Onwuegbuzie, 2007, p. 2).

Information (and meaning) is conveyed through the composition and integration of multiple lines within an image. An example of multiple lines within an image would be geographical maps that use multiple lines, with differentiated line thickness, colors, and weight to portray 3-dimensional information on a 2-dimensional surface (Dickinson et al., 2007). Tufte (2006) noted that "maps show information with differentiated lines all the time, with greater richness" (p. 71). By incorporating differentiated line qualities within data display techniques, we illustrate research information with enhanced clarity, thereby providing a visual summary of the phenomena of interest. After Playfair, Nicol and Pexman (2003, p. 3) delineate "nine different types of figures: bar graphs, line graphs, plots, drawings, combination graphs (which combine graphs or incorporate drawings or photographs), pie graphs, miscellaneous graphs (dendograms and stem-and-leaf plots), charts, and photographs."

Using selected visual display techniques, we developed a visual exploration of different data sets to help identify patterns and discern themes not readily apparent or easily accessible in the numeric or text-only summary format. By sharing the SAS code, which is found in the appendices, and then each resultant graphical output, we provide a visual and practical link between procedure, code, and graphical output.

Pictorial representation of data embodies the best of visual display and information transmission: it organizes and summarizes research data in a visual format (Dickinson, 2009) Indeed, "visual messages that are remembered have the greatest power to inform, to educate, and persuade an individual and a culture" (Lester, 2006, p. vii). Within the visual message, patterns are more readily discerned and themes magnified through visual data exploration and discovery. Creating a visual rendition of research data provides a powerful channel for information exchange. Independently, both qualitative and quantitative research methods yield valuable findings, but may be unable to independently generate a complete and overall Gestalt of meaning. Thus, both numeric and text data benefit from the visual display format, with increased communication of findings, magnification of ideas, and enhanced pattern recognition.

Much as visual ethnography narrates the story of individuals or groups, visual display tells the story of our data. By utilizing mixed methods, with multiple data sources and methods, we combine the strengths of qualitative and quantitative techniques to produce a richer picture of our research phenomena. Combining mixed methods with visual display optimizes research data investigation for transmission of vital information, thereby both enhancing the clarity of and providing support for our research findings. As presented by Ridenour and Newman (2008), all "behavioral research is made up of a combination of qualitative and quantitative constructs," thus advancing the "notion of a qualitative-quantitative research continuum," as opposed to an artificial separation, or dichotomy (Ridenour & Newman, 2008, p. 9).

Using visual display to present research findings of both strands can literally "bridge" the pieces together, creating a visual integration of varied data types and techniques.

Part IV presents graphical examples of findings from QUAL and QUAN strands utilizing visual data displays to integrate findings within mixed methods approaches. Applications in this section provide scenarios including 2-dimensional techniques with the topics of bubble plots, correspondence analysis, choropleth plots, star graphs, and survey research displays with subject responses; and 3-dimensional graphical techniques, including surface maps, prism maps, and block maps. Within each example, we provide a discussion of display techniques based on the purpose of visual display: the organization of data, frequency comparisons that include comparison by unit of analysis and comparison by phenomena of interest. We discuss the current use of geographical reference, using software programs that provide 3-dimensional spatial analysis using location. We also provide ways to compare data over time, using both point-in-time displays and displays for longitudinal analysis; ways to investigate and identify themes and trends within our data; and ways to produce a visual summary of findings to aid in dissemination of research results.

◆ IV. Graphing Applications, Qualitative Data: Envisioning Kinaaldá

This example adapted from Dickinson (2001).

Visual data techniques "have become a prominent approach in qualitative research in general, after they have been used for some time in areas such as visual anthropology" (Banks, 2007, p. viiii). This graphing example focuses on historical data collected by Frisbie (1967) from the Navaho puberty ritual Kinaaldá, which is part of the blessing way. Frisbie conducted a comparative study of the Kinaaldá ritual using accounts from 19 different anthropologists, constructing a gridded chart to compile the individual anthropologists' observations, and the ritual themes mentioned by each person's account. A portion of the recreated grid chart is shown in Table 19.1. The purpose was to conduct a secondary analysis of a historical database, utilizing visual information techniques to display findings and communicate ideas to a new generation of scholars. This study incorporates the original data grid by Frisbie with current icon-driven graphing algorithms to produce an efficient data display.

Table 19.1 Original Kinaaldá Data: Portion of Recreated Grid Chart

Anthropologist	Observed Rituals: Themes Mentioned					
	Kinaaldá as part of the Blessing Way	Kinaaldá as part of the Emergence Myth	Ceremony originated by Changing Women	Instigated by First Man and First Women	Given for Changing Woman	Conducted on Changing Woman's trip to west
Curtis				X	X	
Franciscan Fathers					X	
Wayne & Bailey	X	X		X	X	
Richard			X		X	
Wheelwright	X				X	
Matthews					X	X
Haile	X			X	X	

Anthropologist	Observed Rituals: Themes Mentioned					
	Kinaaldá as part of the Blessing Way	Kinaaldá as part of the Emergence Myth	Ceremony originated by Changing Women	Instigated by First Man and First Women	Given for Changing Woman	Conducted on Changing Woman's trip to west
Goddard				X	X	
A. Leighton (DS)	X					
D. Leighton (TS)					X	
Keith (AM, 1963)				X	X	
Haile (FM, 1932)	X		X		X	
McAllester (FM, 1961)	X		X	X	X	
Johnson (FM, 1963)*			X	X	X	
Johnson (FM, 1963)**						
Johnson (FM, 1963)***						
Johnson (FM, 1964)	X				X	
Johnson (TM, 1964)			X		X	
Haile (SC) 1932	X		X		X	

DATA SOURCE: C.J. Frisbie, 1967.

CONTEXT AND METHODS

Native American (Navaho) ceremonies were first observed and recorded by the Spanish expedition in 1653, and it is quite possible that impermanent sand art portrayals ("dry paintings") were being made even then (Dutton, 1976, p. 7). Many reasons exist, both implicit and implied, for the creation and performance of ritualistic acts of the Navaho people: rituals can be viewed as a form of behavioral response to external events in the life of a person (Kluckhohn, 1942).

Kinaaldá refers to the collective group of rituals and practices associated with the Navaho girls' puberty ceremony. According to Frisbie, "the term for the puberty ceremony is 'Kinaaldá.' Most Navaho use this word to refer to the first menses, alluding to the ceremonial, rather than the physiological event" (Frisbie, 1967, p. 8). Using the data collected by Frisbie (1967) we see graphical displays of observations by each anthropologist: summarizing both the variable frequencies and the means. By graphing how each anthropologist observed and reported the rituals, we can visually discern the similarities and differences between the various accounts of the Kinaaldá puberty ceremonies.

Examples of the variable names include dressing, combing, running, naming, and corn grinding, which are some of the various activities comprising the Navaho puberty ceremonies. Examples of the star graphs constructed with the data results from each anthropologist are shown in Figure 19.2. By using these "small multiples" (Tufte, 1990), we can visually compare the differences and similarities between these 19 different accounts.

During the secondary data analysis, the original data observations were examined, cleaned, and sorted by the researcher during the pre-algorithmic phase. Binary coding of the anthropologist observations was utilized (0 = not observed, 1 = observed),

and descriptive statistics were calculated for each observed Kinaaldá ritual, per anthropologist. The resultant data were then incorporated into the graphing algorithm and postalgorithmic interpretative activities conducted. Star graphs "are a useful way to display multivariate observations with an arbitrary number of variables: each observation is represented as a star-shaped form with one ray for each variable" (Friendly, 1991b, p. 1). Star graphs were created for each of the anthropologist's multivariate ritual observations, with each anthropologist represented by one star graph, as shown in Figure 19.3.

Figure 19.3 Kinaaldá Ritual Observations: Star Graphs

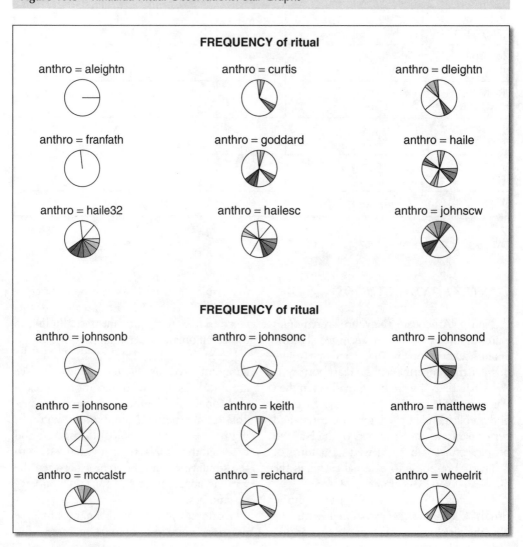

In Figure 19.3, note the similarity of observed rituals by both Goddard and Haile, and the observed ritual similarities between Wheelrite and Haile (32). Within the group, note how different the accounts are by the Fransciscan Fathers and A. Leighton—each account only recorded one observed theme. By looking at the star charts, we can detect similarities and differences in the reported accounts more quickly and more efficiently than by looking at the original gridded data chart with marked responses.

2-DIMENSIONAL GRAPHICAL EXAMPLE: BUBBLE PLOTS

This example adapted from Dickinson, Hines, & Hall (2009).

Our next graphing example shows a 2-dimensional graphing technique called "bubble plots." Bubble plots use a Cartesian coordinate system to display frequencies of the variable of interest. The larger the bubble (diameter), the greater the observed frequency. Our second graphical example is another 2-dimensional technique, correspondence analysis, which is used in survey research displays. Our third graphical examples are two 3-dimensional graphing techniques called surface mapping and prism maps. Both surface mapping and prism maps use geospatial displays to provide a location referent for our numerical data. A 2-dimensional example of graphing using a geographical matrix, choropleth, is also shown using the same mortality data set for comparison purposes.

In 1801, the idea of using a circular image to portray frequency and amount was formalized by William Playfair. These first "statistical charts" illustrated the number of inhabitants in major European cities by a set of hand-drawn circles, with the diameter of the circle indicating population, thus enabling effective size comparison by city. Today's bubble plots enable the same effective frequency comparisons of phenomena of interest but with two pronounced improvements. The first contemporary improvement is the addition of a location-based matrix (Cartesian coordinate system) enabling display of the bubble plots in relation to a second variable.

More importantly, the second improvement is the ability to use computers to draw and replicate the bubble plots quickly and inexpensively. The resultant bubble plots effectively communicate contemporary research findings with both simplicity and elegance, reaching a diverse research audience with information needed for vital decision making. By design, bubble plots are especially effective for categorical data display due to their visual size differential. In this presentation we provide examples, using data on births and deaths, to show how this visual size differential is linked to corresponding data values, resulting in accessible and readily understandable graphical outputs. By utilizing bubble plots to display categorical data, we create a more effective visual means of transmission for research findings, thus enhancing both decision making and interpretation of research outcomes.

Researchers in the social, behavioral, and health sciences "often need to contend with data representing such variables as race, ethnicity, gender, marital status, occupation, state of residence, academic major, blood type, religious affiliation, political affiliation, and presence or absence of some characteristic. These are all considered nominal or categorical variables (Defays, 1988, p. 316), and the process of assigning numbers to elements of these variables is the process of *nominal measurement*" (Dickinson et al., 2009; emphasis in original).

Nominal measurement may be described as the process of grouping units (persons, responses, etc.) into classes or categories so that all of those in a single class are equivalent, or nearly so, with respect to a specific property or attribute. With nominal (categorical) scales, the assigned numbers define each distinct grouping of the attribute and serve merely as a substitute for labels or names. With nominal-level measurement we use only the uniqueness property of numbers, e.g., "1" is distinct from "2," so if object or response A is coded using a "1" and object or response B is coded using a "2," then A and B are different with respect to the attribute. The assigned numbers serve to make categorical distinctions only; each distinct number thus represents a different category. The magnitude of the numbers does not reflect any inherent ordering of the objects or distance among the objects to which the numbers are assigned (Glass & Hopkins, 1996; Hopkins, Hopkins, & Glass, 1996).

Friendly states, "[C]ategorical data means different things in different contexts," including "types of categorical variables, data in case form versus frequency form, frequency data versus count data, and the distinction between explanatory (predictor) and response (criterion) variables" (Friendly, 2000, p. 2). By design, bubble plots are especially effective for categorical data display due to their visual size differential. This visual size differential (bubble diameter) is linked to the corresponding data values, resulting in explanatory graphical output.

This explanatory graphical output is created using the process shown in Appendix 19.1, 2-dimensional bubble plots algorithmic flowchart.

Appendix 19.2 contains the SAS code written to produce the bubble plots from the mortality data set. Note the *blabel* option causes each bubble to be labeled with

the number of deaths associated with that particular observation. Additionally, the *bsize = 12* option invokes a scaling factor of 12 to be utilized when drawing the bubbles. The diameter of the bubbles will be multiplied by a constant factor to increase the size of each bubble within the graphical output, yet maintain the correct proportion (numeric relationship) of data to bubble. The use of the *Axis1 offset* and *Axis2 offset* statements provides "spacing" for the bubbles to keep them from intersecting the x and y axes, resulting in an uninterrupted visual field.

The use of the bubble plot to display data works particularly well with the categorical variables of gender and cause of death. It is easy for the viewer to visually compare the numbers (percentage) and cause of death by looking at the size of the bubble.

Figure 19.4 displays the top 10 causes of death, displayed by cause of death and gender. The 10 most frequently reported causes of death, as recorded by the Centers for Disease Control, are heart disease, malignancies (cancer), accidents, cerebrovascular incidents (stroke), chronic obstructive pulmonary disease and respiratory diseases, diabetes, influenza and pneumonia, suicide, nephritis, and Alzheimer's disease. Note while the top 10 reported causes of death remain the same for both males and females,

Figure 19.4 Top 10 Causes of Death: Percent by Gender

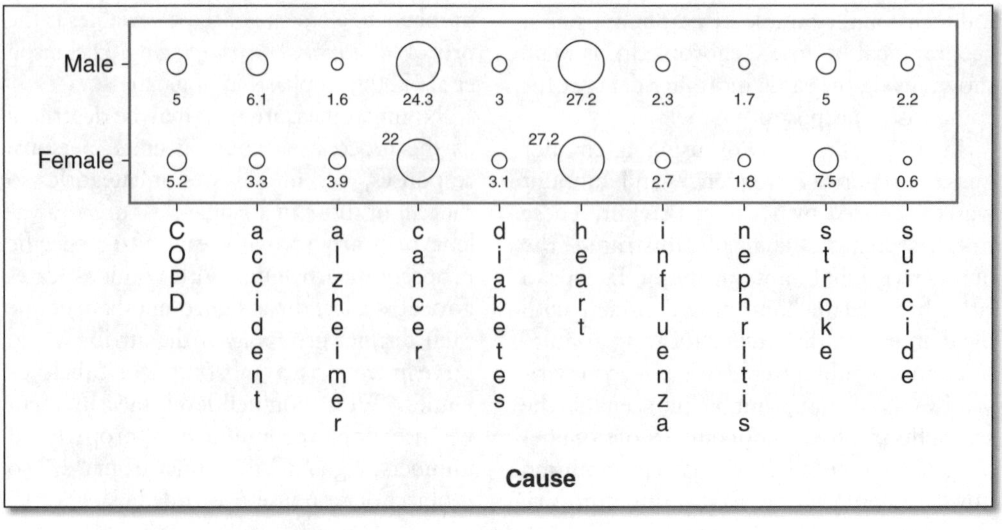

the actual reported percentages differ by category of cause.

Examples of gender differences by cause of death include a lower percentage of females (0.6%) than males (2.2%) committing suicide, and a higher percentage of males (6.1%) than females (3.3%) dying as the result of accidents. A notable exception is the reported incidence of heart disease, which yielded the same percentage (27.2%) for both genders in 2005. By comparing the bubble sizes between genders and category of disease, we can visually discern the ways in which male and female patterns of disease and death are similar, and where the patterns are different.

IMPLICATIONS AND IMPORTANCE

In the public health arena, where timely dissemination of data and treatment strategies is essential for public well-being, bubble plots can be utilized to quickly and efficiently transmit information to both the trained and the naïve viewer. Bubble plots may also prove valuable for data dissemination and interpretation in the social and behavioral sciences where categorical variables within large data sets are common. Bubble plots enable visual comparison of data values across a variety of variables. This visual comparison provides a way for the viewer to detect crucial patterns and trends over time contained within the data set. Thus, bubble plots enable our data to "talk" to us without words, providing a powerful tool for interpretation and dissemination of research results.

2-DIMENSIONAL GRAPHING EXAMPLE: CORRESPONDENCE ANALYSIS

This example adapted from Dickinson & Hall (2008)

Over the past few decades, correspondence analysis has gained "an international reputation as a powerful statistical tool for the graphical analysis of contingency tables" (Beh, 2004, p. 257). Correspondence analysis is a "statistical visualization method for picturing the associations between the levels of a two-way contingency table," with the name being a translation of the French phrase *analyses des correspondences*, denoting a system of correspondence between the elements of two data sets: the goal is "to have a global view of the data that is useful for interpretation"(Lee, 1994, p. 65).

Correspondence analysis (CA) is an exploratory data technique (Hoffman & Franke, 1986) related to both biplot analysis and principal components analysis, yielding a multidimensional representation of the association between the row and the column categories of a two-way contingency table (Friendly, 1991a). Representing complex relationships with graphics requires changing or expanding the familiar visual metaphors typically used for two variables (Friendly, 1991b). Thus, correspondence analysis is designed to show how data deviate from expectation (observed values versus expected values) when the row and column variables are independent (Friendly, 1991a). Correspondence analysis thus produces a 2-dimensional graphical plot of the observed data variation (Wheater, Cook, Clark, Syed, & Bellis, 2003), which is then examined for behavioral overlap between variables. Correspondence analysis, an ordination technique (Palmer, 1993), examines the proportional goodness-of-fit between recorded variable values (Gabriel, 2002), and shows data deviation from expectation within the row and column categories (Friendly, 1991a). A variant of this method, subset correspondence analysis (Greenacre & Pardo, 2006), uses only selected data portions to enter into the analysis and subsequent algorithmic activity. This example focuses on an illustrative scenario utilizing the complete data set.

Visual displays from QUAN data, with correspondence analysis, have previously incorporated QUAN findings quite well (Bazeley, 2010 [this volume]). A second approach utilizing correspondence analysis, to display QUAL findings of observed behaviors, and combine these observations with QUAN data, presenting an integrated visual representation, is detailed here.

Appendix 19.5, Sample SAS Codes, contains the SAS code written to produce each type of two- and three-dimensional graph presented in this chapter. Appendix 19.5f contains the SAS code for the correspondence analysis plotting procedure.

CONTEXT AND METHODS

First, a scenario is provided to illustrate the application of correspondence analysis to a categorical data set. Second, SAS 9.1 code was developed to generate graphical output, demonstrating the PROC CORRESP graphing procedure for categorical data. Finally, practical implications for correspondence analysis are provided. The written scenario is provided below.

CORRESPONDENCE ANALYSIS: SCENARIO

You are the external evaluator for a new museum display consisting of several free-standing, room-like educational exhibits. The museum management would like you to determine how visitors to the museum are interacting with the new exhibits, based on visitors' ages. You decide to record each visitor's age, and then observe how each visitor interacts with the exhibit.

The two categorical variables are thus age group and the observed exhibit behavior. Observed behaviors include looking only at the exhibit from the outside, peeking inside the door to the exhibit space, and entering into the exhibit space. Age grouping was delineated as young (19 years and under), midage (20–39 years), and older (40 and over). Over 1 hour, you observe the visitors (N = 300) in the museum exhibit area.

RESULTS

The correspondence analysis graphical output is shown in Figure 19.5, Museum Behaviors and Ages. In comparison to the traditional chi-square table (numbers only) output, this visual portrayal greatly improves

Figure 19.5 Museum Behaviors and Age

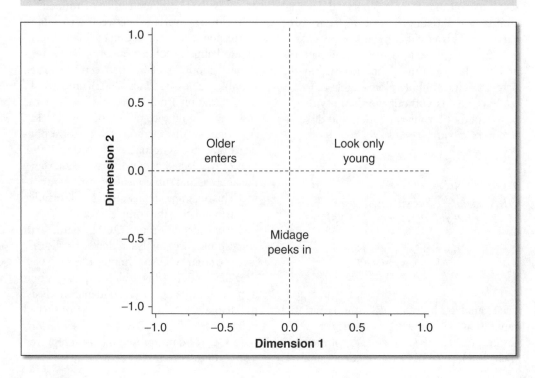

the communication of the underlying correspondence between observed and expected variable information. (For an excellent discussion of traditional frequency tables, see Cody & Smith, 2006.) As shown in Figure 19.5, Dimension 1 depicts the column coordinates of observed behaviors (Columns 1 and 2). Dimension 2 depicts the associated location differences (row coordinates) between museum visitors based on age. The 2-dimensional graphical display combines the row and column coordinates, creating a useful visual summary of the association between the variables of age group and observed behavior.

IMPLICATIONS AND IMPORTANCE

By looking at Figure 19.5, which visually captures the graph of the association between age and behavior, we can determine, based on age group, which museum visitors are likely to look only (if they are young), peek inside (if they are in the mid-age group), or fully enter into the exhibit (if they are older).

This type of visual data summary provides the viewer with a clear understanding of the association between age and behavior recorded in the data. This clear understanding of the relationship between age and behavior might have been masked, however, if we had merely presented the reader with the cross-tabs table of numbers.

While the use of correspondence analysis is relatively new to the educational research field, its "history can be traced back at least 50 years" (Hoffman & Franke, 1986, p. 213). The contemporary application of correspondence analysis to categorical data provides a powerful tool in the arsenal of statistical methodology—a tool that helps interpret and describe relationships between categorical variables. For example, correspondence analysis could help us interpret the measure of association between variables of gender, ethnicity, and school type, variables of agree/disagree for dichotomous survey response categories, and categories of passing/failing for educational assessment instruments.

3-DIMENSIONAL TECHNIQUES: SURFACE MAPS AND PRISM MAPS

This example adapted from Dickinson, Hines, & Onwuegbuzie (2007).

CONTEXT AND METHOD

Federal immigration policy is at the forefront of current public interest and legislative scrutiny across the United States. Questions of economics, ethnicity, and population movement comprise this public discussion. The American Community Survey, released by the United States Census Bureau, offers empirical data by city, state, and region. Using multiple SAS/GRAPH procedures, we developed a visual exploration of the survey response data to help identify patterns and discern themes not readily apparent or easily accessible in the original numeric format.

Variables of interest were selected from two federal databases: the Yearbook of Immigration Statistics and the American Community Survey. Data from each source were input as shown in Appendix 19.3, Algorithmic Flowchart. Variable values were matched by state and year to provide a more complete picture of immigration activity in the United States. The unit of analysis for the data was the state.

Data drawn from these two sources were used to provide visual mappings of areas of concentration that serve as destination points for recent immigrants to the United States, and to show patterns of mobility of the U.S. population within a 1-year period. Both 2- and 3-dimensional graphs were developed: the 2-dimensional graphing procedure produced the choropleth mapping; whereas the 3-dimensional graphing procedures produced block, prism, and surface maps. The GMAP procedure can be invoked to "produce maps, summarize data that vary by physical area, show trends and variations between geographic area, and highlight regional differences or extremes" (SAS Institute, 2004, p. 996). Figure 19.6 is a 2-dimensional

Figure 19.6 Choropleth Map: Persons Obtaining Legal Permanent Resident Status

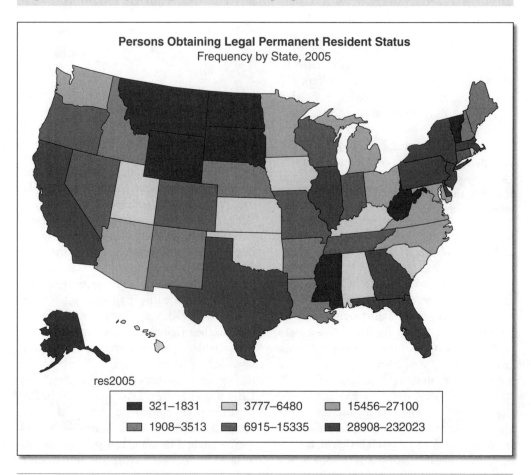

DATA SOURCE: Office of Immigration Statistics

choropleth map, showing persons obtaining legal permanent resident status in the United States. Choropleth maps are a very effective way to show information: they combine the best elements of a bar chart (precise measures with discrete variable units) with the GIS element of spatial representation. Figure 19.7 shows the same data set graphed using a 3-dimensional prism map display. Note the comparative advantage of the "lifted" states—by lifting the states visually "off the page," the differences in states are visually magnified, integrating number, picture, and content in one image. Figure 19.7 is further discussed in the prism maps section of this chapter.

Figure 19.8, a block graph, also combines the familiar bar chart, but with a 3-dimensional twist. Each bar (block) resides in the state it represents, thus integrating location with frequency and narrative. Note how the pattern of nonimmigrant admissions emerges from this figure: the taller blocks are located along the eastern seaboard, and along the southern border with Mexico. This indicates a theme of larger numbers of immigrants moving into these states from their home countries.

While the numeric association of number of nonimmigrant admissions by state was available within the original data table, the inherent relationship of location to immigration frequency was not easily

Figure 19.7 Prism Map Graph

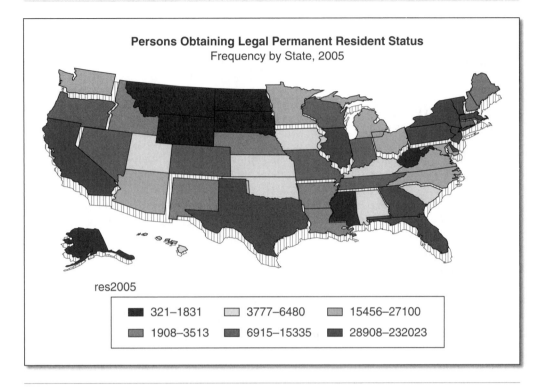

DATA SOURCE: Office of Immigration Statistics

Figure 19.8 Block Graph

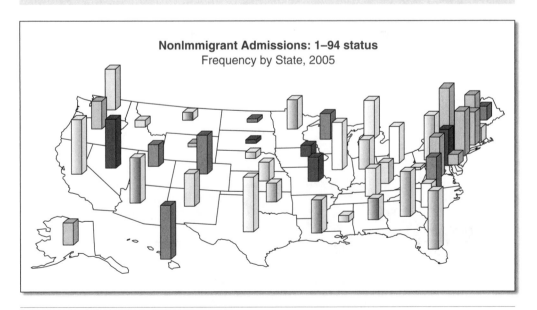

DATA SOURCE: Office of Immigration Statistics

discerned. With the block graph set in a geospatial matrix, we are able to visually integrate the variables of frequency and location, and thus are able to quickly see the location of the largest number of immigrants.

3-DIMENSIONAL EXAMPLE: SURFACE MAPS

This example adapted from Dickinson and colleagues (2007).

PROC GMAP was utilized to combine a surface map of the United States with the corresponding frequencies by state. The frequency of the mobility-by-state is displayed by the height of each graphical element (or spike). There is one spike per state, because state is the unit of analysis. Significantly, each spike base is a polygon. By referencing the distance decay function, we can specify the base width of the spikes that are drawn to display data values, thus modifying the size and summative shape of each spike. These algorithmic procedures are summarized in Appendix 19.4, Surface Map: Changes and Enhancements.

Using the TILT option allows the specification of angle measure (in degrees) for the graphical output. The value of angle measures specified by the TILT option ranges from 0 to 90 degrees [0 ≤ TILT ≤ 90], which allows for movement analogous to picking up a piece of paper from a flat surface and then slowly tilting the page toward you. Therefore, no tilt (TILT = 0) would result in a completely flat (horizontal) view of the page. Increasing the TILT = value allows the viewer to increase the visual differentiation between spikes emerging from the map surface.

Figure 19.9 shows a surface map of persons obtaining legal permanent resident status, by state. Within this surface map, we can see the huge (tall) spikes in the southern border states of California, Florida, and Texas and the New England states. These tall spikes represent extremely large frequencies of people obtaining legal status within each state, with the visual differences in frequency on a national level clearly indicated in the graph.

Figure 19.9 Surface Map: Persons Obtaining Legal Permanent Resident Status

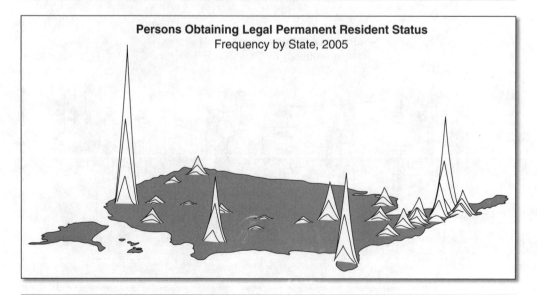

DATA SOURCE: Office of Immigration Statistics

Figure 19.10 shows the mobility of persons across the country, by state. Mobility is seen to be more evenly distributed across the country, as the spike heights are more closely drawn. However, we can distinguish a visual emphasis (greater frequency) of mobility in the western part of the country (higher spikes prevail on the left side of the graph).

Figure 19.10 Surface Map: Mobility by State, 2005

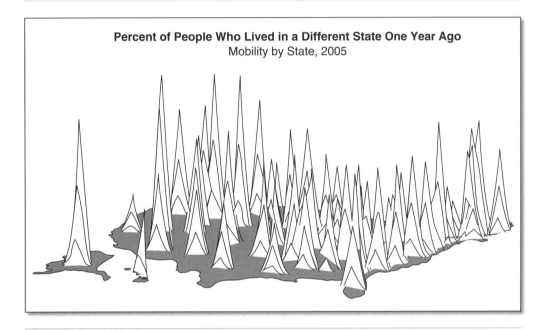

DATA SOURCE: American Community Survey

PROC GMAP—PRISM MAPS EXAMPLE

This example adapted from Dickinson and colleagues (2007).

By using a 3-dimensional coordinate system, we "can label any point in space" (Downing, 1995, p. 36). SAS/GRAPH software envelops three dimensions: "the X axis represents width, the Y-axis represents depth, and the Z-axis represents height" (SAS Institute, 2004, p. 1549). Located at the center of the base grid (corners labeled with coordinate values) is the viewing reference point. This viewing reference point is at the physical intersection of the diagonals, with the coordinate location of (0.5, 0.5, 0). An approximate

illustration is shown in Table 19.2, Prism Map: Coordinate Plane Viewing Position.

By specifying values for XVIEW, YVIEW, and ZVIEW, we can change the viewing position of the coordinate plane from which the prisms emerge. With default XVIEW value = 0.5, an increase in value will push the viewing point along the horizontal (X) axis, to the right. With default value of ZVIEW = 3, any increase in ZVIEW value will raise the viewing point (because the Z-axis represents height).

The value for ZVIEW cannot be negative (less than 0), because that would place the imaginary viewing position underneath the graphical display. To reiterate, if we think of a setting sun, once it reaches the horizon line, the image of the sun disappears. This is

Table 19.2 Prism Map: Coordinate Plane Viewing Position

Aesthetic/Operational Basis for Change	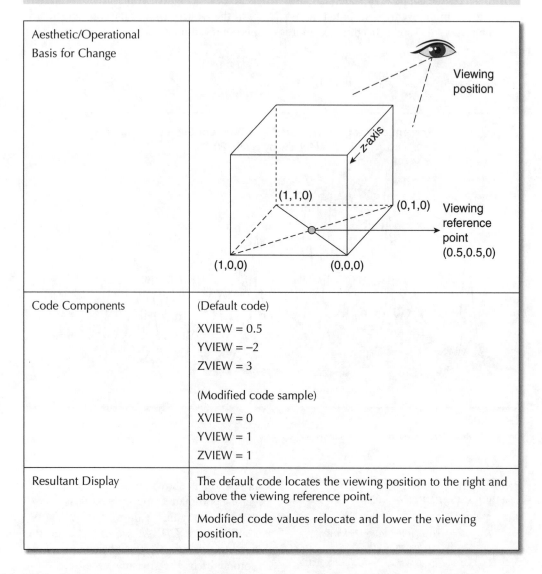
Code Components	(Default code) XVIEW = 0.5 YVIEW = –2 ZVIEW = 3 (Modified code sample) XVIEW = 0 YVIEW = 1 ZVIEW = 1
Resultant Display	The default code locates the viewing position to the right and above the viewing reference point. Modified code values relocate and lower the viewing position.

analogous to the value of ZVIEW: once it reaches 0 (the "horizon line"), it cannot become any smaller (negative number) because the graphical image would disappear from view.

If the light source options are not invoked, "the light source location is the same as the viewing position" (SAS Institute, 2004, p. 1064). Within the prism mapping algorithm, the light source location can be moved horizontally by changing the value assigned to XLIGHT. As the assigned value of XLIGHT increases, the light source location shifts to the right. This subsequently causes the right side of the mapped prisms to be in the "light," and the left side of the prisms to be in the "shade." Therefore, we can alter shadow depth and how much shadow is present (distribution of light) by modifying the SAS code. PROC GMAP has options of XLIGHT and YLIGHT to specify the location coordinates of the imaginary light source within the 3-dimensional (x,y,z) coordinate system. Figure 19.7, Prism Map, shows the resultant graphical display of the legal permanent residents, by state, at one point in time.

IMPLICATIONS AND IMPORTANCE

With increased access to technology and use of advanced graphing software, the "capacity to produce more efficient and easily understood graphical information displays" is a powerful visual tool for data analysis (Dickinson, 2001, p. 4). Indeed, "the overwhelming premise of visual display is that of communication" (Dickinson, 2000, 2002, page 1). Wainer (1992) reminds us of the power of graphical displays, stating the "unrelenting forcefulness inherent in the character of a good graphic is its greatest virtue" (p. 14).

By utilizing 2- and 3-dimensional displays, we were able to highlight immigration and mobility patterns occurring throughout the United States, and produce both surface map and prism map displays. For example, in Figure 19.8, it was easy to see that the geographic areas favored for current immigrant destination are located along the southern border and in the northeastern United States. The visual inventory of immigration activity developed using graphical display techniques provides an effective vehicle of context and content for the composite variable observations of mobility and immigration activity across the United States.

"Maps are important analytical tools" (Rossmo, 2000, p. iv), and these map-based graphical displays can help us discover patterns and recognize important truths about our data not readily apparent in a numeric table or text. Graphs can easily show us patterns that might not have been seen otherwise (Wainer, 1990, 1997b). As Tukey (1972, 1989) declared, the greatest possibilities of visual display lie in the vibrancy and the accessibility of the intended message. Map-based graphics "can display enormous amounts of information in readily understandable form," providing an unspoken, visual message (Rossmo, 2000, p. iv). We have provided examples of powerful map-based techniques for contemporary visual display that yield enhanced transmission of the underlying meaning and message.

ADVANTAGES OF VISUALIZATION IN MIXED METHODS APPLICATIONS

We are "living in a picture-filled world," and there are strong indications that the status of images is improving . . . "for many, understanding of the world is being accomplished, not by reading words, but by reading images" (Lester, 2006, p. 415). Just as grammars of language describe "how words combine in clauses, sentences, and text, visual grammar describes the way in which depicted elements—people, places, and things—combine in visual statements (Kress & van Leeuwen, 2006, p. 1).

There are a number of advantages inherent in the use of visualization: visualization provides "an ability to comprehend huge amounts of data, . . . allows the perception of emergent properties that were not anticipated, . . . often enables problems with the data itself to become apparent, . . . [and] facilitates understanding of both large-scale and small-scale features of the data" (Ware, 2000, p. 3). Visualization of research findings provides a pragmatic way to share mixed methods research in a way that is oriented both to the problem and to the real world, two qualities described by Creswell (2008) as essential elements of pragmatism. Including visualization practices within mixed methods is a logical crossover extension for both, because "images are ubiquitous in society, and because of this, some consideration of visual representation can be potentially included in all studies of society" (Banks, 2007, p. 3).

Images are "instruments of exchange and communication" (Burnett, 2004, p. 18), and traditional applications of graphics to research findings have been rather sparse in nature, showing only variable values without much consideration of context or content. Contemporary applications of visual images to mixed methods reach much higher and further: depicting geospatial variable associations, depicting complex relationships over time, and depicting thematic results, such as interview responses. Geospatial graphics enable comparisons over time to identify shifts and trends; help researchers to identify themes that may not be readily apparent in a nonvisual format, e.g., text data; and enable researchers to combine location of respondents with both qualitative and quantitative modes of inquiry (Dickinson, 2008).

Creswell, Plano Clark, Gutmann, and Hanson (2003) have delineated mixed methods techniques, including sequential explanatory (first quantitative data collection, then qualitative data collection), and sequential exploratory (first qualitative data collection, then quantitative data collection). The use of graphical display can help provide direction and visual documentation for sequential research inquiry. By integrating the two strands (QUAL and QUAN), we can develop meta-inferences, because meta-inference is developed from the integration of the qualitative strand inference and the quantitative strand inference (Tashakkori & Teddlie, 2003). Thus, graphical display can help inform both types of inference by providing a visual delineation and integration of methods.

PRACTICAL RECOMMENDATIONS FOR VISUAL DISPLAY

Graphical display, like mixed research designs, provides an essential multiplicity of investigation, form, and discourse; combining graphical display with these multiple modes of inquiry enhances the narrative power of both (Onwuegbuzie & Dickinson, 2008). Practical recommendations for visual display, as presented by the graphing examples in this chapter, include the following:

a. Provide a naturalistic context for the representation of findings, e.g., indicators of location (immigration example), and indicators of group membership and behaviors (correspondence example).

b. Utilize the visual display type that most efficiently (and simply) portrays the findings.

c. Utilize a uniform color scheme for multivariate data to enable clear comparisons between cases and groups. Grayscale shades may be indicated for an extreme number of cases or variables being represented. For example, a continuum of gray shades may be used to indicate varying levels of an observed attribute or instances of a trend.

d. Clearly label individual cases and groups, as needed, to indicate the unit of analysis. Labels may be placed on the graph itself, or within a legend as supplementary information.

e. Plotting labels may be provided in words, as well as in select symbols, to indicate observed behaviors. For example, the correspondence analysis example uses alphanumeric characters, rather than a standard plotting symbol, to show group behaviors.

f. When using commercially available graphing software, provide illustrative code examples for replication, study, and future use by other researchers.

g. Utilize 3-dimensional graphing methods as indicated, to provide a richer, more defined portrait of the findings for viewers and stakeholders.

As a fundamental principle of mixed methods, "methods should be mixed in a way that has complementary strengths and nonoverlapping weaknesses" (Johnson & Turner, 2003, p. 299). Graphical displays provide these complementary strengths: they have immediate and strong impact and easy flow of information across parallel elements, and they show phenomena, not just numbers (Tukey, 1990). It is this capacity to show phenomena that holds great promise and application to mixed methods approaches, as "visual methods can reveal what was supposed to be concealed, or that which had been unanticipated" (Banks, 2007, p. 33).

Mixed methods research is a powerful synthesis of multiple methods of inquiry, and visual display is a powerful synthesis of data and form. By linking mixed methods and visual display, we fuse inquiry with data and forms to create a richer understanding of our environment. This, then, is our charge for the future: to improve the existing types of display, to create new forms of visual representation, and to connect these new visual forms with research findings to effectively communicate mixed methods findings to a new generation of scholars.

Research Questions and Exercises

Graphical Displays Provide Complementary Strengths

They provide immediate and strong impact and easy flow of information across parallel elements, and they can be used to show phenomena, not merely numbers (Tukey, 1990).

1. Discuss ways in which the graphical capacity to provide information with an immediate and strong impact can be advantageous when disseminating findings from mixed methods research approaches.

2. Discuss ways in which graphical capacity to show information across parallel elements can be applied to mixed methods research approaches.

3. Discuss ways in which graphical capacity to show phenomena can be applied to mixed methods research findings.

4. Tufte (1997) describes three "viewing depths" of graphical displays:

   a. what is seen from a distance (aggregate structure);

   b. what is seen up close and in detail (fine structure of the data); and

   c. what is seen implicitly (What is the idea behind the graphic?).

Select one of the graphing examples from the chapter and evaluate the graph using these three viewing depths.

◆ *Appendices*

Appendix 19.1 2-Dimensional Bubble Plots Algorithm Flowchart

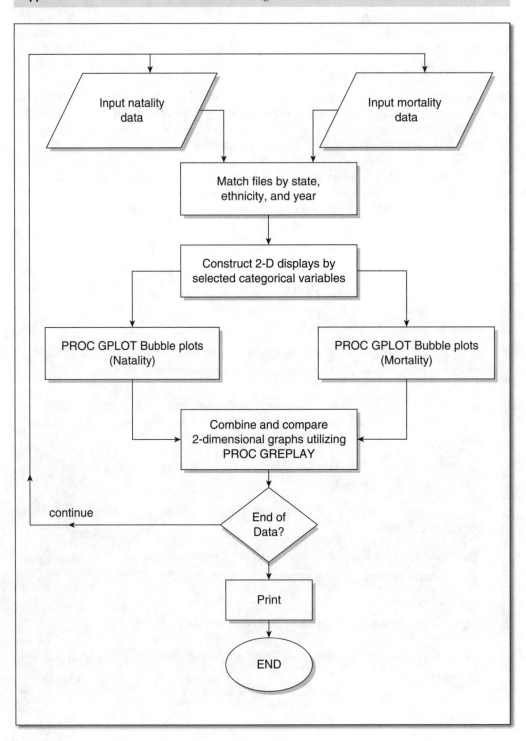

Appendix 19.2   SAS Code for Bubble Plots: Mortality

```
**Causes of Death, SAS 9.1**
**Bubble plots for CDC/NCHS mortality data**
**SGF 2009**
**Dickinson, Hines, Hall**;
************************************************
**reset the graphics environment to new specs **
************************************************,
goptions reset = all gunit = pct border cback = white
        colors = (black blue green red orange brown)
        ftitle = swissb ftext = swiss htitle = 4 htext = 3;

**Data source: Top 10 causes of death by gender: 2004"**
**National Vital Statistics Reports, V. 56 No. 5, 11-20-2007**
**Table D, page 9**
**Cause of death codes from ICD-10: International Causes of Disease, Tenth Revision**;

        data cdc;
                length cause $9;
                input gender $ cause $ deaths percent;
                datalines;
                …
                ;
title1 'Top 10 Causes of Death: Percent by Gender';
*footnote1 h = 2 j = 1 'Source: National Vital Statistics Report, 2007';
                axis1 offset = (5,5)
                        width = 5         value = (height = 4);
                axis2 offset = (7,7)
                         label = none
                         major = (height = 2)   minor = (height = 3)
                         width = 5         value = (height = 4);

                proc gplot data = cdc;
                        bubble gender*cause = percent/haxis = axis1
                        vaxis = axis2     vminor = 1
                        bcolor = blue
                blabel
                        bfont = swissi
                bsize = 10
                        caxis = red;
                        run;
                        quit;
```

Appendix 19.3   Flowchart for 2-and 3-Dimensional Displays: Choropleth, Block, Prism, and Surface

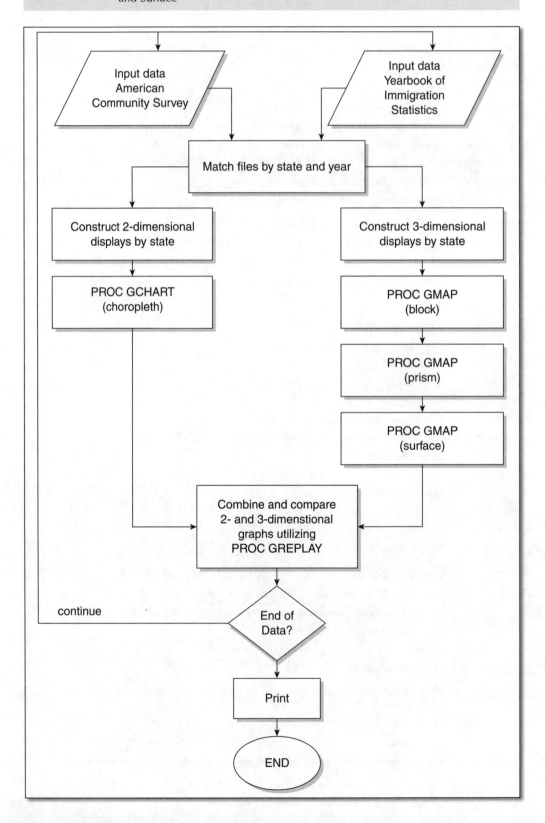

Appendix 19.4 Surface Map: Changes and Enhancements

Surface Map: Changes and Enhancements		
Aesthetic/Operational Basis	Algorithmic Modification	Resultant Display
Spike Size	(Default code) CONSTANT = 10	Base size of spike is determined using default constant value.
• Spike base is a polygon		
• Utilizing distance decay function, $D^k = (x - x^k)^2 + (y - y^k)^k$	(Modified code samples) CONSTANT=5 With constant < default value, spike base value is decreased (spikes emerge from a smaller base).	Base size of spike is modified via decreased constant value.
	CONSTANT=20 With constant > default value, spike base value is increased (spikes emerge from a wider base).	Base size of spike is modified via increased constant value.

Appendix 19.5 Sample SAS Codes

Appendix 19.5a Sample SAS Code: 2-D Choropleth Maps

```
SAS code for Proc GMAP Choropleth maps

/*GRAPH Figure 2*/
/* choropleth map : 2- dimensional PROC GMAP */
/* Define titles and footnotes for map */
title1 'Persons Obtaining Legal Permanent Resident Status';
title2 'Frequency By State, 2005';
footnote j = r 'Data source:Office of Immigration Statistics';

proc gmap map = maps.us data = legalres;
id state;
choro res2005/ coutline = gray;
run;
quit;
```

(Continued)

Appendix 19.5 (Continued)

Appendix 19.5b   Sample SAS Code: Proc GPLOT

```
title1 'American Community Survey'
       justify = center '2005 Report';
       symbol1 font = marker value = U

       color = black;
axis1 order = (0 to 20 by 5)
       label = (angle = 90 'Demographic Frequency')
       minor = none;
axis2 order = (0 to 21 by 1)
       label = ('Ethnicity')
       minor = none;
proc gplot;
plot number*age/vaxis = axis1 haxis = axis2 cframe = grayE2;
run;
quit;
```

Appendix 19.5c   Sample SAS Code Proc GMAP: Block Maps

```
/* Define titles and footnotes for map */
title1 'American Community Survey';
title2 '2005';

proc gmap map = maps.us data = edlevel;
   format sites sitesfmt.;
   id state;
   block educlevl/ discrete area = 1
   shape = block
           coutline = black cblkout = black
           woutline = 3;
run;
quit;
```

Appendix 19.5d Sample SAS Code for Proc GMAP: Surface Maps

```
/*create surface map*/;
/* define titles and footnotes for map */

title1 'American Community Survey';
footnote j = r 'Data source: United States Census Bureau';
proc gmap map = maps.us data = edlevel;
id state;
surface educlvl/cbody = blue nlines =100;
run;
quit;
```

Appendix 19.5e Sample SAS Code for Proc GMAP: Prism Maps

```
/*prism map: 3- dimensional PROC GMAP*/
/* Define titles and footnotes for map */

title1 'Persons Obtaining Legal Permanent Resident Status';
title2 'Frequency By State, 2005';
footnote j = r 'Data source: Office of Immigration Statistics';

proc gmap map = maps.us data = legalres;
id state;
prism res2005/ coutline = gray
               xlight = 5
               xview = .75
               zview = 5;
run;
quit;
```

(Continued)

Appendix 19.5f   SAS Code for Correspondence Analysis (CA)

```
**************************************************;
*Wendy Dickinson and Bruce Hall
*Museum.sas, SAS version 9.1 (2008)
*Modified from Friendly, SAS version 6.0 (1991)
**************************************************;
*input categorical data from visitor observations*;
data museum;
input enters peeksin lookonly agegroup$;
cards;
      10 30 60   young
      30 50 20   midage
      70 20 10   older
             ;

title1 'Museum Behaviors and Age';

**************************************************;
*invoke the correspondence procedure
*define variables
*agegroup is the row variable
*behavior is the column variable
**************************************************;
proc corresp data = museum out = behavior;
var enters peeksin lookonly;
id agegroup;

proc print data = behavior;
var _type_  agegroup dim1 dim2 quality;
run;

data label;
   set behavior;
   xsys = '2'; ysys = '2';
   x = dim1;
   y = dim2;
   text = agegroup;
   size = 1.4;
   function = 'LABEL';
             run;
```

```
****************************************************;
*invoke SAS/GRAPH to create visual display
*using coordinate system
*define axis 1 and axis 2
****************************************************;
        proc gplot data = coord;
                plot dim1 * dim2
                /anno = label frame
                href = 0 vref = 0 lvref = 3 lhref = 3
                vaxis = axis2  haxis = axis1
                vminor = 1 hminor = 1;

                axis1 length = 3 in order = (–1 to 1 by .5)
                        label = (h = 1.3   'Dimension 1');
                axis2 length = 3 in order = (*1 to 1 by .5)
                        label = (h = 1.3  a = 90 r = 0 'Dimension 2');
                        symbol v = none;
        run;
```

◆ References

Banks, M. (2007). *Using visual data in qualitative research*. London: Sage.

Bartke, K. (2005). *2D, 3D, and high-dimensional data and information visualization*. University of Hanover, Germany: Institut fur Wirtschaftsinformatik (IWI).

Beh, E. J. (2004). Simple correspondence analysis: A bibliographic overview. *International Statistical Review*, 72(2), 257–284.

Bertin, J. (1983). *The semiology of graphics*. Translated by William Berg. Madison, WI: University of Wisconsin Press.

Bhowmick, T., Griffin, A. L., MacEachern, A. M., Kluhsman, B. C., & Lengerich, E. J. (2008). Informing geospatial toolset design: Understanding the process of cancer data exploration and analysis. *Health & Place*, 14(3), 576–607.

Burnett, R. (2004). *How images think*. Cambridge, MA: MIT Press.

Cody, R. P., & Smith, J. K. (2006). *Applied statistics and the SAS programming language* (5th ed.). Upper Saddle River, NJ: Pearson Education.

Creswell, J. (2008). *Research design: Qualitative, quantitative, and mixed methods approaches*. Thousand Oaks, CA: Sage.

Creswell, J., Plano Clark, V., Gutmann, M., & Hanson, W. (2003). Advanced mixed methods designs. In A. Tashakkori & C. Teddlie (Eds.), *Handbook of mixed methods in social behavioral research*. Thousand Oaks, CA: Sage.

Defays, D. (1988). Scaling of nominal data. In J. P. Keeves (Ed.), *Educational research, methodology, and measurement: An international handbook*. Oxford, England: Pergamon Press.

Dickie, G. (1997). *Introduction to aesthetics: An analytic approach*. New York: Oxford University Press.

Dickinson, W. B. (2000). *Escaping flatland: Chernoff's faces revisited*. Doctoral thesis. UMI Order Number: AAI9968808. Retrieved from http://portal.acm.org/citation.cfm?id=931541 &jmp=cit&coll=GUIDE&dl=GUIDE&CFID =15596083&CFTOKEN=41111326#CIT

Dickinson, W. B. (2001). *Envisioning* Kinaaldá: *Navaho magic, mystery, and myth*. Retrieved from http://www2.sas.com/proceedings/ sugi25/25/po/25p228.pdf

Dickinson, W. B. (2002). Escaping flatland: Chernoff's faces revisited. *Proceedings of the SAS Users Group International Conference.* Cary, NC: SAS Institute, Inc. Retrieved from http://www2.sas.com/proceedings/sugi26/p195-26.pdf

Dickinson, W. B. (2008). Creating visual displays: Using graphical techniques for exploration, discovery, and dissemination of research findings. Invited paper presented at the 4th Annual Mixed Methods Conference, Fitzwilliam College. Cambridge University, Cambridge, UK, July 21.

Dickinson, W. B. (2009). Number insight and narrative image: Developing statistical analysis strategies utilizing graphical displays of quantitative information. Royal Statistical Society 175th Annual Meeting, Edinburgh: Scotland. Retrieved from http://www.rss.org.uk/pdf/RSS%202009%20abstracts%20booklet.pdf

Dickinson, W. B., & Hall, B. W. (2008, March). PROC CORRESP for categorical data: Correspondence Analysis (CA) for discovery, display, and decision-making. *Proceedings of the SAS Global Forum 2008 Conference* (Paper 227). Cary, NC: SAS Institute. Retrieved from http://www2.sas.com/proceedings/forum2008/227-2008.pdf

Dickinson, W. B., Hines, C., & Hall, B. W. (2009, March). Bubble, bubble: Less toil, no trouble. *Proceedings of the SAS Global Forum 2009 Conference* (Paper 187). Cary, NC: SAS Institute. Retrieved from http://support.sas.com/resources/papers/proceedings09/187-2009.pdf

Dickinson, W. B., Hines, C. V., & Onwuegbuzie, A. J. (2006, March). Graphical analysis of clandestine methamphetamine laboratories utilizing PROC GMAP: A visual inventory of activity across the United States. *Proceedings of the Thirty-first SAS Users Group International Conference* (Paper 136–31). Cary, NC: SAS Institute. Retrieved from http://www2.sas.com/proceedings/sugi31/136-31.pdf

Dickinson, W. B., Hines, C. V., & Onwuegbuzie, A. J. (2007, March). People, pattern, and place: SAS/GRAPH data display of immigration activity across the United States. *Proceedings of the SAS Global Forum 2007 Conference* (Paper 142). Cary, NC: SAS Institute. Retrieved from http://www2.sas.com/proceedings/forum2007/1422007.pdf

Downing, D. (1995). *Dictionary of mathematics terms.* Hauppage, NY: Barron's Educational Series.

Duckeck, J. (2009) *Grotte de Lascaux.* Retrieved from http://www.showcaves.com/english/fr/showcaves/Lascaux.html

Dutton, B. P. (1976). *Navahos and Apaches: The Athabascan people.* Englewood Cliffs, NJ: Prentice Hall.

Frerichs, R. (2001). *John Snow's Map 1 (Broad Street Pump outbreak, 1854).* Los Angeles, CA: UCLA Department of Epidemiology, School of Public Health. Retrieved from http://www.ph.ucla.edu/epi/snow.html

Friendly, M. (1991a). *SAS system for statistical graphics,* 1st ed. Cary, NC: SAS Institute, Inc.

Friendly, M. (1991b). Statistical graphics for multivariate data. *Proceedings of the SAS Users Group International Conference: SUGI 16.* Cary, NC: SAS Institute, Inc. Retrieved from http://www.math.yorku.ca/SCS/sugi/sugi16-paper.html

Friendly, M. (1995). Conceptual and visual models for categorical data. *The American Statistician, 49,* 153–160.

Friendly, M. (2000). Visualizing categorical data. Cary, NC: SAS Institute, Inc.

Friendly, M. (2008). Milestones in the history of thematic cartography, statistical graphics, and data visualization. Retrieved from http://euclid.psych.yorku.ca/SCS/Gallery/milestone/milestone.pdf

Frisbie, C. J. (1967). Kinaaldá: *A study of the Navaho girls' puberty ceremony.* Middleton, CT: Wesleyan University Press.

Glass, G. V., & Hopkins, K. D. (1996). *Statistical methods in education and psychology* (3rd ed.). Needham Heights, MA: Allyn & Bacon.

Gabriel, K. R. (2002). Goodness of fit of biplots and correspondence plots. *Biometrika, 89*(2), 423–436.

Greenacre, M. & Pardo, R. (2006). Subset correspondence analysis: Visualizing relationships among a selected set of response categories from a questionnaire survey. *Sociological Methods and Research, 35*(2), 193–218.

Herdeg, W. (1974). Graphis/diagrams: The graphic visualization of abstract. Zurich, Switzerland: Graphis Press.

Hoffman, D. L., & Franke, G. R. (1986). Correspondence analysis: Graphical representation of categorical data in marketing research. *Journal of Marketing Research, 23*(3), 213–227.

Hopkins, K. D., Hopkins, B. R., & Glass, G. V. (1996). *Basic statistics for the behavioral sciences* (3rd ed.). Needham Heights, MA: Allyn & Bacon.

Ivankova, N. V., Creswell, J. W., & Stick, S. (2007). Using mixed methods sequential explanatory design: From theory to practice. *Field Methods, 18*(1), 3–20.

Johnson, B., & Turner, L. (2003). Data collection strategies in mixed methods research. In A. Tashakkori & C. Teddlie (Eds.), *Handbook of mixed methods in social & behavioral research*. Thousand Oaks, CA: Sage.

Johnson, S. (2006). *The ghost map.* New York: Penguin Group.

Katzer, J., Cook, K., & Crouch, W. (1978). *Evaluating information.* Reading, PA: Addison-Wesley.

Kohler, W. (1967). Gestalt psychology. *Psychological Research, 31*(1), March, pp. XVIII–XXX.

Kress, G. R., & van Leeuwen, T. (2006). *Reading images: The grammar of visual design.* (2nd ed.). New York: Routledge.

Kluckhohn, C. (1942). Myths and rituals: A general theory. *Harvard Theological Review, 35,* 45–79.

Lee, B-L. (1994). *ViSta Corresp: Correspondence analysis with ViSta, the Visual Statistics System. Research Memorandum 94–3.* Chapel Hill: Thurstone Psychometric Laboratory, University of North Carolina.

Lengler, R., & Eppler, M. J. (2007). Towards a periodic table of visualization methods for management. *Proceedings of Graphics and Visualization in Engineering.* University of Lugano, Switzerland. Retrieved from http://www.visual-literacy.org/periodic_table/periodic_table.pdf

Lester, P. M. (2006). *Visual communication* (4th ed.). Belmont, CA: Thomson-Wadsworth.

Mori, G., & Malik, J. (2003). Recognizing objects in adversarial clutter: Breaking a visual CAPTCHA. University of California, Berkeley, CA. Retrieved from http://www.cs.sfu.ca/~mori/research/papers/mori_cvpr03.pdf

Nicol, A. M., & Pexman, P.M. (2003). *Displaying your findings.* American Psychological Association: Washington, DC.

O'Donnell, J. (1998). *Avatars of the world: From papyrus to cyberspace.* Cambridge, MA: Harvard University Press.

Onwuegbuzie, A. J., & Dickinson, W. B. (2008, June). Mixed methods analysis and information visualization: Graphical display for effective communication of research results. *The Qualitative Report, 13*(2), 204–225. Retrieved from http://www.nova.edu/ssss/QR/QR13–2/onwuegbuzie.pdf

Palmer, M. (1993). Putting things in even better order: The advantages of canonical correspondence analysis. *Ecology, 74*(8), 2215–2230.

Playfair, W. (1801 [2005]). *Commercial and political atlas and statistical breviary.* (H. Wainer & I. Spence, Eds.). Cambridge University Press: New York, New York.

Powsner, S. M., & Tufte, E. (1997) Summarizing clinical psychiatric data. *Psychiatric Services, 48,* 1458–1459.

Ridenour, C. S. & Newman, I. (2008). *Mixed methods research: Exploring the interactive continuum.* Carbondale, IL: Southern Illinois University.

Rossmo, D. K. (2000). *Geographic profiling.* Boca Raton, FL: CRC Press.

SAS Institute. (2004). SAS/GRAPH 9.1 Reference: Volumes 1, 2 and 3. Cary, NC: SAS Institute, Inc.

Spence, I. (2005). No humble pie: The origins and usage of a statistical chart. *Journal of Educational and Behavioral Statistics, 30*(Winter), 353–368.

Tashakkori, A., & Teddlie, C. (Eds.) (2003). *Handbook of mixed methods in social & behavioral research.* Thousand Oaks, CA: Sage.

Tufte, E. R. (1983). *The visual display of quantitative information.* Cheshire, CT: Graphics Press.

Tufte, E. R. (1990). *Envisioning information.* Cheshire, CT: Graphics Press.

Tufte, E. R. (1997). *Visual explanations.* Cheshire, CT: Graphics Press.

Tufte, E. R. (2001). *The visual display of quantitative information.* CT: Graphics Press.

Tufte, E. (2006). *Beautiful evidence.* Cheshire, CT: Graphics Press.

Tukey, J. W. (1972). Some graphic and semi-graphic displays. In T. A. Bancroft (Ed.), *Statistical papers in honor of George W. Snedecor* (pp. 293–316). Ames, IA: The Iowa State University Press.

Tukey, J. W. (1977). *Exploratory data analysis.* Reading, MA: Addison-Wesley.

Tukey, J. W. (1989). Data-based graphics: Visual display in the years to come. *Proceedings of the American Statistical Association, 84,* 366–381.

Tukey, J. W. (1990). Data-based graphics: Visual display in the decades to come. *Statistical Science, 5* (3, August, 1990), 327–339. Retrieved from http://www.jstor.org/stable/2245820

Turing, A. M. (1950). Computing machinery and intelligence. Originally published by Oxford University Press on behalf of MIND (the *Journal of the Mind Association*), *59*(236), 433–60. Retrieved from http://www.abelard.org/turpap/turpap.php

von Ahn, L., Blum, M., & Langford, J. (Feb. 2004). Telling humans and computers apart automatically. *Communications of the ACM* 47(2), 56–60. Retrieved from http://www.cs.cmu.edu/~biglou/captcha.pdf

Wainer, H. (1990). Graphical visions from William Playfair to John Tukey. *Statistical Science, 5,* 340–345.

Wainer, H. (1992). Understanding graphics and tables. *Educational Research, 21*(1), 14–23.

Wainer, H. (1997a). *Visual revelations.* Mahwah, NJ: Lawrence Erlbaum Associates, Inc.

Wainer, H. (1997b). Visual revelations. *Chance, 10*(1), 35–37.

Wainer, H. (2005). *Graphic discovery: A trout in the milk and other visual adventures.* Princeton, NJ: Princeton University Press.

Ware, C. (2000). Information visualization: Perception for design. In *Foundation for a Science of Data Visualization* (pp. 1–27). Retrieved from http://www.sfu.ca/media-lab/archive2007/387/Resources/Readings/Ware,%20Colin%20Foundations%20for%20Data%20Vis.pdf

Wertheimer, Max. (1923 [1938]). Laws of organization in perceptual forms. In W. Ellis (Ed. & Trans.), *A source book of Gestalt psychology* (pp. 71–88). London: Routledge & Kegan Paul. (Original work published in 1923 as Untersuchungen zur Lehre von der Gestalt II, in *Psychologische Forschung, 4,* 301–350.) Retrieved from http://psychclassics.yorku.ca/index.htm

Wheater, C. P., Cook, P. A., Clark, P., Syed, Q., & Bellis, M. A. (2003). Re-emerging Syphilis: A detrended correspondence analysis of the behavior of HIV positive and negative gay men. Retrieved from http://www.biomedcentral.com/1471–2458/3/34

United States. (2006). *Department of Homeland Security. Yearbook of Immigration Statistics: 2005.* Washington, DC, U.S. Dept. of Homeland Security, Office of Immigration Statistics.

United States. (2007). United States Immigration Support. Retrieved from http://www.usimmigrationsupport.org/i94.html

United States Census Bureau. (n.d.) American Community Survey. Retrieved from http://www.census.gov/acs/www

Zuk, T., & Carpendale, S. (2006). Theoretical analysis of uncertainty visualizations. Proceedings of SPIE. Retrieved from http://pages.cpsc.ucalgary.ca/~zuk/pub/Zuk_2006_TheoreticalAnalysis.pdf

20

USING Q METHODOLOGY AND Q FACTOR ANALYSIS IN MIXED METHODS RESEARCH

◆ Isadore Newman and Susan Ramlo

Objectives

After reading this chapter, the reader will be able to

- describe and define Q methodology,

- describe and define Q factor analysis,

- identify the historical roots of both Q methodology and Q factor analysis,

- differentiate between Q methodology and Q factor analysis,

- give examples of when it would be appropriate to use Q methodology and Q factor analysis,

- give examples of the types of studies that would involve Q methodology and those that would involve Q factor analysis, and

- identify some strengths and weaknesses for using Q methodology and Q factor analysis as data reduction techniques.

◆ Introduction

The purpose of this chapter is to identify two multivariate techniques that can be used to facilitate the interpretation of mixed methods research. These techniques can aid researchers in answering their research questions by demonstrating how to disaggregate or aggregate their data. More specifically, our purpose is to introduce two multivariate techniques, Q methodology and Q factor analysis, to readers by describing these techniques as well as by giving examples that should assist readers in performing their own Q methodology and Q factor analysis studies. Finally, we discuss how researchers can take their research a step farther by answering more-sophisticated research questions that include groups of people. For instance, these groups, whether derived empirically such as via Q factor analysis or theoretically such as psychosocial stages, can be used as variables within other types of multivariate analyses.

Statistical analyses frequently produce probabilistic conclusions, not absolute truths. The use of these quantitative techniques to aid in the interpretation of qualitative findings is therefore not inconsistent with the ontology of universal laws based on an objective reality. The philosophy that underlies quantitative judgments is based on making statements about relationships, while acknowledging that these measures are not free of error and may be situation or group specific (interactions). This is not inconsistent with the qualitative philosophy that different relationships may exist for different situations, reflecting multiple realities.

The emphasis of this chapter is on how to use sophisticated multivariate data reduction techniques, with an emphasis on Q methodology and Q factor analysis, both of which can be considered to be mixed methodologies. Both Q methodology (McKeown, 2001; Ward, 1963) and Q factor analysis (Burt, 1941; Cattell, 1978) represent approaches for grouping people based on their typologies (profiles).

Creswell (2010 [this volume]) identifies the need for the development of new techniques and procedures to be used in mixed methods research. We strongly agree with this position, but we believe it would be helpful to begin the discussion by considering two techniques that have existed for decades, Q methodology and Q factor analysis. These and other multivariate procedures are frequently not considered or applied to mixed methods and qualitative research.

Q methodology has been discussed in qualitative annals (Brown, 2008; Watts & Stenner, 2005) but also has been designated specifically as a quantitative method (Block, 2008; Brown, 2008; McKeown & Thomas, 1988; Nunnally, 1978). However, Q methodology best fits the framework of mixed methods research as described by Creswell (2010), Tashakkori and Teddlie (1998), Newman and Benz (1998), Ridenour and Newman (2008), and others, as is evidenced by the section dedicated to Q in the edited book *Mixed Methods in Psychology* (Stenner & Stainton-Rogers, 2004). Stenner and Stainton-Rogers (2004) state that Q methodology is such a qualitative–quantitative hybrid that the term "mixed methodology" is not sufficient to describe its position; they suggest the new term "qualiquantology." They base their statements on the idea that the philosophical underpinnings of the Q are a mixture of qualitative and quantitative ideas. Tashakkori and Teddlie (2009) have called this type of hybrid, "inherently mixed." Brown (2008) agrees that with its focus on subjectivity and, therefore, self-referential meaning and interpretation, Q methodology shares many of the focuses of qualitative research while utilizing the type of statistical analyses typically found in quantitative studies.

INTRODUCTION TO Q METHODOLOGY AND Q FACTOR ANALYSIS

R factor analysis and Q methodology parallel, respectively, Newtonian physics (models that mathematically predict the forces and motion in the macroscopic real world) and quantum mechanics (Howard, 2005; Ramlo, 2006; Stephenson, 1982b, 1988). Stephenson expanded on the work of Cyril Burt (the creator of Q factor analysis) and Burt's and his mentor, Charles Spearman, to develop Q methodology. Stephenson was able to blend the concepts of factor analysis with concepts from quantum mechanics (Ramlo, 2006; Stephenson, 1982a, 1982b, 1987, 1988) in order to address his desire to objectively measure subjectivity (Stephenson, Brown, & Brenner, 1972).

Like Cyril Burt, Stephenson learned about factor analysis from its creator, Charles Spearman (Brown, 1998). As a PhD in both psychology and physics, Stephenson was able to blend the concepts of factor analysis with concepts from quantum mechanics, a field of physics that studies particles at the subatomic level where one can never measure the exact location of a particle but instead only can attempt to predict its "behavior." Although connected mathematically, quantum mechanics was less readily accepted as Newtonian laws of motion. Even the great Einstein took issue with some of the ideas of quantum mechanics (Howard, 2005; Sauer, 2008), not unlike some key social science researchers who seemingly disregarded Q methodology, at least in part, due to its subjectivity and, potentially, its mixed methods framework since, as Stenner and Stainton-Rogers (2004) indicate, such a mixed methods hybrid ought to be discomforting. This discomfort emerges from the reorganization of distinct ideas which come together, cross boundaries, and form something new.

A similar discussion between two competing conceptions of research, such as the debate between Newtonian and quantum physics, is found within *Mixed Methods Research: Exploring the Interactive Continuum* (Ridenour & Newman, 2008), in which Ridenour and Newman attempt to connect quantitative and qualitative conceptualizations. As they explain, mixed methods research does not consist of a dichotomy of quantitative and qualitative, but instead represents a third research

model. Q methodology fits well into this idea of mixed methods, although what exactly that model consists of is still in debate (Creswell, 2010; Tashakkori & Teddlie, 2009).

It is important to realize that Q methodology is not simply a statistical technique but, instead, a complete methodology (McKeown & Thomas, 1988; Stephenson, 1953) where the focus is on measuring subjectivity (Brown, 1980, 2008; McKeown & Thomas, 1988; Stephenson, 1953). Thus, Q methodology is a set of procedures, theory, and philosophy that focuses on the study of subjectivity, where subjectivity is typically associated with qualitative research and objectivity is usually associated with quantitative research (Brown, 2008; Stenner & Stainton-Rogers, 2004). Similarly, Q methodology fits into the qualitative framework of naturalistic contextualization of research (Stenner & Stainton-Rogers, 2004). Compared to typical qualitative research, though, Q methodology maintains the relationship among themes within the data as it minimizes the impact of the researcher's frame of reference (Stainton-Rogers, 1995). It does this through complex statistical analysis including correlation and factor analysis (Brown, 1980; Stephenson, 1953).

This sophisticated use of statistics has been what has led to the designation of Q methodology as quantitative (Brown, 2008). Yet within Q methodology aspects of these statistical analyses, especially within the factor analysis, there also exist both qualitative and quantitative aspects (Brown, 2008; Stenner & Stainton-Rogers, 2004). Even the issue within mixed methods studies of how to collect two different strands of data (Creswell, 2010) is not a problem within Q methodology. These mixed methodological aspects of Q will be discussed later in this chapter.

Certainly, Q methodology was not originally identified as a mixed method since, as Creswell (2010) states, mixed method research began around 1988. Perhaps this is why, since its inception 75 years ago when Stephenson first published an article describing Q methodology in *Nature* (Stephenson,

1935), Q methodology has held a controversial position in social science research that has led to its relatively small following (Brown, 1998). It is only recently that Q methodology has become more widely accepted in journals in a variety of disciplines (A. Wolf and S. Ramlo, personal communication, April 29, 2009), possibly due to the greater acceptance of mixed methodology research.

Q factor analysis, which is different from Q methodology, also fits into the conception of mixed methods research. Although Q factor analysis also groups people, it does not include the sorting of items into a grid distribution as a means of measuring subjectivity the way Q methodology does. In other words, the participants' sorting of the statements in Q methodology is what determines the factors and groupings, which makes these categories of operant subjectivity (Brown, 1998). Instead, Cattel (1978) described Q factor analysis as a means of determining dimensions or profiles of people. Within Q factor analysis the factors or groupings are based on various characteristics or data collected, but they are not categories of operant subjectivity such as those in studies involving Q methodology. Even though the techniques are different, sometimes the term "Q factor analysis" is used incorrectly to refer to studies that actually involve Q methodology. Adding to the confusion, the factor analysis of the Q sorts in Q methodology is often referred to as Q factor analysis (McKeown & Thomas, 1988; Stephenson, 1953).

Differences between Q methodology and Q factor analysis are discussed in detail by their respective creators elsewhere (Stephenson & Burt, 1939). Thus, both of these preexisting yet different research approaches fit the new age of social science research that is mixed methods. Specifically, these two methods, Q factor analysis and Q methodology, use sophisticated statistical techniques to reduce large amounts of data. The data collection is typically based on qualitative research, as is the naming of the factors, or groupings of people.

Stephenson presented the idea of Q methodology as a way of investigating people's views of any topic. Thus, Q methodology allows researchers to investigate research questions that involve determining the various views within a group about a specific topic, as well as using those views to investigate how they affect some other aspect of the study.

Q methodology is a measure of subjectivity that represents an individual's feelings, opinions, perspectives, or preferences (Brown, 1980, 2008; McKeown & Thomas, 1988; Siegesmund, 2008; Stenner & Stainton-Rogers, 2004; Stephenson, 1953). This is consistent with qualitative researchers' focus on the investigation of subjectivity (Siegesmund, 2008). Certainly, Q methodology represents a unique way to measure subjectivity (McKeown & Thomas, 1988; Stephenson, 1953) because it allows participants to provide their perspectives by sorting items, typically statements related to the topic, into a sorting grid determined by the researcher. These Q sorts are then analyzed via factor analysis, which allows those of similar views to be grouped into factors. Thus, within Q, people, not items, are grouped and, therefore, researchers must have a sufficient number of items to determine differences among the participants, not a sufficient number of participant to determine differences among the items as is typically required within R factor analysis (Brown, 1980; McKeown & Thomas, 1988; Stephenson, 1953).

PERFORMING A Q METHODOLOGY STUDY

Q studies commence with the development of a collection of items, typically statements or pictures, which is qualitative in design.[1] This collection of items is called the "concourse" within Q methodology, and represents the communications about the topic. These items are typically taken from interviews, focus groups, and other sources of dialogue such as newspapers (McKeown & Thomas, 1988). Often the concourse is extracted via a theme analysis (Strauss & Corbin, 1990). The Q sample, which includes the items for participants to sort, is then selected from the concourse (Brown, 1980; McKeown & Thomas, 1988; Stephenson, 1953). Typically, the Q sample consists of 30 to 60 items selected as representative of the concourse (Brown, 2008). It is the Q sample that is sorted by those participating in a Q study (Brown, 1980, 2008; McKeown & Thomas, 1988; Stephenson, 1953).

The sorting process is inherently subjective because participants judge each Q sample item relative to the others while placing them into a distribution based on a condition of instruction, both of which are provided by the researcher (Brown, 1980; McKeown & Thomas, 1988; Stephenson, 1953). An example would be to have students sort 34 items related to their views of learning in a first-semester college physics course. Each item is presented on an individual strip of paper, which is then placed into the grid shown in Figure 20.1 (Ramlo, 2008a, 2008c). Participants may be interviewed during the sorting process or may be asked to make written comments regarding their sorting selections in order to better inform the researcher's interpretation of the results (Brown, 1980; McKeown & Thomas, 1988).

The analyses of Q sorts involve correlation, factor analysis, and the calculation of factor scores (Brown, 1980, 1986, 2008; Stephenson, 1953). Although sophisticated mathematically, parts of this factor analysis process are qualitative. The first step of the factor analysis process in Q methodology is to select the factor extraction method. Typical software used specifically for Q methodology studies, such as the PQ Method (Brown, 2008; Schmolck, 2002), offers two choices for factor extraction: principal components and Centroid. Principal components analysis is a common extraction method that is frequently used in R factor analysis where there are 1s in the

Figure 20.1 Sample Sorting Grid for a Q Methodology Study

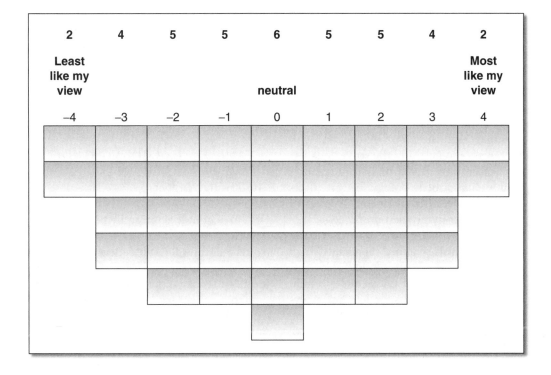

diagonal of the matrix. Conceptually, however, principal components analysis assumes that an individual's sorts are invariant (correlated at 1.00). It is unlikely, however, that a person would sort items in a Q study identically, at two different times, even if the separation of those sorts were only a day or two. Thus, in Q methodology, Centroid is the extraction method of choice. Stephenson (1953) originally designated the Centroid extraction because of the indeterminacy of its solution (one correct solution does not exist among the infinite solutions possible).[2]

In Q methodology software packages, there are two choices for factor rotation available: Varimax and hand rotation. It is the indeterminacy of the Centroid solution that allows the researcher to rotate the factors based on theoretical considerations using hand rotation (Brown, 1980, 1986; Stephenson, 1953). Varimax is the preferred quantitative choice in situations such as R factor analysis because Varimax allows the researcher to produce simple structure, maximizing the eigenvalue for each factor (Stevens, 2002). In this way, Varimax and other similar rotation methods related to simple structure seek to reach a factor structure that is operationally independent of the researcher (Brown, 1980). However, in Q methodology, the researcher is not interested in objectivity but, instead, in subjectivity, including the subjective rotation of factors (Brown, 1980; Stephenson, 1953).[3] Thus, the use of Centroid extraction in conjunction with hand rotation illustrates the strong qualitative aspect of the factor analytic procedures used within Q methodology, because of its focus on subjectivity and its involvement of the researcher in the rotation process.

Following rotation, the researcher must select individuals who are represented by a factor; this is called flagging. In Table 20.1, those who are flagged on factors are indicated with Xs. Factor descriptions and analyses are determined only by those Q sorters who are flagged on that factor (Brown, 1980; McKeown & Thomas, 1988; Schmolck,

2002; Stephenson, 1953). Flagging is described further within the section on factor scores. Flagging sorters for the factors is necessary before the analyses produce a report that involves a variety of tables. Although developed statistically, these tables assist the researcher's description of the various views determined from the factor scores, beyond the types of tables that are generated in more standard statistical packages such as SPSS. These tables will be discussed in detail within the sections that follow. For instance, the sorts of those who are represented by a particular factor are used to create one sort that represents that factor's view, also known as a representative sort (Brown, 1980, 2008; McKeown & Thomas, 1988). In addition, distinguishing factor statements and consensus statements also are identified via the analyses (Brown, 1980; McKeown & Thomas, 1988). Although the analyses of these statements include calculating statistical significance, which is highly quantitative, the interpreting and naming of the factors falls into a more typical qualitative framework (Stenner & Stainton-Rogers, 2004).

In order to best demonstrate the Q methodology research process, in the following section we discuss ongoing studies about how students view their learning in a first-semester physics course, referenced earlier within this chapter. More details of these studies are available via a variety of publications of this research (Ramlo, 2006/2007, 2008a, 2008b, 2008c).

EXAMPLE 1: EXAMINING STUDENT EPISTEMOLOGY WITH Q METHODOLOGY

This example is primarily to describe the creation and revision of a concourse of statements and the subsequent Q sample in an ongoing Q methodology study. In addition, we focus on the analyses of this study and how they are used to interpret perspectives in a specific study, and how that information can be used in additional ways such as correlation and linear regression.

Table 20.1 Factor Matrix With an X Indicating a Defining Sort

	Qsort ID	1	2	3	4
1	CJ24D14	0.05	0.45X	−0.15	−0.24
2	MJ22C17	0.31	0.00	−0.34	−0.28
3	EF19C24	0.29	0.08	−0.75X	0.09
4	SF18A22	0.22	0.26	0.52X	0.19
5	EF19B31	0.59X	0.41	0.01	0.15
6	CJ21C28	−0.24	0.61X	−0.13	0.15
7	MF19C18	0.05	−0.14	0.30X	−0.12
8	ES20C44	0.53X	−0.45	−0.16	0.15
9	MS22C38	−0.28	−0.08	−0.11	0.28
10	CS19A33	0.69X	−0.26	0.27	−0.16
11	MF22D7	−0.09	0.62X	−0.12	−0.06
12	CF19A26	0.63X	0.15	0.06	0.01
13	MS20B24	0.57X	−0.05	−0.40	−0.11
14	SJ35C15	0.12	0.03	0.05	0.17
15	MS21D12	0.02	0.29	−0.12	0.45X
16	SF19B41	0.13	0.28	0.27	0.01
17	MS27A34	0.78X	0.08	0.31	0.15
18	CF20C25	0.32X	−0.03	−0.13	−0.09

NOTES: The Q sort ID in this table contains demographic information; the first letter represents the students' major (C = construction, M = mechanical engineering technology, E = electronic engineering technology, S = surveying & mapping), the second letter represents the students' undergraduate level (F = freshman, S = sophomore, J = junior), the third letter represents the grade received by the student. The first numerical part of the ID represents self-reported age, and the second set of numbers represents the students' score on the FMCE at posttest.

This example begins with the desire of a small group of faculty to investigate students' views of learning and knowledge, also known as personal epistemology (Chan & Elliott, 2004; Hofer & Pintrich, 2002), in a variety of classes at a large, Midwestern public university. This faculty group also sought to compare instructors' beliefs about learning and knowledge to those of their students in these select courses. Using Q methodology allowed them to avoid the lengthy interview process typical of qualitative epistemology studies (Duell & Schommer-Aikins, 2001; Elby & Hammer, 2001; Schraw, Bendixen, & Dunkle, 2002). In addition, Q allowed them to determine the various epistemological views of students, unlike studies that have used Likert-scale surveys (Adams, Perkins, Dubson, Finkelstein, & Wieman, 2005; Halloun & Hestenes, 1998; Perkins, Adams, Pollock, Finkelstein, & Wieman, 2005; Schommer, 1990).

Yet the concourse of statements for the Q methodology study on student epistemology began with the popular Likert survey developed by Schommer (1990), which she developed from interviews. A Q sample of 32 statements was selected from this 72-item questionnaire. Students were required to sort the Q sample statements; analyses of the Q sorts were performed on each class. The results and students' written comments from this initial epistemological study indicated that students typically sorted the Schommer statements—not based on their personal epistemological views but, instead, based on their public epistemology. Lising (2005) differentiated these two views by describing personal epistemology as how someone perceives their own learning and knowledge. Alternatively, someone's public epistemology represents how they view others' epistemology such as scientists or other authorities.

Thus, the preliminary results led Ramlo (2006/2007) to change the wording of these initial Q sample statements to make them more personal. For example, "Learning something really well takes a long time" was changed slightly to "Learning something really well takes me a long time in this course." These changes were intended to stress to students that they were to reflect on their own personal epistemology relative to the course they were taking. Student interviews also were used to develop an additional 22 statements, some replacing Schommer survey items, such that the Q sample increased from 32 to 44 statements. Although other courses and instructors used this revised Q sample, only the results of the physics course's portion of the study are currently available as a journal article (Ramlo, 2006/2007). This aspect of the study allowed the instructors to investigate how their perceptions of students' views of learning in their courses actually compared to the students' views.

However, the physics course investigator wanted to delve more into how students' epistemological views related to their learning of force and motion concepts. Thus, a follow-up study was done with a slightly revised Q sample to better investigate students' experiences in the physics classroom and laboratory (Ramlo, 2008a, 2008c). This Q sample was not used in other courses, which allowed the researcher to change the Q sample such that it targeted learning in the first semester of physics only. This subsequent study demonstrated how Q methodology can be used to investigate college physics students' views of their learning (Ramlo, 2008a, 2008c) and how those views affected their learning of important physics concepts in a first-semester physics course (Ramlo, 2008c). In addition, this study contributed to the already large body of literature on students' learning of force and motion concepts, which has established students' difficulty gaining Newtonian-based understanding of force and motion concepts (Ramlo, 2008d; Redish, Saul, & Steinberg, 2000; Thornton & Sokoloff, 1998).

Although this study further confirmed the connection between learning in physics and students' epistemologies (Halloun & Hestenes, 1998; Hammer & Elby, 2003; Lising & Elby, 2005), the focus of the remainder of this section is to further describe the sorting process and introduce the reader to the type of results produced within a Q methodology study. The four basic types of tables that are generated are (1) factor scores, (2) rank-ordered list of the Q sample statements with z-scores to create a representative sort for each factor, (3) the list of statements that distinguish each factor from the other, and (4) the list of consensus statements that represent agreement among all the factors (Brown, 1980; McKeown & Thomas, 1988). Each of these tables will be described related to the Ramlo 2008 study (Ramlo, 2008a, 2008c)

In this study (Ramlo, 2008a, 2008c), 18 students sorted the 44 statements into the distribution shown in Figure 20.1. Each of these statements was on a separate slip of paper for ease in sorting. The participants sorted these items based on how they viewed their learning in this first-semester physics course.

Each individual sort was entered into PQ Method, one of several software packages designed specifically for analysis of Q sorts (Schmolck, 2002).[4] Only these types of packages provide the types of output reports required to interpret the participants' view on a topic. As Bazeley (2010 [this volume]) suggests, software such as PQ Method is necessary for mixed methods research to effectively integrate different data elements and analyses. Although factor analysis more often fits into the more conventional standard statistical packages such as SPSS, the analysis of the Q sorts requires software that allows the researcher to combine the qualitative and quantitative aspects of such studies. We agree with Onwuegbuzie and Combs (2010 [this volume]) that one of the difficulties of performing mixed methods research is that the researcher must be competent in analyzing both qualitative and quantitative data. However, Q methodology and Q factor analysis actually represent the integration of qualitative and quantitative methods. As Bazeley suggests, this integration allows the researcher to produce findings that are of greater use and to better address the research purpose (Newman, Ridenour, Newman, & DeMarco, 2003). This thinking is supported by the work of a variety of mixed methods researchers (Bazeley, 2010; Creswell, 2010; Onwuegbuzie & Combs, 2010; Tashakkori & Teddlie, 2009).

Within Q methodology, the analyses produce an extensive report with a variety of tables. Four basic types of tables are produced, however. These tables are the basis of the interpretation of the Q sorts and, therefore, the participants' views. The first table is a listing of the factor scores that are used to determine which participants are represented by which factors (views). Each factor represents a similar perspective or worldview of the topic. The other three types of tables produced are specifically for interpreting the views of those represented by each of the perspectives (factors). These tables are for the representative sort for each factor, distinguishing statements for each factor, and statements representing consensus among the factors. Each of these tables is described below in the context of our example on studying students' epistemology in a first-semester physics course.

Table of Factor Scores

The first table, Table 20.1, is the factor matrix for the Ramlo (2008a, 2008c) study discussed here. This table illustrates that four perspectives on learning in this physics course, each represented by a factor, were found in this study. In qualitative research, these factors would be called typologies because they group people of similar views. The table has rows for each sorter that include the sorter's identification and that person's loadings (correlations) with each of the four factors that were retained. If a sorter is primarily represented by one factor, that is indicated by placing an X next to that person's factor score for that particular factor. For instance, in Table 20.1, the sorter in Row 1, CJ24D14, has an X placed next to the factor score of .45 in the Factor 2 column. Thus, as one can see from Table 20.1, Typology / Factor 1 is made up of persons 5, 8, 10, 12, 13, 17, and 18, and Typology / Factor 2 is made up of participants 1, 6, and 11. That means that Factor 2 represents the view held by CJ24D14 along with two other sorters (Row 6, CJ21C28, and Row 11, MF22D7). This is an important table in that it allows us to see that the 18 sorters can be identified as four types via data reduction. However, this table does not explain these types. Other tables must be examined to identify the various views determined and to name these different perspectives. Therefore, to describe these worldviews, we must examine other tables produced from the analyses.

To learn more about those represented by Factor 1, for instance, their Q sort data must be analyzed. The remaining analyses are based on the individual's sorts selected for each factor, shown with the Xs. Participants who do not have an X placed next to a factor score are not represented by any of the four factors and, thus, do not have their sorts included in the analyses. In this way, the factor interpretation follows evaluating the factor scores (McKeown & Thomas, 1988).

Representative Sorts for Each Factor

One sort that represents the views of the people on each factor is created through the analyses. This representative sort is created from the Q sorts of those who were selected as being represented by that factor. This representative sort is created via the listing of all the statements, in rank order of largest positive to largest negative z-score. It is these z-scores that represent each statement's position in the sorting grid (Brown, 1980; McKeown & Thomas, 1988).

The most extreme z-scores (representing the positions toward the outside of the sorting grid) are most useful for interpreting the factor. Table 20.2 lists the top and bottom five statements for Factor 1 in this study. The Q sorts for each person who is represented by Factor 1 were used to create this statement list, which can be used to create a Q sort representing that factor. The ranking of the z-scores was used to determine the grid position, which also is given in the table. Although only the extreme ends of the grid are reported here, the researcher can use the z-scores to create a complete representative sort for this factor, as already mentioned. Similarly, the remaining three factors in this study have statement rankings, based on z-scores, which can be used to create the additional Q sorts that represent these three views.

Representative Q sorts, with focus on those statements on the ends of the grid,

Table 20.2   Factor 1 Tops Five Most Like / Most Unlike Statements

No.	Statement	z-score	Grid Position
12	I like the exactness of math-type subjects.	1.804	4
30	I enjoy solving problems.	1.372	4
10	I can tell when I understand the material in this class.	1.269	3
13	What I learn in this class will help me in other classes.	1.226	3
15	When I don't understand something in my physics lab, I ask another student to help me understand.	1.011	3
7	Learning something really well takes me a long time in this course.	−1.275	−3
16	If I am going to understand something in this course, it will make sense to me right away.	−1.275	−3
5	I have very little control over how much I learn in this course.	−1.310	−3
23	Sometimes I found the lab results hard to truly believe.	−1.369	−4
8	In this course, if I don't understand something quickly, it usually means I won't understand it.	−1.477	−4

were used, in part, for the interpretation of the epistemological views of the students in this study. Because of the importance of the Factor 1 view, we will focus on its interpretation here. From Table 20.2, the most extreme positioned statements for Factor 1 indicate that those represented by this view were reflective, help seeking, and enjoyed math or problem solving. They also saw the relevance of this course to other courses they would take. These students also did not see learning as immediate (disagree with Statements 7, 8, and 16) but did see that they have control over their learning (disagree with Statement 5). These statements allowed us to consider names for this factor or worldview, such as reflective-learners. However, examining the distinguishing statements, which allowed us to differentiate this Factor 1 view from the remaining three, led to other possible names for this view. The next section

describes the use of distinguishing statements in this Q methodology study.

Distinguishing Statements

As previously mentioned, the extensive report produced within Q methodology studies includes tables of distinguishing statements. These tables are created for each factor in the study. Such statements distinguish, here, each factor from the other three at a significance level of .05. Again, our primary interest here concerns Factor 1 so we will only focus on those statements that distinguish Factor 1 from the other three factors found in the study. Table 20.3 contains these statements for Factor 1. Although the representative sort results, such as those given in Table 20.2, are helpful in describing a particular factor's view, the distinguishing statement results provide additional and often insightful information for the researcher. The statements that

Table 20.3 Distinguishing Statements for Factor 1

No	Distinguishing statement	F1 Grid Position	F2 Grid Position	F3 Grid Position	F4 Grid Position
20	When I don't understand something in my physics lab, I ask my instructor to help me understand.	1	0	−4	4
1	I see the ideas of force and motion as coherent and interconnected.*	1	−4	−4	−2
29	I find it hard to learn from our textbook.*	0	4	−3	4
17	Sometimes I just have to accept answers from my professor even though I don't understand them.	−1	2	1	−4
24	Sometimes I find I have problems understanding the terms used in physics.	−2	3	1	1
16	If I am going to understand something in this course, it will make sense to me right away.*	−3	2	2	3
8	In this course, if I don't understand something quickly, it usually means I won't understand it.*	−4	0	3	1

NOTE: These factor 1 statements are different from the other views at the $p < .05$ level; asterisk (*) indicates significance at $p < .01$.

differentiate Factor 1 from the other three views are contained in Table 20.3. It is this table that reveals that Factor 1 students indicated that they sought a coherent view of force and motion (Statement 1) and believed that their learning would take time (Statements 8 and 16). These three statements distinguish this view from the others at the .01 level. In other words, these three statements distinguish Factor 1 from the other factors; it is more certain, therefore, that this difference is not due to chance.

It is important to note that only those represented by this view agreed that they sought coherence for the force and motion concepts and disagreed that learning needed to be immediate (Statement 16). This additional information, in conjunction with the representative sorts from the other views, allowed the researcher to better reveal the epistemology of this Factor 1 perspective on learning in this first-semester physics course. This additional insight allowed the research to select the name of "Reflective learners who sought coherence and found it" for this factor, or view. Describing this view is especially important, given that the Factor 1 view also contains those students who scored highest on the Force and Motion Conceptual Evaluation (FMCE) posttest, thus the additional "and found it" in the view's name. Thus the Factor 1 epistemological view correlates with the only group that had a Newtonian view of force and motion, as will be discussed further in a subsequent section. However, the consensus among the four factors also revealed important insight into the physics students' epistemological views about the course.

Consensus Statements

Consensus statements do not distinguish between any of the factors (Brown, 1980). Thus, in addition to the tables of distinguishing statements for each factor, a table of consensus statements for the factors also is identified in the Q methodology analyses' report. Thus in this study, agreement existed across the four different views about learning

in the physics class. Consensus has allowed researchers to focus on agreement among different views, which can be used to start a dialogue related to commonality, a key idea in organizational change (Ramlo, 2005).

In this way, the consensus yielded additional information related to students' epistemologies. Here, two consensus statements were determined. One of these consensus statements indicated that the physics students agreed that they ask their peers for help in understanding the lab activities. Instructors' observations substantiated this finding. These same students disagreed that they tried to combine ideas across the lab activities. It is worth noting, however, that the lab activities frequently refer to previous activities from earlier labs and that these activities including having students compare their current findings to the findings from earlier activities. Thus the consensus statements here supported the importance of peer interaction among the lab students but indicated that lab materials and instructors needed to focus more on having students combine ideas across the various laboratory activities during the semester.

Correlation of the Epistemological Views With Conceptual Understanding

The true purpose of the Ramlo (2008c) epistemology study, however, was to investigate the relationship between students' views about learning and knowledge and their understanding of force and motion concepts. In other words, discovering the four different views is not the end of our story. Instead, we can relate these world views to the learning of physics concepts. Thus, we had to ask how well this quasi-qualitative outcome, via Q methodology, relates to an important research question within the physics education research community that could not have easily been detectable without Q methodology.

The understanding of force and motion concepts was determined by using the FMCE, an instrument that has been shown to have strong estimates of both validity and reliability (Ramlo, 2008d), at the end of the semester. Thus, the Q methodology aspect of the study allowed the researcher to identify four different factors that represented the four differing epistemologies held by students in the course. The correlations between these factors and the FMCE posttest scores are presented in Table 20.4.

These statistical results indicate that only the Factor 1 epistemological view had a positive correlation (.46) with the FMCE posttest scores. Thus, this view is most interesting in that only this epistemological view represents students who have a Newtonian understanding of force and motion. The remaining three views are negatively correlated with the posttest, and are held by students who did not have a Newtonian understanding of force and motion. Therefore, these correlations suggest more about the epistemological views revealed by the Q methodology aspect of the study. This investigation further demonstrated the strength of Q to investigate views in the research area of conceptual understanding in physics. In addition, it demonstrates how the perspectives revealed within a Q study can be used to investigate how those views are related to other student attributes.

The usefulness of Q methodology has become apparent in other studies with different purposes. Consensus and differing views about the creation of a school of technology at a large Midwestern university were determined using Q methodology that

enabled discussions about organizational change (Ramlo, 2005). The effectiveness of a reading circle professional development experience to help university faculty reflect on their teaching also was determined through a Q methodology study (Ramlo & McConnell, 2008). Thus, using Q methodology to reveal the differing perspectives, as well as consensus, within groups of people can address a large number of research purposes.

EXAMPLE 2: CLASSIFICATION OF INJURED WORKERS IN RELATION TO VOCATIONAL TRAINING WITH Q FACTOR ANALYSIS

Although Q factor analysis is a by-person factor analysis similar to Q methodology, it is not the same as Q methodology. Instead, Q factor analysis only employs one aspect of Stephenson's procedure: the grouping of people with factor analysis. Yet this grouping is not based on participants' sorting of items as it is in Q methodology (Stephenson, 1953; Watts & Stenner, 2005). Q methodology groups people based on subjective data (from the sorts), and Q factor analysis groups people using data that may come from a variety of sources including interviews, observations, surveys, and demographic information. These differences and similarities of Q methodology and Q factor analysis are

Table 20.4 Correlations Between the Factors (Views) and the FMCE Posttest Scores

Factor	Post	Average Posttest score	Std Dev	Number of students
F1	0.463	31	7	7
F2	−0.393	16	11	3
F3	−0.171	21	3	3
F4	−0.318	12	N/A	1

NOTES: The FMCE was used for the posttest and has a maximum of 47 points possible. Only Factor 1 had a positive correlation with the posttest.

demonstrated in Figure 20.2. Specifically, for Q factor analysis, the groupings of people into types are based on the shape of the responses to the various items, as shown in Figure 20.3. In this figure, although Persons 1 and 2 have similar absolute scores overall, they do not represent the same type or profile. Instead, Persons 1 and 3 have similar shapes to their responses; therefore, the Q factor analysis would consider these two persons as representing the same type or profile.

Figure 20.2 Comparison of Q Methodology and Q Factor Analysis

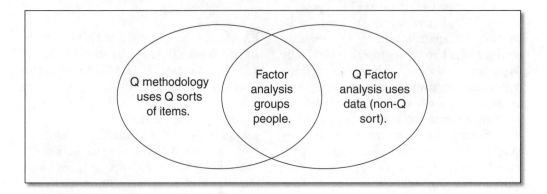

Figure 20.3 Three Persons Representing Two Types / Profiles

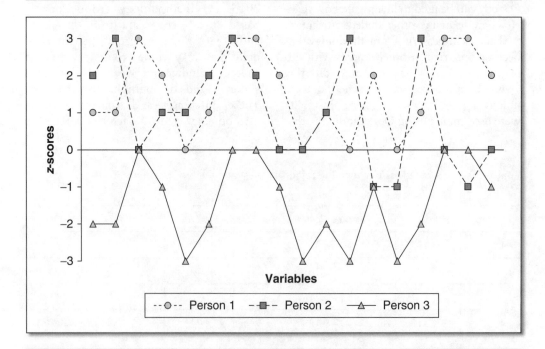

NOTE: The plots of z-scores, called profiles, for three different people are shown here to demonstrate that Persons 1 and 3 have similar profiles and therefore represent one type. Person 2 has a different profile and therefore represents a different type.

Analyses in the example of Q factor analysis described here used QUANAL (Vantubergen, 1975) a program developed for Q methodology.[5] However, unlike a study using Q methodology, the data source was not participants' Q sorts. Instead, the data used within the analyses came from a computer-based assessment and interviews. The computer-assisted vocational assessment system, the Apticom Aptitude Test Battery, has established estimates of validity and reliability and is used for measuring the level of physical functioning of people with disabilities (Alston & Mngadi, 1992). In our example, scores with the Apticom instrument along with age, sex, and type and number of injuries were used to group injured workers into types (Waechter, Newman, & Nolte, 1998).

A number of variations on Q methodology exist in the literature. The Q factor analysis we discuss here involved the mathematical analyses without the Q sort, thus prompting the use of the QUANAL program for analysis with quantified data from the Apticom along with interview and demographic information. The Apticom has 10 scales that were used in a study along with eight other variables (Waechter et al., 1998). Table 20.5, which contains a sample of the type of data used in the Waechter study, will be discussed further in the context of the study. The use of these scales to group people here distinguishes this study from our first example where the data used to group people came from the Q sort. In this current example, the patterns of the

Table 20.5 Descending Array of z-scores for Each Factor Type

Variable	Type I	Type II	Difference
Motor coordination	0.73	−0.54	1.29
Finger dexterity	1.60	0.84	0.76
Manual dexterity	0.90	0.38	0.52
Eye–hand–foot coordination	0.70	0.30	0.40
Back injury	−1.10	−1.07	−0.03
Knee injury	−1.12	−1.08	−0.04
Finger or hand injury	−1.12	−1.08	−0.04
Male or female	−1.11	−1.08	−0.03
Number of injuries	−1.10	−1.05	−0.05
Neck injury	−1.12	−1.05	−0.07
Clerical perception	0.81	0.99	−0.17
Verbal	0.81	1.05	−0.24
Spatial	0.71	1.02	−0.31
Intelligent	0.91	1.31	−0.40
Numerical	0.97	1.44	−0.48
Age	−0.28	0.75	−1.03

NOTE: This table is a subset of items based upon the study by Waechter and colleagues (1998). This specific example of data is useful in demonstrating how Q factor analysis can be used to differentiate between types. Please note that the data presented here are not exactly the same as those presented in Waechter and colleagues (1998).

data were used to classify people creating typologies, sometimes also referred to as profiles or dimensions (Nunnally, 1978).

The purpose of the injured workers study was to develop a process of classifying people who experienced work-related injuries and who were identified for vocational job retraining. Sixty-seven injured workers, 37 males and 30 females, who had their injuries verified, were involved in this study. The data were Q factor analyzed with QUANAL in order to determine similar patterns in the data (see Figure 20.4) that were used to identify the different typologies within the sample. Thus, the analyses are grouping people based on their similar patterns.

In the injured worker study, two types of persons were identified, with 59 of the 67 participants represented by one of the two types. The patterns (shapes) for the two types found, for each of the variables, are represented in Figure 20.4, which shows the z-scores for each variable for Types I and II plotted as a traditional X–Y graph. Table 20.5 contains the data used to create Figures 20.4 and 20.5. The patterns found were used to interpret the two types. This table lists the descending array of z-scores for each of these two types of injured workers by variable type. The difference between the z-scores listed in the fourth column was used to determine which items differentiated one type from the other and to indicate where there were similarities.

Figure 20.4   Q Factor Analysis Results With Two Typologies

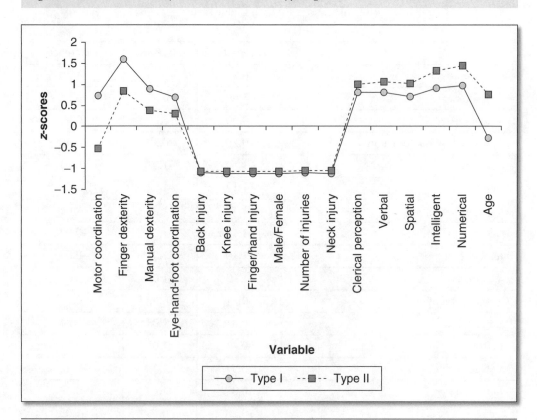

NOTE: Visual representation of the two types, I and II, of injured workers found in the vocational education study using the z-score data from Table 20.5.

Figure 20.5 Injured Workers Study

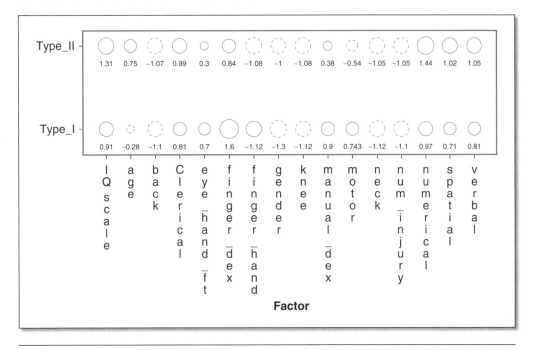

NOTE: Alternative representation of the Table 5 z-score data using this bubble plot presentation provided by Dickinson (2010).

Figure 20.5 is an alternative presentation of the Table 20.5 data. This can be compared to the more traditional graph of the same data illustrated in Figure 20.4. In Figure 20.5, the data are presented using a bubble plot, which is one of the dimensional display formats for data presentation suggested by Dickinson (2010 [this volume]). This type of data visualization tool provides researchers with another way to discern patterns. Although Dickinson presents examples utilizing bubble plots with frequency data, other quantitative measures also may be represented within this format. Specifically, the data displayed in Figure 20.5 use the bubble's (circle) diameter to reflect the z-score values given in Table 20.5 for the two different profiles or types. In other words, the bubble with the largest diameter represents the largest z-score, and so on. Because z-scores can be

positive or negative, these differences must be noted by the patterns used for the bubbles (circles). For instance, in Figure 20.5 the positive z-score bubbles have a solid outline and the negative z-score bubbles have a dashed outline. By observing the distinct pattern differences of the data presented in Figure 20.5, the researcher can discern the two distinct profiles that exist in this study.

From Figures 20.4 and 20.5, as well as from Table 20.5, one can see that Age and the Apticom Motor Coordination scale differentiated between the two types the most. Type I individuals were younger and received a higher score on the Motor Coordination, Finger Dexterity, Motor Dexterity, and Eye–Hand–Foot Coordination scales of the Apticom. Individuals represented by Type II were older, and had higher scores on scales used to measure intelligence, verbal, numerical, and spatial reasoning. The subjects' files also were reviewed to help interpret these findings. This part of the study indicated that Type II individuals were referred to the testing by their attorneys as part of the litigation process against their employers. Since they were older workers, it is not surprising that they also had longer work histories. In addition, these workers refused opportunities to participate in retraining programs. They also had stopped receiving Worker's Compensation, whereas the Type I workers were still receiving assistance. Point biserial correlations also indicated that Type II workers scored lower on several of the dexterity and coordination scales of the Apticom than their Type I counterparts. These results and method of classifying injured workers may allow vocational evaluations to be better informed about the types of injured workers and may improve decision making about screening applications (Waechter et al., 1998).

The method is identical to, but the topic is different from, an earlier Q factor analysis study by Newman (1971) where the views of both Black and White basketball team members were evaluated by grouping the team members and the coach into factors. The data used were from the Subjective Perception Rating Scales, a semantic differential scale, and a behavioral differential scale. Profiles identified for White and Black subjects were then determined from the patterns of responses to these 130 variables. Basically, two profiles or typologies emerged, each representing a different type across these 130 items. These two types were named White Typology and Black Typology since the most discriminating factor between the two factors was race. It turned out that everyone on Type I was Black and everyone on Type II was White, except for one person who loaded similarly on both Types. This person was the coach (Newman, 1971).

With factor analysis, factors are not stable—they are sample specific. They are notoriously unstable. We strongly recommend that when doing a Q or R factor analysis, the sample be split in half to see what types emerge and then to cross validate the types. For example, if four types emerge in the first Q factor analysis and we get five types from the second sample, we could correlate the types from Sample 1 with the types from Sample 2. To the extent that this results in similar types in both samples, we have reason to believe that these types are more stable. From these analyses, we may see, for instance, that only three of the types replicate between the two samples. These three may then be more likely to be more stable, and this may warrant further investigation. The other types may be sample specific. Thus, depending on the research question these may or may not also warrant further investigation. With R factor analysis, other methods tend to be used such as confirmatory factor analysis or Kaisers factor matching techniques (Newman, Dimitrov, & Waechter, 2000).

FUTURE RESEARCH: EXTENDING THE USE OF GROUPS OF PEOPLE

This chapter has demonstrated how sophisticated statistical techniques that are employed by Q factor analysis and Q methodology can effectively reduce large amounts of data that are frequently used in mixed method research. Such data reduction techniques may broaden the researchers' ability to interpret the data in a more efficacious manner. In addition, we also suggest that coupling the groupings with other statistical techniques allows researchers the ability to extend beyond the information they would get by simply grouping. For instance, we could use Chisquares to compare the groups to investigate differences. We also could use these groupings as predictor variables in linear regression models.

To further illustrate this concept, previous studies investigating conceptual understanding have shown that numerous student characteristics play roles in students' learning of force and motion (Ates & Cataloglu, 2007; Dykstra, Boyle, & Monarch, 1992; Ramlo, 2003, 2007a, 2007b; Rowlands, Graham, & Berry, 1998). Thus, to further study the potential impact of the epistemology of physics students described in Ramlo (Ramlo, 2008a, 2008b), we could control variables shown to influence the learning of force and motion concepts. Thus, we could predict the learning of the physics concepts at the end of the course (FMCE posttest scores) in a linear regression model that included the epistemology views (Q methodology factors) along with students' FMCE pretest scores and previous physics course experience. We could then "test" the effect of the epistemological views by comparing, statistically, the full model (the one described above) to the model that includes only the FMCE pretest scores and previous physics course experience, without the epistemology views, to better understand the influence of student epistemologies on their learning while "controlling" the other variables (FMCE pretest and previous physics course work). It is important to remind the reader that although sample size in Q methodology is related to the number of statements sorted, studies using statistical techniques such as linear regression require the researcher to have a sufficiently large sample of people in order to have sufficient statistical power (Cohen, 1988). Thus a larger student sample would be very desirable to conduct the investigation suggested here. However, the current Q methodology study and its suggested further investigation offers the potential of gaining greater insight into physics students' thinking about their learning and knowledge and its potential relationship to student learning, beyond other epistemology studies in physics education that have used Likert-type scales (Adams et al., 2005; Gire,

Price, & Jones, 2007; Halloun & Hestenes, 1998; Perkins et al., 2005; Perkins, Gratny, Adams, Finkelstein, & Wieman, 2006).

Q factor analysis offers researchers a way to create profiles or groupings of people based on patterns of data. These profiles can be used to identify the underlying constructs that can assist in classifying people in a meaningful way. Such profiles also can be used for evaluation purposes, such as the example given about vocational training (Waechter et al., 1998). In that example, further research also may have included using the profiles within linear regression analyses. The researchers could have extended their study by identifying implications drawn from their data that could suggest further direction for their work, based on their analyses. In such a study, a full linear regression model could have the completion of vocational training predicted by each of the worker types (Type 1 or Type 2) and the intervention. The restricted model could "test" the intervention by removing that variable and using only the injured worker type to predict completing vocational training. This new study would then have fewer variables in the models because only the injured worker type is included, omitting all of the variables used to determine these two types. Thus, the number of variables in the models is reduced, which increases the statistical power (Cohen, 1988) and potentially increases the conceptual understanding of the models.

Profiles and perspectives determined with Q factor analysis or Q methodology, respectively, can be used in studies that have purposes beyond simply classifying people into groups. It makes sense to use the types (concepts, constructs, factors) instead of all the individual variables that make up the type, when developing the linear regression models, or when using other statistical techniques. In addition, these profiles could be used to disaggregate data so that researchers could further study a particular group, such as the Type II workers in the vocational education study. More data, such as interview responses, could be collected on others who fit that profile. This could potentially enhance the insight and understanding of the initial findings (Waechter et al., 1998).

Thus, investigations that use Q factor analysis or Q methodology allow researchers to better study the stakeholders from different perspectives. This is frequently important in program evaluation, where there is often value in addressing the various stakeholder groups differently to ascertain their needs, in an attempt to improve the effectiveness of the program (McNeil, Newman, & Steinhauser, 2005). To the extent that the evaluation identifies and communicates with the relevant stakeholder, the more likely it is to be useful and the recommendations implemented. Too often, though, stakeholder groupings are simply based on demographic characteristics such as ethnicity or socioeconomic status. We are suggesting that such variables may not be the most appropriate way to group stakeholders. Instead, Q factor analysis and Q methodology can be used to group people more effectively using profiles that go beyond such surface characteristics. Therefore, these types of profile analyses can provide the evaluators with additional insight into the participants, as demonstrated by Ramlo and others (Newman & Benz, 1987; Ramlo, 2005; Ramlo & McConnell, 2008; Ramlo, McConnell, Duan, & Moore, 2008). In addition, this type of profile analysis can improve communication with the various groups or subgroups. By identifying the specific needs of the various stakeholder groups, evaluators can tailor-fit their services and recommendations, as suggested by McNeil and colleagues (2005). This is likely to make evaluation services more effective and more meaningful to the stakeholders. The benefits of integrating qualitative and quantitative methods in evaluation is a pragmatic approach that is not new and is gaining more widespread use and acceptance (Creswell, 2010; McNeil et al., 2005; Newman & Benz, 1987; Onwuegbuzie & Combs, 2010; Tashakkori & Teddlie, 2009).

◆ Use of Other Multivariate Techniques to Facilitate Interpretation

Certainly, data for grouping can be either quantitative or qualitative. Whichever is used, there always will be some similarity coefficient (such as correlations, distance, z-scores, variability estimates, density functions, etc.) to decide how to group, but one has to understand the strengths and weaknesses of such techniques. There is really no right or wrong approach but it is important to understand the approach that is chosen. Different procedures for grouping people are based in different assumptions. In other words, one has to determine if the principle used for grouping makes logical sense and is aligned with the purpose of the study and the research question. Thus, a researcher would not use height and weight as characteristics to investigate student motivation. Instead, there must be a logical, theoretical link between the characteristics of the individuals studied and the purpose of the study.

This chapter has focused on two specific types of multivariate analyses that we believe demonstrate ways to effectively reduce the huge amount of qualitative variables into profiles that can be used to better investigate research questions. When using multivariate techniques for data reduction, one has to be sensitive to how data are being aggregated or disaggregated to better understand the outcomes. For example, factor analysis can be used to aggregate data that was initially qualitative, to facilitate the interpretation conceptually. Let's assume there are a number of subjects that have been interviewed and that the data from each subject have been initially coded, and let's further assume that four initial codes have emerged. That is, all subjects interviewed talk about clarity, flow, persuasiveness, or resources. As one can see from

Figure 20.6, the coding of the interview of Subject 1 indicates that this subject identified clarity, flow, and persuasiveness, but not resources, yielding a matrix code of 1 1 1 0. The coding of the interview of Subject 2 identified persuasive and resources, yielding a matrix code of 0 0 1 1. All the subjects can be qualitatively coded in a similar manner; these qualitative codings can then be quantitatively coded and placed into a matrix made up of 1s and 0s. The following demonstrates how this could be done.

Figure 20.6 Qualitative Coding "Matrix" From Faculty Interviews Related to Writing for People "subj1" to "subj4"

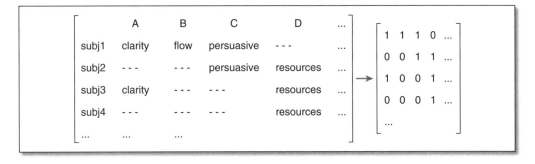

NOTE: Resulting matrix from turning the codes into 1s and 0s based on whether the subject spoke of, for instance, clarity (yes = 1, no = 0).

From this initial coding, qualitative researchers would typically identify different concepts or categories that occur based on how the initial codes logically group together; and the logical groupings of these items is frequently referred to as the themes. This is demonstrated in Figure 20.6 where we have taken the text-codes from Figure 20.6 (A through D), which can be thought of as items, and used them to construct the themes, which can be conceptually thought of as factors. Additionally, we can take these text-codes and convert them into the 1–0 matrix similar to the one shown on the right in Figure 20.6. This is very much what a qualitative researcher might do during the coding process and is where they may end with the development of the emerging themes. This type of table looks similar to a truth table, which an electrical engineer might use to address computer logic or a sociologist might use to investigate complex human phenomenon. However it is more similar to Qualitative Comparative Analysis, known as QCA

(Berg-Schlosser, De Meur, Rihoux, & Ragin, 2009; Ragin, 1987).

We are suggesting that researcher can go back to the 1–0 matrix shown at the right side of Figure 20.6, and factor analyze it to determine what factors emerge from this numerical coding, as shown in Figure 20.7.

Figure 20.7 Matrix for Theme Analysis With Three Themes

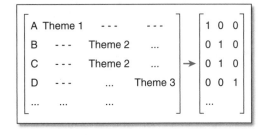

NOTE: These themes can be represented as a matrix, with different items (A, B, C, etc.) forming Themes 1, 2, and 3.

The factor analysis can then be compared to the qualitative theme-analysis. If the factor analysis results do not support these findings, it may suggest a need for the researcher to look at the data in new ways or that the data should be investigated further. Thus, further analysis of qualitative data using quantitative methods can enhance the qualitative research findings.

Finally, we can use similar techniques, once the theme or factors have emerged, to determine which types differentiate between the themes or factors. For example, a discriminate analysis could be performed to better understand how these themes are related to the types found via Q factor analysis. It is important, however, to note that some would take issue with our violating various assumptions by using multivariate statistics as a way to group people and for data reduction. Therefore, it also is important to note that we are not making statistical inferences from samples to populations. Instead, we are using these techniques to help us interpret our data by slicing it in different ways, which allows us to have different perspectives from which the data can be viewed. This may facilitate a better understanding and interpretation of the data.

◆ Conclusions

In this chapter, we have discussed alternative methods to effectively reduce the huge amount of qualitative variables into groupings to better investigate research questions. The suggested techniques discussed, including Q methodology and Q factor analysis, fit into the conception of mixed methods. Specifically, we have focused on the strengths of using multiple quantitative and qualitative techniques to better understand data. We have demonstrated that the qualitative philosophy that different relationships may exist for different situations, reflecting multiple realities, is not inconsistent with using multiple methods.

When these aspects of quantitative and qualitative procedures merge into a mixed methods research, we can enhance our ability to address a variety of new research purposes and questions. As researchers, whether we consider ourselves qualitative, quantitative, or mixed, our ultimate goal is to effectively address our research purpose (Newman et al., 2003) and answer our research questions. The methods discussed here introduce ways to do this that are not typically seen in the research literature at this time.

Research Questions and Exercises

1. Discuss data reduction techniques; include some of the advantages and disadvantages of using them.

2. Discuss univariate and multivariate analysis as data reduction techniques.

3. Describe how Q methodology and Q factor analysis are related and how they are different.

4. Discuss how Q factor analysis and Q methodology may be used to facilitate the interpretation of qualitative research.

◆ Notes

1. A variety of publications provide more detailed explanations of Q methodology (Brown, 1980, 2008; McKeown & Thomas, 1988; Ramlo, 2008a; Stephenson, 1953) and how to perform studies using Q methodology (Brown, 1980, 1986; McKeown & Thomas, 1988; Ramlo, 2008a; Watts & Stenner, 2005).

2. See Brown (1980) for a greater explanation of different extraction methods. Suffice it to say here that Centroid extraction is the preferred method for Q methodology based on philosophical considerations related to the type of rotation promoted by Stephenson (Brown, 1980; Stephenson, 1953).

3. Hand rotation, via a graphical interface, is preferred in cases where it is important to ensure a specific participant is represented by a factor such as an instructor or leader within a group (McKeown & Thomas, 1988). Brown (1986) explained that Centroid extraction of the factors, followed by hand rotation, allows the investigator the opportunity to rotate based upon hunches and to examine the data from a theoretical standpoint. See Brown (1980) for a detailed explanation of hand-rotation procedures.

4. This software is available for free download at http://www.lrz-muenchen.de/~schmolck/qmethod/downpqx.htm

5. This program was previously available only for mainframe computers. An alternative for QUANAL is PQ Method, mentioned previously within this chapter.

◆ References

Adams, W. K., Perkins, K. K., Dubson, M., Finkelstein, N. D., & Wieman, C. E. (2005). The design and validation of the Colorado Learning Attitudes about Science survey. *AIP Conference Proceedings, 790*(1), 45–48.

Alston, R. J., & Mngadi, P. S. (1992). A study of APTICOM's effectiveness in assessing level of physical functioning. *Journal of Rehabilitation, 58*(3), 35.

Ates, S., & Cataloglu, E. (2007). The effects of students' cognitive styles on conceptual understandings and problem-solving skills in introductory mechanics. *Research in Science & Technological Education, 25*(2), 167–178.

Berg-Schlosser, D., De Meur, G., Rihoux, B., & Ragin, C. C. (2009). Qualitative comparative analysis (QCA) as an approach. In B. Rihoux & C. C. Ragin (Eds.), *Configurational comparative methods: Qualitative comparative analysis (QCA) and related techniques* (pp. 1–18). Thousand Oaks, CA: Sage.

Block, J. (2008). *The Q-sort in character appraisal: Encoding subjective impressions of persons quantitatively.* Washington, DC: American Psychological Association.

Brown, S. R. (1980). *Political subjectivity: Applications of Q methodology in political science.* New Haven, CT: Yale University Press.

Brown, S. R. (1986). Q technique and method: Principles and procedures. In W. D. Berry & M. S. Lewis-Beck (Eds.), *New tools for social scientist: Advances and applications in research methods* (pp. 57–76). Beverly Hills, CA: Sage.

Brown, S. R. (1998). *The history and principles of Q methodology in psychology and the social sciences.* Unpublished manuscript. Retrieved May 5, 2009, from http://facstaff.uww.edu/cottlec/QArchive/Bps.htm

Brown, S. R. (2008). Q methodology. In L. M. Given (Ed.), *The Sage encyclopedia of qualitative research methods* (pp. 700–704). Thousand Oaks, CA: Sage.

Burt, C. L. (1941). *The factors of the mind: An introduction to factor-analysis in psychology.* New York: Macmillan.

Cattell, R. B. (1978). *The scientific use of factor analysis in behavioral and life sciences.* New York: Plenum.

Chan, K., & Elliott, R. G. (2004). Relational analysis of personal epistemology and conceptions about teaching and learning. *Teaching and Teacher Education, 20*(8), 817–831.

Cohen, J. (1988). *Statistical power analysis for the behavioral sciences* (2nd ed.). Hillsdale, NJ: Erlbaum.

Duell, O. K., & Schommer-Aikins, M. (2001). Measures of people's beliefs about knowledge and learning. *Educational Psychology Review, 13*(4), 419–449.

Dykstra, D. I., Boyle, C. F., & Monarch, I. A. (1992). Studying conceptual change in learning physics. *Science Education, 76*(6), 615–652.

Elby, A., & Hammer, D. (2001). On the substance of a sophisticated epistemology. *Science Education, 85*(5), 554–567.

Gire, E., Price, E., & Jones, B. (2007). Characterizing the epistemologicai development of physics majors. *AIP Conference Proceedings*, 883(1), 65–68.

Halloun, I., & Hestenes, D. (1998). Interpreting VASS dimensions and profiles for physics students. *Science and Education*, 7(6), 553–577.

Hammer, D., & Elby, A. (2003). Tapping epistemological resources for learning physics. *Journal of the Learning Sciences*, 12(1), 53–90.

Hofer, B. K., & Pintrich, P. R. (2002). *Personal epistemology: The psychology of beliefs about knowledge and knowing*. Mahwah, NJ: Erlbaum.

Howard, D. A. (2005). Albert Einstein as a philosopher of science. *Physics Today*, 58(12), 34–40.

Lising, L. (2005) The impact of epistemology on learning: A case study from introductory physics. *American Journal of Physics*, 73(4), 372–382.

Lising, L., & Elby, A. (2005). The impact of epistemology on learning: A case study from introductory physics. *American Journal of Physics*, 73(4), 372–382.

McKeown, B. (2001). Loss of meaning in Likert scaling: A note on the Q methodological alternative. *Operant Subjectivity*, 24, 201–206.

McKeown, B., & Thomas, D. (1988). *Q methodology*. Newbury Park, CA: Sage.

McNeil, K. A., Newman, I., & Steinhauser, J. (2005). *How to be involved in program evaluation: What every administrator needs to know*. Lanham, MD: Scarecrow Education.

Newman, I. (1971). A multivariate approach to the construction of an attitude battery. Unpublished doctoral dissertation, Southern Illinois University at Carbondale.

Newman, I., & Benz, C. R. (1987). *Multivariate evaluation design: A suggested technique for mental health systems*. Unpublished manuscript. Paper presented to the Ohio Academy of Science, Malone College, Canton, OH.

Newman, I., & Benz, C. R. (1998). *Qualitative-quantitative research methodology: Exploring the interactive continuum*. Carbondale: Southern Illinois University Press.

Newman, I., Dimitrov, D., & Waechter, D. (2000). Factor structure of perceived individualization of instruction: Argument for multiple perspective. *Educational Research Quarterly*, 24, 20–29.

Newman, I., Ridenour, C. S., Newman, C., & DeMarco, G. M. P. Jr. (2003). A typology of research purposes and its relationship to mixed methods. In A. Tashakkori & C. Teddlie (Eds.), *Handbook of mixed methods in social & behavioral research* (pp. 167–188). Thousand Oaks, CA: SAGE.

Nunnally, J. C. (1978). *Psychometric theory* (2nd ed.). New York: McGraw-Hill.

Perkins, K. K., Adams, W. K., Pollock, S. J., Finkelstein, N. D., & Wieman, C. E. (2005). Correlating student beliefs with student learning using the Colorado Learning Attitudes about Science survey. *AIP Conference Proceedings*, 790(1), 61–64.

Perkins, K. K., Gratny, M. M., Adams, W. K., Finkelstein, N. D., & Wieman, C. E. (2006). Towards characterizing the relationship between students' interest in and their beliefs about physics. *AIP Conference Proceedings*, 818(1), 137–140.

Ragin, C. C. (1987). *The comparative method: Moving beyond qualitative and quantitative strategies*. Berkeley: University of California Press.

Ramlo, S. (2003). A multivariate assessment of the effect of the laboratory homework component of a microcomputer-based laboratory for a college freshman physics course. Unpublished doctoral dissertation, The University of Akron, Akron, OH.

Ramlo, S. (2005). An application of Q methodology: Determining college faculty perspectives and consensus regarding the creation of a school of technology. *Journal of Research in Education*, 15(1), 52–69.

Ramlo, S. (2006). A physicist's reflection on Q methodology, quantum mechanics & Stephenson. *Operant Subjectivity*, 29(2), 81–86.

Ramlo, S. (2006/2007). Student views of learning in an introductory college physics course: A study using Q methodology. *Operant Subjectivity*, 30(1 / 2), 52–63.

Ramlo, S. (2007a). Critical thinking and the learning of force and motion concepts. Paper presented at the *American Association of Physics Teachers*, Summer Meeting, Greensboro, NC.

Ramlo, S. (2007b). Physics lab renovation 101. *Physics Teacher, 45*(4), 228–231.

Ramlo, S. (2008a). Determining the various perspectives and consensus within a classroom using Q methodology. *Physics Education Research Conference Proceedings, 1064*(1), 179–182.

Ramlo, S. (2008b). Student perspectives on learning physics and their relationship with learning force and motion concepts: A study using Q methodology. Paper presented at the *Paper Presented at the International Society for the Scientific Study of Subjectivity/ Q Methodology Conference*, Hamilton, Ontario, Canada.

Ramlo, S. (2008c). Student perspectives on learning physics and their relationship with learning force and motion concepts: A study using Q methodology. *Human Subjectivity, 2*(1), 73–90.

Ramlo, S. (2008d). Validity and reliability of the force and motion conceptual evaluation. *American Journal of Physics, 76*(9), 882–886.

Ramlo, S., & McConnell, D. (2008). Perspectives of university faculty regarding faculty reading circles: A study using Q methodology. *Journal of Faculty Development, 22*(1)

Ramlo, S., McConnell, D., Duan, Z., & Moore, F. (2008). Evaluating an inquiry-based bioinformatics course using Q methodology. *Journal of Science Education and Technology, 17*(3), 219–225.

Redish, E. F., Saul, J. M., & Steinberg, R. N. (2000). On the effectiveness of active-engagement microcomputer-based laboratories. *American Journal of Physics, 65*, 45–54.

Ridenour, C. S., & Newman, I. (2008). *Mixed methods research: Exploring the interactive continuum*. Carbondale: Southern Illinois University Press.

Rowlands, S., Graham, T., & Berry, J. (1998). Identifying stumbling blocks in the development of student understanding of moments of forces. *International Journal of Mathematical Education in Science & Technology, 29*(4), 511.

Sauer, T. (2008). Einstein's struggles with quantum theory. *Physics Today, 61*(5), 56–57.

Schmolck, P. (2002). *PQMethod manual mirror.* Unpublished manuscript. Retrieved April 29, 2004, from http://www.rz.unibw-muenchen.de/~p41bsmk/qmethod/

Schommer, M. (1990). Effects of beliefs about the nature of knowledge on comprehension. *Journal of Educational Psychology, 82*, 498–504.

Schraw, G., Bendixen, L. D., & Dunkle, M. E. (2002). Development and validation of the epistemic belief inventory (EBI). In B. K. Hofer & P. R. Pintrich (Eds.), *Personal epistemology: The psychology of beliefs about knowledge and knowing* (pp. 261–277). Mahwah, NJ: Erlbaum.

Siegesmund, R. (2008). Subjectivity. In L. M. Given (Ed.), *The Sage encyclopedia of qualitative research methods* (pp. 843–845). Thousand Oaks, CA: Sage.

Stainton-Rogers, R. (1995). Q methodology. In J. A. Smith, R. Harré & L. van Langenhove (Eds.), *Rethinking methods in psychology* (pp. 178–192). London: Sage.

Stenner, P., & Stainton-Rogers, R. (2004). Q methodology and qualiquantology: The example of discriminating between emotions. In Z. Todd, B. Nerlich, S. McKeown, & D. D. Clarke (Eds.), *Mixing methods in psychology* (pp 101–120). Hove, UK: Psychology Press.

Stephenson, W. (1935). Technique of factor analysis. *Nature, 136*, 297.

Stephenson, W. (1953). *The study of behavior: Q-technique and its methodology.* Chicago: University of Chicago Press.

Stephenson, W. (1982a). Newton's fifth rule and Q methodology: Application to psychoanalysis. *Operant Subjectivity, 5*(4), 127–147.

Stephenson, W. (1982b). Q-methodology, inter-behavioral psychology, and quantum theory. *Psychological Record, 32*(2), 235–248.

Stephenson, W. (1987). *Q methodology: Inter-behavioral and quantum theoretical connections in clinical psychology.* New York; England: Greenwood.

Stephenson, W. (1988). Quantum theory of subjectivity. *Integrative Psychiatry, 6*(3), 180–187.

Stephenson, W., Brown, S. R., & Brenner, D. J. (1972). *Science, psychology, and communication: Essays honoring William Stephenson.* New York: Teachers College Press.

Stephenson, W., & Burt, C. (1939). Alternative views on correlations between persons. *Psychometrika, 4,* 269–281.

Stevens, J. (2002). *Applied multivariate statistics for the social sciences* (4th ed.). Mahwah, NJ: Erlbaum.

Strauss, A. L., & Corbin, J. M. (1990). *Basics of qualitative research: Grounded theory procedures and techniques.* Newbury Park, CA: Sage.

Tashakkori, A., & Teddlie, C. (1998). *Mixed methodology: Combining qualitative and quantitative approaches.* Thousand Oaks, CA: Sage.

Tashakkori, A., & Teddlie, C. (2009). *Foundations of mixed methods research: Integrating quantitative and qualitative approaches in the* social and behavioral sciences. Thousand Oaks, CA: Sage.

Thornton, R. K., & Sokoloff, D. R. (1998). Assessing student learning of Newton's laws: The force and motion conceptual evaluation and the evaluation of active learning laboratory and lecture curricula. *American Journal of Physics, 66*(4), 338–352.

Vantubergen, N. (1975). *QUANAL user's guide (computer program manual).* Lexington: Department of Communication, University of Kentucky.

Waechter, D., Newman, I., & Nolte, D. (1998). Q-factor analysis: The first step in developing typology classifications based upon the Apticom. *Vocational Evaluation and Work Adjustment Journal* (Fall and Winter), 61–66.

Ward, J. H. (1963). Hierarchical grouping to optimize an objective function. *Journal of the American Statistical Association, 58*(301), 236–244.

Watts, S., & Stenner, P. (2005). Doing Q methodology: Theory, method and interpretation. *Qualitative Research in Psychology, 2*(1), 67–91.

ASSESSING THE QUALITY OF MIXED METHODS RESEARCH

Toward a Comprehensive Framework

◆ Alicia O'Cathain

Objectives

- to describe different conceptualizations of quality of mixed methods research;

- to explore gaps within these conceptualizations and contested areas;

- to construct a comprehensive framework for assessing the quality of mixed methods research;

- to test the quality framework by applying it to a mixed methods study; and

- to identify remaining challenges for assessing quality.

How can one judge whether a mixed methods study has been undertaken well or poorly? It is important to assess the quality of mixed methods research, yet currently, there are no accepted criteria for doing so (Creswell & Plano Clark, 2007). A number of scholars have, however, conceptualized the quality of mixed methods research (Bryman, 2006; Bryman, Becker, & Sempik, 2008; Caracelli & Riggin, 1994; Creswell & Plano Clark, 2007; Dellinger & Leech, 2007; O'Cathain, Murphy, & Nicholl, 2008; Onwuegbuzie & Johnson, 2006; Sale & Brazil, 2004; Tashakkori & Teddlie, 2008; Teddlie & Tashakkori, 2003) and indeed have constructed frameworks for quality assessment (Dellinger & Leech, 2007; Teddlie & Tashakkori, 2009). There is a need now to describe these different conceptualizations of quality and identify any gaps in thinking or contested areas, with the aim of producing a comprehensive framework for assessing the quality of mixed methods research.

THE NECESSITY OF A COMPREHENSIVE FRAMEWORK

A framework offers a structured description of a complex issue with the purpose of facilitating understanding. In Chapter 17 of this volume Onwuegbuzie and Combs (2010) set out the reasons why an inclusive framework is necessary for data analysis of mixed methods research. These reasons are highly relevant to a framework for quality assessment, including the need to offer guidance to researchers, to establish a common language, and to provide direction for future development.

To be comprehensive, a framework must include the range of discussions on the topic under study. The framework developed within this chapter is based on a critical review of the literature. The search for literature was wide-ranging to ensure that all disciplines undertaking mixed methods research were represented and that expert thinking in both books and research articles was captured. Constructing the quality framework through a literature review is an approach taken by other researchers addressing the quality of mixed methods research (Pluye, Gagnon, Griffiths, & Johnson-Lafleur, 2009; Sale & Brazil, 2004). Alternative approaches have been taken, in particular conceptualizing quality based on researcher expertise (Teddlie & Tashakkori, 2009) and seeking expert opinion by interviewing individual researchers (Bryman et al., 2008) or undertaking a mapping exercise with a group of researchers (Caracelli & Riggin, 1994). All of these approaches are appropriate and can make complementary contributions to this important topic. With the recent proliferation of methodological publications on mixed methods research, and a growing body of expert researchers, a future priority should be to harness expert opinion through a consensus exercise. Fortunately, this is being addressed through an international Delphi exercise to determine the key quality criteria for mixed methods research (personal communication with Sergi Fabregues Feijoo, assistant professor of qualitative and quantitative research methods, Department of Psychology and Educational Sciences, Open University of Catalonia, Spain).

A comprehensive framework might also be expected to address the needs of the variety of stakeholders who want to assess the quality of mixed methods research (see Figure 21.1). Commissioners of research want to know whether funded studies have addressed the research questions adequately within the allocated resources, that is, delivered the promised goods and gave value for the money. Users of research, such as policymakers, professionals, and lay people, want to know whether they can trust the findings of studies and ultimately take action on them. Research participants want to know whether a study has been a good experience for themselves or others. Teachers of research methods want to communicate core aspects of quality to students of mixed methods research. Researchers want to know

Figure 21.1 Stakeholders Relevant to the Assessment of the Quality of Mixed Methods Research

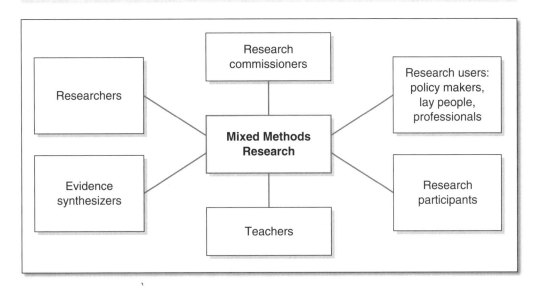

how to design and execute studies that are methodologically sound and credible. Evidence synthesizers want to use a short instrument to help them to grade the quality of studies for inclusion in systematic reviews. Each of these stakeholders has different needs and is likely to be interested in different aspects of the quality of mixed methods research. Although a comprehensive framework will need to accommodate these perspectives, it is unlikely to offer a solution for all these needs. It is also the case that any framework will be shaped by its author and its potential readership; the framework presented here is researcher-focused with the purpose of helping researchers to undertake and assess good mixed methods research.

◆ Reviewing Approaches to Assessing the Quality of Research

Prior to considering the quality of mixed methods research, authors will often describe the accepted criteria for quantitative and qualitative research (Onwuegbuzie & Johnson, 2006; Tashakkori & Teddlie, 2008). This is a useful exercise because it reminds the reader of the established approaches before introducing potential quality criteria for the third methodology (Tashakkori & Teddlie, 2008). In addition, "because researchers collect, analyze, and interpret both forms of data, traditional approaches to validity should not be minimized in mixed methods research" (Creswell & Plano Clark, 2007, p. 146). In this chapter, the discussion of criteria for monomethod studies is deliberately brief to allow more space for discussing mixed methods research. A detailed list of criteria for both qualitative and quantitative research can be found elsewhere (Sale & Brazil, 2004).

QUANTITATIVE RESEARCH

In 2008, Bryman and colleagues presented a set of "traditional criteria for quantitative research" to social policy researchers in the United Kingdom (Bryman et al., 2008). These criteria were validity, reliability, replicability, and generalizability. Some of these are relevant to the measures used within a study, some to the data collection and analysis, and others to the inferences from the study. The social researchers added understandability, transparency, and methods appropriate to the research question as other important quality criteria.

QUALITATIVE RESEARCH

Quality criteria have always been much more contentious for qualitative research. Dellinger and Leech (2007) offer an excellent description of the historical development of such criteria and the differing viewpoints held by researchers from different paradigms, where some researchers adopt criteria from quantitative research and others reject the idea that criteria can be developed for qualitative research. Perhaps the best-known criteria have been developed specifically for qualitative research, addressing the goals of credibility, confirmability, transferability, and dependability (Lincoln & Guba, 1985). Social policy researchers in the United Kingdom added the following to these—transparency, relevance to users, and reflexivity (Bryman et al., 2008).

MIXED METHODS RESEARCH

Three different approaches can be taken to assessing the quality of a mixed methods study: the generic research approach, the individual components approach, and the mixed methods approach.

The Generic Research Approach

Does mixed methods research need its own quality criteria? Surely, it is simply a piece of research, and all research can be assessed in the same way. Assessment can be made of a mixed methods study as a whole, using tools developed for generic use across all study designs including monomethod qualitative studies and monomethod quantitative studies. Eleven tools have been found

that purport to be useful for any design (Katrak, Bialocerkowski, Massy-Westropp, Kumar, & Grimmer, 2004). Evidence synthesizers and users of research may find these helpful because they will need a simple and quick tool to apply to research articles based on a range of research designs to determine whether to include a study within their systematic review (Turner-Stokes, Harding, Sergeant, Lupton, & McPherson, 2006) or take action on the results. Although appealing, generic tools have been found to be too generalist in the nature of their items and to have variable applicability across different research designs (Katrak et al., 2004). In addition, they do not engage with the fact that there may be quality issues specific to mixed methods research. It seems that they do not satisfy the need for quality assessment among most research stakeholders because only evidence synthesizers have applied this type of assessment to mixed methods studies (Turner-Stokes et al., 2006).

The Individual Components Approach

Surely, mixed methods research is simply the sum of its qualitative component and its quantitative component. If so, each component can be assessed to ensure it meets the quality criteria appropriate to that methodology. Bryman describes the use of convergent criteria, where the same criteria are used for both components of a study, and separate criteria, where different criteria are used for each of the qualitative and quantitative components (Bryman, 2006). Researchers taking the latter approach have itemized 33 criteria for assessing qualitative methods and 31 for assessing quantitative methods; they envisaged the final set of mixed methods criteria to be a reduced version of these two lists (Sale & Brazil, 2004). A similar approach has been taken in an evidence synthesis study where the qualitative articles were assessed using criteria deemed appropriate to qualitative research, the quantitative articles were assessed using criteria appropriate to quantitative research, and mixed methods articles were divided into their qualitative and quantitative components and each component assessed separately (Pluye, Grad, Dunikowski, & Stephenson, 2005).

Before considering the usefulness of this approach, two issues are worth exploring. The first is whether it is appropriate to apply criteria to each methodological *approach* or to each *method* used. For example, researchers assessing the quality of a mixed methods study involving focus groups, followed by a survey, might apply criteria developed for qualitative research to the focus group component and quantitative research to the survey. Or they might apply criteria devised specifically for focus groups and those devised specifically for surveys. This latter approach may not be possible because agreed quality criteria are not necessarily available for all methods, and it may also be challenging if five different methods are employed within a single mixed methods project. However it may be necessary if a method in use is always judged by an agreed set of criteria; a key example of this is the randomized controlled trial in health research (Moher et al., 1995).

The second issue involves the assumption made by some researchers that methods are linked to paradigms—quantitative methods to positivism and qualitative methods to constructivism—and therefore the criteria used to assess different methods should also be linked to paradigms (Sale & Brazil, 2004). Researchers have contested the view that methods are linked to paradigms (Bryman, 1988) and thus that different criteria are needed to assess qualitative and quantitative research (Murphy, Dingwall, Greatbatch, Parker, & Watson, 1998). The same criteria may be relevant, although the appropriate means for judging against these criteria may differ because of the research practices employed in different methodological approaches (Murphy et al., 1998). There has been some empirical exploration of whether to use the same criteria for both qualitative and quantitative research, specifically whether quantitative criteria should be applied to qualitative

research (Bryman et al., 2008): 76% of 226 researchers reported that criteria should be separate and different.

So what is the way forward? Quality assessment of the qualitative and quantitative components of a study is essential because each contributes to the study as a whole. It is also important because concerns have been expressed that the quality of one or both components may suffer as a direct consequence of being part of a mixed methods study (Chen, 1997); the resources in terms of time, money, and attention required for a number of methods may lead to the production of research that is underdeveloped or under analyzed (Silverman, 2000; Steckler, Mcleroy, Goodman, Bird, & McCormick, 1992). However, this individual methods approach ignores the fact that there is more to a mixed methods study than its qualitative and quantitative components (Creswell & Plano Clark, 2007). For example, inferences are drawn from the whole mixed methods study—meta-inferences—not simply from each component (Tashakkori & Teddlie, 2008).

The Mixed Methods Approach

Attempts have been made to develop quality criteria that address the whole mixed methods study rather than simply the individual components within it—Bryman (2006) calls this the "bespoke" approach where criteria are developed especially for mixed methods studies. The first documented attempt at this focused on mixed methods evaluation. Researchers identified 94 quality criteria, 20 of which were specific to a mixed methods approach (Caracelli & Riggin, 1994). The 20 mixed methods-specific items clustered into four domains—design, data quality and analysis, bias, and interpretation. Examples of items included whether data transformations were defensible, contradictory findings were explained, and convergent findings were not related to shared bias between methods.

Nearly a decade later, two leading scholars in the field proposed what is still the most comprehensive approach to assessing the quality of mixed methods research (Tashakkori & Teddlie, 2003), and they continued to expand and deepen understanding of their original model (Tashakkori & Teddlie, 2008; Teddlie & Tashakkori, 2009). Tashakkori and Teddlie introduced the concept of *inference quality*, which is a combination of design quality (methodological rigor) and interpretive rigor (authenticity of conclusions from the study). During this period, other researchers produced further conceptualizations of quality, either explicitly building on the Tashakkori and Teddlie model (Dellinger & Leech, 2007; Onwuegbuzie & Johnson, 2006) or undertaking separate endeavors (Creswell & Plano Clark, 2007; O'Cathain et al., 2008).

Onwuegbuzie and Johnson (2006) argued that the Tashakkori and Teddlie model tended to view inference quality as an outcome and that it was essential also to view it as a process, that is, to consider how inferences were drawn as well as the inferences themselves. This led them to add nine types of quality assessment of meta-inferences to the Tashakkori and Teddlie model, including *sample integration legitimation* and *paradigmatic mixing legitimation* (Onwuegbuzie & Johnson, 2006). Teddlie and Tashakkori (2009) did not agree that their conceptualization was limited to quality as an outcome and later argued that they viewed inferences as both processes (steps followed to create meaning) and outcomes (conclusions). Within the same time period, Dellinger and Leech (2007) focused on the meaning of validity in the context of mixed methods research, bringing together Tashakkori and Teddlie's concept of inference quality and Onwuegbuzie and Johnson's nine aspects of quality, while adding their own concept of *foundational element*, which they present as a reflection on researchers' prior understanding of the issue under study. They argue that a researcher's prior understanding of a phenomenon, gained through reviewing the literature, shapes the research study and the findings and interpretation.

Other scholars have taken a "threats minimization" approach (Creswell & Plano Clark, 2007, pp. 145–149), focused on the extent to which attention is paid to the mixed methods knowledge base (Creswell & Plano Clark, 2007, pp. 162–165), or considered the transparency of reporting (O'Cathain et al., 2008). In the first approach, the researcher must consider potential threats to validity that arise during data collection and analysis (Creswell & Plano Clark, 2007). These threats are design specific and include inadequate data transformation in concurrent designs and use of the same sample sizes for qualitative and quantitative data collection in sequential designs. Creswell and Plano Clark (2007) go on to discuss *mixed methods standards*, where the researcher must draw on the mixed methods knowledge base, for example, showing sensitivity to the challenges of using their mixed methods design. O'Cathain and colleagues (2008) constructed quality criteria for the different aspects of mixed methods studies, namely the design, individual components, integration, and inferences. After applying these to a set of mixed methods studies, they concluded that a lack of transparency while reporting studies hindered quality assessment. They developed a set of criteria for good reporting of a mixed methods study (GRAMMS), based on Creswell's (2003) earlier guidance for writing a proposal for a mixed methods study.

The conceptualizations of quality from these six groups of researchers have been used explicitly when constructing a quality framework for mixed methods research (Caracelli & Riggin, 1994; Creswell & Plano Clark, 2007; Dellinger & Leech, 2007; O'Cathain et al., 2008; Onwuegbuzie & Johnson, 2006; Tashakkori & Teddlie, 2008). Given the centrality of Tashakkori and Teddlie's model to the thinking of most of these groups and the comprehensiveness of their approach, it is placed at the core of the framework, and then the contributions of the other five groups are assessed in terms of expanding or challenging this core framework.

Prior to presenting the framework, general issues affecting any framework are explored.

◆ Key Issues to Consider Before Constructing the Framework

The language of quality. Language has been identified as a challenging aspect of mixed methods research in general (Teddlie & Tashakkori, 2003), and this is highly relevant to the assessment of quality. A language has developed over many years for qualitative and quantitative research, and the quality assessment of both. There is an issue about whether researchers should attempt to use this existing language or create a new language for mixed methods research. The difficulty with using existing language is that it is embedded in the politics of research methods, and therefore, the use of a term associated with one methodology may alienate researchers more aligned with the other methodology. The difficulty

with using a new language is that there is yet more terminology for the poor researcher—and other stakeholders—to understand (Figure 21.2). An excellent solution to this dilemma has been proposed, recommending that researchers introduce new terms only when they have good reason to do so (Tashakkori & Teddlie, 2003, p. 673), for example, when existing terms have been overly used or misused.

Researchers have already introduced a number of terms for the concept of quality in mixed methods research. As Maxwell and Mittapalli (2010) point out in Chapter 6 of this volume, *validity* has been rejected by some mixed methods scholars, either because it is overused and therefore meaningless (Teddlie & Tashakkori, 2009) or because it is routinely used in quantitative research and therefore disliked by qualitative researchers (Onwuegbuzie & Johnson, 2006). New language of *inference quality* (Teddlie & Tashakkori, 2009) and *legitimation* (Onwuegbuzie & Johnson, 2006) has been introduced to replace validity as an overarching term. There is, however,

Figure 21.2 The Language of Quality

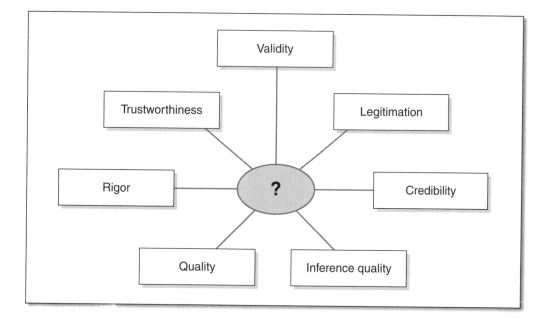

disagreement on this point, with other scholars recommending the continued use of the term *validity* in mixed methods research because it is applied in both qualitative and quantitative research (Creswell & Plano Clark, 2007). There has been further rejection of another overarching term, *rigor,* in favor of *validation* (Giddings & Grant, 2009). The mixed methods community may wish to welcome this diversity, celebrating the variety of language because it reflects a variety of paradigmatic values. However, more consistency of language may facilitate learning and the simple term *quality* might be more helpful for those wishing to assess a mixed methods study as either good or poor.

The assessed and the assessor. When quality is considered, there is an assumption that the completed study is being assessed—either the final report or the publications emerging from a study. However, stakeholders also need to assess the quality of research proposals, and a framework needs also to work in this context. Some researchers have explicitly excluded criteria for a proposal when considering quality (Sale & Brazil, 2004), whereas others have described the content of a good mixed methods proposal (Creswell, 2003). Consideration needs also to be given to the assessor. It cannot be assumed that all assessors will have the expertise to consider all the quality criteria within a framework (Pluye et al., 2009) or that all assessors will share a methodological background or perspective.

One size fits all. Quality criteria may differ by paradigms and mixed methods design (Creswell & Plano Clark, 2007). It is unlikely that any one set of criteria will suit all researchers or all studies; that is, a contingency position will be required (Bryman, 2006).

Paradigms. Quality criteria are likely to depend on researchers' philosophical and political paradigms (Bryman, 2006). For example, researchers undertaking a transformational mixed methods study would want the community affected to be involved in methodological decisions (Mertens, 2003) and judge a study as poor quality if this did not occur. Giddings and Grant (2009) discuss aspects of quality relevant to mixed methods research undertaken in different paradigms, although not all paradigms common to this approach are included, in particular pragmatism. In Chapter 6 of this volume Maxwell and Mittapalli (2010) describe the realist perspective on validity and its value to mixed methods researchers. Researchers from some paradigms may not want to engage with the framework presented below or may value some aspects of the framework more than others, with some rejecting the idea that a framework is desirable or possible.

Design. Can all mixed methods designs be assessed using the same criteria? A number of researchers have pointed out that criteria may need to be design specific (Bryman, 2006; Sale & Brazil, 2004) and indeed have developed design-specific criteria (Creswell & Plano Clark, 2007). Some criteria will be dependent on the purpose of combining methods (completeness or confirmation), the timing of methods (sequential, concurrent), and the priority of methods. For example, if the purpose of a study is triangulation (with the meaning of convergence), then the qualitative and quantitative methods need to be undertaken concurrently and independently (Caracelli & Riggin, 1994). For some dominant–less dominant designs, it has been proposed that the quality criteria associated with the dominant method is used to assess both components of a study (Bryman, 2006). In addition, there is an interesting debate about whether the full set of quality criteria must be applied to the less dominant method of a study. This may be necessary when a less dominant component addresses independently an aspect of the research question. However, when one component is supplementary with a sole aim of supporting the dominant component (for example, the role of a qualitative component is to develop a questionnaire only), it may not be appropriate to subject the supplementary component to full quality assessment. This may not be relevant to some definitions of mixed methods research, which exclude this supplementary use of one method.

◆ Proposing a Quality Framework

Having reviewed the approaches taken by researchers when considering the quality of mixed methods research, Tashakkori and Teddlie (2008) appear to offer the most helpful structure for a framework. As stated earlier, their model is placed at the core of

the framework presented in Figure 21.3 (pages 541–544), with the addition of the contributions of other researchers. The concept of inference quality from the Tashakkori and Teddlie model has been replaced with *quality* because although a research team's inferences—and the quality of data on which they are based—must be assessed, methodological rigor should be assessed independently from inferences because if it is good, then stakeholders outside the research team can develop their own inferences and test the interpretative rigor of them. The framework is structured using Caracelli and Riggin's *domains of quality* because they accommodate the range of quality issues discussed by researchers. The domains and items within them are explained below and applied to a mixed methods study described in Box 21.1.

Example Mixed Methods Study: Evaluation of Evidence-Based Leaflets to Promote Informed Choice in Maternity Care

Ten pairs of leaflets were designed to summarize research evidence and promote informed choice around 10 decisions women face in maternity care. One of each pair was written for women having babies and the other for midwives and other health professionals. Examples of the topics covered were whether to have an ultrasound scan, whether to have the baby in hospital or at home, and which position to adopt during the birth.

A during-trial mixed methods intervention design was used to evaluate the leaflets (Creswell, Fetters, Plano Clark, & Morales, 2009). A randomized controlled trial (RCT) was undertaken to address the effectiveness of the leaflets in promoting women's perceptions of making informed choices during their care. A concurrent ethnographic study focused on how informed choice occurred in maternity care units. The trial was a pragmatic cluster RCT in 10 maternity units in Wales, which is a country within the United Kingdom, with 5 units randomly allocated to receive the leaflets and 5 offering usual care.

The conclusion of the RCT was that the leaflets were not effective in promoting informed choice. The ethnographic study was undertaken in all 10 units, with observation of ante-natal consultations and interviews with women, midwives, and obstetricians. The conclusion of the ethnographic study was that a culture of informed compliance operated rather than one of informed choice, that is, the culture was not conducive to leaflets promoting informed choice.

(Continued)

(Continued)

The study was written up in a final report to funders and in a series of journal articles and book chapters. The key articles were a pair of papers published side by side in the same journal, one reporting the RCT (O'Cathain, Walters, Nicholl, Thomas, & Kirkham, 2002) and one reporting the ethnographic study (Stapleton, Kirkham, & Thomas, 2002).

DOMAIN 1: PLANNING QUALITY

The first domain addresses how well a mixed methods study has been planned. It can be argued that if attention is not paid to planning the study as a mixed methods design then the study may fail to deliver. This domain is applicable to a research proposal and has four items:

1. The *foundational element* was introduced by Dellinger and Leech (2007). They argue that a comprehensible and critical review of the literature is needed to situate the study, with the research question and study design shaped by the literature review. Caracelli and Riggin (1994) also allude to this when they require the design to be guided by a conceptual framework. Foundational element is also important at the end of a study to situate the findings and indeed may sit appropriately under *interpretive rigor*.

2. *Rationale transparency*—offering a justification for using a mixed methods approach—has been recommended by both Caracelli and Riggin (1994) and Creswell (2003). This is particularly important in the context of strategic use of mixed methods research (Bryman 2007; O'Cathain, Murphy, & Nicholl, 2007), where researchers use mixed methods for the purpose of gaining funding, for example, rather than for its intrinsic value for addressing the research question. This strategic use may lead to neglect of one of the study components, a lack of attention to integration, and no attempt at production of meta-inferences. This item is one of many in the framework related to transparency because researchers identify this as an important aspect of quality (Bryman et al., 2008).

3. *Planning transparency* is where key aspects of the study including paradigm, design, data collection, analysis, and reporting are detailed in the proposal. Creswell (2003) offers an excellent framework for writing a proposal for a mixed methods study. Many of the issues he recommends for detailed description in research proposals are also relevant to later domains in the framework presented here.

4. A planned study must be *feasible*. Looking at research proposals of mixed methods studies, evidence has been found of large qualitative components planned for execution in short time frames (O'Cathain et al., 2008). Feasibility is not simply an issue for each component of a study but also for the design; it may not be feasible to complete a sequential mixed methods design within a short time frame. Time is not the only resource of importance; there must be enough money, researchers, and expertise available to deliver the study.

Applying these items to the study described in Box 21.1 is difficult because it is a completed study, and this domain is relevant to researchers wishing to write a good proposal and funding agencies wishing to assess whether a proposal is good. However, rationale transparency should also be apparent at the publication stage of a study. Some explanation is given in the article from the qualitative component of the study of why both a quantitative and a qualitative component were necessary: "The effectiveness of these leaflets has been studied in a

Text continued on page 545.

Figure 21.3 Quality Framework for Mixed Methods Research

Stage of Study	Domains of Quality	Items Within Domain	Definition of Item	Source of Domain and Items
Planning	Planning quality	Foundational element	Comprehensible and critical review of the literature is needed to situate the study and shape both the research question and methods.	Dellinger & Leech (2007)
		Rationale transparency	Justification for using a mixed methods approach is provided.	Caracelli & Riggin (1994) Creswell (2003)
		Planning transparency	Details should be given about the paradigm, planned design, data collection, analysis and reporting according to Creswell's guide for a good proposal.	Creswell (2003)
		Feasibility	The design, and each component, can be undertaken in the resources (time, money, manpower) available.	O'Cathain, Murphy, & Nicholl (2008)
Undertaking	Design quality	Design transparency	Description of design type from known typology, or key aspects of design, if known typologies do not describe design used.	Creswell & Plano Clark (2007) O'Cathain et al. (2008)
		Design suitability	The design is appropriate for addressing the overall research question, matches the reason for combining methods, and is appropriate for the stated paradigm.	Teddlie & Tashakkori (2009) Creswell & Plano Clark (2007) Caracelli & Riggin (1994) Onwuegbuzie & Johnson (2006)
		Design strength	The strengths and weaknesses of methods are considered to minimize shared bias and optimize the breadth and depth of the study.	Caracelli & Riggin (1994) Onwuegbuzie & Johnson (2006)
		Design rigor	Methods are implemented in a way that remains true to the design.	Creswell & Plano Clark (2007) Caracelli & Riggin (1994)

(Continued)

Figure 21.3 (Continued)

Stage of Study	Domains of Quality	Items Within Domain	Definition of Item	Source of Domain and Items
Undertaking	Data quality	Data transparency	Each of the methods is described in sufficient detail, including its role within the study.	Creswell & Plano Clark (2007) O'Cathain et al. (2008)
		Data rigor/design fidelity	The extent to which methods are implemented with rigor.	Creswell & Plano Clark (2007) Teddlie & Tashakkori (2009)
		Sampling adequacy	Sampling technique and sample size for each method are adequate in the context of the design.	Creswell & Plano Clark (2007) Onwuegbuzie & Johnson (2006)
		Analytic adequacy	Data analysis techniques are appropriate for the research question and are undertaken properly.	Teddlie & Tashakkori (2009)
		Analytic integration rigor	Any integration taking place at the analysis stage of a study is robust, e.g., data transformations are defensible.	Caracelli & Riggin (1994) Onwuegbuzie & Johnson (2006) O'Cathain et al. (2008) Creswell & Plano Clark (2007)
Interpreting	Interpretive rigor (Conclusions are based on the findings)	Interpretive transparency	It is clear which findings have emerged from which methods.	O'Cathain et al. (2008)
		Interpretive consistency	Inferences are consistent with the findings on which they are based.	Teddlie & Tashakkori (2009)
		Theoretical consistency	Inferences are consistent with current knowledge or theory.	Teddlie & Tashakkori (2009) Dellinger & Leech (2007)
		Interpretive agreement	Others are likely to reach the same conclusions based on the findings presented, including other researchers and participants.	Teddlie & Tashakkori (2009) Onwuegbuzie & Johnson (2006)

Stage of Study	Domains of Quality	Items Within Domain	Definition of Item	Source of Domain and Items
		Interpretive distinctiveness	Conclusions drawn are more credible than any other conclusions.	Teddlie & Tashakkori (2009)
		Interpretive efficacy	Meta-inferences from the whole study adequately incorporate inferences from the qualitative and quantitative findings and inferences.	Teddlie & Tashakkori (2009) Onwuegbuzie & Johnson (2006) O'Cathain et al. (2008)
		Interpretive bias reduction	Explanations are given for inconsistencies between findings and inferences.	Caracelli & Riggin (1994) Creswell & Plano Clark (2007) Teddlie & Tashakkori (2009)
		Interpretive correspondence	Inferences correspond to the purpose of the study, the overall research question, and the research questions within this.	Teddlie & Tashakkori (2009)
Interpreting	Inference transferability (Where conclusions can be applied to)	Ecological transferability	Transferability to other contexts and settings.	Tashakkori & Teddlie (2003, 2008, 2009)
		Population transferability	Transferability to other groups and individuals.	
		Temporal transferability	Transferability to the future.	
		Theoretical transferability	Transferability to other methods of measuring behavior.	

(Continued)

Figure 21.3 (Continued)

Stage of Study	Domains of Quality	Items Within Domain	Definition of Item	Source of Domain and Items
Disseminating	Reporting quality	Report availability	Study is successfully completed within allocated resources of time, money, and staff.	Datta (1997)
		Reporting transparency	Key aspects of study reported, according to GRAMMS	Caracelli & Riggin (1994) Creswell & Plano Clark (2007) O'Cathain et al. (2008)
		Yield	Whole more than the sum of the parts.	O'Cathain, Murphy, & Nicholl (2007)
Application in the real world	Synthesizability (Of sufficient quality for inclusion in systematic reviews)	15 quality criteria: 6 for qualitative research 3 for quantitative experimental 3 for quantitative observational 3 for mixed methods	An example criterion is "justification of the mixed methods design."	Pluye, Gagnon, Griffiths, & Johnson-Lafleur (2009)
	Utility	Utility quality	The findings are used by consumers and policy makers.	Caracelli & Riggin (1994) Datta (1997) Dellinger & Leech (2007) Onwuegbuzie & Johnson (2006) Tashakkori &Teddlie (2009)

randomized controlled trial. . . . To understand the social context in which the leaflets were used we undertook qualitative research alongside, but independently of, the randomized trial" (p. 639).

DOMAIN 2: DESIGN QUALITY

Design quality is a key component of the Tashakkori and Teddlie model. They propose four criteria within it—design suitability, design fidelity, within-design consistency, and analytic adequacy. In the framework presented in Figure 21.3, design is separated from data collection. Therefore design fidelity and analytic adequacy are moved to Domain 3 on data collection and analysis. Further items, from the work of other researchers, are added to the two remaining Tashakkori and Teddlie criteria:

1. *Design transparency* has been raised as an important aspect of quality in mixed methods studies (Creswell & Plano Clark, 2007; O'Cathain et al., 2008). To offer transparency, a design type may be described from one of the typologies available, or key aspects of the design may be described, given that it is sometimes a challenge to find a design type that fully describes a study in practice. Aspects of design that should be described are priority of approaches, purpose of combining methods, sequencing of methods, and stage at which integration takes place. Creswell and Plano Clark (2007) recommend a visual diagram of the design to facilitate transparency.

2. *Design suitability* or appropriateness has been put forward within the Tashakkori and Teddlie model and by a number of other scholars. The design must be appropriate for addressing the overall research question. Each method must also be appropriate for addressing research questions within the overarching research question. The design must match the stated purpose for combining methods, as well as the research question (Caracelli & Riggin, 1994; Teddlie

& Tashakkori, 2009). Finally, the design must fit with any stated paradigm—called *paradigmatic mixing legitimation* (Onwuegbuzie & Johnson, 2006).

3. *Design strength* is based mainly on items from Caracelli and Riggin (1994), with some input from Onwuegbuzie and Johnson (2006). They are concerned that researchers design studies that optimize breadth (associated with quantitative research) and depth (associated with qualitative research); consciously consider how the weakness of one method is compensated by the strengths of the other (called *weakness minimization legitimation* by Onwuegbuzie & Johnson, 2006); and select methods to minimize shared bias. This may be design specific, for example, that methods used for different but complementary purposes enable a more comprehensive study (Caracelli & Riggin, 1994).

4. *Design rigor* is where the methods are implemented in a way that remains true to the design (Creswell & Plano Clark, 2007). For example, rigor is compromised in triangulation designs if methods are not implemented concurrently and independently (Caracelli & Riggin, 1994). Creswell and Plano Clark (2007) offer design-specific recommendations for attaining rigor in concurrent and sequential designs.

Applying this domain to the example in Box 21.1, the design is not transparent within the journal articles, and the study fails to meet this quality item. The design was a randomized controlled trial and ethnographic study undertaken concurrently with the purpose of complementarity. Within a typology of mixed methods intervention studies, it is now known as a "during-trial" design (Creswell, Fetters, Plano Clark, & Morales, 2009). This design was appropriate for addressing the overall research question of understanding the effectiveness of evidenced-based leaflets in maternity care. However, this overall research question is never stated within the journal articles from the study. The individual questions addressed by the qualitative and quantitative methods are stated, and each method is suitable for addressing its question (see planning quality). The methods fit together, sitting side by side as they address separate but interrelated research questions. The design strength is very good—the trial offers measurement of the effectiveness of the leaflets across five maternity units, and the ethnographic study offers depth of understanding of the culture in which the leaflets were used. The approach to minimization of bias is not obvious for this design. Paradigms are never discussed and therefore paradigmatic legitimation cannot be assessed. The design required that two methods were implemented to a high quality, and this occurred, but generally, design rigor is questionable due to the lack of transparency about the design and therefore the explicit attention paid to design rigor. In particular, did the design require that data sharing occur between qualitative and quantitative researchers throughout the study or only at the interpretation stage? In conclusion, the study is assessed poorly on this domain due to a lack of attention paid generally to the mixed methods design.

DOMAIN 3: DATA QUALITY

The domain of data quality includes data collection and analysis and has five items:

1. *Data transparency* is where each of the methods is described in detail, including its role within the study, data collection, sampling, sample size, and analysis (Creswell & Plano Clark, 2007; O'Cathain et al., 2008).

2. *Data rigor*—or *design fidelity*—concerns the extent to which methods are implemented with rigor (Teddlie & Tashakkori, 2009). Here it is important to consider whether a method has been compromised because it is part of a mixed methods study (O'Cathain et al., 2008). It may not be as developed as it needs to be due to lack of resources. For example, a

Delphi technique only has two rounds because it was part of a sequential mixed methods study, and there was not time for the three rounds considered appropriate for the research question. Creswell and Plano Clark (2007) identify potential threats to validity at the data collection stage of two key mixed methods designs.

3. *Sampling adequacy* is where the sampling technique and sample size are adequate for each method in the context of the design (Creswell & Plano Clark, 2007). This is extremely important for the later domains of interpretive rigor and inference transferability because *sample integration legitimation* impacts on the quality of any meta-inferences (Onwuegbuzie & Johnson, 2006). Researchers may find themselves generalizing their findings inappropriately because they have not paid attention to the type of sample and sample size required for each method (e.g., large random sample for quantitative component) or the relationship between the qualitative and quantitative samples.

4. *Analytic adequacy* means that data analysis techniques are appropriate for the research question and undertaken properly (Teddlie & Tashakkori, 2009). For example, the right statistical tests have been used for the quantitative component.

5. *Analytic integration rigor* applies to the quality of any integration taking place at the analysis stage of a study. This might involve data transformation of qualitative data to quantitative data, or more rarely, quantitative data to qualitative data. It might also involve the use of findings from one component of a study to guide the analysis of another component, or placing both types of data in a matrix for within-case and across-case analysis. It is really a part of analytic adequacy but is presented separately here because so many scholars have identified it as a challenge specific to mixed methods research. Data conversion quality in particular has concerned a number of scholars (Caracelli & Riggin,

1994; Creswell & Plano Clark, 2007), including its impact on meta-inferences (Onwuegbuzie & Johnson, 2006). Helpful guidance is emerging on quantitizing, the most common approach to data conversion (Sandelowski, Voils, & Knafl, 2009).

Applying this domain to the example in Box 21.1, data transparency, data rigor, sampling adequacy, and analytic adequacy all appear to be excellent for each method. There is no integration at the analysis stage, and so the analytic integration rigor item is not relevant. The lack of any integration between components, including inferences from both the qualitative and quantitative findings, means that the effect of sampling adequacy on meta-inferences will be irrelevant for the next two domains.

DOMAIN 4: INTERPRETIVE RIGOR

The quality of inferences is very important to users of research, who must find them credible and trustworthy if they are to take action on them (Tashakkori & Teddlie, 1998). Researchers have considered the complexity of this issue (Miller, 2003), and a call has been made for standards for the evaluation of the accuracy or authenticity of conclusions from mixed methods studies (Tashakkori & Teddlie, 2003). Interpretive rigor considers whether conclusions are based on the findings of the study, with the following eight items:

1. *Interpretive transparency* is where it is clear which findings have emerged from which methods (O'Cathain et al., 2008). Without this, links cannot be made between data quality and inferences.

2. *Interpretive consistency* concerns whether inferences are consistent with the findings on which they are based (Teddlie & Tashakkori, 2009). In addition, a number of inferences may be drawn from a small set of findings, and these inferences must be consistent with each other.

3. *Theoretical consistency* is where the inferences are consistent with current knowledge or theory (Teddlie & Tashakkori, 2009). Dellinger and Leech (2007) acknowledge that their *inferential consistency,* where inferences are consistent with what was already known, is very similar to this.

4. *Interpretive agreement* means that others are likely to reach the same conclusions based on the findings presented, including other researchers and study participants (Teddlie & Tashakkori, 2009). The process by which this is attained may be inside-outside legitimation, where meta-inferences are considered by peer review of an outside party and member checking for an insider view so that inferences do not rely only on the research team (Onwuegbuzie & Johnson, 2006).

5. *Interpretive distinctiveness* considers whether the conclusions drawn are more credible than any other conclusions (Teddlie & Tashakkori, 2009). A researcher must be able to discount other possible interpretations. Strategies for achieving this for the individual components within a mixed methods study include negative case analysis in the qualitative research and controlling for variables in the quantitative research.

6. *Interpretive efficacy* is where the meta-inferences from the whole study adequately incorporate inferences from the qualitative and quantitative findings and inferences (Teddlie & Tashakkori, 2009). Other researchers have given consideration to the balance of inferences from different components of a study (Caracelli & Riggin, 1994; O'Cathain et al., 2008; Onwuegbuzie & Johnson 2006). Onwuegbuzie and Johnson (2006) call an aspect of this *political legitimation* and describe a violation of this when different researchers undertake the qualitative and quantitative components, which then affects the conclusions drawn if one is more powerful or likely to interpret contradictions in data and findings in a particular way. This draws attention to who does the integration (O'Cathain et al., 2008) and also

the extent to which processes of integration are visible within journal articles emerging from a study. Another aspect of what could also be called inference balance is sample integration legitimation, where attention is paid to the way in which individuals are sampled for each component when making meta-inferences (Onwuegbuzie & Johnson, 2006).

7. *Interpretive bias reduction* is a criterion within Tashakkori and Teddlie's interpretive efficacy. It has been drawn out here because a number of researchers have discussed this as an important aspect of quality (Erzberger & Kelle, 2003). Teddlie and Tashakkori (2009) request that explanations are given for inconsistencies between inferences. Caracelli and Riggin (1994) recommend that interpretation of the data collected by different methods should consider bias of the methods, in particular that nonconvergent findings are plausibly explained and that convergent findings are not the result of shared bias between the methods. Further exploration of contradictory findings may be particularly important for concurrent designs (Creswell & Plano Clark, 2007).

8. *Interpretive correspondence* means that inferences correspond to the purpose of the study, the overall research question, and the research questions within this (Teddlie & Tashakkori, 2009). The extent to which the researchers have answered their research question and met any other goals of the research must be assessed.

Applying these to the example in Box 21.1, the study performed well on some of the items within this domain. The interpretive transparency was excellent due to the separate reporting of the qualitative and quantitative components of the study; this made it obvious which findings were related to which methods. There was also interpretive consistency in that inferences were consistent with the findings on which they were based. For the trial, the inference was that the leaflets were not

effective, and the findings clearly showed that there was no clinically significant change in the primary outcome measure and most of the secondary outcome measures; for the ethnography, the inference was that the leaflets were operating in the unhelpful context of informed compliance rather than informed choice, and findings supported this in that health professionals framed information to steer women to specific decisions. There was also interpretive correspondence in that inferences addressed the original research question, and the goal of the research was fulfilled. A very interesting item for this study was theoretical consistency because the inference from the quantitative component was not consistent with current knowledge at the time of publication, in that trials tended to show that these types of decision aids improved decision-making processes. However, explicit attention was paid to this in the journal article, with authors emphasizing that the trial was pragmatic, and previous knowledge was based on explanatory trials. That is, attention to theoretical consistency had shaped the inferences drawn and their reporting.

It was difficult to assess some items in this domain because it was not obvious from reading the articles that interpretive agreement or distinctiveness had occurred. Based on personal knowledge of the study, there was an advisory group of external researchers, maternity care providers, and maternity groups, and there was also peer review of the draft final report, which may have helped to develop interpretive agreement. Interpretive efficacy required balance of inferences from the qualitative and quantitative findings. Because there was no attempt to produce meta-inferences, balance of inferences could not be considered. In conclusion, the interpretive rigor of each component of the study appeared to be very good. However, the lack of attention to meta-inferences was problematic, and thus, the study failed to use the strengths of a mixed methods approach.

DOMAIN 5: INFERENCE TRANSFERABILITY

Tashakkori and Teddlie have proposed the extremely useful concept of inference transferability for mixed methods research—the degree to which the conclusions can be applied to other entities or settings. This is equivalent to *external validity* for quantitative research and *transferability* for qualitative research (Teddlie & Tashakkori, 2003). Inferences can be drawn from each component of a study, with external validity/generalizability considered for the quantitative component and transferability considered for the qualitative component. Mixed methods studies also have meta-inferences, which are the inferences from the whole study rather than simply the individual components. Teddlie and Tashakkori (2009) propose four types of transferability: ecological (transferability to other contexts and settings), population (transferability to other groups and individuals), temporal (transferability to the future), and theoretical (transferability to other methods of measuring behavior).

Taking the example in Box 21.1, inference transferability cannot be considered using the journal articles from the study because the qualitative and quantitative components were published separately. The journal article from the quantitative component paid little attention to generalizability. However, there was transparency of sampling and description of the sample to allow the reader to consider generalizability. The main issue was the sampling of maternity units—there was a mixture of small and large units in a single country, Wales. The study was generalizable to different sizes of maternity units but not necessarily to other countries in the United Kingdom and the rest of the world, unless maternity care operated in a similar way in these countries. Transferability was not considered explicitly in the qualitative article, although there was transparency of sampling and description of participants to allow the reader to draw conclusions about

this. The qualitative component identified the importance of culture within maternity units, which was not conducive to promoting the outcome important to the leaflets. The inference from the quantitative component was that leaflets were not effective in promoting informed choice. The inference from the qualitative component was that the maternity units did not operate a culture of informed choice but rather one of informed compliance. The meta-inference—never explicitly stated in the journal articles emerging from the study–was that leaflets were not effective in maternity units with a culture of informed compliance. The qualitative component offered important information to allow research users to consider whether leaflets might work for them. If they considered that a culture of informed compliance rather than informed choice was in operation in their country, or maternity unit, then they could transfer the findings of the RCT to their context and not purchase leaflets for their service users.

DOMAIN 6: REPORTING QUALITY

1. *Report availability* is a factor in that those who commission research will judge quality by whether a study has been successfully completed, and this has occurred within the allocated resources of time, money, and staff (Datta, 1997). This item is relevant to all types of studies but may be more important to ask of mixed methods research because these studies may be more complex and more expensive than other types. Datta describes a failed mixed methods study where the final comprehensive report was delayed for many years, the cost overrun was high, there was staff burnout, expectations were not met, and only some parts of the study were reported (Datta, 1997).

2. *Reporting transparency* means that key aspects of the study are clearly and explicitly reported. If they are not, then

assessment cannot be made of the above quality domains. Researchers writing up their studies may wish to follow guidelines on good reporting of a mixed methods study (GRAMMS) (O'Cathain et al., 2008). Creswell and Plano Clark (2007) promote the need for attention to key aspects of the mixed methods knowledge base, and underlying this is the need for transparency. Caracelli and Riggin (1994) also identified the need to report findings in a way that maximizes the interest of stakeholders.

3. *Yield* refers to the knowledge gained from a mixed methods study over and above the knowledge gained from undertaking two independent qualitative and quantitative studies (O'Cathain et al., 2007). This may not occur within a study because researchers fail to integrate different components of a study or to make what is learned from integration explicit within their report of a study.

For the example study in Box 21.1, the report was available within a few months of the study ending. The report itself was published by an external body, which increased its availability, and a number of journal articles emerged from the study. Although reporting of each component was transparent within journal articles, there was no transparency of the mixed methods aspects of the study such as design and integration. Therefore, the yield of the study was the sum of its parts. A simple integration of findings to produce a meta-inference from the study would have been of considerable benefit.

DOMAIN 7: SYNTHESIZABILITY

In health research, there is a tradition of synthesizing evidence on the effectiveness of drugs and other treatments. This usually involves systemically searching for all randomized controlled trials of the treatment under study, undertaking a quality assessment of each trial by scoring quality using a validated set of criteria, and either excluding studies of low quality prior to a meta-analysis of remaining studies or ranking studies by quality within the synthesis. Quality assessment is a key part of this process. A number of methodological approaches to synthesizing qualitative studies have emerged (Paterson, Thorne, Canam, & Jillings, 2001). Here, the issue of quality assessment is contested, with concerns that checklists cannot be applied to the diversity of methods within qualitative research and arguments about whether poor quality studies should or should not be excluded from reviews. There is also a recognition of a need to synthesize evidence from a range of study types including those based on qualitative, quantitative, and mixed methods research (Dixon-Woods, Agarwal, Jones, Young, & Sutton, 2005; Pope, Mays, & Popay, 2007). Harden and Thomas (2010) explore this in depth in Chapter 29 of this volume. The term *mixed studies review* has been introduced for this type of synthesis (Pluye et al., 2009). Researchers need to determine whether a mixed methods study is worth including in an evidence synthesis or what weight should be given to it within the synthesis.

Within mixed studies reviews, there is a need to assess articles reporting only qualitative research, only quantitative research, and combinations of both. Pluye and colleagues critically examine the quality appraisal tools that have actually been applied in mixed studies reviews, finding 12 formal quality appraisal procedures used in 17 systematic mixed studies reviews in the health sciences, although no validated checklists were found. From this, they propose a set of 15 quality criteria, with a scoring system. Their aim is a minimum set of criteria for ease of use, rather than an exhaustive list. The criteria include six for application to qualitative studies or the qualitative components of mixed methods studies, six for application to different types of quantitative studies, and three for mixed methods studies for use in conjunction with the qualitative and quantitative criteria.

If the instrument constructed by Pluye and colleagues was applied to the example study in Box 21.1, then the qualitative component and quantitative component would be assessed separately because they were published separately. That is, the three criteria relevant to mixed methods would not be used. When the six criteria for qualitative research are applied to the ethnographic study, five are met; the exception is "discussion of researchers' reflexivity." The qualitative researchers certainly practiced reflexivity, but the word count permitted by the journal was so small that a decision was made not to discuss reflexivity because it was not necessary in the context of the value set of the journal. Two of the three criteria relevant to quantitative experimental research are met when applied to the RCT, with the exception of blinding; blinding was not appropriate because this was a pragmatic trial. Thus, the study scores 5 out of 6 (83%) for the qualitative component and 2 out of 2 (100%) for the quantitative component. If it were assessed as a mixed methods study, it would score 7 out of 8 for its components and 0 out of 3 for the mixed methods aspects, totaling 7 out of 11 (64%).

DOMAIN 8: UTILITY

A number of researchers have put forward the utility of a study as an indicator of quality. Datta (1997) considers whether the results are usable, Caracelli and Riggin (1994) whether the combination of methods informs changes in policy, Onwuegbuzie and Johnson (2006) whether consumers and policy makers use the meta-inferences—called political legitimation—and Dellinger and Leech (2007) whether historically the results are used—called the historical element. Of course, poor research can be used by policy makers, and indeed, Dellinger and Leech propose caution for this reason. A related issue is what Dellinger and Leech (2007) call the consequential element,

which is the social acceptability of the consequences of using findings from a study. An example might be a finding that breast care nurses are not effective in helping young women deal with postoperative care. If policy makers withdraw funding for the service, then this might be seen as unacceptable by some charities and subgroups of the population.

Consideration of the utility of a study is difficult in practice. It may be challenging to associate specific actions by research users with specific studies. Some studies may have an immediate impact because they are newsworthy and therefore disseminated widely. Other studies may contribute quietly to a growing evidence base about a particular issue. In the case of the example of the leaflets in maternity care, a study would have to be made of the continuing use of leaflets and changes in the culture of maternity care, perhaps by considering policy documents in this area or surveying maternity units. Mixed methods scholars have proposed developing a utilization quality audit for the evaluation of utilization quality (Tashakkori & Teddlie, 2009).

ITEMS NOT INCLUDED IN THE FRAMEWORK

Some quality criteria identified have not been included in the framework. For example, Onwuegbuzie and Johnson (2006) propose *sequential legitimation,* where inferences drawn may depend on the sequencing of methods. They suggest that sequencing could be reversed to test this. However, sequencing is chosen to best address the research question—that is, the research question might call for parallel designs—so this solution is limited and therefore is not included in the framework. O'Cathain et al. (2008) discuss the need for expertise in the individual methods within a study. However, the weakness or strength of data collection will be obvious from the reports or journal articles being assessed regardless of the level of expertise present on any research team.

♦ Challenges

Too many criteria. The experience of trying to apply all of the items within this comprehensive framework to a real-life mixed methods study was that it was time consuming and difficult. There is an issue about what one is attempting to do. Researchers can use the whole framework over the life—and afterlife—of a study to ensure they meet the best quality standards. A user of research is more likely to want to know whether the quality of a study is "good enough." In the field of evidence synthesis, devising a minimum rather than comprehensive set of criteria was the goal. There is a need to identify the most important criteria, or at least prioritize them. Prioritization is likely to depend on the paradigm of the decision maker. This makes the planned Delphi study mentioned earlier one of the most important next steps for the development of quality assessment in mixed methods research.

How to assess the individual components. Some authors argue that any quality assessment of mixed methods research must include separate evaluation of the quality of the individual components—where each component is assessed by criteria acceptable to its methodology—as well as a quality assessment of the whole mixed methods study (O'Cathain et al., 2008). Others find this use of three sets of standards cumbersome—indeed, an obstacle—and instead propose an integrated framework that can be applicable to each component as well as to the whole study (Tashakkori & Teddlie, 2008; Teddlie & Tashakkori, 2009). The latter approach is very attractive, and it remains to be seen how acceptable it is to both qualitative and quantitative researchers working together on mixed methods studies.

Competing criteria. A study may meet one criterion and, by doing so, be less likely to meet another criterion. An attempt has been made to assess this when applying the framework to the example in Box 21.1. This issue did not arise but may do so when the framework is tested on more example studies.

Is it really comprehensive? The framework may not include the work of some mixed methods scholars because I failed to find their books or papers. When looking back at the framework now, I already have concerns about the lack of visibility of paradigms, and readers may see more gaps. This chapter is most definitely "toward" a comprehensive framework and has yet to arrive at its destination.

Learning about quality. The quality of mixed methods research needs to be a central part of teaching and training in this approach. Finding ways of consolidating the language of quality in mixed methods research will facilitate learning.

♦ Conclusions

Over the past few years, a number of mixed methods scholars have considered how best to assess the quality of mixed methods research. The work of those who have made the mixed methods aspects of a study central to their assessment has been brought together into a comprehensive framework. This framework consists of eight quality domains and is structured by the journey of a research study from planning through to data collection, interpretation, and use in the real world. It is put forward as a first attempt at a comprehensive framework in the hope that it will be developed further in the future.

Research Questions and Exercises

1. Take the framework and apply it to your own mixed methods study. Test your understanding of each item in the framework and, at the same time, test the framework:

- Are the domains comprehensive?

- Is it possible to assess each item within a domain?

- Does it help you to identify ways of improving your study?

- Can you conclude that your study is a good or a poor mixed methods study?

You may wish to write a paper about this and publish your findings with the aim of contributing to the development of the framework and understanding of how to assess the quality of mixed methods research.

◆ References

Bryman, A. (1988). *Quantity and quality in social research*. London: Routledge.

Bryman, A. (2006). Paradigm peace and the implications for quality. *International Journal of Social Research Methodology, 9*, 111–126.

Bryman, A. (2007). Barriers to integrating quantitative and qualitative research. *Journal of Mixed Methods Research, 1*, 1–18.

Bryman, A., Becker, S., & Sempik, J. (2008). Quality criteria for quantitative, qualitative and mixed methods research. *International Journal of Social Research Methodology, 11*, 261–276.

Caracelli, V. J., & Riggin, L. J. C. (1994). Mixed-method evaluation: Developing quality criteria through concept mapping. *Evaluation Practice, 15*(2), 139–152.

Chen, H. (1997). Applying mixed methods: A dominant methodology for the future? In J. C. Greene & V. J. Caracelli (Eds.), *Advances in mixed-method evaluation: The challenges and benefits of integrating diverse paradigms* (pp. 61–72). San Francisco: Jossey-Bass.

Creswell, J. W. (2003). *Research design: Qualitative, quantitative, and mixed methods approaches* (2nd ed.). London: Sage.

Creswell, J. W., Fetters, M. D., Plano Clark, V. L., & Morales. A. (2009). Mixed methods intervention trials. In S. Andrew & E. J. Halcomb (Eds.), *Mixed methods research for nursing and the health sciences* (pp. 161–180). Chicester, UK: Wiley-Blackwell.

Creswell, J. W., & Plano Clark, V. (2007). *Designing and conducting mixed methods research*. Thousand Oaks, CA: Sage.

Datta, L. (1997). A pragmatic basis for mixed-method designs. In J. C. Greene & V. J. Caracelli (Eds.), *Advances in mixed-method evaluation: The challenges and benefits of integrating diverse paradigms* (pp. 33–46). San Francisco: Jossey-Bass.

Dellinger, A. B., & Leech, N. L. (2007). Toward a unified validation framework in mixed methods research. *Journal of Mixed Methods Research, 1*(4), 309–332.

Dixon-Woods, M., Agarwal, S., Jones, D., Young, B., & Sutton, A. (2005). Synthesising qualitative and quantitative evidence: A review of possible methods. *Journal of Health Services Research and Policy, 10*(1), 45–53.

Erzberger, C., & Kelle, U. (2003). Making inferences in mixed methods: The rules of integration. In A. Tashakkori & C. Teddlie (Eds.), *Handbook of mixed methods in social*

& behavioral research (pp. 457–488). Thousand Oaks, CA: Sage.

Giddings, L. S., & Grant, B. M. (2009). From rigour to trustworthiness: Validating mixed methods. In S. Andrew & E. J. Halcomb (Eds.), *Mixed methods research for nursing and the health sciences* (pp. 119–134). Chicester, UK: Wiley-Blackwell.

Harden, A., & Thomas, J. (2010). Mixed methods and systematic reviews: Examples and emerging issues, In A. Tashakkori & C. Teddlie (Eds.), SAGE *handbook of mixed methods in social & behavioral research* (2nd ed.). Thousand Oaks, CA: Sage.

Katrak, P., Bialocerkowski, A. E., Massy-Westropp, N., Kumar, V. S., & Grimmer, K. A. (2004). A systematic review of the content of critical appraisal tools. *BMC Medical Research Methodology, 4,* 22.

Lincoln, Y. S., & Guba, E. G. (1985). *Naturalistic inquiry.* Newbury Park, CA: Sage.

Maxwell, J. A., & Mittapalli, K. (2010). Realism as a stance for mixed method research. In A. Tashakkori & C. Teddlie (Eds.), SAGE *handbook of mixed methods in social & behavioral research* (2nd ed.). Thousand Oaks, CA: Sage.

Mertens, D. (2003). Mixed methods and the politics of human research: The transformative-emancipatory perspective. In A. Tashakkori & C. Teddlie (Eds.), *Handbook of mixed methods in social and behavioral research* (pp. 135–164). Thousand Oaks, CA: Sage.

Miller, S. (2003). Impact of mixed methods and design on inference quality. In A. Tashakkori & C. Teddlie (Eds.), *Handbook of mixed methods in social & behavioral research* (pp. 423–455). Thousand Oaks, CA: Sage.

Moher, D., Jadad, A. R., Nichol, G., Penman, M., Tugwell, P., & Walsh, S. (1995). Assessing the quality of randomized controlled trials: An annotated bibliography of scales and checklists. *Controlled Clinical Trials, 16*(1), 62–73.

Murphy, E., Dingwall, R., Greatbatch, D., Parker, S., & Watson, P. (1998). *Qualitative research methods in health technology assessment: A review of the literature* (No. 2 (16)): Health Technology Assessment.

O'Cathain, A., Murphy, E., & Nicholl, J. (2007). Why, and how, mixed methods research is undertaken in health services research: A mixed methods study. *BMC Health Services Research, 7,* 85.

O'Cathain, A., Murphy, E., & Nicholl, J. (2008). The quality of mixed methods studies in health services research. *Journal of Health Services Research and Policy, 13*(2), 92–98.

O'Cathain, A., Walters, S. J., Nicholl, J. P., Thomas, K. J., & Kirkham, M. (2002). Use of evidence based leaflets to promote informed choice in maternity care: Randomised controlled trial in everyday practice. *BMJ, 324,* 643–646.

Onwuegbuzie, A., & Combs, J. (2010). Emergent data analysis techniques in mixed methods research: A synthesis. In A. Tashakkori & C. Teddlie (Eds.), SAGE *handbook of mixed methods in social & behavioral research* (2nd ed.). Thousand Oaks, CA: Sage.

Onwuegbuzie, A. J., & Johnson, R. B. (2006). The validity issue in mixed research. *Research in the Schools, 13*(1), 48–63.

Paterson, B. L., Thorne, S. E., Canam, C., & Jillings, C. (2001). *Meta-study of qualitative health research. A practical guide to meta-analysis and meta-synthesis.* London: Sage.

Pluye, P., Gagnon, M., Griffiths, F., & Johnson-Lafleur, J. (2009). A scoring system for appraising mixed methods research, and concomitantly appraising qualitative, quantitative and mixed methods primary studies in mixed studies reviews. *International Journal of Nursing Studies, 46*(4), 529–546.

Pluye, P., Grad, R. M., Dunikowski, L. G., & Stephenson, R. (2005). Impact of clinical information-retrieval technology on physicians: A literature review of quantitative, qualitative and mixed methods studies. *International Journal of Medical Informatics, 74,* 745–768.

Pope, C., Mays, N., & Popay, J. (2007). *Synthesizing qualitative and quantitative health evidence. A guide to methods.* New York: McGraw Hill Open University Press.

Sale, J. E. M., & Brazil, K. (2004). A strategy to identify critical appraisal criteria for primary mixed method studies. *Quality and Quantity, 38*(4), 351–365.

Sandelowski, M., Voils, C. I., Knafl, G. (2009) On quantitizing. *Journal of Mixed Methods Research, 3*(3), 208–222.

Silverman, D. (2000). *Doing qualitative research. A practical handbook*. London: Sage.

Stapleton, H., Kirkham, M., & Thomas, G. (2002). Qualitative study of evidence based leaflets in maternity care. *BMJ, 324,* 639–43.

Steckler, A., Mcleroy, K. R., Goodman, R. M., Bird, S. T., & McCormick, L. (1992). Toward integrating qualitative and quantitative methods: An introduction. *Health Education Quarterly, 19*(1), 1–8.

Tashakkori, A., & Teddlie, C. (1998). *Mixed methodology: Combining qualitative and quantitative approaches*. London: Sage.

Tashakkori, A., & Teddlie, C. (2003). The past and future of mixed methods research: From data triangulation to mixed model designs. In A. Tashakkori & C. Teddlie (Eds.), *Handbook of mixed methods in social & behavioral research* (pp. 671–701). Thousand Oaks, CA: Sage.

Tashakkori, A., & Teddlie, C. (2008). Quality of inferences in mixed methods research. In M. Bergman (Ed.), *Advances in mixed methods research: Theories and applications*. London: Sage.

Tashakkori, A., & Teddlie, C. (2009) Integrating qualitative and quantitative approaches to research. In L. Bicklen & D. Rog (Eds.), *The handbook of applied social research methods* (2nd ed., pp. 283–317). Thousand Oaks, CA: Sage.

Teddlie, C., & Tashakkori, A. (2003). Major issues and controversies in the use of mixed methods in the social and behavioural sciences. In A. Tashakkori & C. Teddlie (Eds.), *Handbook of mixed methods in social & behavioural research* (pp. 3–50). Thousand Oaks, CA: Sage.

Teddlie, C., & Tashakkori, A. (2009). *Foundations of mixed methods research: Integrating quantitative and qualitative approaches in the social and behavioral sciences*. Thousand Oaks: Sage.

Turner-Stokes, L., Harding, R., Sergeant, J., Lupton, C., & McPherson, K. (2006). Generating the evidence base for the National Service Framework (NSF) for long term conditions: A new research typology. *Clinical Medicine, 6,* 91–97.

CONTEMPORARY APPLICATIONS OF MIXED METHODS RESEARCH

22

MEETING THE PRACTICAL CHALLENGES OF MIXED METHODS RESEARCH

◆ Eli Lieber and Thomas S. Weisner

Objectives

Our objectives are to

- describe some of the practical obstacles to the use of mixed methods in social science research;

- discuss some of the ways to overcome those obstacles, including parallel units of analysis, coding decisions, and the value of teams in mixed methods work;

- discuss the nature of mixed methods data and possibilities for their integration; and

- present an example of software that can make the analysis and presentation of qualitative and quantitative evidence easier.

Mixed methods studies use evidence from text, numbers, and other media to understand problems in the social sciences. There are strong conceptual frameworks, designs, and tools available to conduct mixed methods studies. Application of mixed methods is most effective when the various forms of data collected are fully integrated across all phases of a study, but other types of designs are also valuable. Further, the decision to employ a mixed methods approach is only appropriate when such an approach clearly adds value to the study and its findings as compared with the (often easier and less costly) decision to use only text or only numbers or only photos or video. While there are many examples of added value from mixed methods work, there are a number of barriers to doing such work successfully. In this chapter, we describe some of these barriers and offer practical ways to overcome them.

◆ Introduction

Many important problems in the social sciences will benefit from integrating a variety of research methods. Such a strategy can be applied equally well to research in human development, public health, program evaluation, intervention, and any other area where quantitative and/or qualitative methods are employed. Truly mixed methods, when employed well, can bring us closer to a full representation of social phenomena. Mixed methods encourage and support holism, which more richly, authentically, and appropriately represents the true complexity of behaviors as they occur in natural social contexts (Johnson & Onwuegbuzie, 2004; Lieber, 2009; Onwuegbuzie & Leech, 2005; Tashakkori & Teddlie, 2003; Weisner, 1996; Yoshikawa, Weisner, Kalil, & Way, 2008). Further, mixed methods help prevent us from confusing the phenomena themselves that we propose to study (e.g., parenting, diabetes in adolescence, supports for working poor families, beliefs about disabilities in

children, HIV prevention program effectiveness) with the methods we use to represent those phenomena.

Mixed methods approaches seek to capitalize on the complementary nature of qualitative and quantitative methods. The qualitative suite of methods uses words or images—text, discourse, narrative, photographs, video, objects, symbols—to represent the world. The quantitative suite of methods represents the world through the use of numbers and transformations of numbers—variables, graphs, functions, analytic models. The conceptual frameworks for mixed methods designs and analyses using words and numbers are available and increasingly sophisticated (Bernard & Ryan, 1998; Creswell, Plano Clark, Gutmann, & Hanson, 2002; Nastasi, Hitchcock, & Brown, this volume; Pearce, 2002; Teddlie & Tashakkori, 2009; Yoshikawa et al., 2008).

The complementary nature of qualitative and quantitative methods, employed simultaneously or sequentially, is of great value in bringing a wider range of evidence to strengthen and expand our understanding of a phenomenon. Triangulation, expansion, depth, and completeness of evidence from various methodological approaches encourage greater confidence in scientific conclusions for both producers and consumers of research findings. From a practical perspective, having various types of evidence at hand enhances any researcher's ability to discover, understand, and communicate findings to a wide range of audiences. The major challenge is to identify and implement appropriate, effective, and efficient methods that will produce meaningful results that can be communicated in clear and compelling ways to those audiences.

◆ Challenges to Doing Mixed Methods Work

"There are excellent books and courses of instruction dealing with the statistical manipulation of experimental data, but there is little help to be found on the methods of securing adequate and proper data to which to apply statistical procedure" (W. A. McCall as quoted in Campbell & Stanley, 1963, p. 1). Part of our task is to "choose—and often devise—a set of measures . . . that together, transcend one another's methodological vulnerabilities" (McGrath, 1981, p. 207).

THE FALSE QUALITATIVE-QUANTITATIVE DICHOTOMY

Onwuegbuzie and Leech (2005) suggest removing the "Q's" ("qualitative" and "quantitative") because they promote unnecessary boundaries. They suggest instead just the use of methods in the teaching of how to conduct research. Viewing methods on a continuum that can be drawn from in response to the research challenge gives equal status to numbers and words and other ways of representing the world (Dellinger & Leech, 2007; Ercikan & Roth, 2006; Nastasi, Hitchcock, & Brown, this volume; Niglas, this volume). As we move closer to a shared vocabulary and comfort with integrated methods, a more pragmatic appreciation for and flexible application of mixed methods will emerge (Gorard, this volume; Johnson & Onwuegbuzie, 2004; Yoshikawa et al., 2008). Weisner (1996) suggests that *methodocentrism* should be resisted, that all methods are intended to (a) bring us closer to the phenomenon of interest, (b) help us discover truths about the world, (c) produce research findings that are meaningful and valuable to the social sciences, (d) provide findings that are "believable" and supportive of the research claims, and (e) instill confidence in ourselves as researchers and in the audiences to whom we disseminate our work.

CERTAIN TOOLS FOR CERTAIN JOBS

Another belief that limits creative thinking about how methods may be mixed is the notion that particular behaviors or settings are best studied through particular data or methods (e.g., observation, texts, and interviews or Likert-type scales, counts, and levels). Axinn and Pearce (2006) draw a useful distinction between qualitative and quantitative *data* and qualitative and quantitative *analysis*. There is nothing to support the idea that a particular form of data best represents particular behaviors, settings, or programs. Nor is there evidence that qualitative data must be analyzed by only qualitative analysis strategies or that quantitative data must be analyzed by only quantitative analysis strategies (Yoshikawa et al., 2008). Disciplines have often developed histories of practice in which certain topics have been studied using particular methods and so sometimes confuse the study of that topic (fertility, child social behavior, shyness) with the methods (quantitative demography, questionnaire scales, parent reports) typically used by those working in that discipline. Particular topics, behaviors, or settings can be usefully described and assessed using more than one method.

Complementary methods can bring new perspectives in addressing a problem. For example, the study of STD/HIV transmission and prevention has traditionally been the territory of epidemiologists and medical service providers—most of whom are quantitative researchers. Yet, along with an increasing appreciation for the enhancement of program "fit" to the cultural context in which an intervention is deployed, current work in this area increasingly employs qualitative and mixed methods approaches (Lieber et al., 2006; Lieber, Chin, et al., 2009; NIMH Collaborative HIV/STD Prevention Trial Group, 2007a, 2007b).

For example, a large National Institute of Mental Health (NIMH) Collaborative was formed to adapt and implement an STD/HIV transmission prevention program in a variety of locations, including China, Russia, India, Peru, Uganda, and Zimbabwe. Ethnographic methods were used prior to and throughout the project to inform decisions about where best to implement the prevention effort and how to recruit, collect data from, and support participants. Program implementation and program impacts were assessed using both qualitative and quantitative data. As a randomized control trial dealing with serious medical conditions, a range of common quantitative data and biological markers were collected from research participants. At the same time, the ethnographic data were used to adapt the intervention to the specific cultural context in each country, thereby increasing program effectiveness and sustainability.

These program adaptations took place in very different cultures and settings and took on a variety of forms. However, the availability of both qualitative and quantitative data throughout the project allowed for a high level of coordination across the countries for the requisite projectwide analyses. More narrowly focused research could draw on primarily quantitative or qualitative data or move to more fully integrated mixed methods data. There is evidence that in those cases where ethnographic and other qualitative data informed key intervention design decisions, the programs implemented are proving more effective and sustainable.

THE GOLDEN HAMMER

"When all you have is a hammer, everything starts looking like a nail"—in other words, we can rely too much on a particular and familiar tool. Researchers use methods with which they are familiar and have the most skill. Similar to a methodocentric bias, this tendency is analogous to forcing the problem to fit the tool rather than choosing the tool(s) that is most suited to the problem. We view methods as tools, and the adaptive researcher or research team should be prepared to draw on a variety of these tools in response to the specific demands of the research problem. The wider the range of methodological tools you have in your toolkit, the better prepared you are to meet research challenges. The availability of a wider range of tools promotes problem-driven methodological

decisions—decisions that will allow the choices that best fit the circumstances (Creswell & Plano Clark, 2007; Greene, 2007; Onwuegbuzie & Combs, this volume; Onwuegbuzie, Slate, Leech, & Collins, 2009; Plano Clark & Badiee, this volume; Tashakkori & Teddlie, 1998; Yoshikawa, Lowe, et al., 2006).

Here is where common sense and clear goal orientation will benefit researchers as they plan and carry out their work. For example, Johnson, Onwuegbuzie, and Turner (2007) surveyed a number of leaders in the field who each provided their current definition of mixed methods research. These experts' responses spoke mostly to the mixing of qualitative and quantitative methods and included issues of true integration versus parallel application, sequential versus simultaneous application, complementarities, broader and more comprehensive understanding, dealing with validity, and triangulation. What Johnson and colleagues (2007) and many others make clear is that designing and conducting mixed methods research is a balancing act with regard to overall design (Bernard, 1995; Creswell & Plano Clark, 2007; Dellinger & Leech, 2007; Gorard, this volume; Niglas, this volume; Tashakkori & Teddlie, 2003) and sampling (Collins, this volume; Collins, Onwuegbuzie, & Jiao, 2007; Kemper, Stringfield, & Teddlie, 2003; Miles & Huberman, 1994; Tashakkori & Teddlie, 2003; Teddlie & Yu, 2007). How best to do it?

◆ Conceptualizing Mixed Methods Research from Practical Perspectives

Bryman (2006) provides a detailed perspective on the uses of mixed methods research to help answer the question, "How is it done?" Bryman begins with a review of common typologies for how qualitative and quantitative methods are integrated (Greene, Caracelli, & Graham, 1989; Niglas, this volume) and derives 16-plus categories. Bryman's categories all appear in mixed methods research rationale and practice. While each of these categories represents an exemplar from a simpler typology, this more fine-grained viewpoint brings us closer to a picture of why researchers choose to employ various methods and how they are attempting to do so. Mixed methods work may move in phases, be integrated differently in particular studies, generate evidence that can be presented in various forms, and support arguments for the increased validity gained through their use. We believe that this burgeoning field is a natural progression in the social sciences toward a fuller understanding and representation of the naturally rich and complex phenomena we seek to understand. Accordingly, Bryman's breakdown of the reasons for mixed methods strategy and Niglas's (1999, 2001, this volume) "Integrated Multidimensional Continuum of Research Methodology" speak to the wide variety of tools available to a mixed methods researcher. Researchers interested in mixed methods, particularly students and those desiring to add this to their work, frequently say, "I know where to learn *about* qualitative [and sometimes mixed methods] research and theory, but where do you learn *how to do it?*" We turn next to some practical, pragmatic ways to do so.

THE VALUE OF TEAMS

Many of the research programs we advise and consult with through the services we provide via the UCLA Center for Culture and Health, Fieldwork and Qualitative Data Research Laboratory involve multiple investigators and have budgets and timelines that frame opportunities and goals. But these budgets and timelines may also constrain what can be done. For example, staff skill sets sometimes end up being inherited from other studies rather than being specifically tailored to the new study. Further, the research will likely take place

in field settings where circumstances will surely change from what was anticipated. The value of interdisciplinary partnerships, particularly within a respectful environment with colleagues of complementary skills and backgrounds, can be invaluable (Shulha & Wilson, 2003). For most of us who have been trained primarily within one discipline, such collaboration requires all members to step outside the familiar territory of their traditional discipline, hear and respect the approaches of others, and work together to design and carry out the best study that the team is capable of under the circumstances.

The CHILD project team, for example, identified 102 families with a child age 3 or 4 with a developmental delay in Los Angeles. The study focused on understanding how families accommodated their child. How did the child influence the family daily routine; what were the parents' explanatory models for their child's disability; how were any interventions, special education programs, and other services selected, and how did these fit within the family routines; and how did all these features relate to assessments of the child's development over time? The study directors included Ronald Gallimore, an educational, community, and clinical psychologist; Barbara Keogh, special education and psychological assessment; Kazuo Nihira, quantitative methods and measurement in developmental disability; and Weisner, an anthropologist. With funding from the National Institute of Child Health and Human Development (NICHD), this team, along with an interdisciplinary staff from the fields of education, anthropology, psychology, family studies, clinical and intervention work, statistics, and others, followed these children and families for some 20 years.

The team identified patterns of family accommodation through ethnographic observations and qualitative interviews with parents, along with quantitative assessments using questionnaire scales. Children were assessed at three points in time, and educational progress and other clinical data were used to track the children's development. Only through a mixed methods study team could this kind of holistic family and child developmental study have been undertaken (Bernheimer & Weisner, 2007; Gallimore, Coots, Weisner, Garnier, & Guthrie, 1996; Keogh, Bernheimer, Gallimore, & Weisner, 1998; Matheson, Olson, & Weisner, 2007; Weisner, Matheson, Coots, & Bernheimer, 2005).

SITUATION ASSESSMENT AND THE "END GAME"

To maximize the likelihood of project success, start with an audit of study resources and a clear framing of the study goals. The first task is to carry out an open and honest audit of your personnel and other resources. What are the backgrounds of those you are working with? What are their experiences in research similar to and different from the question at hand? Among the team members, what set of skills are available, and what necessary or desired skills are missing? What are the personality characteristics of each individual, and how well are they likely to comfortably fit with and perform for the team? How well are the responsibilities distributed, and is there a central coordinator who will organize task distribution and timing and monitor progress—and is this person in a position of authority that will allow him or her to exercise these responsibilities? And last, how much funding and time do you have to complete the research?

Following the audit, establish a clear definition of the "end game." That is, what is the core research question, what information is sought to address it, and how and to whom will the findings be communicated? The answers to these questions will provide critical guidance from the outset of the project as to decisions about methods, sampling frames, and the breadth and depth of data that can reasonably be expected to be collected. In turn, these decisions determine the evidence you will have available at the

project's end to support the claims you wish to put forward. Reflecting regularly on this end game—the essential evidence to address the research question and communicate findings to primary audiences—will help guide the team toward the most efficient decisions and activities as the real circumstances of the project emerge over time. The practical issues of time constraints, resources (funding, staffing, and time and energy availability), and intended deliverables must be kept in mind as project circumstances rarely proceed as originally expected. Working through these issues early with a research team can help circumvent the following pitfalls: relatively poor-quality data; having poorly managed, disorganized, and confusing data; limiting the type, sophistication, or variety of approaches to data analysis; generating fewer and inferior quality publications and presentations; or ultimately failing to complete the project (House, 1994).

◆ Mixed Methods and the Primary Level of Analysis

In the following sections, we elaborate on a mixed methods conceptual model. The research participant, dyad, family, setting, and so on—whatever the primary unit or level of analysis for a study—is the link that binds the data together (see Figure 22.1).

Figure 22.1 emphasizes the need to focus on the primary level of analysis as the foundation of the data that are collected in a study. Rather than thinking about quantitative and qualitative data as separate pieces of the puzzle to be independently collected and analyzed, a more integrated perspective suggests a focus on the nature of the problem being addressed—the primary research question.

For example, in a study of how the conceptualization and meanings of filial piety may be challenged in modernizing societies, Lieber, Nihira, and Mink (2004) conducted

Figure 22.1 Primary Level of Analysis as Foundation of Mixed Methods Data

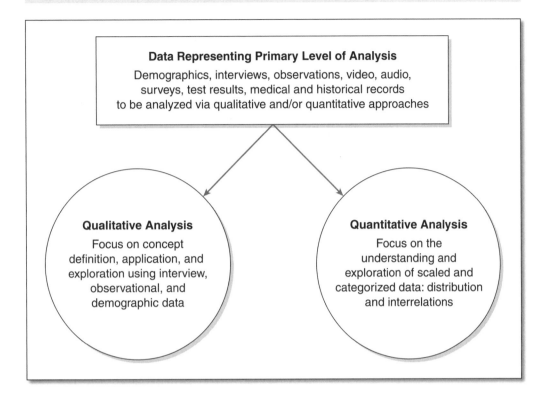

both a traditional factor analysis and a qualitative thematic analysis. The study goal was to explore whether a prominent and long-used measure of filial piety continued to represent filial beliefs and practices in the ways contemporary Chinese immigrants to the United States thought of this core Chinese value. Preliminary qualitative data analysis identified a variety of dimensions suggesting that, in response to modernization and experiences with immigration, filial piety—while continuing to be important and meaningful—was necessarily reframed in order to retain the traditional value but adapted in light of other sociohistorical changes. The factor analysis results of a filial piety scale indicated that, indeed, a unidimensional conceptualization did not properly represent contemporary thinking among U.S. Chinese immigrants. The qualitative data suggested themes that helped interpret the factors. The study

team then used factor scores for individuals to assist in coding the qualitative data. The team then used the distribution of scores for individuals across each of the emerging three filial piety factors as a guide to further analyze the qualitative data, leading to additional findings regarding how and why study participants reconceptualized filial piety as a core Chinese value. This study's findings were only possible due to the integrated mixed methods and the within-subject approach to data collection and analysis. We used EthnoNotes for this study to do the qualitative data analyses and to link these to the quantitative data (SocioCultural Research Consultants, 2008). Figure 22.1 illustrates how, by centering the research on the participant, a variety of approaches to data analysis were available that were continuously guided by the research question.

◆ *Mixed Methods Data Flow, Transformation, and Integration*

Interested in identifying barriers to true integrated methods, Bryman (2007) interviewed 20 social science researchers known for working with mixed methods and asked them to reflect on how they or others carried out mixed methods research. The researchers he talked with reported feeling that, while integrated research design and data collection was not much of a problem, their biggest cause of concern was "bringing together the analysis and interpretation of the quantitative and qualitative data and writing a narrative that linked the analysis and interpretation" (Bryman, 2007, p. 10).

Figure 22.2 provides a practical model for conceptualizing possible mixed methods data flow, transformation, and integration.

In this model, many traditional approaches to qualitative methods can be understood to take place in the leftmost column. For example, fieldwork can generate a variety of data forms to be processed, explored, and analyzed through constant comparison, content, domain, discourse, narrative, or any other qualitative approach. Not all the steps in the leftmost column need to be done in every study, of course. For instance, in many strictly anthropological, ethnographic, or other qualitative studies, activities in this column are the full cycle of a study, leading directly to publication. Similarly, many psychological, physical, biological, or other areas of research that rely predominantly on

Figure 22.2 Conceptual Model of Mixed Methods Data Flow and Analysis

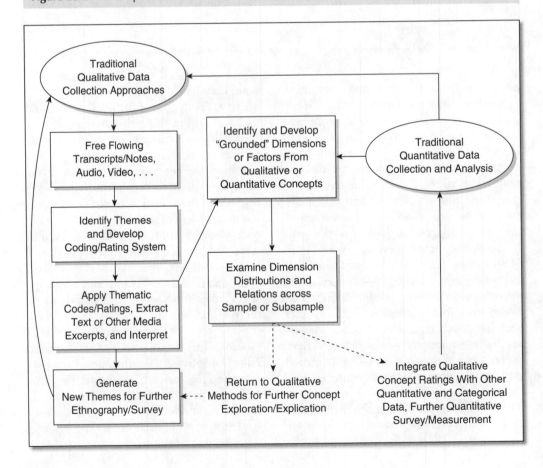

numeric representation of the world are conducted—data collected, analyzed, interpreted, and reported—in purely quantitative ways and so can start and end in the oval labeled "Traditional Quantitative Data Collection and Analysis." However, it is the space between these two traditional approaches that we are most interested in addressing. What are some of the possible connections between the two?

STRATEGIES FOR LINKING DIVERSE DATA TYPES

When it comes to integrating data for both analysis and interpretation, a key question is how to get the data to "speak the same language." The world of words, images, and sound are more flexible than the world of numbers. That is, it is easier to create numeric representations of qualitative content and understand the meaning of the numbers than it is to create qualitative representations of numbers and approach the same richness of understanding.

The Ecocultural Family Interview (EFI) (Bernheimer & Weisner, 2007; Weisner, 2002), and the methods of coding and scoring this interview, illustrate how a transcribed conversation can be used to create reliable scales for use with other quantitative data. The EFI is a guided conversation about the daily routine of life of the participant. Most EFI research to date has focused on parents and children, through a framework that can be used with teachers, health workers, and others. "Walk me through your day. Tell me the first things that happen when you wake up in the morning . . . then what happens next?" The activities that make up the routine are the focus and units for analysis.

Activities as part of a routine are a universal experience that anyone can understand and focus on in a conversation. Activities have features that define them and that can be used to describe and explore them. What tasks are being done? How does it happen—what are the scripts and norms for doing the

activity? Who are the people present, and what are their relationships? What emotions and what degree of engagement in the activity does the informant have? What goals and values are underlying the activity, and what does the activity mean to the person? And how stable and predictable is the daily routine and its associated activities?

Sharing details and experiences in a person's everyday activities opens a window into the circumstances of that person's life and can anchor a rich conversation that can then move in many directions. EFI conversations are usually focused on the specific topics driving a study. A parent raising a child with a disability (such as in the CHILD project described earlier); working poor parents struggling to balance work, parenting, family, and personal concerns in the New Hope study (Duncan, Huston, & Weisner, 2007; Yoshikawa, Weisner, & Lowe, 2006); early literacy experiences and home environments of parents with children in Head Start (Lieber et al., 2007); Mexican American parents and teens in Los Angeles and the issues around family responsibility and obligation (Fuligni & Pedersen, 2002; Fuligni, Weisner, & Gonzalez, 2008); and parents with children with asthma or brain injuries or diabetes are some of the topics of the studies that have used versions of the EFI.

The EFI interview is scored for themes, specific items are developed for each theme that has emerged from the interviews themselves, and then those items are coded and scaled. In any study using the EFI approach, the specific research questions of that study guide the probes and topics on which the interviews are focused. The conversation with parents about their daily routine probes those specific topics in the context of their daily lives. We have found that both the identification of themes (Ryan & Bernard, 2003) and reliable coding using defined scales are relatively easy to develop. The results retain the qualitative discourse and stories of the parents and youth who were interviewed as part of the items' content and definitions of anchor points. The scale scores themselves provide additional information regarding the salience and quality of the daily activities that instantiate those themes and research topics.

The New Hope study illustrates one use of the EFI to evaluate a random-assignment social experiment testing a work-support program in Milwaukee, Wisconsin. The New Hope program was a social contract. If participants worked 30 hours or more a week, they were eligible for a quite rich series of benefits. These benefits included a supplement to their wages that would bring their earnings up to 200% of the poverty level for their family; a subsidized HMO health care benefit for their children; vouchers to use for child care payments to any licensed provider; and assistance in finding or keeping a job, including a community service job for up to six months if needed. A subset of the approximately 1,357 treatment and control participants had at least one child between the ages of 1 and 12, and this group of about 745 was studied during and after the 3-year New Hope program ended. Extensive quantitative data were collected from administrative records, a parent survey completed at three points, assessments of the children's development, and teacher ratings of their school achievement. An ethnographic study randomly sampled about 7% of the overall sample—equal numbers of program and control participants. The ethnographic families were nested within the experimental/ longitudinal design and linked to all the quantitative data collected in the study. EFI-type interviews and more focused, qualitative, open-ended interviews were both used in the qualitative study.

The mixed methods conversation among the New Hope study team continued throughout the 8 years of this longitudinal study. The qualitative data were used to interpret and understand quantitative findings. For example, boys appeared to benefit more in their school behavior and other measures than girls did. One possible reason for this was that parents had greater fears for their boys, who were perceived to face greater risks in their neighborhood; parents described investing somewhat more monitoring time with the boys and placed them in programs somewhat more often. Another example of a mixed methods–produced finding was that participants with only one or, at most, two barriers to being able to work (e.g., no high school diploma, little previous work experience, several young children in the home) benefited more from New Hope than those with no such barriers (the no-barrier group parents were likely already working and continued to do so) or those with several barriers (these parents were unable to work steadily and so could not take up the New Hope offers).

New Hope participants did not differ widely in their commitments to the values of work and trying to provide for their family. As one mother described, "I just want what everyone wants, a good wage, decent job, help for my kids." They did differ in their job search and work tactics, however. Some saw wage work as a way to assemble enough money to take time out for other things they valued more: time at their church, time with their kids, time to rest and recover, and, for some, to deal with personal troubles and conflicts in their lives. The quantitative data on work pathways, child assessments, and school achievement for the participants, and of course their status as having been assigned to the program or control group, were used to place them and their children within the larger study context and provided for the identification and whole-group understanding of many qualitative findings.

TRADITIONAL THEME IDENTIFICATION AND CODING

Prior to the development of a grounded dimensional rating system, a first step is to identify and develop qualitative themes in narrative data (see Ryan & Bernard, 2003, for a variety of approaches) such as was used, for example, in New Hope and with the EFI. Meaningful themes are then developed and defined toward building a traditional qualitative coding system (Miles &

Huberman, 1994). Applying codes to the data through hypothesis testing, evaluation, and refinement then helps determine how and when codes should be applied. This process produces a comprehensive set of codes that represents as much of the meaningful data in the qualitative transcripts and notes as possible and that also helps understand the research question.

We also believe it important to demonstrate acceptable levels of interrater reliability before the code system is applied to the qualitative content (Hruschka et al., 2004; MacQueene, McLellan, Kay, & Milstein, 1998; Miles & Huberman, 1994). This again speaks to the value of teamwork. A team atmosphere that includes open and honest communications around the data collection and coding process will help ensure that the code system and coded content can be clearly communicated to an outside audience. A strong code system description will include code definitions and application criteria that are well understood by all members of the team. Providing Cohen's Kappa coefficients for each code that will be reported and discussed in published work is a rigorous and respected standard to employ. Kappa coefficients and percent agreement data parallel the reporting of Alpha coefficients in quantitative scale data, for example. Kappa is not the only way to measure reliability, of course, and there are nonquantitative ways to ascertain common patterns and themes where this cannot be done for sample size or other reasons.

DEVELOPING "GROUNDED" CODE DIMENSIONS

Developing dimensions from coded qualitative data that can be seamlessly integrated with other quantitative data begins with an exploration and analysis of coded excerpts from the qualitative data. For example, in a study of the home literacy environments of families with young children in Head Start programs, parents were interviewed about a variety of literacy development–supporting activities that took place in their homes (Lieber, Davis, & Weisner, 2009).

One topic that emerged from these interviews was "Pre-Writing Letter Recognition Skills." This topic was then developed into a code that was applied to any data that included reference to the child's inquiry about or recognition of letters in words, whether parents spoke about letters as symbols when reading to the child or observing letters elsewhere, mentioned play with alphabet toys or songs, described child interest in writing or tracing letters, and noted the child's ability to recite the alphabet. After establishing interrater reliability across the research team members and applying the code to all project data, the team sought to develop a further, more elaborated notion of the pre-writing dimension.

The process for accomplishing this first involved extracting all excerpts coded as prewriting. After exploring the excerpts, it was apparent that a range of pre-writing activities took place across the sample. Next, we defined the boundaries and intermediate points along this range of all pre-writing activities. The team then engaged in an iterative pile-sorting exercise to define the points along this pre-writing dimension. Each team member was assigned a small sample of these excerpts and was instructed to sort them into piles differentiating "high," "medium," and "low" levels of pre-writing letter recognition activities. At a team meeting, each member then described his or her definitions for each level and his or her key inclusion or exclusion criteria for assigning an excerpt to a particular level. For example, would a case be assigned a relatively higher rating where there was a lack of detail in the description of the activity or if the activity occurred relatively infrequently? Any disagreements among team members regarding these definitions and decision criteria were resolved until all members felt comfortable and confident about decisions to include or exclude excerpts from each level.

In circumstances where a distribution can be identified, this first step—high, medium, low classification—can be relatively straightforward. For example, in this study, families that reported very little or no activity related to pre-writing activities are easily assigned to the "low" group, those reporting many daily such activity are easily assigned to the "high" group, with the remaining cases being assigned to the (relatively large) "medium" group. The next step was to work with only the "medium" rated excerpts and to repeat the exercise again, distributing the excerpts into "high," "medium," and "low" piles. At this stage, distinguishing the groups becomes more subtle and the task of articulating objective criteria for assignment to each level that is clearly understood and agreed upon by all team members more challenging. This exercise can be repeated any number of times to establish rating dimensions that range from three to more levels. In this study, a five-point dimension was eventually created.

It is critical to document the decision criteria for the rating dimension application, as well as criteria for building a guide for the application of a qualitative code system. This documentation serves as an objective guide for applying the ratings and is often extremely valuable when preparing the methods section of a manuscript. As in the establishment of interrater reliability for code application, independent application of the code dimension to as yet unrated excerpts should be carried out and Cohen's Kappa coefficients calculated for those data. Each individual family now can be assigned a score along this pre-writing dimension based on an average of ratings for all associated letter recognition excerpts that will have been coded for each participant. Along with these rating scales, of course, the parents' interviews and home observational data remained for qualitative analysis and exemplar use in their own right.

LINKING THE MIXED METHODS DATA TOGETHER

The ratings that are assigned to each case based on the grounded dimensions described earlier now allow the qualitative and quantitative data to *speak to each other*. Integrated analyses now can take place (see Figure 22.2). Where created carefully, these dimensions are systematic, reliable, and direct representations of the qualitative data on which they were grounded. The ratings of course do not replace qualitative discourse, stories, and direct observations themselves; all are available for analysis and reporting. Where significant group differences are found from bi- or multivariate analyses, the study can return to the original interviews, now guided by the quantitative findings. It should be noted that the EFI strategy of developing grounded dimensions is just one of many approaches to building from or transforming qualitative content into a form that allows integration with numbers. Alternative approaches that also facilitate this integration include consensus analysis, similarity and dissimilarity coefficients, correspondence analysis, word counts, and multidimensional scaling (Clausen, 1998; Handwerker & Borgatti, 1998; Kruskal & Wish, 1978; Romney, 1999; Weller, 2007).

Any such approach to working with qualitative content that can result in case-specific dimensional ratings, scale scores, ratings, or counts can be used with other numerical data in more traditional quantitative analysis. When chosen appropriately and conducted reliably, these ratings become the link through which the qualitative and quantitative data can be analyzed and interpreted together. These links allow for both unidirectional analysis (e.g., using the qualitative content to confirm or expand on quantitative findings) and iterative bidirectional analysis. Creative and thoughtful uses of these linkages allow the investigator to more truly integrate mixed methods data, analysis, and interpretation.

For example, in the emergent literacy study, the distributions of letter recognition ratings were explored and included in quantitative analyses along with categorical and other quantitative data in the study (Lieber, Davis, Weisner, & Lefkowitz-Burt, 2007). Letter recognition ratings were related to family primary home language, measures of parent reading skills and education, and other qualitative code rating dimensions. Together, these findings revealed various comprehensive sets of home literacy supports for their children. Working back through the distribution of letter recognition ratings to the qualitative content on which they were based provided a richer and more thorough understanding of these patterns (see Figure 22.3). We found a cluster of families with high letter recognition practices across all three household language groups and were able to characterize them qualitatively. Households that were primarily bilingual reported somewhat higher letter recognition practices than those that were either English only or Spanish only—an unanticipated result we turned back to the full data to better understand. Thus, the

quantitative analyses found a number of significant relationships; in turn, the qualitative content allowed for a fuller understanding of these patterns and more comprehensive appreciation for the mechanisms that explained variation in literacy supports as a function of home language.

◆ Tools to Assist the Integration of Mixed Methods Data

One of the major challenges to creative integration and analysis of mixed methods research data stems from a true complexity in the mechanisms through which these data can be managed and queried. There is

Figure 22.3 Letter Recognition Skills Ratings by Primary Household Language

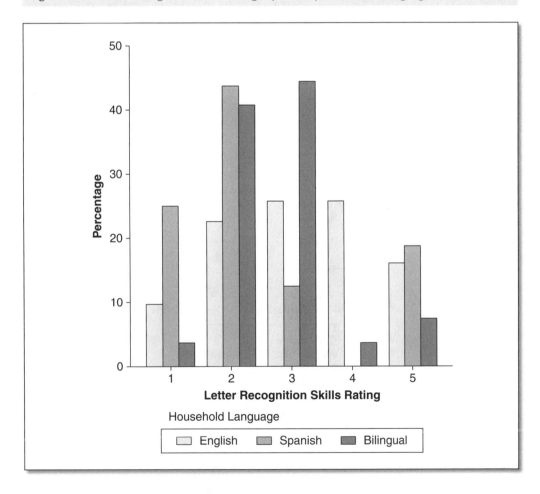

a variety of computer-assisted qualitative data analysis software (CAQDAS) tools available to help manage mixed methods data (see Bazeley, this volume, for further information about computer-assisted mixed methods data analysis). Fundamentally, most of these tools operate as a complex relational database. Users want ease of use, without the tool itself influencing the analysis process and results. This can be daunting for those who do not fully understand how the tools operate and how to capitalize on the available features to extract best answers to their research questions. The effort to integrate qualitative and quantitative data within a database and to understand how to query the system in meaningful and transparent ways is also complex. In this section, we offer an illustration of relational database fundamentals and provide examples of

how such tools can assist in mixed methods research.

Relational database systems operate on the principle of parsimony—the simpler each file (or table) in the system, the more efficiently and flexibly the system can operate. In the Figure 22.4 schematic, there are four primary database files. Each can be thought of as a flat database file common in statistical and spreadsheet software. Through a network of a variety of relations and key variables, these files can remain relatively simple and work together as a more complex system. In this example, the four main files include the following:

1. Descriptors—these are the quantitative and other data that we collect that identify and describe the research participants, settings, communities, dyads

Figure 22.4 Primary Mixed Methods Database Tables and Relationships

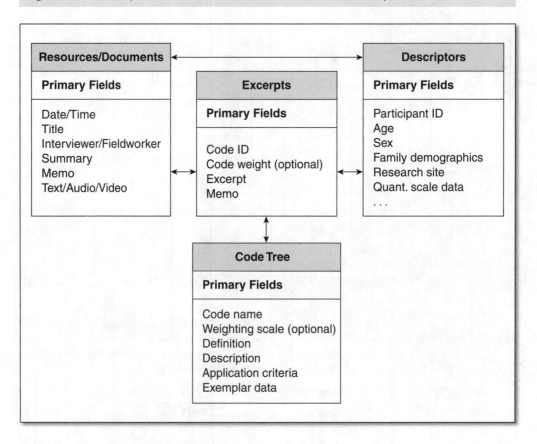

(i.e., everything we know about the source of our data).

2. Resources/Documents—these are the files that contain all the necessary information about a particular qualitative data collection event (i.e., what type of data were collected; time and place of collection; context, thoughts, and procedures through which the data were collected; and the data themselves).

3. Code Tree—this is our coding system that will be used to tag excerpts from the resources and, beyond the code name itself, can serve as a code book and include definitions, application criteria, exemplar data, and rating or weighting systems details.

4. Excerpts—these are the pieces of qualitative information that have been identified within the qualitative data resource as a meaningful block of text, to be tagged by any number of codes from the code tree.

The arrows in Figure 22.4 represent the relationships among the files. The nature of each relationship can vary. For example, the relation between descriptors and resources is a "one-to-many" relationship (i.e., in simple terms, for each participant there can be many interviews). Similarly, the relation between the excerpts and each resource is also a "one-to-many" relationship (i.e., there can be many excerpts from each resource). Preparing a mixed methods database requires three areas of setup. Descriptor and resource data must be created, and the code tree must be specified. Then, prior to an analysis, the resources must be examined, excerpts identified, and codes tagged to the excerpts. Aside from any purely quantitative analysis that may be carried out on the descriptor data, the vast majority of a mixed methods analysis will focus on the excerpts from interviews, field notes, and other text—hence their position at the center of the schematic.

The subsequent operation of the database system capitalizes on the relations among the files. Every piece of data in the system is in some way connected to every other piece of information. With an appreciation for how these systems operate, users are better prepared to extract the information they are looking for and, when searching the database for information, see how complex their queries can be. In its most transparent form, once the data are prepared, the system operates as a filtering, organizing, and presentation tool. If "Letter Recognition Skills," discussed earlier, is a code in the system, the user can, for example, query the database and see all "Letter Recognition" excerpts for individuals of a certain income group, with mother education at or above a particular level, comparing boys and girls, and shown separately for different ethnic or racial groups. Any piece of data, anywhere in the system, can be used as a filter, organizer, or result.

ETHNONOTES AS AN EXAMPLE

There are a variety of software packages available for the analysis of qualitative data, and numeric data can be incorporated into this software (e.g., ATLAS.ti: Muhr, 2004; MAXqda: VERBI Software, 2008). EthnoNotes (SocioCultural Research Consultants, 2008), however, was designed specifically for the analysis of both qualitative and mixed methods data.[1] As a rich Internet application (RIA), more commonly known as Web applications, EthnoNotes is ideal for team research. All system code, associated software, and project data reside entirely on secure commercial servers. Projects may have any number of authorized users (password and encryption protected and with security controls over privileges to view and modify aspects of the database), and all can simultaneously access a project's database using a Web browser from any location, at any time, and with all data being updated in real time. EthnoNotes easily integrates different types of data within a single project. Figure 22.5 presents two screen shots that introduce the basic EthnoNotes project working environment.

Figure 22.5 The EthnoNotes Environment

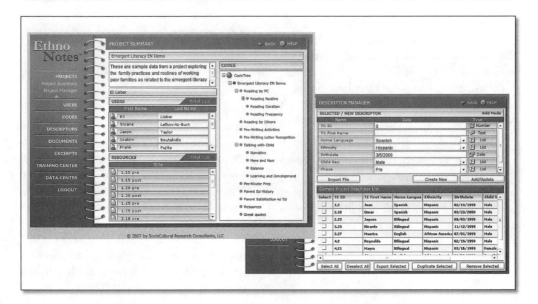

The project summary shows an overview of the project users, documents, and hierarchical code tree. The descriptor manager shows all the variables that were defined for the project and the associated data themselves.

Designed to be as transparent and simple to operate as possible, EthnoNotes features are organized similarly to the relational database schematic presented earlier (see Figure 22.4). Some of the most useful features include the variety of reports (e.g., coding statistics, charting, and code-by-code matrix); the ease of exporting selected results, statistics, and graphs; and a training center that facilitates the development of team interrater reliability. Further, the system is collaborative and dynamic. Any number of team members can be working on different aspects of the project database with real-time updating for all users. For example, if a researcher is generating and exporting charts for presentation at the same time a project assistant is engaged in coding excerpts, the researcher will have immediate access to the new work that can be included when the charts are created.

System transparency and seamless movement from one aspect of the database to another is illustrated in Figure 22.6. These screenshots show the following: (a) a bar chart displaying the frequency of a particular code (pre-writing in the household) for each of three home language descriptors (Spanish, Bilingual, English); (b) by clicking on any of these bars, the database calls up and displays the excerpts coded for all the households in that descriptor (e.g., Spanish-speaking households); (c) by clicking the name of the resource document from which a particular excerpt was extracted, the program presents the excerpt within the entire interview context to look more deeply into the parents' report; and (d) excerpts can then be reopened in the coding window for the addition of new codes to the excerpt that might be now understood as relevant. Codes, excerpts, transcripts, ID information, and all the descriptors and demographics for the sample are similarly linked so that users can look for patterns within charts and tables, codes, transcripts with excerpts, or full document review.

Figure 22.6 EthnoNotes Charting, Exploring, and Coding

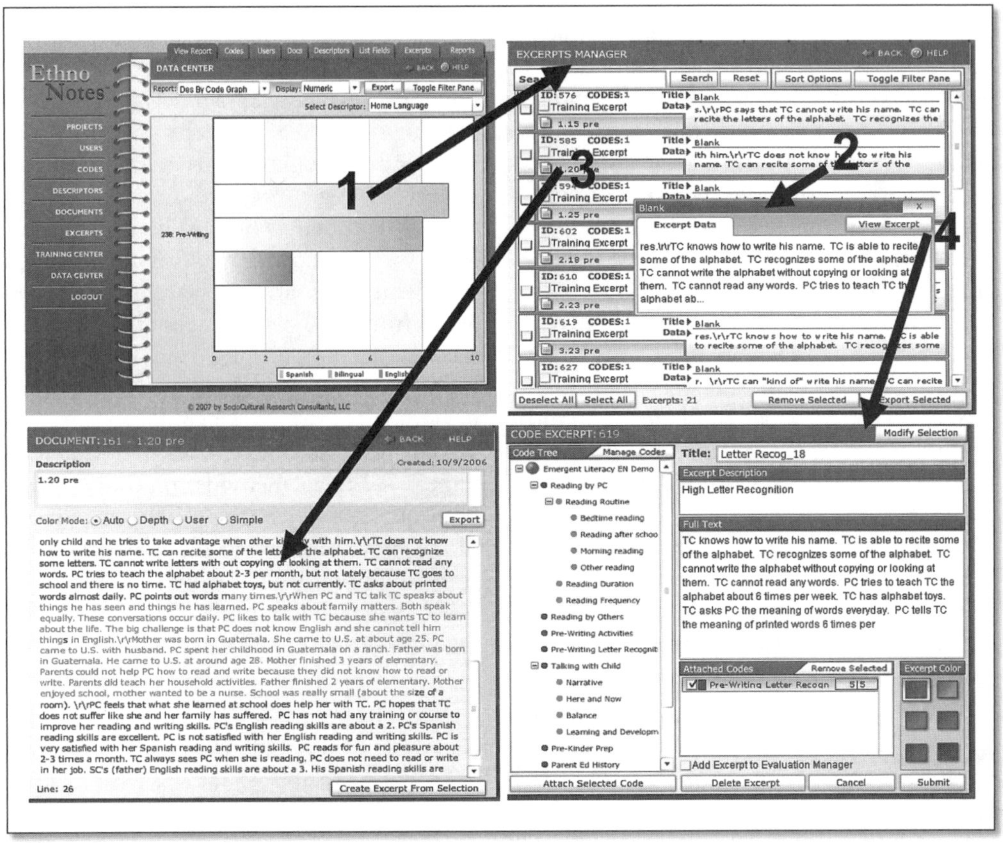

In the illustration, the graph displays how "Pre-Writing" coded excerpts were distributed across families reporting different primary home language. The associated excerpts can be quickly reviewed to better understand the qualitative content in the interviews that differs by home language group in pre-writing activities, and further information can be gleaned by examining the particular excerpts in the context of the full interview data. Note how moving the cursor over a bar on a bar graph displays the interview or field note excerpts that were coded into that category. A click takes the analyst from the quantitative code reflected in the bar graph back to the underlying comments and responses for that code. The same can be done for other graphs and subgroup analyses to address a variety of questions: What did bilingual parents with high to very high codes for home literacy activities say and do? Were these responses different for homes reporting Spanish as their primary language, or for parents whose kids also did well on standardized tests? And so forth.

◆ Presentation and Reporting of Mixed Methods Research

There are at least as many ways to present and report mixed methods research as there are ways to carry it out. With various forms of data to include in the analyses, the mixed methods researcher has a wide variety of approaches to presenting study findings (e.g., charts, tables, statistics, figures, narrative, and quotations). Given the variety of forms reporting may take, describing your methods in detail, complete with justification for key decisions, will go a long way in convincing reviewers and readers of the systematic work behind your approach. These details should include information about the sample, recruitment, procedures, measures (e.g., surveys and interview protocols), levels of analysis and how mixed methods were implemented and integrated, data management and transformation, and code system development and reliability procedures and results. Sharing the specifics of our methods with others will help expand and reinforce confidence and appreciation for how mixed methods work is conducted.

◆ Conclusions

In this chapter, we have suggested solutions for some of the challenges faced by mixed methods researchers. Models for accomplishing such research, such as those offered here and throughout this handbook, can help the field grow. Collaboration with colleagues of differing backgrounds can be an ideal way to move beyond those methods with which they are most familiar. We then learn from and teach each other how to study a common problem and discover new ways to integrate skills. Contemporary technological tools available to serve a mixed methods research team continue to improve. Mixed methods, of course, have been used for generations. The current era offers more systematic models, new software solutions, and a growing network of researchers using improved and more practical mixed methods for the future.

Research Questions and Exercises

1. This chapter discusses three challenges to a broader employment of mixed methods in social science research. Identify and describe each.

2. Discuss the value of teamwork in mixed methods research design.

3. What information can be obtained via an audit of project resources? Following an audit, what decisions may require rethinking, and what are potential costs and benefits?

4. What did the authors mean by the "end game," and how can thinking about these issues help improve the likelihood of success?

5. Discuss the value of establishing reliable coding systems. What can a team working together to demonstrate reliability produce that an individual cannot?

6. What are the procedures for creating empirically based dimensions from qualitative data tagged with particular codes? What types of analyses can these dimensions make possible, and how are they valuable to mixed methods research?

7. Given what the authors present on the nature of relational database systems, discuss the pros and cons of using computer-assisted solutions, for example, EthnoNotes, ATLAS.ti, or others, for the management, analysis, and presentation of mixed methods data.

◆ Note

1. EthnoNotes is a rich Internet application owned, developed, and distributed by SocioCultural Research Consultants, LLC (SCRC). SCRC was founded by the authors, Lieber and Weisner, who both retain a significant financial interest in the company's performance. Although we believe our description of EthnoNotes and its value for mixed methods research is accurate, readers should consider the authors' relationship with SCRC.

◆ References

Axinn, W. G., & Pearce, L. D. (2006). *Mixed method data collection strategies*. New York: Cambridge University Press.

Bernard, H. R. (1995). *Research methods in anthropology: Qualitative and quantitative approaches*. Walnut Creek, CA: AltaMira Press.

Bernard, H. R., & Ryan, G. W. (1998). Text analysis: Qualitative and quantitative methods. In H. R. Bernard (Ed.), *Handbook of methods in cultural anthropology* (pp. 595–646). Walnut Creek, CA: AltaMira Press.

Bernheimer, L. B., & Weisner, T. S. (2007). "Let me just tell you what I do all day . . .": The family story at the center of intervention research and practice. *Infants & Young Children, 20*, 192–201.

Bryman, A. (2006). Integrating quantitative and qualitative research: How is it done? *Qualitative Research, 6*(1), 97–113.

Bryman, A. (2007). Barriers to integrating quantitative and qualitative research. *Journal of Mixed Methods Research, 1*(1), 8–22.

Campbell, D. T., & Stanley, J. C. (1963). *Experimental and quasi-experimental designs for research*. Boston: Houghton Mifflin.

Clausen, S. E. (1998). *Applied correspondence analysis: An introduction*. Thousand Oaks, CA: Sage.

Collins, K. M. T., Onwuegbuzie, A. J., & Jiao, Q. G. (2007). A mixed methods investigation of mixed methods sampling designs in social science research. *Evaluation and Research in Education, 19*, 83–101.

Creswell, J. W., & Plano Clark, V. L. (2007). *Designing and conducting mixed methods research*. Thousand Oaks, CA: Sage.

Creswell, J. W., Plano Clark, V. L., Gutmann, M. L., & Hanson, W. E. (2002). Advanced mixed methods design. In A. Tashakkori and C. Teddlie (Eds.), *Handbook of mixed methods research designs* (pp. 209–239). Thousand Oaks, CA: Sage.

Dellinger, A. B., & Leech, N. L. (2007). Toward a unified validation framework in mixed methods research. *Journal of Mixed Methods Research, 1*(4), 309–332.

Duncan, G. J., Huston, A. C., & Weisner, T. S. (2007). *Higher ground: New hope for the working poor and their children*. New York: Russell Sage.

Ercikan, K., & Roth, W. M. (2006). What good is polarizing research into qualitative and quantitative? *Educational Researcher, 35*(5), 14–23.

Fuligni, A., Weisner, T., & Gonzalez, N. (2008). Family obligation and assistance among adolescents with Mexican backgrounds. NICHD grant proposal.

Fuligni, A. J., & Pedersen, S. (2002). Family obligation and the transition to young adulthood. *Developmental Psychology, 38*(5), 856–868.

Gallimore, R., Coots, J. J., Weisner, T. S., Garnier, H., & Guthrie, G. (1996). Family responses to children with early developmental delays: II. Accommodation intensity and activity in early and middle childhood. *American Journal of Mental Retardation, 101*(3), 215–232.

Greene, J. C. (2007). *Mixed methods in social inquiry*. San Francisco: Jossey-Bass.

Greene, J. C., Caracelli, V. J., & Graham, W. F. (1989). Toward a conceptual framework for mixed-method evaluation designs. *Education Evaluation and Policy Analysis, 11*(3), 255–274.

Handwerker, W. P., & Borgatti, S. P. (1998). Reasoning with numbers. In H. R. Bernard (Ed.), *Handbook of methods in cultural anthropology* (pp. 549–593). Walnut Creek, CA: AltaMira Press.

House, E. R. (1994). Integrating the quantitative and qualitative. *New Directions for Program Evaluation, 61*, 13–22.

Hruschka, D. J., Schwartz, D., St. John, D. C., Picone-Decaro, E., Jenkins, R. A., & Carey, J. W. (2004). Reliability in coding open-ended data: Lessons learned from HIV behavioral research. *Field Methods, 16*(3), 307–331.

Johnson, R. B., & Onwuegbuzie, A. J. (2004). Mixed methods research: A research paradigm whose time has come. *Educational Researcher, 33*(7), 14–26.

Johnson, R. B., Onwuegbuzie, A. J., & Turner, L. A. (2007). Toward a definition of mixed methods research. *Journal of Mixed Methods Research, 1*(2), 112–133.

Kemper, E. A., Stringfield, S., & Teddlie, C. (2003). Mixed methods sampling strategies in social science research. In A. Tashakkori & C. Teddlie (Eds.), *Handbook of mixed methods in social & behavioral research* (pp. 273–296). Thousand Oaks, CA: Sage.

Keogh, B. K., Bernheimer, L. P., Gallimore, R., & Weisner, T. S. (1998). Child and family outcomes over time: A longitudinal perspective on developmental delays. In M. Lewis & C. Feiring (Eds.), *Families, risks, and competence* (pp. 269–287). Mahwah, NJ: Erlbaum.

Kruskal, J. B., & Wish, M. (1978). *Multidimensional scaling*. Beverly Hills, CA: Sage.

Lieber, E. (2009). Mixing qualitative and quantitative methods: Insights into design and analysis issues. *Journal of Ethnographic & Qualitative Research, 3*, 218–227.

Lieber, E., Chin, D., Li, L., Rotheram-Borus, M. J., Detels, R., Wu, Z., Guan, J., & the National Institute of Mental Health (NIMH) Collaborative HIV Prevention Trial Group. (2009). Sociocultural contexts and communication about sex in China: Informing HIV/STD prevention programs. *AIDS Education and Prevention, 21*(6), 415–429.

Lieber, E., Davis, H., & Weisner, T. (2009). *Differences in home literacy environments for English language learners*. Unpublished manuscript. University of California, Los Angeles.

Lieber, E., Davis, H., Weisner, T., & Lefkowitz-Burt, S. (2007, March 29–April 1). *Unpackaging early literacy beliefs and practices of low-income, Latino parents in the US*. Presented at the Society for Research in Child Development (SRCD) Biennial Meeting, Boston.

Lieber, E., Li, L., Wu, Z., Rotheram-Borus, M. J., Guan, J., & the National Institute of Mental Health (NIMH) Collaborative HIV Prevention Trial Group (2006). HIV/AIDS stigmatization fears as health seeking barriers in China. *AIDS and Behavior, 10*(5), 263–271. Available at http://dx.doi.org/10.1007/s10461–005–9047–5

Lieber, E., Nihira, K., & Mink, I. T. (2004). Filial piety, modernization, and the challenges of raising children for Chinese immigrants: Quantitative and qualitative evidence. *Ethos, 32*(3), 324–347.

MacQueen, K. M., McLellan, E., Kay, K., & Milstein, B. (1998). Codebook development for team-based qualitative analysis. *Cultural Anthropology Methods, 10*(2), 31–36.

Matheson, C., Olson, R., & Weisner, T. S. (2007). A good friend is hard to find: Friendship among adolescents with disabilities. *American Journal of Mental Retardation, 112*, 319–329.

McGrath, J. (1981). Dilemmatics: The study of research choices and dilemmas. *American Behavioral Scientist, 25*, 179–210.

Miles, M. B., & Huberman, A. M. (1994). *Qualitative data analysis: An expanded sourcebook*. Thousand Oaks, CA: Sage.

Muhr, Thomas. (2004). *User's manual for ATLAS.ti 5.0*. Scientific Software Development. GmbH, Berlin.

Niglas, K. (1999, September 22–25). *Quantitative and qualitative inquiry in educational research: Is there a paradigmatic difference between them?* Paper presented at the European Conference on Education Research (ECER), Lahti, Finland. Education Line, available at http://www.leeds.ac.uk/educol/

Niglas, K. (2001, September 5–8). *Paradigms and methodology in educational research*. Paper presented at the European Conference on Education Research (ECER), Lille, France. Education Line, available at http://www.leeds.ac.uk/educol/

NIMH Collaborative HIV/STD Prevention Trial Group (Lieber, E., China-Ethnographic methods representative and secondary author) (2007a). Design and integration of ethnography within an international behavior change HIV/sexually transmitted disease prevention trial. *AIDS, 21*(Suppl. 2), S37–S48.

NIMH Collaborative HIV/STD Prevention Trial Group (Lieber, E., China-Ethnographic methods representative and primary author) (2007b). Formative study conducted in five countries to adapt the community popular opinion leader intervention. *AIDS, 21* (Suppl. 2), S91–S98.

Onwuegbuzie, A. J., & Leech, N. L. (2005). Taking the "Q" out of research: Teaching research methodology courses without the divide between quantitative and qualitative paradigms. *Quality and Quantity, 39*, 267–296.

Onwuegbuzie, A. J., Slate, J. R., Leech, N. L., & Collins, K. M. T. (2009). Mixed data analysis: Advanced integration techniques. *International Journal of Multiple Research Approaches, 3*(1), 13–33.

Pearce, L. D. (2002). Integrating survey and ethnographic methods for systematic anomalous case analysis. *Sociological Methodology, 32*(1), 103–132.

Romney, A. K. (1999). Cultural consensus as a statistical model. *Current Anthropology, 40*(Suppl.), S103–S115.

Ryan, G. W., & Bernard, H. R. (2003). Techniques to identify themes. *Field Methods, 15*(1), 85–109.

Shulha, L., & Wilson, R. (2003). Collaborative mixed methods research. In A. Tashakkori and C. Teddlie (Eds.), *Handbook of mixed methods in social & behavioral research* (pp. 639–670). Thousand Oaks, CA: Sage.

SocioCultural Research Consultants. (2008). EthnoNotes Version 1.2, available at http://www.ethnonotes.com

Tashakkori, A., & Teddlie, C. (1998). *Mixed methodology: Combining qualitative and quantitative approaches*. Thousand Oaks, CA: Sage.

Tashakkori, A., & Teddlie, C. (2003). The past and future of mixed methods research: From data triangulation to mixed model designs. In A. Tashakkori & C. Teddlie (Eds.), *Handbook of mixed methods in social & behavioral research* (pp. 671–702). Thousand Oaks, CA: Sage.

Teddlie, C., & Tashakkori, A. (2009). *Foundations of mixed methods research: Integrating quantitative and qualitative techniques in the social and behavioral sciences*. Thousand Oaks, CA: Sage.

Teddlie, C., & Yu, F. (2007). Mixed methods sampling: A typology with examples. *Journal of Mixed Methods Research, 1*(1), 77–100.

VERBI Software. (2008). MAXqda. Consult. Sozialforschung. GmbH, Germany.

Weisner, T. S. (1996). Why ethnography should be the most important method in the study of human development. In R. Jessor, A. Colby, & R. Shweder (Eds.), *Ethnography and human development: Context and meaning in social inquiry* (pp. 305–324). Chicago: University of Chicago Press.

Weisner, T. S. (2002). Ecocultural understanding of children's developmental pathways. *Human Development, 45*, 275–281.

Weisner, T. S., Matheson, C., Coots, J., & Bernheimer, L. (2005). Sustainability of daily routines as a family outcome. In A. Maynard & M. Martini (Eds.), *The psychology of learning in cultural context* (pp. 41–73). New York: Kluwer/Plenum.

Weller, S. C. (2007). Cultural consensus theory: Application and frequently asked questions. *Field Methods, 19*(4), 339–368.

Yoshikawa, H., Lowe, E. D., Bos, J., Weisner, T. S., Nikulina, V., & Hsueh, J. (2006). Do pathways through low-wage work matter for children's development? In H. Yoshikawa, T. S. Weisner, & E. Lowe (Eds.), *Making it work: Low-wage employment, family life, and child development* (pp. 54–73). New York: Russell Sage.

Yoshikawa, H., Weisner, T. S., Kalil, A., & Way, N. (2008). Mixing qualitative and quantitative research in developmental science: Uses and methodological choices. *Developmental Psychology, 44*(2), 344–354.

Yoshikawa, H., Weisner, T. S., & Lowe, E. (Eds.). (2006). *Making it work: Low-wage employment, family life, and child development*. New York: Russell Sage.

23

EMERGING TRENDS IN THE UTILIZATION OF INTEGRATED DESIGNS IN THE SOCIAL, BEHAVIORAL, AND HEALTH SCIENCES

◆ Nataliya Ivankova and Yoko Kawamura

Objectives

To be able to

- delineate the need for the examination of mixed methods application across disciplines;

- discuss the trends and content of mixed methods discipline-related methodological discussions within 2000–2009;

- analyze the trends in adoption of mixed methods empirical research across the years, countries, disciplines, and designs within 2000–2008;

- describe mixed methods application in select disciplines: health and medicine, education, computer sciences, and social work; and

- examine how quantitative and qualitative methods are mixed within integrated designs to achieve meaningful meta-inferences.

◆ Introduction

Mixed methods research is growing in its applications across social, behavioral, and health sciences. With recognition of mixed methods as the "third research paradigm" (Johnson & Onwuegbuzie, 2004, p. 14) or the "third methodological movement" (Teddlie & Tashakkori, 2003, p. 5), mixed methods designs have gained popularity in different disciplines (Tashakkori & Creswell, 2007). This popularity is due to their utility in applied research (Creswell & Plano Clark, 2007), their ability to address the research problem more comprehensively (Teddlie & Tashakkori, 2009), and their focus on generating more valid meta-inferences (Green & Caracelli, 1997). Mixed methods studies offer possibilities for "synergy and knowledge growth that mono-method studies cannot match" (Padgett, 2009, p. 104) and provide opportunities to think creatively and to theorize beyond the quantitative-qualitative divide (Mason, 2006).

Tashakkori and Creswell (2008) identified two parallel factors that underline the development of mixed methods research across disciplines. In some disciplines the researchers felt the need to use all possible methods to answer complex study research questions; in others, the complexity of the social phenomena dictated the need to explore them from various facets and multiple perspectives. The need for the use of integrated designs across disciplines has been also stimulated by calls from the major funding agencies in the United States. In 1999, the Office of Behavioral and Social Science Research of the National Institute of Health issued the guidelines for the use of qualitative methods in health research in which several approaches for combining quantitative and qualitative research were discussed (National Institute of Health, 1999). Similarly, a 2003 National Science Foundation workshop emphasized the development of hybrid methodologies that bring together the strengths of qualitative and quantitative methods (Ragin, Nagel, & White, 2004), while the National Research Council of the National Academy of Sciences specified a sequence of three guiding research questions (qualitative-quantitative-qualitative) for quality educational research (Shavelson & Towne, 2002).

Progress in mixed methods research, however, has been reflected differently across human sciences. The contextual factors demanding the exclusive use of experimental research and randomized control trials to achieve evidence-based outcomes (Ansari, Phillips & Hammick, 2001; Chatterji, 2005; Micari, Light, Calkins, & Streitwieser, 2007) have led to a different degree of adoption of mixed methods approach in the respective fields. In addition, underlying ontological and epistemological assumptions of social, behavioral, and health sciences disciplines dictate the choice of predominant inquiry strategies (Giddings & Grant, 2006; Johnson & Onwuegbuzie, 2004) and have resulted in unique applications of mixed methods designs. Besides, mixed methods practices vary across countries and continents.

Variability of means to combine and integrate quantitative and qualitative methods within one study reflects the complexity of the social world that we attempt to understand and in which we attempt to intervene (Giddings & Grant, 2007). Drawing on a set of available strategies from one discipline might not be sufficient nowadays with increased interdisciplinary and international mixed methods research projects (Gorard, Beng Huat, Smith, & White, 2007; Harkness et al., 2006; Harper, Neubauer, Bangi, & Francisco, 2008; Ungar, Clark, Kwong, Makhnach, & Cameron, 2005). Learning from different practices and employing effective integrative techniques might help mixed methods researchers achieve meaningful inferences in answer to complex research questions. It might also help conceptualize and foresee the methodological developments in the utilization of mixed methods research across disciplines, modifications in basic mixed methods designs to fit the epistemological traditions of various disciplines, and emergence of cross-disciplinary strategies of integrating quantitative and qualitative methods to achieve meaningful inferences. Thus, the intent of this chapter is to examine how mixed methods research is used in different disciplines, to describe the trends and content of the underlying methodological discussions, to analyze the prevailing integrated designs, and to identify the means of mixing quantitative and qualitative methods to achieve quality meta-inferences.

♦ Emergent Methodological Discussions

Consistent search of the five major databases—PubMed, ERIC, PsycInfo, Academic One File, and Academic Search Premier—and two mixed methods journals, the *Journal of Mixed Methods Research* and the *International Journal of Multiple Research Approaches*, from January 2000 to April 2009, yielded 113 peer-reviewed methodological discussions of the use of mixed methods research in different disciplines. These included discussion papers, editorials, and meta-analysis of mixed methods

applications in specific subject areas excluding the articles focused on the general methodological and procedural issues of mixed methods research. Because we were interested in the adoption of mixed methods research across disciplines, we were looking for discussions reflecting the authors' awareness of mixed methods research and intentional use of the terms "mixed method," "mixed-method," or "mixed methods" either in the title or in the abstract. In our analysis, we also considered the discipline and the authors' country of affiliation.

INCREASED INTEREST TO MIXED METHODS RESEARCH

As expected, a consistent growth in the mixed methods methodological discussions is observed since 2000, with 2006 ($n = 26$) and 2008 ($n = 22$) being the most prolific (see Figure 23.1). We assume that publication of the *Handbook of Mixed Methods in the Behavioral & Social Sciences* in 2003 was one of the reasons that account for the significant increase in interest in mixed methods research that has occurred since 2004. Across the countries, the United

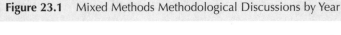

Figure 23.1   Mixed Methods Methodological Discussions by Year

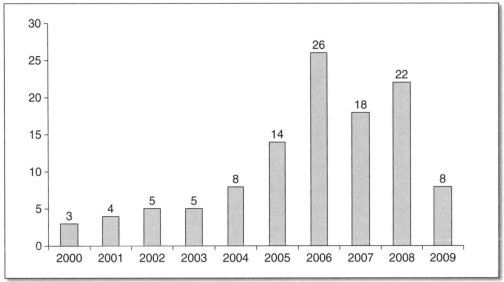

States (*n* = 55) took the lead in mixed methods methodological discussions, with the United Kingdom (*n* = 25), Canada (*n* = 13), and Australia (*n* = 9) following, and covered a range of social, behavioral, and health disciplines (see Figure 23.2). Methodology-related papers have been published consistently over the reviewed period both in the United States and in the United Kingdom, with the numbers steadily increasing each year. By 2009, quite a number of European scholars published at least one mixed methods methodological discussion in the following disciplines: Austria—psychology (Gelo, Braakmann, & Benetka, 2008), Denmark—herd health management (Kristensen, Nielsen, Jensen, Vaarst, & Enevoldsen, 2008), Finland—business (Hurmerinta-Peltomaki & Nummela, 2006), Germany—political studies (Rohlfing, 2008), the Netherlands—communication studies (Geurts & Roosendaal, 2001), Spain—communication studies (Martinez, Dimitriadis, Rubia, Gomez, & de la Fuente,

Figure 23.2   Mixed Methods Methodological Discussions by Year and Country of the First Author's Affiliation

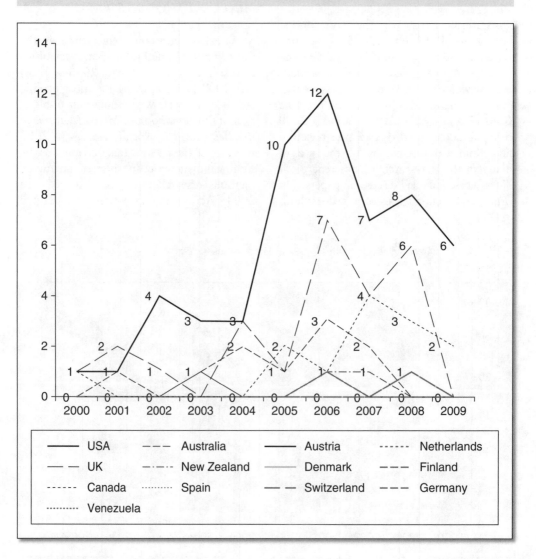

2003; Martinez et al., 2006), and Switzerland—political studies (Doorenspleet & Kopecky, 2008). Scholars from New Zealand and Venezuela also contributed to mixed methods discussions in nursing (Giddings & Grant, 2006, 2007) and education (Niaz, 2008), respectively.

Reasons for Mixed Methods Research

Discipline wise, the use of the mixed methods approach is discussed in publications of scholars from more than 30 disciplines and 10 subject areas (see Table 23.1). Interestingly, about half of the discussions pertain to health and medicine and span such disciplines as health care, nursing, primary care, physical therapy, rehabilitation, palliative care, clinical research, and mental health. The general advantages of mixed methods research as well as its ability to reveal high quality and complex inferences (Rauscher & Greenfield, 2009) are cited as the reasons for the growing interest in mixed methods designs in these disciplines. In the United Kingdom, for example, the primary impetus stems from the extended practice of combining qualitative research with randomized control trials (O'Cathain, Murphy, & Nicholl, 2007). Halcomb and Andrew (2005), from Australia, argued that, due to the complex nature of phenomena investigated by nurses, mixing quantitative and qualitative approaches is necessary to develop nursing knowledge. Similarly, in education, the need for thorough understanding of programs as they take hold in organizational or community settings and the influence of contextual and site-specific variables call for multiple research methods for making generalized causal inferences (Chatterji, 2005). The recent introduction of qualitative methods to the investigation of the issues of inclusion and learning in library and information services to augment quantitative measures prompted an exploration of how mixed methods designs can be used in the evaluation of electronic information services (Dalton & McNicoi, 2004; Fidel,

2008). Niaz (2008) pointed out that quantitative data by itself facilitates progress neither in the physical sciences nor in education. A major argument in favor of mixed methods (integrative) research is that "it provides a rationale for hypotheses/theories/guiding assumptions/presuppositions to compete and provide alternatives" (p. 298).

Although contextual reasons vary across disciplines, the complexity of research objectives, the inductive logic of qualitative inquiry, and the utility of mixed methods designs that allowed for meaningful combinations of quantitative and qualitative methods in a single study seem to be the major factors that caused social, behavioral, and health sciences to embrace mixed methods research. Interestingly, even such quantitatively oriented disciplines as geographical studies and human geographies (Hemming, 2008; Jiang, 2003) and herd health management (Kristensen et al., 2008) refer to mixed methods as a useful methodology to capture the human component, such as an individual's experiences and beliefs, involved in the interpretation of the research results. For example, Kristensen and colleagues illustrated how the results from two projects, a quantitative observational study of risk factors for metritis in Danish dairy cows based on data from the Danish Cattle Database and a semi-structured interview study involving 20 practicing veterinarians, helped validate the relations between herd risk factors and metritis and identify several problems with correctness and validity of data regarding the occurrence of metritis because of differences in case definitions and thresholds for treatments between veterinarians.

Procedural Issues of Mixed Methods Research

The content of the methodological discussions ranges from general issues of mixed methods research, its procedural characteristics and applicability in a certain discipline, to meta-reviews of the mixed

Table 23.1 Mixed Methods Methodological Discussions by Year and Subject Areas

Subject Area	2000	2001	2002	2003	2004	2005	2006	2007	2008	2009	Total
Business	0	0	0	0	0	1	1	0	0	0	2
Communication studies	0	1	0	3	0	0	1	0	0	0	5
Education	2	0	0	0	0	4	7	2	1	1	17
Health and medicine	1	2	2	0	6	5	13	10	10	5	54
Library studies	0	0	0	0	2	0	0	0	1	0	3
Political studies	0	0	0	0	0	1	0	0	2	0	3
Psychology	2	0	0	0	0	2	1	2	3	0	10
Social work	0	0	0	0	0	1	1	1	0	1	4
Sociology	0	0	1	0	1	0	2	3	5	1	13
Women's studies	0	0	1	1	0	0	0	0	0	0	2
Total	5	3	4	4	9	14	26	18	22	8	113

methods design studies in specific subject areas, to the description of a particular strategy viewed as an example of mixed methods designed to achieve research objectives important in this discipline. Quite a few studies are devoted to the procedural issues of mixed methods research and the ways it can be utilized in a specific discipline. For example, Wilkins and Woodgate (2008) addressed the issues of designing a mixed methods study in pediatric oncology nursing research. They referred to the mixed methods literature in both social and health sciences and illustrated the suggested design steps with the concurrent mixed methods study of adolescents' experiences of fatigue and perceptions of its impact on quality of life during and after treatment of cancer. Rauscher and Greenfield (2009) described how three basic mixed methods designs (sequential explanatory, in which qualitative methods follow the quantitative methods; sequential exploratory, in which qualitative methods precede the quantitative methods; and concurrent triangulation, in which both methods are used simultaneously) can be utilized in physical therapy research. Hanson, Creswell, Plano Clark, Petska, and Creswell (2005) identified six different types of mixed methods designs applicable to counseling psychology and outlined the steps and procedures used in these designs. They illustrated the important design features using the studies published in the counseling literature. London, Schwartz, and Scott (2007) demonstrated how mixed methods research, with its integrated sampling, data collection, and data analysis, can yield important and unexpected insights in welfare reform policy research that neither method alone could generate. In education, Li, Marquart, and Zercher (2000) described the practical strategies for conducting mixed methods data analysis in terms of data reduction, transformation, comparison, and interpretation in early childhood intervention research. These "how to" discussions are invaluable in helping researchers accept and apply mixed

methods research in their disciplines. Importantly, several such publications specifically target novice researchers, reaching out to undergraduate students too (Anaf & Sheppard, 2007; Giddings & Grant, 2006).

META-REVIEWS

As the volume of mixed methods discussions grew with the years, the interest to meta-reviews aimed at detailed analysis of published mixed methods research in select disciplines increased as well. We identified 11 such discussions, with 9 being published within 2006–2009. Out of these 11 papers, 4 focused on the comprehensive review of the published studies in the specific field, including quantitative, qualitative, and mixed methods (i.e., studies consisting of quantitative and qualitative components). Classification of research as belonging to quantitative, qualitative, or mixed methods was done based on the type of data collected in the study. The overall number of mixed methods studies comparative to quantitative and qualitative ones found in each field was not large, but taking into consideration a relatively young age of mixed methods research (Teddlie & Tashakkori, 2009), the results are promising: 5% ($n = 22$) in library studies (Fidel, 2008), 14% ($n = 68$) in business (Hurmerinta-Peltomaki & Nummela, 2006), 29% ($n = 207$) in mathematics education (Hart, Smith, Swars, & Smith, 2009), and 15 studies in end-of-life cancer research (Harris et al., 2008). In some areas, mixed methods studies could not be easily identified. For example, in library and information sciences, Fidel (2008) explained that the recognition of mixed methods research by name or as a research method was absent from the articles and from the methodological literature. Hart et al. (2009) reported that often the methods were not explicitly described in the article text, thus prompting them to also consider qualitative data in combination with descriptive statistics as meeting the definition of mixed methods research.

The difficulties in locating the studies that explicitly employed the mixed methods approach in the discipline of interest was also reported by some authors who focused their meta-reviews only on mixed methods empirical studies. The available mixed methods meta-reviews span such disciplines as communication studies (Rocco, Bliss, Gallagher, & Perez-Prado, 2003), family sciences (Plano Clark, Huddleston-Casas, Churchill, Green, & Garrett, 2008), health services (O'Cathain et al., 2007), primary care (Creswell, Fetters, & Ivankova, 2004), school psychology (Powell, Mihalas, Onwuegbuzie, Suldo, & Daley, 2008), and special education (Collins, Onwuegbuzie, & Jiao, 2006; Collins, Onwuegbuzie, & Sutton, 2006). While searching for mixed methods studies, besides the traditional terms "mixed method(s)" (Collins, Onwuegbuzie, & Sutton, 2006; Powell et al., 2008), the researchers often had to use additional search criteria such as "multimethod AND primary care," "qualitative AND quantitative methods AND family medicine" (Creswell et al., 2004), and "quantitative OR survey" and "qualitative OR interview" (Plano Clark et al., 2008) to locate the studies that met their definition of mixed methods research. This is specifically true of the studies published prior to 2003 when the *Handbook of Mixed Methods in the Behavioral and Social Sciences* was released. Creswell and colleagues (2004), for instance, could locate only five studies in primary care that could be classified as mixed methods according to social science criteria. Even in most current reviews, mixed methods research has not been reported as prevalent in the reviewed discipline (Plano Clark et al., 2008; Powell et al., 2008).

The major focus of these meta-analyses was to identify the purposes of and the trends in the use of mixed methods designs, however the approaches differ among the authors. Rocco and colleagues (2003), in

their review of 16 online articles published from 1999 to 2001 in the *Information Technology, Learning and Performance Journal*, distinguish confirmatory and exploratory mixed methods studies based on their primary purpose. Plano Clark and colleagues (2008) pay more attention to the design features and procedural issues in family sciences mixed methods research, differentiating between the studies that used one of the four designs that differ in the sequence and dominance of the quantitative and qualitative methods: "triangulation," "explanatory," "exploratory," and "embedded." Powell and colleagues (2008) reviewed mixed methods studies in school psychology based on the timing of the data collection and analysis (sequential vs. concurrent), priority of each method (quantitative or qualitative dominance), and whether the studies were truly or partially mixed. Two years before, Collins, Onwuegbuzie, and Jiao (2006) discussed 42 studies in school psychology based on a two-dimensional mixed methods sampling model, within which sampling designs can be classified according to the time orientation of the components (concurrent vs. sequential) and the relationship of the qualitative and quantitative samples (identical vs. parallel vs. nested vs. multilevel).

Importantly, few meta-reviews paid attention to how quantitative and qualitative results in mixed methods studies were integrated to achieve meaningful inferences. Mixing or integration is an essential component in mixed methods research. The purpose of mixing is to produce understandings that go beyond the knowledge that is generated by the separate components of the study (O'Cathain et al., 2007). For example, Plano Clark and colleagues (2008) remarked that, consistent with other disciplines, quantitative and qualitative methods were not sufficiently integrated in family sciences mixed methods studies. None of the studies in the reviewed sample had an overarching mixed methods question to guide the whole study.

CROSS-DISCIPLINARY INTEGRATIVE STRATEGIES

More attention to methods integration is observed in the studies that are devoted to the use of mixed methods as a strategy for new ways of achieving better understanding of the research problem. Most often these are mixed methods extensions of the qualitative methods or innovative strategies capitalizing on the traditional uses of mono-methods adopted in the specific discipline. Thus, Micari, Light, Calkins, and Streitwieser (2007) described a mixed methods evaluation model based on the qualitative method phenomenography that can be used to evaluate how learners think in multiple contexts and how their thinking may change over time. In this model, phenomenography, which is a qualitative strategy, generates categories that describe specific conceptions of and approaches to learning in particular contexts that are further tested quantitatively. Similarly, Luck, Jackson, and Usher (2006) categorized case study research in nursing as mixed methods. They argued that because case studies address complex life situations and utilize multiple methods to understand the nature of the case, they could be viewed as "a bridge that spans the research paradigms" (p. 105)—or the mixed methods approach. Lieberman (2005) also presented the joint case study approach with statistical analysis in the nested research designs from a mixed methods perspective. According to the author, this integrated strategy improves the prospects of making valid causal inferences in comparative political studies research.

Several authors (Ansari, Phillips, & Hammick, 2001; Flemming, 2007; Thomas et al., 2004) discussed integrating qualitative research with randomized control trials. Including qualitative methods in systematic reviews of interventions and implementation practices contributes to the overall evidence base generated from "a diverse range of enquiry methods" (Ansari et al., 2001, p. 222). Qualitative methods are seen as beneficial in explaining the process of interventions and how their outcomes were achieved as well as why interventions succeeded or failed. The insights gained from the synthesis of quantitative estimates with the qualitative understanding of people's lives allows for the "exploration of statistical heterogeneity in ways that it would be difficult to imagine in advance" (Thomas et al., 2004, p. 1012).

Concept mapping, another popular qualitative method in health care contexts, is discussed as an example of the mixed methods approach, which combines qualitative group processes (brainstorming, sorting, group interpretation) with a sequence of multivariate statistical analyses (multidimensional scaling, hierarchical cluster analysis) to assess the quality of health care (Trochim & Kane, 2005). The six-step procedure involves the generation of ideas, their sorting and rating by participants, and representation of ideas in maps created based on statistical tests. The integration of qualitative and quantitative techniques allows addressing complex configurations of issues in the health care system. Likewise, the nominal group technique (NGT) used in clinical research is introduced as a mixed methods approach because it can generate both quantitative and qualitative data in addressing clinical practice issues (Potter, Gordon, & Hamer, 2004). The purpose of NGT is to generate information in response to an issue that is then assessed through a group discussion in a highly structured environment. The combination of content analysis and scoring and rating methods during the data analysis provides an in-depth exploration of an issue and enriches evidence-based practice.

Integration of quantitative and qualitative methods was explored at the level of the literature review. Pluye, Gagnon, Griffiths, and Johnson-Lafleur (2009) presented the concept of a mixed methods studies review (MSR), a three-step review technique that concomitantly appraised the methodological quality of the qualitative, quantitative, and mixed methods studies in health sciences. The suggested MSR scoring system capitalizes on the integration of qualitative research into systematic reviews of quantitative studies and synthesizes quantitative and qualitative results of the reviewed studies, building corroborative knowledge based on all types of empirical research.

Finally, the synergistic value of combining quantitative and qualitative methods within a single study when the results are contradictory is the focus of several discussions. Moffatt, White, Mackintosh, and Howel (2006) demonstrated how using mixed methods in health services research can lead to different and sometimes conflicting accounts. They suggested a six-step approach to how such discrepancies could be used to explore quantitative and qualitative data sets more fully. Johnstone (2007) shared a different process of handling conflicting evidence in the mixed methods organizational research. She relied on three theoretical principles that contributed to the trustworthiness of qualitative research: triangulation, clear detailing of method of data collection and analysis, and researcher's reflexivity, which jointly helped researchers determine the relative importance and relevance of the various data in their research.

◆ Current Trends in Use of Mixed Methods Designs

To capture the trends in the use of mixed methods designs across disciplines since 2000, we searched the following major databases—*PubMed, ERIC, PsycINFO, Academic One File,* and *Academic Search Premier*—for mixed methods empirical studies that were published in peer-reviewed journals between January 2000 and April 2009. We focused only on the studies that were intentionally labeled "mixed methods" by the authors, thus showing their awareness of this research approach and their intentional use of the

terms "mixed method," "mixed-method," or "mixed methods" either in the title or in the abstract of the article.

The total number of all the articles picked up as a result of these searches reached about 2,000. After eliminating the overlapping studies across the databases, we scanned the rest for their titles and abstracts to select the empirical studies that met the accepted definition of mixed methods research (Tashakkori & Creswell, 2007) and that had both quantitative and qualitative components reflected in one paper. This way the number of empirical mixed methods studies published between January 2000 and April 2009 was reduced. Since 2009 was not a full year, we decided to exclude 2009 articles and leave only mixed methods studies published within 2000–2008. Thus, 689 mixed methods studies were used for further analysis. This is still an impressive number and just by itself shows the acceptance of mixed methods research across different disciplines. We then coded each study for the discipline, the first author country of affiliation, and mixed methods design used (concurrent vs. sequential).

Similar to methodological articles, the number of published empirical mixed methods studies steadily increased from 2000 to 2008 (see Figure 23.3). Only 10 studies were published in 2000 and 49 in 2004, while 2008 featured 243. By looking at the country of the first author's affiliation, half of the empirical mixed methods studies (*n* = 364) were conducted by researchers from the United States. They were followed by researchers from the United Kingdom (*n* = 141), Canada (*n* = 69), and Australia (*n* = 47), whose contribution was still significant compared with countries other than the United States and the United Kingdom. Besides these four, researchers in 29 countries and Puerto Rico (a special territory of the United States) published mixed methods studies between 2000 and 2008, representing five continents. The same tendency of the increase in the number of mixed methods studies is observed for all countries. It is obvious that researchers in Asian and Pacific countries, as well as Europe, relatively early

Figure 23.3 Mixed Methods Empirical Studies by Year

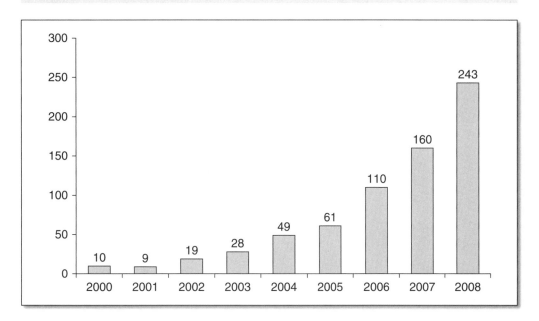

became aware of mixed methods and began to implement it. The movement of utilization of mixed methods in the Middle East and South American countries appeared relatively new, beginning in the last few years (see Figure 23.4).

Across disciplines, 70 fields were identified. However, some mixed methods studies were interdisciplinary, and it was difficult to assign them to a single discipline. In such cases, we referred to the journal names to help prioritize among multiple disciplines. For practical reasons, disciplines were further grouped into 16 subject categories, which are commonly used by libraries in databases classification. The number of studies per subject area varied widely (see Table 23.2), but predominance appeared to be in health and medicine ($n = 326$) and education ($n = 145$). It should be noted that health and medicine could include a wide range of disciplines related to health and medicine, and the areas covered by these disciplines might be broader compared to others. However, while education could cover as wide an area as health and medicine, the outstanding number of health and medicine mixed

methods studies is still noteworthy. This is consistent with the significant number of methodological discussions related to the applications of mixed methods in health and medical disciplines. It seems that the interdisciplinary perspectives required to deal with complexity of problems in the arena of health and medicine might have necessitated the need for a pragmatic approach to research, which demanded utilization of various research methods, including mixed methods. Quite a number of mixed methods studies were revealed in computer sciences ($n = 49$), sociology ($n = 41$), social work ($n = 33$), psychology ($n = 27$), communication studies ($n = 19$), and management ($n = 13$), which demonstrates the utility of mixed methods research across disciplines. Mixed methods studies also can be found in business, justice science, economics, marketing, ecological studies, language and linguistics, library studies, political studies, and women's studies. Looking at the number of the studies in different disciplines year by year, the trends in the increase of the use of mixed methods designs are consistent. Education and health and medicine had a dramatic increase

Figure 23.4 Mixed Methods Empirical Studies by Year and Country of the First Author's Affiliation

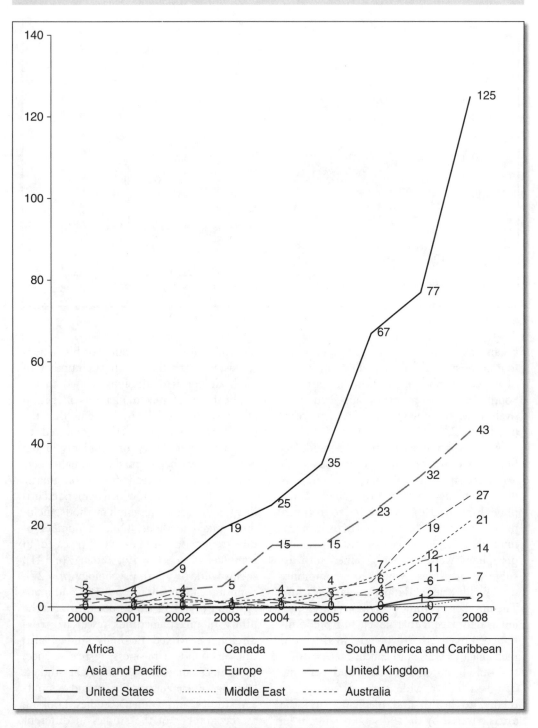

in 2007 and 2008, respectively. Computer sciences, management, and social work consistently increased from relatively early on, while the movement in psychology appeared to begin later and increased more rapidly over the last few years. Overall, utilization of mixed methods has expanded between 2000 and 2008.

Table 23.2 Mixed Methods Empirical Studies by Year and Subject Areas

Subject Area	2000	2001	2002	2003	2004	2005	2006	2007	2008	Total
Business	0	0	0	0	0	0	1	1	0	2
Communication studies	0	0	0	1	1	3	4	4	6	19
Computer sciences	0	0	3	3	2	6	5	10	20	49
Ecological studies	0	1	0	0	0	0	0	2	1	4
Economics	0	0	0	0	0	0	1	1	0	2
Education	2	2	1	4	13	12	19	40	53	146
Health and medicine	6	5	11	13	24	21	58	68	119	325
Justice science	0	0	0	0	1	1	0	4	1	7
Language and linguistics	0	0	0	0	1	0	1	2	4	8
Library studies	0	0	0	0	0	1	1	0	2	4
Management	1	1	0	2	1	2	2	2	2	13
Marketing	0	0	0	0	0	0	1	2	0	3
Political studies	0	0	0	0	0	1	1	0	0	2
Psychology	0	0	0	0	0	7	5	6	9	27
Social work	0	0	3	2	4	3	4	5	12	33
Sociology	1	0	1	3	2	3	7	13	11	41
Women's studies	0	0	0	0	0	1	0	0	3	4
Total	10	9	19	28	49	61	110	160	243	689

The predominant number of studies was reported as two-phase designs, so we also classified the studies according to the type of sequential or concurrent design used based on whether the quantitative and qualitative data were collected and analyzed concurrently or in a sequential order, building from one phase to another. Sometimes the designs were stated by the authors in the article title or abstract. In other cases, we referred to the descriptions of the methods in the article full texts if the design features were not clear. Concurrent mixed methods designs were used in 552 studies, and 125 studies were of a sequential design. Twelve studies were of a more complex design and had more than two quantitative and qualitative strands.

For a more detailed analysis, we decided to focus on the mixed methods studies published in 2008, taking into consideration that this year was the most prolific in the number of mixed methods empirical articles. There was a boost in the methodological discussions since 2006, some major mixed methods books were published, and the journals in different fields became more open to publishing mixed methods research. We believe that all these factors had an impact on the decision to use mixed methods to explore research problems even in the disciplines that favored a monomethod approach.

◆ Application of Mixed Methods Designs in Select Disciplines

The following sections will discuss the use of mixed methods research in health and medicine, education, computer sciences, and social work. We chose health and medicine and education because of the significant number of mixed methods studies in these disciplines. We selected computer sciences due to the lack of meta-analyses in this subject area and the fact that epistemological traditions in this field might provide

some new insight into the applications of mixed methods. We chose social work because of the steady growth of mixed methods studies in this discipline and the predominance of sequential design evaluation projects that methodologically differ from traditional concurrent evaluation studies.

HEALTH AND MEDICINE

Health and medicine counts the greatest number of mixed methods studies and covers various disciplines. The examination of the trends shows a wide variation in the utilization of mixed methods designs and the ways quantitative and qualitative methods are integrated to achieve meta-inferences. We chose two examples from health behavior and nursing to illustrate specific applications of mixed methods in health and medicine.

Fuentes (2008) used a sequential design with qualitative phase informing quantitative phase to explore abused women's risk of getting sexually transmitted infections (STI). The rationale for choosing a mixed methods ("mixed-method" in Fuentes's spelling) approach was that "combining qualitative and quantitative approaches leads to a triangulation of findings and richer detail than either method can generate alone" (p. 1592). In addition, "the findings generated by one method can be used to inform the second (instrumentation, sampling, etc.) while simultaneously expanding the scope and breadth of the study" (p. 1592). In her study, Fuentes wanted to delineate the pathways that link experiences of abused women's lives to heightened risk for sexually transmitted infections (STIs), including HIV/AIDS. To achieve this purpose, she first collected and analyzed the qualitative data, which was followed by the quantitative data collection and analysis. The obtained qualitative data were also used to complement the results from the quantitative study strand. Figure 23.5 presents the visual diagram of Fuentes's study.

Figure 23.5 Sequential Mixed Methods Design With Qualitative Phase Informing Quantitative in Fuentes's (2008) Study

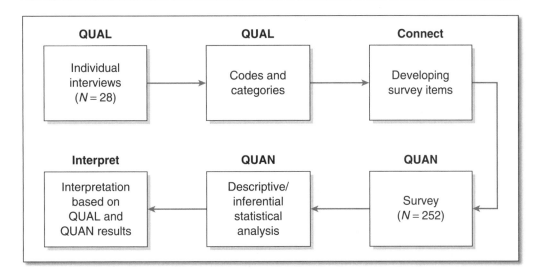

Fuentes (2008) conducted qualitative, in-depth, "life-history" interviews with 28 abused women of different ethnic groups and quantitative structured interviews with 251 abused and nonabused women. The sampling design was borrowed from ethnography and was aimed at searching for cultural variations and preceding life experiences. It was applied in both study strands, utilizing purposive and convenience sampling techniques for qualitative and quantitative data collection. The qualitative data were analyzed using a combination of inductive and deductive text approaches. A preliminary list of codes for sexual risk behaviors was created based on the literature, whereas additional codes regarding other STI/HIV risks were identified and incorporated in the list in the process of coding transcribed interview texts. On the basis of the final code list, a correspondence analysis was performed, in which the influence of ethnicity and abuse on sexual risk was tested by assessing the variations of 28 interviewees' characteristics in responses to the identified sexual risk factors. The findings from the qualitative strand were used to develop the scales to measure specific abuse-generated STI/HIV risk factors along with individuals' abuse conditions in the quantitative study strand.

Quantitative data analysis included three steps. First, reliability and construct validity of the developed measures were assessed. Second, a correspondence analysis was conducted to rigorously assess whether the sexual risk factors identified in the qualitative life-history interview, and further developed in the structured interviews, were related to each other, and to quantify the degree of relationship between each risk factor and the women's levels of experienced violence. Finally, a logistic regression analysis test was conducted to verify to what extent ethnicity might influence abuse-generated sexual risk.

The integration of the quantitative and qualitative methods in this study is evident. The findings from the qualitative strand (life-history interviews) formed the basis of the scales used in the quantitative strand (structured interviews). The findings from the qualitative interviews also were used to support the results from the analyses in the quantitative strand, such as correlation among the various types of abuse and the association between abuse experienced earlier in childhood and in adulthood. Life-history interviews provided additional insights into the nature of abuse, while the results of a logistic regression analysis assessing the relationship of ethnic differences with a likelihood of a history of STI/HIV was consistent with the results of a correspondence analysis of the qualitative data: Women's risk of getting STI/HIV was not related to ethnicity but rather to experience of abuse.

Fuentes (2008) achieved the study purpose by effectively using the findings from the first qualitative strand to create measurement scales and to also provide additional information that helped explain the pathways from abuse and risk for STI/HIV tested women in the second quantitative strand. Both sets of results showed that multiple sexual risk factors that might lead to STI/HIV infection were interrelated, but only the life-history interviews could provide insight on the sequence of risky behaviors. In addition, meta-inferences were created about the complex relationship between the risk of STI/HIV and the severity and frequencies of abuse in women, regardless of their ethnicity or sociodemographic status. In sum, this study illustrates how one method complements another, and the results are compared and contrasted to make stronger inferences even with relatively small sample sizes.

Another study conducted by Shipman and colleagues (2008) employed a concurrent mixed methods design with nested qualitative

component to evaluate the impact of the palliative care education and support programs on the knowledge and confidence of nurses in district nurse (DN) teams. The evaluation was conducted from summative and formative viewpoints, using different types of data for each. The summative component (quantitative strand) focused on measureable effects of the programs on nurses' knowledge, confidence, and perceived competence in the principles and practice of palliative care. This was assessed through a before-and-after educational intervention via postal surveys administered a year apart. A smaller formative evaluation component (qualitative component) focused on nurses' views of the educational programs, particularly their weaknesses and strengths, and was assessed using focus groups and semi-structured telephone interviews. Figure 23.6 presents the visual diagram of the Shipman and colleagues study.

Eight cancer networks in England were randomly selected for the study sites, and the samples for both strands were drawn from the same pool of nurses in DN teams. The postal surveys were sent to 160 members of DN teams in each network, approximating 1,280 nurses in phases one and two of the quantitative strand. In the qualitative strand, one focus group and semi-structured interviews were conducted with a subsample of 39 nurses randomly selected from those who participated in the educational programs.

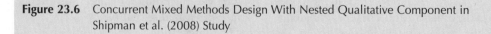

Figure 23.6 Concurrent Mixed Methods Design With Nested Qualitative Component in Shipman et al. (2008) Study

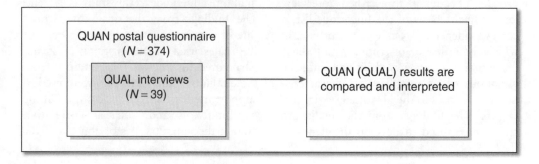

In the quantitative strand, the data from 374 (32% response rate) of nurses who responded to the survey in both years were analyzed using a paired sample *t* test. In addition, exploratory regression analyses were conducted to assess changes in mean scores before and after the educational intervention. The data from qualitative interviews were analyzed using the framework approach, in which a coding scheme was developed based on the analysis of the few transcripts and discussions among the researchers and then applied to coding all the transcripts.

The quantitative results of the mail survey from both years and the qualitative findings from the focus group and semi-structured telephone interviewees were compared and contrasted to assess the effects of the educational programs. The results consistently reported in both strands were increased confidence in palliative care competencies, increased knowledge related to palliative care, and improved palliative care provided by their DN teams after the educational program. The survey results provided additional insight into the factors related to changes in confidence and knowledge; nurses without DN qualifications had the greatest improvements. However, there were contradictory findings in the quantitative and qualitative strands. Although the qualitative findings suggested improved relationship with specialists and family doctors after the educational program, the quantitative results did not indicate statistically significant improvements in such relationships with other medical professionals. However, qualitative results indicated that being able to put "names to faces" (Shipman et al., 2008, p. 501) made it easier for the participants to discuss matters over the phone. Thus, the qualitative findings helped enhance and complement the results from the quantitative strand and contribute to the meta-inferences about the effects of the intervention programs.

The Fuentes (2008) and Shipman and colleagues' (2008) studies are two typical examples of the use of mixed methods designs in health and medicine. Sequential studies in which a qualitative phase is used to create a measurement instrument (e.g., Bass, Ryder, Lammers, Mukaba, & Bolton, 2008; Cotterill, Norton, Avery, Abrams, & Donovan, 2008; Diaz, Rivera, & Bou, 2008; Kulig, Hall, & Kalischuk, 2008) and concurrent designs with a small qualitative component (e.g., Austin & Braidman, 2008; Howell et al., 2008; Mill et al., 2008; Rosen et al., 2008) are popular across health and medical disciplines. However, other mixed methods designs are also observed: concurrent design with an emphasis on the qualitative data (e.g., Gucciardi, Demelo, Offenheim, & Stewart, 2008; Kramer et al., 2008; Luck, Jackson, & Usher, 2008), which are framed more as qualitative studies with a minor quantitative component aimed at augmenting some qualitative findings, and sequential design seeking further understanding of the findings of an initial quantitative strand (e.g., Oblitas & Caufield, 2008; Thomason et al., 2008). Observations, focus group, and individual interviews are common data sources for the qualitative strand, while quantitative strands employ mail and Web surveys and observational checklists. Particularly in nursing, observations are often used to collect qualitative and quantitative data (e.g., Baxter, 2008; Luck, Jackson, & Usher, 2008), while in health care, survey instruments containing both closed- and open-ended questions are quite popular (Gucciardi et al., 2008; Thomas-MacLean et al., 2008). In evaluation of health services, the sampling schemes are expanded to include the perspectives of both the services' users and their providers (e.g., Borlase & Abelson-Mitchell, 2008; Lapane, Waring, Schneider, Dube, & Quilliam, 2008; Liddy et al., 2008).

EDUCATION

Education is another discipline that heavily employed a mixed methods approach. A variation of different concurrent and sequential designs is observed in 29 studies published in 2008. We chose Davis and

Higdon's (2008) study as an illustration because it employed a popular group comparison approach and used multiple types of quantitative and qualitative data. The researchers used a mixed methods ("mixed-method" in Davis and Higton's spelling) concurrent design to examine the influence a school/university induction program had on novice teachers' development in early elementary classrooms. They acknowledged the use of a concurrent design with the purpose of complementarity, putting more emphasis on the quantitative methods. The rationale for collecting both quantitative and qualitative data was "to bring together the strengths of both forms of research to validate the results" (p. 265). Figure 23.7 presents the visual diagram of Davis and Higdon's study.

The sample consisted of 10 first-year elementary teachers; five were teacher fellows—school/university partnership program cohort members—and the other five were not. Five in each group were matched by school sites and/or demographic grade level. The researchers concurrently collected multiple types of quantitative and qualitative data aiming at each type complementing each other to assess a single topic. The quantitative data included structured classroom observations of developmentally appropriate practices during two semesters using the Assessment of Practices in Early Elementary Classrooms measurement instrument and a self-developed survey to rate mentor assistance. The qualitative data consisted of field notes taken during classroom visits, follow-up interviews conducted after the classroom observations in two semesters, semi-structured interviews to explore the induction support participants received from the district and university, as well as their future plans of continuity of teaching.

Although the quantitative and qualitative data were collected in a concurrent manner, analyses were conducted in two phases, with the qualitative strand following the quantitative to provide deeper insight into specific quantitative results. In the quantitative strand, the data were analyzed using the Mann-Whitney U test to

Figure 23.7 Concurrent Mixed Methods Design in Davis and Higdon (2008) Study

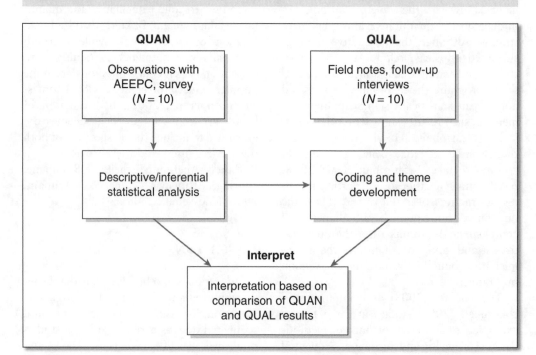

assess the differences between the teacher fellow and non–teacher fellow groups with the effect size of .5. In the qualitative strand analysis, transcribed semi-structured interviews and classroom observation field notes were properly coded by two researchers, and cross-case matrices were developed for two groups to illuminate more clearly how the two groups differed in the quantitative scores for the areas of classroom practices.

Focusing on better integrating the results from two strands, those from the qualitative strand were efficaciously used to closely examine the findings from the quantitative strand, particularly on the greater scores of teacher fellows in the instructional context category (use of materials, instructional methods, and teacher-child language) and the social context category of the classroom practices. Thus, the integration in this study occurred as early as the data analysis stage when the data from the qualitative strand were analyzed to highlight and explain some specific aspects of the quantitative results. This allowed the researchers to achieve more meaningful inferences. The qualitative results provided examples of better practices observed among teacher fellows, and this along with the use of multiple kinds of data, as the authors pointed out, enhanced credibility of the overall study conclusion that the teacher fellows program had a positive influence on novice teachers' classroom practices.

Concurrent designs with multiple data sources are intensively used in education (e.g., Goldman, Reeves, Lauscher, Jarvis-Selinger, & Silver, 2008; Hanbury, Prosser, & Rickinson, 2008; Moseley & Okamoto, 2008). In some studies (e.g., Goldszmidt, Zibrowski, & Weston, 2008; McIlveen, Patton, & Hoare, 2008; Moon & Brighton, 2008; Savage, 2008) more weight was placed on the qualitative data, highlighting the philosophical orientation of the researchers and the tendency toward more constructivist epistemological practices in social science disciplines. For example, Moon and Brighton (2008) conducted a mixed methods study to better understand

the contextual factors influencing primary grade teachers' perceptions and behavior related to talent development in young children. To collect the data, they used a quantitative survey and qualitative case studies. The results from the quantitative and qualitative strands were compared to present the three areas for needed improvement that were found to be equally important from both strands of the study. In Savage's (2008) study, which aimed at investigating the influence of popular/corporate culture texts and discourses on the subjectivities and social lives that young people live every day and the extent to which such influences were critically analyzed in the English classrooms, more inferences are built on the qualitative results from observations and semi-structured interviews with a group of 15- and 16-year-old students in Australia. The quantitative survey data contributed only to assessing the second objective, which was the investigation of the extent to which the influence of popular/corporate culture texts and discourses on the subjectivities and everyday social life were critically analyzed in the English classrooms.

As seen in health and medicine, evaluation studies that used concurrent design with a larger emphasis on the quantitative component were also popular in education (e.g., Anderson & Thorpe, 2008; Hoffman, Badgett, & Parker, 2008; King, 2008). As in Davis and Higdon's (2008) study, Hoffman and colleagues (2008) used a group comparison approach to evaluate the effectiveness of single-sex instruction on achievement outcomes, instructional practices, teacher efficacy, student behaviors, and classroom culture in an urban, at-risk high school. Students grouped based on gender in algebra and English classes were compared with coeducational students. Multiple types of quantitative and qualitative data were collected: standardized test scores, surveys, classroom observations, and individual and focus group interviews. Most of the inferences were generated from the quantitative data analysis. Out of five posted research questions, only one question was addressed through the qualitative data.

Other variations of mixed methods designs were also evident in education, showing varied ways of achieving meta-inferences. These included studies using conversion designs, in which qualitative data were quantitized and analyzed together with other quantitative data to enhance understanding of the trends in the data (e.g., Ainley, Enger, & Kennedy, 2008; Slate, Jones, Wiesman, Alexander, & Saenz, 2008), sequential designs with a qualitative strand following the quantitative (e.g., Goldszmidt et al., 2008; Greene et al., 2008), and sequential designs utilizing a qualitative phase to develop a measurement instrument to be used in the quantitative strand (e.g., Molesworth & Hansen, 2008).

COMPUTER SCIENCES

Mixed methods have been consistently used in computer sciences research since 2002. We chose the study by Feldon and Kafai (2008), who used a concurrent mixed methods design to analyze user activities in the world of avatars, graphic self-representations, in the context of the youth-oriented, informal science education virtual world named Whyville.net. The rationale for choosing a mixed methods approach was to illustrate "the value of using mixed methods to address the methodological and analytical challenges of virtual world research" (p. 578). Specifically, the authors emphasized the meaningfulness of mixed methods inferences because behavioral patterns of the study participants in the virtual world should be meaningfully quantified, as such patterns show the frequencies and types of interactivity and the meaning ascribed to it by the participants. At the same time, qualitative inquiry is necessary to provide contexts, which are key aspects of the interactions in attempting to make generalizable claims about the behavioral patterns of the virtual world users. In the researchers' words, the exploration of complex user experiences in the virtual world "requires an integrated capture and analysis of the data across methods" (p. 581).

The data collection employed two samples. The researchers concurrently collected quantitative data in the form of server logs recording keystroke-level activity over a six-month period and online surveys, and qualitative data in the form of interviews regarding participants' experiences from 595 children between the ages of 8 and 18 who were selected to represent the Whyville.net users in terms of age and gender distributions. They also conducted online and offline ethnographic observations of classroom and after-school environments of a subset of 88 users recruited from 4 participating classrooms and individual interviews with 35 willing participants. The qualitative method was visibly emphasized. Figure 23.8 presents the visual diagram of Feldon and Kafai's study.

Feldon and Kafai (2008) referred to Greene, Caracelli, and Graham's (1989) framework of five purposes of expansion, triangulation, complementarity, initiation, and development that guided their data collection and analysis. Expansion reflected the use of multiple methods to meet the overall goal of the study to provide an integrated perspective on avatars in Whyville.net. Triangulation was used to corroborate the validity of meta-inferences drawn from log files, survey, interviews, and observations to reveal structural constraints, cultural norms, and personal inclusions that affected avatar-related activities. Complementarity was achieved by synthesizing interviews, surveys, and observational data for understanding unique aspects of user interactions around avatars in the shared real and virtual worlds. Development was evident when online ethnography observations were used to inform the development of the categories of Whyville locations, which were then used in a statistical cluster analysis, and when the survey and observational data were used to frame qualitative interview questions. Initiation was realized through a concurrent analysis of the data that revealed some

Figure 23.8   Concurrent Mixed Methods Design in Feldon and Kafai (2008) Study

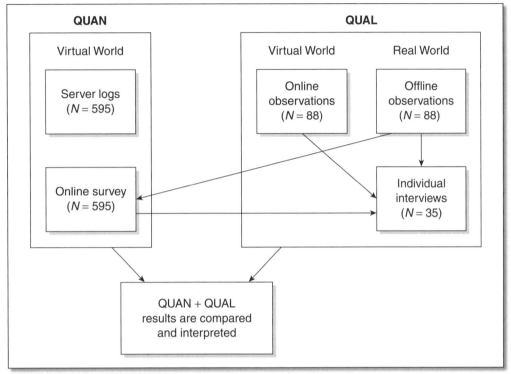

discrepancy in the large proportion of navigation dedicated to avatar-related activities and their moderate effect and value expressed in interviews. Capitalizing on the theoretically grounded integrated use of multiple data sources, Feldon and Kafai's study identified a major user emphasis on avatar appearance and customization that was invariant across user typologies. Sound application of mixed methods procedures produced meta-inferences that were meaningful and useful in the field.

Concurrent design was found to be a predominant mixed methods design used in computer sciences (e.g., Seals, Clanton, Agarwal, Doswell, & Thomas, 2008; Wilhelm, Smith, Walters, Sherrod, & Mulholland, 2008). Of interest is that the researchers typically relied on large samples, used multiple data sources, emphasized qualitative method over quantitative, and utilized some specific Web-enhanced data types. Wilhelm and colleagues (2008),

for example, studied how 188 preservice teachers from three campuses in the United States and in Queensland, Australia, engaged in scientific and mathematical inquiry using Internet forums. The qualitative and quantitative data involved preservice teachers' journals, summative reflections, Internet discussions, final projects, and quantitative inventory to assess their knowledge about the Moon phases. Comparison of the qualitative themes and results from the pre- and post-assessment of the lunar phases concepts allowed the researchers to conclude that Internet discussions with preservice teachers around the world were beneficial for enhancing knowledge of science and mathematics.

Concurrent design was also utilized in a number of evaluation studies of technology projects (e.g., Baki & Veli, 2008; Eteokleous, 2008; Falkman, Gustafsson, Jontell, & Torgersson, 2008; Greenhalgh et al., 2008). Falkman and colleagues (2008) used mixed methods to study the communication patterns of distributed health care professionals in oral medicine. To evaluate the use of Swedish Oral Medicine Web (SOMWeb) and collaboration of professionals via Swedish Oral Medicine Net, the researchers used interviews with nine members of the network, observations of 10 teleconference meetings, and an online questionnaire that was completed by 24 participants. Triangulation of data sources allowed for more enhanced conclusions regarding the system utilization. The introduction of SOMWeb improved the structure of meetings and their discussions; users submitted cases to seek advice on diagnosis or treatment, to show an unusual case, or to create discussion. In addition, three levels of member participation were identified.

A sequential mixed methods design with the qualitative follow-up phase was used by Hossain and Brooks (2008) to develop fuzzy cognitive map (FCM) models to model the adoption of educational software in U.K. secondary schools. The model was developed sequentially in three phases. In the first phase, fully structured interviews conducted with 46 students and staff members were used to construct individual FCMs. In the second phase, individual FCMs were integrated to form one main model. In the third phase, additions and changes to the model were made based on individual semi-structured interviews with each study participant. The complementarity purpose of the qualitative interviews contributed to the credibility of the final model.

SOCIAL WORK

In social work, a mixed methods approach has been predominantly used in evaluation projects. We chose Forrester, Copello, Waissbein, and Pokhrel's (2008) study that used sequential mixed methods design with a small qualitative follow-up phase to evaluate an intensive family prevention service. The service focused on the families in which parents' misuse of substances increased the risk of children's entering care and aimed to improve family function to reduce such risks. The evaluation included two phases: the quantitative quasi-experimental study of care-related outcomes and the qualitative follow-up interviews that were conducted to "shed light" (p. 416) on the quantitative results. Figure 23.9 presents the visual diagram of Forrester et al.'s study.

In the first phase, quantitative information was collected from forms on all children referred to the service between 2000 and 2006 ($N = 279$). Additional information related to care entry was gathered from local authorities. Eighty-nine children who entered the service without a referral formed a comparison group. The statistical analysis of the quantitative data focused on establishing the validity for the comparison group. Chi-square and t tests were used to assess the differences in the outcomes for the intervention and comparison groups. The results indicated the effectiveness of the program: The referred children took longer to enter the service, they spent less time in care and were more likely to be at home at follow-up, which resulted in cost savings. However, these quantitative findings generated the questions that were further addressed in the qualitative follow-up phase: Why did the service tend to produce a delay in care entry rather than preventing it? How did the service produce such positive finding? What lessons can be learned for effective service delivery?

To address these questions, qualitative follow-up semi-structured interviews were conducted with 11 parents and 7 children who had received the program service within the previous 12 months. The interviews with parents revealed six key components that were perceived to be pertinent to the service and accounted for the program effectiveness: a nonjudgmental and understanding approach; good open communication; availability, reliability, and high frequency of contact; helpfulness strategies

Figure 23.9 Sequential Mixed Methods Design With a Qualitative Follow-Up Phase in Forrester et al. (2008) Study

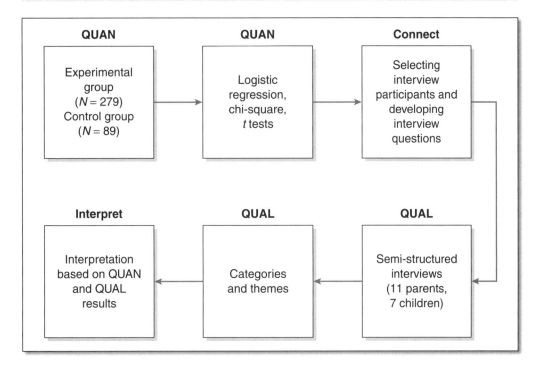

and practical support; support with substance problems; and help with family relationships. Further, interviews with children revealed that their confidence was enhanced as a result of their experiences with the program.

Forrester and colleagues' (2008) study has illustrated how the qualitative interview findings provided insight into the results from the initial quantitative phase and helped explain the reasons for the program effectiveness. Integrating the results from the two strands allowed the researchers to create meta-inferences regarding the program quality and to more thoroughly evaluate its effectiveness.

More social work evaluation projects used sequential mixed methods design. It is apparent that complementarity and development purposes (Greene, et al., 1989) of the sequential design allowed for more enhanced inferences regarding project effectiveness. For example, Abrams, Shannon, and

Sangalang (2008) explored the benefits and limitations of a six-week transition living program for incarcerated youth offenders using a two-phase design. Qualitative follow-up interviews with youth and program staff were used to explain the results of the initial logistic regression analysis and make conclusions about the effectiveness of the program. McWey, Henderson, and Alexander (2008) used the initial quantitative review and power analysis of the foster care court cases in Virginia to identify the number and type of cases for in-depth qualitative case study analysis. This strategy allowed them to select a representative number of cases to evaluate family-court interactions for foster care decisions made across 20 years. In Tassew, Nicola, and Bekele's (2008) international study of the effects of Ethiopia's poverty reduction policy on children's paid and unpaid work, quantitative household survey data results were further explored in qualitative interviews, which helped understand the role of culturally ascribed gendered and age-specific views of children work, parental attitudes, and children's agency in resource allocation plans. To examine the processes and outcomes of parent-worker engagement in child welfare, Altman (2008) began with a qualitative exploration of engagement in one child welfare agency. The qualitative themes informed the collection of the quantitative data from 74 parent-worker dyads in the second phase, which revealed no relationship between engagement and improved case outcomes.

A few evaluation studies followed a concurrent design model in which quantitative and qualitative data were collected and analyzed concurrently (Patrick, Rhoades, Small, & Coatsworrh, 2008; Sanders, Jacobson, & Ting; 2008). Patrick and colleagues (2008) evaluated the implementation of a 10-hour church-based teen parenting intervention program using quantitative surveys at the beginning and end of the program, focus group interviews, and observations. While the survey results revealed the potential benefits of the program, the focus group findings highlighted its advantages and disadvantages, thus providing more validity to the overall study conclusions.

◆ Conclusions

This chapter described the emergent trends in the utilization and adoption of mixed methods research across disciplines by examining discipline-related methodological discussions and analyzing mixed methods empirical studies. Because the selection of empirical studies was limited to five databases, this account should not be viewed as exhaustive but rather as another attempt to contribute to the general discussion of the evolution of mixed methods research in social, behavioral, and health sciences.

The present analysis allows for the conclusion that the movement toward informed application of mixed methods designs in the

majority of disciplines began after 2000, and for many in the last five years. In addition to the practical need to use multiple methods to address complex research situations, this movement was prompted by discipline-related methodological discussions and general advancement of mixed methods in the research community. It is also important that mixed methods research has been increasingly used across five continents, thus becoming international and transcending disciplinary boundaries (Tashakkori & Creswell, 2008). Not all disciplines, however, have equally accepted mixed methods. It seems that interdisciplinary fields that seek understanding of more complex research problems calling for a pragmatic approach to research are more open to variability in the methods and the use of integrated designs. Furthermore, epistemological traditions, research practices, contextual factors, and funding opportunities influence the adoption of mixed methods research in each discipline (Bryman, 2006; Denscombe, 2008; Greene, 2008; Morgan, 2007). In part, the process is impeded by the difficulty in finding publishing outlets for mixed methods studies, particularly those consisting of multiple strands (O'Cathain et al., 2007).

Application of mixed methods across disciplines also has its distinct features in how the methods are integrated and how meta-inferences grounded in both quantitative and qualitative results are created. Even though most of the basic mixed methods designs are utilized across disciplines, they are prioritized differently in some fields, and different roles are assigned to quantitative and qualitative methods within these designs. Discipline-based epistemological practices influence the choice of a mixed methods design and cause its related modifications to better address the specific research situations (e.g., using qualitative methods within randomized control trials or enhancing qualitative case studies with additional quantitative data). Although integration of the quantitative and qualitative methods within these designs pursues the same purposes described in the mixed methods literature (Greene et al., 1989), they are differently utilized and prioritized across disciplines, suggesting a certain degree of the "disciplinarization of mixed-methods" (Rao, 2007, as cited in Tashakkori & Creswell, 2008, p. 3).

Alternatively, the emergence of cross-disciplinary strategies of integrating quantitative and qualitative methods, such as phenomenography, concept mapping, and nominal group technique, indicates the increased utility of mixed methods in achieving meaningful meta-inferences. It also demonstrates how disciplines with different epistemological traditions can inform and enhance each other's mixed methodological practices. Understanding the utilization of integrative designs across disciplines might help researchers in designing and conducting mixed methods studies, particularly if they are engaged in interdisciplinary and international research. It should also help envision the methodological developments in the application of mixed methods across disciplines and the search for the best integration practices in producing quality meta-inferences grounded in the results from both quantitative and qualitative study components.

Research Questions and Exercises

1. What trends of mixed methods research applications do you see in your own discipline and in your country?

2. What factors do you think affect the current trends of mixed methods research applications in your discipline and country?

3. Search for mixed methods empirical studies within your discipline and analyze the trends of mixed methods utilization since 2000. Connect those trends with the major developments in mixed methods research and your discipline.

4. Select a published empirical mixed methods study, discuss its qualitative and quantitative components, and analyze how well the integration of the two served the study purpose.

5. Select published empirical studies of different mixed methods designs and examine how quantitative and qualitative methods are mixed within these designs to achieve meaningful meta-inferences.

◆ References

Abrams, L. S., Shannon, S. K. S., & Sangalang, C. (2008). Transition services for incarcerated youth: A mixed methods evaluation study. *Children and Youth Services Review* 30(5), 522–535.

Ainley, M., Enger, L., & Kennedy, G. (2008). The elusive experience of "Flow": Qualitative and quantitative indicators. *International Journal of Educational Research*, 47, 109–121.

Altman J. C. (2008). A study of engagement in neighborhood-based child welfare services. *Research on Social Work Practice, 18*(6), 555–564.

Anaf, S., & Sheppard, L. (2007). Mixing research methods in health professional degrees: Thoughts for undergraduate students and supervisors. *Qualitative Report, 12*(2), 184–192.

Anderson, E. S., & Thorpe, L. N. (2008). Early interprofessional interactions: Does student age matter? *Journal of Interprofessional Care, 22*(3), 263–283.

Ansari, W., Phillips, C., & Hammick, M. (2001). Collaboration and partnerships: Developing the evidence base. *Health & Social Care in the Community, 9*(4), 15–227.

Austin, A., & Braidman, I. (2008). Support for portfolio in the initial years of the undergraduate medical school curriculum: What do the tutors think? *Medical Teacher, 30(3),* 265–272.

Baki, A., & Veli, E. G. (2008). Evaluation of a Web based mathematics teaching material on the subject of functions. *Computers & Education, 51*(2), 854–863.

Bass, J. K., Ryder, R. W., Lammers, M. C., Mukaba, T. N., & Bolton, P. A. (2008). Post-partum depression in Kinshasa, Democratic Republic of Congo: Validation of a concept using a mixed-methods cross-cultural approach. *Tropical Medicine & International Health, 13*(12), 1534–1542.

Baxter, S. (2008). Assessing pressure ulcer risk in long-term care using Waterlow scale. *Nursing Older People, 20*(7), 34–38.

Borlase, J., & Abelson-Mitchell, N. (2008). User perceptions of the knowledge underpinning practice orientating dial (KUPOD) as a tool to enhance leaning. *Nurse Education in Practice, 8,* 9–19.

Bryman, A. (2006). Integrating quantitative and qualitative research: How is it done? *Qualitative Research, 6*(1), 97–113.

Chatterji, M. (2005). Evidence on "What Works": An argument for extended-term mixed-method (ETMM) evaluation designs. *Educational Researcher, 34*(5), 14–24.

Collins, K. M. T., Onwuegbuzie, A. J., & Jiao, Q. G. (2006). Prevalence of mixed-methods sampling designs in social science research. *Evaluation & Research in Education, 19*(2), 83–101.

Collins, K. M. T., Onwuegbuzie, A. J., & Sutton, I. L. (2006). A model incorporating the rationale and purpose for conducting mixed-methods research in special education and beyond. *Learning Disabilities: A Contemporary Journal, 4*(1), 67–100.

Cotterill, N., Norton, C., Avery, K. N., Abrams, P., & Donovan, J. L. (2008). A patient-centered approach to developing a comprehensive symptom and quality of life assessment of anal incontinence. *Disease of the Colon & Rectum, 51*(1), 82–87.

Creswell, J., Fetters, M., & Ivankova, N. (2004). Designing a mixed methods study in primary care. *Annals of Family Medicine, 2*(1), 7–12.

Creswell, J. W., & Plano Clark, V. L. (2007). *Designing and conducting mixed methods research.* Thousand Oaks, CA: Sage.

Dalton, P., & McNicoi, S. (2004). Balancing the books: Emphasizing the importance of qualitative evaluation for understanding electronic information services. *Library Quarterly, 74*(4), 455–468.

Davis, B., & Higdon, K. (2008). The effects of mentoring/induction support on beginning teachers' practices in early elementary classrooms (K–3). *Journal of Research in Childhood Education, 22*(3), 261–274.

Denscombe, M. (2008). Communities of practice: A research paradigm for the mixed methods approach. *Journal of Mixed Methods Research, 2*(3), 270–283.

Diaz, N. V., Rivera, S. M., & Bou, F. L. (2008). AIDS stigma combinations in a sample of Puerto Rican health professionals: Qualitative and quantitative evidence. *Puerto Rico Health Science Journal, 27*(2), 147–157.

Doorenspleet, R., & Kopecky, P. (2008). Against the odds: Deviant cases of democratization. *Democratization, 15*(4), 697–713.

Eteokleous, N. (2008). Evaluating computer technology integration in a centralized school system. *Computers & Education, 51*(2), 669–686.

Falkman, G., Gustafsson, M., Jontell, M., & Torgersson, O. (2008). SOMWeb: A semantic Web-based system for supporting collaboration of distributed medical communities of practice. *Journal of Medical Internet Research, 10*(3), e25.

Feldon, D., & Kafai, Y. (2008). Mixed methods for mixed reality: Understanding users' avatar activities in virtual world. *Educational Technology Research & Development, 56*(5–6), 575–593.

Fidel, R. (2008). Are we there yet? Mixed methods research in library and information science. *Library & Information Science Research, 30*(4), 265–272.

Flemming, K. (2007). The knowledge base for evidence-based nursing: A role for mixed methods research? *Advances in Nursing Science, 30*(1), 41–51.

Forrester, D., Copello, A., Waissbein, C., & Pokhrel, S. (2008). Evaluation of an intensive family preservation service for families affected by parental substance misuse. *Child Abuse Review, 17,* 410–426.

Fuentes, C. M. (2008). Pathways from interpersonal violence to sexually transmitted infections: A mixed-method study of diverse women. *Journal of Women's Health, 17*(19), 1592–1603.

Gelo, O., Braakmann, D., & Benetka, G. (2008). Quantitative and qualitative research: Beyond the debate. *Integrative Psychological & Behavioral Science, 42,* 266–290.

Geurts P., & Roosendaal, H. (2001). Estimating the direction of innovative change based on theory and mixed methods. *Quality & Quantity, 35*(4), 407–427.

Giddings, L., & Grant, B. (2006). Mixed methods research for the novice researcher. *Contemporary Nurse, 23*(1), 3–11.

Giddings, L., & Grant, B. (2007). A Trojan horse for positivism? *Advances in Nursing Science, 30*(1), 52–60.

Goldman, J., Reeves, S., Lauscher, H. N., Jarvis-Selinger, S., & Silver, I. (2008). Integrating social accountability into continuing education and professional development at medical schools: The case of an institutional collaborative project in Canada. *Journal of Interprofessional Care, 22,* 40–50.

Goldszmidt, M. A., Zibrowski, E. M., & Weston, W. W. (2008). Education scholarship: It's not just a question of "degree." *Medical Teacher, 30,* 34–39.

Gorard, S., Beng Huat, S., Smith, E., & White, P. (2007). What can we do to strengthen the teacher workforce? *International Journal of Lifelong Education, 26*(4), 419–437.

Greene, H. C., O'Connor, K. A., Good, A. J., Ledford, C. C., Peel, B. B., & Zhang, G. (2008). Building a support system toward tenure: Challenges and needs of tenure-track faculty in colleges of education. *Mentoring & Tutoring: Partnership in Learning, 16,* 429–447.

Greene, J. C. (2008). Is mixed methods social inquiry a distinctive methodology? *Journal of Mixed Methods Research, 2*(1), 7–22.

Greene, J. C., & Caracelli, V. J. (Eds.). (1997). Advances in mixed-method evaluation: The challenges and benefits of integrating diverse programs. *New Directions for Evaluation* series, no. 74. San Francisco: Jossey-Bass.

Greene, J. C., Caracelli, V. J., & Graham, W. F. (1989). Toward a conceptual framework for mixed-method evaluation designs. *Educational Evaluation and Policy Analysis, 11*(3), 255–274.

Greenhalgh, T., Stramer, K., Bratan, T., Byrne, E., Mohammad, Y., & Russell, J. (2008). Introduction of shared electronic records: Multi-site case study using diffusion of innovation theory. *BMJ, 337,* a1786.

Gucciardi, E., Demelo, M., Offenheim, M., & Stewart, D. E. (2008). Factors contributing to attrition behavior in diabetes self-management programs: A mixed method approach. *AMC Health Services Research, 8,* 33–43.

Halcomb, E., & Andrew, S. (2005). Triangulation as a method for contemporary nursing research. *Nurse Researcher, 13*(2), 71–82.

Hanbury, A., Prosser, M., & Rickinson, M. (2008). The differential impact of UK accredited teaching development programmes on academics' approaches to teaching. *Studies in Higher Education, 33,* 469–483.

Hanson, W. B., Creswell, J. W., Plano Clark, Y. L., Petska, K. S., & Creswell, D. (2005). Mixed methods research designs in counseling psychology. *Journal of Counseling Psychology, 52*(2), 224–235.

Harkness, S., Moscardino, U., Bermudez, M., Zylicz, P., Welles-Nystrom, B., Blom, M., et al. (2006). Mixed methods in international collaborative research: The experiences of the international study of parents, children, and schools. *Cross-Cultural Research, 40*(1), 65–82.

Harper, G., Neubauer, L., Bangi, A., & Francisco, V. (2008). Transdisciplinary research and evaluation for community health initiatives. *Health Promotion Practice, 9*(4), 328–337.

Harris, F., Kendall, M., Bentley, A., Maguire, R., Worth, A., Murray, S., et al. (2008). Researching experiences of terminal cancer: A systematic review of methodological issues and approaches. *European Journal of Cancer Care, 17*(4), 377–386.

Hart, L., Smith, S., Swars, S., & Smith, M. (2009). An examination of research methods in mathematics education: 1995–2005. *Journal of Mixed Methods Research, 3*(1), 26–41.

Hemming, P. J. (2008). Mixing qualitative research methods in children's geographies. *Area, 40*(2), 152–162.

Hoffman, B. H., Badgett, B. A., & Parker, R. P. (2008). The effect of single-sex instruction in a large, urban, at-risk high school. *Journal of Educational Research, 102,* 15–36.

Hossain, S., & Brooks, L. (2008). Fuzzy cognitive map modelling educational software adoption. *Computers & Education, 51*(4), 1569–1588.

Howell, D. M., Sussman, J., Wiernikowski, J., Pyette, N., Bainbridge, D., O'Brien, M., et al. (2008). A mixed-method evaluation of nurse-led community-based supportive cancer care. *Support Care Cancer, 16,* 1343–1352.

Hurmerinta-Peltomaki, L., & Nummela, N. (2006). Mixed methods in international business research: A value-added perspective. *Management International Review, 46*(4), 439–459.

Jiang, H. (2003). Stories remote sensing images can tell: Integrating remote sensing analysis with ethnographic research in the study of cultural landscapes. *Human Ecology: An Interdisciplinary Journal, 31*(2), 215–232.

Johnson, B., & Onwuegbuzie, A. (2004). Mixed methods research: A research paradigm whose time has come. *Educational Researcher, 33*(7), 14–26.

Johnstone, P. L. (2007). Weighing up triangulating and contradictory evidence in mixed methods organizational research. *International Journal of Multiple Research Approaches, 1*(1), 27–38.

King, A. (2008). Collaborative learning in the music studio. *Music Education Research, 10,* 423–438.

Kramer, M., Schmalenberg, C., Maguire, P., Brewer, B. B., Burke, R., Chmielewski, L., et al. (2008). Structure and practices enabling staff nurses to control their practice. *Western Journal of Nursing Research, 30*(5), 539–559.

Kristensen, E., Nielsen, D., Jensen, L., Vaarst, M., & Enevoldsen, C. (2008). A mixed methods inquiry into the validity of data. *Acta Veterinaria Scandinavica, 50*(30), 30–37.

Kulig, J. C., Hall, B. L., & Kalischuk, R. G. (2008). Bullying perspectives among rural youth: A mixed methods approach. *Rural Remote Health, 8*(2), 923–933.

Lapane, K. L., Waring, M. E., Schneider, K. L., Dube, C., & Quilliam, B. J. (2008). A mixed method study of the merits of e-prescribing drug alerts in primary care. *Journal of General Internal Medicine, 23*(4), 442–446.

Li, S., Marquart, J., & Zercher, C. (2000). Conceptual issues and analytic strategies in mixed-method studies of preschool inclusion. *Journal of Early Intervention, 23*(2), 116–132.

Liddy, C., Dusseault, J. J., Dahrouge, S., Hogg, W., Lemelin, J., & Humbert, J. (2008). Telehomecare for patients with multiple chronic illnesses: Pilot study. *Canadian Family Physician, 54*(1), 58–65.

Lieberman, E. S. (2005). Nested analysis as a mixed-method strategy for comparative research. *American Political Science Review, 99*(3), 435–452.

London, A. S., Schwartz, S., & Scott, E. K. (2007). Combining quantitative and qualitative data in welfare policy evaluations in the United States. *World Development, 35*(2), 342–353.

Luck, L., Jackson, D., & Usher, K. (2006). Case study: A bridge across the paradigms. *Nursing Inquiry, 13*(2), 103–109.

Luck, L., Jackson, D., & Usher, K. (2008). Innocent or culpable? Meaning that emergency department nurses ascribe to individual acts of violence. *Journal of Clinical Nursing,* *17,* 1071–1078.

Martinez, A., Dimitriadis, Y., Gomez-Sanchez, E., Rubia-Avi, B., Jorrin-Abellan, I., & Marcos, J. (2006). Studying participation networks in collaboration using mixed methods. *International Journal of Computer-Supported Collaborative Learning, 1*(3), 383–408.

Martinez, A., Dimitriadis, Y., Rubia, B., Gomez, E., & de la Fuente, P. (2003). Combining qualitative evaluation and social network analysis for the study of classroom social interactions. *Computers & Education, 41*(4), 353–368.

Mason, J. (2006). Mixing methods in a qualitatively driven way. *Qualitative Research, 6*(1), 9–25.

McIlveen, P., Patton, W., & Hoare, P. N. (2008). An interpretative phenomenological analysis of adult clients' experience of "My Career Chapter." *Australian Journal of Career Development, 17*(3), 51–62.

McWey, L. M., Henderson, T. L., & Alexander, J. B. (2008). Parental rights and the foster care system: A glimpse of decision making in Virginia. *Journal of Family Issues, 29*(8), 1031–1050.

Micari, M., Light, G., Calkins, S., & Streitwieser, B. (2007). Assessment beyond performance: Phenomenography in educational evaluation. *American Journal of Evaluation, 28*(4), 458–476.

Mill, J. E., Jackson, R. C., Worthington, C. A., Archibald, C. P., Wong, T., Myers T. et al. (2008). HIV testing and care in Canadian Aboriginal youth: A community based mixed methods study. *BMC Infectious Disease, 8,* 132–144.

Moffatt, S., White, M., Mackintosh, J., & Howel, D. (2006). Using quantitative and qualitative data in health services research: What happens when mixed method findings conflict? *BMC Health Services Research, 6*(28), 1–10.

Molesworth, M., & Hansen, V. (2008). Physical education in primary schools: Classroom teachers' perceptions of benefits and outcomes. *Health Education Journal, 67*(3), 196–207.

Moon, T. R., & Brighton, C. M. (2008). Primary teachers' conceptions of giftedness. *Journal for the Education of the Gifted, 31,* 447–480.

Morgan, D. L. (2007). Paradigms lost and paradigm regained: Methodological implications of combining qualitative and quantitative methods. *Journal of Mixed Methods Research, 1*(1), 48–76.

Moseley, B., & Okamoto, Y. (2008). Identifying fourth graders' understanding of rational number representations: A mixed methods approach. *School Science & Mathematics, 108*(5), 238–250.

National Institute of Health (NIH). (1999). *Qualitative methods in health research: Opportunities and considerations in application and review.* Retrieved May 21, 2009, from http://obssr.od.nih.gov/Publications/Qualitative.pdf

Niaz, M. (2008). A rationale for mixed methods (integrative) research programmes in education. *Journal of Philosophy of Education, 42*(2), 61–68.

Oblitas, F. Y., & Caufield, C. C. (2008). Workplace violence and drug use in women workers in a Peruvian barrio. *International Nursing Review, 54*(4), 339–345.

O'Cathain, A., Murphy, E., & Nicholl, J. (2007). Why, and how, mixed methods research is undertaken in health services research in England: A mixed methods study. *BMC Health Services Research, 7*(85), 1–11.

Padgett, D. (2009). Qualitative and mixed methods in social work knowledge development. *Social Work, 54*(2), 101–105.

Patrick, M. E., Rhoades, B. L., Small, M., & Coatsworrh, J. D. (2008). Faith-placed parenting intervention. *Journal of Community Psychology, 36*(1), 74–80.

Plano Clark, V. L., Huddleston-Casas, C. A., Churchill, S. L., Green, D. O. N., & Garrett, A. L. (2008). Mixed methods approaches in family science research. *Journal of Family Issues, 29*(11), 1543–1566.

Pluye, P., Gagnon, M., Griffiths, F., & Johnson-Lafleur, J. (2009). A scoring system for appraising mixed methods research, and concomitantly appraising qualitative, quantitative and mixed methods primary studies in mixed studies reviews. *International Journal of Nursing Studies 46*, 529–546.

Potter, M., Gordon, S., & Hamer, P. (2004). The nominal group technique: A useful consensus methodology in physiotherapy research. *New Zealand Journal of Physiotherapy, 32*(3), 126–130.

Powell, H., Mihalas, S., Onwuegbuzie, A. J., Suldo, S., & Daley, C. E. (2008). Mixed methods research in school psychology: A mixed methods investigation of trends in the literature. *Psychology in the Schools, 45*(4), 291–309.

Ragin, C. C., Nagel, J., & White, P. (2004). *Workshop on scientific foundations of qualitative research*. National Science Foundation. Retrieved May 21, 2009, from http://www.nsf.gov/pubs/2004/nsf04219/nsf04219.pdf

Rauscher, L., & Greenfield, B. (2009). Advancements in contemporary physical therapy research: Use of mixed methods designs. *Physical Therapy, 89*(1), 91–100.

Rocco, T., Bliss, L., Gallagher, S., & Perez-Prado, A. (2003). Taking the next step: Mixed methods research in organizational systems. *Information Technology, Learning, and Performance, 21*(1), 19–29.

Rohlfing, I. (2008). What you see and what you get: Pitfalls and principles of nested analysis in comparative research. *Comparative Political Studies, 41*(11), 56–60.

Rosen, R. K., Morrow, K. M., Carballo-Diéguez, A., Mantell, A. J. E., Hoffman, S., Gai, F., et al. (2008). Acceptability of Tenofovir gel as a vaginal microbicide among women in a phase I trial: A mixed-methods study. *Journal of Women's Health, 11*, 27–40.

Sanders, S., Jacobson, J. M., & Ting, L. (2008). Preparing for the inevitable: Training social workers to cope with client suicide. *Journal of Teaching in Social Work, 28*(1–2), 1–18.

Savage, G. (2008). Silencing the everyday experiences of youth? Deconstructing issues of subjectivity and popular/corporate culture in the English classroom. *Discourse: Studies in the Cultural Politics of Education, 29*(1), 51–68.

Seals, C. D., Clanton, K., Agarwal, R., Doswell, F., & Thomas, C. M. (2008). Lifelong learning: Becoming computer savvy at a later age. *Educational Gerontology, 34*(12), 1055–1069.

Shavelson, R. J., & Towne, L. (Eds.). (2002). *Scientific research in education*. Committee on Scientific Principles for Education Research, National Research Council.

Shipman, C., Burt, J., Ream, E., Beynon, T., Richardson, A., & Addington-Hall, J. (2008). Improving district nurses' confidence and knowledge in the principles and practice of palliative care. *Journal of Advanced Nursing, 63*(5), 494–505.

Slate, J. R., Jones, C. H., Wiesman, K., Alexander, J., & Saenz, T. (2008). School mission statements and school performance: A mixed research investigation. *New Horizons in Education, 56*(2), 17–27.

Tashakkori, A., & Creswell, J. (2007). The new era of mixed methods. *Journal of Mixed Methods Research, 1*(1), 3–8.

Tashakkori, A., & Creswell, J. (2008). Mixed methodology across disciplines. *Journal of Mixed Methods Research, 2*(1), 3–6.

Tassew, W., Nicola, J., & Bekele, T. (2008). The invisibility of children's paid and unpaid work: Implications for Ethiopia's national poverty reduction policy. *Childhood, 15*(2), 177–201.

Teddlie, C., & Tashakkori, A. (2003). Major issues and controversies in the use of mixed methods in the social and behavioral sciences. In A. Tashakkori & C. Teddlie (Eds.), *Handbook of mixed methods in the behavioral & social sciences* (pp. 3–50). Thousand Oaks, CA: Sage.

Teddlie, C., & Tashakkori, A. (2009). *Foundations of mixed methods research: Integrating quantitative and qualitative approaches in the social and behavioral sciences*. Thousand Oaks, CA: Sage.

Thomas, J., Harden, A., Oakley, A., Oliver, S., Sutcliffe, K., Rees, R., et al. (2004). Integrating qualitative research with trials in systematic reviews. *BMJ, 328*(7446), 1010–1012.

Thomas-MacLean, R. L., Hack, T., Kwan, W., Towers, A., Miedema, B., & Tilley, A. (2008). Arm morbidity and disability after breast cancer: New directions for care. *Oncology Nursing Forum, 35*(1), 65–71.

Thomason, N., Sutcliffe, C. G., Sironjn, B., Sintupat, K., Aramrattana, A., Samuels, A., et al. (2008). Penile modification in young Thai men: Risk environments, procedures and widespread implications for HIV and sexually transmitted infections. *Sex Transmitted Infections, 84,* 195–197.

Trochim, W., & Kane, M. (2005). Concept mapping: An introduction to structured conceptualization in health care. *International Journal for Quality in Health Care, 17*(3), 187–191.

Ungar, M., Clark, S., Kwong, W., Makhnach, A., & Cameron, C. (2005). Studying resilience across cultures. *Journal of Ethnic & Cultural Diversity in Social Work, 14*(3–4), 1–19.

Wilhelm, J. A., Smith, W. S., Walters, K. L., Sherrod, S. E., & Mulholland, J. (2008). Engaging pre-service teachers in multinational, multi-campus scientific and mathematical inquiry. *International Journal of Science & Math Education, 6*(1), 131–162.

Wilkins, K., & Woodgate, R. (2008). Designing a mixed methods study in pediatric oncology nursing research. *Journal of Pediatric Oncology Nursing, 25*(1), 24–33.

24

USING MIXED METHODS IN MONITORING AND EVALUATION

Experiences From International Development

◆ Michael Bamberger, Vijayendra Rao, and Michael Woolcock

Objectives

Upon finishing this chapter, you should be able to

- discuss the current debates on how to evaluate international development interventions;

- identify weaknesses in current approaches to project evaluation and monitoring;

- discuss the potential contribution of mixed methods approaches to strengthening conventional evaluation and monitoring designs;

- show how mixed methods approaches can help overcome budget, time, and data constraints;

(Continued)

(Continued)

- show how mixed methods can strengthen conventional monitoring systems by helping to understand project implementation processes and the influence of contextual factors;

- show how mixed methods can strengthen qualitative evaluation designs;

- identify continuing challenges and areas of opportunity for the use of mixed methods in the evaluation of international development programs; and

- describe three case studies illustrating the application of mixed methods in typical development evaluation contexts.

◆ Introduction

The purpose of this chapter is to review challenges and opportunities for incorporating mixed methods approaches into research and evaluation on the effectiveness and impacts of international development.[1] It draws on the authors' experience over several decades working both in academia and with a wide range of multilateral and bilateral development agencies, nonprofit organizations, and developing country governments on the evaluation of the effectiveness and impacts of development interventions. Development research is informed by current research trends in northern countries, but it is often conducted within very distinct economic, political, cultural, and organizational contexts. While certainly not unique to the international context, many development evaluations are subject to a range of budget, time, data, political, and organizational constraints that tend to be more severe than those faced by researchers working in industrialized nations. Moreover, due to the more limited opportunities to conduct research in developing countries, individual studies or evaluations are often required to address a broader set of questions. So while a researcher in the United States may be able to focus

exclusively on a rigorous summative evaluation designed to address a limited range of questions on quantitative impacts, the same researcher evaluating a major development intervention in Latin America, Africa, or Asia may be asked to address a wider range of summative and formative questions. We argue that the demand for multipurpose evaluations in developing countries opens up opportunities for a broader application of mixed methods approaches than is usually the case in "mainstream" mixed methods research. We hope that this chapter will help readers understand the unique challenges, and also the great opportunities, for strengthening the use of mixed methods in the international development context.

In recent years, there have been increasing demands to measure the effectiveness of international development projects. This demand has emerged in response to two concerns: heightened criticism that most development agencies report only their outputs (e.g., number of teachers trained, kilometers of roads built) rather than outcomes, and concerns that, despite assurances that development resources have contributed to the reduction of illiteracy and poverty, little reliable information has actually been presented to show that this is in fact the case.[2] This has led to a demand for more effective and innovative ways to monitor and evaluate the nature and extent of impacts stemming from development initiatives (Rao & Woolcock, 2003).

Quantitatively oriented development researchers, if not the development community as a whole, have responded enthusiastically to the evaluation challenge. In the last decade there has been an explosion of quantitative impact evaluations of program interventions in international development. This has been driven both by trends within academia and by pressure from international organizations such as the World Bank and has culminated in efforts to adopt the standards and methods of biomedical clinical trials in making knowledge claims about the effectiveness of particular interventions. Some development economists (e.g., Banerjee, 2007; Duflo & Kremer, 2005) have gone so far as to argue that randomized control trials (RCTs) should be central to development practice and that knowledge claims based on alternative approaches are not merely inferior but inherently suspect. Others (Deaton, 2009; Ravallion, 2008), while accepting the central importance of quantitative evaluations, question the exclusive reliance placed by the "randomistas" on randomization and make the case that careful theorizing and tests of hypotheses that derive from theory, along with other types of quantitative methodologies—propensity score matching, careful structural modeling, and instrumental variables—should not be so easily dismissed. The central concern of all these quantitative techniques is with obtaining statistically rigorous counterfactuals.

The strong claims by quantitative development researchers to have the best (the gold standard) or even the only acceptable way to evaluate the effectiveness of development assistance has created a strong reaction from other sectors of the development community.[3] While some argue that randomization is rarely possible in developing countries, that the rigorous designs introduce an inflexibility that makes it difficult to understand the complex environment in which development projects operate or that there are fundamental methodological issues with the approaches, many take the view that randomized and strong statistical designs are only one of a number of approaches to development evaluation. For example, the Network of Networks on Impact Evaluation (NONIE) recently published *NONIE Guidance on Impact Evaluation* (2009), which recognized the importance of rigorous quantitative methods for addressing issues of causal attribution but recommended that evaluators use a mixed methods approach that combines the strengths of a range of quantitative and qualitative methods.[4] In the latest edition of his *Utilization-Focused Evaluation,* Patton (2008) lays out an extensive menu of different evaluation designs that can be used to address different kinds of evaluation questions.

None of the quantitatively oriented development participants in this debate, however, question the singularity of the econometric analysis of survey-based data as the core method of relevance for impact evaluations. Outside the context of impact evaluations, most work by economists on development questions also remains entirely econometric, though there is an increasing (and welcome) trend toward direct engagement in fieldwork and having survey data analyzed by the person(s) who collected it, which in turn has led to a deeper and richer understanding of development problems. However, given that a central challenge in international development is that the decision makers (development economists included) are in the business of studying people separated from themselves by vast distances—social, economic, political, and geographic—there is a strong case for using mixed methods to both help close this distance and more accurately discern how outcomes (positive, negative, or indifferent) are obtained and how any such outcomes vary over time and space (context).

By restricting themselves to the econometric analysis of survey data, development economists are boxed into a Cartesian trap: The questions they ask are constrained by the limitations inherent in the process by which quantitative data from closed-ended questions in surveys are collected (Rao, 2002; Rao & Woolcock, 2003). As such, they are limited in their ability to ask important questions about the social, cultural, and political context within which development problems are embedded. They even miss important aspects of some critical economic issues such as, for instance, the heterogeneity that underlies what are known as "informal" economies (i.e., labor markets that function outside formal salary and wage structures) and tend to overlook marginal markets that are centrally important for policy—such as the market for drugs, political favors, and sex—all of which require a strong degree of rapport with respondents that a short visit to field a questionnaire will not provide. A related criticism (to which we return later) is that many kinds of econometric analysis fail to examine what actually happens during the process of project implementation (the "black box") and consequently are unable to determine the extent to which failure to achieve intended impacts is due to design failure or to implementation failure. In other words, their research questions are being shaped by their data instead of their data being shaped by the questions. A strong case can be made that such questions require a more eclectic approach to data, one that mixes participation; observation; the analysis of text-based information (e.g., from tape recordings of village meetings or newspaper articles); free-ranging, open-ended interviews with key informants and focus groups; and other such types of information that can be loosely called "qualitative data." The name is a bit of a misnomer, however, as a lot of qualitative data can be coded, quantified, and econometrically analyzed. This distinction should therefore be more appropriately made between data collected from structured, closed-ended questions and nonstructured, open-ended modes of inquiry.

Another argument for using mixed methods is that most program assessments have focused on assessing the tangible changes that can be measured over the 3- to 5-year life of most projects and programs funded by international (and national) development agencies. While there are a few large-scale and high-profile impact evaluations that are cited in the literature, most attempts to assess impacts are based on evaluations that are not commissioned until late in the project and that have to be conducted over a short period of time and on a relatively modest budget. This is far from ideal, and concerted efforts need to be made to build impact evaluations into projects from their inception, but it is the reality that evaluators must confront and to which they should be expected to be able to make a constructive and valid contribution; mixed methods can be a useful approach to making such a contribution. Finally, many evaluations, particularly those that are nonquantitative, have a systematic positive bias (Bamberger, 2009c), because the short period that consultants are in the field frequently means that only project beneficiaries and agencies directly involved in project implementation are interviewed, and most of these tend to have a favorable impression of the project (as they are the people who have benefited directly). As such, many project evaluations do not interview anyone who is not a beneficiary or at least is involved in the project. Employing a mixed methods design can help to more accurately identify comparable nonparticipant locations and individuals and specify what a plausible counterfactual—that is, what might have happened to participants were it not for the project—might look like in a given case (Morgan & Winship, 2007).

Finally, there is increasing acceptance of the idea that monitoring is as central to good development practice as evaluation. Where evaluations tell us how well a project worked, monitoring provides real-time feedback, allowing the project to learn by doing and to adjust design to ground-level realities. Evaluations are now broadly perceived as central to development practice and have received a lot of intellectual attention, but scholars and practitioners have paid less attention to monitoring methods. Here again, mixed methods can provide the flexibility to integrate good monitoring practices within evaluation designs.

The response to these contending pressures has been a very lively but as yet unresolved debate on the optimal way to monitor and evaluate the impacts of development assistance. Many aspects of these debates are philosophical and are couched in terms that are inherently contested (and thus will never have a neat resolution), but we argue in this chapter that mixed methods approaches can nonetheless contribute to these debates in substantively important ways. The rest of the chapter proceeds as follows. The first section explores five key issues at the center of debates pertaining to project evaluation in developing countries.[5] The second section moves from first principles to pragmatism, stressing how evaluators can use mixed methods in the less than ideal circumstances they are likely to encounter in the field, and especially in developing countries. The third section focuses on the importance of understanding project processes and contexts and building effective monitoring systems. The fourth section considers some specific ways in which mixed methods can improve qualitative evaluations. Specific case studies of mixed methods evaluation in international development programs are provided in the following section. The final section concludes by considering the ongoing challenges and opportunities for using mixed methods in project evaluation in developing countries.

◆ **Using Mixed Methods in Project Evaluation and Monitoring: Five Key Issues**

Among the many issues that confront program evaluators, at least five speak to the importance of using mixed methods.

The first is the principle that the questions being posed should determine the research methods being used, not the other way around. As noted earlier, while most economists argue that RCTs (with strong quasi-experimental designs as a second best) should be considered the gold standard for impact evaluation (see next point), two counterarguments can be considered.[6] One is that there are many different kinds of development assistance ranging in complexity and scope from the types of clearly defined projects for which conventional impact evaluation models were designed to complex, multicomponent national level programs that involve many donors, numerous national agencies, and line ministries and that often have no clear definition of their scope or intended outcomes and impacts.[7] We argue that the great diversity of projects requires the use of a range of correspondingly different evaluation methodologies, and specifically that strong statistical project level designs are often inappropriate for the more complex, multicomponent programs. We recognize, however, that certain aspects of these complex programs can usefully be subjected to randomized designs (see, e.g., Olken, 2007). The second counterargument is that evaluations are conducted to address a wide range of operational and policy questions—that is, not just average treatment effects—and that, as such, different methodologies are required depending on the specific information needs of particular clients.[8]

Figure 24.1 illustrates how a mixed methods approach can be used for multiple-level analysis (Tashakkori & Teddlie, 2008) of a complex education program that must be assessed simultaneously at the level of the school district, the school, the classroom, and the individual student or teacher. Similar multilevel analysis could be used for the evaluation of multicomponent national level programs.

One of the emerging questions is whether there are alternatives to the statistical counterfactual that can be used in attribution analysis when it is not possible to use a

Figure 24.1   Multilevel Mixed Methods Design: Evaluating Effects of School Reforms on Student Attendance and Performance

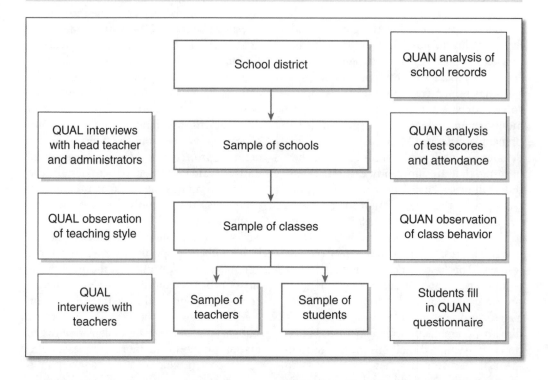

quasi-experimental design with a well-matched comparison group. Most of the alternatives to the strong statistical designs rely on mixed methods approaches that often combine case studies of households, communities, or organizations with key informant interviews and/or focus groups, with the synthesis of available quantitative data sources being used to ensure that the qualitative data is adequately representative and to permit the extrapolation of the findings to other populations. The development of valid alternatives to the statistical counterfactual is still a new and emerging field, one that usually relies on a combination of methods to reconstruct a hypothetical scenario absent the project intervention. Some of the techniques that are used include using two or more program theory models to compare expected outcomes under the intended project design and alternative hypotheses; techniques such as Participatory

Rural Appraisal (PRA) to obtain beneficiary perceptions on causality;[9] concept mapping (Kane & Trochim, 2007); and techniques such as Theory of Change (Morra & Rist, 2009, pp. 150–169). All of these approaches rely on combining different types of data collection and analysis. This field is still in its infancy but, to the extent that strong statistical designs can only be used in a small minority of evaluations, is potentially a very important area for which mixed methods approaches are well suited. Assessing how well these methods work in comparison to randomized impact evaluations is an important area of future research.

The second issue concerns the application of strong statistical designs in development contexts. We will not revisit the ongoing debate about the technical, ethical, political, and practical merits of RCTs and other statistical designs but will only consider contexts in which it has already been agreed to use one or other of these designs. While these designs have significant statistical advantages in terms of the elimination or reduction of project selection and sample selection bias, when used on their own these designs have a number of fundamental weaknesses. We argue that mixed methods can significantly strengthen the validity and operational utility of these designs as well as the design and implementation of more traditional quantitative evaluation strategies using double difference and matching strategies. Indeed, we argue that rigor is not determined solely by the use of a particular method as such but rather the appropriateness of the fit between the nature of the problem being assessed and the particular methods (singular or in combination) deployed in response to it, given prevailing time, political, financial, ethical, and logistical constraints.

The following are some important ways in which mixed methods can contribute to further strengthening these designs:

• Most strong quantitative impact evaluation designs (strong designs, for short) use a pre- and posttest comparison design. Information is usually not collected on the process of project implementation. Understanding "process" is the central concern of monitoring, and we argue that effective monitoring is necessary for effective evaluation. For instance, if the analysis does not find any statistically significant differences between the project and comparison groups, it is not possible to determine whether this is due to *design failure* (the proposed design is not appropriate to achieve the intended objectives in the particular context) or to *implementation failure* (the project was not implemented as planned so it is not possible to assess the validity of the project design or to recommend whether the project should be replicated). A mixed methods approach could incorporate process analysis through the use of qualitative techniques such as participant observation, key informant interviews,

and focus groups to assess the process of project implementation and how this affected program outcomes and impacts. Similarly, the absence of process data precludes analysis of the nature and extent of impact trajectories—that is, whether and how a project is performing not just with respect to a counterfactual but with respect to what theory, evidence, or experience would suggest that particular type of project should be achieving, given how long it has been implemented (Woolcock, 2009). Most evaluations, for example, assume that project impact is monotonic and linear, whereas experience alone would suggest that, for even the most carefully designed and faithfully implemented project, this assumption is not often valid.

• Most traditional evaluation designs rely on a limited number of unidimensional quantitative indicators to measure project impacts and outcomes. However, many constructs (such as poverty, empowerment, community organization, and leadership) are complex and multidimensional, rendering conventional quantitative indicators vulnerable to construct validity issues. Mixed methods can contribute a range of qualitative indicators as well as generating case studies and in-depth interviews to help understand the meaning of the statistical indicators. These indicators can sometimes be aggregated into quantitative measures and thereby incorporated into the statistical analysis.

• Most quantitative data collection methods are not appropriate for collecting information on sensitive topics (such as domestic violence, operation of community and other kinds of organizations, social and cultural factors limiting access to services) or for locating and interviewing difficult to reach groups (e.g., crime bosses, sex workers, members of marginalized social groups). There is a range of mixed methods techniques that can help address these issues.

- Strong designs are usually inflexible, in that the same data collection instrument, measuring the same indicators, must be applied to the same (or an equivalent) sample before and after the project has been implemented. This makes them much less effective for real-time learning by doing and for monitoring. Projects are almost never implemented exactly as planned (Mosse, 2005), and consequently the evaluation design must have the flexibility to adjust to changes in, for example, project treatments and how they are implemented, definition of the target population, and changes in the composition of the control group. Mixed methods can provide a number of rapid feedback techniques to provide this flexibility to adapt to changing circumstances.

- Strong designs are also criticized for ignoring (or being unable to incorporate the range of) the local contexts in which each project is implemented, which in turn can produce significant differences in the outcomes of projects in different locations. Mixed methods can help provide detailed contextual analysis.

- Similarly, RCTs and other quantitative evaluation methods designed to estimate the average treatment effects do not capture heterogeneity in the treatment effect (Deaton, 2009). While there are effective quantitative techniques designed to deal with treatment heterogeneity, qualitative methods can also be a strong aid to understanding how the treatment may have varied across the target population.

- Sample selection for strong designs is often based on the use of existing sample frames that were developed for administrative purposes (such as determining eligibility for targeted government programs). In many cases these sampling frames exclude significant sectors of the population of interest, usually without this being recognized. This is particularly true of regression discontinuity designs that necessarily exclude target populations outside the range of the discontinuity within which the treatment effect is identified. Mixed methods can strengthen sample coverage through a number of techniques such as on-the-ground surveys in selected small areas to help identify people or units that have been excluded (see Collins, this volume).

The third set of issues concern adapting impact evaluation to the real-world contexts and constraints under which most evaluations are conducted in developing countries. While evaluation textbooks provide extensive treatment of rigorous impact evaluation designs—that is, designs that can be conducted in situations where the evaluator has an adequate budget; a reasonable amount of time to design, conduct, and analyze the evaluation findings; access to most of the essential data; and a reasonable degree of political and organization support—most textbooks offer very little advice on how to conduct a methodologically robust impact evaluation when one or more of these conditions do not exist. Most of the recent debates have focused on advocating or criticizing the use of RCTs and strong quasi-experimental designs, and there has been almost no discussion in the literature on how mixed methods can help improve the conduct of impact evaluations in the vast majority of cases where rigorous statistical designs cannot be employed.[10] For many evaluation professionals, particularly those working in developing countries, the debates on the merits and limitations of statistically strong impact evaluation designs are of no more than academic interest, as many may never (and are highly unlikely to) have an opportunity to apply any of these designs during their professional career.[11] (In the following section we discuss how mixed methods evaluation can help adapt evaluation theory to the real-world time, budget, data, and political constraints under which most evaluations are conducted in developing countries.)

A fourth set of issues reflects the widespread concern about the low rate of evaluation utilization (Patton, 2008). Many methodologically sound evaluations are not used or do not contribute to the kinds of changes for which they were commissioned. There are many reasons for this (Bamberger, Mackay, & Ooi, 2004, 2005; Pritchett, 2002), but high among them is the fact that evaluation designs often do not have the flexibility to respond to the priority questions of concern to stakeholders or that the findings were not available when required or did not use a communication style with which clients were comfortable. Often the evaluation paradigm (whether quantitative or qualitative) was not accepted by some of the stakeholders. While mixed methods approaches do not offer a panacea for all of the factors affecting the utilization of evaluation, they can mitigate some of the common causes of low uptake. For example, purely quantitative designs—with their requirement for standardized indicators, samples, and data collection instruments—usually do not have the flexibility to respond to the wide range of questions from different stakeholders, whereas qualitative techniques usually do have this flexibility. Mixed methods can also incorporate process analysis into a conventional pretest and posttest design, thus making it possible to provide regular feedback on issues arising during implementation and to provide initial indications of potential outcomes throughout the life of the project, hence increasing the ability to provide timely response to stakeholder information needs. The collection of both quantitative and qualitative information also makes it possible to use different communication styles for presenting the findings to different audiences. Reports on case studies, perhaps complemented by videos or photographs, can respond to the needs of audiences preferring a human interest focus, while the statistical data can be presented in tables and charts to other more quantitatively oriented stakeholders.

◆ Using Mixed Methods to Conduct Evaluations under Real-World Constraints

When actually conducting evaluations of development projects, one frequently faces one or more of the following political and institutional constraints, all of which affect the ability to design and implement rigorous impact evaluations. First, many evaluations are conducted on a tight budget, which limits the ability to carefully develop and test data collection instruments and which often makes it impossible to use the sample sizes that would be required to detect statistically significant impacts, particularly for the many situations in which even well-designed projects can be expected to produce only a small change.

Second, many evaluations are conducted with a very tight deadline, which limits the time available for data collection and often the amount of time that consultants (many of whom are expensive foreigners) can spend in the field. Another dimension of the time constraint is that evaluators are often asked to assess outcomes or impacts when it is too early in the project cycle to be able to obtain such estimates. A less discussed but equally salient constraint is the limited time that clients and other stakeholders are able, or willing, to discuss the evaluation design or the preliminary findings. Consequently, if program theory models are developed, there will often be very little input from clients, thereby defeating the goal of ensuring that stakeholders are fully engaged in the definition of the program model that is being tested and the output and impact indicators that are being measured.

Third, many evaluations have very limited access to the kinds of data required for constructing baselines or comparison groups. This is particularly problematic in those cases (probably the majority) where the evaluation is not commissioned until late in the project cycle. Frequently no baseline data have been collected on the project group and no attempt was made to identify a plausible comparison group. Sometimes project administrative records or surveys designed for other purposes may provide some data, but often it does not cover the right population, contain the right questions, collect information from the right people (for instance, only the "household head" but not the spouse or other important household members), or refer to the right time period. In other cases, the information is incomplete or of a questionable quality. Another dimension of the data constraint is when the data collection instruments are not well suited for obtaining information on sensitive topics (sexual practices, illegal or illicit sources of income, corruption, or domestic violence) or for identifying and interviewing difficult to reach groups (e.g., those who are HIV positive, drug users, illegal immigrants).

The final set of constraints relate to political and organizational pressures that affect how the evaluation is formulated, designed, implemented, analyzed, and disseminated. These are all influenced, for example, by what issues are studied (and not studied), which groups are interviewed (and not interviewed), what kinds of information are made available (and withheld), who sees the draft report and is asked to comment (and who is not), and how the findings are disseminated. The pressures can range from a subtle hint that "this is not the time to rock the boat" to a categorical instruction from public authorities that it will not be possible to interview families or communities that have not benefited from the project.

Reducing the impact of these constraints requires a concerted effort to change the institutional structure of development assistance. Till this is achieved, the combined influence of these factors can have a major influence on the type of design that can be used, the sample sizes, and the level of methodological rigor (validity) that can be attained. A frequent problem is that the tight budget and the short timeframe that consultants can spend in the field is often considered a justification for only

visiting project sites and only interviewing beneficiaries and stakeholders directly involved in (and usually benefiting from) the project. As a result, many evaluations have a systematic positive bias because they only obtain information from beneficiaries. As these rapid (but flawed) evaluation approaches show funding and implementing agencies in a good light, there has been much less concern about the widespread use of these fundamentally flawed methodologies than might have been expected.

Other common problems include the sample sizes being too small to be able to detect impacts even when they do exist; techniques such as focus groups are often seen as a "quick and dirty" way to capture community or group opinions when there is neither time nor money to conduct sample surveys and when accepted practices for selection of subjects or avoiding bias in data collection and analysis are ignored; attribution is based on comparisons with poorly selected and not very representative control groups; data are only collected from one household member (often whoever is available) even when the study requires that information and opinions are collected from several household members.

Many quantitative evaluation designs are commissioned late in the project cycle and rely on secondary data from previous surveys for the baseline comparison. However, as the secondary surveys were normally commissioned for a different purpose than the project evaluation (e.g., national income and expenditure panel survey, national health or nutrition survey) it will often be found that the surveys do not contain all of the required information (particularly concerning specific information on access to the project), do not collect information from the requisite people, were not conducted at the right time, or do not completely cover the target population. While statistical techniques such as propensity score matching and instrumental variables can help strengthen the match of the project and comparison groups and eliminate some kinds of selection bias, there are a number of challenges that normally cannot be resolved.

In addition to the previously mentioned problems of sample coverage, who was interviewed, and so on, a major challenge frequently concerns missing information on differences between the project and comparison populations that might explain some of the postproject differences (e.g., in income, school test performance, infant mortality) that are assumed to have been produced (at least in part) by the project. For example, the women who apply for small business loans under a microcredit project may mainly come from the small group of women who have the self-confidence and experience to start a business, who have an unusually high degree of control over household decision making, or who have husbands supportive of their economic independence. Most applied econometric analysis tries to downplay the importance of these "unobservables" by assuming they are "time invariant" and consequently can be differenced out by using panel data. However, this assumption is often highly questionable, particularly when the researcher may have no idea what these factors might be.

A final challenge, one that will be discussed in more detail in the following section, concerns the lack of information on what happened during the project implementation process. Projects are rarely implemented according to plan, and often access to services and the quality of the services will be significantly less than planned. Consequently, in explaining why intended outcomes and impacts were not achieved, it is essential to know whether lack of results was due to design failure or whether problems were due to implementation failure. In real-world evaluation contexts, the information is often not available to make this judgment.

HOW CAN MIXED METHODS ADDRESS THESE REAL-WORLD CHALLENGES?

Mixed methods approaches combine quantitative approaches that permit estimates of magnitude and distribution of effects, generalization and tests of statistical differences with qualitative approaches that permit in-depth description, and analysis of processes and patterns of social interaction. These integrated approaches provide the flexibility to fill in gaps in the available information, to use triangulation to strengthen the validity of estimates, and to provide different perspectives on complex, multidimensional phenomena. When working under real-world constraints, a well-designed mixed methods approach can use the available time and resources to maximize the range and validity of information. The following are some of the specific ways that mixed methods can strengthen the impact evaluation design when working with real-world constraints.

Reconstructing Baseline Data. There are a number of qualitative techniques that can be used to reconstruct or to strengthen baseline data. These include recall, key informants, participatory group interview techniques (such as PRA), and the analysis of administrative records (such as school attendance, patient records from health clinics, and sales records from agricultural markets; see Bamberger, 2009a). Ideally a triangulation strategy should be used to increase validity by comparing estimates from different sources. Most of the previously listed sources use purposive, often opportunistic, sampling methods relying on information that is easily accessible, and consequently there are questions of bias or nonrepresentativeness. A mixed methods strategy can include statistical methods either to use random sampling techniques (e.g., to select the schools or clinics) or to assess the potential direction and magnitude of bias.

Observing Unobservables. An important application of the baseline reconstruction techniques is to identify important missing variables from the secondary data sets and to provide estimates of these variables. In the case of the previous microcredit project, techniques such as focus groups or key informant interviews could be used to identify differences between women who did and did not apply for loans that might affect project outcomes (such as successful launch of a small business). If possible, a small sample of beneficiaries and nonbeneficiaries would then be visited to try to reconstruct information on factors such as prior business experience, attitude of the husband to his wife's business initiatives, and self-confidence. If a rapid sample survey is not possible, a second (if less satisfactory) option might be key informant interviews or focus groups providing information on project and nonproject women. As always, the mixed methods approach will include quantitative methods to assess and control for selection bias. Even in strong statistical designs, good qualitative research can also help observe variables that might otherwise be a source of omitted and/or unobserved variable bias and potentially suggest other instrumental variables that could be incorporated into regression analysis.

Identifying a Range of Impact Evaluation Design Options. When real-world constraints make it impossible to use the strongest statistical designs, the evaluator should identify the range of possible design options (going from the most to the least statistically rigorous) and identify which design options are feasible within the prevailing constraints and can achieve an acceptable minimum level of methodological rigor (see following discussion). The possible designs should be assessed in terms of their adequacy for the purposes of the present evaluation, and ways to strengthen validity through the combination of different methods should be considered.

Rapid and Economical Data Collection Methods. There are a number of techniques that can be used to reduce the costs and/or time required for data collection (Bamberger, Rugh, & Mabry, 2006). These include shortening the data collection instrument by eliminating nonessential information, using more economical data collectors (schoolteachers or nurses instead of professional enumerators), collecting information from groups rather than individuals (focus groups and so on), direct observation rather than interviews (e.g., to estimate community travel patterns), using secondary sources, and building required data into project monitoring and similar administrative records. All of these techniques have potential issues of quality and representativeness, and as such it is important to assess these trade-offs between cost/time and validity when defining the data collection strategy.

Threats to Validity of Evaluation Conclusions. While validity should be assessed for all evaluations, these approaches for reducing costs and time and working with less robust evaluation designs significantly increase the range and potential severity of threats to validity. The use of mixed methods also introduces additional validity issues. The use of a threats-to-validity checklist is recommended to systematically assess the potential threats, their severity, and possible measures that can be taken to address them.[12] A key point of using mixed methods, however, is to triangulate data sources so as to check the validity of one instrument against another. Again, even in evaluations deploying strong statistical designs using large household surveys, qualitative methods such as anchoring vignettes (King, Murray, Salomon, & Tandon, 2004) can be used to ensure that survey respondents in different contexts are in fact interpreting questions in the same way.[13]

◆ **Strengthening Monitoring Systems: Understanding Project Processes and Contexts**

Projects are almost never implemented exactly as planned, and there are often significant variations in implementation in different project locations. Consequently, if the analysis finds no statistically significant differences between the change in indicators of intended outcomes/impacts between the project and comparison group, the conventional evaluation designs cannot distinguish between two alternative explanations:

- The project was implemented more or less as planned, so the lack of statistical outcome differences suggests there are weaknesses in the project logic and design (at least for this particular context), and the initial recommendation would be that the project should not be replicated or at least not until it has been redesigned (alternative policy recommendation A in Figure 24.2).

- There were significant problems or deviations during project implementation, so it was not possible to test the logic of the project design. Consequently the initial recommendation might be that another pilot project should be funded with more attention to implementation (alternative policy recommendation B in Figure 24.2).

These two alternatives are shown in Figure 24.2.

A weakness of many conventional impact evaluation designs is that they use a pretest/ posttest comparison group design that only collects data at the start and end of the project and does not examine what happened during the process of project implementation and how this might have affected outcomes. Consequently, as shown in Figure 24.2, these designs are not able to distinguish between the alternative explanations of design failure and implementation failure. Mixed methods designs, by combining statistical analysis with techniques for monitoring implementation, can test both of these hypotheses and hence considerably enhance the operational and policy utility of the evaluation.

Figure 24.3 presents a stylized model that provides a framework for assessing both the quality of project implementation and the level of conformity to the original implementation plan and contextual factors that affect both overall implementation and

Figure 24.2 Alternative Policy Recommendations When Pretest-Posttest Comparisons Find No Statistically Significant Differences in Outcome Indicators

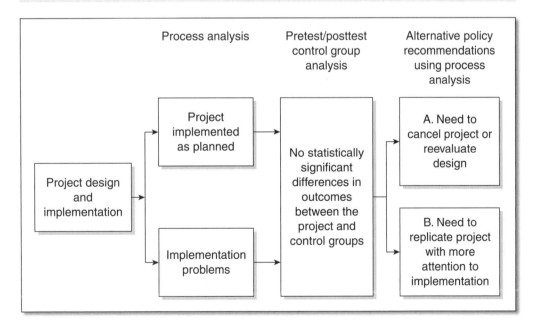

Figure 24.3 Contextual and Process Analysis

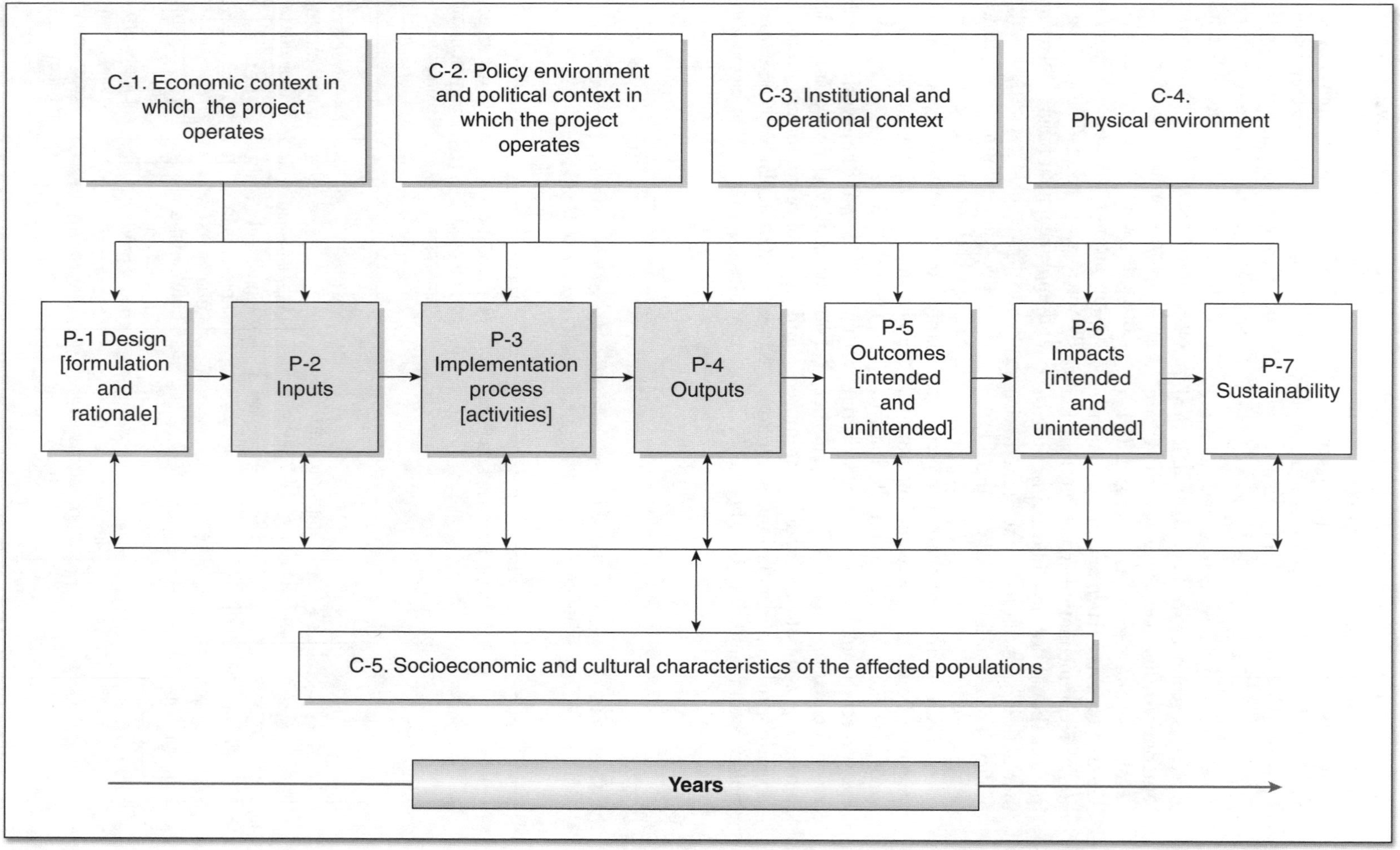

factors explaining variations of performance in different project settings. Steps P-1 through P-7 describe the typical stages of the project implementation process, while boxes C-1 through C-5 identify five sets of contextual factors such as the local, regional, and national economy; the policy and political environment; the institutional and operational environment; the physical environment (droughts, floods, soil erosion, etc.); and the socioeconomic and cultural characteristics of the affected populations that can affect implementation and impacts in different locations.

While some contextual factors can be measured quantitatively (e.g., percentage changes in indicators such as unemployment), others will usually be measured qualitatively (e.g., assessing whether the local political context is supportive of or opposed to the project, or remains neutral; the capacity and performance of local agencies involved in the project).[14] The decision whether to use quantitative and/or qualitative indicators will also depend on data availability, so that in one country opinion polls or citizen report cards may provide detailed statistical data on attitudes toward the performance of public service agencies, while in another country the rating may be based on the opinion of the local consultant or the pooled views of several key informants. For large projects with a longer time horizon and more resources, it may be possible to commission local researchers to conduct an in-depth diagnostic study covering all of these factors, but more commonly the ratings will be based on rapid data collection. Often, mixed methods data transformation techniques will be used so that qualitative ratings are aggregated into dummy variables that can be incorporated into regression analyses (see Onwuegbuzie and Combs, this volume). Where time and resources permit, this can be an iterative process (Figure 24.4) in which researchers return to the field to conduct in-depth analysis to explain how the different contextual factors influence implementation and outcomes.

While contextual analysis examines the influence of external factors, process analysis looks at the internal organizational processes through which the project is implemented. However, this distinction is not rigid, as external factors can affect implementation processes (e.g., political pressures to provide benefits to noneligible groups or problems within partner agencies that can affect the provision of certain services). Process analysis mainly focuses on steps P-2 (inputs), P-3 (processes), and P-4 (outputs). Some of the main sources of information for process analysis are the project's internal monitoring and administrative systems. While in theory a well-functioning monitoring system could provide most of the information required for process analysis, in practice monitoring systems often are seen as having only a narrow accountability function and often only generate a limited set of quantitative indicators.

Figure 24.4 An Iterative Process for Analyzing How Contextual Factors Affect Project Outcomes

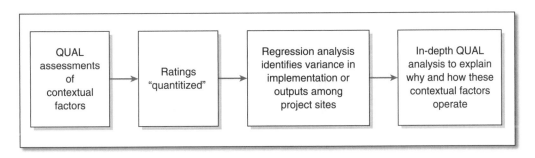

Often (though not always), the quality of the information is poor and relies on self-reporting, where the staff completing the information have an incentive to avoid problems by checking the boxes saying that progress is at least satisfactory. However, even when the quality of data is quite satisfactory, most systems rely on quantitative indicators with little attention given to the quality of the service delivery, how effectively beneficiaries are involved in planning and management, which sectors of the target population do and do not benefit, or the opinions of beneficiaries. A common example of the lack of information on beneficiary participation is the fact that many monitoring systems provide little or no information on differences in male and female participation rates or access to services or similar information for different ethnic groups. As monitoring systems are managed by the implementing agencies, issues such as corruption and major absenteeism (by teachers, medical staff, or office staff) are rarely addressed.

The mixed methods approach to process analysis will build on, and try to strengthen, monitoring and other administrative reporting systems while complementing these with a variety of quantitative and qualitative techniques. These may include participant observation (visiting schools, clinics, small business programs, etc., to observe how they operate); key informant interviews (including a wide range of different types of informant); focus groups; PRA and other participatory group interview techniques; selecting a panel of informants who are visited regularly throughout the life of the project; citizen report card surveys (in which a large and randomly selected sample of the target population are interviewed about their experiences with, and opinions about, public service agencies). It is also possible to make more creative use of administrative records and communications through the use of content analysis, review of e-mails and other internal communications, and analysis of the information and messages provided to the public through posters, notice boards, newsletters, and radio announcements. The information from all of these sources is used to compare how the project was actually implemented with the plan as stated in the operational manual and other planning documents.

The results of the analysis can be used for three complementary purposes. The first is to provide feedback to project management and policymakers to strengthen project implementation and to identify any groups or sectors of the target group that are not fully benefiting (and perhaps to identify noneligible groups that are benefiting). The second purpose is to contribute to the evaluation by helping interpret the extent to which failure to achieve intended outcomes can be attributed to weaknesses in the project design or to problems during implementation. When combined with contextual analysis, this can also help explain differences in outcomes in different project settings.

The third application of the combined process and contextual analysis is to provide guidance on potential project replicability. Conventional statistical evaluation designs match project and comparison groups, which in turn provide a robust analysis of differences between typical project and typical comparison group members but by definition makes it impossible to determine how effectively the positive project outcomes could be generalized to different situations. In other words, the policy recommendation from a conventional statistical impact design would be to say, "If the project were replicated to a very similar population group, these are the results that could be expected." However, the analysis does not permit recommendations on how the project would be likely to perform with different population groups or in different contexts. The combination of contextual and process analysis has the capacity to provide at least some general guidelines on how the project is likely to perform in different settings and with different population groups.

◆ *Using Mixed Methods to Strengthen Qualitative Evaluations*

A frequent criticism of qualitative methods is that they use small and often nonrepresentative samples. Mixed methods approaches offer some strategies for responding to these concerns. For example, even if it is desirable (for whatever reason) to use small samples, researchers can sometimes make careful (and highly strategic) choices about those samples if quantitative information on the larger universe of cases, and thus the nature of the distribution of key variables, is available. For example, selecting a small number of cases that are significantly different, as measured by variables collated in, say, a census or a large household survey, can give qualitative researchers a stronger basis on which to say something about the larger population. Mixed methods sampling has great flexibility to select small samples with a range of different characteristics that can be used to strengthen the understanding and interpretation of quantitative data. Some of the options include selecting extreme cases, selecting cases that are typical of each major group covered by the sample, identifying cases that challenge the research hypotheses or that do not conform to the main patterns, or using reputational sampling to select people that are outstanding or particularly interesting. A well-designed mixed methods data collection and analysis strategy permits a series of iterations whereby statistical findings can be fed back to the qualitative researchers who then generate additional hypotheses or indicators that can be explored statistically and that then generate additional questions to be explored in the field (see Jha, Rao, & Woolcock, 2007; Onwuegbuzie & Combs, this volume).

Dynamic mixed methods designs use and analyze qualitative data quite differently from conventional approaches that only use qualitative methods for initial diagnostic studies to help develop the data collection instruments for the quantitative studies. One practical but little used approach is to reserve a limited amount of time and resources to return to the field once the quantitative analysis has been completed and the draft evaluation report prepared. These resources are used to either provide more descriptive data on particularly interesting findings or to explore inconsistencies in the data (which often lead to some of the most interesting findings). For example, a study of village water management in Indonesia found that all except one of the village water supply systems were managed by women. In the one exception, where it was reported that the water supply was managed by men, it was initially assumed that this was a reporting error, and the initial reaction was to ignore it. However, the local researchers were able to return to this village, and it was discovered that this was the only area in which dairy farming was practiced. In this region only women manage dairy cattle, and as this was a very profitable activity the men agreed to manage the water supply to free their wives to exploit this income-generating opportunity. In none of the other villages did women have opportunities for profitable economic activities, so they were assigned to manage the water supply (Brown, 2000). This proved to be one of the most interesting findings of the study, but it could have easily been overlooked. How many other similarly interesting findings are never discovered because of the lack of a flexible mixed methods design?

With larger sample sizes, mixed methods strategies can also take advantage of new software for analyzing qualitative data that enables reams of coded textual information to be aggregated into more manageable discrete variables. Such techniques have proved useful in analyzing text from newspapers and transcripts of interviews from village meetings (see following discussion, and also Bazeley, this volume). The primary comparative advantage of qualitative methods, however, is their capacity to unpack the details and idiosyncrasies of local contexts and the processes by which different interaction effects play out. This does not mean that large N qualitative work is a contradiction in terms; rather, the larger the N from a qualitative standpoint, the greater the need and opportunity for fruitful engagement with quantitative approaches.

◆ Applying Mixed Methods in International Development Programs

This section discusses some of the special challenges in using mixed methods approaches in project evaluations conducted in developing countries. While mixed methods approaches are becoming more widely accepted among program evaluators in developed countries (although there is still more resistance to their use than is often claimed), there are a number of additional challenges for the application of these approaches in developing countries. Mixed methods designs usually involve additional costs, times, and logistical challenges (particularly when working in remote rural areas) or where there are security issues (meaning that arrival and departure times of the data collectors may have to be coordinated with local security authorities). It is also often the case that the professional divisions among different disciplines and research centers are often much greater, so that building a multidisciplinary team can be more time-consuming and challenging. Many of the central planning and finance ministries that have a major role in approving research have a strong quantitative research tradition and may need to be convinced that the qualitative component of mixed methods is genuine "professional research." Finally, qualitative research is often associated with radical academics or civil society organizations that government agencies fear will deliberately give an antigovernment slant to their evaluation findings (e.g., by using purposive sampling to select individuals or communities that are known to be critical of government programs).

We now present three brief case studies illustrating ways in which mixed methods approaches have been used in developing countries.

INDONESIA: THE KECAMATAN DEVELOPMENT PROJECT

The Kecamatan Development Project (KDP) in Indonesia is one of the world's largest social development projects. Implemented in the aftermath of the Suharto era and the East Asian financial crisis in 1998, KDP was primarily intended as a more efficient and effective mechanism for getting targeted, small-scale development assistance to poor rural communities, but it was also envisioned as a project that could help to nurture the proto-democratic state at the local level. KDP requires villagers to submit proposals for funding to a committee of their peers, thereby establishing a new (and, by design, inclusive) community forum for decision making on development issues (Guggenheim, 2006). Given the salience of conflict as a political and development issue in Indonesia, a key evaluation question is whether these forums are in fact able to complement existing local level institutions for conflict resolution and in the process help villagers acquire a more diverse, peaceful, and effective set of civic skills for mediating local conflict. Such a question does not lend itself to an orthodox stand-alone quantitative or qualitative evaluation, but rather to an innovative mixed methods approach.

In this instance, the team decided to begin with qualitative work, as there was relatively little quantitative data on conflict in Indonesia and even less on the mechanisms (or local processes) by which conflict is initiated, intensified, or resolved.[15] Selecting a small number of appropriate sites from across Indonesia's 3,500 islands and 350 language groups was not an easy task, but the team decided that work should be done in two provinces that were very different (demographically and economically), in regions within those provinces that (according to local experts) demonstrated both a high and low capacity for conflict resolution, and in villages within those regions that were otherwise comparable (as determined by propensity-score matching methods) but that either did or did not participate in KDP. Such a design enabled researchers to be confident that any common themes emerging from across either the program or nonprogram sites were not wholly a product of idiosyncratic regional or institutional capacity factors. Thus quantitative methods were used to help select the appropriate sites for qualitative investigation, which then entailed three months of intensive fieldwork in each of the eight selected villages (two demographically different regions by two high or low capacity provinces by two program or nonprogram villages).

The results from the qualitative work—useful in themselves for understanding process issues and the mechanisms by which local conflicts are created and addressed (see Gibson & Woolcock, 2008)—fed into the design of a new quantitative survey instrument, which will be administered to a large sample of households from the two provinces and used to test the generality of the hypotheses and propositions emerging from the qualitative work. A data set on local conflict was also assembled from local newspapers. Together, the qualitative research (case studies of local conflict, interviews, and observation), the newspaper evidence, data on conflict from national level surveys, and key informant questionnaires provided a broad range of evidence that was used to assess the veracity of (and, where necessary, qualify and contextualize) the general hypotheses regarding the conditions under which KDP could and could not be part of the problem and/or solution to local conflict.

INDIA: PANCHAYAT REFORM

A recent project evaluating the impact of *panchayat* (village government) reform—democratic decentralization in rural India—combines qualitative and quantitative data with a randomized trial.[16] In 1992 the Indian government passed the 73rd amendment to the Indian constitution to give more power to democratically elected village governments (*gram panchayats*—henceforth GPs) by mandating that more funds be transferred to their control and that regular elections be held, with one third of the seats in the village council reserved for women and another third for "scheduled castes and tribes" (groups who have traditionally been targets of discrimination). It was also mandated that a deliberative space—village meetings (*gram sabhas*)—be held at least two times a year to make important decisions such as the selection of beneficiaries for antipoverty programs and discussing village budgets.

It is widely acknowledged that the state of Kerala has been by far the most effective in implementing the 73rd amendment. There were two elements that contributed to this success. The first was that the state government devolved significant resources to the GPs with 40% of the state's expenditures allocated to them; the second element was the "people's campaign," a grassroots training and awareness-raising effort to energize citizens to participate, with knowledge, in the panchayat system. This led to better village plans, widespread and more informed participation, and more accountable government. Kerala is, of course, a special case, with very literate and politically aware citizens (literacy rates are close to 100%). The crucial policy question is whether the Kerala experiment can be replicated in much more challenging and more representative settings.

The northern districts of the neighboring state of Karnataka represent such settings. The literacy rate is about 40%, with high levels of poverty and a feudal social environment with high land inequality. These districts are also known to be beset by corruption and extremely poor governance. If a people's campaign could work in these districts, it could provide an important tool to transform the nature of village democracy in the country by sharply increasing the quality and quantity of citizen participation in the panchayat system and, in turn, have a significant effect on the standard of living. Also, these districts have access to two large national schemes that have substantially increased the funding of GPs, raising the budget of GPs from about 200,000 Indian rupees a year to approximately 4,000,000 rupees. Thus GPs in these districts have fulfilled the first element of the Kerala program—high levels of funding. The evaluation focuses on assessing the impact of the people's campaign. It randomly assigns 50 GPs as "treatment." Another set of GPs, matched to belong to the same county as the treatment GPs and with similar levels of literacy and low-caste populations and randomly chosen within this subset, is selected as "control" GPs. (They are also chosen to be at least one GP away from treatment GPs to avoid treatment spillover problems.)

The "treatment" consists, initially, of a 2-week program conducted by the Karnataka State Institute of Rural Development, which is responsible for all panchayat training in the state and has extensive experience in the field. The program trains citizens in participatory planning processes, deliberative decision making, and disseminates information about the programs and procedures of the panchayat. At the end of 2 weeks, a village meeting is held where priorities are finalized and presented to local bureaucrats. At a meeting with the bureaucrats, an implementation agreement is reached wherein the bureaucrats commit to providing funding and technical support for the selected projects over the course of the year. Following this initial training, the GP is monitored with monthly 2-day visits over a period of 2 years in order to ensure the program's progress.

An extensive quantitative baseline survey was implemented in the 200 treatment and control villages randomly selected from the 100 selected GPs and completed a month prior to the intervention. The survey instruments, developed after several weeks of investigative fieldwork and pretesting, included village-level modules measuring the quality and quantity of public goods, caste and land inequality in the village, and in-depth interviews with village politicians and local officials. Twenty households from each village were also randomly chosen for a household questionnaire assessing socioeconomic status, preferences for public goods, political participation, social networks, and other relevant variables. Two years later, the same sample of villages and households were reinterviewed with identical survey instruments. These pretest and posttest quantitative data provide a gold-standard quantitative assessment of impact using a randomized trial.

To understand "process" issues, however, equal attention was given to in-depth qualitative work. A subset of 5 treatment and 5 control GPs from the quantitative sample was selected purposively for the qualitative investigation. They were selected to compare areas with low and high literacy and different types of administrative variation. A team of qualitative investigators visited these villages for a day or two every week over a 2-year period investigating important dimensions of change: political and social dynamics, corruption, economic changes, and network affiliation, among other things. Under the supervision of two sociologists, the investigators wrote monthly reports assessing these dimensions of change. These reports provide a valuable in-depth look at month-to-month changes in the treatment and control areas that allow the assessment of the quality of the treatment, changes introduced by the treatment, and other changes that have taken place that are unrelated to the treatment. Thus, the qualitative work provides an independent qualitative evaluation of the people's campaign but also supplements findings of the quantitative data.[17]

An important challenge in understanding the nature of the 73rd amendment is to study participation in public village meetings (*gram sabhas*) held to discuss the problems faced by villagers with members of the governing committee. Increases in the quality of this form of village democracy would be a successful indicator of improvements in participation and accountability. To analyze this, a separate study was conducted on a sample of 300 randomly chosen villages across four South Indian states, including Kerala and Karnataka. Retrospective quantitative data on participation in the meetings, however, are very unreliable because people's memories are limited about what may have transpired at a meeting they may have attended. To address this issue, the team decided to record and transcribe village meetings directly. This tactic provided textual information that was analyzed to observe directly changes in participation (see Ban & Rao, 2009; Rao & Sanyal, 2009). Another challenge was in collecting information on inequality at the village level. Some recent work has found that sample-based measures of inequality typically have standard errors that are too high to provide reliable estimates. PRAs were therefore held with one or two groups in the village to obtain measures of land distribution within the village. This approach proved to generate excellent measures of land inequality, and since these are primarily agrarian economies, measures of land inequality should be highly correlated with income inequality. Similar methods were used to collect data on the social heterogeneity of the village. All this PRA information has been quantitatively coded, thus demonstrating that qualitative tools can be used to collect quantitative data. In this example, the fundamental impact assessment design was kept intact, and both qualitative and quantitative data were combined to provide insights into different aspects of interest in the evaluation of the intervention.

ERITREA: COMMUNITY DEVELOPMENT FUND

The Eritrean Community Development Fund (CDF) was launched soon after Eritrea gained independence in the early 1990s, and it had two objectives: developing cost-effective models for the provision of community infrastructure (schools, health care centers, water, environmental protection, veterinary clinics, and feeder roads) and strengthening the participation of the local communities in the selection, implementation, and maintenance of the projects. Separate evaluations were conducted to assess the implementation and impacts of each of the six components. This case describes how mixed methods were used to strengthen the evaluation of the feeder roads component (similar approaches were used to assess the health and education components). Three feeder roads were being constructed, each between 50 and 100 kilometers in length and each serving many small villages that currently had no access to roads suitable for vehicular traffic.

The evaluation was not commissioned until work had already begun on each of the three roads, but none of which had yet been completed (planning and construction took on average around one year, with work often interrupted during the rainy season). The evaluation had a relatively modest budget, and no baseline data had been collected prior to the start of road construction. However, the CDF was intended as a pilot project to assess the efficiency and socioeconomic outcomes of each of the six project components, with the view to considering replication in a follow-up project. Consequently, policymakers were very interested in obtaining initial estimates, albeit only tentative, of the quantitative impacts of each component. Given the rapidly changing economic and social environment during the first decade of independence, it was recognized that the changes observed over the life of the different project components could not be assumed to be due to the project intervention. The need for some kind of simple attribution analysis was recognized, despite the absence of a conventional comparison group.

The possibility that was first considered was to try to identify areas with similar socioeconomic characteristics but that did not have access to a feeder road and that could serve as a comparison group. However, it was concluded, as is often the case with the evaluation of the social and economic impact of roads, that it would be methodologically difficult to identify comparable areas and, in any case, extremely expensive to conduct interviews in these areas, even if they could be found. Consequently, the evaluation used a mixed methods design that combined a number of different data sources and that used triangulation to assess the validity and consistency of information obtained from different sources. The evaluation combined the following elements:

• The evaluation was based on a program theory model that described the steps and processes through which the project was expected to achieve its economic and social impacts and that identified contextual factors that might affect implementation and outcomes. The theory model also strengthened construct validity by explaining more fully the wide range of changes that road construction was expected to achieve so that impacts could be assessed on a set of quantitative and qualitative indicators. Some of the unanticipated outcomes that were identified in this way included strengthened social relations among relatives and friends living in areas that were previously difficult to reach and strengthened and widened informal support networks as people were able to draw on financial, in-kind, and other support from a geographically broader network.

• Quantitative survey data were obtained from a stratified sample of households along the road who were interviewed three times during and after the road construction (the evaluation started too late for a pretest measure).

• The baseline conditions of the project population prior to road construction were reconstructed by combining recall of the time and cost for travel to school, to reach a health center, to transport produce to markets, and to visit government agencies in the nearest towns; with information from key informants (teachers, health workers, community leaders, etc.); and data from secondary sources. Estimates from different sources were triangulated to test for consistency and to strengthen the reliability of the estimates.

• Data on comparison groups, before, during, and after road construction, were obtained from a number of secondary sources. Information on school attendance by sex and age were obtained from the records of a sample of local schools. In some cases, the data also included the villages from which children came so that it was possible to compare this information with recall from the interviews in project villages. Records from local health clinics were obtained on the number of patients attended and the medical services provided. Unfortunately, the records did not permit an analysis of the frequency of visits of individual patients so it was not possible to estimate whether there were a relatively small number of patients making frequent use of the clinics or a much larger number making occasional visits. Most of the local agricultural markets were cooperatives that kept records on the volume of sales (by type of produce and price) for each village, so this provided a valuable comparison group. It was planned to use vehicle registration records to estimate the increase in the number and types of vehicles before and after road construction. However, qualitative observations revealed that many drivers "forgot" to register their vehicles, so this source was not very useful.

• Process analysis was used to document the changes that occurred as road construction progressed. This combined periodic observation of the number of small businesses along the road, changes in the numbers of people traveling, and the proportions on foot, using animal traction, bicycles, and different kinds of vehicles.

• Country-level data on agricultural production and prices, available over a number of years, provided a broader picture and was used to correct for seasonal variations in temperature and rainfall (both between different regions and over time). This was important in order to avoid the error of measuring trends from only two points in time.

All of the data sources were combined to develop relatively robust estimates of a set of social and economic changes in the project areas over the life of the project and to compare these changes with a counterfactual (what would have been the condition of the project areas absent the project) constructed through combining data from a number of secondary sources. The credibility of the estimates of changes that could be (at least partially) attributed to the project intervention was then tested through focus groups with project participants, discussions with key informants, and direct observation of the changes that occurred during project implementation.

This evaluation, conducted with a relatively modest budget and drawing on the kinds of secondary data and recall information that are often available, illustrates how mixed methods designs can offer a promising approach to developing an alternative to the conventional statistical counterfactual, thus strengthening our understanding of the potential impacts of the majority of projects where the conventional counterfactual cannot be applied.

◆ Conclusions

In the final section we discuss both the challenges that continue to affect the introduction of mixed methods approaches as well as some of the areas of opportunity.

CHALLENGES

While dramatic progress has been made in the application of mixed methods in the United States and some other industrial nations, and despite a slow but steady increase in published studies in developing countries, a number of challenges continue to face evaluators wishing to apply mixed methods in the monitoring and evaluation of development projects and policies in these contexts.

A first challenge is the fact that mixed methods have been the evaluation design of choice for many development agencies for many years. However, many of these evaluations used somewhat ad hoc approaches, and most do not apply the kinds of methodological and conceptual rigor that is required by academic journals such as the *Journal of Mixed Method Research*. So the mixed methods approach is not new per se, but the professional, financial, and other resources have usually not been available to increase methodological rigor.

While it is claimed (although not everyone would agree) that the "paradigm wars" are long ended in the United States and Europe and that there is a general acceptance of mixed methods approaches, in many, but certainly not all, developing countries the divisions between quantitative and qualitative researchers are still quite pronounced. In some countries, qualitative researchers tend to be (or are perceived as being) more politically radical than their quantitative colleagues, so this can provide a further complication. Indeed, for precisely this reason, autocratic regimes are often amenable to training engineers and statisticians to help manage the state but are much less sympathetic toward disciplines such as anthropology, sociology, and journalism that might unearth material questioning the claims and legitimacy of the regime. Even in more open societies, this often means that, in practical terms, considerable time and effort is usually required to identify and build a team of local researchers who can work well together on a mixed methods approach. Unfortunately, the planning of many development evaluations does not allow much time for team building, so often the result can be two separate strands of quantitative surveys not very clearly linked to in-depth case studies or other qualitative data collection.

A related challenge in many developing countries has been the fact that most senior officials in central finance and planning agencies have been trained in economics and quantitative methods, and at least until recently many have been suspicious of qualitative methods that are "not really professional research," so many research and consulting agencies have had little incentive to develop a mixed methods capacity. In the last few years, many research agencies have been trying to strengthen their capacity in mixed methods approaches, but this continues to be a weak area.

Another practical problem is the lack of local expertise in mixed methods research in many countries. The more rigid division between quantitatively and qualitatively oriented university faculties also means that in many countries not many courses are offered on mixed methods. It has been our experience that many university-based consulting centers that have a strong track record in quantitative research have found it difficult to integrate a solid qualitative component to their evaluation. Too often a few somewhat ad hoc focus groups are tacked on to the end of the quantitative evaluation with no clear link to the rest of the study.

There are also many practical logistical challenges in applying mixed methods in many development contexts. Many development evaluations require data collection in remote rural areas or in urban areas where security threats makes it more difficult to use the flexible approaches required by mixed methods. For example, in some studies, all data collectors have to be transported together to remote locations, and all need to arrive and leave at the same time so that qualitative interviewers do not have the flexibility to take advantage of invitations to social events such as weddings, parties, and funerals, which are excellent opportunities to observe the community in action. In many countries, police or military authorities may also require exact details on who is to be interviewed.

OPPORTUNITIES

The growing interest in mixed methods, combined with recognition of the special challenges, presents a number of exciting opportunities for strengthening the use of mixed methods in development evaluations. A first area of opportunity is in developing effective monitoring systems. While there is a widespread acceptance that monitoring is essential for good project implementation, much less thought has been given to the design of monitoring systems than to methods to evaluate project impact. Mixed methods, with their ability for the rapid and economical collection of data customized to the characteristics of a particular program and for providing information that can be easily contextualized, can be very helpful in monitoring design.

A second area of opportunity is the fact that strong statistical evaluation designs, even if they are believed to be the best option, can only be applied in a small number of development evaluations. Until this situation changes, the body of literature on how to strengthen evaluation designs for the remaining (i.e., the majority of) evaluations is very limited, and this provides a unique opportunity for developing mixed methods designs that make the most effective use of the many, but often incomplete, sources of quantitative and qualitative information that can be generated. Mixed method designs are intended to address exactly this kind of challenge, and there are strong opportunities for the application of practical, cost-effective mixed methods evaluations.

A third major area of opportunity concerns developing alternatives to the conventional statistical counterfactual. There is now widespread acceptance that the use of randomized trials, and statistically matched project and control designs, can provide a valid counterfactual. More generally, there is an increasing awareness that all development agencies need to be able to address the question, "How do we know that the observed changes in the project population can be attributed to our intervention?" Or, put another way, "How can we estimate what would have been the condition of the project population if our project had not taken place?" We have argued here that techniques such as concept mapping or qualitative group consultation methodologies such as PRA can be used to construct a counterfactual, but this is still a nascent area of research, and no widely accepted alternatives to the conventional counterfactual have yet been found. This is another area of opportunity for mixed methods.

Some of the other areas of opportunity include refining approaches to mixed methods sampling, incorporating process and contextual analysis into strong statistical designs, reconstructing baseline data and using mixed methods to generate more reliable estimates of unobservables in econometric analysis, and improving the extent to which project efficacy is assessed not only with respect to a counterfactual but also to where it should be relative to other projects of a particular type at a given time interval. Furthermore, the development community is moving away from support for individual projects to funding of complex multicomponent, multiagency national level development programs. There is a growing demand for new evaluation methods to assess the outcomes of these complex programs, and these are areas in which mixed methods, with their flexibility to draw on and integrate many different sources of information, can make a valuable contribution.

A final challenge for mixed methods evaluation is to provide guidelines on minimum levels of acceptable methodological rigor when drawing on diverse data sources that are often collected under tight budget and time constraints or where much of the data are collected under difficult circumstances. Conventional threats to validity analysis have still not been widely applied to mixed methods evaluations, and there is an opportunity to develop standards that ensure a satisfactory level of methodological rigor while also being realistic. There is a challenge, on the one hand, of avoiding the "anything goes" approach of some evaluators who believe that given the difficult situations in which they are working they cannot be held accountable to normal standards of rigor, while on the other hand, avoiding the claim of some academic researchers who would apply exactly the same criteria to the assessment of an evaluation of a program to prevent sexual harassment of women in refugee camps as they would to a large federally funded evaluation of education-to-work programs in a U.S. city. At the end of the day, it should only be logical that knowledge claims regarding the efficacy of the diverse range of development projects, in all the diverse contexts in which they are deployed, should be made on the basis of an appropriate corresponding diversity of social science methods and tools.

Research Questions and Exercises

1. What are the main reasons for the increased demand to measure the effectiveness of international development projects? Do similar factors affect the demand for program evaluation in North America and Europe? What are the similarities and differences?

2. What are the main arguments advanced by the advocates and the critics of randomized evaluation designs? Where would you place yourself in this debate?

(Continued)

(Continued)

3. What are the five key issues in project monitoring and evaluation where mixed methods can make an important contribution?

4. What are some of the reasons why the findings of many development agencies have a positive bias? How can mixed methods help control for these biases?

5. What are process analysis and contextual analysis, and why is it important to incorporate them into project and program monitoring? How can mixed methods contribute?

6. How can mixed methods help strengthen qualitative evaluation methods as they are typically applied in development evaluations?

7. Review one (or more) of the case studies described in the chapter. What specific mixed methods approaches were used? Do you believe that these strengthen the methodological rigor of the evaluation and the validity of the findings? Why or why not?

8. How easy would it be to replicate the mixed methods approaches used in these case studies in other development evaluations? What would be some of the main challenges?

◆ Notes

1. The views expressed in this chapter are those of the authors alone and should not be attributed to the respective organizations with which they are affiliated. We thank the *Handbook*'s editors for their helpful comments and our respective collaborators for all that they have taught us on these complex issues over many years.

2. The absence of evidence cuts both ways, of course: Critics also have little empirical basis on which to claim that development projects unambiguously haven't worked.

3. See also the critique of philosophers, such as Cartwright (2007).

4. NONIE is supported by and brings together the Development Assistance Committee of the Organization for Economic Cooperation and Development (DAC) Evaluation Network, the Evaluation Cooperation Group of the multilateral finance institutions, the International Organization for Cooperation in Evaluation, and the UN Evaluation Group.

5. All of these issues are also relevant to the application of mixed methods evaluations in industrialized countries.

6. We will refer to RCT and strong quasi-experimental designs as *strong statistical designs*.

7. Some of the dimensions that can be used for classifying evaluation scenarios include (a) evaluation purpose, (b) level at which the evaluation is conducted, (c) program size or scale, (d) complexity of the evaluand, (e) size of the evaluation budget, (f) stage of the project at which the evaluation is commissioned, (g) duration of the evaluation, (h) who the client is, (i) who will conduct the evaluation, (j) level of required statistical rigor, (k) location of the evaluation design on the QUAN/QUAL continuum, and (l) source of data (primary, secondary, both). See the chapter by Onwuegbuzie and Combs (this volume) for more details of mixed data analysis.

8. Examples of evaluation purpose include (a) generalizability (assessing the feasibility of replicating or scaling up an intervention), (b) developmental (tracking emergent, complex interventions), (c) accountability (ensuring accountability for results), (d) contribution/substitution (assessing the contribution of different donors to comprehensive, collaborative interventions or assessing whether donor funding

produces a net increase in funding for a program or whether this replaces previously allocated government funding). Source: Adapted from NONIE (2009).

9. PRA is a research tool used to engage villagers, many of whom are often illiterate, in tasks such as map drawing and wealth rankings to help formalize issues such as consumption patterns, the spatial and demographic distribution of wealth, changes in income over the seasons, and movements into/out of poverty over time. The key figure is Robert Chambers (see, e.g., Chambers, 1994). For a critical reflection on participatory approaches more generally, see (among others) Brock and McGee (2002).

10. Although no formal statistics are available, the authors estimate that pretest/posttest comparison group designs are used in less than 25% of impact evaluations, and quite probably in less than 10% of cases.

11. One of the authors organizes an annual workshop (International Program for Development Evaluation Training) for 30 to 40 experienced evaluation professionals working in developing countries. Every year he polls them on how many have been involved in a strong statistical evaluation design, and often not a single participant has ever had the opportunity to use one of these designs.

12. A pilot version of a threats-to-validity checklist developed by Bamberger (2009b) is available at http://www.bambergerdevelopment evaluation.org.

13. On the integration of qualitative and quantitative approaches in political science more generally, see Fearon and Laitin (2008).

14. On attempts to assess such political contextual variables, see Barron, Diprose, and Woolcock (2010).

15. The details on this methodological strategy are provided in Barron, Diprose, and Woolcock (2010).

16. Other examples of mixed methods research in India include Rao (2000, 2001); Rao, Gupta, Lokshin, and Jana (2003); and Jha and colleagues (2007).

17. This evaluation is still ongoing, and results are not yet available.

◆ References

Bamberger, M. (2009a). Strengthening impact evaluation designs through the reconstruction of baseline data. *Journal of Development Effectiveness, 1*(1), 37–59.

Bamberger, M. (2009b, June). *Threats to validity checklist.* International Program for Development Evaluation Training workshop on "Conducting Impact Evaluations under Constraints." Carleton University, Ottawa. Available at http://www.bamberger developmentevaluation.org (section on checklists).

Bamberger, M. (2009c, September). *Why do so many evaluations have a positive bias?* Paper presented at the annual conference of the Australasian Evaluation Society, Canberra, Australia. Retrieved February 16, 2010, from http://www.bambergerdevelopment evaluation.org

Bamberger, M., Mackay, K., & Ooi, E. (2004). *Influential evaluations: Evaluations that improved performance and impacts of development programs.* Independent Evaluation Group. Washington, DC: World Bank. Also available at http://www.worldbank.org/ieg/ecd

Bamberger, M., Mackay, K., & Ooi, E. (2005). *Influential evaluations: Detailed case studies.* Independent Evaluation Group. Washington, DC: World Bank. Also available at http://www.worldbank.org/ieg/ecd

Bamberger, M., Rugh, J., & Mabry, L. (2006). *Real world evaluation: Working under budget, time, data and political constraints.* Thousand Oaks, CA: Sage.

Ban, R., & Rao, V. (2009). *Is deliberation equitable? Evidence from transcripts of village meetings in South India* (Policy Research Working Paper No. 4928). Washington, DC: World Bank.

Banerjee, A. (2007). *Making aid work.* Cambridge, MA: MIT Press.

Barron, P., Diprose, R., & Woolcock, M. (2010). *Contesting development: Participatory projects and local conflict dynamics in Indonesia.* New Haven, CT: Yale University Press.

Brock, K., & McGee, R. (2002). *Knowing poverty: Critical reflections on participatory research and policy.* London: Earthscan.

Brown, G. (2000). Evaluating the impact of water supply projects in Indonesia. In M. Bamberger (Ed.), *Integrating quantitative and qualitative research in development projects* (pp. 107–113). Washington, DC: World Bank.

Cartwright, N. (2007). Are RCTs the gold standard? *BioSocieties, 2,* 11–20.

Chambers, R. (1994). The origins and practice of participatory rural appraisal. *World Development, 22*(7), 953–969.

Deaton, A. (2009). *Instruments of development: Randomization in the tropics and the search for the elusive keys to economic development* (Working Paper No. 14690). Cambridge, MA: National Bureau of Economic Research.

Duflo, E., & Kremer, M. (2005). Use of randomization in the evaluation of development effectiveness. In G. Pitman, O. Feinstein, & G. Ingram (Eds.), *Evaluating development effectiveness* (pp. 205–231). New Brunswick, NJ: Transaction.

Fearon, J. D., & Laitin, D. D. (2008). Integrating qualitative and quantitative methods. In J. Box-Steffensmeier, H. Brady, & D. Collier (Eds.). *Oxford handbook of political methodology* (pp. 756–776). New York: Oxford University Press.

Gibson, C., & Woolcock, M. (2008). Empowerment, deliberative development and local level politics in Indonesia: Participatory projects as a source of countervailing power. *Studies in Comparative International Development, 43*(2), 151–180.

Guggenheim, S. E. (2006). Crises and contradictions: Explaining a community development project in Indonesia. In A. Bebbington, S. E. Guggenheim, W. Olson, & M. Woolcock (Eds.), *The search for empowerment: Social capital as idea and practice at the World Bank* (pp. 111–144). Bloomfield, CT: Kumarian Press.

Jha, S., Rao, V., & Woolcock, M. (2007). Governance in the gullies: Democratic responsiveness and community leadership in Delhi's slums. *World Development, 35*(2), 230–46.

Kane, M., & Trochim, W. (2007). *Concept mapping for planning and evaluation.* Thousand Oaks, CA: Sage.

King, G., Murray, C. J. L., Salomon, J. A., & Tandon, A. (2004). Enhancing the validity and cross-cultural comparability of survey research. *American Political Science Review, 98*(1), 191–207.

Morgan, S., & Winship, C. (2007). *Counterfactuals and causal inference: Methods and principles for social research.* New York: Cambridge University Press.

Morra, L., & Rist, R. (2009). *The road to results: Designing and conducting effective development evaluations.* Washington, DC: World Bank.

Mosse, D. (2005). *Cultivating development: An ethnography of aid policy and practice.* London: Pluto Press.

Network of Networks on Impact Evaluation (NONIE). (2009, April). *Impact evaluations and development: NONIE guidance on impact evaluation.* Available at http://www.worldbank.org/ieg/nonie/guidance.html

Olken, B. (2007). Monitoring corruption: Evidence from a field experiment in Indonesia. *Journal of Political Economy, 115*(2), 200–249.

Patton, M. Q. (2008). *Utilization-focused evaluation* (4th ed.). Thousand Oaks, CA: Sage.

Pritchett, L. (2002). It pays to be ignorant: A simple political economy of rigorous program evaluation. *Policy Reform, 5*(4), 251–269.

Rao, V. (2000). Price heterogeneity and real inequality: A case-study of poverty and prices in rural South India. *Review of Income and Wealth, 46*(2), 201–212.

Rao, V. (2001). Celebrations as social investments: Festival expenditures, unit price variation and social status in rural India. *Journal of Development Studies, 37*(1), 71–97.

Rao, V. (2002, May 18). Experiments in participatory econometrics: Improving the connection between economic analysis and the real world. *Economic and Political Weekly, 22*(20), 1887–1891.

Rao, V., Gupta, I., Lokshin, M., & Jana, S. (2003). Sex workers and the cost of safe sex: The compensating differential for condom use in Calcutta. *Journal of Development Economics, 71*(2), 585–603.

Rao, V., & Sanyal, P. (2009). *Dignity through discourse: Poverty and the culture of deliberation in Indian village democracies* (Policy Research Working Paper No. 4924). Washington, DC: World Bank.

Rao, V., & Woolcock, M. (2003). Integrating qualitative and quantitative approaches in program evaluation. In F. J. Bourguignon and L. P. da Silva (Eds.), *The impact of economic policies on poverty and income distribution: Evaluation techniques and tools* (pp. 165–90). New York: Oxford University Press.

Ravallion, M. (2008). Evaluating anti-poverty programs. In P. Schultz and J. Strauss (Eds.), *Handbook of development economics* (Vol. 4, pp. 3787–3846). Amsterdam: North-Holland.

Tashakkori, A., & Teddlie, C. (Eds.). (2008). *Foundations of mixed methods research: Integrating quantitative and qualitative approaches in the social and behavioral sciences.* Thousand Oaks, CA: Sage.

Woolcock, M. (2009). Toward a plurality of methods in project evaluation: A contextualized approach to understanding impact trajectories and efficacy. *Journal of Development Effectiveness, 1*(1), 1–14.

25

TEACHING MIXED METHODS AND ACTION RESEARCH

Pedagogical, Practical,
and Evaluative Considerations

◆ Thomas W. Christ

Objectives

Upon finishing this chapter you should be able to

- distinguish common features of mixed methods and action research;

- use a heading system to organize a research proposal;

- create a methodological map to visually display a research design;

- see how action research can be used to improve curricula and teaching;

- understand how critical realism was used to evaluate mixed methods research; and

- know how a mixed methods course was proposed, developed, and evaluated.

This chapter presents how action research is one form of mixed methods and should be taught as a continuum of philosophical assumptions and methodologies as a way to dispel misconceptions about research being diametrically opposed and incompatible. Introductory and advanced mixed methods research courses were created, evaluated, and improved as a result of numerous action research cycles that include planning, acting, developing, and reflecting. Critical realism was the preferred theoretical lens used by the researcher-teacher to examine the multiple forms of data necessary to refine the courses over numerous reiterative cycles. This chapter highlights several of the teaching strategies and curricula developed as a result of examining and merging the multiple forms of evidence from each cycle that were used to make decisions about how to teach mixed methods research to hundreds of master's and doctoral students.

Tashakkori and Creswell defined mixed methods in their first editorial in the *Journal of Mixed Methods Research* (*JMMR*) as "research in which the investigator collects and analyzes data, integrates the findings, and draws inferences using both qualitative and quantitative approaches or methods in a single study or program of inquiry" (2007, p. 4). Action research, a unique form of mixed methods, adds to Tashakkori and Creswell's definition. Kemmis and McTaggart (1988, p. 1) defined action research as

> a form of collaborative self-reflective enquiry undertaken by participants in social situations in order to improve the rationality and justice of their own social or educational practices, as well as their understanding of these practices and the situations in which these practices are carried out.

Pragmatism is the most commonly cited philosophical orientation associated with the mixed methods and action research movements (Biesta & Burbules, 2003; Bryman, 2006; Howe, 1988; Johnson & Onwuegbuzie, 2004; Morgan, 2007; Reason & Bradbury, 2008; Tashakkori & Teddlie, 1998). Critical and transformative perspectives are also making fast headway (Greene, 2008; Kemmis, 2008; Mertens, 2003). Pragmatism touted in mixed methods as the preferred paradigm rejects the either/or choice of qualitative and quantitative research that perpetuated the paradigm wars. Those who have studied Peirce's, James's, and Dewey's forms of pragmatism understand they are complementary to the conduct of mixed methods research, with its focus on action as the prominent way to create knowledge.

The origins of action research are associated with Kurt Lewin, who coined the following definition: Action research "proceeds in a spiral of steps, each of which is composed of a circle of planning, action, and fact finding about the results of the action" (Lewin, 1946/48, p. 206). Clearly, Dewey's theory of knowledge, concepts of indefinite interactions, knowing as the mode of experience, and the relationship between actions and consequences had influence upon Lewin's action research model. Dewey's pragmatism presents that action is a necessary condition for knowledge and results from thinking and reflection (see Biesta, this volume), which is the prominent feature required of action research. Dewey's and Lewin's theories have had an impact on transformative and intervention-oriented mixed methods research. Teaching action research as a distinct form of mixed methods makes perfect sense. Reason and Bradbury's definition in the *Sage Handbook of Action Research* (2008, p. 4) clarifies this connection:

> Action Research is a participatory process concerned with developing practical knowing in the pursuit of worthwhile human purposes. It seeks to bring together action and reflection, theory and practice, in participation with others, in

pursuit of practical solutions to issues of pressing concern to people, and more generally the flourishing of individual persons and their communities.

This complements Greene and Hall's (this volume) definition of mixed methods as transformative research.

A mixed methods way of thinking, as well exemplified by the dialectic stance, offers opportunities to meaningfully engage with difference as we encounter it in the contexts we study—difference of culture, ethnicity, gender, religion, tradition, and so forth. Because the dialectic stance invites a multiplicity of ways of seeing and ways of knowing into the same study, a multiplicity of different perspectives is engaged, as are diversity and variation in the substance of what is being studied. These differences encompass knowledge claims and value claims alike, because different paradigmatic and methodological traditions embrace different value commitments or, in some cases, eschew a place for values in science all together. (p. 125)

Action-oriented mixed methods research encompasses a family of approaches, individual reflective research with focus on improving one's own teaching practice or living conditions, group-oriented organization development and improvement research, participant-oriented critical and liberating research focusing on imbalance of power, and policy-oriented research practices aimed at making large scale social change (Reason & Bradbury, 2008).

Action, transformative, and critical research have their roots in pragmatism, which rejects a qualitative and quantitative incompatibility stance. Niglas (this volume) first denied the linear or diametrically opposed conceptions of research and the incommensurable paradigm in 1999, expressing that philosophy and methodology fall on a continuum. Biesta (this volume), with a focus on pragmatism, addresses practical and philosophical concerns: practical, defined as "utility of research means for research ends," and a philosophical stance that pragmatism is a "leading contender" in "mixed methods and mixed model" research (p. 96). Creswell (this volume) warns of "paradigms represent rigid categories of information . . . perpetuated by the impermeable, tight boxes drawn around the various philosophical positions" (p. 54).

From a pedagogical stance, teaching postpositivism and constructivism as a dialectic stance from a historical perspective makes sense, but it should not be taught as the way to conceive of research today. Johnson and Gray (this volume) present philosophical and historical perspectives that define five paradigmatic points of view: (a) constructivism, (b) transformative, (c) pragmatism, (d) postpositivism, and (e) positivism. The historical overview helps demonstrate that paradigms fall on a philosophical continuum with practical value. Crotty's (1998) four elements to the research process—(a) epistemology, (b) theoretical perspectives, (c) methodology, and (d) methods—further differentiate paradigms, methodology, and procedures. Presenting a historical overview of the philosophical underpinnings of paradigms helps students to understand they are theories that have influence upon the research process. Creswell (this volume) states that "theory in this placement, resides immediately below the epistemology level, and it helps inform the methodology and methods" (p. 55). Maxwell's interactive research approach (2005), including goals, conceptual framework, methods, validity, and the research questions, also reduces common misconceptions that research is linear and driven by a single paradigm.

Gorard (this volume) presents a compelling argument for teaching students what the term *paradigm* means and how it is commonly misused: "The schismic classifications of qualitative and quantitative work are unjustifiable as paradigms" (p. 249).

Presenting that paradigms are one form of theory that can fit in up to three places in a research cycle—(a) the beginning, as a way to define an intervention and accompanying theories in most confirmatory and action-oriented studies; (b) the middle, in terms of the role of the researcher and his or her own paradigmatic worldview (ontology, epistemology, axiology) with influence on the research process, especially important in exploratory, transformative, and critical research designs; and (c) the end, common to studies that rely on a "grounded theoretical approach to data analysis"—reduces confusion when teaching research (Christ, 2008a, 2008c, 2009a).

Theory should also be expressed to students as a representative model of the phenomenon and as a "series of interconnected ideas that condense and organize knowledge" from the micro, macro, and meso level and as useful for prediction and explanation (Neuman, 2006, p. 50). The interactive nature of mixed methods research and the role of paradigms reinforce that action research is one form of mixed methods that relies on reiterative cycles within the research process (Mertler, 2008). Maxwell's (2005) interactive research design, Gorard's cycle of research (this volume) and Niglas's (this volume) philosophy and methodology continuum all highlight the interactive nature of research. Gorard's definition of research as "a spiral which has no clear beginning or end, in which activities (phases) overlap, can take place simultaneously, and iterate" (p. 241) is a perfect description of action research. Gorard's, Maxwell's, Mertler's and Niglas's models challenge Onwuegbuzie and Teddlie's (2003) early contentions that mixed methods research could be viewed as exploratory and confirmatory, Tashakkori and Teddlie's description of a "third methodological movement" (2003, p. 679), and Johnson and Onwuegbuzie's view that mixed methods is "a third research paradigm" (2004, p. 14).

Pragmatism as the dominant paradigm is a controversial topic and should be presented when teaching mixed methods research. Johnson and Gray's chronological overview (this volume) summarizes eight points: (a) pragmatism rejects dichotomous either/ or thinking; (b) pragmatism emphasizes Dewey's premise that knowledge (epistemology) comes from person-environment interactions; (c) pragmatism recognizes that knowledge is individually and socially created based on empirical evidence; (d) pragmatism embraces ontological pluralism, that multiple theories and perspectives can be true and coexist; (e) pragmatism emphasizes the epistemological position that there are numerous ways to create knowledge: Dewey's conception of warranted assertions challenges the idea that there is a universal truth; (f) pragmatism shows that theories are incomplete but useful for predicting, explaining, and influencing change; (g) pragmatism demonstrates the ontological stance that values are integral in research; and (h) Peirce's capital "T" (Truth) in his definition of pragmatism can only be obtainable at the end of history.

This helps frame two useful concepts for students: First, action research influenced by Dewey's form of pragmatism is mixed methods research as knowledge and is created through action—in essence, a form of confirmatory research in practice. Second, critical realism can be used as a methodological and paradigmatic choice complementary with Dewey's pragmatism when conducting mixed methods. As noted by Maxwell and Mittapalli (this volume), methods are not tied to specific philosophical paradigms but are part of philosophical assumptions (ontology, epistemology, and axiology), which influence the choice of methods and the interactive relationship between philosophy and practice.

Action research requires some form of action, commonly an intervention following a reiterative process of planning, acting, developing, and reflecting (Bradbury, 2007; Greenwood & Levine, 2001; Mertler, 2008). Presenting action research as a series of steps designed to improve social conditions or workforce performance helps students to understand that it is a specific form of mixed methods, a form of transformative research common to business, education, nursing, and social work where multiple sources of numerical and verbal data are combined, reflected upon, and used to make adjustments when conducting an analysis. Typical of action-oriented mixed methods research is the following seven-step cycle:

1. Identifying and limiting the topic. This is usually done by searching the literature, conducting a focus group with identified stakeholders, or observing a social setting.

2. Determining the research, intervention, or action plan. Once the intervention is established, appropriate measures can be matched to the intervention.

3. Administer the intervention and collect appropriate data such as measures, observations, and interviews. Data to be collected should be determined after defining the purpose of the study. For example, in education, data are collected to determine if intervention is improving student performance and teaching praxis.

4. Data analysis. Depending on what form of data are collected, appropriate analysis procedures should be conducted. As action research studies are rarely designed to make broad generalizations, following stringent statistical procedures is not required when analyzing quantitative data. Quantitative data can be examined by comparing trend lines, displays of descriptive statistics, and percentages. Rubrics and rating scales often provide information necessary to determine how to best modify the intervention to meet students needs. Qualitative data such as field notes and interviews can be analyzed using simple sorting and coding techniques. The various forms of data are analyzed and combined using a reiterative process of data analysis to provide the researcher-teacher evidence

necessary to modify and improve the interventions and teaching praxis.

5. Reflection. The researcher-teacher reflects on the findings from the data and identifies potential modifications to the intervention based on insight and input from the participants. This allows for improvements to teaching habits, strategies, and interventions.

6. Modify the intervention. Once the intervention is modified as a result of careful reflection, it is reintroduced, and the cycle repeats three times to be classified as a true action research cycle (i.e., collect and analyze data, reflect on the findings, and modify the intervention). If the action research cycle is conducted for fewer than three reiterations, it should be identified as an arrested action research project.

7. Finally the results are written and disseminated to appropriate stakeholders and those who can gain from the knowledge.

Critical realism is a complementary approach with action-oriented mixed methods research. Maxwell and Mittapalli (this volume) support this contention as they identify that (a) critical realism is compatible with qualitative, quantitative, and mixed research endeavors; (b) methods are not philosophical paradigms, yet philosophical assumptions cannot be ignored when using different methods; (c) the relationship between knowledge and practice is interactive, as knowledge, truth, and values influence the way people conduct, interpret, and disseminate research; (d) paradigm assumptions function as constraints on methods and as lenses for viewing the world; and (e) critical realism should not be considered as an alternative paradigm. Maxwell and Mittapalli's focus on issues of causality, reality, and validity fits well with this researcher-teachers action research project, with its focus on improving pedagogical, practical, and evaluative techniques when teaching mixed methods research, which is discussed in the next section.

◆ Pedagogical Teaching Considerations

Onwuegbuzie and Leech first indicated the importance that "research courses be taught at different levels that simultaneously teach both quantitative and qualitative techniques within a mixed methodological framework" (2005, p. 268). Creswell (2006) advanced this dichotomy by stating that mixed methods incorporates paradigms, philosophical assumptions, and theoretical perspectives, as well as research questions and interpretations. Clearly, paradigmatic considerations are central when teaching mixed methods research. Biesta, Creswell, Greene and Hall, Johnson and Gray, and Niglas (all this volume) refer to pragmatism as a philosophical foundation and not a method. Christ (2008b, 2009a, 2009d) extends the view of pragmatism as a philosophical foundation in mixed methods by indicating that action research shares philosophical underpinnings, methodologies, and design characteristics and thus is and should be taught as a form of mixed methods research. Illustrating that mixed methods research can be exploratory, explanatory, confirmatory, action, transformative, and critical, combined in unique ways, is crucial (Christ, 2009e). Teddlie and Tashakkori (2009) highlight that mixed methods typologies are regularly combined using multiple forms of data blended and merged.

Plano Clark and Badiee (this volume), Gorard (this volume), and Christ (this volume) indicate that the purpose of the study and the research questions are intricately interconnected. Confirmatory mixed research designs are viable options for those who wish to influence policy makers and funding agencies. Action research is regularly utilized by teachers as a way to improve their teaching praxis, student, classroom, and school wide performance and in business as a way to increase productivity, efficiency, and workforce satisfaction. Participatory action research (Rahman, 2008; Swantz, 2008) is commonly used when conducting critical and transformative studies (Greene, 2007; Lykes & Mallona, 2008; Mertens, 2003) designed to improve communities or reduce oppression.

Biesta (this volume) highlights Dewey's theory of action and the relationship between actions and consequences. The way a research question is phrased directly influences the methodological design, data choice, and analysis techniques. Acting as a necessary component in mixed methods research allows the creation of knowledge as a result of blending multiple forms of data when making inferences. Combining critical, action, and/or transformative research is now a viable option, as was combining qualitative and quantitative research over the past two decades, yet little has been published concerning the pedagogical, practical, or evaluative considerations that are important when teaching mixed methods. Interaction of methodology, methods, and paradigms are now becoming increasingly complex, contributing to the challenge of teaching exacerbated by the lack of empirical evidence with a focus on how to effectively teach mixed methods.

Strategies for teaching, including steps to follow when conducting mixed methods research, have recently been published (Christ, 2009a; Collins & O'Cathain, 2009; Creswell, 2009a; Teddlie & Tashakkori, 2009), and others have identified challenges to consider when teaching mixed methods (Onwuegbuzie & Leech, 2005). Christ's article titled "Designing, Teaching, and Evaluating Two Complementary Mixed Methods Research Courses" (2009a) is the only empirically based study that indicates viable strategies and curricula that can be used when teaching mixed methods research.

Creswell, Tashakkori, Jensen, and Shapley (2003) first voiced concerns about teaching qualitative and quantitative methods separately, while Niglas indicated that research should be considered a continuum of philosophy and methodology in

2001. Onwuegbuzie and Leech (2009) also challenged the diametrically opposed way of teaching by advocating for graduate students to learn, use, and appreciate quantitative and qualitative research methodologies simultaneously at different levels within a mixed methods framework.

Teaching students that action research is a form of mixed methods has its share of challenges. Although numerous publications are available that describe action and mixed methods research (Bergman, 2008; Creswell & Plano Clark, 2007; Greene, 2007; Hui & Grossman 2008; Mertler, 2008; Reason & Bradbury, 2008; Ridenour & Newman, 2008; Saks & Allport, 2007; Teddlie & Tashakkori, 2009), no single source identifies that action research is a form of transformative mixed methods that combines multiple forms of data in a single study. Niglas first presented that action research and mixed methods fit within a continuum of philosophy and methodology in 2001. Action research commonly relies on combining, analyzing, and merging multiple forms of qualitative and quantitative data, albeit with the primary intention of making change through action, yet none of the authors in this handbook directly address that action research as a mixed methodology. The question is why?

The purpose for conducting action research fits within the mixed methods continuum, commonly transformative or critical in nature. Participatory action research is one design that fits within the transformative and critical mixed methods continuum concerned with self-investigation by underprivileged and disenfranchised people, which generates action by the people involved, including the outside researcher (Rahman, 2008). Participation is both technique and the epistemological principle inherent in action research, where participants explore their own understanding of their actions and experiences in a less distorted way than what would be created by an outside researcher attempting to capture participants' views. Participatory action research

produces knowledge and action directly useful to the participants, empowering them to understand that they are constructing and using their own knowledge (Reason & Bradbury, 2008).

Action research by design is exploratory, confirmatory, and explanatory, requiring some form of reflexive action (Reason & Torbert, 2001) or intervention with purposeful sampling, not randomized or with the intent to generalize results from a sample to a population. Action research consistently starts as an exploratory design, asking a "how" question with a focus on improving a situation, then moves through cycles of data collection, analysis, and reflection, becoming an explanatory and/or confirmatory design that determines if the actions have an intended effect (Christ, 2009a, 2009c). The action research cycles are sequential, which is clearly a mixed methods design (Creswell & Plano Clark, 2007; Tashakkori & Teddlie, 1998; Teddlie & Tashakkori, 2009). As one form of mixed methods, action research embraces a collaborative and reflective relationship between participants and the researcher conducting activities with an intent to improve social conditions. Action research requires participation that supports purpose and practice (Reason & Bradbury, 2008).

Those interested in determining how empirically derived evidence generated through action research can be used to understand what constitutes effective mixed methods research pedagogy and praxis can look to an example presented in the following section that describes how qualitative and quantitative evidence was collected, analyzed, merged, and reflected on as a way to improve how to teach mixed methods. The researcher-teacher is currently in the curricula development stage of a fifth action research cycle, having examined and chosen new chapters that reflect the latest advancements from this handbook to be used when teaching advanced mixed methods research.

Twelve chapters have been selected from this handbook by the researcher-teacher to update the curricula developed in the fourth iteration of Education Department Curriculum Studies (EDCS) 780 Mixed Methods Research (Christ, 2009a). Many of the strategies from the previous iterations remain, but the curriculum for EDCS 780 will be considerably modified. The next section explains how action research and a critical realist approach were used to refine introductory and advanced mixed methods courses. Constant reflection and action allowed curricula to be improved in the advanced mixed methods class. As with the start of each semester teaching EDCS 780, another action research cycle begins; in this case, the focus will be on updating the curricula to improve the teaching pedagogy, praxis, principles, and methods of instruction.

Numerous action research cycles were used to create and modify two mixed methods research courses developed in 2006. An overview of these cycles is presented in the following sections of this chapter, with the aim of demonstrating how the curricula, strategies, and teaching techniques can be improved through action and reflection. Nine sections of introductory and four of advanced mixed methods classes have now been taught. Each semester, the classes are modified as a result of collecting data and reflecting upon the products. These action research cycles help improve teaching praxis while allowing for the introduction of the latest materials to be infused into the courses.

MIXED METHODS RESEARCH CLASSES

Christ (2009a) indicated that the purpose of a 2-year mixed methods case study was to explain how two courses, Curriculum, Research, and Teaching-EDCS 606 and Mixed Methods Research-EDCS 780, were designed, implemented, evaluated, and improved. Each of these courses was developed following an action research cycle of planning, acting, developing, and reflecting

upon curricula, strategies, and teaching praxis. Multiple forms of evidence were used at each of the action research cycles, the first of which begins by reviewing available resources including syllabi, texts, and journal articles. Once each of the two courses was completed, statistically analyzed anonymous course and faculty evaluations, participant narrations, and the products produced by the students allowed for purposeful and reflective modifications to be performed each semester thereafter. Refinements were based on examining the strengths, challenges, and lessons learned from teaching these classes to a diverse graduate population at a Carnegie ranked research-intensive institution.

Both courses were designed with two goals in mind: to teach a balanced approach of research skills and to support students as they plan and begin to write thesis or dissertation proposals. The University of Hawaii at Manoa's campus has 138 master's and doctoral degree programs. Approximately one fourth of the students who register for the research courses are English as a Second Language learners, adding to the challenge of teaching complex concepts and terminology associated with mixed research methodologies.

TEACHING GOALS AND STRATEGIES

Students in mixed methods research classes were introduced to a nine-step research design strategy used to teach research methods:

1. Defining the topic. Students were taught to concurrently consider (a) their topical interest; (b) the problem under investigation; and (c) the purpose for which the research is intended, and why it is important to determine the purpose before formalizing a tentative overarching research question, choosing a methodology, or designing procedures (Christ, 2008b). Discussions of how

research has multiple overlapping paradigms and numerous potential sources of data help to dispel dialectic paradigmatic thinking and false conceptions that research is a linear process (Christ 2009a). Niglas (this volume) will replace prior readings in the next iteration of EDCS 780, as it highlights that mixed methods research should not be divided into a limited number of paradigms or methodological distinctions, but should be taught as an overlapping continuum of philosophy and methodology.

2. Mental model for mixing. Greene's "mental model" has been defined and presented as the researcher's own "assumptions, understandings, predispositions, and values and beliefs" (Greene, 2007, p. 53) that interact within the research process in both courses. Students in the next iteration of EDCS 780 will read Greene and Hall (this volume) and Mertens, Bledoe, Sullivan, and Wilson (this volume), replacing the Lincoln and Guba chapter in *The Sage Handbook of Qualitative Research* (2005) used to define and defend four fundamental beliefs that form the researchers' worldview: (a) "axiological beliefs about the nature of ethics," (b) "ontological beliefs about the nature of reality," (c) "epistemological beliefs about the nature of knowledge and the relationship between the knower and that which would be known," and (d) "the methodological beliefs about the appropriate methods for a systematic investigation to yield warrantable assertions" (Mertens et al., this volume, p. 194).

Considerable time is spent by students in EDCS 780 discussing, describing, and defending the researcher's worldview and the researcher's role in the research process, concepts critical when conducting mixed action research projects. Extending the definitions of ontology, epistemology, and axiology, students in the next iteration of EDCS 780 will read the Johnson and Gray, Biesta, Greene and Hall, and Niglas chapters in this handbook, with a focus on paradigms as a way to formalize a table that defines their worldview and research topics in relation to

how the data they propose to collect and analyze fit across a continuum of paradigms (postpositivism, pragmatism, constructivism, critical, hermeneutics, transformative, etc.) placed into a matrix that clarifies sampling and integration processes.

3. The design typologies. Triangulation, embedded, explanatory, and exploratory typographies as outlined by Creswell and Plano Clark (2007) continue to be presented. Students are warned that "diversity in potential designs is greater than any typography can adequately encompass" (Maxwell & Loomis, 2003, p. 244) and that "methodologists cannot create a complete taxonomy of mixed methods designs due to the designs' capacity to mutate into other forms" (Teddlie & Tashakkori, 2009, p. 139). Typologies act as decision-making strategies that include multiple methodologies, strands or phases, implementation processes, and processes of integration. The next iteration of EDCS 780 will include Gorard (this volume), which discussed that distinct categories of methods such as qualitative or quantitative should not be taught in isolation. Gorard challenges the widely disseminated concept about creating a third mixed methods paradigm, which he indicates does not help in any way. Advanced students will be asked to reflect on Gorard's argument that all methods involve subjective judgments about less than perfect evidence and that methods imply values and are a matter of personal preference rather than a consequence of the questions being answered.

4. Specifying the reason, rationale, and purpose for conducting mixed methods research. Presenting action-oriented mixed methods designs will continue as many of the students in EDCS 780 are or will become teachers. Action research is a preferable form of teacher research, a way to act and improve praxis and student performance—a philosophy of teaching that extends for a lifetime (Carr & Kemmis, 1983). Participatory action research and critical and transformative mixed methods

designs will continue to be presented to EDCS 780 students as a way to reinforce the concept that there are multiple purposes for conducting mixed methods (Teddlie & Tashakkori, 2009), multimethods (Brewer & Hunter, 1989), embedded (Creswell & Plano Clark, 2007), action-oriented (Reason & Bradbury, 2008), transformative (Greene, 2007), and/or critical research (Lather, 2004). Johnson and Gray (this volume) will replace previously assigned textbook chapters that provided a historical overview of mixed methods. Students in the next iteration of EDCS 780 will be asked to discuss how mixed methods research is an emerging field influenced by philosophical theoretical views reaching back centuries. As Creswell (2009a, p. 101) states,

Some, like myself, focused on the methods of collecting and analyzing data, recognizing that the methods were an integral part of the entire process of research. Others focus on how qualitative and quantitative research flowed into all phases of the research process (the methodologists). Still others focused upon the philosophy. Now we are seeing yet another group emerge—those who combine mixed methods with more traditional designs.

Christ's article "Designing, Teaching and Evaluating Two Mixed Methods Research Courses" (2009a) will be assigned to students in EDCS 780, as it acts as an advanced organizer presenting strategies that will be used over the course of the semester. This article emphasizes teaching research as a creative process by asking students to consider methodologies and methods, combined as necessary, including action, grounded, and transformative approaches that use multiple forms of data logically connected to the purpose as long as the resources and time are available. Many unique research designs have emerged as a result of students' combining various typographies. Two examples of

transformative research designed by students help show that typographies are infinite and ever changing. One methodological graphic organizer is from a high school teacher who successfully proposed a critical action research design where the intervention was a culturally responsive chemistry curricula designed to meet the needs of oppressed Native Hawaiian students (see Figure 25.1). Another was a critical mixed methods study designed to explore what indigenous research means. The design combines auto-ethnography and case studies of other indigenous graduate student researchers (see Figure 25.2, page 654). These methodological concept maps are strategies found to be extremely helpful for students to clarify and formalize their research designs. This practice will continue in future iterations in which students are supplied with a methodological map template (see Figure 25.3, page 655) to be used when designing their study. Methodological maps are quite complementary to visual displays of the results and theoretical models that can be presented in the conclusions. Dickinson (this volume) will be assigned to students in the next iteration of EDCS 780, as it highlights how results and conclusions can be presented as a visual display that helps readers understand complicated interactions and models of phenomena. This technique is especially helpful for English language learners as it presents how themes are merged into a visually represented theoretical model that indicates how the data presented in the conclusions combine, complement, or become divergent.

5. Determining, defining, and modifying the research questions. The critical nature of the research question as the hub in all research designs will continue to rely on an expanded form of Maxwell's (2005) interactive research diagram indicating that five components are constantly working together: the research question, goals, conceptual framework, methods, and validity (Christ & Makarani, 2009). Plano Clark and Badiee's chapter (this volume) will be

Figure 25.1 Critical Action Research Project

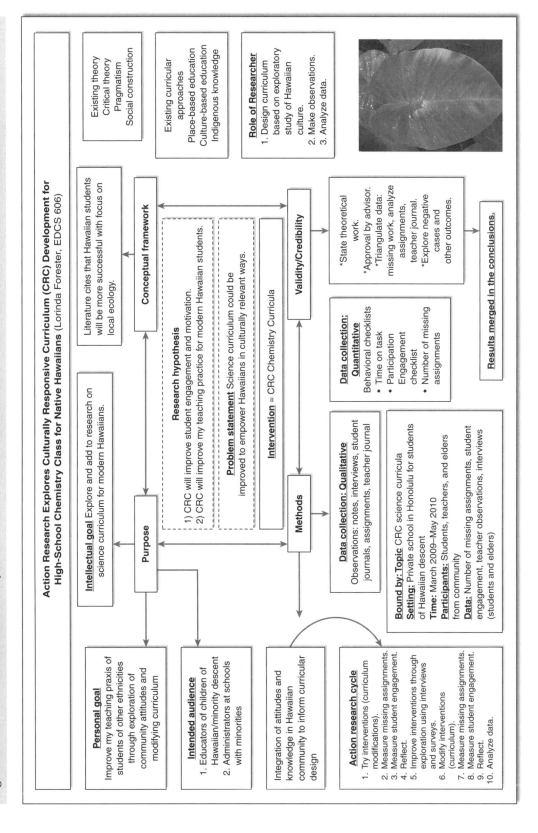

Action Research Explores Culturally Responsive Curriculum (CRC) Development for High-School Chemistry Class for Native Hawaiians (Lorinda Forester, EDCS 606)

Personal goal
Improve my teaching praxis of students of other ethnicities through exploration of community attitudes and modifying curriculum

Intellectual goal Explore and add to research on science curriculum for modern Hawaiians.

Literature cites that Hawaiian students will be more successful with focus on local ecology.

Existing theory
Critical theory
Pragmatism
Social construction

Existing curricular approaches
Place-based education
Culture-based education
Indigenous knowledge

Role of Researcher
1. Design curriculum based on exploratory study of Hawaiian culture.
2. Make observations.
3. Analyze data.

Conceptual framework

Intended audience
1. Educators of children of Hawaiian/minority descent
2. Administrators at schools with minorities

Purpose

Research hypothesis
1) CRC will improve student engagement and motivation.
2) CRC will improve my teaching practice for modern Hawaiian students.

Problem statement Science curriculum could be improved to empower Hawaiians in culturally relevant ways.

Intervention = CRC Chemistry Curricula

Validity/Credibility

*State theoretical work.
*Approval by advisor.
*Triangulate data: missing work, analyze assignments, teacher journal.
*Explore negative cases and other outcomes.

Integration of attitudes and knowledge in Hawaiian community to inform curricular design

Methods

Data collection: Quantitative
Behavioral checklists
• Time on task
• Participation Engagement checklist
• Number of missing assignments

Action research cycle
1. Try interventions (curriculum modifications).
2. Measure missing assignments.
3. Measure student engagement.
4. Reflect.
5. Improve interventions through exploration using interviews and surveys.
6. Modify interventions (curriculum).
7. Measure missing assignments.
8. Measure student engagement.
9. Reflect.
10. Analyze data.

Data collection: Qualitative
Observations: notes, interviews, student journals, assignments, teacher journal

Bound by: Topic CRC science curricula
Setting: Private school in Honolulu for students of Hawaiian descent
Time: March 2009–May 2010
Participants: Students, teachers, and elders from community
Data: Number of missing assignments, student engagement, teacher observations, interviews (students and elders)

Results merged in the conclusions.

Figure 25.2 Critical Mixed Methods Project (Brandy Ann Sato, EDCS 780)

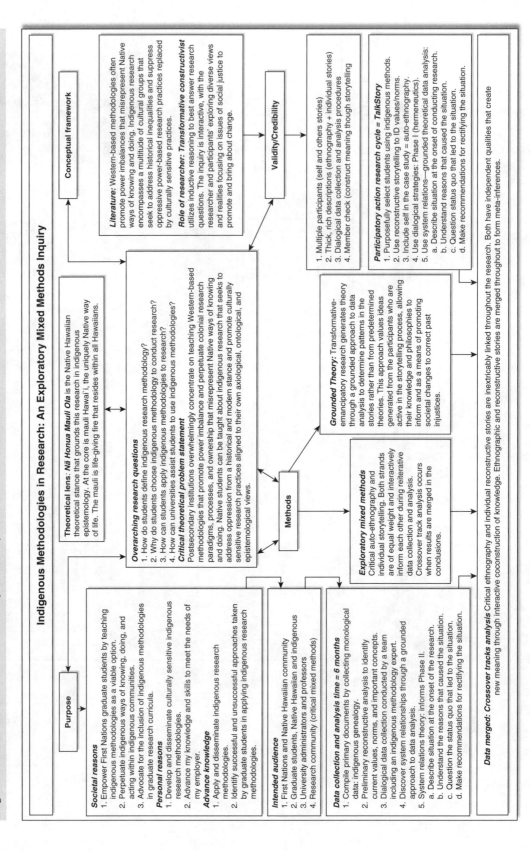

Indigenous Methodologies in Research: An Exploratory Mixed Methods Inquiry

Purpose

Conceptual framework

Theoretical lens: *Nā Honua Mauli Ola* is the Native Hawaiian theoretical stance that grounds this research in indigenous epistemology. At the core is mauli Hawai'i, the uniquely Native way of life. The mauli is life-giving fire that resides within all Hawaiians.

Literature: Western-based methodologies often promote power imbalances that misrepresent Native ways of knowing and doing. Indigenous research encompasses a multitude of cultural groups that seek to address historical inequalities and suppress oppressive power-based research practices replaced by culturally sensitive practices.

Role of researcher: Transformative constructivist utilizes inductive reasoning to best answer research questions. The inquiry is interactive, with the researcher and participants' exploring diverse views and realities focusing on issues of social justice to promote and bring about change.

Validity/Credibility

1. Multiple participants (self and others stories)
2. Thick, rich descriptions (ethnography + individual stories)
3. Dialogical data collection and analysis procedures
4. Member check (construct meaning though storytelling

Participatory action research cycle = TalkStory
1. Purposefully select students using indigenous methods.
2. Use reconstructive storytelling to ID values/norms.
3. Include self in the case study = auto-ethnography.
4. Use dialogical strategies: Phase I. (hermeneutics).
5. Use system relations—grounded theoretical data analysis:
   a. Describe situation at the onset of conducting research.
   b. Understand reasons that caused the situation.
   c. Question status quo that led to the situation.
   d. Make recommendations for rectifying the situation.

Overarching research questions
1. How do students define indigenous research methodology?
2. Why do students choose methodology to conduct research?
3. How can students apply indigenous methodologies to research?
4. How can universities assist students to use indigenous methodologies?

Critical theoretical problem statement
Postsecondary institutions overwhelmingly concentrate on teaching Western-based methodologies that promote power imbalance and perpetuate colonial research paradigms, processes, and ownership that misrepresent Native ways of knowing and doing. Native students can be taught about indigenous research that seeks to address oppression from a historical and modern stance and promote culturally sensitive research practices aligned to their own axiological, ontological, and epistemological views.

Grounded Theory: Transformative-emancipation research generates theory through a grounded approach to data analysis to determine patterns in the stories rather than from predetermined theories. This approach values ideas generated from the participants who are active in the storytelling process, allowing their knowledge and philosophies to inform and as a means of promoting societal changes to correct past injustices.

Methods

Exploratory mixed methods
Critical auto-ethnography and individual storytelling. Both strands are of equal weight and interactively inform each other during reiterative data collection and analysis. Crossover track analysis occurs when results are merged in the conclusions.

Societal reasons
1. Empower First Nations graduate students by teaching indigenous methodologies as a viable option.
2. Perpetuate indigenous ways of knowing, doing, and acting within indigenous communities.
3. Advocate for the inclusion of indigenous methodologies in graduate research curricula.

Personal reasons
1. Develop and disseminate culturally sensitive indigenous research methodologies.
2. Advance my knowledge and skills to meet the needs of my employer.

Advance knowledge
1. Apply and disseminate indigenous research methodologies.
2. Identify successful and unsuccessful approaches taken by graduate students in applying indigenous research methodologies.

Intended audience
1. First Nations and Native Hawaiian community
2. Graduate students, Native Hawaiian and indigenous
3. University administrators and professors
4. Research community (critical mixed methods)

Data collection and analysis time = 6 months
1. Compile primary documents by collecting monological data: indigenous genealogy.
2. Preliminary reconstructive analysis to identify current values, norms, and important concepts.
3. Dialogical data collection conducted by a team including an indigenous methodology expert.
4. Discover system relationships through a grounded approach to data analysis.
5. System relations theory: informs Phase II.
   a. Describe situation at the onset of the research.
   b. Understand the reasons that caused the situation.
   c. Question the status quo that led to the situation.
   d. Make recommendations for rectifying the situation.

Data merged: Crossover tracks analysis Critical ethnography and individual reconstructive stories are inextricably linked throughout the research. Both have independent qualities that create new meaning through interactive coconstruction of knowledge. Ethnographic and reconstructive stories are merged throughout to form meta-inferences.

Figure 25.3 Mixed Methods Template

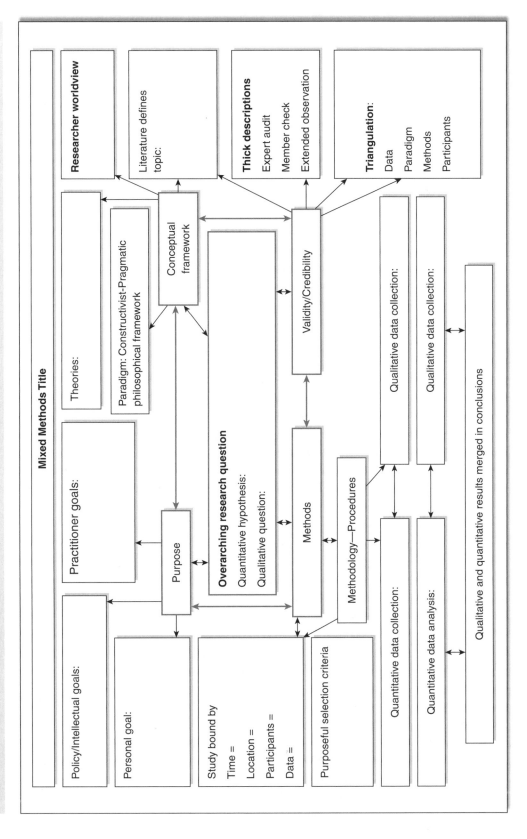

added to the curricula in the next iteration of EDCS 780, opening discussion about the focus of the study, which includes "content area," the broad substantive subject matter of a study; the "purpose," the researcher's primary intent, objectives, and goals; and the "research questions," the questions the researcher is working to answer (p. 276). Emphasis that the research questions should be modifiable in qualitative as well as sequential action mixed methods designs, especially when the focus of the study is exploratory or when the research process is reiterative and evolving continues (Christ, 2007). Plano Clark and Badiee (this volume) indicate that "research questions dictate methods," which will open discussions about how the research question determines methodologies. Students in EDCS 780 will continue to create and refine "overarching and subsumed questions" (Christ, 2009a) as a way to understand how the research questions have influence on the methodological choice by picking a topic and writing exploratory, explanatory, confirmatory, and critical-action oriented research questions.

6. Selecting a mixed methods research design. Students are introduced to the concept that research is reiterative and flexible, philosophy and methodology that falls upon bisecting continuums. They are taught to clearly define the research problem, purpose, and available resources and to identify if the study is exploratory, explanatory, confirmatory, action oriented, transformative, or critical (Christ, 2009a). Teddlie and Tashakkori's typography criteria table (2009, p. 141) will continue to be included as one way for students to consider their topic and an instrument used to indicate why their design is sequential, concurrent, or longitudinal, while Biesta (this volume) will be added in the next iteration of EDCS 780, as it opens discussions about how mixed methods as a "third movement" (Tashakkori & Teddlie, 2003) is potentially another paradigmatic division.

7. Determining sampling strategies. Students in the advanced research class will continue to use Teddlie and Tashakkori's

26 identified sampling techniques as a way to identify the "cases," "materials," and "other elements" (Teddlie & Tashakkori, 2009, p. 181) in their own research design. Collins (this volume) will be added to the next iteration of EDCS 780, as it highlights how stratified, purposeful, random, complete, or convenience sample techniques should be considered for each data strand.

8. Collecting and analyzing data. Clarifying for whom and why the research will be conducted and where the results will be disseminated (Christ, 2009a) will continue to be emphasized in EDCS 780, as it helps students determine what data collection and analysis procedures are necessary. Students consider the major strengths and weaknesses of observations, unobtrusive measures, focus groups, interviews, questionnaires, and tests as presented in Teddlie and Tashakkori's (2009, Table 10.2) text. Students in EDCS 780 will also continue to practice coding raw transcripts and generating models from coded material as a way to understand the grounded approach to data analysis (Christ, 2008a). Students in the next iteration of EDCS 780 will be assigned Onwuegbuzie and Combs chapter (this volume) as a way to open discussion about how, when, and where data should be collected, analyzed, managed, and merged in their own studies.

9. Legitimating inferences and formulating generalizations. Maxwell's (2005) chapter on validity in qualitative research will be maintained in EDCS 780, as it opens discussion about the terms *validity*, *credibility*, and *trustworthiness*. Niglas's observation that "there is a common notion of correctness, and truth value of the research as well as the (trust) worthiness of the results connected to it" (2006, p. 6) and Onwuegbuzie and Johnson's nine types of validity for mixed methods research (2006) will now be summarized in a lecture for the next iteration of EDCS 780. Teddlie and Tashakkori's definition of research inference as "conclusions and interpretations that are made on the basis of collected data in a study" (2009, p. 278, this volume), considering alternatives, and the

process of making, judging, and elaborating data findings as critical in any research project will also be maintained. Students in the next iteration of EDCS 780 will be assigned to read O'Cathain's (this volume) introduction of eight design quality considerations: planning quality, design quality, data quality, interpretive rigor, inference transferability, reporting quality, synthesis ability, and utility.

COURSE EVOLUTION: ACTION RESEARCH

Two mixed methods courses have been developed, taught, evaluated, and refined using action research cycles and critical realism. Curriculum, Research, and Teaching (EDCS 606) was created to introduce the basics of research including qualitative, quantitative, and action-oriented mixed methods to graduate students early in their program. Mixed Methods Research (EDCS 780) was designed as an advanced research option that meets the requirements of the PhD program in all seven College of Education departments. Both courses were first taught in 2007 as an alternative to single method research. The primary goal of designing the courses was to teach skills necessary for determining appropriate methodology and methods (Crotty, 1998) when preparing a thesis or dissertation proposal. Steps outlined in the syllabi act as advanced organizers preparing students to think logically about necessary decisions when framing their proposal. This process was continually developed as a result of teaching 11 semester sections with several hundred students who successfully define and defend applicable research methods, write concise research questions, and propose how to collect, analyze, and blend the appropriate data to answer their research interests. For further detail, see Christ (2009a).

The first iteration of EDCS 780 occurred in fall 2007 and used two texts, Creswell and Plano Clark's (2007) "Designing and Conducting Mixed Methods Research" and Maxwell's (2005) "Qualitative Research Design: An Interactive Approach." These texts were supplemented by several chapters from the first *Handbook of Mixed Methods in Social and Behavioral Research* (Tashakkori & Teddlie, 2003) and a few journal articles. The second iteration of EDCS 780, in fall 2008, added Teddlie and Tashakkori's *Foundations of Mixed Methods Research* (2009) and numerous articles and editorials from *JMMR*. The third iteration, in spring 2009, added chapters from Greene's (2007) *Mixed Methods in Social Inquiry*. The fourth iteration, in summer 2009, was taught as a hybrid class (eight live, eight online activities) and reduced the required number of readings and student presentations. Each class added to the information necessary to make decisions about curricula, strategies, and teaching praxis used in EDCS 780.

The fifth iteration will begin by modifying the curricula developed over the course of 2 years as a result of reflecting on the most helpful readings, which are repetitious, and what should now be removed. The next iteration of EDCS 780 will remove first edition handbook chapters and numerous *JMMR* articles to be replaced by 12 chapters carefully selected by the researcher-teacher from the second edition of this handbook. Class activities in EDCS 780 will continue to include four components to support learning: topical lectures, classroom discussions, student presentations, and triad interactive reading, writing, and data analysis activities.

Student feedback has consistently been used by the researcher-teacher to refine the readings in EDCS 780. Several iterations have revealed that Creswell and Plano Clark's textbook (2007) appealed to students who preferred visual diagrams and tables that summarized topics, whereas Teddlie and Tashakkori's text (2009), according to the students, provided extensive information about certain topics such as typologies, sampling, and inferences. Maxwell's (2005) text, which provides an overview of interactive qualitative research, further supports the planning process. Students in the second iteration of EDCS 780 indicated that the three textbooks were complementary and preferred not to rely upon a single source. The third iteration added Greene's (2007) text and was especially appealing to students who designed participatory, critical, or action-oriented research projects. Students who purchased Creswell's supplemental text "Research Design: Qualitative, Quantitative, and Mixed Methods Approaches" (2009b) indicated that the purpose, research question, and procedure scripts and the chapter on theory were particularly helpful when designing their research proposals. A forced choice rank-order numerical representation of the students' reading preferences was reinforced by comments about the readings during interviews (Christ, 2009b). There was no common preference for a particular textbook among the participants' preferential ranking.

The proposal outline used when teaching EDCS 780 has maintained many of the original features from the first iteration (fall 2007), including the problem, purpose, and research question. The second iteration (fall 2008) included a researcher's worldview and data merging section in the procedures. The third iteration (spring 2008) added the role of theory and expanded the data collection and analysis sections to the basic structure. The fourth iteration (summer 2009) added emphasis upon sampling techniques. Students now write their proposal using a heading system that includes the title, introduction, problem and purpose statement, background justification (literature), the role of theory, overarching and subsumed research questions, methodology statement and visual representation, procedures (role of researcher, bounding the case, qualitative and quantitative data collection, sampling, analysis, merging), and credibility/validity justification (cf. Christ, 2009a).

The proposal outline is designed to create personal relevance and acts as a strategy to teach students how to conceive and write each section of their research proposal. This strategy provides students with the skills necessary to understand and utilize the research components necessary for a multitude of mixed research designs. Unique to EDCS 780 is a writing workshop component where students group into triads to assist each other with drafts, editing, and in some cases analysis and preparation of the results of their dissertations. The heading system and questions (see Appendix 25.1) act as a rubric for students to critique their own proposals as well as others in their triad. The fourth iteration (summer 2009) reduced the number of readings and student chapter presentations and did not include triad editing, which according to the researcher-teacher, reduced the quality of the final product in terms of methodological design and written product. Table 25.1 represents a summary of how the fifth iteration of the class readings will include 12 chapters from this handbook.

Table 25.1 EDCS 780 Mixed Methods Topics, Readings, and Assignments (Fifth Iteration)

EDCS 780	Topic(s)	Chapter(s)* = Presentations	Supporting Materials # = Optional	Written Responses
1.	Introduction to Mixed Methods & History	TT (09), Ch. 1 CP (07), Ch. 1 *MMH2 Ch. 2	*JMMR* 1(1) 3–7 *JMMR* 1(4) 303–308	Research topic: (P, P, RQ, M, D)
2.	Discipline of Mixed Methods Pragmatism and Qualitative Research	TT (09), Ch. 2 M, Chs. 1 & 2 *MMH2 Ch. 3	# HQR Ch. 1 # Patton (99) *Greene (07) Ch. 1	Reflection: Why mixed methods & what paradigms

EDCS 780	Topic(s)	Chapter(s)* = Presentations	Supporting Materials # = Optional	Written Responses
3.	Mixed Methods Traditions Exploratory, Explanatory Confirmatory, Transformative	*CP (07), Ch. 2 *MMH2 Ch. 5 M, Ch. 3 Crotty (98), Ch. 1	JMMR 2(1) 7–22 # HQR Ch. 8	Topical paragraph Diagram design What part QUAN? What part QUAL?
4.	Paradigm and Pragmatism	M, Ch. 4 *MMH2 Ch. 4 *MMH2 Ch. 9	JMMR 1(2) 112–133 *Greene (07), Ch. 2	Strengths & weakness of pragmatism
5.	Visual Representations & Problem Statement	*TT (09), Ch. 5 CP (07), Ch. 5 *MMH2 Ch. 16	JMMR 2(2) 115–120 #Creswell (09), Ch. 5 *Greene (07), Ch. 4	Write & diagram topic: exploratory, confirmatory, action
6.	Supporting Literature Purpose Statement Research Questions	*TT (09), Ch. 6 *MMH2 Ch. 12	#Creswell (09), Ch. 6 Greene (07), Ch. 5	Purpose statement & research questions
7.	Types of Mixed Methods Designs Sampling	*TT (09), Ch. 7 CP (07), Ch. 4 *MMH2 Ch. 14	JMMR 1(3) 212–225 #Creswell (09), Ch. 7 Greene (07). Ch. 6	Midsemester meeting: present diagram to class
8.	Data Analysis	*TT (09), Ch. 8 M, Ch. 5 *MMH2 Ch. 17	JMMR 1(1) 8–22 Greene (07), Ch. 8	Specify in detail data collection
9.	Quality, Credibility, Validity, and Research Design	CP (07), Ch. 5 *M, Ch. 6 *MMH2 Ch. 21	*MMH2 Ch. 20 *Greene (07), Ch. 9	Define mixed methods design & data analysis
10.	Participant Selection and Data Collection	*TT (09), Ch. 9 CP (07) Ch. 6	JMMR 1(3) 226–241 JMMR 1(1) 48–76 #Creswell (09), Ch. 10	Specify forms of credibility/ validity
11.	Qualitative Coding Techniques Critical Realism	*TT (09), Ch. 10 CP (07), Ch. 7 *MMH2 Ch. 15	*MMH2 Ch. 6 Charmaz (06), Ch. 1	Computer coding exercise NVIVO
12.	Theory, Inferences & Validity Issues	*TT (09), Ch. 11 M, Ch. 7 *Newman (06)	JMMR 1(3) 207–211 *Creswell (09), Ch. 3	Theory (3 levels): & worldview

(Continued)

Table 25.1 (Continued)

EDCS 780	Topic(s)	Chapter(s)* = Presentations	Supporting Materials # = Optional	Written Responses
13.	Formatting the Proposal	*TT (09), Ch. 12 *MMH2 Ch. 25 M Appendix 140–158	*Charmaz (06), Ch. 2 Greene (07), Ch. 10	Prob, purp, RQ, methods, proced. analysis sections
14.	Final Write-up to Triad	CP (07), Ch. 8	*Charmaz (06), Ch. 3 *JMMR* 1(2) 107–111	Triad peer review
15.	Final Due			Proposal + map
16.	Presentations			Final paper due

*TT = Teddlie and Tashakkori (2009); CP= Creswell and Plano Clark (2007); MMH2 = this volume (2010); *JMMR*= *Journal of Mixed Methods Research*; M= Maxwell (2005); Patton (1999) = *Health Services Research, 34*(5); Greene (2007) = *Mixed Methods in Social Inquiry*; Creswell (2009b) = *Research Design*; Charmaz (2006) = *Constructing Grounded Theory*.

COURSE EVALUATION METHODOLOGY

The overarching research question used with each iteration of EDCS 780 course development process was, "What do participants in EDCS 780 value about the curricular materials, instructional strategies, and classroom activities as supporting the production of a viable dissertation or thesis proposal?"

Each class was treated as one cycle in the action research process, a single case study (Yin, 2009) linked to previous iterations in terms of data analysis and reflection. The researcher-teacher relied on multiple lenses and perspectives to view the student interactions and their work as evidence of understanding the research process. Three-way feedback—among teacher, student, and peers—was used to modify and improve the proposals and the course in a reiterative

fashion. Dewey's action-oriented pragmatism (Teddlie & Tashakkori, 2009) allows for the combination of an emic and etic perspective, of the researcher-teacher (Mertler, 2008) as an insider using interpretive validity (Maxwell, 2005) while embracing a reflexive lens through which to view and understand the researcher-teacher's "place" in the courses, while interpreting various data sources that make up the iterations summarized and presented here.

Critical realism as a lens is particularly useful, allowing the researcher-teacher to be a social science researcher using both an emic insider perspective, when interpreting data such as interviews and the researcher-teacher reflections, and an etic outsider perspective, when interpreting the statistically analyzed quantitative student ratings of the teacher and the course and descriptive statistical representations of the rank-ordered preferences of assigned curricula.

CRITICAL REALISM
AND ACTION RESEARCH

Critical realism as a theory and a research lens envisions many levels of objective truths (Frauley & Pearce, 2007) that are constructed by looking for relationships and causality (Goff, 2004) in empirically and historically derived evidence collected to explain, describe, and theorize social phenomena. These characteristics make critical realism (Danermark, Ekström, Jakobsen, & Karlsson, 2002) the preferable paradigmatic lens through which to view the evolution of EDCS 780 pedagogy and praxis for two reasons. First, the researcher is also the designer and teacher of the course. Therefore, evidence including anonymous course and faculty evaluations; research proposals evaluated by other staff; and a student-generated, peer-reviewed journal and conference presentations were the "objective" evidence, and the researcher-teacher's reflections, interpretations of the students' work, analysis of anonymous written course ratings, and randomly selected interviews with prior students were deemed to be the "subjective" evidence used to evaluate the effectiveness of the course curricula, strategies, and activities. The course evaluations were particularly helpful when determining what materials and strategies should be used and what could be eliminated when conducting each action research cycle used to update and refine EDCS 780.

Second, critical realism was chosen as a theoretical lens to frame this study, as it relies on the conception that there are levels of objective truths that can be discerned, but finding absolute truths about classroom praxis and pedagogy is impossible. This evaluation concedes that different levels of reality exist, ranging from the objective, which is independent of human understanding, to subjective truths, those that we understand and grasp in the process of meaning making (Frauley & Pearce, 2007).

For the purpose of describing the value of EDCS 780, the real, actual, and empirical are directly related to the mechanisms, events, and experiences that are the foundation of a "generative" (Danermark et al., 2002, p. 163) yet tentative theoretical model that has begun to emerge over the course of five iterations of refining EDCS 780. The emergent model is "descriptive theory" (Danermark et al., 2002, p. 119); that is, it describes the mechanisms—the relationships among the curricula, teaching techniques, strategies, and teacher-student interactions. The objective truths were defined as only the observable and/or measurable outcomes of the course, including the dissertation and thesis proposals and the course and faculty evaluation scales. The subjective truths were defined as the interpretations of the student comments about the curricula and strategies as they were refined over time and the visual representations in the form of methodological maps as reviewed and commented upon by committee members. The researcher-teacher's interpretations of the effectiveness of the strategies that were incorporated and evolved in EDCS 780 were also the subjective truths. These truths were the constructions and interpretations of the "subjective" and "objective" coded, triangulated, reflected, and merged data using "abduction" and "retroduction" techniques to formulate "conceptualizations" (Sayer, 1992, p. 50) about the class pedagogy that in part were influenced by the researcher-teacher's preexisting views of teaching praxis and strategies.

Critical realism as a theoretical lens used to refine the class over time embraces "empirical" evidence, defined as the directly observable actions that have occurred, in this case the course products and outcomes; the "actual," which is comprised of the sum of explanations inferred from data that were collected, combined, and analyzed and the inferences produced; while the "real" (Frauley & Pearce, 2007, p. 16), which cannot be directly observed or theorized, helps explain the structures and processes of the course from the students', faculty's, and researcher-teacher's perspectives.

The critical realist lens used to conduct the course evaluation was based on the ontological tenet that reality exists independently of our knowledge, independent of the mind; although there is a reality out there, it is impossible to determine absolute truth. Thus, critical realism embraces the view that constructed reality is seen through "perceptual filters" (Frauley & Pearce, 2007, p. 4), in this case influenced by teaching and learning theories put into practice that guided the construction and evaluation of the course. The knowledge gained about teaching pedagogy using a critical theoretical lens cannot be identical to what exists, and therefore the descriptions as presented in the findings are understood to be different than factual reality (Danermark et al., 2002).

Critical realism used to frame the description of teacher praxis relied on "abduction" and "retroduction," two forms of inferences. Abduction inferences maintain an explanatory function, a "redescription" or "recontextualization" (Danermark et al., 2002, p. 80) of teaching pedagogy used to gain knowledge about the interconnected workings of the complex social phenomenon that is teaching. Teddlie and Tashakkori's definition of abduction is a "third type of logic" (2009, p. 89), a way to work back from an observed consequence to a probable antecedent to create insights allowing for "inferences about best possible explanations" (Teddlie & Tashakkori, 2009, p. 329). Abduction often begins with a rule, theory, or interpretation when describing a phenomenon, understanding that inferred conclusions are not always logically derived from a premise (Danermark et al., 2002). There can be numerous plausible interpretations (Maxwell, 2005) that allowed the researcher-teacher to explain if the curricula and strategies appeared to help students to evolve as researchers through the process of creating a logical, viable, and meaningful research proposal.

Evaluations during the iteration of EDCS 780 relied on abduction, retroduction, and a pragmatic grounded approach to data analysis (Christ, 2008b) to create a theoretical representation of the students' and researcher-teacher's perceptions about the course praxis. The knowledge gained from the evaluation was stratified across three levels (Danermark et al., 2002); that is, the direct observations were sorted to discern relationships between the operationally defined variables (Creswell, 2008), including curricula used to teach, instructional strategies, and the outcomes specified as applicable research skills necessary to create a viable research proposal. The "objective reality" was a representative model of teaching pedagogy resulting from an analysis of the numerous forms of data linked to create a more complete understanding of how the participants valued EDCS 780. The third level of knowledge that emerged from the analysis of each course over time was a compilation of the indirectly observable data and subsequent inferences analyzed using retroductive analysis to create a representative model of the participant's views of the curricula and teaching strategies used when refining EDCS 780 Mixed Methods Research. In essence, critical realism was the preferred lens when conducting the researcher-teacher evaluation using deductive (statistically analyzed course ratings) and inductive data (proposals, interviews, and teacher reflections), which were combined to create a representative model of the curricula, strategies, and teaching techniques used in the course to promote student success. The constructed model that evolved from the numerous data sources evaluated over time constantly underwent "incremental transformation" (Frauley & Pearce, 2007, p. 5), creating general theories about teaching pedagogy from the evaluations that naturally evolved over the five action research iterations used to develop the course. Thus, the findings from this study are not replicable or generalizable to what could be deduced from teaching the same course tomorrow, but the knowledge gained helped represent a way of viewing the evolution of teaching research, a generally valid set of concepts that were used "when formulating interesting and relevant questions" (Danermark et al., 2002, p. 140) that emerged each time the course was taught.

Ontological, epistemological, and axiological influences on how knowledge was produced, structured, differentiated, stratified, and changed into meanings, representative realities, and processes inferred from the multiple sources of data were pragmatically blended during analysis using more than one theoretical framework to compose a credible and logically deduced representation (Patton, 2002). Although critical realists often use retroduction to show that some explanations are conceived as better than others, in essence, representing lawlike "stable relationships" (Teddlie & Tashakkori, 2009, p. 92), this was not the intent of the explanatory case study of teaching pedagogy. Retroduction used in the evaluation of the course was the preferable way to increase the credibility of a teacher-researcher's analysis of subjective and objective coded, triangulated data, the knowledge that was necessary to set into motion the actions used when conducting the reiterative action research cycles necessary to develop EDCS 780.

Retroduction as a process was used to examine the fundamental structures and properties inherent in the participants' experiences of taking EDCS 780, resulting in both exploratory descriptions and explanatory explanations. The retroductive analysis relied on inductive and deductive reasoning, with discovery used to confirm and verify the best plausible representations and justifications of the participants' learning experiences. The researcher-teacher used critical realism to switch between levels of abstraction, from indirect philosophical and theoretical combined with directly observable evidence, as a way to make meaning, create knowledge, and develop the course. Thus, the abstract interpretations and observable data were combined and related together, back and forth,

blending the abstract and the concrete to help generate a representative understanding of teaching pedagogy and praxis. Clearly, the premises of action research and critical realism are particularly complementary for a researcher-teacher interested in creating and refining curricula, strategies, and her or his own teaching praxis.

Critical realism was used for knowledge production, a way to look at the fundamental properties of teaching pedagogy by examining data for inferred processes and connections. Critical realism in this case focused on what makes the experience of EDCS 780 what it is (Danermark et al., 2002), examining causal relationships between the curricula and the strategies and the products produced during the course, the empirical and the quantifiable, and the meanings created from themes that emerged when analyzing qualitative data combined into a deeper level of the inferred "real" and "actual" (Frauley & Pearce, 2007). Realities of the learning experiences were constructed through sharing meanings underpinned by processes aimed at understanding. Critical realism as a lens combined action constructed knowledge as presented by Dewey in a pragmatic approach to data analysis to gain insight about teaching pedagogy from available data created as a result of teaching. By using abduction and retroduction to examine the data collected over time from the classes, theories that connected praxis and learning could be made. In essence, postpositivist and constructivist methodologies were used to analyze the observable and inferred representations to explore and confirm student and teacher actions in relation to the central phenomenon in this study, that is, the shared experience of how teaching and learning interconnect and function.

BOUNDING THE CASE

This longitudinal action research case study of EDCS 780 Mixed Methods Research is now in the fifth iteration. The classes are offered through the University of Hawaii's College of Education to graduate students and are typically conducted over a 16-week semester, once a week, for 2 1/2 hours with an average class size of nine. Summer 2009 EDCS 780 was conducted as a hybrid class meeting face to face eight times and completing written assignments the other eight times over a 16-week semester. The students are either doctoral or master's level, and the classes are open to all departments throughout the college. The majority of students in EDCS 780 come from the social sciences, special and general education, kinestheology, health sciences, and business. Some prior research coursework or experience is required as a prerequisite for EDCS 780.

RESEARCHER-TEACHER ROLE

The researcher-teacher's epistemology, ontology, and axiology form a worldview (Creswell, 2009b; Maxwell, 2005; Teddlie & Tashakkori, 2009) best described as pragmatic constructivist (Christ, 2008b), which influenced the focus and intent of the study, the design of the research questions, and the multiple forms of data collected to address perceptions of the value of EDCS 780. The researcher-teacher's paradigmatic views (cf. Christ, 2009a) set the stage for this explanatory action research case study of pedagogy, relying on a pragmatic approach to coconstruct knowledge between researcher-teacher and the participants through reflection (Lincoln & Guba 2005; Mertler, 2008).

DATA COLLECTION

The quantitative data consisted of four semester sections of EDCS 780 anonymous 23-item course and faculty evaluation protocols that used a five-point Likert rating scale (1 = Strongly disagree, 5 = Strongly agree) administered to the students by a proctor the

last week of each class (cf. Christ, 2009a). The qualitative data included four anonymous, open-ended questions in the course and faculty evaluation—participant narrations about the texts, journal articles, assignments, and strategies including coding assignments, concept maps, scripts, and proposal criterion used to provide feedback to peers. The students' assignments, the research proposals, and the methodological concept maps were also analyzed to determine if the students were able to transform concepts from the curricula, student presentations, lectures, assignments, and in-class activities into a viable, well-cited, and logical research proposal.

DATA ANALYSES

The 23-item course and faculty evaluation (cf. Christ, 2009a) was analyzed using t tests for significance, comparing each question to the same questions asked of students in the College of Education and across the entire university campus. Descriptive statistics including the mean, standard deviation, number in sample, and frequency were reported.

Four open-ended, anonymous written course and faculty evaluation questions from the four semester sections of 780, interview memos, and classroom observations were summarized following a reiterative-grounded theoretical analysis (cf. Christ 2007, 2008c, for a detailed description of this process). Specifically, the analysis began with the researcher-teacher's reviewing data and taking notes concerning pertinent passages compiled into memos (Charmaz, 2000). Memos are the thoughts and insights of what appears important to the researcher-teacher in the process of reviewing the material generated during data collection and initial analysis (Charmaz, 2006). The memos were also used to identify and highlight quotable written passages that expressed in the words of the participants their thoughts about three categories related to 780: the curricula, strategies, and assignments. Themes and quotes from the three categories were then compared to the 19 quantitative and 4 qualitative items in the course and faculty rating scale, the researcher-teacher's classroom observations, analysis of assignments, final proposals, and student presentations. This reiterative hermeneutic-grounded process of data analysis (Christ, 2006) relied on a four-step sequence: First, sidebar memos indicating location of critical passages used to generate a list of data related to the three constructs: curricula, strategies, assignments. Concepts that emerged repeatedly, were contradictory, or were unique to the three constructs were included in a list for each. Second, the three construct lists were then compiled into a "code report" (Christ, 2008c, p. 28) as a way to examine fit, relevance, and potential quotable passages useful for highlighting emergent themes. Third, main categories, a form of focused coding (Glazer, 1978), were then formulated into a representative model. Finally, the main categories were examined to determine relationships, ongoing and persistent patterns, and themes that emerged directly from the data (Mills, Bonner, & Francis, 2006).

DATA MERGING

Results from the multiple stands of data were merged followed a pragmatic approach (Greene, 2007; Teddlie & Tashakkori, 2009) to representing 780 pedagogy. The reiterative hermeneutic process of data analysis (Christ, 2008a, 2009b) allowed the quantitative and qualitative data sources to be analyzed individually and then combined at the end of each course, repeated each semester, and merged in a final analysis to make meaning of the course praxis, including curricula and strategies that best represent the participants' views (Creswell & Plano Clark, 2007) and as a way to further support the credibility of the researcher-teacher's inferences (Patton, 1999). The

integration process helped the researcher-teacher to draw inductive inferences based on "meaningful and consistent explanations, understandings, conceptual frameworks, and or learning and teaching theories" when integrating (a) knowledge from the literature, (b) concrete observations, and (c) the qualitative and quantitative data results (Tashakkori & Teddlie, 2003, p. 709).

CREDIBILITY/VALIDITY

Four forms of validity as described by Teddlie and Tashakkori (2009), Creswell (2008), Maxwell (2005), Morse (1991), and Patton (1999) were used to enhance the credibility of findings: (a) data triangulation, (b) multiple-analyst triangulation, (c) considering rival conclusions, and (d) expert audit. Mixed-data triangulation (notes, observations, and course and faculty evaluation scales) according to Patton (2002) allowed the researcher-teacher to compare and contrast multiple aspects about the courses. In particular, the emergent themes from the anonymous open-ended questions were compared with the results of the course and faculty evaluation scale. Multiple-analyst credibility occurred when an expert program evaluator, independent of the study, examined emergent themes as a way to compare, corroborate, or refute the researcher-teacher's interpretations. Rival conclusions about the emergent themes were also generated and considered by the researcher-teacher and the outside expert (Patton, 2002). In particular, the results when combined were examined for connections and plausible alternative explanations to determine if the emergent model was a reasonable and accurate representation of EDCS 780 teaching pedagogy.

QUANTITATIVE DATA RESULTS

Analysis of the 19 items from the 780 course and faculty evaluation from the fall

2007 semester class revealed that 75% of the mean score ratings were higher than those of the same items administered to classes throughout the College of Education and that 95% were higher than those from across the university. Four items rated lower than other courses in the College of Education: items 6, "the instructor communicated effectively"; 11, "I felt that the course challenged me intellectually"; 18, "The instructor is willing to meet and help students outside of class"; and 19, "The instructor's feedback about my writing helped me become a better writer." Only item 20, "I was able to get individual help when I needed it," received a class rating lower than other classes at the College of Education and at the university levels. None were statistically significantly different at $p < .05$.

Analysis of the 19-item 780 course and faculty evaluation for the fall 2008 semester revealed that all item mean scores were higher than in other classes at the College of Education and at the university. Items 9, "I developed the ability to carry out original research in this area," and item 19, "The instructor's feedback about my writing helped me become a better writer," were statistically significantly different at $p < .05$.

Analysis of the 19-item 780 course and faculty evaluation for spring 2009 semester revealed no statistically significant difference at $p < .05$. Analysis of the items revealed that 53% of the mean score ratings were higher than those of the same items administered to classes throughout the College of Education and across the university.

QUALITATIVE WRITTEN RESPONSES

The EDCS 780 course and faculty evaluations were anonymously provided by students. One question, "What did you find most valuable and helpful about the course," in the 2007 class resulted in student responses including "The class helped me to outline my project"; "Really good for researchers like me whose research design has both qualitative and quantitative in it. I have really learned a lot about Mixed Methods"; "The final paper"; "The assignments were very relevant to final project & personal research goals"; "Readings"; and "The knowledge and enthusiasm of the instructor." Comments in 2008 to the same question resulted in two emergent themes: "knowledge" and "feedback." One student indicated that the instructor was "very knowledgeable. Individualized feedback on research design was extremely helpful." Another spoke of "systemic knowledge about the subject"; "knowledge, enthusiasm, and ideas" about research designs; and "rich research knowledge" as a resource. Other students indicated that the course value was high for several reasons, including "feedback on assignments," "good syllabus," "awareness of fostering an environment in which students can learn from each other," and the "research assignment feedback."

The question about "concern for the students" revealed themes from the 2007 class responses, including "caring," "flexible," and "helpful." One student stated, "The instructor really seemed to be willing & cared for the students and their needs. He is very knowledgeable and helpful." Another indicated, "He is very flexible in his approach to teaching. He is friendly, I like the way the teacher presents complex ideas in research." Still another observed, "He always checks on us & makes sure that we are keeping up with our work & if we need any help." Others stated that the instructor was "concerned for students" and that they "felt concern-personalization." The same question analyzed in 2008 also revealed "helpful" and "attentive" as themes. Following are evaluations from numerous students in the class: "helpful and encouraging"; "he is enthusiastic"; "excellent regard—gives each specific individual attention"; "he paid attention to every single student, and he is ready to help when we needed it"; and "always willing to help students think through the material."

Quite revealing were the responses to the 2007 question, "What did you find least valuable and helpful about the course?" There were no consistent themes across the comments presented: "Sometimes people in the class didn't have the ability to understand what was being taught and slowed the class down"; "The required texts have different terminology"; "Repeated discussions of other students' topics"; and "Complex subject, perhaps needed more class work + sharing with students." The same question asked in 2008 produced more consistent responses: "None," "Nothing," "Some complicated knowledge." The question, "What changes would you make in the writing assignments?" asked both in 2007 and in 2008 revealed similar responses: "None," "Nothing." One student commented, "I thought the writing and reading assignments were right on, I will use this in the future." Another wrote, "It's good. Step by step." Still another stated, "I would recommend this course to my friends." Not all comments to this question were positive, as should be expected; one student indicated, "More focus in class on assignments. Take student examples and create perfect profiles 'together'—would be possible with only small class." Another student in 780 suggested, "Do student reviews and presentations 1st then other course readings" and "more feedback needed."

PRODUCTS

The researcher-teacher rubric ratings for the student products, including the proposals and visual graphic organizers, were remarkably high for those who read, listened, and modified their weekly assignments and created the methodological maps as required throughout the course. There were a few students who fell short of making excellent progress, which was clearly revealed in their final papers. Numerous student advisors and dissertation and thesis committee members consistently indicated that the student proposals are vastly improved as a result of taking these research courses. This was most prevalent with the English language learners who took multiple research courses and worked to improve their proposals over the course of a year.

Students in 780 indicated that the methodological maps, thesis-dissertation headings with criteria, and method scripts from Creswell's *Research Design* (2009b) were the most helpful strategies for successful completion of their proposals. The researcher-teacher indicated that the assigned chapter presentations with one-page summaries were also of value to the students when citing the course readings in the methods and procedure sections of their proposals, especially for the English language learners. Students who had multiple research classes from the researcher-teacher were at a distinct advantage over their peers, as many of the concepts and strategies had been introduced before, albeit in a limited capacity. Thus, the students were familiar with the structure of the class, assignment expectations, and the way the researcher-teacher taught.

THE FIFTH ITERATION:
NEW COURSE READINGS

Information from the four action research iterations of EDCS 780 have allowed the researcher-teacher to be more knowledgeable about which readings to include from the present edition of this handbook and which readings should be eliminated or offered as supplementary. The next iteration of EDCS 780 will rely on Johnson and Gray (this volume), which eliminates the need to read chapters with the same topic in Teddlie and Tashakkori (2009), Creswell and Plano Clark (2007), and Maxwell (2005). Biesta (this volume) also allows readers to skim chapters with this focus in the assigned textbooks. The four reflective reiterations of EDCS 780 helped the researcher-teacher to determine which chapters were likely to be most appropriate for students at the University of Hawaii, but this will be a decision that each professor must make on determining the prior knowledge students bring to the class and the level for which the research class is intended.

◆ Conclusions

The four action research iterations of EDCS 780 have shown that requiring students to follow a distinct project outline with accompanying methodological diagrams helped them to learn about the strengths and challenges associated with various forms of mixed methods research. By introducing paradigmatic views, terminology, methodological maps, and a rubric with headings for evaluating research early in the semester, the final research proposals were easier for the students to create and were personally relevant to their goals of learning how to successfully conduct their own thesis or dissertation. The researcher-teacher and the students' advisors found that the interactive nature of the weekly activities, organizational strategies, and assignments resulted in much improved proposals. Students in EDCS 780 were able to refine their research topics and prepare proposals that were logical and practical given the restrictions of funding and time as a result of defending how they will "bound" their case.

Students in each iteration of EDCS 780 made excellent progress throughout the semester as long as they completed writing and cited material related to seven basic steps: (a) creating an introduction that defined the topic; (b) including a problem statement identifying the importance backed by citations and applicable statistics; (c) writing a purpose statement identifying the intended audience and why the study is being conducted; (d) citing literature that introduces, aligns, and justifies the

topic, intervention, or theory (beginning, middle, and/or end) and including justification of exploratory, explanatory, confirmatory, action-oriented, critical, or transformative design; (e) using an overarching research question with qualitative and quantitative subquestions in mixed or action research projects; (f) creating a clear methodological statement with accompanying research diagram; and (g) providing replicable procedures including (i) the role of the researcher; (ii) how the study is "bound"; (iii) quantitative and qualitative data sampling, collection, analysis, and merging procedures; and (iv) steps supporting credibility/reliability and potential generalization.

Combining the interactive methodological diagram with the seven-step research outline (cf. Christ, 2009a) has repeatedly been shown to be a viable and efficient way to teach research courses, resulting in a much higher rate of advisor approval than was seen in the past. When students could defend the relationship between the purpose of the research and the intended audience, they wrote much more precise and applicable research questions; they could indicate if the study was exploratory, explanatory, confirmatory, or of a critical prominence; and they could indicate their choice of data, sampling strategies, and weighting of the qualitative and quantitative materials.

Analysis of the weekly assignments indicated value in requiring students to defend the purpose of their research as it helped them choose which research typography is most appropriate for their questions. Student advisors supported the use of the proposal outline and methodological maps as a way to logically organize and defend a project. The advisors also noted that requiring students to justify how the case is "bound," in terms of projected timelines, available resources, and potential to access data sources, reduced the number of proposals that were far beyond the means or skills of the students.

With well over 200 proposals evaluated over the course of 2 years in introductory and advanced mixed methods courses, it is apparent to the researcher-teacher that the strategies incorporated in the courses increased the likelihood that thesis or dissertation proposals would be realistic and viable. All of the students who took EDCS 606 or EDCS 780 were successful at creating a 10- to 15-page proposal with accompanying methodological diagram that could be presented to their adviser or chair for feedback. Faculty in the College of Education who advise students have indicated that the proposal-writing process reduces many of the common research design flaws, potential problems with committee member expectations, and if the scope and breadth of the study is reasonable. The proposal outline and methodological map allow students to receive advice leading to appropriate adjustments before investing too much time in a research proposal that would unlikely be accepted.

In conclusion, the curricula and strategies used in EDCS 780 have consistently improved over the course of 2 years. With the introduction of new chapters from this handbook, a fifth action research cycle will provide information necessary to continue to refine the class readings. In essence, this reiterative process of collecting, analyzing, reflecting, and improving the strategies and curricula is a form of teacher-practitioner action-oriented research that continues as long as the researcher-teacher is interested in improving the curricula, strategies, and his or her own teaching praxis. Student course and faculty evaluations, advisor comments, and the number of proposals accepted shows that the combination of materials and strategies helped students to define and defend viable research projects. From the researcher-teacher's perspective, proposals have improved over the past 2 years for a number of reasons. The researcher-teacher is comfortable that the strategies for EDCS 780 are well developed, but in a new field such as mixed methods, curricula are constantly emerging. This

requires changes to assignments, refining the discussions, and different ways of presenting topics such as paradigms, methodological considerations, ways of conceiving typographies and even the focus of the field, such as either transformative or action oriented.

Although one cannot show a direct correlation between teaching pedagogy and students' performance, the combination of improvements to the curricula, strategies, and teaching praxis have resulted in improved proposals, which from a pragmatic stance is most important. Methodological diagrams as an organizational tool from the perspective of the students, the researcher-teacher, and the students' advisors seem to be the single most powerful strategy in the classes. Electronic feedback, peer editing, and the rubric for evaluating a thesis or dissertation (cf. Christ, 2009a) were also noted to be helpful tools for improving the students' final research proposals.

Most apparent to the researcher-teacher is the daunting and yet exciting challenge of teaching mixed methods research to students from diverse backgrounds. This year approximately one third of the proposals were classroom action oriented; one third qualitative, exploratory, or critical designs; and one third mixed methods. Only a few of the more than 200 students in the introductory and advanced mixed methods classes were interested in conducting survey research, quasi-experimental intervention studies, or single subject designs. This seems to be reflective of the current trend in education. The next iteration of EDCS 780 will include the introduction of Greene and Hall (this volume), which will extend chapters assigned from Greene's textbook (2007). Mertens, Bledsoe, Sullivan, and Wilson (this volume) will extend Mertens's *Journal of Mixed Methods* article (2007). The readings in EDCS 780 are becoming both more focused and more complex. With several lectures focusing on critical, transformative, and action-oriented research theory and methodology, more students are choosing to conduct transformative or critical research studies. The intent of the courses has always been to teach students how to conduct practical and meaningful research while challenging the incompatibility thesis still prevalent in some areas of the social sciences. The researcher-teacher has never tried to convince students to embrace a particular methodological typography, but rather as an alternative to learn about the necessary tools required to design a research study that best answers their research interests. This intent, according to the perspective of the researcher-teacher, the advisors, and the students, has been a success. The students have gained knowledge about the logic behind conducting rigorous multidimensional research, and the intent of creating more knowledgeable researchers, not promoting a specific methodology, seems to have been fulfilled by providing appropriate curricula, strategies, and supports.

This next iteration of EDCS 780 Mixed Methods Research will be exciting, as the *Handbook* provided over a dozen chapters that will be used in the course as a way to present concepts that have been refined by many of the authors for over a decade. Clearly, the chapters provide a level of detail that will be challenging for students. The next iteration of EDCS 780 will be small and restricted to PhD students, an ideal condition to determine if the number of readings are manageable and applicable to the students. As with any action research, data collection, analysis, and reflection will allow the course to constantly change with the inclusion of the most recent information coming from this field. As a researcher-teacher, deep reflection is required to determine how to improve all aspects of praxis. Clearly, action research is ideal for anyone considering how to improve his or her own teaching habits, student performance, strategies, and curricula.

Research Questions and Exercises

1. Using the problem, purpose, research question, and procedures headings from Appendix 25.1, write a two-page outline of a mixed methods or action research proposal.

2. Define why the purpose of the study and the research question are intrinsically linked.

3. What are common characteristics of mixed methods and action research?

4. Why would action research fall under a constructivist paradigm?

5. How does sampling differ when conducting exploratory or explanatory research as compared with confirmatory?

6. Define and defend when you would use the terms *credibility* and *validity* in confirmatory action research and mixed methods designs.

7. Why is critical realism useful when a researcher-teacher is conducting an action research project?

8. Why is reflection important in action research?

9. Defend why teaching research as a continuum is more appropriate than a diametrically opposed or linear research process.

APPENDIX 25.1

Headings and Criteria for a Research Study

♦ **Title**

Indicate the type of design in the title (mixed methods, action, exploratory, explanatory, confirmatory, case study, etc.).

♦ **Introduction**

Define the topic, problem, purpose, and research methodology in the first paragraph. The introduction should provide enough information so readers know what to expect.

♦ **Problem Statement**

• The issue/problem should be addressed and clearly stated immediately.

• Empirical evidence should be provided (i.e., statistics/studies properly cited presenting the problem).

• Topic should pass the reasonable "so what" test.

♦ **Purpose of the Study**

• The purpose statement must be clearly presented and meaningful to others.

• Intended audience should be indicated (practitioners, policy makers, funding agencies).

• Purpose helps define exploratory, explanatory, confirmatory, action, or critical research.

♦ **Background/Significance (Literature Review)**

Literature cited should be directly related and help frame the research project.

• The literature review should emphasize, verify, and convince the readers that a problem exists and that the research is necessary and important.

• Theoretical framework or particular assumptions that drive the study are absolutely necessary in a hypothetical deductive confirmatory study.

♦ **Role of Theory**

• Theory can fit in the beginning (indicated as a basis for your study—establishes that your focus clarifies a preexisting theory that will be used to frame your study), the middle (this is the methodological paradigm—constructivist, pragmatist, postpositivist—which is the theoretical lens you are using for your chosen methodology), and end (theories may be generated [grounded theory] or empirical evidence in the literature may support the data analysis results).

• Theory is often used for confirmatory purposes (explicit with operationally defined terms) or emerges directly from the data in exploratory constructivist qualitative grounded theoretical models.

◆ Research Questions

• The specific research question/hypothesis should be directly related to the problem and purpose of the study (and related to a theory if hypothetical). The research questions should be clearly linked to the topic and limited to a single idea per question.

• Overarching research questions should encompass all methods, followed by subquestions linked to the quantitative and qualitative inquiries.

• The research question(s) should be reasonable given scope, time, researcher skills, and resources. If confirmatory, the questions must be framed as a hypothesis.

◆ Methods

• The methods statement should be a clearly defined paragraph indicating (a) the design (case study, exploratory, explanatory, confirmatory, mixed methods), (b) the combination of methods to be employed, (c) methodological paradigm used to frame the overarching research question, (d) where the methods blend, and (e) justification for methodological selection.

• Include a graphic model of your design (see Figures 25.1, 25.2, and 25.3).

◆ Procedures

Procedures clarify what was/will be done and should be sufficiently explicit to replicate.

• Role of the researcher. Define your paradigmatic stance (constructivist, pragmatist, postpositivist, critical), your relationship to the research (emic-insider-who co-constructs research with participants or etic-outsider-distanced from "subjects" and most concerned with postpositivist conceptions of reliability and validity.

• Bounding the case. Time, location, participants, topic, data collected and analyzed.

• Participants and location. Who you are studying, location, setting, and number of participants or sites, and so on.

• Purposeful selection. Specify criteria for participant and/or site selection.

• Data collection. Separate qualitative and quantitative. Collect data specifically related to the research question and chosen methods determined by the problem and purpose of the study.

• Data analysis. Separate qualitative and quantitative. Data analysis logically flows from the methods. Generally, qualitative (often exploratory) will use a form of coding for themes that can be used to create a model (or theory) that represents the phenomenon in question. Quantitative (often explanatory/confirmatory) relies on statistical analysis. Descriptive statistics of survey results could be used to support a case study, to triangulate findings (confirmatory), or for descriptive (exploratory) purposes.

◆ Credibility/Generalizability/ Reliability

Clearly identify for both qualitative and quantitative methods the procedures for making findings believable. For example, triangulation, multiple cases, member check, internal/external validity, forms of reliability, and alternative explanations. Identify the researcher and participant relationship, potential or inherent biases, and how worldviews (ontology, epistemology, and axiology) may affect representation.

◆ Results

- Clearly state the results that logically follow the research questions, data collection, and analysis.

- Present only information from the data, not opinions or conclusions that cannot be deduced from the presented study.

- Results could be presented in summary format, potentially in graphic representations or in a table format connecting qualitative and quantitative data.

- Results should be directly related to the problem statement, research questions, data collection, and data analysis. If not, there is a flaw in the research design.

◆ Conclusions

Conclusions must be logically related to the specific data collected and literature used in the study. New concepts or problems should not be introduced in the conclusions that could not be deduced directly from the study. The conclusions should logically follow problem, purpose, research question, methods, and results.

◆ Implications

- Implications should be drawn from the literature and the study findings. Implications should be reasonable in context of the study and consider applicability of suggestions.

◆ Limitations

- Limitations should consider alternative explanations and be relevant, based on the research design, and limited to a few pertinent points.

◆ References

Bergman, M. (2008). *Advances in mixed methods research theories and applications.* Thousand Oaks, CA: Sage.

Biesta, G., & Burbules, N. C. (2003). *Pragmatism and educational research.* Lanham, MD: Rowman and Littlefield.

Bradbury, H. (2007). Quality, consequences, and action ability: What action researchers offer the tradition of pragmatism. In W. Pasmore, S. Mohrman, N. Adler, & R. A. Shani (Eds.), *Handbook of Collaborative Management Research.* Thousand Oaks, CA: Sage.

Brewer, J., & Hunter, A. (1989). *Multimethod research: A synthesis of style.* Thousand Oaks, CA: Sage.

Bryman, A. (2006). Paradigm peace and the implications for quality. *International Journal of Social Research Methodology Theory and Practice, 9*(2), 111–126.

Carr, W., & Kemmis, S. (1983). *Becoming critical: Knowing through action research.* Victoria, Australia: Deakin University Press.

Charmaz, K. (2000). *Grounded theory: Objectivist and constructivist methods.* In N. K. Denzin & Y. S. Lincoln (Eds.), *Handbook of qualitative research* (2nd ed., pp. 675–694). Thousand Oaks, CA: Sage.

Charmaz, K. (2006). *Constructing grounded theory: A practical guide through qualitative analysis.* Thousand Oaks, CA: Sage.

Christ, T. (2006). Longitudinal cross case analysis of support services for students with disabilities in postsecondary education. *Dissertation Abstracts International, 67*(05). (UMI N0.3216053)

Christ, T. (2007). A recursive approach to mixed methods research in a longitudinal study of postsecondary education disability support services. *Journal of Mixed Methods Research, 1*(3), 226–241.

Christ, T. (2008a). A cross-case analysis of leadership qualities in three postsecondary disability support centers. *Journal of Ethnographic & Qualitative Research, 2*(4), 223–230.

Christ, T. (2008b, April). *Mixed methods diagram-recursive grounded technique in longitudinal multistage mixed methods study of disability supports: Emerging research questions.* Paper and diagram presented at the 2008 annual meeting of the American Educational Research Association, New York.

Christ, T. (2008c). Technology support services in postsecondary education: A mixed methods study. *Technology and Disability, 20*(1), 25–35.

Christ, T. (2009a). Designing, teaching, and evaluating two complementary mixed methods research courses. *Journal of Mixed Methods Research, 3*(4), 292–325.

Christ, T. (2009b). Interview techniques used in coping and stress mixed methods studies. In K. Collins, T. Onwuegbuzie, & Q. Jiao (Vol. Eds.), *Toward a broader understanding of stress and coping: Mixed methods approaches: Vol. 5. The Research on Stress and Coping in Education* (pp. 391–418). Charlotte, NC: Information Age.

Christ, T. (2009c, February). *Mixed methods and action research in disability studies.* Workshop presented at the 25th annual Pacific Rim Conference, Honolulu, HI.

Christ, T. (2009d). Mixed methods research. In D. Ary, L. Cheser-Jacobs, A. Razavieh, & C. Sorensen (Eds.), *Introduction to Research in Education* (8th ed.). Belmont, CA: Thomson-Wadsworth.

Christ, T. (2009e, February). *Teaching mixed methods and action research.* Paper and diagrams presented at the 2009 Hawaii Educational Research Association, Honolulu, HI.

Christ, T., & Makarani, S. (2009). Teachers' attitudes about teaching English in India: An embedded mixed methods study. *International Journal of Multiple Research Approaches, 3*(1), 73–87.

Collins, K., & O'Cathain, A. (2009). Ten points about mixed methods research to be considered by the novice researcher. *International Journal of Multiple Research Approaches, 3*(1), 2–7.

Creswell, J. (2006, April 7). *Continuing the discourse: Advocates for and challengers to mixed methods research.* Symposium conducted at the American Education Research Association Mixed Methods SIG Business Meeting, San Francisco, CA.

Creswell, J. (2008). *Educational research: Planning, conducting, and evaluating quantitative and qualitative research.* Upper Saddle River, NJ: Merrill Prentice Hall.

Creswell, J. (2009a). Mapping the field of mixed methods research. *Journal of Mixed Methods Research, 3*(2), 95–108.

Creswell, J. (2009b). *Research design: Qualitative, quantitative & mixed methods approaches* (3rd ed.). Thousand Oaks, CA: Sage.

Creswell, J., & Plano Clark, V. (2007) *Designing and conducting mixed methods research.* Thousand Oaks, CA: Sage.

Creswell, J., Tashakkori, A., Jensen, K., & Shapley, K. L. (2003). Teaching mixed methods research: Practices, dilemmas, and challenges. In A. Tashakkori & C. Teddlie (Eds.), *Handbook of mixed methods in social & behavioral research* (pp. 619–637). Thousand Oaks, CA: Sage.

Crotty, M. (1998). *Foundations of social research: Meaning and perspective in the research process.* Thousand Oaks, CA: Sage.

Danermark, B., Ekström, M., Jakobsen, L., & Karlsson, J. C. (2002). *Explaining society: Critical realism in the social sciences.* London: Routledge.

Frauley, J., & Pearce, F. (Eds.). (2007). *Critical realism and the social sciences: Heterodox elaborations.* Toronto: University of Toronto Press.

Glazer, B. (1978). *Theoretical sensitivity.* Mill Valley, CA: Sociology Press.

Goff, R. (2004). *Critical realism, post-positivism and the possibility of knowledge.* London: Routledge.

Greene, J. (2007). *Mixed methods in social inquiry.* San Francisco: Jossey-Bass.

Greene, J. (2008). Is mixed methods social inquiry a distinctive methodology? *Journal of Mixed Methods Research, 2*(1), 7–22.

Greenwood, D., & Levine, M. (2001). Pragmatic action research and the struggle to transform universities into learning communities. In P. Reason & H. Bradbury (Eds.), *Handbook of action research* (pp. 103–113). Thousand Oaks, CA: Sage.

Howe, K. R. (1988). Against the quantitative qualitative incompatibility thesis or dogmas die hard. *Educational Researcher, 17,* 10–16.

Hui, M., & Grossman, D. J. (Eds.). (2008). *Improving teacher education through action research.* New York: Routledge.

Johnson, R., & Onwuegbuzie, A. (2004). Mixed methods research: A research paradigm whose time has come. *Educational Researcher, 33*(7), 14–26.

Kemmis, S. (2008). Critical theory and participatory action research. In P. Reason & H. Bradbury (Eds.), *The Sage handbook of action research* (pp. 121–138). Thousand Oaks, CA: Sage.

Kemmis, S., & McTaggart, R. (Eds.). (1988). *The action research planner* (3rd ed.). Geelong, Australia: Deakin University Press.

Lather, P. (2004). This is your father's paradigm: Government intrusion and the case of qualitative research in education. *Qualitative Inquiry, 10*(1), 15–34.

Lewin, K. (1946/1948). Action research and minority problems. In G. W. Lewin (Ed.), *Resolving social conflicts* (pp. 201–216). New York. Harper & Row.

Lincoln, Y., & Guba, E. (2005). Paradigmatic controversies, contradictions, and emerging confluences. In N. K. Denzin & Y. S. Lincoln (Eds.), *The Sage handbook of qualitative research* (pp. 191–214). Thousand Oaks, CA: Sage.

Lykes, M. B., & Mallona, A. (2008). Towards transformational liberation: Participatory and action research and praxis. In P. Reason & H. Bradbury (Eds.), *Handbook of action research* (pp. 31–48). Thousand Oaks, CA: Sage.

Maxwell, J. (2005). *Qualitative research design: An interactive approach* (3rd ed.). Thousand Oaks, CA: Sage.

Maxwell, J., & Loomis, D. (2003). Mixed methods design: An alternative approach. In A. Tashakkori & C. Teddlie (Eds.), *Handbook of mixed methods in social & behavioral research* (pp. 351–384). Thousand Oaks, CA: Sage.

Mertens, D. (2003). Mixed models and the politics of human research: The transformative-emancipatory perspective. In A. Tashakkori & C. Teddlie (Eds.), *Handbook of mixed methods in social & behavioral research* (pp. 135–166). Thousand Oaks, CA: Sage.

Mertens, D. (2007). Transformative paradigm: Mixed methods and social justice. *Journal of Mixed Methods Research, 1*(2), 212–225.

Mertler, C. (2008). *Action research: Teachers as researchers in the classroom.* (2nd ed.). Thousand Oaks, CA: Sage.

Mills, J., Bonner, A., & Francis, K. (2006). The development of constructivist grounded theory. *International Journal of Qualitative Methods, 5*(1), 1–10.

Morgan, D. (2007). Paradigms lost and pragmatism regained: Methodological implications of combining qualitative and quantitative methods. *Journal of Mixed Methods Research, 1,* 48–76.

Morse, J. M. (1991). Approaches to qualitative and quantitative methodological triangulation. *Nursing Research, 40*(2), 120–123.

Neuman, W. L. (2006). *Basics of social research: Quantitative and qualitative approaches* (3rd ed.). Upper Saddle River, NJ: Prentice Hall.

Niglas, K. (2001, September 5). *Paradigms and methodology in educational research.* Paper presented at the European Conference on Educational Research at the Université Charles de Gaulle, Lille, France.

Niglas, K. (2006). *Introducing the qualitative-quantitative continuum: An alternative view of teaching research methods courses.* Paper and diagrams presented at the 2006 ECER annual meeting, Geneva, Switzerland.

Onwuegbuzie, A., & Johnson, R. (2006). The validity issue in mixed methods research. *Research in the Schools, 13*(1), 48–63.

Onwuegbuzie, A., & Leech, N. (2005). Taking the "Q" out of research: Teaching research methodology courses without the divide between quantitative and qualitative paradigms. *Quality and Quantity: International Journal of Methodology, 39,* 267–296.

Onwuegbuzie, A., & Leech, N. (2009). Lessons learned for teaching mixed research: A framework for novice researchers. *International Journal of Multiple Research Approaches, 3*(1), 105–107.

Onwuegbuzie, A., & Teddlie, C. (2003). A framework for analyzing data in mixed methods research. In A. Tashakkori & C. Teddlie (Eds.), *Handbook of mixed methods in social & behavioral research* (pp. 351–384). Thousand Oaks, CA: Sage.

Patton, M. (1999). Enhancing the quality and credibility of qualitative analysis. *HSR: Health Services Research, 34*(5), 1189–1208.

Patton, M. (2002). *Qualitative research and evaluation methods* (3rd ed.). Thousand Oaks, CA: Sage.

Rahman, M. A. (2008). Some trends in the praxis of participatory action research. In P. Reason & H. Bradbury (Eds.), *Handbook of action research* (pp. 49–62). Thousand Oaks, CA: Sage.

Reason, P., & Bradbury, H. (2008). Introduction. In P. Reason & H. Bradbury (Eds.), *Handbook of action research* (pp. 1–10). Thousand Oaks, CA: Sage.

Reason, P., & Torbert, W. R. (2001). The action turn: Towards a transformative social science. *Concepts and Transformation, 6*(1), 1–37.

Ridenour, C., & Newman, I. (2008). *Mixed methods research: Exploring the interactive continuum*. Carbondale: Southern Illinois University Press.

Saks, M., & Allport, J. (Eds.). (2007). *Researching health: Qualitative, quantitative and mixed methods*. Thousand Oaks, CA: Sage.

Sayer, A. (1992). *Method in social science: A realist approach*. London, Routledge.

Swantz, M. L. (2008). Participatory action research in practice. In P. Reason & H. Bradbury (Eds.), *Handbook of action research* (pp. 31–48). Thousand Oaks, CA: Sage.

Tashakkori, A., & Creswell, J. (2007). Developing publishable mixed methods manuscripts. *Journal of Mixed Methods Research, 1*(2), 107–111.

Tashakkori, A., & Teddlie, C. (1998). *Mixed methodology: Combining the qualitative and quantitative approaches*. Thousand Oaks, CA: Sage.

Tashakkori, A., & Teddlie, C. (Eds.). (2003). *Handbook of mixed methods in social & behavioral research*. Thousand Oaks, CA: Sage.

Teddlie, C., & Tashakkori, A. (2009). *Foundations of mixed methods research: Integrating quantitative and qualitative approaches in the social and behavioral sciences*. Thousand Oaks, CA: Sage.

Yin, R. (2009). *Case study research: Design and methods* (4th ed.). Thousand Oaks, CA: Sage.

26

THE USE OF MIXED METHODS IN BIOGRAPHICAL RESEARCH

◆ Ann Nilsen and Julia Brannen

Objectives

It is intended that this chapter will

- enhance the reader's understanding of biographical methods and their value in the history and developments of social science research and how mixing data and methods have been important over time in this approach;

- extend the use of mixed methods to include a biographical approach; and

- develop an understanding of the different possibilities in which biographical data can be used in mixed methods inquiry.

The study of social change has been a core concern of the social sciences. In particular, sociology has its origins in understanding a changing world, a concern that dates back to the classical studies of the late 19th and early 20th centuries. Of all the different types of data generated that locate the individual in relation to the dimensions of both *time* and *space*, biographical data are the most "qualitative." Kohli (1981) defined a biographical account, or life story, as "the mode by which the individual represents those aspects of his past which are relevant to the present situation, i.e., relevant in terms of the (future-oriented) intentions by which he guides his present actions" (p. 65).[1]

Biographical research requires both intensive and extensive lenses with which to produce knowledge about human lives as they develop over historical time and the life course. Its methods require understanding and interpretation of human experience across time and space while elucidating individual action and engagement in society. Biographical data add an additional layer of complexity to the study of society. Biographical researchers work with a variety of different types of data, including documents such as written autobiographies, letters and diaries (Thomas & Znaniecki, 1958 [1918–20]), interviews, surveys, secondary data (statistical trends, historical accounts) (Bertaux, 1981; Bertaux & Kohli, 1984; Bertaux & Thompson, 1997); and, increasingly, websites, weblogs, and videos (Bornat, 2008; Plummer, 2001).

In this chapter, we will discuss the different developments that have taken place in biographical research from the 1920s to the present and the ways in which the approach has engaged, either explicitly or implicitly, with what can be described as qualitative and quantitative data. Although the language of mixing methods is fairly recent, current debates around mixed methods research have resonances with debates in biographical research that were common in both earlier and current periods. In this chapter, we will reference some of these debates and illustrate them with exemplar studies, then discuss their use of different types of data and methods and their consequences for the framing of the analyses in the publications that were generated from them. We begin by providing an overview of the origins of biographical research and then discuss the ways qualitative and quantitative approaches were combined in biographical research over the

course of the 20th century until the present day. As we will demonstrate, early biographical studies inspired a focus on individual lives as they develop over historical time and life course, not only in sociological studies, but also in related fields such as psychology, social anthropology, and history. The discussion in this chapter, however, is confined to sociology.

In many instances, biographical material has been combined with other sources of data. Whether supplementary sources of information were actually referred to as "data" by the researchers and were an explicit part of the analysis, however, is another matter. We will argue that this needs to be understood in relation to the historical context in which the research was carried out. In this sense, biographical methods should be of interest to those involved in mixed methods research methodology. As in all mixed methods studies, so in biographical research there are different ways of linking data sources. As we will demonstrate, it is not only the definition of the research question that decides how methods are chosen and data are linked, but also the way that social phenomena are conceptualized, the methodological assumptions that are made, and the debates that underpin a study or set of studies at a given historical period. Ontological and epistemological assumptions that are brought to the study need to be considered.

◆ The Biographical Approach: The Polish Peasant in Europe and America

The start of the biographical method is attributed to the work of William I. Thomas and Florian Znaniecki, especially to their study published in *The Polish Peasant in Europe and America*. This is considered to be the first biographical study in sociology; it inspired researchers not only in sociology, but also in all other social science disciplines over the 20th century. The work was published between 1918 and 1920 in five volumes, and republished in

1958 in a two-volume edition, with some changes made to the order of parts and different pagination. Volumes I and II in the original edition concern the peasant primary groups in Poland and their experiences of the rapid industrialization at home and rising rates of migration to America and Germany. Volume III is an autobiography of an immigrant of peasant origin (Wladek). Volume IV is about the development and reorganization of peasant communities in Poland under the new regimes of agriculture and modernization, and Volume V explores the situation of Polish immigrants in the Chicago area, and the disorganization of communities in their new surroundings. There also is a long methodological note in the original Volume I, which Thomas later explained was written after the study had been completed (Blumer, 1979, p. 83).

Thomas met Znaniecki on a field trip to Poland in 1913. Znaniecki then emigrated to the United States after World War I broke out. Together they collected an impressive amount of data of various kinds in their study of Polish migrants. In Poland, they collected newspaper articles, personal letters, archive material, and personal stories. It was the first time that personal documents and biographies in particular had been used as data in an extensive sociological study.

The setting and timing of the development of the biographical approach in these studies are highly significant. At the time, Chicago was the fastest growing North American city; with a huge immigrant population, the city had more than its share of social problems. Social work and sociology in the university were not then separate disciplines, and the approaches that were common in sociology were influential among social workers, also.[2] Empirical sociology in the Chicago department was inspired by pragmatist philosophy (the writings of Peirce, James, Mead, and Dewey). Many of the sociologists in the department saw their purpose as uncovering the conditions of hardship and identifying the causes for the human misery they witnessed in some Chicago communities. Indeed, empirical

sociology was flourishing in the Chicago department at a time when in many other universities sociologists had not moved out of their armchairs. During this period, many Chicago sociologists collected biographies or "cases" as research material. In this context, the term "case" was borrowed from social work; social workers described writing up their clients' life stories as cases (Platt, 1996). The life story approach hence became an important influence in empirical sociology.

W. I. Thomas was a contemporary of another sociologist, Jane Addams, whose work became influential in social work.[3] Addams was the cofounder (with Ellen Gates Starr) of Hull House in Chicago, a charity established in 1889, largely with the help of funding from an heiress, Helen Culver.[4] Hull House was set up to educate and to alleviate the conditions of the poor communities in the city. Many employees of the sociology department—Mead, Thomas, and Dewey, in particular—were associated with the charity work of Hull House. Most, particularly Thomas, also were politically active. This led to unfortunate consequences for his academic career. To make a long story short, he was fired from his position at the university in 1918. By then, the first two volumes of *The Polish Peasant* had been published by the University of Chicago Press. The university broke the contract for the remaining three volumes, however; those volumes were published by a Boston publisher in 1920. Thomas never again obtained a tenured position. His reputation was later restored among the American sociological community, in particular in the Appraisal Proceedings of *The Polish Peasant*, which were conducted at the American Sociological Association in 1938.

◆ The 1938 Appraisal of The Polish Peasant

In 1938, the American Sociological Association held a session where Herbert Blumer, an earlier student of Mead and also of Thomas, gave an extensive review of

The Polish Peasant where both Thomas and Znaniecki were present alongside a number of prominent sociologists.[5] The methodological aspects of the work were a major focus of the debate, which was reproduced verbatim in the published Appraisal Proceedings.

In making sense today of these methodological discussions, it is important to reflect on the historical time in which they took place. Hitler was in power in Germany. Scientists and social scientists were fleeing that country. They rejected the beliefs that underpinned the Third Reich as unscientific as well as unethical. Such a rejection reflected a commitment to a positivist stance on matters of methods and methodology which, in those circumstances, became a liberating and enlightening way of thinking.

The Polish Peasant study combined a variety of data, as mentioned previously, and the researchers' analysis of these was rigorous and thorough. Znaniecki (1934) would later publish a book on his pioneering method which he called *analytic induction*.[6] Values and attitudes were key concepts in Thomas's and Znaniecki's analyses, where values were defined as "the objective cultural elements of social life," and attitudes were defined as "the subjective characteristics of the individual." The researchers' aim was to uncover the "social laws of becoming." Although Thomas distanced himself from this ambition during the proceedings, it nevertheless demonstrates the research climate at that time; some thought social science should become a science alongside the natural sciences and therefore saw the uncovering of laws as important. One of Blumer's conclusions in his review of the work was that Thomas and Znaniecki had not been able to achieve their aim of identifying the "social laws of becoming." This led to a discussion about the relationship between the social and natural sciences, and whether the epistemological foundations of the social sciences should be different from those of the natural sciences.

During the Proceedings, it became clear that the approach to methods and data adopted in *The Polish Peasant* represented challenges for sociology in general. Could subjective accounts be relied on? What methods could be used to overcome subjective biases in the data? How could such data ever become "representative"? By which means could a representative sample of life histories be achieved? How could researchers be sure that those who volunteered their life stories did not have their own agendas and interests? How could subjective accounts be thought to have value beyond the individual story? In grappling with such questions, the panel touched on a number of issues that still haunt what we now call "qualitative research" and what was then referred to as "naturalistic methods."

Replying to challenges about the reliability of biographical, or "subjective," material, W. I. Thomas said,

> there is a collection of about 1000 Swedish case studies along the lines of criminology and psychology which are, on the whole, superior to anything I have seen. . . . In Sweden, all the cases in question are kept under observation and studies for a period of from two to six months. They write their stories themselves, but not extensively. They are interrogated at intervals and sometimes by different persons. The authorities communicate with the persons with whom the subjects have associated—relatives, teachers, landlords, employers, neighbours, etc. The replies are very meticulous since the Swedish state can almost command in this respect. I conceive that this material has an all-round superiority to life histories alone. (Blumer, 1979 [1939], p. 132)

Several points can be made about this quotation. One is the affinity drawn between life stories and case studies, and thus between social workers' involvement with "delinquents," especially young people, and researchers studying these groups. In disciplines other than sociology, such methods became more important over the years following the publication of *The Polish*

Peasant. A second point is that life histories and personal documents were not seen as sufficient material for sociological studies. In one sense, what Thomas proposed here was indeed a mixing of methods! The third point that strikes us today is that the Swedish cases were all "inmates" whose stories could be checked against a variety of sources, thus increasing their individual reliability. However, the respondents were not a volunteer sample but were "command[ed]" to participate by the Swedish state. Studies of such large captive samples of "cases" were later to become common in psychology and related disciplines, including in some early longitudinal studies, as we shall later discuss.

◆ *Empirical Studies and Methodological Discussion in Early Postwar Sociology*

In the interwar period, the main methodological discussions centred on debates about "the case study method" and "the statistical method," while in the postwar period statistical methods gained prominence at the expense of qualitative studies. Discussions focused increasingly on the technicalities of survey methods (Platt, 1996).

During this period, Herbert Blumer was one of the most influential sociologists to engage in debates about methodology. Many of the viewpoints he expressed during the Appraisals Proceedings anticipated his later writings, where he argued against variable-driven research in the social sciences and made a case for a humanistic sociology based on *sensitizing* rather than *definitive* concepts (see, e.g., Blumer, 1954).

However, Blumer was not the only voice to oppose mainstream sociological thought and practice at the time. Foremost amongst the critics of the contemporary trend was C. Wright Mills, who received his doctorate from the University of Wisconsin (1942) on the sociology of knowledge in American pragmatism (Mills, 1966).[7] This body of thought influenced much of his writings in the sociology of knowledge (see, e.g., Mills, 1939, 1940a, 1940b). His ambition for sociology was formulated in an appendix to his most well-known book, *The Sociological Imagination* (Mills 1980 [1959]). This is one of the few texts from the period that set out to describe in great detail how empirical research should be carried out, while also giving good methodological reasons for the practices he recommended.

Although Mills himself did not carry out biographical studies as such, his influence on the field has been very important, especially during the revival of biographical research in the 1970s, as we will discuss later. His vision for the discipline was to combine insights at both macro and micro levels of society, while also applying a processual approach to research questions: that social life must be studied and understood within particular historical periods. Thus, he insisted that equal attention be paid to history and to biography, and that the sociological imagination, which is the power to formulate good research questions, should locate these at the *intersection* of biography and society. In so doing, he proposed a program for the conduct of sociological research that would fulfil the aim of generating knowledge to help people make sense of their lives. He thereby sought to take the discipline out of the grip of *The Theory* (structural functionalism as propounded by Talcott Parsons) on the one hand, and *The Method* (the statistical methods supported by Lazarsfeld and others) on the other (Mills, 1963 [1954]), both of which approaches had gained ground in Anglo-Saxon sociology in this period. In many social sciences, including sociology, large-scale surveys on the one hand and controlled experiments on the other were identified as the new ideal research designs, since they could test hypotheses, which would in time lead to the accumulation of sophisticated bodies of theory, which were seen as essential to the ambition of arriving at social laws.

◆ Life Course Perspectives and Longitudinal Studies

An important development within the quantitative tradition has been the longitudinal and cohort study in which the focus is on temporality and the individual life course of particular groups and cohorts. These studies have considerable narrative potential to provide highly detailed information about individuals (Elliott, 2005); as we shall show, however, these studies require interpretation in relation to historical context.

The affinity between a biographical approach and social work was noted earlier. Participants in longitudinal studies were often "deviants," "delinquents," and other groups of people who for some reason did not fit into the "normal" fabric of society. An early exemplar was carried out by Eleanor and Sheldon Glueck (1930), whose work also was remarked on by Thomas in the Appraisal Proceedings.[8] In 1940, the Gluecks began a second study of 500 delinquent and 500 nondelinquent white boys aged 14 (matched by age, ethnicity, type of neighborhood, and intelligence); they followed them up at 25 and 32 (Glueck & Glueck, 1943, 1950). As Laub and Sampson (1998), who worked on their archived data much later, commented, the data were exceedingly rich; the Gluecks had collected data on a variety of dimensions of juvenile and adult development, including major life course events. Their methods were various: interviews with the respondents and their families, but also with key informants (social workers, school teachers, employers, and neighbors, for example); and official records and criminal histories. This mixed method approach and the rigor of the investigation, together with its longitudinal design, set the study apart from criminological studies that preceded it. However, in the 1940s, the Gluecks had not aimed to integrate the richness and depth of their qualitative and quantitative data. From a methodological and epistemological viewpoint, the study was firmly grounded in a quantitative logic where issues of representativeness, generalization, and reliability were important, and the purpose was to arrive at *causal explanations* and *the ability to predict*. There was no attempt to treat the qualitative data in their own right.

◆ Cohort Studies

A particular form of longitudinal study is the cohort study, which can be defined as "an aggregate of individuals who experienced the same event within the same time interval" (Ryder, 1965, p. 845), the most common of which is the birth cohort. Again, the focus is on the individual, on temporality, and on a concern with social change. One of the most well-known cohort studies is Glen Elder's *Children of the Great Depression*, first published in 1974, and republished in 1999 with an updated last chapter. Inspired by Karl Mannheim's 1928 essay, *On the Problem of Generations*, the purpose of the research was to study how historical context and economic deprivation shaped individuals' lives. The study is based on similar types of material—both qualitative and quantitative—as the Gluecks' studies, but with one main difference: the cases were "ordinary" children. The sample consisted of fifth graders (born around 1920)—84 boys and 83 girls, all of them white, from working- and middle-class backgrounds living in Berkeley and Oakland, California. They were continuously studied over a seven-year period from 1932 to 1939 and contacted again at five different times ending in 1964.[9]

This is indeed an impressive study in terms of the depth and range of data. It stands out from other studies of its time because, as Elder explicitly stated, he chose to study effects of economic deprivation on *theoretical and historical grounds*, and *not* because he sought some decontextualized predictive explanations about how deprivation in childhood would affect individuals over the life course in general (Elder,

1999, p. 6). Elder thus employed a life course–sensitive frame for interpreting the data, as formulated by other earlier advocates of the cohort design (Ryder, 1965). However, in contrast to, e.g., Blumer's approach to sociology, Elder's approach was firmly grounded in a variable logic and in quantitative analysis. However, he did highlight the importance of social and historical context, a viewpoint he shared with those who came to revive the qualitative biographical approach in the same decade in which his groundbreaking study was published (see Bertaux, 1981). Rather than making generalizations about how particular experiences of deprivation in childhood would affect individuals over the life course, irrespective of time and place, Elder concluded that effects of childhood deprivation related not only to the historical circumstances, but also to the points in the life course (age and cohort) in which they experienced it; the children in the Berkeley study were 8 years younger than the children in the Oakland sample, and it was these younger children whose lives were most disrupted by the Depression.

In *Children of the Great Depression*, discussions about methods are placed in an appendix, with detailed accounts about the types of data, methods of data collection, and questions of reliability and validity. Elder relied on a great deal of information about other layers of context. One source of such data was the interviews carried out with the children's mothers. As the following quote indicates, he made use of these interviews, but only for purposes of gaining insights of a general kind, and as illustrations.

> These qualitative materials were found to be an invaluable source of insight and illustrations for the analysis, but they were not sufficiently systematic to permit codification. . . . The staff members who interviewed the mothers also rated them on personal characteristics, using a seven-point scale. (Elder, 1999, p. 367)

The study also relies on information about the different historical periods through which the cohorts lived at various phases in the life course. It can therefore be argued that the interpretation of cohort studies does (and should) involve more than one type of data. Knowledge about the wider historical period is often derived from the literature, archived material, and official statistics; these may only indirectly inform the analysis, however. More often than not, this contextual material is not presented by the researchers as sources of data, much less as mixed methods of analysis. Instead, these data form an invisible aspect of the interpretative process or they are simply referred to as research literature. That this was the situation in the 1970s can be inferred from the following quote from Blumer:

> The jumbling together of naturalistic and nonnaturalistic methods of study has resulted, in my judgment, in a large amount of methodological confusion, a confusion that is more harmful because it is unrecognised. (Blumer, 1979, p. xxvii)

THE REVIVAL OF THE BIOGRAPHICAL METHOD

As Bertaux (1981) remarked, there was a sudden and radical "collapse" in the use of biographical material between the 1940s and the mid 1970s (Bertaux, 1981, p. 5). In the 1978 World Congress of the International Sociological Association in Uppsala, Bertaux arranged a separate session on life course methods that constituted a turning point, putting biographical methods squarely on the sociological map. A publication of the papers from the session has become a standard reference for biographical researchers (Bertaux, 1981).

Debates early in the revival period were similar to those during the Appraisal Proceeding of *The Polish Peasant*. Can personal stories be relied on? Are people telling the truth? How can reliability be checked against other sources of information? Are

684 ◆ *Applications of Mixed Methods Research*

these really scientific data? Wider questions about philosophy of science also were raised, however:

> Biography resets in motion the *Methodenstreit*. It thus presents a unique opportunity for reopening a thorough debate on the subject of the logical, epistemological and methodological foundations of sociology; an occasion for the renewal of thought on the foundations of the social. (Ferrarotti, 1981, p. 21)

The revival of biographical methods thus opened a debate about quantitative and qualitative approaches. The papers in the book edited by Bertaux (1981) make it clear that there are different approaches within biographical research, and that these are mainly related to the researchers' theoretical interests and research questions. Psychologists were mainly interested in the development of individual personality. Historians were interested in oral history and realistic accounts of the past (Hareven, 1978; Thompson, 1978, 1981). Empirical sociologists such as Bertaux, Elder, and Denzin in their chapters in the 1981 book were oriented toward the study of social processes. Seen through their interpretation of the biographical method, they considered it necessary to collect and assemble data and information of different types. However, none of the papers in the book *explicitly* addresses the topic of mixing methods.

Questions of ontology and epistemology dominated debates in biographical research in the 1990s (Nilsen, 2008). Bertaux (1996) took part in the philosophy of science debates of the time about realism versus "idealism" or constructionism, positioning himself as realist, and Fischer-Rosenthal and Rosenthal (1997), among others, positioning themselves in the other camp.[10] From a later vantage point, Miller (2000) saw this dichotomy as simplistic, and instead made a methodological distinction between realist, neopositivist, and narrative approaches.

Bornat (2008) even more recently created a further methodological classification between the biographic-interpretive method, oral history, and narrative analysis.[11] Others, inspired by Strauss and Glaser (1977), distinguished between case histories and case studies: the former focuses on the value of the single life story whereas the latter is concerned with setting the life story in social context (Plummer, 2001). Following the same line of thinking, Roos (1997) discussed the realist-constructionist divide with reference to autobiographies, and made the point that to have sociological merit contextual understanding is essential.

Drawing on the different viewpoints expressed in these writings, we will now give a brief outline of what we consider to be the main characteristics of each biographical approach and their ontological or epistemological standpoints. We will make a distinction between a "contextual approach" on the one hand and an "interpretive approach" on the other. The origins of both approaches to current biographical research can be traced back to the Chicago School (Miller, 2000; Plummer, 2001; Roberts, 2002).

THE CONTEXTUAL APPROACH: LIVES IN SOCIAL CONTEXTS

Studies that adopt this approach (Bertaux, 2003; Bertaux & Kohli, 1984; Bertaux & Thompson, 1997) collect biographical material, mainly by interview, in order to study social change. Informants are usually selected on the basis of age and cohort. While the biographical material is center stage, other types of data are also important, since they provide the necessary context for the analysis of the qualitative material (e.g., Bertaux & Thompson, 1997; Miller, 2000; Roberts, 2002). Inspired by Thomas and Znaniecki's study as well as by the theoretical and methodological writings of Wright Mills (Bertaux, 1981; Roberts, 2002), the focus is on the relationship between wider social change and individual biography, as we have discussed earlier in relation to the classic studies.

In contemporary studies within this tradition, methodological discussions rarely focus on the issue of the "truth" of individual biographical accounts in the way that the early Chicago studies did. This is because their focus is not on single stories, but on the significance of the stories as a whole to understanding the wider social processes under scrutiny. This is not to say that this approach has a simplistic notion of truth and reality or that it takes stories at their face value. The point is rather that the knowledge sought is not only at the individual level (Bertaux, 2003; Bertaux & Thompson, 1997). The approach is realist in that it sees social reality as having consequences beyond individual beliefs. Individual accounts are interpretations, but they are interpretations set within a social *context* of factual events (Bertaux, 2003; Roos, 1997). The focus is therefore rarely only on the way the story is *told*: attention is as much on the features of the lives to which the stories testify (Nilsen, 1996). Each story, or case, adds nuance to the totality, set within the different layers of social context within which the lives are lived. As Bertaux so succinctly put it, "[B]ehind the solo of the human voice one can hear the music of society and culture" (Bertaux, 1990, p. 168). The epistemological standpoint implies that there is reality beyond language and discourse, but that reality must be studied in context, in relation to time and space.

THE INTERPRETIVE APPROACH: NARRATIVES AND TEXTS

Denzin was a key figure in developments of the "narrative turn." A student of Blumer, his early studies were influenced by symbolic interactionism; toward the end of the 1980s, his focus shifted to what he termed "interpretive interactionism," in which discourses and narratives—"stories"—became his main interest.

Ethnographies, biographies, and auto-biographies rest on *stories* which are fictional, narrative accounts of how something happened. Stories are fictions. A *fiction* is something made up or fashioned out of real and imagined events. History, in this sense, is fiction. A *story* has a beginning, a middle, and an end. Stories take the form of texts. They can be transcribed, written down, and studied. They are *narratives* with a plot and a story line that exists independent of the life of the storyteller or *narrator*. Every narrative contains a reason or set of justifications for its telling. (Denzin, 1989, p. 41)

A paradox of the interpretive tradition is that it rests on the same kind of questions that "the positivists" had posed about biographical accounts during the Appraisal Proceedings referred to earlier. Are they truthful? Can they be relied on? Both positivists and constructionists argue that biographies are not truths. However, while an extreme positivist approach would not contest the idea of a reality that can be captured by the "right" type of data and methods, an extreme interpretive perspective would involve questioning whether there is such a thing as reality beyond language—i.e., knowledge about reality expressed in language is the only reality that exists. From these widely different standpoints on questions of philosophy of knowledge, interpretevists and positivists draw very different—yet similar—conclusions about biographical material. Where positivists dismiss these data altogether because they are not "objective" enough, the constructionists see them as parallel to works of fiction that can be analyzed with the same techniques as are literary texts. In either case, they are rendered questionable as far as truth is concerned.

The interpretive approach pays more attention to single stories than does the contextual approach. Plummer, a key exponent of biographical research in the interpretive tradition, makes the following point about why biographical studies are of interest:

> [A]nd what lies at the heart of this enormous outpouring of writing about "the modern human being" is the idea that a highly individuated, self-conscious and unstable identity is replacing the old, stable, unitary self of traditional communities. The new selves are "constructed" through shifts and changes in the modern world, and partly create a new sense of permanent identity crisis. The search for "understanding" and making sense of the self has become a key feature of the modern world. (Plummer, 2001, p. 83)

The focus of attention in this analysis is "inward," on individual narratives rather than "outward," on the wider social context to which the person belongs. This is not to say that social phenomena beyond the individual are of no interest. They are, but the terminology used to refer to society is different from that of a contextual approach. Language and discourse have a key place in the interpretive approach. For example, history is referred to as epochs rather than as specific periods; concepts of "modernity," "late modernity," and "post-modernity" abound (Plummer, 2001).

Notions of context vary between the two approaches; structural dimensions have different meanings. In the contextual approach, age, for instance, refers both to individual experience and interpretation, as well as to age as a structuring element relating to social institutions (Giele & Elder, 1998; Riley, 1987). From an interpretive perspective, Plummer (2001) pointed to the importance of including more than chronological age in interpretations of biographical material; "subjective age (how old the person feels), interpersonal age (how old others think you are) and social age (the age roles you play—so you can 'act much younger—or older—than your age'" (Plummer, 2001, p. 129). All are considered equally important. These ways of addressing age demonstrate

that the research questions addressed from the two epistemological standpoints may vary considerably.

◆ Three Ways of Mixing Methods in Current Studies Using Biographical Methods

In the final section of this chapter, we will discuss ways in which methods are, and can be, mixed in biographical research. We will distinguish between three different ways of integrating data and methods. As we have demonstrated thus far, much of the research that employs the range of biographical methods in the analysis phase integrates inferences made on the basis of different types of data, but often in *implicit* ways. The mixed methods research literature of the recent decade and a half has been influential in making researchers think about the ways in which they can integrate different methods and types of data more *explicitly*. Greene, Caracelli, and Graham (1989, p. 127) were among the first to define ways of integrating data from different methods in mixed methods research designs. They set out a five-fold classification; triangulation where convergence of results is sought arrived at by different methods; complementarity that seeks elaboration, enhancement, and clarification of results from one method with results from another; development that uses the results of one method to develop or inform another method; initiation that seeks to interrogate results from one method with questions or results from another method; and expansion that seeks to extend the breadth and range of inquiry by using different methods for different inquiry components.

Much of the mixed methods research literature refers to studies in which weight is given to both qualitative and quantitative data, albeit in varying proportions (see Cresswell [2003] for an overview). However, as Brannen (1992, 2004) and others (Tashakkori & Teddlie, 1998) have argued, it is more complex than this.

Qualitative and quantitative elements may be introduced into different *phases of the research process*: not only into the research design phase, but also into the fieldwork phase and the phases of interpretation and contextualization. These phases can be distinguished in relation to (a) the context of inquiry, in which methods are chosen to address substantive and theoretical questions, and (b) the context of justification, in which data are discussed in relation to the methods, assumptions, and theories by which they are constituted (Kaplan, 1964).

Some researchers who employ biographical approaches, especially those working within a qualitative interpretive tradition, do not collect more than one type of primary data and therefore do not focus their attention on the methodological aspects of this fact in their data analysis (e.g., see Wengraf, 2001). In some studies, where both quantitative and qualitative data are collected, researchers have tended to make the qualitative data invisible in the analysis, suggesting a lack of systematic integration (Elder, 1999). Some biographical researchers link qualitative studies to existing data sets such as cohort studies or archived data—what we term *linked designs*. Rarely are contemporary cohort studies or longitudinal studies designed with a qualitative study in view, although, in the United Kingdom, at least, with the increasing cost of collecting new data, more linked designs to such studies are expected to take place.

Researchers who carry out cross-national studies involving several countries increasingly use methods and data for the theoretical purpose of addressing a number of layers of social context (micro, meso, and macro). Such an approach underlines the relation between agency and structure and the importance of addressing this relation methodologically (Layder, 1998, p. 14). These contextual layers require the integration of the respective data in the analysis phase. Analysis here therefore typically involves working *across different methods*.

Among researchers working in interpretive traditions, the approach to integration tends to be quite different. For example, those espousing the biographic-interpretive method (Wengraf, 2001) integrate different types of data *within methods*, as we shall describe below. These three ways of mixing methods in biographical studies are now considered. They represent only some among a number of possibilities, however.

LINKED QUANTITATIVE AND QUALITATIVE DESIGNS

Many examples in this category come from the disciplinary intersection between history and sociology. Hareven's historical study of the relationship between work and family in an industrial community in the United States (Hareven, 1982) was one of the earliest to address explicitly issues of combining different data. The material she integrated in her study were "company files and employees' files from Amoskeag, vital records, parish records, insurance records, and linkage with the 1900 census" (Hareven, 1982, pp. 385–386). This massive material was combined with individual interviews. On the differences between surveys and interviews, Hareven observed, "Like surveys, it [a life history] recalls attitudes and perceptions, but, unlike surveys, it places these perceptions in the context of an individual's life history. These perceptions are exceptionally valuable not as individual case histories but as historical, cultural testimonies" (Hareven, 1982, p. 382). Although she did not set out to do a mixed methods research design, she nevertheless integrated both quantitative and qualitative material in the study, and also discussed their methodological implications:

Whereas the quantitative analysis provides structural evidence concerning the organisation and behaviour of kin, the oral-history interviews offer insight into the nature of relationships and their significance to the participants. The empirical analysis reported here—although attempting to weld both types of evidence—at times presents two different levels of historical reality, each derived from a distinct type of data. (Hareven, 1982, p. 371)

Throughout the book, all the types of data are integrated and discussed to explore and explain different layers of contexts of the research questions. This makes Hareven's study one of the first "biographical" studies where data and methods of analysis are fully integrated and the merits of each type of data, together and separately, are explicitly addressed.

Another example where mixed methods have been made an explicit issue of concern is Laub and Sampson's (1998) use of the Gluecks' longitudinal data. Laub and Sampson successfully integrated the original quantitative and qualitative data in the analysis and interpretation, and continued to do so as they followed up the original sample (Laub & Sampson, 1993). Laub and Sampson (1998) described "merg(ing) quantitative and qualitative data to provide a more complex portrait of criminal offending over the life course" (Laub & Sampson, 1998, p. 221) by combining variable-based analysis with data on persons. Their strategy was to select a random subset of cases for intensive qualitative analysis that were consistent with the quantitative data analysis and to explore consistencies and inconsistencies between these according to the different lenses that each data set and method offered. They argued that the approach had two methodological benefits. First, it resulted in the enhancement of quantitative data through recourse to the qualitative life histories that demonstrated the complex processes underlying the persistence of and desistence from crime. Second, by examining residual or "negative cases" that did not fit the quantitative results, the researchers were led to examine "unidentified

pathways into and out of crime" (Laub & Sampson, 1998, p. 222).

Laub and Sampson (1998) reported some additional misgivings about the original data collected by the Gluecks that point to the nature of biographical research and the ways in which the research design of this large-scale longitudinal study failed to address the concern with understanding changes in human lives. In particular, they noted the Gluecks' failure to explore turning points in the life course. Thus, they decided it was important in their own follow up of the Gluecks' sample to adopt a life history approach in their interviews that enabled respondents to reflect retrospectively on the turning points in their life course. They argued that "without qualitative data, discussions of continuity often mask complex and rich qualitative processes" (Sampson & Laub, 1997, quoted in Laub & Sampson, 1998, p. 229). Moreover, like Hareven, they also made the crucial claim for the biographical approach: that the data provide an opportunity for their interpretation in relation to the historical context in which the respondents are studied, in this case the type and level of crime that were prevalent at the time.

As noted above, Paul Thompson and Daniel Bertaux advocated the integration of qualitative and quantitative data (Bertaux & Thompson, 1997). Thompson (2004) noted that one of the key advantages provided by existing large-scale studies is the provision of systematic samples from which to select participants for qualitative study. He gave an account of his attempts to link a qualitative study carried out in the 1990s of growing up in stepfamilies to a birth cohort study (the National Child Development Study), whose participants were born in 1958. Thompson and his colleagues secured a sample of 50 men and women with whom to carry out life story interviews (Gorell Barnes, Thompson, Daniel, & Burchardt, 1997). They specified the criterion that selected respondents from the cohort study should have become stepfamily members between the ages of 7 and 16. Thompson noted that the respondents "had never, over 30 years, been given the chance to tell their own life stories" (Thompson, 2004, p. 249) but that most valued the opportunity to do so. Moreover, Thompson noted that participation in life stories increased participants' cooperation in the next wave of the cohort study, a fact he found reassuring, given the reluctance he encountered among some "guardians" of these large-scale data sets to allow access to other research terms, usually on the grounds that this would jeopardize future response rates.

Significantly, Thompson and his colleagues found that 10 out of the 50 sample members had been classified in the contemporaneous cohort data differently compared with their retrospective life story interview accounts; most had been stepfamily members well before the age of 7 (Gorell Barnes et al., 1997). In order to delve into the reasons for these discrepancies, the research team sought access to the original paper questionnaires but found they no longer existed. Thompson reflected on the importance of the historical context and of the significance of time perspectives on differences between retrospective and contemporaneous biographical data. He also considered who was missing from the quantitative study in terms of the selective effects of taking part in a longitudinal study. He suggested that this latter factor had particular relevance for the research focus on stepfamilies: "Could it be that in order to maintain membership of a longitudinal study . . . you have to have a stable and coherent life?" (Thompson, 2004, p. 251). If this is so, then this reinforces the case for qualitative studies to be linked to national cohorts and longitudinal quantitative studies; in terms of using these both as sampling frames and as a strategy to interrogate these samples by targeting nonparticipants and those who are likely to drop out of such long-term studies.

In the studies by Laub and Sampson (1998), as well as those by Gorell Barnes

and colleagues (1997), qualitative and quantitative biographical data were linked in a mixed methods design. Yet both these examples were studies that were conducted by different teams, at different times, and for different purposes. The benefits of the linkage included the opportunity to pose new critical and theoretically interesting questions to the existing quantitative longitudinal data—the strategy of initiation as defined by Greene and colleagues (1989)—questions, for example, about under what research conditions and historical or life course moments certain life events such as becoming a stepfamily are likely to be or not be reported. A second benefit is that of "completing the picture" or complementarity; by using retrospective biographical interviews, respondents are allowed to interpret their own lives.

INTEGRATION ACROSS METHODS

Particular kinds of research demand multiple data sources. Cross-national research, especially multicountry studies, are a case in point and involve highly explicit research designs.[12] These cross-national research studies typically require researchers to bring into the frame wider policy contexts, existing national and international social trend data, and data about individuals in local and family contexts. Methodological texts give surprisingly little attention to this issue. Indeed, only when the issue of working across different countries is addressed does contextualization come to be seen as a matter deserving special attention (Hantrais, 1999).

A research design for a seven-country cross-national study in which we were both involved used biographical methods, among a range of other methods. Carried out in 2002–05 (Lewis, Brannen, & Nilsen, 2009), it sought to examine the experiences of working parents with young children from their own perspectives and to make sense of their lives in relation to a number of layers of social context: public policies, global economic forces, and the workplaces of parents and their families and communities. The design involved mapping and analyzing public policies and social and economic trend data, carrying out case studies of the organizations in which parents were employed (in a finance company and a social services department in each country), and employing focus groups and biographical interview methods with parents. A variety of data, including documentary data, was collected about parents' workplaces, and interviews with managers at different levels were conducted.

The project's design is an example of an *embedded case study* in which different methods and types of data are integrated. The countries, workplaces, and parents were selected from larger (linked) wholes (Yin, 2003), while clear theoretical rationales were given for the choice of cases at all the contextual levels and in the different phases of the research process; for cases must be "cases of something" (Brannen, Nilsen, & Lewis, 2009; Nilsen & Brannen, 2005). The countries and organizations were selected on the basis of principles of both similarity and difference.

The benefits of adopting this design in relation to the different contextual layers became evident in the analysis of the interview and focus group data with parents. In making sense of the material based on the primary data, especially that written up by the other national teams, we found that the wider context was often missing (Nilsen & Brannen, 2005). To facilitate interpretation, each national team was paired and exchanged drafts of national reports of the organizational case studies and the individual parent case studies, which had been written in English. Each team was asked to report back on these in relation to particular research questions. This meant that the corresponding team had to supply the missing context to help the other team make sense of the data. The eyes of those who stand outside a society are indeed helpful in making manifest what an insider takes as given.

INTEGRATION WITHIN METHODS

The biographic-interpretive method is an example of a method in which the contextual and interpretive data are integrated within *a single research method* (the interview) and are separated in the analysis (Wengraf, 2001). The contextual and interpretive data are then brought together again in the final interpretation. Similar to the approaches to biographical material of Kohli (1981), Nilsen (1996), and others, the biographic-interpretive method is sensitive both to the "told story" (the biographical account), the chronology of the life course, and the historical context of the "lived life" (life histories). The method is justified, however, not in terms of providing contextual understanding for the interpretations that informants themselves provide on their lives. Instead, the rationale is about increasing the explanatory potential of the study by ruling out competing hypotheses and explanations for the individual's life trajectory and the agency of the individual in directing it. This is done through setting up a panel the members of which engage in a close sequential analysis both of the life course sequence and "facts" of the person's life and of the unfolding textual account of the "life story."[13]

Brannen and colleagues employed the biographic-interpretive interview with some adaptations in their study of four-generation families, which examined the ways in which work and care were interwoven in the lives of families and their members across the generations (Brannen, Moss, & Mooney, 2004). They interviewed between five and eight members of 12 families (71 individuals), parents of a young child (under 7), grandparents, and great grandparents.[14] Quoting Thompson (1975) from the study *The Edwardians*, they argued that it was important to look closely at the actions and meanings of individuals that underpinned the grander picture that historians and sociologists created from statistical sources and the documentation of "facts." The full biographic-interpretive method of analysis was not adopted in this study. In analytically distinguishing life course phases and historical change, they found that few research participants referred to the external historical context; that is, they did not stray from the boundaries of their own family and personal lives. Their interpretive accounts, moreover, reflected contemporary normative discourses rather than those of the times in which their life events had occurred. To recreate the historical context, historical knowledge about the relevant periods (the interwar and immediate postwar period, in particular) was brought to bear in the analysis of each interview through the use of historical time lines; this process also was facilitated by the fact that two members of the team were historians by disciplinary origin. Making the links between biography, family generations, and historical time was highly demanding, encompassing as it did the lives of families across the 20th century.

Another example of "integration within methods" is one particular phase of a study in which interviews were combined with life lines. Life lines are graphs where important factual events and phases in an informant's life course are portrayed chronologically in relation to age and historical time. In some studies, such life lines are created with the interviewees after the interview; in other instances, the information is derived from the interview and graphs are drawn by the researcher at a later point (Nilsen, 1994). In the cross-national study (Brannen et al., 2009) that we earlier referred to as an example of "integration across methods," life lines based on the biographical material also were used. They were a valuable resource in comparing cases and contexts cross-nationally. Teams discussed individual life lines relating to the participating countries. In order to elicit similarities and differences and the reasons for these, it was necessary

to draw out the relevant national historical contexts and their institutional specificities in relation to the life course phases and turning points of the interviewees. Researchers native to a country thus came to realize that much of their knowledge about their own national context was taken for granted and implicit; the occasion for interpreting life lines with colleagues without such insider understanding served to make explicit the layers of context that were relevant to understanding the lives of the interviewees (Nilsen & Brannen, 2005). This is an example of a study in which "integration within methods" took place at a particular phase, while as a whole the study can be categorized as an example of "integration across methods."

◆ Conclusions

In this chapter, we have described key developments in and different varieties of biographical research with particular reference to sociology. We have demonstrated that the practice of mixing methods in this type of research has a long history. However, biographical studies have placed emphasis to different degrees on the use of more than one method and data source. Moreover, even those who have used more than one source of data or method have rarely been explicit about issues of method mixing and data integration, and have only recently begun to consider how different methods can contribute to the processes of analysis and interpretation. In some respects, this story is very much the same as for other combinations of methods. Indeed the creation of a clear methodological field of mixed methods research is a recent development that has occurred over the past 15 years.

We began the chapter with a discussion about *The Polish Peasant in Europe and America,* and the study's use of "human documents" (interviews, letters, diaries, public records, and so on). Such practices raised concern at that time because they challenged the very notions of what data and methods in sociology should constitute. In the period between 1930 and 1970, biographical material was largely collected in quantifiable form and based on large samples through the use of surveys and public records. Interviews were regarded as background information only; they were not considered "scientific" (reliable) enough, and thus were used for insights and illustrative purposes despite the systematic basis on which they were often collected. In the late 1970s, there was a revival of biographical methods within sociology. From that time, a whole range of approaches and methods has developed within biographical research. A few approaches have explicitly addressed the issue of mixing methods and integrating different types of data. Others have continued to adopt the more traditional strategy of prioritizing one primary data source and using the research literature and knowledge of the wider context in implicit and often selective or random ways.

As for the future, biographical research (and qualitative research in general) is likely to remain popular in stable societies such as the United Kingdom and Norway (our own countries) because of the importance placed by government on self-regulating citizens and a concern with subjectivities (Alasuutari, Brannen, & Bickman, 2008). It also will continue to be of relevance in societies undergoing rapid change (see the European Sociological Association Network on biographical research). There are a number of developments that lead us to suppose that biographical methods will be an important part of social science research methods in the future not only as a solo method, but also as an important part of a mixed method research strategy. The methods of biographical research are likely to have a particular appeal within the growing field of participatory research which, as the *Handbook* testifies, is an important stimulus for mixed method research (see the chapter by Mertens, 2003, in the *Handbook of Mixed Methods in Social and Behavioral Research*). Another trend suggestive of their increasing importance is the growth in social science training in hypermedia technologies. Yet another is the rising cost of collecting new data and the constraints of ethics committees and procedures. These constraints will mean that new researchers might need to draw on data archives for their material. As archived material grows and becomes more available, and as "e-social science" makes data linkage easier, so the value of biographical material is likely to rise, especially when it can be used in combination with other existing data sources. Finally, as more research funding is devoted to birth cohort studies and very large-scale household panel studies, so the demand for more nuanced forms of explanation will grow.[15] We may indeed see a return to the ambitious aims of some of the classic biographical studies, namely to link qualitative methods to quantitative longitudinal and cohort studies. Such developments and the issues of making explicit the ways of mixing methods and integrating different types of data are addressed, were they to take place, would indeed constitute significant methodological progress.

Research Questions and Exercises

1. What would a biographical approach add to a mixed method study?

2. What biographical method might you employ in your current study?

3. What are the characteristics and aspirations of the stance of pragmatism for the use of biographical methods within mixed methods inquiry?

4. What ontological, epistemological, and theoretical issues might you need to consider in employing a biographical approach in a mixed methods study?

5. How might you analyze the biographical data?

6. How would you go about integrating biographical analysis with other types of data?

7. How might you write up and present such a study?

8. How might the field of mixed methods inquiry be enhanced by the use of biographical methods?

◆ Notes

1. Since we are sociologists, the focus of the chapter is primarily from this perspective. Bertaux (1981), another sociologist, includes two types of biographical accounts: a "life story" told by a person in an interview about his or her own life and a "life history" which is both the person's story but with additional data based upon records and accounts of other informants (Bertaux, 1981, pp. 7–9).

2. The University of Chicago was the first to establish a department of sociology in 1892 with Albion Small as the first chair of department. Chicago was also the first to establish a journal of sociology, *The American Journal of Sociology* (1895).

3. Jane Addams was awarded the Nobel Peace Prize in 1931.

4. Hull House grew in size and scope and became an important inspiration for similar charities across America. The founders, however, were inspired by Toynbee Hall (1885) in London.

5. G. H. Mead defined his approach to sociological studies as "social behaviorism" in contrast to Watson's "behaviorism" which was a very influential school of thought in the early 20th century. Blumer, although much inspired by Mead, did not share his ontological and epistemological viewpoints, however (Lewis & Smith, 1980).

6. This method can be traced as one of the inspirations for grounded theory as formulated by Glaser and Strauss in their 1967 book (Platt, 1996).

7. The title of the thesis was *A Sociological Account of Pragmatism: An Essay on the Sociology of Knowledge*. It was edited by Horowitz and published posthumously in 1966.

8. Glueck and Glueck (1930; *Five Hundred Criminal Careers*) was based on a longitudinal study where a group of inmates was followed from 1911 to 1922, during imprisonment and five years after their release.

9. Mothers were interviewed in 1932, 1934, and 1936; questionnaires were given to children in junior and senior high school (seven times in the period 1932 to 1938); and staff in the schools were required to complete ratings of children's behavior. Fathers were not interviewed. Children filled in questionnaires. Questions were mostly concerned with psychological topics such as attitudes, emotional climate in the home, parent–child relations, and so on. In 1941 and 1948, the sample was contacted again with questions about occupational activity. In 1953–54, the sample of children was interviewed and given physical and psychological assessments. A follow-up in 1957–58 involved biographical interviews with focus on recollections of childhood and adolescence. The last major follow-up was an extensive questionnaire in 1964. Of the whole sample, 76 women and 69 men answered at least one of these follow-ups.

10. *Biography & Society Newsletter*, December 1996 and December 1997.

11. Fritz Schutze, who was writing in Germany in the 1980s and who was greatly influenced by the Chicago School, is usually credited with the development of the biographical interpretive method, later to be refined by Fischer-Rosenthal and Rosenthal (1997) and later in Britain by Tom Wengraf and Prue Chamberlayne (Chamberlayne, Bornat, & Wengraf, 2000).

12. In European Union–funded Framework Programme research, every stage of the research process is broken down into what are known as work packages in which different teams take on responsibilities for leading and carrying out particular tasks.

13. Counterhypothesizing is crucial for enabling the researcher to move beyond their own intuition and common sense and thereby expand the sociological imagination (Wengraf, 2001, p. 258).

14. Interviews were in three parts. In the first part, interviewees were invited to give an account of their lives, with a minimum of guidance and intervention from the interviewer. Encouraged to begin their story where they chose and to use their own words, the interviewees were provided with an opportunity to present their own gestalt (Wengraf, 2001). Some gave stories that lasted more than an hour with no break; others' narratives lasted only minutes. In the second part of the interview, the interviewer invited the respondent to elaborate the initial narrative in relation to salient events or experiences that had figured in it. Finally, using a more traditional semistructured style of interview, the interviewer asked additional questions relating to the specific foci of the study. Depending on interviewees' responses in the first two parts, this could be lengthy or short.

15. In the United Kingdom, the Economic and Social Research Council has recently launched a new national household panel study of 40,000 households, and is proposing to set up a further national birth cohort. In Norway and other Scandinavian countries, it is possible for researchers who have permission to link longitudinal information on individuals from a number of public records.

◆ References

Alasuutari, A., Brannen, J., & Bickman, L. (2008). Introduction. In P. Alasuutari, J. Brannen, & L. Bickman (Eds.) *Handbook of social research* (pp. 1–8). London: Sage.

Bertaux, D. (Ed.) (1981). *Biography and society: The life history approach in the social sciences*. London: Sage.

Bertaux, D. (1990). Oral history approaches to an international social movement. In E. Øyen (Ed.), *Comparative methodology* (pp. 158–170). London: Sage.

Bertaux, D. (1996). A Response to Thierry Kochuyt's "Biographical and empiricist illusions: A reply to recent criticisms." *Biography and Society Newsletter*, (December), 2–6.

Bertaux, D. (2003). On the usefulness of life stories for a realist and meaningful sociology. In R. Humphrey, R. Miller, & E. Zdravomyslova (Eds.), *Biographical research in Eastern Europe: Altered lives and broken biographies* (pp. 39–51). Aldershot, UK: Ashgate.

Bertaux, D., & Kohli, M. (1984). The life history approach: A continental view. *Annual Review of Sociology, 10*, 215–37.

Bertaux, D., & Thompson, P. (1997). Introduction. In D. Bertaux & P. Thompson (Eds.), *Pathways to social class: A qualitative approach to social mobility* (pp. 1–31). Oxford, UK: Clarendon Press.

Blumer, H. (1954). What is wrong with social theory? *American Sociological Review, 19*, 3–10.

Blumer, H. (1979). *Critiques of research in the social sciences: An appraisal of Thomas and Znaniecki's* The Polish Peasant in Europe and America. New Brunswick, NJ: Transaction Books.

Bornat, J. (2008). Biographical methods. In A. Alasuutari, J, Brannen, & L. Bickman (Eds.), *Handbook of Social Research* (pp. 344–357). London: Sage.

Brannen, J. (1992). *Mixing methods: Qualitative and quantitative research*. Aldershot, UK: Ashgate.

Brannen, J. (2004). Working qualitatively and quantitatively. In C. Seale, G. Gobo, J.F. Gubrium, & D. Silverman (Eds.), *Qualitative Research Practice* (pp. 312–327). London: Sage.

Brannen, J., Moss, P., & Mooney, A. (2004) *Working and caring over the twentieth century: Change and continuity in four-generation families*. ESRC Future of Work Series, Basingstoke, UK: Palgrave Macmillan.

Brannen, J., Nilsen, A., & Lewis, S. (2009). Research design and methods: Doing comparative cross-national research. In S. Lewis, J. Brannen, & A. Nilsen (Eds.), *Work, family and organisations in transition: A European perspective* (pp. 17–30). Bristol, UK: Policy Press.

Chamberlayne, P., Bornat, J., & Wengraf, T. (2000). (Eds.). *The turn to biographical methods in the social sciences: Comparative issues and examples*. London: Routledge.

Cresswell, J. W. (2003). *Research design: Qualitative, quantitative, and mixed method approaches*. Thousand Oaks, CA: Sage.

Denzin, N. (1989). *Interpretive biography*. Qualitative Research Methods Series 17. London: Sage.

Elder, G. (1999). *Children of the Great Depression. Social change in life experience*. Oxford, UK: Westview Press. (Originally published in 1974)

Elliott, J. (2005) *Using narrative in social research: Qualitative and quantitative approaches*. London: Sage.

Ferrarotti, F. (1981). On the autonomy of the biographical method. In D. Bertaux (Ed.), *Biography and society: The life history approach in the social sciences* (pp. 19–28). London: Sage.

Fischer-Rosenthal, W., & Rosenthal, G. (1997). Daniel Bertaux's complaint or against false dichotomies in biographical research. *Biography and Society Newsletter*, (December), 5–11.

Giele, J., & Elder, G. (1998). Life course research: Development of a field. In J. Giele & G. Elder (Eds.), *Methods of life course research: Qualitative and quantitative approaches* (pp. 5–27). London: Sage.

Glueck, S., & Glueck, E. (1930). *Five hundred criminal careers*. New York: Alfred A. Knopf.

Glueck, S., & Glueck, E. (1943). *Criminal careers in retrospect*. New York: The Commonwealth Fund.

Glueck, S., & Glueck, E. (1950). *Unravelling juvenile delinquency*. New York: The Commonwealth Fund.

Gorell Barnes, G., Thompson, P., Daniel, G., & Burchardt, N. (1997). *Growing up in step-families*. Oxford, UK: Oxford University Press.

Greene, J. Caracelli, V. J., & Graham, W. F. (1989). Towards a conceptual framework for mixed-method evaluation designs. *Education, Evaluation and Policy Analysis*, 11(3), 255–274.

Hantrais, L. (1999). Contextualisation in cross national comparative research. *International Journal of Social Research. Methodology*, 2, 93–108.

Hareven, T. (1978). Introduction: The historical study of the life course. In T. Hareven (Ed.), *Transitions: The family and the life course in historical perspective* (pp. 1–16). New York: Academic.

Hareven, T. (1982). *Family time and industrial time: The relationship between the family and work in a New England industrial community*. Cambridge, UK: Cambridge University Press.

Kaplan, A. (1964). *The conduct of enquiry: Methodology for behavioral science*. San Francisco: Chandler.

Kohli, M. (1981). Biography: Account, text, method. In D. Bertaux (Ed.), *Biography and society: The life history approach in the social sciences* (pp. 61–75). London: Sage.

Laub, J., & Sampson, R. (1993). Turning points in the life course: Why change matters to the study of crime. *Criminology*, 31, 301–325.

Laub, J., & Sampson, R. (1998). Integrating quantitative and qualitative data. In J. Giele & G. Elder (Eds.), *Methods of life course research* (pp. 213–230). Thousand Oaks, CA: Sage.

Layder, D. (1998). *Sociological practice: Linking theory and social research*. London: Sage.

Lewis, S., Brannen, J., & Nilsen, A. (2009). (Eds.) *Work, family and organisations in transition: A European perspective*. Bristol, UK: Policy Press.

Lewis, D., & Smith, R. (1980). *American sociology and pragmatism: Mead, Chicago sociology and symbolic interaction*. Chicago: University of Chicago Press.

Mertens, D. (2003). Mixed methods and the politics of social research: The transformative-emancipatory perspective. In A. Tashakorri & C. Teddlie (Eds.), *Handbook of mixed methods in social & behavioral research* (pp. 135–164). Thousand Oaks, CA: Sage.

Miller, R. L. (2000). *Researching life stories and family histories*. London: Sage.

Mills, C. Wright. (1939). Language, logic and culture. *American Sociological Review* 4(5), 670–680.

Mills, C. Wright. (1940a). Methodological consequences of the sociology of knowledge. *American Journal of Sociology* (3), 316–330.

Mills, C. Wright. (1940b). Situation actions and vocabularies of motive. *American Sociological Review* 5(6), 904–913.

Mills, C. Wright. (1963). IBM plus reality plus humanism = sociology. In I. L. Horowitz (Ed.), *Power, politics and people: The collected essays of C. Wright Mills* (pp. 568–576). Oxford, UK: Oxford University Press. (Originally published in 1954)

Mills, C. Wright. (1966). *Sociology and pragmatism: Higher learning in America.* New York: Oxford University Press.

Mills, C. Wright. (1980). *The sociological imagination.* London: Penguin Books. (Originally published in 1959)

Nilsen, A. (1994). Life lines—A methodological approach. In G. Bjerren & I. Elgqvist-Saltzman (Eds.), *Gender and education in a life perspective: Lessons from Scandinavia* (pp. 101–115). Avebury, UK: Ashgate.

Nilsen, A. (1996). Stories of life—stories of living: Women's narratives and feminist biography. *NORA, Nordic Journal of Women's Studies, 4*(1), 16–30.

Nilsen, A. (2008). From questions of methods to epistemological issues: The case of biographical research. In P. Alasuutari, J. L. Bickman, J. Brannen (Eds.), *Handbook of Social Research* (pp. 81–95). London: Sage.

Nilsen, A., & Brannen, J. (2005). Interview study consolidated report. Research Report # 8 Manchester Metropolitan University, Research Institute for Health and Social Change, Manchester, UK.

Platt, J. (1996). *A history of sociological research methods in America, 1920–1960.* Cambridge, UK: Cambridge University Press.

Plummer, K. (2001). *Documents of life 2. An invitation to a critical humanism.* London: Sage.

Riley, M. (1987). On the significance of age in sociology. In M. Riley, B. Huber, & B. Hess (Eds.), *Social structures and human lives* (pp. 24–46). London: Sage.

Roberts, B. (2002). *Biographical research.* Buckingham, UK: Open University Press.

Roos, J. P. (1997). Context, authenticity, referentiality, reflexivity: Back to basics in autobiography. In V. Voronov & E. Zdravomyslova (Eds.), *Biographical perspectives on postsocialist societies* (pp. 27–38). St. Petersburg, Russia: Center for Independent Research.

Ryder, N. (1965). The cohort as a concept of social change. *American Sociological Review, 30,* 843–861.

Sampson, R., & Laub, J. (1997) *Crime in the making: Pathways and turning points through life.* Cambridge, MA: Harvard University Press.

Strauss, A., & Glaser, B. (1977). *Anguish. A case history of a dying trajectory.* Oxford, UK: Martin Robertson.

Tashakorri, A., & Teddlie, C. (1998) Introduction to mixed method and mixed model studies in the social and behavioral sciences. In *Mixed methodology: Combining qualitative and quantitative methods* (pp. 3–13). Thousand Oaks, CA: Sage.

Thomas, W. I., & Znaniecki, F. (1958). *The Polish Peasant in Europe and America,* Vol. 1–2. New York: Dover. (Originally published in 1918–1920)

Thompson, P. (1975). *The Edwardians: The remaking of British society.* London: Weidenfeld and Nicolson.

Thompson, P. (1978). *The voice of the past: Oral history.* Oxford, UK: Oxford University Press.

Thompson, P. (1981). Life histories and the analysis of social change. In Bertaux, D. (Ed.), *Biography and society: The life history approach in the social sciences* (pp. 289–306). London: Sage.

Thompson, P. (2004). Researching family and social mobility with two eyes: Some experiences of the interaction between qualitative and quantitative data. *International Journal of Social Research Methodology, 7*(3), 237–259.

Wengraf, T. (2001). *Qualitative research interviewing.* London: Sage.

Yin, R. K. (2003). *Case study research: Design and methods* (3rd ed.) London: Sage.

Znaniecki, F. (1934). *The method of sociology.* New York: Farrar and Rinehart.

27

THE CONTRIBUTION OF MIXED METHODS TO RECENT RESEARCH ON EDUCATIONAL EFFECTIVENESS

◆ Pamela Sammons

Objectives

This chapter seeks to

- examine the potential of mixed methods (MM) designs for the further advancement of educational effectiveness research (EER);

- highlight some of the limitations associated with the paradigmatic divide that has arisen through EER's reliance on largely quantitative (QUAN) methodologies and the postpositivist paradigm, and the largely qualitative (QUAL) methodologies and interpretivist perspectives of those engaged in school improvement (SI) research;

- provide illustrations of the way MM approaches can be used to study complex social phenomena in the social sciences using recent examples of large-scale, longitudinal studies conducted in the EER field; and

- discuss the way QUAN and QUAL data can be analyzed and integrated during the process of research so that new, synergistic understandings can emerge that extend the findings and interpretations that can be achieved from reliance on only one methodological perspective.

◆ Introduction

Teddlie and Sammons (2010) argue that mixed methods (MM) research has emerged as an alternative to the dichotomy of the qualitative (QUAL) and quantitative (QUAN) traditions in the social and behavioral sciences (e.g., Brannen, 1992; Bryman, 1988; Creswell, 1994; Tashakkori & Teddlie, 1998, 2003), and they outline the potential of MM studies to enhance educational effectiveness research (EER). This chapter will discuss the limitations of EER's traditional reliance on studies largely conducted within a single research paradigm and the way MM research can facilitate and enrich the study of EER topics such as school effectiveness (SER), teacher effectiveness (TER), and school improvement (SI).

The first two of the three research examples that will be used to illustrate MM designs in EER in this chapter are associate projects in a recent major educational research program conducted in England. This was called the Teaching and Learning Research Program, a government-funded initiative intended to promote and disseminate educational research that was designed to contribute to the development of evidence-informed policy and practice in different phases of education (for details, see http://www.tlrp.org). The third example was chosen to explore in more depth approaches to the analysis and integration of QUAN and QUAL data adopted in an innovative MM study of successful schools in high-disadvantage contexts in Canada.

The first two of the exemplar studies were conducted by different research teams in which the author was one of several principal investigators, each of whom had different areas of research expertise and experience. The teams adopted MM designs to better address research questions that sought to investigate topics such as preschool influences on children's developmental outcomes, variations in primary teachers' classroom practice, and school and teacher effectiveness; and to

provide robust research evidence and interpretations based on the integration and synthesis of findings drawn from large-scale statistical analyses and those from more detailed case studies of individual institutions or of individual teachers. The teams were of the view that MM designs offered the prospect of providing a richer evidence base and were therefore likely to prove more fruitful in promoting new understandings and contributions to knowledge that would inform policy and practice than would studies relying on approaches from only one research paradigm. The studies involved the combination of statistical prediction and explanation of variation in, for example, children's educational outcomes and the modeling of how these have changed over time, with other case study data including QUAN and QUAL observations of children and teachers, and successive in-depth interviews that provided rich descriptions of practice and explored teachers' perceptions and understandings of their work and identities.

This chapter summarizes and discusses the research designs in the Effective Provision of Pre-school Education (EPPE) project (Sammons et al., 2005; Siraj-Blatchford, Sammons, Sylva, Melhuish, & Taggart, 2006), and in the Variations in Teachers' Work, Lives and Their Effects on Students (VITAE) study (Sammons et al., 2007; Day, Sammons, & Gu, 2008). It focuses on the processes by which two different MM teams worked to enable ongoing dialogue between QUAN and QUAL approaches, including discussion of instruments and data collection, and the integration of analyses and findings over time. The examples show how the different strands of research informed each other in a reciprocal way that may be termed *dialectical*, and the chapter explores how such ways of working helped promote increased interplay in the interpretation of findings to create *synergistic understanding*.

Comparisons also are made with other recent accounts of integrative approaches to MM designs and data analytic strategies in other contexts in the educational effectiveness field (with a special focus on a study of school improvement in difficult circumstances by Jang, McDougall, Pollon, Herbert, & Russell, 2008). In addition, the implications for further development of MM approaches to enquiry and data analysis in EER are discussed.

◆ The Potential of Mixed Methods Studies in Educational Effectiveness Research

Teddlie and Sammons (2010) argue that the flexibility of MM research in simultaneously addressing multiple and diverse research questions through integrated QUAL and QUAN techniques is one of its attractions. They note the growing popularity of MM design despite its fairly late arrival as a third paradigm, citing the phrase "Numbers and a Story" (Spalter-Roth, 2000) to illustrate the appeal of MM research, because the combination of both general statistical findings and thick descriptions of specific cases exemplifying those findings has the potential to generate new insights and increase understanding of EER topics that neither can achieve alone. It is the generation of new knowledge that goes beyond the sum of the individual QUAL and QUAN components that allows MM research to add "extra value" to research studies seeking to better describe, predict, and understand social phenomena, such as the variation in and contributors to differences in educational effectiveness. The integration and synthesis of QUAL and QUAN evidence can foster mutual illumination, and so have the potential to enable the development and testing of additional hypotheses leading to what may be termed new synergistic understandings that add to the explanatory power of MM research. It is argued that MM studies have great potential for the testing and development of EER theories and are also necessary to

inform and support closer links with applied research and evaluations that can promote evidence-based SI initiatives and teacher development programs.

In their contribution to a new book on methodological advances in EER, Teddlie and Sammons (2010) note that much SER and SI research has suffered from the false dichotomy that has arisen between QUAL and QUAN approaches that reflects the legacy of the so-called paradigm wars in social research evident during the past 30 years. This led to the QUAN paradigm becoming primarily associated with larger-scale EER investigations that seek to identify and measure differences in school or teacher effectiveness, and with the statistical prediction and explanation of variance in student outcomes (Sammons, 1996; Scheerens & Bosker, 1997). This also has led to a focus on the development and QUAN testing of theoretical models that seek to account for such variations in educational effectiveness (Creemers & Kyriakides, 2008). By contrast, the QUAL paradigm has mostly been used in SI and teacher development studies and is associated with case studies, action research, and interpretivist approaches to enquiry in SER. Here the focus has been on generating "thick" descriptions and on understanding school and classroom processes and participants' perspectives with limited attention given to investigating the impact of processes on student outcomes.

Statistical criticisms of early examples of SER, such as the classic secondary school study *Fifteen Thousand Hours* in England (Rutter, Maughan, Mortimore, & Ouston, 1979), led to a strong focus on methodological and statistical issues and the use of large samples and more powerful analyses in subsequent EER studies (Sammons, 2006; Sammons & Luyten, 2009). This was greatly facilitated by the development of appropriate multilevel modeling techniques for the study of clustered data that recognized the hierarchical (or nested) structure of much social science data (Bryk &

Raudenbush, 1992; Goldstein, 1995). Studies of student outcomes and school and teacher effects require approaches that recognize the statistical implications associated with the clustering of students in classes, and of classes within schools and other higher-level units such as school boards, local education authorities, or neighborhoods. Over the past quarter century or so, EER has developed increasingly sophisticated approaches for the identification and measurement of the size of teacher and school effects, and the correlates of effective schools (Creemers & Kyriakides, 2008; Scheerens & Bosker, 1997; Teddlie & Reynolds, 2000). It has drawn attention to the importance of contextual influences, cross-level interactions, the study of differential effectiveness, and the use of more complex cross-classified multilevel models to study the continuity of effects across phases, such as primary to secondary school (Goldstein & Sammons, 1997; Leckie, 2009; Teddlie & Reynolds, 2000). Such models also have proved important in developing and testing educational effectiveness theories (Creemers & Kyriakides, 2008).

In contrast to EER, much work in the SI tradition has adopted a largely QUAL focus, involving case studies of particular institutions, such as improving or "turnaround schools" and others that can be viewed as more effective despite disadvantaged contexts. Such research has sought to stimulate and study the processes of change and to explore the perceptions and experiences of participants. SI research has generally paid less attention to the study of student outcomes than has EER (Reynolds & Teddlie, 2000). Several different approaches to promoting SI have been identified as relevant for schools, depending on their organizational history and current performance level (Harris, 2002). Examples of voluntary SI programs include the Improving the Quality of Education for All (IQEA) project (Hopkins & Harris, 1997) and the High Reliability Schools Project (Stringfield, Reynolds, &

Schaffer, 2008). There have been a growing number of evaluations of the impact of various school reform or improvement programs in the United States that have examined the effects on student outcomes (Borman, Hewes, Overman, & Brown, 2003), but these have largely been conducted using QUAN rather than QUAL perspectives and often involve the use of quasi-experimental approaches, including randomized controlled trials.

In order to achieve mutual illumination, such MM studies must be designed to ensure that different phases of QUAN and QUAL data collection and analysis can feed into each other in a productive way that enhances both. They should integrate findings and interpretations to enable metainferences that go beyond and enrich the QUAN and QUAL results considered in isolation. In this way, emerging findings from QUAL interviews, for example, may be used to help shape the topics covered in a largerscale QUAN survey. Following analysis, the survey results may feed into a second round of follow-up interviews in a sequential, iterative cycle. The identification of outlier schools or teachers that are classified as more effective—or, by contrast, less effective—and those that are broadly typical in their effectiveness based on QUAN analyses of student outcomes may be used to help identify a purposive case study sample of schools or teachers for later in-depth investigation using largely QUAL approaches. These case studies, in turn, may suggest additional questions or hypotheses that can be further tested in subsequent analyses using the larger QUAN data sets.

This "to and fro" process of MM research (using inductive and deductive reasoning for ongoing theory generation and testing) represents a cyclical rather than linear approach to enquiry. It suggests that MM researchers are endeavoring to create deeper understandings of a topic rather than to formulate static, constant, linear "truths" or "laws" about a phenomenon; this is deemed more appropriate for the study of educational institutions and processes that are continuously subject to change and so are inherently dynamic in nature. Teddlie and Sammons (2010) suggest that, in general, EER has given too much emphasis to purely large-scale, QUAN methodologies, particularly those involving multilevel modeling approaches to study variations between schools, departments, or classes in the "value added" to student outcomes (Goldstein, 1995). While this has been necessary to enable the development of a sound evidence base on the appropriate measurement of variations in student outcomes and of differences in effectiveness, and to answer important questions concerning the size of school and teacher effects (Creemers & Kyriakides, 2008; Luyten & Sammons, forthcoming; Sammons & Luyten, 2009; Teddlie & Reynolds, 2000), it has led to a stronger focus on producing generalizations, rather than on fostering illumination and understanding of educational effectiveness of value to practitioners. In particular, there has been a focus on identifying the correlates of effectiveness, and on developing and testing models, such as the Comprehensive Model of Educational Effectiveness (Creemers, 1994), and the applicability or generalizability of teacher effectiveness characteristics. By contrast, SI and teacher development research has shown relatively limited interest in measuring the impact of such initiatives on student outcomes and has given a stronger focus on illuminating processes of change, the particularities of context, and institutional histories (Harris, 2002). Such evidence is likely to be of value to practitioners but less useful or usable to policymakers.

The need for greater integration of SER and SI approaches has been identified by a number of authors (Creemers & Reezigt, 1997; Sammons, 1999; Teddlie & Reynolds, 2000). It is argued that MM research is a third paradigm (Johnson & Onwuegbuzie, 2004) that is likely to become increasingly important in EER in the 21st century because it offers approaches that help to bridge the unhelpful QUAL versus QUAN paradigm divide that often separates the EER and SI research communities. In addition, it may encourage greater collaboration in future research studies.

Although much EER is largely situated within the postpositivist QUAN-oriented tradition, there are some examples of QUAL research in TER and SER, and a relatively small but growing number of studies that use MM designs (for example, Day et al., 2008; Day, Sammons, Stobart, Kington, & Gu, 2007; James, Connolly, Dunning, & Elliott, 2006; Jang et al., 2008; MacBeath & Mortimore, 2001; Mortimore, Sammons, Stoll, Lewis, & Ecob, 1988; Sammons, Thomas, & Mortimore, 1997; Teddlie & Stringfield, 1993). Teddlie and Sammons (2010) argue that it is valuable to consider some of the differences between postpositivism and pragmatism as research paradigms. They make comparisons of these approaches in terms of three dimensions seen to be especially relevant to the goal of designing better EER and SI research and evaluations.

1. Methods: Postpositivists utilize QUAN methods primarily, as opposed to pragmatists who utilize both QUAN and QUAL methods as appropriate, given the topic under study.

2. Logic: Postpositivists emphasize deductive logic, especially through the use of the hypothetico-deductive model, as opposed to pragmatists, who ascribe to the "to and fro" characteristic of the inductive/deductive research cycle.

3. The possibility of generalizations: Postpositivists sometimes make nomothetic statements (context- and time-free generalizations) under highly prescribed circumstances, while pragmatists are more inclined toward ideographic statements (specifically focusing on context- and time-bound generalizations).

Rather than maintaining the artificial QUAN versus QUAL opposition evident in the "paradigm wars" between postpositivist and postmodernist approaches, the pragmatic philosophical position underpinning most MM designs focuses on the value and fruitfulness of using evidence from both paradigms to address a broader range of research questions and produce more-robust and more-interesting findings than either approach could do in isolation. It is thus argued that MM research has greater potential to prove of value to both practitioners and the policymakers.

A range of typologies of MM designs can be identified (see Teddlie & Tashakkori, 2006, 2009). Of particular interest to EER and SI studies and evaluations are *multilevel mixed designs* that can be used to examine organizations that have a hierarchical structure such as schools and classrooms (Tashakkori & Teddlie, 1998). This fits well with the emphasis on multilevel modeling evident in much existing EER, because multilevel mixed designs focus on the consequences of clustering in data typical in educational settings and also allow for investigation of the impact of school and neighborhood context. Such multilevel MM designs extend the kinds of research questions that can be addressed via reliance on only the dominant QUAN tradition, particularly in relation to the influence of context. Tashakkori and Teddlie (2003) and Teddlie and Sammons (2010) suggest that *fully integrated mixed designs* are probably the most complete manifestation of MM research designs in which the mixing of the QUAL and QUAN approaches occurs in an interactive manner across all stages of a study.

The further development of EER and SI research is likely to require such multilevel and fully integrated MM designs. The particular teacher effectiveness and preschool research examples included as illustrations in this chapter can be seen to approximate to some extent such designs, although it is not claimed that they have fully achieved the extent of integration proposed in the idealized form outlined by Tashakkori and Teddlie (2003).

◆ Example 1: The Effective Provision of Preschool Education Study

The EPPE project is part of a major longitudinal study (1997–2014) funded by the Department for Children, Schools and Families (DCSF) in England. The study was originally designed to follow young children's development from age 3 to 7 years. Its initial focus was on studying preschool effects, but the research was later extended to follow up the same child sample to age 11, and later into secondary school, investigating outcomes at ages 14 and 16 years (Sylva, Melhuish, Sammons, Siraj-Blatchford, & Taggart, 2008). The original Phase 1 of the EPPE study is the first example of research into the effects of early years education and care to have applied a specific *educational effectiveness* design to investigate the impact of preschool on child outcomes (both cognitive and social behavioral). The questions EPPE sought to answer about "effective" ways to educate and care for young children are both contemporary and practical. The research team brought together researchers and approaches used in different and previously separate research traditions and areas of enquiry—early years, child care, and SER—in a multilevel MM design. This was intended to provide a rigorous analysis that could be presented with both QUAN breadth and QUAL depth to inform policymakers, who had commissioned the study, and practitioners working in early years settings, as well as to contribute to the further development of academic understanding of the influence of preschool on young children and to widen the scope of EER enquiry to the preschool phase (Sammons et al., 2008; Sammons et al., 2004; Siraj-Blatchford et al., 2006; Sylva, Taggart, Melhuish, Sammons, & Siraj-Blatchford, 2007).

Two decades ago, McCartney and Jordan (1990) suggested that the largely separate fields of enquiry (studies of child-care effects and studies of school effects) should be more closely aligned. The EPPE project sought to draw together these two distinct fields of enquiry to investigate the impact of preschool education and care on young children in England at the turn of the millennium. An MM design was judged most appropriate to facilitate this alignment. QUAN analysis was first applied to measure and identify the independent variables of most statistical significance in predicting (explaining in a statistical model) variations in the cognitive progress and social behavioral development of young children during their time in preschool from age 3 years plus to age 5 years at primary school entry, and to investigate the influence of preschools in accounting for variations in young children's progress and development during the preschool period. Multilevel value-added statistical analyses explored variations in the effectiveness of a large sample of 141 individual preschool centers in terms of a range of different child outcomes (Sammons et al., 2005). As well as investigating overall preschool effects, the QUAN phase identified a number of individual "outlier" preschool centers for further in-depth study. The research also undertook a series of QUAL enquiries that both extended and triangulated the explanatory analysis and simultaneously provided the illustrational and practical exemplar resources that were needed in the development of early years' educational practice. These built on the first QUAN analyses that provided evidence to identify centers that were more effective and that had revealed links between QUAN measures of preschool quality and better child outcomes. The subsequent QUAL case studies then sought to illuminate the link between quality and child outcomes and to use thick descriptions and grounded theory to better understand the concept of preschool quality and how it influences child outcomes (for example, via pedagogical practices such as sustained shared thinking).

Research into the effects of preschool education requires longitudinal designs that allow the separation of preschool influences from those related to the individual child's personal and family characteristics and that follow children's developmental trajectories across several years. It also needs to study a wide variety of children, including a range of groups of policy interest (e.g., disadvantaged children, those with special educational needs [SEN]). Such research also should seek to identify and illuminate the educational processes, including pedagogy, associated with positive educational effects on children, and so needs to sample from a wide range of different types of preschool providers and settings while studying individual centers and pedagogical processes in depth. When EPPE was designed, no such MM research had sought to investigate the impact of both types of provision and to identify individual preschool center effects on child outcomes using appropriate longitudinal data sets and a combination of QUAN and QUAL methodologies.

Figure 27.1 provides a simplified overview of the MM approach adopted for the first (preschool) phase of the research. Here the relationships between the QUAN (effectiveness and quality characteristics) and the QUAL (case study) components of the project are summarized. (For further details, see Sammons et al., 2005; Siraj-Blatchford et al., 2006; Siraj-Blatchford & Sylva, 2004). The diagram illustrates the analytical process that was followed in combining these two methodological components. Using the convention adopted by Tashakkori and Teddlie (2003), the rectangular blocks show the QUAN and the ovals show the QUAL stages in the process. The diagram highlights three parallel aspects of analysis: the effectiveness study, the identification of quality characteristics of preschools, and the selected case studies. By conducting two parallel QUAN phases of data collection to address the concepts of preschool effectiveness and quality and then adding a major linked QUAL component to address the concept of quality in

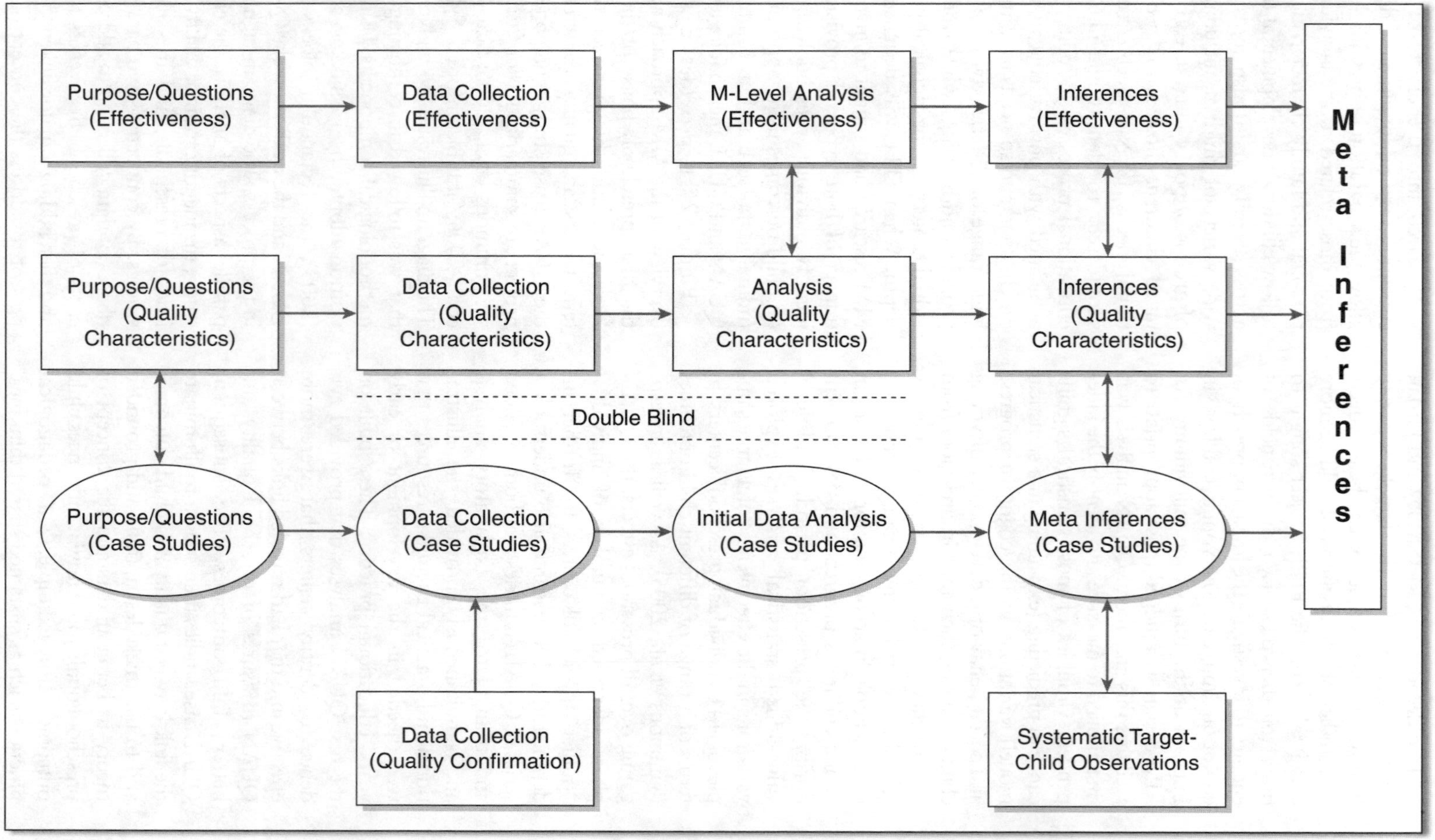

Figure 27.1 Illustration of the Overall Mixed Methods Design of the Effective Provision of Preschool Education Research

more depth via 12 case studies, the research was able to answer a more complex set of research questions about the nature of the influence of preschool on young children's progress and development. These questions cover whether preschool has a measurable impact, its strength, and the extent to which it continues to shape children's later educational trajectories in primary school. In addition, the research was intended to provide rich evidence on the processes by which preschool experiences influence children and, through the findings on and increased understanding of what features of pedagogy and quality predicted better child outcomes, allow the development of new guidance on good practice of value to practitioners.

THE QUANTITATIVE COMPONENT: IDENTIFYING PRESCHOOL EFFECTS

As noted above, EER designs explicitly seek to explore and model the impact of data hierarchies with clustered samples (e.g., where children or young people are grouped into schools or other institutions such as preschool centers). While SER has developed statistical models for the separation of intake and school influences on children's progress using so-called value-added multilevel models (Goldstein, 1995, 1998), at the time EPPE was designed such techniques had not been applied to the preschool sector.

EPPE represents the first large-scale longitudinal attempt to examine the impact of individual preschool centers in promoting different kinds of child outcomes (cognitive and social/behavioral) using value-added analyses (Sammons et al., 2004, 2008). The inclusion of a "home" sample recruited at primary school entry is another important feature because it enables further comparison of the impact of experiencing different types of preschool and different durations of time or quality of provision in a preschool center with a reference group that had no experience of such group care.

The progress and development of EPPE children were followed over 4 years until the children were 7 years old in Phase 1 of the research. Details about the number of sessions registered, duration in months of time in preschool, and attendance also were collected to enable the amount and duration of preschool center experience to be quantified.

Child Assessments

Four common points of assessment were used, tracking children from age 3 years plus to the end of Key Stage 1, so that the longer-term influence of preschool could be followed up to age 7 years (and beyond, in the later extensions to age 16 years). Both cognitive (language, prereading, early number concepts, and later reading and mathematics) and social behavioral outcomes (such as independence and concentration; peer sociability; cooperation and conformity; antisocial behavior; and so on) were assessed, providing a range of QUAN child outcome measures at different ages.

Child and Family Background Characteristics

In-depth parent interviews provided rich information about parents' education, occupation, employment history, and family structure; a very high (97%) response rate was achieved. Details about the child's daycare history and health problems, and parental involvement in educational activities or play (e.g., reading to child, teaching nursery rhymes, and so on), also were collected, and an indicator of the Home Learning Environment (HLE) created (Melhuish et al., 2008).

IDENTIFYING CENTER EFFECTS

The first EER phase of the study explored the impact of child, family, and home environment characteristics on young children's

Figure 27.2 Illustration of the Multilevel Analysis Strategy Used in the Quantitative Component of EPPE Used to Predict Student Outcomes at Different Time Points

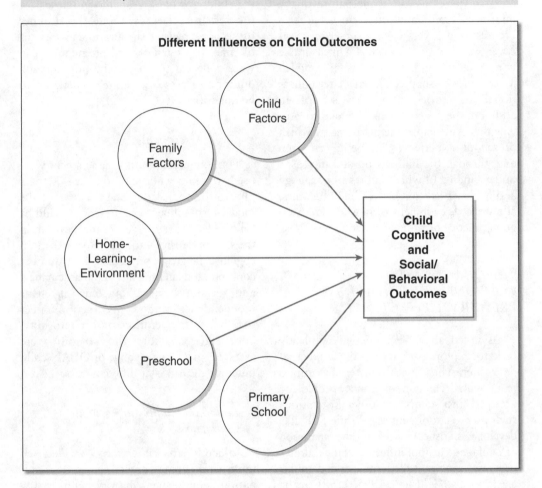

attainment and their social behavior measured at the start of the study age 3 years plus. The second phase focused on progress and development over the preschool period, controlling for children's baseline scores and background influences using multilevel statistical models. Figure 27.2 illustrates the QUAN analysis strategy for studying the influence of different factors (related to the five main groups of interest to the EPPE research) on child outcomes at different time points.

Residual estimates for the 141 individual preschool centers in the sample with associated confidence limits provided indicators of *relative effectiveness* for each center in promoting progress in different child outcome measures. Individual center residuals were classified into five effectiveness categories, ranging from significant positive outlier to significant negative outlier.

Table 27.1 illustrates two contrasting individual preschool center profiles for cognitive outcomes, one classified as broadly more effective in terms of positive outcomes (X) and one classified as broadly less effective (Y), based on the classification of preschool center residuals into five categories, as described above. Similar profiles

Table 27.1 Examples of Two Contrasting Value-Added Center Profiles for Cognitive Outcomes

Center Effectiveness Category	Prereading	Early Number Concepts	Language	Nonverbal Reasoning	Spatial Awareness & Reasoning
Significantly above expected (95% confidence limit)	X				
Above expected (68% confidence limit)			X	X	
As expected	Y	X			X Y
Below expected (68% confidence limit)		Y		Y	
Significantly below expected (95% confidence limit)			Y		

NOTE: **X** shows a typical broadly positive (more effective) individual center profile; **Y** shows a typical broadly negative (less effective) individual center profile.

were constructed for the children's social behavioral outcomes, and both sets of profiles were examined to select center case studies for in-depth investigation using both QUAL and additional QUAN approaches to collect and analyze data (Siraj-Blatchford & Sylva, 2004; Siraj-Blatchford et al., 2003).

QUALITY CHARACTERISTICS

Field officers made regular visits to all 141 centers, maintained notes, observed staff and children, and interviewed center directors. Information also was obtained from the Early Childhood Environment Rating Scale Revised and Extended (ECERS R & ECERS E) (Harms, Clifford, & Cryer, 1998; Sylva, Siraj-Blatchford, & Taggart, 2003). Statistically significant differences in quality measures at the center level within and between types of provider were revealed.

Initially, the multilevel QUAN analysis was conducted independent of, and prior to, the main case study phase to identify individual preschool center effects and to produce individual center profiles that could support the selection of effective and highly effective centers for in-depth study. The QUAN estimates of effectiveness were "qualitized" to create individual preschool center profiles as shown in Table 27.1 and to identify and define two groups of centers, one comprising those that were broadly effective or good at promoting positive child outcomes, and another comprising those that were classed as more effective or excellent, based on the profiles of QUAN results. The explicit link between the QUAL and QUAN through the choice of case study sample centers based on their "qualitized" effectiveness profiles enhanced the ability of the research to produce "meta inferences" based on the integration of findings.

THE QUALITATIVE METHODOLOGICAL COMPONENT: INVESTIGATING CENTER ORGANIZATION AND PEDAGOGICAL PROCESSES

The QUAN component fed into the QUAL in two ways. First, a systematic (although nonlinear) process of "iterative triangulation" characterized much of the general approach in applying the multilevel MM design. Apart from benefits of triangulation in achieving greater internal validity, the research team attempted to work "back and forth between inductive and deductive models of thinking" (Creswell, 1994, p. 178). The regular, weekly meetings of the central team and their varied research backgrounds facilitated this ongoing process of dialogue. Despite this commitment to collaborative practice, it was decided that the initial analysis of the 12 case study preschool centers should be conducted "blind" to avoid any possibility of (subconscious) analytic bias. Therefore, neither the principal QUAL investigator nor any other researcher engaged in the initial QUAL data collection and analysis knew the specific outcomes achieved by each of the 12 selected case study centers, nor did they know which were classed as effective or good and which were classified as highly effective or excellent centers.

CASE STUDIES

The overall aim of the case studies was to explore what helped to make some centers more successful at achieving better child outcomes in particular domains. The QUAL research sought to tease out specific pedagogical and other practices associated with achieving "excellent" outcomes as compared with "good" outcomes. The decision not to compare "excellent" with "poor" performance was intended to maximize the potential impact of the data for use in dissemination and engagement with practitioners. The comparison of excellent with

poor practice was deemed less fruitful and illuminating than was the comparison of good and excellent. The case studies applied a variety of methods of data gathering, including documentary analysis, interviews, and observation.

When all the QUAL data had been initially coded, and "thick descriptions" produced for the individual case study accounts, the "reduced data" were interrogated further seeking pedagogic, process explanations for the cognitive and social outcomes provided by the effectiveness study. (At this point, the QUAL analyses used the information from the QUAN center effectiveness profiles and used the classification of centers into either "good" or "excellent" for contrast.)

The case study analysis was further supported by systematic QUAN target-child and staff observations. Figure 27.3 illustrates the pedagogical model that emerged as a result of the survey of relevant early years' literature and the computer-assisted analysis of rich text QUAL data linked with further QUAN and QUAL analyses of systematic and naturalistic target-child and staff observations.

This example has sought to illustrate the "added value" of using a longitudinal, sequential, integrated multilevel MM research design to study preschool influences. The longitudinal "educational effectiveness" design enabled statistical modeling of the effects of different features of preschool experiences (amount, type, quality, duration of attendance at preschool) on children's attainment and social behavior at different time points, and on children's developmental progress over the preschool period and in primary school.

The EPPE research design was influenced by both pragmatic and philosophical arguments that suggest MM designs incorporating and linking QUAL and QUAN components can offer complementary strengths and minimize the weaknesses associated with reliance on only one paradigm (as argued by Johnson, Onwuegbuzie,

Figure 27.3 The EPPE Model of Effective Pedagogy in the Early Years

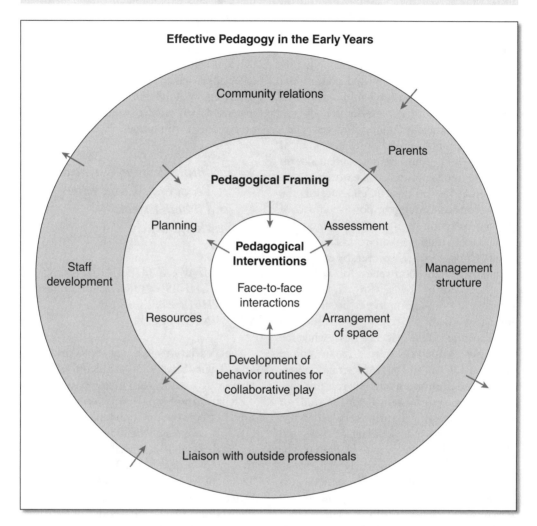

& Turner, 2007). The longitudinal MM effectiveness design brought together a large-scale QUAN survey approach that involved the assessment of young children, and both structured and nonstructured observation of practitioners and children in the in-depth case studies that illuminate and enhance understanding of what constitutes good and excellent preschool practice. Sammons and colleagues (2005) and Siraj-Blatchford and colleagues (2006) claim that the use of MM enabled an innovative study of preschool influence that is more meaningful, and that provides a wider evidence base for both policymakers and practitioners than does reliance on only one form of data gathering and approach to analysis. They argue that complex and pluralistic social contexts demand analysis that is informed by multiple and diverse perspectives. The EPPE conclusions, and EPPE's inferences for both policy and practice, were therefore stronger for having applied an MM approach. On reflection, the EPPE researchers concluded that the study had evolved a dialogic approach to the integration and synthesis of QUAL and QUAN components.

EPPE findings are generally in line with those of a large-scale National Institute of Child Health and Human Development (NICHD) study that was conducted in the United States in a similar time period (NICHD, 2002). However, the NICHD study did not employ an MM educational effectiveness design and so could not investigate the impact of individual preschool centers or illuminate the link between child outcomes and preschool pedagogical processes in depth. The correspondence in findings on the importance of early child care between EPPE and the NICHD suggests the conclusions concerning the positive impact of preschool experience in terms of both quality and quantity (duration) are robust.

EPPE goes further, however, by examining variation in the effectiveness of *individual* preschool centers as well as by exploring the impact of preschool type in England. Interviews with all center managers and parents enriched the evidence base, while the 12 center case studies were a major feature with the QUAL and QUAN strands intersecting and creating an ongoing research dialogue. This proved essential for the study of processes, especially in early years' pedagogy, and to enhance understanding of these and allow theoretical inferences to be drawn. The case studies proved particularly valuable in the development of thick descriptions and explanations and in providing models of effective pedagogical practices. The QUAN analysis had revealed a link between staff qualifications and preschool center quality; due to the stratified random sample, the QUAN analysis could draw generalizations based on the findings to the wider population of preschools in England. The QUAL case studies enhanced understanding of the way staff qualifications contribute to enhanced quality of provision and children's experiences. The case study findings have proved influential in supporting the local authority (LA) development programs for the expanded early years' work force. The QUAN results on preschool effects informed the development of preschool policy in England and

were influential in supporting a major investment in and expansion of preschool provision in England from 2003 onward (Sylva, Melhuish, Sammons, Siraj-Blatchford, & Taggart, 2009; Taggart, Siraj-Blatchford, Sylva, Melhuish, & Sammons, 2008). The MM approach thus enhanced the academic contribution of the research findings and also increased their impact and use by policy and practitioner communities.

◆ *Example 2: The Variations in Teachers' Work, Lives and Their Effects on Students Study*

OVERVIEW OF THE VARIATIONS IN TEACHERS' WORK, LIVES AND THEIR EFFECTS ON STUDENTS STUDY

The Variations in Teachers' Work, Lives and Their Effects on Students (VITAE) project is a study originally based in the TER tradition that was conducted in England between 2001 and 2005 (Day et al., 2007). It adopted a longitudinal MM research design that can be described as complex, iterative, and sequential (Day et al., 2008; Sammons et al., 2007), although the initial plan that involved several distinctive but linked QUAN and QUAL phases did not envisage the extent of iterative integration that evolved in practice over the course of the research.

VITAE was funded by the U.K. government's Department for Children, Schools and Families (DCSF) in England to increase knowledge of effective classroom practice, based on the rationale that "any attempts to sustain initiatives aimed at raising standards in schools and classrooms and to retain high quality teaching are unlikely to succeed without a more comprehensive understanding of teacher effectiveness, its complex configuration and its antecedent" ([UK] Department for Education and Skills Tender Document No. 4/RP/173/99, 6–7).

The research (conducted during 2001–2005) was intended to address topics of policy concern at the turn of the millennium, including improving the quality of teaching, raising standards of student attainment, and supporting retention in the teaching profession.

The DCSF tender document required that teacher effectiveness be linked explicitly to assessed data on students' attainment outcomes and that robust and reliable quantitative data and in-depth qualitative data from a representative sample of LAs and schools should be collected. The funder's requirement indicated that an MM approach to the topic was expected, which concurred with the methodological stance of the research team that was awarded the contract. The VITAE research was conducted with a nationally representative sample of 300 primary (Key Stage 1 and 2) and secondary (Key Stage 3 English and mathematics) teachers working in 100 schools across seven LAs. The schools were selected to be broadly representative of those in England in terms of levels of social disadvantage of student intakes (measured by the indicator percentage of students on free school meals) and current attainment level of the schools in overall national assessment results because such contextual factors were deemed likely to be relevant to a study of teachers' work and their effectiveness.

VITAE sought to describe and analyze influences on teachers' professional and personal lives, their identities, and their effectiveness, and to explore their interconnections. It also investigated associations between the school contexts in which teachers worked and these features. The study approximates to a complex sequential iterative multilevel MM research design (Tashakkori & Teddlie, 2003) involving several linked phases to create case studies of 300 primary and secondary teachers working with classes of students in Years 2, 6, and 9. The field work was conducted over 3 successive academic years and collected a wide range of data through interviews, questionnaire surveys, and assessment data on student attainments in English and mathematics. The team chose to focus on teachers working with students in Years 2, 6, and 9 because these are the years when students in England undertake national assessments in English and mathematics (at ages 7, 11, and 14 years).

Variations among the 300 teachers in their relative effectiveness in promoting students' academic progress were studied using student-level attainment outcome data obtained from central DCSF databases. This was linked with other data on individual students in the classes taught by the teacher sample, including additional student baseline data on English and mathematics from tests selected by the project staff. The use of national data sets had the advantage of reducing research demands on teachers and schools. Even so, the project, conducted over 3 years, involved a considerable commitment from participants. By Year 3, some teachers and schools reduced their participation in the survey and testing component, leading to incomplete QUAN data for some aspects of the 300 individual teacher case studies. The higher demands in terms of data collection and commitment that may be required by longitudinal MM designs in terms of participants' involvement and the resources required need to be balanced against the additional opportunities to examine both potential causal effects and potential causal mechanisms through a richer evidence base (Teddlie & Sammons, forthcoming).

Full findings from the VITAE research are presented elsewhere (Day et al., 2007), and an overview of the study and MM design is given by Sammons and colleagues (2007). This example provides an account of the way the VITAE research sought to move beyond simple integration of QUAN and QUAL approaches to contribute to new knowledge of variations in teachers' work, lives, and effectiveness that used meta-inferences from the combined sources of evidence to create more illuminating "synergistic understanding." It is argued that MM designs that use integrated approaches to produce meta-inferences that result in synergy "hold the potential for enabling the consideration and combination of a greater range of differential data, thus potentially providing opportunities for more nuanced, authentic accounts and explanations of complex realities" (Day et al., 2008, p. 330).

KEY QUESTIONS ADDRESSED BY THE *VARIATIONS IN TEACHERS' WORK, LIVES AND THEIR EFFECTS ON STUDENTS* STUDY

VITAE's overarching aim was to assess variations over time in teacher effectiveness, between different teachers, and for particular teachers, and to identify factors that contribute to variations. It thus recognized the need for a longitudinal approach and explicitly conceptualized teacher effectiveness as a dynamic concept that might vary over time and for different student groups. This is in line with the Dynamic Model of educational effectiveness proposed by Creemers and Kyriakides (2008). Key questions illustrate how MM designs can enhance the scope of traditional QUAN-based EER by allowing studies to address questions that are more complex and wide-ranging:

1. Does teacher effectiveness vary from one year to another and in terms of different student outcomes? Do teachers necessarily become more effective over time?

2. What are the roles of biography and identity?

3. How does school or department leadership influence teachers' practice and their effectiveness?

4. What particular kinds of influence does continuing professional development (CPD) have on teachers' effectiveness?

5. Are teachers equally effective for different student groups or is there differential effectiveness relating (for example) to students' gender or socioeconomic status?

6. Do the factors that influence effectiveness vary for teachers working in different school contexts, or for different kinds of outcomes?

7. Do factors influencing teachers' effectiveness vary across different sectors (primary and secondary) and different age-groups (Key Stage 1, 2, and 3)?

The MM approach benefited from an extensive literature review to develop a clearer conceptual understanding of the dimensions and correlates of teacher effectiveness and teachers' professional development at the start of the VITAE study. This informed both the initial survey of teachers and the first round interviews, and was later extended to include other areas that emerged as important themes as the analysis of the first rounds of QUAL and QUAN empirical data progressed. The review was extended to include the concepts of teacher well-being, professional life phases, identity, resilience, and commitment as these concepts began to emerge as central to understanding the nature of different influences on, and outcomes of, variations in teachers' work and lives and their effectiveness.

DATA COLLECTION

VITAE brought together approaches from two distinctive fields of enquiry: mainly QUAN research on TER and SER, and mainly QUAL research on teachers' work and lives. VITAE sought to integrate these different perspectives in order to better address the central research questions. It chose to focus on following the same 300 teachers over 3 school years, with QUAN-derived measures of student outcomes (academic and affective) relating to successive classes or teaching groups for the same teacher. Thus, the teacher was the focus of longitudinal study rather than the more usual QUAN EER design that follows up various cohorts of students. The issue of change over time in various aspects of teachers' lives and work (including effectiveness, job satisfaction, motivation, and commitment) was explored using student attainment outcome measures, students' views, and teachers' own perceptions and accounts using both initial questionnaire surveys and regular in-depth interviews across 3 years to explore change in these areas over time. Figure 27.4 outlines the sample design.

Two dimensions of teacher effectiveness were investigated: first, teachers' own *perceived effectiveness* (relational) based on self-report, and, second, teachers' *relative effectiveness* (value added) compared with other teachers in the sample using external measures derived from student assessments. The main data concerning perceived effectiveness were collected through twice-yearly semistructured, face-to-face teacher interviews. Measures of teachers' relative

effectiveness were derived from statistical analyses of students' progress and attainment by matching baseline test results at the beginning of the year with students' national curriculum results at the end and exploring the influence of student background characteristics. This enabled differences in the relative "value added" to student progress to be analyzed, using multilevel models that included adjustment for individual student background factors (e.g., age, gender, prior attainment) and student prior attainment at the start of the school year. These multilevel models were used to create teacher-level residual estimates of the difference between students' actual results and those predicted on the basis of the students' intake characteristics and their prior attainments. In each year of the study, the teacher-level

Figure 27.4   Summary of VITAE Sampling Design

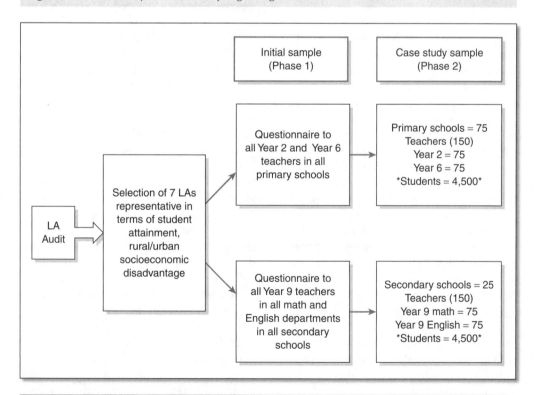

SOURCE: Day, Stobart, et al., 2006, 2007.

NOTE: Data on students' views were collected by survey on a class or teaching group of students for each teacher for three successive school years.

residuals were based on results for a class or teaching group of around 20 to 30 students per teacher.

Student surveys also were conducted in each of the 3 years to gather students' views of their schools and teachers, including features of school and classroom climate as well as attitudes to school and learning. Data reduction techniques (exploratory and confirmatory factor analysis) identified underlying dimensions in the student questionnaire data. These were then tested in multilevel models to investigate the relationships between student attitudes and dimensions related to school and classroom processes and variations in students' academic progress in each of the 3 years.

MOVING FROM INTEGRATION TOWARD METHODOLOGICAL SYNERGY

The VITAE research aims indicated the need for an MM approach that would allow the study to address a set of wide-ranging and more-complex research questions than would have been possible through reliance on methodology associated with only one paradigmatic perspective. The team chose an integrated, sequential MM method approach involving the combination of a range of research techniques rather than a simpler parallel design. The data were collected and analyzed in an iterative and evolving process consistent with the use of grounded theory methods. So, for example, guided by the critical examination of literature at the start of the study, an initial questionnaire for a large sample of teachers across schools in the seven LAs was developed. This questionnaire also was administered to the 300 case study teachers that formed the main focus of the enquiry.

The analysis of data collected from this teacher questionnaire plus the literature review informed the development of first-round and follow-up interview schedules for case study teachers. Emerging findings from the first-year QUAN analysis of the

main student questionnaire was followed up by QUAL group focus interviews with students in a subset of 30% of classes to further explore students' perspectives on their schools and on their teachers' work. In addition, as the QUAN value-added results from the first round (Year 1) of data collection became available, they were fed into the later interviews (Years 2 and 3).

Additional narrative teacher interviews were employed in the third year of the study, drawing on the emerging analyses of the first two rounds of QUAN and QUAL data to explore teachers' retrospective perceptions of and explanations for changes in their perceived effectiveness and in their interpretations of the various factors that shaped this over the last 3 years and the course of their teaching careers. Teachers were asked to construct a timeline indicating critical influences on their perceived effectiveness looking back over their career histories. This retrospective element enhanced the study's focus on change and the ability to provide more-comprehensive evidence for the construction of 300 individual teacher case studies. In constructing each full teacher case study, interview data were incorporated in the form of text. In addition, after thorough analysis using grounded techniques, selected QUAL data were "quantitized." For example, individual researchers made global judgments based on their study of interview and survey responses about each teacher's professional identity, their level of commitment to teaching, and their resilience. These judgments were checked against those made independently by a second researcher using the same data; then teachers were classified accordingly. These classifications were later discussed with teachers to establish whether they accorded with their own views.

The 300 individual teacher case studies were the prime focus of the study and were constructed using four main sources of evidence: teacher interviews, teacher and student questionnaires, and student assessment data. This combination of approaches provided greater opportunities for mapping, analysis, and interpretation to provide understandings of the research area that were more holistic than would have been gained if relying on a single paradigm.

The development of the teacher case studies involved qualitizing QUAN evidence and quantitizing QUAL evidence and allowed the integration and eventual attempts at synthesis of the two in various ways. The outcomes included full individual teacher case studies, summary teacher profiles, and "cameos or pen portraits." Also, via the creation of an overall teacher matrix of themes and attributes, the outcomes enabled further exploration of associations between key attributes (e.g., teacher professional life phase, school context, sector) and other concepts, including effectiveness (perceived and value added), commitment, resilience, and identity. The strengths of the MM strategy include enhanced professional learning of team members through the iterative process of data collection, ongoing analysis, tentative hypothesis generation, and testing and interpretation of results. Day and colleagues (2008) demonstrate how the MM research team attempted to move from conceptual and methodological integration to more-synergistic understandings, which enabled the discovery and

delineation of key findings that were both more enlightening and more robust than would have been the case if one method or another (QUAN or QUAL) had dominated.

An illustration of the iterative nature of the ongoing integration of the QUAN and QUAL MM design is illustrated by the way VITAE changed its conceptualization in response to emerging findings. The initial conceptual framework was based on a model where teacher effectiveness was considered central and was understood to relate to student attitudes, achievements, and attainments, and to be affected by policy, students, and teachers' personal and practice factors. Following the analysis of the initial teacher survey and the first round of interviews with the teacher sample, the team reassessed the initial conceptualization and decided that teachers' selves should be seen as central to the study, instead of the narrower concept of teacher effectiveness. A second conceptual framework grounded in the emerging QUAN and QUAL empirical data was developed, with teachers' identities and professional life phases viewed as key factors that might moderate their commitment and their perceived and relative effectiveness (Figure 27.5).

Figure 27.5 Teachers' Selves as Factors Influencing Effectiveness

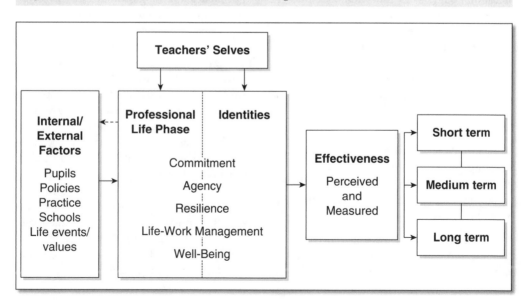

The results from the QUAN, multilevel statistical analyses of teachers' relative effectiveness were initially conducted independently from the QUAL analyses of interview data, but later were incorporated into the initially independent QUAL analyses of teacher case study profiles. These were then used as one of several important attributes in subsequent QUAL analyses in order to understand the potential influences on variations in effectiveness more fully. Discussion of this integration of data (not the integration itself) led to the identification of two key features of teachers' work and lives—professional life phase and identity—which, together, contributed, positively and negatively, to variations among teachers in relation to these features. Investigation of the interaction between these led to hypotheses about their association with teachers' *perceived effectiveness* and, later in the research process, between teachers' commitment and their *relative effectiveness* (measured by value-added analyses).

Three claims that emerged from the research illustrated the processes of moving first to methodological integration and then to attempts at conceptual and methodological synergy. Day and colleagues (2008) argue that neither QUAL nor QUAN analyses in isolation could have led to these new understandings of the links between teachers' professional life phase, identity, commitment, and perceived and value-added effectiveness.

Claim 1: Teachers in later phases of their professional lives are more vulnerable in terms of sustaining their commitment to teaching.

Claim 2: Students of teachers who are sustaining or continuing to build their commitment are more likely to attain results at or above the level expected, regardless of school context.

Claim 3: Teachers do not necessarily become more effective in promoting their students' academic outcomes over time.

A higher proportion of teachers in later career phases, though still a minority, are likely to be relatively less effective in promoting students' academic outcomes.

The significant statistical results in the QUAN analyses supported and extended the emerging findings from QUAL analyses of interview data on variations in teachers' work and lives over the 3 years of the field study. They were supplemented by findings from the retrospective narrative interviews that covered a time frame that was much longer than the 3 years of the field study. When integrated, the data showed differences in commitment and effectiveness between teachers in different phases of their professional lives. The further association of these findings with those of teachers' relative effectiveness, however, suggested not only that teachers in their late career phase are at greater risk of becoming less effective, but also that relative effectiveness is closely associated with teachers' self-reports of their commitment to teaching. Taken together, these three linked findings shed new light on the ways in which teacher effectiveness, commitment, and professional life phase interact and drew attention to the important concept of teacher resilience.

The combination of QUAL and QUAN approaches in a longitudinal study involved several phases of data collection and facilitated ongoing dialogue between data collection approaches and interpretation of findings that fed into each other. This allowed the study to investigate a range of potential direct and indirect influences on teachers' perceived effectiveness, how they managed these in different contexts, and whether there were associations between these and the measurable progress of their students, rather than seeking only to identify particular "cause and effect" relationships. Both statistical and theoretical inferences were thus possible, while the detailed case studies produced more authentic and trustworthy accounts through coconstruction of knowledge with the teachers involved.

The longitudinal nature of the VITAE research posed some challenges in terms of continuity of project staffing and expertise as well as in terms of maintaining the interest and participation of schools and teachers over an extended period. A further limitation was a lack of funding for a proposed classroom observation component, which meant that the research was unable to explore variations in this central dimension of teachers' work and lives. Despite the limitations, the VITAE team found benefits from the MM approach, including the development of research relationships and understandings within the team through regular workshops, which focused on building shared understandings of data analyses, interpretation, and emergent themes. The building of goodwill and mutual support and learning proved to be key factors supporting the processes of conceptual and methodological integration and synergy.

◆ Example 3: Mixed Methods Strategies in Research on School Success in Challenging Circumstances

The Schools With Challenging Circumstances (SCC) project involved collaborative partnerships between two urban school districts in Canada, the Ontario Ministry of Education, and a team of researchers. This project was intended to add to the knowledge base regarding student success in schools facing challenging circumstances, particularly in relation to innovative leadership practices. It sought to address criticisms (discussed by Gray et al., 1999; Teddlie & Reynolds, 2001) that the SI and EER fields had generally neglected the role of context by providing context-rich understandings of a multidimensional construct of SI using MM to provide "evidence based accounts of factors associated with SI in Ontario schools" (Jang et al., 2008, p. 225). The study involved 20 successful elementary

schools selected on the basis of steady improvement in student academic attainment over 3 years (2002–2005), schools that also faced challenging circumstances. The QUAL component of the concurrent MM design involved interviews with teachers, principals, and student and parent focus groups while the QUAN strand involved a survey of principals and teachers.

Jang and colleagues (2008) provide an account of various conceptual and practical challenges in integrative analytic strategies for an MM research study in the SI tradition. The study examines and illustrates the analysis strategies used in a concurrent MM study (McDougall et al., 2006). The researchers argue from a pragmatic stance that rejects dualism by prioritizing research questions over what they term the "traditional assumptive world views" associated with different paradigms. They claim that MM research provides opportunities for stronger meta-inferences due to the use of different types of data sources and their integration. They note Teddlie and Tashakkori's (2006) discussion of conversion and fully integrated MM designs that feature multistrand concurrent approaches where mixing occurs at all stages that go beyond simple convergence across QUAL and QUAN data sources because this is deemed to be insufficient to provide fully integrated meta-inferences.

ANALYTIC STRATEGIES TO PROMOTE INTEGRATION AND CREATE NEW UNDERSTANDINGS

Jang and colleagues (2008) adopted a parallel MM design in which the QUAL and QUAN strands were initially analyzed independently using both thematic (QUAL) and factor (QUAN) analyses for data reduction. They discuss the way results from such initial traditional QUAL or QUAN analyses can be transformed for secondary analyses using another methodological approach from the other paradigm. "For example, quantitative data are converted into narratives that can be analysed qualitatively (qualitizing), and qualitative data are converted to numerical codes that can be statistically analysed (quantitizing)" (Jang et al., 2008, p. 223). Their paper seeks to document and clarify the logic underlying what they refer to as rather "messy" data analytic processes, outlining four additional integrative strategies they used to enhance the quality of the meta-inferences made; these are elaborated below.

Parallel integration for member checking involved participants verifying the investigators' initial interpretations of QUAL data (a strategy also adopted in the VITAE study). Jang and colleagues (2008) engaged principals to check the researchers' preliminary interpretations of three data sets: the QUAL analysis of themes from the interview and focus group data, the QUAN findings of nine underlying factors from the QUAN analysis of the survey data, and the descriptions of school context. It was argued that member checks help to "clarify and contextualize" the data from different research strands, and that this should occur before conducting meta-analyses.

Data transformation for comparison: Jang and colleagues (2008) report that they *qualitized* nine QUAN factors from the survey into narrative descriptions. These were then compared with the QUAL themes. Both overlapping and nonoverlapping aspects of SI were identified after comparing and contrasting the two sets of QUAL themes and QUAN factors. This, they claim, enriched the quality of their overall findings compared with those results derived from either paradigm treated in isolation.

Data consolidation for emergent themes also was applied. Eight integrated themes were found from comparisons of the original and the further reorganized QUAL and QUAN data. Three themes were found to be common across the original QUAL thematic and QUAN factor analyses, but the other five consolidated themes were derived from the further secondary integrative

analyses. Again, this indicates the way new understandings emerged as a direct result of the processes of integration.

Case analysis for the generation of refined case study school profiles also was adopted as a further integrative strategy. This followed procedures suggested by Caracelli and Greene (1993). For each case study, school narrative profiles were written linking QUAL and QUAN evidence. These narratives were compared with the eight consolidated themes that had emerged from the initial integration of QUAL and QUAN data analyses. Iterative analytic processes were used to establish the different ways schools approached specific integrated themes (such as high vs. low parental involvement in successful schools).

Jang and colleagues' (2008) study provides helpful examples of fruitful new approaches to MM research in terms of how best to integrate QUAN and QUAL findings fully, rather than just looking for commonalities across the original QUAL thematic and QUAN statistical analyses. Where inconsistencies were found between QUAL and QUAN evidence, the research team used the opportunity to use integrative analysis approaches involving data consolidation and case analytic strategies to gain an in-depth understanding of the reasons for these inconsistencies. The authors provide examples of the additional learning experienced by research team members derived from engagement with data from an alternative perspective to that they typically had used. They conclude that integrated data analyses require a greater breadth of skills, including both creative imagination and logic. Nonetheless, they note some limitations (due to funding and timescale) to their concurrent MM design and suggest that a fully integrated MM design would have allowed a more comprehensive and illuminating study.

Despite these limitations, Jang and colleagues (2008) conclude that the rich data from their MM concurrent design and the various integrative analytic strategies outlined above allowed the study to gain a more comprehensive understanding of the varying levels of school engagement in aspects associated with school success, and so provide more-convincing explanations for success in challenging circumstances.

> The data analysis involved the iterative process of constantly moving back and forth by revisiting both QUAL and QUAN data. It also was dialogic in that the team members with different experiences took the lead in discussing data analysis strategies. (Jang et al., 2008, p. 224)

◆ Conclusions

This chapter has argued that MM research designs offer the prospect of forging better links between the EER and SI fields that have remained fairly distinct despite the creation of an organization intended to promote interaction between the two fields (the International Congress for School Effectiveness and Improvement) and the publication of specialist journals such as *School Effectiveness and School Improvement* intended to help bridge the divide. Until recently, the reliance on mainly single-paradigm studies, typically only QUAN for the EER field and largely QUAL for SI, has limited the scope for both integration and dialogue (Reynolds & Teddlie, 2000). This has meant that SI work has made less use of EER findings than might have been the case had MM approaches been more widely adopted. Similarly, the lack of focus on measurement issues and student outcomes has reduced the rigor and value of much SI enquiry. The often narrow QUAN focus of EER has likewise limited the extent to which the knowledge base has been able to enhance understanding and to guide practice. The pragmatic philosophical position underlying recent developments in MM research is often described as a new third way alternative to either largely positivist/postpositivist (first

way) or constructivist/interpretivist (second way) approaches to research. Its advantages include the potential to strengthen and link both areas and move away from overreliance on either the postpositivist or, by contrast, postmodern philosophical assumptions associated with these earlier first and second way research traditions.

Teddlie and Sammons (2010) have drawn attention to the need for EER to take more note of MM and QUAL perspectives. In this chapter, three examples have been discussed that seek to illustrate the potential of MM approaches to improve the quality of both SER and TER. In addition, this chapter has highlighted the potential for enriching studies of effective practice in other educational sectors such as the early years. It is seen that MM designs involving research teams with diverse areas of expertise offer the prospect of addressing more-complex and more-interesting research questions and of generating more-fruitful findings and conclusions that are of value to both policymakers and practitioners than is likely to be the case in studies that rely on only QUAL or only QUAN methodologies. Each study illustrates how data integration can take place, the role of narrative case studies (whether of individual preschools, schools, or teachers) that incorporate both QUAL and QUAN findings, and the way additional cycles of analyses that qualitize QUAN data and quantitize QUAL data allow the development of more-powerful meta-analyses and robust conclusions to be drawn through the "to and fro" of analysis involving both inductive and deductive reasoning. Appropriate multilevel MM also allows EER to give greater weight to the context-specific and dynamic nature of many educational processes. It is argued that the greater use of thoughtful and well-framed MM designs also may help to overcome some of the criticisms of EER that have emerged during the last two decades by providing more-powerful and more-illuminating findings of greater value to future policy and practice.

Research Questions and Exercises

1. What are the consequences of the current paradigmatic divide between the EER and SI fields?

2. How far can MM research designs help to overcome some of the limitations of existing EER and SI research approaches?

3. Critically evaluate one or more of the examples of MM research discussed in this chapter. Discuss the way in which the MM approach enabled the authors to address their research aims and questions and the implications of this for the findings and knowledge claims made.

4. Identify the main conceptual and practical challenges facing those seeking to use integrated MM designs, and discuss how these might be addressed based on the three examples outlined in this chapter.

5. Examine the various strategies adopted to approach data analysis in an integrative way in one or more of the example studies in this chapter. How can these strategies support better "meta inferences"?

6. Critically evaluate the evidence that MM approaches and integrative analytic strategies can lead to greater "synergistic" understanding in EER.

7. Identify two examples of EER or SI studies from the existing literature that adopt contrasting methodological approaches (only one QUAN and only one QUAL). Suggest ways in which an MM research design could be adopted to further extend these studies and address a wider range of research questions.

◆ References

Borman, G., Hewes, G., Overman, L., & Brown, S. (2003). Comprehensive school reform and achievement: A meta analysis. *Review of Educational Research, 73*(2), 125–230.

Brannen, J. (1992). *Mixing methods: Quantitative and qualitative research.* Aldershot, UK: Avebury.

Bryk, A. S., & Raudenbush, S. W. (1992). *Hierarchical linear models: Applications and data analysis methods.* Newbury Park, CA: Sage.

Bryman, A. (1988). *Quantity and quality in social research.* London: Unwin Hyman.

Caracelli, V. J., & Greene, J. C. (1993). Data analysis strategies for mixed method evaluation designs. *Educational Evaluation and Policy Analysis, 15,* 195–207.

Creemers, B. P. M. (1994). *The effective classroom.* London: Cassell.

Creemers, B. P. M., & Kyriakides, L. (2008). *The dynamics of educational effectiveness.* London: Routledge Taylor Francis.

Creemers, B. P. M., & Reezigt, G. (1997). School effectiveness and school improvement: Sustaining links. *School Effectiveness and School Improvement, 8*(4), 396–429.

Creswell, J. W. (1994). *Research design: Qualitative and quantitative approaches.* Thousand Oaks, CA: Sage.

Day, C., Sammons, P., & Gu, Q. (2008). Combining qualitative and quantitative methodologies in research on teachers' lives, work, and effectiveness: From integration to synergy. *Educational Researcher, 37*(6), 330–342.

Day, C., Sammons, P., Kington, A., Regan, E., Ko, J., Brown, E., et al. (2008). *Effective classroom practice (ECP): A mixed-method study of influences and outcomes.* End of Award Report submitted to the Economic and Social Research Council, School of Education, The University of Nottingham, Reference No. RES-000–23–1564.

Day, C., Sammons, P., Stobart, G., Kington, A., & Gu, Q. (2007). *Teachers matter.* Milton Keynes: Open University Press.

Goldstein, H. (1995). *Multilevel statistical models* (2nd ed.). London: Edward Arnold.

Goldstein, H. (1998). *Models for reality: New approaches to the understanding of educational processes* (Professorial Lecture Series). London: Institute of Education, University of London.

Goldstein, H., & Sammons, P. (1997). The influence of secondary and junior schools on sixteen year examination performance: A cross-classified multilevel analysis. *School Effectiveness and School Improvement, 8*(2), 219–230.

Gray, J., Hopkins, D., Reynolds, D., Wilcox, B., Farrell, S., & Jesson, D. (1999). *Improving schools: Performance and potential.* Buckingham, UK: Open University Press.

Harms, T., Clifford, M., & Cryer, D. (1998). *Early childhood environmental rating scale, revised edition (ECERS-R).* Williston, VT: Teachers College Press.

Harris, A. (2002). *School improvement: What's in it for schools?* London: Routledge.

Hopkins, D., & Harris, A. (1997). Improving the quality of education for all. *Support for Learning, 12*(4), 147–151.

James, C., Connolly, M., Dunning, G., & Elliott, T. (2006). *How very effective primary schools work.* London: Paul Chapman.

Jang, E., McDougall, D., Pollon, D., Herbert, M., & Russell, P. (2008). Integrative mixed methods data analytic strategies in research on school success in challenging circumstances. *Journal of Mixed Methods Research, 2*(3), 221–247.

Johnson, R. B., & Onwuegbuzie, A. (2004). Mixed methods research: A research paradigm whose time has come. *Educational Researcher, 33*(7), 14–26.

Johnson, R. B., Onwuegbuzie, A., & Turner, L. (2007). Toward a definition of mixed methods research. *Journal of Mixed Methods Research, 1*(2), 112–133.

Leckie, G. (2009). The complexity of school and neighbourhood effects and movements of students on school differences in models of educational achievement. *Journal of the Royal Statistical Society, 172*(3), 537–554.

Luyten, H., & Sammons, P. (forthcoming). Multilevel modelling. In B. P. M. Creemers, L. Kyriakides, & P. Sammons (Eds.), *Methodological advances in educational effectiveness research* (Chapter 11). London: Routledge Taylor Francis.

MacBeath, J., & Mortimore, P. (2001). *Improving school effectiveness.* Buckingham, UK: Open University Press.

McCartney, K., & Jordan, E. (1990). Parallels between research on child care and research on school effects. *Educational Researcher, 19*(1), 24–27.

McDougall, D. E., Gaskell, J., Flessa, J., Kugler, J., Jang, E. E., Herbert, M., et al. (2006). *Improving student achievement in schools facing challenging circumstances.* Toronto, Canada: Ontario Institute for Studies in Education, University of Toronto.

Melhuish, E., Sylva, K., Sammons, P., Siraj-Blatchford, I., Taggart, B., & Phan, M. (2008). Effects of the home learning environment and pre-school center experience upon literacy and numeracy development in early primary school. *Journal of Social Issues, 64,* 157–188.

Mortimore, P., Sammons, P., Stoll, L., Lewis, D., & Ecob, R. (1988). *School matters: The junior years.* Wells, UK: Open Books.

National Institute of Child Health and Human Development (NICHD). (2002). Early child care and children's development prior to school entry: Results from the NICHD Study of Early Child Care. *American Educational Research Journal, 39,* 133–164.

Reynolds, D., & Teddlie, C. (2000). The processes of school effectiveness. In C. Teddlie & D. Reynolds (Eds.), *The international handbook of school effectiveness research* (134–159). London: Falmer Press.

Rutter, M., Maughan, B., Mortimore, P., & Ouston, J. (1979). *Fifteen thousand hours:*

Secondary schools and their effects on children. London: Open Books.

Sammons, P. (1996). Complexities in the judgement of school effectiveness. *Educational Research and Evaluation, 2*(2), 113–149.

Sammons, P. (1999). *School effectiveness research: Coming of age in the 21st century*. Lisse, The Netherlands: Swets & Zeitlinger.

Sammons, P. (2006). The contribution of international studies on educational effectiveness: Current and future directions. *Educational Research and Evaluation, 12*(6), 583–593.

Sammons, P., Anders, Y., Sylva, K., Melhuish, E., Siraj-Blatchford, I., Taggart, B., et al. (2008). Children's cognitive attainment and progress in English primary schools during Key Stage 2: Investigating the potential continuing influences of pre-school education. *Zeitschrift für Erziehungswissenschaften*, 10. Jahrg., Special Issue (Sonderheft) 11/2008, 179–198.

Sammons, P., Day, C., Kington, A., Gu, Q., Stobart, G., & Smees, R. (2007). Exploring variations in teachers' work, lives and their effects on students: Key findings and implications from a longitudinal mixed methods study. *British Educational Research Journal, 33*(5), 681–701.

Sammons, P., Elliot, K., Sylva, K., Melhuish, E., Siraj-Blatchford, I., Taggart, B., et al. (2004). The impact of pre-school on young children's cognitive attainments at entry to reception. *British Educational Research Journal, 30*(5), 691–712.

Sammons, P., & Luyten, H. (2009). Editorial article for special issue on alternative methods for assessing school effects and schooling effects. *School Effectiveness and School Improvement, 20*(2), 133–143.

Sammons, P., Siraj-Blatchford, I., Sylva, K., Melhuish, E., Taggart, B., & Elliot, K. (2005). Investigating the effects of preschool provision: Using mixed methods in the EPPE research. *International Journal of Social Research Methodology, Theory & Practice, 8*(3), 207–224.

Sammons, P., Thomas, S., & Mortimore, P. (1997). *Forging links: Effective schools and effective departments*. London: Paul Chapman.

Scheerens, J., & Bosker, R. (1997). *The foundations of educational effectiveness*. Oxford, UK: Pergamon Press.

Siraj-Blatchford, I., Sammons, P., Sylva, K., Melhuish, E., & Taggart, B. (2006). Educational research and evidence-based policy: The mixed method approach of the EPPE project. *Evaluation and Research in Education, 19*(2), 63–82.

Siraj-Blatchford, I., & Sylva, K. (2004). Researching pedagogy in English pre-schools. *British Education Research Journal, 30*(5), 713–730.

Siraj-Blatchford, I., Sylva, K., Taggart, B., Sammons, P., Melhuish, E. C., & Elliot, K. (2003). The Effective Provision of Pre-school Education (EPPE) Project: Technical Paper 10. *Intensive case studies of practice across the foundation stage*. London: DfES/Institute of Education, University of London.

Spalter-Roth, R. (2000). Gender issues in the use of integrated approaches. In M. Bamberger (Ed.), *Integrating quantitative and qualitative research in development projects* (pp. 47–53). Washington, DC: World Bank.

Stringfield, S., Reynolds, D., & Schaffer E. (2008). *Improving secondary students' academic achievement through a focus on reform reliability*. Research Report for CfBT, Reading, UK: CfBT, http://www.cfbt.com/evidenceforeducation/PDF/High%20Reliability_v5%20FINAL2.pdf

Sylva, K., Melhuish, E., Sammons, P., Siraj-Blatchford, I., & Taggart, B. (2008). Effective Pre-school and Primary Education Project (EPPE 3-11). Final report from the primary phase: Pre-school, school and family influences on children's development during Key Stage 2 (Age 7–11). *DCSF Research Report* RR061, London, Department for Children, Schools & Families.

Sylva, K., Melhuish, E., Sammons, P., Siraj-Blatchford, I., & Taggart, B. (2009). *Early childhood matters: Evidence from the effective pre-school and primary education project*. London: Sage.

Sylva, K., Siraj-Blatchford, I., & Taggart, B. (2003). *Assessing quality in the early years: Early childhood environment rating scale–extension (ECERS-E): Four curricular subscales.* Stoke on Trent, UK: Trentham Books.

Sylva, K., Taggart, B., Melhuish, E., Sammons, P., & Siraj-Blatchford, I. (2007). Changing models of research to inform educational policy. *Research Papers in Education, 22*(2), 155–168.

Taggart, B., Siraj-Blatchford, I., Sylva, K., Melhuish, E., & Sammons, P. (2008). Influencing policy and practice through research on early childhood education. *International Journal of Early Childhood Education, 14*(2), 7–21.

Tashakkori, A., & Teddlie, C. (1998). *Mixed methodology: Combining the qualitative and quantitative approaches.* Thousand Oaks, CA: Sage.

Tashakkori, A., & Teddlie, C. (Eds.). (2003). *Handbook of mixed methods in social and behavioral research.* Thousand Oaks, CA: Sage.

Teddlie, C., & Reynolds, D. (2000). *The international handbook of school effectiveness research.* London: Falmer Press.

Teddlie, C., & Reynolds, D. (2001). Countering the critics: Responses to recent criticism of school effectiveness research. *School Effectiveness and School Improvement, 12*(1), 41–82.

Teddlie, C., & Sammons, P. (2010). Applications of mixed methods to the field of educational effectiveness research. In B. P. M. Creemers, L. Kyriakides, & P. Sammons (Eds.), *Methodological advances in educational effectiveness research.* London: Routledge Taylor & Francis.

Teddlie, C., & Stringfield, C. (1993). *Schools make a difference: Lessons learned from a 10-year study of school effects.* New York: Teachers College Press.

Teddlie, C., & Tashakkori, A. (2006). A general typology of research designs featuring mixed methods. *Research in the Schools, 13*(1), 12–28.

Teddlie, C., & Tashakkori, A. (2009). *The foundations of mixed methods research: Integrating quantitative and qualitative techniques in the social and behavioral sciences.* Thousand Oaks, CA: Sage.

CURRENT PRACTICES AND EMERGING TRENDS IN CONDUCTING MIXED METHODS INTERVENTION STUDIES IN THE HEALTH SCIENCES

◆ Mi-Kyung Song, Margarete Sandelowski, and Mary Beth Happ

Objectives

The goal of this chapter is to advance a methodological conceptualization of the intervention study as a unified, organic entity composed of a series of interlocking qualitative, quantitative observational, and experimental studies. After reading this chapter, you should be able to

- differentiate between experimental and participant-centered intervention studies;

- describe the contributions of qualitative, quantitative observational, and experimental research methods to the development of safe, effective, culturally acceptable, and feasible socially complex interventions;

(Continued)

(Continued)

- describe the components of mixed methods intervention programs of research; and
- discuss the challenges of designing and conducting mixed methods intervention programs of research.

In this chapter, we advance a methodological conceptualization of the intervention study as a unified, organic entity composed of a series of interlocking qualitative, quantitative observational, and experimental studies. We refer to this entity as the mixed methods intervention program of research. Such programs of research are directed toward designing safe, effective, acceptable, and feasible interventions, including therapies, activities, programs, and technologies. We focus here on studies of socially complex interventions (Campbell et al., 2000; Craig et al., 2008; Lindsay, 2004) in the health sciences directed toward individuals or aggregates (e.g., families, communities, group practices, organizations) and targeted to promote health and well-being, prevent disease and its exacerbation, or facilitate peaceful dying and grieving. Although no interventions are simple and all interventions are social, we define socially complex interventions as characterized by greater numbers of interacting components, more difficult behaviors that must be enacted by persons delivering and receiving the intervention, more and variable intervention targets and outcomes, and a greater degree of customization (Craig et al., 2008). Examples include cognitive-behavioral, psychoeducational, social support, and communication interventions.

◆ The Clinical Trial on Trial

The randomized controlled trial (RCT) continues to retain its gold-standard status among the array of research methods used in the health sciences. The control over researchers, subjects, and the research process itself is seen to be foundational to the claim that RCTs produce the best, or most valid, evidence for or against an intervention. When other methods are promoted for the development and evaluation of interventions, it is usually only as before-and-after accessories to the RCT (and, therefore, as frills that can be cut when resources are limited), or only when RCTs cannot be conducted.

Over the past 20 years, however, an important critique literature has emerged that has served to challenge the privileged status of the RCT (e.g., Oakley, 1989; Weinstein, 2004). The critique of the RCT consists of several key elements. First, RCTs are hardly ever conducted according to textbook standards, which calls into question not only their much-touted advantages over other methods, but also whether the RCT exists as anything but an ideal honored more in the breach than in the observance. In actual practice, few RCTs of socially complex interventions fully meet the criteria of random sampling and assignment, creation of mutually exclusive experimental and comparison conditions, double-blinding, and full control over factors likely to influence these conditions and outcomes. If RCTs cannot be ideally practiced, the line between RCTs and other modes of research becomes less distinct and the notion is challenged that a less-than-ideally conducted RCT is better than other kinds of studies conducted closer to the ideals for those studies.

Second, even if they can be conducted according to textbook standards, RCTs are wholly unsuitable for studying socially complex interventions that by virtue of their complexity resist control and standardization. Although RCTs are viewed as the best methodological strategy for optimizing internal validity, the very features that distinguish them may actually pose threats to internal validity. For example, although randomization is supposed to offset the effects of "nuisance variables" that might complicate the interpretation of study outcomes, randomization by itself constitutes a "nuisance variable" encompassing the array of consequences of research participants not being able to choose treatment conditions (Corrigan & Salzer, 2003; Kaptchuk et al., 2009; Thompson, Ritenbaugh, & Nichter, 2009). Not only do both participant and provider treatment preferences interact with randomization; they also may influence participant recruitment and retention in trials (Bower, King, Nazareth, Lampe, & Sibbald, 2005). Furthermore, blinding can be difficult if not impossible to achieve for complex interventions that are visible to participants, observers, data collectors, or trained outcomes raters. For example, in the *Study of Patient–Nurse Effectiveness With Assisted Communication Strategies*, nurses and nonspeaking intensive care unit patients in the intervention phase of this study received communication materials and electronic communication devices that were not present or not available to the usual care (control) cohort (Happ, Sereika, Garrett, & Tate, 2008). Even without information about the intervention or group assignment, trained raters would notice these special items used to facilitate communication in some but not all video-recorded nurse–patient communication interactions.

Third, the very control seen to privilege RCTs over other methods (via reduction of threats to internal validity) also has long been understood to be at odds with the mandate to reduce threats to external validity—that is, with generalizing to the messy, uncontrolled, real world of practice (Brown, 2002; Sidani, Epstein, & Moritz, 2003; ten Have, Coyne, Salzer, & Katz, 2003). Distinguishing between the efficacy of an intervention under the highly controlled conditions of the RCT and the effectiveness of an intervention in the less-controlled world of practice, researchers in the health sciences have increasingly questioned the generalizability and clinical utility of the results of highly controlled trials.

Finally, researchers have increasingly noted that the scientific imperatives and mandates of the RCT are at odds with the ethical imperatives of practice directed toward person-centered care and toward ensuring a patient's right to choose. The standardized one-size-fits-all RCT is seen to favor inappropriately accommodating research participants' preferences, values, and needs to methodological standards.

◆ Toward Participant-Centered Intervention Studies

This critique of the RCT has stimulated calls for participant- or patient-centered intervention studies (Gross & Fogg, 2001; Lauver et al., 2002; Preference Collaborative Review Group, 2008). Such studies incorporate modifications to the design of clinical trials that take into account the distinctive social positions, circumstances, and preferences of the persons toward whom interventions are directed. Key components of participant-centered intervention studies are (a) the customization or tailoring of interventions—in domains such as content, mode and timing of delivery, and dosing—to accommodate the variant of the targeted problem exhibited by research participants and participant characteristics such as gender, race or ethnicity, and cultural values; and (b) the selection of innovative research designs (e.g., preference trials and randomized consent and N of 1 designs; Craig et al., 2008) that accommodate participants' preferences for one or more treatment or control groups. The goal of these modifications is optimization of both internal and external validity—that is, to permit valid scientific inferences to be drawn, while respecting participants' agency and rights.

The overall objective is the development of interventions that are scientifically credible; clinically safe, effective, and feasible; culturally sensitive; and ethically above reproach. Participant-centered intervention programs of research require the full use of an array of diverse methods.

QUANTITATIVE OBSERVATIONAL AND MIXED METHODS ALTERNATIVES TO THE CLINICAL TRIAL

The critique of the RCT has stimulated a new appreciation for what quantitative observational methods can contribute to the development of participant-centered interventions. Researchers have promoted the use of quantitative observational methods as both complementing and moving beyond RCTs (Happ et al., 2008; Morrison et al., 2008). For example, citing the limitations of RCTs, including sampling criteria that exclude patients in need of treatment and time periods too short to identify rare or longer-term adverse events, Silverman (2009) described how observational studies can be directed toward assessing treatment effectiveness and compliance over longer periods in larger and more-diverse samples of patients with shared comorbidities.

Among the limitations of RCTs, the risk of contamination or crossover between treatments can prohibit the use of the experimental design in clinical health services settings. Quasi-experimental alternatives to RCTs, such as pretest–posttest and sequential cohort designs, are used in patient-oriented clinical research to prevent contamination between control (usual care) and intervention groups. Happ and colleagues (2008) described application of a sequential cohort design to test two levels of intervention to improve communication between nurses and critical care patients who are unable to speak. To prevent contamination, three sequential patient–nurse cohorts (baseline, Intervention 1, Intervention 2) were recruited and subsequently studied.

The random assignment standard in RCTs also can present ethical and practical challenges in real-world clinical research. For example, it would be ethically questionable, in a study designed to test the efficacy of an in-hospital program of palliative care consultation, to randomly assign seriously ill hospitalized patients to a control group not receiving this service. Therefore, to determine the impact of palliative care consultation services as a programmatic intervention on outcomes for hospitalized patients, Morrison and colleagues (2008) analyzed 3 years of administrative data from eight hospitals with established palliative care programs. To compensate for the lack of random assignment in this retrospective study, patients receiving palliative care were matched by propensity scores to patients receiving usual care. These researchers used the following design and statistical techniques to reduce potential threats to validity: (a) sample stratification both by site and by vital status prior to propensity score matching; (b) propensity score methods to match patients based on patient characteristics to balance observed covariates; and (c) multivariable techniques to control for non-patient-based characteristics. These techniques were subsequently applied in a multisite prospective observational study of the impact of palliative care consultation on pain and symptom management, rehospitalization, family satisfaction, and cost for hospitalized patients with advanced cancer (NIH, NCI Grant No. R01-CA116227 to D. Meier).

Yeatts and Cready (2007) employed a mixed methods, nonequivalent control group pretest–posttest design to evaluate the effects of work redesign—"empowered" work teams—in long-term care. Participants in this multilevel intervention included certified nurse assistants, nursing home managers, residents, and their family members. Due to the diverse constituents potentially affected by the intervention and the diverse organizational characteristics of nursing homes, it was impractical to randomly assign the five experimental and five control nursing homes. The two groups, instead, were matched on resident and staff characteristics and case-mix (e.g., dedicated Alzheimer's unit). Observations were conducted of more than 270 team meetings, and meeting minutes and managerial responses were reviewed. Analyses of data supported the research proposition that empowered work teams in nursing homes positively affect feelings of empowerment, specifically, certified nurse assistant autonomy and competence. Analyses also demonstrated modest, positive effects on certified nurse assistant performance; resident care and choices; improved procedures, coordination, and cooperation between certified nurse assistants and nurses; and reduced turnover.

QUALITIZING
THE CLINICAL TRIAL

Coincident with the growing critique of the RCT and the call for participant-centered interventions has been the proliferation of qualitative studies in the behavioral and social sciences and the practice disciplines. Most relevant to the focus of this chapter has been the growing number of qualitative and historical studies of the clinical trial itself (e.g., Corrigan & Salzer, 2003; Featherstone & Donovan, 2002; Kaptchuk, 1998; Oudshoorn, 2003; Weinstein, 2004). Also notable is an advocacy literature specifically promoting the incorporation of qualitative research into intervention studies and evidence-based practice (e.g., Barbour, 2000; Sandelowski, 2004). The ascendancy of qualitative research itself likely contributed to the critique of the RCT, because the RCT was typically the standard with which qualitative research was always compared and, not surprisingly, found wholly deficient. Proponents of qualitative research directed their efforts toward challenging the standard itself. Moreover, by virtue of its open-ended methodological focus on preserving the individuality of participant experiences and understanding

the actors' point of view, qualitative research was seen to be already participant centered and, therefore, as offsetting the one-size-fits-all character of the RCT. A spate of literature now exists in which qualitative research methods are described and promoted as enhancing understanding of research participants' views of clinical trials, protecting the rights of trial participants, improving recruitment, facilitating the move from research efficacy to clinical effectiveness, and enhancing the clinical significance of intervention studies and, thereby, the utility and acceptability of interventions in practice settings (e.g., Brett, Heimendinger, Boender, Morin, & Marshall, 2002; Chesla, 2008; de Salis, Tomlin, Toerien, & Donovan, 2008; Donovan et al., 2002; Gamel, Grypdonck, Hengeveld, & Davis, 2001; Miller, Druss, & Rohrbaugh, 2003; Sandelowski, 1996; Sankar, Golin, Simoni, Luborsky, & Pearson, 2006; Schumacher et al., 2005; Verhoef, Casebeer, & Hilsden, 2002).

Even in literature promoting the enhancement and remediation role of qualitative research in intervention studies, however, qualitative research still tends to be depicted not as integral to trial work, but rather as complementary to it. In actual research practice, qualitative research components are still too often not planned, and tacked on without much demonstrable thought given to purpose, sampling, data collection, or data analysis. Forms of qualitative-light research (e.g., adding on a few open-ended questions at the end of a trial) are still done simply to enable researchers to claim that either qualitative or mixed methods research was conducted. Most problematic, qualitative research is essentialized, with no demonstrable recognition that qualitative research itself encompasses a diverse range of methodological approaches suitable for different purposes.

Matching research purpose to type of qualitative method requires a clear sense of how the intervention targeted for a study is to be analytically treated. For example, assessing the treatment fidelity of a behavioral intervention to improve medication adherence via a directed form of qualitative content analysis (Hsieh & Shannon, 2005) of transcripts produced from audio recordings of the intervention sessions as they are delivered implies a view of talk as an index of the intervention. In such studies, fidelity is said to be achieved to the extent that factors such as the content, timing, and dosing of the intervention can be seen to correspond to the manualized instructions for delivering it (Santacroce, Maccarelli, & Grey, 2004). In contrast, the use of an applied form of conversation analysis to ascertain efforts to maintain treatment fidelity implies seeing the intervention as an instance of talk-in-interaction that reflects the institutional practices constituting the intervention study. In conversation analysis, researchers examine features of talk such as turn-taking and repair, conversational openings and closings, and the institutional or social contexts of interaction (ten Have, 2007). Applied conversation analysis in treatment fidelity evaluations might focus on how interventionists maintain the intervention script or repair interruptions to it, or on how those targeted for the intervention accept or resist it. Roberts (2002) used a form of conversation analysis to show the subtle interactional differences between two physicians engaged in the act of recruiting women into a breast cancer treatment clinical trial.

Schumacher and colleagues (2005) described a series of analyses performed on audio-recorded intervention transcripts, intervention logs, field notes, and open-ended evaluation questions collected within an RCT of an individualized education, coaching, and support intervention for pain control intervention with cancer patients. These researchers first used qualitative content analysis to improve understanding of the intervention. A second analysis was performed to determine usefulness of specific pain management tools from the patients' perspective, by categorizing the patients' responses (e.g., positive, negative, or equivocal) and then comparing the frequencies of categorized responses between the intervention and control groups. Finally, criterion-based sampling was used to select patients for whom the intervention outcomes (e.g., pain scores) did not improve; qualitative content analysis was conducted to identify factors impeding acceptance and effectiveness of the intervention.

◆ Challenges of Mixed Methods Intervention Studies and Programs of Research

The renewed appreciation for qualitative and quantitative observational methods in intervention studies is laudable. The challenge, however, is to avoid outmoded binary distinctions between qualitative and quantitative research, and views of qualitative and quantitative observational methods as accessory rather than as central to the intervention study—that is, as only methodological complements to the RCT or as alternatives to the RCT whenever it cannot be used. A more methodologically integrated and dynamic (nonlinear, iterative) view of the intervention program of research is warranted that features the organic unity of the program instead of its methodological parts. Such programs of research are characterized by a view of methods as flexible tools to be accommodated—within the limits of those tools—to specific research aims and questions. Methods are conceived both as "tools for the production of knowledge" (Clarke, 2005, p. 304) and as ways of "interfering with . . . the world" inquirers seek to know (Mol, 2002, p. 155). Such programs of research are characterized also by avoiding the uninformative terms *qualitative* and *(non)quantitative* in favor of explicit descriptions of data collection methods (e.g., ethnographic interview, specific physiologic measure) and data analysis methods (e.g., directed qualitative content analysis, hierarchical regression modeling). Also to be avoided is the terminological morass that defines the mixed methods literature whereby distracting labels for designs substitute for clear explanations of what is planned or was done in a study and why. Not only are these terms uninformative and distracting, but also they reify a view of the world of inquiry as divided into two and perpetuate a view of mixed methods research as a confusing collection of ill-fitting parts. Arguably the single most important impediment to an organic view of mixed methods research is to simplify it as mixes of "qualitative" and "quantitative" elements.

Several challenges exist to conducting strong mixed methods intervention programs of research, characterized by both high "inference quality [and high] transferability" (Teddlie & Tashakkori, 2003, pp. 35–43). Challenges common to all mixed methods studies include the "mixing" of competing philosophical foundations and goals for inquiry, design prerogatives, and principles (Denscombe, 2008), and the different commitments of the members of the multispecialty and multidisciplinary research teams required to conduct such programmatic research (Bergman, 2008; Creswell & Plano Clark, 2007; Greene, 2007; Tashakkori & Teddlie, 2003). Mixed methods studies require accommodating to each other the purposeful sampling, case-oriented, singular focus, and idiographic generalization imperatives typically associated with qualitative research and the probability sampling, variable-oriented, single-dimensionality focus, and formal generalization imperatives typically associated with quantitative research (Collins, Onwuegbuzie, & Jiao, 2007; Sivesind, 1999; Teddlie & Yu, 2007). Foundational to the successful accommodations of these diverse imperatives is addressing the competing and contested understandings of what constitutes validity in scientific research that drive the selection of sampling and data collection and analysis strategies (Dellinger & Leech, 2007; Onwuegbuzie & Johnson, 2006). These challenges are generic to mixed methods research, are the subjects of

the chapters in Parts I and II of this *Handbook*, and are, therefore, not further addressed here.

Of these challenges, however, those most distinctive to conducting mixed methods intervention programs of research concern the timing and "priming effects" (Vitale, Armenakis, & Feild, 2008) of different types of data collection. Mixed methods research designs are defined in large part by the temporal relationship of their component parts: that is, by whether different kinds of sampling—and data collection and analysis—strategies are implemented concurrently or sequentially. Minimizing or, at the very least, accounting for the interventive effects of the temporal placement of techniques is the primary concern in intervention study.

For example, the development of an intervention may call for capturing subtleties of verbal and nonverbal interaction to "distill the active ingredients" of the intervention (Miller et al., 2003), to assess participants' real-time responses to it, or to assess treatment fidelity (i.e., whether it was delivered according to plan). To achieve these research purposes, concurrent data collection via audio or video recordings of intervention sessions may be warranted. Recording all of the sessions with every participant will control for any effects of being recorded on interventionists and participants. Moreover, having a complete data set of these recordings will enable researchers to answer a host of varied research questions concerning the intervention, most notably concerning fidelity and unexpected or adverse outcomes. Indeed, analysis of intervention data collected concurrently with the implementation of an intervention may reveal potential harm from or fatal weaknesses in the intervention and, thereby, prevent adverse events and conserve resources. Participants for whom postintervention outcomes did not improve may be purposively selected for focused analysis to identify weaknesses of the intervention or barriers to effectiveness (Happ, Naylor, & Roe-Prior, 1997; Schumacher et al., 2005).

If recording all sessions is not feasible because of cost or the setting of the intervention (e.g., a hospital emergency department), researchers will have to choose a systematic way to sample which sessions will be recorded to achieve the greatest informational yield. Sample size will depend on whether the analytic goal is to reach informational redundancy, or theoretical or scene saturation. For example, a stratified purposeful sample of sessions may be chosen varying on preselected parameters deemed analytically relevant to the intervention, such as sex, literacy, and severity of problem (Sandelowski, 2000). Up to five cases each may be selected representing every combination of these variables (e.g., if each variable is dichotomized, male, low literacy, low severity; female, low literacy, low severity; male, high literacy, low severity; and so on), for a total of 40 cases. In studies in which all intervention sessions are not recorded, researchers will have to account for this covariate in analyses of the outcomes of the intervention.

If the development of the intervention calls for explaining one or more of the outcomes of the intervention study, sequential data collection and analysis of open-ended and minimally structured interviews or survey questionnaires following completion of the intervention sessions will be warranted. Such sequential data collection and analysis likely will be long as opposed to short term (vis-à-vis the intervention session) because researchers cannot know how any one individual participant fared in response to the intervention—in comparison to all of the other participants—until all of them have completed the measures of the outcomes targeted by the intervention. If researchers want to explain the outcomes of the intervention they tested in the participants who received it, they must be able to select them on the basis of their scores on the outcome measures.

Researchers cannot do this, however, until the last participant has completed those measures, which may be several years after the first participant completed them, which,

in turn, will set up further design choices to address participants' recall of the intervention, and the feasibility and appropriateness of accessing participants after long periods of time. Researchers may choose to collect these data from all participants as soon as they have completed the outcome measures, but that is often not feasible. Alternatively, they may choose to purposefully sample participants on the basis of scores on outcome measures evaluated (a type of criterion sampling), not against the scores of all of the other participants in the study, but rather against normative standards set for those measures (e.g., cutoff scores on a depression inventory indicating presence or absence of clinical depression). Because intervention studies often target more than one outcome, researchers must choose to group participants by their scores on only one of the measures or on combinations of their scores, a choice that may itself require grounded theory or statistical methods to create scoring clusters or profiles.

Complicating the timing problem are the interactive effects of collecting different types of data in the same data collection session. For example, researchers must consider how asking participants to reflect in ethnographic interviews on the experience of decision making during a serious life-threatening illness may influence their responses on a depression measure administered immediately following such an interview. Alternatively, researchers must consider how measures of depression, anxiety, or stress conducted before an intensive interview session may influence participants' reflections during that interview. Separating the conduct of interviews from the administration of standardized tests may be optimal, but also impractical and overly burdensome for research participants. As part of pilot testing of the intervention, different orders of data collection may be tried and then statistically analyzed for their priming effects on each other and on outcome measures. Participants also may be asked to reflect on how and whether their responses to different data collection types influenced each other.

In summary, the temporal features of design have special significance in mixed methods intervention research programs. The quality of the inferences researchers will draw from them and the resources required to conduct them depend on how well they have thought through the benefits and liabilities of concurrent versus sequential data collection.

♦ *Designing Mixed Methods Intervention Studies and Programs of Research*

Mixed methods intervention programs of research consist of studies aimed at (a) developing the theoretical foundation for the intervention and the problem it is intended to mitigate or resolve; (b) pilot testing of the intervention and subsequent evaluation and refinement of the intervention based on the outcomes of the pilot testing; (c) testing of the intervention in controlled conditions (i.e., efficacy studies); and (d) testing of the intervention in real-world settings (i.e., effectiveness studies). As shown in Figure 28.1, conducting a mixed methods intervention program of research is a highly dynamic and iterative process, the nature and direction of which evolve in the course of the program. Researchers tack back and forth among these elements as their results call for refinements in the theoretical foundation for the intervention, in the intervention components, in the persons and outcomes targeted, in the ways these are measured, and as results call for answers to unanticipated questions.

Figure 28.1 Components of Mixed Methods Intervention Programs of Research

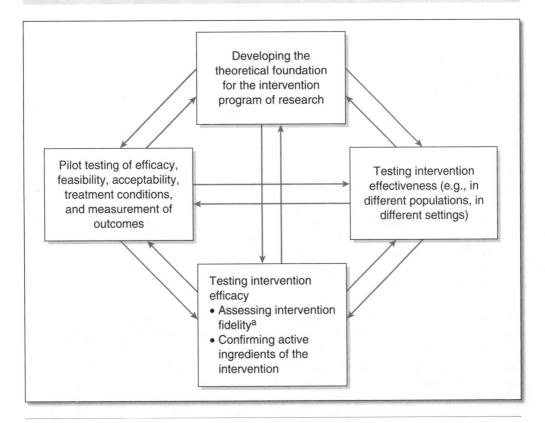

a. Assessing intervention fidelity often begins during pilot testing.

DEVELOPING THE THEORETICAL FOUNDATION FOR THE INTERVENTION PROGRAM OF RESEARCH

The development of effective interventions depends on the identification and deep understanding of the problem deemed to require intervention (e.g., rising morbidity or mortality due to nonadherence to treatment regimens or delay in seeking treatment). This comprehensive understanding is then transformed into a theory of the problem positing causes of the problem, or why it exists (e.g., low self-efficacy, mistrust of healthcare system, lack of knowledge, inability to differentiate symptom cues); for whom it is a problem (e.g., persons in certain social groups, certain healthcare providers or institutions); when (i.e., timing and conditions or circumstances) the problem is most likely to appear (e.g., early in a disease trajectory, under high-stress conditions); and consequences of the problem if it remains unresolved (e.g., continued high morbidity, rising cost to healthcare system). The theory of the problem enables researchers to define those aspects of the problem amenable to change, or subject to intervention (Conn, Rantz, Wipke-Tevis, & Maas, 2001). This theory then directs researchers toward actions that might be used to address those aspects of the problem subject to change and to theorize how and why those actions might work. The development of a sound theoretical foundation for an intervention program of research is the sine qua non for developing effective, translatable, and workable interventions (Sidani & Braden, 1998).

Developing the theoretical foundation for interventions addressing behaviorally and socially complex problems requires multiple and methodologically diverse studies to tap the different dimensions of these problems and potential solutions. This is especially the case if little research has been conducted in the area of interest. For example, Song, DeVito Dabbs, Studer, & Zangle (2008) conducted a series of studies on lung transplant recipients experiencing chronic rejection. They conducted a case study to describe the complex illness trajectory of a lung transplant recipient after the onset of chronic rejection. They sought to determine whether current post-lung-transplant management that was exclusively focused on aggressive treatment would meet the needs of lung recipients and their family caregivers when no proven effective treatment for chronic rejection exists (Song & DeVito Dabbs, 2006). They conducted medical record reviews of 311 lung transplant recipients who developed chronic rejection to examine their rates of morbidity, mortality, and health resource use (Song et al., 2008). They conducted a national survey of palliative care referrals after lung transplantation to describe the prevalence of these referrals for recipients with chronic rejection and the benefits of palliative care in the care of lung transplant recipients (Song, DeVito Dabbs, Studer, & Arnold, 2009). In addition, they conducted a grounded theory study to explore the impact of chronic rejection on clinical management decisions as understood by family and clinician caregivers (Song, DeVito Dabbs, Studer, Arnold, & Pilewski, 2010). The findings from these studies (encompassing the case study, medical record review, survey, and grounded theory) were used to target various dimensions of the problem of interest. Researchers also may select a priori theories of the problem or intervention and then conduct studies to ascertain their utility via qualitative descriptive or grounded theory studies. Alternatively, standardized measures can be used to address various conceptual relations or propositions in those theories.

The development of the theoretical foundation for the intervention to be tested encompasses determination of the critical components of the intervention; outcomes of the intervention against which its success will be evaluated; degree of standardization versus individualization, or customization, required; and determination of its mode of delivery, dose, and timing (Manojlovich & Sidani, 2008; Whittemore & Grey, 2002). Whether drawn from extant theory or newly generated, the intervention theory is directed toward explaining why, how, and under which conditions the intervention effects will likely occur (Conn et al., 2001; Sidani & Braden, 1998). Candidate theories may be drawn from an analysis of the empirical literature on interventions directed toward the target problem. Meta-analysis and other forms of systematic review are useful methods to ascertain the overall effects on targeted outcomes of interventions framed in various theories. For example, Kripalani, Yao, and Haynes (2007) conducted a systematic review to categorize and estimate the effect sizes of interventions to improve medication adherence in chronic medical conditions and identified several types of interventions that were significantly or potentially effective in improving clinical outcomes. Shojania and colleagues (2006) conducted a meta-regression analysis to compare the effects of quality improvement intervention strategies for glycemic control in Type 2 diabetes and concluded that interventions using case management and team change approaches were the most effective.

PILOT TESTING AND REFINING THE INTERVENTION AND ITS THEORETICAL FOUNDATION

Prior to testing of the intervention for its efficacy in controlled conditions and its effectiveness in actual practice settings, pilot studies are conducted to (a) evaluate the efficacy of the intervention; (b) assess the feasibility of the intervention and of the research protocol (including intervention and control conditions); (c) ascertain the acceptability of the intervention to the target population, including its burdens and cultural appropriateness; (d) determine the need for and effects of an attention control condition (i.e., a placebo condition that mimics the amount of time and attention received by the intervention group); and (e) examine the reliability and validity of outcome measures, and their sensitivity to evaluate efficacy. Because comprehensive

pilot testing encompasses such a diverse array of purposes, it requires a diverse repertoire of research methods and data sources from which researchers may choose the ones most suited to those purposes.

For example, descriptive statistical analyses (e.g., frequencies, means, medians, and standard deviations) are commonly used to summarize and evaluate the feasibility of recruitment and retention. Basic content analysis of recruiters' notes for reasons for participant refusal and of data collected in postintervention interviews with participants will yield important information on how researchers can redesign their studies to enhance enrollment and retention. The areas targeted for assessing feasibility and acceptability of treatment conditions may include the constraints on delivering the intervention in a particular setting, the timing (e.g., duration, pacing) of the intervention, the components of the interventionist training protocol, the overall cost of delivering the intervention, the treatment burden for participants and interventionists, participants' perceptions of the quality of interactions during intervention sessions, how well the intervention can be incorporated into participants' lifestyles, intervention fit with cultural values, and the appropriateness of the control condition. Researchers will choose those areas to target for pilot testing most relevant to their specific intervention programs. These areas can be targeted in survey measures (Sidani, Epstein, Bootzin, Moritz, & Miranda, 2009) or in open-ended, moderately structured in-person, telephone, or computer-based interviews.

Mixed methods case study research may embody the most integrated approach to pilot testing, with each participant and all of the data collected from them constituting each case. Case study research is defined here as the intensive empirical study of a relatively small number of cases on a large number of dimensions. When used in pilot testing, a case study approach allows researchers to examine the unique confluence or configuration of factors (e.g., intervention outcomes, perceived acceptability and burden of intervention, severity of problem, and degree of customization of intervention) and how they operate together in each case. The varied configurational comparative methods described in Rihoux and Ragin (2009), and the case study approaches described in Gerring (2007) and Morgan and Morgan (2009), offer a methodological framework different from the one in which pilot testing has typically been staged and one uniquely amenable to a mixed methods intervention program of research. For example, conducting case studies of extreme cases (e.g., selected for very high and very low approval ratings of intervention sessions) may assist researchers to identify how the characteristics of interventionists and participants, the delivery setting, and the content, dose, and timing of the intervention operated together to produce this evaluation. Using a diverse case selection approach, researchers can target the full range of diversity on several dimensions (e.g., combinations of outcomes indicating full, partial, and low efficacy, male and female participants, and burden perceived as high and low).

An additional domain of assessment during the pilot-testing phase is which type of trial design is best suited to the problem being addressed, the nature of the intervention, and the target population. Craig and colleagues (2008) listed five experimental designs for evaluating complex interventions, including: (a) the traditional individually randomized trial, in which persons are randomly allocated to receive either an experimental intervention or an alternative, such as standard treatment, placebo, or remaining on a waiting list; (b) cluster randomized trials, in which groups (e.g., residents in a nursing home) are randomly allocated to either the experimental or the control condition; (c) stepped-wedge design, in which an entire target population receives the intervention, with randomization built into the timing of receipt; (d) preference trials and randomized consent designs, in which treatment allocation is based on patient preferences or randomization occurs before seeking consent; and (e) N of 1 designs, in which individuals undergo the intervention with order and timing decided at random. Stepped-wedge designs may be preferred by groups of persons who do not want to wait for promising interventions, while preference trials allow participants to choose which condition they will enter before giving consent.

Even in traditional individually randomized trials, collecting information on the nature of the control condition will be important. For example, depending on the study context, an attention control condition (whereby participants in a comparison group receive a treatment that mimics the amount of time and attention received by the intervention group but is thought not to have a specific effect on them) may cause resentment and, thereby, negatively affect retention or unnecessarily increase subject burden (Gross, 2005; Hart, 2001). Failing to take account of target group preferences will lead to poor enrollment and retention and, therefore, will lead to a failed intervention program of research. Such information is especially relevant to developing explicit plans mandated by the National Institutes of Health and other funding agencies for recruiting minority populations and other groups typically excluded from intervention studies.

Of all the domains to be addressed in the pilot testing of an intervention, the most relevant to proceeding with the intervention is determining its association with, and efficacy in addressing, the targeted problem. This will be especially challenging when the pilot results show no evidence of efficacy. This result may be a function of the level of treatment fidelity, effects of moderators (e.g., participant characteristics), measurement timing, and sensitivity of outcome measures (Cote & Godin, 2005). Use of narrative or cognitive interviewing in pilot studies may reveal dimensions of the outcome assessment that standardized measures alone cannot identify (McIver, McGartland, & O'Halloran, 2009; Miller et al., 2003; Sandelowski, 1996; Willis, 2005), and may reveal benefits from the intervention not captured in outcome measures (Moffatt, White, Mackintosh, & Howel, 2006).

For example, Song, Ward, and colleagues (2009) designed an RCT pilot-testing the SPIRIT[(CC)1] (Sharing the Patient's Illness Representations to Increase Trust), a psychoeducational intervention with repeated measures that included concurrent assessments via standardized questionnaires and separate interviews with African American dialysis patients and surrogate decision makers at 1 week and 3 months postintervention. The postintervention narrative interviews at 1 week revealed which part of the intervention the participants most valued and which required refinement. Specifically, surrogates most appreciated the opportunity to learn how their loved ones felt about dialysis and end-of-life treatment options; both patients and their surrogates reported that discussions about spiritual aspects of continuing or withdrawing dialysis and end-of-life treatment were lacking during the intervention session. This feedback pertained to the cultural appropriateness of the intervention for the targeted African American population of patients with end-stage renal disease. Additionally, the narrative interviews showed that patients and surrogates held different perceptions about the impact of the intervention. Patients felt relieved after the intervention because they shared their ideas about the burden of illness and life-sustaining measures with their surrogates, and their surrogates were glad that they now gained the knowledge of their loved ones' wishes; however, the surrogates felt that a follow-up would have been helpful to discuss how those wishes could be met. These comments were repeated at 3-month postintervention interviews and confirmed the need for modifications to the intervention. These findings also helped explain why the intervention was shown to be effective in improving the congruence between the patients' end-of-life preferences and the surrogates' understanding of them, but achieved a smaller effect size in improving surrogate decision-making

confidence. On the basis of these findings, the intervention was refined to include an intervention element to explore spiritual representations of illness and end-of-life treatment. Also, an additional session was added to the intervention to assess any need for further discussing patient's expressed end-of-life treatment preferences and to develop plans to inform their healthcare providers and other members of the family of the patient's wishes.

TESTING INTERVENTION EFFICACY

Any alterations made to the theoretical staging, components, and delivery of the intervention made on the basis of pilot studies are then incorporated into the first definitive trial to test the efficacy of the newly refined intervention. Researchers can now select on the basis of empirical evidence the specific population to target; the specific aspect(s) of the problem to target; the specific content, timing, and dosing of the intervention; and the specific research design that will optimize the validity of study outcomes.

Assessing intervention fidelity. A key component of efficacy studies is the assessment of treatment fidelity, or how well the interventionist delivered the intervention as planned (Moncher & Prinz, 1991; Perepletchikova & Kazdin, 2005; Santacroce et al., 2004; Stein, Sargent, & Rafaels, 2007). Treatment fidelity consists of two components: adherence and competence. Adherence is defined as the number of prescribed behaviors shown, while competence is defined as the skillfulness shown in the delivery of the intervention (Carroll et al., 2000; Dumas, Lynch, Laughlin, Phillips, & Prinz, 2001; Moncher & Prinz, 1991). Assessing intervention fidelity is important to discern intervention effects on outcomes and to enhance the implementation of effective interventions in the real world of practice (Bellg et al., 2004; Dumas et al., 2001; Harshbarger, Simmons, Coelho, Sloop, & Collins, 2006).

The study of treatment fidelity requires methods enabling the comparison of the intervention as actually delivered to the pre-scribed plan for delivering it. Both content and process are evaluated. Content fidelity refers to the extent to which each key com-ponent of the intervention was delivered as intended and any unplanned components were delivered. Process fidelity refers to the extent to which effective communication skills were used and how each intervention component was delivered (Dumas et al., 2001). Sources of data include audio- or video-recorded observations of intervention sessions, and structured notes taken by interventionists following intervention ses-sions. Valid means of analyzing these data must then be developed (Stein et al., 2007).

For example, Dabbs and Song developed a tool to assess treatment fidelity to an intervention called Pocket PATH™ (Personal Assistant for Tracking Health) tested in an RCT (NIH, NINR Grant No. R01NR010711–01 to A. DeVito Dabbs). The Pocket PATH™ is a handheld device with custom programs designed to promote self-care behaviors after lung transplantation. Treatment fidelity assessment using this tool includes at least three sources and meth-ods of evaluation: (a) coding audio-recorded intervention sessions; (b) real-time direct observations of selected intervention sessions; and (c) summarizing electronic logs of patient use of device features automatically recorded in individual devices.

Song, Happ, and Sandelowski (2010) illustrated the process of developing a treat-ment fidelity tool and the potential utility in training and monitoring interventionists in delivering the SPIRIT[(CC)] intervention. In this fidelity assessment, interventionists' behaviors in the audio-recorded interven-tion sessions were coded and rated for the overall adherence to intervention content elements and process elements, pacing of intervention delivery, and the overall quality index of intervention delivery. For example, to rate the overall adherence to intervention content elements of the five-step SPIRIT[(CC)] intervention (a total of 30 elements), each prescribed question (a question must be asked by the interventionist to deliver the intervention element) was coded as *attempted* (asked as prescribed but failed to obtain an answer from the patient or surro-gate), *completed* (asked as prescribed and answered), *deviated from* (asked differently and its meaning changed as a result), or *skipped* (no question asked). Then, the overall adherence to intervention content elements was rated using the occurrences of *attempted*, *completed*, *deviated*, and *skipped* elements. These tallies were divided by the total number of elements (30) to com-pute ratios (0–1); a higher score in *com-pleted* indicated higher numbers of intervention elements completed. This tool helped the researchers determine how much deviation or variation from the estab-lished protocol occurred and enhanced the efficiency of training interventionists and monitoring their adherence and competence throughout the clinical trial by periodic and systematic assessment.

Larger programmatic interventions require different methods of fidelity eval-uation that emphasize essential elements or steps of the intervention process. For example, in an evaluation study of a youth mentoring program in Ireland, researchers examined the fidelity of program imple-mentation by reviewing case files and conducting focus groups about program implementation with program staff (Brady & O'Regan, 2009). In the multisite *Study of Palliative Care for Hospitalized Cancer Patients*, manualized training and knowl-edge competency testing is being conducted with all palliative care consultation teams at all sites; all new clinical staff take the UNI-PAC© competency test on their arrival at the institution. Chart audits are conducted on 10 randomly selected patient records each quarter in each clinical site to check adher-ence to clinical quality of care criteria in pal-liative care of cancer patients (NIH, NCI, Grant No. R01-CA116227 to D. Meier).

Confirming active or therapeutic ingredients of intervention. Another key component of efficacy studies is confirming what the active ingredients are in the intervention producing its effects. The active ingredient in a drug is the substance that is pharmacologically active. This term is used in the health sciences intervention literature to refer to intervention components that are responsible for therapeutic effects and changes in the targeted health outcomes.

Confirming active ingredients can be done by examining the associations between the presumed active ingredients and the outcomes. Schmaling, Williams, Schwartz, Ciechanowski, and LoGerfo (2008) first conducted a content analysis of the problem-solving component of a behavioral intervention they had developed to improve depressive symptoms, social activity, and physical activity in elderly people with minor depressive or dysthymic disorder. They then quantified the number of activities scheduled and tested those variables as predictors of the three outcomes. They found that only more activity scheduling was associated with increased physical activity at the 12-month evaluation relative to baseline. The authors concluded that these findings suggest either that the study methodology did not reveal truly existing associations between treatment variables and outcomes or that the presumed active ingredients were not the active ingredients of treatment.

Identifying active ingredients, contributing factors, and inert elements of an intervention is a precursor to intervention translation. Typically, intervention studies are superiority trials (in which two treatments are compared for superiority in effects). There will be increasing need for equivalence or noninferiority trials that test whether the effect of a parsimonious or lean intervention is equivalent or noninferior to that of the full-version intervention (Lovell et al., 2006).

Person-oriented analysis. A quantitative variant of the intensive study of cases is the array of statistical techniques referred to as person-oriented analysis (Bergman & Trost, 2006; Singer, Ryff, Carr, & Magee, 1998;

von Eye & Bogat, 2006). Prominent in life course and human development research, person-oriented analysis is focused on intra- and interindividual differences on the variables selected for study to enable modeling of the "distinct configurations of heterogeneity" that likely exist within a sample (Nurius & Macy, 2008, p. 390). Via prototypical statistical techniques such as profile, class, and cluster analyses, person-oriented methods are useful in ascertaining whether there are "common types or patterned interrelationships that constitute an empirical structure of heterogeneity [or] clusters of theoretically meaningful characteristics . . . shared within subgroups and that distinguish subgroups" (Nurius & Macy, 2008, p. 393). Focused on within-group "coherence" and between-group "distinctiveness" (Nurius & Macy, 2008, p. 397), person-oriented analyses are an important addition to the repertoire of methods in intervention programs of research because they will be useful in showing how intervention outcomes from subgroups or individuals may conflict with outcomes from the overall sample receiving the intervention. This, in turn, will provide important information for customizing and targeting interventions.

TESTING INTERVENTION EFFECTIVENESS

While efficacy studies are focused on the evaluation of interventions in controlled circumstances, effectiveness studies are focused on testing them in real-world settings. This requires delineating how characteristics of the intervention itself, participants, interventionists, and setting operated together to influence each other and intervention outcomes. Such analyses are especially relevant for socially complex interventions that require multiple interactions between intervener(s) and participant(s) over extended periods.

The taxonomy of implementation methods shown in Leeman, Baernholdt, and Sandelowski (2007) offers a framework to guide these analyses. These authors proposed five categories of implementation methods: (a) increasing coordination; (b) raising awareness; (c) persuading individuals to adopt the practice change via interpersonal channels; (d) persuading individuals to adopt the practice change by reinforcing belief that the behavior will lead to desirable results; and (e) increasing behavioral control. This taxonomy encompasses various approaches, such as workshop oversight, pilot testing, performance evaluation, and surveys of individuals' attitudes toward changes and barriers. To select appropriate methods of intervention implementation and then to test it, researchers must clearly describe the intervention comparability with certain settings and populations (e.g., analysis of intervention effects by participants' race, education, and socioeconomic status) and provide information about intervention complexity (e.g., single- vs. multifaceted interventions, patients only vs. patient and caregiver dyads) and essential personnel and material resources required to adapt and implement the intervention (Leeman, Jackson, & Sandelowski, 2006).

Resnick, Gruber-Baldini, and colleagues (2009) translated their restorative care (Res-Care) intervention from the nursing home to assisted living (Res-Care-AL). Modifications for the new setting and population included expanding the theoretical framework from self-efficacy theory to a social-ecological model in which self-efficacy theory guided the interpersonal level concepts and measures (Resnick, Galik, Gruber-Baldini, & Zimmerman, 2009). Interventions were multilevel in both settings; researchers explicated the use and engagement of facility personnel and material resources to conduct the project. Additional measures of nursing assistant knowledge of exercise, resident fear of falling, observation of resident physical activity, and social support for exercise were included. The study translating the intervention to the assisted-living setting was based on information gained from prior qualitative study of how nursing assistants motivate cognitively impaired older adults to participate in restorative care (Galik, Resnick, & Pretzer-Aboff, 2009).

Process tracing as a means of delineating implementation factors. Statistical techniques such as, for instance, regression analyses, t tests, ANOVA, and other equivalent nonparametric analyses are commonly employed to ascertain whether a statistically significant relationship exists between an intervention and the one or more outcomes targeted by that intervention. These techniques are oriented largely toward establishing that a relationship exists, not toward explaining why it exists, or why the intervention may have failed to produce targeted outcomes. Because they share a focus on the intensive study of particulars, both qualitative and case study research have been advanced as the methods of choice for establishing causal mechanism (Edwards, Dattilio, & Bromley, 2004; Maxwell, 2004a, 2004b).

Mixed methods research, by common definition, encompasses disparate and noncomparable data sets. As described in Gerring (2007), Harding, Fox, and Mehta (2002), and Mahoney (1999), process tracing is a means of assessing causality (especially causal mechanism) with multiple types of evidence constituting noncomparable individual observations. Although achieving functional as opposed to cosmetic integration of diverse data sets continues to receive much attention in the mixed methods research literature (Bergman, 2008; Driscoll, Appiah-Yeboah, Salib, & Rupert, 2007; Happ, Dabbs, Tate, Hricik, & Erlen, 2006; Onwuegbuzie & Teddlie, 2003), how this is to be achieved is still debated. The mechanisms involved, and the gains and losses of information entailed, in transforming diverse data sets into each other— commonly referred to as the quantitizing of qualitative data and the qualitizing of quantitative data—have yet to be fully examined (Sandelowski, Voils, & Knafl, 2009). The full explanation of study findings through the use of mixed methods, however, is largely dependent on the extent to which researchers "genuinely integrate" the analysis and interpretation of data (Bryman, 2007, p. 8).

Process tracing directly addresses the challenge of how to meaningfully assemble all of the disparate information about a case into coherence to establish causality. As socially complex interventions typically entail intervention contacts or measurements of outcomes over a period of time, their study can be conceived as longitudinal. Process tracing involves long causal chains contributing to an outcome in a single case (i.e., $X_1 \rightarrow X_2 \rightarrow X_3 \rightarrow X_4 \rightarrow X_n \rightarrow Y$), as opposed to multiple instances of $X_1 \rightarrow Y$ (Gerring, 2007). Entailing a series of N = 1 observations, process tracing is foundational to narrative or historical explanation in that a targeted outcome is viewed as the product of a unique, temporally ordered, and sequentially unfolding series of events. Process tracing is especially useful to assess causality when temporal sequencing, particular events, and path dependence must be accounted for; therefore, it is useful in explaining how the many factors involved in testing and implementing an intervention come together to yield outcomes. Cases (individuals or aggregates receiving the intervention and all of the data collected from and about them) may be selected for process tracing to explain, for example, their typicality or atypicality vis-à-vis all the other cases studied.

◆ Conclusions

Mixed methods intervention programs of research paradoxically require a mindset less focused on mixing methods and more focused on what makes sense in developing the interventions that will resolve problems in real-world settings. They require knowledge of the opportunities, limits, and diversity in application of methods and the imagination to configure them into method assemblages (Law, 2004), uniquely fitting to the particular intervention program as it unfolds.

Research Questions and Exercises

Select a problem in your discipline subject to intervention.

1. How would you go about developing a theory of that problem and a theory of how to resolve it?

2. What information do you need to acquire concerning the key stakeholders and settings affected by the problem?

3. How would you go about acquiring this information?

4. How would you handle the timing and priming effects of a mixed methods approach to conducting intervention development and testing studies?

5. To what extent and at what point in your studies should your intervention be modified based on the findings from those studies?

◆ Note

1. (cc): Creative Commons.

◆ References

Barbour, R. S. (2000). The role of qualitative research in broadening the "evidence base" for clinical practice. *Journal of Evaluation in Clinical Practice, 6*(2), 155–163.

Bellg, A. J., Borrelli, B., Resnick, B., Hecht, J., Minicucci, D. S., Ory, M., et al. (2004). Enhancing treatment fidelity in health behavior change studies: Best practices and recommendations from the NIH Behavior Change Consortium. *Health Psychology, 23*(5), 443–451.

Bergman, L., & Trost, K. (2006). The person-oriented versus the variable-oriented approach: Are they complementary, opposites, or exploring different worlds? *Merrill-Palmer Quarterly, 52*(3), 377–389.

Bergman, M. M. (2008). *Advances in mixed methods research.* Los Angeles: Sage.

Bower, P., King, M., Nazareth, I., Lampe, F., & Sibbald, B. (2005). Patient preferences in randomised controlled trials: Conceptual framework and implications for research. *Social Science & Medicine, 61*(3), 685–695.

Brady, B., & O'Regan, C. (2009). Meeting the challenge of doing an RCT evaluation of youth mentoring in Ireland. *Journal of Mixed Methods Research, 3*(3), 265–280.

Brett, J. A., Heimendinger, J., Boender, C., Morin, C., & Marshall, J. A. (2002). Using ethnography to improve intervention design. *American Journal of Health Promotion, 16*(6), 331–340.

Brown, S. J. (2002). Nursing intervention studies: A descriptive analysis of issues important to clinicians. *Research in Nursing & Health, 25*(4), 317–327.

Bryman, A. (2007). Barriers to integrating quantitative and qualitative research. *Journal of Mixed Methods Research, 1*(1), 8–22.

Campbell, M., Fitzpatrick, R., Haines, A., Kinmonth, A. L., Sandercock, P., Spiegelhalter, D., et al. (2000). Framework for design and evaluation of complex interventions to improve health. *British Medical Journal, 321*(7262), 694–696.

Carroll, K. M., Nich, C., Sifry, R. L., Nuro, K. F., Frankforter, T. L., Ball, S. A., et al. (2000). A general system for evaluating therapist adherence and competence in psychotherapy research in the addictions. *Drug and Alcohol Dependence, 57*(3), 225–238.

Chesla, C. A. (2008). Translational research: Essential contributions from interpretive nursing science. *Research in Nursing & Health, 31*(4), 381–390.

Clarke, A. E. (2005). *Situational analysis: Grounded theory after the postmodern turn.* Thousand Oaks, CA: Sage.

Collins, K. M., Onwuegbuzie, A. J., & Jiao, Q. G. (2007). A mixed methods investigation of mixed methods sampling designs in social and health science research. *Journal of Mixed Methods Research, 1*(3), 267–294.

Conn, V. S., Rantz, M. J., Wipke-Tevis, D. D., & Maas, M. L. (2001). Designing effective nursing interventions. *Research in Nursing & Health, 24*(5), 433–442.

Corrigan, P. W., & Salzer, M. S. (2003). The conflict between random assignment and treatment preference: Implications for internal validity. *Evaluation and Program Planning, 26*(2), 109–121.

Cote, J. K., & Godin, G. (2005). Efficacy of interventions in improving adherence to antiretroviral therapy. *International Journal of STD & AIDS, 16*(5), 335–343.

Craig, P., Dieppe, P., Mcintyre, S., Mitchie, S., Nazareth, I., & Petticrew, M. (2008). Developing and evaluating complex interventions: The new Medical Research Council guidance. *British Medical Journal, 337,* 979–983.

Creswell, J. W., & Plano Clark, V. L. (2007). *Designing and conducting mixed methods research.* Thousand Oaks, CA: Sage.

Dellinger, A. B., & Leech, N. L. (2007). Toward a unified validation framework in mixed methods research. *Journal of Mixed Methods Research*, *1*(4), 309–332.

Denscombe, M. (2008). Communities of practice: A research paradigm for the mixed methods approach. *Journal of Mixed Methods Research*, *2*(3), 270–283.

de Salis, I., Tomlin, Z., Toerien, M., & Donovan, J. (2008). Using qualitative research methods to improve recruitment to randomized controlled trials: The Quartet study. *Journal of Health Services Research & Policy*, *13*(Suppl. 3), 92–96.

Donovan, J., Mills, N., Smith, M., Brindle, L., Jacoby, A., Peters, T., et al. (2002). Quality improvement report: Improving design and conduct of randomised trials by embedding them in qualitative research: ProtecT (prostate testing for cancer and treatment) study. Commentary: Presenting unbiased information to patients can be difficult. *British Medical Journal*, *325*(7367), 766–770.

Driscoll, D., Appiah-Yeboah, A., Salib, P., & Rupert, D. J. (2007). Merging qualitative and quantitative data in mixed methods research: How to and why not. *Ecological and Environmental Anthropology*, *3*(1), 19–28.

Dumas, J. E., Lynch, A. M., Laughlin, J. E., Phillips, S. E., & Prinz, R. J. (2001). Promoting intervention fidelity: Conceptual issues, methods, and preliminary results from the EARLY ALLIANCE prevention trial. *American Journal of Preventive Medicine*, *20*(1 Suppl.), 38–47.

Edwards, D. J., Dattilio, F. M., & Bromley, D. B. (2004). Developing evidence-based practice: The role of case-based research. *Professional Psychology: Research and Practice*, *35*(6), 589–597.

Featherstone, K., & Donovan, J. L. (2002). "Why don't they just tell me straight, why allocate it?" The struggle to make sense of participating in a randomised controlled trial. *Social Science & Medicine*, *55*(5), 709–719.

Galik, E. M., Resnick, B., & Pretzer-Aboff, I. (2009). "Knowing what makes them tick": Motivating cognitively impaired older adults to participate in restorative care. *International Journal of Nursing Practice*, *15*(1), 48–55.

Gamel, C., Grypdonck, M., Hengeveld, M., & Davis, B. (2001). A method to develop a nursing intervention: The contribution of qualitative studies to the process. *Journal of Advanced Nursing*, *33*(6), 806–819.

Gerring, J. (2007). *Case study research: Principles and practices*. New York: Cambridge University Press.

Greene, J. C. (2007). *Mixed methods in social inquiry*. San Francisco: Jossey-Bass.

Gross, D. (2005). On the merits of attention-control groups. *Research in Nursing & Health*, *28*(2), 93–94.

Gross, D., & Fogg, L. (2001). Clinical trials in the 21st century: The case for participant-centered research. *Research in Nursing & Health*, *24*(6), 530–539.

Happ, M. B., Dabbs, A. D., Tate, J., Hricik, A., & Erlen, J. (2006). Exemplars of mixed methods data combination and analysis. *Nursing Research*, *55*(2 Suppl.), S43–S49.

Happ, M. B., Naylor, M. D., & Roe-Prior, P. (1997). Factors contributing to rehospitalization of elderly patients with heart failure. *Journal of Cardiovascular Nursing*, *11*(4), 75–84.

Happ, M. B., Sereika, S., Garrett, K., & Tate, J. (2008). Use of the quasi-experimental sequential cohort design in the Study of Patient-Nurse Effectiveness With Assisted Communication Strategies (SPEACS). *Contemporary Clinical Trials*, *29*(5), 801–808.

Harding, D. J., Fox, C., & Mehta, J. D. (2002). Studying rare events through qualitative case studies: Lessons from a study of rampage school shootings. *Sociological Methods & Research*, *31*(2), 174–217.

Harshbarger, C., Simmons, G., Coelho, H., Sloop, K., & Collins, C. (2006). An empirical assessment of implementation, adaptation, and tailoring: The evaluation of CDC's National Diffusion of VOICES/VOCES. *AIDS Education and Prevention*, *18*(4 Suppl. A), 184–197.

Hart, A. (2001). Randomized controlled trials: The control group dilemma revisited. *Complementary Therapies in Medicine*, 9(1), 40–44.

Hsieh, H. F., & Shannon, S. E. (2005). Three approaches to qualitative content analysis. *Qualitative Health Research*, 15(9), 1277–1288.

Kaptchuk, T. J. (1998). Intentional ignorance: A history of blind assessment and placebo controls in medicine. *Bulletin of History of Medicine*, 72(3), 389–433.

Kaptchuk, T. J., Shaw, J., Kerr, C. E., Conboy, L. A., Kelley, J. M., Csordas, T. J., et al. (2009). "Maybe I made up the whole thing": Placebos and patients' experiences in a randomized controlled trial. *Culture, Medicine, and Psychiatry*, 33(3), 382–411.

Kripalani, S., Yao, X., & Haynes, R. B. (2007). Interventions to enhance medication adherence in chronic medical conditions: A systematic review. *Archives of Internal Medicine*, 167(6), 540–550.

Lauver, D. R., Ward, S. E., Heidrich, S. M., Keller, M. L., Bowers, B. J., Brennan, P. F., et al. (2002). Patient-centered interventions. *Research in Nursing & Health*, 25(4), 246–255.

Law, J. (2004). *After method: Mess in social science research*. London: Routledge.

Leeman, J., Baernholdt, M., & Sandelowski, M. (2007). Developing a theory-based taxonomy of methods for implementing change in practice. *Journal of Advanced Nursing*, 58(2), 191–200.

Leeman, J., Jackson, B., & Sandelowski, M. (2006). An evaluation of how well research reports support the use of findings in practice. *Journal of Nursing Scholarship*, 38(2), 171–177.

Lindsay, B. (2004). Randomized controlled trials of socially complex nursing interventions: Creating bias and unreliability? *Journal of Advanced Nursing*, 45(1), 84–94.

Lovell, K., Cox, D., Haddock, G., Jones, C., Raines, D., Garvey, R., et al. (2006). Telephone administered cognitive behaviour therapy for treatment of obsessive compulsive disorder: Randomised controlled non-inferiority trial. *British Medical Journal*, 333(7574), 883.

Mahoney, J. (1999). Nominal, ordinal, and narrative appraisal in macrocausal analysis. *American Journal of Sociology*, 104(4), 1154–1196.

Manojlovich, M., & Sidani, S. (2008). Nurse dose: What's in a concept? *Research in Nursing & Health*, 31(4), 310–319.

Maxwell, J. A. (2004a). Causal explanation, qualitative research, and scientific inquiry in education. *Educational Researcher*, 33(2), 3–11.

Maxwell, J. A. (2004b). Using qualitative methods for causal explanation. *Field Methods*, 16(3), 243–264.

McIver, S., McGartland, M., & O'Halloran, P. (2009). "Overeating is not about the food": Women describe their experience of a yoga treatment program for binge eating. *Qualitative Health Research*, 19(9), 1234–1245.

Miller, C. L., Druss, B. G., & Rohrbaugh, R. M. (2003). Using qualitative methods to distill the active ingredients of a multifaceted intervention. *Psychiatric Services*, 54(4), 568–571.

Moffatt, S., White, M., Mackintosh, J., & Howel, D. (2006). Using quantitative and qualitative data in health services research—What happens when mixed method findings conflict? *BMC Health Services Research* (*Open Access journal*). Retrieved September 24, 2009, from http://www.biomedcentral.com/content/pdf/1472-6963-6-28.pdf

Mol, A. (2002). *The body multiple: Ontology in medical practice*. Durham, NC: Duke University Press.

Moncher, F., & Prinz, R. (1991). Treatment fidelity in outcome studies. *Clinical Psychology Review*, 11(3), 247–266.

Morgan, D. L., & Morgan, R. K. (2009). *Single-case research methods for the behavioral and health sciences*. Los Angeles: Sage.

Morrison, R. S., Penrod, J. D., Cassel, J. B., Caust-Ellenbogen, M., Litke, A., Spragens, L., et al. (2008). Cost savings associated with U.S. hospital palliative care consultation programs. *Archives of Internal Medicine,* *168*(16), 1783–1790.

Nurius, P. S., & Macy, R. J. (2008). Heterogeneity among violence-exposed women: Applying person-oriented research methods. *Journal of Interpersonal Violence,* *23*(3), 389–415.

Oakley, A. (1989). Who's afraid of the randomized controlled trial? Some dilemmas of the scientific method and "good" research practice. *Women & Health,* *15*(4), 25–59.

Onwuegbuzie, A. J., & Johnson, R. B. (2006). The validity issue in mixed research. *Research in the Schools, 13*(1), 48–63.

Onwuegbuzie, A. J., & Teddlie, C. (2003). A framework for analyzing data in mixed methods research. In A. Tashakkori & C. Teddlie (Eds.), *Handbook of mixed methods in social and behavioral research* (pp. 351–383). Thousand Oaks, CA: Sage.

Oudshoorn, N. (2003). Clinical trials as a cultural niche in which to configure the gender identities of users: The case of male contraceptive development. In N. Oudshoorn & T. Pinch (Eds.), *How users matter: The co-construction of users and technologies* (pp. 209–227). Cambridge, MA: MIT Press.

Perepletchikova, F., & Kazdin, A. E. (2005). Treatment integrity and therapeutic change: Issues and research recommendations. *Clinical Psychology: Science and Practice, 12*(4), 365–383.

Preference Collaborative Review Group. (2008). Patients' preferences within randomised trials: Systematic review and patient level meta-analysis. *British Medical Journal, 337,* a1864.

Resnick, B., Galik, E., Gruber-Baldini, A. L., & Zimmerman, S. (2009). Implementing a restorative care philosophy of care in assisted living: Pilot testing of Res-Care-AL. *Journal of the American Academy of Nurse Practitioners, 21*(2), 123–133.

Resnick, B., Gruber-Baldini, A. L., Zimmerman, S., Galik, E., Pretzer-Aboff, I., Russ, K., et al. (2009). Nursing home resident outcomes from the Res-Care intervention. *Journal*

of the American Geriatrics Society, 57(7), 1156–1165.

Rihoux, B., & Ragin, C. C. (2009). *Configurational comparative methods: Qualitative Comparative Analysis (QCA) and related techniques.* Thousand Oaks, CA: Sage.

Roberts, F. (2002). Qualitative differences among cancer clinical trial explanations. *Social Science & Medicine, 55*(11), 1947–1955.

Sandelowski, M. (1996). Using qualitative methods in intervention studies. *Research in Nursing & Health, 19*(4), 359–364.

Sandelowski, M. (2000). Combining qualitative and quantitative sampling, data collection, and analysis techniques in mixed-method studies. *Research in Nursing & Health, 23*(3), 246–255.

Sandelowski, M. (2004). Using qualitative research. *Qualitative Health Research, 14*(10), 1366–1386.

Sandelowski, M., Voils, C. I., & Knafl, G. (2009). On quantitizing. *Journal of Mixed Methods Research, 3*(3), 208–222.

Sankar, A., Golin, C., Simoni, J. M., Luborsky, M., & Pearson, C. (2006). How qualitative methods contribute to understanding combination antiretroviral therapy adherence. *Journal of Acquired Immune Deficiency Syndrome, 43*(Suppl. 1), S54–S68.

Santacroce, S. J., Maccarelli, L. M., & Grey, M. (2004). Intervention fidelity. *Nursing Research, 53*(1), 63–66.

Schmaling, K. B., Williams, B., Schwartz, S., Ciechanowski, P., & LoGerfo, J. (2008). The content of behavior therapy for depression demonstrates few associations with treatment outcome among low-income, medically ill older adults. *Behavior Therapy, 39*(4), 360–365.

Schumacher, K. L., Koresawa, S., West, C., Dodd, M., Paul, S. M., Tripathy, D., et al. (2005). Qualitative research contribution to a randomized clinical trial. *Research in Nursing & Health, 28*(3), 268–280.

Shojania, K. G., Ranji, S. R., McDonald, K. M., Grimshaw, J. M., Sundaram, V., Rushakoff, R. J., et al. (2006). Effects of quality improvement strategies for Type 2 diabetes on glycemic control: A meta-regression analysis. *Journal of the American Medical Association*, 296(4), 427–440.

Sidani, S., & Braden, C. J. (1998). *Evaluating nursing interventions: A theory-driven approach*. Thousand Oaks, CA: Sage.

Sidani, S., Epstein, D. R., Bootzin, R. R., Moritz, P., & Miranda, J. (2009). Assessment of preferences for treatment: Validation of a measure. *Research in Nursing & Health*, 32(4), 419–431.

Sidani, S., Epstein, D. R., & Moritz, P. (2003). An alternative paradigm for clinical nursing research: An exemplar. *Research in Nursing & Health*, 26(3), 244–255.

Silverman, S. L. (2009). From randomized controlled trials to observational studies. *American Journal of Medicine*, 122(2), 114–120.

Singer, B., Ryff, C. D., Carr, D., & Magee, W. J. (1998). Linking life histories and mental health: A person-centered strategy. *Sociological Methodology*, 28(1), 1–51.

Sivesind, K. H. (1999). Structured, qualitative comparison: Between singularity and single-dimensionality. *Quality & Quantity*, 33(4), 361–380.

Song, M. K., & DeVito Dabbs, A. J. (2006). Advance care planning after lung transplantation: A case of missed opportunities. *Progress in Transplantation*, 16(3), 222–225.

Song, M. K., DeVito Dabbs, A., Studer, S. M., & Arnold, R. M. (2009). Palliative care referrals after lung transplantation in major transplant centers in the United States. *Critical Care Medicine*, 37(4), 1288–1292.

Song, M. K., DeVito Dabbs, A., Studer, S. M., Arnold, R. M., & Pilewski, J. M. (2010). Exploring the meaning of chronic rejection after lung transplantation and its impact on clinical management: The perspectives of family and clinician caregivers. *Journal of Pain and Symptom Management*. Manuscript in press.

Song, M. K., DeVito Dabbs, A., Studer, S. M., & Zangle, S. E. (2008). Course of illness after the onset of chronic rejection in lung transplant recipients. *American Journal of Critical Care*, 17(3), 246–253.

Song, M. K., Happ, M. B., & Sandelowski, M. (2010). Development of a tool to assess fidelity to a psycho-educational intervention. *Journal of Advanced Nursing*, 66(3), 673–682.

Song, M. K., Ward, S. E., Happ, M. B., Piraino, B., Donovan, H. S., Shields, A. M., et al. (2009). Randomized controlled trial of SPIRIT: An effective approach to preparing African American dialysis patients and families for end-of-life. *Research in Nursing & Health*, 32, 260–273.

Stein, K. F., Sargent, J. T., & Rafaels, N. (2007). Intervention research: Establishing fidelity of the independent variable in nursing clinical trials. *Nursing Research*, 56(1), 54–62.

Tashakkori, A., & Teddlie, C. (2003). *Handbook of mixed methods in social and behavioral research*. Thousand Oaks, CA: Sage.

Teddlie, C., & Tashakkori, A. (2003). Major issues and controversies in the use of mixed methods in the social and behavioral sciences. In A. Tashakkori & C. Teddlie (Eds.), *Handbook of mixed methods in social & behavioral research* (pp. 3–50). Thousand Oaks, CA: Sage.

Teddlie, C., & Yu, F. (2007). Mixed methods sampling: A typology with examples. *Journal of Mixed Methods Research*, 1(1), 77–100.

ten Have, P. (2007). *Doing conversation analysis: A practical guide*. London: Sage.

ten Have, T. R., Coyne, J., Salzer, M., & Katz, I. (2003). Research to improve the quality of care for depression: Alternatives to the simple randomized clinical trial. *General Hospital Psychiatry*, 25(2), 115–123.

Thompson, J. J., Ritenbaugh, C., & Nichter, M. (2009). Reconsidering the placebo response from a broad anthropological perspective. *Culture, Medicine, and Psychiatry*, 33(1), 112–152.

Verhoef, M. J., Casebeer, A. L., & Hilsden, R. J. (2002). Assessing efficacy of complementary medicine: Adding qualitative research methods to the "Gold Standard." *Journal of*

Alternative and Complementary Medicine, 8(3), 275–281.

Vitale, D. C., Armenakis, A. A., & Feild, H. S. (2008). Integrating qualitative and quantitative methods for organizational diagnosis: Possible priming effects? *Journal of Mixed Methods Research*, 2(1), 87–105.

von Eye, A., & Bogat, G. A. (2006). Person-oriented and variable-oriented research: Concepts, results, and development. *Merrill-Palmer Quarterly*, 52, 390–420.

Weinstein, M. (2004). Randomized design and the myth of certain knowledge: Guinea pig narratives and cultural critique. *Qualitative Inquiry*, 10(2), 246–260.

Whittemore, R., & Grey, M. (2002). The systematic development of nursing interventions. *Journal of Nursing Scholarship*, 34(2), 115–120.

Willis, G. (2005). *Cognitive interviewing: A tool for improving questionnaire design.* Thousand Oaks, CA: Sage.

Yeatts, D. E., & Cready, C. M. (2007). Consequences of empowered CNA teams in nursing home settings: A longitudinal assessment. *Gerontologist*, 47(3), 323–339.

29

MIXED METHODS AND SYSTEMATIC REVIEWS

Examples and Emerging Issues

◆ Angela Harden and James Thomas

Objectives

Upon finishing this chapter, you should be able to

- recognize a systematic review as a piece of research;

- outline the major steps involved in a systematic review;

- discuss the major dimensions of difference between systematic reviews;

- distinguish between mono-method and mixed methods systematic reviews;

- discuss the strengths and limitations of "mono-method" reviews and "mixed methods" reviews;

(Continued)

(Continued)

- compare and contrast Critical Interpretive Synthesis, Realist Synthesis, Meta-narrative review, Bayesian synthesis, and the model of mixed methods review used as a worked example in this chapter;

- describe the paradigmatic stance underpinning the above approaches;

- identify difficulties with the use of the terms *qualitative* and *quantitative* within a mixed methods systematic review; and

- write a proposal or plan for conducting a mixed methods systematic review.

This chapter focuses on the use of mixed methods to bring together and integrate existing qualitative and quantitative research findings within a systematic review. Although systematic reviews—reviews of research that use rigorous and explicit methods to identify and integrate findings from multiple studies—have become an established methodology in recent years, mixed methods systematic reviews are only just emerging as a distinct category. In line with many authors writing about mixed methods in primary research, we see the use of mixed methods in systematic reviews as being influenced by several factors, such as paradigm and philosophical assumptions or the available skills within a research team, but a key driver ought to be the review questions. We thus offer a working definition of a mixed methods systematic review as a review that combines the findings of qualitative and quantitative studies within a single review in order to address overlapping or complementary questions. In this chapter, we provide an introduction to the role of mixed methods in systematic reviews, present a framework for designing and conducting such reviews, illustrate this framework using a worked example, and suggest future directions for mixed methods and systematic reviews. First,

however, we outline in more detail the principles and methods of systematic reviews and highlight the benefits of including diverse study types within them.

◆ What Is a Systematic Review?

Just like primary research, literature reviews come in many different shapes and forms. Literature reviews, for example, can serve many different purposes. They can help us work out what research has already been done and where research gaps lie; develop a new argument or perspective on a topic; identify the types of methods and theories that have been applied in a field; shed light on contradictory findings from similar studies; assess generalizability and consistency of relationships across studies; synthesize evidence about the effects of interventions; provide a shortcut to the research literature on a particular topic; bridge the gap between research, policy, and practice; and avoid duplication of effort and the considerable costs of embarking on new studies that may not be needed (Cooper & Hedges, 1994; Hart, 1998; Light & Pillemer, 1984; Mulrow, 1994; Petticrew

& Roberts, 2006). As Gough and Elbourne (2002) have noted, literature reviews are considered by some to be a useful strategy in the accumulation of knowledge (e.g., Cooper & Hedges, 1994; Light & Pillemer, 1984), while others see reviews as a way to "recast" the literature by analyzing how research is historically and socially located within particular (dominant) conceptual frameworks (e.g., Lather, 1999; Livingston, 1999).

Systematic reviews are one particular category or subset of literature reviews that have become an important part of the move in recent years to evidence-informed policy and practice (EIPP). They can provide policymakers and practitioners with a rigorous and transparent shortcut to the voluminous research literature, reduce an overreliance on single studies, and shed light on contradictory findings from different research studies.

Chalmers and Haynes (1994, p. 863) predicted that "a substantial proportion of current notions about the effects of healthcare will be changed" when the research community "synthesises existing evidence thoroughly" by using systematic reviews. There is now a substantial body of evidence that supports these predictions in health care and beyond. These include interventions thought to be useful but later exposed in systematic reviews as harmful, such as the use of human albumin for the emergency treatment of burns and shock (Roberts, 2000), and the "scared straight" intervention, which increased crime among young people (Peterosino, Turpin-Peterosino, & Buehler, 2003); interventions thought to be useless but later exposed as beneficial, such as corticosteroids to prevent complications from premature birth (Crowley, 1996); and interventions thought to be useful that have yet to be demonstrated as such when the evidence for them is reviewed in a systematic way, such as sex education for the prevention of teenage pregnancy (DiCenso, Guyatt, Willan, & Griffith, 2002).

A defining feature of a systematic review is the application of an explicit method to conduct the review. In other words, a systematic review is a piece of research that follows standard stages and methods. A systematic review starts with a research question, but its participants are research studies rather than people. Systematic reviews have a sampling stage (searching and screening for studies), a data collection stage (often called coding or data extraction), and a data analysis stage (often called the synthesis). Some authors have described a crucial feature of a systematic review as the application of the scientific method to uncover and minimize bias and error in the selection and treatment of studies (Chalmers, Hedges, & Cooper, 2002; EPPI-Centre, 2006; Mulrow, 1994; Petticrew & Roberts, 2006). For these authors, concepts of "bias" and "error" are central to systematic reviews because they may lead to distorted or erroneous review results. In research, "bias" usually refers to any kind of systematic error introduced into research procedures—for example, when research is either consciously or unconsciously designed in ways that support prior beliefs—whereas "error" refers to random mistakes (e.g., failure of a tape recorder when collecting data in an interview study) (Hammersley & Gomm, 1997; Juni, Altman, & Egger, 2001; Peersman, Oliver, & Oakley, 2001; Shadish, Cook, & Campbell, 2002; Wallace, 1971). In systematic reviews, attempts are made to minimize the introduction of bias and error into the review process by, for example, identifying as much as possible of all the relevant research to avoid a selective sample of studies, or using standardized data collection protocols so that each study in the review is treated in the same way (Higgins & Green, 2009; Stock, 1994; White, 1994). Attempts also are made to uncover bias and error in the individual studies included in the review by assessing their quality; those of lower quality are sometimes excluded or given less weight (Higgins & Green, 2009; Juni et al., 2001; Wortman, 1994).

Systematic review guidelines and handbooks often outline a set of discrete steps and processes to follow as an ideal type or standard for a reviewer to strive for (e.g., Campbell Collaboration, 2001; Cooper & Hedges, 1994; EPPI-Centre, 2006; Higgins & Green, 2009; Centre for Reviews and Dissemination, 2009; Petticrew & Roberts, 2006). These steps and processes can be specified in advance in a review protocol that states what is to be done and why. Ideally, both the review protocol and the final review report are subjected to peer review and made available for public scrutiny. Some systematic review guidelines recommend methods to protect against or uncover bias at the very beginning of the review process when deciding on the question or hypothesis for review (e.g., EPPI-Centre, 2006; Jackson et al., 2005). Making review methods explicit and transparent can facilitate accountability and debate, replication, and review updates (Gough & Elbourne, 2002).

An important stage in a systematic review is the synthesis, where the findings of the included studies are integrated to answer the review question. In comparison to other stages of the systematic review, such as searching and quality assessment, defining what synthesis is and describing the processes involved is difficult. Synthesis is defined in the *Oxford English Dictionary* as "the process or result of building up separate elements, especially ideas, into a connected whole, especially a theory or system." In systematic reviews, "ideas" are usually the findings of research; the "building up" of findings from individual studies into a "connected whole" in a systematic review ideally should be guided by rigorous and explicit procedures. Statistical meta-analysis is one such rigorous and explicit method of synthesis that can be used when findings from studies are in a numerical form (Deeks, Altman, & Bradburn, 2001; Lipsey & Wilson, 2001). In reviews that ask questions about the effects of interventions, the appropriate use of statistical meta-analysis—which is used to "pool" the

effect sizes from individual trials—can estimate the average balance of benefit and harm from an intervention with greater power and precision than can less formal synthesis techniques such as simple "vote counting" (Bushman, 1994). Alternative methods for synthesis, which do not rely on statistical summaries, are underdeveloped, although there is currently much ongoing work to address this. For example, Popay et al. (2006, p. 5) have produced guidance on "narrative synthesis," a textual approach to synthesis that "tells the story of the findings of included studies." There also is substantial activity around developing methods to synthesize qualitative research, which we describe below.

A useful concept in methodological debates surrounding synthesis is whether the approach that is being taken can be conceptualized as "integrative" or "interpretative" (Dixon-Woods, Agarwal, Jones, Young, & Sutton, 2005). An integrative review attempts to summarize the contents of multiple studies and minimizes any interpretation on the part of the reviewer. The studies in these syntheses would be relatively homogeneous; the assumption made is that their research paradigms are commensurate. Systematic reviews of quantitative research (e.g., trials) that employ statistical meta-analysis are considered to be using an integrative mode of synthesis. An "interpretive" synthesis, on the other hand, is explicitly about the reviewer *interpreting* the data. While based on the research in the review, its findings depend on the judgment of the reviewer to pick out the most salient aspects of the studies in order to create a synthesis that is uniquely the reviewer's own. The issue of replicability is one that is often discussed in the context of systematic reviews of quantitative research, with the assumption being that, given the same parameters, different researchers would follow the same methods, identify the same studies, and come to the same conclusions. Whether or not this assumption is justified in the context of many systematic reviews of social research, it is something that is explicitly not claimed by authors of interpretive syntheses. (In practice, all reviews, whether of quantitative or qualitative research, tend to have interpretative and integrative aspects, but usually emphasize one more than the other.)

◆ Qualitative Research and Systematic Reviews

Up until around 10 years ago, the focus of systematic reviews was on trials and other sorts of evaluation designs to answer questions about the effects of interventions. (This type of research is often characterized as "quantitative" research.) There is now an emerging genre of systematic reviewing activity developed specifically for qualitative research. Systematic reviews of qualitative research have been used predominantly to explore issues of context, process, and meaning, and to understand health and social issues from the perspective of the people under study. Examples of reviews include experiences of elders being discharged from the hospital (Fisher, Qureshi, Hardyman, & Homewood, 2006); experiences of teenage mothers in the United Kingdom (McDermott & Graham, 2005); and experiences of people with diabetes and the care they receive (Campbell et al., 2003). In these reviews, the study findings to be synthesized are concepts, themes, and theories, rather than effect sizes and confidence intervals.

Various methods have been developed for the systematic review of qualitative research. These are often linked to analysis strategies or approaches for primary research, and include meta-ethnography (Britten et al., 2002; Campbell et al., 2003; Noblit & Hare, 1988), "qualitative meta-synthesis" (Sandelowski & Barroso, 2003; Thorne, Jenson, Kearney, Noblit, & Sandelowski, 2004), "meta-study of qualitative research" (Paterson, Thorne, Canam, & Jillings, 2001; Thorne et al., 2002), thematic synthesis (Thomas &

Harden, 2008), and formal grounded theory (Kearney, 1998). We will discuss the characteristics of some of these methods here, since they are all concerned with combining primary studies that may have used different (qualitative) methods.

While systematic reviews of qualitative research vary in approach and method as much as primary qualitative research varies, there are many commonalities, too. All approaches involve the comparison, or "translation," of concepts, themes, or theories between studies. In some approaches (e.g., meta-ethnography and thematic synthesis), this activity is mostly confined to the content of the primary studies that are included in the review. Other approaches take a broader perspective (e.g., meta-narrative and critical interpretive synthesis) and include in this process an attempt to locate the various research studies being synthesized within the disciplinary context or paradigm within which they were originally conducted. All approaches carry out some assessment of the quality of research they are including, though the precise detail of how this is done in practice differs between methods. This process is related to how differences between studies are explored and explained. Some approaches relate this to the quality of the individual studies, whereas others attempt to explain differences in terms of their disciplinary context.

Qualitative syntheses also differ from one another in their approach to "going beyond," or developing new constructs and theories from, the studies they contain. An *integrative* synthesis may not aim to develop new theory at all, aiming simply to summarize, for example, what the participants in different studies are saying, and to identify any points of conflict. An *interpretive* synthesis might aim to develop new theories that attempt to explain, for example, why the participants in the studies contained in that synthesis thought or felt what they did. Some methods aim to do both (e.g., meta-ethnography and thematic synthesis), by beginning with an aggregation, to "translate" the findings of studies into a common language before moving on to interpretation, in order to answer a specific research question.

Given that there is so much similarity between different approaches to synthesizing qualitative research, one might wonder why there are so many different methods. In a recent critical overview of methods for qualitative synthesis, Barnett-Page and Thomas (2009) (one of the authors of this chapter) address this question, arguing that, to some extent, the proliferation of methods and terminology masks some of their common underlying properties and makes it difficult to identify important differences. They conclude, however, that there are genuine differences in approach that can be explained by taking account of the epistemological foundations of each method. They divide the methods into two broad camps: idealist, that err more toward social constructivist viewpoints; and realist, that assume the existence of an external reality, albeit with the acceptance that research can only ever be a representation of that reality. Idealist approaches are characterized by being flexible in their approach to identifying and assessing the quality of the literature they contain, and they are more likely to aim to locate it within its disciplinary context. Realist approaches follow methods that are similar to systematic reviews of quantitative research, having prespecified search strategies and predetermined inclusion and quality criteria. In addition, they are less likely to use the paradigm within which the primary research was conducted as part of their analysis.

◆ Systematic Reviews and Diverse Study Types

Perhaps mirroring the history of the development of primary research methodology, it has taken time for the utility of synthesizing qualitative research to be generally acknowledged. Whether qualitative or quantitative, however, "mono-method" systematic reviews have limitations that will be recognizable to anyone familiar with mixed methods literature. Some of these limitations might best be summarized in the phrase "But what else do we know?" A meta-analysis will provide a good (if the primary studies are good) estimate of the balance of benefit and harm of a particular intervention. Without the inclusion of good qualitative research, though, it will have little to say about whether participants found a given intervention acceptable or appropriate. Some reviewers have searched for a limited type of research (often randomized controlled trials) and have not identified any that meet the criteria for inclusion in their review. Their review is therefore "empty"; while empty reviews can record important gaps in the evidence base, they do not tell the reader what might be learned from the research that was excluded on methodological grounds. (In 2007, 14% of the reviews on the Cochrane Library were "empty.")[1] Likewise, reviews of qualitative research are unable to say, for example, *how much* better intervention A was than intervention B, though they will be able to tell us how appropriate the interventions were thought to be, or how people conceptualized the problem in question.

"Empty" Cochrane and other types of reviews have been a key driver in the move to include a wider range of evidence alongside trials in reviews. Discussing the inclusion of qualitative research in particular, Dixon-Woods, Fitzpatrick, and Roberts (2001) highlight the following reasons for including qualitative research alongside trials in systematic reviews: to help define relevant and meaningful outcomes, to explain and explore statistical findings on the effectiveness of interventions, to generate hypotheses to test, and to explore intervention implementation issues.

Perhaps the most important limitation of mono-method reviews is that they do not answer the range of questions that are asked of reviews. Some authors highlight this issue when discussing the reasons for using mixed methods in primary research (e.g., Brannen, 2005; Johnson & Onwuegbuzie, 2004). In the case of systematic reviews—which are usually, but not always, linked to a policy or practice concern—the reason is because the question asked of the reviewer requires that he or she draw on different types of research. At the least, this requires the reviewer to consider how to synthesize primary research studies that used different methods. This consideration may then lead in turn to the reviewer needing to use mixed methods in order to synthesize those methods. For example, a "What works?" question, which may be adequately addressed by a statistical meta-analysis of trials, is often extended to include "What works and why, for whom, and in what circumstances?" which clearly requires the inclusion of a wider variety of study types. As Mays, Pope, and Popay (2005) have noted in relation to research for decision making in health services management, the questions posed by and asked of systematic reviews tend to be multifaceted and complex.

There is now a significant body of work on the theoretical and practical issues surrounding the inclusion, generally, of diverse study types in systematic reviews and, specifically, on the inclusion of qualitative research alongside trials in reviews (e.g., Dixon-Woods et al., 2001; Dixon-Woods et al., 2006; Harden & Thomas, 2005; Pawson, 2006; Popay, 2005; Pope, Mays, & Popay, 2007; Thomas et al., 2004). Reviewers have addressed the challenge of synthesizing diverse primary studies in two ways. Some have developed essentially the same method to account for different types of primary study, whereas others have used different (mixed) methods to synthesize different types of research within the same review.

Examples of reviewers developing one method that can account for diversity in primary studies are Critical Interpretive Synthesis (Dixon-Woods et al., 2006) and Realist Synthesis (Pawson, 2006). Examples of reviewers developing mixed methods to synthesize diverse primary studies are

Bayesian meta-analysis (Roberts, Dixon-Woods, Fitzpatrick, Abrams, & Jones, 2002), meta-narrative (Greenhalgh et al., 2005), and the method outlined in the next section of this chapter.

In Critical Interpretive Synthesis and Realist Synthesis (even though this method is named "realist" synthesis, it probably belongs on the "idealist" side of the spectrum described earlier), reviewer judgment and interpretation are critical. Neither originator of these methods spells out how, for example, studies are to be assessed or synthesized; the reviewer must assess the reliability and salience of a study in the context of review that is being undertaken. Likewise, the precise method of synthesis is not stated in detail, but is something for reviewers, or review teams, to develop as the review progresses. In Critical Interpretive Synthesis, the aim is to develop a *synthesizing argument* from the, potentially, diverse literature in the review. By integrating studies across the review, a "coherent theoretical framework comprising a network of constructs and the relationships between them" (Dixon-Woods et al., 2006, p. 5) is developed. The key distinguishing feature of this method, compared with others (apart from meta-narrative review), is that the synthesis is *critical*. It questions the way in which the authors of its included studies conceptualize and construct the phenomenon under consideration, and it uses this as the foundation for developing its argument.

The development of an argument, or theory, is also the purpose of a Realist Synthesis. In this method, the unit of analysis is not an intervention but the *mechanism* or *theory of change* by which different interventions are thought to work. Thus, instead of replications of exactly the same intervention, a reviewer seeks out examples of the same theoretical mechanism in different situations. In so doing, the reviewer is able to construct a theory of his or her own—one that explains how and why a given theoretical mechanism works for different people in different contexts. Sometimes called a "middle range theory"

(Merton, 1968), this theory then can contribute to the refinement of other theories and so advance sociological theory in general. This examination of other middle-range theories in the light of what has come out of a review is an interesting example of mixing methods. From evaluations of individual interventions, the reviewer builds up a theory of how a given mechanism works in different situations. Having converted their "metric" from, for example, means and standard deviations into theory, they are then able to generalize beyond their specific case and consider how their middle-range theory relates to others.

The aim of a meta-narrative review is to plot the "unfolding 'storyline' of a research tradition over time" (Greenhalgh et al., 2005, p. 417). Conceptually similar to a Critical Interpretive Synthesis, this method takes as its starting point Kuhn's theory of scientific paradigms, which posits that groups of researchers work together within particular communities at particular times with agreed rules and procedures for investigating and understanding the world. According to Kuhn, these paradigms are essentially incommensurable; thus, when synthesizing the development of a theory, it is essential to take this into account. Trisha Greenhalgh and her colleagues (2005) used this theory as their organizing framework in a synthesis of research on the diffusion of innovations in health service organizations. When examining a relevant study in their review, their starting point was to identify in which body of research—which paradigm—it had originated. They then developed separate syntheses of research within each paradigm before exploring commonalities and contradictions between them. In contrast to Critical Interpretive Synthesis, in which the quality of studies is determined by reviewer judgment, studies in a meta-narrative review are appraised according to the standards that pertained to studies within that paradigm. Differences in findings between paradigms could then be explored systematically by, in the words of the authors, converting them into "data"

with the conclusions originating from each paradigm being treated as cases.

In a study that adopted a Bayesian analysis to examine the factors that affect the update of infant immunization, Karen Roberts and her colleagues (2002) sought out both qualitative and quantitative research. They found that both types of research were able to tell them which factors (might) affect the reasons why parents do and do not have their children vaccinated, but that neither body of research contained all the factors that they identified. In order to combine the qualitative and quantitative research, they essentially "quantified" the qualitative research by converting qualitative estimates of the importance of each factor into a quantitative probability. These probabilities gave them "priors" for their Bayesian analysis, which enabled them to modify estimates about the relative importance of each factor in parents' decisions from the quantitative studies in the light of those from the qualitative. This method depends on good correspondence between the factors identified in the two bodies of literature, however: while the qualitative studies identified 11 factors affecting immunization uptake, only 5 of these also were variables in the quantitative studies, and so the mixed methods synthesis was not able to use some of the factors present in the qualitative studies.

The approach described above—of using the outcomes of a synthesis of qualitative research to inform a statistical analysis of quantitative studies—is also the basis for the mixed methods example to which we now turn.

◆ The Evolution of One Mixed Methods Approach to Systematic Reviews

Our approach to mixed methods reviews evolved out of a program of work to advance evidence-informed health promotion and public health. This long-running research program is funded by the English Department of Health (DH) in the United Kingdom; it is conducted at the Evidence for Policy and Practice Information and Co-ordinating Centre at the Social Science Research Unit, Institute of Education, University of London. A large part of this program is the conduct of a series of policy-relevant systematic reviews on the promotion of children's and young people's health. Mental health, physical activity, and healthy eating have all been areas of policy priority for the DH. Recently, there has been concern over a relatively high prevalence of mental health problems and suicide among young people; interest in promoting physical activity and healthy eating has stemmed from rising levels of obesity, poor diet, and low levels of physical activity. In response, we offered a series of reviews that synthesized evidence on the effectiveness and appropriateness of interventions to promote health and suggestions for the kinds of interventions that could be tested in the future.

Each review began with the question, "What is known about the barriers to and facilitators of, for example, young people's participation in physical activity?" From the outset, all of these reviews were designed to integrate both "quantitative" and "qualitative" research. There was much intellectual curiosity among the research team with respect to how we could integrate different types of research within the reviews; this curiosity was supported by policymakers' acknowledgment of the need to extend the evidence base in public health to incorporate a wider variety of study types beyond trials and other kinds of evaluation studies (Department of Health, 2001). The UK government also was committed to listening to and involving patients and the public in the design of new interventions and public services (Department of Health, 1999).

At the beginning of the review series, it was hypothesized that barriers and facilitators could be identified from (a) "intervention" studies (e.g., trials) distinguishing between effective, ineffective, and harmful interventions; and (b) "nonintervention"

studies analyzing factors associated with mental health, physical activity, and healthy eating. A variety of research designs and methods were anticipated to make up the category of nonintervention studies, ranging from large-scale surveys and epidemiological analyses of large data sets to "qualitative" studies examining people's perspectives and experiences through in-depth interviews or focus groups. As the review series progressed, we focused our efforts on these latter types of studies in the nonintervention category. Previous work by the research team had indicated that intervention research was largely conducted without reference to the substantial literatures documenting the perspectives and experiences of the public who are targeted by the interventions being researched (Harden & Oliver, 2001). We saw this as a significant gap in the evidence base underpinning health promotion and public health and wanted to address this by bringing the two sets of literature together. As noted earlier, our policy colleagues also were interested in public and patient perspectives.

In the absence of an established methodology to draw on to conduct these reviews, our approach evolved largely by getting on and "doing" the work, alongside engaging with and responding to the scientific and policy feedback on our review protocols and each completed review product, and keeping a close eye on the emerging literature on integrating diverse study types in systematic reviews. We were guided, however, by several key principles: transparency (we wanted to be explicit about the methods we used to integrate different types of studies); error avoidance (we employed various strategies to enhance the rigor of our reviews); user involvement (we consulted and negotiated with policymakers at several points throughout the review process to ensure that the review would be both relevant to their needs and scientifically robust); matching and adapting review methods according to the study type under review; a complementary rather than competing view of qualitative and quantitative research; and a commitment to learning from the experiences of the intended targets of the policies and practices under review.

These principles shaped the general framework for conducting our mixed methods approach (Figure 29.1).

Figure 29.1 A Mixed Methods Approach to Conducting a Systematic Review of Diverse Study Types

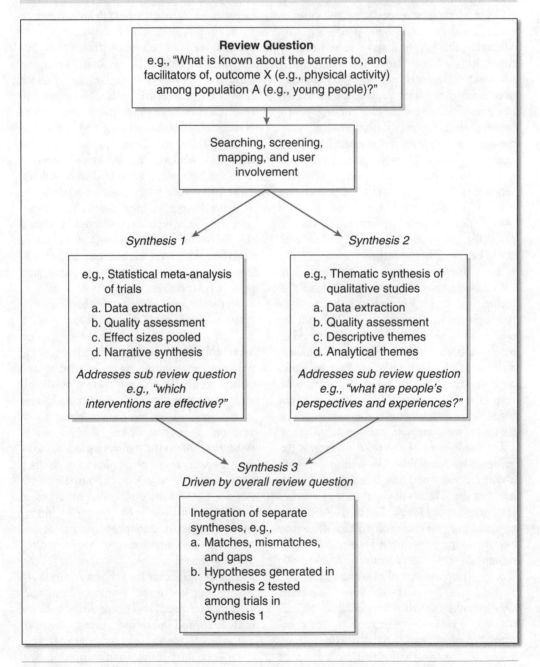

SOURCE: Adapted from Harden et al., 2004; and Oliver et al., 2005.

There are at least two ways in which this is a mixed methods approach. First, the reviews include different types of studies. In the reviews we have conducted so far, the different types of studies that are included have been mainly trials evaluating the effects of interventions (which might be considered to be quantitative studies because they, for example, collect numerical data and use statistical methods to analyze the data), and qualitative and other types of studies of people's perspectives and experiences. Second, we use different types of methods to conduct the reviews. As illustrated in Figure 29.1, we conduct three separate syntheses, each using different methods. The first synthesis uses a statistical meta-analysis to pool the effect sizes from trials (a "quantitative" synthesis). The second synthesis uses qualitative methods to synthesize the findings of qualitative and other types of studies focused on people's perspectives and experiences of the topic under review (a "qualitative" synthesis). The third synthesis (a "cross-study" synthesis) integrates the findings of the first and second syntheses.

Despite the above innovations, we did retain many of the features of traditional systematic review methodology. All the reviews were conducted according to the standard stages of a systematic review (e.g., Cooper & Hedges, 1994; Higgins & Green, 2009): setting a well-formulated review question, establishing the scope and boundaries of the review (inclusion and exclusion criteria), developing a review protocol, searching comprehensively for studies, describing the key features of included studies, assessing their quality, and synthesizing their findings. Methods were adapted as necessary to accommodate different study types, however. For example, trials and qualitative research were assessed using different sets of quality criteria appropriate for each, data on study findings were extracted using data collection tools tailored to each type of study, and different methods of synthesis were used. In addition to these stages, potential users of the review were involved in decision-making processes about review questions and scope

by means of advisory or steering groups. The reviews also were conducted according to a two-stage process: (i) a descriptive mapping stage and (ii) an in-depth review stage. User involvement and a two-stage process are particular features of an EPPI-Centre review (e.g., EPPI-Centre, 2006; Peersman, Harden, & Oliver, 1999; Thomas & Harden, 2003). The descriptive mapping stage is undertaken after searching and screening have been completed. Included studies are coded according to a standardized coding strategy to build up a detailed description of existing research activity relevant to answering a particular review question. The in-depth review stage moves beyond description to assess methodological quality and synthesize findings. The production of a descriptive map can facilitate further user involvement. If a large number of studies have been identified in the map, users can help to select criteria to identify a smaller set of studies for in-depth review.

In the following section, we provide a worked example of our approach to mixed methods reviews. We describe each of the three syntheses in our mixed methods approach in more detail, focusing in particular on the third synthesis that integrates the findings from the "quantitative" and "qualitative" arms of the review. To illustrate the methods, we use one of the reviews from our series, specifically the review focused on children and healthy eating. The full details of this review are reported in Thomas et al. (2003). Further discussion and reflection on the methods can be found in Thomas and colleagues (2004), Harden and Thomas (2005), Oliver and colleagues (2005), and Thomas and Harden (2008).

◆ Conducting a Mixed Methods Systematic Review

REVIEW QUESTIONS, SEARCHING, AND MAPPING

As noted above, our review on the topic of children and healthy eating was commissioned by the English Department of Health in the United Kingdom; its purpose was to inform policy about how to encourage children to eat healthily in the light of recent surveys highlighting that British children were eating less than half the recommended five portions of fruit and vegetables per day. Our overarching review question, "What are the barriers to and facilitators of healthy eating among children aged 4 to 10 years old?," was followed by the following three subquestions: (1) Which interventions are effective in promoting healthy eating among children?; (2) What are children's perspectives on, and experiences of, healthy eating?; and (3) What are the implications of questions (1) and (2) for intervention development?

After exhaustive searches of databases, Web sites, and journals, we identified and mapped 193 relevant studies (10 reviews, 33 nonintervention studies, and 150 evaluation studies). In consultation with our advisory groups, we focused the review on 33 of the evaluation studies that had employed a control or comparison group (trials) to examine the impact of interventions on children's fruit and vegetable consumption and on 8 of the nonintervention studies that had examined children's own perspectives and experience on healthy eating. Most of the latter studies were qualitative in nature.

DATA EXTRACTION AND QUALITY ASSESSMENT

The two sets of studies went through separate and independent procedures for extracting data on study findings and characteristics, quality assessment, and synthesis. For the trials, data were extracted using a standardized coding tool that covered aims; theoretical and empirical background; characteristics of the intervention and study population; and effect sizes and associated p values and confidence

intervals. Trial quality was assessed according to whether the intervention and control or comparison groups were equivalent, both pre- and posttest data on outcomes were presented, and all intended outcomes were reported upon.

For the qualitative and other types of studies assessing children's perspectives, data were extracted using a standardized tool that covered the aims of the study, theoretical and empirical background, characteristics of the study population, and study findings. It is not a straightforward task to extract the findings of qualitative studies. Findings may be found in the form of themes, concepts, theories, interpretations, or simple narrative summaries of the data; these may appear in several different places in a research report. In our review, we defined study findings to be all of the text labeled as "results" or "findings" in study reports. We were, however, also mindful of capturing findings appearing in study abstracts and discussions. We entered all study findings verbatim into a software package for qualitative analysis. The quality of these studies was assessed using 12 criteria based on those criteria commonly cited to assess qualitative research in the literature. These criteria covered the quality of reporting, the use of strategies to enhance rigor, and the extent to which children's perspectives and experiences had been privileged in the study.

SYNTHESIS OF TRIALS USING STATISTICAL META-ANALYSIS

Following established methods for statistical meta-analysis (e.g., Lipsey & Wilson, 2001), the effect sizes from trials were pooled to answer the first subquestion of our review regarding the effectiveness of interventions in promoting healthy eating (Figure 29.2). In this synthesis, we were working with one specific outcome

Figure 29.2 A Forest Plot Illustrating the Results of a Statistical Meta-Analysis of Trials of Interventions to Promote Healthy Eating on Children's Intake of Fruit and Vegetables

Item	Effect (Confidence Interval)	Weight	Size
Fruit and vegetable intake: core set			
Anderson et al. (2000)	0.46 (0.00, 0.92)	4.8	120
Auld et al. (1998)	0.48 (0.03, 0.94)	4.8	445
Auld et al. (1999)	0.53 (−0.12, 1.18)	2.8	647
Baranowski et al. (2000)	0.12 (−0.05, 0.30)	11.7	1172
Cullen et al. (1997)	0.26 (−0.03, 0.55)	8.2	210
Epstein et al. (2001)	1.02 (0.17, 1.86)	1.8	25
Gortmaker et al. (1999)	0.36 (0.10, 0.62)	9.1	336
Henry et al. (2001)	0.16 (−0.45, 0.77)	3.2	42
Hopper et al. (1996)	0.44 (0.12, 0.75)	7.6	97
Parcel et al. (1989)	−0.11 (−0.29, 0.08)	11.6	352
Perry, Bishop, et al. (1998)	0.15 (−0.08, 0.38)	10.1	408
Perry, Lytle, et al. (1998)	0.02 (−0.11, 0.14)	13.4	1186
Reynolds et al. (2000)	0.35 (0.15, 0.56)	10.8	1512
	0.23 (0.11, 0.35)		

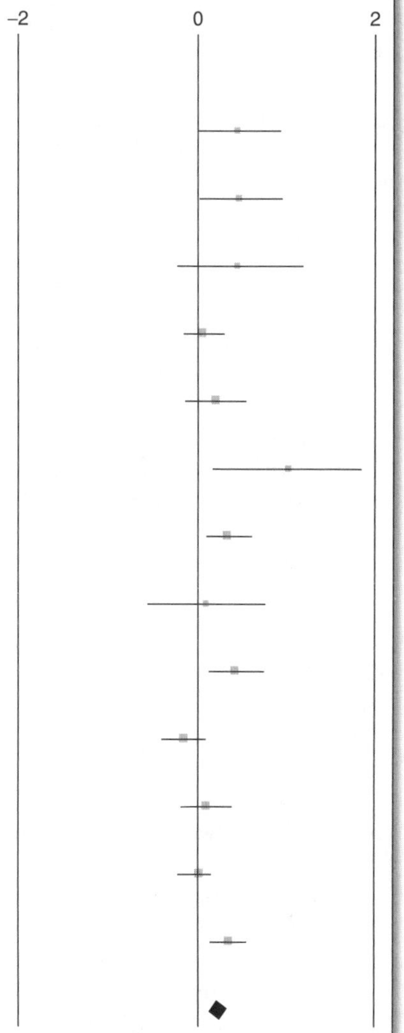

category—children's intake of fruit and vegetables calculated in terms of portions per day. The pooled effect size shown at the bottom of Figure 29.2 indicates that, on average, the interventions were able to increase fruit and vegetable consumption by approximately half a portion per day.

There was significant variation between the results of individual studies. For example, one study (Epstein et al., 2001) found that the intervention led to an increase of nearly two portions of fruit and vegetables per day, while another study (Parcel, Simons-Morton, O'Hara,

Baranowski, & Wilson, 1989) found a decrease in consumption as a result of the intervention.

The interventions evaluated across the studies generally combined education about healthy eating with exposure, or access, to fruit and vegetables through, for example, changes made to school menus. The variation in effect sizes between studies (heterogeneity) was explored by carrying out subgroup analyses on a limited range of categories, specified in advance (e.g., study quality, study design, setting and type of intervention). We found that this a priori analysis was not able to shed much light on the observed differences in effect sizes between the studies. We also undertook an exploratory narrative analysis that compared characteristics of interventions showing harmful effects, no effects, or positive effects. Although this revealed several potential explanations, these were necessarily very speculative since it was difficult to avoid data dredging.

SYNTHESIS OF QUALITATIVE STUDIES USING THEMATIC SYNTHESIS

As noted earlier, the "raw data" for this synthesis was all of the text from study reports that was labeled "findings" or "results." This had been entered verbatim into a qualitative analysis software package and was subjected to thematic synthesis. Thematic synthesis is conducted in three main stages: (1) the coding of text "line by line," (2) the development of "descriptive themes," and (3) the generation of "analytical themes" (Thomas & Harden, 2008). The starting point for the first two stages of the analysis was the findings of the studies themselves without reference to our review questions. In the third stage, we returned to our review question. This was a crucial step in preparation for the third cross-study synthesis.

(1) Coding Text "Line by Line"

Three reviewers independently coded each line of text according to its meaning and content. Codes were structured, either in a tree form or as "free" codes—without a hierarchical structure. Thirty-six codes were created (e.g., "Children prefer fruit to vegetables," "Why eat healthily?," "Bad foods = nice, healthy foods = awful"); every sentence of text had at least one code applied, and most were categorized using several codes. The use of line-by-line coding enabled us to undertake what has been described as one of the key tasks in the synthesis of qualitative research: the *translation* of concepts from one study to another (Noblit & Hare, 1988).

(2) Development of Descriptive Themes

Once all of the text had been coded, we looked for similarities and differences between the codes in order to start grouping them. New codes were created at this stage to capture the meaning of groups of initial codes. This process resulted in a hierarchical tree structure with a total of 12 descriptive themes (Figure 29.3). This tree was divided into two layers. These layers organized themes into those focused on children's understandings of healthy eating or influences on children's food choices.

A draft summary of the findings across the studies organized by the 12 descriptive themes was then written by one of the review authors. Two other review authors commented on this draft and a final consensus was reached. At this stage, we had remained very close to the original findings of the studies and had produced a summary of their content. The findings of each study had been combined into a whole via a listing of themes that described children's perspectives on healthy eating. As noted earlier in this chapter, here we were working primarily within an integrative mode of synthesis.

Figure 29.3 The Set of Descriptive Themes Derived From a Thematic Synthesis of Studies of Children's Perspectives and Experiences of Healthy Eating

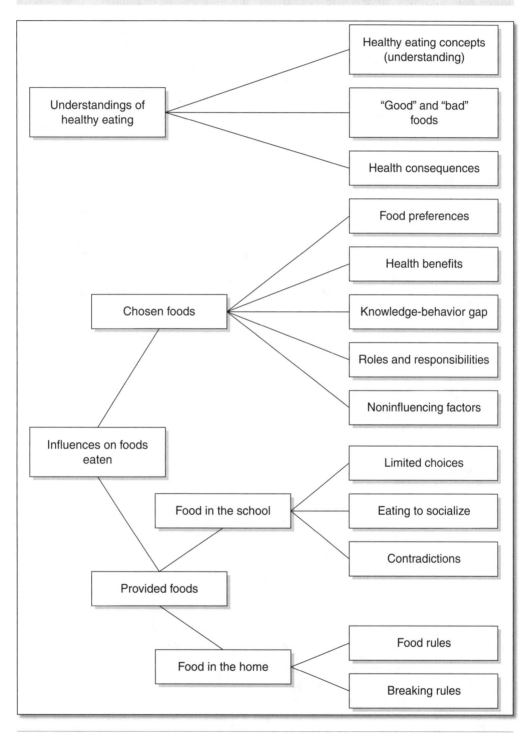

SOURCE: Thomas et al., 2003.

We had not yet "gone beyond" the findings of the primary studies and generated additional concepts, understandings, or hypotheses.

(3) Generation of Analytical Themes

The next stage of the synthesis involved examining the descriptive themes (and their associated data) in the light of our review question. We inferred from them barriers to and facilitators of healthy eating and implications for intervention development. Here we had switched to an *interpretive* mode of synthesis. We were interpreting the data in front of us using our review questions and associated assumptions and principles as our interpretive framework. This is equivalent to the stage in meta-ethnography in which third-order interpretations are constructed. A total of six analytical themes emerged from this process. These six analytical themes, together with implications for interventions, are shown in Figure 29.4.

Using terminology from meta-ethnography, each analytical theme can be seen as capturing a "line of argument." By way of illustration, five of the initial descriptive themes covered influences on children's own choice of foods (food preferences, perceptions of health benefits, knowledge-behavior gap, roles and responsibilities, noninfluencing factors). From these, reviewers inferred several barriers and implications for intervention development. Children identified readily that taste was the major concern for them when selecting food, and that health was either a secondary factor or, in some cases, a reason for rejecting food ("All the things that are bad for you are nice and all the things that are good for you are awful" (Dixey, Sahota, Atwal, & Turner, 2001, p. 73). They did not see purchasing fruit for health reasons as being a legitimate use of their pocket money. "That is what parents are there for." Children wanted to use their pocket money to buy sweets that could be

Figure 29.4 Analytical Themes and Examples of Implications for Interventions Generated From a Thematic Synthesis of Studies of Children's Perspectives and Experiences of Healthy Eating

1. Children don't see it as their role to be interested in health.	Brand fruit and vegetables as "tasty" rather than "healthy".
2. Children do not see future health consequences as personally relevant or credible. ———→	Reduce health emphasis of messages. Do not promote fruit and vegetables in the same way within the same intervention.
3. Fruit, vegetables, and confectionary have very different meanings for children.	Create situations for children to have ownership over their food choices.
4. Children actively seek ways to exercise their own choices with regard to foods. ———→	Ensure messages promoting fruit and vegetables are supported by appropriate access to fruit and vegetables.
5. Children value eating as a social occasion.	
6. Children recognize contradiction between what is promoted and what is provided.	

SOURCE: Thomas et al., 2003

enjoyed with friends. These perspectives indicated to us that branding fruit and vegetables as "tasty" rather than "healthy" might be more effective in increasing consumption. The following quote from a child in one of the studies illustrates this point incisively: "All adverts for healthy stuff go on about healthy things. The adverts for unhealthy things tell you how nice they taste" (Dixey et al., 2001, p. 75). We captured this line of argument in the *analytical themes* entitled, "Children do not see it as their role to be interested in health" and "Children do not see messages about future health as personally relevant or credible."

CROSS-STUDY SYNTHESIS

The analytical themes and associated implications for interventions were the starting point for the integration of the "qualitative" and "quantitative" phases of the review. The integration was carried out in two main stages. First, we examined all of the interventions evaluated by the trials to assess the extent to which they addressed or incorporated the implications for interventions that we had derived from studies of children's perspectives. The results of this analysis were charted within a conceptual and methodological matrix (Figure 29.5). This enabled us to identify interventions that had addressed the implications of interventions derived from children's perspectives (matches), interventions that did not address the implications of interventions derived from children's perspectives (mismatches), and implications for intervention development that had not yet been tested for their effectiveness (research gaps). The matrix also recorded the quality of the intervention studies so that further research gaps could be identified (e.g., interventions may have addressed one or more of the implications for intervention development but may not have been soundly evaluated yet).

In other words, this comparative analysis, which juxtaposed the findings from the first synthesis against the findings of the second, identified which interventions matched children's perspectives and experiences and revealed the aspects of children's views that have been ignored (or were unknown) by those developing

Figure 29.5 Extract From a Conceptual and Methodological Matrix Used to Conduct a Cross-Study Synthesis in Mixed Methods Review on Children and Healthy Eating

Implications for interventions derived from thematic synthesis	Trials of interventions from the statistical meta-analysis	
	Good quality	*Other*
Do not promote fruit and vegetables in the same way	0	0
Brand fruit and vegetables as an "exciting" or child-relevant product, as well as a "tasty" one	5	5
Reduce health emphasis in messages to promote fruit and vegetables, particularly those which concern future health	6	6

SOURCE: Adapted from Thomas et al., 2004.

and evaluating interventions. We listed the recommendations for interventions down the left-hand side of the matrix and then noted which interventions actually built on the recommendations and those that did not. We used the good quality trials to assess whether or not there was evidence to support the children's views, whether the evidence was contrary to what the children were suggesting, or whether there was a gap in available evidence. The interventions that had not been evaluated well were identified as building on a potentially fruitful facilitator and were recommended for rigorous evaluation. The first row in Figure 29.5 indicates a research gap.

The cross-study synthesis was pushed one step further in the second stage. When we had sufficient numbers of well-evaluated

interventions that either matched or did not match our implications for interventions, we were able to test whether interventions that matched children's perspectives showed bigger effect sizes than those that did not. For example, in the third recommendation in Figure 29.5—to reduce the emphasis on health—we identified five well-evaluated interventions. Two of these provided results on the same outcome so we were able to conduct a statistical subgroup analysis dividing the studies between those that emphasized health messages and those that did not (Figure 29.6).

We were able to conduct standard statistical tests to test whether we had identified a statistically significant difference. In this case, we found that interventions that had little or no emphasis on health messages showed greater increases in children's

Figure 29.6   Subgroup Analysis Testing a Hypothesis Derived From a Thematic Synthesis Within a Statistical Meta-Analysis

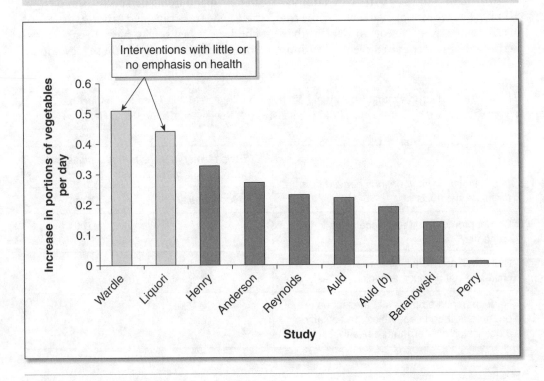

SOURCE: Reproduced from Thomas et al., 2004.

vegetable intake than did those interventions that had a substantial emphasis on health. However, we were cautious in interpreting the findings of these tests; the method might be considered to be a good way of generating hypotheses for future interventions to test, rather than for determining critical policy or practice decisions.

◆ Mixed Methods Designs and Systematic Reviews

The inclusion of diverse study types in systematic reviews has largely developed independently of the methodological literature around mixed methods (for exceptions, see Harden & Thomas, 2005; and Sandelowski, Voils, & Barroso, 2006). In Chapter 2, John Creswell discussed two milestone writings in mixed methods, identifying two significant issues: the necessity of addressing the "paradigmatic foundations" of the approach taken, and the importance of documenting "procedures" when discussing mixed methods approaches. We will first discuss our conclusions on the paradigmatic implications of the above approach and then move on to thinking about its procedures.

Creswell also outlined a taxonomy of paradigm stances that is becoming a de facto standard in the mixed methods literature, suggesting that the "paradigm debate," which asserted that work undertaken in different paradigms is incommensurable, has diminished. His list of paradigm stances is as follows:

> The paradigms are different and therefore cannot be mixed (incommensurable stance); the paradigms are independent and can be mixed and matched in various combinations (a-paradigmatic stance); the paradigms are not incompatible, but they are different and should be kept separate in mixed methods research (complementary strengths stance); the paradigms are different in important ways, and this

difference can lead to useful tensions and insights (a dialectic stance) and should be honored; a single paradigm provides the foundation for mixed methods, and this foundation may be found in pragmatism or a transformative-emancipatory perspective (an alternative paradigm stance); paradigms can be mixed in a study and linked to the type of design being used (design stance); and paradigms are embedded or intertwined with substantive theories in mixed methods (substantive theory stance). (Creswell, 2010 [this volume], p. 54)

As mentioned above, mixing methods in the context of systematic reviews involves two kinds of mixed methods: those already established in the primary research that is being synthesized and those being used to conduct the synthesis. Within each separate synthesis, our approach could be described as taking an "a-paradigmatic" stance with respect to the studies they contain. We have tended to treat the studies *within* each synthesis as being broadly commensurable and not requiring differential treatment. This approach might be criticized if it led, for example, to the findings of an ethnography being combined with a piece of advocacy, without regard for their different foundations. In a recent qualitative synthesis of children's perspectives about body size, shape, and weight, we came across this very issue and were faced with combining studies that came from an essentially psychological discipline with those that took a sociological stance (Rees, Oliver, Woodman, & Thomas, 2009). In this case, we decided that it was appropriate to conduct two separate syntheses, since it appeared that the nature of these studies' findings were qualitatively different from one another. In the case of the example described above, we found that the qualitative and other types of studies of children's perspectives were relatively homogeneous in terms of their theoretical and disciplinary background. The majority were underpinned by a health promotion perspective that explicitly aimed to gather the views of children to inform interventions to promote healthy eating.

While our stance *within* syntheses might be considered a-paradigmatic in certain cases, our approach to the third synthesis, the cross-study synthesis, is more complex. Within syntheses, we clearly see the paradigms as being independent, requiring separate methods of synthesis but also being complementary: the review is stronger for having both types of research present. However, the stance taken in the cross-study synthesis can most closely be described as dialectic in that we use the findings of one synthesis (qualitative) to interrogate the other (quantitative). Though using different methods, the meta-narrative review of Greenhalgh and colleagues (2005) also takes a dialectical stance, aiming to explore and explain differences between study findings in terms of their different paradigms. These two mixed paradigm approaches contrast with other models for mixed research synthesis. Neither Critical Interpretive Synthesis nor Realist Synthesis use different methods when combining studies from different research traditions. Instead, they set the interpretive judgment of the reviewer at center stage and use this "common denominator" to combine study findings (an "alternative" or "single paradigm" stance). The Bayesian approach we described earlier would be described also as taking an "alternative paradigm" stance (a Bayesian one). Certainly, when considering the paradigmatic foundations of different methods of synthesis, it is important to bear in mind that the different methods were developed for different purposes by different teams of researchers. Thus, Thomas Kuhn's notion of "scholarly communities" may well be a useful organizing framework when considering these different approaches to synthesis (Kuhn, 1970).

As well as the paradigmatic issues, we also should observe that there are sociopolitical motivations underpinning our selection of study types in these reviews. We include the qualitative and other types of studies of people's perspectives and experiences, because we think it is important that the voices of those who are at the receiving end of interventions be heard and that they be taken into account when interventions and research are planned. We include trials to assess the effectiveness of interventions because we think that it is important that policy and practice be informed by the best available evidence, and that syntheses of these types of study offer the most reliable answers to effectiveness questions.

(As a side observation, we have found it difficult to use the terms *qualitative* and *quantitative* to describe studies. On the quantitative side, we have preferred to use the more precise term *trials* to describe our studies of interest. On the qualitative side, our studies of interest have actually encompassed a variety of study types that have included surveys as well as qualitative designs such as interviews and focus groups. Within our research team, we used the nomenclature *views studies* as shorthand to describe studies of people's perspectives and experiences. The term *qualitative* is actually quite difficult to define in relation to actual studies and is sometimes an ill-suited descriptor of the studies in a synthesis. The studies in our reviews were selected for their ability to answer a given question, rather than for characteristics of their research methodology. This requirement to develop a new language is in accordance with Creswell's observations in Chapter 2 of this volume, that mixed methods research is creating a new language for itself. In our case, this is not in order to distinguish what we are doing from other approaches, but because the existing terminology did not describe what we were doing adequately.)

We now turn to a consideration of the procedures used in our mixed methods systematic reviews. Greene (2008) describes the main distinctions between mixed methods as being along the axis of independence/interaction between methods, the relative status they are awarded, and the timing of their use within the research process. The relative independence of the different syntheses in our reviews depends on which stage in the research process we are considering. This stems from the dialectical nature of the final synthesis: We want to develop an argument from the independent syntheses that is resolved within the cross-study synthesis. The two syntheses therefore have little interaction before they each have come to their own conclusions. The synthesis of "views" studies of potential recipients of interventions are used to frame the cross-study synthesis, giving this a very strong design, both conceptually and statistically. The framework afforded by the "views" synthesis gives the statistical subgroup analyses (which are not protected by any randomization in the original studies) a clear empirical rationale as well as protecting the reviewer from "data dredging" for statistically significant results. The two types of syntheses are thus accorded equal status, with each contributing the strengths of its particular tradition.

◆ Conclusions

In this chapter, we have described the principles and methods of systematic reviews, highlighting how these types of reviews are pieces of research in their own right. We have applied a mixed methods lens to our discussion of reviews, outlining the strengths and weaknesses of mono-methods reviews, and we have argued that including diverse types of research in reviews can increase their relevance to policy and practice when broad multifaceted questions are asked. We have introduced an emerging category of systematic review that we have developed, which adopts a mixed methods approach to including diverse study types within it; and we have contrasted this with other review models that use a single approach to synthesize diverse study types. Through a worked example, we have illustrated the assumptions and procedures involved in mixed methods reviews. This worked example demonstrates how a number of questions can be addressed in the same review with a particular emphasis on questions that require integration of estimates of the average balance of benefit and harm from interventions with qualitative understanding from people's perspectives and experiences of the health or social issues under study. Our approach facilitates a critical analysis of intervention studies from the perspective of those targeted by interventions. We also demonstrate how our mixed methods reviews preserve the integrity of the findings of different types of studies within a complementary rather than competitive framework.

Our approach to conducting a mixed methods systematic review has so far been characterized by a sequential mixed methods design in which "qualitative" and "quantitative" data and modes of analysis have equal weight. It also largely has consisted of including two main types of studies within it. However, there is great potential in this approach to vary the number of different types of studies to be included, and hence potentially to increase the numbers of syntheses that are conducted independently and then brought together. There is also potential to vary the sequencing of the syntheses. For example, it may be fruitful to conduct a synthesis of qualitative studies prior to conducting a statistical meta-analysis in order to inform the scope and boundaries of the analysis and to determine the variables for a subgroup analysis. Since the methodology of systematic reviews is rapidly developing, we expect to see more and more reviews that attempt to integrate diverse study types within them. We look forward to reflecting further on how the mixed methods literature can help to shape and understand these developments.

Research Questions and Exercises

1. Compare and contrast traditional literature reviews with systematic reviews and explain the ways in which systematic reviews are pieces of research.

2. What is the relationship between systematic reviews and evidence-informed policy and practice (EIPP)?

3. Discuss the developments that have occurred in (a) the review and synthesis of qualitative research and (b) the review and synthesis of diverse types of research.

4. Using a bibliographic database or GOOGLE Scholar, identify a review that employs statistical meta-analysis and a review that employs meta-ethnography. Identify which review uses an integrative logic and which uses an interpretive logic. Does either of them use both?

5. Choose a topic relevant to your field of practice or study and identify (a) one review that conducts a statistical meta-analysis, and (b) one review that uses meta-ethnography or another synthesis method for qualitative research. What does each review contribute to your understanding of the topic in question?

6. Write a short essay evaluating the strengths and weaknesses of mono-method reviews and mixed methods reviews.

7. Identify two reviews using different mixed methods approaches discussed in this chapter. Write a short essay that compares the approaches used. Focus your attention on the paradigmatic stances adopted by each as well as on the procedures used.

◆ Note

1. Retrieved from http://www.imbi.uni-freiburg.de/OJS/cca/index.php/cca/article/view/5034

◆ References

Anderson, A. S., Hetherington, M., Adamson, A., Porteous, L., Higgins, C., Foster, E., et al. (2000). *The development and evaluation of a novel school-based intervention to increase fruit and vegetable intake in children*. London: Food Standards Agency.

Auld, G. W., Romaniello, C., Heimendinger, J., Hambidge, C., & Hambidge, M. (1998). Outcomes from a school-based nutrition education program using resource teachers and cross-disciplinary models. *Journal of Nutrition Education, 30,* 268–280.

Auld, G. W., Romaniello, C., Heimendinger, J., Hambidge, C., & Hambidge, M. (1999). Outcomes from a school-based nutrition education program alternating special resource teachers and classroom teachers. *Journal of School Health, 69,* 403–408.

Baranowski, T., Davis, M., Resnicow, K., Baranowski, J., Doyle, C., Lin, L. S., et al. (2000). Gimme 5 fruit, juice, and vegetables for fun and health: Outcome evaluation. *Health Education and Behavior, 27,* 96–111.

Barnett-Page, E., & Thomas, J. (2009). Methods for the synthesis of qualitative research: A critical review. *BMC Medical Research Methodology, 9,* 59. doi:10.1186/1471-2288-9-59.

Brannen, J. (2005). Mixing methods: The entry of qualitative and quantitative approaches into the research process. *International*

Journal of Social Research Methodology, 8(3), 173–184.

Britten, N., Campbell, R., Pope, C., Donovan, J., Morgan, M., & Pill, R. (2002). Using meta ethnography to synthesize qualitative research: A worked example. *Journal of Health Services Research and Policy, 7,* 209–215.

Bushman, B. (1994). Vote counting procedures in meta-analysis. In H. Cooper & L. Hedges (Eds.), *The Handbook of Research Synthesis* (pp. 193–214). New York: Russell Sage Foundation.

Campbell, R., Pound, P., Pope, C., Britten, N., Pill, R., Morgan, M., et al. (2003). Evaluating meta-ethnography: A synthesis of qualitative research on lay experiences of diabetes and diabetes care. *Social Science and Medicine, 56,* 671–684.

Campbell Collaboration. (2001). *Campbell Systematic Reviews: Guidelines for the eparation of review protocols* (version 1.0). Retrieved from http://www.campbellcollaboration .org/artman2/uploads/1/C2_Protocols_guide lines.pdf

Centre for Reviews and Dissemination. (2009). *Systematic reviews: CRD's guidance for undertaking reviews in health care.* York, UK: University of York.

Chalmers, I., & Haynes, B. (1994). Systematic reviews: Reporting, updating and correcting systematic reviews of the effects of healthcare. *British Medical Journal, 309,* 862–865.

Chalmers, I., Hedges, L., & Cooper, H. (2002). A brief history of research synthesis. *Evaluation and the Health Professions, 25,* 12–37.

Cooper, H., & Hedges, L. (1994). *The handbook of research synthesis.* New York: Russell Sage Foundation.

Creswell, J. W. (2010). Mapping the developing landscape of mixed methods research. In A. Tashakkori & C. Teddlie (Eds.), *SAGE handbook of mixed methods in social & behavioral research* (2nd ed., pp. 45–68). Thousand Oaks, CA: Sage.

Crowley, P. (1996). Prophylactic corticosteroids for preterm birth. *The Cochrane Database of Systematic Reviews* (1), CD000065.

Cullen, K. W., Bartholomew, L. K., & Parcel, G. S. (1997). Girl scouting: An effective channel for nutrition education. *Journal of Nutrition Education, 29,* 86–91.

Deeks, J., Altman, D., & Bradburn, M. (2001). Statistical methods for examining heterogeneity and combining results from several studies in meta-analysis. In M. Egger, G. Davey-Smith, & D. Altman (Eds.), *Systematic reviews in health care: Meta-analysis in context* (pp. 285–312). London: BMJ Publishing.

Department of Health. (1999). *Patient and public involvement in the new NHS.* London: The Stationery Office.

Department of Health. (2001). *A research and development strategy for public health.* London: The Stationery Office.

DiCenso, A., Guyatt, G., Willan, A., & Griffith, L. (2002). Interventions to reduce unintended teenage pregnancies in adolescents: A systematic review of randomised controlled trials. *British Medical Journal, 324,* 1426–1434.

Dixey, R., Sahota, P., Atwal, S., & Turner, A. (2001). Children talking about healthy eating: Data from focus groups with 300 9–11-year-olds. *Nutrition Bulletin, 26,* 71–79.

Dixon-Woods, M., Agarwal, S., Jones, D., Young, B., & Sutton, A. (2005). Synthesising qualitative and quantitative evidence: A review of possible methods. *Journal of Health Services Research and Policy, 10,* 45–53.

Dixon-Woods, M., Bonas, S., Booth, A., Jones, D., Miller, T., Sutton, A., et al. (2006). How can systematic reviews incorporate qualitative research? A critical perspective. *Qualitative Research, 6,* 27–44.

Dixon-Woods, M., Caver, D., Agarwal, S. et al. (2006). Conducting a critical interpretive synthesis of the literature on access to healthcare by vulnerable groups. *BMC Medical Research Methodology* 6(35). doi:10.1186/ 1471-2288-6-35

Dixon-Woods, M., Fitzpatrick, R., & Roberts, K. (2001). Including qualitative research in systematic reviews: Problems and opportunities. *Journal of Evaluation in Clinical Practice, 7,* 125–133.

EPPI-Centre. (2006). *EPPI-Centre methods for conducting systematic reviews.* London: EPPI-Centre, Social Science Research Unit, Institute of Education, University of London.

Epstein, L. H., Gordy, C. C., Raynor, H. A., Beddome, M., Kilanowski, C. K., & Paluch, R. (2001). Increasing fruit and vegetable intake and decreasing fat and sugar intake in families at risk for childhood obesity. *Obesity Research, 9,* 171–178.

Fisher, M., Qureshi, H., Hardyman, W., & Homewood, J. (2006). *Using qualitative research in systematic reviews: Older people's views of hospital discharge.* London: Social Care Institute for Excellence.

Gortmaker, S. L., Cheung, L. W., Peterson, K. E., Chomitz, G., Cradle, J. H., Dart, H., et al. (1999). Impact of a school-based interdisciplinary intervention on diet and physical activity among urban primary school children: Eat well and keep moving. *Archives of Pediatrics and Adolescent Medicine, 153,* 975–983.

Gough, D., & Elbourne, D. (2002). Systematic research synthesis to inform policy, practice and democratic debate. *Social Policy and Society, 1,* 225–236.

Greene, J. (2008). Is mixed methods social inquiry a distinctive methodology? *Journal of Mixed Methods Research, 2,* 7–22.

Greenhalgh, T., Robert, G., Macfarlane, F., Bate, P., Kyriakidou, O., & Peacock, R. (2005). Storylines of research in diffusion of innovation: A meta-narrative approach to systematic review. *Social Science & Medicine, 61*(2), 417–430.

Hammersley, M., & Gomm, R. (1997). Bias in social research. *Sociological Research Online, 2.* Retrieved from http://www .socresonline.org.uk/2/1/2.html

Harden, A., Garcia, J., Oliver, S., Rees, R., Shepherd, J., Brunton, G., et al. (2004). Applying systematic review methods to studies of people's views: An example from public health. *Journal of Epidemiology and Community Health, 58,* 794–800.

Harden, A., & Oliver, S. (2001). Who's listening? Systematically reviewing for ethics and empowerment. In S. Oliver & G. Peersman (Eds.), *Using research for effective health promotion* (pp. 123–137). Buckingham, UK: Open University Press.

Harden, A., & Thomas, J. (2005). Methodological issues in combining diverse study types in systematic reviews. *International Journal of Social Research Methods, 8,* 257–271.

Hart, C. (1998). *Doing a literature review: Releasing the social science research imagination.* London: Sage.

Henry, J., Warren, J., Bradshaw, S., Perwaiz, S., & Lightowler, H. (2001). *Family centred, school-based intervention for the prevention of obesity in primary school-aged children.* Oxford, UK: Oxford Brookes University.

Higgins, J., & Green, S. (Eds.). (2009). *Cochrane handbook for systematic reviews of interventions 5.0.2* [updated September 2009]. Retrieved from http://www.cochrane-handbook.org/

Hopper, C. A., Munoz, K. D., Gruber, M. B., MacConnie, S., Schonfeldt, B., & Shunk, T. (1996). A school-based cardiovascular exercise and nutrition program with parent participation: An evaluation study. *Children's Health Care, 25,* 221–235.

Jackson, N., Waters, E., Anderson, L., Bailie, R., Brunton, G., Hawe, P., et al. (2005). Criteria for the systematic review of health promotion and public health interventions. *Health Promotion International, 20,* 367–374.

Johnson, R., & Onwuegbuzie, A. (2004). Mixed methods research: A research paradigm whose time has come? *Educational Researcher, 33,* 14–26.

Juni, P., Altman, D., & Egger, M. (2001). Assessing the quality of controlled clinical trials. *British Medical Journal, 323,* 42–46.

Kearney, M. (1998). Ready-to-wear: Discovering formal grounded theory. *Research in Nursing and Health, 21,* 179–186.

Kuhn, T. (1970). *The structure of scientific revolutions* (2nd ed.). Chicago: University of Chicago Press.

Lather, P. (1999). To be of use: The work of reviewing. *Review of Educational Research, 69,* 2–7.

Light, R., & Pillemer, D. (1984). *Summing up: The science of reviewing research.* Cambridge, MA: Harvard University Press.

Lipsey, M., & Wilson, D. (2001). *Practical meta-analysis.* Thousand Oaks, CA: Sage.

Livingston, G. (1999). Beyond watching over established ways: A review as recasting the literature, recasting the lived. *Review of Educational Research, 69,* 9–19.

Mays, N., Pope, C., & Popay, J. (2005). Systematically reviewing qualitative and quantitative evidence to inform management and policy-making in the health field. *Journal of Health Services Research and Policy, 10,* S1:6–S1:20.

McDermott, E., & Graham, H. (2005). Resilient young mothering: Social inequalities, late modernity and the "problem" of "teenage" motherhood. *Journal of Youth Studies, 8,* 59–79.

Merton, R. K. (1968). *Social theory and social structure.* New York: Free Press.

Mulrow, C. (1994). Systematic reviews: Rationale for systematic reviews. *British Medical Journal, 309,* 597–599.

Noblit, G., & Hare, R. (1988). *Meta-ethnography: Synthesizing qualitative studies.* London: Sage.

Oliver, S., Harden, A., Rees, R., Shepherd, J., Brunton, G., Garcia, J., et al. (2005). An emerging framework for integrating different types of evidence in systematic reviews for public policy. *Evaluation, 11,* 428–466.

Parcel, G. S., Simons-Morton, B. G., O'Hara, N. M., Baranowski, T., & Wilson, B. (1989). School promotion of healthful diet and physical activity: Impact on learning outcomes and self-reported behavior. *Health Education Quarterly, 16,* 181–199.

Paterson, B., Thorne, S., Canam, C., & Jillings, C. (2001). *Meta-study of qualitative health research.* Thousand Oaks, CA: Sage.

Pawson, R. (2006). *Evidence-based policy: A realist perspective.* London: Sage.

Peersman, G., Harden, A., & Oliver, S. (1999). *Effectiveness reviews in health promotion.* London: EPPI-Centre, Social Science Research Unit.

Peersman, G., Oliver, S., & Oakley, A. (2001). Systematic reviews of effectiveness. In S. Oliver & G. Peersman (Eds.), *Using research for effective health promotion* (pp. 96–108). Buckingham, UK: Open University.

Perry, C. L., Bishop, D. B., Taylor, G., Murray, D. M., Mays, R. W., Dudovitz, B. S., et al. (1998). Changing fruit and vegetable consumption among children: The 5-a-Day Power Plus program in St. Paul, Minnesota.

American Journal of Public Health, 88, 603–609.

Perry, C. L., Lytle, L. A., Feldman, H., Nicklas, T., Stone, E., Zive, M., et al. (1998). Effects of the Child and Adolescent Trial for Cardiovascular Health (CATCH) on fruit and vegetable intake. *Journal of Nutrition Education, 30,* 354–360.

Peterosino, A., Turpin-Peterosino, C., & Buehler, J. (2003). Scared straight and other juvenile awareness programs for preventing juvenile delinquency: A systematic review of the randomized experimental evidence. *The ANNALS of the American Academy of Political and Social Science, 589,* 41–62.

Petticrew, M., & Roberts, H. (2006). *Systematic reviews in the social sciences: A practical guide.* Oxford, UK: Blackwell Publishing.

Popay, J. (2005). Moving beyond floccinaucinihilipilification: Enhancing the utility of systematic reviews. *Journal of Clinical Epidemiology, 58,* 1079–1080.

Popay, J., Roberts, H., Sowden, A., Petticrew, M., Aari, L., Roen, K., et al. (2006). *Guidance on the conduct of narrative synthesis in systematic reviews: A product from the ESRC Methods Programme.* Lancaster, UK: Institute for Health Research, Lancaster University.

Pope, C., Mays, N., & Popay, J. (2007). *Synthesizing qualitative and quantitative evidence: A guide to methods.* Milton Keynes, UK: Open University Press.

Rees, R., Oliver, K., Woodman, J., & Thomas, J. (2009). *Children's views about obesity, body size, shape and weight: A systematic review.* London: EPPI Centre, Social Science Research Unit, Institute of Education, University of London.

Reynolds, K. D., Franklin, F. A., Binkley, D., Raczynski, J. M., Harrington, K. F., Kirk, K. A., et al. (2000). Increasing the fruit and vegetable consumption of fourth-graders: Results from the High 5 project. *Preventive Medicine, 30,* 309–319.

Roberts, I. (2000). Randomized trials or the test of time? The story of human albumin administration. *Evaluation and Research in Education, 14,* 231–236.

Roberts, K., Dixon-Woods, M., Fitzpatrick, R., Abrams, K., & Jones, D. (2002). Factors affecting uptake of childhood immunisation: A Bayesian synthesis of qualitative and quantitative evidence. *The Lancet, 360,* 1596–1599.

Sandelowski, M., & Barroso, J. (2003). Creating metasummaries of qualitative findings. *Nursing Research, 52,* 226–233.

Sandelowski, M., Voils, C., & Barroso, J. (2006). Defining and designing mixed research synthesis studies. *Research in the Schools, 13,* 29–40.

Shadish, W., Cook, T., & Campbell, D. (2002). *Experimental and quasi-experimental design.* Boston: Houghton-Mifflin.

Stock, W. (1994). Systematic coding for research synthesis. In H. Cooper & L. Hedges (Eds.), *The handbook of research synthesis.* New York: Russell Sage Foundation.

Thomas, J., & Harden, A. (2003). Practical systems for systematic reviews of research to inform policy and practice in education. In L. Anderson & N. Bennett (Eds.), *Evidence-informed policy and practice in educational leadership and management: Applications and controversies* (pp. 39–54). London: Paul Chapman Publishing.

Thomas, J., & Harden, A. (2008). Methods for the thematic synthesis of qualitative research in systematic reviews. *BMC Medical Research Methods, 8,* 45.

Thomas, J., Harden, A., Oakley, A., Oliver, S., Sutcliffe, K., Rees, R., et al. (2004). Integrating qualitative research with trials in systematic reviews: An example from public health. *British Medical Journal, 328,* 1010–1012.

Thomas, J., Sutcliffe, K., Harden, A., Oakley, A., Oliver, S., Rees, R., et al. (2003). *Children and healthy eating: A systematic review of barriers and facilitators.* London: EPPI-Centre, Social Science Research Unit, Institute of Education, University of London.

Thorne, S., Jenson, L., Kearney, M. H., Noblit, G., & Sandelowski, M. (2004). Qualitative metasynthesis: Reflections on methodological orientation and ideological agenda. *Qualitative Health Research, 14,* 1342–1365.

Thorne, S., Paterson, B., Acorn, S., Canam, C., Joachim, G., & Jillings, C. (2002). Chronic illness experience: Insights from a metastudy. *Qualitative Health Research, 12,* 437–452.

Wallace, W. (1971). *The logic of science in sociology.* Chicago: Aldine-Atherton.

White, H. (1994). Scientific communication and literature retrieval. In H. Cooper & L. Hedges (Eds.), *The handbook of research synthesis.* New York: Russell Sage Foundation.

Wortman, P. (1994). Judging research quality. In H. Cooper & L. Hedges (Eds.), *The handbook of research synthesis* (pp. 97–110). New York: Russell Sage Foundation.

30

FUNDING AND PUBLISHING INTEGRATED STUDIES

Writing Effective Mixed Methods Manuscripts and Grant Proposals

◆ Britt Dahlberg, Marsha N. Wittink, and Joseph J. Gallo

Objectives

This chapter will

- list and describe the components and function of each section of a mixed methods manuscript being prepared for publication;

- list and describe the components and function of each section of a mixed methods proposal;

- identify three strategies to "get in the mind of the reviewer" of papers and proposals; and

- discuss the role of the "punch line" paragraphs in a proposal (at the end of the background, at the end of the preliminary work, and at the end of the research design).

◆ *Writing for Funding and Publication*

> By throwing our occasional
> Thoughts on Paper, we more read-
> ily discover the Defects of our
> Opinions, or we digest them
> better, and find new Arguments to
> support them. This I sometimes
> practice, but such Pieces are fit
> only to be seen by Friends.
>
> Benjamin Franklin (1752)

Benjamin Franklin had the right idea: Good writing requires hard work. Rarely is our writing ready for "prime time" on our first try. Writing requires rewriting and editing based on constructive comments from others. Too often writing can seem such hard work that potential writers never get started. Think for a moment why we want to write for publication in the first place. Most persons in academic positions are expected to publish in their field—publishing is an important part of building a national and international reputation. As well, effective writing will be more persuasive in proposals seeking funding than writing that is not clear or that does not have a "force" and direction. Though academic success would be reason enough for writing, Franklin understood that the process of writing helps us hone our ideas. Writing for publication refines our ideas through the peer-review process, pushing your field and the scope of human knowledge and understanding forward.

In this chapter, we provide readers with practical suggestions for successfully publishing and funding mixed methods studies. With attention and respect to flexibility and applicability in different disciplines, we provide a template for manuscripts and grant proposals that we have developed and found effective in our own work. Our approach is designed to overcome some of the previously identified challenges researchers have faced in successfully publishing and funding

mixed methods studies (Committee on Facilitating Interdisciplinary Research, 2004). This chapter is designed to enable both junior and experienced investigators to reflect on writing and the review process, and on ways to overcome common challenges in order to effectively communicate their mixed methods work.

Our research on mental health has motivated us to mix methods because interventions developed through traditional research paradigms have not had the hoped-for public health impact, and because there is a need for new social and behavioral science approaches to mental health interventions (Glass & McAtee, 2006). Widespread dissatisfaction with current models of service delivery (e.g., patients who do not want treatment for depression, lack of cultural relevance of current paradigms, interventions that are not sustainable in practice) were outlined by the NIMH *Strategic Plan* (National Institute of Mental Health, 2008), the IOM *Quality Chasm* reports (Committee on Crossing the Quality Chasm: Adaptation to Mental Health and Addictive Disorders, 2006; Institute of Medicine, 2001), and the Surgeon General (U.S. Department of Health and Human Services, 1999, 2001). In most clinical research, the biomedical model guides the questions and methods employed (*etic*, or external scientific explanations), as well as strategies that may have been developed for groups other than the groups to which they are applied. In contrast, obtaining the insider perspective (or *emic* view) seeks to understand the patient's point of view, employing methods that are designed to elicit the patient's cultural model of illness and health. We draw on our experience in successfully publishing work in the biomedical field and mental health services research across methods, including articles employing (a) *statistical models* (e.g., Bogner & Gallo, 2004; Bogner, Lin, & Morales, 2006; Wittink, Morales, et al., 2008), (b) *qualitative methods* (e.g., Switzer, Wittink, Karsch, & Barg, 2006; Wittink et al., 2008; Wittink, Dahlberg, Biruk, & Barg, 2008), and (c) *mixed methods* (e.g., Barg et al., 2006;

Bogner, Cahill, Frauenhoffer, & Barg, 2009; Cahill, Lewis, Barg, & Bogner, 2009; Dahlberg, Barg, Gallo, & Wittink, 2009; Wittink, Barg, & Gallo, 2006; Wittink, Joo, Lewis, & Barg, 2009). We mix methods in order to draw from both *etic* and *emic* understandings in devising ways to redesign the delivery of mental health services. The strategies we describe in this chapter reflect our own work and training. We recognize that different fields may have developed specific ways to carry out and present research results (e.g., readers of an anthropology journal may have a very different set of expectations than readers of a psychology journal or a medical journal). Writers are wise to examine examples of publications from the journals that reach an intended audience (or audiences). There are many paths to successful publication and funding. We set forth "a" way we have found useful, but we make no pretense of providing readers with "the" way to write proposals and papers. We welcome comments and ideas from readers.

A point worth making early and often concerns the need to be clear in mixed methods research about the epistemological assumptions we have made in carrying out our research. Doing so is particularly important in writing the results from mixed methods studies because often we must educate reviewers who are primarily schooled and socialized in one field, method, or stance, whose expectations for what constitutes "good work" may differ from our own. We hasten to add, however, that the epistemological questions are present in all research whether acknowledged or not: Confusing a statistical model of reality with reality itself may be the most common example. We recognize the tension represented by the conventional division between "qualitative" and "quantitative" methods but emphasize at the outset the need for clarity in how the research question drives the data collection, data analysis, and inference methods we have chosen (Bergman, 2008). This book provides many discussions and examples linking epistemology, reflexivity, and the

nature of knowledge to methodological considerations, so we do not need to revisit them here (for example, see Chapters 4–7 and 10, this volume). Instead, our task is to provide the reader with tangible strategies to use at the point where the epistemological rubber meets the road—with publication and grant funding. In this chapter, we present (1) a strategy for the structure of a mixed methods paper, (2) an approach to the mixed methods research proposal, (3) comments on the peer-review process and on responding to reviews of papers and proposals, and (4) how to get in the mind of the reviewer.

◆ The Research Publication

STRATEGY FOR THE STRUCTURE OF MIXED METHODS PAPERS

In this section, we set forth a strategy for the structure of mixed methods papers, recognizing that our comments often apply to papers even when mixed methods were not applied, and keeping in mind that conventions and styles of communication differ across disciplines. In addition to publishing a mixed methods paper that makes both qualitative and quantitative findings available to readers in a single paper, as we emphasize here, other approaches to integrated publishing are possible (Stange, Crabtree, & Miller, 2006). For example, investigators may publish in different journals with clear citations to each other, may publish linked papers in the same journal, or may publish a standalone paper that makes inferences across a set of papers describing a body of work that employs mixed methods.

A framework for the structure of a paper does not stifle creativity—a plan enhances creativity. Imagine an artist who works on a canvas of a given size who must plan the work so that no one element of the painting takes up the entire canvas: We would not take up the entire canvas with an apple when painting a still life. No one would argue that the individuality of the artist fails to come through because of planning to include all the fruits in the finished painting. The manuscript is the canvas. Some journals permit a larger canvas than others, so if you are able to write with a particular journal in mind you can lay out the tasks that need to be accomplished accordingly. Writing a paper or a grant proposal can be a daunting task. Having a structure aforethought enhances writing because the writer can focus on one sentence or one paragraph at a time, shifting back and forth between the details and the whole. A structure is not a formula for all occasions, but using a game plan can be especially helpful when writers at any level of experience begin to write.

Work from a detailed outline, perhaps using a framework like the one we provide in this chapter. Then the task is reduced to writing paragraphs, each of which has a job, rather than writing an entire paper from beginning to end. In general, the length of a journal article will be about 3,000 words for *Archives of Internal Medicine* and many medical journals,

6,000 words for *Anthropology and Medicine*, 8,000 words for *Social Science & Medicine* or *Medical Anthropology Quarterly*, and 10,000 words or more for an anthropology journal such as *Ethos*. With 200 to 250 words per double-spaced page, and 2 paragraphs per page, this works out to be a range of 12 pages of text (24 paragraphs to spend) for a 3,000-word paper to about 40 pages of text (80 paragraphs to spend) for a 10,000-word paper. Writing and style conventions vary according to the journal; a good practice is to read several papers from the journal to which you want to send your manuscript and to seek advice from experienced persons who have published papers.

We discuss the construction of the paper in four sections: Introduction, Methods, Results, and Discussion. The sections do not need to be written in the order in which they appear; for instance, the Results section can be a good place to begin writing the paper (Box 30.1). We conclude with

BOX 30.1

Tips for Writing

o Work from an outline.

o Strive for parallel construction in the methods, results, and discussion.

o Use the active voice.

o First person is okay.

o Search and edit your writing to remove unnecessary or ambiguous "these," "there," "those," "them," "this," and "it."

o Suppress the internal critic when writing the initial drafts.

o Do not necessarily write the first sections first.

o Use headings as guideposts to the reader.

o Write transitional sentences and paragraphs to tell what's coming next.

o Cut and paste in real space, not just virtual space. Spread the grant out to make sure the sections relate to one another clearly.

o Find a critical reader and get critical feedback.

o Start with the "one-pager" for proposals to refine the aims and obtain feedback.

Figure 30.1 Outline for One Possible Structure of a Manuscript

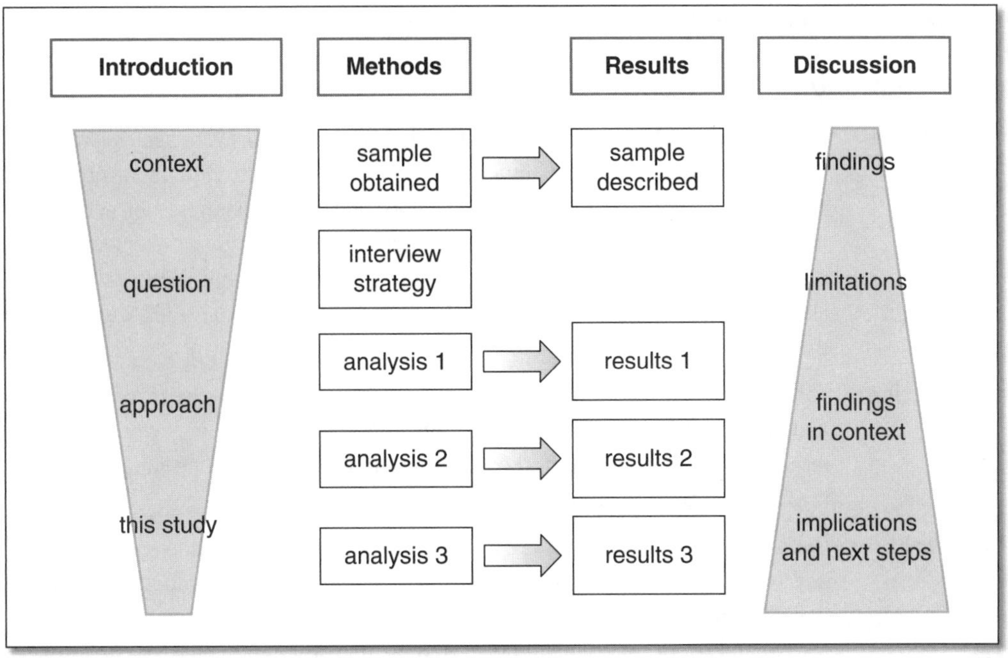

NOTE: In this example, the Introduction sketches broad themes leading to the specific research question, approach taken, and study to be described. The Methods and Results sections have parallel constructions. The Discussion section expands from the findings of the specific study to the implications for the wider field.

some comments on writing the Abstract section, which we generally leave until last.

Figure 30.1 illustrates a general outline for most papers. The Introduction section is depicted as a narrowing funnel, since one construction of the Introduction starts with providing the reader with a context for the work, describes the research question, lays out the approach taken, and ends with a statement of the goals of the particular work to be reported.

The Methods and Results sections are shown with parallel construction, as we discuss below. In our example outline, the Discussion section turns the funnel of the Introduction upside down, starting with the particulars of the reported study, discussing limitations, putting the study in context of prior work, and concluding with the implications of the work and next steps. The mirrored structures of the Introduction and Discussion sections (wide-to-narrow funnel and narrow-to-wide funnel) help to tie the paper together and to place the paper squarely within a particular literature or field by beginning and ending with discussion of the broader literature of which this article will be a part, and connecting that literature to this particular study and to the findings in the middle.

Introduction Section

The job of the Introduction is to draw the reader into the research so that the reader (and, importantly, the reviewer) will appreciate the contribution the paper will make to the field if published. One organization for the Introduction starts with the context for

BOX 30.2

Example of the Structure of the Introduction

INTRODUCTION

Context: The primary health-care setting plays a key role for older adults with depression.... Nevertheless, evidence on the quality of care for older adults with depression in primary care suggests that often their depression is not diagnosed or actively managed.... Several previous studies have linked patient-physician communication to important health outcomes and adherence to treatments. When patients like the way their physician communicates with them, they are more likely to heed the physician's recommendations.

Question: For depression, how patients perceive the communication between physician and patient becomes particularly salient, because patients may not readily reveal their feelings or accept the diagnosis, and they may be unwilling to take medicine or seek counseling.

Approach: Our study focuses on the patient's view of the interactions with their physicians and is based on an integrated mixed methods design that includes elements derived from both quantitative and qualitative traditions, alternating hypothesis-testing and hypothesis-generating strategies. This design allowed us to link the themes regarding how patients talk to their physicians with personal characteristics and standard measures of distress.

The study: Our work differs from previous studies of communication ... in that most previous work focuses on the interaction ... at a specific visit and underemphasizes the patient's contribution to and perspective on the active production of the diagnostic process. In this study, we wanted to understand aspects of the physician–patient relationship (as perceived by the patient) that may influence the way patients communicate about depression. (Wittink et al., 2006)

the work, expresses the research question or topic to be addressed, spells out the conceptual framework or epistemological approach of the authors, and anticipates the specific study to be described in subsequent sections (see Figure 30.1 and Box 30.2). We will review each of these roles of the Introduction here. Throughout our discussion of manuscript structure, we will talk of the roles played by the "first paragraph" or "second paragraph" of a section; keep in mind, however, that these "paragraphs" could in fact be performed by two sentences or two pages, depending on the "size of your canvas" set by the journal's word limit. A "paragraph," then, refers here to an important *piece* of

your mixed methods manuscript (which may often be a paragraph in length).

CONTEXT

The Introduction will typically begin with a description of context: Why is the problem addressed in the paper important to your audience? How have others addressed the same issue? What makes this paper new and different? This could be a place to give some history of the problem, such as with a brief description of prior attempts to solve it. The way mixed methods contribute to the approach can be discussed here. For example, the introduction of the mixed methods article mapped in Box 30.2 begins by describing the importance of the primary care setting for treating depression in older adults, but sets up the specific context for the article (the problem) by describing a body of literature that has shown that depression among older adults is often not diagnosed or actively managed. The statement of the problem sets the stage for the use of methods from different epistemological frameworks.

There are usually multiple ways of framing a paper. For example, we might describe the problem as the negative impact of depression on the functioning of older adults (Biruk & Barg, in press), the challenges faced by older adults with both depression and other illnesses such as heart disease (Bogner, Dahlberg, de Vries, Cahill, & Barg, 2008), or whether doctors identify depression among older adults (Gallo, Bogner, Morales, & Ford, 2005). For the paper quoted in Box 30.2, we selected lack of diagnosis and management of depression in primary care settings as the starting point framing the article. The context often begins fairly broadly (the top of the funnel, Figure 30.1), but may be quickly narrowed down to the more specific context of the study. In the example in Box 30.2, the broad context of poor diagnosis and management was narrowed to the more specific focus on doctor–patient communication. The two issues are linked by a literature review showing that lack of diagnosis and active management are partly due to problems around communication. For a good discussion of how to start and frame the Introduction, see *Effective Writing for Engineers, Managers, Scientists*, by Tichy (1988).

QUESTION

Next, the specific problem is narrowed further into the question of the study. In this example (Box 30.2), the article moves from doctor communication in general to the question of how patients perceive communication with their doctor. Notice that by starting with the broad issue—the context—the funnel structure has linked the specific

question of this study to an issue of broader significance to the journal's audience. Locating the question at this place in the structure gives it the force of growing directly out of a major problem significant to your audience and sets the stage for introduction of your own study, which can now introduce your approach and what differentiates your paper from others.

APPROACH

Placing description of the approach next emphasizes that the methods we employ grow out of the question we want to answer: The question drives the methods, and not the other way around. Even though a standard format calls for a detailed description of the methods in the Methods section, consider providing a brief nontechnical discussion of the methods here. At the end of the Introduction, tell readers, What is the point of view you bring to your research? What conceptual framework? What lens? Here is the place to describe and give the reason for the theoretical framework and methodology you use and to provide an initial signal to the reader of how your questions and methods line up. A brief description of the methods used near the end of the Introduction may be particularly useful for a mixed methods manuscript because the methodological approach may be innovative and unfamiliar to reviewers.

Simply stating that using mixed methods ensures that the weaknesses and strengths of different approaches counterbalance each other is not sufficient as a rationale for mixing methods. Being explicit about your approach to the question allows you to emphasize the connection between your methods, theory, and research question. Explain what insights are made possible by mixing methods that would be inaccessible through either method alone. Tashakkori and Teddlie provide an excellent summary of the rationale behind much mixed methods research as well as ways to gauge the quality of inference from mixed methods studies (Tashakkori & Teddlie, 2008). They describe seven purposes for mixed methods studies: (1) *complementarity* (gaining complementary views about a phenomenon or relationship); (2) *completeness* (obtaining a complete picture of the phenomenon or relationship); (3) *development* (questions for one strand of research emerging from inference from another strand); (4) *expansion* (explaining results derived from a previous strand of a study); (5) *corroboration or confirmation* (assessing credibility of inferences across strands); (6) *compensation* (one approach compensating for the weaknesses of another approach); and (7) *diversity* (obtaining divergent views of the same phenomenon or relationship). In the example presented in Box 30.2, we briefly described our methodology as "alternating hypothesis-testing and hypothesis-generating strategies" and explained, "This design allowed us to link the themes regarding how patients talk to their physicians with personal characteristics and standard measures of distress," a goal that derived from the research context and question to obtain a more complete picture of the phenomenon under study. The explanation of the epistemological framework should make it clear how the theory and rationale for the approach influenced the selection of the mixed methods employed, the analysis of the data, and the inferences that emerge, and it sets the tone and force of writing for the rest of the paper.

THE STUDY

In the last paragraph of the Introduction, state explicitly how your study differs from others and contributes to the literature. Do not leave it to the reviewer to figure out what is new or how the findings would contribute to the field (innovation and contribution to the field will typically be criteria for selecting the manuscript for publication). Provide the "one-sentence literature review," that is, "Our study differs from others in x, y, and z" with citations after x, y, and z. Or, "Although prior studies have done x (provide citations for these studies), our study is the first to do y." In the first example in Box 30.3, we began by arguing that "most prior studies" have had one focus but we had identified a gap our study would fill. In the second example, we summarized a large literature in a lengthier one-sentence literature review, grouping different approaches in sections of the sentence in order to summarize the myriad approaches others have taken to understanding the phenomenon of interest. (Later in that paper, we contrasted those approaches in detail with our own.) Remember that the time you spend (or rather, the *words* you spend) on summing up the relevant literature will depend on the overall canvas size: You might provide one sentence in the Introduction for a 2,500-word article or several pages in a 10,000-word article.

BOX 30.3

Examples of the One-Sentence Literature Review

[M]ost prior studies focused either on patients' and family members' beliefs about causes of coronary heart disease (references) or the causal attributions of depression (references) and do not comment on the coexistence of conditions. . . . [In this study] we sought to understand older patients' perspectives regarding the relationship between depression and heart disease in order to lay the groundwork for designing integrated interventions. (Bogner et al., 2008)

Anthropologists have studied nerves as a symbol and social tool, folk idiom or lay idiom of distress (references), an ineffective idiom of distress (references), a folk ailment (references), a folk illness (references) . . . and as social commentary (references). . . . Nonetheless, a purely constructivist approach ignores aspects of the process and experience of distress encompassed by nerves. (Dahlberg et al., 2009)

◆ *Methods Section*

A common sequence for the methods section might be a description of how participants were sampled and how the data were collected (e.g., interview strategies, measurements employed), and an explanation of the strategy for data analysis. In some cases, the methods section begins with a short overview of the study.

SAMPLING STRATEGY

The job of this paragraph is to (1) describe how the participants were identified and recruited for the study, (2) provide eligibility criteria, and (3) acknowledge that the study was approved by the Institutional Review Board (IRB) at your institution. Description of the sample can come later, in the Results section. In our experience, it is particularly important to explain the rationale for your sampling strategy in a mixed methods manuscript. Reviewers often have a very narrow view of what constitutes scientific sampling (one that differs between fields), so this is another place where you must carefully educate the reviewer of not only *how* you sampled, but *why* you used that sampling strategy, how the sampling strategy is supported by theory, and how the sampling strategy is consistent with the purpose of your study (Glaser & Strauss, 1967). Cite other studies that have used a similar approach in your field, for example, "We used purposive sampling in order to be sure to include people who . . . Purposive sampling is a strategy designed to . . . [here cite a main description of the approach], and has been used by researchers to . . . [cite examples]." Also, it can be useful to contrast the purposes of your approach with more "standard" approaches reviewers might be expecting, such as, "Unlike a random sampling approach which is designed to . . . , purposive sampling is used in order to . . ." Providing a rationale for decisions shows you have considered other approaches and intentionally selected the strategy you describe.

If you use a purposive sampling approach, provide details about the process—that is, What characteristics did you use to select participants and why? For example, Barg and colleagues (2006; see also Box 30.4) laid out in detail how purposive sampling unfolded. Note again, this is an instance where the research process was iterative, but the paper can still be organized into discrete sections typical of the journal to which you send your manuscript. In this case, although the process of sampling and transcript analysis was iterative, we described sampling and analysis in separate sections for clarity, but also explained how the pieces were interrelated at various places in the paper. If you have information on people who refused participation, incorporate that here.

BOX 30.4

Example Description of Purposive Sampling in a Mixed Methods Manuscript

We used a purposive sampling strategy in order to select participants for Spectrum II [the second stage of the study]. We selected at random an initial subsample of 8 participants from the pool of available participants to be interviewed. After reviewing eight transcripts from this initial group, we began to form ideas for selection criteria for the next subsample. In the first group of transcripts, participants expressed a preference for

(Continued)

(Continued)

a diagnosis of anxiety over a diagnosis of depression. Some denied the presence of depression but acknowledged the presence of anxiety and the need to treat it. Therefore, the sampling criteria for the next subsample included persons with high or low depression scores and high anxiety scores. Subsequent subsamples, based on ongoing discussion of transcripts, included persons with a family history of depression, persons for whom there was discordance between the level of depressive symptoms and the doctor's opinion about whether the person was depressed, men with relatively good physical functioning, and the oldest participants in Spectrum I [the first phase of the study]. In addition to these sampling criteria, we purposively sampled to achieve an equal number of African American and White participants. (Barg et al., 2006)

DATA COLLECTION

After describing how the sample was selected, the next pieces of the Methods section will describe how data were collected. Data collection can be separated into different types of approaches (each described in its own section and heading). For example, you might use sections with headings such as "Structured Interview" discussing measures employed, and "Semistructured Interview" discussing open-ended interview procedures. Sections addressing data collection will differ depending on your study and the overall structure you choose for illustrating how you mixed methods. Depending on the space allotted and how explicitly you need to describe your mixed methods approach, you may want to tell readers directly about how you are organizing your methods, such as is illustrated in Box 30.5.

BOX 30.5

Example of Data Collection Section Opening Statement and Subsections for Three Modes of Data Collection, Each With Its Own Heading and Paragraph

Our data consisted of both text and numbers, reflecting the differing epistemological frameworks we used. Here we discuss the strategies under three rubrics: freelisting; semi-structured interviews; and structured interviews employing standardized closed-ended questions tapping into the constructs of interest.

Freelisting. At the start of each interview we collected freelists . . .

Semistructured interviews. . . . [W]e asked participants to respond to vignettes and open-ended questions about depression . . .

Structured interviews. . . . [W]e obtained information on age, gender . . . using standard questions . . . (Barg et al., 2006)

Interview Strategy

When our strategy has included both standardized instruments and approaches that are more open-ended, we have found clarity by writing about the data collection process under headings such as "Interview Strategy" or "Semistructured Interview," and another labeled as "Measurement Strategy" or "Structured Interview." The Interview Strategy section is a place to describe how the semistructured interviews were carried out; here, you want to say who conducted the interviews, describe the procedure for training interviewers, give a summary of the interview guide and guidelines on probing (Were interviewers encouraged to probe into topics raised by participants? Was the goal to hold informal conversation-like interviews? Or was the intention to stick closely to a fixed interview guide?), and say where the interviews were held (e.g., participant's home, doctor's office, public setting).

Measurement Strategy

The "Measurement Strategy" section will describe each of the survey instruments used to measure the domains of interest. If the manuscript only uses survey measures and demographic questions in order to describe the sample, one paragraph summarizing the questions and measurements used may suffice. If the manuscript has more-extensive analysis of survey results across different domains (such as exploring the relationship between social support and depression), you may want to provide a paragraph describing the measurement instruments employed for each domain, and organize according to the conceptual framework guiding the research. Include only measures relevant to the research question at hand rather than listing every measure collected in the study; including off-topic measures will just confuse readers and distract them from the salient points of your argument. Make sure, however, that you discuss all measures and data collection strategies used to collect the data reported in the article: Nothing should appear in the Results section that was not described in the Data Collection section, and vice versa.

DATA ANALYSIS

The "Data Analysis" (or "Analytic Strategy") section describes the steps you took in analyzing data obtained through the data collection strategies described above, and which resulted in the findings you will present in the Results section below. Nothing should come up later in the manuscript (i.e., in the Results or Discussion sections) that is not explained here. The Data Analysis section may include things such as a description of the statistical analyses you performed, or how you coded transcripts to arrive at the themes you discuss in the Results section, as well as an account of integrative or iterative analyses across data collected through different methods.

When writing about an iterative data analytic process, keep in mind that the inherently linear structure of the written manuscript differs from the often lengthy, cyclical, and organic process of research and analysis, and that your readers do not need an account that goes completely in time order. A sequential account can be hard for readers to follow and makes it particularly difficult to determine where exactly the results presented are coming from. Instead, once you have completed your analyses, consider different ways of laying out a *description of* that analytic process that will include all the important information readers need to know in order to evaluate your findings in light of your methods, but also which makes the process more readily transparent in the written format.

One way of organizing the data analysis is into sections based on the type of data collected, for instance a section on the statistical analyses used for analysis of survey data, and a section on the approach used for interpreting transcripts from semistructured interviews. A technique that can help organize the

Data Analysis section clearly, particularly when you have used an iterative or linked approach in which the data analysis strategy for one set of data was predicated on what you found in an earlier analytic stage, is to talk about the process in terms of numbered "phases" or "steps." Then you can describe *Phase 1* in the Data Analysis section, and refer to *Phase 1* in the Results section ("In Phase 1, we discovered that . . ."). For examples of mixed methods manuscripts using phases to structure data analysis and results, see "Unwritten Rules of Talking to Doctors" (Wittink et al., 2006) and "Older Primary Care Patient Views Regarding Antidepressants" (Bogner et al., 2009).

For mixed methods manuscripts in particular, explicitly discussing the connections between analytic approaches in this section can be especially helpful. In other words, although the data collection strategy might be described in separate paragraphs, as in Box 30.5, linking the strategies and the plans for inference across methods should be explicitly described in the Data Analysis section. Were structured interviews planned to be developed based on findings from open-ended interviews? Did you compare groups statistically based on characteristics identified as salient through open-ended interviews? Did you ask in-depth questions of respondents based on statistical findings? If you lay out the section in terms of numbered phases or methods, you can describe the connections between those methods at the opening of the Data Analysis section, or in an additional closing section about analysis across methods, labeling the integration of methods as a final analytic phase.

The Data Analysis section provides the reader with criteria for judging the quality of your data collection and data analysis techniques for factors such as reliability and trustworthiness (Tashakkori & Teddlie, 2008). Examples might include measures of goodness-of-fit for statistical models, reliability of standard measures employed, provision of specific guidelines for assessing when saturation was reached, or descriptions of your strategies for text analysis.

Consider what evidence reviewers will be expecting regarding the confidence they should place in your methods. Reviewers are apt to evaluate methods in light of their own background, which may hold very different epistemological and practical assumptions from the approach you use. To help reviewers judge your research on its own terms, let them know what assumptions the tests of reliability or trustworthiness make and how your methods line up with your research question. Other chapters in this volume discuss strategies for gauging the quality of the inference from mixed methods studies; the job of the Data Analysis section of the manuscript is to provide reviewers with evidence that the inferences you make from the work are solid.

◆ Results Section

The Results section typically begins with a description of the characteristics of the people included in the study. The rest of the Results can be organized into subsections that line up with the sections of the data analysis description (Figure 30.1). The Methods and Results sections should have parallel structures. For example, if the data collection strategy was organized into (a) structured interviews and (b) semistructured interviews, and the Data Analysis (or Analytic Strategy) section was organized into (a) statistical analyses and (b) analysis of semistructured interviews, and possibly (c) integrated analysis across methods, the Results section might be organized into (a) results of statistical analysis, (b) themes from semistructured interviews, and (c) results from analyses across both methods.

SAMPLE CHARACTERISTICS

In medicine, reviewers expect some description of the sample that involves demographic characteristics such as age, gender, ethnicity, marital status, and level of educational attainment, plus clinical characteristics, but we recognize the tacit assumptions behind describing people in this way (Morse, 2008). Nevertheless, in general the first paragraph, with a heading "Sample Characteristics," provides a description of the sample, or a description of the setting of the research. Table 1 of a paper generally provides a detailed description of the sample (a summary of the findings gathered through the measures described in the Measurement Strategy section of Methods above; in this paragraph, briefly summarize those characteristics). See other articles in the journal to which you plan to submit your article to get a feel for the information typically covered.

SUBHEADINGS IN PARALLEL CONSTRUCTION TO THE METHODS SECTION

Remember that the structure of the manuscript itself helps communicate your study and argument to readers. Headings and subheadings are guideposts to the reader. Use headings that correspond to the sections of the analysis paragraph for each phase or step of the work being presented. For example, use of regression models described in one phase of the Data Analysis section might correspond to a paragraph with the heading "Regression Models" in the Results section. A data collection strategy employing semistructured interviews would be described in the Methods section, a description of how the data would be analyzed in the Data Analysis section, and corresponding subheadings in the Results section (e.g., "Text Analysis") would complete the parallel construction. As mentioned above, laying out "phases" or "steps" can help the reader to understand the methodology and to line up the results with the methods, while facilitating discussion of iterative approaches that are often part of mixed methods studies (e.g., how Step 2 is built on Step 1). Tell your readers explicitly that although you first present results from different strands

separately, the analytic process was an iterative mixed methods design (reflected in a summary at the end of the Results section that presents an integrated analysis, as described next).

INTEGRATED PRESENTATION OF MIXED METHODS RESULTS

One of the benefits of mixing methods in a single study is the ability to perform analysis *across* data collected from different methods. Even if you opt to organize your Methods and Results sections into sections according to data collection methods or phases, you can employ an additional final section in the Results section that explicitly links the results from each method. There are numerous ways of describing results and making inferences from different strands, and we discuss a few strategies here. For simplicity, we describe these in terms of "qualitative" and "quantitative" findings, using these imprecise labels as placeholders for the specific methods you use in your study.

Strategy 1: Present quantitative results within the description of qualitative results. This approach organizes the Results section according to themes found from qualitative methods (e.g., open-ended interviews). As an example, in Cahill and colleagues (2009), "You Don't Want to Burden Them: Older Adults' Views on Family Involvement in Care," authors compared the characteristics of participants who raised particular themes and discussed these when describing the theme. Here is an excerpt from one theme's section in the Results:

> Ten of the 23 older respondents (43%) thought their children were busy with their own lives and should not be burdened with their parents' health problems. . . . The 10 older adults expressing the theme, "They have children of their own" had low levels of functioning as indicated by scores on the physical function (45.0) and role physical (43.1)

scales of the SF-36 and received 4.8 hours of help per week from family members. (Cahill et al., 2009, p. 10)

The relevance of differences between characteristics of participants raising each of the various themes was further explicated in the Discussion section of the paper.

Strategy 2: Present the description of themes from in-depth interviews first, then provide a single separate section (with subheading) describing the variation in characteristics of participants who raised each theme. A table to illustrate the comparisons is useful, in which case the paragraph can serve to briefly describe and highlight the main patterns reported in the table. For examples, see Bogner and colleagues (2009), "Older Primary Care Patient Views Regarding Antidepressants: A Mixed Methods Approach," or Wittink and colleagues (2006), "Unwritten Rules of Talking to Doctors About Depression: Integrating Qualitative and Quantitative Methods." An outline of the Wittink and colleagues (2006) results structure is shown in Box 30.6.

BOX 30.6

Example of Results Section Structure for Integrated Mixed Methods Approach (Strategy 2)

RESULTS

Sample characteristics

In all, 53 patients from the 102 who participated in semistructured interviews considered themselves to have been depressed.... Table 2 compares the characteristics of patients whom the physician rated as depressed with the patients who were not rated as depressed....

Themes that emerged in semistructured interviews

Several themes emerged from careful review of the transcripts. We describe four major themes selected for their clinical importance....

"My doctor just picked it up"

In several of the transcripts patients expressed a belief that their physicians are able to "pick up" on depression....

"I'm a good patient"

This theme emerged when patients discussed what the physician thinks of them....

"They just check out your heart and things"

Several patients mentioned that physicians focus mostly on the physical issues and tend to ignore emotional ones....

"They'll just send you to a psychiatrist"

This theme connotes that patients feel any discussion of emotional issues will lead to a referral to a psychiatrist....

Patient characteristics and themes

Table 2 displays characteristics of patients according to the themes.... All of the patients who discussed the theme of "my doctor just picks it up" were women and were concordant with their physicians on the diagnosis of depression. Few of the patients who brought up the "good patient" [theme] were rated by their physician as depressed (3 out of 8), and most were women (6 of 8). (Wittink et al., 2006)

NOTE: See text for details.

Strategy 3: Present findings from each method separately in the Results section (using subheadings), and present the integrated analysis in a Summary section located either at the end of the Results section or in the Discussion section. The first sentence of a new subsection can help show the links between data analytic steps (if there were links) and between the findings resulting from them; for example, the Barg and colleagues (2006) article on loneliness separates presentation of results into (1) sample characteristics, (2) salient terms identified through the freelisting method, (3) themes from semistructured interviews, and (4) statistical analysis of survey report of depression and loneliness. However, the sections are linked through transition statements; for example, the "Themes" section begins by showing that the analysis of semistructured interviews grew out of insights derived from the freelists: "Because loneliness played such a significant role in the definition of depression in the freelists, we examined the semistructured interviews in order to better understand the concept" (Barg et al., 2006, p. S334).

Strategy 4: Label the different Results sections as ordered "steps" or "phases" to highlight how each phase builds on insights drawn from previous phases of the research. This language helps you refer clearly through numbering but, like the transition sentences in Strategy 3 above, highlights connections between data analytic steps. For example, consider how your quantitative results provided clues leading to qualitative analysis (or how the quantitative results were unable to answer the research question, and thus prompted you to search qualitative data for an answer), and vice versa.

Across all of these strategies or any other format you decide on, keep in mind that dividing up the results with subheadings and sections (based on different methods of data analysis or collection, or on different stages of the study) does not preclude you from creating links across sections. We view the sections and their headings as *facilitating* discussion of such links, because you have created labels for different parts you will use to refer consistently to particular data and insights gained from different methods. The sections help organize the findings, but each section also can include some mention of other sections, or comment on how the findings refine, alter, or support the findings that came in the preceding sections. Comments also can be organized into a final summary section of the results, which is explicitly focused on "integrating findings" or analysis across methods (and should have an appropriate heading indicating the summary or integrative function of the concluding Results section). The structure of the paper contributes to the communication of complex ideas and approaches.

◆ Discussion Section

THE FIRST PARAGRAPH: STATE THE FINDINGS

Use the first paragraph of the Discussion to say what you did and to state your most important findings (i.e., provide a brief summary of your paper thus far). You also might describe here how mixed methods were needed in order to arrive at the insights and findings that emerged. Picture the funnel again (Figure 30.1). Unlike the Introduction, the Discussion section begins with the "narrow end" up—the findings from this study—and widens into a larger discussion of what those findings mean in terms of the broader literature and the field.

THE SECOND PARAGRAPH: LIMITATIONS

The second paragraph of the Discussion can be the limitations paragraph. Although some writers place the limitations discussion at the very end of the paper, the advantage of placing it here is that your article ends on a strong note, with its conclusions, rather than ending with a "disclaimer" about all its possible drawbacks. Present the principal limitations as well as ways in which you tried to mitigate each limitation. For example, the limitations section in Dahlberg and colleagues (2009), "Bridging Psychiatric and Anthropological Approaches: The Case of 'Nerves' in the United States," noted,

> *Although* our approach does not allow us to generalize about the prevalence of nerves, *it does provide* a more in-depth understanding of the cultural model for nerves and its variable usage because we were able to observe ways respondents spontaneously used the model. (Dahlberg et al., 2009; emphasis added)

In this sentence, we begin by addressing one critique a statistically minded reviewer raised in reading a mixed methods paper; namely, that we did not use a random-sampling and survey-question design to pursue our investigation of how older adults thought about "bad nerves" in relation to depression. Though we begin by acknowledging what our approach does not allow us to do (make a statement from this study about prevalence), we couple this limitation

with the strengths of our approach: "It does provide a more in-depth understanding of the cultural model." Essentially, we have taken what a reviewer of the submitted manuscript identified as a "limitation" and used the opportunity to remind the reader of the published paper—who may think along the same lines as the reviewer—to evaluate our sampling strategy in the light of our specific research question rather than according to a general notion that all samples need to be "random" to yield useful information.

For mixed methods articles in particular, the limitations section may be a place to again highlight what distinguishes your methodological–epistemological approach, and what its strengths are. If you used statistical comparisons to generate hypotheses and not to test them, let readers know. Tell readers how you intentionally used your methods, *especially* when those uses are likely to differ from the uses to which reviewers are accustomed. The limitations section of a manuscript is much like the "alternative approaches considered" section in a grant proposal: The purpose is to show reviewers and readers you thought of possible threats to the inferences you want to make, how you have attempted to address threats to your inferences, and *why* you chose the approach you did.

SUBSEQUENT PARAGRAPHS: FINDINGS IN CONTEXT

After describing limitations, repeat the findings. "Despite limitations, our study deserves attention because x, y, and z" (perhaps the same factors you mentioned in the Introduction as factors that set your work apart from others). Review the literature more thoroughly here than in the Introduction. You may have quickly summarized past literature in the Introduction to highlight what distinguishes your article and how the past literature called for your research. Revisit some of those articles here, but provide a thoughtful review—do not just repeat what others have reported. What synthesis can you provide *across* these various studies and in relation to the findings you have just presented in this manuscript?

The approach to the literature review will differ for journals from different fields. In response to our own submitted manuscripts across a range of fields, we note that quantitatively focused clinical journals seemed to expect the Discussion section to compare and contrast whether studies have "replicated" the same findings, or have found discrepancies. In contrast, social science journals emphasizing qualitative work were more inviting to meta-analysis across studies, asking how past findings and theories could help shed light on the findings from our research. For journals whose readers expect comparing and contrasting, consider details about how others carried out the work. How did the samples differ? What do you make of findings based on those differences? For example, what are the implications when one study focused only on in-hospital patients, whereas another study sampled people from neighborhood venues? What about interviews conducted by the patient's physician in the doctor's office, versus interviews conducted by a research assistant in the participant's home? How might such design differences have shaped the reported findings? In the social science arena, you may focus more on differences in the theoretical perspectives taken by each study, as well as implications of the body of findings as a whole for theoretical development. Journals are geared to audiences who have different notions about the outcomes of the research presented (e.g., understanding whether something about the sample accounts for differing response to treatment vs. expanding conceptual development of a field by explicating the boundaries of a concept, such as perceptions of racism).

THE LAST PARAGRAPH: IMPLICATIONS AND NEXT STEPS

The last paragraph should put the study in context, describe its importance and implications, and state what is next. The "implications" will differ greatly depending on your audience (i.e., depending on the jour-

nal), and depending on the problem you set up as the main context for this particular manuscript. Generally speaking, a clinical journal will seek practical implications—that is, how should clinical practice be changed in light of your findings (what tips do you have for physicians, for example?), or how might interventions be designed to test your findings and seek to improve health outcomes? Other journals might instead be seeking theoretical implications germane to their particular field; for *Medical Anthropology Quarterly*, for example, you may conclude by commenting on the implications of your manuscript for theory development within the field of medical anthropology.

For the conclusion, ask, What is new about this article? If your research raises more questions about the phenomenon under study or about the strengths and limitations of the methods employed, spell out the questions as next steps. The ubiquitous "Future research should explore . . . " statement need not be a throw-away comment. Rather, use the opportunity to articulate the next steps you would undertake in your own line of research so that over time your publications will tell a story. At the same time, you can invite others to pick up where you left off—to move the field forward.

◆ *Abstract*

Some readers will only read the abstract. While journals may not be available to everyone, with Internet access anyone can read your abstract (e.g., via PubMed). Although the Abstract is the first section of a paper, we recommend writing it last. The abstract provides a concise summary of the background of the problem, the approach used to answer the research question, results, inferences, and implications. We have found that writing this succinct summary of the entire work is often easiest *after* having written out the details of the manuscript; after all, the Abstract section should express not the logic you began with when you sat down to write, but rather the final insights you arrived at after completing your analysis and writing.

Spend some time polishing the abstract so it is concise and grabs the reader's attention (the same is true for designing a title). Also give some thought to selecting key words because they will play a role in the indexing of your article and in shaping who is likely to find your article when searching or browsing. You may want to use the term *mixed methods* in the title, abstract, or key words, especially if part of the article's intent is to reflect on the insights available through mixed methods. Each journal tends to have a precise word limit and format

required for abstracts, so read the directions for authors and check abstracts from several articles published in that journal to identify the abstract's format and style conventions.

◆ The Research Proposal

The mixed methods research proposal shares many issues and strategies in common with the mixed methods manuscript described above, but some features differ significantly. We provide a common outline for a research proposal in Figure 30.2. The

Figure 30.2   Outline for One Possible Structure of a Mixed Methods Grant Proposal

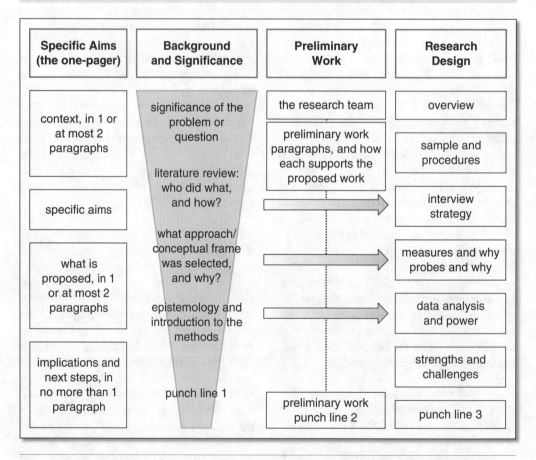

NOTE: The first page describes the entire grant in summary form. The background and significance statement has a funnel structure and prepares the reader by mapping to the research design. Preliminary work provides evidence of the teamwork, feasibility, and research that led to the proposal. Strategically placed punch-line paragraphs summarize the preceding section and transition to the next. Applications to NIH must specifically address innovation.

instructions of the agency, foundation, or institute from whom you are requesting funds provide your canvas—read and follow the instructions with care.

Readers should be aware that as we go to press the National Institutes of Health (NIH) has revised the structure of the application. Comments here are even more salient to the new format, which is leaner and more aligned with the criteria reviewers are asked to use in rating the application for the investigator-initiated R01. Specifically, the specific aims should be 1 page and the research plan 12 pages (it was 25 pages). The research plan must include the following sections: Significance, Innovation, Approach, and Preliminary Work. The shorter application means the writing has to grab the reader with the significance of the question, the innovation of the ideas, and the force and direction of the argument. Continually updated instructions can be accessed at http:// grants.nih.gov/grants/funding/phs398/phs 398.html

SPECIFIC AIMS: THE "ONE-PAGER"

At the NIH, most proposals begin with "specific aims," but other organizations may use the term *objectives* or *goals*. We begin with a "one-pager"—a summary of the research that can be used in the process of developing the ideas in the proposal that then becomes the first page of the grant proposal (the first section of NIH grants is the "Specific Aims" section). The one-pager consists of four sections, each about one paragraph in length (Figure 30.2): (1) a background statement (the background and significance section of the grant proposal, in miniature) and what has led to this proposal, (2) the specific aims, (3) a description of what is proposed, and (4) implications and next steps. This page sets the stage for the proposal; we refine this page before working on the rest of the application.

The specific aims should be as explicit and clear as possible; sometimes it may be useful to think of each aim as having a

corresponding phase of data collection and analysis, so one aim might have primarily a "quantitative" focus and another a "qualitative" focus. The aims should follow directly from the preceding background paragraph. Specific aims associated with quantitative work are often expressed with key verbs such as "to determine," "to estimate," "to compare," or "to test," while qualitative aims are often expressed as "to explore," "to understand," or "to develop."

We use the one-pager in several ways. First, we refine the specific aims and what is proposed by circulating the one-pager to co-investigators. Doing so taps the expertise of collaborators and gets everyone on board about the scope of the proposed project. Second, the one-pager can be used to interact with foundation or NIH staff. The one-pager introduces them to the ideas in the project and provides them with an opportunity to provide specific feedback about the project, instead of general comments that do not help hone the ideas. Ask colleagues, other scholars in the field, and a program officer to share their reactions to the one-pager. Using the one-pager as a springboard for discussion with others can help you identify problem areas, fill in details that are not clear, and solidify the rationale for the approaches that are proposed. Keeping track of the decisions made along the way can be incorporated into the proposal in discussion of alternative approaches considered (labeled "strengths and challenges" in Figure 30.2). If you can get a quick response from the funding agency, you may learn things to address in the grant proposal prior to sending it out for review (helping you "get in the mind of the reviewer"; see Getting in the Mind of the Reviewer section below).

BACKGROUND AND SIGNIFICANCE SECTION

The Background and Significance section of the proposal might have a structure like the Introduction to papers as discussed above: Here the funnel points directly to why this project was proposed now and with the approaches selected (summarized in a paragraph labeled "punch line 1" in Figure 30.2). The purpose of the punch line paragraph is to summarize the field, to repeat the important points you have made earlier, and to sharpen the focus on why the question and what you are proposing is important and compelling.

Several pitfalls are common to all proposals, but are particularly salient in mixed method work. Do not assume the reviewer will see what is innovative in your proposal or will know why you have selected the approach you did. Common mistakes are assuming reviewers will be familiar with the importance of the problem or question you are tackling, failing to mention or cite alternative approaches and the rationale for selection of one approach over another (see Box 30.7 for an example of providing a rationale for how sampling would be accomplished), and not specifying the conceptual framework or lens that guides the research. Address epistemological issues explicitly. Stating that your proposal is innovative because of the use of mixed methods will not be compelling without making clear the specific links between theory, your questions, and the methods you have chosen. Offer a clear conceptual model, and show how your conceptual framework or the lens with which you approach your question frames the sampling design, methods, data analysis, and ways you expect to draw inferences. Having a clear conceptual framework or model is not inconsistent with an inductive approach. Even when the research requires openness to emerging themes, reviewers may expect you to provide some prediction of what you might find.

BOX 30.7

Example Sampling Rationale From Mixed Methods Grant Proposal

(1) Although qualitative research sometimes calls for random sampling, more often deliberately nonrandom samples that allow for credible, but time and context-bound results, are selected. **(2)** The logic of a purposive sample lies in selecting people who can provide the most information for the question under study (Glaser & Strauss, 1967; Kemper, Stringfield, & Teddlie, 2003). **(3)** We justify this approach because disparities in mental health care across ethnic minorities persist and require attention to the diversity of views on depression and pathways to care. We take a public health approach, trying to reach the many older adults who typically do not receive or engage in treatment. **(4)** We propose the use of purposive sampling (or "theoretical," i.e., theory-developing, sampling) as we have in peer-reviewed work (Barg et al., 2006; Dahlberg et al., 2009; Switzer et al., 2006; Wittink et al., 2006) in order to discover the range of concepts and their overlap and to inform identification of older adults who could benefit from treatment. Based on our prior work, we estimate the random sample interview will take no more than 45 minutes and the purposive sample interview no more than 90 minutes.

Role of each sentence

1. Addresses reviewer expectations and specifies why an alternative approach is taken

2. Explains the rationale of the sampling approach and provides citations to show basis in the literature

3. Connects the standard reason for the sampling technique with the particular reason it was selected for this study

4. Shows that we are experienced with the approach and illustrates ways we have used it

As in a mixed methods paper where introducing methods early can be useful, we often bring up the methods in the concluding section of the background statement (to educate the reviewers so that the rationale for the methods is clear before the reviewer must absorb what is often a more technical treatment of the methods in the Research Design section). Know who the reviewers will be, not only in terms of the disciplinary approaches they might bring to their reading of the proposal, but also their names and whether their work has any relevance to the work you have proposed. Being aware of your audience for the grant proposal also means paying attention to what the agency expects to get out of the grant. Are their primary goals to advance health through the development of new interventions, or to develop new theories and knowledge in a particular field? Read through the agency's mission statements as well as instructions and advice to researchers for grant proposals. Pay attention to the checklist of features they are looking for and the review criteria to be employed, and use the granting agency's own language to explicitly tell reviewers *how* your grant proposal meets those criteria.

PRELIMINARY WORK SECTION

Your proposal must convince reviewers you can successfully carry out the study. For mixed methods research in which you plan to collaborate with colleagues across disciplines, you need to show reviewers that you have developed working relationships that bode well for the proposed work. Good collegial relationships can be demonstrated through your track record (Do you have

publications together? Have you worked together on projects before? Have you been meeting regularly?). The preliminary work section (Figure 30.2) can be organized so that each publication, finding, or collaboration that pertains to the proposed work is covered by a paragraph. While a specific collaboration might not be on topic for the current grant proposal, a description in the Preliminary Work section of the results of the collaboration provides evidence the collaborative relationships are solid. We conclude each paragraph with a sentence making explicit how the preliminary work presented supports the proposed work (rather than leaving it to the reviewer to figure out how). Summarize the preliminary work section with a summary ("punch line 2" in Figure 30.2). The purpose of the punch line paragraph at the end of the Preliminary Work section is to state how the preliminary work led to the work you are proposing and will describe in the following sections.

RESEARCH DESIGN SECTION

The description of the research design can take many of the same strategies from the writing of a manuscript (e.g., precision in describing how sampling will be carried out). Reviewers will expect enough detail to evaluate the quality of the inferences that you will be able to make. As indicated by the arrows from left to right across the middle of Figure 30.2, the research design should logically follow from the literature in the background statement. Training of interviewers and the procedures they will follow should be carefully explained. A common pitfall of R21 or R34 proposals (NIH intervention development applications) concerns failure to have specific links to how what is learned from a qualitative phase (typically, focus groups) will be used to inform the next steps of the research. In other words, proposals may fail to convey, through the use of precise explanations and examples, how the qualitative data will influence the subsequent phase of the research. Mixed procedures for interviewing or for data analysis might be described separately but with a specific description of how the strands will be linked. Applications to NIH must incorporate specific headings in the Research Plan: Significance, Innovation, and Approach.

Near the end of the proposal, we place a paragraph discussing strengths and challenges. Here a description of alternative approaches considered or how potential threats to the ability to carry out the project are mitigated will demonstrate to reviewers that you have anticipated their comments. The craft of writing the proposal incorporates describing limitations in a way that demonstrates the limitations were not avoidable and that the limitations are outweighed by the advantages of the chosen methods. Even though different people may contribute sections of the grant proposal, make sure all of the pieces and details fit together. You want the grant proposal to read like a cohesive product of a working group, not as independently written pieces pasted together. The purpose of "punch line 3" (Figure 30.2) is to bring the reviewer back to the research question and to remind the reviewer of the significance and importance of the proposed work.

LINKS IN A CHAIN: MAKING THE PROPOSAL COMPELLING

One of the most common faults reviewers find with proposals is that the components are not clearly linked. A premise of this chapter is that we can improve the process of writing by considering a structure that permits us to focus on one component of the product at a time: Each paragraph has a job

to do. As the proposal fills out, considering the "forest" in addition to the "trees" brings the grant proposal into alignment so that the sections map well to one another. Use a real desktop and actual cutting and pasting as needed: that is, print the grant proposal and lay out the pages so you can *see* its full structure. Cut the pieces and move them physically to place them in the grant proposal where they belong conceptually, and tape them down. This can facilitate making changes on the computer later, and it helps you see the "forest" of the document: What sections are included and what role do they play in the whole? Is the arrangement sensible, and does it give cohesion and force to the proposal? When each section relates closely to the foundation laid out in the Background and Significance section, particularly given a well-specified conceptual framework underlying the research, the grant proposal reads "tight"—there are no loose ends; the writing has "force" and is compelling.

◆ Breathing Deeply: Peer Review and Response for Papers and Proposals

Reading the comments of reviewers can sometimes cause the most experienced investigators to question their choice of a career. If your paper has been rejected, do not lose heart—almost every idea has a home. If your paper has been rejected after being sent off for review, you will have received some comments from reviewers, and it is wise to consider the comments carefully, as painful as this can sometimes be. Remember, when you send the paper to another journal it is possible one of the reviewers may be the same; even if that is not the case, other reviewers may bring up the same criticisms. Perhaps the paper was very good but the reviewers and editor thought the paper was not suitable for the audience of that specific journal. If you are submitting to the best journals in a field, expect rejection, but that does not mean you should not aim high.

If the decision was "revise and resubmit," you should make a list of the reviewers' comments in the outline of a letter (Box 30.8), and then cool off. When you are ready, consider and draft your responses, point by point, but only turn to the manuscript when you have gone through and responded to each point. Deal with contrasting or contradictory comments from reviewers by juxtaposition. Often the editor will provide guidance about the direction the revision should take, but, if not, juxtapose the contrary recommendations and then give your rationale for the course you choose. Focusing on the response first makes the process of revision of the manuscript more efficient and deliberate: The letter with initial responses provides a way for collaborators and mentors to get on board and contribute to how the manuscript should be modified (it is much easier to change direction in the letter than in the manuscript). Note that a response in the letter does not necessarily imply that the manuscript has to change. Sometimes providing the information requested by a reviewer in the letter is enough. An example might be when a reviewer asks for a study detail that has been addressed in another publication. Be sure to reiterate the positive comments reviewers made when providing your response and to thank them for their work (Box 30.8).

◆ Getting in the Mind of the Reviewer

For both manuscripts and grant proposals, it is important to consider your reviewers. Who are they? What fields are they from? How are they likely to read and respond to your work? and What biases, concerns, and questions are likely to be on their minds while reading? Has the organization and formatting of the manuscript or proposal reflected your thinking clearly? Is the argument easy to follow? Does the reviewer have to search for key ideas in densely packed text? Try to anticipate and address such questions head on in the article or grant proposal. For instance, if you know most of the reviewers are anthropologists who will likely be less familiar with quantitative methods (or may have particular biases against these methods), anticipate those questions and critiques and preemptively address them. Have you considered the appropriate background in anthropology that pertains to your study? Even if they do not agree with you, your readers are likely to find your work more convincing if they see you have already considered the critiques they want to bring up while reading. If writing for a medical journal, you need to bring in a discussion of the epistemology underlying your methods, but perhaps not to the same degree or in the same way as for other audiences. In all cases, make explicit what you include and what you leave out, based on the anticipated audience.

In a manuscript, probably a paragraph overall will suffice for addressing biases and educating reviewers on your methods and approach. In the discussion above, we noted that there are places throughout the manuscript to address your audience, such as by introducing the methods in the Introduction (to help educate the reviewer) and by describing alternative approaches considered and the strengths and weaknesses of methods in the limitations section. Similar concepts apply for grant proposals. In the grant proposal, your goal is to convince reviewers that you have chosen an appropriate approach likely to generate new and useful knowledge in the field. Some of the same strategies, such as explicitly describing alternative approaches considered and the reasons you chose particular methods, are equally helpful in grant proposals.

BOX 30.8

Example of a Letter to Accompany a Manuscript That Has Been Revised and Resubmitted for Review

Dear Dr. Smith:

Attached is a revision of the paper entitled "ABC." We appreciate the opportunity to respond to your comments as well as to the reviewers' comments. In this letter, we have outlined changes made in response to each point raised in the review. In the revised version of the manuscript, we tried to balance the additional information requested by reviewers with the need to shorten the manuscript. We have shortened the text of the paper to xxxx words (was xxxx words). Modifications to the manuscript have been underlined in the text.

Editor's comments

We appreciate your comment, which acknowledges that our findings are of potential value; we have revised the paper based on your recommendations.

1. There are numerous questions the reviewers raise about the usage of certain terms....

   The use of the term in the paper has been clarified on page xx.

2. The question of ethnicity....

   You raise an important issue, which we discuss further in the response to Reviewer 1, Point 2 below.

Reviewer 1

We appreciated the reviewer's comments: "The authors have tapped into a well-designed...." We respond to the comments of Reviewer 1 below.

1. INTRODUCTION: Would expand the review of....

   Keeping in mind the need to reduce the length of the manuscript, a discussion of...has been added to the literature review on page 5.

2. ...

Reviewer 2

We appreciated the reviewer's extensive comments on the importance of the paper: "This is a very interesting manuscript...." Below, we respond to the comments of Reviewer 2.

1. It takes a fairly careful read to realize....

   The reviewer makes an excellent suggestion....

2. ...

(Continued)

(Continued)

The time and care with which you and the referees have reviewed our manuscript is very much appreciated. We believe that the paper is stronger as a result. We hope that the changes will be satisfactory and that the paper will be suitable for publication. Please do not hesitate to contact me if you have any questions about the response, or if I can be of further assistance to you in your role as editor.

Sincerely,

While many of the following points apply to all manuscripts, we summarize ideas of particular significance for mixed methods articles:

- Describe your methods at the end of the Introduction section; this serves at least two functions. First, a description of methods here links your theoretical approach to the methods you have employed. Second, a description of how the methods work in nontechnical terms lays the groundwork for a more technical account in the Methods section (educating reviewers who may be unfamiliar with the method).

- Be explicit about why you are using mixed methods, linking theory, your question, the research design, and how you will make inferences (Tashakkori & Teddlie, 2008).

- Provide a clear justification for your chosen sampling strategy (Glaser & Strauss, 1967).

- Write clearly. Mixed methods studies are often iterative, not linear, with connections between data collection and data analysis of different data types. This poses challenges for a clear presentation of the study methods and results. Our recommendations for increasing clarity include

  ✓ parallel structure,
  ✓ components of study design labeled as numbered phases or steps, and

  ✓ transition paragraphs that alert the reader about how you will present the methods and results provided.

- Describe alternative study designs considered, and reiterate the strengths of your particular mixed methods approach.

- When attempting to publish qualitative data in journals representing fields with typically 4,000 words or less allotted to a paper, consider condensed ways to present results. Examples include presenting quotes in text boxes or tables, or presenting a summary of the themes visually (e.g., see diagram in Bogner et al., 2008).

- Be explicit about the significance of the study for different fields: Within the Discussion section, include sections addressing theoretical implications, methodological implications, and practical implications.

- Anticipate questions. Crossing epistemological boundaries means assumptions need to be explicitly addressed at the outset and reflected in the data collection methods, the analytic strategy, and the presentation and interpretation of results.

We should keep in mind that challenges in writing about mixed methods can be turned to advantage. All good research ought to be carried out with an awareness of the particular perspective and assumptions on which it is built; working across disciplinary and epistemological boundaries helps make our assumptions more visible, gives us practice in communicating and defending clearly the assumptions of our field, and pushes us to find new ways of considering problems from across different perspectives.

◆ Conclusions

Perhaps the strategies we have used for publishing papers and writing proposals were only, as Franklin said, "fit to be seen by Friends." Nevertheless, we welcome comments from other investigators about approaches to writing mixed methods manuscripts and proposals they have found successful. All research benefits from a clear design stemming from an explicit and well-thought-out theoretical perspective. Researchers face particular challenges in mixing methods, and in publishing and funding such studies. Consideration of the epistemological issues involved in mixing methods and working across disciplinary boundaries is essential for conducting good mixed methods studies, but such work heightens the need to address the task of writing. In some sense, the words of Benjamin Franklin with which we began are particularly true for mixed methods research, and for any work that sets off in untraveled directions: We write in order to clarify our thoughts. Writing as a task is distinct, but not separable, from conducting mixed methods research. Writing has a rhythm and process all its own, but it is through writing that our ideas become clear, and that new ways of pushing forward the boundaries of methodological and theoretical development are elucidated. Though writing takes time and effort, once we realize that the process is slow for anyone, we can begin with a basic structure, and thus free ourselves to take writing one step at a time until we find ourselves polishing a manuscript ready for publication, or a grant proposal worthy of funding.

◆ Research Questions and Exercises

Select a mixed methods paper in your field (e.g., from the *Journal of Mixed Methods Research*) or from the references listed at the end of the chapter. Look carefully at the structure of the Introduction, Methods, Results, and Discussion sections. Compare and contrast the approach taken by the authors with the suggested strategies discussed in the chapter. What strategies seem effective? What alternatives would you suggest to the authors?

Obtain a draft or funded grant proposal. Create an outline of the proposal and compare the outline with the structure of the proposal provided in the chapter. Compare and contrast the approach taken by the investigators with the suggested structure and strategies discussed in the chapter. What strategies seemed effective? What alternatives would you suggest to the investigators in terms of how the ideas are presented?

◆ Recommended Resources

WEB SITES

http://mulford.meduohio.edu/instr/

Links to Web sites that provide instructions to authors for more than 3,500 journals in the health and life sciences. All links are to primary sources—that is, to publishers and organizations with editorial responsibilities for the titles.

http://cms.csr.nih.gov/Resources forApplicants/InsidetheNIHGrant ReviewProcessVideo.htm

The Center for Scientific Review has produced a video of a mock study section meeting to provide an inside look at how NIH grant applications are reviewed for scientific and technical merit.

http://grants.nih.gov/grants/funding/phs398/phs398.html

Instructions for the new NIH application and a description of the review process, which should be consulted when preparing an NIH application.

USEFUL SOURCES WHEN WRITING

Graff, G., & Birkenstein, C. (Eds.). (2006). *They say, I say: The moves that matter in academic writing.* New York: W. W. Norton.

Office of Behavioral and Social Sciences Research. (2001). *Qualitative methods in health research: Opportunities and considerations in application and review.* Bethesda, MD: National Institutes of Health. http://obssr.od.nih.gov/pdf/Qualitative.pdf

Sandelowski, M. (2003). Tables or tableaux? The challenges of writing and reading mixed methods studies. In A. Tashakkori & C. Teddlie (Eds.), *Handbook of mixed methods in social and behavioral research.* Thousand Oaks, CA: Sage.

Scheier, L. M., & Dewey, W. L. (Eds.). (2008). *The complete writing guide to NIH behavioral science grants.* New York: Oxford University Press.

Strunk, W., Jr., & White, E. B. (2000). *The elements of style* (4th ed.). Boston: Allyn & Bacon.

Tashakkori, A., & Teddlie, C. (2008). Quality of inferences in mixed methods research: Calling for an integrative framework. In M. M. Bergman (Ed.), *Advances in mixed methods research* (pp. 100–119). London: Sage.

◆ Acknowledgments

I am indebted to colleagues at the Johns Hopkins University who taught me to write and gave me a sound footing in the world of research (James C. Anthony, PhD, and William W. Eaton, PhD) and to a wonderful colleague at the University of Pennsylvania who opened my eyes to a whole new way of thinking (Frances K. Barg, PhD).—Joseph J. Gallo

◆ References

Barg, F. K., Huss-Ashmore, R., Wittink, M. N., Murray, G. F., Bogner, H. R., & Gallo, J. J. (2006). A mixed methods approach to understand loneliness and depression in older adults. *Journal of Gerontology: Social Sciences, 61*(6), S329–S339.

Bergman, M. M. (2008). The straw men of the qualitative-quantitative divide and their influence on mixed methods research. In M. M. Bergman (Ed.), *Advances in mixed methods research* (pp. 11–21). London: Sage.

Biruk, C., & Barg, F. K. (in press). "I wasn't that type of person": The role of physical pain in stories of suffering and self. *Medical Anthropology Quarterly.*

Bogner, H. R., Cahill, E., Frauenhoffer, C., & Barg, F. K. (2009). Older primary care patient views regarding antidepressants: A mixed methods approach. *Journal of Mental Health, 18*(1), 57–64.

Bogner, H. R., Dahlberg, B., de Vries, H. F., Cahill, E., & Barg, F. K. (2008). Older patients' views on the relationship between depression and heart disease. *Family Medicine, 40*(9), 652–657.

Bogner, H. R., & Gallo, J. J. (2004). Are higher rates of depression in women accounted for by differential symptom reporting? *Social Psychiatry and Psychiatric Epidemiology, 39*(2), 126–131.

Bogner, H. R., Lin, J. Y., & Morales, K. H. (2006). Patterns of early adherence to the antidepressant Citalopram among primary care patients: The PROSPECT study. *International Journal of Psychiatry in Medicine, 36*(1), 103–119.

Cahill, E. C., Lewis, L., Barg, F. K., & Bogner, H. R. (2009). "You don't want to burden them": Older adults' views on family involvement in care. *Journal of Family Nursing, 15*, 295–317.

Committee on Crossing the Quality Chasm: Adaptation to Mental Health and Addictive Disorders. (2006). *Improving the quality of care for mental and substance-use conditions: Quality chasm series.* Washington, DC: National Academies Press.

Committee on Facilitating Interdisciplinary Research. (2004). *Facilitating interdisciplinary research.* Washington, DC: National Academies Press.

Dahlberg, B., Barg, F. K., Gallo, J. J., & Wittink, M. N. (2009). Bridging psychiatric and anthropological approaches: The case of "nerves" in the United States. *Ethos, 37,* 283–313.

Gallo, J. J., Bogner, H. R., Morales, K. H., & Ford, D. E. (2005). Patient ethnicity and the identification and active management of depression in late life. *Archives of Internal Medicine, 165*(17), 1962–1968.

Glaser, B. G., & Strauss, A. L. (1967). *The discovery of grounded theory: Strategies for qualitative research.* New York: Aldine Publishing.

Glass, T. A., & McAtee, M. (2006). Behavioral science at the crossroads in public health: Extending horizons, envisioning the future. *Social Science & Medicine, 62,* 1650–1671.

Institute of Medicine. (2001). *Crossing the quality chasm: A new health system for the 21st century.* Washington, DC: National Academies Press.

Kemper, E. A., Stringfield, S., & Teddlie, C. (2003). Mixed methods sampling: Strategies in social science research. In A. Tashakkori & C. Teddlie (Eds.), *Handbook of mixed methods in social and behavioral research* (pp. 273–296). Thousand Oaks, CA: Sage.

Morse, J. M. (2008). "What's your favorite color?" Reporting irrelevant demographics in qualitative research. *Qualitative Health Research, 18*(3), 299–300.

National Institute of Mental Health. (2008). *National Institute of Mental Health strategic plan.* Washington, DC: Author.

Stange, K. C., Crabtree, B. F., & Miller, W. L. (2006). Publishing multimethod research. *Annals of Family Medicine, 4,* 292–294.

Switzer, J., Wittink, M., Karsch, B. B., & Barg, F. K. (2006). "Pull yourself up by your bootstraps": A response to depression in older adults. *Qualitative Health Research, 16*(9), 1207–1216.

Tashakkori, A., & Teddlie, C. (2008). Quality of inferences in mixed methods research: Calling for an integrative framework. In M. M. Bergman (Ed.), *Advances in mixed methods research* (pp. 100–119). London: Sage.

Tichy, H. J. (1988). *Effective writing for engineers, managers, scientists* (2nd ed.). New York: John Wiley & Sons.

U.S. Department of Health and Human Services. (1999). *Mental health: A report of the surgeon general—older adults and mental health.* Rockville, MD: U.S. Department of Health and Human Services, Substance Abuse and Mental Health Services Administration, Center for Mental Health Services, National Institutes of Health, National Institute of Mental Health.

U.S. Department of Health and Human Services. (2001). *Mental health: Culture, race and ethnicity. A supplement to mental health: A report of the surgeon general.* Rockville, MD: U.S. Department of Health and Human Services, Substance Abuse and Mental Health Services Administration, Center for Mental Health Services.

Wittink, M. N., Barg, F. K., & Gallo, J. J. (2006). Unwritten rules of talking to doctors about depression: Integrating qualitative and quantitative methods. *Annals of Family Medicine, 4*(4), 302–309.

Wittink, M. N., Dahlberg, B., Biruk, C., & Barg, F. K. (2008). How older adults combine medical and experiential notions of depression. *Qualitative Health Research, 18*(9), 1174–1183.

Wittink, M. N., Joo, J. H., Lewis, L. M., & Barg, F. K. (2009). Losing faith and using faith: Older African Americans discuss spirituality, religious activities, and depression. *Journal of General Internal Medicine, 24*(3), 402–407.

Wittink, M., Morales, K. H., Meoni, L. A., Ford, D. E., Wang, N. Y., Klag, M. J., et al. (2008). Stability of preferences for end-of-life treatment after 3 years of follow-up: The Johns Hopkins Precursors Study. *Archives of Internal Medicine, 168,* 2125–2130.

EPILOGUE

Current Developments and Emerging Trends in Integrated Research Methodology

◆ Abbas Tashakkori and Charles Teddlie

Here we are, at the end of our journey through mixed methods, or is it the beginning?

(Tashakkori & Teddlie, 2003c, p. 671)

In the preface to this volume, we shared with you some of our experiences in what we called a "journey in time" while we worked on the two editions of the *Handbook* (Tashakkori & Teddlie, 2003a, and the current volume). It has been a challenging and enriching journey, indeed. Once again, we find ourselves simultaneously at the end and in the beginning of a fantastic and enriching journey. The second edition of the *Handbook* has been another window to the continuously evolving landscape of integrated methodology. We would like to share with our readers some of our experiences and observations within that landscape.

The mixed methods community, as it has been called by various scholars (Denscombe, 2008; Morgan, 2007; Tashakkori, 2009), has gone through a relatively rapid growth spurt. Scholars writing within the two volumes of the *Handbook,* and outside of it, have repeatedly pointed to the fact that mixed methods is not new; its practices have deep-seated roots in social science research and evaluation. On the other hand, it is not old either; it has acquired a formal methodology that did not exist before and is subscribed to by an emerging community of practitioners and methodologists across the disciplines. In the process of developing a distinct identity, as compared with the other major communities of researchers in the social and human sciences, mixed methods has been adopted as the de facto third alternative, or "third methodological movement."

An examination of the chapters in this *Handbook* clearly demonstrates the existence of a distinct nomenclature, methodology, and utilization potential. We believe that mixed methods started from a judicious rejection of the false dichotomy between the two dominant research communities of the 1990s (qualitative and quantitative). Mixed methods researchers and evaluators have clearly been dissatisfied with the legitimacy of the dichotomized methodology of social and behavioral research methodology and its reliance on monolithic conceptual/philosophical foundations. From early writers on to the current *Handbook* authors, mixed methodologists have rebelled against the false dichotomy and have been criticized for it by some.

We consider the formation of the mixed methods research (MMR) community a third methodological movement with a distinct and traceable developmental trajectory.[1] There is a core of common ideas that binds the community together and constructs an identity for the scholars in the community. We reviewed some of them in Chapter 1 of this volume, including the rejection of the dichotomy of the QUAL and QUAN approaches/methods and the promotion of methodological eclecticism. Recently, fundamental disagreements have also been surfacing within the community. One seems to be centered on the importance or value of the *convergence* of ideas that comes through developing bridges

between diverse conceptualizations of mixed methods, nomenclature, design issues, and methodology. As we also discussed in Chapter 1 of this volume, we believe that *diversity* of ideas is a major strength of mixed methods. But, on the other hand, disparate and unrelated conceptual models, nomenclature, design classifications, and so forth might do more harm than good due to the increased possibility of duplicating ideas, inconsistent terminology, chaotic classifications, and burdensome pedagogy.

◆ The Landscape of an Emerging Field of MMR

In Chapter 2 of this volume, John Creswell (2010; Table 2.1) provided an insightful comparison of three perspectives in MMR. The value of such a map (and topical areas within its domains) is that it presents a conceptual structure for mixed methods scholars. We further the discussion here by comparing the three broad areas of this *Handbook* with the five general domains presented by Creswell (2009) and the four domains presented in Jennifer Greene's (2008) framework. Our comparisons are meant simply to describe similarities and differences among the three ways of conceptualizing mixed methods.

Figure 31.1 presents the three overlapping circles that diagram the contents of the *Handbook* (previously described in Figure 1.1): Conceptual Orientations (Philosophical, Theoretical, Sociopolitical), Issues Regarding Methods and Methodology, and Contemporary Applications of MMR. Creswell presents further information about his five domains (Creswell, 2009) and Greene's (2008) four domains in Table 2.1 of this volume, which may be valuable for the reader to refer to throughout this discussion.

There are more similarities among the three perspectives than differences, which points to somewhat of a consensus among

Figure 31.1 Overlapping Components of an Emerging "Map" of Mixed Methods Research

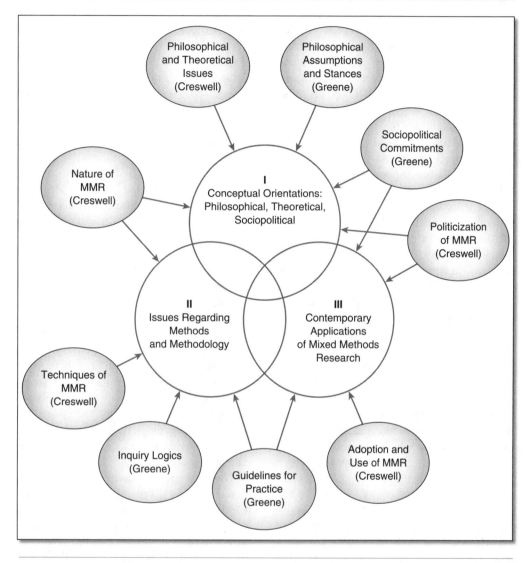

NOTE: Circles I, II, and III represent the three sections of this volume. References are to Greene (2006, 2008) and Creswell (2009, 2010 [this volume]).

these broad conceptualizations of the field. For example, the topics contained in Circle 1 in Figure 31.1 (Conceptual Orientations) are very similar to what Creswell (2009) referred to as Philosophical and Theoretical Issues and what Greene (2008) called Philosophical Assumptions and Stances (refer to Table 2.1 in this volume). All three perspectives consider these conceptual and

philosophical issues to be a continuing part of the future of MMR, as further illustrated by the various contemporary versions of those topics discussed in Part I of the *Handbook*.

Similarly, the topics contained in Circle II in Figure 31.1 (Issues Regarding Methods and Methodology) are very similar to what Creswell (2009) referred to as Techniques of Mixed Methods Research and Greene (2008) called Inquiry Logics and Guidelines for Practice. All three perspectives consider discussions of these issues (e.g., mixed methods sampling, designs) to be a continuing part of the future of MMR, which is hardly surprising; we are, after all, discussing the field of MMR. Ongoing innovations in the particular methods and overall methodology of MMR will probably always dominate the field.

The topics discussed in Circle III in Figure 31.1 (Contemporary Applications of Mixed Methods Research) are similar to those topics discussed by Creswell (2009) in his domain entitled Adoption and Use of MMR. Issues in this rather broad domain include a wide variety of topics such as the application of mixed methods across disciplinary boundaries, pedagogical issues, logistical issues (such as collaboration), and so forth. These issues also describe part of what Greene (2008) calls Guidelines for Practice, such as discussions across different disciplines and fields of applied practice.

While the similarities among these three basic perspectives are strong, there are also a few interesting differences. One of Creswell's (2009) domains is the Nature of Mixed Methods, which focuses largely on language and definitional issues, which we have also featured (e.g., Teddlie & Tashakkori, 2003; also in Chapter 1 of this volume). In the current *Handbook,* discussions related to the language or nomenclature of MMR are located in both Part I, which emphasizes conceptual terminology, and Part II, which concentrates on definitions related to methods. Whether a separate domain is needed for the "essence or nature of MMR" or whether these topics can be subsumed within the conceptual and methodological/methods domains remains an unresolved issue.

Even more interesting are the topics that Greene (2008) calls Sociopolitical Commitments and Creswell (2009) refers to as Politicization of Mixed Methods Research.

For Greene (2008, p. 19), sociopolitical commitments involve "whose interests are served by the inquiry and what political stances and value commitments are advanced." Although Greene (2008, p. 10) acknowledges that the Sociopolitical Commitments domain is *not independent* of her Philosophical Assumptions and Stances domain, she emphasizes its importance as a distinctive and different part of what we have been referring to as the "map" of MMR.

Creswell's (2009) discussion of the Politicization of Mixed Methods Research includes topics such as deconstructing and justifying mixed methods, as well as funding issues. In his chapter for this *Handbook,* Creswell concludes that political issues have had an uneven assessment in the field, which he plans to address more directly in future writings. Almost all direct discussion of the sociopolitical component of MMR in the *Handbook* is found in Part I and involves authors' statements regarding their values or axiological orientations and how those affect the way in which they conduct their research in applied fields of study (e.g., Hesse-Biber in Chapter 7; Mertens, Bledsoe, Sullivan, & Wilson in Chapter 8). Therefore, we believe that topics within the sociopolitical domain may be best conceptualized as existing within the overlap between Conceptual Orientations (Circle I) and Contemporary Application (Circle III). Said differently, much of what has been discussed under this topic is related to purposes of conducting research (changing lives, creating change, etc.) and utilization of the attained understandings in order to reach these purposes.

Thus, the field of MMR could be conceptualized in three broad domains (conceptual, methods and methodology, and applications, plus their overlaps) or could include other domains such as the nature of mixed methods and sociopolitical commitments. Also, standards of quality might be considered one of these emerging domains, generating much discussion and debate in the past few years. It includes both the quality of evidence (data, results), the quality of inferences made on the basis of such evidence, and the utilization of the final outcomes. This last component (utilization for policy and practice) might also be conceptualized as an intersection of two or more of the main domains. The emergence of these or other domains will signify that they are of great importance to the field and generate new directions for the field.

One major benefit of developing a map of the field is that it then allows researchers from throughout the social and behavioral sciences to locate their work within domains associated with MMR. Each of the domains of MMR can be further divided into distinct topical areas, which can then generate even more specific lines of research or inquiry. These specified topical areas and lines of inquiry could then have the effect of directing researchers toward studies similar to their own areas of interest. Such a map with specified lines of research could have great heuristic value because these distinct research areas often result in increasingly more complex findings and serve as the catalyst for new interdisciplinary research projects.

We believe that the field of MMR is at a point where its major domains can be categorized into more specific topics and lines of research. For example, Creswell (2009) analyzed a set of 30 topics that emerged from notes he had taken on manuscripts submitted to the *Journal of Mixed Methods Research,* and he assigned each of those topics to one or another of the five domains in his map of the field. He then categorized each of the papers given at the 2008 Mixed Methods Conference at Cambridge University into one of the 30 topical areas. Some members of his list of topics were not represented by any papers at the conference (e.g., joint displays of quantitative and qualitative data), while other topics were represented by multiple papers (e.g., fields and disciplines using mixed methods, which had 20 papers assigned to it).

A major goal of practitioners of MMR over the next few years should be to develop a comprehensive list of topics associated with the domains of MMR because this would help to organize the field and to generate more original research associated with the recognized topics. This task is obviously well beyond the scope of this chapter, but we thought it would be instructive to briefly examine a sample of topics and associated lines of inquiry within the three MMR domains that structure this *Handbook.*

An obvious topical area within the conceptual orientations domain is the role of pragmatism as a philosophical foundation for MMR. Writings regarding pragmatism and MMR have been published for more than 20 years (e.g., Howe, 1988; Maxcy, 2003; Tashakkori & Teddlie, 1998), but they have become increasingly more sophisticated over the past few years as scholars have tried to more precisely define how pragmatism can serve as a philosophical foundation for MMR and exactly what variant of pragmatism is most appropriate for consideration in the field (e.g., Biesta, 2010 [this volume]; Greene & Hall, 2010 [this volume]; Johnson & Onwuegbuzie, 2004). We foresee a continuing evolution of this topical area with specific lines of inquiry (e.g., Is there a specific type of pragmatism that is most appropriate for use in MMR? If so what are its characteristics? and so forth) developing over time.

Another potential topical area within the conceptual orientations domain is the use of abduction or abductive logic in MMR. This topic is being written about more frequently in the general literature as an alternative to the well-known hypothetico-deductive and inductive logics (e.g., Haig, 2005) and has been mentioned specifically with regard to MMR (e.g., Erzberger & Kelle, 2003; Morgan, 2007).

There are several obvious broad topics within the methods and methodology domain, most of which are addressed in Part II of this *Handbook:* the nature of research questions in MMR, the types of designs used, sampling strategies, data analysis, issues regarding assessing the quality of inferences, and so forth. A chapter in the first *Handbook* (Kemper, Stringfield, & Teddlie, 2003) was among the first to discuss mixed methods sampling strategies, and several articles and chapters have followed, adding greatly to our understanding of this broad topical area within MMR (e.g., Collins, Onwuegbuzie, & Jiao, 2007; Onwuegbuzie & Collins, 2007; Teddlie & Yu, 2007). Collins's review of advanced mixed methods sampling strategies in Chapter 15 included discussion of several lines of inquiry that could be pursued further, including factors associated with determining the optimal sample size for MMR, developing a terminology or "language" for mixed methods sampling, comparing existing typologies of MMR sampling techniques, determining criteria for judging the quality of mixed method sampling procedures, and so forth.

The third domain, contemporary applications of MMR, is very broad and not as well delineated as the other two. One very large topical area is the use of MMR in different disciplines or fields: In the first edition of the *Handbook,* chapters covered several broad disciplines (e.g., sociology, psychology, nursing, evaluation, health sciences, education), whereas in the second edition, the focus is on more specialized subfields within larger disciplines such as intervention research in the health sciences, international development evaluation, and educational effectiveness research. Further development of MMR in some of these disciplines might come from discussions of how mixed methods enables researchers to examine issues in those fields in ways that traditional QUAN methods cannot alone (e.g., Sammons, 2010; Song, Sandelowski, & Happ, 2010 [both in this volume]). For example, Yoshikawa, Weisner, Kalil, & Way (2008) described six research circumstances in developmental psychology where mixed methods was particularly suitable including assessing constructs that are difficult to measure using either set of methods alone, estimating and understanding developmental change at multiple time scales, and exploring causal associations and their mechanisms.

There are several other topics in the applications of MMR domains that are developing a growing literature: pedagogical issues, collaborative and other team approaches, writing mixed methods research (MMR), mixed methods funding, and so forth. One of the most interesting applied mixed methods topical areas is that concerned with *incidence rates* (counts of the absolute number of MMR articles published per year) and *prevalence rates* (the proportion of research studies published in a given field that are mixed in nature), which was briefly described in Chapter 1. Chapter 23, by Ivankova and Kawamura, is an excellent example of this literature, which documents some interesting trends in the incidence rates of mixed research published from 2000 to 2008. The topic of incidence and prevalence rates could generate several separate lines of inquiry, some associated with methodological issues such as what actually should "count" as a mixed methods study.

The emerging maps presented by Creswell in Chapter 2 and by us in this chapter may serve not only as a guide for conceptualizing studies and locating them within the MM context but also as a road map for identifying controversies and unresolved issues. Such a road map has the potential to also generate new directions for mixed methods.

◆ Challenges and Controversial Issues in Mixed Methods

In Chapter 1 of this volume, we examined some of the important and often controversial issues in mixed methodology in some detail. We argued that some of the burning issues we discussed in 2003 have been resolved, while other issues have emerged, which is certainly a healthy attribute of an evolving field of methodology. One controversy that has been resolved is the definition of mixed methods, for which there is now a broad consensus, although some scholars may still prefer the specifics of their own definitions. Other issues have changed shape over time. For example, although mixed methodologists have constructed a basic nomenclature, a mushrooming of new terms is making it increasingly difficult for researchers to understand each other's work.

We find it invigorating to witness the lively debates and discourses within and outside of the community of mixed methods scholars. Many important issues need further exploration by the community as discussed in Chapter 1. After reading the work of contributors to the *Handbook,* we summarize in this chapter some of the most important ones that need more systematic discussion in the future. The issues we will expand on or address in this chapter are mainly related to the following:

- necessity of convergence in core ideas
- conceptual stances in MMR
- quality standards for MMR
- the language of MMR
- design issues in MMR
- utilization of MMR for policy and practice

This list is not exhaustive by any means, but it includes the areas in more urgent need of discussion and resolution. By focusing on these issues, rather than avoiding them, we hope to stimulate more extended discussions and discourse. We believe that such an open and informed discourse will strengthen the community, at least by better informing the skeptics both within and outside the mixed methods community regarding these issues.

THE NECESSITY OF CONVERGENCE IN CORE IDEAS

Some members of the community of mixed methods scholars consider a call for creating bridges and being mindful of mushrooming inconsistent conceptual frameworks as a premature attempt to impose uniformity (e.g., see Mertens, 2010), at best, or silencing of diverse perspectives, at worst. For example, Freshwater (2007), Greene (2007; Greene & Hall, 2010), and others have expressed concern that MMR is prematurely headed toward some "fixed" unity or consensus for social inquiry that will preclude the consideration of and respect for multiple approaches to that inquiry. Freshwater (2007) criticizes the "idolatry of integration and coherence," which she sees as "rife throughout nursing and the healthcare literature" (p. 141). This concern is akin to the apprehension that Smith and Heshusius (1986) voiced over two decades ago about "closing down the conversation" with regard to the quantitative-qualitative debate.

We can understand this concern intellectually; one of the characteristics of MMR is "an emphasis on diversity at all levels of the research enterprise," but we don't see MMR as becoming a static unified approach toward social inquiry that will stifle diverse viewpoints concerning that inquiry. Without question, the jury is still out on this issue. On one hand, there is a need for the development and expansion of a core group of conceptual and methodological ideas that may potentially bind together the community of mixed methods researchers. On the other hand, the mixed methods community should stay open to new ideas in the theoretical, methodological, and utilization realms. We do not see these two perspectives as mutually exclusive. Perhaps, as the interpersonal and political tensions within the mixed methods community subside over time, we will be able to achieve both.

As might be expected, during the 1990s, most writers considered mixed methods to be in its infancy. More recent writings have referred to its adolescence. These developmental classifications inherently assume that one day, mixed methods will mature. One might imagine such a mature state to include well articulated world-views, internally consistent concepts, parsimonious design blueprints, clearly implementable data analysis tools, flexible pathways for making inferences, and general guidelines for assessing and ensuring the quality of assertions that are made on the basis of the findings. Nothing in such a naively idealistic mature state remotely indicates that the findings of mixed methods studies would not (or should not) be used to improve the lives of those who are studied, both directly and indirectly. Neither does this envisioned interconnected state imply the exclusion of new areas of inquiry, in terms of both discipline and context (e.g., attention to those whom Mertens, 2010, p. 4, calls "unheard voices").

CONCEPTUALIZATION OF MIXED METHODS

Most MMR scholars can agree with paradigm pluralism as a starting point, but then they have to (a) consider what the alternative paradigmatic positions are and (b) ascertain which of the alternative positions is most closely related to their own perspective. The following three paradigmatic positions[2] are the most widely accepted in contemporary MMR and are all described in Part I of the *Handbook*:

- pragmatism and its interpretations,

- frameworks associated with the axiological assumption, and

- the dialectic stance, which involves using multiple assumptive frameworks within the same study.

The following section briefly reviews contemporary perspectives (as reflected in the *Handbook* and other sources) regarding these three conceptual orientations.

Many researchers who use MMR have an affinity for *pragmatism* as the paradigm of choice. This affinity is a historical one, going back to Howe's (1988) postulation of the compatibility thesis as a product of pragmatism that allows for the use of MMR. The pragmatic approach to philosophical issues is appealing to many researchers in the applied social sciences, who use a kind of "everyday pragmatism" (Biesta, 2010) in their solution of problems in their research and evaluation projects.

As MMR has matured, a more *philosophically nuanced pragmatism* has emerged (e.g., Biesta, 2010; Greene & Hall, 2010; Johnson & Onwuegbuzie, 2004). This pragmatism asks, "Apart from the rejection of the either-or, what does pragmatism mean for MMR?" We briefly describe three recent interpretations of philosophical pragmatism that appear to have advanced the conversation.

Johnson and colleagues have ventured into a kind of "paradigm or systems building" with regard to *philosophical pragmatism*. Johnson and Onwuegbuzie (2004) presented 21 characteristics of pragmatism in an effort to more completely delineate what the important tenets of this philosophy are and how they relate to MMR. In recent writing, Johnson (2009, p. 456) defined *dialectical pragmatism* as a "supportive philosophy for mixed methods research" that combines classical pragmatism with Greene's (2007) dialectic approach.

In contrast, Biesta (2010) contends that "pragmatism should not be understood as a philosophical position among others, but rather as a set of philosophical tools that can be used to address problems" (p. 97). Biesta concludes that Deweyan pragmatism has made a major contribution by eliminating the epistemological dualism of objectivity/ subjectivity:

This is tremendously important for the field of mixed methods research as it does away with alleged hierarchies between different approaches and rather helps to make the case that different approaches generate *different* outcomes, *different* connections between doing and undergoing, between actions and consequences, so that we always need to judge our knowledge claims pragmatically. (p. 113; italics in original)

Thus, Biesta's (2010) philosophical pragmatism leads us to understand that no methodological approach is intrinsically better than another in terms of generating knowledge. We have to evaluate the results from our research studies in terms of how good a job we did in selecting, using, and integrating all the available methodological tools.

Greene (2007) referred to pragmatism as the *alternative paradigm* that promotes the active mixing of methods and integration of research findings. Greene and Hall (2010) further described how thinking pragmatically affects the manner in which mixed researchers conduct their research and use results from it by describing a hypothetical researcher, Juan. For Greene and Hall and others (e.g., Johnson & Onwuegbuzie, 2004), pragmatism results in a problem-solving, action-oriented inquiry process based on a commitment to democratic values and progress.

Mertens (2007) identified four basic assumptions associated with paradigms: axiological, epistemological, ontological, and methodological. Mertens, Bledsoe, Sullivan, and Wilson (2010 [this volume]) further described the *axiological assumption,* which "takes precedence and serves as a basis for articulating the other three belief systems because the transformative paradigm emerged from the need to be more explicit about how researchers can address issues of social justice" (p. 195).

In discussions of pragmatism, the philosophical issues that tend to be emphasized are epistemological in nature concerning topics such as what is knowledge, how is it acquired, and the relationship between the knower and that which would be known. On the other hand, scholars working within transformative or critical frameworks (e.g., feminism) give precedence to axiological considerations, which center on the nature of value judgments. This *axiological assumption* means that scholars working within transformative/critical frameworks have a different perspective on the use of research methods. For these scholars, mixed methods are tools that are used in the service of the value systems, which are of foremost importance to their perspectives.

The *dialectic stance* assumes that all paradigms have something to offer and that the use of multiple paradigms contributes to greater understanding of the phenomenon under study. The dialectic stance calls for the juxtaposition of multiple assumptive frameworks within the same research study. Greene and Hall (2010) describe the dialectical way of thinking through the hypothetical researcher Michelle.

An essential aspect of Greene's dialectical way of thinking is that she is directing attention away from the so-called incommensurable attributes of paradigms and toward different and distinctive (but not inherently incompatible) attributes such as distance-closeness, outside-insider, and so forth. The dialectical tensions that Greene (2007; Greene & Caracelli, 2003) emphasize include value neutrality and value commitment, emic and etic, particularity and generality, social constructions and physical traces, and so forth.

QUALITY STANDARDS FOR MIXED METHODS STUDIES

A growing body of literature seems to be evolving around the issues of quality in MMR. There are multiple frameworks for assessing quality, with common and unique elements that are not necessarily consistent with each other. Inconsistencies occur in several areas: linguistic (i.e., labeling the same standard or concept differently), conceptual (i.e., disagreeing on what exactly is important to evaluate), procedural (i.e., lack of agreement on the necessity of evaluating the components of a study/design separately from each other), and consequential (i.e., is it necessary to evaluate a mixed methods study in terms of how the final inferences are used for policy and practice?). The procedural controversies are also rooted in the fact that standards of quality are not the same for QUAL and QUAN components of mixed methods studies.

We believe that the discussions of quality are probably easier to reconcile by examining mixed methods as a systemic attempt to answer research questions. Such a systemic attempt at making meaning would include *inputs, processes,* and *outcomes* of inquiry. Consequently, it is necessary to evaluate *these three elements* of a research project separately but in an interrelated manner, recognizing that the three might not always be operating in a temporal linear manner (e.g., in a sequential design, the inputs to a new strand of a study stem from the outcomes of a previous strand). In a mixed methods project, the inputs are ideas (questions, prior knowledge), cultural knowledge, contextual information (e.g., field notes), and systematically collected QUAL and QUAN data. The process (of answering and meaning making) includes the analysis of all the collected data by summarizing, categorizing, linking, comparing, contrasting, and integrating all available evidence. Obviously, this process includes statistical analysis of numerical (including quantitized) data and holistic (including thematic and phenomenological) analysis of other data.

A higher order part of the process of making inferences also includes comparing and contrasting the aggregated outcomes (both the findings and the inferences) from QUAL and QUAN components of a study. The ultimate goal of all of this is to attain a global understanding of the phenomenon or behavior under investigation, as well as understanding the relationship between parts of the evidence and between each part and the whole. The final outcomes are a set of conclusions (e.g., mental images, explanations) as answers to the research questions, as well as the consequences of these conclusions (e.g., recommendations, guidelines) for policy and practice.

An evaluation of a mixed methods study must examine these three elements almost independently. There is no doubt that vaguely conceptualized questions lead to a vaguely defined and inconsistent research design, poor analysis, and inferior outcomes. Similarly, if the process of collecting and analyzing data is ill conceived, the final outcomes (results and conclusions) will be unsatisfactory. Finally, despite a well-articulated mixed methods question, and a well-implemented process of data collection and analysis, one might interpret the findings inappropriately, leading to low-quality inferences. It should be evident that the quality of each of these three components (inputs, processes, and outcomes) is highly dependent on the quality of previous ones, but it must also be assessed/audited in its own terms because the standards for assessing quality are not necessarily the same for all three.

A traditional approach to quality evaluation in mixed methods has been to evaluate the components of the QUAL strand using those criteria known in the QUAL literature and the QUAN strand using those from the QUAN literature. Despite its simplicity and the appeal of keeping everything compartmentalized and neat, a mixed methods project is not a simple juxtaposition of two types of results. In a mixed methods study, inputs to the process interact with each other, making it difficult to clearly differentiate the components of research questions that are predominantly QUAN from those that are QUAL. This is more clearly seen in overarching mixed questions in which asking, "Is the research question of this study of high quality?" might be impossible to answer by using separate standards from QUAL and QUAN traditions. We think Plano Clark and Badiee's Chapter 12 discussion of research questions in MMR provides an excellent starting point for our development of quality standards.

Examining and evaluating the other inputs to the process of problem solving or meaning making is equally crucial. Certainly, QUAL and QUAN traditions are often in sharp disagreement about what is acceptable as research evidence (i.e., data, information) and what is considered to be credible evidence. Much of what QUAL researchers consider as evidence is discarded or ignored by QUAN investigators. Examples of such evidence are personal observations, field notes, cultural expectancies, and participants' anecdotal reactions to the study. In Chapter 21, O'Cathain provides an excellent review of some of the issues in this regard, before trying to develop a comprehensive framework for auditing mixed methods studies. For a mixed methods researcher, credible evidence is pragmatically assessed with a close focus on how well it paves the path to finding credible answers to research questions. Evidence leading to uncertain conclusions about a phenomenon or behavior lacks quality. This, however, does not negate the fact that credible evidence might also be poorly analyzed and misinterpreted, leading to poor answers or inferences.

In Chapter 1, we summarized some of the issues related to making conclusions in mixed methods studies. Following our previous work, we used the term *inference* as both the process of making sense out of the results of a study and the outcome of such process (conclusions). Also, we used the terms *inference quality* and *inference transferability* as possible terms to denote the quality of conclusions and the degree to which these conclusions may be applicable to other (receiving) settings, individuals, time periods, and ways of conceptualizing the events and behaviors under investigation. Although we have presented these components in a linear manner, in practice they are anything but. Making sense consists of a back-and-forth process until a level of certainty is achieved about the conclusions that explain a part of the results or answer a part of the question. That certainty is directly related to standards of quality for assessing the intermediate and the final conclusions. A question of considerable interest is, then, "What constitutes a reasonable/believable mixed methods inference?" The community of mixed methods scholars has wrestled with the attributes of credible inferences and proposed various standards (what we call quality audits) for assessing each. O'Cathain's Chapter 21 is a big step forward in that direction. Her proposed framework includes evaluating studies in eight domains ranging from planning stage to utilization of outcomes for practice and policy.

It is hard to foresee the degree to which O'Cathain's comprehensive framework will create order in the rather chaotic literature of mixed methods quality. There is much promise in the framework, at least as a first attempt toward creating bridges between competing systems. On the other hand, the framework itself adds to the controversy by including new components and concepts that might be controversial. Some of the questions that need answers about the framework are the following: Does *design transparency* in Domain 2 indicate naming a specific design from current typologies or clearly conveying the procedures for the mixed methods study? Or is *sampling adequacy* in Domain 3 an attribute of the collected data or an attribute of the design? Despite these and other questions, the framework provides an excellent tool for further discussion and expansion or modification.

A criticism of MMR has been related to the quality of the writing of some articles and chapters in the field. In Chapter 11 of this volume, Leech conducted interviews with early developers of the field (Bryman, Creswell, Greene, Morse), who concluded that authors need to do a better job of (a) expressing where their research fits within the current MMR literature; (b) presenting their own definition of MMR; (c) explaining where and how the mixing of methods (or approaches?) occurred in their research; and (d) explicitly describing their philosophical orientation. Some of these components of quality are also addressed in contemporary frameworks, including that of O'Cathain (2010 [this volume]). There seems to be a broad consensus among scholars about the need for clarity and transparency of communicating one's purpose, questions, design, analysis, integration process, and possible answers to the research questions. The importance of stating one's philosophical orientation, as a quality standard for mixed methods studies, is probably less agreed-upon. One reason for this lack of consensus is that historically, some (or even most) mixed methods studies have been aparadigmatic in nature (we have called this a bottom-up approach to MMR).

Aiding our future discussions of both of these issues (clarity of communication; necessity of stating one's philosophical approach) is the availability of the preliminary maps of the field (Creswell, 2009, 2010; our own in Figure 31.1). These maps include the domains, topics, and some lines of inquiry that should help authors in "locating" themselves within the field and communicating their location. The multiple definitions of MMR presented by Johnson, Onwuegbuzie, and Turner (2007) should help authors in describing their own perspectives, while the design typologies synthesized by Nastasi, Hitchcock, and Brown (2010 [this volume]) present several precursor, basic, and complex typologies for MMR, which are also summarized in other sources (e.g., Teddlie & Tashakkori, 2009). Furthermore, the explicit delineation of at least three philosophical orientations in the field (pragmatism, frameworks associated with the axiological assumption, the dialectic stance) with other emerging alternatives (e.g., critical realism described by Maxwell & Mittapalli, 2010; Christ, 2010 [both in this volume]) provides authors with alternative philosophical orientations from which to choose and then make explicit in their writings, if it is deemed necessary by them (authors) or the community.

THE LANGUAGE OF MMR

A common criticism of the recent developments in mixed methods is the lack of agreement on a language for terms used in integrated studies (e.g., Bryman, 2008). As we also mentioned in Chapter 1, much of this issue stems from the fact that in the past decade, mixed methodologists have developed many mixed methods terms as vehicles for expressing their often unique ways of addressing methodological or philosophical challenges. As might be expected, without a systematic effort toward linking these conceptualizations, there are inconsistencies in this emerging nomenclature, including (a) having a number of different definitions for the same term and (b) having a number of different names for the same concept. The field of MMR has been fortunate to have a number of gifted methodologists writing on a variety of topics simultaneously over the past few years, and the result has been the generation of several very important works, each using somewhat different terminology. The time is ripe for linking these diverse ideas and creating at least a core of partially shared nomenclature.

Several chapters in Part II of this *Handbook* have tried to generate such common frameworks for large methodological domains such as mixed methods design, sampling, and analysis. Perhaps the terms used in these chapters (plus other recent syntheses of additional topics within MMR) can serve as the starting point for the development of a comprehensive dictionary of MMR terms. Such an entity would do much to organize and further the development of the field.[3] For those concerned about premature convergence regarding the meanings of controversial terms, alternative perspectives could be provided and explained, as Schwandt (1997) did in his dictionary of QUAL inquiry.

DESIGN TYPOLOGIES IN MMR

Design typology is perhaps the most explored area of mixed methods and at the same time the most confusing aspect of it. Mixed methods scholars have complained about the fact that there are too many sub-types of designs, often labeled differently by different authors and treated as static blue-prints for research projects. We share this frustration, even within our own conceptual-ization of designs in the past decade. In Chapter 1, we discussed how our way of conceptualizing mixed methods designs has evolved between 1998 and 2010. After going through many iterations, and on the basis of ongoing examination of mixed methods studies in the past 20 years, we are now ready to adopt three basic and one complex *families* of designs, each with the capability of taking different shapes as a project devel-ops (see Tashakkori, Brown, & Borghese, 2009; Tashakkori & Newman, in press). We have called the three basic families sequential, parallel, and conversion mixed methods designs. Within each family, we have identified three subgroups based on data sources (same/subsample, multisample, multilevel samples). Integrating multiple components of this 3 × 3 matrix is a fourth family of designs that we have called *fully integrated*. All four families are conceptual-ized as processes that evolve during the course of a study, indicating that the investi-gator might start with one plan and change the design as he or she proceeds on the basis of emerging changes in the problem or the logistical difficulties in the field. Such changes might occur within each family or across families (i.e., from one family to another, often leading to a fully integrated mixed methods design).

In the light of broad diversity and some-times inconsistency of design types, Nastasi et al. undertake the enormous task, in Chapter 13, of linking them to each other and developing an overarching framework that can systematically contain and differentiate them. In addition to an excellent review of the similarities and differences between design typologies, Nastasi et al. provide a framework that could be a starting point toward a shared conceptualization of mixed methods designs. They have created a "typology of design typologies" (not a term they used) by placing mixed methods design typologies into six cat-egories. Three of these categories (basic typologies) are framed on single dimensions (number of strands, priority of data, stages in which mixing occurs). The other three (com-plex typologies) have focused on "approach to integration" by employing multiple dimen-sions from basic typologies, integrating approaches at multiple stages of research in an iterative manner, and synergetic mixing (pre-dominantly in the interpretation of the results) as a gestalt (our label) leading to an under-standing that is bigger than the sum of its (QUAL and QUAN) components. As an umbrella overarching other typologies, they offer an "inclusive framework" that is built on the idea of synergy between QUAL and QUAN approaches, teamwork, and partici-patory research in fully integrated mixed methods designs.

The Nastasi et al. (2010) framework is by no means an end to the controversies in multiplicity of design typologies and inconsistencies/contradictions within and between them. It is, on the other hand, a starting point for continuing the efforts for bridging or consolidating diverse per-spectives into consistent and parsimo-nious frameworks for mixed methods studies.

THE UTILIZATION OF MIXED METHODS

Undoubtedly, in the past two decades, there has been a sharp increase in the general awareness about the necessity and appropri-ateness of mixed methods for answering some research questions. Consequently, funding agencies have been encouraging (and sometimes demanding) MMR. Skillful presentation of these trends, and many examples of such studies, may be found in various chapters of this *Handbook*. For example, Ivankova and Kawamura (Chapter 23) and Song, Sandelowski, and Happ (Chapter 28) summarize many such studies in social, behavioral, and health sciences. Dahlberg, Wittink, and Gallo (Chapter 30) also provide examples and add strategies for pursuing funding for MMR. These examples (and others throughout the *Handbook*) and funding opportunities are clear indications of the widespread utilization of mixed methods across disciplines and types of problems and serve as prototypes for investigators to adopt or to modify for adoption.

Despite the increase in the sheer number of studies using mixed methods, it is difficult to assess the degree to which this trend has led, or will potentially lead, to more effective use of research outcomes for policy and practice. This is certainly an area of investigation for the future. A fundamental assumption about MMR in social, behavioral, and health research is that it provides a better (broader, more credible) understanding of the phenomena under investigation than a dichotomous QUAL/QUAN approach. Consequently, it is also assumed that, because of its potential for broader understanding of social issues, it provides more robust opportunities for devising policies and practices to implement positive change. Implicit and explicit traces of this assumption may be found in many chapters in this *Handbook*. We will briefly review a few of them, with the hope of sensitizing the reader to finding more.

Bamberger, Rao, and Woolcock in Chapter 24 present many examples of effective use of mixed methods in international development, rural sociology, and related large-scale policy fields. There is a clear indication of the fundamental assumption mentioned above: that better understanding and more comprehensive inferences might lead to better policy decisions. One also finds an interesting added assumption in their presentation. They suggest that "a central challenge in international development is that the decision makers (development economists included) are in the business of studying people separated from themselves by vast distances—social, economic, political, and geographic" (Bamberger, Rao, &

Woolcock, 2010 [this volume], p. 615). Their explicit assumption is that by virtue of helping to close this distance, and also by revealing "*how* outcomes (positive, negative, or indifferent) are obtained and how any such outcomes vary over time and space (context)" (p. 615, italics added), mixed methods improves the chances of making the right policies to improve social conditions (at least in the developing world, within the context of their reviewed studies). In Chapter 8, Mertens et al. provide other examples of participatory research in international development. We hope that future policy analysis studies will undertake the task of assessing the impact of these integrated studies on the implemented policies in the field.

Mertens et al. (2010) add another angle to the assumption of greater policy and practice effectiveness. Their implicit assumption is that mixed methods can potentially change the lives of underprivileged populations by giving them voice in conducting studies. It is assumed that this is achieved by including the participants (participatory perspective through forming community involvement and partnerships) in a dynamic process of designing, data collection and analysis, interpretation of the findings, and effective policy and practice decisions. They provide examples of such studies and demonstrate how QUAL and QUAN approaches are used in tandem for better understanding of issues rooted in inequality of power and opportunities. The implicit assumption is that the outcomes (conclusions, understandings, policy suggestions) have been stronger than what would have been obtained via traditional QUAN or QUAL approaches. Developing a popular mentoring program at the university is presented as one such effective policy and practice outcome.

Perhaps one of the most important controversies regarding the use of research for policy and practice occurred during the Bush-Cheney administration as a result of a distinctly postpositivist QUAN orientation in the U.S. Department of Education. Manifestations of that orientation included the passage of the No Child Left Behind Act (2001), which contained a detailed definition of "scientifically based research" and required federal grantees to expend their research funds on "evidence-based strategies" (Feur, Towne, & Shavelson, 2002). The passage of the Education Sciences Reform Act of 2002 included the standard that causal relationships could be claimed "only in random assigned experiments or other designs (to the extent such designs substantially eliminate plausible competing explanations for the obtained results)" (Eisenhart & Towne, 2003, p. 36). Results of strictly controlled experimental studies and randomized trials were advocated (and required) as the main (or sometimes only) acceptable outcomes for use in policy and practice. Much of the research from the educational and behavioral sciences was deemed unfit for policy and practice use because researchers had not included randomized experiments in their designs, and this included virtually all the QUAL-oriented literature.

A review of pro and con arguments about this issue is beyond the scope of this chapter (Howe, 2004; Song et al., 2010, present some of these). However, responses to these pro and con arguments are clearly linked to our discussions of mixed methods utilization. A new explicit or implicit assumption has emerged among many researchers that mixed methods might provide an alternative to the qualitative-quantitative dichotomy by providing for more credible studies of "participant-centered interventions" (Song et al., 2010, p. 728). In Dahlberg et al.'s (2010 [this volume]) words, "Our research on mental health has motivated us to mix methods because interventions developed through traditional research paradigms have not had the hoped-for public health impact" (p. 776). Challenges resulting from this assumption are well articulated in Song et al. (2010) and do not need further discussion

here. However, the fundamental assumption (that mixed methods studies provide more clear, credible, and effective policy and practice utilization) remains to be explored in future studies.

Another important issue regarding utilization concerns pedagogy and mentorship of research methods (in general) in social and behavioral sciences. We and other scholars have repeatedly suggested that an effective and appropriate way to teach research methods and to mentor young scholars is to use mixed methods. We continue to advocate that using mixed methods will enhance the future capability and readiness of our young scholars to use the best methods (and approaches) to solve crucial and often complex social and behavioral problems (e.g., Tashakkori & Teddlie, 2003b). A number of recent texts have used the mixed methods approach to teaching research (e.g., Creswell & Plano Clark, 2007; Greene, 2007; Johnson & Christensen, 2008; Morse & Niehaus, 2010; Ridenour & Newman, 2008; Teddlie & Tashakkori, 2009).

A final comment regarding utilization of mixed methods pertains to what is broadly called action research. Although this idea was initially suggested by Kurt Lewin as a broad-based approach to using research for improving social policies, some of the textbooks present it with a purely QUAL or QUAN approach. Action research is conceptualized as a systematic practice of collecting, analyzing, and interpreting evidence to improve one's professional effectiveness. Within such a conceptualization, it cannot be anything but mixed. Action research is, in our view, a fertile ground for using mixed methods. Christ's Chapter 25 in this volume presents an excellent review of many perspectives on this type of research, including its use for developing effective mixed methods pedagogy. An interesting question for future discussion and development would be how to conduct action research within a mixed methods framework. A related area needing further development concerns how to teach action research courses using a mixed methods framework.

◆ Critiques of Mixed Methods Research

Some of the most highly related and frequently mentioned criticisms of MMR pertain to the costs of conducting it, unrealistic expectations regarding an individual researcher's competence in both QUAL and QUAN methodology, complexity of putting together teams to carry out such research when groups (rather than individuals) conduct MMR, and (last, but not least) the impossibility of an individual or even a team's examining issues from different perspectives/worldviews.

We believe that the employment of QUAL, QUAN, or MMR approaches in any given study depends on the research questions that are being addressed and that many issues are best and most efficiently answered using either the QUAN-only or QUAL-only approach. Mixed methods should be used only when necessary to adequately answer the research questions, because the mixed approach is inherently more expensive and probably more time-consuming than the QUAL- or QUAN-alone orientations. Mixed studies take longer to conduct, which is an issue for doctoral students, as well as researchers operating under stringent timelines to complete contracted work (e.g., Sammons, 2010). All the same, if the research questions clearly call for it, or if there is compelling expectation that mixed methods might provide better answers, the cost and the time constraints are secondary. In other words, if there is a strong possibility that one might get incomplete and unsatisfactory answers, shorter and less expensive paths that provide such answers are not desirable.

As for those who do the research, there is concern that a minimal competence model

or methodological bilingualism is "superficial, perhaps even unworkable" (Denzin, 2008, p. 322). We believe that a good social-behavioral researcher *must* be competent in the full spectrum of research methods and approaches in order to be able to select the best pathways for answering research questions. It is fully possible to educate our young scholars for such a broad competency *only if* they are mentored by scholars who themselves are competent in the full spectrum and are open to searching for the most suitable and parsimonious methods and approaches. There are ample examples of dissertations, program evaluation results, and published work by single investigators to support the possibility of this. We presented an argument in Chapter 1 for a team approach, in which each researcher in a mixed study has a *minimum level of competency* in QUAL and QUAN methods, plus expertise in one or the other (e.g., Shulha & Wilson, 2003). Even when the research is conducted by a team of scholars consisting of individuals with QUAL or QUAN subspecializations, every member of the team needs minimum competencies in the full spectrum of research methods. Competency in and familiarity with both types of research allow team members to communicate effectively because they have a common methodological language with at least a workable number of conceptual similarities. Once again, there are ample examples of successful team projects. We presented some examples in Chapter 1, and others are found in Lieber and Weisner's Chapter 22, Sammons's Chapter 27, and elsewhere. Also, many of the field studies conducted by international organizations consist of such teams. Chapter 24 by Bamberger et al. provides summaries of some of these studies.

From a historical perspective, the most common criticism of MMR has been based on the incompatibility thesis. The thesis stated that it is inappropriate to mix QUAL and QUAN methods in the same study due to epistemological differences between the paradigms, which are purportedly related to them (e.g., Howe, 1988). We discussed this in Chapter 1, under the heading of *methodological eclecticism,* which contends that we are free to combine the best methodological tools in answering our research questions. While the philosophical justification for methodological eclecticism is important, the historical argument against the incompatibility thesis is probably more compelling: Researchers have been fruitfully combining QUAL and QUAN methods throughout the history of the social and behavioral sciences, resulting in multilayered research that is distinct from either QUAL or QUAN research alone.

The issue of examining problems via different lenses and worldviews (what we call *approaches,* as compared with *methods*) is probably more contentious (also see Morgan, 2007). Some authors have clearly criticized mixed methods for advocating this possibility. Our own reaction to this pessimism is rooted in our belief in mixed methods as a humanistic methodology closely mimicking our everyday human problem solving. We believe that neither the QUAL nor QUAN approaches truly parallel human exploration and problem solving. In everyday life, we do not wake up each day reminding ourselves that we are going to be "objective" today, and "subjective" tomorrow, or "compassionate" today and "aloof" tomorrow, and so forth. We see mixed methods as an extension of everyday sense making. Everyday problem solvers (naive researchers) use multiple approaches (similar to QUAL and QUAN pathways) concurrently or closely in sequence and examine a variety of sources of evidence in decision making (and in forming impressions). In everyday problem solving and meaning making, we question the credibility of the existing evidence on which our impressions are based. (We might not do a satisfactory job in these evaluations, but we do the job, nevertheless!) We evaluate the conclusions and decisions that emerge in response to this active process of seeking, evaluating, organizing, and interpreting the evidence.

Although using a different type of data, more sophisticated methods of analysis, and more stringent standards of evidence and inference, a mixed methods researcher (the *methodological connoisseur* described earlier) follows the same general path, characterized by a reliance on diverse sources of evidence. Mixed methods is much more amenable to this humanistic conceptualization of the research process than the other two monolithic methodological approaches/movements. Incompatibility issues are irrelevant within such a humanistic framework.

Criticisms from the QUAL and postmodern communities (e.g., Denzin & Lincoln, 2005; Howe, 2004; Giddings, 2006; Sale, Lohfeld, & Brazil, 2002) have involved several related issues, which have in turn been addressed by the MMR community (e.g., Creswell, Shope, Plano Clark, & Green, 2006; Teddlie, Tashakkori, & Johnson, 2008). Perhaps the most salient of these issues is the concern that MMR subordinates QUAL methods to a secondary position to QUAN methods. As noted throughout this *Handbook* and elsewhere (e.g., Teddlie & Tashakkori, in press), the literature of mixed methods is peppered with examples of using QUAL methods in highly credible and substantial ways. We contend that the overwhelming majority of truly mixed research involves a thorough integration of both types of methods and approaches to problem solving. Also confirming this is the recent literature (e.g., Creswell et al., 2006; Denzin, 2008; Teddlie & Tashakkori, in press) indicating that the QUAL and mixed methods communities can be involved in a productive discourse respectful of diverse viewpoints and cognizant of our many points of agreement.

Undoubtedly, the MMR and QUAL communities are both outside the mainstream in certain fields still dominated by postpositivism, such as psychology in the United States. In a study recently conducted by Alise and Teddlie (in press), the prevalence rate for QUAN studies in four elite journals in psychology was 93%, with the other 7% classified as mixed. Thus, in these highly QUAN-oriented journals, the only way that QUAL research was introduced has been though mixed method research. Politically, there is an assumed kinship between the QUAL and MMR communities in trying to introduce methodological diversity into highly traditional QUAN disciplines.

Another contemporary criticism of MMR, which was discussed in Chapter 1, concerns the relative overemphasis on topics associated with foundations (conceptual issues) and design typologies and the relative lack of emphasis on analytical techniques that support integration (e.g., Bazeley, 2009). We believe that these trends are beginning to change for a variety of reasons. For example, the emphasis on conceptual issues was to be expected in the early stages of the development of MMR as different scholars put forth their theoretical positions in the quest for a single or alternative paradigm that embraces mixed methods and is "not troubled by issues of incommensurable philosophical assumptions" (Greene, 2007, p. 82). There is now a general agreement among many mixed methods researchers that multiple paradigms may be associated with mixed methods, and four distinct philosophical positions have been fully articulated (pragmatism, frameworks associated with the axiological assumption, the dialectic stance, and critical realism). Although conceptual issues will always play a role in MMR, it is likely that there will be relatively less attention paid to them in the future than in the past 20 years.

Similarly, a great deal of attention has been paid to design typologies thus far in the history of MMR, with the result that there are at least a half dozen often referenced typologies, plus some integrated frameworks (e.g., O'Cathain, 2010). The value of design typologies is that they provide researchers with viable options to choose from and modify when they are planning their own MMR studies. Researchers doing MMR now have a wide

variety of viable design typologies from which to select. It seems likely that the design typology component of MMR is at least partially saturated; that is, new advances will be made in the integration and use of design typologies in MMR, but relatively less attention will be paid to this issue in the future.

On the other hand, we identified several trends in Chapter 1 that indicate an increasing emphasis on analytical issues in MMR: the publication of a number of syntheses of analytical techniques in MMR (including the comprehensive "meta-framework of mixed analysis strategies" proposed by Onwuegbuzie & Combs, 2010 [this volume]); the dramatic discovery of distinct mixed methods analytical techniques as exemplified by Box 1.2, which demonstrates a trend that appears to be continuing; the generation of new mixed methods techniques that borrow from or adapt existing procedures (e.g., Bergman, 2010; Newman & Ramlo, 2010 [both in this volume]); the application of analytical techniques used in either the QUAL or QUAN tradition in developing analogous techniques within the other tradition (e.g., Greene, 2007; Teddlie & Tashakkori, 2009); and computerized analysis of MMR data sources and analyses (e.g., Bazeley, 2003, 2010a [this volume], 2010b). It appears to us that the field of MMR is ready for an exponential growth in the discovery and utilization of new analytical techniques especially driven by advances in the computerized integration of data initially identified as QUAL or QUAN.

A final criticism of MMR concerns what some believe to be its overreliance on typologies. Bazeley (2010b) recently criticized the "North American fascination with typologies (which I find to be of little interest or value)" (p. 80). This criticism echoes that of Maxwell and Loomis (2003), who developed an interactive model of research design in which the components of a study are interrelated in a network, or web. The components of the design (research questions, purposes, conceptual framework, methods, validity) connect with and influence one another. Design maps can be generated that analyze mixed methods projects in terms of how the components are integrated, rather than in terms of which design from a predetermined set of possibilities the study best matches. There are several complex typologies in this *Handbook* (e.g., Nastasi et al., Chapter 13; O'Cathain, Chapter 21; Onwuegbuzie & Combs, Chapter 17) that attempt to integrate broad methodological areas in MMR. Alternatives to the typological approach might be valuable, but they have seldom emerged in MMR to date.

◆ **Challenges and Emerging Trends**

Many of the challenges facing the MMR community have their roots, and their remedies, in the processes associated with educating new researchers to be familiar with the full spectrum of research methods (QUAL and QUAN, integrated) and to have a broad understanding of the theoretical and philosophical foundations of these approaches. The "first generation" of instructors of mixed methods courses are preparing researchers who should be minimally competent in both QUAN and QUAL methods, as well as soloists whose first research project (their dissertation) might be a complex mixed methods study (e.g., Ivankova, 2004; Schulenberg, 2004). A challenge facing that generation is how to cover the core QUAL, QUAN, and MMR concepts and methods in a minimum number of courses. An active literature is developing in this area (e.g., Christ, 2009; Creswell, Tashakkori, Jensen, & Shapley, 2003; Earley, 2007; Tashakkori & Teddlie, 2003b), which includes details on how to develop and teach MMR courses (also, see Christ, 2010).

Although there is an increasing diversity in journals' openness to publishing mixed methods articles, the challenges of publishing such articles are still present. Mixed methods articles, by default, must present the findings of both QUAL and QUAN data analysis and integrate them into coherent and meaningful meta-inferences. Including all of this in the relatively limited space allowed by the journals is a challenge for mixed methods researchers. There are various strategies to deal with these problems, from submitting to journals that devote greater space to mixed methods papers, to publishing the two components in separate journals and then linking them in a third article. Details of these strategies are expertly discussed by Dahlberg et al. in Chapter 30. Facilitating these strategies is the emergence of new computer programs for data analysis (see Bazeley, 2010a), sophisticated graphic presentations (see Dickinson, 2010 [this volume]), and a diverse set of studies in the literature, removing the necessity of explaining all details of methods and procedures in mixed studies.

A closely related challenge for publishing mixed methods studies is the need for better educated and more methodologically sophisticated journal reviewers. We receive numerous communications from authors whose manuscripts or grant proposals have been rejected because the reviewers were not knowledgeable about mixed methods concepts or methodology. We hope that this problem loses its intensity as the new generations of scholars emerge as "stewards of the research enterprise" in social, behavioral, and health sciences (Tashakkori & Creswell, 2008). However, educating such an emerging community of stewards and providing mentorship for it (and the current reviewer community) is a formidable challenge for the mixed methods community.

Perhaps as a consequence of the emergence of the new community of stewards, funding opportunities for mixed methods studies have substantially increased over the past few years. There is a general understanding among funding agencies that many complex questions require a meaningful integration of multiple QUAL and QUAN evidence. As discussed by Dahlberg et al. (2010), foundations, governmental agencies, and nongovernmental organizations are familiar with MMR and encourage proposals that use it. We hope that, as the literature of credible and strong mixed methods studies continues to expand, recognition of its potential will also increase within funding agencies and policy-making bodies.

An interesting trend in the past decade has been the emergence of meta-reviews and meta-analysis of mixed methods studies, for the purpose of identifying how these studies were conducted. We predict a shift in the direction of future studies in this area, from simply verifying their existence and providing prototype examples or profiles, to more critical stances regarding the worth of studies. There is widespread agreement that mixed methods studies cost more and are more time-consuming. There is a clear need for exploring the functional utility of mixed methods studies in a value-added policy and practice framework. We need studies to assess the degree to which better policies are formulated and better practices are being employed by professionals as a result of the added time, effort, and cost associated with mixed methods.

◆ Notes

1. There is also disagreement regarding this issue. For example, the Web page of the annual Mixed Methods Conference states, "Whilst it is debatable whether it is a third methodological movement, there is a consensus that its emergence was in response to the limitations of the sole use of quantitative or qualitative methods." (from http://www.healthcareconferences.leeds .ac.uk/community/, retrieved January 21, 2010).

2. Critical realism (Maxwell & Mittapalli, 2010 this [volume]) has recently been proposed as another framework for the use of mixed methods, but its description is beyond the scope of

this chapter. See Christ's (2010 [this volume]) detailed description of how he used critical realism in his development of a mixed methods research course.

3. Burke Johnson influenced our thoughts with regard to the value of generating a dictionary for MMR.

◆ References

Alise, M. A., & Teddlie, C. (in press). A continuation of the paradigm wars? Prevalence rates of methodological approaches across the social/behavioral sciences. Manuscript accepted for publication in the *Journal of Mixed Methods Research*.

Bamberger, M., Rao, V., & Woolcock, M. (2010). Using mixed methods in monitoring and evaluation: Experiences from international development evaluation. In A. Tashakkori & C. Teddlie (Eds.), *SAGE handbook of mixed methods in social & behavioral research* (2nd ed.). Thousand Oaks, CA: Sage.

Bazeley, P. (2003). Computerized data analysis for mixed methods research. In A. Tashakkori & C. Teddlie (Eds.), *Handbook of mixed methods in social and behavioral research* (pp. 385–422). Thousand Oaks, CA: Sage.

Bazeley, P. (2009). Integrating data analyses in mixed methods research. *Journal of Mixed Methods Research, 3*(3), 203–207.

Bazeley, P. (2010a). Computer-assisted integration of mixed methods data sources and analysis. In A. Tashakkori & C. Teddlie (Eds.), *SAGE handbook of mixed methods in social & behavioral research* (2nd ed.). Thousand Oaks, CA: Sage.

Bazeley, P. (2010b). Review of the book *The mixed methods reader. Journal of Mixed Methods Research, 4*(1), 79–81.

Bergman, M. M. (2010). Hermeneutic content analysis: Textual and audiovisual analyses within a mixed methods framework. In A. Tashakkori & C. Teddlie (Eds.), *SAGE handbook of mixed methods in social & behavioral research* (2nd ed.). Thousand Oaks, CA: Sage.

Biesta, G. (2010). Pragmatism and the philosophical foundations of mixed methods research. In A. Tashakkori & C. Teddlie (Eds.), *SAGE handbook of mixed methods in social & behavioral research* (2nd ed.). Thousand Oaks, CA: Sage.

Bryman, A. (2008). Why do researchers combine quantitative and qualitative research? In M. M. Bergman (Ed.), *Advances in mixed methods research: Theories and applications* (pp. 87–100). London: Sage.

Christ, T. W. (2009). Designing, teaching, and evaluating two complementary mixed methods research courses. *Journal of Mixed Methods Research, 3*(4), 292–325.

Christ, T. (2010). Teaching mixed methods and action research: Pedagogical, practical, and evaluative considerations. In A. Tashakkori & C. Teddlie (Eds.), *SAGE handbook of mixed methods in social & behavioral research* (2nd ed.). Thousand Oaks, CA: Sage.

Collins, K. M. T., Onwuegbuzie, A. T., & Jiao, Q. C. (2007). A mixed methods investigation of mixed methods sampling designs in social and health science research. *Journal of Mixed Methods Research, 1*(3), 267–294.

Creswell, J. W. (2009). Mapping the field of mixed methods research. *Journal of Mixed Methods Reseach, 3*(2), 95–108.

Creswell, J. W. (2010). Mapping the developing landscape of mixed methods research. In A. Tashakkori & C. Teddlie (Eds.), *SAGE handbook of mixed methods in social & behavioral research* (2nd ed.). Thousand Oaks, CA: Sage.

Creswell, J. W., & Plano Clark, V. (2007). *Designing and conducting mixed methods research*. Thousand Oaks, CA: Sage.

Creswell, J. W., Shope, R., Plano Clark, V., & Green, D. (2006). How interpretive qualitative research extends mixed methods research. *Research in the Schools, 13*(1), 1–11.

Creswell, J. W., Tashakkori, A., Jensen, K., & Shapley, K. (2003). Teaching mixed methods research: Practice, dilemmas, and challenges. In A. Tashakkori & C. Teddlie (Eds.), *Handbook of mixed methods in social and behavioral research* (pp. 619–638). Thousand Oaks, CA: Sage.

Dahlberg, B., Wittink, M. N., & Gallo, J. J. (2010). Funding and publishing integrated studies: Writing effective mixed methods manuscripts and grant proposals. In A. Tashakkori & C. Teddlie (Eds.), *SAGE handbook of mixed methods in social & behavioral research* (2nd ed., pp. 775–802). Thousand Oaks, CA: Sage.

Denscombe, M. (2008). Communities of practice: A research paradigm for the mixed methods approach. *Journal of Mixed Methods Research, 2*, 270–283.

Denzin, N. K. (2008). The new paradigm dialogs and qualitative inquiry. *International Journal of Qualitative Studies in Education, 21*, 315–325.

Denzin, N. K., & Lincoln, Y. S. (2005). Introduction: The discipline and practice of qualitative research. In N. K. Denzin & Y. S. Lincoln (Eds.), *Handbook of qualitative research* (3rd ed., pp. 1–32). Thousand Oaks, CA: Sage.

Dickinson, W. B. (2010). Visual displays for mixed methods findings. In A. Tashakkori & C. Teddlie (Eds.), *SAGE handbook of mixed methods in social & behavioral research* (2nd ed.). Thousand Oaks, CA: Sage.

Earley, M. A. (2007). Developing a syllabus for a mixed methods research course. *International Journal of Social Research Methodology, 10*(2), 145–162.

Eisenhart, M., & Towne, L. (2003). Contestation and change in national policy on "scientifically based" education research. *Educational Researcher, 32*(7), 31–38.

Erzberger, C., & Kelle, U. (2003). Making inferences in mixed methods: The rules of integration. In A. Tashakkori & C. Teddlie (Eds.), *Handbook of mixed methods in social and behavioral research* (pp. 457–490). Thousand Oaks, CA: Sage.

Feur, M. J., Towne, L., & Shavelson, R. J. (2002). Scientific culture and educational research. *Educational Researcher, 31*(8), 4–14.

Freshwater, D. (2007). *Reading* mixed methods research: Contexts for criticism. *Journal of Mixed Methods Research, 1*(2), 134–146.

Giddings, L. S. (2006). Mixed-methods research: Positivism dressed in drag? *Journal of Research in Nursing, 11*(3), 195–203.

Greene, J. C. (2006). Toward a methodology of mixed methods social inquiry. *Research in Schools, 13*(1), 93–99.

Greene, J. C. (2007). *Mixing methods in social inquiry.* San Francisco: Jossey-Bass.

Greene, J. C. (2008). Is mixed methods social inquiry a distinctive methodology? *Journal of Mixed Methods Research, 2*(1), 7–22.

Greene, J. C., & Caracelli, V. J. (2003). Making paradigmatic sense of mixed-method practice. In A. Tashakkori & C. Teddlie (Eds.), *Handbook of mixed methods in social and behavioral research* (pp. 91–110). Thousand Oaks, CA: Sage.

Greene, J., & Hall, J. (2010). Dialectics and pragmatism: Being of consequence. In A. Tashakkori & C. Teddlie (Eds.), *SAGE handbook of mixed methods in social & behavioral research* (2nd ed.). Thousand Oaks, CA: Sage.

Haig, B. D. (2005). An abductive theory of scientific method. *Psychological Methods, 10*(4), 371–388.

Howe, K. R. (1988). Against the quantitative-qualitative incompatibility thesis or dogmas die hard. *Educational Researcher, 17,* 10–16.

Howe, K. R. (2004). A critique of experimentalism. *Qualitative Inquiry, 10*(1), 42–61.

Ivankova, N. V. (2004). *Students' persistence in the University of Nebraska–Lincoln distributed doctoral program in Educational Leadership in Higher Education: A mixed methods study.* Unpublished dissertation, University of Nebraska–Lincoln.

Johnson, R. B. (2009). Toward a more inclusive "scientific research in education." *Educational Researcher, 38,* 449–457.

Johnson, R. B., & Christensen, L. B. (2008). *Educational research: Quantitative, qualitative, and mixed approaches* (3rd ed.). Thousand Oaks, CA: Sage.

Johnson, R. B., & Onwuegbuzie, A. (2004). Mixed methods research: A research paradigm whose time has come. *Educational Researcher, 33*(7), 14–26.

Johnson, R. B., Onwuegbuzie, A. J., & Turner, L. A. (2007). Toward a definition of mixed methods research. *Journal of Mixed Methods Research, 1*(2), 112–133.

Kemper, E. A., Stringfield, S., & Teddlie, C. (2003). Mixed methods sampling: Strategies in social science research. In A. Tashakkori & C. Teddlie (Eds.), *Handbook of mixed methods in social and behavioral research* (pp. 273–296). Thousand Oaks, CA: Sage.

Maxcy, S. (2003). Pragmatic threads in mixed methods research in the social sciences: The search for multiple modes of inquiry and the end of the philosophy of formalism. In A. Tashakkori & C. Teddlie (Eds.), *Handbook of mixed methods in social and behavioral research* (pp. 51–90). Thousand Oaks, CA: Sage.

Maxwell, J., & Loomis, D. (2003). Mixed methods design: An alternative approach. In A. Tashakkori & C. Teddlie (Eds.), *Handbook of mixed methods in social and behavioral research* (pp. 241–272). Thousand Oaks, CA: Sage.

Maxwell, J. A., & Mittapalli, K. (2010). Realism as a stance for mixed method research. In A. Tashakkori & C. Teddlie (Eds.), *SAGE handbook of mixed methods in social & behavioral research* (2nd ed.). Thousand Oaks, CA: Sage.

Mertens, D. M. (2007). Transformative paradigm: Mixed methods and social justice. *Journal of Mixed Methods Research, 1*(3), 212–225.

Mertens, D. (2010). Divergence and mixed methods. *Journal of Mixed Methods Research, 4*(1), 3–5.

Mertens, D. M., Bledsoe, K. L., Sullivan, M., & Wilson, A. (2010). Utilization of mixed methods for transformative purposes. In A. Tashakkori & C. Teddlie (Eds.), *SAGE handbook of mixed methods in social & behavioral research* (2nd ed.). Thousand Oaks, CA: Sage.

Morgan, D. (2007). Paradigms lost and pragmatism regained: Methodological implications of combining qualitative and quantitative methods. *Journal of Mixed Methods Research, 1*(1), 48–76.

Morse, J., & Niehaus, L. (2010). *Mixed method design: Principles and procedures.* Walnut Creek, CA: Left Coast Press.

Nastasi, B. K., Hitchcock, J. H., & Brown, L. M. (2010). An inclusive framework for conceptualizing mixed methods design typologies: Moving toward fully integrated synergistic research models. In A. Tashakkori & C. Teddlie (Eds.), *SAGE handbook of mixed methods in social & behavioral research* (2nd ed.). Thousand Oaks, CA: Sage.

Newman, I., & Ramlo, S. (2010). Using Q methodology and Q factor analysis in mixed methods research. In A. Tashakkori & C. Teddlie (Eds.), *SAGE handbook of mixed methods in social & behavioral research* (2nd ed.). Thousand Oaks, CA: Sage.

O'Cathain, A. (2010). Assessing the quality of mixed methods research: Toward a comprehensive framework. In A. Tashakkori & C. Teddlie (Eds.), *SAGE handbook of mixed methods in social & behavioral research* (2nd ed.). Thousand Oaks, CA: Sage.

Onwuegbuzie, A. J., & Collins, K. M. T. (2007). A typology of mixed methods sampling designs in social science research. *The Qualitative Report, 12*(2), 281–316. Retrieved May 15, 2009, from http://www.nova.edu/ssss/QR/QR12-2/Onwuegbuzie2.pdf

Onwuegbuzie, A. J., & Combs, J. P. (2010). Emergent data analysis techniques in mixed methods research: A synthesis. In A. Tashakkori & C. Teddlie (Eds.), *SAGE handbook of mixed methods in social & behavioral research* (2nd ed., pp. 397–430). Thousand Oaks, CA: Sage.

Ridenour, C. S., & Newman, I. (2008). *Mixed methods research: Exploring the interactive continuum.* Carbondale: Southern Illinois University Press.

Sale, J., Lohfeld, L., & Brazil, K. (2002). Revisiting the qualitative-quantitative debate: Implications for mixed-methods research. *Quality and Quantity, 36,* 43–53.

Sammons, P. (2010). The contribution of mixed methods to recent research on educational effectiveness. In A. Tashakkori & C. Teddlie (Eds.), *SAGE handbook of mixed methods in social & behavioral research* (2nd ed.). Thousand Oaks, CA: Sage.

Schulenberg, J. L. (2004). *Policing young offenders: A multi-method analysis of vari-ations in police discretion.* Waterloo, ON: University of Waterloo.

Schwandt, T. (1997). *Qualitative inquiry: A dictionary of terms.* Thousand Oaks, CA: Sage.

Shulha, L., & Wilson, R. (2003). Collaborative mixed methods research. In A. Tashakkori & C. Teddlie (Eds.), *Handbook of mixed methods in social and behavioral research* (pp. 639–670). Thousand Oaks, CA: Sage.

Smith, J. K., & Heshusius, L. (1986). Closing down the conversation: The end of the quantitative-qualitative debate among educational researchers. *Educational Researcher, 15,* 4–12.

Song, M.-K., Sandelowski, M., & Happ, M. B. (2010). Current practices and emerging trends in conducting mixed methods intervention studies in the health sciences. In A. Tashakkori & C. Teddlie (Eds.), *SAGE handbook of mixed methods in social & behavioral research* (2nd ed.). Thousand Oaks, CA: Sage.

Tashakkori, A. (2009). Are we there yet? The state of the mixed methods community. *Journal of Mixed Methods Research, 3*(4), 287–291.

Tashakkori, A., Brown, L. M., & Borghese, P. (2009). Integrated methods for studying a systemic conceptualization of stress and coping. In K. Collins, A. J. Onwuegbuzie, & Q. G. Jiao (Eds.), *Toward a broader understanding of stress and coping: Mixed methods approaches* (Research on Stress and Coping in Education Series, Vol. 5). Charlotte, NC: Information Age Publishing.

Tashakkori, A., & Creswell, J. (2008). Envisioning the future stewards of the social-behavioral research enterprise. *Journal of Mixed Methods Research, 2*(4), 291–295.

Tashakkori, A., & Newman, I. (in press). Mixed methods: Integrating quantitative and qualitative approaches to research. In B. McGaw, E. Baker, & P. P. Peterson (Eds.), *International encyclopedia of education* (3rd ed.). Oxford, UK: Elsevier.

Tashakkori, A., & Teddlie, C. (1998). *Mixed methodology: Combining the qualitative and quantitative approaches.* Thousand Oaks, CA: Sage.

Tashakkori, A., & Teddlie, C. (Eds.). (2003a). *Handbook of mixed methods in social and behavioral research*. Thousand Oaks, CA: Sage.

Tashakkori, A., & Teddlie, C. (2003b). Issues and dilemmas in teaching research methods courses in social and behavioral sciences: U.S. perspective. *International Journal of Social Research Methodology, 6,* 61–77.

Tashakkori, A., & Teddlie, C. (2003c). The past and future of mixed methods research: From data triangulation to mixed model designs. In A. Tashakkori & C. Teddlie (Eds.), *Handbook of mixed methods in social and behavioral research* (pp. 671–702). Thousand Oaks, CA: Sage.

Teddlie, C., & Tashakkori, A. (2003). Major issues and controversies in the use of mixed methods in the social and behavioral sciences. In A. Tashakkori & C. Teddlie (Eds.), *Handbook of mixed methods in social and behavioral research* (pp. 3–50). Thousand Oaks, CA: Sage.

Teddlie, C., & Tashakkori, A. (2009). *The foundations of mixed methods research: Integrating quantitative and qualitative techniques in the social and behavioral sciences.* Thousand Oaks, CA: Sage.

Teddlie, C., & Tashakkori, A. (in press). Mixed methods: Contemporary issues in an emerging field. In N. K. Denzin & Y. S. Lincoln (Eds.), *Handbook of qualitative research* (4th ed.). Thousand Oaks, CA: Sage.

Teddlie, C., Tashakkori, A., & Johnson, B. (2008). Emergent techniques in the gathering and analysis of mixed methods data. In S. Hesse-Biber & P. Leavy (Eds.), *Handbook of emergent methods in social research* (pp. 389–413). New York: Guilford Press.

Teddlie, C., & Yu, F. (2007). Mixed methods sampling: A typology with examples. *Journal of Mixed Methods Research, 1*(1), 77–100.

Yoshikawa, H., Weisner, T. D., Kalil, A., & Way, N. (2008). Mixing qualitative and quantitative research in developmental science: Uses and methodological choices. *Developmental Psychology, 33*(7), 344–354.

AUTHOR INDEX

SUBJECT INDEX

ABOUT THE EDITORS

Abbas Tashakkori (PhD, Social Psychology, University of North Carolina at Chapel Hill) is the chairperson of the Department of Educational Psychology and professor of research and evaluation methodology at the University of North Texas. He was a Distinguished Frost Professor of Research and Evaluation Methodology at Florida International University until 2009. He has published extensively in social and behavioral sciences on attitudes and self-perceptions, bilingual and minority issues, education and social mobility, educational effectiveness evaluation, and research methodology. His scholarly work includes four authored or edited books, numerous journal articles and book chapters, and presentations and keynote speeches at national and international meetings. He has served as a Founding Chair of the Mixed Methods Special Interest Group (SIG) of the American Educational Research Association (AERA) and was the Founding Editor (with John Creswell) of the *Journal of Mixed Methods Research*.

His latest book in progress is entitled *Practical Guide for Planning and Conducting Integrated Research in Behavioral and Social Research* (Guilford, with Charles Teddlie).

Charles Teddlie (PhD, Social Psychology, University of North Carolina at Chapel Hill) is a distinguished professor emeritus in the College of Education at Louisiana State University. Since 1986, he has been the co-owner and evaluation director of K. T. Associates, which conducts mixed methods research and evaluation studies in the United States and other countries. His major writing interests are mixed methods research, educational effectiveness research, and equity issues in education. He recently completed a review of the Black–White achievement gap that integrated the cultural, sociological, psychological, genetic, and educational literatures related to that topic. He has produced numerous articles and chapters in education, psychology, and evaluation and has coauthored or coedited a dozen books, including *Schools Make a Difference: Lessons Learned From a Ten-Year Study of School Effects* (1993), *Forty Years After the Brown Decision: The Current and Future Sociological Implications of School Desegregation* (1997), *The International Handbook of School Effectiveness Research* (2000), and three books on mixed methods research (with Abbas Tashakkori), including *Foundations of Mixed Methods Research* (2009).

ABOUT THE CONTRIBUTORS

Manijeh Badiee (MA, St. Edwards University) is a doctoral student in counseling psychology at the University of Nebraska–Lincoln. She works as a research assistant in the Office of Qualitative and Mixed Methods Research. She plans on becoming a professor and aspires to further knowledge on Iranian and Iranian-American populations. Other research interests include global women's empowerment and transformative research methods. She is currently the student representative of the International Section of Division 17, Counseling Psychology, and served as cochair, with Sherry Wang, of the Student Committee for Division 52, International Psychology.

Michael Bamberger (PhD, London School of Economics) earned his doctorate in sociology. After a decade working in urban community development and social program evaluation with nongovernmental organizations in Latin America, he spent 20 years with the World Bank evaluating social and economic development programs, organizing evaluation training, and working in the Gender and Development Department. Since retiring, he has consulted with more than 15 international development agencies and developing country governments on program evaluation and evaluation capacity development. He is on the faculty of the International Program for Development Evaluation Training (IPDET) and on the editorial board of a number of leading evaluation journals. He has published widely on program evaluation through books, technical guidelines, training manuals, and professional journals on a variety of evaluation topics, including conducting impact evaluations under real-world constraints, reconstruction of baseline data, evaluation utilization, mixed method evaluation, and the institutionalization of impact evaluation systems in developing countries.

Pat Bazeley (PhD, Macquarie University) provides assistance and time out (and good food) to local and international researchers from a wide range of disciplines at her research retreat at Bowral, in the Southern Highlands of New South Wales. She also holds senior, part-time appointments in Research Centres at the University of New South Wales and at the Australian Catholic University, and has served as an associate editor for the *Journal of Mixed Methods Research*. Her particular expertise is in helping researchers make sense of both quantitative and qualitative data and in using computer software for management and analysis of data. Her publications focus on qualitative and mixed methods data analysis, and on the development and performance of researchers.

Manfred Max Bergman (PhD, University of Cambridge) holds the chair in methodology and political sociology at the University of Basel, Switzerland, and is currently visiting professor at the Universities of Johannesburg and Witwatersrand in South Africa. His substantive research interests include discrimination and inequality in education and employment. He teaches and applies qualitative, quantitative, and mixed methods designs. He recently edited *Advances in Mixed Method Research* (Sage, 2008) and *Mobilities and Inequality* (with Ohnmacht and Maksim, 2009) and is editor of the *Swiss Journal of Sociology* and the *Journal of Mixed Methods Research* (with Mertens; Sage).

Gert Biesta (PhD, Leiden University, the Netherlands) is professor of education at the Stirling Institute of Education, University of Stirling, Scotland, and visiting professor for education and democratic citizenship at Mälardalen University, Sweden. His research focuses on the theory and philosophy of education, democratic education and civic learning, and the philosophy and theory of educational research and its relationships with policy and practice. Recent books include *Pragmatism and Educational Research* (with Nicholas C. Burbules; 2003); *Beyond Learning: Democratic Education for a Human Future* (2006); *Democracy, Education and the Moral Life* (coedited with Michael Katz and Susan Verducci; 2008); *Rethinking Contexts for Learning and Teaching* (coedited with Richard Edwards and Mary Thorpe; 2008);

Derrida, Deconstruction and the Politics of Pedagogy (with Michael A. Peters; 2008); and *Good Education in an Age of Measurement: Ethics, Politics, Democracy* (2010).

Katrina L. Bledsoe (PhD, Claremont Graduate University) is a senior research manager at Walter R. McDonald & Associates, Inc., and project director of the national evaluation of the Comprehensive Community Mental Health Services for Children and Their Families Program, which is funded by the Center for Mental Health Services of the Substance Abuse and Mental Health Services Administration. Dr. Bledsoe specializes in applied social psychology, community-based and theory-driven program evaluation, cultural contexts, and multicultural behavioral health. Dr. Bledsoe has more than 15 years of experience in research and evaluation using participatory evaluation approaches such as democratic, transdisciplinary, and empowerment evaluation. Dr. Bledsoe is the author of articles and chapters featured in the *American Journal of Evaluation*, *The Handbook of Ethics for Research in the Social Sciences*, and *When Research Studies Go off the Rails: Solutions and Prevention Strategies*, and work forthcoming in the edited book *Qualitative Inquiry in the Practice of Evaluation*.

Julia Brannen (PhD, University of London) is professor of sociology of the family in the Institute of Education, University of London, and adjunct professor in the Department of Sociology, University of Bergen, Norway. Her writing on methodological issues extends over many years and includes *Mixing Methods: Qualitative and Quantitative Research* (1992) and *The Handbook of Social Research* (Sage, 2008). She is a contributor to a number of methods texts including Seale and others, *Qualitative Research in Practice* (Sage, 2004) and Bergman, *Advances in Mixed Methods Research* (Sage, 2008). In the course of a long career in research, both British and cross-national, she has also employed biographical methods extensively in her work on intergenerational relations in families and employed comparative methods in European cross-national studies on work and family life. She is a cofounder and coeditor of the *International Journal of Social Research Methodology* (www.tandf.co.uk); currently, she is an associate editor of the *Journal of Mixed Methods Research*.

Lisa M. Brown (PhD, Pacific Graduate School of Psychology) is a licensed clinical psychologist and an associate professor in the Department of Aging and Mental Health Disparities, Florida Mental Health Institute, College of Behavioral and Community Sciences, University of South Florida. Dr. Brown is interested in how people cope with adverse personal or societal life events. Her clinical and research focus is on aging, health, disasters, and long-term care. She teaches courses and seminars on assessment, intervention, and disasters. She recently coedited *Psychology of Terrorism* (2007). She serves on the Disaster Mental Health Subcommittee of the National Biodefense Science Board Federal Advisory Committee and as the assistant clinical director of the Florida Crisis Consortium, Florida Department of Health.

Thomas W. Christ (PhD, University of Hawai'i) is a research specialist for the Center on Disability Studies and is a research, evaluation, and theory teacher in the Curriculum Studies Department at the University of Hawai'i. His current research focus includes mixed methods and action research pedagogy, student, program, and organization evaluations, international education reform, and curricula theory and development. Thomas was a school psychologist and special educator in public schools for 10 years before teaching and conducting research at the university level. Thomas's publications include mixed and action research methodologies, postsecondary support services, technology, leadership,

and program evaluations. His international research includes education transformation in post-Soviet Kyrgyzstan and Hungary; his North American research includes a longitudinal evaluation of grieving and coping strategies seen in families who had a firefighter perish in 09/11, tiered writing strategies (RtI) designed to improve literacy, and dual enrollment in secondary and postsecondary education for students with disabilities.

Kathleen M. T. Collins (PhD, University of California Santa Barbara) is an associate professor in the Department of Curriculum and Instruction at the University of Arkansas at Fayetteville. Dr. Collins's interests are in research methodological issues as they pertain to mixed research, special populations, and the identification and assessment of literacy problems of post-secondary students. She has published more than 60 research articles, book chapters, and encyclopedia chapters, and has presented more than 70 research papers at international, national, and regional conferences. She is lead editor of a mixed methods book entitled *Toward a Broader Understanding of Stress and Coping: Mixed Methods Approaches* (2010). Also, she is co-writing a book, *Mixed Research: A Step-by-Step Guide*.

Julie P. Combs (EdD, Texas A&M University–Commerce) is assistant professor in the Educational Leadership and Counseling Department at Sam Houston State University. Previously, she worked as a school principal for 10 years at an award-winning school. She teaches academic writing, program evaluation, and research methods courses in the doctoral program and teaches various leadership courses in the principal certification program. In addition to maintaining an active research agenda focused on stress and coping, academic writing, and the role of the school principal, she has made more than 75 international, national, state, and local presentations, one half of which include consultations with schools and districts. She has written more than 30 journal articles and six book chapters and has cowritten the books *Managing Conflict: 50 Strategies for School Leaders* and *Examining What We Do to Improve Our Schools: Eight Steps From Analysis to Action*. In addition, she has recently served as an associate editor of *Educational Researcher*.

John W. Creswell (PhD, University of Iowa) is professor of educational psychology at the University of Nebraska–Lincoln; teaches courses and writes about mixed methods research, qualitative methodology, and general research design; and has held an endowed chair in research methodology. He has been at Nebraska for 30 years and is the author of 12 books, many of which focus on alternative types of research designs, comparisons of different qualitative methodologies, and the nature and use of mixed methods research. His books are read around the world by audiences in the social sciences, education, and the health sciences. In addition, he has directed the Office of Qualitative and Mixed Methods Research at Nebraska, which provides support for scholars incorporating qualitative and mixed methods research into projects for extramural funding. He served as the founding coeditor for a Sage journal, *Journal of Mixed Methods Research*, and he has been an adjunct professor of family medicine at the University of Michigan and assisted investigators in the Veterans Administration health sciences on research methodology. In 2008, he was a Senior Fulbright Scholar to South Africa, lecturing in education and the health sciences.

Britt Dahlberg (BA, University of Pennsylvania) is a PhD student in anthropology and works as a research coordinator on interdisciplinary studies about depression and aging in the Department of Family Medicine and Community Health. She is interested in exploring connections between culture and mental health, and in developing the theoretical and methodological tools needed to explore these complex relationships. Her work to date has focused on how older adults conceptualize and experience depression and depression diagnoses, older adults' strategies for treating depression, and how cultural models about distress arise in response to and shape personal experience.

Wendy B. Dickinson (PhD, University of South Florida) is a liberal arts instructor at Ringling College of Art and Design, teaching geometry, visual anthropology, and visual mathematics (statistics and graphical display). Her doctorate is in curriculum and instruction, with an emphasis in educational measurement and research, and with a cognate in fine arts. As a practicing studio artist, Wendy has exhibited her 2- and 3-dimensional prints and book arts in more than 90 regional, state, and national venues. Dr. Dickinson served as president of the Florida Educational Research Association (2008-2009), is contributing editor for *Anthropology News* (2007–2010), was named a Fellow of the Royal Statistical Society (2008), and provides expertise as external evaluator for federal granting agencies. Wendy Dickinson has made more than 100 refereed presentations at regional, national, and international research conferences in research areas of statistical methodology, authentic assessment, evaluation, graphical display, and computer programming.

Joseph J. Gallo (MD, Pennsylvania State University, MPH, Johns Hopkins University) is professor in the Department of Family Medicine and Community Health at the University of Pennsylvania. He was an NIMH/NIA postdoctoral fellow in psychiatric epidemiology at the Johns Hopkins University and was the project director for the 13-year follow-up of the Baltimore sample of the NIMH Epidemiologic Catchment Area Program in 1994. He is principal investigator of the "spectrum of depression in late life," a set of linked studies employing mixed methods to investigate depression in late life from the older adult's point of view. He leads a long-term follow-up of the depression and health service use outcomes of a practice-randomized trial of depression management in primary care. He serves on the editorial boards of the *International Journal of Psychiatry in Medicine*, the *Journal of Mixed Methods Research*, and the *American Journal of Geriatric Psychiatry*.

Stephen Gorard (PhD, Cardiff University) holds the centrally funded chair in education research at the University of Birmingham, UK. His research is focused on issues of equity, especially in educational opportunities and outcomes, and on the effectiveness of educational systems. Recent project topics include assessing the impact of schools on childrens' notions of justice (*Equity in Education*, 2010), widening participation in learning (*Overcoming the Barriers to Higher Education*, 2007), the role of technology in lifelong learning (*Adult Learning in the Digital Age*, 2006), and teacher supply and retention (*Teacher Supply: The Key Issues*, 2006). He is particularly interested in the process and quality of research, having recently led the UK ESRC Research Capacity-Building Network, and an ESRC Researcher Development Initiative to improve the understanding of randomized controlled trials in social science. He is the author of hundreds of pieces on research methods and is editor of *Quantitative Research in Education* (Sage, 2008).

Robert Gray (PhD, University of Alabama) is director of the Program for the Enhancement of Teaching and Learning at the University of South Alabama. He holds a PhD in instructional technology from the University of Alabama and has a strong background in English, having completed his bachelor's and master's at the University of Alabama and his doctoral coursework at Michigan State University. He has taught at the University of Alabama, Michigan State, Troy State, and the University of South Alabama. He has presented at several national and international conferences on innovative approaches to the use of streaming media in instruction and on reconceptualizing interaction in online courses. He is currently coediting a book entitled *Technology Integration in Higher Education: Social and Organizational Aspects*, and he has published two books of poetry, *I Wish That I Were Langston Hughes* and *DREW: Poems From Blue Water*.

Jennifer C. Greene (PhD, Stanford University) is currently a professor of educational psychology at the University of Illinois at Urbana-Champaign. Her scholarship focuses on making evaluation useful and socially responsible, both in theory and in practice, and her research emphasizes the development of alternative approaches to evaluation—notably, qualitative, participatory, and mixed methods approaches. Greene has held leadership positions in the American Evaluation Association and the American Educational Research Association. She served as coeditor-in-chief of New Directions for Evaluation, from 1997 to 2004. She also coedited the 2006 Sage *Handbook on Evaluation* and was the author of *Mixed Methods in Social Inquiry* (Sage, 2007). In 2003, she received AEA's Lazarsfeld award for contributions to evaluation theory. She is currently president-elect of the American Evaluation Association for 2011.

Jori N. Hall (PhD, University of Illinois, Champaign-Urbana) is assistant professor in the Department of Lifelong Education, Administration and Policy, and Education Policy and Evaluation Center Fellow in the College of Education at the University of Georgia. She teaches graduate courses, advancing theory and practice related to mixed methods inquiry and qualitative research. Her evaluation practice focuses on programs for science, technology, engineering, and mathematics education and school improvement. Her current research examines educational accountability and a school's capacity to respond to accountability mechanisms.

Mary Beth Happ (PhD, University of Pennsylvania) is a professor of nursing in the Department of Nursing Acute and Tertiary Care at the University of Pittsburgh (primary) and the University of Pittsburgh Center for Bioethics and Health Law. Dr. Happ's program of research is focused on improving communication in the care of seriously ill hospitalized adults, primarily in the care of patients who are unable to speak. She is the recipient of a Mid-Career Award from the National Institute of Nursing Research, National Institutes of Health (5K24-NR010244, 2007–2010) to study symptom management, patient–caregiver communication, and outcomes in the ICU. She is a principal investigator of a study funded by the Robert Wood Johnson Foundation Interdisciplinary Nursing Quality Research Initiative (2009–2011) to test an intervention to improve patient communication and quality outcomes in the ICU. Dr. Happ has published numerous methodological papers and mixed methods research reports and has conducted mixed methods research workshops internationally.

Angela Harden (PhD, University of London) is professor of community and family health at the Institute of Health and Human Development at the University of East London. She is a social scientist with expertise in public health and evidence-informed policy and practice. She has nearly 20 years experience in mixed methods research on the health and well-being of children and young people and the communities in which they live. She has also developed innovative methods to synthesize data from diverse study types within systematic reviews. She has published widely on these topics and is a co-convenor of the Cochrane Collaboration's Qualitative Research Methods Group. Angela was previously an associate director of the EPPI-Centre at the Social Science Research Unit, Institute of Education. She now directs a program of research linked to improving health in the East End of London.

Sharlene Nagy Hesse-Biber (PhD, University of Michigan) is professor of sociology, Boston College. Her monograph, *Am I Thin Enough Yet?* (1996), was selected as one of *Choice Magazine*'s best academic books for 1996. She is author of *The Cult of Thinness* (2007) and *Mixed Methods Research: Merging Theory With Practice* (2010). She is the coauthor of *Working Women in America* (2005) and *The Practice of Qualitative Research* (Sage, 2006, 2011). She is coeditor of *Feminist Approaches to Theory and Methodology* (1999), *Approaches to Qualitative Research* (2004), *Feminist Perspectives on Social Research* (2004), *Emergent Methods in Social Research* (Sage, 2006), and *The Handbook of Emergent Methods* (2008). She is editor of *The Handbook of Feminist Research* (Sage, 2007; this book was an AESA Critics' Choice Award winner and was selected one of *Choice Magazine*'s Outstanding Academic titles for 2007) and *The Handbook of Emergent Technologies* (2011). She is co-developer of HyperRESEARCH, a software tool for analyzing qualitative data, and a transcription software tool, HyperTranscribe (www.researchware.com).

John H. Hitchcock (PhD, University at Albany SUNY), prior to joining the Educational Studies Department at Ohio University, worked as a research consultant in the Washington, D.C., area. He is experienced with research design, program evaluation, project management, and providing technical assistance to educators and clinicians. His professional interests lie in developing educational and psychological interventions for minority groups in the United States and in international settings, special education research, experimental design, and mixed method (i.e., quantitative and qualitative) designs. He is currently serving as a co–principal investigator of two federally funded randomized controlled trials and continues to work on a multiyear research program that utilizes mixed methods designs to develop assessment and intervention services for children in Sri Lanka.

He is a member of the American Education Research Association and the American Evaluation Association, is an education affiliate of the Campbell Collaboration, and is on the editorial board of *Learning Disabilities Research and Practice*.

Nataliya V. Ivankova (PhD, University of Nebraska-Lincoln) is associate professor at the Department of Human Studies and Department of Health Care Organization and Policy at the University of Alabama at Birmingham (UAB). She also works as associate scientist at the UAB Center for Educational Accountability. Her expertise is in qualitative inquiry and mixed methods research and their applications in social, behavioral, and health sciences. She teaches campus-based and online graduate level applied research methods courses; mentors doctoral students in their dissertation research in education, health, nursing, and medicine; and serves as consultant and coinvestigator on funded research projects. Dr. Ivankova's scholarship includes peer-reviewed presentations and publications dealing with methodological issues of applying qualitative and mixed methods research across disciplines, as well as teaching applied research methods in the computer-mediated learning environment.

Burke Johnson (PhD, University of Georgia) is a professor in the Department of Professional Studies at the University of South Alabama. He holds three master's degrees (psychology, sociology, and public administration). His PhD is from the REMS Program (Research, Evaluation, Measurement, and Statistics) at the University of Georgia. He is first author of *Educational Research: Quantitative, Qualitative, and Mixed Approaches* (Sage, 2008), and second author of *Research Methods, Design, and Analysis* (2010). He is author or coauthor of numerous articles and chapters. He recently completed his term as an associate editor with the *Journal of Mixed Methods Research*. He was guest editor of a special issue on mixed methods

research in Research in the Schools (http://www.msera.org/rits_131.htm) and is working on a special issue on mixed methods research with the American Behavioral Scientist. His current interests are in research methodology (especially mixed) and the history and philosophy of social science.

Yoko Kawamura (MPH, PhD, University of Alabama at Birmingham) specializes in health education and health communication. At the University of Alabama at Birmingham, School of Public Health, she, utilizing mixed methods, completed her dissertation research. She is now associate professor at Kumamoto University, Center for Policy Studies, Japan. She currently works on projects dealing with various health issues, such as rural health, health-related information delivery, and maternal and child health, in community settings, in which mixed methods are particularly useful.

Nancy L. Leech (PhD, Colorado State University) is an associate professor at the University of Colorado Denver. Dr. Leech is currently teaching master's- and PhD-level courses in research, statistics, and measurement. Her area of research is promoting new developments and better understandings in applied qualitative, quantitative, and mixed methodologies. To date, she has published more than 45 articles in referred journals and is coauthor of four books: *SPSS for Introductory Statistics: Use and Interpretation* (3rd ed.; 2007), *SPSS for Intermediate Statistics: Use and Interpretation* (3rd ed.; 2008), *Research Methods in Applied Settings: An Integrated Approach to Design and Analysis* (2nd ed.; 2009), and the forthcoming mixed research text, *Mixed Research: A Step-by-Step Guide* (in press). Dr. Leech has made more than 40 presentations at regional, national, and international conferences.

Eli Lieber (PhD, University of Illinois, Champaign-Urbana) is an associate research psychologist in the Department of Psychiatry, University of California at Los Angeles, and codirector, Fieldwork and Qualitative Data Research Laboratory, at the same institution. With primary interests in developing and applying strategies for integrated (mixed methods) social science research, his research typically involves a cultural perspective with attention to public health issues (e.g., HIV/STD prevention, mental health) and families facing unique challenges (e.g., literacy, immigration, or diabetes). Much of this interest stems from his work in Taiwan and continued collaboration on cross-cultural studies of health, motivation, parenting, and family adaptation. A quantitative psychologist, he works extensively with colleagues from many disciplines integrating quantitative and qualitative methods. He has a particular interest in maximizing technologies in research, with his help in the development of EthnoNotes being a primary example. He received his doctorate in 1996.

Joseph A. Maxwell (PhD, University of Chicago) is a professor in the College of Education and Human Development at George Mason University, where he teaches courses on research design and methods. He is the author of *Qualitative Research Design: An Interactive Approach* (Sage, 2nd ed., 2005) and a chapter on designing mixed methods studies (with Diane Loomis) in the first edition of the *Handbook of Mixed Methods in Social and Behavioral Research* (Sage, 2003), as well as papers on qualitative and mixed methodology, sociocultural theory, Native American societies, and medical education. His current research focuses on using qualitative research for causal explanation, the value of philosophic realism for qualitative and mixed methods research, and the importance of diversity and dialogue among research paradigms and methods. His doctorate is in anthropology.

Donna M. Mertens (PhD, University of Kentucky), a professor in the Department of Educational Foundations and Research, Gallaudet University, Washington, D.C., teaches graduate-level research methods and program evaluation to deaf and hearing students in education, administration, psychology, social work, audiology, and international development. The major focus of her work is the blending of issues of social justice and human rights with research and evaluation frameworks and methods. She is the coeditor of the *Journal of Mixed Methods Research* (Max Bergman, coeditor). A past president (1998) of the American Evaluation Association, she provided leadership for AEA's Diversity Initiative, Graduate Internship for Evaluators of Color, and the International Organization for Cooperation in Evaluation. She is the author and editor of several books, including *Research and Evaluation in Education and Psychology: Integrating Diversity With Quantitative, Qualitative, and Mixed Methods* (Sage, 3rd ed., 2010), *Transformative Research and Evaluation* (Guilford Press, 2009), *Handbook of Social Research Ethics* (coedited with Pauline Ginsberg; Sage, 2009), and *Research and Evaluation Methods in Special Education* (with John McLaughlin; Corwin Press, 2004).

Kavita Mittapalli (PhD, George Mason University) is an education research and program evaluation consultant in the Washington, D.C., area. In addition to providing consultancy to various for-profit, and non-profit organizations and state education agencies, she works as an adjunct faculty at Argosy University (Washington, D.C., campus) where she teaches academic writing and methods courses and serves on several dissertation committees. She received her doctorate in research methodology (education) in May 2008. Dr. Mittapalli presents at various conferences and publishes in peer-reviewed journals. In April 2009, she published a book, *What Makes Public School Teachers Stay, Leave or Become Non-teachers* (2009). This work was based on her dissertation.

Janice M. Morse (PhD Nursing, PhD Anthropology, University of Utah) is a professor and Presidential Endowed Chair at the University of Utah College of Nursing, and Professor Emeritus, University of Alberta, Canada. She was the founding director of the International Institute for Qualitative Methodology (IIQM), University of Alberta; was founding editor for the *International Journal of Qualitative Methods*; and, since 1991, has served as the founding editor for *Qualitative Health Research*. Morse is the recipient of the Episteme Award (Sigma Theta Tau) and honorary doctorates from the University of Newcastle (Australia) and Athabasca University (Canada). She is the author of 350 articles and 15 books on qualitative research methods, suffering, comforting, and patient falls. Her most recent book (with Linda Niehaus) is *Mixed Method Design: Principles and Procedure* (2009).

Bonnie Kaul Nastasi (PhD, Kent State University) is an associate professor in the Department of Psychology, School of Science and Engineering, at Tulane University. Dr. Nastasi's research focuses on the use of mixed methods designs to develop and evaluate culturally appropriate assessment and intervention approaches for promoting mental health and reducing health risks such as sexually transmitted infections (STIs) and HIV, both in the United States and internationally. She has worked in Sri Lanka since 1995 on development of school-based programs to promote psychological well-being and is currently directing a multicountry study of psychological well-being of children and adolescents with research partners in 12 countries. She has worked in India since 2001 as one of the principal investigators of an interdisciplinary public health research program to prevent STIs among married men and women living in the slums of Mumbai. Dr. Nastasi is the current president of Division 16 (School Psychology) of the American Psychological Association.

Isadore Newman (PhD, Southern Illinois University, Carbondale) is the director of research and graduate studies in the College of Education at Florida International University, where he teaches advanced statistics and multivariate analyses. He is an Emeritus Distinguished Professor at The University of Akron, where he also taught research courses. Specializing in mixed methodology and the general linear model, he has served on more than 300 dissertation committees, been the author of approximately 130 refereed articles and 13 books and monographs, evaluated more than $10 million in single- and multi-site grants, and presented more than 300 nationally refereed conference papers. Dr. Newman is also an adjunct professor at North East Ohio Universities College of Medicine. He has been editor and served on the editorial board of numerous journals. In 1999, he was the recipient of the Southern Illinois University, Carbondale, College of Education Alumni Achievement Award. While at The University of Akron, he received both the College and University Outstanding Teaching Award. He also received an Outstanding Reviewer Award in 2010 from the AERA Educational Researcher, and he is on the Scientific Advisory Board of the Kronos Longevity Research Institute.

Katrin Niglas (PhD, Tallinn University, Estonia) is a professor of data analysis in the Institute of Informatics at Tallinn University. She has taught various data analysis and research methods courses for 15 years. After getting a teacher training diploma and earning a master's of art degree in Estonia, Katrin Niglas studied at the University of Cambridge and earned a master's of philosophy degree in educational research in 1999. In her doctoral dissertation in educational sciences, defended in 2004, she focused on the combined use of qualitative and quantitative methods in educational research. This topic continues to be her main writing interest. During her career she has taken part in various research projects on the fields of education, social sciences, and humanities as an expert in methodology and data analysis.

She has held several administrative positions at Tallinn University and has been successful in leading a number of international research and development projects. Niglas is a member of the editorial board of the *Journal of Mixed Methods Research*, as well as of the *International Journal of Multiple Research Approaches*.

Ann Nilsen (Dr. Philos, University of Bergen, Norway) is professor of sociology at the Department of Sociology, University of Bergen, Norway. Her doctorate is in sociology. She also has been visiting professorial scholar at the Institute of Education, University of London, and visiting professor at the Department of Sociology, University of Uppsala, Sweden. She has done research and published in different areas of sociology with particular emphasis on methodological issues in biographical studies and life course research. She was editor and coeditor of the *Journal of Sociology (Sosiologisk tidsskrift)* from 1997 to 2002. She has held research grants from the Norwegian Research Council and from the European Union. Recent publications include articles in *Sociology* and *Sociological Review*.

Alicia O'Cathain (PhD, University of Sheffield) is Professor of Health Services Research at the School of Health and Related Research, University of Sheffield, UK. She has worked in health services research for over 20 years with interests in measuring patients' views of services, evaluating new services, and combining qualitative and quantitative methods in health research. She is currently leading mixed methods research studies evaluating telephone access to urgent care, the use of qualitative research in randomized controlled trials and measuring the patient view of the emergency and urgent care system. She is an Associate Editor of the *Journal of Mixed Methods Research* and an editorial board member of the *International Journal of Multiple Research Approaches*.

Anthony J. Onwuegbuzie (PhD, University of South Carolina) is professor in the Department of Educational Leadership and Counseling at Sam Houston State University. He teaches doctoral-level courses in qualitative research, quantitative research, and mixed research. His research areas primarily involve social and behavioral science topics, including disadvantaged and underserved populations such as minorities, children living in war zones, students with special needs, and juvenile delinquents. Additionally, he writes extensively on qualitative, quantitative, and mixed methodological topics applicable to multiple disciplines within the social and behavioral sciences field. Dr. Onwuegbuzie has secured the publication of more than 230 refereed journal articles, 50 book or encyclopedia chapters, one book which he wrote, and one which he coedited. He is lead author of a book titled *Mixed Research: A Step-by-Step Guide* (2010). Also, he has made more than 500 presentations and keynote addresses worldwide. Dr. Onwuegbuzie has served as editor of *Educational Researcher* and is coeditor of *Research in the Schools*.

Vicki L. Plano Clark (PhD, University of Nebraska–Lincoln) is director of the Office of Qualitative and Mixed Methods Research, a service and research unit that provides methodological support for funded projects at the University of Nebraska–Lincoln (UNL). She is also a research assistant professor in the Quantitative, Qualitative, and Psychometric Methods program housed in UNL's Department of Educational Psychology. She teaches research methods courses, including foundations of educational research, qualitative research, and mixed methods research. Her publications include the books *Designing and Conducting Mixed Methods Research* (Sage, 2007), *The Mixed Methods Reader* (Sage, 2008), and *Understanding Research: A Consumer's Guide* (2010), which she cowrote with John W. Creswell. Her writings focus on methodological discussions about procedural issues that arise when implementing different mixed methods designs and disciplinary contexts for conducting mixed methods studies, such as education, family research, counseling psychology, and primary care medicine. She currently serves as an associate editor for the *Journal of Mixed Methods Research*.

Susan Ramlo (PhD, The University of Akron) is a former industrial physicist who currently holds the titles of Professor of General Technology: Physics, and Professor of Education at The University of Akron. She also is adjunct graduate faculty within the Physics Department at Kent State University. Ramlo has been recognized for her teaching excellence and has received The University of Akron Outstanding Teacher–Scholar Award, the Northeast Ohio Council on Higher Education Award for Teaching Excellence, and *Ohio Magazine*'s Excellence in Education recognition and is listed in *Who's Who Among America's Teachers*. Her research focuses on applications of Q Methodology and the learning of concepts in physics. Ramlo has served as a reviewer of numerous journals, including *The Physics Teacher* and the *Physics Education Research Conference Proceedings*. She is on the editorial boards of *Operant Subjectivity: The International Journal of Q Methodology* and *Human Subjectivity*. She is the president of the International Society for the Scientific Study of Subjectivity.

Vijayendra Rao (PhD, University of Pennsylvania) is a lead economist in the Development Research Group of the World Bank. He integrates his training in economics with theories and methods from sociology and political science to study the social, cultural, and political context of extreme poverty in developing countries. Dr. Rao's current work examines the determinants of citizen engagement in poor societies and the interrelationship between social and economic mobility, with a goal toward understanding how best to improve living standards and well-being. Dr. Rao obtained a BA from St. Xavier's College (Bombay) and a PhD (Economics) from the University of Pennsylvania, and he worked at the

University of Chicago, the University of Michigan, and Williams College before joining the World Bank. He serves on the editorial boards of four journals and the Social Development Board of the World Bank, and is an advisory committee member of the Canadian Institute for Advanced Research.

Pamela Sammons (PhD, Council for National Academic Awards) is a professor of education at the Department of Education, University of Oxford and is course director of the MSc in Educational Research Methodology there. Previously she was a professor at the University of Nottingham and spent 11 years at the Institute of Education, University of London where she was coordinating director of its International School Effectiveness & Improvement Centre. She has been involved in educational research for the past 30 years, with a special focus on school effectiveness and improvement, leadership, and equity in education. Pam has conducted many studies of primary and secondary schools and their influence on pupils and has a special interest in mixed methods research. She was coauthor of *School Matters* (Open Books, 1988), a seminal study of primary schools in inner London; and principal investigator for *Forging Links: Effective Schools & Effective Departments* (Paul Chapman, 1997). She was a codirector of the VITAE DCSF funded research on variations in teachers' work, lives and their effects on students (*Teachers Matter*, OUP, 2006) and is a principal investigator of the Effective Provision of Pre-school and Primary school longitudinal research (*Early Childhood Matters*, Routledge, 2010).

Margarete Sandelowski (PhD, Case Western Reserve University) is Cary C. Boshamer Distinguished Professor and director of the summer programs in qualitative research at the University of North Carolina at Chapel Hill School of Nursing. She is currently principal investigator of a study, funded by the National Institute of Nursing Research, National Institutes of Health (5R01 NR004907, 2005–2010), to develop methods to synthesize qualitative and quantitative research findings. Recent publications include "On Quantitizing" (with Voils and Knafl; *Journal of Mixed Methods Research*, 2009); "Making Sense of Qualitative and Quantitative Findings in Mixed Research Synthesis Studies" (with Voils, Barros, and Hasselblad; *Field Methods*, 2008); and "Bayesian Data Augmentation Methods for the Synthesis of Qualitative and Quantitative Research Findings" (with Crandell, Voils, and Chang; *Quality & Quantity*, in press).

Mi-Kyung Song (PhD, University of Wisconsin-Madison) is assistant professor of nursing at the University of North Carolina at Chapel Hill and faculty fellow at the Parr Center for Ethics, the University of North Carolina at Chapel Hill. Her research focuses on improving end-of-life and palliative care for patients with serious chronic illness and their caregivers. She currently serves as principal investigator of a clinical trial (R01NR011464, 2009–2014) to test a communication intervention to clarify goals of care, prepare for end-of-life decision making, and reduce psychological distress for patients with end-stage renal disease and their caregivers. She has also conducted a series of studies to describe the illness course and experiences of lung-transplant recipients and family caregivers after the onset of chronic rejection. This work has led her to design and test an outpatient-based palliative care intervention for lung transplant recipients who experience chronic rejection and their caregivers.

Martin Sullivan (PhD, University of Auckland) is a senior lecturer at the School of Health and Social Services, Massey University, Palmerston North, New Zealand, where he teaches and coordinates a postgraduate program in disability studies. He was awarded his PhD in 1997 and was made a Winston Churchill Fellow in 2000 for his work on the development of disability studies in the United Kingdom. He has published widely on disability, is chair of Advocacy Manawatu (a citizen advocacy

organization for disabled people), was part of the expert panel that reviewed and set guidelines for the disability research funded by the Health Research Council of New Zealand, and was a ministerial appointment for 6 years to the National Ethics Advisory Committee.

James Thomas (PhD, University of London) is reader in social policy and associate director of the EPPI-Centre in the Social Science Research Unit, Institute of Education, London. He is director of the EPPI-Centre's Reviews Facility for the Department of Health, England, and undertakes systematic reviews across a range of policy areas to support the department. He has specialized in developing methods for research synthesis, in particular for qualitative and mixed methods reviews and in using emerging information technologies in research. He leads a module on synthesis and critical appraisal on the EPPI-Centre's MSc in Evidence for Public Policy and Practice, and he designed and cowrote the Centre's in-house reviewing software, EPPI-Reviewer.

Thomas S. Weisner (PhD, Harvard University) is professor of anthropology, Departments of Psychiatry (Semel Institute, Center for Culture and Health) and Anthropology at the University of California, Los Angeles. His research and teaching interests are in culture and human development; medical, psychological, and cultural studies of families and children at risk; mixed methods; and evidence-informed policy. He has done fieldwork with the Abaluyia of Kenya, native Hawai'ians, countercultural U.S. families, U.S. families with children with disabilities, and working poor families in the United States. His bachelor's of art is from Reed College, and his doctorate is in social relations and anthropology. He is the author or editor of *Higher Ground: New Hope for the Working Poor and Their Children* (with Greg Duncan and Aletha Huston, 2007); *Making It Work: Low-Wage Employment, Family Life and Child Development* (with Hiro Yoshikawa & Edward Lowe, 2006);

and *Discovering Successful Pathways in Children's Development: New Methods in the Study of Childhood and Family Life* (2005).

Amy Wilson (PhD, Gallaudet University) is an associate professor at Gallaudet University in Washington, D.C., and program director of the Graduate School's International Development program, which focuses on the inclusion of people with disabilities in development assistance programs and in nongovernmental, federal, and faith-based development organizations both in the United States and overseas. Dr. Wilson teaches deaf and hearing students research and evaluation, theory and practice of international development, micropolitics, and disability and international development. Dr. Wilson evaluates and advises organizations and agencies about the inclusiveness and effectiveness of their programs. She specializes in inclusive participation for disabled and deaf populations, gender equity for girls and women with disabilities, advocacy on behalf of the global disability rights agenda, and training new development workers. Dr. Wilson uses participatory evaluation approaches in community-based settings and has written several chapters and articles about disability and development in developing countries.

Marsha N. Wittink (MD, Jefferson Medical School; MBE, University of Pennsylvania) is an assistant professor in the Department of Family Medicine and Community Health and a senior scholar in the Center for Clinical Epidemiology and Biostatistics at the University of Pennsylvania. Her research combines methods derived from epidemiology, medical anthropology, and decision science to study how and why patients and physicians make particular treatment decisions. Her work focuses on the assessment and stability of treatment preferences in relation to treatment behavior and explanatory models of disease with the goal of developing tailored treatments in the primary care setting. She earned a patient-oriented career development grant (K23) and has an R34 from the National Institute of Mental Health to develop methods to tailor depression treatment services to the needs of older adults. She teaches mixed methods for the University of Pennsylvania's Center for Public Health Initiatives Winter Institute.

Michael Woolcock (PhD, Brown University) is senior social scientist in the Development Research Group at the World Bank, where he has worked since 1998. From 2007 to 2009 he was on external service leave as professor of social science and development policy at the University of Manchester, and founding research director of its Brooks World Poverty Institute. From 2000 to 2006 he taught part-time at Harvard University's Kennedy School of Government. He is an Australian national, his doctorate is in comparative historical sociology, and he is currently working on local justice reform issues in several countries in the Asia-Pacific region. He has been a member of three World Development Report teams and serves on the editorial board of three journals, including the *Journal of Mixed Methods Research*.